# Lecture Notes in Computer Science 13532

More information about this series at https://link.springer.com/bookseries/558

Elias Pimenidis · Plamen Angelov ·
Chrisina Jayne · Antonios Papaleonidas ·
Mehmet Aydin (Eds.)

# Artificial Neural Networks and Machine Learning – ICANN 2022

31st International Conference on Artificial Neural Networks
Bristol, UK, September 6–9, 2022
Proceedings, Part IV

Springer

*Editors*
Elias Pimenidis ⓘ
University of the West of England
Bristol, UK

Plamen Angelov ⓘ
Lancaster University
Lancaster, UK

Chrisina Jayne ⓘ
Digital Innovation
Teesside University
Middlesbrough, UK

Antonios Papaleonidas ⓘ
Democritus University of Thrace
Xanthi, Greece

Mehmet Aydin ⓘ
The University of the West of England
Bristol, UK

ISSN 0302-9743 ISSN 1611-3349 (electronic)
Lecture Notes in Computer Science
ISBN 978-3-031-15936-7 ISBN 978-3-031-15937-4 (eBook)
https://doi.org/10.1007/978-3-031-15937-4

This Springer imprint is published by the registered company Springer Nature Switzerland AG
The registered company address is: Gewerbestrasse 11, 6330 Cham, Switzerland

# Preface

The International Conference on Artificial Neural Networks has entered this year its fourth decade. After two years of disturbance the conference has returned in a hybrid mode with delegates attending on site and remotely via an immersive online space. In 2022 the 31st ICANN was organized under the auspices of the European Neural Networks Society (ENNS) and hosted by the University of the West of England, in Bristol, United Kingdom.

The event attracted a large number and wide range of new and established researchers from five continents and 27 countries in total. The delegates came from Australia, Belgium, Brazil, Canada, China, Czech Republic, Egypt, Finland, France, Germany, Greece, India, Israel, Italy, Japan, Mexico, Morocco, New Zealand, Norway, Portugal, Slovakia, Spain, Sweden, Switzerland, Turkey, UK, and USA.

The research themes explored all innovative pathways in the wider area of Neural Networks and Machine Learning. There were 561 papers submitted. These were reviewed by at least two reviewers with the average number of reviews being 3 per paper. The quality of the submitted work was very high and the program committee chairs had the challenge and delight to be able to select 259 papers in total to be presented orally at the conference. These papers are included in the four volumes of these proceedings. Out of the selected papers, 255 were regular papers, with an additional four submissions accepted for presentation as extended abstracts. These, despite their short length, represent future concepts that promise very high quality research outputs, and the program committee agreed to offer the authors the opportunity to share their ideas with the delegates of the conference.

The papers included in these four volumes of the Lecture Notes in Computer Science series addressed a variety of topics, representing a wide breadth of research, not just in the area of Artificial Neural Networks but in related AI topics themes too: Deep Learning, Neural Network Theory, Neural Network Models, Recurrent Networks, Reinforcement Learning, Natural Language Processing, Generative Models, Graphical Models, Supervised Learning, Image Processing, CNN, Evolutionary Neural Networks, Unsupervised NN, Relational Learning, Image Processing, Recommender Systems, and Features Based Learning.

The conference delegates benefited from the inspiring keynote speeches by four distinguished invited speakers, details of which are given below.

**Agnieszka Wykowska** leads the unit Social Cognition in Human-Robot Interaction at the Italian Institute of Technology, Genoa, Italy. Her background is cognitive neuroscience with a Ph.D. in psychology from Ludwig Maximilian University Munich. In 2016 she was awarded an ERC Starting grant for InStance: Intentional Stance for Social Attunement, which addresses the question of attribution of intentionality to robots. She is Editor-in-Chief of the International Journal of Social Robotics. She is the President of the European Society for Cognitive and Affective Neuroscience (ESCAN). She is a delegate to the European Research Area (ERA) Forum, and a member of ELLIS (European Lab for Learning and Intelligent Systems). Her research bridges psychology, cognitive neuroscience, robotics and healthcare. Among other work her team develops robot-assisted training protocols to help children diagnosed with autism-spectrum disorder improve social skills.

**Věra Kůrková** is a senior scientist in the Institute of Computer Science of the Czech Academy of Sciences. She received a Ph.D. in mathematics from Charles University, Prague, and a Dr. Sc. in theoretical computer science from the Czech Academy of Sciences, from which she received the Bolzano Medal for her contribution to mathematical sciences. Her main interests are the mathematical theory of neurocomputing and machine learning. She has served as president of the European Neural Network Society (ENNS), and she is a member of the editorial boards of the journals Neural Networks, Neural Processing Letters, and Applied and Computational Harmonic Analysis. She has been involved in the organization of many conferences, among them ICANN 2008 and 2001.

**The Anh Han** is a professor of Computer Science and head of the Centre for Digital Innovation, Teesside University. His research covers several topics in AI and interdisciplinary research, including evolutionary game theory, behavioural and cognitive modelling, agent-based simulations, knowledge representation and reasoning, and AI safety. He has published over 100 peer-reviewed articles in top-tier conferences (AAAI, IJCAI, AAMAS) and journals. He regularly serves in the program committees of top-tier AI conferences, and he is on the editorial boards of several journals (Adaptive Behavior, PLOS One, Frontiers in AI and Robotics, Entropy). He has been awarded prestigious research fellowships and grants from the Future of Life Institute, the Leverhulme Trust Foundation, and FWO Belgium.

**Lyndon Smith** is a professor in the Centre for Machine Vision, University of the West of England, Bristol. He has over 28 years of research experience in the field of Computer Simulation and Machine Vision, with particular emphasis on 3D analysis of complex surface textures and object morphologies. A strong area of ongoing research is the development of deep learning for vision-based solutions for complex problems, the automation of which had been previously considered intractable. This is leading to strong industrial impact in a number of sectors.

September 2022

Plamen Angelov
Mehmet Aydin
Chrisina Jayne
Elias Pimenidis

# Organization

## General Chairs

Elias Pimenidis      University of the West of England, UK
Angelo Cangelosi      University of Manchester, UK

## Organizing Committee Chairs

Tim Brailsford      University of the West of England, UK
Larry Bull      University of the West of England, UK

## Honorary Chairs

Stefan Wermter (ENNS President)      University of Hamburg, Germany
Igor Farkaš      FMPI, Comenius University in Bratislava, Slovakia

## Program Committee Chairs

Plamen Angelov      Lancaster University, UK
Mehmet Aydin      University of the West of England, UK
Chrisina Jayne      Teesside University, UK
Elias Pimenidis      University of the West of England, UK

## Communication Chairs

Paolo Masulli      ENNS, Technical University of Denmark
Kristína Malinovská      FMPI, Comenius University in Bratislava, Slovakia
Antonios Papaleonidas      Democritus University of Thrace, Greece

## Steering Committee

Jérémie Cabessa      Université Versailles Saint-Quentin-en-Yvelines, France
Włodzisław Duch      Nicolaus Copernicus University, Torun, Poland
Igor Farkaš      Comenius University, Bratislava, Slovakia
Matthias Kerzel      Universität Hamburg, Germany
Věra Kůrková      Czech Academy of Sciences, Prague, Czechia

| | |
|---|---|
| Alessandra Lintas | Université de Lausanne, Switzerland |
| Paolo Masulli | iMotions A/S, Copenhagen, Denmark |
| Alessio Micheli | University of Pisa, Italy |
| Erkki Oja | Aalto University, Finland |
| Sebastian Otte | Universität Tübingen, Germany |
| Jaakko Peltonen | Tampere University, Finland |
| Antonio J. Pons | Universitat Politècnica de Catalunya, Barcelona, Spain |
| Igor V. Tetko | Helmholtz Zentrum München, Germany |
| Alessandro E. P. Villa | Université de Lausanne, Switzerland |
| Roseli Wedemann | Universidade do Estado do Rio de Janeiro, Brazil |
| Stefan Wermter | Universität Hamburg, Germany |

## Local Organizing Committee

| | |
|---|---|
| Nathan Duran | University of the West of England, UK |
| Haixia Liu | University of the West of England, UK |
| Zaheer Khan | University of the West of England, UK |
| Antonios Papaleonidas | Democritus University of Thrace, Greece |
| Nikolaos Polatidis | Brighton University, UK |
| Antisthenis Tsompanas | University of the West of England, UK |

## Hybrid Facilitation and Moderation Committee

| | |
|---|---|
| Anastasios Panagiotis Psathas | Democritus University of Thrace, Greece |
| Dimitris Boudas | Democritus University of Thrace, Greece |
| Ioanna-Maria Erentzi | Democritus University of Thrace, Greece |
| Ioannis Skopelitis | Democritus University of Thrace, Greece |
| Lambros Kazelis | Democritus University of Thrace, Greece |
| Leandros Tsatsaronis | Democritus University of Thrace, Greece |
| Nikiforos Mpotzoris | Democritus University of Thrace, Greece |
| Nikos Zervis | Democritus University of Thrace, Greece |
| Odysseas Tsonos | Hellenic Open University, Greece |
| Panagiotis Restos | Democritus University of Thrace, Greece |
| Tassos Giannakopoulos | Democritus University of Thrace, Greece |
| Vasilis Kokkinos | Democritus University of Thrace, Greece |

## Program Committee

| | |
|---|---|
| Abdelhamid Bouchachia | Bournemouth University, UK |
| Abdur Rakib | University of the West of England, UK |
| Abraham Yosipof | College of Law and Business, Israel |
| Akihiro Inokuchi | Kwansei Gakuin University, Japan |

Alaa Zain                          Hosei University, Japan
Albert Bifet                       LTCI, Telecom ParisTech, France
Alejandro Cabana                   Universidad Autónoma de Madrid, Spain
Alexander Claman                   University of Miami, USA
Alexander Gepperth                 ENSTA ParisTech, France
Alexander Ilin                     Aalto University, Finland
Alexander Kovalenko                Czech Technical University in Prague, Czechia
Alexander Krawczyk                 HAW Fulda, Germany
Ali Zoljodi                        MDU, Sweden
Aluizio Araújo                     Universidade Federal de Pernambuco, Brazil
Amit Kumar Kundu                   University of Maryland, College Park, USA
An Xu                              Donghua University, China
Anastasios Panagiotis Psathas      Democritus University of Thrace, Greece
André Artelt                       Bielefeld University, Germany
Andre de Carvalho                  University of São Paulo, Brazil
Andrea Castellani                  Bielefeld University - CITEC, Germany
Andrea Galassi                     University of Bologna, Italy
Angelo Cangelosi                   University of Manchester, UK
Anmol Biswas                       Indian Institute of Technology, Mumbai, India
Anna Jenul                         Norwegian University of Life Sciences, Norway
Annie DeForge                      Bentley University, USA
Anselm Haselhoff                   Hochschule Ruhr West, Germany
Antisthenis Tsompanas              University of the West of England, UK
Antonio García-Díaz                Université libre de Bruxelles (ULB), Belgium
Antonio Pons                       Universitat Politècnica de Catalunya, Spain
Antonios Papaleonidas              Democritus University of Thrace, Greece
Argyris Kalogeratos                CMLA, ENS Cachan, France
Asada                              Osaka University, Japan
Asei Akanuma                       Goldsmiths College, University of London, UK
Atsushi Koike                      Tohoku University, Japan
Baris Serhan                       University of Manchester, UK
Barkha Javed                       University of the West of England, UK
Benedikt Bagus                     Hochschule Fulda, Germany
Benyuan Liu                        University of Massachusetts, Lowell, USA
Bernhard Pfahringer                University of Waikato, New Zealand
Bi Yan-Qing                        National University of Defense Technology,
                                     China
Binyi Wu                           TU Dresden, Germany
Binyu Zhao                         Harbin Institute of Technology, China
Bo Mei                             Texas Christian University, USA
Boyu Diao                          ict, China
Cao Hongye                         Northwestern Polytechnical University, China

| | |
|---|---|
| Carsten Marr | German Research Center for Environmental Health, Germany |
| Chao Ma | Hong Kong Polytechnic University, Hong Kong, China |
| Cheng Feng | Fujitsu R&D Center, China |
| Ching-Chia Kao | Academia Sinica, Taiwan |
| Chrisina Jayne | Teesside University, UK |
| Christian Bauckhage | Fraunhofer IAIS, Sankt Augustin, Germany |
| Christian Oliva | Universidad Autónoma de Madrid, Spain |
| Christoph Linse | Universität zu Lübeck, Germany |
| Chuan Lu | Aberystwyth University, UK |
| Chuang Yu | University of Manchester, UK |
| Chunhong Cao | Xiangtan University, China |
| Chun-Shien Lu | Academia Sinica, Taiwan |
| Claudio Bellei | Elliptic, UK |
| Claudio Gallicchio | University of Pisa, Italy |
| Claudio Giorgio Giancaterino | Catholic University of Milan, Italy |
| Connor Gäde | University of Hamburg, Germany |
| Constantine Dovrolis | Georgia Institute of Technology, USA |
| Cornelius Weber | University of Hamburg, Germany |
| Coşku Can Horuz | University of Tübingen, Germany |
| Cui Wang | Macao Polytechnic University, China |
| Dan Fisher | University of North Carolina, Wilmington, USA |
| Daniel Kluvanec | Durham University, UK |
| David Dembinsky | German Research Center for Artificial Intelligence, Germany |
| David Martínez | DataSpartan Ltd., UK |
| Dayananda Herurkar | DFKI, Germany |
| Denise Gorse | University College London, UK |
| Dennis Becker | Lüneburg University, Germany |
| Dimitrios Bountas | Democritus University of Thrace, Greece |
| Dimitrios Michail | Harokopio University of Athens, Greece |
| Diyuan Lu | Frankfurt Institute for Advanced Studies, Germany |
| D. J. McMoran | University of North Carolina, Wilmington, USA |
| Domenico Tortorella | University of Pisa, Italy |
| Dominique Mercier | German Research Center for Artificial Intelligence, Germany |
| Doron Nevo | Bar-Ilan University, Israel |
| Douglas Nyabuga | Donghua University, China |
| Efe Bozkir | University of Tübingen, Germany |
| Eisuke Ito | Ritsumeikan University, Japan |

| | |
|---|---|
| Elias Pimenidis | University of the West of England, UK |
| Fabian Hinder | Bielefeld University, Germany |
| Fanglin Chen | Harbin Institute of Technology, Shenzhen, China |
| Fares Abawi | University of Hamburg, Germany |
| Federico Tavella | University of Manchester, UK |
| Feixiang Zhou | University of Leicester, UK |
| Feng Wei | York University, Canada |
| Florence Dupin de Saint-Cyr | IRIT, Université Paul Sabatier, France |
| Francesco Semeraro | University of Manchester, UK |
| Francois Blayo | Neoinstinct, Switzerland |
| Frank Gyan Okyere | Rothamsted Research, UK |
| Frederic Alexandre | Inria, France |
| Gang Yang | Renmin University, China |
| Giannis Nikolentzos | Athens University of Economics and Business, Greece |
| Gonzalo Martínez-Muñoz | Universidad Autónoma de Madrid, Spain |
| Grégory Bourguin | LISIC/ULCO, France |
| Guillermo Martín-Sánchez | Graduate Training Center of Neuroscience, Germany |
| Gulustan Dogan | University of North Carolina, Wilmington, USA |
| Habib Khan | Islamia College Peshawar, Pakistan |
| Hafez Farazi | University of Bonn, Germany |
| Haixia Liu | University of the West of England, UK |
| Haizhou Du | Shanghai University of Electric Power, China |
| Hang Gao | Institute of Software, Chinese Academy of Sciences, China |
| Haopeng Chen | Shanghai Jiao Tong University, China |
| Hazrat Ali | Hamad Bin Khalifa University, Qatar |
| Heitor Gomes | University of Waikato, New Zealand |
| Hideaki Yamamoto | Tohoku University, Japan |
| Hina Afridi | NTNU, Norway |
| Hiroyoshi Ito | University of Tsukuba, Japan |
| Hisham Ihshaish | University of the West of England, UK |
| Hong Qing Yu | University of Bedfordshire, UK |
| Hongchao Gao | South China University of Technology, China |
| Honggang Zhang | University of Massachusetts, Boston, USA |
| Hugo Eduardo Camacho Cruz | Universidad Autónoma de Tamaulipas, Mexico |
| Hugues Bersini | Université libre de Bruxelles, Belgium |
| Huifang Ma | Northwest Normal University, China |
| Huiyu Zhou | University of Leicester, UK |
| Hy Dang | Texas Christian University, USA |
| Igor Farkaš | Comenius University in Bratislava, Slovakia |

| | |
|---|---|
| Ioannis Pierros | Aristotle University of Thessaloniki, Greece |
| Iveta Bečková | Comenius University in Bratislava, Slovakia |
| Jae Hee Lee | University of Hamburg, Germany |
| James J. Q. Yu | Southern University of Science and Technology, Hong Kong, China |
| James Msonda | Aberystwyth University, UK |
| Jan Faigl | Czech Technical University in Prague, Czechia |
| Jan Feber | Czech Technical University in Prague, Czechia |
| Jan Kalina | Czech Academy of Sciences, Czechia |
| Jérémie Cabessa | University Paris 2, France |
| Jia Cai | Guangdong University of Finance & Economics, China |
| Jiajun Liu | CSIRO, Australia |
| Jianhua Xu | Nanjing Normal University, China |
| Jian-Wei Liu | China University of Petroleum, Beijing, China |
| Jianyong Chen | Shenzhen University, Shenzhen, China |
| Jichao Bi | Zhejiang University, China |
| Jie Shao | University of Science and Technology, Chengdu, China |
| Jim Smith | University of the West of England, UK |
| Jing Yang | Hefei University of Technology, China |
| Jingyi Yuan | Arizona State University, USA |
| Jingyun Jia | Florida Institute of Technology, USA |
| Johannes Brinkrolf | CITEC Centre of Excellence, Germany |
| Jonathan Jakob | Bielefeld University, Germany |
| Jonathan Lawry | University of Bristol, UK |
| Jonathan Mojoo | Hiroshima University, Japan |
| Jordi Cosp-Vilella | Universitat Politècnica de Catalunya, Spain |
| Jordi Madrenas | Universitat Politècnica de Catalunya, Spain |
| Joseph Jaja | University of Maryland, USA |
| Juan Liu | Wuhan University, China |
| K. L. Eddie Law | Macao Polytechnic University, Macao, China |
| Kamran Soomro | University of the West of England, UK |
| Katsiaryna Haitsiukevich | Aalto University, Finland |
| Kenneth Co | Imperial College London, UK |
| Koji Kyoda | RIKEN Center for Biosystems Dynamics Research, Japan |
| Koloud Alkhamaiseh | Western Michigan University, USA |
| Kostadin Cvejoski | Fraunhofer IAIS, Sankt Augustin, Germany |
| Kostantinos Demertzis | Democritus University of Thrace, Greece |
| Kristian Hovde Liland | Norwegian University of Life Sciences, Norway |
| Kuntal Ghosh | Indian Statistical Institute, India |

| | |
|---|---|
| Larry Bull | University of the West of England, UK |
| Lei Luo | Kansas State University, USA |
| Leiping Jie | Hong Kong Baptist University, Hong Kong, China |
| Lian Yahong | Dalian University of Technology, China |
| Liang Ge | Chongqing University, China |
| Liang Zhao | Dalian University of Technology, China |
| Liang Zhao | University of São Paulo, Brazil |
| Lingfei Dai | ICT - CAS, China |
| Linlin Shen | Shenzhen University, China |
| Lu Wang | Macao Polytechnic University, Macao |
| Luca Oneto | University of Genoa, Italy |
| Luca Raggioli | University of Manchester, UK |
| Luís A. Alexandre | UBI and NOVA LINCS, Portugal |
| Luis Lago | Universidad Autónoma de Madrid, Spain |
| Lun-Ing Zhang | China University of Petroleum, Beijing, China |
| Magda Friedjungová | Czech Technical University in Prague, Czechia |
| Manon Dampfhoffer | Université Grenoble Alpes, France |
| Marc Wenninger | Technische Hochschule Rosenheim, Germany |
| Marcello Trovati | Edge Hill University, UK |
| Marco Perez Hernandez | University of the West of England, UK |
| Maria Papadaki | University of Derby, UK |
| Marika Kaden | HS Mittweida, Germany |
| Markus Kollmann | Heinrich Heine Universität, Germany |
| Marta Romeo | University of Manchester, UK |
| Martin Butz | University of Tübingen, Germany |
| Martin Ferianc | University College London, UK |
| Masanari Kimura | ZOZO Research, Japan |
| Masoud Daneshtalab | Mälardalen University, Sweden |
| Matthew Evanusa | University of Maryland, USA |
| Matthias Karlbauer | University of Tübingen, Germany |
| Matthias Kerzel | University of Hamburg, Germany |
| Mattias Dahl | Blekinge Institute of Technology, Sweden |
| Md Delwar Hossain | Nara Institute of Science and Technology, Japan |
| Mehmet Emin Aydin | University of the West of England, UK |
| Mihaela Oprea | University Petroleum-Gas of Ploiesti, Romania |
| Mohammad Loni | MDU, Sweden |
| Moritz Wolter | University of Bonn, Germany |
| Mu Hua | University of Lincoln, UK |
| Muhammad Usama Javaid | Eura Nova, Belgium |
| Nashwa El-Bendary | Arab Academy for Science, Technology & Maritime Transport, Egypt |
| Nathan Duran | University of the West of England, UK |

| | |
|---|---|
| Nermeen Abou Baker | Hochschule Ruhr West, Germany |
| Nikolaos Polatidis | University of Brighton, UK |
| Oleg Bakhteev | MIPT, Russia |
| Olga Grebenkova | Moscow Institute of Physics and Technology (MIPT), Russia |
| Or Elroy | CLB, Israel |
| Ozan Özdemir | University of Hamburg, Germany |
| Paulo Cortez | University of Minho, Portugal |
| Plamen Angelov | Lancaster University, UK |
| Rafet Durgut | Bandirma Onyedi Eylul University, Turkey |
| Roman Moucek | University of West Bohemia, Czechia |
| Roseli S. Wedemann | Universidade do Estado do Rio de Janeiro, Brazil |
| Ruijun Feng | Zhejiang University of Finance and Economics, China |
| Saikat Chakraborty | Kalinga Institute of Industrial Technology (KIIT), India |
| Sajjad Heydari | University of Manitoba, Winnipeg, Canada |
| Sander Bohte | CWI, Netherlands |
| Sandrine Mouysset | IRIT, France |
| Sebastián Basterrech | VSB-Technical University of Ostrava, Czechia |
| Sebastian Otte | University of Tübingen, Germany |
| Senwei Liang | Purdue University, USA |
| Shelan Jeawak | University of the West of England, UK |
| Shoubin Dong | South China University of Technology, China |
| Sidi Yang | RI-MUHC, Canada |
| Song Guo | Xi'an University of Architecture and Technology, China |
| Songlin Du | Southeast University, China |
| Stefan Wermter | University of Hamburg, Germany |
| Steve Battle | University of the West of England, UK |
| Sven Behnke | University of Bonn, Germany |
| Takaharu Yaguchi | Kobe University, Japan |
| Takeshi Ikenaga | Waseda University, Japan |
| Tang Kai | Toshiba, China |
| Tetsuya Hoya | Nihon University, Japan |
| Tianlin Zhang | University of the Chinese Academy of Sciences, China |
| Tieke He | Nanjing University, China |
| Tim Brailsford | University of the West of England, UK |
| Ting Bai | Hefei University of Technology, China |
| Toby Breckon | Durham University, UK |
| Varun Ojha | University of Reading, UK |

| | |
|---|---|
| Wenxin Yu | Southwest University of Science and Technology, China |
| Xi Cheng | Nanjing University of Science and Technology, China |
| Xia Feng | Civil Aviation University, China |
| Xian Zhong | Wuhan University of Technology, China |
| Xiang Zhang | National University of Defense Technology, China |
| Xiaoqing Liu | Kyushu University, Japan |
| Xiumei Li | Hangzhou Normal University, China |
| Xizhan Gao | University of Jinan, China |
| Xuan Yang | Shenzhen University, China |
| Yan Chen | Chinese Academy of Sciences, China |
| Yangguang Cui | East China Normal University, China |
| Yapeng Gao | University of Tübingen, Germany |
| Yaxi Chen | Wuhan University, China |
| Yiannis Aloimonos | University of Maryland, USA |
| Yihao Luo | Huazhong University of Science and Technology, China |
| Yipeng Yu | Tencent, China |
| Yuan Li | Academy of Military Science, China |
| Yuanyuan Chen | Sichuan University, China |
| Yuchen Zheng | Shihezi University, China |
| Yuchun Fang | Shanghai University, China |
| Yue Gao | Beijing University of Posts and Telecommunications, China |
| Yuji Kawai | Osaka University, Japan |
| Zhaoxiang Zang | China Three Gorges University, China |
| Zhaoyun Ding | National University of Defense Technology, China |
| Zhengfeng Yang | East China Normal University, Shanghai, China |
| Zhenjie Yao | CMCC, China |
| Zhiping Lai | Fudan University, China |
| Zhiqiang Zhang | Hosei University, Japan |
| Zhixin Li | Guangxi Normal University, China |
| Zhongnan Zhang | Xiamen University, China |

# Contents – Part IV

Analysing the Predictivity of Features to Characterise the Search Space . . . . . . .    1
   *Rafet Durgut, Mehmet Emin Aydin, Hisham Ihshaish, and Abdur Rakib*

Boosting Feature-Aware Network for Salient Object Detection . . . . . . . . . . . . . .   14
   *Jianwei Zheng, Yubin Gu, Yuchao Feng, Jinshan Xu, and Meiyu Zhang*

Continual Learning Based on Knowledge Distillation and Representation
Learning . . . . . . . . . . . . . . . . . . . . . . . . . . . . . . . . . . . . . . . . . . . . . . . . . . . . . . . . . . .   27
   *Xiu-yan Chen, Jian-wei Liu, and Wen-tao Li*

Deep Feature Learning for Medical Acoustics . . . . . . . . . . . . . . . . . . . . . . . . . . .   39
   *Alessandro Maria Poirè, Federico Simonetta, and Stavros Ntalampiras*

Feature Fusion Distillation . . . . . . . . . . . . . . . . . . . . . . . . . . . . . . . . . . . . . . . . . . . .   51
   *Chao Tan and Jie Liu*

Feature Recalibration Network for Salient Object Detection . . . . . . . . . . . . . . . .   64
   *Zhenshan Tan and Xiaodong Gu*

Feature Selection for Trustworthy Regression Using Higher Moments . . . . . . . . .   76
   *Fabian Hinder, Johannes Brinkrolf, and Barbara Hammer*

Fire Detection Based on Improved-YOLOv5s . . . . . . . . . . . . . . . . . . . . . . . . . . .   88
   *Mengdong Zhou, Jianjun Li, and Shuai Liu*

Heterogeneous Graph Neural Network for Multi-behavior
Feature-Interaction Recommendation . . . . . . . . . . . . . . . . . . . . . . . . . . . . . . . . . .  101
   *Li Ma, Zheng Chen, Yingxun Fu, and Yang Li*

JointFusionNet: Parallel Learning Human Structural Local and Global
Joint Features for 3D Human Pose Estimation . . . . . . . . . . . . . . . . . . . . . . . . . . .  113
   *Zhiwei Yuan, Yaping Yan, Songlin Du, and Takeshi Ikenaga*

Multi-scale Feature Extraction and Fusion for Online Knowledge
Distillation . . . . . . . . . . . . . . . . . . . . . . . . . . . . . . . . . . . . . . . . . . . . . . . . . . . . . . . . . .  126
   *Panpan Zou, Yinglei Teng, and Tao Niu*

Multi-scale Vertical Cross-layer Feature Aggregation and Attention
Fusion Network for Object Detection . . . . . . . . . . . . . . . . . . . . . . . . . . . . . . . . . .  139
   *Wenting Gao, Xiaojuan Li, Yu Han, and Yue Liu*

Multi-spectral Dynamic Feature Encoding Network for Image Demoiréing  ....    151
  Qiang Dai, Xi Cheng, and Li Zhang

Ranking Feature-Block Importance in Artificial Multiblock Neural
Networks .........................................................    163
  Anna Jenul, Stefan Schrunner, Bao Ngoc Huynh, Runar Helin,
  Cecilia Marie Futsæther, Kristian Hovde Liland, and Oliver Tomic

Robust Sparse Learning Based Sensor Array Optimization for Multi-feature
Fusion Classification .....................................................    176
  Leilei Zhao, Fengchun Tian, Junhui Qian, Ran Liu, and Anyan Jiang

Stimulates Potential for Knowledge Distillation ..........................    187
  Haifeng Qing, Jialiang Tang, Xiaoyan Yang, Xinlei Huang,
  Honglin Zhu, and Ning Jiang

Adaptive Compatibility Matrix for Superpixel-CRF .......................    199
  Boquan Zhou and Chunpeng Li

BERT-Based Scientific Paper Quality Prediction ..........................    212
  Taiki Sasaki, Yasuaki Ito, Koji Nakano, and Akihiko Kasagi

Effective ML-Block and Weighted IoU Loss for Object Detection ............    224
  Zhenxin Yuan, Xin Xiao, Shuai Zhao, Linlin Jiang, and Zhongtao Li

FedNet2Net: Saving Communication and Computations in Federated
Learning with Model Growing .........................................    236
  Amit Kumar Kundu and Joseph Jaja

Reject Options for Incremental Regression Scenarios ......................    248
  Jonathan Jakob, Martina Hasenjäger, and Barbara Hammer

Stream-Based Active Learning with Verification Latency in Non-stationary
Environments .........................................................    260
  Andrea Castellani, Sebastian Schmitt, and Barbara Hammer

StTime-Net: Combining both Historical and Textual Factors for Stock
Movement Prediction ..................................................    273
  Hy Dang, Minh Nguyen, and Bo Mei

Subspace Clustering Multi-module Self-organizing Maps with Two-Stage
Learning .............................................................    285
  Marcondes R. da Silva Júnior and Aluizio F. R. Araújo

SVM Ensembles on a Budget ........................................ 297
    David Nevado, Gonzalo Martínez-Muñoz, and Alberto Suárez

The Parallelization and Optimization of K-means Algorithm Based
on MGPUSim ..................................................... 309
    Zhangbin Mo, Yaobin Wang, Qingming Zhang, Guangbing Zhang,
    Mingfeng Guo, Yaqing Zhang, and Chao Shen

Two-Dimensional Encoding Method for Neural Synthesis of Tabular
Transformation by Example ........................................ 321
    Yoshifumi Ujibashi and Atsuhiro Takasu

Variational Autoencoders for Anomaly Detection in Respiratory Sounds ....... 333
    Michele Cozzatti, Federico Simonetta, and Stavros Ntalampiras

An Innovate Hybrid Approach for Residence Price Using Fuzzy C-Means
and Machine Learning Techniques .................................. 346
    Antonios Papaleonidas, Konstantinos Lykostratis,
    Anastasios Panagiotis Psathas, Lazaros Iliadis, and Maria Giannopoulou

Contrastive Learning for Session-Based Recommendation ................... 358
    Yan Chen, Wanhui Qian, Dongqin Liu, Yipeng Su, Yan Zhou,
    Jizhong Han, and Ruixuan Li

Discriminative and Robust Analysis Dictionary Learning for Pattern
Classification ................................................... 370
    Kun Jiang, Lei Zhu, and Zheng Liu

Domain Adaptive Semantic Segmentation by Fine-Grained Alignment ...... 383
    Zhixin Li, Wei Li, and Jia Zhang

Hypergraph Variational Autoencoder for Multimodal Semi-supervised
Representation Learning ........................................... 395
    Jingquan Liu, Xiaoyong Du, Yuanzhe Li, and Weidong Hu

Intention-Aware Frequency Domain Transformer Networks for Video
Prediction ...................................................... 407
    Hafez Farazi and Sven Behnke

Knowledge-Aware Self-supervised Graph Representation Learning
for Recommendation .............................................. 420
    Yeheng Sun, Jinghua Zhu, and Heran Xi

Meta-Style: Few-Shot Learning Dataset for Social Media Field ............. 433
    Yuncong Peng, Boyi Fu, and Xiaolin Qin

Problem Classification for Tailored Helpdesk Auto-replies . . . . . . . . . . . . . . . . .  445
  *Reece Nicholls, Ryan Fellows, Steve Battle, and Hisham Ihshaish*

Self-Enhancer: A Self-supervised Framework for Low-Supervision,
Drifted Data with Significant Missing Values . . . . . . . . . . . . . . . . . . . . . . . . . . .  455
  *Yu Chen and Peter Flach*

Self-supervised Anomaly Detection by Self-distillation and Negative
Sampling . . . . . . . . . . . . . . . . . . . . . . . . . . . . . . . . . . . . . . . . . . . . . . . . . . . . . . . .  459
  *Nima Rafiee, Rahil Gholamipoor, Nikolas Adaloglou, Simon Jaxy,
  Julius Ramakers, and Markus Kollmann*

Self-supervised Detransformation Autoencoder for Representation
Learning in Open Set Recognition . . . . . . . . . . . . . . . . . . . . . . . . . . . . . . . . . . . .  471
  *Jingyun Jia and Philip K. Chan*

Supervised Learning for Convolutional Neural Network with Barlow Twins . . . .  484
  *Ramyaa Murugan, Jonathan Mojoo, and Takio Kurita*

Using Multiple Heads to Subsize Meta-memorization Problem . . . . . . . . . . . . . . .  496
  *Lu Wang and K. L. Eddie Law*

Video Motion Perception for Self-supervised Representation Learning . . . . . . . .  508
  *Wei Li, Dezhao Luo, Bo Fang, Xiaoni Li, Yu Zhou, and Weiping Wang*

A Differentiable Architecture Search Approach for Few-Shot Image
Classification . . . . . . . . . . . . . . . . . . . . . . . . . . . . . . . . . . . . . . . . . . . . . . . . . . . . . .  521
  *Chunmao He, Lingyun Zhang, Songqing Huang, and Pingjian Zhang*

AFS: Attention Using First and Second Order Information to Enrich
Features . . . . . . . . . . . . . . . . . . . . . . . . . . . . . . . . . . . . . . . . . . . . . . . . . . . . . . . . . . .  533
  *Yan Zuo, Junjie Lv, and Huiwei Wang*

Autonomous Driving Model Defense Study on Hijacking Adversarial
Attack . . . . . . . . . . . . . . . . . . . . . . . . . . . . . . . . . . . . . . . . . . . . . . . . . . . . . . . . . . . . .  546
  *Kabid Hassan Shibly, Md. Delwar Hossain, Hiroyuki Inoue,
  Yuzo Taenaka, and Youki Kadobayashi*

Chinese Character Style Transfer Model Based on Convolutional Neural
Network . . . . . . . . . . . . . . . . . . . . . . . . . . . . . . . . . . . . . . . . . . . . . . . . . . . . . . . . . . .  558
  *Weiran Chen, Chunping Liu, and Yi Ji*

CNN-Transformer Hybrid Architecture for Early Fire Detection . . . . . . . . . . . . .  570
  *Chenyue Yang, Yixuan Pan, Yichao Cao, and Xiaobo Lu*

DeepArtist: A Dual-Stream Network for Painter Classification
of Highly-Varying Image Resolutions .................................... 582
*Doron Nevo, Eli O. David, and Nathan S. Netanyahu*

Dual Branch Network Towards Accurate Printed Mathematical Expression
Recognition .............................................................. 594
*Yuqing Wang, Zhenyu Weng, Zhaokun Zhou, Shuaijian Ji, Zhongjie Ye,
and Yuesheng Zhu*

Efficient Search of Multiple Neural Architectures with Different
Complexities via Importance Sampling .................................... 607
*Yuhei Noda, Shota Saito, and Shinichi Shirakawa*

End-to-End Large-Scale Image Retrieval Network with Convolution
and Vision Transformers ................................................. 620
*Qing Zhang, Feilong Bao, Xiangdong Su, Weihua Wang,
and Guanglai Gao*

Ensemble Ranking for Image Retrieval via Deep Hash ..................... 633
*Donggen Li, Dawei Dai, Hongyuan Shan, Shunyin Xia, and Yulong Xia*

Examining the Proximity of Adversarial Examples to Class Manifolds
in Deep Networks ....................................................... 645
*Štefan Pócoš, Iveta Bečková, and Igor Farkaš*

Gesture MNIST: A New Free-Hand Gesture Dataset ....................... 657
*Monika Schak and Alexander Gepperth*

GH-CNN: A New CNN for Coherent Hierarchical Classification ............ 669
*Mona-Sabrine Mayouf and Florence Dupin de Saint-Cyr*

Hyperspectral Endoscopy Using Deep Learning for Laryngeal Cancer
Segmentation ........................................................... 682
*Felix Meyer-Veit, Rania Rayyes, Andreas O. H. Gerstner, and Jochen Steil*

Image Super-Resolution Using Deep RCSA Network ...................... 695
*Yuheng Cao and Mengjie Zhou*

Lip Reading Using Deformable 3D Convolution and Channel-Temporal
Attention .............................................................. 707
*Chen Peng, Jun Li, Jie Chai, Zhongqiu Zhao, Housen Zhang,
and Weidong Tian*

Loop Closure Detection Based on Siamese ConvNet Features
and Geometrical Verification for Visual SLAM .......................... 719
  Zhe Chen, Xiaofeng Zhang, Yaojun Ou, and Mei Wang

Multi-Sensor Data Fusion for Short-Term Traffic Flow Prediction:
A Novel Multi-Channel Data Structure Integrated with Mixed-Pointwise
Convolution and Channel Attention Mechanism .......................... 731
  Ruijun Feng and Mingzhou Chen

Neural Architecture Search for Low-Precision Neural Networks ............. 743
  Binyi Wu, Bernd Waschneck, and Christian Mayr

RegionDrop: Fast Human Pose Estimation Using Annotation-Aware
Spatial Sparsity ...................................................... 756
  Youki Sada, Seiya Shibata, Yuki Kobayashi, and Takashi Takenaka

SDCN: A Species-Disease Hybrid Convolutional Neural Network
for Plant Disease Recognition ......................................... 769
  Yiqi Yang

TFCNs: A CNN-Transformer Hybrid Network for Medical Image
Segmentation ......................................................... 781
  Zihan Li, Dihan Li, Cangbai Xu, Weice Wang, Qingqi Hong, Qingde Li,
  and Jie Tian

Author Index ........................................................ 793

# Analysing the Predictivity of Features to Characterise the Search Space

Rafet Durgut[1], Mehmet Emin Aydin[2(✉)], Hisham Ihshaish[2],
and Abdur Rakib[2,3]

[1] Bandirma Onyedi Eylul University, Bandirma, Turkey
rdurgut@bandirma.edu.tr
[2] University of the West of England, Bristol, UK
{mehmet.aydin,hisham.ihshaish,rakib.abdur}@uwe.ac.uk
[3] Centre for Future Transport and Cities, Coventry University, Coventry, UK
rakib.abdur@coventry.ac.uk

**Abstract.** Exploring search spaces is one of the most unpredictable challenges that has attracted the interest of researchers for decades. One way to handle unpredictability is to characterise the search spaces and take actions accordingly. A well-characterised search space can assist in mapping the problem states to a set of operators for generating new problem states. In this paper, a landscape analysis-based set of features has been analysed using the most renown machine learning approaches to determine the optimal feature set. However, in order to deal with problem complexity and induce commonality for transferring experience across domains, the selection of the most representative features remains crucial. The proposed approach analyses the predictivity of a set of features in order to determine the best categorization.

**Keywords:** Feature analysis · Search space characterisation · Supervised machine learning

## 1 Introduction

Optimisation is the process of searching for the best fitting solution within a solution space. Search process uses instruments to achieve moving between the neighbouring solutions by the means of neighbourhood functions, also know as operators. Operators produce new solutions, but the replacement of the produced solutions or promoting them into the recognised population of solutions retains substantial challenges. Various metaheuristic approaches instrumentalise different approaches to promote the produced solutions [19]. Many studies drive focus on the characteristics of search space and the fitness landscape with which more information extracted through can be used for better promotion rules and higher success rate [8].

This work is supported by TUBITAK, Turkey, with sponsoring for Dr Durgut's research visit hosted by UWE Bristol, UK.

Adaptive operator selection appears to be another useful avenue to maintain diversity and richness in the search process in order to avoid potential local optima points [7]. This approach is usually applied with population-based metaheuristics, i.e., evolutionary algorithms [20] and swarm intelligence algorithms [3]. The compelling challenge always enforces to pay more attention in the way how to build the adaptive selection scheme and which kind of information to use in opting the most suitable operators.

Fitness landscape studies have been attractive for a long time with which more auxiliary information can be extracted and used for identification of the search and the characterisation of the search space. More details can be found in one of latest reviews [8]. Such auxiliary information can be utilised to harvest for representative and discriminating features to characterise the search circumstances, while, previously, the problem state has been used to help characterise the search circumstances [3,4], but, the approach was not scalable for different size of problem instances due to strong dependency to the problem size. This study is expected to support to hypothesise a scalable approach through a bespoke set of features.

The aim of this study is to pave an avenue to identify the best set of predictive features in characterising the search space and fitness landscape so as to make the most efficient decision in selecting the relevant actions such as activating the best fitting/productive neighbourhood function. Predictive analysis is expected to let us dive-down in the causal effects the behaviours of neighbourhood functions in producing the neighbouring solutions. Details of predictive analysis have been introduced in [14].

The rest of this paper is organised as follows; Sect. 2 provides the relevant background and related work, while Sect. 3 introduces the details of fitness landscape information items used previously, and selected for use in this study including population-based and individual-based measures. Section 4 includes experimental details of the relevant discussions, and Sect. 5 concludes and outlines future work.

## 2   Related Work

Data-driven and bottom-up approaches – using data analysis – in characterisation of unknown problems have been eased and facilitated with the introduction of big-data, which escalated to dealing with huge number of data instances and features. The search spaces in optimisation domain is known as an-predictable and dynamic processes, where the search space size increases exponentially as the number of dimensions grows. Attempts to characterise such search spaces faces increasing the computational complexity of most learning algorithms - for which the number of input features and sample size are critical parameters. In order to reduce the space and computational complexities, the number of features of a given problem should be reduced [5]. Many predictors benefit from the feature selection process since it reduces overfitting and improves accuracy, among other things [2]. In the literature [12,23], fitness landscape analysis has been shown to be an effective technique for analysing the hardness of an optimization problem by extracting its features. Here, we review some existing approaches that are most closely related to the work proposed in this paper.

In [23], the notion of population evolvability is introduced as an extension of dynamic fitness landscape analysis. The authors assumes a population-based algorithm for sampling, two metrics are then defined for a population of solutions and a set of neighbours from one iteration of the algorithm. Because of the exploration process that occurs during each generation, population evolvability can be a very expensive operation. To avoid a computationally intensive operation, the work suggests that the number of sampled generations must be carefully defined. In [12], a very similar approach has been proposed to apply population evolvability in a hyper-heuristic, named Dynamic Population-Evolvability based Multi-objective Hyper-heuristic. In [21], the authors proposed a differential evolution (DE) with an adaptive mutation operator based on fitness landscape, where a random forest based on fitness landscape is implemented for an adaptive mutation operator that selects DE's mutation strategy online. Similarly, in both [17] and [18], DE embedded with an adaptive operator selection (AOS) mechanism based on landscape analysis for continues functional optimisation problems.

A survey by Malan [13] summarises recent advances in landscape analysis, including a variety of novel landscape analysis approaches and studies on sampling and measure robustness. it drives attention on landscape analysis applications for complex problems and explaining algorithm behaviour, as well as algorithm performance prediction and automated algorithm configuration and selection. In [22], the authors propose a continuous state Markov Decision Process (MDP) model to select crossover operators based on the states during evolutionary search. For AOS, they propose employing a self-organizing neural network. Unlike the Reinforcement Learning technique, which models AOS as a discrete state MDP, their neural network approach is better suited to models of AOS that have continuous states and discrete actions. However, usually MDP based model computationally expensive due to the state space explosion problem.

The majority of these studies have considered population-based landscape metrics to characterise the situation, while some have considered individual-based measures. In this study, we attempt to use both population and individual-based metrics side-by-side and to evaluate the impact of each upon the prediction results in order to consider a wide-range of information aspects in characterisation of search space. In addition, the state-of-the-art literature implemented approaches to solve functional optimisation problems, which are significantly different from combinatorial problems with respect to predictability and characterisation of fitness landscape. We attempt to solve two combinatorial problems (binary in this case), which can be seen more un-predictable in this respect.

## 3   Landscape Features

Fitness landscape analysis provides representative information, which can be used in characterisation of the search space and the position of the problem state in hand. A vast literature has been developed over last few decades that can be utilised in selecting the most representative information. The relevant literature can be found in [8, 15, 16].

Diversity is one of very important aspects of swarms to help characterise the states [6], while Wang et al. [23] discuss evolvability of populations with dynamic landscape structure.

A number of features can be retrieved from state of art literature as listed in tables below Table 1 and Table 2. The population-based metrics – considered as feature– are listed in Table 1 with corresponding calculation details. The first 5 metrics, $\{psd, pfd, pnb, pic, pai\}$, have been collected from [22] and implemented for (i.e. adjusted to) artificial bee colony algorithm (ABC), which is one of very recently developed highly reputed swarm intelligence algorithm [10]. The metrics calculated based on distance measure have been binarised using Hamming distance as in [6] in order to adjust them to binary problem solving. The metrics, $\{pcv, pcr, eap, app\}$, are introduced and proposed in [23] with sound demonstration, while $atn$ is obtained from the trail index used in ABC and utilised to measure/observe the iteration-wise hardness in problem solving. In addition, $pdd$ is picked up from [1] to calculate the distance between two farthest individuals with in a population/swarm.

The literature includes more metrics calculated through local search procedures. However, these kind of features, i.e. metrics, have been left out due to the scope of the study. In fact, it is known that access to preliminary information on search is not easy, hence, we encompass the change in instant search in formation online decision making.

The base notation of population-based features is as follows. Let $P = \{p_i | i = 0, 1, ..., N\}$ be the set of parent solutions and $C = \{c_i | i = 0, 1, ..., N\}$ be the set of children solutions reproduced from $P$, where each solution has $D$ dimensions. Also, let $F^p = \{f_i^p | i = 0, 1, ..., N\}$ be the set of parent fitness values and $F^c = \{f_i^c | i = 0, 1, ..., N\}$ be set of children fitness values. $g_{best}$ represents the best solution has found by so far and $p_{best}$ represents the best solution in the current population.

On the other hand, a number of metrics – features – can be obtained from the auxiliary information of individual solution, which seem to serve efficiently in individual-specific aspects with which the operators can act upon significantly on case basis. The individual-related features are tabulated in Table 2, which are mostly proposed by [22] except $itn$, which is introduced in this study first time. Among these features, the success rate for operator $i$ is calculated with $osr_i = \frac{sc_i}{tc_i}$, where $sr$ is success counter and $tc$ is total usage counter.

## 4    Experimental Results

This experimental results have been collected over multiple runs of an Artificial Bee Colony algorithm bespoke in earlier studies embedded with a pool of operators selected each time a new solution is generated randomly selecting the operators to execute. Each successful move achieved whilst the execution of the algorithm has been picked up as a successful case and labelled accordingly.

**Table 1.** Population-based features

| Feature | Formula |
|---|---|
| Population solution diversity | $psd = \frac{\sum_{i=0}^{n-1} \sum_{j=i+1}^{n} \|p_i - p_j\|}{D^{\frac{n(n-1)}{2}}}$ |
| Population fitness deviation | $pfd = \frac{\sum_{i=0}^{n-1} \sum_{j=i+1}^{n} \|f_i^P - f_j^P\|}{\frac{n(n-1)}{2}}$ |
| Population of new best children | $pnb = \frac{|c_i| f_i^c > f_i^P|}{N}$ |
| Proportion of new improving children | $pic = \frac{|c_i| f_i^c > g_{best}|}{N}$ |
| Proportion of amount of improvements | $pai = \frac{(f_i^c - f_i^P)/f_i^c | f_i^c > f_i^P}{N}$ |
| Proportion of convergence velocity | $pcv = \frac{E[max(F^c) - max(F^P)]}{max(F^P)}$ |
| Proportion of convergence reliability | $pcr = \frac{E[\|x^* - x_t\| - \|x^* - x_{t+1}\|]}{D}$ |
| Evolutionary ability of population | $eap = \sum_{i \in N^*} \frac{\sigma(P)|f^*(P) - f(Cf_i)}{N}$ |
| Evolvability of population | $evp = eap \times pic$ |
| Proportion of average trial number | $atn = \frac{\sum_i^n tn_i}{N}$ |
| The diameter of population | $pdd = max_{i,j \in \{P,C\}} \|p_i - c_i\|$ |

**Table 2.** Individual solution-based features

| Feature | Formula |
|---|---|
| Distance between $g_{best}$ and parent solutions | $idg = \frac{\|x^* - p_i\|}{D}$ |
| Distance between parent and child solutions | $idp = \frac{\|p_i - c_i\|}{D}$ |
| Fitness gap between $g_{best}$ and child solutions | $ifg = (f^{x^*} - f_i^c)/f^{x^*}$ |
| Fitness gap between the parent and the offspring | $ifp = (f_i^c - f_i^P)/f_i^c$ |
| Distance between $p_{best}$ and parent solutions | $idb = \frac{\|p_{best} - p_i\|}{D}$ |
| Distance between $p_{worst}$ and parent solutions | $idw = \frac{\|p_{worst} - p_i\|}{D}$ |
| Proportion of trial number | $itn = \frac{trial_i}{trial_{max}}$ |

Two well-known combinatorial optimisation problems have been considered as test-bed; One-Max [9] as unimodal and Set Union Knapsack (SUKP) [11] as multi-model problems. The size of benchmark problems taken under consideration for One-Max and SUKP are 1000 and 500, respectively, while the maximum number of iterations are 150 and 500, respectively.

The preliminary experimentation demonstrated that the level of hardness and complexity very much depends on the progress of search process, hence, the whole search period is divided into three phases since it is expected that the behaviour of the operators would vary significantly over the time and stage of iterations, relevant analysis is provided in upcoming subsection.

## 4.1   Feature Exploratory Analysis

A set of exploratory analyses are conducted to explore both the relevance of input features as well as their relative importance to the task of operator selection—the latter is discussed further in Sect. 4.2. The tests are evaluated for each phase of the search process, separately. That is, given the set of all input features, $A$, the aim is to examine if a subset $A' \in A$ is associated with the *target* success operators, corresponding to each search phase. The assumption made here is based on whether feature membership for $A'$ is consistent, which in turn can be used to indicate the features most prevalent at predicting *success* operators, per search phase, and if comparable across the two different optimisation problems.

The first test evaluated the strength of linear relationship between input features relative to each search phase, as shown in Fig. 1 for One-Max problem and in Fig. 2 for SUKP.

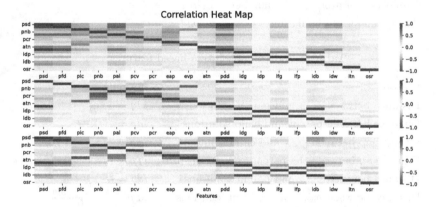

**Fig. 1.** Pearson correlation coefficient matrix for the features applied to One-Max problem. The matrices are ordered top-down per search phase; 1 top and 3 down.

There is clearly apparent linearity – as additionally expected, both positive as well as negative– among different groups of features in both optimisation problems. The strength of relationship furthermore exhibits variability across the different search phases. Generally, whilst relative strength of association can be indicative for feature selection processes, further evaluation of feature importance relative to operator selection is essential, nonetheless. In particular, where membership in $A'$ can be relatively stable across the two optimisation problems, we examine if the selected subset of features can learn the target variables, i.e. *success* operators, associated with each problem, correctly.

Accordingly, for both the One-Max and SUKP problems, the Chi-square $(\chi^2)$ test – a test on whether two variables are related or independent from one another– is conducted to examine the dependency of the response variable (*success* operator) on the set of input features. $\chi^2$ statistic, computed for each feature-class pair, provides a score on the relative dependency between the values

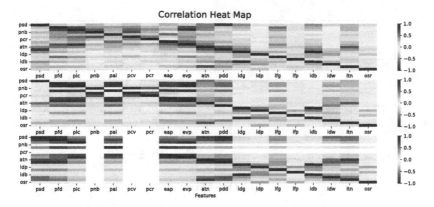

**Fig. 2.** Pearson correlation coefficient matrix for the features applied to SUKP problem. The matrices are ordered top-down per search phase

of each attribute and the different target classes. The attributes of higher values for the $\chi^2$ statistic can be said to have more importance at the task of predicting the target class, i.e. search operator, and usually as a result are selected as the input features in classification tasks.

The resulted ranking of input features relative to both optimisation problems is shown in Fig. 3. Whilst these seem to exhibit differences in importance across the two problems; namely there appears to be a higher number of relevant features in SUKP compared to those in One-Max, there is nonetheless an interesting overlap between both regarding a subset of (dominant) input features {$idp$, $ifp$, $osr$}, as well as an agreement on the relative irrelevance of further features to search operators. This additionally persists across the three search phases corresponding to both examined problems. Although such finding can result primitive – not the least conclusive given the nature of the examined problems –, the resulted similarity can nonetheless be critical to examining potential prospects leading to learning a solution path (or important features) from one problem to another.

## 4.2 Operator Classification

To assess the possible transferability of selected features from one search domain to another, the prediction of the different *success* operators at each search phase corresponding to the two different optimisation problems is subsequently evaluated. The *success* of operators relative to each search problem and phase are shown in Table 3. This provides the setting for a supervised classification task in which problem features are the independent variables and the corresponding *success* operators are the target class.

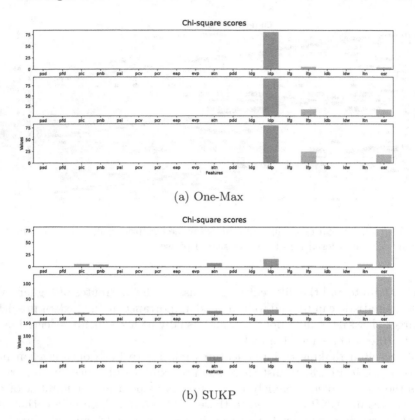

(a) One-Max

(b) SUKP

**Fig. 3.** Chi-square statistic rank for input features on successful search operators. Again, in both (a) and (b), ranking is ordered top-down per search phase.

**Table 3.** Success of operators for One-Max and SUKP search problems.

| Problem | Operator | Phase 1 | Phase 2 | Phase 3 | Mean |
|---------|----------|---------|---------|---------|------|
| One Max | OP 0 | 306 | 375 | 357 | 346.00 |
| | OP 1 | 234 | 218 | 235 | 229.00 |
| | OP 2 | 304 | 405 | 456 | 388.33 |
| | OP 3 | 323 | 328 | 316 | 322.33 |
| SUKP | OP 0 | 104 | 200 | 245 | 183.00 |
| | OP 1 | 494 | 150 | 89 | 244.33 |
| | OP 2 | 1397 | 1368 | 1487 | 1,417.33 |
| | OP 3 | 916 | 777 | 649 | 780.67 |

Three classifiers are applied to predict the *success* operators; a multilayer perceptron (MLP) with one hidden layer (feedforward ANN with 'adam' solver), Support Vector Machine (SVM) classifier with radial basis function (rbf) kernel and a Random Forest classifiers of size 200. All models have been used in classification tasks very widely for decades, and the particular choice for RF and SVM was additionally due to their ability to provide explicit feature importance ranking alongside their prediction, which we aim to utilise in the proposed hypothesis. We report the accuracy score as the prediction measure of accuracy in Table 4.

**Table 4.** The accuracy results for both problem types achieved by machine learning approaches across 3 phases

|         | One Max | | | SUKP | | |
|---------|------|------|------|------|------|------|
|         | RF | SVM | MLP | RF | SVM | MLP |
| Phase 1 | 0.79 | 0.52 | 0.70 | 0.71 | 0.62 | 0.68 |
| Phase 2 | 0.85 | 0.63 | 0.73 | 0.79 | 0.72 | 0.75 |
| Phase 3 | 0.84 | 0.65 | 0.71 | 0.83 | 0.77 | 0.80 |
| Mean    | 0.83 | 0.60 | 0.71 | 0.77 | 0.71 | 0.74 |

Interestingly, the performance of the classifiers on both optimisation problems is relatively comparable. With the exception of SVM on One-Max which seems to be underperforming that on SUKP, the predictability of success operators from both individual as well as population domain features is consistent. It should be noted that the reported performance of the three classifiers can be tuned for further optimisation, which we aim at providing in a further study. In this study, however, the aim is to examine whether predictability of *success* operators can be achieved with a subset of input features learnt in different search problem(s). In such a way the relative importance of input features for the classification tasks are computed and compared; the weighted coefficients of feature vectors in the SVM classifier as well as the importance of features from the resulted Random Forest classifier, normalised across the 200 Decision Trees between 0 and 1. The results are shown in Fig. 4 for the One-Max problem and Fig. 5 for SUKP.

Once again the results show promising findings as a subset of features can be seen to have similar relative importance across both search problems. In fact this emphasises the suggestion, as observed earlier in the Chi-sqaure test results, that there seems to be a subset of *effective* features, like $A'$, to the task of operator selection that can be transferable from one problem to another. Worth mentioning that in both Fig. 4 and Fig. 5, the relative feature importance is computed for the whole set of features, as the SVM considers weighing all input attributes, and the RF calculates class impurity – relative Shannon entropy– weighted by the probability of reaching the target class (*success* operator) corresponding to all features as these are re-sampled across 200 trees, and subsequently their scores normalised. That is to say that in selecting the subset of *effective* features, their relative importance should be considered rather than the values assigned to them.

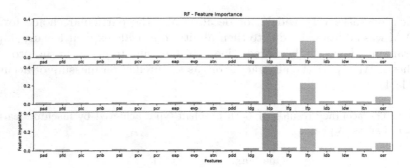

(a) Feature importance calculated with Random Forest

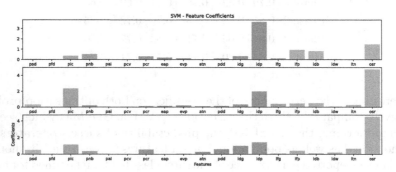

(b) Features coefficients calculated with SVM

**Fig. 4.** Feature importance ranking for One-Max problem.

The assessment on what specific features are most prevalent to the *success* operator selection, and why can be 'overenthusiastic' at this stage, especially so as this would require extensive characterisation of both search problems, which will be evaluated further in a later study. Here, however, the argument on finding a transferable $A'$ from one search problem to another seems plausible. For this, the extent of predictability (solution quality) and robustness as features are reduced and transferred across different search domains should be examined further.

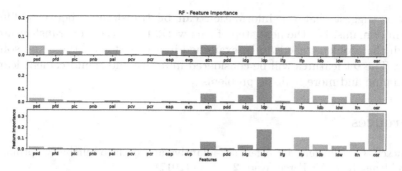

(a) Features importance calculated with Random Forest

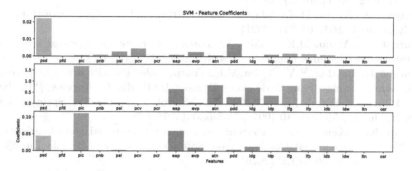

(b) Feature coefficients calculated with SVM

**Fig. 5.** Feature importance ranking for SUKP problem.

## 5    Conclusions and Future Work

This paper presents an exploratory and a predictive analysis in order to reveal the impacts and domination of a set of features considered for characterisation of search spaces in optimisation domain. The idea is to identify the set of the most impactful and prominent features that best represent a problem state and its standing within its neighbourhood so that the best fitting neighbourhood function among many alternatives can be selected to generate the next problem state avoiding local optima for higher efficiency in search process. A swarm intelligence algorithm – artificial bee colony – has been used with a pool of neighbourhood functions, i.e. operators, to solve two different types of combinatorial optimisation problems utilising an adaptive operator selection scheme. The set of most prominent features are elicited through a rank of weights using statistical and machine learning methods. The analysis demonstrated that a set of features mostly including individual features are found to be more discriminative than those of population-based metrics.

The interesting preliminary outcome of the study is that the most effective features have been mostly the same even if the problem domain has changed.

This can suggest that the information can be transferable between different problem domains. For the next step of this work, the success of transfer learning through the problems needs to be examined in terms of robustness and solution quality. The set features will be considered in active and reinforcement learning for dynamic and more realistic problems.

# References

1. Anescu, G., Ulmeanu, P.: A fast self-adaptive approach to reliability optimization problems. Rev. Air Force Acad. **2**, 23–30 (2017)
2. Chandrashekar, G., Sahin, F.: A survey on feature selection methods. Comput. Electr. Eng. **40**(1), 16–28 (2014)
3. Durgut, R., Aydin, M.E.: Adaptive binary artificial bee colony algorithm. Appl. Soft Comput. **101**, 107054 (2021)
4. Durgut, R., Aydin, M.E., Rakib, A.: Transfer learning for operator selection: a reinforcement learning approach. Algorithms **15**(1), 24 (2022)
5. Durgut, R., Baydilli, Y.Y., Aydin, M.E.: Feature selection with artificial bee colony algorithms for classifying Parkinson's diseases. In: Iliadis, L., Angelov, P.P., Jayne, C., Pimenidis, E. (eds.) EANN 2020. PINNS, vol. 2, pp. 338–351. Springer, Cham (2020). https://doi.org/10.1007/978-3-030-48791-1_26
6. Erwin, K., Engelbrecht, A.: Diversity measures for set-based meta-heuristics. In: 2020 7th International Conference on Soft Computing & Machine Intelligence (ISCMI), pp. 45–50. IEEE (2020)
7. Fialho, Á.: Adaptive operator selection for optimization. Ph.D. thesis, Université Paris Sud-Paris XI (2010)
8. Fragata, I., Blanckaert, A., Louro, M.A.D., Liberles, D.A., Bank, C.: Evolution in the light of fitness landscape theory. Trends Ecol. Evol. **34**(1), 69–82 (2019)
9. Goëffon, A., Lardeux, F.: Optimal one-max strategy with dynamic island models. In: 2011 IEEE 23rd International Conference on Tools with Artificial Intelligence, pp. 485–488. IEEE (2011)
10. Karaboga, D., Gorkemli, B., Ozturk, C., Karaboga, N.: A comprehensive survey: artificial bee colony (abc) algorithm and applications. Artif. Intell. Rev. **42**(1), 21–57 (2014)
11. Lin, G., Guan, J., Li, Z., Feng, H.: A hybrid binary particle swarm optimization with tabu search for the set-union knapsack problem. Exp. Syst. Appl. **135**, 201–211 (2019)
12. Macias-Escobar, T.E., Cruz-Reyes, L., Dorronsoro, B., Fraire-Huacuja, H., Rangel-Valdez, N., Gómez-Santillán, C.: Application of population evolvability in a hyper-heuristic for dynamic multi-objective optimization. Technol. Econ. Dev. Econ. **25**(5), 1–28 (2019)
13. Malan, K.M.: A survey of advances in landscape analysis for optimisation. Algorithms **14**(2) (2021). https://www.mdpi.com/1999-4893/14/2/40
14. Nyce, C.: Predictive analytics white paper, SL: American institute for chartered property casualty underwriters. Insurance Institute of America p. 1 (2007)
15. Ochoa, G., Malan, K.: Recent advances in fitness landscape analysis. In: Proceedings of the Genetic and Evolutionary Computation Conference Companion, pp. 1077–1094 (2019)
16. Pitzer, E., Affenzeller, M.: A comprehensive survey on fitness landscape analysis. Recent Advances in Intelligent Engineering Systems pp. 161–191 (2012)

17. Sallam, K.M., Elsayed, S.M., Sarker, R.A., Essam, D.L.: Landscape-based adaptive operator selection mechanism for differential evolution. Inf. Sci. **418**, 383–404 (2017)
18. Sallam, K.M., Elsayed, S.M., Sarker, R.A., Essam, D.L.: Landscape-assisted multi-operator differential evolution for solving constrained optimization problems. Exp. Syst. Appl. **162** (2020)
19. Sotoudeh-Anvari, A., Hafezalkotob, A.: A bibliography of metaheuristics-review from 2009 to 2015. Int. J. Knowl.-Based Intell. Eng. Syst. **22**(1), 83–95 (2018)
20. Sun, G., Yang, B., Yang, Z., Xu, G.: An adaptive differential evolution with combined strategy for global numerical optimization. Soft Comput. **24**(9), 6277–6296 (2020)
21. Tan, Z., Li, K., Wang, Y.: Differential evolution with adaptive mutation strategy based on fitness landscape analysis. Inf. Sci. **549**, 142–163 (2021)
22. Teng, T.-H., Handoko, S.D., Lau, H.C.: Self-organizing neural network for adaptive operator selection in evolutionary search. In: Festa, P., Sellmann, M., Vanschoren, J. (eds.) LION 2016. LNCS, vol. 10079, pp. 187–202. Springer, Cham (2016). https://doi.org/10.1007/978-3-319-50349-3_13
23. Wang, M., Li, B., Zhang, G., Yao, X.: Population evolvability: dynamic fitness landscape analysis for population-based metaheuristic algorithms. IEEE Trans. Evol. Comput. **22**(4), 550–563 (2017)

# Boosting Feature-Aware Network for Salient Object Detection

Jianwei Zheng(ID), Yubin Gu, Yuchao Feng, Jinshan Xu, and Meiyu Zhang(✉)

Zhejiang University of Technology, Hangzhou 310023, China
zmy@zjut.edu.cn

**Abstract.** Deep convolutional neural networks have demonstrated competitive performance in salient object detection. To capture more precise saliency maps, recent approaches mainly concentrate on aggregating deep features from convolutional networks and introducing edge supervision for a guarantee of compact targets. Though significant progress has been accomplished, the problems of low-contrast by targets against backgrounds and the inconsistency of object size are still challenging to tackle. To relieve these troubles, we propose a boosting feature-aware network (BFANet) following a dual-stream architecture, including an object sub-network for salient objects detection and a boundary guidance sub-network supervised by enhanced labels for edge detection. Specifically, for the interesting yet low-confidence areas, we mold a boosting feature-aware module (BFAM) hammering at suppressing the background while highlighting the weak features. In addition, considering the different responses of channels to output, we present a weighted aggregation block (WAB) to strengthen the significant channel features and recalibrate channel-wise feature responses. Extensive experiments on five benchmark datasets demonstrate that our proposed model outperforms most other state-of-the-art methods.

**Keywords:** Salient object detection · Multi-level feature · Information fusion · Edge supervision

## 1 Introduction

Salient object detection (SOD), as a usual preprocessing step of most computer vision tasks such as visual tracking, aims at capturing and locating the most visually attractive components in the visual media. In SOD, the main obstacles lie in the low contrast of salient objects against backgrounds and the complicacy of the scenes. Most conventional methods adopt hand-crafted features to predict the saliency area. Though clear saliency maps can be achieved from these schemes, the applicability is limited to scenes with desired backgrounds and evident objects. Recently, the study of SOD is seeing a paradigm shift, as CNN-based methods push aside the hand-crafted models. Many CNN-based methods [12, 20] have achieved compelling performance using different feature mining and

E. Pimenidis et al. (Eds.): ICANN 2022, LNCS 13532, pp. 14–26, 2022.
https://doi.org/10.1007/978-3-031-15937-4_2

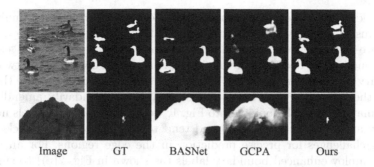

Image          GT          BASNet          GCPA          Ours

**Fig. 1.** Some comparative examples of different methods.

fusion mechanisms. Unfortunately, due to the convolutional and pooling layers of deep networks, CNNs may destroy the boundary details or omit valuable information of saliency objects. Furthermore, features extracted by deep networks may not agree appropriately with SOD task, resulting in inaccurate non-salient pixels or missed target regions, especially in complex scenes with low-contrast and tiny objects. Recently, more methods [2, 21] consider edges as supervision to decorate models. Though significant improvement has been achieved, the performance is not steady, especially when the pixel distribution of edge regions is sparse. Additionally, making deeper use of high-level semantic information is also an important offshoot to capture saliency objects. To this end, different decoders have been designed to handle high-level features, with significant progress being made. Nevertheless, the existing approaches do not fully capitalize on the elaborate characteristics of different levels and ignore the relationship between them, resulting in the tricky detection of tiny objects and low confidence regions.

Figure 1 presents some comparative results of different methods in complex scenarios. As shown, for the low-contrast and tiny objects (e.g., Fig. 1, row 2), two state-of-the-art (SOTA) approaches, e.g., BASNet [11] and GCPA [1], are unable to obtain correct results suffering from the negative influence of misleading background. Similarly, for the multiple salient objects in the first row of Fig. 1, only ghost shadows in the designated location can be detected by these two SOTAs.

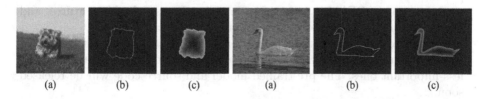

(a)          (b)          (c)          (a)          (b)          (c)

**Fig. 2.** (a) is the images, (b) represents the pure edge labels, and (c) means the enhanced edge labels.

To tackle the problems mentioned above, designing an effective multi-level features fusion strategy is of importance. In this paper, we propose a boosting feature-aware network using a dual-stream architecture and an "encoder-decoder" mode. The overall model mainly consists of an object sub-network and a boundary guidance sub-network. While the former is used to capture the main body of the salient targets, the latter is capable of secondarily amending the saliency maps. By deeply looking into Fig. 1, we observe that the pixels near the boundary are unevenly distributed and tend to blend in with the background, incurring challenges for precise prediction in the edge regions. For an alleviation, we employ enhanced boundary labels (as shown in Fig. 2(c)) to supervise the boundary sub-network, by which more attention would be drawn to pixels around the edge regions rather than the pure edge labels. Besides, in the face of variable size and the number of targets, approaches with coarse fusion [2,17] strategies are not competent to obtain satisfying results. Therefore, it is necessary to develop effective feature fusion strategies to improve the robustness of models. On this purpose, in this paper, we develop a novel multi-level multi-scale features fusion module, namely boosting feature-aware module (BFAM). Specifically, as shown in Fig. 3, three BFAMs are used in the object sub-network refining the mainbody features. Functionally, BFAMs integrate and refine multi-level features from a global perspective, improving information representation to detect hard-to-find cues and suppress interference features. Subsequently, a weighted aggregation block (WAB) is deployed to reweight each feature channel, which highlights the valuable features for further enhancing global awareness. Finally, the output features of the two sub-networks are fused to obtain more convincing saliency maps. Since the two sub-network tasks have exclusive properties, we adopt a mixed loss strategy for training. To sum up, the main contributions of this paper are as follows:

- We design a novel model involving two sub-networks, i.e., boundary guidance sub-network and object sub-network, as well as a novel multi-level features fusion scheme. The boundary sub-network is supervised by enhanced boundary labels, detecting edge regions and providing more contextual information. The object sub-network is proposed to discover the intrinsic features and predict the main saliency maps.
- To remedy the limited receptive field inherited by typical convolution and pooling operation, we propose a novel multi-level multi-scale features fusion module, namely BFAM, which refines and heightens valuable features, and boosts feature-aware to detect trickily predictable features.
- We also introduce a weighted aggregation block that can reweight the multi-channel features, emphasizing the most valuable features and penalizing the less important ones. The pre-trained model and source code will be released soon.

## 2   Related Work

Many methods for detecting salient objects in an image have been proposed in recent years. Manual features such as contrast, boundary background and others were used in the early approaches to predict salient maps using bottom-up patterns. Due to the limitations of conventional methods in dealing with complex situations, recent CNN-based methods have shown great potential, greatly surpassing early methods. Long et al. [9] firstly proposed a fully convolution network (FCN) to predict the semantic label of each pixel. More recently, most attempts for pixel-wise saliency detection have been conducted. Wang et al. [14] designed a recurrent FCN structure for saliency detection. Hou et al. [4] proposed a short-connection based on HED [18] to integrate multi-level features to address the scale-space issue. And in [19], authors aggregated multi-level features into multiple resolutions and then assembled these feature maps by a bi-directional aggregation approach. Inspired by the above proposed methods, effective fusion of multi-level multi-scale features is very important for SOD, so we propose a novel fusion strategy in this paper. In addition, researchers have found that introducing object edge information helps the SOD task, so relevant methods [6,10,13,21] employing edge information are starting to surface. Different from most other methods that employ edge cues, we employ the enhanced edge label to supervise the edge sub-network and design the decoding module for the characteristics of edge detection.

## 3   Proposed Model

### 3.1   Overall Framework

The overall framework of our BFANet is shown in Fig. 3, which mainly involves a dual-stream decoder structure including an object branch and a boundary guidance branch. The backbone of the encoder is implemented by Resnet-50 [3] for multi-level features extraction. Note Res-1 has relatively high resolution and contributes little to the final performance, so we omit this block in decoder for computation save. Four-level features generated from Res-2 to Res-5 are sufficient for our study and denoted as $R_2$ to $R_5$, respectively. These four level features are then respectively transferred to the boundary and object sub-network. The object sub-network further consists of two modules, i.e., BFAMs and WABs, boosting feature awareness by integrating multi-level multi-scale features. Note BFAMs hammer at further refining input features and is able to compensate for the limited information recovery capability of common CNNs. The output of each BFAM is passed to the corresponding WAB that recalibrates channel-wise feature responses. With the upsampling operation, the outputs of the consecutive WABs are summed and the last features are fused with the features generated from the boundary guidance sub-network. Finally, the saliency map is obtained through two consecutive $3 \times 3$ convolution layers.

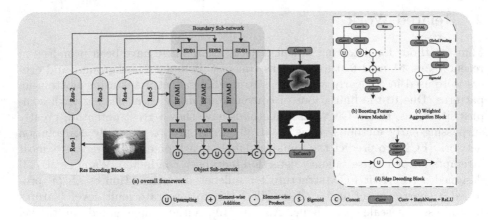

**Fig. 3.** (a) is the overall architecture of our model, (b) represents BFAM, and (c) is WAB in object sub-network. (d) means EDB in boundary sub-network.

## 3.2 Edge Guidance Sub-network

Introducing edge information helps to provide more contextual information, yet the practical performance depends heavily on the quality of the given boundary maps. Specifically, using pure edge labels as [11] may be suboptimal due to the negligence of adjacent pixels surrounding the edge contour. In other words, not only the pixels on the edge line but also the nearby pixels would contribute positively to the saliency detection. To this end, we generate enhanced boundary labels by processing masks using a distance transformation algorithm like [15], rendering a more balanced pixel distribution and drawing more attention to the edge regions. Note the crude fusion methods, such as simple concatenation or upsampling, might introduce impurity features and would further incur learning errors. In view of these points, we devise an edge decoding block (EDB, as shown in Fig. 3(d)) with skip connection that integrates multi-level multi-scale features including the low-level features with detailed information and the high-level features with global attention information. Such an exquisite design can make the edge branch contain more detailed features and semantic features, learn to obtain a higher-quality edge map, and then improve the detection quality of the object branch. Intuitively, this block promotes a better feature representation of boundaries. The output of each EDB can be formulated as:

$$R_i^c = conv_1(conv_3(R_i)), \quad i = 2, 3, 4, 5, \tag{1}$$

$$EDB_i = \begin{cases} conv_3(Up(R_5^c) \oplus R_4^c), & i = 1 \\ conv_3(Up(EDB_1) \oplus R_3^c), & i = 2 \\ conv_3(Up(EDB_2) \oplus R_2^c), & i = 3 \end{cases} \tag{2}$$

where $conv_3$ is a $3 \times 3$ convolution layer. For simplicity, the parameters in the convolution operation, the activation function and the batch normalization operations are omitted in formulations. $Up(*)$ is bilinear interpolation operation aiming at up-sampling $*$ to matched size, and $\oplus$ is element-wise addition. $R_i^c$ represents the compressed backbone feature from $R_i$. Finally, edge predictions are obtained by $EDB_3$ through a $3 \times 3$ convolution layer and a sigmoid function, followed by a resizing operation to the initial image size.

### 3.3   Object Sub-network

Multi-level multi-scale features fusion is a natural idea since low-level features contain more detailed information and high-level features hold more semantic information. However, owing to the inappropriate feature fusion schemes and short-range dependencies originating from common convolution and pooling layers, existing methods may generate internal discontinuities and further lead to erroneous or missed predictions. To resolve these issues, we design two effective modules at the object decoding stage.

**Boosting Feature-Aware Module:** To adapt to the changing conditions, effectively fusing multi-level multi-scale features and making full use of features with different attributes are of importance. However, convolutional blocks are conventionally stacked layer-by-layer, which may not serve the purpose. To this end, we build the BFAM module (as shown in Fig. 3(b)) to effectively integrate multi-level features which can refine and heighten features for feature awareness boosting by utilizing the multiplication and addition operator. In detail, the BFAM multiplies high-level features having more semantic information and low-level features having more detailed information to refine similar feature information, instead of merging the low-level features directly. This operation can improve the response of valuable features and reduce noise feature interference. Furthermore, multi-level features have complementary information, and we add them together to enrich the feature map. Finally, the added feature is passed through two convolution layers to improve the learning ability. By doing so, it is possible to perceive both the full view and the accurate positioning of objects. We call this process as boosting multi-level features awareness. Each output of BFAM can be formulated as follows:

$$M_i' = \begin{cases} R_4 \oplus \{Up(conv_1(R_5)) \odot R_4\} \oplus Up(conv_1(R_5)) & i = 1 \\ R_3 \oplus \{Up(conv_1(M_1)) \odot R_3\} \oplus Up(conv_1(M_1)) & i = 2 \\ R_2 \oplus \{Up(conv_1(M_2)) \odot R_2\} \oplus Up(conv_1(M_2)) & i = 3 \end{cases}, \quad (3)$$

$$M_i = conv_1(conv_3(M_i')), \quad (4)$$

where $\odot$ is the element-wise product and $R_i$ is the output of the corresponding backbone block. Besides, $conv_1$ is a convolution layer with $1 \times 1$ kernel size for changing the number of feature channels.

**Weighted Aggregation Block:** For the purpose of adapting to the fluctuations of object shape and size, existing methods tend to sum multi-scale features along the channel dimension for final predictions. However, the high-level features may not be fully activated and beneficial to object recovery. Similar as Ref. [5], the WABs, as shown in Fig. 3(c), are designed to aggregate the multi-scale side-outputs from BFAMs and transfer the more globally representations to high-level layers respectively. In each WAB, global average pooling is used firstly to aggregate the global semantic information, followed by two $1 \times 1$ convolution layers with different nonlinearity activation functions, estimating layer relevance and generating weights along different channels. The learned weights are then multiplied by the outputs to produce more representative features.

### 3.4 Loss Function

Inspired by BASNet [11], we adopt a mixed loss scheme that engages IoU and BCE to train our model, where BCE is used to maintain a smooth gradient of the loss function and IoU is employed to draw more attention to the structure of objects. Since the two terms are functionally different and possess their individual properties, we jointly use both of these two for generating the loss of object sub-network. However, for the boundary sub-network, we only adopt BCE to learn the loss since the enhanced boundary labels are not binary, which is required by the IoU metric. Specifically, the definition of BCE is as follows:

$$\ell_{bce} = -\sum_{i=1}^{N} [G(i) \log(P(i)) + (1 - G(i)) \log(1 - P(i))], \tag{5}$$

where $G(i)$ denotes the label of the pixel in $i$ and $P(i)$ is the predicted maps. $N$ is the number of pixels. Besides, the IoU loss can be defined as:

$$\ell_{iou} = 1 - \frac{\sum\limits_{i=1}^{N} [G(i) * P(i)]}{\sum\limits_{i=1}^{N} [G(i) + P(i) - G(i) * P(i)]}. \tag{6}$$

In addition, the importance of the two sub-networks is intuitively different, so we use a parameter to balance the two sub-losses:

$$L_{total} = \alpha \ell_{bce}(E,B) + (1-\alpha) [\ell_{bce}(P,G) + \ell_{iou}(P,G)], \tag{7}$$

where $E$ denotes the edge label and $B$ represents the predicted boundary map. $G$ means the ground-truth and $P$ is the predicted saliency map. $\alpha$ is set as 0.3 at the training stage.

## 4     Experimental Results

### 4.1     Datasets and Evaluation Metrics

We employ five benchmark datasets, including DUTS, ECSSD, DUT-OMRON, HKU-IS, and PASCAL-S, to evaluate the effectiveness of our proposal. For numerical comparison, we use two metrics that are widely adopted for quality investigation of resultant maps, including the Mean Absolute Error (MAE), the max F-measure (maxF, $\beta^2$ is set as 0.3 for all comparison models). In addition, we also draw the Precision-Recall (PR) curves to visually show the cross-comparison of performance.

## 4.2  Implementation Details

Note the DUTS dataset has been pre-split into DUT-TR for training and DUT-TE for testing. To investigate the generalization of all competing approaches, DUTS-TR is consistently used for model optimization. For better robustness, certain augmentation strategy is also adopted. The ResNet-50 pre-trained on ImageNet is used as backbone, among which we use only Res-1 to Res-5 for our model. Linear decay, warm-up strategies, and stochastic gradient descent optimizer are used at the training stage. Weight decay and Momentum are set to 0.0005 and 0.9, respectively. Training batchsize is set to 32. We utilize the Pytorch and Nvidia TITAN V to implement our model. During testing, our model takes an average of 0.02 s to process per input image.

## 4.3  Comparison with the State-of-the-Arts

We compare the results of our method with 11 state-of-the-art methods, including GCPANet [1], CANet [12], LDF [15], ITSD [22], MLMS [16], BASNet [11], CPD-R [17], Pool Net [7], AFNet [2], SAMNet [8], and PAGRNet [20]. For a fair comparison, all the saliency images participating in the comparison are provided by the original authors or computed by their released source codes. The evaluation metrics are also computed with the same code.

**Quantitative Comparisons:** The comparison results are listed in Table 2, among which the best results are highlighted in boldface and the second-best results are styled in italics. As shown in the table, our proposed model ranks first almost in all cells. Although LDF achieves the highest value in terms of maxF on DUTS-TE and ECSSD, its improvement over our model is marginal and it lags behind our model in all other cases. Furthermore, we also calculate the parameter quantities and GFLOPs of each approach and the comparison result shows that our model has certain advantages in both. The PR curves are shown in Fig. 4 for an intuitive comparison, which also confirms the superiority of our model.

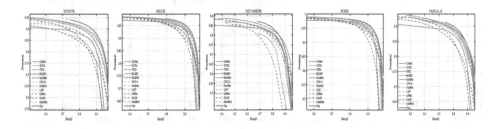

**Fig. 4.** PR curves for all compared methods on five benchmark datasets.

To further validate the performance of our method specifically for small object detection, we conduct the experiments on three selected sub-datasets on DUTS-TE. Specifically, the number of positive pixels of the label accounted respectively for 30%, 20% and 10% of the total image pixels. The resultant metrics are shown in Table 1, which again demonstrate the better performance of our method and verify the elaborate design of BFAM, WAB and the edge sub-network.

**Table 1.** Comparison amongst our method, GCPA and LDF on the three sub-datasets of DUTS-TE.

| Positive pixel ratio | Methods | | | | | |
|---|---|---|---|---|---|---|
| | Our | | GCPA | | LDF | |
| | MAE | maxF | MAE | maxF | MAE | maxF |
| ≤30% | 0.029 | 0.892 | 0.035 | 0.880 | 0.031 | 0.890 |
| ≤20% | 0.026 | 0.887 | 0.033 | 0.873 | 0.027 | 0.887 |
| ≤10% | 0.023 | 0.866 | 0.029 | 0.847 | 0.025 | 0.863 |

**Visual Comparisons:** For visual comparison, the qualitative results on several example images are given in Fig. 5. We select various scenes for this experiments, including a light-colored cat blended in a bright window and a dark curtain, an inconspicuous car located at the bottom margin, a view of man's back in complex surroundings, a huge target almost filling the image, and a tiny window far away. It can be easily observed that our proposed method not only locates and detects the saliency objects clearly, but also well restrains the background noises in these scenes.

**Table 2.** Numerical metrics of all competing models. The best outcome is styled in bold, while the second-best outcome is styled in italics. The higher the maxF, the better; the lower the MAE, the better.

| Method | Params (M) | GFLOPs | Datasets | | | | | | | | | |
|---|---|---|---|---|---|---|---|---|---|---|---|---|
| | | | DUTS-TE | | ECSSD | | HKU-IS | | PASCAL-S | | DUT-O | |
| | | | maxF | MAE | maxF | MAE | maxF | MAE | maxF | MAE | maxF | MAE |
| Our | 32.12 | 9.28 | .897 | **.033** | .948 | **.033** | **.942** | **.026** | **.875** | **.059** | **.830** | **.049** |
| CANet | - | - | .876 | .044 | .938 | .044 | .930 | .037 | .866 | .072 | .810 | .058 |
| SAMNet | 1.33 | 0.6 | .836 | .058 | .928 | .050 | .915 | .045 | .839 | .090 | .803 | .065 |
| GCPANet | 34.76 | 67.06 | .888 | .038 | .948 | .035 | .938 | .031 | .869 | .061 | .812 | .056 |
| LDF | 25.15 | 8.25 | **.898** | .034 | **.950** | .034 | .939 | .027 | .873 | .059 | .820 | .051 |
| ITSD | 26.47 | 12.59 | .883 | .041 | .947 | .034 | .934 | .031 | .870 | .065 | .821 | .061 |
| MLMS | 72.24 | - | .843 | .045 | .882 | .038 | .920 | .034 | .869 | .067 | .780 | .055 |
| BASNet | 87.06 | 127.4 | .860 | .048 | .942 | .037 | .928 | .032 | .854 | .075 | .805 | .056 |
| CPD-R | 47.85 | 14.67 | .865 | .043 | .887 | .037 | .925 | .034 | .859 | .070 | .797 | .056 |
| PoolNet | 68.26 | 49.56 | .880 | .040 | .944 | .039 | .933 | .032 | .863 | .074 | .808 | .056 |
| AFNet | 34.3 | - | .863 | .046 | .935 | .042 | .923 | .036 | .863 | .070 | .797 | .057 |
| PAGRNet | - | - | .854 | .055 | .927 | .061 | .918 | .048 | .847 | .089 | .771 | .071 |

## 4.4    Ablation Studies

In this subsection, we explore the effect of different parts in the proposed model over two datasets and show the results under different settings. The quantitative and qualitative results are given in Table 3 and Fig. 6, respectively.

**Effectiveness of Enhanced Boundary Label:** Introducing edge information is helpful for salient object detection. However, using pure edge labels is considered to be insufficient since it neglects the positive roles of the pixels near the boundary. To verify this point, we use the backbone network bonded with only object sub-network (without BFAMs and WABs) as a baseline. The results in the first three rows of Table 3(a,b,c) show an incremental trend, which demonstrates the superiority of enhanced boundary labels over pure edge labels. Moreover, we have employed the enhanced edge labels for other supervised learning model such as EGNet [21], the results show that MAE on the DUTS-TE has dropped by 6.51%. In addition, MAE decreased by an average of 5.75% on LDF [15].

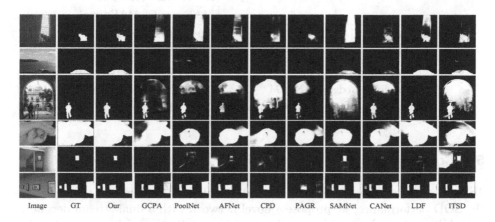

**Fig. 5.** Visual comparisons with some other models.

**Effectiveness of BFAM and WAB:** By sequentially adding BFAM and WAB, the upward performance can be easily observed from Table 3(c), (d) and (e), which further verifies the positive behaviors of our proposed modules. The saliency maps presented in Fig. 6 also confirm the numerical results. Evidently, our final model produces results with more smooth contours and complete targets, compared with broken edges and missed pixels generated by other competitors. These results demonstrate that our proposed method is more effective for fusing multi-scale and multi-level features information and boosting feature awareness.

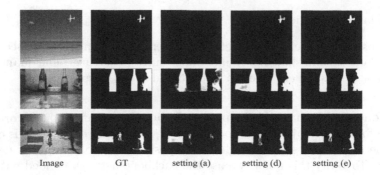

Image     GT     setting (a)     setting (d)     setting (e)

**Fig. 6.** Comparison of visual results for different model settings. Settings (a), (d) and (e) correspond to the model settings in Table 3, respectively.

**Table 3.** The quantitative results. "†" denotes using enhanced boundary labels.

| Model settings | Datasets | | | |
|---|---|---|---|---|
| | DUTS-TE | | HKU-IS | |
| | MAE | avgF | MAE | avgF |
| (a) Baseline | 0.044 | 0.796 | 0.033 | 0.895 |
| (b) Baseline + edge | 0.041 | 0.804 | 0.033 | 0.899 |
| (c) Baseline + edge† | 0.039 | 0.820 | 0.031 | 0.907 |
| (d) Baseline + edge† + BFAM | 0.035 | 0.837 | 0.028 | 0.915 |
| (e) Baseline + edge† + BFAM + WAB | 0.033 | 0.850 | 0.026 | 0.920 |

## 5 Conclusion

To cope with the cases of low-contrast and complicated background that plagues the SOD performance, we propose a novel network with a dual-stream decoder, containing a boundary guidance sub-network as well as an object sub-network. Supervised by the enhanced boundary labels, boundary guidance sub-network learns edge information that provides more contextual information for precise detection. In addition, to mine multi-scale multi-level features and promote weak features for detecting more accurate regions, we propose BFAM that fuses cross-features effectively in the object sub-network. Finally, different from other models that simply merge the half-produced maps, we introduce WAB to reweight each channel for highlighting the more valuable features. Extensive experimental results demonstrate that our method achieves the SOTA performance, especially in complex cases with tiny or inconspicuous objects.

**Acknowledgements.** This work is supported in part by the National Key Research and Development Program of China under Grant 2018YFE0126100, in part by the National Natural Science Foundation of China under the Grant No. 62073293 and

61602413, and in part by the Open Research Projects of Zhejiang Laboratory under Grant 2019KD0AD01/007.

# References

1. Chen, Z., Xu, Q., Cong, R., Huang, Q.: Global context-aware progressive aggregation network for salient object detection. In: Proceedings of the AAAI Conference on Artificial Intelligence, vol. 34, pp. 10599–10606 (2020)
2. Feng, M., Lu, H., Ding, E.: Attentive feedback network for boundary-aware salient object detection. In: Proceedings of the IEEE/CVF Conference on Computer Vision and Pattern Recognition, pp. 1623–1632 (2019)
3. He, K., Zhang, X., Ren, S., Sun, J.: Deep residual learning for image recognition. In: Proceedings of the IEEE Conference on Computer Vision and Pattern Recognition, pp. 770–778 (2016)
4. Hou, Q., Cheng, M.M., Hu, X., Borji, A., Tu, Z., Torr, P.H.: Deeply supervised salient object detection with short connections. In: Proceedings of the IEEE Conference on Computer Vision and Pattern Recognition, pp. 3203–3212 (2017)
5. Hu, J., Shen, L., Sun, G.: Squeeze-and-excitation networks. In: Proceedings of the IEEE Conference on Computer Vision and Pattern Recognition, pp. 7132–7141 (2018)
6. Li, X., Yang, F., Cheng, H., Liu, W., Shen, D.: Contour knowledge transfer for salient object detection. In: Ferrari, V., Hebert, M., Sminchisescu, C., Weiss, Y. (eds.) ECCV 2018. LNCS, vol. 11219, pp. 370–385. Springer, Cham (2018). https://doi.org/10.1007/978-3-030-01267-0_22
7. Liu, J.J., Hou, Q., Cheng, M.M., Feng, J., Jiang, J.: A simple pooling-based design for real-time salient object detection. In: Proceedings of the IEEE/CVF Conference on Computer Vision and Pattern Recognition, pp. 3917–3926 (2019)
8. Liu, Y., Zhang, X.Y., Bian, J.W., Zhang, L., Cheng, M.M.: SAMNet: stereoscopically attentive multi-scale network for lightweight salient object detection. IEEE Trans. Image Process. **30**, 3804–3814 (2021)
9. Long, J., Shelhamer, E., Darrell, T.: Fully convolutional networks for semantic segmentation. In: Proceedings of the IEEE Conference on Computer Vision and Pattern Recognition, pp. 3431–3440 (2015)
10. Luo, Z., Mishra, A., Achkar, A., Eichel, J., Li, S., Jodoin, P.M.: Non-local deep features for salient object detection. In: Proceedings of the IEEE Conference on Computer Vision and Pattern Recognition, pp. 6609–6617 (2017)
11. Qin, X., Zhang, Z., Huang, C., Gao, C., Dehghan, M., Jagersand, M.: Basnet: boundary-aware salient object detection. In: Proceedings of the IEEE/CVF Conference on Computer Vision and Pattern Recognition, pp. 7479–7489 (2019)
12. Ren, Q., Lu, S., Zhang, J., Hu, R.: Salient object detection by fusing local and global contexts. IEEE Trans. Multim. **23**, 1442–1453 (2020)
13. Tan, Z., Hua, Y., Gu, X.: Salient object detection with edge recalibration. In: Farkaš, I., Masulli, P., Wermter, S. (eds.) ICANN 2020. LNCS, vol. 12396, pp. 724–735. Springer, Cham (2020). https://doi.org/10.1007/978-3-030-61609-0_57
14. Wang, L., Wang, L., Lu, H., Zhang, P., Ruan, X.: Saliency detection with recurrent fully convolutional networks. In: Leibe, B., Matas, J., Sebe, N., Welling, M. (eds.) ECCV 2016. LNCS, vol. 9908, pp. 825–841. Springer, Cham (2016). https://doi.org/10.1007/978-3-319-46493-0_50

15. Wei, J., Wang, S., Wu, Z., Su, C., Huang, Q., Tian, Q.: Label decoupling framework for salient object detection. In: Proceedings of the IEEE/CVF Conference on Computer Vision and Pattern Recognition, pp. 13025–13034 (2020)
16. Wu, R., Feng, M., Guan, W., Wang, D., Lu, H., Ding, E.: A mutual learning method for salient object detection with intertwined multi-supervision. In: Proceedings of the IEEE/CVF Conference on Computer Vision and Pattern Recognition, pp. 8150–8159 (2019)
17. Wu, Z., Su, L., Huang, Q.: Cascaded partial decoder for fast and accurate salient object detection. In: Proceedings of the IEEE/CVF Conference on Computer Vision and Pattern Recognition, pp. 3907–3916 (2019)
18. Xie, S., Tu, Z.: Holistically-nested edge detection. In: Proceedings of the IEEE International Conference on Computer Vision, pp. 1395–1403 (2015)
19. Zhang, P., Wang, D., Lu, H., Wang, H., Ruan, X.: Amulet: aggregating multi-level convolutional features for salient object detection. In: Proceedings of the IEEE International Conference on Computer Vision, pp. 202–211 (2017)
20. Zhang, X., Wang, T., Qi, J., Lu, H., Wang, G.: Progressive attention guided recurrent network for salient object detection. In: Proceedings of the IEEE Conference on Computer Vision and Pattern Recognition, pp. 714–722 (2018)
21. Zhao, J.X., Liu, J.J., Fan, D.P., Cao, Y., Yang, J., Cheng, M.M.: EGNet: edge guidance network for salient object detection. In: Proceedings of the IEEE/CVF International Conference on Computer Vision, pp. 8779–8788 (2019)
22. Zhou, H., Xie, X., Lai, J.H., Chen, Z., Yang, L.: Interactive two-stream decoder for accurate and fast saliency detection. In: Proceedings of the IEEE/CVF Conference on Computer Vision and Pattern Recognition, pp. 9141–9150 (2020)

# Continual Learning Based on Knowledge Distillation and Representation Learning

Xiu-yan Chen, Jian-wei Liu$^{(\boxtimes)}$ (iD), and Wen-tao Li

Department of Automation, College of Information Science and Engineering,
China University of Petroleum, Beijing, Beijing 102249, China
liujw@cup.edu.cn

**Abstract.** In recent years, continual learning that is more in line with real-world scenarios has received more attention. In order to solve the catastrophic forgetting problem in continual learning, researchers have put forward various solutions, which are simply summarized into three types: network structure-based methods, rehearsal-based methods and regularization-based methods. Inspired by pseudo-rehearsal and regularization methods, we propose a novel Continual Learning Based on Knowledge Distillation and Representation Learning (KRCL) model, which employs Beta-VAE as a representation learning module to extract a shared representation of learned tasks. In addition, Beta-VAE is also used as a generative model to generate pseudo samples of historical task, and KRCL trains the pseudo samples of the previous tasks together with the data of the current task, and then combines the knowledge distillation process to extract the dark knowledge from the old task model to alleviate the catastrophic forgetting. We compare KRCL with the Finetune, LWF, IRCL and KRCL_real baseline methods on four benchmark datasets. The result shows that the KRCL model achieves state-of-the-art performance in standard continual learning tasks.

**Keywords:** Continual learning · Class incremental learning · Representation learning · Knowledge distillation · Catastrophic forgetting

## 1 Introduction

In the past few years, continual learning has attracted much attention, but the concept of continual learning can be traced back to the 1990s [18]. Continual learning studies the problem of learning from an infinite stream of data, and one of its goals is to incrementally extend the acquired knowledge and apply it to future learning [2]. However, realistic scenario data streams are often non-stationary data, which can lead to catastrophic forgetting when continual learning is incrementally acquiring new knowledge. The so-called catastrophic forgetting means that after learning new knowledge, the model's performance on the old knowledge will drop sharply, or even completely forget the old knowledge.

E. Pimenidis et al. (Eds.): ICANN 2022, LNCS 13532, pp. 27–38, 2022.
https://doi.org/10.1007/978-3-031-15937-4_3

Despite the great success of deep learning today, continual learning remains a long-term challenge. The current neural network learning paradigm relies on a large number of annotated training samples and performs well in many classification tasks. However, this learning scheme assumes that all samples are available during the training phase. Although zero-based retraining avoids catastrophic forgetting, this approach is inefficient and hinders real-time learning of new data. This limitation also represents the main drawback of the latest deep neural network models.

Many methods have been proposed to solve the problem of catastrophic forgetting, and there are three main categories: network structure-based methods, rehearsal-based methods, and regularization-based methods. Network structure-based methods is limited to task incremental scenarios, and is more suitable for learning long sequence tasks when the model capacity is not constrained and the best performance is prioritized. The representative models of this type of methods includes Progressive Neural Nets (PNN) [16], Dynamic expandable network (DEN) [20], Packnet [12], etc. Rehearsal-based methods based on rehearsal stores samples in their original format, or uses generative models to generate pseudo samples. If pseudo-sample is used, it is called a pseudo-rehearsal based method. Representative models of these methods include incremental classifier and representation learning (iCaRL) [15], Gradient episodic memory for continual learning (GEM) [11], etc. Regularization-based methods based on regularization avoids storing the original input, prioritizes privacy, and reduces memory requirements. The representative models based on regularization methods include Learning without Forgetting (LWF) [10], Elastic Weight Consolidation (EWC) [7], Memory Aware Synapses (MAS) [1], etc.

Based on existing solutions of catastrophic forgetting in continual learning, in this paper, we propose a novel method based on pseudo-rehearsal and regularization, called Continual Learning Based on Knowledge Distillation and Representation Learning (KRCL). The model mainly uses pseudo-rehearsal and knowledge distillation techniques, combined with the Beta-VAE model in representation learning to solve the class incremental learning problems. Specifically, the Beta-VAE encoder disentangles the invariant representation of the data, and uses it in conjunction with a specific representation to learn sequential tasks. The decoder generates the pseudo-sample and uses it for training in the next task. Finally, knowledge distillation techniques are used to extract dark knowledge from the model and generate distillation losses to constrain the training process of the model.

In summary, the main contributions of this paper are as follows:

(1) Using Beta-VAE to disentangle the learned representations into invariant representations and specific representations, which helps to better grasp the fundamental information in continuous training tasks.
(2) Add the ground truth labels of the data to the Beta-VAE decoder, and use the decoder to generate pseudo-sample for the training of the next task. This is so-called pseudo-rehearsal.

(3) Knowledge distillation techniques are introduced to extract dark knowledge from trained models of old tasks (also known as teacher models), and construct distillation losses in combination with models of the current task. The distillation loss is added to the classifier loss to constrain model training, which plays a key role in alleviating catastrophic forgetting.

The rest of this paper is organized as follows: in Sect. 2, we present a brief introduction to class incremental learning scenarios, Beta-VAE and knowledge distillation. Section 3 details the proposed KRCL model and in Sect. 4, we provide comparisons to four baseline methods on four benchmark datasets.

## 2   Related Works

### 2.1   Class Incremental Learning

Class incremental learning, as a subclass of continual learning [13], is distinguished by the fact that the dataset of class incremental learning consists of sequences of tasks with increasing categories. Now suppose there is a sequence of tasks $\{1, 2, \ldots, t, \ldots, T_{total}\}$ with a total number of tasks $T_{total}$, and each task $t$ has a corresponding training dataset,

$$D^t = \left\{ \left( x_i^t, y_i^t \right) \right\}_{i=1}^{N^t} \tag{1}$$

where $x_i^t$ is the $i$ th training instance, $y_i^t$ is the corresponding ground truth label, and $N^t$ is the number of training samples (it is worth mentioning that there are no overlapping categories between different tasks). The class incremental learning training process starts from task 1, followed by task 2, until all tasks are trained. And the data $D^1, D^2, \ldots, D^{t-1}$ of the previous tasks are not allowed to be accessed when training task $t$. The goal of class incremental learning is not only to acquire the knowledge in the current task, but also to retain the knowledge learned in the previous tasks.

### 2.2   Beta-VAE

A Variational Autoencoder (VAE) is a type of likelihood-based generative model [6]. It consists of an encoder and a decoder. Given the observed data $x$, the joint distribution $p_\theta(x, z) = p_\theta(x \mid z) p_\theta(z)$ is defined, where $z$ is a latent representation. The encoder generates $z$ by model $q_\phi(z \mid x)$ using $x$. The decoder model $p_\theta(x \mid z)$ generates the reconstructed data $x'$ using $z$. The objective function of VAE is:

$$\mathcal{L}_{VAE}(\theta, \phi) = E_{q_\phi(z|x)}[\log p_\theta(x \mid z)] - D_{KL}\left(q_\phi(z \mid x) \| p_\theta(z)\right) \tag{2}$$

where, the first term is the log-likelihood of the reconstructed data sampled from the approximate posterior distribution $q_\phi(z \mid x)$; the second term is the Kullback-Leibler divergence between the approximate posterior distribution $q_\phi(z \mid x)$ and the prior distribution $p_\theta(z)$.

Beta-VAE [4] is a variant of VAE that modifies VAE by introducing hyper-parameter $\beta$. Its objective function is:

$$\mathcal{L}_{Beta\_VAE}(\theta, \phi) = E_{q_\phi(z|x)}[\log p_\theta(x \mid z)] - \beta D_{KL}(q_\phi(z \mid x) \| p_\theta(z)) \quad (3)$$

### 2.3  Knowledge Distillation

Knowledge distillation is a compression technique [5] that trains a smaller student model by learning from a larger teacher model, extracting the dark knowledge from the teacher model to optimize the student model. In supervised learning, classification models are typically trained to predict a class by maximizing the estimated probability of truth labels. Thus, a standard training goal includes minimizing the cross-entropy loss between the predicted and true labels. In [5], the cross-entropy loss is calculated using a softmax function with temperature:

$$softmax_\varsigma(a_i) = \frac{\exp(a_i/\varsigma)}{\sum_j \exp(a_j/\varsigma)} \quad (4)$$

where, $a_i$ is the output value of a neural network, usually called logits; $\varsigma$ is the distillation temperature, usually taken as 2.

## 3  Model and Methodology

### 3.1  KRCL Model

The KRCL model proposed in this paper has three modules, Representation Learning Module (RLM), Knowledge Distillation Module (KDM) and Classification Module (CM). RLM is mainly composed of encoder and decoder of Beta-VAE. The encoder encodes the training data into invariant representations, and the decoder decodes the invariant representations into pseudo-samples. KDM is mainly composed of teacher model, which contains old encoder, old specific representation learner (essentially VAE encoder) and old classifier. The first two parts encode training data into old invariant representations and old specific representations, respectively. CM is mainly composed of specific representation learner and classifier. The former encodes training data into specific representations, and the latter combines the specific and invariant representations to generate predict value. More details are shown in the KRCL model architecture in Fig. 1. To better understand the three modules, we present the training process of the KRCL model in two stages as follows:

**Stage 1:** This stage trains task 1, since there is no model trained by the old task, KDM is not required for this stage of training. First, the training data $x^{1\text{-}tr}$ enters the encoder $E^1$ of RLM to generate the invariant representation $z_I^1$. Next, $z_I^1$ is combined with the training sample labels (TSL) and then passed through the decoder $D^1$ to generate the pseudo-sample $\hat{x}^1$ (also the reconstructed sample $x^{1'}$). Then, it enters the specific representation learner $S^1$ of CM to obtain the specific representation $z_S^1$. Finally, $z_I^1$ and $z_S^1$ are concatenated and passed through the classifier $C^1$ to obtain the predict value $\hat{y}^1$.

**Stage 2:** This stage trains task 2 to task $T_{total}$. The model trained in the previous task is used as the teacher model for the next task. After the training of task 1, we obtain the teacher model for task 2. In the same way, after the training of task 2 is completed, the teacher model of task 3 is obtained. By analogy, the teacher model can be obtained during the training process of task 4 to task $T_{total}$. This stage is as follows: when training task $t$ ($t = 2, 3, \ldots, T_{total}$), the training samples $x^{t\_tr}$ consist of task $t$ samples and task $t-1$ pseudo-samples. The operations of training samples in CM and RLM are the same as stage 1. For KDM, the training samples are passed through the old encoder $E_{old}^{t-1}$ and the old specific representation learner $S_{old}^{t-1}$ to generate the old invariant representation $z_{old\_I}^{t-1}$ and the old specific representation $z_{old\_S}^{t-1}$. Combine them and send them to the old classifier $C_{old}^{t-1}$ to get the old predict value $\hat{y}_{old}^{t-1}$. Finally, the old predict value are used to generate the distillation loss.

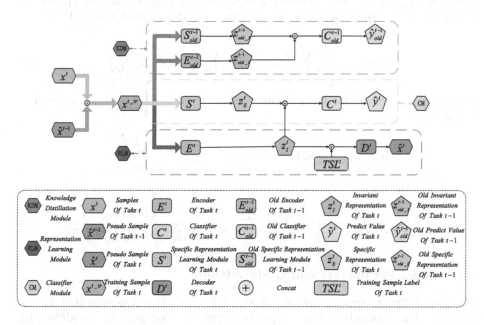

**Fig. 1.** KRCL model architecture. The contents surrounded by purple, light blue and red dashed boxes correspond to the three key modules of the KRCL model, where purple represents the knowledge distillation module, light blue represents the classification module, and red represents the representation learning module. The positive hexagon points to the three key modules, the regular hexagon to the training data, the pentagon to the learned representation, the quadrilateral to the neural network learning module, and the circle to the connection operation. The specific meanings of these graphs are explained in more detail at the bottom of the figure. (Color figure online)

## 3.2   KRCL Loss Function

The loss function of task $t$ of KRCL model mainly includes two parts: conditional Beta-VAE loss function $loss^t_{Beta\_VAE}$ and classifier loss function $loss^t_c$. The former consists of reconstruction loss $loss^t_{rec}$ and KL divergence $loss^t_{KL}$,

$$loss^t_{Beta\_VAE} = loss^t_{rec} + \beta \cdot loss^t_{KL} \qquad (5)$$

where, $loss^t_{rec}$ is the mean squared error between training samples and reconstructed samples; Parameter $\beta$ is a hyperparameter; $loss^t_{KL}$ is the KL divergence between probability distribution of the invariant representation and conditional invariant representation probability distribution under the training samples for task $t$.

The latter consists of $loss^t_{true}$ and $loss^t_{dis}$,

$$loss^t_c = loss^t_{true} + \lambda \cdot loss^t_{dis} \qquad (6)$$

where, $loss^t_{true}$ is the cross-entropy loss between ground truth label and predicted value; $\lambda$ is a hyperparameter; $loss^t_{dis}$ is distillation loss, generated by KDM,

$$loss^t_{dis} = \sum_{i=1}^{N^t} \sum_{j=1}^{2t} \left( \hat{y}^{t-1}_{old\_soft\_\varsigma} \right)_{ij} \log \left( \left( \hat{y}^t_{soft\_\varsigma} \right)_{ij} \right) \qquad (7)$$

where, $\varsigma$ is the distillation temperature; $(\hat{y}^t_{soft\_\varsigma})_{ij}$ and $(\hat{y}^{t-1}_{old\_soft\_\varsigma})_{ij}$ are detailed as follows:

$$\left( \hat{y}^t_{soft\_\varsigma} \right)_{ij} = soft\max{}_{\_\varsigma} \left( \hat{y}^t_i \right) = \frac{\exp \left( \hat{y}^t_{ij}/\varsigma \right)}{\sum_{k=1}^{2t} \exp \left( \hat{y}^t_{ik}/\varsigma \right)} \qquad (8)$$

$$\left( \hat{y}^{t-1}_{old\_soft\_\varsigma} \right)_{ij} = softmax_{\_\varsigma} \left( \left( \hat{y}^{t-1}_{old} \right)_i \right) = \frac{\exp \left( \left( \hat{y}^{t-1}_{old} \right)_{ij} /\varsigma \right)}{\sum_{k=1}^{2t} \exp \left( \left( \hat{y}^{t-1}_{old} \right)_{ik} /\varsigma \right)} \qquad (9)$$

## 3.3   Model Parameters and Update Rules

The KRCL model consists of an encoder with variational parameters $\Phi_{E^t}$, a decoder with parameters $\Phi_{D^t}$, a specific representation learning module with parameters $\Phi_{S^t}$, and a classifier with parameters $\Phi_{C^t}$. The objective function of learning classifier is as follows:

$$min_{\Phi_{E^t},\Phi_{D^t}} loss^t_{Beta\_VAE}(\Phi_{E^t}, \Phi_{D^t}; z^t_S, z^t_I, x^{t\_tr}) \qquad (10)$$

$$min_{\Phi_{S^t},\Phi_{C^t}} loss^t_c(\Phi_{S^t}, \Phi_{C^t}; z^t_S, z^t_I, x^{t\_tr}) \qquad (11)$$

**Table 1.** The selected parameters for KRCL model on four datasets.

| Datasets | $\lambda$ | $\varsigma$ | $\beta$ |
|---|---|---|---|
| Split MNIST | 2.0 | 2.0 | 1.0 |
| Split FashionMNIST | 1.3 | 2.0 | 2.2 |
| Split SVHN | 12.0 | 2.0 | 1.0 |
| Split CIFAR10 | 16.0 | 2.0 | 2.6 |

The updating rules of parameters are as follows:

$$-Grad\left(loss^t_{Beta\_VAE}\right) \overset{update}{\Rightarrow} \Phi_{E^t}$$

$$-Grad\left(loss^t_{Beta\_VAE}\right) \overset{update}{\Rightarrow} \Phi_{D^t}$$

$$-Grad\left(loss^t_c\right) \overset{update}{\Rightarrow} \Phi_{s^t}$$

$$-Grad\left(loss^t_c\right) \overset{update}{\Rightarrow} \Phi_{C^t}$$

(12)

where $Grad(\cdot)$ represents the gradient operator.

## 4 Experimental Comparison

### 4.1 Benchmark Datasets

**Split MNIST Dataset:** MNIST dataset [9] is a large database of handwritten digits, which contains a training set of 60,000 pictures and a test set of 10,000 pictures. The Split MNIST dataset divides the MNIST dataset into different categories of 5 tasks.

**Split FashionMNIST Dataset:** FashionMNIST dataset [19] is a clothing dataset that contains 70,000 gray-scale images, including a training set of 60,000 examples and a test set of 10,000 examples. The Split FashionMNIST dataset divides the FashionMNIST datasets into 5 tasks according to different categories.

**Split SVHN Dataset:** SVHN dataset [14] is a dataset that recognizes Arabic numerals in images. The training set contains 73257 pictures, the test set contains 26032 pictures, and there are 531131 additional pictures. The Split SVHN dataset divides the SVHN dataset into 5 tasks according to different categories.

**Split CIFAR10 Dataset:** CIFAR10 dataset [8] is a color image dataset closer to a pervasive object. A total of 10 categories of RGB color images are included: Airplane, Automobile, Bird, Cat, Deer, Dog, Frog, Horse, Ship and Truck. The Split CIFAR10 dataset divides CIFAR10 dataset into five tasks according to different classes.

## 4.2    Baseline Methods

Finetune [3], LWF [10], IRCL [17] and KRCL_real are selected as baseline methods to compare with our proposed KRCL model.

**Table 2.** Experimental result table.

| Split MNIST | | | | Split fashion MNIST | | | |
|---|---|---|---|---|---|---|---|
| Baselines | ACC % | BWT | LA % | Baselines | ACC % | BWT | LA % |
| Finetune | $19.41 \pm 0.49$ | $-79.84 \pm 1.35$ | $98.24 \pm 0.12$ | Finetune | $20.22 \pm 0.32$ | $-79.37 \pm 1.87$ | $98.59 \pm 0.22$ |
| LWF | $44.82 \pm 0.35$ | $-6.14 \pm 0.98$ | $49.96 \pm 0.53$ | LWF | $45.45 \pm 0.13$ | $-22.85 \pm 1.23$ | $67.30 \pm 0.87$ |
| IRCL | $85.07 \pm 0.21$ | $-13.16 \pm 0.87$ | $97.23 \pm 0.22$ | IRCL | $76.83 \pm 0.38$ | $-19.46 \pm 1.02$ | $95.29 \pm 0.12$ |
| KRCL | $89.36 \pm 0.34$ | $3.59 \pm 0.52$ | $84.58 \pm 0.24$ | KRCL | $79.39 \pm 0.23$ | $-9.49 \pm 0.13$ | $87.88 \pm 0.28$ |
| KRCL_real | $90.58 \pm 0.17$ | $2.91 \pm 1.13$ | $86.67 \pm 0.23$ | KRCL_real | $68.37 \pm 0.35$ | $-23.54 \pm 0.13$ | $90.91 \pm 0.29$ |
| Split SVHN | | | | Split CIFAR10 | | | |
| Baselines | ACC % | BWT | LA % | Baselines | ACC % | BWT | LA % |
| Finetune | $19.31 \pm 0.34$ | $-79.25 \pm 1.12$ | $97.56 \pm 0.09$ | Finetune | $18.97 \pm 0.23$ | $-74.78 \pm 1.02$ | $92.75 \pm 0.12$ |
| LWF | $39.44 \pm 0.15$ | $-37.02 \pm 0.49$ | $75.46 \pm 0.23$ | LWF | $25.65 \pm 0.10$ | $-13.64 \pm 0.92$ | $38.29 \pm 0.98$ |
| IRCL | $20.70 \pm 0.21$ | $-77.62 \pm 1.24$ | $97.32 \pm 0.11$ | IRCL | $18.98 \pm 0.34$ | $-73.31 \pm 1.29$ | $91.29 \pm 0.20$ |
| KRCL | $62.75 \pm 0.23$ | $-8.31 \pm 0.74$ | $70.10 \pm 0.42$ | KRCL | $31.42 \pm 0.25$ | $-28.00 \pm 1.05$ | $58.42 \pm 0.79$ |
| KRCL_real | $85.87 \pm 0.35$ | $10.37 \pm 0.82$ | $74.50 \pm 0.56$ | KRCL_real | $54.46 \pm 0.21$ | $4.45 \pm 0.16$ | $49.01 \pm 0.91$ |

**Finetune:** Finetune is a basic model in a continual learning environment without memory unit or any regularization term. When a new task arrives, the current task model initializes with the parameters of the previous task.

**LWF:** LWF (Learning Without Forgetting) is a classical continual learning model that maintains the performance of previous tasks by introducing knowledge distillation technology.

**IRCL:** IRCL is a pseudo-rehearsal-based approach in which class invariant representations are obtained from conditional generative models and used jointly with specific representations to learn sequential tasks.

**KRCL_real:** KRCL_Real is based on the KRCL model, which replaces the pseudo samples generated by the decoder with real samples as a baseline method.

### 4.3    Network Architecture

In this experiment, Fully connected neural network(FC) and AlexNet are used. Split MNIST and Split FashonMNIST are single-channel images, so FC is used. While Split SVHN and Split CIFAR10 are three-channel, AlexNet is used. For Split MNIST and Split Fashion MNIST datasets, the network structures of encoder, decoder, classifier and specific representation learner are FC. Their number of hidden layer neurons is 300, 300, 40 and 20 respectively. For Split SVHN and Split CIFAR10 datasets, encoder and specific representation learner use standard AlexNet structure, decoder and classifier both use FC. In Split SVHN, the number of hidden layer neurons of encoder and classifier are 40 and 30, respectively. In Split CIFAR10, 55 and 35 respectively.

## 4.4   Evaluation Metrics

We use three evaluation metrics to verify the performance of the proposed method, i.e., Average Accuracy (ACC), Backward Transfer Metric (BWT) [11] and Learning Accuracy (LA). The specific calculation formulas as follows:

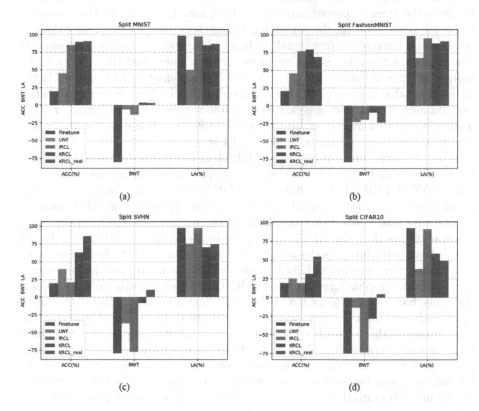

**Fig. 2.** Histogram of experimental results.

$$ACC = \frac{1}{T_{total}} \sum_{i=1}^{T_{total}} A_{T_{total},i} \tag{13}$$

$$BWT = \frac{1}{T_{total} - 1} \sum_{i=1}^{T_{total}-1} A_{T_{total},i} - A_{i,i} \tag{14}$$

$$LA = \frac{1}{T_{total}} \sum_{i=1}^{T_{total}} A_{i,i} \tag{15}$$

where $T_{total}$ is the total number of tasks, and $A_{j,i}$ denotes the accuracy of the task after the task $j$ in the task learning sequence.

## 4.5   Experimental Results and Analysis

According to the experimental results, it is found that different datasets are more sensitive to the three hyperparameters ($\lambda$, $\varsigma$ and $\beta$), so we designed a parameter tuning experiment to select the best hyperparameters of the four datasets. A more detailed procedure is as follows: we assume that the effects between the three hyperparameters can be ignored, first select the parameter to be adjusted, then fix the remaining parameters, and set different values for the selected parameters from small to large (0.01–100) to conduct experiments. The experiment was repeated five times for each value, and the value with the highest average accuracy was taken as the best parameter. The optimal hyperparameter table is shown in Table 1. According to the best hyperparameters of each dataset, experiments are carried out on four baselines, each group of experiments is repeated five times, and the average value is taken as the final result. The final results are shown in Table 2 and Fig. 2.

From the experimental results, the KRCL model performed superiorly on all three metrics and was much better than other three baseline methods (Fine-tune, LWF and IRCL) on both ACC and BWT metrics (the bigger the better). In addition, the improvement of ACC reflects the superiority of KRCL model in mitigating catastrophic forgetting. In addition, we can also find from the experimental results that the KRCL_real model outperforms the KRCL model and is the best performing model among all baseline methods, which reflects the superior performance of the KRCL model on the one hand, and the better mitigation of catastrophic forgetting by the KRCL_real model using real samples on the other hand. It should be noted that KRCL_real is not the best ACC on the Split FashionMNIST dataset, which we attribute to the effect of hyperparameters. However, the focus of our model is not to adjust the parameters to make every dataset perform best, but simply to experimentally verify the correctness and superiority of our theory. Obviously, the experimental results do show the advantage of our innovation in solving the catastrophic forgetting problem, so we did not delve into the performance of KRCL_real on the Split FashionMNIST dataset.

## 5   Conclusions and Future Works

In this paper, we propose the KRCL model to alleviate the catastrophic forgetting problem on the class incremental learning settings by introducing knowledge distillation and pseudo-rehearsal techniques. Experimental results show that, The KRCL model has a certain degree of improvement over other baseline methods based only on regularization or pseudo-rehearsal methods. It can better alleviate catastrophic forgetting problems on simple datasets and achieve excellent experimental results, and can alleviate to a certain extent on particularly complex datasets.

Based on the experimental results, the quality of the pseudo samples generated by the decoder has a relatively large impact on the effect of the model. In the future, we can consider using models such as GAN to generate better pseudo samples and thus improve the effectiveness of the model.

**Acknowledgement.** This work was supported by the Science Foundation of China University of Petroleum, Beijing (No. 2462020YXZZ023).

# References

1. Aljundi, R., Babiloni, F., Elhoseiny, M., Rohrbach, M., Tuytelaars, T.: Memory aware synapses: learning what (not) to forget. In: Ferrari, V., Hebert, M., Sminchisescu, C., Weiss, Y. (eds.) ECCV 2018. LNCS, vol. 11207, pp. 144–161. Springer, Cham (2018). https://doi.org/10.1007/978-3-030-01219-9_9
2. Delange, M., et al.: A continual learning survey: defying forgetting in classification tasks. IEEE Trans. Pattern Anal. Mach. Intell. **44**(7), 3366–3385 (2021)
3. Girshick, R., Donahue, J., Darrell, T., Malik, J.: Rich feature hierarchies for accurate object detection and semantic segmentation. In: Proceedings of the IEEE Conference on Computer Vision and Pattern Recognition, pp. 580–587 (2014)
4. Higgins, I., et al.: beta-VAE: learning basic visual concepts with a constrained variational framework (2016)
5. Hinton, G., Vinyals, O., Dean, J., et al.: Distilling the knowledge in a neural network, **2**(7). arXiv preprint arXiv:1503.02531 (2015)
6. Kingma, D.P., Welling, M.: Auto-encoding variational bayes. arXiv preprint arXiv:1312.6114 (2013)
7. Kirkpatrick, J., et al.: Overcoming catastrophic forgetting in neural networks. Proc. Natl. Acad. Sci. **114**(13), 3521–3526 (2017)
8. Krizhevsky, A., Hinton, G., et al.: Learning multiple layers of features from tiny images (2009)
9. LeCun, Y.: The MNIST database of handwritten digits (1998). http://yann.lecun.com/exdb/mnist/
10. Li, Z., Hoiem, D.: Learning without forgetting. IEEE Trans. Pattern Anal. Mach. Intell. **40**(12), 2935–2947 (2017)
11. Lopez-Paz, D., Ranzato, M.: Gradient episodic memory for continual learning. In: Advances in Neural Information Processing Systems, vol. 30 (2017)
12. Mallya, A., Lazebnik, S.: PackNet: adding multiple tasks to a single network by iterative pruning. In: Proceedings of the IEEE Conference on Computer Vision and Pattern Recognition, pp. 7765–7773 (2018)
13. Masana, M., Liu, X., Twardowski, B., Menta, M., Bagdanov, A.D., van de Weijer, J.: Class-incremental learning: survey and performance evaluation on image classification. arXiv preprint arXiv:2010.15277 (2020)
14. Netzer, Y., Wang, T., Coates, A., Bissacco, A., Wu, B., Ng, A.Y.: Reading digits in natural images with unsupervised feature learning (2011)
15. Rebuffi, S.A., Kolesnikov, A., Sperl, G., Lampert, C.H.: iCaRL: incremental classifier and representation learning. In: Proceedings of the IEEE Conference on Computer Vision and Pattern Recognition, pp. 2001–2010 (2017)
16. Rusu, A.A., et al.: Progressive neural networks. arXiv preprint arXiv:1606.04671 (2016)
17. Sokar, G., Mocanu, D.C., Pechenizkiy, M.: Learning invariant representation for continual learning. arXiv preprint arXiv:2101.06162 (2021)

18. Thrun, S.: Lifelong learning algorithms. In: Thrun, S., Pratt, L. (eds.) Learning to Learn, pp. 181–209. Springer, Boston (1998). https://doi.org/10.1007/978-1-4615-5529-2_8
19. Xiao, H., Rasul, K., Vollgraf, R.: Fashion-MNIST: a novel image dataset for benchmarking machine learning algorithms. arXiv preprint arXiv:1708.07747 (2017)
20. Yoon, J., Yang, E., Lee, J., Hwang, S.J.: Lifelong learning with dynamically expandable networks. arXiv preprint arXiv:1708.01547 (2017)

# Deep Feature Learning for Medical Acoustics

Alessandro Maria Poirè, Federico Simonetta⑩, and Stavros Ntalampiras(✉)⑩

LIM – Music Informatics Laboratory, Department of Computer Science,
University of Milano, Milan, Italy
stavros.ntalampiras@unimi.it
https://www.lim.di.unimi.it/

**Abstract.** The purpose of this paper is to compare different learnable frontends in medical acoustics tasks. A framework has been implemented to classify human respiratory sounds and heartbeats in two categories, i.e. healthy or affected by pathologies. After obtaining two suitable datasets, we proceeded to classify the sounds using two learnable state-of-art frontends – LEAF and nnAudio – plus a non-learnable baseline frontend, i.e. Mel-filterbanks. The computed features are then fed into two different CNN models, namely VGG16 and EfficientNet. The frontends are carefully benchmarked in terms of the number of parameters, computational resources, and effectiveness.

This work demonstrates how the integration of learnable frontends in neuralaudio classification systems may improve performance, especially in the field of medical acoustics. However, the usage of such frameworks makes the needed amount of data even larger. Consequently, they are useful if the amount of data available for training is adequately large to assist the feature learning process.

## 1 Introduction

Cardiovascular and respiratory diseases are the leading cause of mortality worldwide; it is estimated that in 2019 17.9 million people died due to cardiovascular diseases, representing the first and second cause of death worldwide (32 % of all deaths worldwide), followed by respiratory disease [23,24]. Therefore, considerable efforts have been devoted to research for the improvement of the early diagnosis and routine monitoring of patients with cardiovascular and respiratory diseases. A large portion of the research has focused on the auscultation of respiratory sounds and heart tones. Indeed, these diseases, such as asthma, COPD, pneumonia, heart murmurs, heart valve abnormalities, and arrhythmia, are associated with distinct sound patterns. Such abnormal breathing sounds in the lungs are called adventitious sounds [24]. A similar phenomenon can be observed relatively to abnormal blood flows in the heart, which can also cause characteristics noises.

To the purpose of screening these cardiovascular and respiratory diseases, cardiac auscultation by phonocardiograms (PCG) and pulmonary auscultation

E. Pimenidis et al. (Eds.): ICANN 2022, LNCS 13532, pp. 39–50, 2022.
https://doi.org/10.1007/978-3-031-15937-4_4

are among the most important tools. The auscultation happens via an electronic stethoscope capable of digitally recording PCGs and respiratory sounds. However, this process is based on the availability of an expert as well as on his degree of competence. Thus, the need to automate the diagnosis process has arisen in recent years, bringing the development of algorithms able of classifying heart or pulmonary sounds. Such algorithms are usually based on Machine Learning technologies with the aim of assisting physicians in the diagnosis of health diseases, as well as providing patients with effective auto-diagnosis tools where physicians are not available [15,16].

Artificial Neural Networks (ANN) comprise the most used approach for the classification of heart and pulmonary sounds [5]. ANNs require discriminating features of the signal as input; usually such features are time-frequency representations of an audio signal, such as spectrograms, Mel spectrograms and Mel-frequency cepstral coefficient (MFCC) [1,9,13]. Recent studies, regarding sound classification in general, show that using Log-Mel spectrograms has significant improvements on the efficiency of the neural network [7,18]. Some studies also adopted Wavelet-based representations, but such features were only little explored compared to FFT-based ones [6].

The goal of this work is the comparison of various frontends, i.e. feature-extraction methods. Indeed, various frontends for neural features extraction were recently proposed in the field of audio signal processing. Specifically, two learnable frontends for audio processing received a large attention – LEAF and nnAudio [4,25]. Both the two frontends allow to compute time-frequency representations specifically crafted for the learning problem. This study aims at assessing if the learned features can improve the efficiency of ANN for Medical Acoustics and therefore we compare them to a standard representation method based on Log-Mel-spectrograms.

The contributions of this work are:

- a binary classification method for respiratory and heartbeat sounds;
- comparison of LEAF and nnAudio frameworks with traditional hand-crafted features for audio processing;
- efficiency and effectiveness benchmarks of different feature extraction strategies using different types of Neural Networks;

To the sake of reproducibility, the source-code used for this work is fully available online[1].

## 2   The Considered Frontends

As mentioned above, the purpose of this paper is to compare two learnable frontends, LEAF and nnAudio. LEAF and nnAudio are features extractors that, unlike Mel-filterbank, are completely trainable during the neural network training process. Interestingly, all audio features extraction operations, such as filtering, pooling, compression and normalization are learnable.

---

[1] https://github.com/LIMUNIMI/Feature-Learning-Medical-Acoustics.

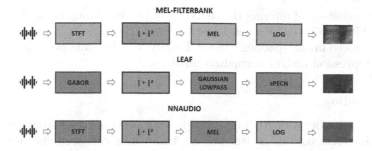

**Fig. 1.** Breakdown of Mel-filterbanks, LEAF and nnAudio frontends. Orange boxes are fixed, while computations in blue boxes are learnable. Grey boxes represent activation functions. (Color figure online)

Log-Mel spectrograms are the most used time-frequency representation for neural classification tasks in the field of medical acoustics [1,11,12,14,21]; it is for this reason that they have been chosen as a baseline for comparing representations produced by learnable frontends.

The three frontends are depicted in Fig. 1.

## 2.1 Mel-filterbanks

Mel-filterbank is a fixed frontend that receives waveforms as an input, and produces Log-Mel spectrograms as output. It is fixed because the parameters that control it are non-learnable, that is, they do not change during the training of the network.

A Mel-filterbank is applied to an audio excerpt to obtain the Log-Mel spectrograms. More specifically, we first compute the spectrogram of the audio excerpt using the squared modulus of the short-term Fourier transform (STFT). Then, the spectrogram is passed through a bank of triangular bandpass filters, spaced logarithmically according to the Mel scale. The Mel scale is designed to replicate the non-linearity of human pitch perception. Finally, to reflect the non-linearity of the human loudness sensitivity, the resulting coefficients are passed through a logarithmic compression.

Log-Mel spectrograms have various parameters that should be finely tuned, adding a large number of hyper-parameters to the resulting pipeline and making the designing of Machine Learning methods more complex.

## 2.2 LEAF

LEAF (LEarnable Audio Frontend) [25] is a neural network-based frontend to extract features such as Mel spectrograms. Being a neural network, it can be trained inside any neural architecture to discover task-specific features, adding only a few parameters to the model. This frontend learns all operations of audio features extraction, from filtering to pooling, compression and normalization.

In the first stage of filtering the sound wave passed through a bank of Gabor bandpass filters followed by a non-linearity. Then, the temporal resolution of the signal is reduced in the "pooling" phase. Finally, the dynamic range is optimized with a compression and/or normalization stage.

## 2.3  nnAudio

nnAudio (neural network Audio) [4] is a neural network based frontend able to extract Mel spectrograms as features. nnAudio uses convolutional neural networks to perform the conversion from time domain to frequency domain, and it can be trained together with any classifier.

As input, nnAudio receives a waveform from which it extracts the Mel-spectrogram via a learnable process. The frontend first computes the STFT using a Convolutional Neural Network, and then applies a bank of Mel filters. The values of the Mel filter bank are used to initialize the weights of a single-layer fully-connected neural network. Each time step of the STFT is sent in this fully-connected layer initialized with Mel weights. The Mel filter bank therefore must only be created during the initialization of the neural network. All of these weights are trainable.

# 3  Models

To test the frontends under different conditions, two different well-known CNNs were chosen for the classification phase: *EfficientNet-B0* and *VGG16* [19,20].

## 3.1  EfficientNet

The EfficientNet models are a family of artificial neural networks where the basic building block is the Mobile Inverted Bottleneck Conv Block (MBConv). The Efficient-Net family includes 8 models (from B0 to B7): as the number increases, the complexity of the network increases. The main idea of EfficientNet is to start from one simple, compact and computationally efficient structure, and gradually increasing its complexity. Unlike other CNN models, EfficientNet uses a new activation feature known as Swish, rather than the classic ReLU function. The "lightweight" version of EfficientNet (EfficientNetB0, with ∼4M parameters) has been adopted as first classifier.

## 3.2  VGG

The VGG16 version of VGG was adopted as another classifier. VGG stands for Visual Geometry Group; It is a standard multi-level CNN architecture. According to the number of layers, the various versions of VGG are named, for example VGG11 has 11 layers, VGG16 has 16 layers, VGG19 has 19 layers and so on.

VGG16 is a deep 16-layer neural network; this means that it is quite large, and has a total of about 138 million parameters. However, its architecture is relatively simple and straightforward.

**Table 1.** Statistics on the datasets used

|  |  | Respiratory sound database [2] | Heartbeat physio-net database [3] |
|---|---|---|---|
| Normal samples | Train set | 2732 | 20461 |
|  | Validation set | 546 | 4092 |
|  | Test set | 364 | 2728 |
|  | **Total** | **3642** | **27281** |
| Abnormal Samples | Train set | 2442 | 5284 |
|  | Validation set | 488 | 1057 |
|  | Test set | 326 | 704 |
|  | **Total** | **3256** | **7045** |
| Total |  | **6898** | **34326** |

# 4   Datasets

In order to compare the proposed frontends, tests were performed for two different medical acoustics tasks: anomaly detection in respiratory sounds and in heartbeat recordings. The datasets differ in content and quantity of elements, so that frontends can be tested under different conditions.

Table 1 shows summary statistics about the used datasets.

## 4.1   Respiratory Dataset

The first database is the Respiratory Sound database [2], created to support the scientific challenge organized at the International Conference on Biomedical Health Informatics - ICBHI 2017 [8].

The database consists of a total of 5.5 h of records containing 6898 respiratory cycles, of which 1864 contain crackles, 886 contain wheezes and 506 contain both crackles and wheezes.

The total number of audio samples was 920, obtained from 126 participants. The recordings were collected using heterogeneous equipment and their duration ranged from 10 to 90 s. For each audio recording, the time-mark list of start and end time of each respiratory cycle is provided. The sampling frequency of the recordings varies, with values of 4 kHz, 10 kHz or 44.1 kHz; in the preprocessing phase they are resampled at 4 kHz. It is currently the largest publicly available respiratory sound database.

The level of noises – cough, speech, heartbeat, etc. – in some breathing cycles is relatively high representing real-life conditions very well. Respiratory cycles were noted by experts, dividing them into four categories: crackles, wheezes, a combination of them, or no adventitious sounds.

In this work we have chosen to use only two labels: normal and abnormal. The normal class covers sounds categorized as non-adventitious, while the abnormal class includes sounds containing crackles, wheezes, or a combination of them. In this way, the two resulting classes are more balanced, accounting 3642 normal sounds and 3256 abnormal cycles.

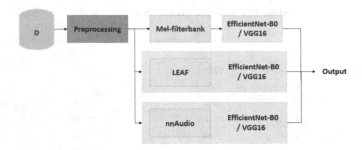

**Fig. 2.** General scheme of the neural network architecture.

## 4.2 Heartbeat Dataset

The second database is the Heartbeat Physio-Net Database [3], created specifically for the 2016 PhysioNet Computing in Cardiology (CinC) Challenge [17].

This database contains a total of 3153 heart sound recordings from 764 healthy and pathological patients. The recordings have a duration from 5 to 120 s, obtaining about 25 h of sound material. All audio samples were recorded with a sampling rate of 2 kHz or resampled to the same rate. In the database there are recordings labeled as unsure, i.e. with a very low signal quality. These audio samples were omitted from the test, leaving a total of 2872 recordings for the training, validation and testing phases. All phonocardiograms in the database are categorized into two types: normal and abnormal. Recordings with the normal label come from healthy patients, while those with the abnormal label come from patients with pathologies such as coronary artery disease and heart valve defects (mitral valve prolapse syndrome, mitral regurgitation, aortic regurgitation, aortic stenosis and valve surgery).

As in the Respiratory Database, the data includes not only "clean" heart sounds, but also very noisy recordings, providing an accurate representation of real life conditions.

## 5   Experiments

This section describes the experiments performed to compare the various frontends and models described in Sects. 2 and 3. The generic workflow is shown in Fig. 2.

### 5.1   Pre-processing

Pre-processing included segmentation, filtering, resampling, and padding.

For the respiratory database, the samples were segmented following the time-marks annotations indicating each respiratory cycle – see Sect. 4.1. For instance, the audio file 107_2b5_Pr_mc_AKGC417L.wav is 8.97 s long; it has been segmented according to the indicated time-marks thus producing 4 audio files: file_1.wav

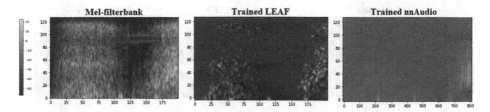

**Fig. 3.** Features learned on a sample from the Respiratory Sound Database [2] by LEAF and nnAudio compared with classical Mel-spectrograms.

(from 0.077 to 1.411 of the original file), `file_2.wav` (from 1.411 to 3.863), `file_3.wav` (from 3.863 to 6.601) and `file_4.wav` (from 6.601 to 8.97).

For the heartbeat database, instead, the individual audio files of variable length (from 6 to 120 s) were segmented into 2-s files. For instance, a file initially lasting 10 s is split into 5 files of 2 s each. In this way, the total number of samples becomes 34326.

Subsequently, the audio files obtained from the segmentation phase are filtered through a 12th order Butterworth band-pass filter, with cut-off frequencies [120–1800] Hz for the respiratory database, and [25, 400] Hz for the heartbeat database. This eliminates the components of sound caused by coughing, intestinal noises, stethoscope movement and speech.

All audio files were then resampled at 4 KHz (only in the Respiratory dataset, the Heartbeat dataset was already sampled at 4 kHz) and truncated or zero-padded so that they lasted exactly 2 s.

### 5.2    System Parameterization

To better compare the frontends considered, the same hyper-parameters were used in the tests.

In all three frontends, after various experiments, it was decided to use a window length of 30 ms, with a window stride of 10 ms. The frequency range of the Mel filters was set at [100, 2000] Hz in the tests with respiratory dataset, and [25, 1000] Hz in the tests with heratbeat dataset. 128 Mel-filters were used. Only in the LEAF frontend some parameters have been changed in respect to their factory defaut values; specifically, in the PCEN compression layer, the alpha and root parameters that control the amount of compression applied, respectively alpha = 2, root = 4.

In the VGG16 classifier, two dropout layers with a value of 0.5 have been added between the last two fully connected layers. The dropout layer prevents the co-adaptation of a neural network, disabling some nodes of the network during the training phase with a specific probability (0.5 in this case). In EfficientNetB0 the drop connect rate parameter has also been changed, setting it to 0.5.

The training was carried out considering a period of 300 epochs for the heartbeat test, and 200 epochs for the respiratory test. The batch size was set at 64,

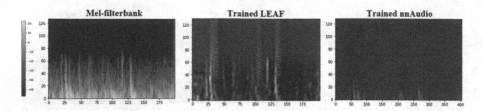

**Fig. 4.** Features learned on a sample from the heartbeat physio-net database [3] by LEAF and nnAudio compared with classical Mel-spectrograms.

while the learning rate as set at $1e-5$, and ADAM was chosen as weight-update algorithm.

We empirically found an optimal split size using 75% of the dataset for the train set, 15% for the validation set, and 10% for the test set.

Examples of features learned on the two datasets are shown in Figs. 3 and 4.

## 6    Results

In order to compare the proposed frontends, two tests with two different datasets were formulated: "Test 1 - Respiratory" and "Test 2 - Heartbeat". The datasets differ in content and quantity of elements, so the frontends can be tested under different conditions.

The evaluation metrics used in this study are balanced accuracy, True Positive Rate (TPR) and True Negative Rate (TNR):

$$BalancedAccuracy = \frac{TPR + TNR}{2}$$
$$TPR = \frac{TruePositive}{TruePositive + FalseNegative} \qquad (1)$$
$$TNR = \frac{TrueNegative}{TrueNegative + FalsePositive}$$

**Table 2.** McNemar p-values corrected with Bonferroni-Holm method.

|            | Mel-LEAF   | Mel-nnAudio | LEAF-nnAudio |
|------------|------------|-------------|--------------|
| Resp. Eff. | 0.2010     | 0.0500      | 0.5263       |
| Resp. VGG  | 0.3998     | 0.0366      | 0.3998       |
| Heart. Eff.| 9.8515e–07 | 0.4194      | 2.6648e–05   |
| Heart. VGG | 1.1219e–03 | 9.1734e–09  | 7.1666e–03   |

## 6.1 Test 1 - Respiratory

As shown in Tables 3 and 4, VGG16 always achieves better results than EfficientNet. However, using VGG16, the differences between the three frontends are larger, acheiving 6% of difference in accuracy between nnAudio and Mel-filterbank.

Surprisingly, we found that with VGG16 the baseline method outperforms the learnable frontends, proving the well-design of old Log-Mel spectrograms compared to newer neural network frameworks.

When EfficientNet is used, instead, a small difference emerges that awards the learnable frontends, especially nnAudio; however, McNemar test with Bonferroni-Holm correction finds no statistically significant difference among the three.

Specific p-values are shown in Table 2.

## 6.2 Test 2 - Heartbeat

Even in this scenario VGG16 was better than EfficientNet in all the tests. Nevertheless and contrarily to the respiratory task, the Mel-filterbank was surpassed by both nnAudio and LEAF.

Tables 5 and 6 show that LEAF achieves the better accuracy using both VGG16 and EfficientNet. However, when using EfficientNet, the best TNR was achieved by nnAudio. Note that TNR is particularly important in first-screening diagnosis, because low TNR is associated with a high false negative rate, meaning that false negatives are common. When a false negative prediction happens, the therapeutic intervention may be delayed with catastrophic consequences.

Specific p-values are shown in Table 2.

## 6.3 Overall

Comparing the results obtained from the two tests Test 1 and Test 2, we note that the best scores were achieved in Test 2 (Heartbeat), with the LEAF frontend. We theorize that LEAF performed better in Test 2 than Test 1 due to the size of the phonocardiogram database, which is much larger than the respiratory sound database.

**Table 3.** Comparison results using VGG16 as classifier on the ICBHI dataset [2]. Only Mel-filterbank and nnAudio accuracies show a statistical significance ($p \sim 0.04$ using McNemar with Bonferroni-Holm correction).

| % | Balanced accuracy | TPR | TNR |
|---|---|---|---|
| Mel-filterbank | **80.21** | **81.42** | **79.01** |
| LEAF | 77.47 | 80.87 | 74.07 |
| nnAudio | 74.12 | 77.86 | 70.37 |

**Table 4.** Comparison results using EfficientNet-B0 as classifier on the ICBHI dataset [2]. Only Mel-filterbank and nnAudio accuracies show a small significance ($p \sim 0.05$ using McNemar with Bonferroni-Holm correction).

| % | Balanced accuracy | TPR | TNR |
|---|---|---|---|
| Mel-filterbank | 61.05 | 62.84 | **59.26** |
| LEAF | 61.40 | 66.94 | 55.86 |
| nnAudio | **61.74** | **68.85** | 54.63 |

**Table 5.** Comparison results using VGG16 as classifier on the heart beats dataset [3]. All p-values between accuracies are $<<0.05$ (McNemar with Bonferroni-Holm correction)

| % | Balanced accuracy | TPR | TNR |
|---|---|---|---|
| Mel-filterbank | 90.71 | **96.22** | 85.20 |
| LEAF | **92.29** | 95.29 | **89.30** |
| nnAudio | 91.41 | 93.64 | 89.16 |

Moreover, the different balancing of the two databases is probably the reason why TPR and TNR are more distant in Test 2 than in Test 1. Indeed, the Respiratory database has the most balanced classes compared to the Heartbeat database – see Table 1.

In general, the 3 frontends learn different features, as shown in Figs. 3 and 4. Namely, nnAudio learns more sparse representations that focus on low frequencies. On the contrary, LEAF learns representations less sparse and well distributed across the frequency space. Compared with classical Mel-filterbanks, both of them seems to learn specific characteristics that are relevant for the classification. We theorize that LEAF learned features work by extracting discriminative local descriptors in the time-frequency space similarly to audio fingerprint algorithms [10, 22]. nnAudio, instead, extracts blurred regions that are likely less characteristics of the single excerpt. Moreover, LEAF manages to handle both positive and negative values, while nnAudio's activation functions only return non-negative values, thus deleting possibly useful information.

**Table 6.** Comparison results using EfficientNet-B0 as classifier on the heart beats dataset [3]. All comparisons of accuracies revealed stastical significance except between Mel-filterbank and nnAudio (McNemar test with Bonferroni-Holm correction).

| % | Balanced accuracy | TPR | TNR |
|---|---|---|---|
| Mel-filterbank | 81.12 | 90.92 | 71.33 |
| LEAF | **84.36** | **95.40** | 73.31 |
| nnAudio | 83.51 | 92.52 | **74.50** |

# 7 Conclusion

This work has shown how the integration of learnable frontends in classification systems with convolutional neural networks can improve results in the field of medical acoustics. The tests carried out show that learnable frontends are particularly useful when there is a sufficient amount of available data (Test 2), while using small data-sets (Test 1) prevent them from learning accurate features to surpass the classic hand-crafted methods.

The proposed method therefore stands as a valid alternative to traditional feature extraction methods as long as they are used in contexts with a large amount of data available.

# References

1. Acharya, J., Basu, A.: Deep neural network for respiratory sound classification in wearable devices enabled by patient specific model tuning. IEEE Trans. Biomed. Circuits Syst. (2020)
2. Rocha, B.M., et al.: An open access database for the evaluation of respiratory sound classification algorithms. Physiol. Meas. **40**, 035001 (2019)
3. Liu, C., et al.: An open access database for the evaluation of heart sound algorithms. Physiol. Meas. **37**, 2181 (2016)
4. Cheuk, K.W., Anderson, H., Agres, K., Herremans, D.: nnaudio: An on-the-fly GPU audio to spectrogram conversion toolbox using 1d convolutional neural networks. IEEE Access (2020)
5. Clifford, G.D., et al.: Classification of normal/abnormal heart sound recordings: the physionet/computing in cardiology challenge 2016. PhysioNet (2016)
6. Serbes, G., Ulukaya, Khaya, Y.P.: An Automated Lung Sound Preprocessing and Classification System Based on Spectral Analysis Methods. Precision Medicine Powered by pHealth and Connected Health, Springer, Singapore (2018). https://www.springerprofessional.de/en/an-automated-lung-sound-preprocessing-and-classification-system-/15232246
7. Huzaifah, M.: Comparison of time-frequency representations for environmental sound classification using convolutional neural networks. arXiv:1706.07156v1 (2017)
8. ICBHI: ICBHI 2017 challenge. https://bhichallenge.med.auth.gr/ICBHI_2017_Challenge. Accessed 10 2021
9. Kamarulafizam, I., Salleh, S., Jamaludin, M.N.: Heart sound analysis using MFCC and time frequency distribution. In: 3rd Kuala Lumpur International Conference on Biomedical Engineering 2006, pp. 402–405 (2007)
10. Ke, Y., Hoiem, D., Sukthankar, R.: Computer vision for music identification. In: 2005 IEEE Computer Society Conference on Computer Vision and Pattern Recognition (CVPR 2005) vol. 1, pp. 597–604 (2005)
11. Meghanani, A., Anoop, C.S., Ramakrishnan, A.G.: An exploration of log-mel spectrogram and MFCC features for Alzheimer's dementia recognition from spontaneous speech. In: IEEE Spoken Language Technology Workshop (SLT) (2021). https://doi.org/10.1109/SLT48900.2021.9383491
12. Mukherjee, U., Pancholi, S.: A visual domain transfer learning approach for heartbeat sound classification (2021). https://doi.org/10.48550/ARXIV.2107.13237

13. Nakamura, N., Yamashita, M., Matsunaga, S.: Detection of patients considering observation frequency of continuous and discontinuous adventitious sounds in lung sounds. In: Proceedings of the Annual International Conference of the IEEE Engineering in Medicine and Biology Society (2016)

14. Nguyen, T., Pernkopf, F.: Lung sound classification using snapshot ensemble of convolutional neural networks. In: 2020 42nd Annual International Conference of the IEEE Engineering in Medicine Biology Society (EMBC) (2020). https://doi.org/10.1109/EMBC44109.2020.9176076

15. Ntalampiras, S.: Collaborative framework for automatic classification of respiratory sounds. IET Signal Process. **14**(4), 223–228 (2020). https://doi.org/10.1049/iet-spr.2019.0487

16. Ntalampiras, S.: Identification of anomalous phonocardiograms based on universal probabilistic modeling. IEEE Lett. Comput. Soc. **3**(2), 50–53 (2020). https://doi.org/10.1109/LOCS.2020.3014306

17. PhysioNet: Classification of heart sound recordings: The physionet/computing in cardiology challenge 2016. https://physionet.org/content/challenge-2016/1.0.0/. Accessed 10 2021

18. Purwins, H., Li, B., Virtanen, T., Schluter, J., Chang, S.Y., Sainath, T.: Deep learning for audio signal processing. IEEE J. Sel. Topics Signal Process. **13**(2), 206–219 (2019). https://doi.org/10.1109/jstsp.2019.2908700

19. Simonyan, K., Zisserman, A.: Very deep convolutional networks for large-scale image recognition. arXiv:1409.1556v6 (2015)

20. Tan, M., Le, Q.V.: EfficientNet: rethinking model scaling for convolutional neural networks. arXiv:1905.11946v5 (2020)

21. Ul Haq, H.F.D., et al.: Efficientnet optimization on heartbeats sound classification. In: 2021 5th International Conference on Informatics and Computational Sciences (ICICoS) (2021). https://doi.org/10.1109/ICICoS53627.2021.9651818

22. Wang, A.: An industrial strength audio search algorithm. In: ISMIR (2003)

23. WHO: The top 10 causes of death. https://www.who.int/news-room/fact-sheets/detail/the-top-10-causes-of-death. Accessed 03 2022

24. WHO: World statistics on cardiovascular disease. https://www.who.int/news-room/fact-sheets/detail/cardiovascular-diseases-(cvds). Accessed 03 2022

25. Zeghidour, N., Teboul, O., de Chaumont Quitry, F., Tagliasacchi, M.: Leaf: a learnable frontend for audio classification. In: ICLR (2021)

# Feature Fusion Distillation

Chao Tan[1,2] and Jie Liu[1,2(✉)]

[1] Science and Parallel and Distributed Processing Laboratory,
National University of Defense Technology, Changsha 410073, China
liujie@nudt.edu.cn
[2] Laboratory of Software Engineering for Complex Systems,
National University of Defense Technology, Changsha 410073, China

**Abstract.** Most recent efforts made in knowledge distillation (KD) can be credited to filling the representation gap between the cumbersome teacher and its light student. In general, the soft targets, the intermediate feature representation in hidden layers, or a couple of them from the teacher serve as the supervisory signal to educate the student. However, previous works aligned hidden layers one on one and cannot make full use of rich context knowledge. To this end, we propose a Feature Fusion Module (FFM) to concatenate diverse feature maps from different layers to aggregate knowledge as the to-be-distilled dark knowledge. Moreover, to hedge the adverse effects of the fused feature maps, we devise an Asymmetric Switch Function (ASF) to make the transfer process more reliable. The combination of FFM and ASF is termed Feature Fusion Distillation (FFD). Experiments of image classification, object detection, and semantic segmentation on individual benchmarks show FFD jointly assist the student in achieving encouraging performance. It is worth mentioning that when the teacher is ResNet34, the ultimately educated student ResNet18 achieves 71.40% top-1 accuracy on ImageNet-1K.

**Keywords:** Neural network compression · Knowledge distillation · Knowledge transfer

## 1 Introduction

Hinton *et al.* [13] introduced the concept of knowledge distillation (KD) and explored the teacher-student paradigm for network compression. Following this novel idea, KD based approaches directly train a light network (student), which mimics its original cumbersome network (teacher). However, only transferring soft targets as [13] would limit the performance of output distillation. To make full use of teacher's knowledge, as shown in Fig. 1(a), several approaches [23,32] transfer teacher knowledge by using hidden layers knowledge. So, this framework is used as the basic framework in this paper. Moreover, KD is widely used for specific applications. For example, prior research has been conducted on face recognition [8,29], image retrieval [17], cross-modal task [9,31], neural machine translation [26] and speech recognition [1,3].

© The Author(s), under exclusive license to Springer Nature Switzerland AG 2022
E. Pimenidis et al. (Eds.): ICANN 2022, LNCS 13532, pp. 51–63, 2022.
https://doi.org/10.1007/978-3-031-15937-4_5

However, as shown in Fig. 1(a), teacher transfers its knowledge one on one in most of the previous approaches. As demonstrated in [34], the projections from each level (low/mid/high) show the hierarchical nature of the features in the network. For example, low-level features show the corners and other edge/color conjunctions, while high-level features are more related to entire objects with significant pose. So, traditional transfer pattern limited the interactivity between different levels.

This drawback motivates us to collect both diverse intermediate features in hidden layers from the teacher as dark knowledge via a *Feature Fusion Module* (FFD). For clarity, FFD is shown in Fig. 1(b), where its way to extract the to-be-distilled dark knowledge is very different from the traditional method. Though more knowledge of the teacher is utilized via the FFD, the empirical analysis shows that the student not only needs to learn negative values of feature maps but also needs to avoid the adverse effects from the negative values of the teacher. So, an *Asymmetric Switch Function* (ASF) is developed to reduce the side effect of dark knowledge due to the large negative activations. The combination of FFM and ASF is termed Feature Fusion Distillation (FFD).

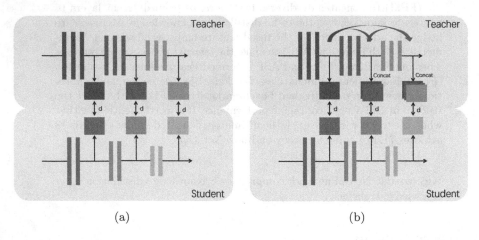

(a)                                                              (b)

**Fig. 1.** (a) The general knowledge transfer architecture. (b) The proposed knowledge transfer architecture. Different colors mean the feature maps distilled from different layers.

The contributions in this paper can be summarized as follows:

1. A novel feature fusion module is introduced to make the best use of the teacher's hidden layers knowledge;
2. An asymmetric switch function is proposed to eliminate the harmful knowledge from the teacher;
3. Experiments of image classification on both CIFAR-100 [16] and ImageNet-1K [24], object detection on VOC 2007 [7], and semantic segmentation on VOC 2012 Aug [6] demonstrate the efficacy of FFD.

# 2   Related Work

Hinton *et al.* [13] introduced the concept of KD for model compression and acceleration, where soft targets of the teacher network are used to educate the student network. Compared with hard targets, soft targets contain the information about inter-class correlations. Consequently, the student network can get relatively better performance. Henceforth, KD becomes an important branch of model compression and acceleration, then amounts of efforts have been made. The differences of such methods primarily lie in two aspects: knowledge representation and transfer skill.

For knowledge representation, the core is to aggregate feature representation from the teacher network as dark knowledge to educate the student. Build off [13], Romero *et al.* [23] utilized intermediate representation in hidden layers of the teacher to make the student better mimic. Yim *et al.* [32] intended to leverage the flow of solution procedure (FSP) matrix between the layers from the teacher as knowledge representation. To educate the student effectively, Kim *et al.* [15] exploited convolutional operations to paraphrase teacher knowledge. Afterwards, Huang *et al.* [14] compared the distributions of neuron selectivity patterns between teacher and student. In [20,22,28], they investigated the correlation between multiple instances as the interaction way between teacher and student. Tian *et al.* [27] used contrastive learning to help the student capture the teacher's knowledge.

For transfer skill, the involved techniques primarily consider how to help the student absorb the teacher's knowledge to the utmost. In general, the basic skill is to employ the squared loss to evaluate the feature similarity between teacher and student. Heo *et al.* [12]. proposed a knowledge transfer method by transferring activation boundaries of hidden neurons. Afterwards, Heo *et al.* [11] moved the distillation position to the front of the ReLU layer and minimized a new distance function, called partial $L_2$ distance, to realize knowledge transfer. Yue *et al.* [33] tried to match the teacher's channels with student's without convolutional operation. Afterwards, Passalis *et al.* [21] and Chen *et al.* [4] automatically assigned proper target layers of the teacher model for each student layer.

# 3   Method

## 3.1   Feature Fusion Module

Zagoruyko and Komodakis [34] pointed out the projections from each level (low/mid/high) show the hierarchical nature of the features in the network. For example, low-level features show the corners and other edge/color conjunctions. Besides, high-level features are more related to entire objects with significant pose. Specifically, we show the Grad-cam++ [2] visualization. As Grad-cam++ visualizes the regions where the network has considered important, in Fig. 2, we compare the results of a model on different levels. It can be observed that low-/mid-level feature maps pay much more attention on the edge of objects. While high-level maps concentrate more on entire objects. Based on this, feature maps on different levels can be mutually complementary. However, previous works just aligned hidden layers one on one and cannot make full use of rich context knowledge. By this insight, we devise FFM to extract diverse intermediate features as rich knowledge in a simple concatenation manner, which is a necessity for a qualified teacher. In this way, context knowledge can be leveraged.

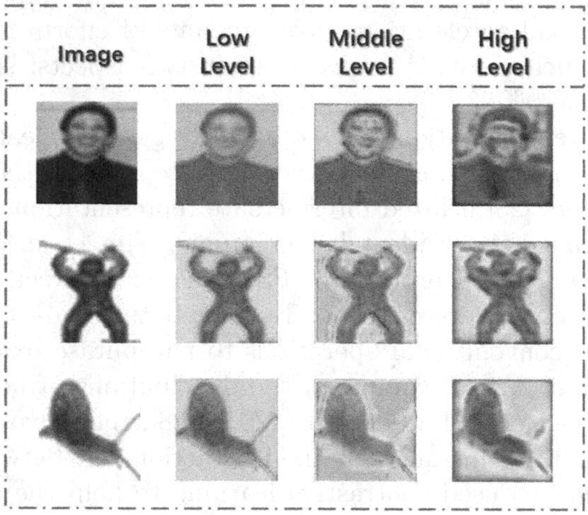

**Fig. 2.** The Grad-cam++ visualization on different levels.

Following [11], the intermediate features are acquired before ReLU. This distillation position enables the student to touch the preserved knowledge of the teacher before it passes through ReLU. The selected hidden layer in the teacher network outputs the corresponding feature map matrix $\mathbf{F} \in \mathbf{R}^{h \times w \times c}$, where $h$, $w$ and $c$ represent the height, width and the number of channels, respectively. Using the given notations, FFM can be described as:

$$
\begin{aligned}
\mathbf{F}'_1 &= \psi\left\{\eta\left(\mathbf{F}_1\right)\right\}, \\
\mathbf{F}'_2 &= \psi\left\{\eta\left(\mathbf{F}_1\right), \eta\left(\mathbf{F}_2\right)\right\}, \\
&\cdots, \\
\mathbf{F}'_l &= \psi\left\{\eta\left(\mathbf{F}_1\right), \eta\left(\mathbf{F}_2\right), \cdots, \eta\left(\mathbf{F}_l\right)\right\}.
\end{aligned}
\tag{1}
$$

where $l$ represents the number of those selected hidden layers and could vary from different visual tasks. In our empirical studies, $l = 3$ is suited for image classification on CIFAR-10 [16] and CIFAR-100 [16], while $l = 4$ is better on ImageNet [24]. $\eta(\cdot)$ means the adaptive function of each distilled feature map before they are combined. To fuse the feature maps with different dimensions more simply and efficiently, the AdaptiveAvgPool2d function is used to resize them to the same size. Afterwards, the concatenation acts as $\psi(\cdot)$ to aggregate different layer-wise feature maps altogether. The element-wise summation as another generic alternative to fusing layer-wise features is not considered here.

This is because it requires layer-wise feature maps to be the same channels, which might not be best. As in Eq. (1), $\mathbf{F}'_l$ is the fused feature map, which corresponds to the $l$-th layer feature maps of the student.

## 3.2 Asymmetric Switch Function

As there is some harmful knowledge lurked in feature maps, especially in feature maps before ReLU, none of the transformations over the teacher's feature maps might hurt the KD process. So, we investigate ASF used to transform the teacher's feature maps to further improve the efficacy of FFM. As FFM transfer the knowledge before ReLU, the switch function should be changed considering ReLU. In the feature maps of the teacher, the positive values are actually used for the network which implies that the positive responses of the teacher should be transferred by their exact values. However, since the negative values are filtered out by ReLU, learning from all the negative values could not always be helpful for the student. However, negative values are not. For these values in the teacher are negative, if the student's value is higher than the target value, it should be reduced, but if the student's value is lower than the target value, it does not need to be increased since negatives are equally blocked by ReLU regardless of their values. Furthermore, as mentioned in [12], to transfer the activation boundary accurately, it is required to amplify the negligible values near the activation boundary. So, we propose a switch function to suspend negative values and transfer the activation boundary accurately. The concrete form of ASF is

$$\delta(x) = \begin{cases} n & x < 0 \\ \max(x, m) & x \geq 0, \end{cases} \qquad (2)$$

where $m$ is a positive value and $n$ is a negative one. In Fig. 3(a), the activation boundaries are determined by the lines $y = 1$ and $y = -1$. However, the teacher's knowledge can not be well represented in this rigid setting. In Fig. 3(b), only a negative boundary is fixed [12]. In principle, the positive part also needs the counterpart for activation boundaries. As in Fig. 3(c), ASF shares the merits of the previous two switch functions, thus it not only magnifies the tiny values around zero to transfer activation boundaries but also suspends the adverse values. Note that the predefined parameters $m$ and $n$ are defined as the channel-by-channel expectation of the positive and negative values, respectively. Given that the $c$-th channel of the teacher's fused feature map is $F_l^{c'}$, the $m^c$ and $n^c$ of a channel can be calculated from the expectation values of all the training data as follows.

$$\begin{aligned} m^c &= \mathrm{E}\left[F_l^{c'} | F_l^{c'} \geq 0\right], \\ n^c &= \mathrm{E}\left[F_l^{c'} | F_l^{c'} < 0\right]. \end{aligned} \qquad (3)$$

The expectation values can be calculated via the parameters of the batch normalization layer before the distillation position. Appendix A contains the process of calculation. ASF obtains channel-wise margin value without sampling and averaging on training process. As a result, ASF $\delta(\cdot)$ generates the target value as the ultimate knowledge representation to educate the student network.

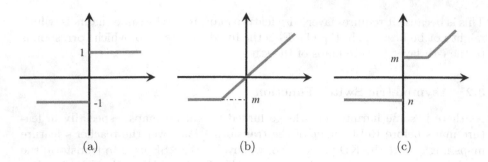

**Fig. 3.** (a) Switch function of [12]. (b) Switch function of [11]. (c) ASF.

### 3.3   Total Loss Function

Since the distillation position is before ReLU, the ReLU should be taken into account in designing FFD. For the target value, the positive part should be transferred to the student in an exact way. However, the negative part is not done. If the source value of the student is greater than the negative target value, it should be diminished to amplify the negligible values. But if the source value is less than or equal to the negative target value, it does not need to be added since the negative source value is blocked by the ReLU. Suppose that both source value and target value are $\mathbf{T}$ and $\mathbf{S} \in \mathbf{R}^{h \times w \times c}$, respectively, then the $i$-th component of $\mathbf{T}$ and $\mathbf{S}$ are $T_i$ and $S_i$, respectively, and the distance function $d$ is defined as follows.

$$d = \sum_i^{h \times w \times c} \begin{cases} 0 & \text{if } S_i \leq T_i = n, \\ (T_i - S_i)^2 & \text{otherwise.} \end{cases} \tag{4}$$

In terms of FFD, $\eta(\cdot)$ and $\psi(\cdot)$ are used as the adaptive function and FFM. ASF is $\delta(\cdot)$ is. A regressor $\gamma(\cdot)$ comprising a convolutional layer and a batch normalization layer to align the student's feature maps with the teacher's. Besides, $d(\cdot)$ is the distance function to evaluate the learning effect. Then, the calculating flow of distillation loss is

$$L_{distill} = d\left(\delta\left(\psi\left(\eta\left(\mathbf{F}_T\right)\right)\right), \gamma\left(\mathbf{F}_S\right)\right), \tag{5}$$

where $\mathbf{F}_T$ and $\mathbf{F}_S$ are input feature maps of the teacher and student network, respectively. Yet, several points of the distillation loss are non-differentiable. The non-differentiable points of the function will never appear in practice [36]. $L_{task}$ is task-specific. Consequently, the total loss function can be described as

$$L_{total} = L_{task} + \lambda L_{distill}. \tag{6}$$

## 4   Experiments

### 4.1   Image Classification (CIFAR-100)

CIFAR-100 contains 50K training images and 10K test images, both of which have 100 classes. In recent distillation literature, CIFAR-100 is a widely used benchmark for classification performance evaluation. To make the results convincing, FFD should work well with different network architectures. For training convergence and efficiency, different types of ResNet [10] and WideResNet [35] are chosen in this section. Each experiment is trained around 200 epochs with an initial learning rate of 0.1, which is divided by 10 at epoch 100 and epoch 150, respectively. The hyperparameter $\lambda$ in Eq. (6) is set to $6e^{-4}$. The top-1 accuracy acts as the evaluation metric. The hyperparameters of the other methods can be referred to [27].

Table 1 report the results of different methods. The results of the KD model with FFD substantially surpass the state-of-the-art counterparts. The margins range from 0.10% to 3.17%, then the average value is 1.39%. Compared with the student's 'Baseline', the average increase reaches 2.94%. Particularly, when both the teacher and the student are built off ResNet110 and ResNet32, respectively, training the student network with FFD can excel the teacher network in many cases. Notably, in two cases the student even outperforms the teacher network. Therefore, FFD can work well to distill either the same architecture network or the different structure network with some expected performance gain.

**Table 1.** Top-1 accuracy (%) of the student and the corresponding teacher exploited by different KD methods on CIFAR-100 dataset. Of them, 'Baseline' represents the result without distillation.

| Teacher | WRN40-2 | WRN40-2 | WRN22-4 | WRN22-4 | ResNet56 | ResNet110 | ResNet110 |
|---|---|---|---|---|---|---|---|
| Baseline | 75.91 | 75.91 | 77.56 | 77.56 | 72.98 | 73.79 | 73.79 |
| Student | WRN16-2 | WRN40-1 | WRN10-4 | WRN22-2 | ResNet20 | ResNet20 | ResNet32 |
| Baseline | 73.26 | 71.68 | 71.41 | 73.92 | 68.76 | 68.76 | 70.79 |
| KD [13] | 74.81 | 73.06 | 73.52 | 76.35 | 71.19 | 70.56 | 72.79 |
| FitNet [23] | 73.50 | 72.17 | 72.93 | 74.12 | 69.89 | 69.50 | 71.19 |
| AT [34] | 73.33 | 72.23 | 73.20 | 74.78 | 70.30 | 70.08 | 72.06 |
| FSP [32] | 73.54 | n/a | 72.87 | n/a | 69.94 | 70.08 | 71.39 |
| CC [22] | 73.31 | 71.98 | 72.93 | 74.65 | 69.98 | 69.90 | 71.86 |
| SP [28] | 73.69 | 71.91 | 72.93 | 74.87 | 70.00 | 69.88 | 71.65 |
| CO [11] | 75.23 | 73.75 | 73.97 | 76.77 | 70.06 | 70.33 | 73.28 |
| CRD [27] | 75.56 | 73.95 | 74.28 | 76.97 | 71.06 | 70.92 | 73.62 |
| SSKD [30] | 75.80 | 74.12 | 74.20 | 77.02 | 71.11 | 71.24 | 73.85 |
| FFD | **75.91** | **74.45** | **74.59** | **77.34** | **71.29** | **71.65** | **73.95** |

## 4.2 Image Classification (ImageNet-1K)

To convince the ones of the efficacy of FFD, we further conduct our experiments on ImageNet-1K, which is a larger dataset made up of 1.2M training images and 50K test images. ResNet34 is selected as the teacher network and ResNet18 is the student. The parameters ratio of the student to the teacher is 53.63%. For a fair comparison, we directly use the off-shelf pre-trained model as the teacher network. The experiment performs 100 epochs in total with an initial learning rate of 0.1, which is gradually reduced by dividing itself by 10 at epoch 30, epoch 60 and epoch 90 in order. The hyperparameter $\lambda$ is set to $6e^{-5}$. Both top-1 and top-5 accuracy are viewed as the evaluation metrics. The settings of the compared other methods are suggested from [27].

To compare with FFD, we select four other counterparts, which have shown sound performance in Sect. 4.1. According to Table 2, the 'Baseline' gap between the teacher and student network is 3.55%, in terms of the top-1 accuracy. FFD can reduce this gap by 1.64%, which is obviously superior to the other methods. So is the top-5 accuracy of FFD.

**Table 2.** Top-1 and top-5 accuracy (%) of the student network ResNet18 on ImageNet dataset. 'Baseline' stands for the results without distillation.

|  | ResNet34 Baseline | ResNet18 Baseline | KD [13] | CC [22] | SP [28] | CO [11] | SSKD [30] | FFD |
|---|---|---|---|---|---|---|---|---|
| Top-1 | 73.31 | 69.76 | 70.70 | 70.61 | 70.64 | 70.96 | 71.27 | **71.40** |
| Top-5 | 91.42 | 89.08 | 89.85 | 89.59 | 89.70 | 90.05 | 90.22 | **90.42** |

### 4.3 Object Detection

In this section, another computer vision task, object detection, is used to further verify the effectiveness of our work. We distill a high-speed detector termed Single Shot Detector (SSD) [18] with FFD. PASCAL VOC 2007 trainval and test dataset are used to train and evaluate the smaller SSD. The backbone of SSD in this section is pre-trained by ImageNet-1K. The starting learning rate is set to $1e^{-3}$ then divided by 0.1 at 80K iterations and 100K iterations, a total of 120K iterations with a batch size of 16. We assign $3e^{-5}$ to the hyperparameter $\lambda$.

Table 3 shows the mAP of FFD. ResNet is widely used as the backbone of SSD. The teacher network is based on ResNet50. There are two student networks which are based on ResNet34 and ResNet18. The parameters ratios are 38.21% and 63.76%, respectively. In the case of ResNet34, the mAP of FFD is greater than the 'Baseline' and [5] by 2.91% and 0.60%. Particularly, it is even greater than the teacher's mAP. As for the ResNet18, the mAP increases by 1.45% and 0.51%. Regardless of the compression ratio, the student networks in experiments are enhanced. Obviously, when the student's capacity is closer to the teacher's, performance improvement tends to be more significant.

### 4.4 Semantic Segmentation

Similar to the goal of the above object detection experiments, semantic segmentation is another visual task. We select DeepLabV3+ [7] as our model architecture. For the teacher network, we choose ResNet101 as the backbone. And ResNet50 and MobileNetV2 [25] are used as the student network, respectively.

**Table 3.** Object detection results of SSD300 on PASCAL VOC 2007 dataset. The mean average precision (mAP) serves to stand for the results. 'Baseline' represents the result without distillation.

|         | Networks     | Methods  | mAP (%) |
|---------|--------------|----------|---------|
| Teacher | ResNet50-SSD | Baseline | 79.52   |
| Student | ResNet34-SSD | Baseline | 76.93   |
|         |              | [5]      | 79.24   |
|         |              | FFD      | **79.84** |
|         | ResNet18-SSD | Baseline | 70.10   |
|         |              | [5]      | 71.04   |
|         |              | FFD      | **71.55** |

All these backbones are pre-trained on ImageNet. FFD is based on the PAS-CAL VOC 2012 Aug dataset. Each image is cropped to the same size $513 \times 513$, which are largest in any other tasks and more challenging. The learning rate decreases in a polynomial curve. All the compared models are trained around 30K iterations with a batch size of 16. The hyperparameter $\lambda$ is set to $1e^{-6}$.

Results are displayed in Table 4. The performance is measured in terms of pixel intersection-over-union averaged with 21 classes (mIOU). No matter whether the student share has the same architectural style as the teacher or not, FFD remarkably enhances the performance of the student. Without surprise, the same network architecture can induce better results. No matter in which cases FFD is a generic approach for improving other KD models.

**Table 4.** Semantic segmentation results of DeepLabV3+ in PASCAL VOC 2012 Aug dataset. The performance is measured in terms of pixel intersection-over-union averaged (mIOU). 'Baseline' represents the result without distillation.

|         | Backbones   | Methods  | mIOU (%) |
|---------|-------------|----------|----------|
| Teacher | ResNet110   | Baseline | 78.33    |
| Student | ResNet50    | Baseline | 74.11    |
|         |             | [19]     | 76.12    |
|         |             | FFD      | **76.92** |
|         | MobileNetV2 | Baseline | 71.13    |
|         |             | [19]     | 72.61    |
|         |             | FFD      | **73.24** |

## 5   Ablation Study

In this section, the ablation study is conducted to help further understand FFD. The ablation study is conducted by in order adding the layer-wise feature maps gradually to observe how the aggregated context knowledge affects performance. We select CIFAR-100 and ImageNet-1K for image classification tasks. Three kinds of teacher-student networks are adopted, which are recorded in Table 5. Implementation details and evaluation metrics are introduced in Sect. 4.1 and Sect. 4.2.

**Table 5.** Experiments settings with several network architectures on CIFAR-100 and ImageNet-1K.

| Setup | Dataset | Teacher | Student | Teacher params | Student params | Parameters ratio |
|-------|---------|---------|---------|----------------|----------------|------------------|
| (a) | CIFAR-100 | WRN22-4 | WRN10-4 | 4.32M | 1.22M | 28.24% |
| (b) | | WRN22-4 | WRN22-2 | 4.32M | 1.09M | 25.23% |
| (c) | | WRN22-4 | ResNet20 | 4.32M | 0.28M | 6.48% |
| (d) | ImageNet-1K | ResNet34 | ResNet18 | 21.80M | 11.69M | 53.62% |

The results are shown in Table 6. The 'Baseline' is not trained as in [23]. It can be observed that considering all the ablation components can improve the performance of the fundamental KD model to different degrees. Thus, FFM and ASF are indispensable roles for KD.

**Table 6.** Ablation study of FFD. The results are evaluated by the top-1 accuracy (%). The values in bracket denote the improvement by adding a layer-wise feature maps of FFD.

| Setup | Baseline | Feature fusion module | Asymmetric switch function |
|-------|----------|-----------------------|----------------------------|
| (a) | 73.99 | 74.23(+0.24) | 74.59(+0.36) |
| (b) | 76.81 | 77.09(+0.28) | 77.34(+0.25) |
| (c) | 69.00 | 69.49(+0.49) | 70.77(+1.38) |
| (d) | 70.66 | 71.05(+0.39) | 71.40(+0.35) |

# 6   Conclusion

In this paper, we make an improvement for knowledge distillation (KD) by a Feature Fusion Module (FFM) and an Asymmetric Switch Function (ASF) are proposed. The combination of FFM and ASF is termed Feature Fusion Distillation (FFD). FFD is evaluated on three visual tasks including image classification, object detection and semantic segmentation. In particular for image classification, FFD shows its performance superior to the state-of-the-art methods and even better than the teacher model on standard benchmark datasets. Particularly, when the teacher is ResNet34, the top-1 accuracy of the student ResNet18 is greater than that of baseline by 1.64% on ImageNet-1K. Meanwhile, in the case of object detection and semantic segmentation, the efficacy of the educated student significantly excels its baseline. These results imply that FFD including knowledge representation and transfer skill can boost the KD model and also be applied for many fields in practice.

# Appendix

## A  Margin Value

When the feature maps are before ReLU, the batch-norm layer determine the distribution of feature $F_l^{c'}$ in a batch. Batch norm layer normalizes the feature for each channel to a gaussian distribution with a specific mean $\mu$ and variance $\sigma$. In other words,

$$F_l^{c'} \sim \mathcal{N}(\mu, \sigma). \tag{7}$$

The value of mean and variance $(\mu, \sigma)$ of each channel correspond to the parameters $(\beta, \gamma)$ of the batch-norm layer. So, it can be obtained by analyzing the teacher network. Using the distribution of $F_l^{c'}$, we can directly calculate the margin value.

$$m = \frac{1}{Z} \int_0^\infty \frac{x}{\sqrt{2\pi}\sigma} e^{-\frac{(x-\mu)^2}{2\sigma^2}} dx. \tag{8}$$

The expectation can be obtained from integration using pdf of gaussian distribution, where the range is smaller than zero. The result of the integration can be expressed in simple form using the cdf function $\Phi(\cdot)$ of normal distribution.

$$m = \frac{\sigma e^{-\mu^2/2\sigma^2}}{\sqrt{2\pi}\Phi(-\mu/\sigma)}. \tag{9}$$

As $m + n = \mu$, then, $n$ can be calculated as follows.

$$n = \mu - \frac{\sigma e^{-\mu^2/2\sigma^2}}{\sqrt{2\pi}\Phi(-\mu/\sigma)}. \tag{10}$$

# References

1. Aguilar, G., Ling, Y., Zhang, Y., Yao, B., Fan, X., Guo, C.: Knowledge distillation from internal representations. In: AAAI, pp. 7350–7357 (2020)
2. Chattopadhay, A., Sarkar, A., Howlader, P., Balasubramanian, V.N.: Grad-cam++: generalized gradient-based visual explanations for deep convolutional networks. In: 2018 IEEE Winter Conference on Applications of Computer Vision (WACV), pp. 839–847. IEEE (2018)
3. Chebotar, Y., Waters, A.: Distilling knowledge from ensembles of neural networks for speech recognition. In: Interspeech, pp. 3439–3443 (2016)
4. Chen, D., Mei, J.P., Zhang, Y., Wang, C., Wang, Z., Feng, Y., Chen, C.: Cross-layer distillation with semantic calibration. In: Proceedings of the AAAI Conference on Artificial Intelligence, vol. 35, pp. 7028–7036 (2021)

5. Chen, G., Choi, W., Yu, X., Han, T., Chandraker, M.: Learning efficient object detection models with knowledge distillation. In: Advances in Neural Information Processing Systems, pp. 742–751 (2017)

6. Chen, L.-C., Zhu, Y., Papandreou, G., Schroff, F., Adam, H.: Encoder-decoder with atrous separable convolution for semantic image segmentation. In: Ferrari, V., Hebert, M., Sminchisescu, C., Weiss, Y. (eds.) ECCV 2018. LNCS, vol. 11211, pp. 833–851. Springer, Cham (2018). https://doi.org/10.1007/978-3-030-01234-2_49

7. Everingham, M., Eslami, S.A., Van Gool, L., Williams, C.K., Winn, J., Zisserman, A.: The pascal visual object classes challenge: a retrospective. Int. J. Comput. Vision **111**(1), 98–136 (2015)

8. Ge, S., Zhao, S., Li, C., Li, J.: Low-resolution face recognition in the wild via selective knowledge distillation. IEEE Trans. Image Process. **28**(4), 2051–2062 (2018)

9. Gupta, S., Hoffman, J., Malik, J.: Cross modal distillation for supervision transfer. In: Proceedings of the IEEE Conference on Computer Vision and Pattern Recognition, pp. 2827–2836 (2016)

10. He, K., Zhang, X., Ren, S., Sun, J.: Deep residual learning for image recognition. In: Proceedings of the IEEE Conference on Computer Vision and Pattern Recognition, pp. 770–778 (2016)

11. Heo, B., Kim, J., Yun, S., Park, H., Kwak, N., Choi, J.Y.: A comprehensive overhaul of feature distillation. In: Proceedings of the IEEE International Conference on Computer Vision, pp. 1921–1930 (2019)

12. Heo, B., Lee, M., Yun, S., Choi, J.Y.: Knowledge transfer via distillation of activation boundaries formed by hidden neurons. In: Proceedings of the AAAI Conference on Artificial Intelligence, vol. 33, pp. 3779–3787 (2019)

13. Hinton, G., Vinyals, O., Dean, J.: Distilling the knowledge in a neural network. arXiv preprint arXiv:1503.02531 (2015)

14. Huang, Z., Wang, N.: Like what you like: Knowledge distill via neuron selectivity transfer. arXiv preprint arXiv:1707.01219 (2017)

15. Kim, J., Park, S., Kwak, N.: Paraphrasing complex network: network compression via factor transfer. In: Advances in Neural Information Processing Systems, pp. 2760–2769 (2018)

16. Krizhevsky, A., et al.: Learning multiple layers of features from tiny images. Technical report (2009)

17. Liu, Q., Xie, L., Wang, H., Yuille, A.L.: Semantic-aware knowledge preservation for zero-shot sketch-based image retrieval. In: Proceedings of the IEEE International Conference on Computer Vision, pp. 3662–3671 (2019)

18. Liu, W., et al.: SSD: single shot multibox detector. In: Leibe, B., Matas, J., Sebe, N., Welling, M. (eds.) ECCV 2016. LNCS, vol. 9905, pp. 21–37. Springer, Cham (2016). https://doi.org/10.1007/978-3-319-46448-0_2

19. Liu, Y., Chen, K., Liu, C., Qin, Z., Luo, Z., Wang, J.: Structured knowledge distillation for semantic segmentation. In: Proceedings of the IEEE Conference on Computer Vision and Pattern Recognition, pp. 2604–2613 (2019)

20. Park, W., Kim, D., Lu, Y., Cho, M.: Relational knowledge distillation. In: Proceedings of the IEEE Conference on Computer Vision and Pattern Recognition, pp. 3967–3976 (2019)

21. Passalis, N., Tzelepi, M., Tefas, A.: Heterogeneous knowledge distillation using information flow modeling. In: Proceedings of the IEEE/CVF Conference on Computer Vision and Pattern Recognition, pp. 2339–2348 (2020)

22. Peng, B., et al.: Correlation congruence for knowledge distillation. In: Proceedings of the IEEE International Conference on Computer Vision, pp. 5007–5016 (2019)

23. Romero, A., Ballas, N., Kahou, S.E., Chassang, A., Gatta, C., Bengio, Y.: Fitnets: hints for thin deep nets. arXiv preprint arXiv:1412.6550 (2014)
24. Russakovsky, O., et al.: ImageNet large scale visual recognition challenge. Int. J. Comput. Vision **115**(3), 211–252 (2015)
25. Sandler, M., Howard, A., Zhu, M., Zhmoginov, A., Chen, L.C.: Mobilenetv 2: inverted residuals and linear bottlenecks. In: Proceedings of the IEEE Conference on Computer Vision and Pattern Recognition, pp. 4510–4520 (2018)
26. Tan, X., Ren, Y., He, D., Qin, T., Zhao, Z., Liu, T.Y.: Multilingual neural machine translation with knowledge distillation. arXiv preprint arXiv:1902.10461 (2019)
27. Tian, Y., Krishnan, D., Isola, P.: Contrastive representation distillation. arXiv preprint arXiv:1910.10699 (2019)
28. Tung, F., Mori, G.: Similarity-preserving knowledge distillation. In: Proceedings of the IEEE International Conference on Computer Vision, pp. 1365–1374 (2019)
29. Wang, M., Liu, R., Hajime, N., Narishige, A., Uchida, H., Matsunami, T.: Improved knowledge distillation for training fast low resolution face recognition model. In: Proceedings of the IEEE International Conference on Computer Vision Workshops (2019)
30. Xu, G., Liu, Z., Li, X., Loy, C.C.: Knowledge distillation meets self-supervision. In: Vedaldi, A., Bischof, H., Brox, T., Frahm, J.-M. (eds.) ECCV 2020. LNCS, vol. 12354, pp. 588–604. Springer, Cham (2020). https://doi.org/10.1007/978-3-030-58545-7_34
31. Ye, H.J., Lu, S., Zhan, D.C.: Distilling cross-task knowledge via relationship matching. In: Proceedings of the IEEE/CVF Conference on Computer Vision and Pattern Recognition, pp. 12396–12405 (2020)
32. Yim, J., Joo, D., Bae, J., Kim, J.: A gift from knowledge distillation: fast optimization, network minimization and transfer learning. In: Proceedings of the IEEE Conference on Computer Vision and Pattern Recognition, pp. 4133–4141 (2017)
33. Yue, K., Deng, J., Zhou, F.: Matching guided distillation. In: Vedaldi, A., Bischof, H., Brox, T., Frahm, J.-M. (eds.) ECCV 2020. LNCS, vol. 12360, pp. 312–328. Springer, Cham (2020). https://doi.org/10.1007/978-3-030-58555-6_19
34. Zagoruyko, S., Komodakis, N.: Paying more attention to attention: improving the performance of convolutional neural networks via attention transfer. arXiv preprint arXiv:1612.03928 (2016)
35. Zagoruyko, S., Komodakis, N.: Wide residual networks. arXiv preprint arXiv:1605.07146 (2016)
36. Zhou, H., Alvarez, J.M., Porikli, F.: Less is more: towards compact CNNs. In: Leibe, B., Matas, J., Sebe, N., Welling, M. (eds.) ECCV 2016. LNCS, vol. 9908, pp. 662–677. Springer, Cham (2016). https://doi.org/10.1007/978-3-319-46493-0_40

# Feature Recalibration Network for Salient Object Detection

Zhenshan Tan[ID] and Xiaodong Gu[(✉)][ID]

Department of Electronic Engineering, Fudan University, Shanghai 200433, China
{zstan19,xdgu}@fudan.edu.cn

**Abstract.** Learning-based models have demonstrated the superiority of extracting and aggregating saliency features. However, we observe that most off-the-shelf methods mainly focus on the calibration of decoder features while ignore the recalibration of vital encoder features. Moreover, the fusion between encoder features and decoder features, and the transfer between boundary features and saliency features deserve further study. To address the above issues, we propose a feature recalibration network (FRCNet) which consists of a consistency recalibration module (CRC) and a multi-source feature recalibration module (MSFRC). Specifically, intersection and union mechanisms in CRC are embedded after the decoder unit to recalibrate the consistency of encoder and decoder features. By the aid of the special designed mechanisms, CRC can suppress the useless external superfluous information and enhance the useful internal saliency information. MSFRC is designed to aggregate multi-source features and reduce parameter imbalance between saliency features and boundary features. Compared with previous methods, more layers are applied to generate boundary features, which sufficiently leverage the complementary features between edges and saliency. Besides, it is difficult to predict the pixels around the boundary because of the unbalanced distribution of edges. Consequently, we propose an edge recalibration loss (ERC) to further recalibrate the equivocal boundary features by paying more attention to salient edges. In addition, we also explore a compact network (cFRC-Net) that improves the performance without extra parameters. Experimental results on five widely used datasets show that the FRCNet achieves consistently superior performances under various evaluation metrics. Furthermore, FRCNet runs at the speed of around 30 fps on a single GPU.

**Keywords:** Salient object detection · Feature recalibration · Edge recalibration loss

## 1 Introduction

Salient Object Detection (SOD) aims at locating the most attractive regions of images or videos and is used as the pre-processing procedure for downstream vision tasks [1,2]. Earlier SOD algorithms mainly rely on hand-crafted features such as background prior, color contrast and contextual cue to extract salient

E. Pimenidis et al. (Eds.): ICANN 2022, LNCS 13532, pp. 64–75, 2022.
https://doi.org/10.1007/978-3-031-15937-4_6

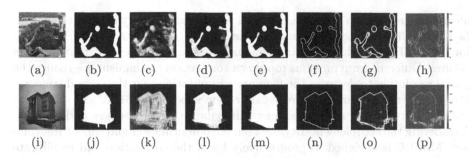

**Fig. 1.** Feature fusion and loss difference. (a) (i): images, (b) (j): ground truths, (c) (k): encoder features, (d) (l): decoder features, (e) (m): fusion features, (f) (n): edges directly from fusion features, (g) (o): generated edges from network, (h) (p): error maps of (f) (g) and (n) (o).

objects. However, these unsupervised stimuli-driven algorithms hardly capture high-level semantic features and are not robust to detect salient object in challenging complex background. In recent years, convolutional neural networks have been introduced to SOD and achieve best results on many benchmark datasets [5,8,10–13,15,18]. One representative network is U-net-like [9] structure, which significantly improves the resulting saliency maps. More recently, boundary features are integrated to convolutional features to predict more reliable saliency structure [19].

There are still three main challenges in SOD. Firstly, most of the previous works mainly focus on the construction of decoder features and various effective connection. However, the reconstruction of important encoder features and the fusion between encoder and decoder features remain scarce. As shown in Fig. 1 (c) (k), the raw encoder features are coarse and blur, which may mislead the subsequent feature transfer. Secondly, the aggregation of boundary features and saliency features has not been comprehensively studied. In fact, the correlation and difference between edges and saliency directly determine the performance of the generated saliency maps. Moreover, because the boundary features are less than the saliency features, conventional feature fusion methods may lead to parameter imbalance [19]. Finally, at present, boundary features are applied to refine the saliency features. Most of the existing methods generate boundary features from several convolutional layers after saliency features [19,21]. Nevertheless, the boundary features from the previous saliency convolutional layer may be changed during the process of feature transfer (see Fig. 1 (h) (p)). Therefore, when the saliency feature is supervised, the boundary features extracted from the saliency features should be supervised simultaneously, aiming at recalibrating the structure of saliency maps.

To address the above challenges, we propose a feature recalibration network (FRCNet) for accurate and fast SOD. In a specific, for the first issue, we propose a consistency recalibration module (CRC). CRC adopts an intersection and union mechanism, in which intersection mechanism is used to filter noise information and union mechanism is used to enhance saliency information. With the help of CRC, the noises are removed and the coarse edges are refined. In addition, after CRC, top-down feature refinement is adopted to aggregate multi-level features. Different from previous top-down connection mechanism, we reduce the spatial resolution to decrease the memory computation. For the second issue, we introduce a multi-source feature recalibration module (MSFRC) to aggregate multiple features and reduce parameter imbalance between edges and saliency. Considering the complementarity between edge information and salient information, MSFRC is designed to progressively learn the correlation and recalibrate the difference between boundary features and saliency features. In addition, more boundary feature layers help balance the parameters between edges and saliency. For the final issue, we propose an edge recalibration loss (ERC) to further recalibrate the boundary features directly from the saliency features. Because the pixels around the edges are hard to predict and discriminate, paying more attention to these edge pixels can refine the resulting saliency maps. In ERC, the edge pixels are given the maximum attention, then the saliency maps, and finally the background. The specially designed loss can lead the network to focus on the edges and further enhance the detection of saliency structure.

Experimental results on five popular datasets show that the proposed FRC-Net achieves consistently superior performance in comparison with other state-of-the-arts. The visual assessment verifies the results. Besides, the ablation studies demonstrate the effectiveness of each proposed module. FRCNet runs at around 30 fps on a single NVIDIA 2080Ti GPU. The codes will be released. In a word, the main contributions can be highlighted as follows.

- We propose a consistency recalibration module to recalibrate the encoder features and the decoder features, which is able to refine the coarse encoder features and selectively aggregate encoder features and decoder features.
- We propose a multi-source feature recalibration module to aggregate multi-source features and reduce parameter imbalance, which progressively learns the correlation and recalibrates the difference between edges and saliency.
- A novel edge recalibration loss is designed to guide the network to focus on the edge information and refine the coarse edges.
- Visual and objective assessments on five datasets show that the proposed FRCNet can achieve consistently superior performance, which verifies the superiority of the proposed model.

## 2    Proposed Method

As illustrated in Fig. 2, we propose a consistency recalibration module to aggregate encoder features and decoder features, which can suppress the useless information and enhance useful information. To progressively couple the complementarity and reduce parameter imbalance, we propose a multi-source feature recalibration module to aggregate multi-source features. To recalibrate the saliency edges, we design a novel edge recalibration loss to focus on the refinement of the edges.

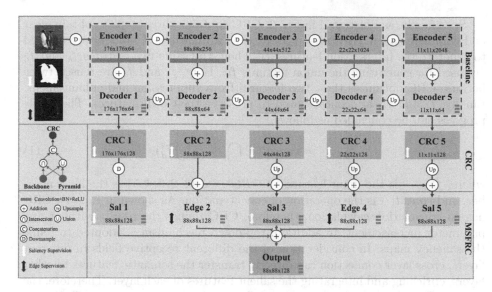

**Fig. 2.** Overall architecture. Baseline includes an encoder network and a decoder network. ResNet-50 is adopted as the encoder network and a U-net-like structure is used as the decoder network. CRC: Consistency recalibration module. MSFRC: Multi-source feature recalibration module.

## 2.1 Consistency Recalibration Module

At first, inspired by U-net-like [9] structure, a typical encoder-decoder network is adopted in this paper to generate the baseline features. Then, we propose consistency recalibration module (CRC) to refine both encoder features $f_e \in R^{H \times W \times C}$ and decoder features $f_d \in R^{H \times W \times C}$. As shown in Fig. 1, $f_e$ contains lots of details such as textures and edges, while lacks enough semantic information. On the contrary, $f_d$ extracts rich semantic features with coarse edges. The possible reason is that $f_e$ is close to the input and the receptive fields are small. While $f_d$ has relatively large receptive fields but goes through too many downpoolings and upsamplings, which leads to the loss or the extra of information.

Therefore, intersection and union mechanisms are applied in CRC to filter the noises and enhance the semantic features. Intersection mechanism picks up the most confident pixels and suppresses the noise pixels. However, some salient pixels especially around the edges may be corroded as well. Consequently, union mechanism is designed to enhance the internal saliency features. The union mechanism enhances the confident pixels in both encoder and decoder features, meanwhile, the indefinite pixels are enhanced as well. Based on the intersection and union mechanisms, the background noises are suppressed and the foreground information are strengthened. Therefore, the intersection and union are designed to refine the features instead of conventional encoder features and decoder features.

Specifically, as illustrated in Fig. 2, CRC contains three steps to obtain clear and complete saliency features. Firstly, the two features $f_e$ and $f_d$ are applied to generate the intersection features $f_I$. Then, the same two features $f_e$ and $f_d$ are used for generating the union features $f_U$. Here, $f_e$ and $f_d$ are reused twice because CRC optimizes these two features from suppression and enhancement. Finally, $f_I$ and $f_U$ are concatenated to preserve their own features. The whole progress can be concluded as follows.

$$f^i_{CRC_{in}} = concat(f^i_e \bigcap f^i_d, f^i_e \bigcup f^i_d), \tag{1}$$

where, $f^i_{CRC_{in}}$ is the input features of $CRC^i$, $i \in \{1, 2, 3, 4, 5\}$ is the layer number, and $concat(\cdot)$ is the operation of concatenation. As shown in Eq. (1), CRC has no convolution calculation, therefore, CRC refines the results without any parameter increasement. In addition, top-down mechanism is adopted to refine the saliency maps. In consideration of the different receptive fields in different layers, cross layer connection can directly transfer the semantic features to other layers, enriching and integrating the salient features of each layer. Therefore, the final CRC features can be denoted as follows.

$$f^i_{CRC_{out}} = \begin{cases} down(f^i_{CRC_{in}}), & i = 1 \\ down(f^1_{CRC_{in}}) + f^i_{CRC_{in}}, & i = 2 \\ down(f^1_{CRC_{in}}) + up(f^i_{CRC_{in}}), & i = other \end{cases} \tag{2}$$

where, $f^i_{CRC_{out}}$ is the output features of $CRC^i$, $down(\cdot)$ denotes the bilinear downsampling operation and $up(\cdot)$ denotes the bilinear upsampling operation. Finally, $f^i_{CRC_{out}}$ is supervised by saliency ground truth after a $1 \times 1$ channel adjustment layer.

## 2.2 Multi-source Feature Recalibration Module

Multi-source feature recalibration (MSFRC) is divided into two steps. The first step is to progressively learn the correlation and recalibrate the difference between edges and saliency, and the second step is to integrate boundary features and saliency features. As illustrated in Fig. 2, there are three feature changes in the first step of MSFRC, which brings more correlation information and difference information. In addition, previous methods [19] introduce boundary features as auxiliary supervision, however, they only use one of the convolutional blocks to generate boundary features, which may lead to parameter imbalance. The larger the saliency parameter is, the more attention the network pays to saliency, while the boundary features with less parameters are easily ignored. Note that the boundary features should not be larger than the saliency features, which may lead to put the cart before the horse.

For the first step, the 1-th block, the 3-th block and the 5-th block are supervised by saliency, which generate the saliency features. The 2-th block and the 4-th block are supervised by edges, which generate the boundary features. Because of back propagation, each layer has potential feature transfer even though there is no direct layer-to-layer connection. Therefore, the boundary features are generated between every saliency layer, which force the network to learn the correlation and recalibrate the diversity. Besides, the saliency layers are more than the edge layers, which ensures the advantage of saliency. For the second step, different layers are aggregated to a whole layer by addition. Two boundary feature layers in MSFRC increase the proportion of edges, which reduces the parameter imbalance.

Specifically, the features $f^i_{CRC_{out}}$ from CRC are transferred to MSFRC, and each $f^i_{CRC_{out}}$ goes through three convolutional layers with batch normalization and ReLU activation function. Then, the five feature maps in MSFRC are added to aggregate multi-level features. The resolution and the channel are unchanged during the process. The whole process can be denoted as follows.

$$f^i_{MSFRC} = F^3_2(\sum_{i=1}^{5} F^3_1(f^i_{CRC_{out}}; \theta^3_1); \theta^3_2), \tag{3}$$

where, $F^3_1$ and $F^3_2$ are the combination of three convolution, batch normalization and ReLU. $\theta^3_1$ and $\theta^3_2$ are the parameters of $F^3_1$ and $F^3_2$. Finally, if $i = 1, 3, 5$, $f^i_{MSFRC}$ is supervised by saliency ground truth after a $1 \times 1$ channel adjustment layer. If $i = 2, 4$, $f^i_{MSFRC}$ is supervised by edge ground truth after a $1 \times 1$ channel adjustment layer.

## 2.3   Loss Function

In mathematical optimization, loss function represents the degree of inconsistency between the predicted value and the ground truth value. In this paper, loss function is divided into saliency loss function and edge loss function.

**Saliency Loss Function.** Currently, most of the methods adopt edge supervision to refine the salient edges. However, the boundary features are usually generated after multiple convolutional layers, which may lead to the feature inconsistency between edge and saliency. Even though in MSFRC, the feature inconsistency is applied to correct the possible errors occurred in previous layers, the salient edges directly from saliency feature layers still need to refine. Therefore, we propose an edge recalibration loss function (ERC) as follows.

$$L^{(s)}_{ERC} = \begin{cases} -\sum_{(m,n)} [\gamma MGlogP], \\ \qquad\qquad if \ M = 1, G = 1 \\ -\sum_{(m,n)} [(1 - \gamma)(1 - M)GlogP], \\ \qquad\qquad if \ M = 0, G = 1 \\ -\sum_{(m,n)} [\gamma M(1 - G)log(1 - P)], \\ \qquad\qquad if \ M = 1, G = 0 \\ -\sum_{(m,n)} [(1 - \gamma)(1 - M)(1 - G)log(1 - P)], \\ \qquad\qquad if \ M = 0, G = 0 \end{cases} \tag{4}$$

where, $L_{ERC}^{(s)}$ is the loss of $s$-th layer. $M$, $G$, $P$ represent the abbreviations $M(m, n)$, $G(m, n)$, $P(m, n)$, respectively. $M(m, n) \in \{0, 1\}$ is the edge ground truth of the pixels $(m, n)$, $\gamma$ is a hyper parameter which controls the edge superiority and we set $\gamma$ to 0.75 in this paper. $G(m, n) \in \{0, 1\}$ is the saliency ground truth and $P(m, n)$ is the predicted saliency probability. Equation 4 means the saliency features are constrained directly by the edge ground truth. Considering the sparsity of edge, we expand the edges in a $3 \times 3$ neighborhood. Consequently, Eq. 4 can be concluded as Eq. 5.

$$L_{ERC}^{(s)} = - \sum_{(m,n)} [(\gamma(M \oplus \boldsymbol{B}) + (1 - \gamma)(1 - (M \oplus \boldsymbol{B}))) \tag{5}$$
$$(G log P + (1 - G)(1 - log P))],$$

where, $\boldsymbol{B}$ is a $3 \times 3$ matrix with all 1, and $M \oplus \boldsymbol{B} = \{m, n | \boldsymbol{B}_{mn} \bigcap M \neq \varnothing\}$ denotes the morphological dilation. For all pixels, ERC first pays more attention to the salient edges, then the saliency and finally the background. ERC has two superiorities. On the one hand, ERC is used for recalibrating the salient edges directly from salient features, which helps the network detect the edges of saliency features. On the other hand, the saliency features and the boundary features of them are optimized simultaneously, which means ERC can balance the two to some extent. Equation 5 means ERC loss mainly focuses on the saliency structure. Therefore, the optimization based on foreground and background should be considered as well. We adopt BCE loss and Dice loss [6] to further optimize the network.

$$L_{BCE}^{(s)} = - \sum_{(m,n)} [G log P + (1 - G)(1 - log P)], \tag{6}$$

$$L_{Dice}^{(s)} = 1 - \frac{\sum_{(m,n)} GP}{\sum_{(m,n)} [G + P]} \tag{7}$$

**Edge Loss Function.** The edges generated in MSFRC are supervised by weighted BCE loss. Different from BCE loss, weighted BCE loss considers the sparsity difference between foreground pixels and background pixels. Weighted BCE loss is shown in Eq. 8.

$$L_{wBCE}^{(e)} = - \sum_{(m,n)} [\omega G log P + (1 - G)(1 - log P)], \tag{8}$$

where, $L_{wBCE}^{(e)}$ is the loss of $e$-th layer. $\omega$ is the abbreviation $\omega(m, n)$ and we set $\omega(m, n) = \frac{\#0\{m,n\}}{\#1\{m,n\}}$, in which $\#0\{m, n\}$ (or $\#1\{m, n\}$) is the number of 0 (or 1). Compared with the background, the sparse edge foreground are assigned higher weights by $\omega$. The hybrid loss can be denoted as follows.

$$L = \sum_{s=1}^{S} [L_{ERC}^{(s)} + L_{BCE}^{(s)} + L_{Dice}^{(s)}] + \sum_{e=1}^{E} L_{wBCE}^{(e)}, \tag{9}$$

where, $S$ and $E$ represent the layer number and are set as 9 and 2, respectively.

**Table 1.** Comparison with state-of-the-art methods. max F-measure ($F_M$, larger is better), max E-measure ($E_M$, larger is better) and S-measure ($S_m$, larger is better) are applied to evaluate the performance. Values with bold fonts indicate the best performance of all results.

| Methods | ECSSD | | | DUT-OMRON | | | PASCAL-S | | | DUTS-Test | | | HKU-IS | | |
|---|---|---|---|---|---|---|---|---|---|---|---|---|---|---|---|
| | $F_M$ | $E_M$ | $S_m$ | $F_M$ | $E_M$ | $S_m$ | $F_M$ | $E_M$ | $S_m$ | $F_M$ | $E_M$ | $S_m$ | $F_M$ | $E_M$ | $S_m$ |
| HRSOD | .932 | .925 | .887 | .743 | .796 | .761 | .846 | .858 | .815 | .835 | .878 | .823 | .910 | .932 | .877 |
| EGNet | .947 | .954 | .924 | .815 | .863 | .838 | .865 | .886 | .851 | .889 | .922 | .885 | .935 | .957 | .917 |
| SCRN | .950 | .955 | .926 | .811 | .875 | .836 | .877 | .904 | **.868** | .888 | .925 | .885 | .934 | .955 | .916 |
| AFNet | .935 | .946 | .913 | .797 | .856 | .825 | .858 | .890 | .847 | .863 | .908 | .866 | .923 | .948 | .905 |
| MLMS | .928 | .916 | .911 | .774 | .839 | .809 | .864 | .847 | .845 | .852 | .863 | .862 | .920 | .938 | .907 |
| BASNet | .942 | .950 | .915 | .805 | .871 | .836 | .854 | .881 | .837 | .859 | .902 | .866 | .928 | .951 | .909 |
| CPD | .939 | .950 | .917 | .797 | .868 | .825 | .859 | .885 | .847 | .865 | .914 | .869 | .925 | .950 | .905 |
| GateNet | .945 | .951 | .919 | .818 | .872 | .837 | .869 | .898 | .857 | .888 | .926 | .885 | .933 | .954 | .914 |
| F3Net | .945 | .953 | .923 | .813 | .867 | .838 | .872 | .897 | .860 | .891 | .926 | .888 | .937 | .957 | .917 |
| ITSD | .947 | .957 | .924 | .821 | .878 | .840 | .870 | .901 | .858 | .883 | .929 | .885 | .934 | .959 | .917 |
| MINet | .947 | .956 | .924 | .810 | .865 | .832 | .867 | .897 | .855 | .884 | .926 | .884 | .935 | .959 | .919 |
| cFRCNet | .944 | .953 | .924 | .821 | .879 | .841 | .872 | .900 | .861 | .887 | .929 | .886 | .933 | .954 | .912 |
| FRCNet | **.951** | **.958** | **.928** | **.828** | **.885** | **.849** | **.879** | **.905** | .865 | **.893** | **.932** | **.890** | **.938** | **.960** | **.920** |

# 3 Experiments

## 3.1 Datasets and Evaluation Metrics

The performance of FRCNet is evaluated on five benchmark datasets: DUT-OMRON with 5168 difficult images, DUTS-test with 5019 complex images, PASCAL-S with 850 images, ECSSD with 1000 images and HKU-IS with 4447 images. Same as the current methods, DUTS-train is used as the training dataset.

Three widely used metrics are applied to evaluate the performance of FRC-Net and other state-of-the-art methods. The first one is maximal F-measure, which has been adopted in most of SOD methods. E-measure [4] and structural similarity measure [3] are widely used metrics in recent years.

## 3.2 Implementation Details

We train FRCNet on DUTS-train dataset following previous works. For a fair comparison, ResNet-50 and U-net-like structure [9] are used as the encoder network and the decoder network, respectively. The whole framework is implemented in PyTorch on an NVIDIA 2080Ti GPU and FRCNet is trained end-to-end. We utilize stochastic gradient descent (SGD) optimizer and the hyper parameters are set as follows: maximum learning rate = 0.005, weight decay = 0.0005, momentum = 0.9. In addition, the learning rate is adjusted by warm-up and linear decay strategies. We train FRCNet for 100 epochs with a batchsize of 32. We do not use any pre-processing or post-processing techniques. The source code will be released.

### 3.3    Comparison with the State-of-the-Art

**Quantitative Comparison.** We compare the proposed FRCNet against 12 state-of-the-art SOD methods, including HRSOD [18], AFNet [5], MLMSNet [15], BASNet [8], SCRN [17], EGNet [19], CPD [16], GateNet [20], F3Net [14], ITSD [21], MINet [7]. For a fair comparison, the saliency maps of the above methods are provided by the authors. As illustrated in Table 1, FRCNet outperforms other methods across five datasets, especially with respect to MaxF metrics. Besides, we also remove all the parameters of MSFRC (cFRCNet). Therefore, the model size is the baseline size. We can observe that cFRCNet also achieves competitive results. This verifies that our CRC and MSFRC are effective.

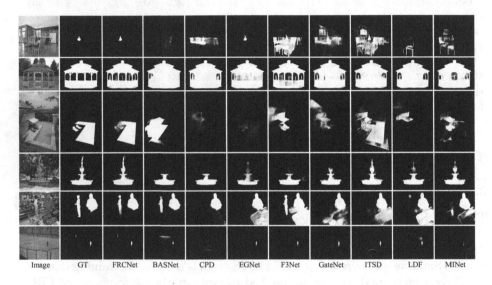

Image    GT    FRCNet    BASNet    CPD    EGNet    F3Net    GateNet    ITSD    LDF    MINet

**Fig. 3.** Visual comparison with state-of-the-art methods.

**Visual Comparison.** As illustrated in Fig. 3, we visualize some results of FRCNet and 9 typical methods for saving room. The resulting saliency maps of FRCNet achieve superior performance, which are closer to the ground truth in visual. Specifically, with the help of CRC, our model not only enhances the salient regions, but also suppresses the background noises (see Fig. 3 row 1, 2 and 3). By the aid of the complementarity of saliency features and boundary features in MSFRC, FRCNet is able to generate more accurate and complete saliency maps even though in the complex background (see Fig. 3 row 4, 5 and 6). Furthermore, FRCNet achieves these results without any pre-processing or post-processing.

### 3.4    Ablation Studies

In this paper, there is one hyper parameter (*i.e.*, $\gamma$) to be determined. $\gamma$ is used in ERC loss function to adjust the weights of boundary features. Obviously, $\gamma$

**Table 2.** Ablation study on different modules optimized by BCE loss. Baseline: the baseline network.

| Baseline | CRC | MSFRC | ECSSD | | | DUT-OMRON | | | PASCAL-S | | |
|---|---|---|---|---|---|---|---|---|---|---|---|
| | | | $F_M$ | $E_M$ | $S_m$ | $F_M$ | $E_M$ | $S_m$ | $F_M$ | $E_M$ | $S_m$ |
| ✓ | | | .914 | .921 | .897 | .763 | .805 | .789 | .816 | .829 | .803 |
| ✓ | ✓ | | .921 | .928 | .904 | .774 | .818 | .802 | .825 | .844 | .812 |
| ✓ | | ✓ | .931 | .937 | .910 | .790 | .837 | .812 | .839 | .861 | .823 |
| ✓ | ✓ | ✓ | **.938** | **.943** | **.918** | **.803** | **.845** | **.823** | **.852** | **.875** | **.835** |

**Table 3.** Ablation study on different losses.

| ωBCE | BCE | Dice | ERC | ECSSD | | | DUT-OMRON | | | PASCAL-S | | |
|---|---|---|---|---|---|---|---|---|---|---|---|---|
| | | | | $F_M$ | $E_M$ | $S_m$ | $F_M$ | $E_M$ | $S_m$ | $F_M$ | $E_M$ | $S_m$ |
| ✓ | ✓ | | | .942 | .945 | .920 | .807 | .856 | .831 | .857 | .879 | .840 |
| ✓ | | ✓ | | .933 | .938 | .912 | .791 | .847 | .820 | .842 | .864 | .826 |
| ✓ | | | ✓ | .944 | .951 | .922 | .811 | .860 | .835 | .861 | .886 | .846 |
| ✓ | ✓ | ✓ | | .946 | .949 | .925 | .818 | .869 | .839 | .862 | .892 | .851 |
| ✓ | | ✓ | ✓ | .947 | .951 | .927 | .822 | .873 | .841 | .866 | .896 | .854 |
| ✓ | ✓ | | ✓ | .948 | .954 | .926 | .824 | .878 | .844 | .871 | .900 | .860 |
| ✓ | ✓ | ✓ | ✓ | **.951** | **.958** | **.928** | **.828** | **.885** | **.849** | **.879** | **.905** | **.865** |

should be larger than 0.5, which assigns higher weights to the edges. When $\gamma = 1$, ERC will only optimize the edges without the saliency features. As mentioned above, ERC should detect the edges and saliency simultaneously. Therefore, the value of $\gamma$ should be between 0.5 and 1. If $\gamma$ is close to 0.5, ERC prefers to detect the saliency. In contrast, if $\gamma$ is close to 1, ERC prefers to detect the edges. Therefore, we set $\gamma$ to 0.75, which balances the assigned weights between boundary features and saliency features.

To validate the effectiveness of each key module, a series of detailed analysis is conducted on DUT-OMRON dataset under various metrics. As shown in Table 2 and Table 3, the ablation study is divided into loss function part and module part. For module ablation, we observe that both CRC and MSFRC can refine the results. Furthermore, the combination of CRC and MSFRC achieves superior qualitative results. For loss ablation, the hybrid loss achieves the best performance. Besides, the single ERC loss performs better than the single BCE loss and Dice loss. The results in Table 2 and Table 3 verify the effectiveness of the proposed modules and losses.

## 4    Conclusion

In this paper, a novel model FRCNet is proposed for accurate and fast SOD. Firstly, to suppress the external noises and enhance the internal salient object, we introduce the intersection and union mechanisms to CRC to recalibrate the consistency of encoder and decoder features. Secondly, to learn the correlation and recalibrate the difference between boundary features and saliency features, MSFRC is proposed to sufficiently couple the complementary features between edges and saliency by alternate feature transfer. Besides, MSFRC can reduce parameter imbalance and effectively aggregate different source features to refine the resulting saliency maps. Finally, to further guide the network to focus on the edges, we propose an ERC loss to recalibrate the equivocal edge pixels. Experimental results on five datasets demonstrate that the proposed FRCNet can achieve consistently superior performance under various metrics.

**Acknowledgements.** This work was supported in part by National Natural Science Foundation of China under grant 62176062.

# References

1. Chen, C., Tan, Z., Cheng, Q., et al.: UTC: a unified transformer with inter-task contrastive learning for visual dialog. In: Proceedings of the IEEE/CVF Conference on Computer Vision and Pattern Recognition, New Orleans, pp. 18103–18112. IEEE (2022)
2. Cheng, Q., Tan, Z., Wen, K., et al.: Semantic pre-alignment and ranking learning with unified framework for cross-modal retrieval. IEEE Trans. Circuits Syst. Video Technol. (2022)
3. Fan, D., Cheng, M., Liu, Y., et al.: Structure-measure: a new way to evaluate foreground maps. In: Proceedings of the IEEE International Conference on Computer Vision, Hawaii, pp. 4548–4557. IEEE (2017)
4. Fan, D., Gong, C., Cao, Y., et al.: Enhanced-alignment measure for binary foreground map evaluation. In: Proceedings of the International Joint Conference on Artificial Intelligence (2018)
5. Feng, M., Lu, H., Ding, E.: Attentive feedback network for boundary-aware salient object detection. In: Proceedings of the IEEE International Conference on Computer Vision, California, pp. 1623–1632. IEEE (2019)
6. Fidon, L., et al.: Generalised wasserstein dice score for imbalanced multi-class segmentation using holistic convolutional networks. In: Crimi, A., Bakas, S., Kuijf, H., Menze, B., Reyes, M. (eds.) BrainLes 2017. LNCS, vol. 10670, pp. 64–76. Springer, Cham (2018). https://doi.org/10.1007/978-3-319-75238-9_6
7. Pang, Y., Zhao, X., Zhang, L., et al.: Multi-scale interactive network for salient object detection. In: Proceedings of the IEEE International Conference on Computer Vision, Seattle, pp. 9413–9422. IEEE (2020)
8. Qin, X., Zhang, Z., Huang, C., et al.: BASNet: boundary-aware salient object detection. In: Proceedings of the IEEE International Conference on Computer Vision, California, pp. 7479–7489. IEEE (2019)
9. Ronneberger, O., Fischer, P., Brox, T.: U-Net: convolutional networks for biomedical image segmentation. In: Navab, N., Hornegger, J., Wells, W.M., Frangi, A.F. (eds.) MICCAI 2015. LNCS, vol. 9351, pp. 234–241. Springer, Cham (2015). https://doi.org/10.1007/978-3-319-24574-4_28
10. Tan, Z., Hua, Y., Gu, X.: Salient object detection with edge recalibration. In: Farkaš, I., Masulli, P., Wermter, S. (eds.) ICANN 2020. LNCS, vol. 12396, pp. 724–735. Springer, Cham (2020). https://doi.org/10.1007/978-3-030-61609-0_57

11. Tan, Z., Gu, X.: Scale balance network for accurate salient object detection. In: Proceedings of the International Joint Conference on Neural Networks, Glasgow, pp. 1–7. IEEE (2020)
12. Tan, Z., Gu, X.: Depth scale balance saliency detection with connective feature pyramid and edge guidance. Appl. Intell. **51**(8), 5775–5792 (2021)
13. Tan, Z., Gu, X.: Co-saliency detection with intra-group two-stage group semantics propagation and inter-group contrastive learning. Knowl.-Based Syst. **252**, 109356 (2022)
14. Wei, J., Wang, S., Huang, Q.: F3Net: fusion, feedback and focus for salient object detection. In: Proceedings of the AAAI Conference on Artificial Intelligence, pp. 12321–12328 (2020)
15. Wu, R., Feng, M., Guan, W., et al.: A mutual learning method for salient object detection with intertwined multi-supervision. In: Proceedings of the IEEE International Conference on Computer Vision, California, pp. 8150–8159. IEEE (2019)
16. Wu, Z., Su, L., Huang, Q.: Cascaded partial decoder for fast and accurate salient object detection. In: Proceedings of the IEEE International Conference on Computer Vision, California, pp. 3907–3916. IEEE (2019)
17. Wu, Z., Su, L., Huang, Q.: Stacked cross refinement network for edge-aware salient object detection. In: Proceedings of the IEEE International Conference on Computer Vision, California, pp. 7264–7273. IEEE (2019)
18. Zeng, Y., Zhang, P., Zhang, J., et al.: Towards high-resolution salient object detection. In: Proceedings of the IEEE International Conference on Computer Vision, Seoul, pp. 7234–7243. IEEE (2019)
19. Zhao, J., Liu, J., Fan, D., et al.: EGNet: edge guidance network for salient object detection. In: Proceedings of the IEEE International Conference on Computer Vision, California, pp. 8779–8788. IEEE (2019)
20. Zhao, X., Pang, Y., Zhang, L., Lu, H., Zhang, L.: Suppress and balance: a simple gated network for salient object detection. In: Vedaldi, A., Bischof, H., Brox, T., Frahm, J.-M. (eds.) ECCV 2020. LNCS, vol. 12347, pp. 35–51. Springer, Cham (2020). https://doi.org/10.1007/978-3-030-58536-5_3
21. Zhou, H., Xie, X., Lai, J., et al.: Interactive two-stream decoder for accurate and fast saliency detection. In: Proceedings of the IEEE International Conference on Computer Vision, Seattle, pp. 9141–9150. IEEE (2020)

# Feature Selection for Trustworthy Regression Using Higher Moments

Fabian Hinder$^{(\boxtimes)}$, Johannes Brinkrolf, and Barbara Hammer

Cognitive Interaction Technology (CITEC), Bielefeld University,
Inspiration 1, 33619 Bielefeld, Germany
{fhinder,jbrinkro,bhammer}@techfak.uni-bielefeld.de

**Abstract.** Feature Selection is one of the most relevant preprocessing techniques in machine learning. Yet, it is usually only considered in the context of classification tasks. Although many methods designed for classification can be carried over to regression tasks, they usually lack some of the theoretical guarantees, that are provided for classification. In particular, reject-option and certainty measures or, more generally, operations which depend on the posterior distribution rather than its expectation only, are not supported. As machine learning is increasingly used in all areas of the daily life including high risk areas like medicine, such tools are essential. In this work, we focus on the problem how to extend feature selection techniques, such that certainty measures are taken into consideration during the selection process. We show that every method which is applicable in multi-value regression can be extended to take into account the complete distribution by making use of higher moments. We prove that the resulting method can be applied to preserve various certainty measures for regression tasks, including variance and confidence intervals, and we demonstrate this in example applications.

**Keywords:** Feature selection · Feature relevance · Trustworthy regression · Higher moments · Non-parametric methods

## 1 Introduction

As machine learning systems become more and more relevant in every day life, including critical infrastructure, medical applications, autonomous driving, etc., the demand for trustworthy AI becomes increasingly relevant [5,12,15]. Many existing approaches including feature selection technologies mainly focus on improving model precision or efficiency and often ignore the model confidence [11]. This is particularly problematic if critical decisions are based on possibly insufficient predictions e.g. due to statistical fluctuations in the (training) data or a small sample size. Popular approaches that tackle such restrictions per design include, e.g., reject-options [5,14,15], background classification [12],

Funding in the frame of the BMWi project KI-Marktplatz, 01MK20007E, is gratefully acknowledged.

or confidence intervals [15]. These methods rely on quantities which are derived from the conditional label distribution or posterior rather than the expected prediction only.

Issues regarding trustworthiness or certainty can be amplified if relevant information is removed during preprossessing steps or ignored by analysis tools. Feature selection is a common preprocessing technique that has a high risk for such mistakes, by removing features that are not relevant to model accuracy but could be critical to trustworthiness. A simple example to show this point is given by the regression task $y = x_1 + x_2\varepsilon$ where $\varepsilon$ is independent Gaussian noise. In this case a simple feature selection that only pays attention to the mean value would consider $x_2$ to be irrelevant, although it is of high relevance for the certainty of the prediction. Currently, many common feature selection methods suffer from this problem.

In this contribution, we provide a theoretical framework that allows us to understand the discrepancy between accuracy-based feature selection methods and those that take the entire posterior, including model certainty, into account. We relate this challenge to feature relevance theory. Thereon, we derive a simple extension to standard feature selection methods and analysis techniques that extends the selection objective to consider the entire posterior, thus including all certainty related quantities. The model can efficiently be implemented based on the higher moments of the label variable.

This paper is organized as follows: First, we recall common certainty measures for regression and discuss their strength and weaknesses (Sect. 2). Then, we recall the definition of classical feature relevance (Sect. 3.1) and provide a new definition that focuses on performance (Sect. 3.2). We recall several feature selection methods from the literature and set them into the context of the theoretical framework provided before (Sect. 4) and compare the relevance notions on a theoretical level (Sect. 5) and derive new approach to deal with them (Sect. 6). We conclude our work by a numerical evaluation of our criterion (Sect. 7) and summarize our findings (Sect. 8).

## 2   Trustworthy Regression

As it is a common assumption in classification that the classes are rather well separated, a very common assumption in regression tasks is that the noise is independent of the data (see Fig. 1a). Both assumptions can be violated in practical applications, leading to the need for confidence or certainty measures to avoid misleading over-precise results.

In classification, one commonly used type are reject options: If a probabilistic classification model predicts very comparable likelihoods for more than one most likely class then the model refuses to perform the prediction [14]. This idea has been extended by adding a "background class" that has a low uniform density everywhere, which allows the model to identify regions where there is insufficient data to make a trustworthy prediction [12].

Under the common assumption that the conditional label $y \mid X$ follows an unimodal distributed, e.g. normal distribution, we can extend the idea of reject

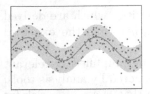 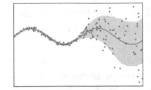 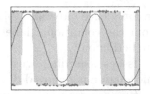

(a) Common regression example with independent Gaussian noise.

(b) Regression example with dependent Gaussian noise.

(c) Regression on bimodal distribution with dependent mean.

**Fig. 1.** Regression examples with comparable MSE but different levels of trustworthyness. Graphic shows data points (blue), regression line (blue), and 10%–90%-quantiles (red). (Color figure online)

options to regression tasks by estimating not only the mean value but also a confidence interval. Similar to reject options for classification, the model can reject a sample if the confidence interval is too large [15] or present the interval to the user to allow them to make an informed decision.

We illustrate the idea of confidence bounds in Fig. 1. Although, the MSE is comparable in all three cases, only in the case of Fig. 1a it is also a valid measure for the model certainty. In case of Fig. 1b, the variance drastically increases to the right, so that the model certainty heavily depends on the considered point. In case of Fig. 1c, the estimation of the mean value is very precise, however, as the distribution is not unimodal, the conditional mean itself is misleading. In all three cases the 10%–90%-quantile area provides a good insight into the specific certainty issue.

*(Conditional) Variance (and Higher Moments):* A common way to quantify the certainty of a measurement is offered by its (conditional) variance. In the case of normal distributed noise, the variance fully represents the uncertainty. However, in cases where the uncertainty depends on the input value, it might be more reasonable to consider conditional variance $\text{Var}(y \mid X) = \mathbb{E}[(y - \mathbb{E}[y \mid X])^2 \mid X]$. It has been successfully used in the context of regression with reject option [15], for example. Notice that conditional variance can easily be estimated using a second model to estimate $\mathbb{E}[y^2 \mid X]$ based on a mean squared error loss.

Albeit the variance offers a suitable certainty measure under the assumption of normal distributed noise, higher moments like skewness or kurtosis can help to understand the peculiarities of more general distributions. For example, if overestimating the true value is less problematic than underestimating it, skewness can offer important information. As another example if an estimation error is critical in extreme cases only, it might be sufficient to take care of the tail distribution – such information is provided by the kurtosis of the distribution.

*Quantiles:* One drawback of moment-based confidence measures is that they are sometimes hard to interpret in a specific setup. Quantiles provide an alternative in such cases: since they are the level points of the cumulative distribution function (cdf), their interpretation is straight forward. As in the case of moments, several estimation methods exist. However, as those are based on a different loss function [9] not every model can be used in a straight forward fashion. Another drawback of quantiles in comparison to moments is that they provide information of a single point of the distribution only. In particular, they do not take information regarding the tail distribution into account.

## 3    Feature Relevance

We will now recall the notion of feature relevance. We consider classification and regression over $\mathbb{R}^d$ to $\{c_1, \ldots, c_m\}$ and $\mathbb{R}$, respectively, with pairs of random variables $(\mathbf{X}, Y)$, corresponding to data and label. We refer to the $i$-th feature of $\mathbf{X}$ as $X_i$. For a set $R = \{r_1, \ldots, r_n\} \subseteq \{1, \ldots, d\}$, we denote the sub-vector containing all features in $R$ as $X_R = (X_{r_1}, \ldots, X_{r_n})$. We also make use of the shorthand notation $C_i = \{i\}^C$ and $X_{C_i}$ for the subset and sub-vector of all features except $i$. In the next two section we will first recall the notion of feature relevance from the literature and then extend it as needed.

### 3.1    Feature Relevance for Classification

We recall the notion of relevance of a feature to the label variable $Y$ as given by [7]. Roughly speaking, a feature $X_i$ is relevant, if it provides information regarding $Y$. More formally, feature relevance is defined as follows:

**Definition 1.** *A feature $X_i$ is* relevant *to $Y$ if and only if there exists a set $R \subseteq C_i$ such that $X_i$ and $Y$ are not independent given $X_R$, i.e.*

$$Y \not\perp\!\!\!\perp X_i \mid X_R.$$

*A relevant feature is called* strongly relevant, *if and only if we may choose $R = C_i$, otherwise it is called* weakly relevant. *A feature that is not relevant is called* irrelevant.

Some authors prefer a slightly different but equivalent definition of strong and weak relevance:

**Corollary 1.** *A feature $X_i$ is strong relevant if and only if $Y$ is not conditionally independent of $X_i$ given the remaining features, i.e. $Y \not\perp\!\!\!\perp X_i \mid X_{C_i}$. It is weakly relevant if and only if it can be made relevant by restricting the feature set, i.e. there exists a proper subset of features $R \subsetneq C_i$ for which $X_i$ is strong relevant.*

As pointed out in [4], the distinction between strong and weak relevance is inspired by the observation that some features may carry redundant information regarding $Y$. As an example, consider the case where two features are identical copies of each other, i.e. $\mathbf{X} = (X_1, X_2, X_2)$. Supposing that $Y$ can be predicted using $X_1 + X_2$, then the first feature is clearly relevant. The other features carry relevant information but they are redundant and only one of those is required. In the framework of Definition 1, the first feature is strongly relevant, while features two and three are weakly relevant.

In the context of feature relevance, two problems are of particular interest: the minimal-optimal problem and the all-relevant problem.

The *minimal-optimal* problem refers to the problem of finding a smallest set of features, that are relevant to the Bayesian classifier and contain all important information. Hence adding further features does not improve the prediction accuracy for $Y$. It can be shown that there exists exactly one such minimal set for strictly positive distributions [10], which is equivalent to the set of strongly relevant features. When it comes to feature selection, one is usually interested in a minimal feature set.

The *all-relevant* problem refers to the problem of identifying all features relevant to $Y$. It was shown that this problem needs exhaustive search for general distributions [10]. Under assumptions on the distribution exact but computational expensive algorithms exist. Due to this restriction, other model based approaches were designed to find approximate solutions [4,8,13].

## 3.2   Feature Relevance for (MSE-)Regression

Although the definition of relevance given above can be applied to regression tasks, and is often referred to in the literature [3,8,13], it is usually approximated by a simpler form in practical applications, at least for regression tasks. The term of statistical independence is empirically tested only by considering a "decrease of the loss of the model", i.e. a feature $X_i$ is relevant if it contains information that may help to predict $Y$. For universal MSE-regression models, this can be formalized as follows:

**Definition 2.** *A feature $X_i$ is $\mathbb{E}$-relevant to $Y$ if and only if there exists a set $R \subseteq C_i$, such that the conditioning of $Y$ on $X_i$ and $X_i, X_R$ differ, i.e.*

$$\mathbb{E}[Y \mid X_i, X_R] \neq \mathbb{E}[Y \mid X_R].$$

*A $\mathbb{E}$-relevant feature is called* strongly $\mathbb{E}$-relevant *if and only if we may choose $R = C_i$, otherwise it is called* weakly $\mathbb{E}$-relevant*. A feature that is not $\mathbb{E}$-relevant is called $\mathbb{E}$-irrelevant.*

Notice that the first formulation of weak and strong relevance (Corollary 1) carries over to weak and strong $\mathbb{E}$-relevance.

A key observation in this context is that (conditional) variance and bias are decreasing if the set of considered features is increased. As a consequence we observe that for the optimal model $f_X^*(x) = \mathbb{E}[Y \mid X = x]$ it holds

$$\mathrm{MSE}(f_{X_i, X_R}^*) \leq \mathrm{MSE}(f_{X_R}^*)$$

and equality holds for all $R$ if and only if $X_i$ is $\mathbb{E}$-irrelevant. However, one can easily construct an example of a strongly-relevant but $\mathbb{E}$-irrelevant feature:

  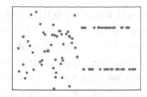

(a) Sample drawn from distribution of Example 1.

(b) Sample drawn from distribution of Example 2

(c) Sample drawn from distribution of Example 3

**Fig. 2.** Example distributions. Axis are $x_1$ and $y$, $\alpha$-channel is $x_2$ (if present).

*Example 1.* Let $\mathbf{X} = (X_1, X_2)$ be a $\mathbb{R}^2$-valued random variable, $\varepsilon \sim \mathcal{N}(0, 1)$ an independent standard normal distributed random variable, $f : \mathbb{R} \to \mathbb{R}$ be some function. If we set $Y = f(X_1) + X_2\varepsilon$, then it holds $\mathbb{E}[Y \mid \mathbf{X}] = f(X_1) + X_2\mathbb{E}[\varepsilon] = f(X_1)$. So $X_2$ is $\mathbb{E}$-irrelevant, but since $\mathrm{Var}(Y \mid \mathbf{X}) = X_2^2$, $X_2$ is strong relevant.

We illustrate the distribution in this example in Fig. 2a. Notice that this example shows that $\mathbb{E}$-relevance is not sufficient for trustworthy regression, as only the first feature is relevant for the prediction, the second feature, however, is very important to estimate the certainty of the prediction. This gives rise to the question under which circumstances we lose information regarding the certainty of a model if we apply feature selection based on the notion of $\mathbb{E}$-relevance. As it turns out, this is a problem which is specific to regression tasks.

Furthermore, the question occurs, how the properties of relevance and $\mathbb{E}$-relevance are related in general. We will consider this question in Sect. 5.

## 4    Feature Selection Methods

In the following, we will discuss some classical feature selection methods from the literature and consider them in the context of the definition of relevance and $\mathbb{E}$-relevance and all-relevant and minimal-optimal problem, respectively. Notice that we will concentrate on wrapper methods which derive a relevance measure from an underlying model, as our approach is based on a transformation of the labels for the prediction task at hand, to select the features.

*Recursive Feature Elimination (RFE)* [3] is based on models that assign importances to features. This can be the feature weight, as in the case of linear models, or an implicit quantity, such as feature importance in case of decision trees or random forests. The algorithm proceeds in a recursive fashion: starting with all features, the model is trained and the feature with the smallest importance value is remove. This procedure is repeated until a certain number of features is obtained. Thereby, the desired number of features can either be predefined by the user or determined by cross-validation.

As RFE does not directly consider the features but only importances assigned by the model its relation to relevance or $\mathbb{E}$-relevance is unclear. However, if it is used together with models that rely on an optimization of the MSE, only $\mathbb{E}$-relevance is considered. This model dependence also makes it hard to determine precisely the set of features RFE aims for, as not all models can process all information equivalently well. Furthermore, it also depends on whether the model is sparse, in which case we will obtain a model dependent analog to the minimal-optimal set, or not, in which case we are closer to the all-relevant set.

*Sequential Feature Selection (SFS)* [2] works similar to RFE in the sense that it either removes ("backward") or adds ("forward") features in a recursive fashion. However, instead of relying on the model to obtain the feature importance, cross-validation is used. It can be shown that "backward" and "forward" procedure do not lead to the same results, in general.

As in the case of RFE, it is neither clear whether relevant or $\mathbb{E}$-relevant features are found. However, in case of "backward" direction, features that are not necessarily relevant for the model are assigned a small value. Hence one can consider SFS as a minimal-optimal search strategy.

*Boruta* [8] uses the feature importance assigned by a learning model, most commonly a random forest. However, in contrast to RFE it adds a randomly permuted versions of the features, dubbed as "shadow-features". These are irrelevant for the prediction of the label by design. As a consequence, any feature that is ranked less important than a shadow feature cannot be relevant. A relevance ranking is then obtained by repeating the steps several time and then performing a statistical analysis.

Boruta is presented as an all-relevant search by the authors. Since it relies on the model error, it aims for $\mathbb{E}$-relevant features in the sense of Definition 2.

## 5   On the Relation of Relevance Notions

As already shown in Example 1, the notions of relevance and $\mathbb{E}$-relevance are not equivalent. Indeed, as suggested above the notion of relevance is stronger, in the sense that $\mathbb{E}$-relevance implies relevance. However, it is also true that under certain circumstances, e.g. in case of binary classification, both notions are equivalent. This justifies the usage of methods that aim for $\mathbb{E}$-relevance from a theoretical point of view in the case of classification problems. Furthermore, it also shows that in the case of classification, standard feature selection methods do not deteriorate trustworthiness of a model.

**Theorem 1.** *Let $\mathbf{X}$ and $Y$ be random variables. If $X_i$ is (weakly/strongly) $\mathbb{E}$-relevant, then it is (weakly/strongly) relevant. Conversely if $X_i$ is irrelevant, then it is $\mathbb{E}$-irrelevant.*

*Furthermore, if $Y \mid X_R$ is Bernoulli distributed (or more general the set of all distributions can be parametrized by their mean value) for all R, then the notions of (weak/strong) relevance and (weak/strong) $\mathbb{E}$-relevant coincide.*

*Proof.* It suffices to show the first statement in the case where $X_i$ is strongly $\mathbb{E}$-relevant. In case of weak $\mathbb{E}$-relevance, we reduce to the set $R$ for which $i$ is strongly $\mathbb{E}$-relevant (Corollary 1), the converse statement for irrelevance follows directly from the definition. Let $X_i$ be strongly $\mathbb{E}$-relevant and assume that it is not strongly relevant. By the rules of conditional expectation regarding independence it then holds $\mathbb{E}[Y \mid X_i, X_{C_i}] = \mathbb{E}[Y \mid X_{C_i}]$ which is a contradiction.

For the second statement, it again suffices to show that strong relevance implies strong $\mathbb{E}$-relevance. Let $X_i$ be strongly relevant and assume that it is not strongly $\mathbb{E}$-relevant. Then $\mathbb{E}[Y \mid X_i, X_{C_i}] = \mathbb{E}[Y \mid X_{C_i}]$, but since expectation is (by assumption) the only parameter of $\mathbb{P}_{Y\mid X_R}$ for all $R$, this implies that $\mathbb{P}_{Y\mid X_i, X_{C_i}} = \mathbb{P}_{Y\mid X_{C_i}}$ which is equivalent to conditional independence and therefore a contradiction.

Considering Theorem 1, one might ask for which type of distribution the notion of relevance and $\mathbb{E}$-relevance coincide. However, as shown by Example 1 this does not hold even for very simple distributions. Indeed, equality basically only holds in the described case. In particular, for the simplest regression task the notion actually do coincide:

**Corollary 2.** *If there exists a function $f$ such that $Y \mid \mathbf{X} = f(\mathbf{X}) + \varepsilon$, where $\varepsilon \sim \mathcal{N}(0, \sigma)$ is independent, normal distributed noise, the notions of (weakly/strong) relevance and (weakly/strong) $\mathbb{E}$-relevant coincide.*

However, in this case the certainty is independent of $\mathbf{X}$ and thus of no interest. For every set that contains more than two points there exists a distribution for which equality no longer holds:

*Example 2.* Let $\mathbf{X} = (X_1) \sim \mathcal{U}([-1, 1])$ a uniformly distributed random variable and $\sigma$ be an independent Bernoulli distributed random variable with mean value $1/2$. Set $Y = 2\sigma - 1$ if $X_1 > 0$ and $Y = 0$ otherwise. Then $Y$ is supported on three points only. Furthermore, since $\mathbb{E}[Y \mid \mathbf{X}] = 0 = \mathbb{E}[Y]$ it follows that $X_1$ is not $\mathbb{E}$-relevant, but the value of the conditional variance implies that $X_1$ is relevant.

We illustrate this example in Fig. 2b. As restricting the considered distributions yields only trivial solutions, we are looking for a way that allows us to relate relevance and $\mathbb{E}$-relevance. Considering Example 1 and 2, the size of the variance may provide a sufficient criterion. However, it is easy to construct an example where this is no longer the case:

*Example 3.* Consider the same setup as in Example 2 and let $\varepsilon$ be an independent standard normal distributed random variable. Set $Y' = \varepsilon(1 - |Y|) + Y$. Clearly $\mathbb{E}[Y' \mid \mathbf{X}] = \mathbb{E}[Y'] = 0$, furthermore $\mathrm{Var}(Y' \mid \mathbf{X}) = 1$.

Instead of considering only the first two moments, i.e. mean and variance, we can also consider the higher moments which solves the problem:

**Theorem 2.** *Let $Y$ be a real-valued random variable. Assume $Y$ is compactly supported or fulfills Carleman's condition [1]. If $X_i$ is (weakly/strongly) relevant to $Y$ then there exists a $k$ such that $X_i$ is (weakly/strongly) $\mathbb{E}$-relevant to $Y^k$.*

*Proof.* It is again suffices to show the case where $X_i$ is strongly relevant (see the proof of Theorem 1). As $X_i$ is strongly relevant it holds $Y \not\perp X_i \mid X_{C_i}$ which is equivalent to $\mathbb{P}_{Y|X_i,X_{C_i}} \neq \mathbb{P}_{Y|X_{C_i}}$, i.e. there exists a set $C$ such that $\mathbb{P}_{Y|X_i,X_{C_i}}(C) \neq \mathbb{P}_{Y|X_{C_i}}(C)$ as $L^1$-functions. Denote the conditionals (with and without $X_i$) difference by $f(x_i, x_r) = \mathbb{P}_{Y|X_i=x_i,X_{C_i}=x_r}(C) - \mathbb{P}_{Y|X_{C_i}=x_r}(C)$. As $f \neq 0$, we may find a set $A \times B \subset \mathbb{R} \times \mathbb{R}^{d-1}$ on which $f$ has positive expectation, i.e. $\mathbb{E}[f, A \times B] > 0$, using a monotonous class argument. As $\mathbb{E}[f \mid X_{C_i}] = 0$, it follows that $\mathbb{E}[f, A \times B] = -\mathbb{E}[f, A^C \times B]$ and thus $\mathbb{P}_{Y|X_i \in A, X_{C_i} \in B} \neq \mathbb{P}_{Y|X_i \in A^C, X_{C_i} \in B}$. If $Y$ is compactly supported, the statement follows by applying Weierstrass's approximation theorem. To use Carleman's condition observe that either $\mathbb{P}_{Y|X_i \in A, X_{C_i} \in B^C} = \mathbb{P}_{Y|X_i \in A^C, X_{C_i} \in B^C}$, in which case we may replace $B$ by $\mathbb{R}^{d-1}$, or it does not hold, so that we end up with two pairs of distributions, each with a global split along $X_i$. As Carleman's condition holds globally for $Y$, it follows by Jensen's inequality that it holds for at least one of the two/four distributions, which is then uniquely determined by its moments. Notice that this suffices to show the statement since the partner distributions either fulfills the condition, too, in which case the uniqueness applies, or it does not, in which case the moments have to be different.

Notice that Theorem 2 allows us to connect relevance and $\mathbb{E}$-relevance of a higher dimensional problem, using a transformation of the labels. We will derive an algorithmic solution from this observation in the next section.

# 6    Application: Moment Feature Relevance

By applying Theorem 2 we connect the task to determine relevant and $\mathbb{E}$-relevant features. For this purpose, we perform relevance analysis for the regression task with respect to the label vector $(Y, Y^2, \ldots, Y^d)$ rather than $Y$ [6]. One can also use a different transformation, e.g. based on the Legendre polynomials or a Fourier transformation, which can be beneficial in practice. Indeed, if $Y$ is compactly supported, any function basis can be used. We refer to this method as *Moment Feature Relevance*.

Although we have to take $d \to \infty$ to monitor relevance, considering the first $d$ moments is usually sufficient in practice due to noise and estimation errors. Indeed, we can quantify the error by following corollary of [6, Theorem 2] which shows that for large $d$ only features with small impact on the label are missed:

**Corollary 3.** *Let $Y$ be a $[-1,1]$-valued random variable and assume that $\mathbb{E}[Y^k \mid \mathbf{X}] = \mathbb{E}[Y^k \mid X_{C_i}]$ for all $k \leq d$. Then it holds*

$$\int_0^1 \left| F^{-1}_{Y|X_{C_i}}(q) - F^{-1}_{Y|\mathbf{X}}(q) \right| \mathrm{d}q = \int_{-\infty}^{\infty} \left| F_{Y|X_{C_i}}(y) - F_{Y|\mathbf{X}}(y) \right| \mathrm{d}y \leq \sqrt{\frac{16}{2d-1}},$$

*where $F_{Y|\mathbf{X}}$, $F^{-1}_{Y|\mathbf{X}}$, $F_{Y|X_{C_i}}$, and $F^{-1}_{Y|X_{C_i}}$ denote the cdf and quantile function (i.e. inverse cdf) of $\mathbb{P}_{Y|\mathbf{X}}$ and $\mathbb{P}_{Y|X_{C_i}}$, respectively.*

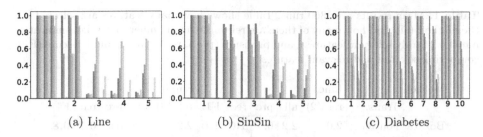

(a) Line                    (b) SinSin                    (c) Diabetes

**Fig. 3.** Mean probability to select a feature (1–5/1–10) for used datatasets, selection methods, and transformations. Block order: Boruta (blue), REF (orange), SFS (green). In block order (dark to light): Fourier, Legendre, Moment, Raw. (Color figure online)

Notice that this result connects the two confidence measures considered in Sect. 2. In particular, when computing the feature relevances using the moment technique, we also take care of the quantiles. Furthermore, notice that though Corollary 3 formally require $Y$ to take values in $[-1, 1]$, the statement can also be applied in the case where $Y$ takes on any values in $\mathbb{R}$ using a suitable preprocessing function like tanh.

## 7  Empirical Evaluation

We empirically evaluate our method. The method uses a label transformation followed by a standard feature selection on the resulting (multi-)regression problem (see Sect. 6 for details). We use two theoretical datasets with ground truth, i.e. the relevant features are known. Further, we use one real world dataset. We use the following feature selection methods: SFS (backward search, predefined number of features), RFE (using cross-validation to determine number of features), and Boruta (default parameters). We use the following moment transformations: Fourier $(y \mapsto (\exp(k\pi \mathrm{i} y))_{k=-d}^{d})$, Legendre $(y \mapsto (L_k(y))_{k=1}^{d}$, where $L_k$ denotes the Legendre polynomial of degree $k$), Moment: $(y \mapsto (y^k)_{k=1}^{d})$, and Raw $(y \mapsto y,$ i.e. the base case without transformation). In all cases, we choose $d = 5$ as suggested in [6] and random forests as base model. Before the transformation, $Y$ is normalized to the interval $-1$ and $1$.

For the theoretical data, $\mathbf{X}$ follows a 5-dimensional uniform distribution. $Y$ is distributed according to

$$\text{Line: } Y = 8X_1 - (36X_2^2 - 36X_2 + 1)\varepsilon$$
$$\text{SinSin: } Y = \sin(2\pi X_1 - \pi) + 3\sin(2\pi X_2 - \pi)\sin(2\pi X_3 - \pi)\varepsilon,$$

whereby $\varepsilon \sim \mathcal{N}(0, 1)$ is an independent standard normal distribution. As can be seen $X_1$ and $X_2$ are relevant for Line, and $X_1, X_2$, and $X_3$ relevant for SinSin. In both cases only $X_1$ is E-relevant. Notice that the all-relevant and minimal-optimal feature sets coincide. To evaluate the method we compare the feature set selected by the method and the set of relevant features. The results are presented in Fig. 3a, b, and in Table 1. The Fourier transformation works best over

**Table 1.** Mean results over 300 runs. Table shows how many features are selected by the method (all) and how many of them are relevant (rel., number in brackets indicates number of truly relevant features), and precision (prc.), recall (rec.), and F1-score (F1) comparing selected and relevant features.

| Method | | Line | | | | | SinSin | | | | |
|---|---|---|---|---|---|---|---|---|---|---|---|
| | Trans. | rel. (2) | all | prc | rec | F1 | rel. (3) | all | prc | rec | F1 |
| Boruta | Fourier | 2.0 | 2.2 | 0.9 | **1.0** | **1.0** | 2.2 | 2.4 | 0.9 | **0.7** | **0.8** |
| | Legendre | 1.5 | 1.7 | 0.9 | 0.8 | 0.8 | 1.0 | 1.1 | 1.0 | 0.3 | 0.5 |
| | Moment | 1.0 | 1.1 | 0.9 | 0.5 | 0.6 | 1.0 | 1.1 | 1.0 | 0.3 | 0.5 |
| | Raw | 1.0 | 1.2 | 0.9 | 0.5 | 0.6 | 1.0 | 1.1 | 1.0 | 0.3 | 0.5 |
| RFE | Fourier | 2.0 | 2.9 | **0.8** | **1.0** | **0.9** | 2.8 | 3.5 | **0.8** | **0.9** | **0.9** |
| | Legendre | 2.0 | 3.2 | 0.7 | **1.0** | 0.8 | 2.7 | 4.3 | 0.7 | **0.9** | 0.7 |
| | Moment | 1.5 | 3.7 | 0.5 | 0.8 | 0.5 | 2.4 | 4.0 | 0.6 | 0.8 | 0.7 |
| | Raw | 1.5 | 3.6 | 0.5 | 0.8 | 0.6 | 2.1 | 3.5 | 0.7 | 0.7 | 0.6 |
| SFS | Fourier | 2.0 | 2.0 | **1.0** | **1.0** | **1.0** | 2.8 | 3.0 | **0.9** | **0.9** | **0.9** |
| | Legendre | 2.0 | 2.0 | **1.0** | **1.0** | **1.0** | 2.5 | 3.0 | 0.8 | 0.8 | 0.8 |
| | Moment | 1.7 | 2.0 | 0.9 | 0.9 | 0.9 | 2.3 | 3.0 | 0.8 | 0.8 | 0.8 |
| | Raw | 1.3 | 2.0 | 0.6 | 0.6 | 0.6 | 2.0 | 3.0 | 0.7 | 0.7 | 0.7 |

all selection methods, followed by the Legendre transformation, which however seems to be less compatible with Boruta and RFE on SinSin. Simple moments seem to work with SFS, only. Furthermore, without moments (Raw) all methods are only capable of identifying the $\mathbb{E}$-relevant features, the probability of detecting the other relevant features is random.

We also apply the method to the UCI benchmark diabetes. We evaluate the method by splitting the dataset in two halves (50%), one for selecting the features and the remaining to score the selection using the test error (5-fold, 2/3–1/3 train test split) of a quantile regression model ($q = 0.05, 0.10, 0.25, 0.50, 0.75, 0.90, 0.95$) on the selected features only. The selection probability for Boruta and REF are very comparable (see Fig. 3c). SFS considers features 1, 2, 5, 6, and 8 less relevant. The scores of all methods are comparable and well inside the range of statistical fluctuations.

## 8    Conclusion

In this paper, we considered the problem of feature selection for trustworthy regression. We showed that feature relevance is a suitable relevance notion to take confidence intervals into account. We established a formal framework that allows us to connect feature selection via wrapper methods and feature relevance. Using this, we showed that commonly used wrapper methods are not sufficient for detecting all features that are needed if confidence is a target. We suggested and evaluated an extension via a label transformation to solve this problem.

# References

1. Akhiezer, N.I.: The Classical Moment Problem and Some Related Questions in Analysis. SIAM, Philadelphia (2020)
2. Chandrashekar, G., Sahin, F.: A survey on feature selection methods. Comput. Electr. Eng. **40**(1), 16–28 (2014). https://doi.org/10.1007/s10462-021-10072-6
3. Guyon, I., Weston, J., Barnhill, S., Vapnik, V.: Gene selection for cancer classification using support vector machines. Mach. Learn. **46**(1), 389–422 (2002). https://doi.org/10.1023/A:1012487302797
4. Göpfert, C., Pfannschmidt, L., Göpfert, J.P., Hammer, B.: Interpretation of linear classifiers by means of feature relevance bounds. Neurocomputing **298**, 69–79 (2018). https://doi.org/10.1016/j.neucom.2017.11.074
5. Hendrickx, K., Perini, L., Van der Plas, D., Meert, W., Davis, J.: Machine learning with a reject option: A survey. arXiv preprint arXiv:2107.11277 (2021)
6. Hinder, F., Vaquet, V., Brinkrolf, J., Hammer, B.: Fast non-parametric conditional density estimation using moment trees. In: 2021 IEEE Symposium Series on Computational Intelligence (SSCI), pp. 1–7 (2021). https://doi.org/10.1109/SSCI50451.2021.9660031
7. Kohavi, R., John, G.H.: Wrappers for feature subset selection. Artif. Intell. **97**(1), 273– 324 (1997). https://doi.org/10.1016/S0004-3702(97)00043-X, relevance
8. Kursa, M.B., Rudnicki, W.R.: Feature selection with the Boruta package. J. Stat. Softw. **36**(11), 1–13 (2010). https://doi.org/10.18637/jss.v036.i11
9. Meinshausen, N., Ridgeway, G.: Quantile regression forests. J. Mach. Learn. Res. **7**(6), 983–999 (2006)
10. Nilsson, R., Peña, J., Björkegren, J., Tegner, J.: Consistent feature selection for pattern recognition in polynomial time. J. Mach. Learn. Res. **8**, 589–612 (2007)
11. Osborne, J.W., Waters, E.: Four assumptions of multiple regression that researchers should always test. Pract. Assess. Res. Eval. **8**(1), 2 (2002)
12. Perello-Nieto, M., Filho, T.D.M.E.S., Kull, M., Flach, P.: Background check: a general technique to build more reliable and versatile classifiers. In: 2016 IEEE 16th International Conference on Data Mining (ICDM), pp. 1143–1148 (2016). https://doi.org/10.1109/ICDM.2016.0150
13. Pfannschmidt, L., Hammer, B.: Sequential feature classification in the context of redundancies. CoRR **abs/2004.00658** (2020). https://arxiv.org/abs/2004.00658
14. Villmann, T., et al.: Self-adjusting reject options in prototype based classification. In: Merényi, E., Mendenhall, M.J., O'Driscoll, P. (eds.) Advances in Self-Organizing Maps and Learning Vector Quantization. AISC, vol. 428, pp. 269–279. Springer, Cham (2016). https://doi.org/10.1007/978-3-319-28518-4_24
15. Zaoui, A., Denis, C., Hebiri, M.: Regression with reject option and application to KNN. In: Larochelle, H., Ranzato, M., Hadsell, R., Balcan, M.F., Lin, H. (eds.) Advances in Neural Information Processing Systems, vol. 33, pp. 20073–20082. Curran Associates, Inc. (2020)

# Fire Detection Based on Improved-YOLOv5s

Mengdong Zhou, Jianjun Li, and Shuai Liu[(✉)]

Central South University of Forestry and Technology, Changsha 410004, China
xifang99@126.com

**Abstract.** Forest fires have a very bad impact on the natural environment and human beings. To protect the environment and enhance human safety, it is important to detect the source of a fire before it spreads. The existing fire detection algorithms have a weak generalization and do not fully consider the influence of fire target size on detection. To enhance the ability of fire detection of different sizes, ground fire data and Unmanned Aerial Vehicle (UAV) forest fire data are combined in this paper. To improve the detection accuracy of the model, a cosine annealing algorithm, label smoothing, and multi-scale training are introduced. The experimental results show that the Improved-YOLOv5s model proposed in this paper has strong generalization and a good detection effect for different sizes of fires. The mean Average Precision (mAP) value reaches 88.7%, 8% higher than that of YOLOv5s mAP. The proposed model has the advantages of strong generalization and high precision.

**Keywords:** Fire detection · YOLOv5 · Cosine annealing

## 1 Introduction

Forests are known as the "lungs of the earth". As a kind of natural ecosystem, forests can regulate climate, purify the air and maintain ecological balance [1]. However, in recent years, frequent forest fires have inflicted devastating blows on many forest ecosystems, not only burning trees, affecting soil quality, but also having a significant impact on human society [2, 3]. After the flame spreads, it is difficult to carry out fire fighting work, so it is very important to find the fire source in time [4].

There are two approaches to fire detection: sensor-based and vision-based. Sensor-based fire detection requires close activation of sensors to collect sensitive information on the fire scene. The fire alarm detection system designed by Dasari [5] uses a smoke sensor and a flame sensor to detect the flame and uses the global mobile communication system to notify the user remotely. Noureddine [6] uses a unimodal approach to detect fires (the sensed data is scalar in nature, such as temperature and humidity). Due to the high cost of sensor-based detection systems and complex detection conditions [7], vision-based detection systems have fast response, wide-coverage, and low deployment costs [8]. Therefore, vision-based fire detection has attracted more and more attention.

In the early development of computer vision, machine learning algorithms flourished, and the development of fire detection was accompanied by machine learning methods. Mithira et al. [9] used a Bayesian classifier and Support Vector Machine (SVM) classifier

E. Pimenidis et al. (Eds.): ICANN 2022, LNCS 13532, pp. 88–100, 2022.
https://doi.org/10.1007/978-3-031-15937-4_8

to analyze the features of the Histogram of Oriented Gradient (HOG) extracted from images. To achieve higher detection accuracy; Jin and Lu [10] extracted the fire motion information and color information and improved the Local Binary Pattern (LBP) features in the color information to achieve better detection performance. Mishra et al. [11] achieved accurate and efficient prediction by combining RGB, $YC_bC_r$, and CIE-LAB color features. Wahyono et al. [12] proposed a new framework for fire detection based on color, motion, and shape features combined with machine learning techniques to accelerate detection speed while maintaining accuracy. Although machine learning can achieve good detection results, it still cannot get rid of the shortcomings of manual extraction. Fire detection is faced with the problem of background complexity and target diversity, which makes it impossible for humans to discover the deep features hidden in pixel information with naked eyes [13, 14]. The emergence of the deep learning method brings a new development path to fire detection.

Deep learning methods can realize automatic feature extraction, which makes flame detection based on image classification more efficient [15]. Existing object detection algorithms can be roughly divided into two categories: two-stage algorithms and one-stage algorithms. The algorithm of the two-stage is to locate first and then classify; the algorithm of the one-stage completes two tasks at the same time. Zhang [16] adopted Faster Regional Convolutional Neural Network (Faster R-CNN) to detect wildland forest fire smoke, avoiding the complex manual feature extraction process in traditional video smoke detection methods. Barmpoutis [17] combined Faster R-CNN with multi-dimensional texture analysis, and the detection accuracy was improved. Saponara [18] developed a detection technique using R-CNN to measure smoke and fire features in restricted video surveillance environments. These two-stage algorithms, although high in accuracy, are slow in detection. To address this problem, efficient object detection frameworks (one-stage algorithms) are proposed, such as You Only Look Once (YOLO) and Single Shot MultiBox Detector (SSD). Wu [19] judged that the one-stage algorithm has a better real-time performance by comparing the ability of Faster R-CNN, YOLOv3, and SSD to detect fire. Wang [20] proposed a lightweight fire detection model using MobileNetV3 to replace the backbone network of YOLOv4, and the inference speed was accelerated by 3 times. Xu [21] integrated YOLOv5 and EfficientDet to complete the fire detection process, while using EfficientNet to learn global information, the detection performance was improved by 2.5%–10.9%. Since forest fire detection needs to take into account the accuracy and speed, this paper improves the YOLOv5 network on this premise.

The main contributions of this paper are as follows:

- To improve the detection accuracy, the Focus module in the backbone network is replaced by the Convolution layer, the BatchNorm layer, and the Sigmoid Weighted Liner Unit layer (CBS);
- To speed up the inference process of the model, the Spatial Pyramid Pooling (SPP) module is upgraded to the Spatial Pyramid Pooling Faster (SPPF) module;
- Use the cosine annealing algorithm and the warm-up learning rate decay strategy to replace the original linear decay strategy to make the model more effective;
- Label smoothing is used to prevent overfitting;
- Use multi-scale training to improve the detection accuracy of the model.

## 2  Method

### 2.1  Data Collection and Preprocessing

**Data Collection.** To enhance the generalization ability of the model, the dataset in this paper contains flames of different shooting heights, different forest scenes, different times, and different burning ranges. The large number of pictures taken by drones included in it ensure the model's ability to detect small flames.

Due to the scarcity of public fire datasets, this paper collected three sets of public datasets for experiments, namely the public datasets of the Computer Vision and Pattern Recognition Laboratory of Keimyung University in Korea [22], the FIRESENSE database [23], and the public datasets of Durham University. The dataset [24], with a total of 2059 images (Fig. 1a). To enhance the generalization effect of the model and improve the detection ability of the model for small target flames, the data set also contains 1853 pieces of UAV forest flame data published by Northern Arizona University, Fire Luminosity Airborne-based Machine learning Evaluation (FLAME) [25] (Fig. 1b), and 1549 flame data of the drone data taken by ourselves (Fig. 1c). The final experimental data has a total of 5461 flame pictures.

Images are marked with "fire" using LabelME software to generate XML files. In the experiment, the data set is divided into the training set, validation set, and test set according to the ratio of 8:1:1.

a                               b                               c

**Fig. 1.** Dataset example, where a is ordinary fire data, b is FLAME drone data, and c is our drone data.

**Data Preprocessing.** To further enhance the generalization of the model, we preprocess the images using mosaic data augmentation. Mosaic data enhancement is to stitch four pictures into one picture, and these four pictures are randomly flipped, scaled, color gamut changed, and panned (Fig. 2). The probability of image scaling and flipping is 50%, the probability of hue, saturation, and brightness in the color gamut change is 1.5%, 70%, and 40%, respectively, and the probability of panning is 10%.

The uneven distribution of small objects in the dataset on the images will lead to insufficient training. After using mosaic data enhancement, the distribution of small targets will become uniform, so mosaic data enhancement can improve the detection ability of small targets.

**Fig. 2.** Mosaic data augmentation.

## 2.2 Network Model

YOLOv5 is the latest YOLO network, which achieves the effect of fast detection speed and high detection accuracy. It is mainly composed of the backbone network, neck, and head. In this experiment, we fine-tuned the network structure of YOLOv5, replacing the Focus module in the backbone network with the CBS module, and the SPP module in the neck with the SPPF module. The overall network model is shown in Fig. 3.

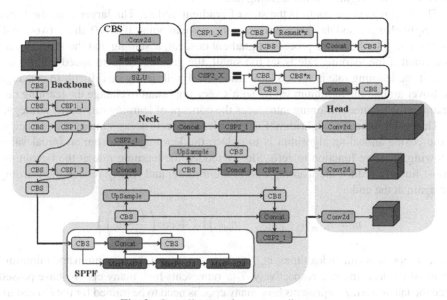

**Fig. 3.** Overall network structure diagram.

**SPPF.** The SPPF module is called fast spatial pyramid pooling, which can transform feature maps of arbitrary size into feature vectors of fixed size. Compared with the SPP module, SPPF (see Fig. 4) divides the features obtained through the maximum pooling layer into two parts, one is used for final splicing and the other is continued pooling, and features of different levels are obtained through different sub-pooling. The final effect of both SPP and SPPF is to obtain eigenvectors of fixed size, but SPPF is about 4 times faster.

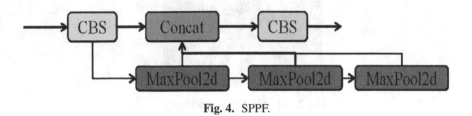

**Fig. 4.** SPPF.

## 2.3   Cosine Annealing + Warm-Up

In the training of the deep learning algorithm, the method of gradient descent is adopted to optimize the model, and the standard weight update formula is Eq. 1:

$$W+ = \alpha * gradient \tag{1}$$

where $W$ is the weight; $\alpha$ is the learning rate.

The learning rate $\alpha$ controls the step of gradient update. The larger $\alpha$ is, the faster the weight changes and the faster it reaches the optimal point. If $\alpha$ is 0, the network will stop updating. In the whole process of gradient descent, assuming that the learning rate is constant if the learning rate is set too small, the gradient descent speed will be too slow; if the learning rate is set too large, the model will finally be difficult to converge and hover around the minimum value. So it's very important to change the learning rate dynamically. So model training introduces the concept of learning rate decay strategy.

The cosine annealing algorithm (Eq. 2) is a learning rate decay strategy. The principle of the cosine annealing algorithm is to reduce the learning rate from an initial value following a cosine function to zero. Slowly reduce the learning rate at the beginning, almost linearly reduce the learning rate in the middle, and slowly reduce the learning rate again at the end.

$$\eta_t = \eta_{min}^i + \frac{1}{2}\left(\eta_{max}^i - \eta_{min}^i\right)\left(1 + cos\left(\frac{T_{cur}}{T_i}\pi\right)\right) \tag{2}$$

where, $i$ represents the index times, $\eta_{max}^i$ and $\eta_{min}^i$ represent the maximum and minimum values of the learning rate respectively. $T_{cur}$ represents how many epochs have passed since the last restart. $T_i$ represents how many epochs need to be trained for the $i$ th restart.

Warm-Up is a way to warm up the learning rate. Since the model weight is randomly generated at the beginning of training, if the learning rate is too large at this time, the model will be oscillated (unstable). If Warm-Up is selected, the learning rate at the beginning of training will be small, and the model will gradually stabilize. The pre-set learning rate is used for training, which makes the model convergence speed faster and the model effect better. We combine the two methods to obtain the learning rate transformation of this experiment (see Fig. 5).

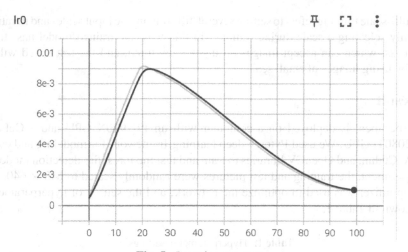

**Fig. 5.** Learning rate curve.

## 2.4 Label Smoothing

Because the samples of the dataset are manually labeled, there are usually a small number of incorrect labels, which can affect the prediction effect. Label smoothing is to assume that there may be errors in the label in the training process, avoid "excessive" trust in the label of the training sample, and improve the problem of poor generalization ability.

Label smoothing (Eq. 3–4) combines uniform distribution and replaces the traditional one-hot encoded label vector $y_{hot}$ with the new label vector $\hat{y}_i$:

$$\hat{y}_i = y_{hot} * (1 - \alpha) + \alpha/K \tag{3}$$

$$\hat{y}_i = \begin{cases} 1 - \alpha, & i = \text{target} \\ \alpha/K, & i \neq \text{target} \end{cases} \tag{4}$$

where $K$ is the number of label categories and $\alpha$ is the hyperparameter that determines the smoothness quantity, $\alpha$ is a small hyperparameter (generally 0.1).

Distribution of label smoothing is equivalent to adding noise to the real distribution, which prevents the model from being too confident about the correct labels and reduces the difference between the output values of positive and negative samples, thus avoiding over-fitting and improving the generalization ability of the model.

## 2.5 Multi-scale

Multi-scale training has been proven to be an effective way to improve performance. The size of the input image has a great influence on the performance of the detection model. In the basic network part, the feature image is often generated tens of times smaller than the original image, resulting in the feature description of small objects not easy to be captured by the detection network. By inputting larger and larger images for training, the robustness of the detection model to object size can be improved to a certain extent.

Multi-scale training refers to setting several different image input scales and iterations randomly selecting a scale during training. In this way, the trained model has strong robustness, which can accept images of any size as input, and the test speed will be faster by using images of small scale.

## 3 Result

The experiment is deployed on a computer with an I9-7920X CPU and a GeForce RTX 2080Ti GPU. We used Pytorch deep learning framework for modeling and called CUDA, Cudnn, and OpenCV libraries to train and test the forest fire detection model. In the experiment, the training and test pictures were randomly scaled to 640 × 640. The SGD optimizer was used to optimize the network, and the setting of hyperparameters was shown in Table 1.

**Table 1.** Hyperparameter settings.

| Parameter value | Parameter value |
|---|---|
| Learning rate (lr) | 0.01 |
| Warm Up epochs | 3.0 |
| Warm Up momentum | 0.8 |
| Warm Up bias lr | 0.1 |
| Momentum | 0.937 |
| Batch size | 16 |
| Number of iterations | 100 |

### 3.1 Evaluation Index Calculation Formula

To compare the difference in detection effect among different models, three evaluation indexes, precision (Eq. 5), recall (Eq. 6), and mAP (Eq. 7), are introduced to quantitatively compare model performance.

$$Precision = \frac{TP}{TP + FP} \tag{5}$$

$$Recall = \frac{TP}{TP + FN} \tag{6}$$

$$mAP = \sum_{k=1}^{N} P(k)\Delta R(k) \tag{7}$$

Among them, True Positive (TP) means that the sample is positive and the prediction result is positive, False Negative (FN) means that the sample is positive and the prediction result is negative, and FP (False Positive) means that the sample is negative and the prediction result is positive. In Eq. 7, N represents the number of all pictures in the test set, P(k) represents the value of Precision when k pictures can be recognized, and $\Delta R(k)$ represents that the number of recognized pictures changes from k $-1$ to k time (by adjusting the threshold) the change of the recall value.

## 3.2  Results Presentation

To compare the progress of each modification on the experiment, we conducted five control experiments, and each control experiment was modified by one step based on the previous one. Since adding the modified method name directly after the model name will cause the name to be too large. Therefore, letters A~E are used to represent different control experiments. The correspondence between letters A~E and experiments is shown in Table 2.

**Table 2.**  Correspondence between letters and models

| Letter | Model |
| --- | --- |
| A | YOLOv5s |
| B | YOLOv5s + CBS + SSPF |
| C | YOLOv5s + CBS + SSPF + cosine annealing |
| D | YOLOv5s + CBS + SSPF + cosine annealing + label smoothing |
| E (Our model) | YOLOv5s + CBS + SSPF + cosine annealing + label smoothing + multi-scale |

Figure 6 is a curve of the evaluation index as the number of training iterations increases. As can be seen from the figure, Experiment E as a whole is the best performing model in terms of precision, recall, and mAP. The original model is the worst in any aspect, so it can be concluded that our modification is very helpful to improve the detection effect.

To show the improvement of the model more intuitively, Table 3 shows the result data of the four evaluation indicators, where mAP_0.5 represents the average accuracy of the model when the threshold is 0.5, and mAP_0.5:0.95 represents the average accuracy of the model when the threshold is 0.95. It can be seen from the table that compared with the previous set of experiments, the precision of experiments B, C, and E is improved, but the recall remains unchanged, which proves that modifying the model structure, using the cosine annealing algorithm and setting multi-scale can reduce the false detection rate, that is, the target that is not a flame is not detected as a flame, which enhances the detection ability of similar targets. The recall value of experiment D is increased and the precision is decreased, which proves that label smoothing improves the overall detection level, and thus improves the false detection rate, but overall the improvement of flame detection is still stronger, so the mAP increases. In general, mAP is 8% higher than that of YOLOv5s, which is a great improvement. Among them, the cosine annealing algorithm contributes the most to the improvement of the model detection effect.

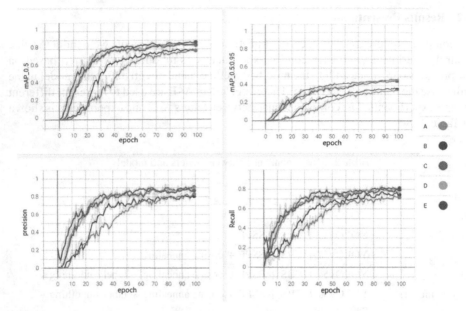

**Fig. 6.** Change curve of evaluation indexes.

**Table 3.** Comparison of evaluation index results.

| Model | Precision | Recall | mAP_0.5 | mAP_0.5:0.95 |
|---|---|---|---|---|
| YOLOv5s | 0.77804 | 0.7834 | 0.80621 | 0.35018 |
| YOLOv5s + CBS + SSPF | 0.81124 | 0.78409 | 0.81004 | 0.36408 |
| YOLOv5s + CBS + SSPF + cosine annealing | 0.90271 | 0.78409 | 0.85961 | 0.44868 |
| YOLOv5s + CBS + SSPF + cosine annealing + label smoothing | 0.87013 | 0.81439 | 0.86947 | 0.45218 |
| YOLOv5s + CBS + SSPF + cosine annealing + label smoothing + multi-scale (Our model) | 0.94685 | 0.81061 | 0.88712 | 0.45584 |

To demonstrate the detection ability of the model for objects of different sizes in different environments, Tables 4 and 5 show the detection effects of the five models on common datasets and UAV datasets. Among them, Table 4 shows the detection effect of ordinary flame data, and Table 5 shows the detection effect of UAV data. From the table, it can be seen that experiment E is better in terms of both the number of detections and the accuracy. Especially in the UAV image, the flame target is too small and easy to be missed, and the missed detection rate of the model in this paper is the lowest.

**Table 4.** Detection results of normal data.

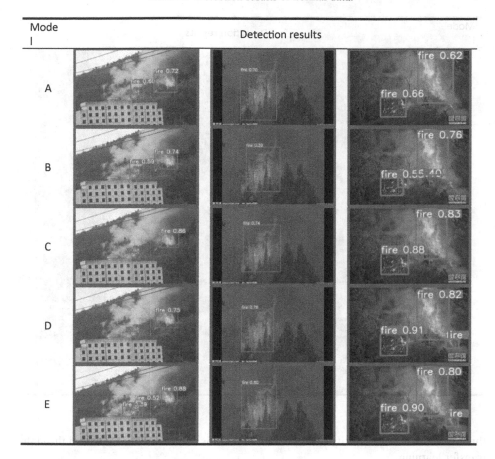

| Mode l | Detection results |
|--------|-------------------|
| A | |
| B | |
| C | |
| D | |
| E | |

## 4 Discussion

In Sect. 3.2, we discuss the application performance of Improved-YOLOv5s in different scenarios. The Improved-YOLOv5s model proposed in this paper has achieved good results in detecting targets of different scales, targets in different environments, and targets from different angles. It not only provides real-time detection but also has good robustness in practical applications. Nonetheless, we found that there are still problems of false detection of fire-like objects and missed detection of severely occluded objects during testing. This phenomenon may be caused by the variability of flames and the complexity of fire spread in the actual environment. It is worth mentioning that this is also an urgent problem to be solved by current object detection models [26]. Encouragingly, these difficulties are not insurmountable. A more powerful feature extraction network [27, 28] or an attention mechanism [29] can be selected to enhance the learning ability of the model. In future work, the structure of the Improved-YOLOv5s model will be further optimized, and the focus will be on the image feature extraction stage. It is hoped

**Table 5.** Detection results of UAV data.

| Model | Detection results |
|-------|-------------------|
| A | |
| B | |
| C | |
| D | |
| E | |

that the generalization ability of Improved-YOLOv5s can be further improved through transfer learning.

## 5   Conclusion

Forest is an important natural resource, it is very important to grasp the prevention and control of forest fire. In this paper, we put forward a forest fire detection model with strong generalization, which is convenient for the follow-up fire fighting work. To improve the detection effect of the model, the Focus module and SPP module are modified structurally. Cosine annealing algorithm, label smoothing, and multi-scale training are introduced in the training. Compared with the original network, the mAP of the modified network is improved by 8%. In the future, we will further study the characteristic differences between fires and similar targets to further improve the model accuracy and speed up detection.

# References

1. Muys, B.: Forest Ecosystem Services. Encyclopedia of the UN Sustainable Development Goals (2020)
2. Holden, S.R., Rogers, B.M., Treseder, K.K., Randerson, J.T.: Fire severity influences the response of soil microbes to a boreal forest fire. Environ. Res. Lett. **11**, 035004–035004 (2016). https://doi.org/10.1088/1748-9326/11/3/035004
3. Matin, M.A., Chitale, V.S., Murthy, M.S.R., Uddin, K., Bajracharya, B., Pradhan, S.: Understanding forest fire patterns and risk in Nepal using remote sensing, geographic information system and historical fire data. Int. J. Wildland Fire **26**, 276–286 (2017). https://doi.org/10.1071/wf16056
4. Bo, P.: Research on Classification of Forest Fire Risk Based on GIS Technology in Xichang City, Sichuan Province (2021)
5. Premsai, D., Reddy, G.K.J., Gudipalli, A.: Forest fire detection using wireless sensor networks. Int. J. Smart Sens. Intell. Syst. **13**, 1–8 (2020). https://doi.org/10.21307/ijssis-2020-006
6. Noureddine, H., Bouabdellah, K.: Field Experiment Testbed for Forest Fire Detection using Wireless Multimedia Sensor Network (2020). https://doi.org/10.2174/2210327909666619021 9120432
7. Varela, N., Díaz-Martinez, J.L., Ospino, A., Zelaya, N.A.L.: Wireless sensor network for forest fire detection. FNC/MobiSPC (2020). https://doi.org/10.1016/j.procs.2020.07.061
8. Bouakkaz, F., Ali, W., Derdour, M.: Forest fire detection using wireless multimedia sensor networks and image compression. Immunotechnology **20**, 57–63 (2021). https://doi.org/10.18280/i2m.200108
9. Mithira, S., Kavi, S., Ilakiya, S.: Efficient Fire Detection Using Hog Feature Extraction In Machine Learning (2020)
10. Jin, S., Lu, X.: Vision-based forest fire detection using machine learning. In: Proceedings of the 3rd International Conference on Computer Science and Application Engineering (2019). https://doi.org/10.1145/3331453.3361659
11. Mishra, R., Gupta, L., Gurbani, N., Shivhare, S.N.: Image-based forest fire detection using bagging of color models. In: Khanna, A., Gupta, D., Bhattacharyya, S., Hassanien, A.E., Anand, S., Jaiswal, A. (eds.) International Conference on Innovative Computing and Communications. AISC, vol. 1394, pp. 477–486. Springer, Singapore (2022). https://doi.org/10.1007/978-981-16-3071-2_38
12. Wahyono, Harjoko, A., Dharmawan, A., Adhinata, F.D., Kosala, G., Jo, K.-H.: Real-time forest fire detection framework based on artificial intelligence using color probability model and motion feature analysis. Fire (2022). https://doi.org/10.3390/fire5010023
13. Nazarenko, E., Varkentin, V., Polyakova, T.: Features of application of machine learning methods for classification of network traffic (features, advantages, disadvantages). In: 2019 International Multi-Conference on Industrial Engineering and Modern Technologies (FarEastCon), pp. 1–5 (2019). https://doi.org/10.1109/fareastcon.2019.8934236
14. Bhoomika, C.H., Rakshitha, B.H.: A survey on machine learning. Int. J. Eng. Appl. Sci. Technol. (2021)
15. Goodfellow, I.J., Bengio, Y., Courville, A.C.: Deep learning. Nature **521**, 436–444 (2015)
16. Zhang, Q.X., et al.: Wildland forest fire smoke detection based on faster R-CNN using synthetic smoke images. Procedia Eng. **211**, 441–446 (2018)
17. Barmpoutis, P., Dimitropoulos, K., Kaza, K., Grammalidis, N.: Fire detection from images using faster R-CNN and multidimensional texture analysis. In: ICASSP 2019 - 2019 IEEE International Conference on Acoustics, Speech and Signal Processing (ICASSP), pp. 8301–8305 (2019)

18. Saponara, S., Elhanashi, A.E., Gagliardi, A.: Exploiting R-CNN for video smoke/fire sensing in antifire surveillance indoor and outdoor systems for smart cities. In: 2020 IEEE International Conference on Smart Computing (SMARTCOMP). IEEE (2020)

19. Wu, S., Zhang, L.: Using popular object detection methods for real time forest fire detection. In: 2018 11th International Symposium on Computational Intelligence and Design (ISCID), vol. 1, pp. 280–284 (2018). https://doi.org/10.1109/iscid.2018.00070

20. Wang, S., et al.: Forest fire detection based on lightweight yolo. In: 2021 33rd Chinese Control and Decision Conference (CCDC), pp. 1560–1565 (2021). https://doi.org/10.1109/ccdc52312.2021.9601362

21. Xu, R., Lin, H.-X., Kang, L., Cao, L., Liu, Y.: A forest fire detection system based on ensemble learning. Forests **12**, 217 (2021). https://doi.org/10.3390/f12020217

22. Ko, B.C., Ham, S.J., Nam, J.Y.: Modeling and formalization of fuzzy finite automata for detection of irregular fire flames. IEEE Trans. Circuits Syst. Video Technol. **21**, 1903–1912 (2011). https://doi.org/10.1109/tcsvt.2011.2157190

23. Grammalidis, N., Dimitropoulos, K., Cetin, E.: FIRESENSE Database of Videos for Flame and Smoke Detection. Zenodo (2017). https://doi.org/10.5281/zenodo.836749

24. Dunnings, Andy Fire Image Data Set for Dunnings 2018 Study - PNG Still Image Set. Durham University

25. Shamsoshoara, A., Afghah, F., Razi, A., Zheng, L., Fulé, P., Blasch, E.: The FLAME dataset: aerial imagery pile burn detection using drones (UAVs). https://doi.org/10.1016/j.comnet.2021.108001

26. Muhammad, K., Ahmad, J., Mehmood, I., Rho, S., Baik, S.W.: Convolutional neural networks based fire detection in surveillance videos. IEEE Access **6**, 18174–18183 (2018). https://doi.org/10.1109/ACCESS.2018.2812835

27. Chen, Z., Yang, J.-C., Chen, L., Jiao, H.: Garbage classification system based on improved ShuffleNet v2. Resources, Conservation and Recycling (2022)

28. Ding, X., Zhang, X., Ma, N., Han, J., Ding, G., Sun, J.: RepVGG: making VGG-style ConvNets great again. In: 2021 IEEE/CVF Conference on Computer Vision and Pattern Recognition (CVPR), pp. 13728–13737 (2021)

29. Liu, Z., et al.: Swin transformer: hierarchical vision transformer using shifted windows. In: 2021 IEEE/CVF International Conference on Computer Vision (ICCV), pp. 9992–10002 (2021)

# Heterogeneous Graph Neural Network for Multi-behavior Feature-Interaction Recommendation

Li Ma, Zheng Chen, Yingxun Fu, and Yang Li[✉]

North China University of Technology, Shijingshan District, Beijing, China
liyang17@mails.jlu.edu.cn

**Abstract.** Graph neural network has great advantage in learning vector representation of users and items for modern recommender systems. Modeling user-item interaction bipartite graph is helpful for learning the collaborative signals between users and items. However, this modeling scheme ignores the influence of the objectively existing attribute information of item itself, and cannot well explain why users focus on items.

A feature interaction-based graph convolutional collaborative filtering algorithm, Attention Interaction Graph Collaborative Filtering (ATGCF) is proposed to address the limitations of existing works in this paper. It can deeply explore user preferences for multi-feature items. Firstly, we inject user and multi-feature into a user-feature interaction layer composed of multi-head-attention and fully connected layers to capture the user potential preference for multi-feature. Then we build a user-features-item bipartite graph and design the corresponding graph aggregation layer to obtain the high-order connectivity between the three. Experiment results on three real-world datasets verify the effectiveness of our model in exploiting multi-feature data, and ATGCF algorithm outperforms the other baselines in terms of recall, precision and NDCG evaluation metrics. Moreover, further experiments demonstrate that our model can achieve better results with less data.

**Keywords:** Multi-head attention · Feature interaction · Collaborative filtering · Heterogeneous graph networks · Recommendation system

## 1 Introduction

Personalized recommender system has been widely used to deal with the problem of information overload [1]. Collaborative filtering (CF) [2], the most widely used recommendation model can mine user preference and estimate preference based on existing historical behavior data such as purchases and browsing. Traditional CF models [3] are designed to directly model the relationship between users and items, which can directly bring benefits to the platform, such as movie recommendations and music recommendations. However, in real-world applications, this may lead to serious data sparsity issue. For example, in movie software, it is often difficult to achieve better results by building a CF for recommendation only through user click behavior. In other words, recommender

© The Author(s), under exclusive license to Springer Nature Switzerland AG 2022
E. Pimenidis et al. (Eds.): ICANN 2022, LNCS 13532, pp. 101–112, 2022.
https://doi.org/10.1007/978-3-031-15937-4_9

system should have the ability to utilize richer information, including interrelated movie features. Learning different feature combinations can help our model to more accurately predict the objects that users may interact with in the future.

Existing researches [4] has explored this task from two perspectives. The first category tries to mine information in the form of matrix factorization. [5] models the relationship between users and items directly through the historical interaction matrix and embedding the user vector and item vector through the dot product of the two vectors. Neural Collaborative Filtering (NCF) [6] replaces the interaction function of MF by introducing a deep learning method, so that the model can adaptively learn high-order vector representations of users and items. The second category considers modeling user historical behavior as a graph structure. [7] encodes the collaborative information between the user and the item, so that the model can learn the collaborative information hidden in the historical interaction among user and item to represent the behavioral similarity between users and items. [8] captures user preferences for each interacted item by adding node-level attention. However, these algorithms face the following two problems. First, only modeling user-item interactions will lead to very sparse data and seriously affect the recommendation effect. Especially for users with few interactive items, the noisy data may prevent the model from learning effective information from sparse historical behaviors. Second, only using user and item data will lose very rich attributes information. The items that the user has interacted with may have a certain similarity in features. For example, the user has watched more romantic anime movies in the past period of time, indicating that the user has a preference for romantic anime to a certain extent, so these multi-feature should be fully utilized.

To address them, we propose to construct a unified heterogeneous graph based on multi-features interaction. Firstly, we use users, items, features represented as nodes, and different types of behaviors represented as multiple types of edges of the graph to model user-feature and user-item-feature relationships, respectively. Secondly, we design a new user-item-features message passing graph recommendation model, Attention Interaction Graph Collaborative Filtering (ATGCF), which takes into account the historical interaction between users and items, also models the historical behavior response of user to the item feature preferences. To be more specific, we design a user and multi-feature interaction layer by utilizing user and features information to capture the preference information between user and features. Finally, we design user-item-features propagation layers, which helps to capture different CF semantics of item and multi-features similarity for user and enhance the learning for node embeddings. To summarize, our work makes the following contributions:

- We model the user-item-feature heterogeneous bipartite graph from the real scene and mine user preferences for multi-feature.
- We propose the Attention Interaction Graph Collaborative Filtering (ATGCF) model which can capture the internal associations between user and item features more accurately.
- We conduct experimental analysis on three public large-scale datasets. The performance of our proposed model is significantly improved compared to the other baselines in terms of accuracy, recall, and NDCG.

# 2 Methodology

## 2.1 Heterogeneous Bipartite Graph

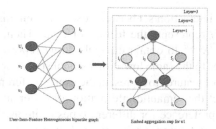

User-Item-Feature Heterogeneous bipartite graph          Embed aggregation step for u1

**Fig. 1.** Representation of the user-item-feature heterogeneous bipartite graph, and how users obtain information of all types of nodes as the network aggregates.

The heterogeneous bipartite graph shows the heterogeneity of the user next-hop node, and we describe the specific method of generating the graph in Fig. 1. First, we can obtain the user-item pair $\langle U, I \rangle$ through the historical interaction information. Meanwhile, we generate the item-feature pair $\langle I, F \rangle$ according to the attribute column of the item, and then the user-feature pair $\langle U, F \rangle$ can be obtained through the item as an intermediary. On the basis of obtaining the above information, the matrix R can be generated. Finally, the adjacency matrix $A$ of our generated graph.

$$A = \begin{bmatrix} 0 & R \\ R^T & 0 \end{bmatrix} \tag{1}$$

The concatenation matrix representation of the adjacency matrix $A$ obtained should satisfy $A = A^T$. That is to say, it satisfies $A = D^{\frac{1}{2}} \Lambda D^{-\frac{1}{2}}$, i.e. the graph volume operator in ATGCF satisfies the definition of Laplacian operator in GCN [9]. We refer to the mainstream recommendation model [10] to map users, items, features node into a vector. The final preference of each user for an item is predicted by finally learning embedding representation vector.

## 2.2 User-Features Interaction

In recommendation scenarios, such as movie recommendation and product recommendation. It is difficult for us to obtain the contextual information of the user, but the contextual information of the item can be obtained effectively. Our goal is to model the user's own preference for such items. First, we define the context of the item as where $n$ represents the number of contextual features, and $d$ represents the dimension of contextual features. However, in the absence of clear user features and item features, the user embedding will be inconsistent with the item embedding, which will make the model unable to train normally. Therefore, we obtain the user feature initialization by averaging the sum of all the features of the items that the user has interacted with according to the historical interaction information between user and item. Expressed as:

$$F_u = \frac{1}{sum(R_{ui} \in E)} \left( \sum_{i \in R_{ui}} F_i \right) \tag{2}$$

where $R_{ui}$ represents the interaction set between user and item history, $sum()$ represents the total number, and $F_i$ represents the feature of item. Then, we define the feature embedding matrix $e_f \in R^{n \times d}$ to obtain the embedding representation of the feature. We map different features to the same low-dimensional space for convenience, and then combine different forms of features to represent the user's preference for different feature combinations and extract the semantic information of different feature combinations. We construct the user's preference for different types of items through the multi-head attention model [11]. Specifically, we use multi-head attention to analyze which items are more in line with the user preference. We map the embedded representations of users and features and user features to a low-dimensional space of the same dimension so that we can model higher-order interaction representations between users and different features. Next, we will elaborate on how we define it. First, we define the representation of different item feature combinations, the specific definitions are as follows:

$$\alpha_{i,m}^h = \frac{exp\left(\psi^{(h)}(F_u^i, F_u^m)\right)}{\sum_{l=1}^M exp\left(\psi^{(h)}(F_u^i, F_l^m)\right)} \tag{3}$$

where $i$ and $m$ represent the currently calculated user features, $h$ represents the set number of heads, and $M$ represents the total number of item features. $\psi^{(h)}(F_u^i, F_u^m) = <W_q^{(h)}F_u^i, W_k^{(h)}F_u^m>$ is the size of the correlation coefficient between current user feature $i$ and user feature $m$. $W_q^{(h)}$ and $W_k^{(h)}$ are weights. The final correlation coefficient between user feature $i$ and user feature $m$ on each head $h$ is normalized by (3) and then expressed as $\alpha_{i,m}^h$. The feature-interaction is expressed as:

$$e_{ui}^m = \sum_{h=1}^H \sum_{k=1}^M \alpha_{F_u^m, F_u^i}^{(h)} (W_V^{(h)} e_{F_u^i}) \tag{4}$$

where $W_V^{(h)}$ is weight, $e_{ui}^m$ represents the interactive embedding representation of user feature $i$ and user feature $m$. Then we can define a user preference for different user feature interaction embedding. Its definition is shown as following:

$$\alpha_u^m = \sum_{h=1}^H \frac{exp\left(\psi^{(h)}(e_u, e_u^m)\right)}{\sum_{l=1}^M exp\left(\psi^{(h)}(e_u, e_l^m)\right)} \tag{5}$$

where $\psi^{(h)}(e_u, e_u^m)$ represents the user preference for each interaction feature, $h$ represents the number of heads, and $m$ represents the total number of feature combinations. The finally learned result represents the user preference for the current combined feature. It is expressed as:

$$e_{F_u} = ReLU \left( \sum_{h=1}^h \sum_{l=1}^M \alpha_u^{m(h)} \left( W_V^{(h)} e_u^{m(h)} \right) \right) \tag{6}$$

where $ReLU()$ represents the nonlinear activation function, $\alpha_u^{m(h)}$ and $e_u^{m(h)}$ represent the preference coefficient and preference vector on each head.

## 2.3  Graph Neural Network Aggregation Layer

The historical interaction information between users and items is a reliable source of user preference information, and we refer to the method of [6] to model the user's higher-order preference for items and item features by considering the features of the items. The specific graph convolution operation is shown as follows:

$$m_{u \leftarrow i}^{(k)} = \frac{1}{\sqrt{|N_u||N_i|}}(W_1^{(k)} e_i^{(k-1)} + W_2^{(k)} e_{F_i}^{(k-1)} + W_3^{(k)}((e_i^{(k-1)} \oplus e_{F_i}^{(k-1)}) \odot e_u^{(k-1)})) \quad (7)$$

$$m_{i \leftarrow u}^{(k)} = \frac{1}{\sqrt{|N_u||N_i|}}(W_1^{(k)} e_u^{(k-1)} + W_2^{(k)} e_{F_u}^{(k-1)} + W_3^{(k)}((e_i^{(k-1)} \oplus e_{F_i}^{(k-1)}) \odot e_u^{(k-1)}))$$

$$\qquad (8)$$

where $e_{F_i}$, $e_{F_u}$ denote the item and feature embedding of the user, $W_1$, $W_2$, $W_3$ denote the coefficient matrix of the science department, $e_i$ denotes the embedding representation of the item, and $k$ denotes the current number of layers. Through the stacking of multi-layer networks, the model can learn the influence of multi-hop neighbors on current node. Meanwhile, the model updates the state representation of current node according to the state of multi-hop neighbors at last. After passing through the stacking of $K$ layers, vector representation of users and items can be displayed as:

$$e_u^{(K)} = ReLU\left(m_{u \leftarrow u}^{(K)} + \sum_{i \in N_n} m_{u \leftarrow i}^{(K)}\right), \quad e_i^{(K)} = ReLU\left(m_{i \leftarrow i}^{(K)} + \sum_{i \in N_u} m_{i \leftarrow u}^{(K)}\right) \quad (9)$$

where the final learned user vector is denoted as $e_u$, and the item embedding is denoted as $e_i$. It should be noted that after combining item features and item features indirectly represented by item features, the dimensions of user embedding $e_u$ and item embedding $e_i$ are updated from the original $R^{n \times d}$ set to $R^{n \times 2d}$.

## 2.4  Prediction Layer

After the above propagation, we learn the user preference for each item. This is very meaningful. We can clearly understand why users choose this item and also learn that items with this attribute are of interest to users. Then, we express the user preference for items of each attribute by making points between the user embedded representation and the embedded representation of items with different attributes.

$$y_{ATGCF}(u, i, f) = e_u^T e_i \quad (10)$$

The user preference for different types of items can be expressed in a variety of ways. For example, calculating the distance between each embedding is used to represent the user's preference for different kinds of items. In this paper, we use the dot product [9] which was often used in existing researches.

## 2.5  Model Training

The overall model process is shown in Fig. 2. We use the BPR [12] loss to train the model. For each user, we calculate the preference for positive and negative samples, and then update the learnable parameters according to the difference between positive and negative samples. The overall loss is calculated as follows:

$$Loss = \sum_{(u,i,j)\in O} -ln\sigma\left(y_{ui} - y_{uj}\right) + \lambda\|\Theta\|^2 \tag{11}$$

where $O = \{(u, i, j)|(u, i) \in R^+, (u, j) \in R^-\}$ represents the paired training samples, and $\langle u, i \rangle$ represents the set of positive samples and $\langle u, j \rangle$ represents the set of negative samples. $\sigma()$ represents the activation function, and $\Theta$ represents the trainable parameters in the model and $\lambda$ controls the $L_2$ regularization strength to prevent overfitting. The optimizer chooses Adam [13] in our proposed algorithm.

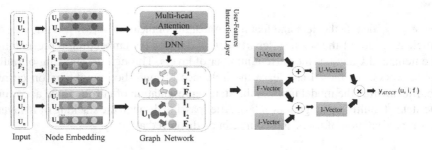

**Fig. 2.** An illustration of ATGCF model architecture

## 2.6  Complexity Analysis

In terms of complexity, the ATGCF model is simpler than the traditional CF model. Assuming our input matrix dimension is $R^{d \times d}$, the number of layers is L, and the number of nodes is $n$. Compared to MF which is the most concise embedding based on the recommendation model, our ATGCF only uses $d_l^2$ level parameters in the graph convolution layer. The overall complexity is $O(n^2d + dd_{l-1})$. The additional cost of such model parameters is almost zero and negligible, considering that L is usually a number less than or equal to 3, and $d_l$ is typically set as the embedding size, which is much smaller than the number of users and items.

## 3  Experiment

### 3.1  Dataset Description

To evaluate the effectiveness of ATGCF, we conduct experiments on three benchmark datasets: Amine, MovieLens-1m, and Amazon-book, which are publicly accessible and vary in terms of domain, size, and sparsity. We summarize the statistics of three datasets in Table 1.

**Amine:** This is a dataset from Kaggle website for anime recommendation. For each user we keep at least 20 more interactions.

**MovieLens-1m:** A public movie recommendation dataset for scientific research [14].

**Amazon-Book:** This is a widely used product recommendation dataset [15]. Similarly, it is also guaranteed that each user interacts with at least 20 items.

**Table 1.** Statistics of the datasets.

| Dataset | #Users | #Items | #Interactions |
|---|---|---|---|
| Amine | 15506 | 34325 | 2601998 |
| MovieLens-1m | 6040 | 5953 | 1000209 |
| Amazon-Book | 51639 | 84355 | 2648963 |

We consider each interaction directly observed in the training set to be recorded as a positive instance and randomly sample as a negative sample from the set of items that user has never interacted with.

## 3.2 Experimental Settings

**Evaluation Metrics.** For each method the output the user's preference scores over all the items. To evaluate the effectiveness of top-K recommendation and preference ranking, we adopt three widely-used evaluation protocols: recall@K, precision@K and ndcg@K. We evaluate the results of our model under different K values. We demonstrate the average metrics for all users in datasets.

To demonstrate the effectiveness, we compare our proposed NGCF with the following baselines:

- **ItemCF:** The algorithm learns item representations based on the historical interaction records of user items, considers that similar item vector representations are close, and finally recommends items based on similarity.
- **MF:** This is matrix factorization optimized by the Bayesian personalized ranking (BPR) loss, which exploits the user-item direct interactions only as the target value of interaction function.
- **NeuMF:** The method is a state-of-the-art neural CF model which uses multiple hidden layers above the element-wise and concatenation of user and item embeddings to capture their non-linear feature interactions.
- **NGCF:** NGCF is the state-of-the-art graph neural network model which has some special design to fit graph neural network into recommender system. Here only target behavior is used to build the user-item bipartite graph.
- **PUP [8]:** The state-of-the-art graph neural network model which has some special design to fit sensitivity of a user on item price. Effectively establish the potential relationship between user to commodity and commodity to price.

**Parameters Settings.** Our ATGCF is implemented in Pytorch. The embedding size is fixed to 64 for all models. We optimize all models with Adam optimizer, and the batch size is 4096. In terms of hyperparameters, we apply a grid search for hyperparameters: the learning rate is tuned amongst [0.0001, 0.0005, 0.001, 0.005], and for baseline models we randomly select 80% of historical interactions of each user to constitute the training set, and treat the remaining as the test set. When training ATGCF, we found that only 10% of the data is needed to achieve the best results. It demonstrates that our model has good performance in the face of small samples. $L_2$ normalization coefficient is tuned in [1e7, 1e6, 1e5, 1e4, 1e3].

## 3.3  Overall Performance

We compare the performance of our proposed algorithm ATGCF with all other baselines. The results on three datasets are reported on Table 2, Table 3 and Table 4. From the results, we have the following observations.

**Model Effectiveness.** Based on these tables, we find that our ATGCF overperforms all baselines substantially on all Recall@K, Precision@K and NDCG@K metrics. The average improvement of our model to the best baseline is 5.62%, 3.95% and 5.20% for Recall, Precision and NDCG on the Amine dataset; 3.60%, 5.95% and 6.00% on MovieLens-1m dataset; 4.07%, 6.80% and 4.30% on Amazon-Book dataset, which justifies the effectiveness of our model.

**Table 2.** Comparisons on Amine and improvement comparing with the best baseline.

| Method | Recall@20 | Recall@30 | Recall@40 | Recall@50 | Precisio@10 | Precisio@20 | Ndcg@20 |
|--------|-----------|-----------|-----------|-----------|-------------|-------------|---------|
| ItemCF | 0.0286 | 0.0304 | 0.0401 | 0.0412 | 0.0260 | 0.0201 | 0.0115 |
| MF | 0.0354 | 0.0446 | 0.0524 | 0.0644 | 0.0311 | 0.0231 | 0.0214 |
| NCF | 0.0402 | 0.0542 | 0.0644 | 0.0685 | 0.0342 | 0.0256 | 0.0256 |
| NGCF | 0.0434 | **0.0580** | 0.0669 | 0.0772 | **0.0358** | 0.0294 | 0.0294 |
| PUP | **0.0482** | 0.0574 | **0.0684** | **0.0784** | 0.0336 | **0.0296** | **0.0304** |
| ATGCF | **0.0535** | **0.0616** | **0.0702** | **0.0806** | **0.0372** | **0.0308** | **0.0320** |
| Improve | **10.9%** | **6.2%** | **2.6%** | **2.8%** | **3.9%** | **4.0%** | **5.2%** |

**Table 3.** Comparisons on MovieLens-1m and improvement comparing with the best baseline.

| Method | Recall@20 | Recall@30 | Recall@40 | Recall@50 | Precisio@10 | Precisio@20 | Ndcg@20 |
|--------|-----------|-----------|-----------|-----------|-------------|-------------|---------|
| ItemCF | 0.0214 | 0.0238 | 0.0446 | 0.0512 | 0.0332 | 0.0327 | 0.0396 |
| MF | 0.0384 | 0.0425 | 0.0584 | 0.0748 | 0.0559 | 0.0445 | 0.0425 |
| NCF | 0.0401 | 0.0554 | 0.0644 | 0.0864 | 0.0532 | 0.0496 | 0.0489 |
| NGCF | 0.0443 | 0.0647 | 0.0839 | 0.1026 | **0.0604** | 0.0584 | 0.0504 |
| PUP | **0.0455** | **0.0665** | **0.0856** | **0.1048** | 0.0588 | **0.0596** | **0.0548** |
| ATGCF | **0.0482** | **0.0689** | **0.0884** | **0.1070** | **0.0645** | **0.0627** | **0.0581** |
| Improve | 5.9% | 3.6% | 3.2% | 2.0% | 6.7% | 5.2% | 6.0% |

**Table 4.** Comparisons on Amazon-Book and improvement comparing with the best baseline.

| Method | Recall@20 | Recall@30 | Recall@40 | Recall@50 | Precisio@10 | Precisio@20 | Ndcg@20 |
|--------|-----------|-----------|-----------|-----------|-------------|-------------|---------|
| ItemCF | 0.0184 | 0.0196 | 0.0312 | 0.0452 | 0.0186 | 0.0195 | 0.0356 |
| MF | 0.0250 | 0.0267 | 0.0524 | 0.0624 | 0.0254 | 0.0201 | 0.0518 |
| NCF | 0.0265 | 0.0288 | 0.0644 | 0.0665 | 0.0262 | 0.0225 | 0.0542 |
| NGCF | 0.0348 | 0.0387 | 0.0669 | 0.0731 | **0.0328** | 0.0257 | **0.0630** |
| PUP | **0.0382** | **0.0415** | **0.0684** | **0.0754** | 0.0316 | **0.0285** | 0.0624 |
| ATGCF | **0.0408** | **0.0426** | **0.0713** | **0.0775** | **0.0358** | **0.0298** | **0.0651** |
| Improve | 6.8% | 2.6% | 4.2% | 2.7% | 9.1% | 4.5% | 4.3% |

**Multi-features Models Work Well.** In the comparison of MF, NCF, and NGCF, we can find that adding item features information into predicting (PUP and ATGCF) can improve the performance. And through the results, we find that ATGCF outperforms PUP on average by 10.9% on Recall@20, 4% on Precision@20, and 5.2% on NDCG@20, which also shows that multi-feature fusion will be better than single-feature fusion.

**Our Model is the Best Model that can Mine Users' Potential Preferences for Items with Multi-features.** Comparing with the graph neural network models that can extract user potential preferences such as NGCF and PUP, our ATGCF performs the best. That can be explained in two folds. In terms of item preference, neither NGCF nor PUP has uncovered the user deep preference for interacted items, which may lead to the loss of some information in original data. In terms of feature processing, PUP only considers the impact of a single feature (price) on user selection and does not comprehensively consider the situation of multi-features. Fortunately, our ATGCF fully considers the influence of multiple features on user selection, and can dig out the user preference for different mixed features.

## 3.4 Model Analysis

As the feature interaction propagation layer plays a pivotal role in ATGCF, we investigate its impact on the performance. We first explore the impact of different feature embedding methods on the model, and then study the performance of ATGCF with different proportions of training data.

**ATGCF-F.** Learning by directly adding the features of items and then integrating them into the network. The method neither understands user preferences for different features nor the impact of different feature combinations.

**ATGCF-IF.** Learning the user's preference for each item feature by using the self-attention mechanism. On the basis of considering features, the user's preferences for different features are considered.

**ATGCF.** Modeling user preferences for different interaction features based on consideration of different feature preferences. The user preference for different feature combination items is learned through the multi-head attention mechanism plus MLP.

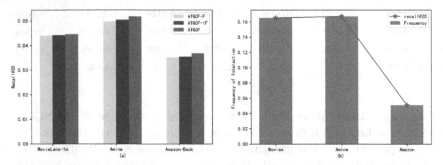

**Fig. 3.** (a) The influence of different feature extraction components on ATGCF, (b) The sensitivity analysis of ATGCF to user's feature preference under different interaction frequencies.

In order to analyze the necessity of each feature selection method, we use the three methods (ATGCF-F, ATGCF-IF and ATGCF) to extract the user preferences for different item features. The results are shown in Fig. 3(a), the effect of learning interaction features from the results is significantly better than that of using the attention mechanism to learn the users preference for item features. Meanwhile, using the attention mechanism to learn the user's preference for different items also achieve better performance than simply adding item features. Therefore, the mechanism we design to learn user preferences for items with different combinations of features is necessary and can obtain better performance.

Meanwhile, we analyze the sensitivity of ATGCF to features. We use the total number of interactions in the dataset divided by the number of users in the dataset (emphasizing the role of features) define the user interaction frequency, and obtain the interaction frequency size of MovieLens-1m 165, Amine 167 and Amazon-Book 51, separately. As long as the interaction frequency is high, it means that we can extract more user's selection history of items. Moreover, we can more accurately extract the user's preference for item features. The experimental results are shown in Fig. 3(b). The higher the interaction frequency of the dataset, the better the effect of the ATGCF model. It also demonstrates the sensitivity of our model to item features and the rationality of our model design.

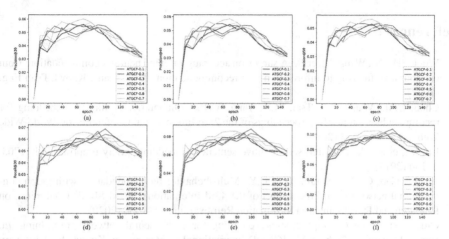

**Fig. 4.** Analysis of the recall and accuracy results of ATGCF with different training ratios in MovieLens-1m.

We evaluate the performance of our proposed algorithm with different training ratios and find that ATGCF requires less training data and achieve better performance. As shown in Fig. 4, the ordinate represents the performance value achieved by each method. The decimal at the end of each method in the lower right corner represents the ratio of the training samples to the total dataset. We find that while the ratio of 0.5 performs the best, ATGCF also achieves relatively good performance with a ratio of 0.1. The baseline model achieves the best effectiveness at a ratio of 0.7–0.8 [8]. The results indicates that even with little user interaction data, better recommendations can be made to users on the premise of understanding user preferences for item features. However, as the number of training increases, overfitting will occur, and we guess that the model fits unrepresentative features due to too many training times.

## 4   Conclusion

In this work, we study the feature interaction graph neural network recommendation model, and propose a graph neural network model ATGCF. We inject user and multi-features into a user-features interaction layer composed of multi-head-attention and fully connected layers to capture the user potential preference for multi-features. Then we build a user-features-item bipartite graph and design the corresponding graph aggregation layer to obtain the high-order connectivity among user, features and items. Ultimately, experiments on three public datasets demonstrate that our model outperforms the best baseline model in 4.43%, 5.56% and 5.16% for Recall, Precision and NDCG.

**Acknowledgement.** This work was supported by National Key R&D Program of China (2018YFB1800302), Natural Science Foundation of China (62001007), Beijing Natural Science Foundation (KZ201810009011, 4202020, L192021, 4212018), Re-search Start-up Fund of North China University of Technology and Jilin Province Science and Technology Development Plan Project (20190201180JC, 20200401076GX).

# References

1. Wu, L., He, X., Wang, X., et al.: A survey on accuracy-oriented neural recommendation: from collaborative filtering to information-rich recommendation. IEEE Trans. Knowl. Data Eng. (2022)
2. Chen, C.M., Wang, C.J., Tsai, M.F., Yang, Y.H.: Collaborative similarity embedding for recommender systems. In: Proceedings of the 28th International Conference on World Wide Web, pp. 2637–2643 (2019)
3. Lin, Z., et al.: A structured self-attentive sentence embedding. arXiv preprint arXiv:1703. 03130 (2017)
4. Jin, B., Gao, C., He, X., Jin, D., Li, Y.: Multi-behavior recommendation with graph convolutional networks. In: Proceedings of the 43rd International ACM SIGIR Conference on Research and Development in Information Retrieval, pp. 659–668 (2020)
5. Qiu, J., et al.: GCC: graph contrastive coding for graph neural network pre-training. In: Proceedings of the 26th ACM SIGKDD International Conference on Knowledge Discovery and Data Mining, pp. 1150–1160 (2020)
6. He, X., Liao, L., Zhang, H., Nie, L., Hu, X., Chua, T.S.: Neural collaborative filtering. In: Proceedings of the 26th International Conference on World Wide Web, pp. 173–182 (2017)
7. He, R., McAuley, J.: Ups and downs: modeling the visual evolution of fashion trends with one-class collaborative filtering. In: Proceedings of the 25th International Conference on World Wide Web, pp. 507–517 (2016)
8. Zheng, Y., Gao, C., He, X., Li, Y., Jin, D.: Price-aware recommendation with graph convolutional networks. In: Proceedings of IEEE 36th International Conference on Data Engineering, pp. 133–144 (2020)
9. Berg, R., Kipf, T.N., Welling, M.: Graph convolutional matrix completion. arXiv preprint arXiv:1706.02263 (2017)
10. Cao, Y., Wang, X., He, X., Hu, Z., Chua, T.S.: Unifying knowledge graph learning and recommendation: towards a better understanding of user preferences. In: Proceedings of the 28th International Conference on World Wide Web, pp. 151–161 (2019)
11. Vaswani, A., et al.: Attention is all you need. In: Advances in Neural Information Processing Systems 30 (2017)
12. Rendle, S., Freudenthaler, C., Gantner, Z., Schmidt-Thieme, L.: BPR: Bayesian personalized ranking from implicit feedback. arXiv preprint arXiv:1205.2618 (2012)
13. Kingma, D.P., Ba, J.: Adam: a method for stochastic optimization. arXiv preprint arXiv:1412. 6980 (2014)
14. Harper, F.M., Konstan, J.A.: The movielens datasets: history and context. ACM Trans. Interact. Intell. Syst. **5**(4), 1–19 (2015)
15. Ricci, F., Rokach, L., Shapira, B.: Introduction to recommender systems handbook. In: Ricci, F., Rokach, L., Shapira, B., Kantor, P.B. (eds.) Recommender Systems Handbook, pp. 1–35. Springer, Boston, MA (2011). https://doi.org/10.1007/978-0-387-85820-3_1

# JointFusionNet: Parallel Learning Human Structural Local and Global Joint Features for 3D Human Pose Estimation

Zhiwei Yuan[1], Yaping Yan[1], Songlin Du[1(✉)], and Takeshi Ikenaga[2]

[1] Southeast University, Nanjing 210096, China
sdu@seu.edu.cn
[2] Waseda University, Kitakyushu 808-0135, Japan

**Abstract.** 3D human pose estimation plays important roles in various human-machine interactive applications, but how to efficiently utilize the joint structural global and local features of human pose in deep-learning-based methods has always been a challenge. In this paper, we propose a parallel structural global and local joint features fusion network based on inspiring observation pattern of human pose. To be specific, it is observed that there are common similar global features and local features in human pose cross actions. Therefore, we design global-local capture modules separately to capture features and finally fuse them. The proposed parallel global and local joint features fusion network, entitled JointFusionNet, significantly improve state-of-the-art models on both intra-scenario H36M and cross-scenario 3DPW datasets and lead to appreciable improvements in poses with more similar local features. Notably, it yields an overall improvement of 3.4 mm in MPJPE (relative 6.8% improvement) over the previous best feature fusion based method [22] on H36M dataset in 3D human pose estimation.

**Keywords:** 3D human pose estimation · Human structural joint features · Feature fusion

## 1 Introduction

Human pose estimation (HPE), aiming to build human body representation (such as body skeleton and body shape), is a longstanding computer vision problem. 3D Human pose estimation has been applied to numerous applications, including motion recognition and analysis, human-computer interaction, virtual reality (VR), security identification and so on. However, this task is extremely challenging due to 1) the deep ambiguity in 2D-to-3D space transformation where a 2D keypoint corresponds to multiple 3D poses, 2) the insufficiency of labeled dataset due to the high cost of obtaining labels and 3) self-occlusion of human pose. Thanks to the success of deep neural networks, the generalization performance of the deep-learning-based method has risen sharply [13,16,25], making it have a broader prospect.

E. Pimenidis et al. (Eds.): ICANN 2022, LNCS 13532, pp. 113–125, 2022.
https://doi.org/10.1007/978-3-031-15937-4_10

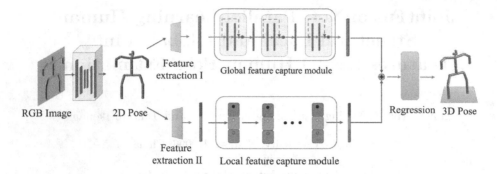

**Fig. 1.** Architecture of our proposed global-local features fusion network for 3D human pose estimation. Parallel full-connection module and group-connection module capture the global and local features of human pose respectively.

Improving the generalization performance of deep-learning-based 3D human pose estimation models is still a challenging problem. Surprisingly, we found some inspiring observations in the existing 3D human pose estimator: the prediction errors of keypoints of the human body have a high correlation with the structure of human pose, as shown in Fig. 2. Different human pose cross actions have high similarities in local features, and there are some samples as shown in Fig. 2(c). These inspiring observations indicate that there are communal global features in human pose cross actions, and regular similar local features existing in pose of different action categories. Whether it is possible to design a model based on this inspiring pattern for 3D human pose estimation.

To realize this idea, we designed a parallel fusion network where full-connection network and group-connection network learn to capture global-feature and local-feature of human pose, respectively. In this work, full-connection network connect all the input features and output features indiscriminately to learn the global information. Group-connection network connect the input features and output features in the group with global information representation to focus on learning the local information of human pose. Based on this motivation, a parallel fusion network which learn human structural local and global joint features (JointFusionNet) is designed for 3D human pose estimation, as shown in Fig. 1.

In extensive comparisons to state-of-the-art techniques, JointFusionNet exhibits performance considerably on 3D human pose estimation. More importantly, experiments show that JointFusionNet can not only outperform previous work, but elevate huge performance on pose with more similar local features, such as Sit, Greet and Phone. Moreover, various ablation studies validate our proposed approach. The main contributions are summarized as follows:

- The methods of global and local features capture modules are proposed respectively to model human pose based on inspiring observation.
- A network structure that fuses the global and local joint features of human pose is designed to improve the estimation performance.

- Extensive comparisons and various ablation studies to validate our proposed JointFusionNet for single-frame 3D human pose estimation.

## 2  Related Works

Extensive research has been conducted on 3D human pose estimation and global-local features fusion. In the following, we briefly review methods that are related to our approach.

### 2.1  3D Human Pose Estimation

Existing deep-learning-based 3D pose estimation methods mainly follow two frameworks: end-to-end methods and two-stage methods. End-to-end methods regress 3D pose directly from the input image [15], which is extremely expensive to acquire labeled datasets, although those methods avoid error accumulation in two stages. Thanks to the high accuracy of 2D pose estimators, the two-stage method has become a major popular solution for 3D human pose estimation. The two-stage methods [13,25,26] first employ off-the-shelf 2D pose estimators to extract 2D pose from the input image and then establish the mapping from 2D pose to 3D pose. Simultaneously, considering the sequence information in video, Pavllo *et al.* [16] proposed a network that combines multi-frame sequence information for pose estimation. The methods of multi-view fusion [5] are also applied to 3D human pose estimation due to the natural existence of multiple-view cameras or sensors in the dataset or reality. Furthermore, the transform network based on the attention mechanism [10] is also used to mine spatial and temporal information in 3D human pose estimation. Simultaneously, lacking diversity in existing labeled 3D human pose dataset restricts the generalization ability of deep learning based methods. Therefore, Li *et al.* [9] proposed a method to synthesize massive paired 2D-3D human skeletons with evolution strategy. JointPose [21] further jointly performs pose network estimation and data augmentation by designing a reward/penalty strategy for effective joint training. In this paper, we focus on the universal transformation from 2D pose to 3D pose in the two-stage method, as much as possible to fuse the global and local features of human pose at the same time.

### 2.2  Global-Local Features Fusion

The method of considering global and local features has long been applied to deep learning models, such as part-based branching network [17] for 2D human pose estimation. Martinez *et al.* [13] proposed a simple yet effective full connection network to learn the mapping relationship of 2D-3D space, in which the keypoints are fully connected but do not pay attention to local connection features. Based on the connection relationship of the graph model, Ma *et al.* [11] proposed a pose estimation model considering context node information, which does not consider local groups based on human pose structure information. Zeng *et al.* [22] proposed a grouping and reorganization pose estimation model based on the local group of human structure information, which does not fully consider the global information of human pose. In this paper, we consider the global and local joint features of the human pose in parallel, hence propose JointFusionNet that fuses global and local features for 3D human pose estimation.

## 3   Method

In this section, we propose global- and local-feature capture module to learn the observed patterns of human pose and design a parallel fusion network for 3D human pose estimation.

### 3.1   Inspiring Pattern of Human Pose

The inspiring and regular observed patterns in human pose be applied to 3D human pose estimation models. Pattern I is the estimation performance pattern cross keypoints in existing 3D human pose estimator [22]: the estimation performance cross keypoints are not only quite different, but also show a regular pattern, as shown in Fig. 2(a) and Fig. 2(b). Pattern II is the similar local features of human pose: different human pose cross actions have specific similarities in local features. Here are some examples in H36M, as shown in Fig. 2(c).

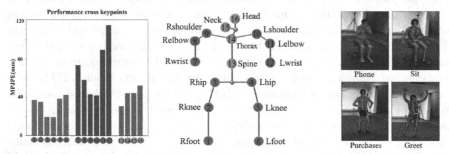

(a) Keypoints performance  (b) Keypoints of human pose  (c) Example pose in H36M

**Fig. 2.** Inspiring observation pattern in human pose.

**Pattern of estimation performance cross keypoints** reveals that the performance of keypoints has a great correlation with the structure of human pose. The closer the keypoints to the center of the human body (like hip, shoulder and spine), the smaller the estimation error; the further away from the part (like foot, wrist and head), the greater the error compared to a structurally adjacent keypoint. The keypoints with low error represent global features of human pose, which are related to all the keypoints of human pose; The keypoints with high error represent local features of human pose, which are related to only part of keypoints. Based on Pattern I, also considering the partitioning of human pose used in [14], the keypoints of human pose are divided into groups, for example, 3 groups in different colors in Fig. 2(a) and Fig. 2(b).

**Pattern of similar local features of human pose** reveals that different human pose cross actions have high similarities in local features. Considering the structure and kinematics of human pose, the local features are limited and appear repeatedly in different actions. For example, the local feature of Sitting in the lower body appears in the action categories of Phone; the local feature of standing in the lower body appears in action of Purchases, Greet and so on. Further, the group of local features are not strongly related to each other, for example, the posture of the arm and of the legs are not highly correlated.

## 3.2  Global and Local Features Fusion

Inspired by the observed pattern of estimation error cross keypoints and similar local features of human pose, we explore this pattern to design the architecture of 3D pose estimation network, and proposed JointFusionNet, as shown in Fig. 1. In JointFusionNet, the 2D pose of the RGB image is estimated by the existing 2D human pose estimator, then full connection module and group connection module capture the global and local features of human pose. Finally, these features are fused and regressed to 3D pose.

We propose the global-local feature capture module, as shown in Fig. 3, to learn to capture global feature information and local feature information of human pose. Then a parallel structure is used to design the fusion network that fuses the learned features.

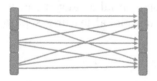    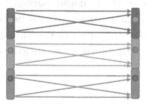

(a) Full-connection layer network (FCN)    (b) Group-connection layer network (GCN)

**Fig. 3.** Global-local features capture module

**Global feature capture module** is a full-connection layer network (FCN) [13], learning the global features of human pose when processing the encoding vector representing the global information of the human body, as shown in Fig. 3(a). It can be noted that in the global feature capture module, each output features and each intermediate feature is connected to all of the input features indiscriminately, allowing it to learn the global information represented by each feature. Simultaneously, residual connections [4] are used as a technique to improve generalization performance.

**Local feature capture module** is a group-connection layer network (GCN) with Low-Dimensional Global Context (LDGC) [22], learning the local features of human pose when processing the encoding vector representing the group local information of the human body, as shown in Fig. 3(b). According to the observed patterns in the human body and previous researches [14,22], we divide the keypoints into groups, which are used to capture the local features of human pose. And Low-Dimensional Global Context is used to learn to represent the relationship between local features and the whole pose.

Given the keypoints of 2D human pose $X = \{X_i | i, ..., N\} \in \mathbb{R}^{2N}$, where $N$ is the number of keypoints. Formally, the global feature of human pose can be expressed as

$$F_{global} = FCN(X). \tag{1}$$

Then the keypoints can be divided into $k$ groups $X^k = \{X_i^k | i, ..., N_k\} \in \mathrm{R}^{2N}$, where $k$ represents the number of groups, and $N_k$ represents the number of keypoints in $k^{th}$ group. The local feature of human pose can be expressed as

$$F_{local}^k = GCN^k(X^k), \tag{2}$$

where $F_{local}^k$ represents local feature in $k^{th}$ group.

**Arrangement of Feature Capture Modules.** Full connection module and group connection module capture the global and local features of human pose respectively. When the representations of global features and local features are determined, how to fuse these two features becomes a key issue. At this time, the global-feature capture module and the local-feature capture module can be placed in a parallel or sequential manner, as shown in Fig. 4. Based on the previous feature fusion based method [22] and our research experiments, the parallel arrangement gives a better result than a sequential arrangement, which means learning the information of local features and global features separately and then conducting the fusion of the two.

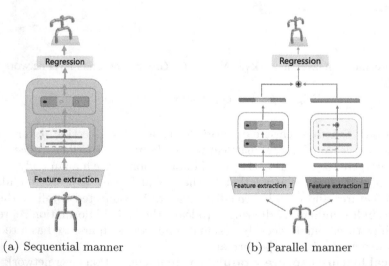

(a) Sequential manner             (b) Parallel manner

**Fig. 4.** Conceptual difference arrangement of full connection module and group connection module.

**Table 1.** The MPJPE (mm) of the SOTA methods on the H36M dataset under protocol #1 and protocol #2, respectively. Best performance is marked with bold font. Dim: representation dimension.

| Method authors | | Performance | | | | | | | | | | | | | | | |
|---|---|---|---|---|---|---|---|---|---|---|---|---|---|---|---|---|---|
| Protocol #1 | | Dire | Disc | Eat | Greet | Phone | Photo | Pose | Purch | Sit | SitD | Smoke | Wait | WalkD | Walk | WalkP | **Avg** |
| Zhou et al. [26] | ICCV'17 | 54.8 | 60.7 | 58.2 | 71.4 | 62.0 | 65.5 | 53.8 | 55.6 | 75.2 | 111.6 | 64.2 | 66.1 | 51.4 | 63.2 | 55.3 | 64.9 |
| Martinez et al. [13] | ICCV'17 | 51.8 | 56.2 | 58.1 | 59.0 | 69.5 | 78.4 | 55.2 | 58.1 | 74.0 | 94.6 | 62.3 | 59.1 | 65.1 | 49.5 | 52.4 | 62.9 |
| Pavlakos et al. [16] | CVPR'18 | 48.5 | 54.4 | 54.4 | 52.0 | 59.4 | 65.3 | 49.9 | 52.9 | 65.8 | 71.1 | 56.6 | 52.9 | 60.9 | 44.7 | 47.8 | 56.2 |
| Yang et al. [20] | CVPR'18 | 51.5 | 58.9 | 50.4 | 57.0 | 62.1 | 65.4 | 49.8 | 52.7 | 69.2 | 85.2 | 57.4 | 58.4 | 43.6 | 60.1 | 47.7 | 58.6 |
| Zhao et al. [25] | CVPR'19 | 47.3 | 60.7 | 51.4 | 60.5 | 61.1 | **49.9** | 47.3 | 68.1 | 86.2 | **55.0** | 67.8 | 61.0 | 42.1 | 60.6 | 45.3 | 57.6 |
| Iskakov et al. [7] | ICCV'19 | 41.9 | 49.2 | 46.9 | 47.6 | 50.7 | 57.9 | 41.2 | 50.9 | 57.3 | 74.9 | 48.6 | 44.3 | **41.3** | 52.8 | 42.7 | 49.9 |
| Wang et al. [18] | ICCV'19 | 44.7 | 48.9 | 47.0 | 49.0 | 56.4 | 67.7 | 48.7 | 47.0 | 63.0 | 78.1 | 51.1 | 50.1 | 54.5 | 40.1 | 43.0 | 52.6 |
| Ci et al. (LCN) [2] | ICCV'19 | 46.8 | 52.3 | 44.7 | 50.4 | 52.9 | 68.9 | 49.6 | 46.4 | 60.2 | 78.9 | 51.2 | 50.0 | 54.8 | 40.4 | 43.3 | 52.7 |
| Pavllo et al. [16] | CVPR'19 | 47.1 | 50.6 | 49.0 | 51.8 | 53.6 | 61.4 | 49.4 | 47.4 | 59.3 | 67.4 | 52.4 | 49.5 | 55.3 | 39.5 | 42.7 | 51.8 |
| Cai et al. [1] | ICCV'19 | 46.5 | 48.8 | 47.6 | 50.9 | 52.9 | 61.3 | 48.3 | 45.8 | 59.2 | 64.4 | 51.2 | 48.4 | 53.5 | 39.2 | 41.2 | 50.6 |
| Zeng et al. [22] | ECCV'20 | 44.5 | 48.2 | 47.1 | 47.8 | 51.2 | 56.8 | 50.1 | 45.6 | 59.9 | 66.4 | 52.1 | 45.3 | 54.2 | 39.1 | 40.3 | 49.9 |
| Li et al. [9] | CVPR'20 | 45.6 | **44.6** | 49.3 | 49.3 | 52.5 | 58.5 | 46.4 | 44.3 | 53.8 | 67.5 | 49.4 | 46.1 | 52.5 | 41.4 | 44.4 | 49.7 |
| Xu et al. [19] | CVPR'20 | 40.6 | 47.1 | 45.7 | 46.6 | 50.7 | 63.1 | **45.0** | 47.7 | 56.3 | 63.9 | 49.4 | 46.5 | 51.9 | 38.1 | 42.3 | 49.2 |
| Gong et al. [3] | CVPR'21 | – | – | – | – | – | – | – | – | – | – | – | – | – | – | – | 50.2 |
| Zeng et al. [23] | ICCV'21 | 43.1 | 50.4 | **43.9** | 45.3 | 46.1 | 57.0 | 46.3 | 47.6 | 56.3 | 61.5 | 47.7 | 47.4 | 53.5 | 35.4 | **37.3** | 47.9 |
| Zhan et al. [24] | CVPR'22 | 44.7 | 48.7 | 48.7 | 48.4 | 51.0 | 59.9 | 46.8 | 46.9 | 58.7 | 61.7 | 50.2 | 46.4 | 51.5 | 38.6 | 41.8 | 49.7 |
| Ours (Dim: 2048) | | 38.7 | 46.7 | 50.5 | 40.6 | 45.1 | 62.9 | 47.2 | 40.0 | 43.0 | 76.7 | 47.3 | 42.0 | 48.3 | 35.9 | 41.9 | 47.1 |
| Ours (Dim: 4096) | | **37.3** | 47.9 | 49.6 | **38.8** | **43.7** | 62.6 | 45.9 | **37.9** | **41.6** | 80.4 | **45.6** | **41.7** | 51.2 | **33.6** | 39.6 | **46.5** |
| Protocol #2 | | Dire | Disc | Eat | Greet | Phone | Photo | Pose | Purch | Sit | SitD | Smoke | Wait | WalkD | Walk | WalkP | **Avg** |
| Martinez et al. [13] | ICCV'17 | 39.5 | 43.2 | 46.4 | 47.0 | 51.0 | 56.0 | 41.4 | 40.6 | 56.5 | 69.4 | 49.2 | 45.0 | 49.5 | 38.0 | 43.1 | 47.7 |
| Pavlakos et al. [16] | CVPR'18 | 34.7 | 39.8 | 41.8 | 38.6 | 42.5 | 47.5 | 38.0 | 36.6 | 50.7 | 56.8 | 42.6 | 39.6 | 43.9 | 32.1 | 36.5 | 41.8 |
| Yang et al. [20] | CVPR'18 | **26.9** | 30.9 | **36.3** | 39.9 | 43.9 | 47.4 | **28.8** | **29.4** | 36.9 | 58.4 | 41.5 | 30.5 | **29.5** | 42.5 | 32.2 | 37.7 |
| Wang et al. [18] | ICCV'19 | 33.6 | 38.1 | 37.6 | 38.5 | 43.4 | 48.8 | 36.0 | 35.7 | 51.1 | 63.1 | 41.0 | 38.6 | 40.9 | 30.3 | 34.1 | 40.7 |
| Ci et al. (LCN) [2] | ICCV'19 | 36.9 | 41.6 | 38.0 | 41.0 | 41.9 | 51.1 | 38.2 | 37.6 | 49.1 | 62.1 | 43.1 | 39.9 | 43.5 | 32.2 | 37.0 | 42.2 |
| Pavllo et al. [16] | CVPR'19 | 36.0 | 38.7 | 38.0 | 41.7 | 40.1 | 45.9 | 37.1 | 35.4 | 46.8 | 53.4 | 41.4 | 36.9 | 43.1 | 30.3 | 34.8 | 40.0 |
| Cai et al. [1] | ICCV'19 | 36.8 | 38.7 | 38.2 | 41.7 | 40.7 | 46.8 | 37.9 | 35.6 | 47.6 | 51.7 | 41.3 | 36.8 | 42.7 | 31.0 | 34.7 | 40.2 |
| sXu et al. [19] | CVPR'20 | 33.6 | 37.4 | 37.0 | 37.6 | 39.2 | 46.4 | 34.3 | 35.4 | 45.1 | 52.1 | 40.1 | 35.5 | 42.1 | 29.8 | 35.3 | 38.9 |
| Li et al. [9] | CVPR'20 | 34.2 | **34.6** | 37.3 | 39.3 | 38.5 | 45.6 | 34.5 | 32.7 | 40.5 | **51.3** | 37.7 | 35.4 | 39.9 | 29.9 | 34.5 | 37.7 |
| Gong et al. [3] | CVPR'21 | – | – | – | – | – | – | – | – | – | – | – | – | – | – | – | 39.1 |
| Ours (Dim: 2048) | | 28.8 | 40.0 | 40.0 | 34.4 | 49.2 | **33.2** | 32.0 | 31.4 | 32.4 | 60.1 | 37.7 | 28.8 | 41.0 | 28.5 | 33.9 | 36.8 |
| Ours (Dim: 4096) | | 27.4 | 39.1 | 38.3 | **33.4** | **31.5** | 47.3 | 31.0 | 30.1 | **31.5** | 63.5 | **36.0** | **27.6** | 42.5 | **26.9** | **31.9** | **35.9** |

# 4   Experiments

In this section, we quantitatively evaluate the effectiveness of JointFusionNet and visualize the observed patterns and further explain the performance of JointFusionNet cross actions. The ablation study analyzes the effects of global and local features, representation dimension, and grouping strategy.

## 4.1   Datasets, Evaluation Metrics and Details

**Human3.6M** [6] is a large benchmark widely used for 3D human pose estimation with 11 professional actors collected by the motion sensor. Following conventional works, data from 5 actors (subject 1, 5, 6, 7, 8) are used for training, and data from other 2 actors (subject 9, 11) are used for testing. We use MPJPE and PA-MPJPE for evaluation.

**3DPW** [12] is the first dataset in the wild with more complicated motions and scenes for 3D human pose estimation evaluation. To verify generalization of the proposed method, we use its test set for evaluation with MPJPE and PA-MPJPE as metric.

**Evaluation Metrics.** Following convention, we use the mean per joint position error (MPJPE) [6] for evaluation, as follows

$$MPJPE = \frac{1}{N} \sum_{i=1}^{N} \|J_i - J_i^*\|_2, \tag{3}$$

where $N$ is the number of all joints, $J_i$ and $J_i^*$ are respectively the groundtruth position and the estimated position of the $i$th joint. Protocol #1 was directly calculated, Protocol #2 (Procrustes Analysis MPJPE, PA-MPJPE) was calculated after rigid transformation.

**Implementation Details.** To train the 3D human pose estimation network, we adopt Adam optimizer [8] with a learning rate initialized as 0.001 and decays at the rate of 0.95 after each epoch. We train JointFusionNet model for 60 epoches in PyTorch framework on NVIDIA RTX 2080 Ti GPU.

### 4.2    Comparison with State-of-the-Art Methods

In this setting, we use the 2D pose detected by off-the-shelf 2D pose estimator as input of JointFusionNet, and set the representation dimension to 4096, grouping strategy to 5. We first compare our proposed method with the state-of-the-art methods using the standard subject protocol under Protocol #1 and Protocol #2. Table 1 shows that JointFusionNet yields an overall improvement over state-of-the-art methods, indicating strong generalization ability for 3D human pose estimation.

### 4.3    Cross-dataset Results on 3DPW

In this setting, we examine cross-dataset generalization ability of JointFusion-Net by training the model on the Human3.6M training set and evaluating on the 3DPW test set. The performance of JointFusionNet is generally outperforming than that of previous work by a large margin. Notably, it yields an overall improvement of 14.8 mm (relative 13.8% improvement) over the previous best method [2] on 3DPW dataset. As shown in Table 2, proposed approach achieves the best cross-data generalization performance.

**Table 2.** Performance on the 3DPW test set

| Method authors | | Performance | |
|---|---|---|---|
| | | Protocol #1 | Protocol #2 |
| Martinez et al. (FCN) [13] | ICCV'17 | 159.8 | 113.3 |
| Pavllo et al. (1-frame) [16] | CVPR'19 | – | 146.3 |
| Zhao et al. (SemGCN) (1-frame) [25] | CVPR'19 | – | 152.3 |
| Ci et al. (LCN) [2] | ICCV'19 | 191.5 | 107.6 |
| Cai et al. (ST-GCN) (1-frame) [1] | ICCV'19 | – | 154.3 |
| Zeng et al. [22] | ECCV'20 | 169.0 | 110.7 |
| Gong et al. (PoseAug) (1-frame) [3] | CVPR'21 | – | 130.3 |
| Ours | | **123.1** | **92.8** |

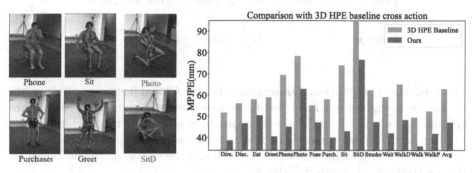

(a) Example pose in H36M          (b) Comparison with 3D HPE Baseline

**Fig. 5.** A visualization of example pose with huge and light improvement compared with 3D HPE Baseline cross actions.

## 4.4 Visualization and Explanation

This section visualizes some example human pose with local similar features in H36M and explains the performance comparison between JointFusionNet and 3D HPE Baseline method cross actions, as shown in Fig. 5. The local feature of sitting in the lower body and standing in the lower body appear in different action categories similarly. Correspondingly, the estimation performance of action (Such as Sit and Phone) that has more similar local features has a huge improvement (relative 26.4%, 36.8% improvement over the 3D HPE Baseline method [13]). On the contrary, there is still an improvement in the performance of actions with relatively less similar local features (Such as Photo and SitD), though it is difficult for JointFusionNet to fully learn the relationship between global and local features of the action with few local similar features.

### 4.5   Ablation Study

**Effect of Global and Local Features.** In proposed JointFusionNet, the global-feature capture module and local-feature capture module focu on learning global and local features of human pose respectively. Therefore, this set of experiments explores the role of the global features and local features separately. This experiments use global-feature capture module, local-feature capture module and parallel global-local-feature capture module to capture features, respectively. Compared to capturing the global or local features individually, the proposed global-local features fusion network is more efficient, as shown in Table 3.

**Table 3.** Performance under capturing different features

| Representation features | Global | Local | Global and Local |
|---|---|---|---|
| Protocol #1 | 62.9 | 49.9 | **46.5** |
| Protocol #2 | 47.7 | 38.7 | **35.9** |

**Effect of Representation Dimension.** In the Global-feature capture module, we use a high-dimensional feature representation of human pose. In this experiment, we set different representations to explore the effect of representation dimension. Higher-dimensional features represent the potential to learn to capture more complex interconnections, although inevitably pose challenges to network training, as shown in Table 4.

**Table 4.** Performance under different representation dimensions

| Representation dimensions | 1024 | 2048 | 4096 | 5120 |
|---|---|---|---|---|
| Protocol #1 | 47.80 | 47.12 | **46.50** | 46.89 |
| Protocol #2 | 37.67 | 36.75 | **35.86** | 36.61 |

**Effect of Grouping Strategy.** We compare the results of using different numbers of local groups in Table 5. Although there can be more and complex grouping strategies, we only set 3 commonly used strategies to explore the effect of grouping strategy. The way of grouping reveals the structural information of the human body. It is shown that the performance is best when the grouping method is consistent with intuitive perception, which indicates that a strong physical relationship among joints in a group is a prerequisite for learning effective local features.

Table 5. Performance under different grouping strategies

| Group | 5 | 3 | 2 |
|---|---|---|---|
| Protocol #1 | 46.50 | **46.25** | 46.53 |
| Protocol #2 | **35.86** | 35.88 | 36.16 |

# 5    Conclusion

In this paper, we proposed JointFusionNet, a structural global and local joint features fusion approach based on inspiring observation patterns, which improves generalization performance in 3D human pose estimation. The key idea is to design a parallel fusion network that captures global-features and local-features for more effective learning. Experimental results and ablation studies show that JointFusionNet outperforms state-of-the-art techniques, especially for poses with more similar local features.

**Acknowledgment.** This work was jointly supported by the National Natural Science Foundation of China under grant 62001110, the Natural Science Foundation of Jiangsu Province under grant BK20200353, and the "Zhishan Young Scholar" Program of Southeast University.

# References

1. Cai, Y., et al.: Exploiting spatial-temporal relationships for 3D pose estimation via graph convolutional networks. In: Proceedings of the IEEE/CVF International Conference on Computer Vision (ICCV), pp. 2272–2281 (2019). https://doi.org/10.1109/ICCV.2019.00236
2. Ci, H., Wang, C., Ma, X., Wang, Y.: Optimizing network structure for 3D human pose estimation. In: Proceedings of the IEEE/CVF International Conference on Computer Vision (ICCV), pp. 2262–2271 (2019). https://doi.org/10.1109/ICCV.2019.00235
3. Gong, K., Zhang, J., Feng, J.: PoseAug: a differentiable pose augmentation framework for 3D human pose estimation. In: Proceedings of the IEEE/CVF Conference on Computer Vision and Pattern Recognition (CVPR), pp. 8575–8584 (2021)
4. He, K., Zhang, X., Ren, S., Sun, J.: Deep residual learning for image recognition. In: Proceedings of the IEEE/CVF Conference on Computer Vision and Pattern Recognition (CVPR), pp. 770–778 (2016). https://doi.org/10.1109/CVPR.2016.90
5. He, Y., Yan, R., Fragkiadaki, K., Yu, S.I.: Epipolar transformers. In: Proceedings of the IEEE/CVF Conference on Computer Vision and Pattern Recognition (CVPR), pp. 7776–7785 (2020). https://doi.org/10.1109/CVPR42600.2020.00780
6. Ionescu, C., Papava, D., Olaru, V., Sminchisescu, C.: Human3.6M: large scale datasets and predictive methods for 3D human sensing in natural environments. IEEE Trans. Pattern Anal. Mach. Intell. **36**(7), 1325–1339 (2014). https://doi.org/10.1109/TPAMI.2013.248
7. Iskakov, K., Burkov, E., Lempitsky, V., Malkov, Y.: Learnable triangulation of human pose. In: Proceedings of the IEEE/CVF International Conference on Computer Vision (ICCV), pp. 7717–7726 (2019). https://doi.org/10.1109/ICCV.2019.00781

8.  Kingma, D.P., Ba, J.: Adam: A method for stochastic optimization. arXiv preprint arXiv:1412.6980 (2014)
9.  Li, S., Ke, L., Pratama, K., Tai, Y.W., Tang, C.K., Cheng, K.T.: Cascaded deep monocular 3D human pose estimation with evolutionary training data. In: Proceedings of the IEEE/CVF Conference on Computer Vision and Pattern Recognition, pp. 6173–6183 (2020)
10. Li, W., Liu, H., Tang, H., Wang, P., Van Gool, L.: MHFormer: Multi-hypothesis transformer for 3D human pose estimation. arXiv preprint arXiv:2111.12707 (2021)
11. Ma, X., Su, J., Wang, C., Ci, H., Wang, Y.: Context modeling in 3D human pose estimation: a unified perspective. In: Proceedings of the IEEE/CVF Conference on Computer Vision and Pattern Recognition (CVPR), pp. 6234–6243 (2021). https://doi.org/10.1109/CVPR46437.2021.00617
12. von Marcard, T., Henschel, R., Black, M., Rosenhahn, B., Pons-Moll, G.: Recovering accurate 3D human pose in the wild using IMUs and a moving camera. In: Proceedings of the European Conference on Computer Vision (ECCV), pp. 601–617 (2018)
13. Martinez, J., Hossain, R., Romero, J., Little, J.J.: A simple yet effective baseline for 3D human pose estimation. In: Proceedings of the IEEE/CVF International Conference on Computer Vision (ICCV), pp. 2659–2668 (2017). https://doi.org/10.1109/ICCV.2017.288
14. Park, S., Kwak, N.: 3D human pose estimation with relational networks. CoRR abs/1805.08961 (2018). http://arxiv.org/abs/1805.08961
15. Pavlakos, G., Zhou, X., Daniilidis, K.: Ordinal depth supervision for 3D human pose estimation. In: 2018 IEEE/CVF Conference on Computer Vision and Pattern Recognition, pp. 7307–7316 (2018). https://doi.org/10.1109/CVPR.2018.00763
16. Pavllo, D., Feichtenhofer, C., Grangier, D., Auli, M.: 3D human pose estimation in video with temporal convolutions and semi-supervised training. In: Proceedings of the IEEE/CVF Conference on Computer Vision and Pattern Recognition (CVPR), pp. 7745–7754 (2019). https://doi.org/10.1109/CVPR.2019.00794
17. Tang, W., Wu, Y.: Does learning specific features for related parts help human pose estimation? In: Proceedings of the IEEE/CVF Conference on Computer Vision and Pattern Recognition (CVPR), pp. 1107–1116 (2019). https://doi.org/10.1109/CVPR.2019.00120
18. Wang, J., Huang, S., Wang, X., Tao, D.: Not all parts are created equal: 3D pose estimation by modeling bi-directional dependencies of body parts. In: Proceedings of the IEEE/CVF International Conference on Computer Vision (ICCV), pp. 7771–7780 (2019)
19. Xu, J., Yu, Z., Ni, B., Yang, J., Yang, X., Zhang, W.: Deep kinematics analysis for monocular 3D human pose estimation. In: Proceedings of the IEEE/CVF Conference on Computer Vision and Pattern Recognition (CVPR), pp. 896–905 (2020). https://doi.org/10.1109/CVPR42600.2020.00098
20. Yang, W., Ouyang, W., Wang, X., Ren, J., Li, H., Wang, X.: 3D human pose estimation in the wild by adversarial learning. In: Proceedings of the IEEE/CVF Conference on Computer Vision and Pattern Recognition (CVPR), pp. 5255–5264 (2018).https://doi.org/10.1109/CVPR.2018.00551
21. Yuan, Z., Du, S.: JointPose: jointly optimizing evolutionary data augmentation and prediction neural network for 3D human pose estimation. In: Farkaš, I., Masulli, P., Otte, S., Wermter, S. (eds.) ICANN 2021, Part III. LNCS, vol. 12893, pp. 368–379. Springer, Cham (2021). https://doi.org/10.1007/978-3-030-86365-4_30

22. Zeng, A., Sun, X., Huang, F., Liu, M., Xu, Q., Lin, S.: SRNet: improving generalization in 3D human pose estimation with a split-and-recombine approach. In: Proceedings of the European Conference on Computer Vision (ECCV), pp. 507–523 (2020)
23. Zeng, A., Sun, X., Yang, L., Zhao, N., Liu, M., Xu, Q.: Learning skeletal graph neural networks for hard 3D pose estimation. In: Proceedings of the IEEE/CVF International Conference on Computer Vision (ICCV), pp. 11436–11445 (2021)
24. Zhan, Y., Li, F., Weng, R., Choi, W.: Ray3D: ray-based 3D human pose estimation for monocular absolute 3D localization (2022). https://doi.org/10.48550/ARXIV.2203.11471, http://arxiv.org/abs/2203.11471
25. Zhao, L., Peng, X., Tian, Y., Kapadia, M., Metaxas, D.N.: Semantic graph convolutional networks for 3D human pose regression. In: Proceedings of the IEEE/CVF Conference on Computer Vision and Pattern Recognition (CVPR), pp. 3425–3435 (2019)
26. Zhou, X., Huang, Q., Sun, X., Xue, X., Wei, Y.: Towards 3D human pose estimation in the wild: a weakly-supervised approach. In: Proceedings of the IEEE/CVF International Conference on Computer Vision (ICCV), pp. 398–407 (2017). https://doi.org/10.1109/ICCV.2017.51

# Multi-scale Feature Extraction and Fusion for Online Knowledge Distillation

Panpan Zou[1] , Yinglei Teng[1,2]([envelope]) , and Tao Niu[1]

[1] Beijing University of Posts and Telecommunications, Beijing, China
{zoupanpan,lilytengtt,tasakim}@bupt.edu.cn
[2] Beijing Key Laboratory of Space-Ground Interconnection and Convergence,
Beijing, China

**Abstract.** Online knowledge distillation conducts knowledge transfer among all student models to alleviate the reliance on pre-trained models. However, existing online methods rely heavily on the prediction distributions and neglect the further exploration of the representational knowledge. In this paper, we propose a novel Multi-scale Feature Extraction and Fusion method (MFEF) for online knowledge distillation, which comprises three key components: Multi-scale Feature Extraction, Dual-attention and Feature Fusion, towards generating more informative feature maps for distillation. The multi-scale feature extraction exploiting divide-and-concatenate in channel dimension is proposed to improve the multi-scale representation ability of feature maps. To obtain more accurate information, we design a dual-attention to strengthen the important channel and spatial regions adaptively. Moreover, we aggregate and fuse the former processed feature maps via feature fusion to assist the training of student models. Extensive experiments on CIFAR-10, CIFAR-100, and CINIC-10 show that MFEF transfers more beneficial representational knowledge for distillation and outperforms alternative methods among various network architectures.

**Keywords:** Knowledge distillation · Multi-scale · Feature fusion

## 1 Introduction

Driven by the advances in algorithms, computing power, and big data, deep learning has achieved remarkable breakthroughs in various vision tasks [11, 12,15]. Increasing the network depth or width is often the key point to further improve the performance of deep neural networks. However, these models with millions of parameters demand high computational costs and huge storage requirements, making it challenging to deploy them in resource-limited or low latency scenarios. For instance, mobile phones and Internet of Things (IoT)

---

This work was supported in part by the National Key R&D Program of China (No. 2021YFB3300100), and the National Natural Science Foundation of China (No. 62171062).

devices. To address this problem, extensive research has been carried out to develop a lightweight model while simultaneously keeping negligible model accuracy degradation in performance. These efforts can typically be classified into network pruning, parameter quantization, low-rank approximation, and knowledge distillation.

Knowledge distillation (KD) has been demonstrated as an effective technique for model compression. The vanilla KD [8] method adopts a two-stage training strategy, where knowledge is transferred from the pre-trained high-capacity teacher model to a compact student model via aligning prediction distributions or feature representations [16], also known as the offline distillation. Drawbacks of these methods include the fact that the high-capacity teacher is not always available, even if they are, higher computational cost and training time of the complex teacher also cannot be avoided. In addition, KD suffers from model capacity gap when the size difference is large between the student and teacher model [13].

Online knowledge distillation (OKD) [6,9,23,24] has been developed to alleviate the above issue. This paradigm is more attractive for the reason that instead of using a pre-trained high-performance teacher, it breaks the presupposed specific strong-weak relationship and simplifies the training process to an end-to-end one-stage fashion. All models are trained simultaneously by learning from each other across the training process. In the other words, knowledge is distilled and shared among all networks. Compared to the offline KD, the online KD achieves superior performance while keeping a more straightforward structure. However, popular methods concentrate on transferring logit information as soft targets in common. Although the soft targets carry richer information than one-hot labels, it is relatively unitary to make use of only the logit. Since feature maps can provide rich information about the perception, channel and spatial correlations, simply aligning or fusing cannot take full advantage of the meaningful feature representation.

In this paper, to alleviate the aforementioned limitation, we propose a novel Multi-scale Feature Extraction and Fusion method (MFEF) for online knowledge distillation, including three key components, i.e., multi-scale feature extraction, dual-attention, and feature fusion. In order to obtain more beneficial representational knowledge for distillation, we first get multi-scale features which can focus on both local details and global regions by multiple divide and concatenate operations. Then, students are guided to learn more accurate features by introducing dual-attention which boosts the representation power of important channel and spatial regions while suppressing unnecessary regions. Finally, we utilize feature fusion to integrate the acquired feature maps and feed them into a fusion classifier to assist the learning of student models.

To summarize, the main contributions of this paper are:

– We propose a novel Multi-scale Feature Extraction and Fusion method (MFEF) for online knowledge distillation, which integrates the feature representation with soft targets for distillation.

- We first introduce multi-scale feature extraction to improve the multi-scale representation ability of the features and provide richer information apart from simply alignment. Then the dual-attention is proposed to generate more accurate features. Furthermore, we use feature fusion to fuse the enhanced knowledge, which can improve the generalization ability for distillation.
- Extensive experiments on CIFAR-10/100 [10] and CINIC-10 [3] verify that the proposed MFEF can effectively enhance the multi-scale representation power of features and generate more informative knowledge for distillation.

## 2    Related Work

Many efforts have been conducted with regard to knowledge distillation and vision tasks. In this section, we will give a comprehensive description of the related literature.

### 2.1    Traditional Knowledge Distillation

The idea of transferring the knowledge from a cumbersome model to a smaller model without a significant drop in accuracy is derived from [1]. Traditional KD works in a two-stage fashion which needs a pre-trained teacher. [16] first introduces intermediate features from hidden layers, the main idea is to match the feature activations of the student and teacher model. [25] combines attention with distillation to further exploit more accurate information. [19] explores the relationships between layers by mimicking the teacher's flow matrices using the inner product. In [17], the adversarial training scheme is utilized to enable the student and teacher networks to learn the true data distribution. [13] introduces a teacher assistant to mitigate the capacity gap between the teacher model and student model. In [7], it proposes to use the activation boundaries formed by hidden neurons for distillation.

### 2.2    Online Knowledge Distillation

Online knowledge distillation has emerged to further improve the performance of the student model and eliminate the dependency on high-capacity teacher models which are time-consuming and costly. In this paradigm, student models learn mutually by sharing the predictions throughout the training process. [23] is a representative method in which multiple networks work in a collaborative way. Each network imitates the peer network's class probabilities using Kullback-Leibler divergence. [6] further extends DML to construct an ensemble logit as the teacher by averaging a group of students' predictions to improve generalization ability. A fusion module is introduced to train a fusion classifier to guide the training of sub-networks in [9]. [26] adds a gate module to generate the importance score for each branch and build a stronger teacher. [2] proposes two-level distillation between multiple auxiliary peers and a group leader to enhance diversity among student models. In terms of architecture designing, [18] forms

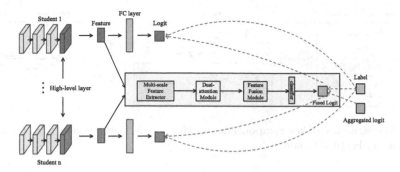

**Fig. 1.** An overview of Multi-scale Feature Extraction and Fusion (MFEF) for Online knowledge distillation. The output of high-level layer is sent to three key components (i) Multi-scale Feature Extraction: Enhance the multi-scale representation ability of feature maps. (ii) Dual-attention: Use channel and spatial attention to strengthen informative regions. (iii) Feature Fusion: Integrate knowledge among stuent models and futher improve the generalization ability.

the student model via replacing the standard convolution with cheap convolution operations. Student and teacher models share the same networks in [22], where knowledge is distilled within the network itself and knowledge from the deeper portions of the network is distilled into shallow ones.

### 2.3 Multi-scale Feature

Multi-scale feature representations are of critical importance to many vision tasks. Some concurrent works focus on promoting the capability of models by utilizing multi-scale features. [5] constructs hierarchical residual-like connections within a residual block to represent multi-scale features at a granular level. [4] uses pyramidal convolution including four levels of different kernel sizes to generate multi-scale features. Similarly, [21] integrates information at different scales via pyramidal convolution structure for the channel-wise feature maps. A flexible and efficient hierarchical-split block is used in [20] to capture multi-scale features. [14] adopts atrous spatial pyramid pooling to probes convolutional features on multiple scales for semantic image segmentation.

## 3 Proposed Method

In this section, we describe the framework and loss function in detail. An overview of MFEF is illustrated in Fig. 1. Different from the existing KD methods, MFEF digs deeper into the information provided by feature maps including multi-scale representation ability and the channel and spatial attention.

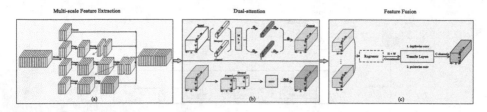

**Fig. 2.** The structure of key components: (a) Multi-scale feature extraction. (b) Dual-attention. (c) Feature Fusion

## 3.1  Problem Definition

The key idea of knowledge distillation is that soft targets contain the dark knowledge which can be used as a supervisor to transfer knowledge to the student model. Given a labeled dataset $D\{x_i, y_i\}_{i=1}^N$, with $N$ samples, $x_i$ is the $i$th input sample and $y_i \in \{1, 2, ..., M\}$ is the corresponding ground-truth label. $M$ is the total number of classes in the dataset. Consider $n$ student models $\{S_j\}_{j=1}^n$, the logit produced by the last fully connected layer of the student $S_j$ is denoted as $z_j = \{z_j^1, z_j^2, ..., z_j^M\}$. Then the probability of the $j$th student for the sample $x_i$ over the $m$th class $p_j^m(x_i)$ can be estimated by a softmax function,

$$p_j^m(x_i) = \frac{\exp(z_j^m/T)}{\sum_{m=1}^M \exp(z_j^m/T)}, \tag{1}$$

where $T$ is the temperature which produces a more softened probability distribution as it increases. Specifically, when $T = 1$, it is defined as the original softmax output, we consider writing it as $p_j^m(x_i)$; otherwise it is rewritten as $\tilde{p}_j^m(x_i)$. For multi-class classification, the objective is to minimize the cross-entropy loss between the softmax outputs and the ground-truth labels,

$$L_j^{CE} = -\sum_{i=1}^N \sum_{m=1}^M l_i \log(p_j^m(x_i)), \tag{2}$$

where $l_i = 1$ if $y_i = m$, and 0 otherwise. Knowledge transfer is facilitated by matching the softened probability of the student model $\tilde{p}_j^m(x_i)$ and the teacher model $\tilde{p}_t^m(x_i)$. We introduce the distillation loss of $j - th$ student model in the form of Kullback-Leibler Divergence

$$L_j^D = \sum_{i=1}^N \sum_{j=1}^M \tilde{p}_t^m(x_i) \log \frac{\tilde{p}_t^m(x_i)}{\tilde{p}_j^m(x_i)}. \tag{3}$$

## 3.2  MFEF Framework

From a global perspective, the main idea of MFEF is to enhance the multi-scale representation power of feature maps and generate more informative knowledge for distillation. The details of each key component are explained in the following.

**Multi-scale Feature Extraction.** Aligning the soft targets of teacher and student models enhances the model generalization, but it ignores the feature maps which contain rich information. In addition to the soft targets, inspired by [20], we introduce multi-scale feature extraction to generate multi-scale features which are of significant importance for vision tasks. As shown in Fig. 2(a), the extraction includes multiple divide and concatenate operations in the channel dimension to enhance the information flow between different groups. We use the feature maps of the last layer as the input for the reason it has high-level semantic information which is richer and specific. For the convenience of notation, we name the feature map of the $j$th student model as $F_j$ and the extraction as $E$. $D$ and $C$ represent the divide and concatenate operations, respectively. First, $F_j$ is divided into $p$ groups $\{F_{j1}, F_{j2}, ..., F_{jp}\}$. The first group $F_{j1}$ is output straightforward and the second part is sent to a convolution operation and then is divided into two sub-groups $D_{21}$ and $D_{22}$. One of them is exported to the output and the other is concatenated with the next part. The rest other than the last group follows the concatenate-convolution-export-divide procedure. The last part does not need the divide operation. We define the output as

$$E(F_j) = C(F_{j1}, D_{22}, D_{32}, ..., Conv(C(F_{jp}, D_{p-1,1}))). \tag{4}$$

The multi-scale feature extraction can generate feature maps that contain multiple scales of receptive fields. The more features are concatenated, the larger the receptive field is. Larger receptive fields can capture global information while the smaller ones can focus on details. Such a combination can generate more meaningful feature maps to improve the performance of distillation.

**Dual-Attention.** After the extraction, we utilize dual-attention to dig deeper into the feature maps (see Fig. 2(b)). Channel and spatial attention focus on "what" and "where" are important, and we apply them in a sequential manner. We denote the multi-scale feature map $E(F_j) \in \mathbb{R}^{C \times H \times W}$ as the input, where $C$, $H$, $W$ represent its channel numbers, height, and width, respectively. Average-pooling and max-pooling are used in combination to obtain finer attention.

For channel attention, we denote $a_c, m_c \in \mathbb{R}^{C \times 1 \times 1}$ as the vectors after average-pooling and max-pooling. The weight $w_c \in \mathbb{R}^{C \times 1 \times 1}$ of channel is

$$w_c = \sigma(W(a_c))) + (W(m_c))), \tag{5}$$

where the symbol $\sigma$ denotes the Sigmoid function, $W$ is the weight of a multi-layer perceptron (MLP). The channel attention output $AT_j^c$ is

$$AT_j^c = w_c \otimes F_M, \tag{6}$$

where $\otimes$ refers to element-wise multiplication. Similarly, we denote the average-pooling and max-pooling vector $a_s, m_s \in \mathbb{R}^{1 \times H \times W}$, $w_s \in \mathbb{R}^{1 \times H \times W}$ is

$$w_s = \sigma(conv(a_s; m_s)), \tag{7}$$

where *conv* represents a convolution operation. The output $AT_j^s$ is

$$AT_j^s = w_s \otimes AT_j^c, \tag{8}$$

Dual-attention can strengthen the informative channel and spatial regions while suppressing the less important ones and thus generate more informative outputs which can focus on useful regions within a context adaptively.

**Feature Fusion.** We propose feature fusion to aggregate and maximize the usage of the student models' information. The structure of it is illustrated in Fig. 2(c). Specifically, we first concatenate the meaningful feature maps of students that have been processed previously, i.e., $\{AT_1^s, AT_2^s, ..., AT_j^s\}$. If the resolutions of the feature maps are different, we apply a convolutional regressor to make them identical. Then we concatenate them and sent the results to the transfer layers which consist of a sequence of depthwise and pointwise convolution operations. Finally, we fuse the student models' feature information and feed it into a fusion classifier which is supervised by ground truth labels.

### 3.3   Loss Function

The cross-entropy loss of the $j$th student and the fused classifier is $L_j^{CE}$ and $L_f^{CE}$, respectively, as described in Eq. (2). We further define the aggregated logit of students as $z_a^m = \frac{1}{n}\sum_{j=1}^n z_j^m$ and probability as $p_a^m$. The fusion classifier is trained with KL divergence

$$L_a^D = L_a^{KL}(\tilde{p}_a^m, \tilde{p}_f^m), \tag{9}$$

This loss is used to transfer the knowledge of the student models to the fusion classifier. Then the fusion classifier facilitate the knowledge which contains informative feature representations transferring back to the student models via minimizing the distillation loss

$$L_f^D = \sum_{j=1}^n L_f^{KL}(\tilde{p}_f^m, \tilde{p}_j^m), \tag{10}$$

Finally, we derive the total training objective as

$$L_{total} = L_{CE} + T^2 L_D. \tag{11}$$

where $L_{CE}$ is the sum of cross-entropy of students and fused classifier. $L_D$ refers to the sum of $L_a^D$ and $L_f^D$. Because the gradients produced by the soft targets are scaled by $1/T^2$, thus $L_D$ is multiplied with $T^2$ to keep the contributions of $L_{CE}$ and $L_D$ roughly balanced.

## 4    Experiment

In this section, we conduct comprehensive experiments to evaluate the performance of MFEF on three datasets and various widely-used neural networks. We choose various related methods under different settings for comparison and show the results to demonstrate that MFEF generalizes well among different numbers and types of models. Finally, evaluation of each component are carried out.

**Table 1.** Comparisons with closely related methods on CIFAR 10 and CIFAR-100 with seven different networks. Top-1 error rates (%) are reported. Two same student models are used for each method. FFL-S and MFEF-S refer to the results of the student model, and FFL and MFEF refer the results of fused classifiers.

| Dataset | Network | Baseline | KD | DML | FFL-S | FFL | MFEF-S | MFEF |
|---------|---------|----------|------|-------|-------|-------|--------|-------|
| CIFAR-10 | ResNet-20 | 7.32 | 7.18 | 6.63 | 6.49 | 6.22 | **6.38** | **6.08** |
| | ResNet-32 | 6.77 | 6.69 | 6.52 | 6.06 | 5.78 | **5.59** | **5.41** |
| | ResNet-56 | 6.30 | 6.14 | 5.82 | 5.46 | 5.26 | **5.28** | **4.82** |
| | ResNet-110 | 5.64 | 5.47 | 5.21 | 5.18 | 4.83 | **4.81** | **4.52** |
| | WRN-16-2 | 6.78 | 6.40 | 5.49 | 6.09 | 5.97 | **5.33** | **4.99** |
| | WRN-40-2 | 5.34 | 5.24 | 4.72 | 4.75 | 4.60 | **4.51** | **4.02** |
| | DenseNet40-12 | 6.87 | 6.81 | 6.50 | 6.72 | 6.24 | **5.79** | **5.30** |
| CIFAR-100 | ResNet-20 | 31.08 | 29.94 | 29.61 | 28.56 | 26.87 | **28.46** | **26.30** |
| | ResNet-32 | 30.34 | 29.82 | 26.89 | 27.06 | 25.56 | **26.36** | **24.84** |
| | ResNet-56 | 29.31 | 28.61 | 25.51 | 24.85 | 23.53 | **24.22** | **23.15** |
| | ResNet-110 | 26.30 | 25.67 | 24.49 | 23.95 | 22.79 | **23.37** | **22.16** |
| | WRN-16-2 | 27.74 | 26.78 | 26.16 | 25.72 | 24.74 | **24.66** | **22.93** |
| | WRN-40-2 | 25.13 | 24.43 | 22.77 | 22.06 | 21.05 | **21.76** | **20.60** |
| | DenseNet40-12 | 28.97 | 28.74 | 26.94 | 27.21 | 24.76 | **26.81** | **24.27** |

### 4.1    Experiment Settings

**Datasets and Architecture.** We incorporate three image classification datasets in the following evaluations. (1) CIFAR-10 which contains 60000 colored natural images (50000 training samples and 10000 test samples) over 10 classes. (2) CIFAR-100 consists of 60000 images (50000 training samples and 10000 test samples) drawn from 100 classes. (3) CINIC-10 consists of images from both CIFAR and ImageNet. It is more challenging than CIFAR-10. It contains 90000 train samples and 90000 test samples. For CIFAR-10/100, there are seven popular networks used, namely ResNet-20, ResNet-32, ResNet-56, ResNet-110, WRN-16-2, WRN-40-2, and DenseNet-40-12. For CINIC-10, we use MobileNetV2 and ResNet-18 following the settings in [3].

**Settings.** We apply horizontal flips and random crop from an image padded by 4 pixels for data augmentation in training. We use SGD as the optimizer with

Nesterov momentum 0.9, weight decay of 1e–4 for student models and 1e–5 for fusion and mini-batch size of 128. The models are trained for 300 epochs for all datasets. We set the initial learning rate to 0.1 and is multiplied by 0.1 at 150, 225 epochs. We set the temperature $T$ to 3 empirically and $\alpha = 80$ for ramp-up weighting. For the case of student models have same architecture, the low-level layers are shared following [2]. When output channels of the feature maps are different, the feature fusion is designed to match the smaller one. For fair comparison, we set the number of student models to two. The top-1 error rate (%) of the best student over 3 runs is reported.

## 4.2    Experiment Results

**Results on CIFAR-10/100.** As shown in Table 1, we evaluate the effectiveness of MFEF on CIFAR-10 and CIFAR-100 based on several popular networks. Since our goal is to distill more powerful feature representations for online distillation, we compare MFEF with the offline KD, logit-only online method DML, and fusion-only method FFL. For the offline KD, it employs a pre-trained ResNet-110 as the teacher model. For DML, we report the top-1 error rate of the best student. FFL-S and MFEF-S represent the results of the best student and FFL and MFEF indicate the results of the fused classifier.

The results clearly show the performance advantages of our MFEF. Specifically, MFEF improves by approximately 1% and 2% of the backbone networks. MFEF also achieves the best top-1 error rate compared with the closely related online distillation methods. For instance, on CIFAR-10, MFEF-S achieves lower error rates than FFL-S by approximately 0.5%, 0.8%, and 1% on ResNet-32, WRN-16-2, and DensNet-40-12, respectively. MFEF improves FFL by about 1% on WRN-16-2 and DensNet-40-12; While on CIFAR-100, MFEF achieves 0.6%, 0.7%, and 1% increase on ResNet-56, ResNet -32, and WRN-16-2, respectively. MFEF is higher by about 1.8% on WRN-16-2 compared with FFL. These improvements attribute to the integration of the multi-scale feature extraction and the attention mechanism and the feature fusion of student models.

**Table 2.** Top-1 error rate (%) comparison with FFL on CINIC-10.

| Network | Baseline | FFL-S | FFL | MFEF-S | MFEF |
|---|---|---|---|---|---|
| MobileNetV2 | 18.07 | 17.85 | 16.10 | **17.56** | **15.66** |
| ResNet-18 | 13.94 | 13.33 | 12.67 | **13.22** | **12.39** |

**Results on CINIC-10.** In this section, we compare the top-1 error rate of MFEF with FFL based on MobileNetV2 and ResNet-18. As shown in Table 2, FFL and MFEF both reduces the error rate of the baseline and MFEF shows higher improvement of performance in both student models and fused classifier. In case of MobileNetV2, MFEF improves by around 0.5%, 0.3%, and 0.4%

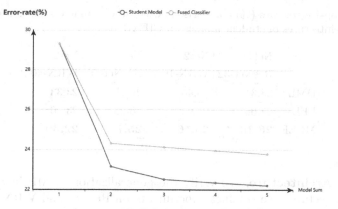

**Fig. 3.** Evaluating the impact of expansion of student models on CIFAR-100 using ResNet-56.

compared to the baseline and FFL for student model and fused classifier. Based on these experiments, we could confirm that thanks to the enhancement of the multi-scale representation power, higher-quality knowledge is transferred among all student models and consequently achieves a lower error rate than others.

**Table 3.** Top-1 error rate (%) comparisons with other online distillation methods for training three students model on CIFAR-100. ONE and ONE-E refer to the results of the student models and the gated ensemble teacher.

| Method | ResNet-32 | ResNet-56 |
|--------|-----------|-----------|
| ONE    | 26.64     | 24.63     |
| FFL-S  | 26.30     | 24.51     |
| MFEF-S | **26.04** | **24.12** |
| ONE-E  | 24.75     | 23.27     |
| FFL    | 24.31     | 23.20     |
| MFEF   | **24.03** | **22.51** |

**Expansion of Student Models.** The impact of increasing the number of student models is illustrated in Fig. 3. We conduct experiments on ResNet-56. Not surprisingly, the performance of both students and the fusion classifier improves as the number of student models increases. When the student models expanded to 3, MFEF still performs competitively against ONE and FFL, as shown in Table 3. We can see that MFEF-S achieves an approximately 0.3% and 0.6% performance improvement on ResNet-32 compared to FFL-S and ONE-S, respectively. The fusion classifier yields an about 0.7% and 0.8% improvement on ResNet-56 superior to ONE and FFL.

**Table 4.** Top-1 error rate (%) comparisons with other online distillation methods for different architectures of student models on CIFAR-100.

|  | Net1 | Net2 | Net1 | Net2 |
|---|---|---|---|---|
|  | ResNet-32 | WRN-16-2 | ResNet-56 | WRN-40-2 |
| DML | 28.31 | 26.45 | 26.75 | 23.33 |
| FFL | 27.06 | 25.93 | 26.23 | 23.06 |
| MFEF | **26.38** | **25.16** | **25.7** | **22.39** |

**Different Architecture.** To verify the generalization of MFEF on different model architectures, we conduct experiments on ResNet and WRN in Table 4. We set ResNet as Net1 and WRN as Net2. MFEF shows better performance than DML and FFL in both Net1 and Net2. An interesting observation is that when MFEF is applied, the smaller network (Net1) improves significantly compared to the larger one. For example, when compared with DML, MFEF is higher by about 2% and 1.3% on ResNet-32 and WRN-16-2. This is because MFEF can aggregate and fuse all networks' feature maps and transfer the informative knowledge of the larger network to the smaller one better.

**Table 5.** Evaluating the effectiveness of each component on CIFAR-100 using ResNet-110.

| Case | Component | Student | Fused |
|---|---|---|---|
| A | Backbone | 26.30 | – |
| B | Backbone+MSFE | 24.35 | – |
| C | Backbone+OKD | 24.79 | – |
| D | Backbone+MSFE+OKD | 23.54 | 22.54 |
| E | Backbone+MSFE+DA+OKD | 23.37 | 22.16 |

**Component Effectiveness Evaluation.** To further validate the benefit of each component, we conduct various ablation studies on CIFAR-100 on ResNet-110. Specifically, we perform experiments in five cases of ablations. As shown in Table 5, Case A refers to the model trained from scratch. Case B and C refer to the network where only the multi-scale feature extraction (MSFE) and OKD are included. And they improved by around 2% and 1.5% compared to the backbone. When both MSFE and OKD are applied in Case D, the student model achieves a higher accuracy by around 2.8% compared to Case A. When we get rid of MSFE from Case D (Case C), the performance decrease sharply by about 1.3%, which confirms the usefulness of the MSFE. Dual-attention (DA) is added in Case E based on Case D. This increases the performance by around 0.2% and 0.4% of the student models and the fused classifier, respectively, and it has more influence on the fused classifier. The improvements manifest that MSFE has a more significant impact on the model performance, which is mainly attributed to the enhancement of the multi-scale representation ability.

## 5    Conclusion

We present a novel Multi-scale Feature Extraction and Fusion method (MFEF) for online knowledge distillation. It integrates multi-scale extraction and attention mechanism into a unified feature fusion framework. Different from existing online knowledge distillation methods, we enhance the multi-scale representation ability of the feature maps and then fuse them from student models to assist the training process by transferring more informative knowledge. Extensive experiments based on three datasets show the superiority of our method compared to prior works. Results on various networks also demonstrate that the proposed method can be broadly applied to a variety of architectures from a very small scale to a large one.

## References

1. Bucilă, C., Caruana, R., Niculescu-Mizil, A.: Model compression. In: Proceedings of the 12th ACM SIGKDD International Conference on Knowledge Discovery and Data Mining, pp. 535–541 (2006)
2. Chen, D., Mei, J.P., Wang, C., Feng, Y., Chen, C.: Online knowledge distillation with diverse peers. In: Proceedings of the AAAI Conference on Artificial Intelligence, vol. 34, pp. 3430–3437 (2020)
3. Darlow, L.N., Crowley, E.J., Antoniou, A., Storkey, A.J.: CINIC-10 is not ImageNet or CIFAR-10. arXiv preprint arXiv:1810.03505 (2018)
4. Duta, I.C., Liu, L., Zhu, F., Shao, L.: Pyramidal convolution: rethinking convolutional neural networks for visual recognition. arXiv preprint arXiv:2006.11538 (2020)
5. Gao, S.H., Cheng, M.M., Zhao, K., Zhang, X.Y., Yang, M.H., Torr, P.: Res2Net: a new multi-scale backbone architecture. IEEE Trans. Pattern Anal. Mach. Intell. **43**(2), 652–662 (2019)
6. Guo, Q., et al.: Online knowledge distillation via collaborative learning. In: Proceedings of the IEEE/CVF Conference on Computer Vision and Pattern Recognition, pp. 11020–11029 (2020)
7. Heo, B., Lee, M., Yun, S., Choi, J.Y.: Knowledge transfer via distillation of activation boundaries formed by hidden neurons. In: Proceedings of the AAAI Conference on Artificial Intelligence, vol. 33, pp. 3779–3787 (2019)
8. Hinton, G., Vinyals, O., Dean, J., et al.: Distilling the knowledge in a neural network. arXiv preprint arXiv:1503.02531, vol. 2, no. 7 (2015)
9. Kim, J., Hyun, M., Chung, I., Kwak, N.: Feature fusion for online mutual knowledge distillation. In: 2020 25th International Conference on Pattern Recognition (ICPR), pp. 4619–4625. IEEE (2021)
10. Krizhevsky, A., Hinton, G., et al.: Learning multiple layers of features from tiny images (2009)
11. Krizhevsky, A., Sutskever, I., Hinton, G.E.: Imagenet classification with deep convolutional neural networks. In: Advances in Neural Information Processing Systems, vol. 25 (2012)

12. Long, J., Shelhamer, E., Darrell, T.: Fully convolutional networks for semantic segmentation. In: Proceedings of the IEEE Conference on Computer Vision and Pattern Recognition, pp. 3431–3440 (2015)
13. Mirzadeh, S.I., Farajtabar, M., Li, A., Levine, N., Matsukawa, A., Ghasemzadeh, H.: Improved knowledge distillation via teacher assistant. In: Proceedings of the AAAI Conference on Artificial Intelligence, vol. 34, pp. 5191–5198 (2020)
14. Redmon, J., Farhadi, A.: Yolov3: an incremental improvement. arXiv preprint arXiv:1804.02767 (2018)
15. Ren, S., He, K., Girshick, R., Sun, J.: Faster R-CNN: towards real-time object detection with region proposal networks. In: Advances in Neural Information Processing Systems, vol. 28 (2015)
16. Romero, A., Ballas, N., Kahou, S.E., Chassang, A., Gatta, C., Bengio, Y.: Fitnets: hints for thin deep nets. arXiv preprint arXiv:1412.6550 (2014)
17. Wang, X., Zhang, R., Sun, Y., Qi, J.: KDGAN: knowledge distillation with generative adversarial networks. In: Advances in Neural Information Processing Systems, vol. 31 (2018)
18. Xie, J., Lin, S., Zhang, Y., Luo, L.: Training convolutional neural networks with cheap convolutions and online distillation. arXiv preprint arXiv:1909.13063 (2019)
19. Yim, J., Joo, D., Bae, J., Kim, J.: A gift from knowledge distillation: Fast optimization, network minimization and transfer learning. In: Proceedings of the IEEE Conference on Computer Vision and Pattern Recognition, pp. 4133–4141 (2017)
20. Yuan, P., et al.: HS-ResNet: hierarchical-split block on convolutional neural network. arXiv preprint arXiv:2010.07621 (2020)
21. Zhang, H., Zu, K., Lu, J., Zou, Y., Meng, D.: EPSANet: an efficient pyramid split attention block on convolutional neural network. arxiv 2021. arXiv preprint arXiv:2105.14447 (2021)
22. Zhang, L., Song, J., Gao, A., Chen, J., Bao, C., Ma, K.: Be your own teacher: improve the performance of convolutional neural networks via self distillation. In: Proceedings of the IEEE/CVF International Conference on Computer Vision, pp. 3713–3722 (2019)
23. Zhang, Y., Xiang, T., Hospedales, T.M., Lu, H.: Deep mutual learning. In: Proceedings of the IEEE Conference on Computer Vision and Pattern Recognition, pp. 4320–4328 (2018)
24. Zhou, G., Fan, Y., Cui, R., Bian, W., Zhu, X., Gai, K.: Rocket launching: a universal and efficient framework for training well-performing light net. In: Proceedings of the AAAI Conference on Artificial Intelligence, vol. 32 (2018)
25. Zhou, Z., Zhuge, C., Guan, X., Liu, W.: Channel distillation: channel-wise attention for knowledge distillation. arXiv preprint arXiv:2006.01683 (2020)
26. Zhu, X., Gong, S., et al.: Knowledge distillation by on-the-fly native ensemble. In: Advances in Neural Information Processing Systems, vol. 31 (2018)

# Multi-scale Vertical Cross-layer Feature Aggregation and Attention Fusion Network for Object Detection

Wenting Gao[ID], Xiaojuan Li[ID], Yu Han[ID], and Yue Liu[✉][ID]

Beijing Engineering Research Center of Mixed Reality and Advanced Display, School of Optics and Photonics, Beijing Institute of Technology, Beijing 100081, China
liuyue@bit.edu.cn

**Abstract.** Scale imbalance is one of the primary limitations for object detection. To tackle such a problem, existing methods such as FPN usually integrate the features at different scales, which suffers from the inconsistence of different high-level and low-level features due to the straightforward combination. In this paper, we propose a multi-scale vertical cross-layer feature aggregation and attention fusion network which not only has bottom-up and top-down pathways with lateral connections, but also adds cross-layer paths in the vertical direction. The proposed method can boost information flow and shorten the information path between high-level and low-level features. An attention fusion module is also introduced to obtain the internal correlation between local, global and contextual information of other feature layers. In order to optimize the anchor configurations, a differential evolution algorithm is employed to reconfigure the ratios and scales of anchors. Experimental results show that the proposed method achieves superior detection performance on the public dataset PASCAL VOC.

**Keywords:** Deep learning · Object detection · Attention mechanism

## 1 Introduction

Object detection is an important and challenging task in such computer vision applications as unmanned vehicles, augmented reality and face recognition. Current state-of-art object detection methods can be mainly grouped into two-stage and one-stage detection. For two-stage detection, the detection problem is divided into two processes: region proposal and detection, which generally takes longer to obtain the final results and has a more complicated architecture. In contrary, one-stage detections have been tuned for speed, their accuracy meanwhile trails for two-stage detections.

Scale imbalance occurs in cases of overexpression of certain sizes of the objects or input bounding boxes in the dataset, which greatly affects the overall detection performance. Many deep learning object detectors obtain visual features from input images by employing backbone convolutional networks. However, only such backbones lead to the limitation of the spatial down-sampling rate for the high-level features, which are insufficient for the object detection task. Although FPN was proposed to address

© The Author(s), under exclusive license to Springer Nature Switzerland AG 2022
E. Pimenidis et al. (Eds.): ICANN 2022, LNCS 13532, pp. 139–150, 2022.
https://doi.org/10.1007/978-3-031-15937-4_12

this issue via utilizing the pyramidal of a CNN network and implementing a top-down path through lateral connections, it still suffers from a significant drawback as a result of the direct merger of the features collected from the backbone network, where the contribution of the feature maps from different level for the object in input image should differ. Therefore, the features from different layers are supposed to be integrated in a coordinated manner, which helps to reduce the inconsistency during the prediction.

In this paper, we propose a multi-scale vertical cross-layer feature aggregation and attention fusion network for object detection. We make further improvements on the basis of RetinaNet. On the one hand, we address the scale imbalance problem in object detection by introducing a multi-scale vertical cross-layer feature aggregation network and hence allow the features to reach the layers in which the predictions occur in a faster way. In order to promote the top-down and bottom-up flow of feature information, we exploit several additional vertical cross-layer pathways along with a bottom-up and a top-down pathway that up-samples abstract features into high-resolution features. On the other hand, we propose an attention fusion module based on the principle of self-attention mechanism [13] and Non-local block [14], which enables the target feature maps to obtain mutual relation from other feature maps and to capture the internal correlation between local, global and contextual information. In addition, we employ a differential evolution algorithm to reconfigure the ratios and scales of anchors on the train set. Experimental results show that the proposed method achieves better performance than majority of state-of-art object detectors on the public dataset Pascal VOC.

## 2    Related Work

**Two-Stage Detections.** R-CNN [1] was the first algorithm that transfered classification tasks to object detection. It adopts selective search [2] to yield about 2000 region proposals for every image. Fast R-CNN [3] took the advantages of R-CNN and SPPNet [4], enabling simultaneous training of a detector and a bounding box regressor under the same network configurations. Faster R-CNN [5] further improved the detection speed and accuracy by introducing a convolutional neural network called Region Proposal Network (RPN). Numerous extensions to this framework have also been proposed [6, 7].

**One-Stage Detections.** YOLO [8] reframed the whole detection problem as a regression problem and used one topmost feature map for classification and localization. SSD [9] designed various default anchors boxes for multi-resolution features to naturally handle objects of various sizes. In general, one-stage detections always fail to achieve the accuracy of two-stage detections. Lin [10] found that the extreme foreground-background class imbalance during the training process is the major cause, so a new loss function called Focal Loss has been introduced through reducing the loss contribution from easy examples. RetinaNet achieves better performance in accuracy and speed than the two-stage detectors.

**Feature Fusion.** Features at different scales possess different characteristics. Features in shallower layers tend to contain more spatial information such as edges and contours, whereas the high-level features represent stronger invariance and more semantic information. Thus, it is vital to integrate the deep and shallow features in a CNN model. Lin et al. [11] proposed Feature Pyramid Networks (FPN), which significantly improves the performance of detection by utilizing the hierarchy of a convolutional network and several lateral path are added to implement the bottom-up and top-down pathway. Despite its benefits, the impact of the feature map from different resolution of the feature hierarchy differs and results in the feature-level problem. Several methods aiming to improve the pyramidal features collected by FPN have also been proposed [12, 13]. Therefore, the focus of this work is to mitigate the feature-level imbalance problem by proposing novel architectures.

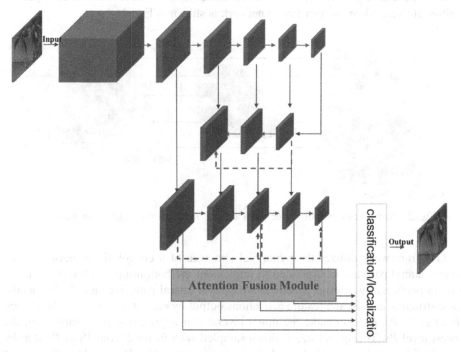

**Fig. 1.** Architecture of multi-scale vertical cross-layer feature aggregation and attention fusion network for object detection.

## 3 Architecture of Proposed Network

Higher layers from multiple feature maps with different resolutions contain more abstract and semantic information whereas the lower layers indicate more spatial information in the images. Large objects are typically associated with high-lever feature maps and small objects are associated with low-level feature maps. When detecting objects with feature pyramids, the contradiction among features from different levels prevents the improvements of performance and weakens the effect of the feature pyramids. The features from different layers are supposed to be integrated in a coordinated manner. Therefore, the detector could utilize qualitative feature information sufficiently. Figure 1 shows the framework of the proposed multi-scale vertical cross-layer feature aggregation and attention fusion detection network, which is primarily composed of three parts: the backbone feature extraction network (ResNet-50), the multi-scale vertical cross-layer feature aggregation network and the attention fusion module.

### 3.1   Multi-scale Vertical Cross-Layer Feature Aggregation Network

The multi-scale vertical cross-layer feature aggregation network is designed to further enhance the feature gathered by FPN and sufficiently employ these features. The specific multi-scale vertical cross-layer fusion network is shown in Fig. 2.

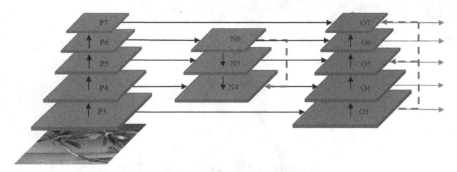

**Fig. 2.** Architecture of multi-scale vertical cross-layer feature aggregation network.

Our framework utilizes the pyramidal structure of a convolutional network, and several lateral path are incorporated to implement the bottom-up and top-down pathway. In particular, we design a vertical cross-layer lateral path. We take ResNet as the basic structure and use the feature activations output by each stage's last residual block $\{P_3, P_4, P_5, P_6, P_7\}$ to denote the initial layers. Our aggregation path starts from the lowest level $P_3$. The spatial size is down-sampled with factor 2 from $P_3$ to $P_7$ step by step. Besides, each pyramid channel dimension is set to 256. We use $\{N_4, N_5, N_6\}$ to denote feature levels generated by FPN. $\{O_3, O_4, O_5, O_6, O_7\}$ are final set of feature maps to perform prediction. We first adopt a $3 \times 3$ convolutional layer with stride 2 to down-sample high-resolution maps $O_i$ to the size of $O_{i+1}$. Then each element of feature map $N_{i+1}$ and the down-sampled map $O_i'$ are added through lateral connection. Finally, the fused feature map $O_{i+1}$ passes through a $3 \times 3$ convolutional layer to generate the subsequent feature map.

On the basis of the above structure, three cross-layer connections are added in the vertical direction, including one top-down and two bottom-up vertical connections. This is important since the features from the initial layers have rich information about localization and the upper layers have more semantic information. Comparative experimental results show that the vertical cross-layer network can indeed further help the network to obtain a comprehensive understanding of the fused feature information by repeatedly extracting deep and shallow features in a CNN model. At the end, features at different levels are fused by using attention fusion module.

## 3.2 Attention Fusion Module

We introduce an attention fusion module to integrate multi-level features instead of simply using element-wise sum or concatenation. In attention fusion module, important features are given greater concerns to guide the network to focus on feature layer regions with greater contribution, which also enables the network to keep useful information for combination. The attention fusion module is inspired by and based on Non-local [14] and self-attention [15], which are designed capture relationships of local, global and contextual information from other feature maps via non-local operations. According to the definition of non-local mean operation, the generic non-local operation in deep neural networks is:

$$y_i = \frac{1}{C(x)} \sum_{\forall j} f(x_i, x_j) g(x_j) \tag{1}$$

where $x$ is the input feature layer and $y$ is the output feature layer. $f(x_i, x_j)$ denotes the similarity between $i$ and all $j$. The function $g$ is used to calculate the representation of the input feature in $j$. Finally, the result is normalized by a factor $C(x)$. We further improve and apply the operation to the field of object detection. We define an improved non-local operation for object detection as:

$$y_i = \frac{1}{C(x)} \sum_{\forall j} f(x_i, a_j) g(x_j) \tag{2}$$

where $x$ is the input feature layer as the target feature map and $a$ is the feature layer at other level as the auxiliary feature map. $f(x_i, a_j)$ denotes the similarity between $x$ in position $i$ and $a$ in position $j$. Our attention fusion module is shown in Fig. 3. If we assume the target feature map as $T \in R^{C \times N}$ and the auxiliary feature map at other level as $A \in R^{C \times N'}$. The auxiliary feature map first goes through a nearest-interpolation or a $3 \times 3$ convolutional layer with stride 2 to change the spatial size. Therefore, $A' \in R^{C \times N}$. $N$ is the total amount of positions in a feature map, $N = H \times W$, $C$ is the channel dimension. In this module, we consistently use channel 256 of feature maps. $A'$ is the auxiliary feature map after conducting a resizing operation.

The target feature map $T$ and the auxiliary feature map $A'$ are transformed to the corresponding feature space by $\theta(x) = W_\theta x, \varphi(x) = W_\varphi x$ and $g(x) = W_g x$, where $W_\theta, W_\varphi$ and $W_g$ are the weight matrix to be learned. It can be implemented by $1 \times 1$ convolution. The dimension of channels for $W_\theta, W_\varphi$ and $W_g$ are set to be half of $C$. The $f(x_i, a_j)$ is defined as a dot-product similarity $r_{i,j} = \theta(x_i)^T \varphi(a_j)$, where $r_{i,j}$ is the similarity response of $a$ in position $j$ and $x$ in position $i$. Since $C(x) = \sum_{\forall j} r_{i,j}$, we have:

$$s_{i,j} = \frac{1}{C(x)} f(x_i, a_j) = \frac{e^{\theta(x_i)^T \varphi(a_j)}}{\sum_{\forall j} e^{\theta(x_i)^T \varphi(a_j)}} \tag{3}$$

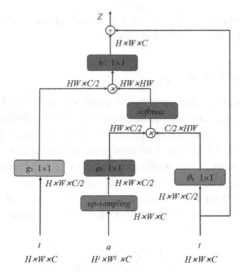

**Fig. 3.** Architecture of attention fusion module.

where $s_{i,j}$ becomes the softmax computation along the position $j$ in $a$ and $i$ in $x$. Then, we can obtain the output feature $Z \in R^{C \times N}$ by adding a residual connection:

$$z_i = W_h y_i + x_i \tag{4}$$

where $z_i$ is the feature of the output feature on position $i$, $y_i$ is given in Eq. (2). We add a residual connection "$+x_i$" to make it easier to carry out without interfering the original effects (e.g., if $W_h$ is initialized as zero). Figure 4 shows how to incorporate the attention fusion module with our proposed multi-scale vertical cross-layer feature aggregation network, each output feature map is used for object detection following the same pipeline of RetinaNet.

$$Output = z(A_1, T) + z(A_2, T) + z(A_3, T) + z(T, T) \tag{5}$$

where $z(\cdot)$ denotes the fused feature map from target and auxiliary feature maps. $A_1, A_2$ and $A_3$ are both auxiliary feature maps.

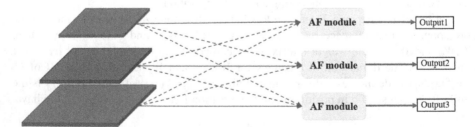

**Fig. 4.** Illustration of the attention module. The attention module takes all levels of feature layers as the input feature layers.

The attention fusion module enables the target feature map to acquire long-range dependencies of local, global and contextual information from other feature maps. It also alleviates the vanishing-gradient problem in backpropagation.

### 3.3 Anchor Optimization Strategy

The concept of anchor box is proposed in Faster R-CNN [5], where anchors are a group of predefined bounding boxes placed on the feature map at different aspect ratios and scales, and then the detection box based on these references is predicted. Through training, the original anchor boxes are adjusted according to the IoU scores thus obtaining more accurate prediction results.

The scale and size are key parameters for anchor boxes. In Faster R-CNN [5], three sizes ($128^2$, $256^2$, $512^2$) and three aspect ratios (1:1, 1:2, 2:1) are selected by heuristic design method. The anchor sizes in RetinaNet [10] are set to [32, 64, 128, 256, 512] corresponding to the five feature layers from $P_3$ to $P_7$ in the feature pyramid, and each anchor size corresponds to three aspect ratios and three scales respectively. It is difficult to optimize the size of anchor box because it is related to the setting of multi-scale feature fusion network in the CNN model. However, the aspect ratio and scale ratio parameters of the anchor box can be optimized and improved. When being applied to a dataset with its own features, the shape of the anchor box needs to be adaptively adjusted to improve accuracy.

Once the anchor shapes are determined, the parameters will not be changed during training. Accordingly, inferior performance in specific areas may result from improper design of the anchor shapes may result.

Inspired by [16], we exploit differential evolution algorithm to reconfigure the ratios and scales of anchors on the train set. The anchor box optimization problem can be transformed into a constrained optimization problem based on the overlapping area of the anchor box and the ground truth, and can be solved efficiently by global searching. We establish a single-objective constrained optimization model as:

$$\min f(x) = \sum_{i=0}^{N} (1 - \max v_i(s, r))^2 \log(\max v_i(s, r)) \tag{6}$$

where $N$ indicates the amount of anchor boxes, $v_i$ is the overlap score between the anchor box and the ground truths in $i$, $r \in [1, 4]$, $s \in [0.4, 2]$. Then we can find the global optimal solution for the three sets of aspect ratios and scales to determine the optimization strategy for anchor box assignment.

The parameters of the differential evolutionary algorithm are set as follows: the population size $N_p$ is 200, the crossover probability $C_r$ is 0.3, the differential weight $F$ is 0.5. When initializing the population of candidate solutions, the scales are bounded to a range of [0.4, 2] and the ratios are bounded in [1, 4]. The final anchor optimization configurations are shown in Table 1.

**Table 1.** Table of anchor configurations.

| Parameters | Original | After |
|---|---|---|
| Anchor size | [32, 64, 128, 256, 512] | [32, 64, 128, 256, 512] |
| Strides | [8, 16, 32,64, 128] | [8, 16, 32, 64, 128] |
| Ratios | [0.5, 1.0, 2] | [0.433, 1.0, 2.311] |
| Scales | [1, 1.26, 1.59] | [0.529, 0.864, 1.295] |

These optimized configurations can cover more scale range of small objects and better fit with the ground truth, which are then used for training the detector.

## 4 Experiment

### 4.1 Implementation Details

The network model is evaluated on the PASCAL VOC [17] 2007 + 2012 dataset, which contains 16,551 images in the train + val set and 4,952 images in the test set. We train our model on 4*RTX 2080Ti GPU and choose the pre-trained ResNet-50 on ImageNet as the backbone. The training process can be grouped into freezing and unfreezing stage. In the first stage, we freeze the base network and only train the extra layers where the batch size is set to 32. We initialize the learning rate as 0.001 and decay the learning rate of each parameter by every epoch. For the second stage, we train the whole network including the backbone where the batch size is set to 16 and the learning rate is set to 0.0001. We use mAP as a measure of our experimental results.

### 4.2 Comparison with Other Methods

We conduct experiments with our multi-scale vertical cross-layer feature aggregation and attention fusion network and other state-of-art methods on the public dataset PASCAL VOC.

The experimental detection results in Table 2 and Table 3 show that the detection accuracy of our proposed multi-scale vertical cross-layer feature aggregation and attention fusion network can reach 86.77% on the VOC2007 test set, which is equivalent to the improvement of 3.56% for the original RetinaNet. Comparison with the two-stage method such as Faster R-CNN shows that the multi-scale vertical cross-layer feature aggregation and attention fusion network has significant superiority both in speed and accuracy.

Since we follow the Focal Loss function in RetinaNet, the detection speed is slower than other one-stage object detection algorithms. In addition, our method performs better on the detection of small objects. For instance, the mAPs of bird, bottle and plant are 89.41%, 71.27% and 59.79% respectively, which confirms that our method enables the handling of the scale imbalance problem and is superior to the other methods on small objects.

**Table 2.** VOC 2007 test detection mAP (%) and average precision.

| Method | Faster R-CNN | SSD | RFBnet | YOLO V3 | RetinaNet | Ours |
|---|---|---|---|---|---|---|
| mAP (%) | 80.35 | 78.55 | 79.86 | 83.5 | 83.21 | **86.77** |
| Aeroplane | 82.63 | 81.33 | 82.41 | **94.41** | 88.05 | 91.58 |
| Bike | 88.69 | 87.4 | 88.2 | 90.03 | 90.58 | **92.56** |
| Bird | 80.71 | 77.45 | 80.32 | 85.58 | 87.65 | **89.41** |
| Boat | 70.79 | 69.78 | 72.46 | 64.27 | 74.56 | **82.04** |
| Bottle | 61.16 | 47.63 | 52.75 | **80.79** | 67.52 | 71.27 |
| Bus | 87.14 | 86.12 | 87.07 | **95.98** | 89.39 | 92.09 |
| Car | 88.8 | 88.42 | 88.28 | 86.8 | 91.84 | **93.61** |
| Cat | 91.91 | 89.09 | 90.97 | 90.41 | 94.42 | **96.02** |
| Chair | 62.4 | 61.6 | 59.72 | **74.99** | 61.39 | 68.89 |
| Cow | 84.24 | 84.11 | 84.73 | 73.23 | 89.41 | **92.05** |
| Table | 76.82 | 78.93 | 77.65 | **79.98** | 76.32 | 79.12 |
| Dog | 89.8 | 86.93 | 87.48 | 87.36 | 93.45 | **94.69** |
| Horse | 90.08 | 89.34 | 88.7 | 91.71 | 91.09 | **93.34** |
| Motorbike | 85.58 | 85.71 | 87.83 | 90.33 | 89.11 | **92.39** |
| Person | 85.2 | 80.15 | 81.34 | **90.66** | 86.8 | 87.34 |
| Plant | 51.4 | 50.12 | 55.3 | 59.37 | 53.26 | **59.79** |
| Sheep | 81.76 | 79.53 | 80.87 | 71.65 | 87.46 | **91.12** |
| Sofa | 79.18 | 82.61 | 80.56 | 84.27 | 78.32 | **85.55** |
| Train | 88.35 | 88.59 | 88.4 | 92.25 | 88.1 | **93.01** |
| Tvmonitor | 80.15 | 76.24 | 82.24 | 85.91 | 85.55 | **89.43** |

**Table 3.** Comparison of state-of-the-art small networks over parameters, mAP and FPS.

| Method | Backbone | mAP (%) | Parameters (M) | FPS |
|---|---|---|---|---|
| SSD | VGG | **78.55** | 99.76 | 58.03 |
| RFBnet | VGG | **79.86** | 151.42 | 41.07 |
| YOLO V3 | Darknet | **83.50** | 236.32 | 38.19 |
| Faster R-CNN | Resnet-50 | **80.35** | 522.91 | 13.03 |
| RetinaNet | Resnet-50 | **83.21** | 144.84 | 21.49 |
| Ours | Resnet-50 | **86.77** | 147.59 | 19.15 |

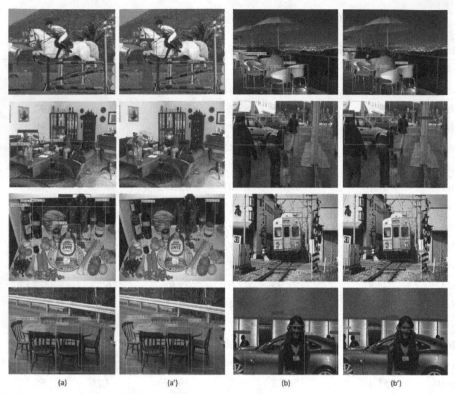

**Fig. 5.** Detection examples on VOC2007 testing set with RetinaNet and our proposed method. (a) and (b) are the detection results of ours.

Figure 5 presents the comparison of the detection examples on VOC2007 testing set of the proposed method in this paper and the RetinaNet, which indicates that the proposed method has a much superior detection performance than the RetinaNet and further validates the effectiveness of our method.

### 4.3  Ablation Study

We conduct comprehensive ablation experiment on a baseline of RetinaNet for object detection. The ablation experimental results are illustrated in Table 4.

On the VOC dataset, when only using the multi-scale vertical cross-layer feature aggregation network, the mAP improves by 0.9%. The extra addition cross-layer may boost information flow in object detection framework. However, the impact of the high- and low-level features varies for different resolution in a feature hierarchy. Integrating multi-level feature using element-wise sum or concatenation may cause spatial inconsistency. The mAP is raised to 85.11% after combining the multi-scale vertical cross-layer feature aggregation network and attention fusion module, which improves by 1.08% over RetinaNet with multi-scale vertical cross-layer feature aggregation network. The

**Table 4.** Ablation experiment for multi-scale vertical cross-layer feature aggregation and attention fusion network on the PASCAL VOC2007 testing set.

| Component | | | | |
|---|---|---|---|---|
| Multi-scale vertical cross-layer feature aggregation network | Baseline | √ | √ | √ |
| Attention fusion | | | √ | √ |
| Anchor optimization | | | | √ |
| mAP (%) | 83.21 | 84.11 | 85.19 | **86.77** |
| Parameters (M) | 144.84 | 147.09 | 147.59 | 147.59 |

attention fusion module allows for efficient fusion in a feature hierarchy and avoids spatial contradictions.

The mAP is improved by 1.58% after applying the optimized anchor configuration. The results prove that the three components proposed in this paper do not affect each other's performance, and the combined use of them will yield the greatest performance. The combination of multi-scale vertical cross-layer feature aggregation network and attention fusion helps to learn comprehensive understanding to the scale change of objects and handle the feature-level scale imbalance problem. The size and aspect ratio of the target vary for different datasets, and setting the parameters of the anchor box according to the actual situation is beneficial to improve the IoU at detection, which in turn improves the detection performance.

The complexity of the network increases slightly with each additional module, which can be shown by the change in the number of model parameters, but the increase in complexity is acceptable when compared to the performance improvement.

## 5 Conclusion

In this work, we identify scale imbalance as great obstacle preventing object detection task from fully utilizing the information of features. To address this issue, we propose a multi-scale vertical cross-layer feature aggregation and attention fusion network, which allows the combination of features from different layers to be coordinated and boosts information flow. We design several vertical cross-layer pathways to shorten the information path between lower layers and higher features. Besides, the attention fusion module helps to acquire long-range dependencies between different feature maps, which thus reduces the spatial contradictions between layers in a feature hierarchy. In order to pursue superior performance, we further employ a differential evolution algorithm to reconfigure the ratios and scales of anchors. Experimental results prove the effectiveness of our structure, which significantly improves strong baselines with tiny inference overhead. The mAP of our network model on PASCAL VOC2007 can reach to 86.77%, which achieves state-of-art accuracy.

**Acknowledgments.** This work was supported by the Key-Area Research and Development Program of Guangdong Province (No.2019B010149001) and the National Natural Science Foundation of China (No. 61960206007, No. 61731003) and the 111 Project (B18005).

# References

1. Girshick, R., Donahue, J., Darrell, T., Malik, J.: Rich feature hierarchies for accurate object detection and semantic segmentation. In: Proceedings of the IEEE Conference on Computer Vision and Pattern Recognition, pp. 580–587 (2014)
2. Uijlings, J.R., Van De Sande, K.E., Gevers, T., Smeulders, A.W.: Selective search for object recognition. Int. J. Comput. Vision **104**(2), 154–171 (2013)
3. Girshick, R.: Fast R-CNN. In: Proceedings of the IEEE International Conference on Computer Vision, pp. 1440–1448 (2015)
4. He, K., Zhang, X., Ren, S., Sun, J.: Spatial pyramid pooling in deep convolutional networks for visual recognition. IEEE Trans. Pattern Anal. Mach. Intell. **37**(9), 1904–1916 (2015)
5. Ren, S., He, K., Girshick, R., Sun, J.: Faster R-CNN: towards real-time object detection with region proposal networks. Adv. Neural Inf. Process. Syst. **28**, 1–9 (2015)
6. Dai, J., Li, Y., He, K., Sun, J.: R-FCN: object detection via region-based fully convolutional networks. Adv. Neural Inf. Process. Syst. **29**, 1–9 (2016)
7. Cai, Z., Vasconcelos, N.: Cascade R-CNN: delving into high quality object detection. In: Proceedings of the IEEE Conference on Computer Vision and Pattern Recognition, pp. 6154–6162 (2018)
8. Redmon, J., Divvala, S., Girshick, R., Farhadi, A.: You only look once: unified, real-time object detection. In: Proceedings of the IEEE Conference on Computer Vision and Pattern Recognition, pp. 779–788 (2016)
9. Liu, W., et al.: SSD: single shot multibox detector. In: Leibe, B., Matas, J., Sebe, N., Welling, M. (eds.) Computer Vision – ECCV 2016. LNCS, vol. 9905, pp. 21–37. Springer, Cham (2016). https://doi.org/10.1007/978-3-319-46448-0_2
10. Lin, T.Y., Goyal, P., Girshick, R., He, K., Dollár, P.: Focal loss for dense object detection. In: Proceedings of the IEEE International Conference on Computer Vision, pp. 2980–2988 (2017)
11. Lin, T.Y., Dollár, P., Girshick, R., He, K., Hariharan, B., Belongie, S.: Feature pyramid networks for object detection. In: Proceedings of the IEEE Conference on Computer Vision and Pattern Recognition, pp. 2117–2125 (2017)
12. Liu, S., Qi, L., Qin, H., Shi, J., Jia, J.: Path aggregation network for instance segmentation. In: Proceedings of the IEEE Conference on Computer Vision and Pattern Recognition, pp. 8759–8768 (2018)
13. Pang, J., Chen, K., Shi, J., Feng, H., Ouyang, W., Lin, D.: Libra R-CNN: towards balanced learning for object detection. In: Proceedings of the IEEE/CVF Conference on Computer Vision and Pattern Recognition, pp. 821–830 (2019)
14. Wang, X., Girshick, R., Gupta, A., He, K.: Non-local neural networks. In Proceedings of the IEEE Conference on Computer Vision and Pattern Recognition, pp. 7794–7803 (2018)
15. Zhang, H., Goodfellow, I., Metaxas, D., Odena, A.: Self-attention generative adversarial networks. In: International Conference on Machine Learning, pp. 7354–7363. PMLR (2019)
16. Zlocha, M., Dou, Q., Glocker, B.: Improving RetinaNet for CT lesion detection with dense masks from weak RECIST labels. In: Shen, D., et al. (eds.) Medical Image Computing and Computer Assisted Intervention – MICCAI 2019. LNCS, vol. 11769, pp. 402–410. Springer, Cham (2019). https://doi.org/10.1007/978-3-030-32226-7_45

# Multi-spectral Dynamic Feature Encoding Network for Image Demoiréing

Qiang Dai[1], Xi Cheng[2], and Li Zhang[1]($\boxtimes$)

[1] School of Computer Science and Technology,
Soochow University, Suzhou 215006, Jiangsu, China
zhangliml@suda.edu.cn
[2] School of Computer Science and Engineering, Nanjing University of Science
and Technology, Nanjing 210094, China
chengx@njust.edu.cn

**Abstract.** Moiré often appears when photographing textured objects, which can seriously degrade the quality of the captured photos. Due to the wide distribution of moiré and the dynamic nature of the moiré textures, it is difficult to effectively remove the moiré patterns. In this paper, we propose a multi-spectral dynamic feature encoding (MSDFE) network for image demoiréing. To solve the issue of moiré with distributed frequency spectrum, we design a multi-spectral dynamic feature encoding module to dynamically encode moiré textures. To remedy the issue of moiré textures with dynamic nature, we utilize a multi-scale network structure to process moiré images at different spatial resolutions. Extensive experimental results indicate that our proposed MSDFE outperforms the state-of-the-art in terms of fidelity and perceptual on benchmarks.

**Keywords:** Image demoiréing · Moiré pattern · Multi-spectral dynamic feature encoding

## 1 Introduction

Moiré usually appears in the form of colored stripes, ripples, or curves and is sensitive to shooting distance and camera orientation, which seriously degrades the visual quality of captured images. A common example of causing moiré is to shoot digital screens with a smartphone. More specially, digital screens are composed of liquid crystal display (LCD), which has a similar texture structure to the color filter array (CFA) of the digital camera's sensor. As a result, the imperfect alignment between them causes moiré.

Unlike other image restoration problems, such as denoising [22], super-resolution [5,15], and deblurring [12,14], a moiré pattern on images is dynamic and has a broad frequency distribution, which covers both the low-frequency part and the high-frequency parts. As a result, the broad frequency spectrum and the dynamic texture of moiré are the two main challenges in image demoiréing [3].

E. Pimenidis et al. (Eds.): ICANN 2022, LNCS 13532, pp. 151–162, 2022.
https://doi.org/10.1007/978-3-031-15937-4_13

Recently, many methods based on convolutional neural network (CNN) [2,3,6,7,19] have been proposed to remove moiré patterns of different frequency bands. A multi-scale network architecture was typically used in these demoiréing methods to obtain dynamic representations of moiré patterns, which facilitates the modeling of moiré patterns with different spatial frequencies and different resolutions. We also utilize a multi-scale design with three branches in our proposed model, which learns the parameters of each branch and aggregates the results at different branches to produce the final output. Furthermore, a progressive upsampling strategy was employed in our model to smoothly increase the resolution.

However, existing methods cannot handle the dynamic nature of moiré textures, and none of them tried to model moiré patterns explicitly. In this paper, we propose a multi-spectral dynamic feature encoding (MSDFE) network for image demoiréing. In our model, we leverage a multi-spectral dynamic feature encoding module to encode moiré patterns, which helps the model learn the frequency prior to moiré patterns and restore moiré images clearly.

## 2    Proposed Method

### 2.1    Overall Network Architecture

As shown in Fig. 1, we construct a three-branch convolutional network to dispose of demoiréing tasks. On Branch 1, we first utilize three learnable convolutional layers to downsample and encode original moiré images, which can be described as:

$$D_1 = \bigtriangledown(I) = W_3(W_2(\delta^p W_1(I))), \tag{1}$$

where $\bigtriangledown$ denotes the downsampling block, $D_1$ is the output of the first downsampling block, $W_i$ means the parameters of the $i$-th convolution layers in the downsampling block, $\delta^p$ is the activation function of parametric rectified linear units (PReLU) [8], and $I$ is the input image.

Branch 1 makes use of 2 residual blocks and increases channel attention. In addition, the resolution of Branch 1 is half of the original input image. The whole process of Branch 1 can be described as follows:

$$F_1 = \triangle(MD_2(MD_1(D_1)) + D_1), \tag{2}$$

where $F_1$ is the output of Branch 1, $\triangle$ denotes the upsampling block with subpixel convolution [18], and $MD_i$ means the $i$-th dynamic feature encoding residual block with multi-spectral channel attention, whose structure is shown in Fig. 4. We will explain the operation of multi-spectral channel attention in Sect. 2.3.

Both Branches 2 and 3 have a similar structure as Branch 1 except the number of residual blocks. The calculation processes of Branches 2 and 3 can be expressed as follows:

$$F_i = \triangle(NL(MD_k \cdots (MD_1(D_{i-1}))) + D_{i-1}), \tag{3}$$

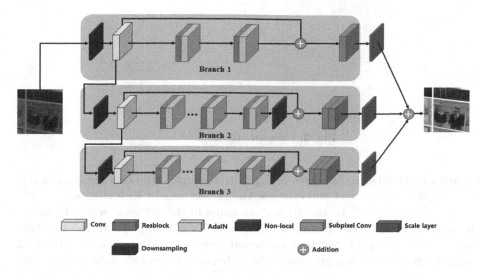

**Fig. 1.** Overall architecture of our proposed MSDFE.

where $F_i$ means the output of the $i$-th branch, $k$ is the number of multi-spectral dynamic feature encoding residual blocks, $NL(\cdot)$ denotes the region-level non-local operation [4] at the end of the current branch, which could help the model learn self-similarity; $D_{i-1}$ is the downsampled feature maps from the $i-1$-th branch, whose resolution is higher.

## 2.2  DCT and Channel Attention

In this section, we describe DCT and channel attention.

**DCT.** Usually, DCT is used for data or image compression. DCT can convert the signal in the spatial domain to the frequency domain due to its strong energy concentration property. Specially, we utilize the two-dimensional DCT (2D-DCT) [1]. For an image $I \in \mathbb{R}^{H \times W}$ with a height of $H$ and a width of $W$, 2D-DCT can be described as:

$$\Psi(h, w) = 2DDCT_{h,w}(I) = \sum_{u=0}^{H-1} \sum_{v=0}^{W-1} I_{u,v} \beta_{u,v}(h, w),$$
$$h \in \{0, 1, \cdots, H-1\}, w \in \{0, 1, \cdots, W-1\}, \tag{4}$$

where $\Psi(h, w)$ denotes the 2D-DCT frequency spectrum at $(h, w)$, $2DDCT_{h,w}$ is the 2D-DCT function, $I_{u,v}$ is the pixel of image $I$ at $(u, v)$, $h \in \{0, 1, \cdots, H-1\}$, $w \in \{0, 1, \cdots, W-1\}$, and the basis function $\beta_{u,v}(h, w)$ has the form

$$\beta_{u,v}(h, w) = cos\left(\frac{\pi h}{H}\left(u + \frac{1}{2}\right)\right) cos\left(\frac{\pi w}{W}\left(v + \frac{1}{2}\right)\right) \tag{5}$$

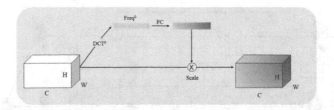

**Fig. 2.** Channel attention (CA).

**Channel Attention.** As shown in Fig. 2, the channel attention mechanism [16] uses a scalar to represent and evaluate the importance of each channel.

Let $X \in \mathbb{R}^{H \times W \times C}$ be the 2D feature maps in the network, where $C$ means the number of channels, $H$ and $W$ denote the height and the width of feature maps. Qin et al. [16] found that the scalar representation in channel attention could be treated as a compression problem because it has to represent the whole channel while only one scalar can be used. From this perspective, the channel attention can be expressed as:

$$\gamma = sigmoid(fc(\Gamma_{compress}(X))), \tag{6}$$

where $\gamma \in \mathbb{R}^C$ denotes the channel attention vector, $sigmoid$ means the Sigmoid function, $fc$ represents a mapping function, such as a fully connected layer or a 1D convolution, and $\Gamma_{compress} : \mathbb{R}^{H \times W \times C} \to \mathbb{R}^C$ is a compression method.

After obtaining the attention vector of all $C$ channels, the attention value will scale the corresponding input $X$. This process could be calculated as:

$$\overline{X}'_c = \gamma_c X'_c, c \in \{0, 1, \cdots C - 1\}, \tag{7}$$

where $\overline{X}'_c$ denotes the output of attention mechanism, $\gamma_c$ represents the $c$-th element of attention vector, and $X'_c$ means the $c$-th channel of the input $X$.

### 2.3  Multi-spectral Channel Attention (MSCA)

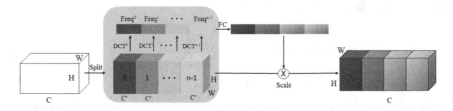

**Fig. 3.** Multi-spectral channel attention (MSCA [16]).

Given the input $X \in \mathbb{R}^{H \times W \times C}$, it will be divided into $n$ parts: $[X^0, X^1, \cdots, X^{n-1}]$ along the channel dimension, where $X^j \in \mathbb{R}^{H \times W \times C'}, C' =$

$\frac{C}{n}$. For each part, a corresponding 2D-DCT frequency component is assigned. This can be formulated as:

$$Freq^j = \Gamma_{compress}(2DDCT_{h_j,w_j}(X^j)),\tag{8}$$

where $[h_j, w_j]$ are the frequency component 2D indices corresponding to $X^j$, $Freq^j \in \mathbb{R}^{C'}$ is the $C'$ dimensional vector after the compression. More especially, the compression vector could be acquired by concatenating all the dimensional vectors, which can be calculated as:

$$Freq = concat([Freq^0, Freq^1, \cdots, Freq^{n-1}]),\tag{9}$$

where $Freq \in \mathbb{R}^C$ denotes the multi-spectral vector. In fact, the MSCA can be described as [16]:

$$MSCA = sigmoid(fc(Freq)),\tag{10}$$

The channel information after compression is effectively enriched for representation, and the overall illustration of the MSCA is shown in Fig. 3.

## 2.4   Multi-spectral Dynamic Feature Encoding (MSDFE)

We encode image feature maps at different spatial resolutions using three branches with various scales. We also add MSCA [16] and adaptive instance normalization (AdaIN) [10] in each branch. In addition, the residual block [9] is used to model the difference between clean and moiré images at each feature level and frequency band.

Afterwards, we calculate the mean value and the variance of the obtained MSCA feature maps in the $i$-th encoding layer as:

$$\hat{\mu}_i = \frac{1}{HW} \sum_{u=1}^{H} \sum_{v=1}^{W} X^i_{uv},\tag{11}$$

and

$$\hat{\sigma}_i^2 = \frac{1}{HW} \sum_{u=1}^{H} \sum_{v=1}^{W} (X^i_{uv} - \mu_i)^2,\tag{12}$$

where $H$ and $W$ denote the height and width of the MSCA feature map, $\hat{\mu}_i$ and $\hat{\sigma}_i^2$ are the mean value and the variance of the MSCA feature map from the $i$-th encoding layer in the multi-spectral dynamic feature encoding branch, respectively.

We utilize statistical values that we calculate from moiré patterns to dynamically adjust the statistical characteristics (i.e. mean and variance) of each branch via AdaIN as following:

$$X^{i+1} = \frac{X^i - \mu_i}{\sqrt{\sigma_i^2 + \epsilon}} \sqrt{\hat{\sigma}_i^2} + \hat{\mu}_i,\tag{13}$$

where $X^i$ denotes the feature maps from the $i$-th residual block in each branch, $\mu_i$ and $\sigma_i^2$ mean the statistical information from the multi-spectral dynamic feature encoding branch.

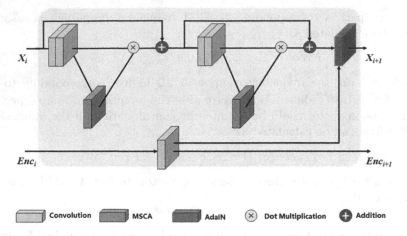

**Fig. 4.** Multi-spectral channel attention dynamic feature encoding residual block, where MSCA denotes the multi-spectral channel attention.

### 2.5 Loss Function

In terms of the loss function, Lai et al. [13] found that using the general $L_2$ loss in image restoration would make the image over smooth. To make demoiréd images more visually pleasing, we refer to the Charbonnier loss proposed by Lai et al., which can be calculated as the following:

$$Loss_{char} = \frac{1}{B} \sum_{i=1}^{B} \sqrt{(I_i - \hat{I}_i)^2 + \varepsilon^2},$$ (14)

where $B$ denotes the batch size of the input, $\varepsilon$ is a parameter in the Charbonnier penalty and is empirically set to 0.001, and $I_i$ and $\hat{I}_i$ are the ground truth and generated demoiréd image, respectively.

Besides, we also utilize the $L_1$ wavelet loss proposed by Cheng et al. [3] to address moiré patterns with different spatial frequencies, which has the form:

$$Loss_{wav} = \frac{1}{B} \sum_{i=1}^{B} \sqrt{\left(\Gamma_{wav}(\hat{I}_i) - \Gamma_{wav}(I_i)\right)^2 + \xi^2},$$ (15)

where $\xi$ is a positive parameter, which is set to $10^{-6}$ in our experiments; $\Gamma_{wav}$ is the wavelet decomposition function with four decomposed bands.

In the end, we calculate the total loss as follows:

$$Loss_{total} = Loss_{char} + \alpha Loss_{wav}$$ (16)

in which $0 < \alpha \leq 1$ is a trade-off factor. In experiments, we set $\alpha = 0.6$ referring to Ref. [3].

# 3 Experiments

## 3.1 Datasets and Training Details

We have conducted extensive experiments on two public datasets: the LCD-Moiré dataset [20] and the Sun [19] moiré dataset. Moreover, MSDFE is built by using PyTorch1.9 with CUDA11.0 and accelerated by applying two NVIDIA TITAN_RTX GPUs with data-parallel. Specially, the Adam optimizer is used to minimize the loss function to train the model, and the learning rate with an initial value of $10^{-4}$ is reduced by 10 times for every 30 epochs. The network is fully trained for 60 epochs.

## 3.2 Comparison with State-of-the-Arts

To evaluate the gap between generated moiré-free images and ground truths, we use the peak signal-to-noise ratio (PSNR) and structural similarity (SSIM) as the performance indicators.

We compare our proposed MSDFE with recent deep-learning-based demoiréing methods, including Islab [21], DMCNN [19], MSFE [6], MopNet [7], MDDM [2] and MDDM+ [3]. Besides, we take VDSR [11], DnCNN [22] and UNet [17] into our benchmark test.

Table 1 lists the demoiréing results on the LCDMoiré dataset, where the best and second-best values are in bold and underlined types, respectively. It can be seen on the LCDMoiré dataset, our MSDFE can achieve the best PSNR and SSIM among compared methods. The best PSNR is 44.10 dB obtained by MSDFE, which is 0.66 dB higher than the second-best value. The SSIM of MSDFE is slightly higher than that of MDDM+. Table 2 shows the demoiréing results on the Sun moiré dataset. The results on the Sun moiré dataset indicate that our MSDFE can achieve 30.14 dB in PSNR and 0.897 in SSIM that are significantly better than and compared to the state-of-the-arts, respectively.

**Table 1.** Comparison of PSNR and SSIM among DnCNN [22], VDSR [11], UNet [17], MSFE [6], DMCNN [19], MDDM [2], Islab [21], MDDM+ [3] and MSDFE on LCDMoiré dataset.

|  | DnCNN | VDSR | UNET | MSFE | DMCNN | MDDM | Islab | MDDM+ | MSDFE |
|---|---|---|---|---|---|---|---|---|---|
| PSNR (dB) | 29.08 | 32.36 | 34.84 | 36.66 | 37.41 | 42.49 | 42.90 | <u>43.44</u> | **44.10** |
| SSIM | 0.906 | 0.964 | 0.971 | 0.981 | 0.982 | 0.994 | 0.995 | <u>0.996</u> | **0.997** |

## 3.3 Visual Results

The visual results of our proposed MSDFE are compared with the recently proposed methods, including DnCNN [22], MSFE [6], DMCNN [19], and MDDM+ [3]. The visual results on some images from the LCDMoiré and Sun datasets are shown in Fig. 5 and Fig. 6, respectively.

**Table 2.** Comparison of PSNR and SSIM among DnCNN [22], VDSR [11], UNet [17], MSFE [6], DMCNN [19], MopNet [7], MDDM [2], MDDM+ [3] and MSDFE on Sun dataset.

|            | DnCNN | VDSR  | UNET  | MSFE  | DMCNN | MopNet | MDDM  | MDDM+ | MSDFE |
|------------|-------|-------|-------|-------|-------|--------|-------|-------|-------|
| PSNR (dB)  | 24.14 | 24.68 | 26.49 | 25.31 | 26.77 | 27.75  | 28.11 | <u>30.03</u> | **30.14** |
| SSIM       | 0.834 | 0.837 | 0.864 | 0.837 | 0.871 | 0.895  | 0.895 | **0.897** | **0.897** |

Each row in Fig. 5 shows the moire image, demoiréing results obtained by five methods, and the ground truth from left to right, where the area in a red square is taken as the zoom-in part such that we can compare the details of results. It can be easily found that our proposed MSDFE can restore moiré details and provide the clearest results, and the compared methods have a bad performance for generating blocking artifacts and incorrect color tunes. Furthermore, these methods are ineffective in removing low-frequency moiré patterns.

In Fig. 6, the three images from the Sun dataset are photos taken from real-world objects. Thus, the demoiréing task on the Sun dataset is more difficult than that on the LCDMoiré dataset consisting of computer-rendered images.

We can easily find that our MSDFE recovers correct color tunes, while other methods fail to do although they remove most of the moiré patterns. The above visual results on LCDMoiré and Sun datasets indicate that our proposed MSDFE outperforms the state-of-the-art methods.

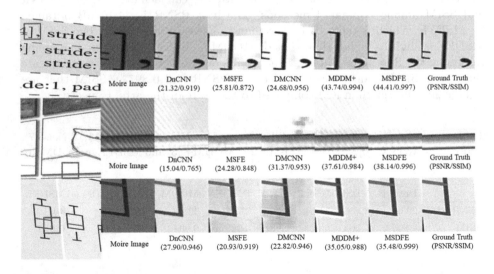

**Fig. 5.** Visual comparison on the LCDMoiré dataset.

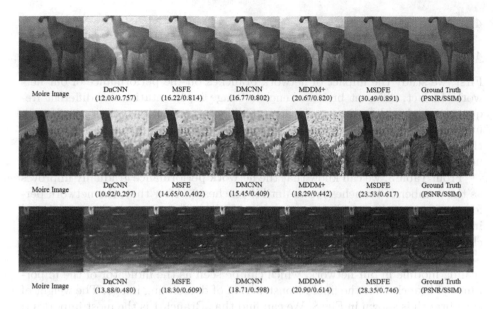

**Fig. 6.** Visual comparison on the Sun dataset.

## 3.4 Model Parameters

In this part, we compare our MSDFE with seven demoiréing methods on the model performance and the model parameters. Parameters are an indicator to measure the size of a model, an efficient network would have an impressive performance with a relatively small number of parameters. Figure 7 shows the performance vs. the number of parameters of compared methods on the LCD-Moiré dataset. From Fig. 7, we can see that MSDFE (red dot) can achieve the best results only with a relatively small number of parameters.

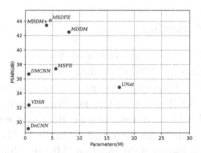

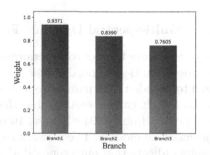

**Fig. 7.** PSNR vs. parameter number for eight methods on LCDMoiré dataset (Color figure online)

**Fig. 8.** Weight of branches.

# 4  Ablation Study

## 4.1  Network Branches

First, we study the impact of network branches on the performance of our network. In fact, different branches encode image representations at different frequencies and address image features at different resolutions; thus, the branch number in the network greatly influences its performance and size. Table 3 lists the network performance and size on the LCDMoiré dataset, where the size of network is measured by parameter number.

From Table 3, we can know that the network performance gradually improves as the number of branches grows until it reaches 3. After that, the network performance starts decreasing because too many branches cause the loss of detailed information in images. As a result, the network with 3 branches is the optimal choice.

In addition, the weight of each branch can be automatically learned by the scaling module in our network, which can be seen as the indicator of the importance of branches for the final reconstruction of demoiréing image. The weight of each branch is shown in Fig. 8. We can find that Branch 1 is the most important; thus, a branch with higher resolution is of greater importance.

**Table 3.** Network performance and parameters of MSDFE with different branches.

| Branch | PSNR (dB) | Parameter (M) |
|--------|-----------|---------------|
| 1 | 36.04 | 1.14 |
| 2 | 38.96 | 2.45 |
| 3 | 44.10 | 3.91 |
| 4 | 43.71 | 5.51 |
| 5 | 43.55 | 7.27 |

## 4.2  Multi-spectral Dynamic Feature Encoding

Next, we study the network performance and complexity with and without our proposed multi-spectral dynamic feature encoding. This encoding way is leveraged to encode the dynamic properties of moiré. Experimental results are shown in Table 4. It can be easily found that the PSNR score of the network output is improved from 40.93 dB to 44.10 dB on the LCDMoiré dataset after adding the encoding module. The network parameters also can be found in Table 4. The results indicate that our proposed MSDFE is a lightweight module. MSDFE has a great performance improvement but a small parameter number increase, say 0.55 M.

**Table 4.** Network performance and parameters of baseline and MSDFE.

| Structure | PSNR (dB) | Parameter (M) |
|-----------|-----------|---------------|
| Baseline  | 40.93     | 3.36          |
| MSDFE     | 44.10     | 3.91          |

# 5  Conclusion

Demoiréing is more challenging than other image restoration tasks because of its variability and dynamics. In this paper, we propose MSDFE for image demoiréing. The multi-scale network structure of MSDFE can help our model remove moiré in different frequency bands and retain more image details. Besides, we leverage a multi-spectral dynamic feature encoding module to encode moiré patterns dynamically, which makes the model adapt to the transient nature of the moiré patterns. Experimental results indicate that the model achieves 3.17 dB higher in PSNR after adding the multi-spectral dynamic feature encoding module. In addition, our proposed MSDFE significantly outperforms state-of-the-art methods and can remove moiré patterns effectively.

# References

1. Ahmed, N., Natarajan, T., Rao, K.R.: Discrete cosine transform. IEEE Trans. Comput. **100**(1), 90–93 (1974)
2. Cheng, X., Fu, Z., Yang, J.: Multi-scale dynamic feature encoding network for image demoiréing. In: 2019 IEEE/CVF International Conference on Computer Vision Workshop (ICCVW), pp. 3486–3493. IEEE (2019)
3. Cheng, X., Fu, Z., Yang, J.: Improved multi-scale dynamic feature encoding network for image demoiréing. Pattern Recogn. **116**, 107970 (2021)
4. Dai, T., Cai, J., Zhang, Y., Xia, S.T., Zhang, L.: Second-order attention network for single image super-resolution. In: Proceedings of the IEEE/CVF Conference on Computer Vision and Pattern Recognition, pp. 11065–11074 (2019)
5. Dong, C., Loy, C.C., He, K., Tang, X.: Image super-resolution using deep convolutional networks. IEEE Trans. Pattern Anal. Mach. Intell. **38**(2), 295–307 (2015)
6. Gao, T., Guo, Y., Zheng, X., Wang, Q., Luo, X.: Moiré pattern removal with multi-scale feature enhancing network. In: 2019 IEEE International Conference on Multimedia & Expo Workshops (ICMEW), pp. 240–245. IEEE (2019)
7. He, B., Wang, C., Shi, B., Duan, L.Y.: Mop moire patterns using mopnet. In: Proceedings of the IEEE/CVF International Conference on Computer Vision, pp. 2424–2432 (2019)
8. He, K., Zhang, X., Ren, S., Sun, J.: Delving deep into rectifiers: surpassing human-level performance on imagenet classification. In: Proceedings of the IEEE International Conference on Computer Vision, pp. 1026–1034 (2015)
9. He, K., Zhang, X., Ren, S., Sun, J.: Deep residual learning for image recognition. In: Proceedings of the IEEE Conference on Computer Vision and Pattern Recognition, pp. 770–778 (2016)

10. Huang, X., Belongie, S.: Arbitrary style transfer in real-time with adaptive instance normalization. In: Proceedings of the IEEE International Conference on Computer Vision, pp. 1501–1510 (2017)
11. Kim, J., Lee, J.K., Lee, K.M.: Accurate image super-resolution using very deep convolutional networks. In: Proceedings of the IEEE Conference on Computer Vision and Pattern Recognition, pp. 1646–1654 (2016)
12. Kupyn, O., Budzan, V., Mykhailych, M., Mishkin, D., Matas, J.: Deblurgan: blind motion deblurring using conditional adversarial networks. In: Proceedings of the IEEE Conference on Computer Vision and Pattern Recognition, pp. 8183–8192 (2018)
13. Lai, W.S., Huang, J.B., Ahuja, N., Yang, M.H.: Deep laplacian pyramid networks for fast and accurate super-resolution. In: Proceedings of the IEEE Conference on Computer Vision and Pattern Recognition, pp. 624–632 (2017)
14. Li, T., et al.: A new design in iterative image deblurring for improved robustness and performance. Pattern Recogn. **90**, 134–146 (2019)
15. Qian, Z., Huang, K., Wang, Q.F., Xiao, J., Zhang, R.: Generative adversarial classifier for handwriting characters super-resolution. Pattern Recogn. **107**, 107453 (2020)
16. Qin, Z., Zhang, P., Wu, F., Li, X.: FcaNet: frequency channel attention networks. In: Proceedings of the IEEE/CVF International Conference on Computer Vision, pp. 783–792 (2021)
17. Ronneberger, O., Fischer, P., Brox, T.: U-Net: convolutional networks for biomedical image segmentation. In: Navab, N., Hornegger, J., Wells, W.M., Frangi, A.F. (eds.) MICCAI 2015. LNCS, vol. 9351, pp. 234–241. Springer, Cham (2015). https://doi.org/10.1007/978-3-319-24574-4_28
18. Shi, W., et al.: Real-time single image and video super-resolution using an efficient sub-pixel convolutional neural network. In: Proceedings of the IEEE Conference on Computer Vision and Pattern Recognition, pp. 1874–1883 (2016)
19. Sun, Y., Yu, Y., Wang, W.: Moiré photo restoration using multiresolution convolutional neural networks. IEEE Trans. Image Process. **27**(8), 4160–4172 (2018)
20. Yuan, S., Timofte, R., Slabaugh, G., Leonardis, A.: Aim 2019 challenge on image demoireing: dataset and study. In: 2019 IEEE/CVF International Conference on Computer Vision Workshop (ICCVW), pp. 3526–3533. IEEE (2019)
21. Yuan, S., et al.: Aim 2019 challenge on image demoireing: methods and results. In: 2019 IEEE/CVF International Conference on Computer Vision Workshop (ICCVW), pp. 3534–3545. IEEE (2019)
22. Zhang, K., Zuo, W., Chen, Y., Meng, D., Zhang, L.: Beyond a gaussian denoiser: residual learning of deep CNN for image denoising. IEEE Trans. Image Process. **26**(7), 3142–3155 (2017)

# Ranking Feature-Block Importance in Artificial Multiblock Neural Networks

Anna Jenul[✉][ID], Stefan Schrunner[ID], Bao Ngoc Huynh[ID], Runar Helin[ID], Cecilia Marie Futsæther[ID], Kristian Hovde Liland[ID], and Oliver Tomic[ID]

Norwegian University of Life Sciences, Universitetstunet 3, 1432 Ås, Norway
{anna.jenul,stefan.schrunner,ngoc.huynh.bao,runar.helin,
cecilia.futsaether,kristian.liland,oliver.tomic}@nmbu.no

**Abstract.** In artificial neural networks, understanding the contributions of input features on the prediction fosters model explainability and delivers relevant information about the dataset. While typical setups for feature importance ranking assess input features individually, in this study, we go one step further and rank the importance of groups of features, denoted as feature-blocks. A feature-block can contain features of a specific type or features derived from a particular source, which are presented to the neural network in separate input branches (multiblock ANNs). This work presents three methods pursuing distinct strategies to rank feature-blocks in multiblock ANNs by their importance: (1) a composite strategy building on individual feature importance rankings, (2) a knock-in, and (3) a knock-out strategy. While the composite strategy builds on state-of-the-art feature importance rankings, knock-in and knock-out strategies evaluate the block as a whole via a mutual information criterion. Our experiments consist of a simulation study validating all three approaches, followed by a case study on two distinct real-world datasets to compare the strategies. We conclude that each strategy has its merits for specific application scenarios.

**Keywords:** Feature-block importance · Importance ranking · Multiblock neural network · Explainability · Mutual information

## 1 Introduction

In machine learning, datasets with an intrinsic block-wise input structure are common; blocks may represent distinct data sources or features of different types and are frequently present in datasets from industry [7], biology [3], or healthcare [5]. For example, in healthcare, heterogeneous data blocks like patient histology, genetics, clinical data, and image data are combined in outcome prediction models. However, good prediction models do not necessarily depend equally on each block. Instead, some blocks may be redundant or non-informative. Identifying the key data sources in multi-source treatment outcome models promises to deliver new insights into the behavior of black-box models like ANNs. In particular, potential benefits include improving model explainability, reducing costly

© The Author(s), under exclusive license to Springer Nature Switzerland AG 2022
E. Pimenidis et al. (Eds.): ICANN 2022, LNCS 13532, pp. 163–175, 2022.
https://doi.org/10.1007/978-3-031-15937-4_14

data acquisitions that do not contribute to the model prediction, and allowing domain experts to explore latent relations in the data. Thus, there is a need to measure the importances of feature-blocks, denoted as feature-block importance ranking (BIR).

In order to exploit the internal structure of the block-wise data in neural networks, a multiblock ANN (M-ANN) architecture is used. As depicted in Fig. 1, the M-ANN consists of a separate input branch for each block, a concatenation layer to merge information from all branches, and a blender network to map the information to the model output. The architecture allows for any type of network layer, depth, activation, or other network parameters, including the special case where the concatenation layer equals the input layer (block branches of depth 0).

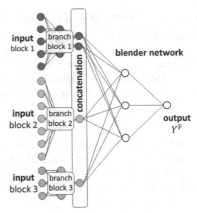

**Fig. 1.** M-ANN architecture.

Ranking individual features by their importances (feature importance ranking, FIR) has been studied for different types of ANNs [8,14,15]. An extensive evaluation [9] showed that versions of the variational gradient method (VarGrad) [1,2] outperformed competitors such as guided backprop and integrated gradients. For BIR, however, a combination of features in one block may accumulate a larger amount of information than each feature separately due to informative non-linear relations between features. Hence, using FIR might oversimplify the problem of measuring block importance since interactions between features of the same block are disregarded. Nevertheless, the strategy of reducing BIR to a simple summary metric (sum, mean, max) over FIR scores is considered in our evaluation.

A related problem to FIR is feature selection, where the input dimensionality is reduced to the most influential features as part of the preprocessing. Feature selection is widely studied in ANNs. Furthermore, specialized feature selectors can account for block structures like UBayFS [11] or groupLasso [16]. Conceptually, these feature selectors aim to improve model performance and classify an entire block as important/unimportant in a binary way before model training. In contrast, our BIR problem is considered a post-processing procedure, focusing on analyzing the model after training without influence on the model performance.[1]

This study presents and discusses three distinct approaches to quantify the importance of feature-blocks in M-ANNs. While exploiting the flexibility of ANNs and their capacities to learn complex underlying patterns in the data, the

---

[1] BIR may be used for block feature selection if deployed as filter method—however, this aspect is beyond the scope of the present work.

discussed methods aim to deliver insights into the trained network's dependence structure on the distinct input blocks and thereby foster model explainability. We propose three paradigms for BIR: a block is considered as important if

1. it consists of features with high FIR scores (composition strategy), or
2. it explains a large part of the network output (knock-in strategy), or
3. its removal significantly changes the network output (knock-out strategy).

We evaluate and discuss the proposed paradigms in a simulation study and present two case studies on real-world datasets, where the behaviors of the proposed ranking strategies become apparent.

In the following, bold letters denote vectors and matrices; non-bold letters denote scalars, functions or sets. Square brackets denote index sets $[n] = \{1, \ldots, n\}$.

## 2  Block Importance Ranking Methods

We assume data input $x$ from some feature space $D \subset \mathbb{R}^N$, $N \in \mathbb{N}$, following a probability distribution $X \sim P_X$, and a univariate target variable $y \in T \subset \mathbb{R}$ following a probability distribution $Y \sim P_Y$. Given training data $(x, y) \in D_{\text{train}} \times T_{\text{train}} \subset D \times T$, model parameters $w \in W \subset \mathbb{R}^M$, $M \in \mathbb{N}$, are trained with respect to some loss term $e : D \times T \to \mathbb{R}^+$,

$$w^* = \min_{w \in W} e\left(f_w(x), y\right),$$

where the ANN is a function $f_w : D \to T$ given weights $w$.

In an M-ANN architecture, see Fig. 1, the block structure of the model input is represented by a direct sum of subspaces $D = \bigoplus_{b=1}^{B} D_b$, each corresponding to one block $b \in [B]$ with dimension $N_b = \dim(D_b)$, $N = \sum_{b=1}^{B} N_b$. Each block enters a distinct branch of the network that processes the block input. Afterwards, the outputs of all branches are merged in a concatenation layer, which consists of $n_b$ nodes associated with each block $b$, respectively. A so-called blender network $f_w^{\text{blender}}$ connects the concatenation layer to the network output. Network training is performed using backpropagation, where all block branches and the blender network are trained simultaneously in an end-to-end manner.

### 2.1  Composite Strategy

Our first paradigm composes block importance measures from FIR in a direct way. As a prototype of state-of-the-art FIR methods, we use VarGrad [2]. Var-Grad builds on the idea that variations of an important feature provoke measurable variations in the output. Under the assumption that features are on a common scale, we estimate the gradient of the function $f_w$ with respect to each feature by adding small random perturbations in the input layer. A large variance in the gradient indicates that the network output depends strongly on a feature, i.e., the feature is important. We denote the importance of feature $n \in [N]$ as quantified by VarGrad, by $\alpha_n \in \mathbb{R}^+$.

To translate the feature-wise importance measure to feature-blocks in M-ANNs, we deploy a summary metric $\varphi$ over all single-feature importances in a block $b \in [B]$. Thus, block importances $\gamma_\varphi^{(b)}$ are defined as

$$\gamma_\varphi^{(b)} = \varphi(\alpha_1^{(b)}, \ldots, \alpha_{N_b}^{(b)}), \tag{1}$$

where $\alpha_n^{(b)}$ denotes the $n^{\text{th}}$ feature associated with the $b^{\text{th}}$ block. Intuitive choices for $\varphi$ are either the sum, mean, or maximum operator, denoted as $\varphi_{\text{sum}}$, $\varphi_{\text{mean}}$, or $\varphi_{\text{max}}$, respectively. Rankings based on mean and sum are equal, if all blocks contain the same number of features. Operators $\varphi_{\text{sum}}$ and $\varphi_{\text{mean}}$ accumulate the individual feature importances: a block with multiple features of high average importances is preferred over blocks with few top features and numerous unimportant features. In contrast, $\varphi_{\text{max}}$ compares the top-performing features out of each block, while neglecting all other's contributions. Statistical properties of block importance quantifiers implementing the composite strategy are transmitted from (i) the feature importance ranking method and (ii) the summary metric. Since this approach cannot capture between-feature relations, potentially impacting the importance of a block, we suggest two other paradigms.

## 2.2    Knock-In Strategy

The knock-in strategy is inspired by work on the information bottleneck [4], demonstrating that node activations can be exploited for model interpretation in ANNs. In the concatenation layer of the M-ANN (Fig. 1), where information from the blocks enters the blender network, activations are of particular importance since they represent an encoding of the block information. When passing model input $x$ through the network, we denote the activation of the $n$th node associated with block $b \in [B]$ in the concatenation layer by $c_{b,n}(x)$, $n \in [n_b]$. The average activation of the $n$th node in block $b \in [B]$ across all training data $x \in D_{\text{train}}$ is denoted by $\bar{c}_{b,n}$.

For BIR, we compute a pseudo-output by passing data of only one block $b$ through the network. For this purpose, we introduce a pseudo-input $v^{(b)}(x)$ as

$$v_{b',n}^{(b)}(x) = \begin{cases} c_{b',n}(x) & \text{if } b' = b \\ \bar{c}_{b',n} & \text{otherwise,} \end{cases} \tag{2}$$

where $b' \in [B]$, and $n \in [n_b]$. By propagating pseudo-input $v^{(b)}(x)$ through the blender network, we obtain the pseudo-output $f_w^{\text{blender}}(v^{(b)}(x))$. The main assumption behind the knock-in strategy is that high agreement between output $f_w(x)$ and pseudo-output $f_w^{\text{blender}}(v^{(b)}(x))$ indicates a high importance of block $b$, since information from $b$ is sufficient to recover most of the model output. In contrast, a large discrepancy between the two quantities indicates low explanatory power of the block $b$, and thus, a lower block importance. The concept to generate knock-in pseudo-outputs is illustrated in Fig. 2.

We implement the knock-in concept via the mutual information (MI) [6], an information-theoretic measure to quantify the level of joint information between two discrete random variables $Z$ and $Z'$, defined as

$$\mathrm{MI}(Z, Z') = \sum_z \sum_{z'} p_{Z,Z'}(z,z') \log_2 \left( \frac{p_{Z,Z'}(z,z')}{p_Z(z)p_{Z'}(z')} \right).$$

If $Z$ and $Z'$ are independent, $\mathrm{MI}(Z, Z')$ is 0. Otherwise, $\mathrm{MI}(Z, Z')$ is positive, where a high value indicates a large overlap in information. To quantify the joint and marginal distributions of continuous variables $Z$ and $Z'$, two-dimensional and one-dimensional histograms can be used as non-parametric estimators for $p_{Z,Z'}$, $p_Z$, and $p_{Z'}$, respectively. We denote the number of equidistant histogram bins along each axis by $\ell \in \mathbb{N}$. It follows from the properties of entropy [6] that an upper bound to $\mathrm{MI}(Z, Z')$ is given by $\log_2(\ell)$.

As shown in Fig. 2, the random variable of (full) model output, $Y^{\mathrm{F}} = f_w(X)$, and the random variable of the pseudo-output with respect to block $b$, $Y^{(b)} = f_w^{\mathrm{blender}}(v^{(b)}(X))$, where $X$ follows the input distribution $P_X$, are used to measure knock-in (KI) block importance as

$$\gamma_{\mathrm{KI}}^{(b)} = \frac{\mathrm{MI}(Y^{\mathrm{F}}, Y^{(b)})}{\log_2(\ell)}. \tag{3}$$

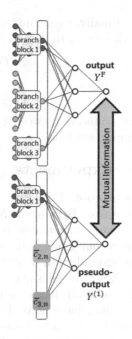

**Fig. 2.** Knock-in strategy: Pseudo-outputs for feature-block $b = 1$ are generated by activating block $b$, while imputing averaged activations for all other blocks.

## 2.3   Knock-Out Strategy

The knock-out paradigm is an ablation procedure where one block at a time is removed from the model in order to measure the impact of the remaining blocks. We pursue a similar approach as in the knock-in paradigm and specify knock-out pseudo-inputs $v^{(-b)}(x)$ as

$$v_{b',n}^{(-b)}(x) = \begin{cases} \bar{c}_{b',n} & \text{if } b' = b \\ c_{b',n}(x) & \text{otherwise,} \end{cases} \tag{4}$$

for an arbitrary block $b \in [B]$. Thus, the definition in Eq. 4 represents an opposite behavior of Eq. 2 in the knock-in case. In analogy to the knock-in notation, we denote the random variable of pseudo-outputs with respect to $v^{(-b)}$ as $Y^{(-b)} = f_w^{\mathrm{blender}}(v^{(-b)}(X))$. The knock-out concept is illustrated in Fig. 3. In contrast to knock-in, we assume that leaving out block $b$ having a relevant impact on the final output delivers a more dissimilar pseudo-output to the full output since relevant information is lost. Removing an unimportant block preserves the relevant information and delivers a pseudo-output similar to the full output.

Finally, we define the importance of block $b \in [B]$ with respect to the knock-out strategy (KO) as

$$\gamma_{\text{KO}}^{(b)} = \frac{\log_2(\ell) - \text{MI}(Y^{\text{F}}, Y^{(-b)})}{\log_2(\ell)}. \quad (5)$$

For both, KI and KO, importance scores $\gamma_{\text{KI}}^{(b)}$ and $\gamma_{\text{KO}}^{(b)}$ are bounded between 0 (unimportant block) and 1 (important block).

## 3    Experiments

As a proof of concept, we conduct two experiments to assess BIR in M-ANNs. The first experiment involves six simulated, non-linear regression problems, where our simulation setup delivers information on the ground truth block importances. This experiment verifies that our suggested measures can identify the ground truth block rankings, defined by their corresponding paradigms. Real-world datasets are evaluated in two case studies in experiment 2, where no exact ground truth block ranking is available. Instead, we compare BIR strategies to each other.

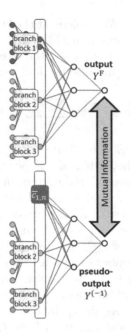

**Fig. 3.** Knock-out strategy: Pseudo-outputs are generated by activating all but one blocks.

### 3.1    Simulation Experiment

We simulate a synthetic datasets along with six distinct target functions, denoted as setups S1a–S1c and S2a–S2c. The dataset consists of $N = 256$ features, divided randomly into $B = 8$ blocks (B1–B8) à $N_b = 32$ features. The sample size is set to $|D_{\text{train}}| = 10\,000$ and $|D_{\text{test}}| = 10\,000$. All features are simulated from a multivariate normal distribution with mean vector $\boldsymbol{\mu} = \boldsymbol{0}$ and a randomized covariance matrix $\boldsymbol{\Sigma}$; hence a non-trivial correlation structure is imposed.[2]

Setups S1a–S1c and S2a–S2c differ in the parameters used to compute the non-linear target variable $y$, which is simulated via a noisy linear combination of the squared features with coefficient matrix $\boldsymbol{\beta}^{(b)} \in \mathbb{R}^{N_b \times N_b}$, given as

$$y = \underbrace{\sum_{b=1}^{8} \boldsymbol{x}^T \boldsymbol{\beta}^{(b)} \boldsymbol{x}}_{g(\boldsymbol{x})} + \varepsilon_{\text{noise}}, \text{ where}$$

$$\varepsilon_{\text{noise}} \underset{\text{i.i.d.}}{\sim} \mathcal{N}\left(0, \sigma_{\text{noise}}^2\right), \text{ and}$$

$$\boldsymbol{\beta}^{(b)} = \begin{pmatrix} \beta_{\text{imp}} & 0 & \cdots & 0 & 0 & \cdots & 0 \\ \beta_{\text{int}} & \beta_{\text{imp}} & \vdots & 0 & 0 & \vdots & 0 \\ & \cdots & & \ddots & & & \\ \beta_{\text{int}} & \beta_{\text{int}} & \beta_{\text{imp}} & 0 & 0 \\ 0 & 0 & 0 & 0 & 0 \\ & \cdots & & & & \ddots & \\ 0 & 0 & 0 & 0 & 0 \end{pmatrix}. \quad (6)$$

---

[2] Code and details on simulation and network architecture are available at https://github.com/annajenul/Block_Importance_Quantification.

**Table 1.** Specifications for matrix $\beta^{(b)}$: block importance is steered via count $N_{imp}$, coefficient $\beta_{imp}$, and interaction $\beta_{int}$ of the important features.

| Setup | Block | | | | | | | | | | | | | |
|---|---|---|---|---|---|---|---|---|---|---|---|---|---|---|
| | B1 | | | B2 | | | ... | B7 | | | B8 | | | |
| | $N_{imp}$ | $\beta_{imp}$ | $\beta_{int}$ | $N_{imp}$ | $\beta_{imp}$ | $\beta_{int}$ | ... | $N_{imp}$ | $\beta_{imp}$ | $\beta_{int}$ | $N_{imp}$ | $\beta_{imp}$ | $\beta_{int}$ | |
| S1a | 2 | 7 | 0 | 2 | 6 | 0 | ... | 2 | 1 | 0 | 0 | 0 | 0 | |
| S1b | 7 | 2 | 0 | 6 | 2 | 0 | ... | 1 | 2 | 0 | 0 | 0 | 0 | |
| S1c | 1 | 7 | 0 | 2 | 6 | 0 | ... | 7 | 1 | 0 | 0 | 0 | 0 | |
| S2a | 2 | 7 | 1 | 2 | 6 | 1 | ... | 2 | 1 | 1 | 0 | 0 | 1 | |
| S2b | 7 | 2 | 1 | 6 | 2 | 1 | ... | 1 | 2 | 1 | 0 | 0 | 1 | |
| S2c | 1 | 7 | 1 | 2 | 6 | 1 | ... | 7 | 1 | 1 | 0 | 0 | 1 | |

The matrix $\beta^{(b)} \in \mathbb{R}^{N_b \times N_b}$ contains an $N_{imp} \times N_{imp}$ quadratic sub-matrix consisting of coefficients $\beta_{imp}$ of important features, i.e. features with relevant contribution to the target, and interactions $\beta_{int}$. The noise parameter $\sigma_{noise}$ is set to 10% of the standard deviation of the linear combination $g(x)$ across the generated samples $x$. As shown in Table 1, block importances are varied between the setups and as follows

– S1a: varying coefficients of important features, but constant counts;
– S1b: varying counts of important features, but constant coefficients;
– S1c: varying counts and coefficients of important features;
– S2a–S2c: same as S1a–S1c, but with interaction terms between features.

Due to the randomized correlation matrix of the feature generation, unimportant features may be correlated with important features, as well as with the target $y$.

For each setup, we trained the described M-ANN model in 30 independent runs with distinct weight initializations after data standardization. Since BIR methods are deployed post-hoc and assume a model with appropriate performance, runs with poor performances (R2 < 0.8) were excluded from the analysis after outlier removal. Hence, the number of model runs in the analysis was 20 (S1a, S1b, S2a, S2b), 18 (S1c), and 19 (S2c), respectively. The remaining models achieved an average performance of $\geq$0.9 (R2 score) and $\leq$0.2 (RMSEIQR: root mean squared error scaled by inter-quartile range) on the test set.

For evaluation, importance scores across all model runs were tested for significant differences using a pairwise Wilcoxon-test with Bonferroni correction. If the p-value in a comparison between two blocks was above a significance level of 0.01, both were counted as tie. Figure 4 illustrates the distributions of BIR scores after min-max-normalization by setup and method, along with rankings (colors) based on significant group differences. All methods discovered the intrinsic ranking in dataset S1a. In dataset S1b, knock-in, knock-out, and VarGrad-mean identified the ranking by underlying important feature counts $N_{imp}$, while VarGrad-max failed to deliver a significant distinction between blocks with higher counts of

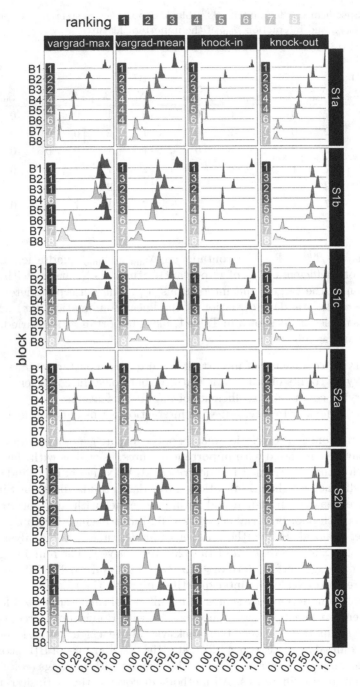

**Fig. 4.** Distributions of the normalized BIR scores across model runs. Rankings are indicated by colors and refer to significant group differences based on a pairwise Wilcoxon-test (significance level 0.01).

**Table 2.** Averaged Spearman's rank correlation coefficients comparing each ranking to the ground truth BIR for each paradigm across model runs. Standard deviations were $\leq 0.03$ for S1a, S1b, S2a and S2b, and $\leq 0.06$ for S1c and S2c.

| Paradigm | Dataset | | | | | |
| --- | --- | --- | --- | --- | --- | --- |
| | S1a | S1b | S1c | S2a | S2b | S2c |
| Composite (VarGrad-max) | 0.97 | 0.58 | 0.93 | 0.98 | 0.58 | 0.91 |
| Composite (VarGrad-mean) | 0.98 | 0.95 | 0.96 | 0.97 | 0.95 | −0.40 |
| Knock-in | 0.99 | 0.98 | 0.85 | 0.97 | 0.99 | 0.89 |
| Knock-out | 0.99 | 0.98 | 0.81 | 0.99 | 0.99 | 0.89 |

important features. For dataset S1c, VarGrad-max mostly ranked by underlying $\beta_{\mathrm{imp}}$ and ignored $N_{\mathrm{imp}}$, while knock-in, knock-out and VarGrad-mean delivered trade-offs between counts $N_{\mathrm{imp}}$ and coefficients $\beta_{\mathrm{imp}}$ of important features. In setups S2a, S2b, and S2c with between-feature interactions, the same rankings as in S1a, S1b, and S1c could be obtained by all methods with negligible deviations. Hence, we conclude that all metrics remain stable in more complex scenarios.

We further validated the paradigms by comparing the results to their corresponding ground truth block importances, determined by the real coefficients in the simulation setup. For the composite max and mean paradigms, the corresponding maxima and means over $\beta^{(b)}$, were used as references. Ground truth importances for knock-in (KI), and knock-out (KO) were based on the explained variances of the single block $b$ in the underlying linear combination, given as

$$KI_b = \mathbb{E}\left( y - \left( \boldsymbol{x}^{(b)} \right)^T \boldsymbol{\beta}^{(b)} \boldsymbol{x}^{(b)} \right), \text{ and } KO_b = \mathbb{E}\left( y - \sum_{\substack{b'=1 \\ b' \neq b}}^{8} \left( \boldsymbol{x}^{(b')} \right)^T \boldsymbol{\beta}^{(b')} \boldsymbol{x}^{(b')} \right),$$

where $\boldsymbol{x}^{(b)}$ denotes projection of input $\boldsymbol{x}$ on the subspace of block $b$, $D_b$. The comparison between the rankings based on (average) predicted importance scores and ground truth rankings was made using Spearman's correlation coefficient, see Table 2. With two exceptions, all correlation values were at a high level, indicating that our methods accurately predicted the ground truth. Spearman's correlation coefficient is not representative in S1b, and S2b with respect to the maximum metric since the ground truth ranking is equal for blocks B1–B7. In S2c VarGrad-mean is distracted by decreasing $\beta_{\mathrm{imp}}$ and an increasing number of interaction terms, although underlying block importances are in increasing order with respect to the mean metric.

## 3.2   Real-World Experiment

Since verification on simulated data showed that the presented approaches match the ground truth according to their paradigms, we deployed the methods on two real-world datasets, where underlying block importance is unknown. Prior to analysis, both datasets were standardized on the trained data. Again, we trained 30 independent model runs.

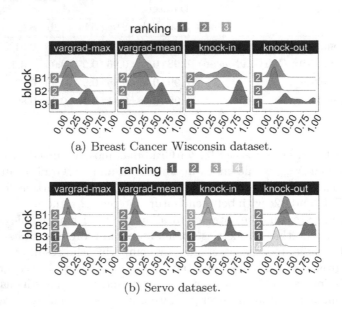

(a) Breast Cancer Wisconsin dataset.

(b) Servo dataset.

**Fig. 5.** Distributions of normalized BIR scores in experiment 2 across model runs.

The Breast Cancer Wisconsin dataset (BCW) [13] describes a binary classification problem (malignant or benign tumor) and consists of 569 samples (398 train, 171 test) and three blocks with ten features each, representing groups of distinct feature characteristics (mean values, standard deviations, and extreme values of measured parameters). The average performance was 0.95 (accuracy) and 0.96 (F1 score) without outliers. The average scores and rankings delivered by BIR methods are shown in Fig. 5a. All four paradigms discovered that block 3 is dominant, which agrees with previous research on the dataset [10]. However, knock-in was the only method that distinguished between the importances of B1 and B2. According to [10], block B1 contains overlapping information with B3, while B2 is rather non-informative. Thus, the experiment underlines a difference between knock-in and knock-out rankings in the presence of redundancies.

Servo [12] is a dataset containing 167 samples (120 train, 47 test), a univariate, numeric target variable, and four features, two of which are categorical variables with four levels each, and two are numerical variables. Each feature was assigned its own block. One-hot encoding was performed for the two blocks containing categorical features, leading to two blocks (B1 and B2) of four binary features, each. Blocks corresponding to numerical features (B3 and B4) contain one feature each. In the 30 M-ANN model runs, an average performance of 0.21 (RMSEIQR) and 0.87 (R2) was obtained without outliers. Figure 5b shows that for all four paradigms, block B3 was most important. While VarGrad methods delivered a binary ranking, knock-in and knock-out suggested a ranking with 3 and 4 distinct importance levels, respectively—thus, the level of detail was higher in the MI-based rankings compared to VarGrad methods.

# 4  Discussion

Our experiments demonstrated several differences between the proposed strategies. While the composite strategy evaluates features individually and depends on two user-selected parameters (the feature-wise ranking scheme and the summary metric), the knock-in and knock-out strategies consider each block a closed unit. They require no selection of a summary statistic. MI-based rankings deliver a score in $[0, 1]$, while VarGrad has no upper bound. However, the discretization associated with the mutual information calculation may influence the importance scores and, thus, the rankings by knock-in and knock-out. All strategies are applicable for multivariate target variables, as well. However, an MI-based comparison between outputs and pseudo-outputs is prone to suffer from the curse of dimensionality since higher-dimensional probability distributions are compared to each other. On the contrary, the vanishing gradient problem can influence VarGrad in deep ANN architectures. All approaches delivered accurate experimental results, but only knock-in and knock-out provided a consistent ranking of blocks with minor importance in dominant blocks, such as for the servo dataset.

Even though knock-in and knock-out rely on the same concept of assessing pseudo-outputs related to each block, their properties and interpretations differ. The knock-in strategy determines whether a block can deliver a reasonable target description independently from the remaining blocks. This interpretation of block importance evaluates the performance achieved if we reduce the model to solely one block at a time. In contrast, knock-out quantifies whether the contribution of a block can be compensated by any other block. If two blocks contain redundant information about the target, knock-in delivers high values for both blocks since each block individually has high explanatory power. In contrast, knock-out penalizes redundant blocks since each of them can be removed without loss of information. This property became evident in the BCW experiment, where B3 was dominant but shared overlapping information with B1: knock-in was the only approach that discovered the higher information content in B1 compared to the uninformative B2.

# 5  Conclusion

We have demonstrated three strategies to rank the importance of feature-blocks as post-processing in ANNs with block-wise input structure. The composite strategy, which is a direct generalization of feature-wise importance rankings, provided promising results in most cases, but selecting the correct summary statistic was crucial. Knock-in and knock-out strategies, implemented using an information-theoretic measure on the model outputs, delivered a trade-off between the extremes of maximum and mean feature importance in the composite case. All methods uncovered the true block importance with high accuracy and delivered new insights into the ANN's behavior. Still, computing multiple proposed metrics is advantageous for making informative block ranking decisions.

**Acknowledgment.** The authors gratefully acknowledge the financial support from internal funding scheme at Norwegian University of Life Sciences (project number 1211130114), which financed the international stay at the University of British Columbia, and thereby fostered the completion of this work.

# References

1. Adebayo, J., Gilmer, J., Goodfellow, I., Kim, B.: Local explanation methods for deep neural networks lack sensitivity to parameter values. arXiv (2018)
2. Adebayo, J., Gilmer, J., Muelly, M., Goodfellow, I., Hardt, M., Kim, B.: Sanity checks for saliency maps. In: Advances in Neural Information Processing Systems, vol. 31 (2018)
3. Alnemer, L.M., et al.: Multiple sources classification of gene position on chromosomes using statistical significance of individual classification results. In: International Conference on Machine Learning and Applications and Workshops, vol. 1, pp. 7–12 (2011). https://doi.org/10.1109/ICMLA.2011.101
4. Amjad, R.A., Geiger, B.C.: Learning representations for neural network-based classification using the information bottleneck principle. IEEE Trans. Pattern Anal. Mach. Intell. **42**(9), 2225–2239 (2019). https://doi.org/10.1109/TPAMI.2019.2909031
5. Cao, B., He, L., Kong, X., Philip, S.Y., Hao, Z., Ragin, A.B.: Tensor-based multiview feature selection with applications to brain diseases. In: IEEE International Conference on Data Mining, pp. 40–49 (2014)
6. Cover, T., Thomas, J.: Elements of Information Theory. Wiley, Hoboken (2012)
7. Dagnely, P., Tourwé, T., Tsiporkova, E.: Annotating the performance of industrial assets via relevancy estimation of event logs. In: IEEE International Conference on Machine Learning and Applications (ICMLA), pp. 1261–1268 (2018). https://doi.org/10.1109/ICMLA.2018.00205
8. Ghorbani, A., Abid, A., Zou, J.: Interpretation of neural networks is fragile. In: AAAI Conference on Artificial Intelligence, vol. 33, pp. 3681–3688 (2019)
9. Hooker, S., Erhan, D., Kindermans, P.J., Kim, B.: A benchmark for interpretability methods in deep neural networks. In: Advances in Neural Information Processing Systems, vol. 32 (2019)
10. Jenul, A., Schrunner, S., Liland, K.H., Indahl, U.G., Futsæther, C.M., Tomic, O.: Rent-repeated elastic net technique for feature selection. IEEE Access **9**, 152333–152346 (2021)
11. Jenul, A., Schrunner, S., Pilz, J., Tomic, O.: A User-Guided Bayesian Framework for Ensemble Feature Selection in Life Science Applications (UBayFS). arXiv (2021)
12. Quinlan, J.R.: Combining instance-based and model-based learning. In: International Conference on Machine Learning, pp. 236–243 (1993)

13. Street, W.N., Wolberg, W.H., Mangasarian, O.L.: Nuclear feature extraction for breast tumor diagnosis. In: Acharya, R.S., Goldgof, D.B. (eds.) Biomedical Image Processing and Biomedical Visualization, vol. 1905, pp. 861–870. SPIE (1993). https://doi.org/10.1117/12.148698
14. Wojtas, M., Chen, K.: Feature importance ranking for deep learning. Adv. Neural. Inf. Process. Syst. **33**, 5105–5114 (2020)
15. Yu, R., et al.: NISP: pruning networks borisusing neuron importance score propagation. In: IEEE Conference on Computer Vision and Pattern Recognition, pp. 9194–9203 (2018)
16. Yuan, M., Lin, Y.: Model selection and estimation in regression with grouped variables. J. Roy. Stat. Soc. Ser. B (Stat. Methodol.) **68**(1), 49–67 (2006)

# Robust Sparse Learning Based Sensor Array Optimization for Multi-feature Fusion Classification

Leilei Zhao[1] , Fengchun Tian[2]([⊠]) , Junhui Qian[1] , Ran Liu[3] ,
and Anyan Jiang[1]

[1] School of Microelectronics and Communication Engineering, Chongqing University,
Chongqing 400044, China
{leileizhao,junhuiq,20161202003}@cqu.edu.cn
[2] Chongqing Key Laboratory of Bio-perception and Intelligent Information
Processing, Chongqing University, Chongqing 400044, China
fengchuntian@cqu.edu.cn
[3] College of Computer Science, Chongqing University, Chongqing 400044, China
rliu@cqu.edu.cn

**Abstract.** In this paper, we propose a robust sensor array optimization method based on sparse learning for multi-feature fusion data classification. The proposed approach contains three key characteristics. First, it considers the intrinsic group structure among features by combining an $\ell_{F,1}$ norm regularizer design and least squares regression framework. Second, in sensor selection, insignificant feature groups can be eliminated by grouped row sparse coefficients generated by the model, while the $\varepsilon$-dragging trick is introduced to improve the classification ability. Third, an efficient alternating iteration algorithm is presented to optimize the convex objective function. The results compared with the other classical methods on gas sensor array data sets demonstrate that the proposed method can effectively reduce the number of sensors with higher classification accuracy.

**Keywords:** Sensor array optimization · Sparse learning · Multiple feature fusion

## 1 Introduction

Gas sensor array is an important part of classical electronic nose systems, which converts different gases into different electrical signals thus enabling pattern recognition [5]. The time series signals of the sensor response are usually represented in a low-dimensional way by feature extraction [13]. However, in practice, some sensors in the array are useless for gas detection because they do not respond to the target gas or are heavily disturbed by noise, then the corresponding extracted features will be redundant for pattern recognition task. The

This work is founded by the Natural Science Foundation of China (No. 62171066).

optimization of the sensor array, i.e., the selection of the optimal sensor combination, will improve the accuracy of pattern recognition [8]. In addition, it will also reduce the complexity and cost of the subsequent system design.

Sensor array optimization is usually performed by combining feature selection methods due to their similar purpose [7,9,11]. In [7], three types of feature selection methods, t-statistics, Fisher's criterion and minimum redundancy maximum relevance, were used to select the most informative features, experimental results show that performance of electronic nose system was improved by 6–10%. In [9], five methods were used to optimize sensor array, then linear discriminant analysis (LDA) achieved the best experimental results, with a 9.6% increase in recognition rate while reducing the number of sensors by 10. Most of the above methods obtain the sensor importance ranking by evaluating the importance of individual features, but the best combination of features is not necessarily composed of the best features. In many scenarios, especially where multiple features are extracted for each sensor, considering the correlation among features is more valuable for selecting the optimal feature set.

Recently, sparse learning based feature selection methods have received considerable attention due to its good performance and interpretability [2–4]. In these methods, the $\ell_p$ norm or $\ell_{p,q}$ norm regularization terms is often used, which forces important features to have large coefficients and unimportant features to have small or zero coefficients, thus completing the selection of important features. Specially, in [4], the joint $\ell_{2,1}$ norms minimization was designed for multiclass classification problems, it selects features across all data points with joint sparsity. In [3], sparse group LASSO was used to select most informative features and thus improve the accuracy of the binary classification problem. The group structure between features is considered in group LASSO-based approaches, but the $\ell_1$ norm in them is commonly used to constrain variables in vector form. The $\ell_{2,1}$ norm-based methods eliminate unimportant features by generating row sparse solutions, but does not consider the correlation between features.

Motivated by the previous works, in this paper, we propose a robust sensor array optimization method (RSAO) for multi-feature fusion data classification by combining the least squares regression framework and an $\ell_{F,1}$ norm regularizer design. When each sensor is characterized by multiple features, there are clear group structures divided by sensor category among the features. Therefore, the $\ell_{F,1}$ norm regularizer is designed to enforce unimportant feature groups to have small or zero coefficients, and then the corresponding sensors can be removed. Compared with traditional methods, the proposed method takes into account the intrinsic relevance of features and selects important sensors by directly scoring the feature groups. Besides, to improve the discriminative ability of the model, we further introduce the $\varepsilon$-dragging technique proposed in [12] to increase the inter-class distance. Meanwhile, an efficient alternating iteration algorithm is presented to solve the convex optimization problem. Experimental results on the gas sensor data sets show that the sensor combinations selected by the proposed method have better classification accuracy than the other conventional methods.

The rest of the paper is organized as follows. In Sect. 2, we present the proposed method and its optimization algorithm. In Sect. 3, we report experimental results. Finally, conclusions are offered in Sect. 4.

## 2  The Proposed Method

In this section, we propose a robust sensor array optimization method by combining an $\ell_{F,1}$ norm regularizer design and least squares regression framework. Meanwhile, an efficient iterative algorithm is presented to optimize the convex objective function.

### 2.1  $\ell_{F,1}$ Norm Regularization Term

Here we first summarize the common norms for vectors and matrices. For any vector $\mathbf{x} = [x_1, x_2, \ldots, x_n]^T$, its $\ell_1$ norm and $\ell_2$ norm are

$$\|\mathbf{x}\|_1 = \sum_{i=1}^{n} |x_i| \tag{1}$$

$$\|\mathbf{x}\|_2 = \sqrt{x_1^2 + x_2^2 + \cdots + x_n^2}. \tag{2}$$

For any matrix $\mathbf{X} \in \mathbb{R}^{n \times d}$, its $i$-th row and $j$-th column element is denoted as $X_{ij}$, then its Frobenius norm and $\ell_{2,1}$ norm can be calculated by

$$\|\mathbf{X}\|_F = (\sum_{i=1}^{n} \sum_{j=1}^{d} X_{ij}^2)^{1/2} \tag{3}$$

$$\|\mathbf{X}\|_{2,1} = \sum_{i=1}^{n} \sqrt{\sum_{j=1}^{d} X_{ij}^2}. \tag{4}$$

Models based on $\ell_1$ norm regularizer can usually generate sparse solutions, and based on similar principles, row sparse solutions can also be generated for models based on $\ell_{2,1}$ norm regularizer. To enable a model to produce grouped row sparse solutions, we design the $\ell_{F,1}$ norm as follows.

Suppose $\mathbf{X} \in \mathbb{R}^{n \times d}$ is the feature fusion matrix extracted from the sensor array response values, and $d$ features can be divided into $m$ groups by sensor category, that is, $\mathbf{X}$ is divided into $m$ block matrices by column $\mathbf{X} = [\mathbf{X}_1, \mathbf{X}_2, \ldots, \mathbf{X}_m]$, where $n$ and $m$ are the number of samples and sensors, respectively. Correspondingly, the transformation matrix $\mathbf{W}$ can also be divided into $m$ block matrices by row $\mathbf{W} = [\mathbf{W}_1^T, \mathbf{W}_2^T, \ldots, \mathbf{W}_m^T]^T$, and then we define $\ell_{F,1}$ norm of matrix as

$$\|\mathbf{W}\|_{F,1} = \sum_{s=1}^{m} \|\mathbf{W}_s\|_F \tag{5}$$

Obviously, $\|\cdot\|_{F,1}$ is a norm due to satisfying the positive definiteness, absolute homogeneity and triangle inequality.

## 2.2   Sensor Selection Model

For binary classification problems, the $\ell_1$ norm-based models are often used to select important features, such as LASSO model

$$\min_{\mathbf{w}} \|\mathbf{Xw} + \mathbf{1}b - \mathbf{y}\|_2^2 + \lambda \|\mathbf{w}\|_1 \tag{6}$$

where $\mathbf{1}$ is a vector with all elements one. In multi-class classification problems, class label vector $\mathbf{y}_i$ is usually transformed into matrix consisting of "0/1" element by one-hot coding. At this point, feature selection can be accomplished by using $\ell_{2,1}$ norm-based models, such as

$$\min_{\mathbf{W}} \|\mathbf{XW} + \mathbf{1b}^T - \mathbf{Y}\|_F^2 + \lambda \|\mathbf{W}\|_{2,1}. \tag{7}$$

Usually, traditional feature selection methods obtain the importance ranking of sensors by scoring individual features, in which the intrinsic structure between features is not considered. However, in many sensor array optimization tasks, each sensor is represented by multiple features, it is valuable to consider the group structure among features divided by sensor type. Therefore, following the least squares regression framework, we propose a novel sensor array optimization method for multi-feature fusion data classification by using the $\ell_{F,1}$ norm regularizer as follows:

$$\min_{\mathbf{W}} \|\mathbf{XW} + \mathbf{1b}^T - \mathbf{Y}\|_F^2 + \lambda \|\mathbf{W}\|_{F,1}. \tag{8}$$

In Eq. (8), the intrinsic group structure of the features is considered and the unimportant feature groups are forced to have small or zero coefficients, so that the corresponding sensors are removed. In addition, to increase the robustness of the model, the Frobenius norm is replaced by the $\ell_{2,1}$ norm, while the $\varepsilon$-dragging trick is introduced to improve the discriminative performance of the model, and finally we obtain a robust sensor array optimization method (RSAO) as follows:

$$\min_{\mathbf{M,W,b}} \|\mathbf{XW} + \mathbf{1b}^T - \mathbf{Y} - \mathbf{E} \odot \mathbf{M}\|_{2,1} + \lambda \|\mathbf{W}\|_{F,1} \tag{9}$$

where symbol $\odot$ represents Hadamard product of matrix, matrix $\mathbf{M}$ consists of positive elements, $\lambda$ is a positive regularized parameter, and matrix $\mathbf{E}$ is defined as

$$E_{ij} = \begin{cases} +1, & \text{if } Y_{ij} = 1 \\ -1, & \text{if } Y_{ij} = 0. \end{cases} \tag{10}$$

In sensor selection process, the proposed method uses $\|\mathbf{W}_i\|_F$ as a score for the feature subset $\mathbf{X}_i$ to obtain the importance ranking of the sensors, which is more efficient and has better interpretability.

## 2.3 Model Optimization

Clearly, there are three unknown variables to learn in Eq. (9), so we present an alternating iteration algorithm to solve it. First, given $\mathbf{M}$, let $\tilde{\mathbf{Y}} = \mathbf{Y} + \mathbf{E} \odot \mathbf{M}$, we will solve the following problem

$$\min_{\mathbf{W},\mathbf{b}} \|\mathbf{XW} + \mathbf{1b}^T - \tilde{\mathbf{Y}}\|_{2,1} + \lambda\|\mathbf{W}\|_{F,1}. \tag{11}$$

Since problem (11) has no analytical solution, we present an efficient iterative algorithm to solve for $\mathbf{W}$ and $\mathbf{b}$.

Let $J(\mathbf{W},\mathbf{b})$ be objective function of problem (11), taking the derivative of the function $J(\mathbf{W},\mathbf{b})$ with respect to $\mathbf{W}$ and $\mathbf{b}$, we have

$$\frac{\partial J(\mathbf{W},\mathbf{b})}{\partial \mathbf{W}} = \mathbf{X}^T\mathbf{U}_1(\mathbf{XW} + \mathbf{1b}^T - \mathbf{Y}) + \lambda\mathbf{U}_2\mathbf{W} \tag{12}$$

$$\frac{\partial J(\mathbf{W},\mathbf{b})}{\partial \mathbf{b}^T} = \mathbf{1}^T\mathbf{U}_1(\mathbf{XW} + \mathbf{1b}^T - \mathbf{Y}) \tag{13}$$

where $\mathbf{U}_1$ and $\mathbf{U}_2$ are diagonal matrix, and their diagonal elements are

$$U_1^{tt} = \frac{1}{\|\mathbf{e}_t\|_2}, \quad t = 1, 2\ldots, n \tag{14}$$

$$U_2^{ii} = \frac{1}{\|\mathbf{W}_j\|_F}, \mathbf{w}_i \in \mathbf{W}_j, j = 1, 2\ldots, m \tag{15}$$

where $\mathbf{e}_t$ is $t$-th row of matrix $\mathbf{XW} + \mathbf{1b}^T - \tilde{\mathbf{Y}}$ and $\mathbf{w}_i$ is $i$-th row of matrix $\mathbf{W}$. Setting Eq. (13) equal to zero, we can get

$$\mathbf{b}^T = c\mathbf{1}^T\mathbf{U}_1(\mathbf{Y} - \mathbf{XW}) \tag{16}$$

where $c$ is equal to $(\mathbf{1}^T\mathbf{U}_1\mathbf{1})^{-1}$. Then setting Eq. (12) equal to zero and using Eq. (16), we can obtain

$$\mathbf{W} = (\mathbf{X}^T\mathbf{LX} + \lambda\mathbf{U}_2)^{-1}\mathbf{X}^T\mathbf{LY} \tag{17}$$

where $\mathbf{L} = \mathbf{U}_1 - c\mathbf{U}_1\mathbf{1}\mathbf{1}^T\mathbf{U}_1$. Note that the computation of $\mathbf{U}_1$ and $\mathbf{U}_2$ depends on $\mathbf{W}$ and $\mathbf{b}$, so $\mathbf{W}$ and $\mathbf{b}$ can be iteratively updated by using $\mathbf{U}_1$ and $\mathbf{U}_2$ from the previous step.

Second, we perform the optimization of $\mathbf{M}$. Given $\mathbf{W}$ and $\mathbf{b}$, let $\mathbf{T} = \mathbf{XW} + \mathbf{1b}^T - \mathbf{Y}$, then we need to solve the following problem

$$\min_{\mathbf{M}} \|\mathbf{T} - \mathbf{E} \odot \mathbf{M}\|_{2,1} \tag{18}$$

this problem can be decomposed into subproblems by row

$$\min_{\mathbf{m}_i} \|\mathbf{t}_i - \mathbf{e}_i \odot \mathbf{m}_i\|_2, \quad i = 1, 2\cdots, n \tag{19}$$

where $\mathbf{t}_i$, $\mathbf{e}_i$, and $\mathbf{m}_i$, are $i$-th row of the matrix $\mathbf{T}$, $\mathbf{E}$, and $\mathbf{M}$, respectively.

Let $J(\mathbf{m}_i)$ be objective function of problem (19), taking the derivative of $J(\mathbf{m}_i)$ with respect to $M_{ij}$, we have

$$\frac{\partial J(\mathbf{m}_i)}{\partial M_{ij}} = \frac{E_{ij}T_{ij} - M_{ij}}{\|\mathbf{t}_i - \mathbf{e}_i \odot \mathbf{m}_i\|_2} \qquad (20)$$

and set it equal to zero, we obtain

$$M_{ij} = max\{0, E_{ij}T_{ij}\} \qquad (21)$$

where $M_{ij}$, $E_{ij}$, and $T_{ij}$ are $i$-th row and $j$-th column of the matrix $\mathbf{M}$, $\mathbf{E}$, and $\mathbf{T}$, respectively. So the solution of problem (18) can be write as

$$\mathbf{M} = max\{\mathbf{0}, \mathbf{E} \odot \mathbf{T}\} \qquad (22)$$

In short, we present an alternating iterative method to solve problem (9), and it mainly includes two steps. First, optimize vector $\mathbf{b}$ and matrix $\mathbf{W}$ with fixed matrix $\mathbf{M}$ according to Eq. (16) and Eq. (17); Second, optimize matrix $\mathbf{M}$ with fixed vector $\mathbf{b}$ and matrix $\mathbf{W}$ according to Eq. (22). The proposed iterative algorithm is summarized as Algorithm 1.

---

**Algorithm 1.** RSS for Sensor Selection

---

**Input:** feature matrix $\mathbf{X} \in \mathbb{R}^{n \times d}$ with divided into m groups by column, label matrix $\mathbf{Y} \in \mathbb{R}^{n \times k}$, parameters $\lambda$.
**Output:** indices of the first $s$ sensors
1: initialize $\mathbf{M}$, $\mathbf{W}$ and $\mathbf{b}$ for solving Eq. (9)
2: **while not converged do**
3:   $\tilde{\mathbf{Y}} = \mathbf{Y} + \mathbf{E} \odot \mathbf{M}$
4:   **while not converged do**
5:     calculate $\mathbf{U}_1$ and $\mathbf{U}_2$ according to Eq. (14) and (15)
6:     calculate $\mathbf{b}^T = c\mathbf{1}^T\mathbf{U}_1(\mathbf{Y} - \mathbf{X}\mathbf{W})$
7:     calculate $\mathbf{W} = (\mathbf{X}^T\mathbf{L}\mathbf{X} + \lambda\mathbf{U}_2)^{-1}\mathbf{X}^T\mathbf{L}\mathbf{Y}$
8:   **end while**
9:   $\mathbf{T} = \mathbf{X}\mathbf{W} + \mathbf{1}\mathbf{b}^T - \mathbf{Y}$
10:   $\mathbf{M} = max\{\mathbf{0}, \mathbf{E} \odot \mathbf{T}\}$
11: **end while**
12: calculate $\|\mathbf{W}_i\|_F$ as an importance score of the $i$-th sensor
13: sort the scores in descending order and output the first $s$ indices

---

## 2.4   Complexity Analysis

The computational cost of Algorithm 1 is mainly concentrated in three parts due to matrix inverse and matrix product calculation. In step 6, the complexity of calculating $\mathbf{b}$ is $O(n^2k + ndk)$, where $n$ and $k$ are the number of samples and classes, $d$ is the dimension of features. In step 7, the complexity of calculating

$\mathbf{W}$ is $O(n^2d + nd^2 + ndk + d^3 + d^2k)$. The sum of the complexity of computing $\mathbf{W}$ and $\mathbf{b}$ is $O(n^2d + nd^2 + ndk + d^3 + d^2k + n^2k)$. In step 9, the complexity of calculating $\mathbf{XW}$ is $O(ndk)$. Since the number of classes is much smaller than the number of samples and the feature dimension, neglecting the lower order quantities, the total computational complexity of algorithm 1 is $O(\tau(n^2d + d^3))$, where $\tau$ is the number of iterations.

# 3   Experiment

In this section, we evaluate the proposed method on gas sensor array data sets while comparing other classical methods.

## 3.1   Data Sets

We provide a brief description of all the data sets used in the experiments as follows. Note that three data sets are from the UCI Machine Learning Repository and the corresponding papers are cited.

Gas sensor array under flow modulation data set (GSAFM) [15]: this data set was collected from an array of 16 metal-oxide gas sensors under gas flow modulation conditions. It contains four categories and a total of 58 samples. Each sample included 16 time series (one time series per sensor),and then 27 features contain one maximum features, 13 high-frequency features and 13 low-frequency features extracted from each time series as corresponding sensor features, so each sample has 432 features.

Gas sensor array drift data set (GSAD) [6,10]: this data set was collected from an array of 16 chemical sensors exposed six gases. Its first batch contains six classes and a total of 445 samples. Each sample contains 16 time series, four steady-state features and four dynamic features are extracted from each time series, thus each sample is characterized by 128 features.

Gas sensors for home activity monitoring data set (GSHAM) [1]: this data set has recorded time series signals of eight gas sensors in response to wine, banana and background activity. It contains three classes and a total of 100 samples. After the time series signals are filtered by FIR low-pass filter, each sensor signal is represented by three features, minimum, average, and minimum slope, i.e., each sample contains 24 features.

## 3.2   Experiments Settings

We will compare our method, RSAO, with the classical T-test [7], LDA [9], MI [14] and ERFS [4]. All data are normalized by Z-score method. Classification accuracy is used to evaluate the performance of the selected sensors. A linear

SVM classifier is trained on the training set, and then its classification accuracy on the test set is calculated by the function fitcsvm in Matlab. For all data sets, ten times five-fold cross-validation is performed, i.e., 50 classification accuracies are obtained, and finally we present the average accuracy and standard deviation of the different methods to compare.

In ERFS and RSAO, the regularization parameter $\lambda$ needs to be tuned. In addition, the regularization parameter $C$ in SVM needs to be tuned for all methods. In each experiment, the optimal parameters are selected by the grid search method with three-fold cross validation as the evaluation criterion based on the training set. The candidate set for log value of parameter $\lambda$ is $\{-2, -1, 0, 1, 2, 3, 4\}$ and the candidate set for log value of parameter $C$ is $\{-3, -2, -1, 0, 1, 2, 3\}$.

## 3.3 Comparison of Classification Accuracy

Figure 1 presents the relationship between the classification accuracy and the number of sensors selected by the five methods. It can be seen that the proposed method surpasses the other methods in most points. Table 1 presents the classification accuracies of the raw sensor array features and the optimized sensor array features, as well as the corresponding number of selected sensors. It can be seen that the classification accuracy has been significantly improved after sensor array optimization, and the proposed method achieves better accuracy than other methods while fewer sensors are selected. In addition, Fig. 2 presents the variation of the values of the objective function (11) and the objective function (9) with the number of iterations in the proposed optimization algorithm. It can be seen that the objective function values are monotonically decreasing and are convergent after fewer iteration steps.

**Table 1.** Optimal classification accuracy and corresponding number of selected sensors after executing sensor array optimization.

| Method | Gas sensor array data sets | | | | | |
| --- | --- | --- | --- | --- | --- | --- |
| | GSAFM | | GSAD | | GSHAM | |
| | Number of sensor | Accuracy | Number of sensor | Accuracy | Number of sensor | Accuracy |
| Raw | 16 | 0.8986 ± 0.0845 | 16 | 0.9755 ± 0.0130 | 8 | 0.7464 ± 0.0972 |
| Ttest | 13 | 0.9050 ± 0.0934 | 6 | 0.9744 ± 0.0174 | 7 | 0.7499 ± 0.0848 |
| MI | 9 | 0.9145 ± 0.0846 | 5 | 0.9746 ± 0.0184 | 6 | 0.7546 ± 0.0933 |
| LDA | 8 | 0.9209 ± 0.0693 | 7 | 0.9733 ± 0.0150 | 5 | 0.7646 ± 0.0842 |
| ERFS | 8 | 0.9221 ± 0.0821 | 7 | 0.9760 ± 0.0137 | 7 | 0.7479 ± 0.07781 |
| RSAO | 5 | **0.9300 ± 0.0675** | 5 | **0.9764 ± 0.0156** | 3 | **0.7650 ± 0.1000** |

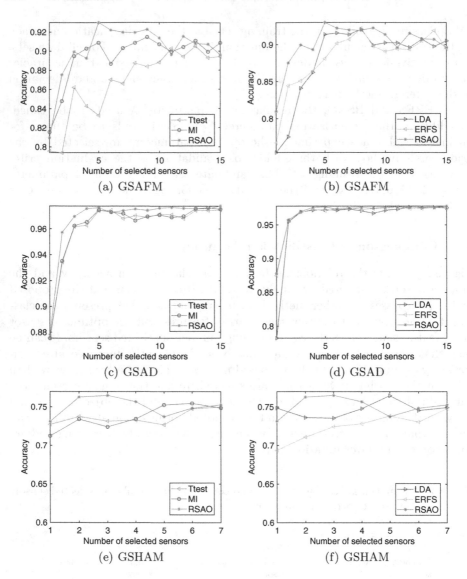

**Fig. 1.** Relationship between classification accuracy and the number of selected sensors on the three gas sensor array data sets.

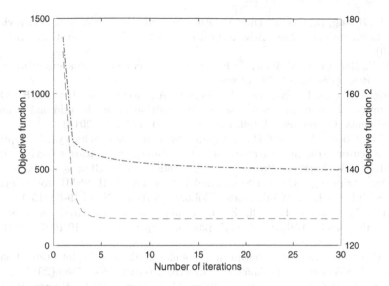

**Fig. 2.** Relationship between the objective function value and the number of algorithm iterations.

## 4    Conclusion and Future Work

In this paper, we propose a novel sensor array optimization method for multi-feature fusion data classification. The intrinsic group structure of the sensor features is considered by combining a least squares regression framework and an $\ell_{F,1}$ norm regularization design. Experimental results on the gas sensor array data sets demonstrate that the proposed method can effectively improve the classification accuracy while reducing the number of sensors compared to other classical methods.

However, the work in this paper has a limitation that it is only evaluated on gas sensor array data sets. In the future, the generalization of the proposed method will be validated for more feature fusion tasks, such as EEG signals, machine fault detection, radar array signals, etc.

## References

1. Huerta, R., Mosqueiro, T., Fonollosa, J., Rulkov, N.F., Rodriguez-Lujan, I.: Online decorrelation of humidity and temperature in chemical sensors for continuous monitoring. Chemometr. Intell. Lab. Syst. **157**, 169–176 (2016)
2. Li, J., et al.: Feature selection: a data perspective. ACM Comput. Surv. (CSUR) **50**(6), 1–45 (2017)
3. Liu, B., et al.: Lung cancer detection via breath by electronic nose enhanced with a sparse group feature selection approach. Sens. Actuators B Chem. **339**, 129896 (2021)

4. Nie, F., Huang, H., Cai, X., Ding, C.: Efficient and robust feature selection via joint $\ell 2$, 1-norms minimization. Adv. Neural Information Process. Syst. **23**, 1813–1821 (2010)
5. Röck, F., Barsan, N., Weimar, U.: Electronic nose: current status and future trends. Chem. Rev. **108**(2), 705–725 (2008)
6. Rodriguez-Lujan, I., Fonollosa, J., Vergara, A., Homer, M., Huerta, R.: On the calibration of sensor arrays for pattern recognition using the minimal number of experiments. Chemometr. Intell. Lab. Syst. **130**, 123–134 (2014)
7. Saha, P., Ghorai, S., Tudu, B., Bandyopadhyay, R., Bhattacharyya, N.: Optimization of sensor array in electronic nose by combinational feature selection method. In: Mason, A., Mukhopadhyay, S.C., Jayasundera, K.P., Bhattacharyya, N. (eds.) Sensing Technology: Current Status and Future Trends II. SSMI, vol. 8, pp. 189–205. Springer, Cham (2014). https://doi.org/10.1007/978-3-319-02315-1_9
8. Scott, S.M., James, D., Ali, Z.: Data analysis for electronic nose systems. Microchimi. Acta **156**(3), 183–207 (2006). https://doi.org/10.1007/s00604-006-0623-9
9. Sun, H., et al.: Sensor array optimization of electronic nose for detection of bacteria in wound infection. IEEE Trans. Ind. Electron. **64**(9), 7350–7358 (2017)
10. Vergara, A., Vembu, S., Ayhan, T., Ryan, M.A., Homer, M.L., Huerta, R.: Chemical gas sensor drift compensation using classifier ensembles. Sens. Actuators B Chem. **166**, 320–329 (2012)
11. Wei, G., Zhao, J., Yu, Z., Feng, Y., Li, G., Sun, X.: An effective gas sensor array optimization method based on random forest. In: 2018 IEEE SENSORS, pp. 1–4. IEEE (2018)
12. Xiang, S., Nie, F., Meng, G., Pan, C., Zhang, C.: Discriminative least squares regression for multiclass classification and feature selection. IEEE Trans. Neural Netw Learn. Syst. **23**(11), 1738–1754 (2012)
13. Yan, J., et al.: Electronic nose feature extraction methods: A review. Sensors **15**(11), 27804–27831 (2015)
14. Zhou, J., Welling, C.M., Kawadiya, S., Deshusses, M.A., Grego, S., Chakrabarty, K.: Sensor-array optimization based on mutual information for sanitation-related malodor alerts. In: 2019 IEEE Biomedical Circuits and Systems Conference (BioCAS), pp. 1–4. IEEE (2019)
15. Ziyatdinov, A., Fonollosa, J., Fernandez, L., Gutierrez-Galvez, A., Marco, S., Perera, A.: Bioinspired early detection through gas flow modulation in chemo-sensory systems. Sens. Actuators B Chem. **206**, 538–547 (2015)

# Stimulates Potential for Knowledge Distillation

Haifeng Qing, Jialiang Tang, Xiaoyan Yang, Xinlei Huang, Honglin Zhu, and Ning Jiang[✉]

School of Computer Science and Technology, Southwest University of Science and Technology, Mianyang, Sichuan 621000, China
jiangning@swust.edu.cn

**Abstract.** In knowledge distillation, numerous methods devote to exploring effective knowledge to guide the training of the small student network. However, these approaches ignore inspiring the student network's own capability, a small student network also has the potential to achieve comparable performance to a large teacher network. We propose a new framework named stimulates the potential for knowledge distillation (SPKD). The SPKD framework consists of two components, 1) residual-based local feature normalization (LFNR), and 2) the local feature normalized extraction (LFNE). LFNR can enhance the competitiveness of local areas of feature maps by adding to the student network and can make better use of local areas with rich information. On the other hand, the stimulated local features are more expressive. LFNE extracts local representational features from the teacher network; the obtained local features are transferred to the student to guide the student network learning. Extensive experimental results demonstrate that our SPKD has achieved significant classification results on the benchmark datasets CIFAR-10 and CIFAR-100.

**Keywords:** Knowledge distillation · Local feature normalization · Residual structure

## 1 Introduction

In 2015 [3], Hinton et al. proposed a network training method called Knowledge Distillation (KD) that allows small networks to mimic the behavior of high-capacity parametric networks by setting a distillation loss. All negative labels are treated uniformly during traditional training. That is to say, this new training method makes each sample bring more information to students than the conventional training method. A classic teacher-student structure was established, and various effective methods were proposed to seek to feed the student network with more effective information in the teacher network. For example, Zagoruyko et al. [7] encode output decisions, such as image classification [5,12] to obtain the regions of most interest in the input to narrow the distance between the student and teacher network attention maps. Peng et al. [8] believe that a certain vector of students to fit the vector of the teacher network, whether it is

© The Author(s), under exclusive license to Springer Nature Switzerland AG 2022
E. Pimenidis et al. (Eds.): ICANN 2022, LNCS 13532, pp. 187–198, 2022.
https://doi.org/10.1007/978-3-031-15937-4_16

kl scatter or European distance, is only a mapping between the vectors, due to the original difference between the teacher network and the student network, so should not only learn the difference between the teacher network and the student network of a single sample vector but also should learn the correlation between the two samples. The idea that the relationships between migrated samples (structural information) would be superior to migrating individual sample features is presented in 2019 [5]. Which convey the structural relationships of the outputs rather than the individual outputs themselves. We propose to revisit the knowledge distillation.

The above method extracts different categories of information from the teacher network to guide students in training. But these approach does not make good use of the potential of the student network itself. In recent years, several methods have been proposed to improve specific capabilities of the network. For example, adding local response normalization (LRN) [14] to Alexnet to create a competition mechanism can improve the generalization ability of the network. And the addition of an external structure Convolutional Block Attention Module (CBMA) [5] to improve the network's ability to pay attention to sensitive information. In the paper [9], a method called Local Feature Normalization (LFN) is proposed to enhance local feature competition. It can effectively improve the processing capacity of the network for local features.

Based on these inspirations, we propose a distillation framework that stimulates the potential for knowledge distillation (SPKD). SPKD stimulates the potential of the network itself to improve performance, and the framework is implemented by two components (see Fig. 1). LFNR and LFNE, where LFNR stimulates the network by adding a residual structure in the student network to enhance the processing power of local features, LFNR consists of three parts, of which we propose SLFN guides network training by comparing the differences in local information between the feature graph between the teacher and the student network. The contributions of our proposed approach are summarized below:

1. We propose to use a new residual structure LFNR. To stimulate the learning ability of the network itself, and to improve the performance of the network for classification tasks without affecting the overall parameters of the network.
2. We propose a new framework for extracting local features LFNE, It can enable the teacher network to better guide the student network to learn the local feature processing ability.
3. Through a large number of experiments, We demonstrated that the SPKD framework stimulates the potential of student networks themselves and demonstrates the effectiveness of LFNE and LFNR.

## 2   Related Literature

We discuss related works in knowledge distillation and Normalization in this section. In both areas, various approaches have been proposed over the past few years. We summarize them as follows.

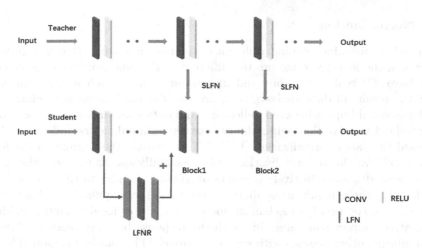

**Fig. 1.** Added LFNR to the student network. The input of the residual structure is fixed as the output of the first layer of the network after convolution. Normalize local features to stimulate students' ability to process local information. SLFN is part of the LFNE and focuses on calculating the difference in local areas of the feature map.

## 2.1   Knowledge Distillation

The knowledge distillation [1,3,6] used for model compression is similar to the way humans learn. Inspired by this, current methods of knowledge distillation have been extended to teacher-student learning, mutual learning, assisted teaching, lifelong learning, and self-study. Hinton et al. [3] transferring fine-grained knowledge from large-scale training models to training small-scale models have increased the speed and efficiency of its learning, and the classification effect of confusing instances in small-grained tasks has been enhanced. Zhang et al. [6] explore improving the performance of deep neural networks by mutual distillation in the same/different untrained networks. This method obtains a compact network with better performance than the network extracted from a strong network by a static teacher. Smith et al. [1] proposes a new DFCIL incremental distillation strategy that provides an improved cross-entropy training and importance-weighted feature distillation. By inverting a frozen copy of the learning classification model, the image is synthesized for training, so that the model can not forget the knowledge of previous tasks and replay the data previously trained. Kim et al. [4] are more effective strategies to soften hard targets by providing high-quality confidence estimates.

We build on the teacher-student structure by adding new structures to stimulate the learning ability of the network itself. As far as we know, this method has not been done before.

## 2.2 Normalization

In the field of machine learning, different evaluation indicators (that is, different features in the feature vector are the different evaluation indicators described) often have different dimensions and dimensional units. Such a situation will affect the results of data analysis, the purpose of normalization is to eliminate the dimensional impact between indicators, and data standardization processing is carried out to solve the comparability between data indicators. Ioffe et al. [11] proposed the batch normalization (BN). BN normalizes the neurons in the features to achieve global normalization and successfully speeds up the training of neural networks, and effectively prevents overfitting. Similar to LFN, a method of enhancing the generalization ability of the model was applied to Alxnet [12] by creating a competitive mechanism for the activity of local neurons, making the relatively larger pair values in which the response becomes relatively large, and inhibiting other neurons with smaller feedback. This method is named local response normalization (LRN). For BN, the error rate is higher when the batch size is small because the calculation results of the BN layer rely on the data of the current batch. When the match size is small (such as 2 or 4), the mean and variance of the match data are poorly represented, so the final result is also more significant. In the field of image stylization, the discovery of Instance Normalization (IN) [2] differs from BN's emphasis on normalizing each match to ensure consistent data distribution. Tending to produce results that rely primarily on an image instance, normalizing width and height can accelerate model convergence and maintain independence between each image instance. Our residual structure is based on Local Feature Normalization [9].

We note that knowledge distillation of the teacher-student architecture is a fairly interpretable and transparent topic. Starting from the structure of teachers and students, we have explored a distillation method that gives structural changes to the network and stimulates the learning of students' networks. As far as we know, this method has not been done before.

# 3   Approach

In this section, we will introduce two components of the SPKD framework. How LFNR handles feature mappings, and related formulas. Describes the composition of the LFNE. Instructions on how to use LFNR finally.

## 3.1   Residual-Based Local Feature Normalization

We aim to stimulate the potential of the network itself and thus improve the network's performance. Recent literature suggests that enhancing the network's ability to process local information is critical in classification tasks. And normalization method is to limit the processing data to a specific range and summarizes the statistical distribution of a unified sample. From a collection perspective, high-expression regions are categorized into a category when dealing

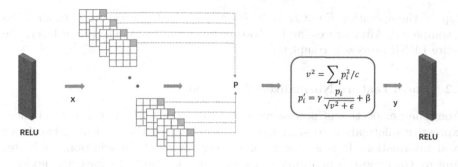

**Fig. 2.** The process of the LFNR to normalize the feature. RELU gives the feature map $x$, and $x$ is normalized to $y$ by LFN, $y$ contains H × W number of local feature vector $p$, the LFN is normalizing $p$ along the channel dimension to get the Normalized feature diagram. Again as an input to the RELU.

with attributes. In [9], LFN is proposed, and LFN can effectively strengthen the competition between local positions and contains a small number of parameters. Inspired by LFN, We proposed the LFNR. This residual structure is constructed in a form similar to a "sandwich", with the LFN layer in the middle of two layers of RELU [10]. By means of the residual structure, we can prevent LFN from destroying the global information of the feature map. RELU can eliminate the LFN layer's negative incentives to the network. The specific operation is as follows.

As shown in (see Fig. 2), to better explain our method, we set the feature map after the output of the Relu layer as a 4D tensor $x \in R^{B*C*H*W}$. B is the batchsize, C is the channel number of $x$, and H, W is the width and height of $x$. $y \in R^{B*C*H*W}$ is obtained by $x$ after processing by LFN. We assume that local normalization processes a set of vectors $p = \{p_1, p_2, ...p_n\}$ for the same location of the feature figure y. $n$ represents the number of feature channels. y contains H × W number of such local feature value vector. The mean square is calculated as follows:

$$v^2 = \sum_i^n p_i^2/n \tag{1}$$

Through the mean square, the competition of local characteristics is effectively strengthened, followed by normalization to normalize the data to a unified interval, reducing the degree of data divergence and reducing the network's learning difficulty.

$$p_i^{'} = f\left(p_i\right) = \frac{p_i}{\sqrt{x^2 + \epsilon}} \tag{2}$$

$\epsilon$ is a small normal number that prevents the occurrence of a denominator of zero. On top of Eq. 2, add two trainable parameters as follows.

$$p_i^{'} = f\left(p\right) = \gamma \frac{p_i}{\sqrt{x^2 + \epsilon}} + \beta \tag{3}$$

Repeat the operation Eq. 3 H * W times, and the local feature normalization is completed. After processing the feature map again through a Relu layer, the entire LFNR process is completed.

## 3.2   Local Feature Normalized Extraction

From the perspective of processing feature mapping, LFNR can extract more expressive information to stimulate the potential of the student network for local information. It is a process of self-improvement. In addition, to better improve the network's performance for classification tasks, we have also added a guided process. Therefore, we propose a method of comparing the middle layer information of teachers and students, called spatial local feature normalization (SLFN). Based on SLFN, We propose a framework for extracting local features for transmission and local feature normalization extraction (LFNE). We divide the teacher-student network into three blocks (see Fig. 1), and the output of each block is used as the source of SLFN extraction information. The specific implementation of LFNE is as follows.

To further illustrate our approach. We note $F_t$ and $F_s$ represent the set of feature representations of teacher and student respectively, $n$ represents the number of groups in the middle of the comparison. $F_t = \left(f_t^1, f_t^2 ... f_t^n\right)$, $F_s = \left(f_s^1, f_s^2 ... f_s^n\right)$, there into $f_i \in R^{C*H*W}$. After extracting the feature map of the middle layer of the teacher and student network, we use the processing method of the LFN layer to process the feature map. $F_{t'} \in R^{n*C*H*W}$, $F_{s'}$ too.

$$F_{t'} = LFN\left(F_t\right) \tag{4}$$

$$F_{s'} = LFN\left(F_s\right) \tag{5}$$

Further, in order to better extract local information, we compress the number of channels of the same block output feature map into one by maximizing pooling. We claim that regional information in the same location on different feature maps corresponds. This allows for richer local feature information. $F_{t_{max}} = \left(f_{t_{max}}^1, f_{t_{max}}^2 .. f_{t_{max}}^n\right)$, $F_{t_{max}} \in R^{n*H*W}$. $F_{s_{max}}$ too.

$$F_{t_{max}} = MAXPOOL\left(F_{t'}\right) \tag{6}$$

$$F_{s_{max}} = MAXPOOL\left(F_{s'}\right) \tag{7}$$

k We then use the mean squared difference (MSE) to calculate the difference between the feature plots to guide the training of the network.

$$L_{LSFN} = MSE\left(F_{s_{max}} - F_{t_{max}}\right)$$
$$= \frac{\sum_i^n \left(f_{s_{max}}^i - f_{t_{max}}^i\right)^2}{n}$$

Then, the optimization goal of SPKD is to minimize the following loss function:

$$L_{LFNE} = \alpha L_{KD} + (1 - \alpha) L_{CE} + \beta L_{SLFN} \tag{8}$$

where $L_{CE}$ is the cross-entropy loss, $L_{KD}$ [3] is knowledge distillation loss, $\alpha$ and $\beta$ two hyperparameters that balance instance consistency and local feature normalization.

## 3.3   How to Use Structure

This section will discuss in detail how LFN-based residual structures can be applied to convolutional neural networks. We give a plot of two types of teacher-student networks to illustrate where we should add our structure. As shown in Fig. 3, taking the student network as a Resnet network as an example, the input data passes through the first layer of convolution and then gives the output into the residual structure based on LFN. To make the residual structure better work with our SLFN, we only added the feature map after the three-layer structure CONV, BN, and RELU on the front end of the Resnet network. WRN is similar to this principle. The input also comes from the first layer of the network CONV, which is then returned to the network after passing through LFNR. LFNR is only suitable for placement in shallow layers, and placing it in the middle and tail ends of the network destroys the overall information of the feature map.

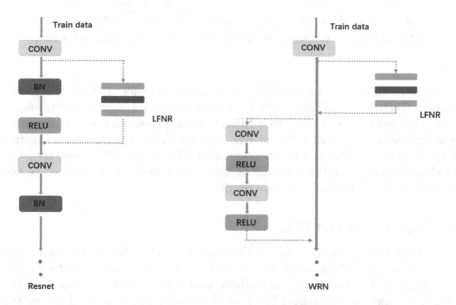

**Fig. 3.** The LFRN acts on the location of the network structure, giving a graph of WRN and Resnet. Both structures are the first layer of the network for the input of LFNR.

## 4    Experiment

In this section, we take a series of experiments on CIFAR-10 and CIFAR-100 to demonstrate the effectiveness of LFNR and LFNE. Ablation experiments were conducted to understand the role of the system components for experiments with the CIFAR dataset. Our configuration regarding the experiment is optimized CNN with random gradient descent SGD and set the learning rate, weight decay, and the momentum are set as 0.1, $5 \times 10^{-4}$ and 0.9, The batchsize is fixed as 128. And take a data-enhanced approach to datasets. Includes random cropping, flipping, and filling.

### 4.1    Experiments on CIFAR-10

We first implement experiments on the CIFAR-10 [14] dataset, The dataset has a total of 60,000 color images, which are $32 \times 32$ and are divided into 10 classes with 6,000 figures in each category. There are 50,000 for training, which constitutes 5 training batches, each batch of 10,000 figures, another 10,000 for testing, forming a separate batch.

**Table 1.** SPKD verified accuracy results on the CIFAR-10 dataset. The accuracy of the comparison method comes from the papers of other authors

| Teacher | Student | Teacher | Student | KD [3] | SPKD |
|---------|---------|---------|---------|--------|------|
| WRN40-2, 2.2M | WRN16-2, 0.7M | 94.73% | 93.69% | 93.92% | **94.22%** |
| WRN40-1, 0.6M | WRN16-1, 0.2M | 93.42% | 91.23% | 91.61% | **91.85%** |

As shown in Table 1, on the CIFAR-10 dataset, we picked WRN [13] as the network structure for validating SPKD. A total of two sets of experiments are set up. Experimental results show that SPKD can improve the student network's accuracy and compare it with the KD method. After using SPKD, the two groups of networks obtained an accuracy of 94.22% and 91.85%, respectively. It can effectively improve the accuracy of the student network. Compared to the KD, Our method also achieves good results.

### 4.2    Experiments on CIFAR-100

The CIFAR-100 [14] dataset has 100 classes. Each class has 600 color images in the size of $32 \times 32$, of which 500 are training sets and 100 are test sets. For each image, it has two labels, fine labels, and coarse labels, representing the fine-grained and coarse-grained labels of the image, respectively. That is, the CIFAR100 dataset is hierarchical and speaks volumes about the performance of the network Compare to CIFAR-10.

We selected the Resnet [18] and WRN to experiment on the CIFAR-100 dataset. The starting learning rate is set as 0.1 and divided by ten at 150, 180, and 210 epochs, a total of 240 epochs. Our experimental setup is to compare SPKD with other methods in the field. Explore how SPKD behaves on complex data sets. And two different sets of teacher and student networks were selected to prove the effectiveness of SPKD in different structures. In Table 2, SPKD can make WRN40-2 training WRN16-2 perform better than other methods. Only in Resnet32 × 4 training Resnet8 × 4, the effect is not as good as CRD.

**Table 2.** SPKD verified accuracy results on the CIFAR-100 dataset. The accuracy of the comparison method comes from the papers of other authors.

| Teacher | Resnet32 × 4 | WRN40-2 |
|---------|--------------|---------|
| Student | Resnet8 × 4 | WRN16-2 |
| KD [3] | 73.33% | 74.92% |
| AT [7] | 73.44% | 74.08% |
| CC [8] | 72.97% | 73.56% |
| SP [17] | 72.94% | 73.83% |
| VID [19] | 73.09% | 74.11% |
| RKD [5] | 71.90% | 73.35% |
| PKT [16] | 73.64% | 74.54% |
| NST [19] | 73.30% | 73.68% |
| CRD [20] | **75.51%** | 75.48% |
| SPKD | 74.80% | **75.52%** |

## 4.3   Ablation Experiments

In this section, we conduct ablation experiments. The dataset of the experiment is still CIFAR-100, and the purpose of the experiment here is to understand the role and effect of the components of the system we proposed. Therefore, the experiment is divided into the following two groups.

**LFNR Athentication.** We have selected two sets of network architectures, and Table 3 summarizes the improvement in network accuracy brought about by the use of LFNR in conjunction with different loss functions. LFNR+AT improves the accuracy of WRN16-2 and Resnet8 × 4 by 0.31% and 0.47%, respectively. For WRN40-2, LFNR and SP, CC, VID, RKD, PKT, NST improved the network accuracy by 0.36%, 0.27%, 0.38%, 0.81%, 0.72%, and 0.28%, respectively. Overall, our LFNR works well with other loss functions. What's more, LFNR does not greatly increase the number of parameters in the network, and the number of parameters in the WRN16-2 student network structure increases by 512. The total number of parameters WRN16-2 is 600,000. Interestingly, We found that LCNR was more effective when used in conjunction with PCT and RKD. We believe that the reason is that PKT and RKD are related to a method of knowledge extraction about features. But this needs to be further experimentally proven.

**Table 3.** The data in the experimental results of LFNR and other loss functions on CIFAR-100.() represent the accuracy rate before the LFNR was added. The accuracy of the comparison method comes from the papers of other authors. The data in bold font is the accuracy after adding LFNR

| Teacher Student | WRN40-2 WRN16-2 | Resnet32 × 4 Resnet8 × 4 |
|---|---|---|
| LFNR+AT | **74.71%** (74.08%) | **73.91%** (73.44%) |
| LFNR+SP | **74.19%** (73.83%) | **73.61%** (72.94%) |
| LFNR+CC | **73.83%** (73.56%) | **73.15%** (72.97%) |
| LFNR+VID | **74.49%** (74.11%) | **73.28%** (73.09%) |
| LFNR+RKD | **74.14%** (73.35%) | **72.41%** (71.90%) |
| LFNR+PKT | **75.17%** (74.54%) | **74.74%** (73.64%) |
| LFNR+NST | **73.96%** (73.68%) | **74.04%** (73.30%) |

**LFNE Authentication.** In this section, we verify with the loss function we propose. Explore whether a function has an effect. The experiment selects two different architecture networks, and the hyperparameters set by the experiment are $\alpha = 0.9$, $\beta = 2$. Select CIFAR-100 for the dataset. LFNE increased by 0.4% and 1.31% on the basis of KD, respectively training WRN16-2, Resnet8 × 4. The results are displayed in Table 4. And compared with other methods, the network accuracy improved by LFNE is also the highest.

**Table 4.** Ablation experiments on LFNE to compare whether LFNE has an effect.

| Teacher Student | Resnet32 × 4 Resnet8 × 4 | WRN40-2 WRN16-2 |
|---|---|---|
| KD | 73.33% | 74.92% |
| AT | 73.44% | 74.08% |
| CC | 72.97% | 73.56% |
| SP | 72.94% | 73.83% |
| VID | 73.09% | 74.11% |
| RKD | 71.90% | 73.35% |
| PKT | 73.64% | 74.54% |
| NST | 73.30% | 73.68% |
| LFNE | **74.64%** | **75.40%** |

## 5    Conclusion

In this study, we propose a knowledge distillation framework (SPKD) to stimulate the potential of student networks to leverage their abilities to improve network performance. Extensive experiments show that SPKD can enhance the performance of student networks. We demonstrate that LFNR and LFNE can be effectively applied to networks by analyzing two system components in the SPKD framework. We believe that with further theoretical analysis of the SPKD framework and more attention to the student network itself, there will be more improvements and applications of SPKD.

**Acknowledgement.** This research is supported by Sichuan Science and Technology Program (No. 2022YFG0324), SWUST Doctoral Foundation under Grant 19zx7102.

# References

1. Smith, J., et al.: Always be dreaming: a new approach for data-free class-incremental learning. In: Proceedings of the IEEE/CVF International Conference on Computer Vision (2021)
2. Ulyanov, D., Vedaldi, A., Lempitsky, V.: Instance normalization: The missing ingredient for fast stylization. arXiv preprint arXiv:1607.08022 (2016)
3. Hinton, G., Vinyals, O., Dean, J.: Distilling the knowledge in a neural network. arXiv preprint arXiv:1503.02531 (2015)
4. Kim, K., et al.: Self-knowledge distillation: A simple way for better generalization. arXiv preprint arXiv:2006.12000 (2020)
5. Park, W., et al.: Relational knowledge distillation. In: Proceedings of the IEEE/CVF Conference on Computer Vision and Pattern Recognition (2019)
6. Zhang, Y., et al.: Deep mutual learning. In: Proceedings of the IEEE Conference on Computer Vision and Pattern Recognition (2018)
7. Zagoruyko, S., Komodakis, N.: Paying more attention to attention: Improving the performance of convolutional neural networks via attention transfer. arXiv preprint arXiv:1612.03928 (2016)
8. Peng, B., et al.: Correlation congruence for knowledge distillation. In: Proceedings of the IEEE/CVF International Conference on Computer Vision (2019)
9. Jiang, N., Tang, J., Yu, W., Zhou, J.: Local feature normalization. In: Qiu, H., Zhang, C., Fei, Z., Qiu, M., Kung, S.-Y. (eds.) KSEM 2021, Part II. LNCS (LNAI), vol. 12816, pp. 228–239. Springer, Cham (2021). https://doi.org/10.1007/978-3-030-82147-0_19
10. Glorot, X., Bordes, A., Bengio, Y.: Deep sparse rectifier neural networks. In: Proceedings of the Fourteenth International Conference on Artificial Intelligence and Statistics, pp. 315–323 (2011)
11. Ioffe, S., Szegedy, C.: Batch normalization: accelerating deep network training by reducing internal covariate shift (2015)
12. Krizhevsky, A., Sutskever, I., Hinton, G.E.: ImageNet classification with deep convolutional neural networks. In: Advances in Neural Information Processing Systems, pp. 1097–1105 (2012)
13. Zagoruyko, S., Komodakis, N.: Wide residual networks. arXiv preprint arXiv:1605.07146 (2016)
14. Krizhevsky, A., Hinton, G., et al.: Learning multiple layers of features from tiny
15. Hadsell, R., Chopra, S., LeCun, Y.: Dimensionality reduction by learning an invariant mapping. In: 2006 IEEE Computer Society Conference on Computer Vision and Pattern Recognition (CVPR 2006), vol. 2. IEEE (2006). Images (2009)
16. Passalis, N., Tefas, A.: Probabilistic knowledge transfer for deep representation learning. CoRR, abs/1803.10837 (2018)

17. Tung, F., Mori, G.: Similarity-preserving knowledge distillation. In: Proceedings of the IEEE/CVF International Conference on Computer Vision (2019)
18. He, K., et al.: Deep residual learning for image recognition. In: Proceedings of the IEEE Conference on Computer Vision and Pattern Recognition 2016, pp. 1097–1105 (2012)
19. Huang, Z., Wang, N.: Like what you like: Knowledge distill via neuron selectivity transfer. arXiv preprint arXiv:1707.01219 (2017)
20. Tian, Y., Krishnan, D., Isola, P.: Contrastive representation distillation. arXiv preprint arXiv:1910.10699 (2019)

# Adaptive Compatibility Matrix
# for Superpixel-CRF

Boquan Zhou[1](✉) and Chunpeng Li[2]

[1] School of Computer Science (National Pilot Software Engineering School), Beijing University of Posts and Telecommunications, Beijing 100876, China
lovelyfrog@bupt.edu.cn
[2] Chinese Institute for Brain Research, Beijing 102206, China
lichunpeng@cibr.ac.cn

**Abstract.** Compatibility Matrix plays a very important role in Fully-connected pairwise Conditional Random Field (full-CRF). However, former studies often fix it on any dataset or make too strong assumptions, which may cause abnormal object co-occurrence in image segmentation. The reason lies on the fixed compatibility matrix will give both normal objects co-occurrence and abnormal objects co-occurrence the same penalty. In this paper, we propose an adaptive compatibility matrix to replace the fixed compatibility matrix in full-CRF. Based on a weaker assumption of local independence, we propose the algorithm for adaptive compatibility matrix to learn from the dataset. In order to decrease the high computational complexity of full-CRF and maintain the accuracy at the same time, we build superpixel-CRF with adaptive compatibility matrix and propose the corresponding method to solve it. Our experiments demonstrate that the adaptive compatibility matrix improves the accuracy of full-CRF. The expansion in superpixel-CRF not only reduces the complexity but also performs well on the results.

**Keywords:** CRF · Image segmentation · Adaptive compatibility matrix

## 1 Introduction

The goal of multi-class image segmentation is to classify each pixel in an image to a label and split the image into different semantic patches, which is one of the most challenging problems in computer vision. Multi-class image segmentation is widely used in many applications such as video surveillance [4], object recognition [6], autopilot [5], etc.

A commonly used approach to solve segmentation problem is modelling each pixel as a node and an image as a graph. The segmentation problem is converted to a maximum a posteriori (MAP) inference defined over pixels or image patches [9,11,14,18,20]. The potentials in CRF incorporate pairwise potentials that model contextual relationships between object classes. However, former studies [3,13] often fixed the compatibility matrix in pairwise potentials, where the penalties between normal co-occurrence objects and abnormal co-occurrence objects are equal. That will cause some abnormal objects to appear together (Fig. 1). In order to solve that problem, we propose an adaptive compatibility matrix learned from the dataset to substitute the fixed compatibility matrix. In [8,20] people build local connected CRF, however it can not model long-range connections. For modeling long-range connections, [13] first builds the full-CRF. For solving CRF, traditional discrete optimization methods such as graph cut: $\alpha$-expansion [3] or tree reweighted message passing(TRW) [12] work well for local connected CRF, but are too expensive for full-CRF. In [13], they develop an approximate optimization algorithm that is sublinear in the number of pairwise potentials. It is based on mean field inference, which is a local technique and the solution can be arbitrarily far from the optimum [10]. As a result, in [22] they develop an efficient graph cut optimization for full-CRF, assuming that image pixels have been tessellated into superpixels, and the weight of an edge between two pixels depends only on the superpixels these pixels belong to. The new superpixel-CRF decreases the computational complexity greatly and guarantees that the result will have the approximation factor of two, however it still suffers from the abnormal objects co-occurrence problem. In order to solve that problem, we fuse adaptive compatibility matrix into superpixel-CRF. Our contributions lie on 2 aspects: 1. We propose an adaptive compatibility matrix that is learned from the dataset by variational method based on local-independence, which can relieve the abnormal object co-occurrence problem in pixel-CRF. 2. We introduce the adaptive compatibility matrix into superpixel-CRF, which decreases the computation time greatly than pixel-CRF and relieve the abnormal object co-occurrence problem of the original superpixel-CRF.

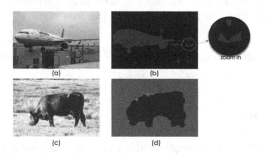

**Fig. 1.** Examples of abnormal objects co-occurrence. (a, c) is the original image, (b, d) is the corresponding segmentation result of potts model. (b) is the segmentation result of (a), black represents the background, red represents aeroplane, blue represents boat. (d) is the segmentation result of (c), green represents grass, dark blue represents cow, light blue represents sheep, orange represents face. (Color figure online)

## 2  Related Work

### 2.1  CRF and Superpixel-CRF

CRF is a kind of statistical modeling methods often applied in pattern recognition and machine learning. CRF models are composed of unary potentials and pairwise potentials on pixels or superpixels. There are many methods for solving sparsely connected CRF, such as iterative conditional modes(ICM) [21], TRW [12] and graph cut(expansion move, swap move) [3]. For densely connected CRF, mean field inference in [13] can solve it with fast speed; However, the result can be far from global minimum. [10] points that discrete optimization methods based on graph-cut can work better. To decrease computational complexity, in [2,17,23], they transform from pixel level to superpixel level. In [22], they consider that the weight of an edge between two pixels depends only on the superpixels they belong to, but the use of potts model [3] as compatibility function will cause the abnormal objects co-occurrence problem.

### 2.2  Compatibility Function

As an import part of overall potential, pairwise potential models relationship between two nodes. Pairwise potential consists of two parts: weight between two nodes and compatibility function $\mu(a,b)$ between two labels classified to these two nodes. In [15,20], they use potts model as compatibility matrix which is very simple: $\mu(a,b) = 1$ if $a \neq b$ else 0. In [21], they use truncated distance as compatibility value between two labels. No matter the potts model or truncated distance, they are all fixed values with no difference between different datasets. [13] makes an assumption that all nodes are independent and get their compatibility function, which is too strong because the pixels in an image are connected with each other and can not simply considered as independent. All the above compatibility function will cause the abnormal objects to appear. To be more precise, only two pixels are considered independent during the process of iteration in our study which maintain the connections between other pixels. In this article, we map compatibility function to a matrix $M$ called compatibility matrix with $\mu(a,b)$ mapped to $M_{ab}$. With the compatibility matrix, the equations and the optimization problem will become more concise.

## 3  Preliminary

Consider an image $\mathbf{I}$ which is defined over all its pixels $\{I_1, I_2, ...I_N\}$, and a random field $\mathbf{X}$ which is defined over all its labels $\{X_1, X_2, ..., X_N\}$, where $N$ is the number of pixels. $I_i$ means the image vector of pixel $i$ in $\mathbf{I}$, and $X_i$ means the corresponding label of pixel $i$ in $\mathbf{X}$. Based on the graph $G$ constructed, the probability of $\mathbf{X}$ given $\mathbf{I}$ can be computed [16]:

$$P_G(\mathbf{X}|\mathbf{I}) = \frac{1}{Z(\mathbf{I})} \cdot \exp(-E(\mathbf{X}|\mathbf{I})) \tag{1}$$

To simplify the notation, the subscript $G$ and the condition $\mathbf{I}$ are omitted: $P(\mathbf{X}) = \frac{1}{Z} \cdot \exp(-E(\mathbf{X}))$. The $E(\mathbf{X})$ in $P$ means the overall potentials:

$$E(\mathbf{X}) = \sum_i f_u(x_i) + \sum_{i,j} f_p(x_i, x_j) \qquad (2)$$

$f_u(x_i)$ means the unary potential of pixel $i$, which is computed from an independent classifier. $f_p(x_i, x_j)$ means the pairwise potential between pixel $i$ and pixel $j$, which is defined as [13]

$$f_p(x_i = a, x_j = b) = w_{ij} \cdot \mu(a, b) \qquad (3)$$

where the $w_{ij}$ means the weight between pixel $i$ and pixel $j$, which is defined as

$$w_{ij} = \lambda_1 \cdot \exp\left(-\frac{||p_i - p_j||^2}{2\theta_1^2}\right) + \lambda_2 \cdot \exp\left(-\frac{||I_i - I_j||^2}{2\theta_2^2}\right) \qquad (4)$$

where $p_i$ means the position of pixel $i$, and $I_i$ means the image vector or pixel $i$. $\mu(a, b)$ is the compatibility function that measures the penalty between any two pixels $i$ and $j$ classified as label $a$ and $b$. In the potts model, if $a \neq b$, $\mu(a, b) = 1$ else 0.

## 4   Adaptive Compatibility Matrix

We substitute the compatibility function with compatibility matrix $\mathbf{M}$ for two reasons: one is the simplicity in notation, the other is that any value in the matrix is the penalty that two pixels classified to the two labels represented by the row and column of the value and you can observe the penalty visually in the heatmap of $\mathbf{M}$. Former studies often use the fixed compatibility matrix such as potts model [22]. However, using the fixed compatibility matrix will cause abnormal objects co-occurrence problem as Fig. 1 shows. In Fig. 1(a), some parts of aeroplane are classified as boat and in Fig. 1(d), some parts of cow are classified as sheep and face. The reason lies on two aspects. The first aspect is the unary classifier, which will give these places classified as boat low unary potentials. The second aspect is the compatibility matrix $\mathbf{M}$ of potts model, which considers the penalty that aeroplane-background co-occurrence and boat-background co-occurrence is the same, and the aeroplane-aeroplane co-occurrence is only tiny smaller than aeroplane-boat co-occurrence. As a result, some pixels will be classified as boats.

If the compatibility matrix is learned from the dataset, we will know which objects are less likely to appear together and give them bigger penalties. Then the abnormal objects co-occurrence problem can be get rid of. In order to learn the matrix, the following optimization problem needs to be focused on:

$$\arg\max_{\mathbf{M}} \prod_{i=1}^{K} P(\mathbf{T}^{(i)}|\mathbf{I}^{(i)}, \mathbf{M}) \qquad (5)$$

where $K$ is the size of our train dataset, $\mathbf{T}^{(i)}$ is the true label of image $\mathbf{I}^{(i)}$. After some transformations, we can get the loss $\mathcal{L}(\mathbf{M}) = \sum_{i=1}^{K} -log(P(\mathbf{T}^{(i)}|\mathbf{I}^{(i)}, \mathbf{M}))$ and the optimization problem becomes:

$$\arg \min_{\mathbf{M}} \mathcal{L}(\mathbf{M}) \tag{6}$$

However, it is impossible to get the analytic solution of $M$(as it's a transcendental equation). We need use stochastic gradient descent to optimize it gradually. For the sake of simplicity, we consider the loss on one image $\mathbf{I}$ and compute the partial derivative for $M_{ab}$:

$$\frac{\partial \mathcal{L}}{\partial M_{ab}} = \sum_{i,j} w_{ij} \cdot \left[ 1_{t_i=a} \cdot 1_{t_j=b} - \sum_{\mathbf{X}} P(\mathbf{X}) 1_{x_i=a} \cdot 1_{x_j=b} \right] \tag{7}$$

where $1_{x_i=a}$ means if $x_i = a$ it equals 1 otherwise 0.

However, the complexity of computing the $\sum_{\mathbf{X}} P(\mathbf{X}) 1_{x_i=a} \cdot 1_{x_j=b}$ is huge. If there are a total of $B$ categories of labels, the time complexity will be $O(B^N)$. As a result, some approximations need to be considered to $P(\mathbf{X})$ and the computation need to be simplified. We can write $\sum_{\mathbf{X}} P(\mathbf{X}) 1_{x_i=a} \cdot 1_{x_j=b}$ as this form: $\sum_{\mathbf{X}} P(x_1, ... x_i = a, ..., x_j = b, ..., x_N)$, and then $P(x_i = a, x_j = b)$.

The overall energy $E(\mathbf{X})$ can be written as:

$$E(\mathbf{X}) = E(x_i, x_j) + E_{o.t}^{i,j}(\mathbf{X}) \tag{8}$$

where $E(x_i, x_j) = f_u(x_i) + f_u(x_j) + f_p(x_i, x_j)$, and $E_{o.t}^{i,j}(\mathbf{X})$ are all other terms in $E(\mathbf{X})$ except $E(x_i, x_j)$. Then we can get :

$$p(x_i = a, x_j = b) = \frac{\exp[-E(x_i = a, x_j = b)] \cdot \sum_{\mathbf{X}-x_i-x_j} \exp[-E_{o.t}^{i,j}(\mathbf{X})]}{Z} \tag{9}$$

In [13], they use mean field which considers that the classifications of all pixels are independent, and then they get the compatibility matrix. Obviously this assumption is too strong because in the real world, the classification is not independent at all. Instead we make a weaker assumption that the classifications of pixel $i$ and $j$ are independent, then $P(x_i = a, x_j = b) = P(x_i = a) \cdot P(x_j = b)$. We consider the approximation distribution as $Q(x_i, x_j)$. In order to get $Q(x_i, x_j)$, we minimize the KL divergence $D_{KL}(Q||P)$. Let $\sum_{\mathbf{X}-x_i-x_j} \exp[-E_{o.t}^{i,j}(\mathbf{X})]$ be $h(x_i = a, x_j = b)$. For solving this variational problem, we will get:

$$L(Q_i, Q_j) = \sum_{x_i, x_j} Q(x_i, x_j)[E(x_i, x_j) - \ln h(x_i, x_j)]$$
$$+ \sum_{x_i=1}^{M} [Q_i(x_i) - \lambda_i] \ln Q_i(x_i) + \sum_{x_j=1}^{M} [Q_j(x_j) - \lambda_j] \ln Q_j(x_j) \tag{10}$$

Using Euler-Lagrange equation we will have:

$$\frac{\partial L}{\partial Q_i} = \ln Q_i(x_i) + 1 - \lambda_i + \sum_{x_j} Q_j(x_j)[E(x_i, x_j) - \ln h(x_i, x_j)] \tag{11}$$

Then $Q_i(x_i)$ can be computed:

$$Q_i(x_i) = \frac{1}{Z} \cdot \exp[-\sum_{x_j} Q_j(x_j)E(x_i,x_j)] \cdot \exp[\sum_{x_j} Q_j(x_j)\ln h(x_i,x_j)] \quad (12)$$

For any label $a$, compared with the other terms in $h(x_i = a, x_j)$, the $\sum_n f_p(x_i = a, x_n)$ is much smaller for one order of magnitude. As a result, we can omit it. Then for any $x_i$, $\exp[\sum_{x_j} Q_j(x_j)\ln h(x_i,x_j)]$ will be the same. Finally we will get:

$$Q_i(x_i) = \frac{1}{Z} \cdot \exp[-\sum_{x_j} Q_j(x_j)E(x_i,x_j)] \quad (13)$$

where $Z_i$ is the normalization factor. Then it needs to be solved iteratively. After getting the approximation distribution $Q$, we can compute the partial derivative with respect to $M_{ab}$. The details can be seen in Algorithm 1. Then the adaptive compatibility matrix $\mathbf{M}$ can be updated iteratively. It is easy to prove that the pairwise potential with $M$ satisfies semi-metric [3], then we can use $\alpha$-expansion to solve the CRF.

---

**Algorithm 1** Variational Method: Calculate $\frac{\partial \mathcal{L}}{\partial \mathbf{M}}$

---

1: **for** each $i \in [1, N]$ **do**
2:     initialize $Q_i^{new}(x_i) = \frac{\exp[-f_u(x_i)]}{Z_i}$
3: **end for**
4: **for** each $a \in [1, B]$ **do**
5:     **for** each $b \in [a+1, B]$ **do**
6:         **for** each $i, j \in [1, N]$ **do**
7:             $Q_i^{old} = 0$;
8:             **while** $\max |Q_i^{new} - Q_i^{old}| > \epsilon$ **do**
9:                 $Q_i^{old} = Q_i^{new}$
10:                **for** each $x_i \in [1, B]$ **do**
11:                    $Q_i^{new}(x_i)$
12:                    $= \frac{\exp\left[-f_u(x_i) - \sum_{j;j>i}\sum_{x_j} f_p(x_i,x_j)Q_j^{old}(x_j)\right]}{Z_i}$
13:                **end for**
14:            **end while**
15:        **end for**
16:        $\frac{\partial \mathcal{L}}{\partial M_{ab}} = \sum_{i,j} w_{ij} \left[ \mathbb{1}_{a=T_i} \cdot \mathbb{1}_{b=T_j} - Q_i(a) \cdot Q_j(b) \right]$
17:    **end for**
18: **end for**

---

## 5   Apply Adaptive Compatibility Matrix to Superpixel CRF

Solving full-CRF via graph-cut is very expensive especially when the resolution of the image is high. However, compared with mean field, graph cut works significantly better on the quality of solution [10]. In [22], they first try the superpixel-CRF, and use graph cut to solve it which decreases the computation time greatly. However, the accuracy also declines and it still suffers from the abnormal object co-occurrence problem. In order to relieve that problem, we introduce the adaptive compatibility matrix to superpixel-CRF. The pixels in the superpixel are similar to each other, as a result,the weights between any two pixels in one superpixel can be considered as the same which are called inner weights. Also, the weights between any pixel in one superpixel $s$ and any pixel in another superpixel $t$ can be considered as the same too, which are called outer weights. For two pixels $i$ and $j$ in the same superpixel, the inner weight is defined as

$$w_{ij} = \lambda_1 \exp(-\frac{\sigma_i^2}{2\beta_1^2})$$

where the $\sigma_i^2$ is the intensity variance of the superpixel that $i$ belongs to. For two pixels $i$ and $j$ that belong to two different superpixels $S(i)$ and $S(j)$, the outer weight is defined as

$$w_{ij} = \lambda_1 \exp(-\frac{|d_i - d_j|^2}{2\beta_2^2}) + \lambda_2 \exp(-\frac{|\mu_i - \mu_j|^2}{2\beta_3^2})$$

where $d_i$ and $\mu_i$ are the center and the intensity mean of the superpixel $S(i)$. We consider the binary class first, and then expand it to multi-class.

## 5.1   Binary Class

In this section, the energy function is assumed to contain two classes $\mathcal{L} = \{0, 1\}$. For the notation simplicity, we put the unary potential $f_u(x_i = 1) = f_u(x_i = 1) - f_u(x_i = 0)$, and $f_u(x_i = 0) = 0$ which is equivalent to the original problem.

The compatibility matrix for the binary class is:

$$\begin{bmatrix} 0 & M_{01} \\ M_{01} & 0 \end{bmatrix}$$

Consider the superpixel $s$ and $t$, we assume that pixel $p, q \in P_s, a \in P_t$, where $P_s, P_t$ is the pixel set of superpixel $s$ and $t$. Assume that $n_s$ is the number of pixels in $P_s$, $y_s$ is the number of pixels that are assigned as 1 in $P_s$. Then the inner weight inside $P_s$ is $M_{01}w_{pq}(n_s - y_s)$, the outer weight between $P_s$ and $P_t$ is $M_{01}w_{pa}[y_s(n_t - y_t) + y_t(n_s - y_s)]$. Let $g_s(y_s)$ be the unary potential of superpixel $s$ which contains the unary potentials of all the pixels and all the pairwise potentials in $s$, $o(p)$ as the ranking of pixel $p$'s original unary potential in the superpixel that it belongs to (if $p$ has the least unary energy in the superpixel, then $o(p) = 1$), then:

$$g_s(y_s) = M_{01}w_{pq}y_s(n_s - y_s) + \sum_{p \in P_s, o(p) \leq y_s} f_u(x_p = 1) \tag{14}$$

The pairwise potential $V_{st}$ between superpixel $s$ and $t$ which contains all the pairwise potentials between any pixels in $s$ and $t$ is:

$$V_{st} = M_{01}w_{pq}[y_s(n_t - y_t) + y_t(n_s - y_s)] \tag{15}$$

After $M_{01}w_{pq}(y_s n_t - y_t^2)$ transferred into $g_s(y_s)$ and $M_{01}w_{pq}(y_t n_s - y_t^2)$ transferred into $g_t(y_t)$, $V_{st}$ equals $M_{01}w_{pq}(y_s - y_t)^2$ which satisfies semi-metric. Then the overall potential will be:

$$g(y) = \sum_{s \in S} g_s(y_s) + \sum_{s,t \in S} V_{st}(y_s, y_t) \tag{16}$$

which can be solved easily via $\alpha$-expansion.

## 5.2    Multi-class

Multi-class problem is our ultimate task and the knowledge in binary-class can be expanded to Multi-class. In each iteration, we only consider one label $\alpha$. Assume that the result of the last iteration is $\mathbf{X}_{old}$, the pixels can be split into two parts: $x_i^{old} \neq \alpha$ and $x_i^{old} = \alpha$. For each pixel $i$, we define a binary-class classification $z_i$. The result after this iteration is defined as $\mathbf{X}$ and the relationship between $\mathbf{Z}$ and $\mathbf{X}$ is:

$$\begin{cases} z_i = 0, & \text{if } x_i = x_i^{old} \\ z_i = 1, & \text{if } x_i = \alpha \end{cases} \tag{17}$$

Then the new unary potential $h_u$ of $\mathbf{Z}$ will be defined as: $h_u(z_i = 0) = f_u(x_i = x_i^{old}), h_u(z_i = 1) = f_u(x_i = \alpha)$. The new pairwise potential will be:

$$h_p(z_i = 1, z_j = 1) = 0 \tag{18}$$

$$h_p(z_i = 0, z_j = 0) = \begin{cases} 0, & \text{if } x_i^{old} = x_j^{old} \\ w_{ij} \cdot M_{x_i^{old} x_j^{old}}, & \text{if } x_i^{old} \neq x_j^{old} \end{cases} \tag{19}$$

$$h_p(z_i = 0, z_j = 1) = w_{ij} \cdot M_{x_i^{old} \alpha} \tag{20}$$

However, when $z_i = 0, z_j = 0$ and $x_i^{old} \neq x_j^{old}$, the pairwise potential is not 0, which does not satisfy the requirement of semi-metric. As a result, we need to do some transformations. After some terms are transferred from pairwise terms to unary terms, we get the new unary potential and new pairwise potential.

$$h_u(z_i = 0) = f_u(x_i = x_i^{old}) + \frac{1}{2} \sum_{j; x_i^{old} \neq x_j^{old}} w_{ij} \cdot (M_{x_i^{old} x_j^{old}} - 2M_{x_j^{old} \alpha}) \tag{21}$$

$$h_u(z_i = 1) = f_u(x_i = \alpha) \tag{22}$$

$$h_p(z_i, z_j | z_i = z_j) = 0 \tag{23}$$

$$h(z_i, z_j | z_i \neq z_j) = \begin{cases} w_{ij} \cdot M_{x_i^{old} \alpha}, & x_i^{old} = x_j^{old} \\ \frac{1}{2} w_{ij} \cdot [2M_{x_i^{old} \alpha} + 2M_{x_j^{old} \alpha} - M_{x_i^{old} x_j^{old}}], & x_i^{old} \neq x_j^{old} \end{cases}$$

$$(24)$$

After that, the new potentials are equivalent to the original ones and the current pairwise potentials satisfy semi-metric. Then the method in binary class can be used to transform the CRF from pixel level to superpixel level and the multi-class problem can be solved iteratively.

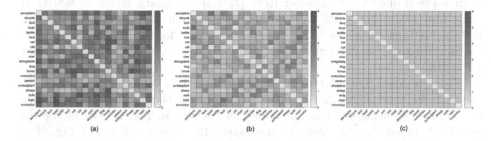

**Fig. 2.** Visualization of three compatibility matrices from VOC. (a) is the adaptive compatibility matrix using out method. (b) is the compatibility matrix using mean field. (c) is the compatibility matrix of potts model.

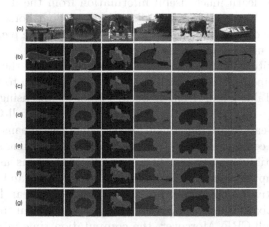

**Fig. 3.** The left 3 images are from VOC and the right 3 images are from MSRC-21. (a) Original images. (b) Ground truth. (c)–(e) Segmentation from fixed compatibility matrix, compatibility matrix computed by mean field and adaptive compatibility matrix of full-CRF. (f)–(g) Segmentation from fixed compatibility matrix and adaptive compatibility matrix of superpixel-CRF.

# 6   Experiments

We conduct many experiments on two standard benchmarks to see the improvement of the segmentation result. The first is PASCAL VOC 2012 (VOC) [7] which contains 1928 color images. The images in VOC are approximately $500 \times 300$ and there are 21 object class labels. The second is the MSRC-21 dataset [19], which consists of 591 color images of size $320 \times 213$ with corresponding ground truth labelings of 21 object classes. The experiment environment is person computer with Intel-i5 processor and 8G memory. The unary terms of VOC come from a pre-trained CNN classifier from [1] and the unary terms of MSRC-21 come from textonBoost [20]. We use SLIC [2] to compute superpixels, approximately 1000 per image for VOC and 800 per image for MSRC-21. To evaluate the performance, we compute the mean IOU for VOC and the pixel accuracy for MSRC-21.

First we learn the adaptive compatibility matrix of VOC and MSRC-21 respectively, using Algorithm 1. The heatmap of the three compatibility matrices from VOC using different methods can be seen in Fig. 2. The larger the penalty between the two labels is, the darker the square will be. In Fig. 2(a), it can be seen that the penalty of aeroplane-boat occurrence becomes more prominent than 1 which will solve the aeroplane-boat occurrence problem. Other than aeroplane-boat, the penalty of many abnormal objects co-occurrence also increase. Compared to our adaptive compatibility matrix, the matrix learned by mean field can not learn much useful information from the dataset. For many pairs of abnormal objects such as aeroplane-bicycle, boat-horse and bus-dining table, our adaptive compatibility matrix will give them large penalties while the matrix learned by mean field can not perform that well.

Then we substitute the fixed compatibility matrix with the learned matrix in full-CRF and superpixel-CRF with the use of $\alpha$-expansion to get the segmentation result. In Table 1 and Table 2, potts model means using full-CRF with fixed compatibility matrix in [3], mean field means using full-CRF with compatibility matrix learned by mean field in [13], adaptive means using full-CRF with our adaptive compatibility matrix, sp+origin means using superpixel-CRF with fixed compatibility matrix in [22], sp+adaptive means using superpixel-CRF with our adaptive compatibility matrix. From Table 1 and Table 2, we can see that the adaptive compatibility matrix increases the mean IOU of VOC by 2 points and the pixel accuracy of MSRC-21 by 2 points than the fixed compatibility matrix in full-CRF. Moreover, the computation time of superpixel-CRF decreases greatly than full-CRF and superpixel-CRF with our adaptive compatibility matrix obtain good performance close to full-CRF. The visual result of three methods on full-CRF can be seen in Fig. 3(c, d, e) and two methods on superpixel-CRF can be seen in Fig. 3(f, g).

**Table 1.** The comparisons of mIoU and computation time of 5 methods on PASCAL VOC 2012.

|             | mIoU | Computation time |
|-------------|------|------------------|
| Potts model | 71   | 4.1 min          |
| Mean field  | 72   | 4.2 min          |
| Adaptive    | **73** | 4.8 min        |
| sp+origin   | 69   | 3.1 s            |
| sp+adaptive | 71   | 3.9 s            |

**Table 2.** The comparisons of pixel accuracy and computation time of 5 methods on MSRC-21.

|             | Pixel accuracy | Computation |
|-------------|----------------|-------------|
| Potts model | 80             | 3.8 min     |
| Mean field  | 81             | 3.9 min     |
| Adaptive    | **82**         | 4.6 min     |
| sp+origin   | 77             | 2.8 s       |
| sp+adaptive | 80             | 3.7 s       |

# 7   Conclusions

In this paper, we propose the adaptive compatibility matrix of pairwise potential based on local-independence assumption and the corresponding algorithm to learn it from dataset. By introducing the adaptive compatibility matrix to full-CRF, we relieve the abnormal objects co-occurrence problem. However, the computation speed of solving full-CRF is too slow. Superpixel-CRF can be solved efficiently but due to the use of fixed compatibility matrix, it still suffers from the abnormal objects co-occurrence problem. As a result,we introduce the adaptive compatibility matrix to superpixel-CRF, and propose the corresponding method to solve it. The experiments show that superpixel-CRF with adaptive compatibility matrix not only decreases the computation time greatly but also alleviates the abnormal object co-occurrence problem and improves the performance.

# References

1. Vedaldi, A., Gupta, K.L.: MatConvNet: CNNs for MATLAB (2016). http://www.vlfeat.org/matconvnet/pretrained/
2. Achanta, R., Shaji, A., Smith, K., Lucchi, A., Fua, P., Süsstrunk, S.: SLIC superpixels compared to state-of-the-art superpixel methods. IEEE Trans. Pattern Anal. Mach. Intell. **34**(11), 2274–2282 (2012). https://doi.org/10.1109/TPAMI.2012.120
3. Boykov, Y., Veksler, O., Zabih, R.: Fast approximate energy minimization via graph cuts. IEEE Trans. Pattern Anal. Mach. Intell. **23**(11), 1222–1239 (2001)

4. Cao, X., Gao, S., Chen, L., Wang, Y.: Ship recognition method combined with image segmentation and deep learning feature extraction in video surveillance. Multimedia Tools Appl. **79**(13), 9177–9192 (2020). https://doi.org/10.1007/s11042-018-7138-3

5. De Croon, G., De Wagter, C., Remes, B., Ruijsink, R.: Sky segmentation approach to obstacle avoidance. In: 2011 Aerospace Conference, pp. 1–16. IEEE (2011)

6. Delmerico, J.A., David, P., Corso, J.J.: Building facade detection, segmentation, and parameter estimation for mobile robot localization and guidance. In: 2011 IEEE/RSJ International Conference on Intelligent Robots and Systems, pp. 1632–1639. IEEE (2011)

7. Everingham, M., Van Gool, L., Williams, C.K.I., Winn, J., Zisserman, A.: The PASCAL Visual Object Classes Challenge 2012 (VOC2012) Results (2012). http://www.pascal-network.org/challenges/VOC/voc2012/workshop/index.html

8. Fulkerson, B., Vedaldi, A., Soatto, S.: Class segmentation and object localization with superpixel neighborhoods. In: 2009 IEEE 12th International Conference on Computer Vision, pp. 670–677. IEEE (2009)

9. He, X., Zemel, R., Carreira-Perpinan, M.: Multiscale conditional random fields for image labeling. In: Proceedings of the 2004 IEEE Computer Society Conference on Computer Vision and Pattern Recognition, CVPR 2004, vol. 2, pp. II-II (2004). https://doi.org/10.1109/CVPR.2004.1315232

10. Kappes, J., et al.: A comparative study of modern inference techniques for discrete energy minimization problems. In: Proceedings of the IEEE Conference on Computer Vision and Pattern Recognition, pp. 1328–1335 (2013)

11. Kohli, P., Torr, P.H., et al.: Robust higher order potentials for enforcing label consistency. Int. J. Comput. Vis. **82**(3), 302–324 (2009). https://doi.org/10.1007/s11263-008-0202-0

12. Kolmogorov, V., Schoenemann, T.: Generalized sequential tree-reweighted message passing (2012)

13. Krähenbühl, P., Koltun, V.: Efficient inference in fully connected CRFs with gaussian edge potentials. Adv. Neural Inf. Process. Syst. **24**, 109–117 (2011)

14. Kumar, S., Hebert, M.: A hierarchical field framework for unified context-based classification. In: Tenth IEEE International Conference on Computer Vision (ICCV 2005) Volume 1, vol. 2, pp. 1284–1291 (2005). https://doi.org/10.1109/ICCV.2005.9

15. Ladický, L., Russell, C., Kohli, P., Torr, P.H.: Associative hierarchical CRFs for object class image segmentation. In: 2009 IEEE 12th International Conference on Computer Vision, pp. 739–746 (2009). https://doi.org/10.1109/ICCV.2009.5459248

16. Lafferty, J., McCallum, A., Pereira, F.C.: Conditional random fields: Probabilistic models for segmenting and labeling sequence data (2001)

17. Levinshtein, A., Stere, A., Kutulakos, K.N., Fleet, D.J., Dickinson, S.J., Siddiqi, K.: TurboPixels: fast superpixels using geometric flows. IEEE Trans. Pattern Anal. Mach. Intell. **31**(12), 2290–2297 (2009). https://doi.org/10.1109/TPAMI.2009.96

18. Rabinovich, A., Vedaldi, A., Galleguillos, C., Wiewiora, E., Belongie, S.: Objects in context. In: 2007 IEEE 11th International Conference on Computer Vision, pp. 1–8 (2007). https://doi.org/10.1109/ICCV.2007.4408986

19. Shotton, J., Winn, J., Rother, C., Criminisi, A.: *TextonBoost*: joint appearance, shape and context modeling for multi-class object recognition and segmentation. In: Leonardis, A., Bischof, H., Pinz, A. (eds.) ECCV 2006, Part I. LNCS, vol. 3951, pp. 1–15. Springer, Heidelberg (2006). https://doi.org/10.1007/11744023_1

20. Shotton, J., Winn, J., Rother, C., Criminisi, A.: TextonBoost for image under-standing: multi-class object recognition and segmentation by jointly modeling tex-ture, layout, and context **81**, 2–23 (2009)
21. Szeliski, R., et al.: A comparative study of energy minimization methods for Markov random fields with smoothness-based priors. IEEE Trans. Pattern Anal. Mach. Intell. **30**(6), 1068–1080 (2008)
22. Veksler, O.: Efficient graph cut optimization for full CRFs with quantized edges. IEEE Trans. Pattern Anal. Mach. Intell. **42**(4), 1005–1012 (2020)
23. Veksler, O., Boykov, Y., Mehrani, P.: Superpixels and supervoxels in an energy optimization framework. In: Daniilidis, K., Maragos, P., Paragios, N. (eds.) ECCV 2010, Part V. LNCS, vol. 6315, pp. 211–224. Springer, Heidelberg (2010). https://doi.org/10.1007/978-3-642-15555-0_16

# BERT-Based Scientific Paper Quality Prediction

Taiki Sasaki[1], Yasuaki Ito[1(✉)], Koji Nakano[1], and Akihiko Kasagi[2]

[1] Graduate School of Advanced Science and Engineering, Hiroshima University,
Higashihiroshima, Japan
{taiki,yasuaki,nakano}@cs.hiroshima-u.ac.jp
[2] Fujitsu Ltd., Tokyo, Japan
kasagi.akihiko@fujitsu.com

**Abstract.** In recent years, scholarly databases have made many scientific papers available on the Internet. While these databases facilitate access to excellent papers, they also increase the possibility of encountering inferior papers. However, it is difficult to predict the quality of a paper just from a glance at the paper. In this paper, we propose a machine learning approach to predicting the quality of scientific papers. Specifically, we predict the quality of an article by classifying for the abstract of the paper whether the article is included in a superior journal or not. The proposed model is trained using a BERT-based model widely used in natural language processing. After training, we achieved a test accuracy of 95.1% and 89.6% in medicine and computer science, respectively. In addition, the results of the classification are visualized by evaluating the sentence combinations in the abstract to clarify the details of the classification.

**Keywords:** Paper quality prediction · Machine learning · BERT

## 1 Introduction

Text classification is a fundamental problem in natural language processing (NLP), and it has been applied in various fields such as translation, dialogue response, sentiment analysis, and summarization. In recent years, machine learning models have been widely used for text classification [20]. In these approaches, the text is input to a machine learning model and it is trained to classify the text. In NLP using machine learning, recurrent neural networks (RNNs) such as long short-term memory (LSTM) with recursive structures have often been used in natural processing using machine learning. However, these models require sequential processing from the beginning to the end of a sentence, which prevents parallel computation. This is a critical drawback for training networks, which generally require a large amount of time. For this problem, the Transformer was proposed [22]. By introducing the self-attention structure, Transformer can achieve the same or better performance as RNNs without recursive structure.

© The Author(s), under exclusive license to Springer Nature Switzerland AG 2022
E. Pimenidis et al. (Eds.): ICANN 2022, LNCS 13532, pp. 212–223, 2022.
https://doi.org/10.1007/978-3-031-15937-4_18

The Transformer processes the inputs simultaneously and computes the attention weights among them. This allows the network to be trained on large data sets using parallel processing. Also, BERT (Bidirectional Encoder Representations from Transformers) [13] utilizing Transformer technology is one of the most successful models currently available; the performance of natural language processing using machine learning has been greatly improved by BERT.

The main contribution of this paper is to propose a method for predicting the quality of scholarly papers using machine learning. Recently, many scientific papers have been available on the Internet through PubMed [4], Web of Science [7], Google Scholar [2], and others. While they have made it easier to browse superior papers, they have also increased the chances of encountering inferior papers. Generally, the number of citations is used as an indicator of the superiority of a paper. However, it is not easy to predict quality simply by the number of citations alone, as it is highly dependent on the time of publication, and moreover, it is impossible to predict a paper before submission. Therefore, in this paper, we consider papers published in superior journals to be superior papers and papers published in less superior journals to be less superior papers. Furthermore, we consider the abstracts of papers published in these journals to be similar, thus predicting the quality of papers based on the abstracts. Based on the above idea, in the proposed approach, the quality prediction of papers is obtained as a classification problem for the abstracts of papers. Specifically, the proposed method uses a BERT-based model to classify whether an article is included in the upper or the lower-ranked journal in the Average Journal Impact Factor Percentile [1] from its abstract. In this paper, we show that different datasets of pre-training of the proposed BERT-based model affect classification accuracy. The results of training the models show that the models can classify whether the input abstracts are from superior or less superior journals with a test accuracy of 95.1% and 89.6% in the field of medicine and computer science, respectively.

As related work, studies predicting the quality of academic papers have been conducted [8,16]. In those studies, there are mainly two types of approaches of prediction. One is to predict the quality of a paper based only on its content, using the title, abstract, text, figures, tables, references, and appearance of the paper [10,14,19,21,24]. The other is to estimate the quality based on the contents of the paper as well as additional information outside of the paper, such as author reputations, impact factor of the journal in which the paper was published, cited papers and the citation network composed of them [9,11,12,17,25]. Unlike the above methods, the proposed method classifies whether or not the content of an abstract is that of a superior journal. This classification is inspired by the idea that papers in a good journal have well-described abstracts. The proposed approach does not aim to judge the excellence of the research, but focuses on the quality of writing of the papers.

The rest of this paper is organized as follows. We briefly introduce BERT in Sect. 2. In Sect. 3, we show our proposed machine learning approach using the BERT-based model, and experimental results are presented in Sect. 4. Finally, we conclude the paper in Sect. 5.

## 2   BERT

*Bidirectional Encoder Representations from Transformers* (BERT) [13] is one of the state-of-the-art machine learning techniques based on Transformer [22] for NLP. The technique includes model structures and learning approaches. In this section, we briefly introduce the technique.

Figure 1 illustrates an outline of the structure of the BERT model. Given an input sequence of $N$ words, each word is converted to a token and then each of them is mapped to a vector data of size $k$ by word embedding. After that, $L$ transformer encoder blocks transform the tokens to contain more accurate information. Each Transformer encoder block based on the encoder of the Transformer has $A$ attention heads and $H$ hidden layers. The BERT model has configurations of various sizes, and typical models and their number of parameters are shown in Table 1. Users can choose whether to use all of the output of the last Transformer encoder block or the part of one for final classification. Usually, it is sufficient to use only the first output for classification tasks, and the final classification result is obtained using the classifier based on the first output as shown in the figure.

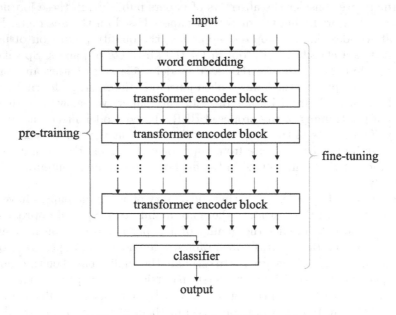

**Fig. 1.** Structure of the BERT model

The training of BERT models consists of two phases: *pre-training phase* and *fine-tuning phase*. In general, the pre-training phase involves training the model on a large corpus such as Wikipedia. On the other hand, in the fine-tuning phase, the weight parameters obtained in pre-training are used as initial values for the model, and training is performed on the target task. This phase can often be completed with much less computation than the pre-training phase. We give an explanation about these phases as follows.

**Table 1.** Model configuration of BERT models

| Model | $L$ | $H$ | $A$ | Parameters |
|-------|-----|-----|-----|------------|
| BERT-tiny | 2 | 128 | 2 | 4,386,050 |
| BERT-mini | 4 | 256 | 4 | 11,170,817 |
| BERT-small | 4 | 512 | 8 | 28,764,161 |
| BERT-medium | 8 | 512 | 8 | 41,373,697 |
| BERT-base | 12 | 768 | 12 | 109,483,009 |

The network training in the pre-training phase is unsupervised and consists of two tasks, *masked language model* (MLM) and *next sentence prediction* (NSP). In this training, we train only on word embedding and transformer encoder blocks. In MLM, we input sentences of tokens with some of them masked to train the model to predict the original tokens. In NSP, we input two sentences concatenated to train the model to predict whether the two sentences are consecutive or not. When selecting two sentences, 50% of the input is actually consecutive sentences and the other 50% is randomly selected from the data set. By training on a large number of sentences for these two tasks, we obtain a model that can capture the features of the sentences. Since the computational cost of pre-training is enormous, we can utilize BERT models already trained on massive corpora such as Wikipedia, BookCorpus, and MEDLINE/PubMed [6,23], and often employ these models for the following fine-tuning phase.

In the fine-tuning phase, we train the whole network on the target task. The model obtained in the above pre-training is used as the initial values and trained as supervised learning. In general, this training requires fewer iterations than the pre-training. In the proposed method, the pre-trained model is trained as a classification problem.

# 3 Proposed Quality Prediction of Scientific Papers

This section presents the proposed method, the BERT model for predicting the quality of papers as a classification problem, the utilized dataset, and the classifier.

## 3.1 Dataset of Scientific Papers

In this work, we use the semantic scholar open research corpus (S2ORC) [5,18] version 20200705v1 as a dataset of scientific papers. S2ORC is used for natural language processing and text mining research. The dataset contains 136M paper data, of which 12M are full-text papers, covering various fields of research. In this study, we employ abstracts of papers in the fields of medicine and computer science from the data set.

## 3.2 Quality Classification of Papers

In order to predict the quality of papers, we introduce the Average Journal Impact Factor Percentile (Average JIF Percentile) provided by Journal Citation

Reports [1] as the metric of article quality. JIF Percentile is a metric that indicates the top percentage of journals in a given field in terms of impact factor in that field. JIF Percentile is obtained by the following formula [3]:

$$\frac{N - R + 0.5}{N}, \tag{1}$$

where $N$ is the number of journals in the category and $R$ is the descending rank. Average JIF Percentile is the average of the JIF Percentile values of the target fields, which takes into account the fact that the target fields cover multiple fields. In this study, we consider predicting the quality of papers as a classification problem. Let $J_U$ be the set of journals whose Average JIF Percentile is 0.8 or higher, and $J_L$ denote the set of journals whose Average JIF Percentile is 0.2 or lower. In the classification problem, given an abstract of a paper, we classify whether the paper is included in $J_U$ or $J_L$. The reader might think that if the journals in a particular field are biased toward either of $J_U$ and $J_L$, then this classification problem would lead to a different classification problem of whether a paper is in a particular field or not. Tables 2 and 3 are the 10 journals with the most papers in $J_U$ and $J_L$ for medicine and computer science, respectively. According to the tables, there is no significant unbalance in the fields of papers included in $J_U$ and $J_L$, respectively. This means that this classification problem cannot be correctly classified only by finding papers in a specific field.

**Table 2.** Journals with the most papers for medicine

| (a) 10 journals with the most papers in $J_U$ | | |
|---|---|---|
| Journal | #papers | % |
| Nature Communications | 19744 | 6.67 |
| Nanoscale | 17215 | 5.82 |
| Nutrients | 9582 | 3.24 |
| JAMA Internal Medicine | 9535 | 3.22 |
| JAMA Pediatrics | 7813 | 2.64 |
| Small | 7377 | 2.49 |
| eLife | 7188 | 2.43 |
| PLoS Genetics | 6088 | 2.06 |
| PLoS Neglected Tropical Diseases | 6028 | 2.04 |
| PLoS Pathogens | 5871 | 1.98 |
| (b) 10 journals with the most papers in $J_L$ | | |
| Journal | #papers | % |
| European Journal of Hospital Pharmacy-Science and Practice | 3687 | 3.64 |
| Vascular and Endovascular Surgery | 3460 | 3.41 |
| Natural Product Communications | 3162 | 3.12 |
| Therapeutic Innovation & Regulatory Science | 2758 | 2.72 |
| Indian Journal of Psychiatry | 2101 | 2.07 |
| Psychiatria Danubina | 1842 | 1.82 |
| Journal of Traditional Chinese Medicine | 1800 | 1.77 |
| Indian Journal of Surgery | 1699 | 1.68 |
| Australasian Psychiatry | 1660 | 1.64 |
| Oncology Research and Treatment | 1616 | 1.59 |

**Table 3.** Journals with the most papers for computer science

| (a) 10 journals with the most papers in $J_U$ | | |
|---|---|---|
| Journal | #papers | % |
| PLoS Computational Biology | 4279 | 9.23 |
| IEEE Transactions on Industrial Informatics | 3113 | 6.71 |
| IEEE Transactions on Smart Grid | 3038 | 6.55 |
| IEEE Transactions on Information Forensics and Security | 2183 | 4.71 |
| IEEE Transactions on Neural Networks and Learning Systems | 2121 | 4.57 |
| IEEE Transactions on Cybernetics | 1994 | 4.30 |
| IEEE Internet of Things Journal | 1990 | 4.29 |
| IEEE Robotics and Automation Letters | 1915 | 4.13 |
| IEEE Transactions on Robotics | 1762 | 3.80 |
| IEEE Wireless Communications Letters | 1730 | 3.73 |
| (b) 10 journals with the most papers in $J_L$ | | |
| Journal | #papers | % |
| International Journal of Distributed Sensor Networks | 3461 | 15.92 |
| Security and Communication Networks | 1997 | 9.19 |
| Journal of Internet Technology | 1612 | 7.42 |
| Turkish Journal of Electrical Engineering and Computer Sciences | 1393 | 6.41 |
| International Journal on Artificial Intelligence Tools | 1007 | 4.63 |
| Journal of Semiconductor Technology and Science | 797 | 3.67 |
| Electronics and Communications in Japan | 754 | 3.47 |
| Journal of Medical and Biological Engineering | 724 | 3.33 |
| International Journal on Software Tools for Technology Transfer | 720 | 3.31 |
| Cognitive Processing | 628 | 2.89 |

### 3.3 BERT-Based Model of Quality Prediction of Scientific Papers

The proposed BERT-based model of quality prediction of scientific papers is the structure shown in Fig. 1. The classifier has an input that corresponds to the first token in the output of the last transformer encoder block and outputs the classification result. The model including the classifier is trained in the fine-tuning phase to output 1 if the input abstract is included in $J_U$ and 0 if it is included in $J_L$. The classifier uses a fully connected layer with one output channel and a sigmoid function as the activation function. We note that since the problem targeted by the proposed model is to classify peer-reviewed papers, this is a more difficult problem than the classification problem that predicts acceptance and non-acceptance for publishing [10,24].

## 4 Experimental Results

In this section, we show the methodology for training models for predicting paper quality as the target task, and evaluate the resulting models. In this study, we train models to predict the quality from abstracts for two research fields, medicine and computer science. In the proposed approach, three types of models have been employed as the BERT-models trained in the pre-training phase. Two of them are pre-trained models from the TensorFlow Hub [6], one trained on the Wikipedia and BookCoups datasets, and the other trained on the MEDLINE/PubMed datasets. Please refer [6] for the already pre-trained models on the Wikipedia and BookCoups datasets and the MEDLINE/PubMed datasets. Since the pre-trained model sizes available in the TensorFlow Hub vary by dataset, we experiment with the BERT-tiny, BERT-mini, BERT-small, and BERT-base models for the Wikipedia and BookCoups datasets, and the BERT-base model for the MEDLINE/PubMed datasets. The remaining one is a model that we trained by ourselves using the abstracts of papers in S2ORC [5]. On the other hand, in the fine-tuning phase, we fine-tune the models on abstracts of papers in S2ORC. In the following, we show the details of the training in the pre-training phase and the fine-tuning phase.

## 4.1   Training in the Pre-training Phase on Abstracts from S2ORC

Here, we show the training of the BERT models on all abstracts in the S2ORC dataset trained from scratch. The BERT-based models were trained using MLM and NSP tasks shown in Sect. 2. Each model was trained for 3,000,000 steps, with a batch size of 8, and a maximum input size 512. The training is optimized by Adam with learning rate of 0.0001, $\beta_1 = 0.9$, $\beta_2 = 0.999$, $L_2$ weight decay of 0.01, learning rate warmup over the first 10,000 steps, and linear decay of the learning rate. We use GELU [15] as the activation function and the sum of the likelihood of MLM and NSP as the training loss.

## 4.2   Training in the Fine-Tuning Phase

The training in the fine-tuning phase was performed using each model trained in the pre-training phase as initial values of weights. In the experiment, models were trained on S2ORC dataset from two fields, medicine and computer science, respectively. The number of papers in each field of training data and test data is shown in Table 4. Each model was trained for 50 epochs, with a batch size of 64, and a maximum input size 512. The training is optimized by AdamW with a learning rate of 0.00003, $L_2$ weight decay of 0.01, learning rate warm-up over the first 10,000 steps, and linear decay of the learning rate. We use GELU as the activation function and the binary cross-entropy loss as the training loss.

**Table 4.** The number of abstracts from S2ORC dataset in the fine-tuning phase

|  | Medicine | | Computer science | |
|---|---|---|---|---|
|  | $J_U$ | $J_L$ | $J_U$ | $J_L$ |
| Training data | 294,840 | 100,416 | 47,381 | 21,737 |
| Test data | 1,000 | 1,000 | 1,000 | 1,000 |

## 4.3   The Test Accuracy of Prediction of the Trained Model

Table 5 shows the test accuracy of prediction of the trained models for each research field. The table shows that for both fields, the larger models are more accurate, and the model pre-trained on MEDLINE/PubMed dataset is the most accurate. The reason for the lower accuracy when using the S2ORC dataset for pre-training despite having the same scholarly articles as the MED-LINE/PubMed dataset is due to the smaller size of the dataset compared to the other two datasets. As a result of training the model, we achieved a test accuracy of 95.1% in the medical field and 89.6% in the computer science field. As shown in Tables 2 and 3, since there is little unevenness in fields between $J_U$ and $J_L$ journals, this result implies that the model does not classify papers by finding specific research fields from their abstracts, but can perform the classification in terms of abstract presentation.

**Table 5.** The test accuracy of prediction

| Pre-training dataset | Model | Medicine | Computer science |
|---|---|---|---|
| Wikipedia and BookCorpus | BERT-tiny | 0.9014 | 0.8280 |
| | BERT-mini | 0.9254 | 0.8380 |
| | BERT-small | 0.9265 | 0.8519 |
| | BERT-medium | 0.9290 | 0.8610 |
| | BERT-base | 0.9304 | 0.8769 |
| MEDLINE/PubMed | BERT-base | **0.9509** | **0.8955** |
| S2ORC | BERT-tiny | 0.8805 | 0.8285 |
| | BERT-mini | 0.9114 | 0.8365 |
| | BERT-small | 0.9170 | 0.8455 |
| | BERT-medium | 0.9260 | 0.8530 |
| | BERT-base | 0.9370 | 0.8625 |

## 4.4   Detailed Analysis of the Prediction

To clarify the classification details of the proposed model, we performed the classification on subsets of the sentences in the abstract. Specifically, Tables 6 and 7 show the results of the classification performed on the $i$-th to $j$-th sentences for two abstracts sampled from $J_U$ and $J_L$, respectively. We note that these two abstracts are simply sampled from each dataset and are not meant to judge their quality of them. The classification results are the top right values of the table, 0.9736 and 0.0429, respectively, indicating that the model correctly classifies each. Also, the values of the diagonal elements indicate the output values of each sentence evaluated on itself. From the table, it appears that the proposed model outputs the final result by considering multiple sentences, although both abstracts contain sentences with large and small values. Focusing on the output values of single sentences, there are sentences with high or low values, but the final estimated results seem to be evaluated by considering multiple sentences. In addition, the proposed model may be used as a supporting tool when writing papers, since the output as shown in Tables 6 and 7 provides at-a-glance information on good and bad descriptions in abstracts.

**Table 6.** Detailed analysis for an abstract in $J_U$ sampled from computer science papers in S2ORC [18]

(a) abstract in $J_U$

1. Deeper neural networks are more difficult to train.
2. We present a residual learning framework to ease the training of networks that are substantially deeper than those used previously.
3. We explicitly reformulate the layers as learning residual functions with reference to the layer inputs, instead of learning unreferenced functions.
4. We provide comprehensive empirical evidence showing that these residual networks are easier to optimize, and can gain accuracy from considerably increased depth.
5. On the ImageNet dataset we evaluate residual nets with a depth of up to 152 layers-8x deeper than VGG nets but still having lower complexity.
6. An ensemble of these residual nets achieves 3.57% error on the ImageNet test set.
7. This result won the 1st place on the ILSVRC 2015 classification task.
8. We also present analysis on CIFAR-10 with 100 and 1000 layers.
9. The depth of representations is of central importance for many visual recognition tasks.
10. Solely due to our extremely deep representations, we obtain a 28% relative improvement on the COCO object detection dataset.
11. Deep residual nets are foundations of our submissions to ILSVRC & COCO 2015 competitions, where we also won the 1st places on the tasks of ImageNet detection, ImageNet localization, COCO detection, and COCO segmentation.

(b) Output values of the model for the $i$-th to $j$-th sentences

| $i$ \ $j$ | 1 | 2 | 3 | 4 | 5 | 6 | 7 | 8 | 9 | 10 | 11 |
|---|---|---|---|---|---|---|---|---|---|---|---|
| 1 | 0.9494 | 0.9146 | 0.9662 | 0.9832 | 0.9221 | 0.9062 | 0.8776 | 0.9218 | 0.9732 | 0.9837 | 0.9736 |
| 2 | | 0.9128 | 0.9336 | 0.9424 | 0.9250 | 0.9306 | 0.9035 | 0.9492 | 0.9766 | 0.9873 | 0.9740 |
| 3 | | | 0.9324 | 0.9837 | 0.9020 | 0.8694 | 0.8283 | 0.8847 | 0.9532 | 0.9764 | 0.9623 |
| 4 | | | | 0.9762 | 0.6459 | 0.5470 | 0.4694 | 0.6045 | 0.7709 | 0.8799 | 0.8965 |
| 5 | | | | | 0.3641 | 0.2645 | 0.1109 | 0.1645 | 0.2636 | 0.6235 | 0.8059 |
| 6 | | | | | | 0.3372 | 0.1311 | 0.2202 | 0.3566 | 0.6363 | 0.7867 |
| 7 | | | | | | | 0.3083 | 0.3480 | 0.3527 | 0.8034 | 0.8298 |
| 8 | | | | | | | | 0.1070 | 0.4168 | 0.8924 | 0.7935 |
| 9 | | | | | | | | | 0.9597 | 0.9852 | 0.8694 |
| 10 | | | | | | | | | | 0.9813 | 0.8248 |
| 11 | | | | | | | | | | | 0.9170 |

**Table 7.** Detailed analysis for an abstract in $J_L$ sampled from computer science papers in S2ORC [18]

(a) abstract in $J_L$

1. GPUs are one of the most prevalent platforms for accelerating general-purpose workloads due to their intuitive programming model, computing capacity, and cost-effectiveness.
2. GPUs rely on massive multi-threading and fast context switching to overlap computations with memory operations.
3. Among the diverse GPU workloads, there exists a class of kernels that fail to maintain a sufficient number of active warps to hide the latency of memory operations, and thus suffer from frequent stalling.
4. We observe that these kernels will benefit from increased levels of Instruction-Level Parallelism and we propose a novel architecture with lightweight Out-Of-Order execution capability.
5. To minimize hardware overheads, we carefully design our extension to highly re-use the existing micro-architectural structures.
6. We show that the proposed architecture outperforms traditional platforms by 15 to 46 percent on average for low occupancy kernels, with an area overhead of 0.74 to 3.94 percent.
7. Finally, we prove the potential of our proposal as a GPU u-arch alternative, by providing a 5 percent speedup over a wide collection of 63 general-purpose kernels with as little as 0.74 percent area overhead.

(b) Output values of the model for the $i$-th to $j$-th sentences

| | $j$ | | | | | | |
|---|---|---|---|---|---|---|---|
| $i$ | 1 | 2 | 3 | 4 | 5 | 6 | 7 |
| 1 | 0.0209 | 0.0159 | 0.0082 | 0.0054 | 0.0044 | 0.0116 | 0.0429 |
| 2 | | 0.0700 | 0.1192 | 0.0123 | 0.0064 | 0.0110 | 0.0497 |
| 3 | | | 0.0188 | 0.0084 | 0.0055 | 0.0115 | 0.0110 |
| 4 | | | | 0.9172 | 0.4710 | 0.3974 | 0.3587 |
| 5 | | | | | 0.2333 | 0.4810 | 0.4205 |
| 6 | | | | | | 0.7966 | 0.4325 |
| 7 | | | | | | | 0.4937 |

## 5 Conclusions

In this paper, we proposed a method for predicting the quality of scholarly papers using machine learning. We predict the quality of papers as a classification problem for the abstracts of papers whether the paper is included in superior journals or less superior journals. We used BERT-based models and trained them on several datasets. As a result of our experiment, we showed that different datasets of pre-training of the proposed BERT-based model affect classification accuracy. Also, the results of training the models showed that the models could classify whether the input abstracts are from superior or less superior journals with a test accuracy of 95.1% and 89.6% in the field of medicine and computer science, respectively. Furthermore, by evaluating the sentence combinations in the abstracts, we clarified the details of the classification results and visualized them.

# References

1. Journal Impact Factor: Journal Citation Reports Science Edition (Clarivate Analytics 2021). https://jcr.clarivate.com/
2. Google Scholar. https://scholar.google.co.jp/
3. Journal Impact Factor Percentile. https://help.incites.clarivate.com/incitesLive JCR/glossaryAZgroup/g8/9586-TRS.html
4. PubMed. https://pubmed.ncbi.nlm.nih.gov/
5. S2ORC. https://github.com/allenai/s2orc
6. TensorFlow Hub. https://tfhub.dev/
7. Web of Science. https://clarivate.jp/training/web-of-science/
8. Bai, X., Liu, H., Zhang, F., Ning, Z., Kong, X., Lee, I., Xia, F.: An overview on evaluating and predicting scholarly article impact. Information **8**(3), 73 (2017). https://doi.org/10.3390/info8030073
9. Bai, X., Zhang, F., Lee, I.: Predicting the citations of scholarly paper. J. Inform. **13**(1), 407–418 (2019). https://doi.org/10.1016/j.joi.2019.01.010
10. Maillette de Buy Wenniger, G., van Dongen, T., Aedmaa, E., Kruitbosch, H.T., Valentijn, E.A., Schomaker, L.: Structure-tags improve text classification for scholarly document quality prediction. In: Proceedings of the First Workshop on Scholarly Document Processing, pp. 158–167 (2020). https://doi.org/10.18653/v1/2020.sdp-1.18, https://aclanthology.org/2020.sdp-1.18
11. Castillo, C., Donato, D., Gionis, A.: Estimating number of citations using author reputation. In: Proceeding of the 14th International Conference on String Processing and Information Retrieval, pp. 107–117 (2007)
12. Davletov, F., Aydin, A.S., Cakmak, A.: High impact academic paper prediction using temporal and topological features. In: Proceedings of the 23rd ACM International Conference on Information and Knowledge Management, pp. 491–498 (2014)
13. Devlin, J., Chang, M.W., Lee, K., Toutanova, K.: BERT: pre-training of deep bidirectional transformers for language understanding. In: Proceedings of the 2019 Conference of the North American Chapter of the Association for Computational Linguistics: Human Language Technologies, vol. 1 (Long and Short Papers), pp. 4171–4186 (2019). https://doi.org/10.18653/v1/N19-1423
14. van Dongen, T., Maillette de Buy Wenniger, G., Schomaker, L.: SChuBERT: scholarly document chunks with BERT-encoding boost citation count prediction. In: Proceedings of the First Workshop on Scholarly Document Processing. Association for Computational Linguistics (2020). https://doi.org/10.18653/v1/2020.sdp-1.17
15. Hendrycks, D., Gimpel, K.: Gaussian error linear units (GELUs) (2020)
16. Hou, J., Pan, H., Guo, T., Lee, I., Kong, X., Xia, F.: Prediction methods and applications in the science of science: a survey. Comput. Sci. Rev. **34**, 100197 (2019). https://doi.org/10.1016/j.cosrev.2019.100197
17. Livne, A., Adar, E., Teevan, J., Dumais, S.: Predicting citation counts using text and graph mining. In: iConference 2013, Workshop on Computational Scientometrics: Theory and Application, February 2013
18. Lo, K., Wang, L.L., Neumann, M., Kinney, R., Weld, D.: S2ORC: the semantic scholar open research corpus. In: Proceedings of the 58th Annual Meeting of the Association for Computational Linguistics, pp. 4969–4983. Association for Computational Linguistics (2020). https://doi.org/10.18653/v1/2020.acl-main.447
19. Ma, A., Liu, Y., Xu, X., Dong, T.: A deep-learning based citation count prediction model with paper metadata semantic features. Scientometrics **126**(8), 6803–6823 (2021). https://doi.org/10.1007/s11192-021-04033-7

20. Otter, D.W., Medina, J.R., Kalita, J.K.: A survey of the usages of deep learning for natural language processing. IEEE Trans. Neural Netw. Learn. Syst. **32**(2), 604–624 (2021). https://doi.org/10.1109/TNNLS.2020.2979670

21. Shen, A., Salehi, B., Qi, J., Baldwin, T.: A multimodal approach to assessing document quality. J. Artif. Intell. Res. **68**, 607–632 (2020). https://doi.org/10.1613/jair.1.11647

22. Vaswani, A., et al.: Attention is all you need. In: Advances in Neural Information Processing Systems, vol. 30 (2017)

23. Wolf, T., et al.: Transformers: state-of-the-art natural language processing. In: Proceedings of the 2020 Conference on Empirical Methods in Natural Language Processing: System Demonstrations, pp. 38–45 (2020)

24. Yang, P., Sun, X., Li, W., Ma, S.: Automatic academic paper rating based on modularized hierarchical convolutional neural network. In: Proceedings of the 56th Annual Meeting of the Association for Computational Linguistics, vol. 2: Short Papers, pp. 496–502 (2018). https://doi.org/10.18653/v1/P18-2079

25. Zhao, Q., Feng, X.: Utilizing citation network structure to predict paper citation counts: a deep learning approach. J. Inform. **16**(1), 101235 (2022). https://doi.org/10.1016/j.joi.2021.101235

# Effective ML-Block and Weighted IoU Loss for Object Detection

Zhenxin Yuan[1], Xin Xiao[1], Shuai Zhao[2], Linlin Jiang[1], and Zhongtao Li[1(✉)]

[1] School of Information Science and Engineering,
University of Jinan, Jinan 250022, China
`ise_lizt@ujn.edu.cn`
[2] Jinan Housing and Urban-Rural Development Bureau, Jinan, China

**Abstract.** In computer vision tasks, better performance of the transformer model is due to self-attention mechanism and learning of global information. However, it also largely increases parameters and calculations. In this paper, we propose the following problems. (1) How to build a lighter module that integrates CNN and Transformer? We propose the ML-block module in this paper. Especially, for one thing, reducing the number of channels after the convolution module; for another, spatial attention is introduced after the ML-block input layer to reduce the loss caused by information fusion. (2) Small object detection problem in one-stage object detector. We propose weighted IoU loss in this paper. According to the object size, it adaptively weighs the IoU loss to improve the performance of the detector. We adopt YOLOX-s as the baseline through sufficient experiments on PASCAL VOC data sets and COCOmini data sets to demonstrate the effectiveness of our methods, and AP increases by 1.1% and 3.3%.

**Keywords:** Object detection · ML-block · Transformer · Weighted IoU loss

## 1 Introduction

Localization is one of the tasks for object detection, and localization accuracy has a great challenge. It is closely related to the prediction of the anchor box. The definition of loss function directly affects the effect of model parameter training.

Generally speaking, there are mainly methods to solve the problem of predicting box localization. One is to enhance feature fusion and improve the feature extraction ability of neural networks. For example, the feature pyramid [9,12] integrates the feature information of different layers and solves the multi-scale feature problem. Second, extract detailed feature information by increasing the resolution of the image. In addition, the convolutional neural network is limited by the size of the convolution kernel and often cannot achieve the learning of global information. Transformer adopts multi-head attention to capture global contextual information to extract more powerful features. Therefore, in the feature fusion layer, the fusion of the underlying visual information learned by CNN

E. Pimenidis et al. (Eds.): ICANN 2022, LNCS 13532, pp. 224–235, 2022.
https://doi.org/10.1007/978-3-031-15937-4_19

and the feature between the visual elements and objects learned by Transformer will improve the performance of the detector.

In one-stage detection algorithm, the localization of small objects is a great challenge. The MS COCO [11] dataset divides the object size into three categories, with 32 and 96 as the boundaries, namely small, medium and large objects. Those less than 32 are small objects, those greater than 32 and less than 96 are medium objects, and the others are large objects. The detection accuracy of small objects affects the effect of the entire detector. Experimental results show that the detection accuracy of small objects is often less than 1/2 of large objects. In this paper, we propose an exponential function weighted method adaptive to different object scales. From the perspective of the loss function, we increase penalties for small objects under the condition without increasing the number of additional parameters. Determine whether it is a small object according to the object scale and dynamically increase the penalty value for different scales of objects.

The contribution of work is summarized as follows:

1. Weighted IoU loss. Adaptively penalize small objects according to the size of the object box.
2. ML-block. Enhanced feature map learning contextual information module in feature fusion layer.
3. The experimental results on PASCAL VOC and COCO datasets prove that the proposed method can achieve better performance.

## 2    Related Work

### 2.1    Box Regression Loss

In the field of object detection, Intersection over Union was widely used to evaluate the loss between predict box and the ground truth box. UnitBox [24] introduced Intersection over Union (IoU) as the metric of predict box and the ground truth box, and it divided predict box into positive samples and negative samples. Based on IoU, Generalized Intersection over Union [19] considered the overlap area and the non-overlapping area, which solved the problem of no overlap between predict box and the ground truth box. Due to the contain phenomenon between predict box and the ground truth box, Distance-IoU [26] considered the distance of the center point. Complete-IoU [26] considered not only the overlap area and the distance of the center point but also the aspect ratio of them.

### 2.2    One-Stage Object Detectors

One-stage detector [1,3,13,15–17] was more efficient than two-stage detector [6,18]. However, class imbalance and small objects detection were important factors affecting accuracy. The proposal of the feature pyramid [4,9,12] effectively strengthened feature fusion between various layers, and it has improved detection accuracy to a certain extent. Focal Loss [10] reduced the proportion of easy negative examples in training and improved the learning of hard examples. Hence, it solved class imbalance and improved the accuracy of the one-stage detector. The resolution of the input sample was reduced with a deeper convolutional layer.

For one thing, multi-scale [2] training allowed the model to adapt to different input sizes and better learn the characteristics of different objects. For another, enhanced feature extraction and contextual information can also improve the detection ability of small objects [8,21,22,25]. CoT block [7] was a transformer-style architecture. It strengthened the capacity of visual representation by capturing the static context among neighbor keys. In addition, the learning of global information also contributed to the robustness of small object detection. However, the above methods of enhanced feature fusion and contextual information increased model parameters and calculations. On the premise of enhancing feature fusion and contextual information, reducing the increase of model parameters and calculations is very meaningful.

## 3   Approach

### 3.1   Weighted IoU Loss

When testing the trained model, it is often found that average precision(AP) of small objects is less than $1/2$ of medium and large objects, so small objects are also an important factor affecting the accuracy of AP. Improving contextual awareness of small objects increases the complexity of the model and the number of parameters and calculations. From the whole training of the model, it is a process of constantly solving the optimal value, and the loss function greatly affects the direction of model learning.

From this point of view, based on YOLOX [3], an adaptive weighted process is added to the calculation of box regression; the design of the loss function tilts to the direction with the lowest loss of small objects and increases the adaptability of the whole network structure for small objects, so as to improve the learning ability of the model for small objects.

$$L_{IoU} = \sum 1 - IoU \tag{1}$$

$$L_{IoU(YOLOX)} = \sum 1 - IoU^2 \tag{2}$$

$$L_{WIoU} = \sum \Phi(z)\left(1 - IoU^2\right) \tag{3}$$

$$\Phi(z) = 1 + e^{\alpha\sqrt{z}} \tag{4}$$

Calculating IoU in the baseline (YOLOX) is Eq. 2, which reduces IoU by squaring and increases the value of Box loss to achieve better learning results for the model. In the process of model training, multi-scale training is adopted

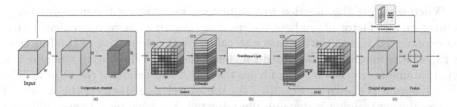

**Fig. 1.** ML-block. (a) Compression channel. Reduce the number of channels by $1 \times 1$ convolution. (b) Unfold: Cut the feature map into Patch. Fold: Inverse operation of unfold. Restore the extracted sliding local area block into batch tensor form. TransformerLight: Heads in multi-head attention to $1/2$ and neurons of the multilayer perceptron to $2/3$ compared with the MobileViT block. (c) Channel alignment: The channel of the restored feature map is the same as the input channel. Fusion: Adopt add operation replace concatenate operation. Spatial Attention Module: Use spatial attention to weight the input to reduce information loss of direct addition.

to change the size of the object input. It improves the learning of object feature information and enhances model robustness for different sizes of objects. However, it is necessary to make the model focus more on the small object features that are hard to learn when calculating the loss. And how to better define the loss of detection result and better play the effect of multi-scale training is important. In response to this problem, we propose to weight the loss according to the size of object, aiming to improve the model's perception of small objects and parameter learning capabilities, as shown in Eq. 3.

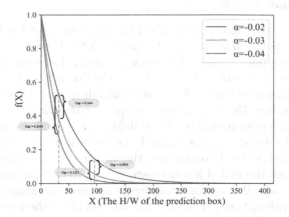

**Fig. 2.** The image of the function $f(x) = e^{\alpha X}$. When $\alpha$ takes different values, it corresponds to different mapping values, indicating the strength of the weighting of the small object.

When selecting the function to weight loss, we consider the mapping range of function and factor of gradient backpropagation. It is more convenient to use the exponential function with base e to calculate the derivative of the function. In Eq. 4, $\Phi$ represents the weighted IoU loss function (WIoU loss), where $\alpha$ is a hyperparameter, $z = w \times h$ (w and h are the width and height of the object). The effect diagram is shown in Fig. 3(d). As the object size changes, the weight of the loss during training is dynamically adjusted. We have tested three different hyperparameters $\alpha$ respectively, and the results are shown in Table 1. According to the standard of small objects, we select the exponential function as the weighted IoU loss function. By scaling the exponential function, the weighted value is within 0–1, and the three detection scales (small, medium and large) can be distinguished. The degree of distinction is shown in Fig. 2.

**Table 1.** The effectiveness of the model on VOC2007 test set when the hyperparameter $\alpha$ takes different values.

| Baseline | Param ($\alpha$) | AP (%) |
|---|---|---|
| YOLOX-s | - | 62.2 |
| | [0.3 0.2 0.1] | 62.4 (+**0.2**) |
| | −0.04 | 62.5 (+**0.3**) |
| | −0.03 | 62.6 (+**0.4**) |
| | −0.02 | 62.8 (+**0.6**) |

## 3.2 MobileLight Block

The feature extraction ability of the model is important for the final detection task. In the feature fusion layer of the baseline, PANet is used to fuse features of different scales in a bottom-up and top-down manner. However, due to convolution's local feature extraction characteristics, the far-away information is often ignored, which makes the feature fusion layer unable to exert its maximum effect.

Here we introduce the transformer, adopt global information to fill in the limitations of the convolutional receptive field, and expand the network's focus area. Because the backbone has learned the feature information, the feature fusion layer is mainly used to enhance the interaction of global information. We aim to enhance the global feature learning and reduce the module's weight. However, the introduction of the transformer has brought about an increase in parameters and calculations. Although the MobileViT method greatly decreases the consumption of Transformer parameters and calculations, it still puts a lot of pressure on the model. MobileViT adopts properties similar to convolution without considering position coding. We analyze the structure of MobileViT block, operations similar to convolution must be performed first when entering the Transformer structure, operations like unfolding, matrix multiplication, and folding. We found a phenomenon that the number of channels of the input feature map affects the complexity of mobileViT. Therefore, we compress the channels to

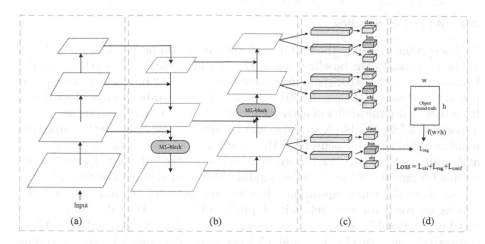

**Fig. 3.** Network structure. We add ML-block to two high-resolution branches to enhance extraction of global contextual information. (a) Backbone. (b) Feature Pyramid Networks. (c) Detection head. (d) Loss function.

1/2 before they enter. After block calculation is completed, the input dimension is restored by convolution to ensure the alignment of the channels calculated later. In the Transformer module, heads in multi-head attention to 1/2 and neurons of the multilayer perceptron to 2/3 compared with the MobileViT block. Reduce the weight of ML-block through the above operations. In ML-block, if the input is directly added to the result of the Transformer operation, it will cause a certain loss of information. To solve this problem, we add spatial attention to the input branch to weigh the spatial information. The method achieves the purpose of reducing information loss. The network structure is shown in Fig. 3.

We also found that the concatenate operation will increase the number of channels when combining convolution and transformer in MobileViT block. Generally, it is necessary to perform $1 \times 1$ convolution after the concatenate operation to enhance the fusion. Therefore, we use add operation instead of the concatenate operation. In the case of the same number of channels, a convolution kernel is shared, and the calculation amount of add is 1/2 of concatenation, thereby reducing the cost calculation of the model. The ML-block module is shown in Fig. 1.

## 4   Experiments

### 4.1   Experimental Setup

We train 300 epochs on PASCAL VOC and COCOmini data sets, use the VOC2007 test set and COCO val-2017 as verification sets. We take AP (averaged AP at IoUs from 0.5 to 0.95 with an interval of 0.05) and $AP_{50}$ (AP at IoU threshold 0.5) as our evaluation indicators. We adopt the SGD training method, and the initial learning rate is 0.01.

## 4.2 Ablation Studies

In this section, we study the overall performance of adding WIoU and ML-block in the baseline. In the baseline, IoU is the box loss calculation method. On the basis of unchanging other structures in the baseline, a dynamic adaptive weighted penalty is added to IOUloss. In this work, we add two ML-blocks to feature fusion layer to enhance the ability of extracting contextual information. Considering the impact of adding ML-block on the model parameters, we respectively reduce the number of hidden layer neurons in the multilayer perceptron of the transformer and heads in the multi-head attention. To reduce the calculation amount and parameter amount of the ML-block module, the input channel is reduced to 1/2.

To show the superimposition effect of our methods, we have trained 300 epochs on cocomini data sets with input resolution of $416 \times 416$ and verified in COCO val-2017. As shown in Table 4, after adding WIoU, AP and AP50, respectively, increased by 0.4% and 0.5% compared with baseline. We are adding two ML-block modules alone to feature fusion layer, AP and $AP_{50}$, respectively, increased by 0.9% and 0.8% compared with baseline. When stacking WIoU and ML-block, AP and $AP_{50}$ increase significantly, respectively, increase by 1.2% and 1.3% compared with baseline. Therefore, the effectiveness of our proposed methods is verified (Table 2).

**Table 2.** The effectiveness of AP and $AP_{50}$ using the WIoU and ML-block respectively on COCO val-2017. The input resolution is $416 \times 416$.

| Baseline | WIoU | ML-block | AP (%) | $AP_{50}$ |
|----------|------|----------|--------|-----------|
| YOLOX-s  |      |          | 30.1   | 46.6      |
|          | ✓    |          | 30.5   | 47.1      |
|          |      | ✓        | 31.0   | 47.4      |
|          | ✓    | ✓        | **31.3** | **47.9** |

## 4.3 Evaluation on PASCAL VOC

In order to demonstrate the effectiveness of WIoU, we select three hyperparameters respectively to test. According to the classification criteria of small, medium, and large objects in the coco data sets, we set the hyperparameter $\alpha$. We carry out a fixed weighting method for three different types of objects, small, medium, and large objects set to 0.3, 0.2 and 0.1, respectively. By relatively increasing the detection loss of small objects, the learning ability of the entire network structure for small objects is improved. The training results of PASCAL VOC2007 and PASCAL VOC2012 data sets show that compared with the baseline, the model AP increases by 0.2%, demonstrating the effectiveness of the loss penalty for small objects.

Therefore, we adopt the scaled exponential function to weight and penalize small objects. Three $\alpha$ function images are shown in Fig. 2. As seen from the

**Table 3.** The effectiveness of different object detectors on VOC2007 test set after using WIoU.

| Method | Method | AP (%) |
|---|---|---|
| YOLOv4-tiny [1] | - | 52.6 |
| | WIoU | 53.9(+1.3) |
| YOLOv5-s [5] | - | 58.5 |
| | WIoU | 58.8(+0.3) |
| YOLOX-s [3] | - | 62.2 |
| | WIoU | 62.8(+0.6) |

image, when $\alpha = -0.02$, the function corresponding to the three object scales has a larger distinguishment. When X equals to 32, the difference with other values of $\alpha$ is 0.1444 and 0.2493 respectively. When X equals to 96, the difference with other values of $\alpha$ is 0.0905 and 0.1251. As $\alpha$ increases, the segmentation of small, medium, and large objects becomes more and more obvious. We attempt three parameters on the PASCAL VOC data sets, and the training results are shown in Table 1. When $\alpha$ equals to $-0.02$, the performance for AP is largely improved by 0.6%. At the same time, as $\alpha$ increases, the AP increase trend becomes more and more obvious. In order to demonstrate the effectiveness of our method, we conduct experiments on different networks. As shown in Table 3, the AP increases by 1.3% on the YOLOv4-tiny model. The AP increases by 0.3% on the YOLOv5s model. On the baseline [3], the AP increases by 0.6%. These experimental results demonstrate the effectiveness of WIoU. Therefore, by means of adaptive weighted, weighting the IoU loss according to the size of different detection objects is good for enhancing the sensitivity of parameters to small objects and promoting the learning of the entire network parameters, thereby improving the overall detection performance of the network.

**Table 4.** Comparison of the accuracy and the speed of different modules at the feature fusion layer on VOC2007 test set.

| Method | Size | FPS (1080Ti) | AP (%) | Parameters (M) | GFLOPs | Latency (ms) |
|---|---|---|---|---|---|---|
| - | 416 | **66.7** | 62.8 | 8.95 | 11.28 | 15.00 |
| CBAM [23] | 416 | 63.4 | 62.9(+0.1) | 9.02(+0.07) | 11.28 | 15.76 |
| CoT [7] | 416 | 64.5 | 63.1(+0.3) | 11.24(+2.29) | 13.34 | 15.49 |
| MobileViT [14] | 416 | 62.9 | 63.5(+0.7) | 12.48(+3.53) | 15.58 | 15.90 |
| MobileViT C/2 | 416 | 65.6 | 63.3(+0.5) | 11.66(+2.71) | 14.94 | 15.23 |
| MobileViT H/2 | 416 | 64.4 | 63.3(+0.5) | 10.20(+1.25) | 12.96 | 15.52 |
| ML-block | 416 | 63.6 | **63.5(+0.7)** | 10.41(+1.39) | 13.25 | 15.61 |

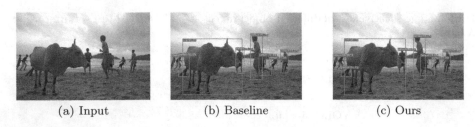

(a) Input                (b) Baseline                (c) Ours

**Fig. 4.** Detection example using WIoU and ML-block. (a) Input. (b) YOLOX-s. (c) YOLOX-s with WIoU and ML-block.

To demonstrate the effectiveness of ML-block compared to other modules, after adding WIoU loss, we respectively compared the effectiveness of CBAM, CoT block, and MobileViT in extracting contextual information at the feature fusion layer. As shown in Table 4, the amount of parameters and calculations vastly increase under the condition of adding new modules. Among them, due to the characteristics of the Transformer, AP of the MobileViT module has the most significant improvement, and the amount of parameters and calculations have also vastly increased. Therefore, we reduce the number of feature channels of the input MobileViT block to $1/2$, heads in multi-head attention to $1/2$, and neurons of the multilayer perceptron to $1/2$ compared with the original MobileViT block. At the same time, AP decreases by 0.2%, and the amount of parameters has decreased by 0.88M. When we replace concatenate operation with add operation, the number of neurons in the multilayer perceptron reduces to $2/3$ of the original. Compared with the MobileViT block, AP decreases by 0.2%, and parameters are also decreased by 2.28M. When adding spatial attention to the input, AP of the ML-block reaches the level of MobileViT, and the parameter quantity is decreased by 2.07M. The latency and GFLOPs are lower than those of MobileViT. So we found that when the two feature tensors are added, spatial attention is used to enhance adequate spatial information, which is helpful for the effective fusion of features and the reduction of information loss. Therefore, compared with the baseline, AP of the ML-block is increased by 0.7%, achieving a balance between accuracy and parameters.

## 4.4   Evaluation on COCOmini

To demonstrate the method's effectiveness on more categories of data sets, we involve COCOmini [20] in comparative analysis. COCOmini is a subset of COCO train2017, which contains 25K images. We train on COCOmini and use COCO val-2017 (including 5K images) to demonstrate the generalization ability of our method. Based on the baseline training strategy. Here, we have conducted three comparative experiments of baseline: adding WIoU loss, adding ML-block module, adding WIoU loss and ML-block module simultaneously, and trained all models on COCOmini for 300 epochs.

As shown in Table 5, we tested the model at three different resolutions. When adding WIoU loss to the baseline with the input resolution is $416 \times 416$, AP and

**Table 5.** Comparison of the accuracy of different method and resolution on COCO val-2017. We select all the models trained on 300 epochs for fair comparison.

| Method | Size | AP (%) | $AP_{50}$ | $AP_{75}$ | $AP_S$ | $AP_M$ | $AP_L$ |
|---|---|---|---|---|---|---|---|
| YOLOX-s | 416 | 30.1 | 46.6 | 31.7 | 13.3 | 32.6 | 43.3 |
| | 512 | 31.1 | 47.9 | 33.1 | 15.9 | 34.5 | 41.3 |
| | 608 | 31.4 | 49.1 | 33.5 | 18.0 | 35.2 | 39.2 |
| YOLOX-s + WIoU | 416 | 30.5 | 47.1 | 32.3 | 13.2 | 33.4 | 43.5 |
| | 512 | 31.1 | 48.1 | 33.2 | 15.7 | 34.6 | 40.7 |
| | 608 | 31.6 | 49.3 | 33.8 | 18.5 | 35.6 | 39.1 |
| YOLOX-s + ML-block | 416 | 31.0 | 47.4 | 32.7 | 13.7 | 33.6 | **45.0** |
| | 512 | 31.8 | 48.6 | 33.5 | 15.2 | 35.2 | 42.9 |
| | 608 | 32.0 | 49.4 | 34.1 | 18.2 | 35.9 | 40.9 |
| YOLOX-s + WIoU + ML-block | 416 | 31.3 | 47.9 | 33.2 | 13.5 | 34.1 | 44.8 |
| | 512 | 32.5 | 49.5 | 34.6 | 16.5 | 35.8 | 43.3 |
| | 608 | **33.4** | **50.3** | **35.8** | **18.5** | **36.7** | 43.0 |

$AP_{50}$ increase by 0.4% and 0.5%, respectively. When the input resolution is $512 \times 512$, the $AP_{50}$ slightly increases by 0.2% under the condition without any additional parameters.

Under the condition of adding WIoU loss and ML-block module to the baseline simultaneously, the parameters only increase by 1.27M. When the input resolution is $416 \times 416$, AP and $AP_{50}$ increase by 1.2% and 1.3%, respectively. When the input resolution is $608 \times 608$, AP and $AP_{50}$ are significantly improved, increased by 3.3% and 3.7%, respectively. As shown in Fig. 4(c), the model has a higher degree of discrimination between object and background, improving detection ability. At the same time, the detection confidence in Fig. 4(c) is higher than in Fig. 4(b). In the feature fusion layer, the use of Transformer to enhance global contextual information is beneficial to improve the characterization ability of the feature map after fusion. Extensive experiments on COCOmini data sets have shown that WIoU loss and ML-block module can substantially enhance the detector's accuracy.

## 5   Conclusion

In this work, we propose two methods to improve object detector performance: WIoU and ML-block. The ML-block solves the problem of insufficient contextual information learning in the feature fusion layer of one-stage detector. According to the object size, the IoU loss is weighted and penalized to improve the learning ability for small targets. Using yolox-s as the baseline, extensive experiments on COCOmini data sets and PASCAL VOC data sets have shown that WIoU and ML-block can substantially improve the model's performance.

# References

1. Bochkovskiy, A., Wang, C.Y., Liao, H.Y.M.: Yolov4: optimal speed and accuracy of object detection. arXiv preprint arXiv:2004.10934 (2020)
2. Chen, Y., et al.: Dynamic scale training for object detection. arXiv preprint arXiv:2004.12432 (2020)
3. Ge, Z., Liu, S., Wang, F., Li, Z., Sun, J.: Yolox: exceeding yolo series in 2021. arXiv preprint arXiv:2107.08430 (2021)
4. Ghiasi, G., Lin, T.Y., Pang, R., Le, Q.V.: NAS-FPN: learning scalable feature pyramid architecture for object detection. In: CVPR (2019)
5. Glenn-Jocher, R., et al.: yolov5 (2021). https://github.com/ultralytics/yolov5
6. He, K., Gkioxari, G., Dollár, P., Girshick, R.: Mask R-CNN. In: ICCV (2017)
7. Li, Y., Yao, T., Pan, Y., Mei, T.: Contextual transformer networks for visual recognition. arXiv preprint arXiv:2107.12292 (2021)
8. Lim, J.S., Astrid, M., Yoon, H.J., Lee, S.I.: Small object detection using context and attention. In: 2021 International Conference on Artificial Intelligence in Information and Communication (ICAIIC), pp. 181–186. IEEE (2021)
9. Lin, T.Y., Dollár, P., Girshick, R., He, K., Hariharan, B., Belongie, S.: Feature pyramid networks for object detection. In: CVPR (2017)
10. Lin, T.Y., Goyal, P., Girshick, R., He, K., Dollár, P.: Focal loss for dense object detection. In: ICCV (2017)
11. Lin, T.-Y., et al.: Microsoft COCO: common objects in context. In: Fleet, D., Pajdla, T., Schiele, B., Tuytelaars, T. (eds.) ECCV 2014. LNCS, vol. 8693, pp. 740–755. Springer, Cham (2014). https://doi.org/10.1007/978-3-319-10602-1_48
12. Liu, S., Qi, L., Qin, H., Shi, J., Jia, J.: Path aggregation network for instance segmentation. In: CVPR (2018)
13. Liu, W., et al.: SSD: single shot multibox detector. In: Leibe, B., Matas, J., Sebe, N., Welling, M. (eds.) ECCV 2016. LNCS, vol. 9905, pp. 21–37. Springer, Cham (2016). https://doi.org/10.1007/978-3-319-46448-0_2
14. Mehta, S., Rastegari, M.: Mobilevit: Light-weight, general-purpose, and mobile-friendly vision transformer. arXiv preprint arXiv:2110.02178 (2021)
15. Redmon, J., Divvala, S., Girshick, R., Farhadi, A.: You only look once: Unified, real-time object detection. In: CVPR (2016)
16. Redmon, J., Farhadi, A.: Yolo9000: better, faster, stronger. In: CVPR (2017)
17. Redmon, J., Farhadi, A.: Yolov3: an incremental improvement. arXiv preprint arXiv:1804.02767 (2018)
18. Ren, S., He, K., Girshick, R., Sun, J.: Faster R-CNN: towards real-time object detection with region proposal networks. In: NeurIPS (2015)
19. Rezatofighi, H., Tsoi, N., Gwak, J., Sadeghian, A., Reid, I., Savarese, S.: Generalized intersection over union: a metric and a loss for bounding box regression. In: Proceedings of the IEEE/CVF Conference on Computer Vision and Pattern Recognition, pp. 658–666 (2019)
20. Samet, N., Hicsonmez, S., Akbas, E.: HoughNet: integrating near and long-range evidence for bottom-up object detection. In: Vedaldi, A., Bischof, H., Brox, T., Frahm, J.-M. (eds.) ECCV 2020. LNCS, vol. 12370, pp. 406–423. Springer, Cham (2020). https://doi.org/10.1007/978-3-030-58595-2_25
21. Tang, Y., Gu, B., Jiang, B.: Research on feature enhancement for small object detection. In: Journal of Physics: Conference Series, vol. 2006, p. 012036. IOP Publishing (2021)

22. Wang, Q., Zhang, H., Hong, X., Zhou, Q.: Small object detection based on modified FSSD and model compression. arXiv preprint arXiv:2108.10503 (2021)
23. Woo, S., Park, J., Lee, J.-Y., Kweon, I.S.: CBAM: convolutional block attention module. In: Ferrari, V., Hebert, M., Sminchisescu, C., Weiss, Y. (eds.) ECCV 2018. LNCS, vol. 11211, pp. 3–19. Springer, Cham (2018). https://doi.org/10.1007/978-3-030-01234-2_1
24. Yu, J., Jiang, Y., Wang, Z., Cao, Z., Huang, T.: Unitbox: an advanced object detection network. In: Proceedings of the 24th ACM international conference on Multimedia, pp. 516–520 (2016)
25. Zhang, H., Hong, X., Zhu, L.: Detecting small objects in thermal images using single-shot detector. Autom. Control Comput. Sci. **55**(2), 202–211 (2021)
26. Zheng, Z., Wang, P., Liu, W., Li, J., Ye, R., Ren, D.: Distance-IOU loss: faster and better learning for bounding box regression. In: Proceedings of the AAAI Conference on Artificial Intelligence, vol. 34, pp. 12993–13000 (2020)

# FedNet2Net: Saving Communication and Computations in Federated Learning with Model Growing

Amit Kumar Kundu[✉] and Joseph Jaja

University of Maryland, College Park, MD 20742, USA
{amit314,josephj}@umd.edu

**Abstract.** Federated learning (FL) is a recently developed area of machine learning, in which the private data of a large number of distributed clients is used to develop a global model under the coordination of a central server without explicitly exposing the data. The standard FL strategy has a number of significant bottlenecks including large communication requirements and high impact on the clients' resources. Several strategies have been described in the literature trying to address these issues. In this paper, a novel scheme based on the notion of "model growing" is proposed. Initially, the server deploys a small model of low complexity, which is trained to capture the data complexity during the initial set of rounds. When the performance of such a model saturates, the server switches to a larger model with the help of *function-preserving transformations*. The model complexity increases as more data is processed by the clients, and the overall process continues until the desired performance is achieved. Therefore, the most complex model is broadcast only at the final stage in our approach resulting in substantial reduction in communication cost and client computational requirements. The proposed approach is tested extensively on three standard benchmarks and is shown to achieve substantial reduction in communication and client computation while achieving comparable accuracy when compared to the current most effective strategies.

**Keywords:** Communication efficiency · Federated learning · Function preserving transformation

## 1 Introduction

Federated learning (FL) is a new machine learning (ML) paradigm that enables the training of a model by utilizing private data distributed across many clients governed by a central server [16]. In contrast to the traditional ML, where all samples are stored in a single place, FL assumes that the data are generated and collected by many distributed, independent clients. Therefore, the overall data is

---

Partially supported by a DOD contract to the University of Maryland Institute for Advanced Computer Studies.

expected to be heterogeneous and non-IID (Identically and Independently Distributed). In training, the server broadcasts the current global model to a set of randomly selected clients. Each selected client locally trains the received model with its private data and sends the updates to the server. The server aggregates the updates on the current model using federated averaging. This constitutes a single communication round. This procedure is repeated for many communication rounds, where in each round the randomly selected clients advance the training, until convergence is achieved. FL has been growing in importance especially with the emergence of edge computing and AI on the edge due to the massive deployment of IoT devices and advances in communication and networking systems [23,30].

In the most general setting, the standard FL strategy has a number of significant bottlenecks that need to be addressed before it can be widely used in practice. These bottlenecks include data heterogeneity [5], unreliable and variable rate connectivity [16], uneven and relatively limited client resources [8], high communication requirement, and high impact on the clients' resources. Strategies to address these bottlenecks is suggested in the literature, see for example [11] but here we focus our attention on the two bottlenecks of communication requirements and the limited client resources.

Three approaches have been suggested to reduce the communication requirement and achieve comparable performance to the standard FL. The first, as in [6,18,28], relies on quantization methods; the second relies on the sparsification of the model update as in [12]; and the third approach broadcasts smaller networks to improve communication efficiency [13,27].

Another constraint is the relatively limited resources available at the clients. In general, whenever a state-of-the-art model is required to capture the global heterogeneous data complexity, FL induces a significant computational overhead on the clients. Therefore, we should aim at reducing the computational requirements on the clients. In [3], federated dropout is introduced in which random sub-networks of the entire model are broadcast thereby reducing communication bandwidth and computational resources.

The main contributions of this paper are:

- A novel strategy called FedNet2Net is introduced in which we start with a small initial model, and gradually enlarge the model to capture the increasing complexity of the data processed by the clients and improve accuracy.
- Function preserving transformations are used to switch from one model to the next once the performance of the current model saturates. Our switching is efficient and ensures a continuous improvement in accuracy as long as the inherent complexity of the data increases.
- FedNet2Net is shown through extensive experiments to result in large savings in the amounts of computation and communication compared to several of the best known strategies.
- FedNet2Net can be used to adaptively terminate at the smallest possible model that achieves the desired accuracy.

The rest of the paper is organized as follows. Section 2 provides an overview of techniques related to reducing the communication and client resources, while Sect. 3 describes our approach in details. Section 4 introduces the benchmarks used for evaluation and describes the details of our model implementations. We present and discuss the results in Sect. 5 and we conclude in Sect. 6.

## 2    Related Work

Since the introduction of federated averaging [19], reducing communication bandwidth and local computation has received a great deal of interest in the community. Most of the work tried to improve communication efficiency, which can be broadly categorized into model compression based techniques [6,15,18,20,21,28,31], update sparsification based techniques [12] or broadcasting smaller networks [10,13,27]. Model compression techniques involve mainly quantization [6,18,28], compressed sensing [15], low rank approximation [20] and tensor decomposition [31]. The approach in [12] combines sparsification of gradient updates with quantization for reducing the client-to-server communication cost. Model pruning technique has been used for communicating smaller networks, for example by applying the lottery ticket hypothesis for pruning [10,13]. The work in [17] partitions the model into local parameters for representation learning and global parameters for broadcasting by training the whole model locally. Significant savings is not expected from models having fully connected (FC) layers at the bottom as they possess most of the parameters of the entire model. Moreover, for testing new client data, the scheme needs to pass the data through all local models and ensemble the outputs, which is not suitable in practice. Some of the works avoid communicating the entire model by replacing it with either logits from model outputs as in [9,22] or binary masks as in [14].

The above schemes mostly improve communication efficiency but do not deal directly with possible computation savings at the client side. To achieve this objective, the typical approach used is mainly focused on broadcasting a sub-network to clients. For example, federated dropout [3] and adaptive federated dropout [1] randomly drop out a fixed percentage of units or filters to broadcast a sub-network combined with lossy compression at each round. Unlike the other knowledge distillation based methods, the approach in [7] trains small models on clients and transfers their knowledge to a large server-side model. The approach used in [14] only communicates and learns personalized binary masks, while freezing the model parameters. This idea, however, restricts the model to update its weights. On the other hand, the method described in HeteroFL [5] broadcasts submodels to clients based on their computation capability assuming that this knowledge is present to the server. All the discussed methods consider a single global model throughout the entire training. We just found out that a concurrently developed method in [26] progressively adds randomly initialized layers (or blocks) from the final model architecture with new classification layers at specific intervals. We expect this scheme to result in a drop of performance at the beginning of each stage and hence, we believe its performance will be significantly lower than ours.

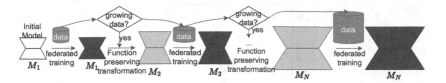

**Fig. 1.** Overview of the FedNet2Net training.

# 3 Proposed Approach

We develop a modified training scheme to make the local training computationally much less demanding and reduce the communication requirement while maintaining accuracy. We observe that to achieve a state-of-the-art accuracy, a model needs to capture the essential characteristics of the global data held in the clients, which are known only after the participation of a large number of clients. However, it is not necessary to broadcast such a model throughout the entire training. At the beginning, the model starts with a small amount of data available at relatively few clients, and then progresses with additional information after each round of FL. Intuitively, a model with much lower complexity can be deployed at the beginning and then, we can exploit transfer learning strategies to transfer the knowledge from a lower complexity model to a higher complexity model. In this way, the complexity of the model grows as the data complexity increases, until we reach a final model that can capture the global data.

Our approach is based on transfer learning, but in a different way than standard transfer learning in which the top layers of a student network are directly copied from a teacher network [29]. Instead, the strategy of function-preserving transformations introduced in [4] is utilized, where the student network is initialized in such a way that it represents the same function as the teacher but with different parameterization. We start federated training with a small network. As the training proceeds and more data from clients are exposed, the model is enlarged using two transformations. The first is Net2Widernet, which replaces a model with an equivalent model that is wider, i.e. the student model will have a larger number of units at a certain layer(s). The second operation is Net2DeeperNet, which replaces a model with an equivalent deeper model. These two transformations constitute the essential components of Net2Net. Each transformation preserves the function of the network. After initializing the student network that has the same function as the teacher network, the student network is trained further to improve performance, and once no improvement is detected, the network is enlarged using the Net2Net transformations. We call our scheme FedNet2Net after the Net2Net methodology. Details are presented next.

Let us assume model 1 to model $N$, $\{M_1, M_2, ..., M_N\}$ are of increasing complexity, where $M_1$ is a model having the fewest number of layers and units. $M_N$ is a model that can capture the entire data fairly well, and could have the same architecture as deployed in the standard federated training. $M_1$ through $M_N$ are designed in such a way that for two consecutive models $M_i$ and $M_{i+1}$,

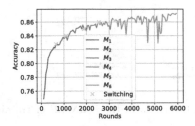

**Fig. 2.** Model switching in FedNet2Net training using the EMNIST dataset

the architecture of $M_{i+1}$ has either increased the number of layers or increased the number of units in some layer(s) or both compared to $M_i$, as enlarging the model width or depth is proven to be effective in improving accuracy [7]. Figure 1 presents the overview of FedNet2Net training. During each stage, the model is deployed after enlarging it by applying a functional preserving transformation to meet the growing data complexity without degradation in performance. In this way, we continue to train a model until its progress saturates after which we switch to the next model. Figure 2 shows the model switching in FedNet2Net training. We observe that since the highest complexity model is broadcast only at the final stage, we achieve a large reduction in communication bandwidth and clients' computational requirements while achieving similar performance as in the standard FL. In a federated setting, FedNet2Net can be a life long learner and can adapt over a long period of time [24].

We now describe how the transformation is function preserving and how to apply the transformation to transfer knowledge from $M_i$ to $M_{i+1}$. The student network $M_{i+1}$ has either increased the number of layers or increased the number of units in some layer(s) compared to $M_i$. In the case of Net2DeeperNet, to insert a FC layer to $M_i$, we initialize the weights of the inserted layer as the identity matrix. To insert a convolutional layer, we initialize the kernel as the identity filter. Similarly, Net2WiderNet operation replaces a layer with a wider layer while preserving the function value, that is more units for FC layers, or more filters for convolutional layers. For a convolutional kernel $K_l$ of shape $(w_l, h_l, i_l, o_l)$, $w_l$ and $h_l$ denote filter width and height, and $i_l, o_l$ are the number of input and output channels of layer $l$. To widen this kernel $\hat{K}_l$ having a shape of $(w_l, h_l, i_l, \hat{o}_l)$, where $\hat{o}_l > o_l$, a random mapping is considered as follows:

$$G_l(j) = \begin{cases} j, & \text{if } 1 \leq j \leq o_l \\ \text{random sampling from } \{1, 2, ..., o_l\}, & \text{if } o_l \leq j \leq \hat{o}_l \end{cases}$$

Then the new kernel becomes $\hat{K}_l[x, y, i, j] = K_l[x, y, i, G_l(j)]$. Therefore, the first $o_l$ number of output channels are directly copied while the rest of the output channels are randomly sampled and copied to the new kernel. For preserving the function value, the next layer kernel $K_{l+1}$ is also reduced due to the replication in its input. The new kernel $\hat{K}_{l+1}$ is given as $\hat{K}_{l+1}[x, y, j, k] = \frac{K_{l+1}[x, y, G_l(j), k]}{|\{z | G_l(z) = G_l(j)\}|}$. Similar transformation can be realized for FC layers. More details regarding the transformations appear in [4]. This operation preserves the function value, that is, for any sample, the function value of the model before and after the transformation remains the same. As we have dropout layers in our models, no extra noise adding is needed for advancing the training since the dropout technique achieves the same goal.

We now address the issue of when to switch to a larger model.

**Switching Policy.** For the server to decide when to switch from one model to the next, we adopt a switching policy based on the model loss. As the loss at each round fluctuates significantly due to training and random selection of clients, we calculate the window-based loss at $t$-th round and then compare it to another window of a certain time lag $L$ as follows.

$$S_t = \frac{1}{N} \sum_{i=1}^{N} \text{loss}[t - i - L] - \frac{1}{N} \sum_{i=1}^{N} \text{loss}[t - i] \tag{1}$$

where loss[$i$] is the weighted average of local model losses from clients at $i$-th round, $L$ is the time lag between two consecutive windows of size $N$. In other words, we compute the running average of losses for $N$ rounds of the earlier past and the recent past and take the difference. This measure captures the progress in training based on the loss over the time window. If $S_t$ is not above a certain threshold, then switching to a larger model is performed. Given that the clients are selected randomly during each round, our measure to use the average loss over a window stabilizes the switching decision process. A new model is trained for at least $N + L$ rounds before determining the next switching decision. The thresholds are tuned to get the best possible results. A similar switching policy can be realized by using the validation accuracy evaluated at the server; however this assumes that there is a public validation dataset available at the server.

# 4     Datasets and Detailed Model Implementations

In this section, we present brief descriptions of the datasets and the detailed model sequences used to conduct various experiments.

## 4.1     Data Description

In order to evaluate the proposed training approach, three benchmark datasets namely, EMNIST, CIFAR-10, and MNIST are used. For federated training, the training sets in MNIST and CIFAR10 are randomly divided into 100 clients. The EMNIST dataset is an extension of the MNIST, which consists of 671585 images of 62 classes split into 3400 unbalanced non-IID clients [2].

## 4.2     Performance Evaluation

To evaluate FedNet2Net, we implement and compare the following five methods.

1. **FedAvg:** Federated averaging [19] with traditional dropout layer. Here, we add a dropout layer [25] after each convolutional and FC layer. Dropping out of units or filters is performed inside clients.
2. **FD:** Federated dropout [3]. Because of broadcasting smaller subnetworks, some amount of communication and computation are saved compared to FedAvg. We consider FedAvg and FD as the baseline methods.
3. **HeteroFL** [5]: We uniformly sample computation level of each client at each round from 5 different levels.
4. **FedNet2Net (FNN):** This is our approach with traditional dropout layer.
5. **FedNet2Net-FD (FNN-FD):** Our approach is combined with federated dropout to reduce further communication and computation. Here, dropout is applied to all models except the smaller ones.

For performance evaluation, we plot the accuracy against total communication of all methods and the reduction in average communication per round versus the accuracy of our approaches over the baselines. The second plot can be used to determine the communication saved for a desired accuracy, and to determine the number of clients that can participate at a round. While not mentioned explicitly, similar reduction in the amount of computations is achieved since the models used are much smaller for the majority of the rounds (if not all). All methods are trained for 6000 rounds and for convenience, the test accuracy is recorded after every 50 rounds.

### 4.3    Parameters for Switching

As mentioned before, we switch from one model to a larger one when we detect that the training improvement is below a certain threshold over a running window, as described by the Eq. (1). We use $N = 100$ and $L = 300$ for all datasets. The thresholds for consecutive switching are listed in Table 1. The switching is decided at the server, and hence, no extra computation or communication is incurred at the client side.

### 4.4    Model Description and Hyper-parameters

The hyperparameters and models for FedAvg, FD and the final stage of FedNet2Net are set as suggested in [3]. The learning rates and the number of clients per round are listed in Table 1. The number of epochs per round is set to 1

**Table 1.** Thresholds for five consecutive switchings and hyperparameters for three datasets.

| Dataset | Thresholds for policy Eq. (1) | Learning rate | Clients per round |
|---------|-------------------------------|---------------|-------------------|
| EMNIST  | $[0.08, 0.04, 0.02, 0.01, 0.005]$ | 0.035 | 35 |
| CIFAR10 | $[0.12, 0.11, 0.10, 0.09, 0.08]$ | 0.05 | 10 |
| MNIST   | $[0.04, 0.02, 0.01, 0.005, 0.0025]$ | 0.015 | 10 |

**Table 2.** Consecutive models of FedNet2Net training for the EMNIST and MNIST datasets. The number of units are written in parenthesis. For MNIST, we use the same architectures except each classification layer has 10 units and the number of units in the second last layer is 128 for models 1–4, 256 for model 5 and 512 for model 6. Kernel size is $5 \times 5$.

| Model number | Architecture | Para- meters |
|---|---|---|
| Model 1 | Conv2D(16) → maxpool(4,4) → FC(512) → FC(62) | 434K |
| Model 2 | **Conv2D(32)** → maxpool(4,4) → FC(512) → FC(62) | 836K |
| Model 3 | Conv2D(32) → maxpool(2,2) → **Conv2D(32)** → maxpool(2,2) → FC(512) → FC(62) | 862K |
| Model 4 | Conv2D(32) → maxpool(2,2) → **Conv2D(64)** → maxpool(2,2) → FC(512) → FC(62) | 1.7M |
| Model 5 | Conv2D(32) → maxpool(2,2) → Conv2D(64) → maxpool(2,2) → **FC(1024)** → FC(62) | 3.3M |
| Model 6 | Conv2D(32) → maxpool(2,2) → Conv2D(64) → maxpool(2,2) → **FC(2048)** → FC(62) | 6.6M |

and the batch size for local training is 10. SGD optimizer and sparse categorical cross-entropy loss are used. Dropout rate is set to 0.125. The sequence of models used in FedNet2Net are presented in Tables 2 and 3 along with the number of parameters in each model. Changes in consecutive models are highlighted. RELU activation and dropout is applied after each convolutional and FC layer except the last classification layer, where a softmax activation is applied.

## 5   Results

Figure 3 compares the performance between FedNet2Net and the baseline methods using the model loss based switching policy. The figures on the left present the accuracy against total communication (in bits) with switching positions in our approach. We observe that for any fixed amount of communication, Fed-Net2Net achieves higher and occasionally equal accuracy compared to FedAvg, federated dropout and HeteroFL; the only exception is the performance of Het-eroFL on CIFAR10 at the high accuracy end, which we believe is due to adding batch normalization layers in HeteroFL, which boosted the training. Otherwise, HeteroFL training is highly unstable.

The figures on the right present the percentage reduction in communication per round of FNN over FedAvg, FNN-FD over FD, FD over FedAvg, HeteroFL over FedAvg and FNN-FD over FedAvg. It is observed that, at the slightly lower accuracy regions than the best possible, the percentage savings is approximately more than 90% per round. This saving remains constant for most of the accuracy regions. At the higher accuracy region, the percentage savings starts to drop, which intuitively makes sense as we are switching to larger models to capture the growing data complexity. Moreover, the reduction of FD and HeteroFL over

**Table 3.** Consecutive models in FedNet2Net for CIFAR10. Kernel size is $3 \times 3$ everywhere except the last two convolutional layers of model 6, where it is $1 \times 1$.

| Model number | Architecture | Parameters |
|---|---|---|
| Model 1 | Conv2D(32) $\to$ maxpool(3,3) $\to$ Conv2D(64) $\to$ maxpool(3,3) $\to$ Conv2D(10) $\to$ GlobalAveragePooling2D (GAP) $\to$ FC(10) | 20K |
| Model 2 | Conv2D(32) $\to$ **Conv2D(32)** $\to$ maxpool(3,3) $\to$ Conv2D(64) $\to$ **Conv2D(64)** $\to$ maxpool(3,3) $\to$ Conv2D(10) $\to$ GAP $\to$ FC(10) | 66K |
| Model 3 | **Conv2D(64)** $\to$ **Conv2D(64)** $\to$ maxpool(3,3) $\to$ **Conv2D(128)** $\to$ **Conv2D(128)** $\to$ maxpool(3,3) $\to$ Conv2D(10) $\to$ GAP $\to$ FC(10) | 262K |
| Model 4 | **Conv2D(96)** $\to$ **Conv2D(96)** $\to$ maxpool(3,3) $\to$ **Conv2D(192)** $\to$ **Conv2D(192)** $\to$ maxpool(3,3) $\to$ Conv2D(10) $\to$ GAP $\to$ FC(10) | 586K |
| Model 5 | Conv2D(96) $\to$ Conv2D(96) $\to$ maxpool(3,3) $\to$ Conv2D(192) $\to$ Conv2D(192) $\to$ maxpool(3,3) $\to$ **Conv2D(192)** $\to$ Conv2D(10) $\to$ GAP $\to$ FC(10) | 918K |
| Model 6 | Conv2D(96) $\to$ Conv2D(96) $\to$ maxpool(3,3) $\to$ Conv2D(192) $\to$ Conv2D(192) $\to$ maxpool(3,3) $\to$ Conv2D(192) $\to$ **Conv2D(192)** $\to$ Conv2D(10) $\to$ GAP $\to$ FC(10) | 955K |

FedAvg remains the same for all accuracies as they broadcast roughly the same number of parameters at all rounds. However, additional per round communication savings is achieved by combining FedNet2Net with FD. Similar reduction is achieved when we separated a validation set from the training data to measure validation accuracy for making switching decisions. Therefore, our training approach based on model growing reduces significant amount of communication per round. Moreover, as our approach starts from a significantly small model and gets transformed into a higher capacity model, it opens the opportunity to adapt the model as data complexity grows.

**Effect of Choosing the Different Set of Intermediate Models.** Given the final model, we implement FedNet2net with a different set of intermediate models to show the effect of choosing them differently. For EMNIST, we implement FedNet2Net with sets of 6 and 8 models (FNN-6 and FNN-8), and the results are presented in Fig. 4. FNN-8 has a smaller starting network than FNN-6. We observe that FNN-8 performs better than FNN-6 in terms of communication reductions. This is intuitive as the final model is broadcast for lesser number of rounds. Similarly for CIFAR10, we implement FedNet2Net by changing some of the intermediate models mentioned in Table 3. The reductions achieved is almost the same as in Fig. 3(b). We omitted the figure due to space limitations.

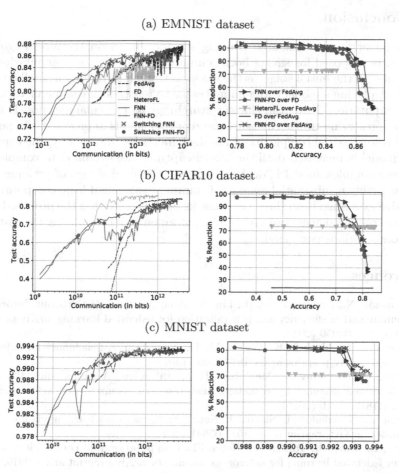

**Fig. 3.** Accuracy against communication of the FedAvg, FD, HeteroFL, FedNet2Net and FedNet2Net-FD (left), and percentage reduction in communication per round of FedNet2Net, FD and HeteroFL over FedAvg (right). The markings in the left figures indicate the switching positions based on policy Eq. (1). Accuracies fluctuate due to training from randomly selected clients at each round.

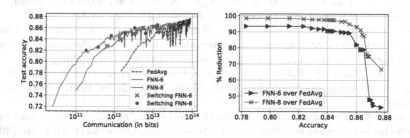

**Fig. 4.** Performance comparison of FedNet2Net with different set of intermediate models for the EMNIST dataset.

# 6   Conclusion

In this paper, a new federated training scheme, based on the model growing strategy, is proposed for saving both communication cost and computations at the clients. At the initial stage, as the model is trained using only a small amount of data, deploying a model with minimal capacity saves both communication and local computation. Next, the efficient switchings to the enlarged models using function-preserving transformations ensure a continuous improvement in performance as long as the complexity of the data increases. In this way, the capacity of the model is increased until the model captures the overall data complexity. The most complex model is deployed only at the final stages of training, and thereby, saving a substantial amount of communication and local computations. Extensive experiments on three benchmarks demonstrate that the proposed Fed-Net2Net training scheme can save significant amount of communication cost and local computations per round.

# References

1. Bouacida, N., Hou, J., Zang, H., Liu, X.: Adaptive federated dropout: Improving communication efficiency and generalization for federated learning. arXiv preprint arXiv:2011.04050 (2020)
2. Caldas, S., Duddu, S.M.K., Wu, P., Li, T., et al.: Leaf: A benchmark for federated settings. arXiv preprint arXiv:1812.01097 (2018)
3. Caldas, S., Konečny, J., McMahan, H.B., Talwalkar, A.: Expanding the reach of federated learning by reducing client resource requirements. arXiv preprint arXiv:1812.07210 (2018)
4. Chen, T., Goodfellow, I., Shlens, J.: Net2Net: Accelerating learning via knowledge transfer. arXiv preprint arXiv:1511.05641 (2015)
5. Diao, E., Ding, J., Tarokh, V.: HeteroFL: Computation and communication efficient federated learning for heterogeneous clients. arXiv preprint arXiv:2010.01264 (2020)
6. Elkordy, A.R., Avestimehr, A.S.: HeteroSAg: secure aggregation with heterogeneous quantization in federated learning. IEEE Trans. Commun. (2022)
7. He, C., Annavaram, M., Avestimehr, S.: Group knowledge transfer: federated learning of large CNNs at the edge. Adv. Neural Inf. Process. Syst. (NeurIPS) **33**, 14068–14080 (2020)
8. Imteaj, A., Thakker, U., Wang, S., et al.: A survey on federated learning for resource- constrained IoT devices. IEEE IoT J. **9**(1), 1–24 (2021)
9. Itahara, S., Nishio, T., Koda, Y., Morikura, M., et al.: Distillation-based semi-supervised federated learning for communication-efficient collaborative training with non-IID private data. arXiv preprint arXiv:2008.06180 (2020)
10. Jiang, Y., Wang, S., Valls, V., Ko, B.J., et al.: Model pruning enables efficient federated learning on edge devices. IEEE Trans. Neural Netw. Learn. Syst. (NNLS) (2022)
11. Kairouz, P., McMahan, H.B., Avent, B., Bellet, A., et al.: Advances and open problems in federated learning. Found. Trends Mach. Learn. **14**(1–2), 1–210 (2021)
12. Konečnỳ, J., McMahan, H.B., Yu, F.X., Richtárik, P., et al.: Federated learning: Strategies for improving communication efficiency. arXiv preprint arXiv:1610.05492 (2016)

13. Li, A., Sun, J., Wang, B., Duan, L., et al.: LotteryFL: empower edge intelligence with personalized and communication-efficient federated learning. In: IEEE/ACM Symposium on Edge Computing, pp. 68–79 (2021)
14. Li, A., Sun, J., Zeng, X., Zhang, M., et al.: FedMask: joint computation and communication-efficient personalized federated learning via heterogeneous masking. In: 19th ACM Conference on Embedded Networked Sensor Systems, pp. 42–55 (2021)
15. Li, C., Li, G., Varshney, P.K.: Communication-efficient federated learning based on compressed sensing. IEEE IoT J. **8**(20), 15531–15541 (2021)
16. Li, T., Sahu, A.K., Talwalkar, A., Smith, V.: Federated learning: challenges, methods, and future directions. IEEE Signal Process. Mag. **37**(3), 50–60 (2020). https://doi.org/10.1007/978-3-030-85559-8_13
17. Liang, P.P., Liu, T., Ziyin, L., Salakhutdinov, R., et al.: Think locally, act globally: Federated learning with local and global representations. arXiv preprint arXiv:2001.01523 (2020)
18. Mao, Y., Zhao, Z., Yan, G., Liu, Y., et al.: Communication efficient federated learning with adaptive quantization. ACM Trans. Intell. Syst. Technol. (2021)
19. McMahan, B., Moore, E., Ramage, D., Hampson, S., et al.: Communication-efficient learning of deep networks from decentralized data. In: Artificial Intelligence and Statistics, pp. 1273–1282 (2017)
20. Qiao, Z., Yu, X., Zhang, J., Letaief, K.B.: Communication-efficient federated learning with dual-side low-rank compression. arXiv preprint arXiv:2104.12416 (2021)
21. Rothchild, D., Panda, A., Ullah, E., Ivkin, N., et al.: FetchSGD: communication-efficient federated learning with sketching. In: 37th International Conference on Machine Learning, vol. 119, pp. 8253–8265 (2020)
22. Sattler, F., Marban, A., Rischke, R., Samek, W.: Communication-efficient federated distillation. arXiv preprint arXiv:2012.00632 (2020)
23. Savazzi, S., Nicoli, M., Rampa, V.: Federated learning with cooperating devices: a consensus approach for massive IoT networks. IEEE IoT J. **7**(5), 4641–4654 (2020)
24. Silver, D.L., Yang, Q., Li, L.: Lifelong machine learning systems: beyond learning algorithms. In: 2013 AAAI Spring Symposium Series (2013)
25. Srivastava, N., Hinton, G., Krizhevsky, A., Sutskever, I., et al.: Dropout: a simple way to prevent neural networks from overfitting. J. Mach. Learn. Res. **15**(1), 1929–1958 (2014)
26. Wang, H.P., Stich, S.U., He, Y., Fritz, M.: ProgFed: effective, communication, and computation efficient federated learning by progressive training. In: International Conference on Machine Learning, pp. 23034–23054 (2022)
27. Wu, C., Wu, F., Lyu, L., Huang, Y., et al.: Communication-efficient federated learning via knowledge distillation. Nat. Commun. **13**(1), 1–8 (2022)
28. Xu, J., Du, W., Jin, Y., He, W., et al.: Ternary compression for communication-efficient federated learning. IEEE Trans. NNLS (2020)
29. Yosinski, J., Clune, J., Bengio, Y., Lipson, H.: How transferable are features in deep neural networks? In: Advances in NeurIPS, vol. 27 (2014)
30. Yu, R., Li, P.: Toward resource-efficient federated learning in mobile edge computing. IEEE Netw. **35**(1), 148–155 (2021)
31. Zheng, H., Gao, M., Chen, Z., Feng, X.: A distributed hierarchical deep computation model for federated learning in edge computing. IEEE Trans. Industr. Inf. **17**(12), 7946–7956 (2021)

# Reject Options for Incremental Regression Scenarios

Jonathan Jakob[1(✉)], Martina Hasenjäger[2], and Barbara Hammer[1]

[1] Bielefeld University, Bielefeld, Germany
`jjakob@techfak.uni-bielefeld.de`
[2] Honda Research Institute, Offenbach, Germany

**Abstract.** Machine learning with a reject option is the empowerment of an algorithm to abstain from prediction when the outcome is likely to be inaccurate. Although the topic has been investigated in the literature already some time ago, it has not lost any of its relevance as machine learning models are increasingly delivered to the market. At present, most work on reject strategies addresses classification tasks. Moreover, the majority of approaches deals with classical batch learning scenarios. In this publication, in contrast, we study the important problem of reject options for incremental online regression tasks. We propose different strategies to model this problem and evaluate different approaches, both in a theoretical and a real world setting from the domain of human motion prediction; from the methods which we evaluate, a clear winner emerges as regards accuracy and efficiency.

**Keywords:** Reject option · Incremental learning · Online regression

## 1 Introduction

In machine learning a reject option is the ability of an algorithm to abstain from prediction when the outcome is likely to be inaccurate [8]. Classification with reject option has already been studied many decades ago [3], and it has been proven that certainty-based rejection offers an optimal strategy, provided the underlying probability distributions are known. In practice, this strategy is usually approximated based on suitable surrogates, since the true probability distribution is not known [2,6,9]. However, most reject option applications from the literature have been proposed for classification tasks.

In this contribution, we are interested in reject options for regression tasks such as arise in online time series prediction. Only a few reject option systems for regression tasks have been published recently. In the work [12] the authors propose a new uncertainty function for regression called *Blend-Var*. The approach tackles the rejection problem from a risk-coverage point of view and measures the variance of multiple predictions on an input image that was rotated, reflected or shifted. [7] introduces *SelectiveNet*, an approach where a deep neural network with two separated heads (one for prediction and one for rejection) is trained end-to-end in a single model. The work [1] presents a neural framework, that is based on a generalized meta-loss function. It revolves around the simultaneous training of two neural networks, one for prediction and the other for rejection. Finally, [4] proposes a reject scheme which targets general prescription methods based on an extended cost functions, incorporating costs for rejection, and controls the reject strategy by an explicit adaptive output value, indicating whether the current input should be rejected. Here, regression or classification prescriptions are trained simultaneously to the reject indicator output.

However, all of these approaches deal with reject options in an offline setting; i.e., training data are given prior to training, and the regression model together with the reject strategy can be trained based on these batch training data. We, on the other hand, are interested in reject options for incremental regression tasks. Incremental learning tasks learn from a stream of data which arrive continuously over time rather than a priorly available batch of training data [16]. This is an important scenario e.g. in the context of lifelong learning, where models need to be continuously adapted to a possibly changing environment, or product personalization, where a smart device needs to be adapted to the specific demands of a user to enable full functionality.

In the specific setup which we consider in this contribution, the motivation stems from an application of learning schemes for an optimization of control of exoskeletons. Modern exoskeleton robots utilize machine learning to facilitate the prediction of upcoming movements in order to provide adequate support for the user. Hereby, incremental algorithms can be of great help because they can automatically adapt to new movement patterns [17,23]. However, the adaption usually takes some time. In such settings, no support in a smooth movement is better than applying the wrong support; hence it can be beneficial to realize incremental learning with reject option in places that outcasts those samples of a novel movement pattern that are highly afflicted by errors in the prediction forecast. Therefore, in this contribution, we investigate how reject options can be facilitated that work next to an incremental algorithm and ideally reject only the initiate samples of new concepts in the data stream so that the underlying regressor has time to adapt itself. We propose different approaches for this task and evaluate the different methods in a scenario which incorporates movement patterns measured in a realistic environment and with different individuals. We will demonstrate that one modeling in particular shows very promising results.

This paper is structured as follows: The next section explains the problem setting. Afterwards, we introduce the different rejection approaches that we compare. Then, the design of our experiments is revealed and subsequently the results are presented. Finally, the last section concludes the paper.

## 2 Problem Setting

We use incremental regression to predict a data stream one instance after another. Hereby, we define a data stream $S = \{s_1, s_2, s_3, ..., s_t\}$ as a potentially infinite set of data points $s_i \in \mathbb{R}^n$. The task is predicting the vector $s_{t+1}$ from previous instances of the stream. An incremental model is an algorithm that receives a data stream instance after instance and instantaneously generates a sequence of models $h_1, h_2, h_3, ..., h_t$ which are used for next step prediction, i.e. $h_{i-1}(s_i)$ should approximate the value $s_{i+1}$ based on the function $h_{i-1}$ that acts on the current instance and predicts the value of the next instance of the data stream. After that, the true value $s_{i+1}$ is revealed and a new model $h_i$ is learned. To evaluate this regression task, the *Interleaved train test error (ITTE)* is applied:

$$E(S) = \sqrt{\frac{1}{t} \sum_{i=1}^{t} (h_{i-1}(s_i) - s_{i+1})^2}$$

ITTE measures the *Root Mean Squared Error (RMSE)* over every model $h_i$ up to time $t$. By $E(s_t)$ we refer to the sequence of errors rather than the average.

Furthermore, a *Reject Option* in an incremental learning scheme is a function $r(s_i, E(s_i)) \rightarrow \{0, 1\}$, that acts on the current input data or the local error of the model $h_{i-1}$, i.e. a subpart or summary statistics of $E(s_i)$, and produces an indicator that governs whether the current sample is rejected or not. To evaluate the rejection function, we can refer to the ITTE over all non rejected samples. This should be compared to the percentage of points which are rejected, since these two quantities typically form a Pareto front: good reject strategies should result in an improved remaining ITTE the more samples are rejected.

## 3    Rejection Models

We evaluate four different approaches for a Reject Option in incremental regression. All of these approaches are agnostic to the underlying regression algorithm and can be used in combination with any online regression model. Based on the findings in [11], we use a simple kNN regressor to conduct our experiments, since it displayed competitive and particularly robust results in that work.

### 3.1    Drift Rejection

The first rejection is based on drift detection. It monitors the local errors of the underlying regression model on the incoming data stream and applies a standard drift detection algorithm to detect changes in those error values, using any drift detection technology [10]. The reasoning behind this is, that when changes in the error occur, e.g. the error increases, the algorithm does not perform well in this area of the data stream and therefore samples should be rejected until the algorithm has learned to deal with the current concept. Here, any drift detection method from the literature can be used. We opted for the Page-Hinkley drift detector [21] and its implementation from the online library River [18]. To determine, how long samples should be rejected once drift has been detected, we use a simple strategy, that monitors the overall mean error on the data stream, and compares it to the rolling mean of the last $n$ samples. When the rolling mean falls under the long term mean, we stop the rejection and the drift detector is activated again. The hyperparameters that can be adjusted in this approach are the threshold for drift detection of the Page-Hinkley algorithm and a value $\alpha$, that scales the long term mean used to determine the end of a rejection phase.

### 3.2  Local Outlier Probabilities Rejector

The next two approaches are based on Local Outlier Probabilities (LoOP) [13]. LoOP is a local density based outlier detection method that provides outlier scores in the range [0,1]. We use LoOP for two different rejection approaches.

**LoOP Data.** In the first approach we apply LoOP to the input data. Unlike drift-based rejection, which targets critical time steps, this approach targets points in space which are unknown by the current model. When a new concept manifests itself in the stream, LoOP should assing high outlier probabilities to these input samples. Since, the underlying incremental regressor has not learned the new concept yet, these samples should be rejected until enoug of them have been processed, rendering them not outliers anymore.

**LoOP Error.** The second approach, like the drift rejector, applies LoOP to the error stream generated by the underlying regressor. The idea is that unknown error profiles indicate regions of high insecurity of the process where prediction should be rejected. If the error values increase, they become outliers and should be labeled as such by higher outlier probabilities. So, in theory, samples with high error values are rejected until the error decreases into normal ranges again.

In both variants, the hyperparameter that governs the rejection rate is a cutoff probability $\beta$ that defines the threshold from which to reject samples.

### 3.3  Baseline Rejection

The last rejection strategy is a simple baseline approach. It monitors the long term mean error over the whole data stream and rejects all samples that exhibit a local error higher than the mean. Hence rejection takes place based on the recent observed error. Here, the hyperparameter is a value $\gamma$ that scales the long term mean in order to facilitate various rejection rates.

## 4  Experiments

As stated previously, we use a kNN regression model which incrementally acts on time windows as underlying model. We use two distinct types of data sets. Theoretical benchmark data with known ground truth and data from a real world scenario from the domain of online human motion prediction.

### 4.1  Chaotic Time Series Data

For the theoretical part, we create special benchmark data sets from chaotic systems. We use the Lorenz system [14] along with the Roessler system [22] as well as the Tinkerbell map [20] along with the Duffing map [5] to create four new benchmark data sets. Hereby, the Lorenz and Roessler systems are three

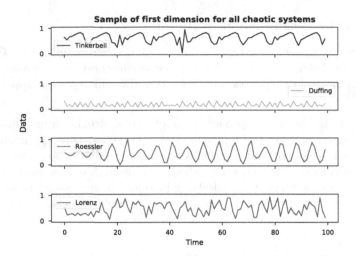

**Fig. 1.** Example plot of the first 100 data points in the first dimension for all chaotic systems. The first row shows the Tinkerbell map, the second row shows the Duffing map, the third row shows the Roessler system, the last row shows the Lorenz system.

dimensional, while the Tinkerbell and Duffing map are two dimensional data streams. Figure 1 shows the expansion of the first 100 data points in a stream created from each of the chaotic systems. Our benchmark data sets are created from the raw streams in the following way. Data streams holding 2000 instances of the three dimensional Lorenz and Roessler systems are glued together in alternate fashion, to form a data set with two sudden change points of which the latter initiates the reoccurring of the first system for a second time. The same is done for the two dimensional Tinkerbell and Duffing maps, leading to four data sets of 6000 data points each. Figure 2 shows a sample plot of the Roessler-Lorenz data set.

## 4.2   Real World Data

For the real world part, we use data from the NEWBEE database [15]. This data was created at the Honda Research Institute Europe and comprises human gait recordings from 20 participants that completed three different walk courses with various terrains, such as stairs, slopes and level walk. The data was recorded using full body xsens suits as well as insole trackers. We use a subset of this database comprising of four different persons on the course-A track, where we only use the lower body features of acceleration and angular momentum in three directions. This leads to an input space of 42 features.

## 4.3   RMSE-Reject Curves

We evaluate and compare the different rejection approaches by means of Root Mean Squared Error (RMSE) - reject curves [19]. This means, that we compute

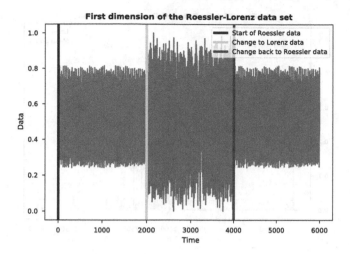

**Fig. 2.** Example plot of the first dimension of the Roessler-Lorenz data set. The first 2000 samples are taken from the Roessler system, followed by another 2000 points from the Lorenz system. In the end another change point back to the Roessler system is induced.

the rejected samples for a wide range of possible hyperparameters in order to acquire runs with different rates of rejection. Then, we plot the RMSE of the non rejected samples per rejection rate and evaluate the algorithms by comparing the curves. Different RMSE-reject curves for a given data set all start at the same point in the plot. This point is given by the RMSE of the underlying regressor on the total data set, i.e. on a run with 0% rejection. As the rejection rate increases, the RMSE on the non rejected data samples drops, until it reaches 0, for a 100% rejection. This means, that algorithms with lower curves outperform those with higher curves because they exhibit a lower RMSE for the same rejection rates.

### 4.4   Chaotic Data Experiment

In the first experiment we evaluate the four rejection approaches on the chaotic data sets. It is important to note, that all sets have different internal complexities, i.e. they exhibit different levels of difficulty for the underlying regressor. For the two dimensional systems, the Tinkerbell map is easier than the Duffing map, while for the three dimensional systems, the Roessler expansion is easier than the Lorenz expansion. Overall, the Lorenz system is the hardest to predict.

All chaotic data sets consist of two different chaotic expansions, one sandwiched in between the other. This means, that the underlying incremental regressor first learns one system and then suddenly has to switch to learning the next system. This clear and sudden switch creates a situation that is very suitable for the deployment of a reject option. Ideally, a rejection approach should reject the initial samples of the new system because the underlying regressor needs time

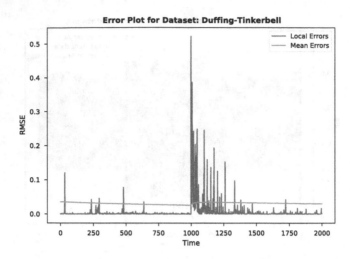

**Fig. 3.** Error plot for the chaotic experiment on the Duffing-Tinkerbell data set.

to adequately learn it and return accurate predictions. This, then should lead to a reduction in RMSE compared to a setting without rejection.

An example of the error progression of the underlying regressor for the Duffing-Tinkerbell data set is given in Fig. 3. We pre-train the regressor on 1000 samples and plot the local errors and accumulating mean errors on the subsequent 2000 samples. Hence the onset of the Tinkerbell expansion is located at time step $t = 1000$. One can observe, that the local errors increase drastically here and then gradually decrease as the regressor adapts to the new system.

### 4.5  Real World Data Experiment

In the second experiment we evaluate the different approaches in a real world setting. Here, data is complex and exhibits a high degree of noise. This leads to a scenario, where the local errors fluctuate strongly over the whole series.

An example is shown in Fig. 4. It shows the error progression for the NEW-BEE CourseA Person 1 data set in the same fashion as Fig. 3. One can observe, that changes in the underlying pattern, given for example at time steps $t = 300$ and $t = 1300$, are not leading to dramatic error spikes as in the chaotic data. Instead, the behaviour of the error values is a lot more coherent, which renders it harder to work on with error based rejection approaches.

## 5  Results

In this section, we first report the results for both experiments by means of RMSE-reject curves. Afterwards, we evaluate the effect of different rejection rates as the relative reduction of the RMSE compared to a scenario without rejection in tabular form.

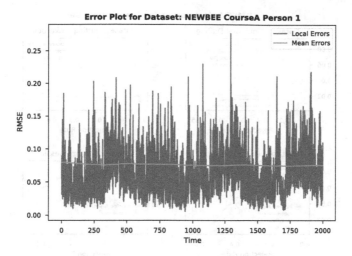

**Fig. 4.** Error plot for the real world experiment on the NEWBEE CourseA Person 1 data set.

## 5.1   Chaotic Data Results

The results for the chaotic data experiment are visualized in Fig. 5. The plots show the RMSE-reject curves of all rejection approaches for all chaotic data sets. The first thing to note is, that both LoOP approaches do not seem to work very well, meaning, they do not reduce the error substantially even when the rejection rate increases dramatically. In the case of LoOP Error this can be explained by the fact, that the error values do not spread out over a large space. Therefore, only the first few high errors are classified as outliers while the then slowly diminishing error values form their own group, and thus are not perceived as outliers anymore. The LoOP Data approach on the other hand does not work well because the different chaotic expansions do not seem to be very far apart in input space.

The Page-Hinkley rejector is the best performing approach on three out of the four data sets and tied for first place on the remaining one.

The baseline works rather well, but only on the Tinkerbell-Duffing and the Roessler-Lorenz data sets. These are those sets, where the easier chaotic expansion is intercepted by the harder one. Instead, when the harder expansion comes first, the baseline does not work well because it tracks the mean error over the whole sequence and therefore is faced with a gradually reducing error in the interception part, leading to none adequate rejections.

Another observation to note is the behaviour of the approaches with regard to granularity. Hereby, the baseline shows the most agile behaviour, meaning that it is possible to tweak its hyperparameters in such a way as to enable the realization of a wide array of rejection rates. The Page-Hinkley approach on the other hand, does not come with such a fine granularity. Due to its reliance on active drift detection it can only realize larger spaced rejection rates. Similarly,

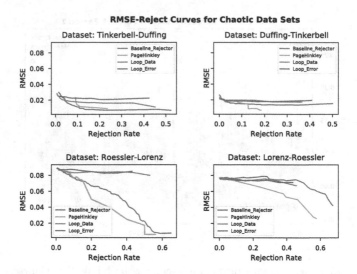

**Fig. 5.** RMSE-Rejection Curves for all rejection methods on the four chaotic data sets.

the LoOP approaches can not match the baseline in terms of agility with regard to the space of rejection rates.

## 5.2  Real World Data Results

The RMSE-reject curves of the real world data experiment are visualized in Fig. 6. Again, and for the same reason as in the previous experiment, the LoOP error approach does not yield good results. Interestingly, the LoOP Data rejector now becomes the second best performing system, tying for first place on two out of the four data sets and coming in second on the remaining ones. This can be explained by the much more complex input space, where clear differences of the samples can now manifest themselves.

Same as in the previous experiment, the Page-Hinkley rejector is the best performing approach, although it is tied for first place with the LoOP Data system on two out of four data sets.

The baseline shows more ambiguous results. It is the worst performer on one data set but matches the performance of LoOP Data in another one. For the remaining ones it is clear, that it does not match LoOP Data and Page-Hinkley.

## 5.3  Tabular Evaluation

Here, we evaluate the previous experiments by means of the reduction in RMSE for different rejection rates compared to a scenario without rejection. The results are listed in Table 1. This table shows the mean reduction of RMSE on the chaotic and real world data sets for four distinct rejection rates. As observed previously, the Page-Hinkley approach wins outright in all categories. On the

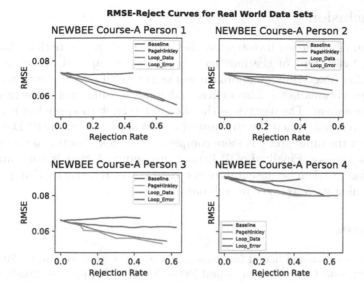

**Fig. 6.** RMSE-Rejection Curves for all rejection methods on the four real world data sets.

chaotic data sets, it is followed by the baseline, while the LoOP systems come in last. However, on the real world data, the results of the baseline diminish and it gets overtaken by the LoOP Data approach.

Furthermore, one can observe, that the rejection works much better on the chaotic data sets than on the real world setting. This is probably due to the fact, that those sets are a lot less complex and less noisy than the real world data sets. However, the Page-Hinkley approach still manages a reduction between 10% and 20% on various rejection rates. In our opinion, this is a very promising result with high relevance in practice.

**Table 1.** Relative reduction in RMSE (in %) for different rejection rates. All values have been averaged over all chaotic and real world data sets respectively.

| Rejectors | Data sets and rejection rates | | | | | | | |
|---|---|---|---|---|---|---|---|---|
| | Chaotic data | | | | Real world data | | | |
| | 20% | 30% | 40% | 50% | 20% | 30% | 40% | 50% |
| LoOP Error | 22.23 | 20.53 | 20.28 | 20.28 | 1.78 | 2.12 | 2.12 | 2.12 |
| LoOP Data | 24.56 | 25.94 | 28.52 | 33.66 | 7.55 | 10.22 | 12.89 | 14.65 |
| Page-Hinkley | 52.24 | 58.08 | 64.85 | 73.38 | 10.39 | 14.75 | 16.92 | 19.79 |
| Baseline | 40.00 | 42.31 | 47.47 | 54.70 | 4.21 | 5.83 | 7.51 | 9.05 |

# 6   Conclusion

In this contribution we investigated the problem of reject options for online regression tasks. Out of the four models that we compared one clear winner emerged. The Page-Hinkley approach works very well on easy data with clear rejection conditions but it also delivers adequate results in a more messy real world environment. The baseline is the cheapest version to apply but it can only deliver good results when the circumstances are appropriate. LoOP Data works better when the input space is more complex and a clear discrimination of input samples is possible. Finally, LoOP Error is an approach that is not suitable for the rejection problem because it does not yield better RMSEs for rising rejection rates, meaning its rejections are sub par.

# References

1. Asif, A.: Generalized neural framework for learning with rejection. In: 2020 International Joint Conference on Neural Networks (IJCNN), pp. 1–8 (2020). https://doi.org/10.1109/IJCNN48605.2020.9206612
2. Bartlett, P.L., Wegkamp, M.H.: Classification with a reject option using a hinge loss. J. Mach. Learn. Res. **9**, 1823–1840 (2008). https://dl.acm.org/citation.cfm?id=1442792
3. Chow, C.: On optimum error and reject trade-off. IEEE Trans. Inf. Theory **16**, 41–46 (1970)
4. Denis, C., Hebiri, M., Zaoui, A.: Regression with reject option and application to KNN (2021)
5. Duffing, G., Emde, F.: Erzwungene schwingungen bei veränderlicher eigenfrequenz und ihre technische bedeutung
6. Fischer, L., Hammer, B., Wersing, H.: Optimal local rejection for classifiers. Neurocomputing **214**, 445–457 (2016). https://doi.org/10.1016/j.neucom.2016.06.038
7. Geifman, Y., El-Yaniv, R.: SelectiveNet: a deep neural network with an integrated reject option (2019)
8. Hendrickx, K., Perini, L., der Plas, D.V., Meert, W., Davis, J.: Machine learning with a reject option: a survey. CoRR abs/2107.11277 (2021). https://arxiv.org/abs/2107.11277
9. Herbei, R., Wegkamp, M.H.: Classification with reject option. Can. J. Stat./La Revue Canadienne de Statistique **34**(4), 709–721 (2006). https://www.jstor.org/stable/20445230
10. Hinder, F., Artelt, A., Hammer, B.: Towards non-parametric drift detection via dynamic adapting window independence drift detection (DAWIDD). In: Proceedings of the 37th International Conference on Machine Learning, ICML 2020, 13–18 July 2020, Virtual Event. Proceedings of Machine Learning Research, vol. 119, pp. 4249–4259. PMLR (2020). https://proceedings.mlr.press/v119/hinder20a.html
11. Jakob, J., Hasenjäger, M., Hammer, B.: On the suitability of incremental learning for regression tasks in exoskeleton control. In: IEEE Symposium on Computational Intelligence in Data Mining (CIDM). IEEE, December 2021
12. Jiang, W., Zhao, Y., Wang, Z.: Risk-controlled selective prediction for regression deep neural network models. In: 2020 International Joint Conference on Neural Networks (IJCNN), pp. 1–8 (2020). https://doi.org/10.1109/IJCNN48605.2020.9207676

13. Kriegel, H., Kröger, P., Schubert, E., Zimek, A.: Loop: local outlier probabilities (2009)
14. Lorenz, E.: Deterministic nonperiodic flow. Journal of the atmospheric sciences 20, 130–41.1. Prog. Phys. Geogr. Earth Environ. **32**(4), 475–480 (2008). https://doi.org/10.1177/0309133308091948
15. Losing, V., Hasenjaeger, M.: NEWBEE: a multi-modal gait database of natural everyday-walk in an urban environment. Sci. Data (2022, submitted)
16. Losing, V., Hammer, B., Wersing, H.: Incremental on-line learning: a review and comparison of state of the art algorithms. Neurocomputing **275**, 1261–1274 (2018). https://doi.org/10.1016/j.neucom.2017.06.084
17. Losing, V., Yoshikawa, T., Hasenjäger, M., Hammer, B., Wersing, H.: Personalized online learning of whole-body motion classes using multiple inertial measurement units. In: International Conference on Robotics and Automation, ICRA 2019, Montreal, QC, Canada, 20–24 May 2019, pp. 9530–9536. IEEE (2019). https://doi.org/10.1109/ICRA.2019.8794251
18. Montiel, J., et al.: River: machine learning for streaming data in python. J. Mach. Learn. Res. **22**(110), 1–8 (2021). https://jmlr.org/papers/v22/20-1380.html
19. Nadeem, M.S.A., Zucker, J.D., Hanczar, B.: Accuracy-rejection curves (ARCS) for comparing classification methods with a reject option. In: Machine Learning in Systems Biology, pp. 65–81. PMLR (2009)
20. Nusse, H., Yorke, J.: Dynamics: Numerical Explorations. Springer, New York (1997)
21. Page, E.S.: Continuous inspection schemes. Biometrika **41**(1–2), 100–115 (1954). https://doi.org/10.1093/biomet/41.1-2.100
22. Rössler, O.: An equation for continuous chaos. Phys. Lett. A **57**(5), 397–398 (1976). https://doi.org/10.1016/0375-9601(76)90101-8. https://www.sciencedirect.com/science/article/pii/0375960176901018
23. Tijjani, I., Kumar, S., Boukheddimi, M.: A survey on design and control of lower extremity exoskeletons for bipedal walking. Appl. Sci. **12**(5) (2022). https://doi.org/10.3390/app12052395. https://www.mdpi.com/2076-3417/12/5/2395

# Stream-Based Active Learning
# with Verification Latency
# in Non-stationary Environments

Andrea Castellani[1]([✉]) [ID], Sebastian Schmitt[2] [ID], and Barbara Hammer[1] [ID]

[1] Bielefeld University, Bielefeld, Germany
{acastellani,bhammer}@techfak.uni-bielefeld.de
[2] Honda Research Institute Europe, Offenbach, Germany
sebastian.schmitt@honda-ri.de

**Abstract.** Data stream classification is an important problem in the field of machine learning. Due to the non-stationary nature of the data where the underlying distribution changes over time (*concept drift*), the model needs to continuously adapt to new data statistics. Stream-based Active Learning (AL) approaches address this problem by interactively querying a human expert to provide new data labels for the most recent samples, within a limited budget. Existing AL strategies assume that labels are immediately available, while in a real-world scenario the expert requires time to provide a queried label (*verification latency*), and by the time the requested labels arrive they may not be relevant anymore. In this article, we investigate the influence of finite, time-variable, and unknown verification delay, in the presence of concept drift on AL approaches. We propose *PRopagate (PR)*, a latency independent utility estimator which also predicts the requested, but not yet known, labels. Furthermore, we propose a drift-dependent dynamic budget strategy, which uses a variable distribution of the labelling budget over time, after a detected drift. Thorough experimental evaluation, with both synthetic and real-world non-stationary datasets, and different settings of verification latency and budget are conducted and analyzed. We empirically show that the proposed method consistently outperforms the state-of-the-art. Additionally, we demonstrate that with variable budget allocation in time, it is possible to boost the performance of AL strategies, without increasing the overall labeling budget.

**Keywords:** Streaming active learning · Verification latency · Concept drift · Online learning

## 1 Introduction

The growing digitization of industrial processes leads to an ever-increasing data stream recorded by many sensors. In potentially critical settings, there is an interest to continuously monitor the data stream and analyze data samples at

E. Pimenidis et al. (Eds.): ICANN 2022, LNCS 13532, pp. 260–272, 2022.
https://doi.org/10.1007/978-3-031-15937-4_22

the time they are recorded e.g., in order to detect failing machines or deter-mine the current operating state of a machine in a factory setting. Data-driven online machine learning techniques can address such tasks, but require labeled data samples for task-specific training [6]. Realistic data streams are often non-stationary and the underlying data statistics might change over time, so-called *concept drifts* [9]. This can render labels and trained models outdated (in partic-ular in the case of so-called real concept drift) and leads to the need to manually relabel data samples and retrain models continuously.

Stream-based Active Learning (AL) approaches address this problem by interactively querying an oracle e.g., a human expert, to provide new data labels for particularly informative training samples which arrive over time. Since acquir-ing new labels is costly, models typically operate based on an only limited total budget for new labels. Therefore, a utility function is employed to determine which of the incoming data samples should be labelled. The most useful samples are queried as far as the labeling budget, which is defined as the percentage of the data samples that can be labeled per time unit, allows for it [24].

Most existing AL strategies assume that labels are immediately available after data samples have been queried [16,24]. However, this is unrealistic if labels cannot be calculated automatically and human experts need to be involved. As an example, in a typical factory setting, data samples for which labels are required within an AL strategy are collected over some time period. Then an expert inspects the current batch of data samples in infrequent intervals and provides some or all labels. Hence a queried label is available after some time period only, the so-called *verification latency* [14].The verification latency varies from sample to sample and it is unknown a priori. The presence of verification latency can be particularly problematic for machine learning approaches which deal with streaming data subject to concept drift, because a label might already be wrong when it arrives. To the best of our knowledge, the effect of unknown verification latency on AL strategies is currently widely unexplored [18]. Further, most AL strategies assume a homogeneous budget over time, albeit label requests might be particularly beneficial right after a detected drift event [12,24].

In this work, we explore the influence of verification latency in the presence of concept drift in AL. We investigate limitations of existing AL strategies to estimate the utility of the current sample under a priori unknown verification latency. We focus on two aspects to improve this performance: (1) A novel utility estimator called PRopagate (PR), which concentrates on the feature space to infer the still unknown labels of queried samples, which is model-agnostic and latency independent. (2) A dynamic budget allocation scheme, which distributes the overall labelling budget inhomogeneously over time as soon as driven a drift is detected. In the following, we investigate the performance of unsupervised and semi-supervised drift detectors under the effect of verification latency. We test the performance by a thorough evaluation of several synthetic and real-world non-stationary datasets, with several realistic settings of verification delay, and we compare the proposed strategies against the State-Of-The-Art (SOTA) [18].

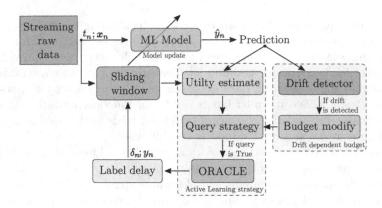

**Fig. 1.** Proposed stream-based Active Learning (AL) framework.

## 2    Related Work

*Verification latency* was introduced in [14] considering three different variants: *null latency* refers to a label for a selected sample arriving instantaneously – this is the most common setting for AL in the literature; *extreme latency*, i.e. the label is never available – this setting is getting a lot of attention recently [21]; and *intermediate latency*, with a finite delay between sample selection and label arrival – this is common in many real-world applications, but has received only little attention in the literature [18]. In [10], the authors list research questions and approaches addressing verification latency in streaming data, but do not consider AL strategies. AL strategies are considered in [13,17,19], where delayed labels are directly incorporated to the training loop of various models. A utility estimation method similar to the one proposed here is considered in [18] which addresses the effect of delayed labels. Yet the work makes unrealistic assumptions about the label delay, e.g., fixed delay which is also known a priori; the authors point out the necessity for more research on generalizations thereof [18,20].

Drift detection in presence of verification latency is getting some attention in recent years [6,16]. Semi-supervised drift detection methods are rather prominent, which monitor the performance of the queried labeled in a specific task [12,24]. But, with large verification delay recent labels might be lacking, leading to degraded performance of semi-supervised detection methods. Unsupervised drift detectors within a AL strategy is introduced in [22]. An adaptive labelling budget, where labeling ratio increases after a drift, was studied in [12]. However, *null latency* is assumed and semi-supervised drift detectors are used, which may not work in case of finite verification latency.

## 3    Proposed Active Learning Framework

The processing flow for the proposed AL framework is shown in Fig. 1. Let $\mathcal{D}$ be a data stream, $\mathcal{D} = \{(t_n, \boldsymbol{x}_n) \mid n \in \mathbb{N}\}$, where each data sample is a $d$-dimensional feature vector $x_n$, which arrives at time $t_n$. We consider a classification task where label $y_n$ for the data sample can be actively obtained by querying an oracle. The learning model is blindly updated at each time step $t_n$ using data (samples and available labels) from the sliding window of the latest $l \in \mathbb{N}$ time steps $\mathcal{T}_n = [t_{n-l}, t_n]$. First, the utility of the current sample $x_n$ is quantified based on the available information contained in the sliding window $\mathcal{T}_n$. Then, the query strategy determines whether the data sample is queried or not, based on its utility and the budget [22]. The currently available budget $B(t)$, with $0 \leq B(t_n) \leq 1$, is expressed as the probability that a data sample could be selected for querying at all. The output of the querying strategy is realized as a Boolean variable $a_n$. If the label is queried, $a_n =$ True, then $x_n$ is given to the oracle, so its label will be provided at the time $t_n + \delta_n$ and the sliding window $\mathcal{T}_n$ will be updated with the label information. The delay $\delta_n$ is called *verification latency*. In parallel to the utility calculation, a drift detector is employed. In case concept drift is detected, the budget for the query strategy is first increased substantially for a certain period of time, to adapt faster to the new data statistics. After a while, when the model has hopefully adapted to the new data distribution, the budget is decreased to not exceed the number of total labeled samples, and later it returns to its nominal value.

## 3.1  Proposed Utility Estimator: PRopagate Labels

In a classical AL strategy, labels that have been queried, but are not yet available due to the verification latency $\delta_n$, would be ignored. As the utility function determining which samples to query is also not updated during that time, this leads to an oversampling of high utility regions for querying. A schematic example is shown in Fig. 2 where the utility (taken as classification confidence) already led to submitting samples $\hat{x}_1$ and $\hat{x}_2$ to the oracle. Without labels, the current sample $x_n$ would also have high utility and be a likely candidate for requesting its label. However, as soon as a label arrives for $\hat{x}_1$ or $\hat{x}_2$, not much information can be gained by obtaining the label of $x_n$.

As a solution to this problem, we propose to PRopagate (PR) the spatial information of the queried labels to the neighboring unlabeled queried data samples, an idea inspired by [18]. We estimate a still missing label with a weighted majority vote of the label of its $k$-Nearest Neighbor labels, restricted to samples from the sliding window $\mathcal{T}_n$. The weight for each nearest neighbor depends on the arrival time of the labels via $w_{i,j} = \exp\left(-\lambda(t_i - t_j)^2\right)$, where $t_i$ and $t_j$ are respectively the timestamp of the queried sample and its neighbor $j$, with $j = 1 \ldots k$. Therefore, weights for newer labels are larger than older labels, which reflects that newer labels are less likely to be outdated as compared to older ones. Finally, the decision boundaries of the classifier are updated using the true and predicted labels, and the utility of the current sample $x_n$ is calculated.

In Fig. 2 is shown an example of the proposed method (with $k = 3$), the samples with requested but not yet arrived label have their neighbors highlighted. The marker size of their neighbors is proportional to $w$. The samples $\hat{x}_0$ and $\hat{x}_2$ are assigned respectively to classes red and blue, since all their labeled neighbors

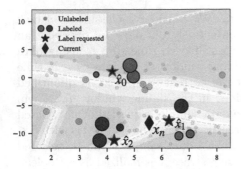 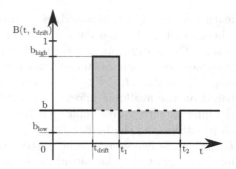

**Fig. 2.** Schematic classifier decision regions. Colored circles represent labelled data samples. The background color is the model confidence for each class. Circle size indicates weight $w_{i,j}$ where larger implies more recent. (Color figure online)

**Fig. 3.** Drift detection driven budget distribution $B(t, t_{drift})$.

belong to those classes. The sample $\hat{x}_1$, even if the majority of its neighbors belong to the red class, is assigned to the blue class, due to of the weight strategy.

### 3.2  Proposed Budget Strategy: Dynamic Budget Allocation

In order to increase the performance for non-stationary data streams we include feedback between the AL strategy and the concept drift detection module. We propose to use a concept drift-dependent distribution of the labeling budget over time, without exceeding the global budget limit for the complete data stream, i.e. the total number of queried labels. We employ a piece-wise constant budget function $B(t, t_{drift})$,

$$B(t, t_{drift}) = \begin{cases} b_{\text{high}} & \text{if } t_{drift} < t < t_1 \\ b_{\text{low}} & \text{if } t_1 < t < t_2 \\ b & \text{otherwise} \end{cases}, \tag{1}$$

which is sketched in Fig. 3. After a detected drift, the budget increases to $b_{\text{high}}$ for a time period $t_1 - t_{drift}$, and then decreases to $b_{\text{low}}$ for a time period $t_2 - t_1$. After the time $\Delta T = t_2 - t_{drift}$ the budget is back to $b$, which is the value for no detected drift. In order to have the same total number of queries to the oracle with and without drift, not all parameters of this budget can be chosen freely, but the condition $\int_{t_{drift}}^{t_{drift} + \Delta T} B(t)\, dt \overset{!}{=} b\Delta T$ needs to be fulfilled. Given am overall budget $b$, we freely adjust parameters $b_{\text{high}}$, $b_{\text{low}}$ and $\Delta T$, which leads to the time points $t_1$ and $t_2$:

$$t_1 = t_{drift} + \Delta T \frac{b - b_{\text{low}}}{b_{\text{high}} - b_{\text{low}}}, \quad t_2 = t_1 + \Delta T \frac{b_{\text{high}} - b}{b_{\text{high}} - b_{\text{low}}} \tag{2}$$

---

**Algorithm 1:** Proposed stream-based AL framework

---

**Require:** Classifier $f$, drift detector $\Psi$, utility function $UL$, query strategy $QS$,
          budget function $B$ , budget parameters $b_{high}$, $b_{low}$, $\Delta T$

1  $f, \Psi, UL, QS \leftarrow$ initialize
2  $t_1, t_2 \leftarrow$ Eq. (2)
3  $t_{drift} \leftarrow +\infty$
4  **for** $n$ in $1, \ldots$ **do**
5      $(t_n, x_n) \leftarrow$ retrieve new data sample from data stream
6      $\hat{y}_n = f(x_n)$                                 // *Get label prediction*
7      **if** $\Psi(\mathcal{T}_n) =$ True **then**
8         $t_{drift} = t_n$                             // *Drift detected*
9
10     $b_n \leftarrow B(t_n, t_{drift})$       // *Eq. (1): Drift dependent budget modification*
11     $u_n \leftarrow UL(x_n, \hat{y}_n, \mathcal{T}_n, f)$           // *Get utility for current sample*
12     $a_n \leftarrow QS(b_b, u_n)$                   // *Query sample*
13     **if** $a_n = True$ **then**
14        ask oracle for label of $x_{n'}$ (label $y_n$ will be provided at $t_n + \delta_n$)
15
16     $\mathcal{T} \leftarrow (t_n, x_n, y_n)$             // *Update sliding training window*
17     $f, \Psi \leftarrow$ update with $\mathcal{T}$
18 **end**

---

In this way, the total rate of labels queried by the AL strategy is the same as with constant budget $b$. Yet it is inhomogeneously distributed, i.e., after a drift, the labelling budget is substantially increased. This leads to a quicker model update but needs to be compensated by reducing the budget later on to arrive at the same average label rate.

## 4 Experimental Setup

We perform all the experiments with the proposed stream-based AL framework sketched in Algorithm 1. We evaluate the proposed method on synthetic and real-world datasets, listed in Table 1. For benchmarking purposes, concept drift is artificially introduced and controlled after 50% of the data stream, by corrupting the most informative features in a gradual manner, as described in [2].

We evaluate the model with the prequential evaluation [8] (test-then-train) over all instances of the data stream. We use the Parzen Window Classifier (PWC). In order to make a fair comparison with the existing literature, we follow the benchmark framework of [18]. The classifier is first initialized with the first 100 samples of each data stream, then it is trained used a sliding window of $l = 500$ samples. As stream-based querying strategies, we use *Split* [24] and *Probabilistic Active Learning (PAL)* [11]. We also use the baseline strategy *Random Selection (rand)*, that randomly samples instances according to the given budget. We compare the proposed sample utility estimation strategy (PR) to the current SOTA introduced in [18], which is referred to as '*forgetting and simulating incoming labels with bagging (FS.B)*'.

Table 1. Details of the data streams used for training.

| Dataset | Instances | Features | Classes | Data type | Drift type |
|---------|-----------|----------|---------|-----------|------------|
| *RBF_2_2* [18] | 4000 | 2 | 2 | Synthetic | Induced |
| *RBF_10_4* [18] | 4000 | 10 | 4 | | |
| *hyperplane* [7] | 4000 | 2 | 2 | | |
| *stagger* [7] | 4000 | 2 | 2 | | |
| *wine* [2] | 6497 | 12 | 2 | Real-world | Induced |
| *digits08* [2] | 1499 | 16 | 2 | | |
| *digits17* [2] | 1457 | 16 | 2 | | |
| *Luxembourg* [23] | 1901 | 31 | 2 | Real-world | Unknown |
| *Weather* [5] | 18159 | 8 | 2 | | |

We investigate the influence of variable verification latency by sampling the actual delay $\delta_n$ for each label query from a predefined distribution. We tested two representative distributions, a uniform distribution with $\delta_n \sim \mathcal{U}(50, 50 + \delta)$, and a truncated normal distribution, $\delta_n \sim \max(0, \mathcal{N}(\delta, 50))$ (truncation refers to the fact that we set a negative delay to zero). We tested various parameter values for $\delta = [0, 50, 100, 150, 200, 300]$, and several budgets levels $b$ of 5%, 10%, 15%, 20%, 25%, 40%, 50%, 75% and 100% as an upper bound of performance. Unless explicitly reported, we set the number of neighbors for the label propagation to $k = 3$ and the weighting coefficient of $\lambda = 0.01$. The budget modification time is set to $\Delta T = 1000$ and modified budgets are $b_{\text{high}} = 4b$ and $b_{\text{low}} = b/2$. We use two popular semi-supervised drift detection algorithms, Drift Detection Model (DDM) [7] and Adaptive Windowing (ADWIN) [1]. These act only using the labeled samples coming from the active learning [12]. We also employ the unsupervised Hellinger Distance Drift Detection Model (HDDDM) drift detection method [4], operating directly on data samples in the feature space of the input data. For each algorithm and dataset, we monitor the accuracy of the whole data stream. All experiments have been repeated 50 times with different random seeds. The source code used in the experiments is publicly available on http://github.com/Castel44/AL_delay.

## 5    Results and Discussion

Due to space restrictions, we report only a representative subset of all results, which clearly demonstrate the qualitative trends obtained in all the experiments.

**Effect of Unknown Label Delay in Existing AL Strategies.** The SOTA utility estimator for AL strategies requires knowledge of the verification latency in advance. We analyze the performance of the *FS.B+pal* strategy [18], under the influence of verification latency sampled from the truncated normal distribution, $\delta_n \sim \max(0, \mathcal{N}(\delta, 50))$, where the parameter value $\delta$ is unknown in advance. In the experiments, when the expected latency $\hat{\delta}$ of *FS.B+pal* is not equal to the

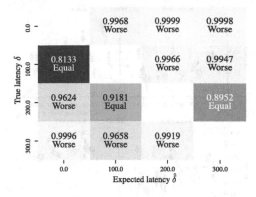

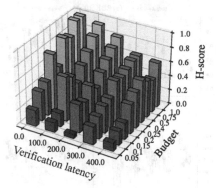

**Fig. 4.** P-values for *FS.B+pal* with true latency vs expected latency.

**Fig. 5.** Semi-supervised drift detector (ADWIN) performance.

true latency, $\delta \neq \hat{\delta}$, we witness an average accuracy drop of 0.87%, with 95% confidence interval (0.21%–2.15%). For each value of true latency $\delta$, we compare the performance obtained with the correct match of the true latency against expected latency values. In Fig. 4, we report p-values of the non-parametric statistical *Mann-Whitney U-Test* [15] with $\alpha$ level of 0.05 for the dataset *RBF_4_10* based on the null hypothesis that the performance is not affected by differing latencies. It can be clearly observed that there are statistical differences when the actual and the expected latency differ, and the null hypothesis is rejected for most of the combinations.

**Experimental Results with Proposed Utility Estimator PR.** We compare the performance achieved with the proposed PR, against the SOTA utility estimator FS.B [18]. We combine it with two popular query strategies, *split* [24] and *pal* [11]. Figure 6 shows the results with low (5%) and medium (25%) budget for different levels of varying verification latency $\delta_n \sim \max(0, \mathcal{N}(\delta, 50))$. Note that in this case even with $\delta = 0$, about half of the labels arrive with some delay. To compare PR to the best possible SOTA algorithm, we use the real expected latency $\hat{\delta} = \delta$ for the latter. As upper limit on the performance, the dashed red line shows the results when every data sample is labeled, i.e. 100% budget. As expected, the classification accuracy decreases with the increase of the verification latency. The proposed utility estimator consistently outperforms the SOTA for the same querying strategies. The best performance is achieved combining the PR utility estimator with the *pal* AL strategy. Also, for $\delta = 0$ the PR slightly outperform the SOTA. Because the SOTA assumes zero delay, leading to reduced performance, while the PR utility estimator makes no assumption on the expected delay. This confirms the expectation that using the current classification model to estimate the latest queried labels, as done in the *FS.B* query estimation [18], leads to reduced performance in case of drift, while relying on the recently sampled labels utilizes the available information more efficiently. It is

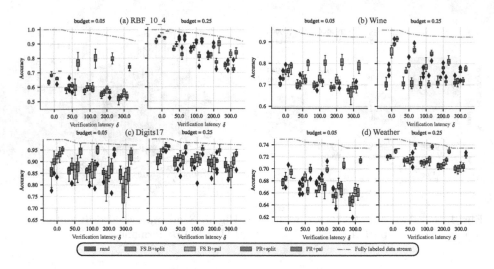

**Fig. 6.** Results with fixed budget distribution.

interesting to note that already for 25% budget the proposed method comes close to the best cases with 100% budget for the three datasets RBF_10_4, Digits17 and Weather.

**Drift Detection Performance.** In AL strategies, semi-supervised drift detectors can be used to monitor the error rate of the requested labeled samples [12,24]. We empirically show that under the influence of verification delay, and low budget, such drift detectors have low performance. Either the drift is not detected, or it is detected too late, when the model already recovered due to the AL process. We use the H-score [2] as drift detection metric, as it takes in account the real detection of a change event and its detection delay. In Fig. 5 we report the ADWIN detection performance on the dataset RBF_10_4. A good level of performance ($H > 0.75$) is only achieved with budget above 0.25, and with latency less than 200. Hence, hereafter, we use the unsupervised drift detector (HDDDM) which is independent of budget or latency, and it is able to promptly detect the drifts in the distribution of the feature space.

**Drift Detection Driven Budget Distribution.** In Fig. 7, we report the performance of the proposed AL framework with dynamic budget allocation after a detected drift, as described in Eq. (1). We compare it to using a fixed static budget $b$, where the total number of queried labeled sample is the same in both approaches. Again, the red dashed line is the upper bound of performance, obtained with a fully labeled data stream. For readability, we only report the best performing query strategy (*pal*) of Fig. 6, and we compare the proposed PR with *FS.B* utility estimator. It is clear that the dynamic budget allocation, after a detected drift, increases the performance for both approaches considerably (crosses compared to full circles). Also, the proposed method for label propagation consistently outperforms the SOTA. Remarkable, the proposed budget

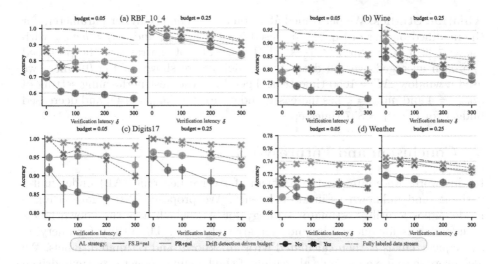

**Fig. 7.** Results of the proposed drift detection driven budget distribution.

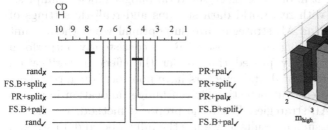

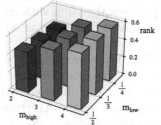

**Fig. 8.** Critical distance diagram summarizing all experiments.

**Fig. 9.** Average performance rank of modified budget hyper-parameters.

strategy is able to obtain accuracy level comparable to using a 100% labeled data stream, with as little as 5% of labeled data. This demonstrates that by carefully labeling instances, we are able to achieve competitive model accuracy with much lower cost.

As a summary, in order to assess the statistical significance of the results, we use the Friedman non-parameteric test with 0.05 confidence level, followed by Nemenyi post-hoc test. We report in Fig. 8 the critical differences plot [3] of our experiments, accumulated over all the datasets, budget and latency levels. The querying strategies combined with the proposed utility estimator (PR) are significantly better than the SOTA counterpart. The AL strategies using the proposed drift driven budget distribution (subscript ✓) are in all cases significantly better than the corresponding methods with the static budget allocation (subscript ✗).

**Ablation Studies.** We performed ablation studies on the hyper-parameters for the modified budget of Eq. (1) and used $b_{high} = b\, m_{high}$ and $b_{low} = b\, m_{low}$ with $m_{high} \in [2, 3, 4]$ and $m_{low} \in [\frac{1}{2}, \frac{1}{3}, \frac{1}{4}]$. The results of the rank of the proposed approach averaged over all datasets and delays are shown in Fig. 9, where we used a window $\Delta T = 1000$ timesteps. Therefore, the best performing setting of $m_{high} = 4$ and $m_{low} = \frac{1}{2}$ has increased budget for $t_1 - t_{drift} = 143$, and decreased budget for $t_2 - t_1 = 857$ timesteps.

## 6  Conclusion and Future Work

In this work, we addressed the problem of Active Learning (AL) under finite, variable, and unknown verification latency. We proposed PRopagate (PR), a model-agnostic utility estimator strategy for AL, which uses the known labels to infer labels for queried but not yet arrived labels. The utility for querying subsequent labels is then calculated with all, known and estimated, labels. We also propose to use a dynamic allocation of the labeling budget over time, driven by the detection of concept drift events. After a drift detection, we increase the budget, then we decrease it in order to meet the total budget labeled samples.

Experimental results with real-world data streams and realistic settings of latency, showed that existing AL strategies are sub-optimal when the amount of latency is unknown. By using the proposed PR we consistently outperform the SOTA. We also empirically proved that under the effect of verification latency, semi-supervised concept drifts detectors have poor performance. Then, we proved that the proposed drift detection driven budget allocation improves the performance of the AL strategies. With the proposed method, we showed that is possible to achieve similar results as we use the fully labeled data stream, with as little as 5% of labeled samples. We thoroughly analyzed the dependency of the introduced hyperparameters and identified a range of values for robust and good operation.

Even though the proposed methods are model-agnostic, for this article, we only used the Parzen Window Classifier, and we used the classification confidence as utility measure. In future, we extend to apply the proposed method to semi-supervised Deep Learning classifiers and to use other utility measures e.g. information gain. As shown, the dynamic budget strategy works well in the current setting, where only one abrupt drift occurs. An open question for future work is the investigation of the proposed approach in situations where multiply drifts might occur during the dynamic budget adjustment period, or where a continuous drift occurs over a longer period of time.

## References

1. Bifet, A., Gavalda, R.: Learning from time-changing data with adaptive windowing. In: SIAM International Conference on Data Mining (2007)
2. Castellani, A., Schmitt, S., Hammer, B.: Task-sensitive concept drift detector with constraint embedding. In: IEEE Symposium Series on Computational Intelligence (SSCI) (2021)

3. Demšar, J.: Statistical comparisons of classifiers over multiple data sets. J. Mach. Learn. Res. **7**, 1–30 (2006)

4. Ditzler, G., Polikar, R.: Hellinger distance based drift detection for nonstationary environments. In: 2011 IEEE Symposium on Computational Intelligence in Dynamic and Uncertain Environments (CIDUE) (2011)

5. Ditzler, G., Polikar, R.: Incremental learning of concept drift from streaming imbalanced data. IEEE Trans. Knowl. Data Eng. **25**, 2283–2301 (2013)

6. Fahy, C., Yang, S., Gongora, M.: Scarcity of labels in non-stationary data streams: a survey. ACM Comput. Surv. (CSUR) **55**(2), 1–39 (2022)

7. Gama, J., Medas, P., Castillo, G., Rodrigues, P.: Learning with drift detection. In: Bazzan, A.L.C., Labidi, S. (eds.) SBIA 2004. LNCS (LNAI), vol. 3171, pp. 286–295. Springer, Heidelberg (2004). https://doi.org/10.1007/978-3-540-28645-5_29

8. Gama, J., Sebastião, R., Rodrigues, P.P.: Issues in evaluation of stream learning algorithms. In: KDD (2009)

9. Gama, J., Žliobaitė, I., Bifet, A., Pechenizkiy, M., Bouchachia, A.: A survey on concept drift adaptation. ACM Comput. Surv. (CSUR) **46**, 1–37 (2014)

10. Gomes, H.M., Read, J., Bifet, A., Barddal, J.P., Gama, J.: Machine learning for streaming data: state of the art, challenges, and opportunities. SIGKDD Explor. **21**, 6–22 (2019)

11. Kottke, D., Krempl, G., Spiliopoulou, M.: Probabilistic active learning in datastreams. In: Fromont, E., De Bie, T., van Leeuwen, M. (eds.) IDA 2015. LNCS, vol. 9385, pp. 145–157. Springer, Cham (2015). https://doi.org/10.1007/978-3-319-24465-5_13

12. Krawczyk, B., Pfahringer, B., Wozniak, M.: Combining active learning with concept drift detection for data stream mining. In: 2018 IEEE International Conference on Big Data (2018)

13. Kuncheva, L.I., Sánchez, J.S.: Nearest neighbour classifiers for streaming data with delayed labelling. In: 2008 IEEE International Conference on Data Mining (2008)

14. Marrs, G.R., Hickey, R.J., Black, M.M.: The impact of latency on online classification learning with concept drift. In: Bi, Y., Williams, M.-A. (eds.) KSEM 2010. LNCS (LNAI), vol. 6291, pp. 459–469. Springer, Heidelberg (2010). https://doi.org/10.1007/978-3-642-15280-1_42

15. McKnight, P.E., Najab, J.: Mann-Whitney u test. The Corsini encyclopedia of psychology (2010)

16. Mohamad, S., Mouchaweh, M.S., Bouchachia, A.: Active learning for data streams under concept drift and concept evolution. In: STREAMEVOLV@ECML-PKDD (2016)

17. Parreira, P.H., Prati, R.C.: Naive importance weighting for data stream with intermediate latency. In: 2021 IEEE Symposium Series on Computational Intelligence (SSCI) (2021)

18. Pham, T., Kottke, D., Krempl, G., Sick, B.: Stream-based active learning for sliding windows under the influence of verification latency. Mach. Learn. 1–26 (2021). https://doi.org/10.1007/s10994-021-06099-z

19. Plasse, J., Adams, N.M.: Handling delayed labels in temporally evolving data streams. In: 2016 IEEE International Conference on Big Data (2016)

20. Serrao, E., Spiliopoulou, M.: Active stream learning with an oracle of unknown availability for sentiment prediction. In: IAL@PKDD/ECML (2018)

21. Umer, M., Polikar, R.: Comparative analysis of extreme verification latency learning algorithms. ArXiv abs/2011.14917 (2020)

22. Žliobaitė, I.: Change with delayed labeling: when is it detectable? In: 2010 IEEE International Conference on Data Mining Workshops (2010)
23. Žliobaitė, I.: Combining similarity in time and space for training set formation under concept drift. Intell. Data Anal. **15**, 589–611 (2011)
24. Žliobaitė, I., Bifet, A., Pfahringer, B., Holmes, G.: Active learning with drifting streaming data. IEEE Trans. Neural Netw. Learn. Syst. **25**, 27–39 (2014)

# StTime-Net: Combining both Historical and Textual Factors for Stock Movement Prediction

Hy Dang[1]([✉]), Minh Nguyen[2], and Bo Mei[1]

[1] Texas Christian University, Fort Worth, TX 76129, USA
hy.dang@tcu.edu
[2] University of Minnesota, Twin Cities, Minneapolis, MN 55455, USA

**Abstract.** With the development of modern technology, machine learning has become the most popular tool for analyzing financial and numerical data. It has great potential to forecast stock prices. The proper prediction of future stock prices helps investors to increase their chances of earning more profits. As a result, many research papers using machine learning and deep learning in stock price prediction have been conducted. However, most researchers only focus on the past price categories of the stock market without considering other essential types of information, which include the articles about a company and how people talk about a company on social media. Thus, in this paper, we apply machine learning and deep learning methods to predict the future stock market through both numerical data and textual information. The textual information is based on analyzing tweets about the companies. Moreover, we adopt Time2Vec [13] to learn a vector representation of time. We show that our method (StTime-Net) is a more suitable approach for stock movement prediction.

**Keywords:** Stock prediction · Machine learning · Classification problem

## 1 Introduction

The prediction of stock price movement is an active research area worldwide due to its importance for quantitative analysts and investment companies [15]. The main challenge that many researchers face is the volatility and non-stationary nature of stock price, making it difficult to make a correct prediction.

According to [18], the factors that influence the stock market the most were the past performance of the company's stock, policies, earnings and potential developments. On the other hand, the loyalty to the company's products, rumors, and expected losses in other investments are the least influencing factors [18]. In other words, fundamental analysis (FA) and technical analysis (TA) are the two main methods which influence the decisions in the market [26]. FA uses the publicly available information about the stock to analyze the company and

© The Author(s), under exclusive license to Springer Nature Switzerland AG 2022
E. Pimenidis et al. (Eds.): ICANN 2022, LNCS 13532, pp. 273–284, 2022.
https://doi.org/10.1007/978-3-031-15937-4_23

extract insights [26]. In contrast, TA employs various technical factors to the available history of the stock prices to retrieve a decision [26].

However, most research regarding predicting stock price movement treats stock movement prediction as a time series problem because of the nature of stock prices, which is driven by new information and follows a random walk pattern [17]. Moreover, price signals only are lack of the understandings of influences of sudden events or news [27]. Therefore, a more modern viewpoint should adopt the information from social media, which can play an essential role in the stock market. For instance, Tweets from people on Twitter might contain important information about stock movement, which can be utilized to predict returns [22]. Based on this idea, in recent years, there have been several research projects involving sentiment analysis to predict and analyze the movement of the stock [11]. The conventional approach and analyzing the Twitter posts approach have achieved some possible results related to the dependence between stock price and Twitter information [25]. However, there has not been much research combining these two fields and utilizing the advantages of information among these two. By combining these two types of information, we can tackle some problems of market information and correlations of information to the stock price prediction.

We propose Stock Time Neural Network (StTime-Net), which is a combination method that learns features from historical prices and social media information. This model captures valuable features in both fields through an advanced deep learning model to predict the movement of the stock. Through varied experiments, we show the effectiveness of this model through this research problem. The remainder of this paper is organized as follows. Section 2 explains the related work to the stock market prediction. Section 3, 4 discusses how we formulate the problem and dataset setup as a categorical classification problem. The architectures are then presented in Sect. 5. Moreover, our results, discussions and future work are then presented in Sect. 6 and Sect. 7, respectively.

## 2   Related Work

Previously, researchers have conducted various projects and derived problems related to stock price prediction with different methods. There are some effective approaches, for instance, the theoretical approach. The theoretical approach includes quantitative models like Modern Portfolio Theory [10] or Black-Scholes model [2].

Moreover, most related works were based on TA, using historical prices for prediction. However, with the rise of the Artificial Intelligent field, Machine learning has been adopted and implemented to solve this task. There were different systems of Deep Learning models that achieved high accuracy for financial analysis [28]. The autoregressive integrated moving average model (ARIMA) [4] as a part of a hybrid model associated with neural network was implemented by Zhang et al. [32] to forecast stocks.

With the time series characteristic of stock price data [16], many related approaches have been implemented to address this problem. Lu et al. [16] uses a forecasting method based on CNN-LSTM to predict the stock price. Another example of time series analysis was a model proposed in Moghaddam et al. [19], which utilized the day of the week as a feature. Moreover, Ghosh et al. [8] implemented random forests and LSTM networks to forecast movements of stock prices for intraday trading. Furthermore, Qiu et al. [24] implemented an attention mechanism in LSTM, improving the stock price predictions task. These examples show potential approaches to employ the analysis of stock prediction.

Another analysis used to predict future movements and prices of stock is FA. Recently, this method has been adopted in many research to extend the ways for this problem. For example, Joshi et al. [12] created three classification models (RF, SVM, and Naive Bayes) to categorize the news articles to be positive or negative. From that, we can study the correlation between news and stock trends [12]. In addition, an approach proposed in of Latent Dirichlet Allocation (LDA) followed by Naive Bayes classification shows that the volatility movements are more predictable when using financial news than using asset price movements [1]. Another research conducted in [20] proved the importance of FA in predicting future stock returns.

Researchers have tried to employ both the significant values of both TA and FA. Xu et al. [31] proposed StockNet, a deep generative model to predict the stock movement. They considered both sources from both fundamental and technical information [31]. By comparing with existing methods and techniques, StockNet achieved significant results and accuracies for stock prediction. Moreover, to compare our result, we also adopted StockNet dataset from [31]. To analyze the textual information, we implemented the encoder architecture from Transformer architecture proposed in [29], which is a network architecture based on attention mechanisms. The architecture has reached state of the art in translation task [29]. Additionally, most recurrent neural networks (RNN) have achieved significant results on various modeling problems. However, these RNN models do not consider time as a feature [13]. The Time2Vec is proposed in [13], which is used as a method to improve the performance of problems that consume time. Thus, we tried to utilize the advantage of Time2Vec in our historical information to retrieve more features involving time.

## 3   Problem Formulation

The purpose is to predict the stock movement of a stock on a trading day $d$ with the information during the interval $[t - \Delta t, t - 1]$ where $\Delta t$ is the day range.

Following [31], we treat the problem as a binary classification problem where the outputs of a model are either 1, representing an increase in stock price, or 0, representing a decrease in stock price. In more generalize form,

$$Y = \begin{cases} 1 & \text{if } (p_d^c > p_{d-1}^c) \\ 0 & \text{otherwise} \end{cases} \tag{1}$$

where $p_d^c$ denotes the adjusted closing price. This information is widely used to predict the movement of stock [30, 31].

## 4    Dataset Setup

As mentioned in Sect. 2, we adopted the StockNet dataset. The dataset includes 88 stocks from 9 industries mentioned in [31]. The time interval is a two-year period from 01/01/2014 to 01/01/2016. The author of the dataset sets two lower and upper thresholds, which are $-0.5\%$ and $0.55\%$, respectively, to remove exceptionally minor movement ratios. In detail, if the movement ratio of a sample $\leq -0.5\%$, it is classified as negative movement and labeled with 0. On the other hand, if the movement ratio of a sample $\geq 0.55\%$, it is classi-fied as positive movement and labeled with 1. We remove these data points by eliminating $38.72\%$ of the dataset, returning $49.78\%$ and $50.22\%$ with labels 0 and 1, respectively. We split the dataset into the training set, validation set, and test set with the ratio 70:10:20 with 20339 movements for the training set from 01/01/2014 to 08/01/2015, 2555 movements for the validation set from 08/01/2015 to 10/01/2015, and 3720 movements for the test set from the rest in the time interval. The dataset has two main components: a Twitter dataset and a price dataset. The price dataset is built from Yahoo Finance[1], and the Twitter dataset. Moreover, we also adapt the trading-day alignment proposed in [31] to eliminate non-eligible trading days.

## 5    Methodology

### 5.1    Price Encoder

The historical price information plays a crucial role in the indications of future movements. Therefore, we try to encode some useful features from price data. The Price Encoder in Fig. 1 represents our encoding step for price inputs. We implemented Gated Recurrent Unit (GRU) [6] and Long Short Term Memory (LSTM) [7] to capture the sequential correlation among days in the interval $\Delta t$. We implement these techniques to overcome the suffer from short-term memory from Recurrent Neural Networks [7]. According to [7], with a longer sequence, the architecture may not carry all necessary information to the next steps. There-fore, LSTM's and GRU's are the potential solutions to this problem where their internal mechanisms can regulate the flow of information. The output of GRU and LSTM on day i are presented as:

$$h_t = GRU(p_t, h_{t-1})$$
$$h_t = LSTM(p_t, h_{t-1})$$

where, $p_t$ is the price vector on day t, which composed of closing price, the highest price and the lowest price or a vector of $p_t = [p_t^c, p_t^h, p_t^l]$. $h_t$ is the hidden state retrieved through the layer on day t. The price vectors are normalized with its last adjusted closing price:

$$p_t^{\text{norm}} = \frac{p_t}{p_{t-1}^c}$$

---

[1] https://finance.yahoo.com/industries.

However, from our experiment, GRU layer returns better results compare to LSTM layer in this problem. Therefore, we adopt GRU as our unit for the architecture. Moreover, the stock trend is affected among days. Therefore, we uses the temporal attention suggested in [27,31] to learn the weights of days and generate feature representation.

**Time2Vec.** Time2Vec is a learnable vector representation of time [13]. Moreover, Kazemi et al. [13] has proved that Time2Vec is invariant to time rescaling. In addition, it can capture periodic behavior. With the effectiveness of Time2Vec, we try to implement this technique in our model to extend the features of historical price and capture the representation of time. The formulation of Time2Vec is proposed in [13]:

$$t2v_i(t) = \begin{cases} \omega_i t + \phi_i & \text{if } i = 0 \\ \alpha(\omega_i t + \phi_i) & \text{if } 1 \leq i \leq k \end{cases}$$

where $t2v_i(t)$ is the ith element of t2v(t), $\alpha$ is a periodic function and in our case, we choose cosine as our function. $\omega$ and $\phi$ are the frequency and phase-shift of the periodic function, respectively. After generating the representation vector by Time2Vec, we concatenate the extracted feature with the price feature in the encoder as shown in Fig. 1.

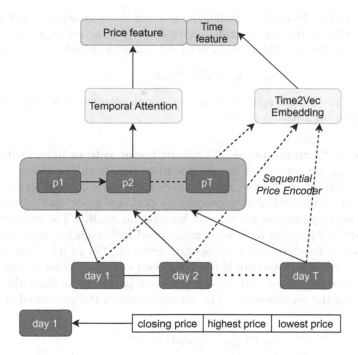

**Fig. 1.** Price encoder

## 5.2 Text Information Encoder

The Textual Information Encoder (TIE) or Text Encoder encodes features and information from textual data generated from the Twitter dataset. Twitter information can offer useful representations of the financial market. Moreover, Twitter public sentiments are used widely in research [22]. Our model uses the TIE to extract a feature vector as Text feature in Fig. 2 using information from Twitter.

**Tweet Embedding.** We implemented different embedding methods such as Global Vectors for Word Representation (GloVe) [23], and fastText [3]. Through our experiment, the pretrained GloVe[2] model achieves more potential results in this type of problem. Thus, we encode the Twitter information via GloVe.

**Sequential Text Encoder.** To learn the representation of information during the day, we need a technique to encode all features in a time interval. We also utilized GRU for sequential text encoder, which is represented by:

$$h_i = GRU(q_i, h_{i-1})$$

where $h_i$ are the hidden state from tweet i from a day through sequential encoder and $q_i$ is the Twitter information ith during the day.

**Sequential Day Encoder.** Similarly, to learn the representation of information from different days in the time interval, we need a technique to encode all features. We utilized GRU for sequential day encoder, which is represented by:

$$h_t = GRU(q_t, h_{t-1})$$

where $h_t$ are the hidden state from day t through sequential day encoder and $q_t$ is the Twitter information in day t.

**Transformer Encoder Layer.** To encode useful features from Twitter information. We implemented Transformer Encoder Layer from Transformer architecture [29]. According to [29], the Transformer architecture is based on an attention mechanism to retrieve global dependencies between input and output. Moreover, it achieves promising accuracy in translation quality. The encoder part of Transformer architecture includes a multi-head self-attention mechanism with a position-wise fully connect feed-forward network [29]. In addition, the benefit of Transformer architecture is the positional encoding, when it replaces the recurrence or convolution part, to capture some information about the position of elements in the sequence [29]. The author proposes the positional encoder as follows:

$$PE_{p,2i} = \sin(p/10000^{2i/d_m})$$
$$PE_{p,2i+1} = \cos(p/10000^{2i/d_m})$$

---

[2] https://nlp.stanford.edu/projects/glove/.

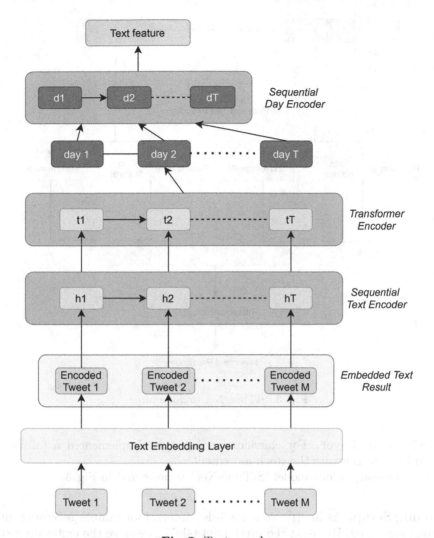

**Fig. 2.** Text encoder

where $p$ is the position of the token in the sequence, and $i$ is the dimension, and $d_m$ is the dimension of the output. The text encoder architecture is visualized in Fig. 2.

## 5.3   Combined Encoder

To predict the movement prediction, we combined the encoded features from Price Encoder and Text Encoder through concatenation.

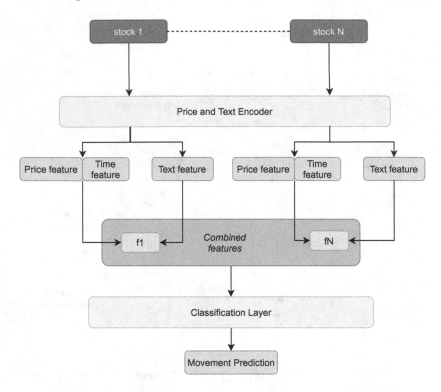

**Fig. 3.** StTime-Net architecture

**Classification Layer.** For classification layer, we implemented a fully connected layer to generate the stock movement.

The summary of our model (StTime-Net) is presented in Fig. 3.

**Training Setup.** As in [31], we use a 5-day interval for sample generation and a batch size of 32. By using the pretrained GloVe, we have the embedding size to 50. We initialized weight matrices in the model with Xavier Initialization [9]. To train the model, we use an Adam optimizer [14] and the cross entropy loss with binary classification represented as:

$$L_{cel} = -(y\log(p) + (1-y)\log(1-p)) \tag{2}$$

where y is the true movement of the stock price.

### 5.4   Metrics and Optimizer

To measure the accuracy, we utilize the metrics of accuracy and the Matthews Correlation Coefficient (MCC), which is a reasonable way of calculation [5].

# 6    Evaluation and Results

## 6.1    Baselines

We compare our model with other baselines to examine the accuracy. Beside some baselines as below, we also considered our model with different variations such as:

- **StTime-Net-TECH:** The StTime-Net uses only historical prices.
- **StTime-Net-FUND:** The StTime-Net uses only tweet information.
- **StTime-Net-FULL:** The StTime-Net uses both information from historical prices and Twitter.

**Technical Analysis:** These methods only use the textual dataset.

- **RAND:** Random guess as the movement is positive or negative.
- **ARIMA:** Autoregressive Integrated Moving Average [4].

**Fundamental Analysis:** These methods only use the historical dataset.

- **Random Forest** Random Forests classifier for Twitter dataset [22].
- **TSLDA** Topic Sentiment Latent Dirichlet Allocation model [21].

**Full Analysis:** These methods consider both historical dataset and textual dataset.

- **StockNet:** We considered different variations of StockNet proposed in [31] including:
  - TECHNICALANALYST: The StockNet model uses only historical prices.
  - FUNDAMENTALANALYST: The StockNet model uses only tweet information.
  - HEDGEFUNDANALYST: The StockNet model uses both information from historical prices and Twitter.

**Table 1.** Results.

| Analysis types | Baseline models | Accuracy |
|---|---|---|
| Technical analysis | RAND | 50.9 |
| | ARIMA [4] | 51.4 |
| | StockNet-TECHNICALANALYST [31] | 54.96 |
| | **StTime-Net-TECH** | **56.4** |
| Fundamental analysis | Random Forest [22] | 53.1 |
| | TSLDA [21] | 54.1 |
| | **StockNet-FUNDAMENTALANALYST** [31] | **58.2** |
| | StTime-Net-FUND | 56.3 |
| Combined analysis | **StockNet-HEDGEFUNDANALYST** [31] | **58.2** |
| | StTime-Net-FULL | 57.4 |

## 6.2    Discussion

As mentioned in previous sections, the stock market is difficult to predict, and a small improvement can lead to significant profit returns [31]. Moreover, [21] mentioned that the 56% of accuracy hits a promising result for predicting stock movement. Through the performance presented in Table 1, we compare our model with other baselines from different perspectives (considering only historical information, only twitter information, and both information). We show that for TA, our variation achieved the best result among others in this analysis type. It shows that the Time2Vec technique is a potential approach for this problem. Although not achieving the best result in FA and full analysis (combining all information), StTime-Net still achieves a promising accuracy with 56.4% and 57.4% in order. These values are higher than the 56% degree of accuracy. For this reason, our model can be implemented as another method for stock movement prediction. Moreover, StTime-Net can still achieve a reasonable MCC score. We also show that the combination of both FA and TA can yield a potential result and can be used simultaneously for analysis.

## 7    Conclusion and Future Work

We examined stock movement prediction using the natural language processing approach, Time2Vec, and both FA and TA. We showed the effectiveness of our proposed StTime-Net model as an another approach for this type of problem. For future research direction, we plan to examine other types of text encoder. Moreover, according to Sawhney et al. [27], the inner stock relations are also important, which directly affect the stock movement and stock market [27]. For example, there are many companies that share similar trends during a period of time because of their characteristics or relations. Therefore, further work is to capture the stock relations among companies into the analysis.

## References

1. Atkins, A., Niranjan, M., Gerding, E.: Financial news predicts stock market volatility better than close price. J. Finance Data Sci. **4**(2), 120–137 (2018)
2. Black, F., Scholes, M.: The pricing of options and corporate liabilities. In: World Scientific Reference on Contingent Claims Analysis in Corporate Finance: Volume 1: Foundations of CCA and Equity Valuation, pp. 3–21. World Scientific (2019)
3. Bojanowski, P., Grave, E., Joulin, A., Mikolov, T.: Enriching word vectors with subword information. Trans. Assoc. Comput. Linguist. **5**, 135–146 (2017)
4. Brown, R.G.: Smoothing, Forecasting and Prediction of Discrete Time Series. Courier Corporation (2004)
5. Chicco, D., Jurman, G.: The advantages of the Matthews correlation coefficient (MCC) over F1 score and accuracy in binary classification evaluation. BMC Genomics **21**(1), 1–13 (2020). https://doi.org/10.1186/s12864-019-6413-7
6. Cho, K., et al.: Learning phrase representations using RNN encoder-decoder for statistical machine translation. arXiv preprint arXiv:1406.1078 (2014)

7.  Gers, F.: Long short-term memory in recurrent neural networks. Ph.D. thesis, Verlag nicht ermittelbar (2001)
8.  Ghosh, P., Neufeld, A., Sahoo, J.K.: Forecasting directional movements of stock prices for intraday trading using LSTM and random forests. arXiv preprint arXiv:2004.10178 (2020)
9.  Glorot, X., Bengio, Y.: Understanding the difficulty of training deep feedforward neural networks. In: Proceedings of the Thirteenth International Conference on Artificial Intelligence and Statistics, pp. 249–256. JMLR Workshop and Conference Proceedings (2010)
10. Goetzmann, W.N., Brown, S.J., Gruber, M.J., Elton, E.J.: Modern Portfolio Theory and Investment Analysis, vol. 237. Wiley, Hoboken (2014)
11. Gupta, R., Chen, M.: Sentiment analysis for stock price prediction. In: 2020 IEEE Conference on Multimedia Information Processing and Retrieval (MIPR), pp. 213–218 (2020). https://doi.org/10.1109/MIPR49039.2020.00051
12. Kalyani, J., Bharathi, P., Jyothi, P., et al.: Stock trend prediction using news sentiment analysis. arXiv preprint arXiv:1607.01958 (2016)
13. Kazemi, S.M., et al.: Time2Vec: learning a vector representation of time. arXiv preprint arXiv:1907.05321 (2019)
14. Kingma, D.P., Ba, J.: Adam: a method for stochastic optimization. arXiv preprint arXiv:1412.6980 (2014)
15. Li, X., Li, Y., Yang, H., Yang, L., Liu, X.Y.: DP-LSTM: differential privacy-inspired LSTM for stock prediction using financial news. arXiv preprint arXiv:1912.10806 (2019)
16. Lu, W., Li, J., Li, Y., Sun, A., Wang, J.: A CNN-LSTM-based model to forecast stock prices. Complexity 2020 (2020)
17. Malkiel, B.G.: A Random Walk Down Wall Street: Including a Life-Cycle Guide to Personal Investing. WW Norton & Company (1999)
18. Marshal, O.T.: Factors influencing investment decisions in capital market: a study of individual investors in Nigeria. Organ. Mark. Emerg. Econ. 4(1), 141–161 (2013). https://doi.org/10.15388/omee.2013.4.1.14263. https://www.journals.vu.lt/omee/article/view/14263
19. Moghaddam, A.H., Moghaddam, M.H., Esfandyari, M.: Stock market index prediction using artificial neural network. J. Econ. Finance Adm. Sci. 21(41), 89–93 (2016)
20. Muhammad, S., Ali, G.: The relationship between fundamental analysis and stock returns based on the panel data analysis; evidence from Karachi stock exchange (KSE). Res. J. Finance Account. 9(3), 84–96 (2018)
21. Nguyen, T.H., Shirai, K.: Topic modeling based sentiment analysis on social media for stock market prediction. In: Proceedings of the 53rd Annual Meeting of the Association for Computational Linguistics and the 7th International Joint Conference on Natural Language Processing (Volume 1: Long Papers), pp. 1354–1364 (2015)
22. Pagolu, V.S., Reddy, K.N., Panda, G., Majhi, B.: Sentiment analysis of Twitter data for predicting stock market movements. In: 2016 International Conference on Signal Processing, Communication, Power and Embedded System (SCOPES), pp. 1345–1350. IEEE (2016)
23. Pennington, J., Socher, R., Manning, C.D.: GloVe: global vectors for word representation. In: Proceedings of the 2014 Conference on Empirical Methods in Natural Language Processing (EMNLP), pp. 1532–1543 (2014)
24. Qiu, J., Wang, B., Zhou, C.: Forecasting stock prices with long-short term memory neural network based on attention mechanism. PLoS ONE 15(1), e0227222 (2020)

25. Ranco, G., Aleksovski, D., Caldarelli, G., Grčar, M., Mozetič, I.: The effects of Twitter sentiment on stock price returns. PLoS ONE **10**(9), e0138441 (2015)
26. Renu, I.R., Christie, P.: Fundamental analysis versus technical analysis-a comparative review. Int. J. Recent Sci. Res. **9**(1), 23009–23013 (2018)
27. Sawhney, R., Agarwal, S., Wadhwa, A., Shah, R.R.: Deep attentive learning for stock movement prediction from social media text and company correlations (2020)
28. Shen, J., Shafiq, M.O.: Short-term stock market price trend prediction using a comprehensive deep learning system. J. Big Data **7**(1), 1–33 (2020). https://doi.org/10.1186/s40537-020-00333-6
29. Vaswani, A., et al.: Attention is all you need. In: Advances in Neural Information Processing Systems, pp. 5998–6008 (2017)
30. Xie, B., Passonneau, R., Wu, L., Creamer, G.G.: Semantic frames to predict stock price movement. In: Proceedings of the 51st Annual Meeting of the Association for Computational Linguistics, pp. 873–883 (2013)
31. Xu, Y., Cohen, S.B.: Stock movement prediction from tweets and historical prices. In: Proceedings of the 56th Annual Meeting of the Association for Computational Linguistics (Volume 1: Long Papers), pp. 1970–1979 (2018)
32. Zhang, G.P.: Time series forecasting using a hybrid ARIMA and neural network model. Neurocomputing **50**, 159–175 (2003)

# Subspace Clustering Multi-module Self-organizing Maps with Two-Stage Learning

Marcondes R. da Silva Júnior$^{(\boxtimes)}$ ⬡ and Aluizio F. R. Araújo ⬡

Center of Informatics, Federal University of Pernambuco, Recife, Brazil
{mrsj,aluizioa}@cin.ufpe.br

**Abstract.** Clustering complexity increases with the number of categories and sub-categories and with data dimensionality. In this case, the distance metrics lose discrimination power with the growth of such dimensionality. Thus, we propose a multiple-module soft subspace clustering algorithm called Subspace Clustering Multi-Module Self-Organizing Maps (SC-MuSOM) that produces a map for each category. Moreover, SC-MuSOM learns a relevance coefficient for each dimension of each cluster handling the dimensionality curse. This fast-training model has a second learning stage in which the cluster prototypes are finely tuned considering the spatial resemblance between cluster centers. We validated the model with data mining sets from UCI Repository and computer vision data. Our experiments suggest that SC-MuSOM is competitive with other state-of-the-art models for the tested problems.

**Keywords:** Subspace clustering · High-dimensional data · Self-organizing maps · Multiple-model clustering · Fine-tuning stage

## 1 Introduction

High-dimensional data originating from images, videos, and texts have been increasingly used in machine learning. With the increasing availability of cheap storage and the rising use of sensor data, we notice substantial data growth in both volume and dimensionality. Data sets with many attributes are referred to as high dimensional. Their complexity turn them hard to handle, therefore, suitable computational tools are needed to process such type of data [1].

An important difficulty in the categorization of high-dimensional data is the progressive reduction of the discriminant capacity of dissimilarity distances caused by the growth of dimensionality [2], therefore data can be miscategorized. Thus, previous works accomplished dimensionality reduction by creating new dimensions through combinations of the original attributes. Such a dimensionality decrease provokes loss of information, even yet preserving information about irrelevant dimensions [3,4].

We thank FACEPE (Fundação de Amparo à Ciência e Tecnologia do Estado de Pernambuco) for financial support project.

E. Pimenidis et al. (Eds.): ICANN 2022, LNCS 13532, pp. 285–296, 2022.
https://doi.org/10.1007/978-3-031-15937-4_24

We propose a simple solution, called Subspace Clustering Multi-Module Self-Organizing Maps (SC-MuSOM), that can effectively cluster high-dimensional data reducing the curse dimensionality problem through decomposition of the learning process and use of dimension relevance for identifying the more significant attributes for each cluster. Moreover, such a model has a significantly lower computational cost when compared with state-of-art models.

Our model is made up of Self-organizing Maps (SOM) modules. The model design entails a multi-module architecture in which each module is trained only with instances of the same category. In spite of having a number of modules, this is not an assembly model, hence, the most active unit of all modules determines the category of an input pattern. In the training stage, a relevance vector associated with each node is updated at the end of each epoch. Such relevancies weigh the importance of each dimension as a discriminant attribute for a cluster. Therefore, the most discriminating features for each category count more on the distance metrics than on the less relevant attributes. Furthermore, SC-MuSOM has a second learning stage that aims to reduce the miscategorization of some patterns due to spatial proximity between prototypes of different categories. A mutual moving-away movement of close prototypes typifying different clusters is carried out to reduce the odds of errors.

In sum, the proposed model differs from the original SOM mainly in:

– Use of multiple modules to reduce the losses of the curse of dimensionality;
– Use of relevance to weigh each attribute in the distance calculation;
– Use of a refinement stage moving apart prototypes of different categories;
– Definition of a second learning stage for refinement of the clustering method.

In Sect. 2, the subspace clustering and learning refinement are defined and some papers on them are briefly discussed. Section 3 presents SC-MuSOM. In Sect. 4, we show the experimental results and their analysis. Finally, Sect. 5 concludes the paper and makes some suggestions for future research.

## 2 Self-organizing Maps and High-Dimensional Data Clustering

This section briefly discusses clustering for high-dimensional data, algorithms based on SOM for categorization of that type of data, and, subspace clustering and methods for learning refinement.

### 2.1 Clustering of High-Dimensional Data

Clustering consists of the process of partitioning unlabeled datasets into groups of similar elements. Each cluster comprises patterns more similar to one another according to a given measure than patterns belonging to other groups [2]. Data clustering is a technique useful in many types of problems such as data mining in which solid knowledge can be extracted from apparently unstructured data. When analyzing data with high-dimensionality, data having a few dozens to many thousands of dimensions, the ordinary distance measures often lose their discriminative capacity, thus, clustering performance is negatively impacted by that. As a consequence, clustering methods based on traditional distance measures often fail to achieve acceptable performance since many feature dimensions may be irrelevant or redundant to certain clusters [2].

Pioneer methods reduce the data dimensionality or use a parsimonious Gaussian mixture model (GMM) to overcome the curse of dimensionality. Very often, the reduction of dimensionality is followed by a classical clustering method. Dimension reduction techniques typically employ feature extraction and feature selection for generate new variables preserving most of the global information. The parsimonious models require the estimation of some parameters. Such models allow clustering methods based on the expectation-maximization.

Subspace Clustering (SC) algorithms identify different subspaces to determine distinct clusters. Their two main types are Hard Subspace Clustering (HSC) and Soft Subspace Clustering (SSC) [5]. HSC algorithms, identify the exact subspaces for different clusters and assign 1 or zero to each relevance. In turn, SSC algorithms perform clustering by assigning a real-valued weight to each feature (attribute) of each cluster to weigh its importance to that particular cluster [2]. Such algorithms are classified as conventional SSC (CSSC), independent SSC (ISSC), and extended SSC (XSSC). In CSSC, all clusters share the same subspace and a common weight vector. The weight vectors in ISSC are determined independently for each cluster. XSSC was developed by extending CSSC or ISSC algorithms for some specific purposes or introducing new mechanisms to enhance clustering performance [5].

## 2.2 Self-organizing Maps for Subspace Clustering

The SOM and LVQ are prototype-based neural network models. They use a distance measure to select the cluster prototypes to be updated. Euclidean distance tends to lose its discriminating power as the number of attributes increases. So, there are LVQ and SOM-based models that assign a weight, the relevance [6], to each attribute differentiating the importance of each dimension for each cluster. The proposed algorithms obtain relevance attributes in the learning process.

Some recent LVQ models were recently proposed for subspace clustering. GMLVQ and GLVQ had their activation function step modified for improving the categorization process [7]. Intuitive indications of feature relevancies for a given model's decision can be provided by metric-learning approaches, such as GRLVQ [6] that adapts a diagonal matrix, scaling the relevance of the input features. Generalizations that use a full matrix, such as in GMLVQ [8] exist, however, a single global quadratic matrix remains the most common choice. A few approaches extend this setting to non-global matrices, such as LGRLVQ [9] and LGMLVQ [8]. However, they allow only one matrix per prototype, which corresponds to one metric per Voronoi cell in the input space. The mentioned LVQ-based methods are up-to-date alternatives that assign relevance to attributes to make the distance metrics more discriminating.

Also, some SOM-based approaches were proposed, we can mention Dimension Selective Self-organizing Map (DSSOM) [10], Local Adaptive Receptive Field Dimension Selective Self-organizing Map (LARFDSSOM) [11], Local Adaptive Receptive Field Dimension Selective Self-organizing Map 2 (LARFDSSOM2) [4], and Soft Subspace Neural Gas for Data Stream Clustering (S2G-Stream) [12]. DSSOM can find clusters and identify their relevant dimensions, simultaneously with the self-organizing process. The next models are time-varying structure SOM, TVS-SOM [13]. LARFSSOM is characterized by a structure of nodes that change according to the defined level of resemblance between a pattern and the prototype of the category it belongs to. LARFSSOM2 is a version that improves learning capacity by refining the relevance accuracy. S2G-Stream algorithm is based on growing neural gas. The authors proposed two models of feature and block weighting (global and local), a method for SSC on an evolving data stream. We returned to the original SOM with a fixed structure as a simple solver for the same class of problems.

## 2.3   Learning Enhancement

Several adaptations were proposed to the original SOM to ameliorate categorization. Some of them were accuracy-oriented for high-dimensional data such as a type of assembly of SOMs [14]. The method connects the output of a SOM to the input of the next SOM. It also utilizes the characteristic of high-dimensional data insensitivity to update the values of dimensions. Another approach is a hierarchical categorization in which patterns that have imprecise categorization can undergo further training with different data composition from initial training to refine a solution [15]. SOM-based model performance can be improved with a second process of weight adjustment. Bi-organization local refinement [16] organizes the data by defining an appropriate representation and metric such that they respect the smoothness and structure underlying the data.

Many changes were proposed to the original SOM to ameliorate categorization. Some of them were accuracy-oriented for high-dimensional data such as a type of assembly of SOMs [14]. In this approach, each SOM is trained with some different criteria and after training all expert SOMs, the output is determined by a criterion considering the specialists. Cascaded SOM is an extension of classical SOM [14] in which multiple SOMs are connected in series, the so-called cascaded structure. The method connects the output of a SOM to the input of the next SOM. It also utilizes the characteristic of high-dimensional data insensitivity to update the values of dimensions.

Another approach is hierarchical categorization, in which patterns that have imprecise categorization can undergo further training with different data compositions from initial training to refine a solution. Hierarchical sparse subspace clustering (HESSC) [15] deals with high-dimensional and highly mixed data robustly and quickly. The algorithm performs a hierarchical subspace clustering and it determines the number of clusters.

SOM-based model performance can be improved with a second process of weight adjustment. Bi-organization local refinement [16] organizes the data by defining an appropriate representation and metric such that they respect the smoothness and structure underlying the data. They also aim to generalize the joint clustering of observations and features, in the case the data does not fall into clear disjoint groups. The process consists of an iterative refinement procedure that exploits the co-dependencies between features and observations.

The learning process of SC-MuSOM is fully based on SOM. Thus, we train each SOM module with patterns belonging to a particular category. Moreover, the learning process has two stages: the first training stage is based on the original SOM and the second stage modifies locally the Voronoi regions.

## 3    Subspace Clustering Multi-module Self-organizing Maps (SC-MuSOM)

LVQ and SOM are prototype-based competitive algorithms with supervised and unsupervised learning. Both algorithms typically compress any-dimensional data into a two-dimensional grid, however, only SOM takes taking into account data topology. LVQ employs labels in the training stage, the weights update can approximate or distance a prototype from an input pattern depending on if the categorization is correct or not [17]. SOM determines clusters based on the instances similarities and dissimilarities. Some previous studies suggest that supervised learning achieves superior performance than unsupervised learning for small training sets.

The proposed model is composed of multiple modules, each one consisting of a self-organizing map (SOM) trained for data clustering of a particular category, thus, there are as many SOM modules as the number of categories. Each SOM undergoes unsupervised training with samples belonging to a single category. Any node of each SOM module learns a prototype vector and a relevance vector associated with it. A second learning stage, the refinement phase, consists of mutual repelling of very close pairs of nodes belonging to different categories, closeness determined by distances below a threshold. Such distancing aims to increase the spatial separations of the different categories. After the two-stage training, each input pattern is presented to all SOM modules. The module with the winning node determines the category of the input instance.

After the two-stage learning process, each input pattern is presented to all SOM modules. The module with the winning node determines the category of the input instance.

### 3.1    The Description of SC-MuSOM

SC-MuSOM is formed by multiple modules of one-dimensional SOMs, each one defines a subcluster of a given category. For each SOM module, the weight vectors associated with each node are initialized as the arithmetic average of the instances of that category added to a random noise ranging within the interval $[-0.01 + 0.01]$ for each attribute. The relevance vector of each node is initialized as the complement of the variance vector (Eq. 1) of all instances of a considered category. The calculation of the relevancies is an interactive process that takes into consideration this instantaneous term of relevance (a function of the variance) to update the current relevance of each dimension. The relevance value of each attribute weighs its distance component. Thus, dimensions with lower variance tend to be more relevant to determine the distance between an input vector and the subcluster centers (Eq. 2). Relevancies contribute to the calculation of distance so that certain attributes have greater importance without loss of information in a process of dimensionality reduction.

$$\mathbf{r}_k = (1 - variance(\mathbf{x}_k)) \tag{1}$$

$$d_r(\mathbf{x}_t, \mathbf{c}_k) = \sqrt{\sum \mathbf{r}_k(\mathbf{x}_{in} - \mathbf{c}_k)^2} \tag{2}$$

A SOM module groups any input pattern into a subcluster of a determined category. In any module, the winner node ($w$) is determined by the smallest Euclidean distance between an input pattern ($\mathbf{x}_{in}$) and each weight vector $\mathbf{c}_k$ in cluster C (Eq. 3). In the training stage, the winner is searched among the nodes of the SOM module for each category. After the learning stage, any winner is the most active node of all categories. Algorithm 1 shows the first training stage.

$$\|\mathbf{x}_{in} - \mathbf{c}_w\| = \min_{k \in C} d_r(\mathbf{x}_{in}, \mathbf{c}_k) \tag{3}$$

The weight updating runs separately for each module, one by one, i.e., only the module of the input pattern category is updated. For all input vectors closest to $c_w$, a weight vector is adjusted with learning rate $\eta(t)$ and neighborhood function $h_w(t)$ as shown in Eqs. 4, 5, and 6. The excitation equation employs the relevance diagonal matrix $\mathbf{R}_k$, the relevancies form the main diagonal, in the update process.

$$\mathbf{c}_k(n + 1) = \mathbf{c}_k(n) + \eta(n) \cdot h_w(n) \cdot \mathbf{R}_k [\mathbf{x}_{in} - \mathbf{c}_k(n)] \tag{4}$$

$$\eta = \eta(0) \cdot e^{-\frac{n}{\tau_\eta}} \tag{5}$$

$$h_w(n) = h_0 e^{-\frac{\|\mathbf{c}_k - \mathbf{c}_w\|^2}{\sigma^2(n)}} \tag{6}$$

The neighborhood function, $h_w$ decreases when the distance between $c_k$ and $c_w$ increases. We employed a Gaussian function to describe a topological neighborhood that shrinks with time due to the time varying dispersion term ($\sigma(n)$) defined by Eqs. 7.

$$\sigma(n) = \sigma_0 \cdot e^{-\frac{n}{\tau}} \tag{7}$$

For each epoch, all patterns are presented in random order, for each SOM module. At the end of each epoch, the values of all relevancies are updated. For relevance calculation, initially, all training patterns referring to each SOM are evaluated and the node closest to each pattern is determined by Eq. 2. The new relevance (at time instant n + 1) associated with a node is calculated as a function of an instantaneous relevance (Eq. 1) that considers all patterns belonging to a subcluster. Each pair, weight vector and relevance vector, is associated with a subcluster, represented by a node. The weights are updated with each presentation of a new pattern whereas the relevancies are only updated at the end of each epoch.

The refinement procedure increases the distance between the closest prototypes of subcategories belonging to different categories. In this stage, the algorithm does not change the relevance vector since it is not affected by this slight movement. The relocation process runs for all nodes that have a distance below a threshold.

Algorithm 2 shows the refinement process, the second stage of learning. Initially, the cosines of the angles of all pairs of weight vectors belonging to different categories are calculated. Then, the pairs of nodes that are close enough and belong to different categories are selected for the separation process. The chosen distance metric is the cosine similarity metric [18]. Oppositely to the Euclidean distance, in the cosine similarity, the furthermost vectors have a value nearby zero whereas the closest vectors have cosine neighboring 1. For a pair of vectors $\mathbf{c}_k$ and $\mathbf{c}_m$, $\mathbf{c}_k$ is moved away from $\mathbf{c}_m$ (Eq. 8), movement determined by the minus sign in it. An analogous movement of $\mathbf{c}_m$ with respect to $\mathbf{c}_k$ is carried out swapping the roles of each vector in Eq. 8. The learning rate $\alpha$ is smaller than the rate $\eta$ at the end of the first learning stage of learning. Equation 8 continues to use relevance in the weight refinement process, as in the Eq. 4.

$$\mathbf{c}_k(n + 1) = \mathbf{c}_k(n) + \alpha(n) \cdot \mathbf{R}_k \left[\mathbf{c}_m - \mathbf{c}_k(n)\right] \tag{8}$$

$$\alpha = \alpha(0) \cdot e^{-\frac{n}{\tau_\alpha}} \tag{9}$$

The categorization of an input vector is determined by the most active node in all SOM modules. This node determines the subcategory, therefore the category, to which the input belongs to. Clustering accuracy is calculated by the percentage of samples correctly categorized.

## 3.2   The Pseudo-code

The SC-MuSOM pseudo-code has two stages. The first stage, Algorithm 1, consists of module-by-module training. The updating of the relevance only occurs after all weights adjustment of an epoch.

Then, the pairs of nodes that have a cosine distance greater than a given threshold are selected to be pushed away. This process of calculating distance and moving away is repeated until the selected pairs are below the threshold (Algorithm 2).

---

**Algorithm 1.** SC-MuSOM-Stage1

---

1: Initialize all $c_{kj}(0)$ with mean and noise insertion of $[-0.01 +0.01]$ and learning parameters $\eta(0)$, $h_0$, $\sigma_0$, $\tau$, $\tau_\eta$, $T$;
2: **for** $t = 0$ to $T$ **do**
3:     **for all** $x_t$ patterns from the category training set **do**
4:         Present pattern $x_t$ at time $t$.
5:         Select the winning node for $x_t$ by Eq. 3.
6:         Update the weights for all nodes by Eq. 4.
7:         Set $t = t + 1$;
8:     **end for**
9:     Update the relevancies for all nodes by Eq. 1.
10:     Update the learning rate, $\eta(t)$, by Eq. 5.
11:     Update the topological neighborhood, $\sigma(t)$, by Eq. 7.
12: **end for**

---

---

**Algorithm 2.** SC-MuSOM-Stage2

---

1: Initialize $\alpha(0)$ and $Th$;
2: **for** $t = 0$ to $T$ **do**
3:     Calculate cosine distances from all nodes to all nodes.
4:     Selects pairs of nodes of different categories that have a cosine distance above a threshold $Th$.
5:     Updating the pair or the pairs selects pushing each other away by 8.
6:     Set $t = t + 1$;
7: **end for**

---

## 4 Experiments

SC-MuSOM was tested with data mining and high-dimensional computer vision sets for performance assessment. We have run 10 rounds of tests with different random initializations for which we present the average performances with their standard deviations. We compared SC-MuSOM performance with those achieved by previously published articles. For a fair comparison, the number of executions for each algorithm follows that specified for published papers.

### 4.1 Datasets and Setups

The datasets Digits, Ionosphere, Iris, and Image Segmentation belong to the UCI repository [19]. The computer vision datasets include USPS [20], Scenes-15 [21] and Caltech-101 [22]. Table 1 shows the number of patterns ($n_p$), attributes ($n_a$), and categories ($n_c$) of each dataset and the type of each dataset.

The four data mining sets have low or medium dimensionality, ranging from 4 to 64 attributes. Such sets vary from 150 to 2,306 patterns divided into 2 to 10 categories. The patterns in the tree remaining sets have 256 to 1,080 attributes. Such high-dimensional data sets have 4,885 to 9,298 patterns that are categorized into 10 to 101 groups.

The digits data is composed of images. The Ionosphere set contains data on electrons in the ionosphere. The Iris dataset describes 3 different types of the plant Iris. The Image Segmentation dataset encodes several attributes of image regions. The USPS dataset stores images of handwritten digits. The Scene-15 dataset is formed by images for 15 outdoor scenes whereas the Caltech-101 dataset keeps images of objects belonging to 101 categories. For the Scenes-15 and Caltech-101 databases, features were extracted using a deep learning strategy through VGG-19 [24], a deep neural network. The output of the VGG-19 is a vector of 4,096 attributes.

**Table 1.** Datasets

| Dataset | $n_p$ | $n_a$ | $n_c$ | Type |
|---|---|---|---|---|
| Digits | 1,797 | 64 | 10 | Data mining |
| Ionosphere | 351 | 34 | 2 | Data mining |
| Iris | 150 | 4 | 3 | Data mining |
| Image segmentation | 2,306 | 16 | 7 | Data mining |
| USPS | 9,298 | 256 | 10 | Computer vision |
| Scenes-15 | 4,885 | 1,024 | 15 | Computer vision |
| Caltech-101 | 8,677 | 1,080 | 101 | Computer vision |

## 4.2 Results

The performance of prototype-based models is shown in Table 2. SC-MuSOM performance is compared with the LGMLVQ [8] and KNN methods for low or medium-dimensional datasets. SC-MuSOM performance is also compared with those of KNN, deep-learning, and SOM-based soft subspace clustering methods (ETLMSC [23] and LARFDSSOM2 [4]) and the results are shown in Table 3. The tables bring mean accuracy values and their standard deviation. The numbers of the compared methods were collected in their original publications.

**Table 2.** Results for small and medium dimensional databases compared with KNN and LGMLVQ.

| Dataset | KNN | LGMLVQ | SC-MuSOM (1 stage) | SC-MuSOM (2 stages) |
|---|---|---|---|---|
| Digits | 94 (0.75) | 87 (1.68) | **97.09 (0.18)** | **97.09 (0.18)** |
| Ionosphere | 77 (4.68) | 76 (3.75) | 89.09 (4.12) | **89.32 (5.67)** |
| Iris | 93 (3.40) | 93 (2.98) | 96.49 (2.56) | **96.49 (2.53)** |
| Image Seg. | 93 (0.39) | **94 (0.64)** | 90.43 (4.88) | 91.90 (5.96) |
| USPS | 94 (0.25) | **95 (0.27)** | 94.07 (0.21) | 94.17 (0.25) |

**Table 3.** Results for high-dimensional databases compared with KNN, ETLMSC, and LARFDSSOM2.

| Dataset | KNN | ETLMSC | LARFDSSOM2 | SC-MuSOM (1 stage) | SC-MuSOM (2 stages) |
|---------|-----|--------|------------|---------------------|----------------------|
| Scenes-15 | 76.75 (1.08) | 87.80 (0.2) | 89.07 (0.2) | 89.32 (0.15) | **89.34 (0.14)** |
| Caltech-101 | 60.07 (1.98) | 63.9 (0.4) | 65.41 (0.89) | 74.47 (0.2) | **74.50 (0.2)** |

### 4.3 Comparisons

We have not implemented the comparison methods shown in Table 2 and Table 3, therefore, the results in the tables are those reported in the literature.

SC-MuSOM reached the best performance for Digits, Ionosphere, Iris, Scenes-15 and Caltech-101 datasets. The performance of SC-MuSOM for USPS dataset was slightly below that of LGMLVQ. For the Image Segmentation dataset, SC-MuSOM achieved a performance inferior to KNN and LGMLVQ. The Image Segmentation dataset has a peculiar characteristic, its training data entails only 10% of the total set of patterns while the other sets have above 45% of the total of patterns used for training. The SOM compared to the LVQ tends to lose performance when the percentage of training data in relation to the total set of patterns is reduced [17].

An extension of the original LVQ model, LGMLVQ employs a complete relevance matrix in the similarity measure [8]. We consider a distance generalization that can explain the correlations between the attributes. SC-MuSOM only uses the calculation of feature vectors, being computationally less expensive in comparison with LGMLVQ.

The refinement stage of our algorithm marginally improves the performance of some of the tested databases. We apply the Mann-Whitney statistical test to verify whether the numerical differences are statistically significant. Such an analysis indicated that for 4 out of the 7 datasets, stage 2 presented statistically relevant improvements.

The promising results of the proposed method are due to the specialization in multi-modules of the SOM networks together with the use of relevances to make the distance metric discrimination more robust because of the curse of the dimensionality. The second stage of learning also contributes to a little performance improvement, this stage has a more significant impact on data mining bases than computer vision. The refinement stage is a low computational cost procedure that can marginally improve the results.

## 5    Discussion and Conclusion

Our proposed model, SC-MuSOM, has multiple SOM modules, one for each category of datasets used in the experiments. The first learning stage determines the clusters and their prototypes using the relevance vectors that assign different importance to the attributes. In the second stage, nodes of different categories that are overlapped are moved away from each other. This second stage improves slightly the model accuracy.

SC-MuSOM is a soft subspace clustering (SSC) method that determines continuous values for relevancies ranging from zero to one. SC-MuSOM performs feature weighting to establish the relative prominence of each attribute regarding each category: the higher the relevance, the more important the attribute.

The refinement stage is characterized by the modification of the weight vectors by a low learning rate to separate further overlapping Voronoi regions between nodes of different modules. In some data mining and computer vision datasets, we notice a small improvement in accuracy compared to only the first stage of learning.

The model has a number of nodes established by the designer, however, the number of sub-categories may vary from category to category. This can make some nodes unnecessary. These nodes do increase the cost of running the algorithm. A potential improvement for this limitation is to employ a time-varying topology to increase the number of subcategories (nodes) for each category only if necessary. Something welcome to speed up the processing would be a massively parallel implementation of SC-MuSOM with GPUs or multi-core CPUs, another potential topic for future research.

# References

1. Assent, I.: Clustering high dimensional data. Wiley Interdisc. Rev. Data Min. Knowl. Discov. **2**, 340–350 (2012)
2. Liu, C., Xie, J., Zhao, Q., Xie, Q., Liu, C.: Novel evolutionary multi-objective soft subspace clustering algorithm for credit risk assessment. Expert Syst. Appl. **138**, 112827 (2019)
3. Pereira, R.B., Plastino, A., Zadrozny, B., Merschmann, L.H.: Categorizing feature selection methods for multi-label classification. Artif. Intell. Rev. **49**, 57–78 (2018). https://doi.org/10.1007/s10462-016-9516-4
4. Araújo, A.F.R., Antonino, V.O., Ponce-Guevara, K.L.: Self-organizing subspace clustering for high-dimensional and multi-view data. Neural Netw. **130**, 253–268 (2020)
5. Deng, Z., Choi, K.S., Jiang, Y., Wang, J., Wang, S.: A survey on soft subspace clustering. Inf. Sci. **348**, 84–106 (2016)
6. Hammer, B., Villmann, T.: Generalized relevance learning vector quantization. J. Int. Neural Netw. Soc. **15**, 1059–68 (2002)
7. Melchert, F., Bani, G., Seiffert, U., Biehl, M.: Adaptive basis functions for prototype-based classification of functional data. Neural Comput. Appl. **32**, 18213–18223 (2020). https://doi.org/10.1007/s00521-019-04299-2
8. Schneider, P., Biehl, M., Hammer, B.: Adaptive relevance matrices in learning vector quantization. Neural Comput. **21**, 3532–3561 (2009)
9. Hammer, B., Schleif, F.M., Villmann, T.: On the generalization ability of prototype-based classifiers with local relevance determination. Citeseer (2005)
10. Bassani, H.F., Araújo, A.F.R.: Dimension selective self-organizing maps for clustering high dimensional data. In: The International Joint Conference on Neural Networks, pp. 1–8. IEEE (2012)

11. Bassani, H.F., Araújo, A.F.R.: Dimension selective self-organizing maps with time-varying structure for subspace and projected clustering. IEEE Trans. Neural Netw. Learn. Syst. **26**(3), 458–471 (2015)
12. Attaoui, M.O., Attaoui, M.O., Azzag, H., Lebbah, M., Keskes, N.: Subspace data stream clustering with global and local weighting models. Neural Comput. Appl. **33**(8), 3691–3712 (2021). https://doi.org/10.1007/s00521-020-05184-z
13. Araújo, A.F.R., Rego, R.L.: Self-organizing maps with a time-varying structure. ACM Comput. Surv. **46**(1), 7:1–7:38 (2013)
14. Hua, W., Lingfei, M.: Clustering ensemble model based on self-organizing map network. Comput. Intell. Neurosci. **2020** (2020)
15. Shahi, K.R., et al.: Hierarchical sparse subspace clustering (HESSC): an automatic approach for hyperspectral image analysis. Remote Sens. **12**(15), 2421 (2020)
16. Mishne, G., Talmon, R., Cohen, I., Coifman, R.R., Kluger, Y.: Data-driven tree transforms and metrics. IEEE Trans. Sig. Inf. Process. Netw. **4**(3), 451–466 (2017)
17. Goren-Bar, D., Kuflik, T.: Supporting user-subjective categorization with self-organizing maps and learning vector quantization. J. Am. Soc. Inf. Sci. Technol. **56**(4), 345–355 (2005)
18. Rahutomo, F., Kitasuka, T., Aritsugi, M.: Semantic cosine similarity. In: International Student Conference on Advanced Science and Technology, ICAST, vol. 4, no. 1 (2012)
19. Dua, D., Graff, C.: UCI machine learning repository (2017). https://archive.ics.uci.edu/ml/index.php
20. Hull, J.J.: A database for handwritten text recognition research. IEEE Trans. Pattern Anal. Mach. Intell. **16**(5), 550–554 (1994)
21. Fei-Fei, L., Perona, P.: A Bayesian hierarchical model for learning natural scene categories. In: 2005 IEEE Computer Society Conference on Computer Vision and Pattern Recognition, vol. 2, pp. 524–531 (2005)
22. Fei-Fei, L., Fergus, R., Perona, P.: Learning generative visual models from few training examples: an incremental bayesian approach tested on 101 object categories. In: Conference on Computer Vision and Pattern Recognition Workshop, p. 178 (2004)
23. Wu, J., Lin, Z., Zha, H.: Essential tensor learning for multi-view spectral clustering. IEEE Trans. Image Process. **28**(12), 5910–5922 (2019)
24. Simonyan, K., Zisserman, A.: Very deep convolutional networks for large-scale image recognition. In: International Conference on Learning Representations (2015)

# SVM Ensembles on a Budget

David Nevado, Gonzalo Martínez-Muñoz(✉) [ID], and Alberto Suárez [ID]

Escuela Politécnica Superior, Dpto. de Ingeniería Informática, Universidad Autónoma de Madrid, C/Francisco Tomás y Valiente, 11, 28049 Madrid, Spain
{gonzalo.martinez,alberto.suarez}@uam.es

**Abstract.** This paper presents a model to train an ensemble of SVMs that achieves better generalization performance at a lower computational training cost than a single SVM. The idea of the proposed model is, instead of training a single SVM on the whole dataset, to train a diverse set of simpler SVMs. Specifically, the proposed algorithm creates $B$ subensembles of $T$ SVMs using a different set of hyper-parameters in each subensemble. Then, in order to gain more diversity, the $T$ SVMs of each of the subsensembles are trained on a different $1/T$ disjoint fraction of the training set. The paper presents an extensive analysis of the computational training complexity of the algorithm. The experiments show that for any given computational budget, the presented method obtains a better generalization performance than a single SVM.

**Keywords:** SVM · Ensembles of classifiers · Computational complexity

## 1 Introduction

Support Vector Machines (SVM) are among the most accurate machine learning methods for classification problems [1,5]. In spite of their excellent performance, they are costly to train. A cost that can be higher than quadratic with respect to the number of training instances [3]. Furthermore, the generalization capacity of an SVM is very sensitive to the actual values of its hyperparameters [4]. These are typically determined by a computationally expensive cross-validation search. For these reasons, the practical application of SVM's in large problems is limited. Ensembles of classifiers are a way to improve the performance of SVMs [7,8,10,12]. Several strategies focus only in generating diverse SVMs for improving the accuracy of the model (for instance by using different kernels [12]). Other strategies are boosting-based optimization ensembles [7,8]. Other works focus both in diversification and optimization [10]. However, the accuracy improvements are in general small as SVM are very stable classifiers [8].

In this work we present a novel architecture to build SVM ensembles with a low computational training complexity that can achieve similar or better accuracies than a single SVM trained on the complete dataset. In particular, given a limited training time budget, the proposed ensembles can have higher accuracy than a single SVM. In order to achieve this, a combination of two techniques is

E. Pimenidis et al. (Eds.): ICANN 2022, LNCS 13532, pp. 297–308, 2022.
https://doi.org/10.1007/978-3-031-15937-4_25

used: Hyperparameter diversification and structured subsampling. These strategies serve to introduce the variability among the base SVMs that is needed to build an effective ensemble. Subsampling, in particular, not only fulfills this purpose of diversification, but also reduces the computational complexity of the training process. In addition, a detailed analysis of the computational cost of the proposed method is carried out.

## 2   Structured Subbagging for SVM Ensembles

In order to achieve hyperparameter diversification, the proposed ensemble is composed of $B$ subensembles of SVMs. The SVMs within each subensemble use an RBF kernel and are built using the same combination of hyperparameters $(C, \gamma)$. However, each one of them is trained using a different random subset of size $tp \cdot N_{train}$, where $tp$ is a hyperparameter of the ensemble that stands for *train proportion*. Hence, we need to generate $B$ pairs of hyper-parameters $\{(C_b, \gamma_b)\}_{b=1}^{B}, \{(C_b, \gamma_b); b = 1, \ldots, B\}$, one for each subensemble. Each of these pairs $(C_b, \gamma_b)$ is obtained by performing an exhaustive grid search with 2-fold cross-validation over an independent partition $\mathcal{D}_b$, sampled from the training set, $\mathcal{D}_{train}$. These partitions $\mathcal{D}_b$ have $2 \cdot N \cdot tp$ instances. In this way, during the grid search each SVM is trained on a sample of size $N \cdot tp$, the same number of instances on which each base SVM will be trained later. Having set the size of the partitions for searching for the hyper-parameters, $\mathcal{D}_b$, we distinguish two possible scenarios: If $tp \cdot B \leq 1/2$ then it is possible to extract from the training set $\mathcal{D}_{train}$, $B$ disjoint subsets with $2 \cdot N \cdot tp$ instances each. If we have $tp \cdot B > 1/2$ then it is not possible to make such partitions. In this case we take $B$ subsets of $2 \cdot N \cdot tp$ instances drawn from $\mathcal{D}_{train}$ uniformly at random without replacement.

Once the hyper-parameter pairs, $\{(C_b, \gamma_b)\}_{b=1}^{B}$, have been selected, $B$ subensembles of SVMs are trained as follows: For each pair $(C_b, \gamma_b)$ of hyper-parameters, the training set is randomly divided into $T = 1/tp$ disjoint subsets, $\{\mathcal{D}_t\}_{t=1}^{T}$, that is, $\mathcal{D}_{train} = \bigcup_{t=1}^{T} \mathcal{D}_t$. Then, one SVM with hyper-parameters $(C_b, \gamma_b)$ is trained on each subset $\mathcal{D}_t$ for $t = 1, \ldots, T$. After iterating over the $B$ hyper-parameter subsets and the $T = 1/tp$ subsets, a total of $B \cdot T$ SVMs will form the final ensemble. The complete pseudocode for this training procedure is detailed in Algorithm 1.

Note that in the ensemble method proposed in this work, the base models are trained on datasets that are extracted with a certain structure. Specifically, instead of using random sampling as in standard bagging or similar methods, the original dataset is partitioned into disjoint sets (see line 8 Algorithm 1). By training each base learners on one of these disjoint subsets of the original training set, we expect to maximize the diversity of the base classifiers, and thus improve the benefits of aggregation. Furthermore, this method guarantees that all the samples available for training are used, which should limit the loss of information in the bootstap process and lead to an improved predictive performance. This is presented in the section on experiments. In order to validate these expected effects, an experiment is carried out to compare the differences of accuracy between ensembles built with the structured sampling strategy introduced in this work and standard subbagging.

---

**Algorithm 1:** SVM Ensemble training.

---

**Input:** $\mathcal{D}_{train} = \{(\mathbf{x}_i, y_i)\}_{i=1}^{N_{train}}$    % Training set
$\qquad B$    % Number of subensembles
$\qquad tp$    % Train proportion
$\qquad grid$    % Hyperparameter grid

**Output:** $E$    % Ensemble

**1** if $tp \cdot B \leq 1/2$ then
**2** $\quad \mid \{\mathcal{D}_b\}_{b=1}^{B} \leftarrow$ Extract from $\mathcal{D}_{train}$ $B$ disjoint subsets of size $2 \cdot tp \cdot N_{train}$.
**3** else
**4** $\quad \mid \{\mathcal{D}_b\}_{b=1}^{B} \leftarrow$ Extract from $\mathcal{D}_{train}$ $B$ subsets of size $2 \cdot tp \cdot N_{train}$ drawn
$\qquad$ uniformly at random.
**5** $T = 1/tp$
**6** foreach $b \leftarrow 1$ to $B$ do
**7** $\quad \mid (C_b, \gamma_b) \leftarrow GridSearch(\mathcal{D}_b, folds = 2, grid)$
**8** $\quad \mid \{\mathcal{D}_t\}_{t=1}^{T} \leftarrow$ Split $\mathcal{D}_{train}$ into $T$ disjoint subsets of size $tp \cdot N_{train}$
**9** $\quad \mid$ foreach $t \leftarrow 1$ to $T$ do
**10** $\quad \mid \quad \mid$ % Train SVM with hyperparameters $(C_b, \gamma_b)$ and data $\mathcal{D}_t$
**11** $\quad \mid \quad \mid c_{b,t} \leftarrow SVM(\mathcal{D}_t, (C_b, \gamma_b))$
**12** $E(\cdot) = \underset{y \in \mathcal{Y}}{\operatorname{argmax}} \sum_{b=1, t=1}^{B,T} \mathbb{1}[c_{b,t}(\cdot) = y]$
**13** return $E$

---

The characteristics of ensemble learning algorithm depends on two hyperparameters $B$ and $tp$, whose role we now review

- The ensemble consists in $B$ subensembles. Each of these subensembles is composed of SVMs that are built using the same hyperparameters $(C, \gamma)$. Therefore the SVMs within the same subensemble only differ in the data they are trained on. Exploratory experiments show that $B = 10$ is a good choice for most cases.
- The $tp$ (*train proportion*) hyperparameter determines both the fraction of training samples that are used to build each base SVM of the ensemble and the number of SVMs to be combined in each subensemble. By design, each of the $T = 1/tp$ individual SVMs within a subensemble is built on a disjoint partition of the training set with $tp \cdot N_{train}$ instances. In this way, all training instances are used once for building each subensemble. In addition, since the datasets are disjoint, the diversity of SVMs should increase, an effect that is expected to improve the benefits of aggregation. Lower values of $tp$ correspond to larger ensembles of SVMs trained on fewer instances. Higher values of $tp$ correspond to smaller ensembles, with SVMs trained on larger samples. In the limit case, $tp = 1$, only one SVM is trained using the whole dataset, which is equivalent to training a single SVM. The higher limit for possible values of $T$ (low $tp$) is determined by the number of instances of the training set

$N_{train}$. In this way, $tp$ provides a way to balance between the strength of the individual classifiers and the size of the ensemble. Generally, $tp \in (0, 0.25]$ is a range of values that provide good performance.

Notice that the values of these hyperparameters jointly determine the size of the complete ensemble: With $B$ subensembles each of size $1/tp$ we get a total ensemble size of $B/tp$.

## 3    Training Complexity of the Proposed Model

The training complexity of the proposed model can be expressed as a function of four factors: $N_{train}$, $GSize$, $B$ and $tp$, where $N_{train}$ is number of samples of the training set, $(B, tp)$ are the hyper-parameters of the model described in the previous section and $GSize$ is the size of the grid over which the hyperparameters $(C, \gamma)$ are selected. In what follows, we assume that the cost of training an SVM on a dataset with $N$ instances is $\approx \mathcal{O}(N^2)$, even though there is empirical evidence that it can be higher than quadratic [3]. Breaking down the training algorithm in its phases we get: Hyperparameters selection and base SVMs training.

The hyperparameters selection consists in an exhaustive 2-fold cross-validation search performed over the grid with folds of size $tp \cdot N_{train}$. This process is repeated $B$ times. Ignoring the evaluation cost of the SVMs in the grid search, we get the following complexity for this phase

$$B \cdot 2 \cdot GSize \cdot \mathcal{O}(tp^2 \cdot N_{train}^2). \tag{1}$$

In the base SVMs training phase, the ensemble is formed by $B/tp$ SVMs trained on $tp \cdot N_{train}$ samples. The resulting cost is

$$B \cdot \frac{1}{tp} \cdot \mathcal{O}(tp^2 \cdot N_{train}^2). \tag{2}$$

Adding up these costs we get an estimate of the overall complexity of the model

$$Cost = B \cdot \mathcal{O}(tp^2 \cdot N_{train}^2)(2 \cdot GSize + \frac{1}{tp}). \tag{3}$$

In most situations, we will have $2 \cdot GSize > 1/tp$. This implies that the search of hyperparameters phase is more demanding than training the base learners. The opposite can also happen for low values of $tp$, which may be adequate for very large datasets. This could also happen if the hyperparameter space is explored with alternative techniques such as Bayesian optimization [11], randomization or partial optimization [10] that lower the cost of exploring the hyperparameter grid. Considering that $T = 1/tp$, the final expression for the training complexity is

$$Cost = \mathcal{O}(B \cdot tp^2 \cdot N_{train}^2 \cdot (2GSize + T)). \tag{4}$$

We can read this complexity as number of subensembles $(B)$ times the training complexity of training a single SVM $(tp^2 \cdot N_{train}^2)$ times the number of trained SVMs $(2GSize + T)$ in each subensemble.

To put this results in perspective, we now detail the computational cost for training a single SVM on the whole training dataset for which a grid search is performed to tune its hyperparameters. We will assume an exhaustive grid search of $K$-fold cross-validation. As before, in this estimation we will ignore the evaluation cost of the SVMs during the grid search process.

The grid search involves the creation of $(GSize \cdot K)$ SVMs, each of them trained on a fraction $(K-1)/K$ of the data. Hence, the total cost of this phase is:

$$ GSize \cdot K \cdot \mathcal{O}\left(\left(\frac{K-1}{K}\right)^2 N_{train}^2\right), \tag{5} $$

and the cost of training the final SVM on the selected combination of hyperparameters is

$$ \mathcal{O}\left(N_{train}^2\right). \tag{6} $$

In this case, it is clear that the hyperparameter tuning phase is the dominant term in the overall cost. Therefore we can write the estimation for the training cost of the single SVM as

$$ SVM\_Cost = \mathcal{O}\left(GSize \cdot \frac{(K-1)^2}{K} \cdot N_{train}^2\right). \tag{7} $$

From the expressions (4) and (7) we observe that the training complexity for both models scale quadratically with the number of instances on the train set. If we suppose that $GSize > T$ (as is often the case), the ratio between the complexity of the proposed ensemble and a single SVM is

$$ \mathcal{O}\left(\frac{K \cdot B \cdot tp^2}{(K-1)^2}\right). \tag{8} $$

This indicates that even though their training complexity have an equivalent asymptotic growth, the ensemble training cost can be adjusted using hyperparameter $B$ and $tp$ to achieve significant speedups. In Sect. 4, we present the results of an empirical evaluation to validate the complexity estimations presented in this section.

## 4  Experimental Evaluation

We now present the results of the experiments carried out to assess the generalization accuracy of the proposed ensemble as well as its complexity estimations. The comparison was carried out in six relatively large datasets for a single SVM: three synthetic datasets and three real datasets. The synthetic datasets [2] used are: *Twonorm*, *Threenorm* and *Ringnorm*. The real datasets (*Magic04, Bank Marketing* [9] and *Adult*) are taken form the UCI repository [6]. We did not considered larger datasets because training a single SVMs on datasets with more instances was unfeasible.

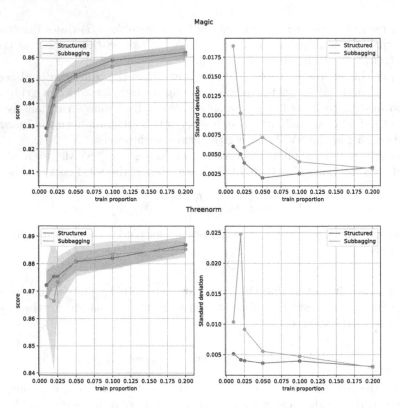

**Fig. 1.** Average accuracy (left column) and standard deviation (right) for structured sampling and subbagging models

Some basic preprocessing has been applied to the data as part of the training pipeline. Both Adult and Bank datasets have some categorical attributes. These attributes were transformed into numerical features using one-hot encoding. In the 6 problems all features were standardized to 0 mean and 1 standard deviation. All time measurements have been taken from single-threaded executions on an Intel(R) Core(TM) i5-7200U CPU @ 2.50 GHz with 8 GB RAM. All the hyperparameter searches for the SVMs were done using the grid $C = 2^q$, $\gamma = 2^p$ with $q = -5, -3, \ldots, 15$; $p = -15, -13, \ldots, 3$ following [10].

### 4.1 Comparison of Structured and Non-structured Sampling

In this first experiment, the way the data is sampled in the proposed method is analyzed. The proposed method samples the data with a *structure* by creating random disjoint sets in order to generate the base SVMs (line 8, Algorithm 1). In this experiment we compare this proposal with standard random sampling without replacement. That is, the same algorithm as the one shown in Algorithm 1 is used but substituting line 8 by the generation of random samples without replacement of size $tp \cdot N_{train}$ (*subbagging*). For this test the ensembles

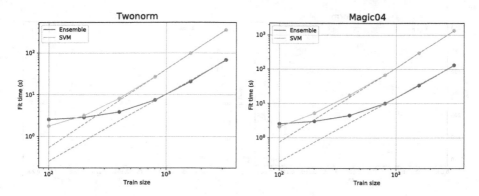

**Fig. 2.** Average training time. Both axis are in log scale. The red dashed line is a linear fit to the log-log data. (Color figure online)

were evaluated with different values for the hyperparameter $tp$: $[0.01, 0.02, 0.025, 0.05, 0.1, 0.2]$. The hyperparameter $B$ remained fixed for both models at $B = 10$. The mean and standard deviations reported are the average over 20 independent executions.

Figure 1 shows the results for a representation of the analyzed datasets. Similar results are obtained in the other datasets. The plots on the left column of Fig. 1 display the average accuracy of the models with respect to $tp$ with the standard deviation shown as a shaded region around the mean values. The values of the standard deviation are also represented on the plots shown on the right column.

These results show that the average accuracy achieved using the proposed method with structured sampling is more accurate than subbagging for most values of $tp$, although the differences are in general small. More importantly, the structured model produces results that are more stable than regular subbagging. This can be seen from the standard deviation plots where the standard deviation for subbagging is generally higher that the one of the structured model. This difference is more noticeable in general for low values of $tp$. In the following experiments, we will use only the proposed structured type of sampling.

## 4.2 Training Complexity

In these experiments, we study the training time complexity for the proposed ensemble and for the single SVM as a function of the size of the training set $N_{train}$ and as a function of hyperparameter $tp$. These tests have been carried out for two datasets: Magic04 and Twonorm. The reported results are averages over 10 independent executions.

In the first analysis, we study the impact of $N_{train}$. For the proposed ensemble, we have fixed $B = 10$ and $tp = 0.2$. For the SVM, we used 10-fold cross-validation in the grid search, i.e. $K = 10$. Both models use the same grid with $GSize = 110$ as defined above. The models have been evaluated for the follow-

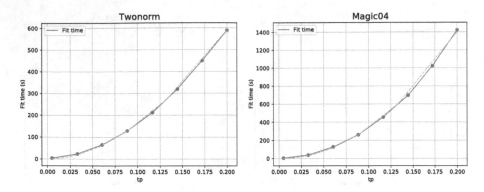

**Fig. 3.** Average training time of the SVM ensemble. The red dashed line indicates a linear fit to the log-log of the data. (Color figure online)

ing training sizes $N_{train}$ = 100, 200, 400, 800, 1600, 3200. The limitations of our workstation prevented us from using higher values of $N_{train}$ as the cost for training a single SVM became too high. Nonetheless, the selected values provide enough data to identify the asymptotic growth of both algorithms.

The results of this experiment are presented in Fig. 2 using a logarithmic scale in both axis. The plots show the execution training time in seconds with respect to $N_{train}$ for the proposed ensemble (blue solid line) and for the single SVM trained on the whole dataset (orange solid line). Both training times include the hyperparameter search as previously described. The red dashed lines represents a linear fit to the data excluding the first 3 points in order to capture the asymptotic behavior of the sequences. The slope of these lines are 1.60, 1.88 for the ensemble and the SVM respectively in Twonorm and 1.86, 2.16 in Magic04. All four slopes show values close to 2, which indicates that the complexity of both models with respect to the training size is approximately quadratic as predicted in previous sections. It is also worth noting that there is a substantial difference between the training times in both problems. The training cost in the Magic04 dataset for training the single SVM and the SVM ensemble is, respectively, 3.7 and 1.9 times higher that their cost in Twonorm. This shows that training time for both models is very problem dependent.

In a second experiment we analyze the training time of the proposed ensemble as a function of hyperparameter $tp$. The parameter $B$ and the training set size $N_{train}$ are fixed with values $B = 10$, $N_{train} = 10000$. The ensemble is evaluated at 8 evenly spaced values of $tp$ between 0.005 and 0.2.

The results of this experiment are presented Fig. 3 with a solid blue line. In addition, the plots show with a dashed red line the linear fit to the log-log data excluding the first 3 points in order to capture the asymptotic tendency of the curve. The slopes of these lines are 1.88 in Twonorm and 2.08 in Magic04. These results show the quadratic growth of the training time with respect to $tp$, which confirms the cost estimation we obtained in the previous section with respect to $tp$ (see Eq. 4).

## 4.3    Accuracy

In this set of experiments the relation between training time and generalization accuracy of the models is analyzed in detail. Each experiment realization involves the following steps: (i) For each of the non-synthetic problems, $N_{train} = 10000$ training instances are selected at random and the rest of the data is used as test set. For the synthetic datasets, two sets of 10000 instances are sampled randomly as training and testing sets; (ii) With the available training data, a set of ensembles of SVMs and a set of single SVMs are trained such that they require different training computational budgets. For a single SVM the most natural way of adjusting to these constraints is to reduce the number of instances used for training. In this way, the SVM uses only a fraction of the available training set. Specifically, for the Single SVM model the training subset evaluated sizes, $N_{train}$, are: [200, 500, 1000, 2000, 3500, 5000, 10000] for all problems except for Adult, for which the last value (10000) was not evaluated due to computational limitations of our workstation. For the ensemble, the parameters $B$ and $tp$ can be reduced to adjust to the constraints while using all the available data. In these tests we only modify $tp$ and leave $B$ fixed at a value that generally yields good results $B = 10$. For the ensemble model the evaluated $tp$ values are: [0.01, 0.025, 0.05, 0.1, 0.2, 0.25]; (iii) Finally all trained models were evaluated in the same left out test set. The scores presented are the result of averaging 20 independent executions. The training time measurements are the result of averaging 4 executions. The reason for this difference in the number of repetitions is twofold: Firstly, time measurements are more stable and therefore increasing the number of repetitions does not improve the precision of the measurement. Secondly, measuring the training times is delicate as they must be taken in a controlled environment with a single thread executions. All time measurements are done in a single thread process in order to attain a clear over all estimation of the total computational resources needed.

Figure 4 represents the average generalization accuracy obtained by each model (vertical axis) with respect to the corresponding training time required to train the models (horizontal axis) represented in logarithmic scale. The standard deviation of the accuracy is represented by a shaded region around the mean. The numerical figures for these plots are also presented in Table 1 for the different values of $tp$ and training size for the ensemble (left part of the table) and single SVM respectively (right part).

The main observation that we extract from these plots is that for a fixed training time budget, the ensemble consistently outperforms the single SVM. The differences between their accuracies is specially significant for the cases with limited time budgets (<100 s). Comparing maximum scores, regardless of the training time, we observe that the ensemble has the highest score in 3 datasets: Adult, Twonorm and Ringnorm, while the SVM has the highest score in the other 3. However, the highest scores of the SVM are always achieved for $N_{train} = 10000$, which involve very large training times (all above 10000 s). Comparing the training times in these datasets of the highest scores achieved by each model, we observe that the SVM training time is 7.6, 36.8 and 6.6 higher that the

**Table 1.** Average scores and training times of ensemble and single SVM.

| Dataset | SVM ensemble | | | Single SVM | | |
|---|---|---|---|---|---|---|
| | tp | Score | Time (s) | $N_{train}$ | Score | Time (s) |
| Magic04 | 0.010 | 82.82 ± 0.63 | 6.40 ± 0.20 | 200 | 80.65 ± 1.51 | 4.80 ± 0.37 |
| | 0.025 | 84.72 ± 0.31 | 22.54 ± 1.28 | 500 | 83.27 ± 0.76 | 25.81 ± 2.44 |
| | 0.050 | 85.34 ± 0.31 | 77.34 ± 0.47 | 1000 | 84.60 ± 0.34 | 102.87 ± 1.18 |
| | 0.100 | 85.80 ± 0.29 | 306.35 ± 3.05 | 2000 | 85.41 ± 0.27 | 437.49 ± 57.67 |
| | 0.200 | 86.10 ± 0.38 | 1462.35 ± 118.66 | 3500 | 85.88 ± 0.21 | 1445.34 ± 53.12 |
| | 0.250 | 86.30 ± 0.23 | 1991.58 ± 13.51 | 5000 | 86.14 ± 0.20 | 3145.13 ± 129.61 |
| | | | | 10000 | 86.58 ± 0.21 | 15127.35 ± 514.01 |
| Bank | 0.010 | 88.33 ± 0.05 | 7.13 ± 0.03 | 200 | 88.03 ± 0.90 | 5.68 ± 0.11 |
| | 0.025 | 89.29 ± 0.40 | 26.84 ± 0.20 | 500 | 88.86 ± 0.53 | 28.44 ± 1.08 |
| | 0.050 | 89.89 ± 0.20 | 92.52 ± 0.33 | 1000 | 89.29 ± 0.41 | 102.69 ± 1.55 |
| | 0.100 | 89.93 ± 0.18 | 341.74 ± 1.84 | 2000 | 89.65 ± 0.25 | 392.08 ± 7.23 |
| | 0.200 | 89.83 ± 0.27 | 1304.53 ± 9.86 | 3500 | 89.72 ± 0.24 | 1190.67 ± 19.23 |
| | 0.250 | 89.90 ± 0.22 | 2023.25 ± 30.18 | 5000 | 89.76 ± 0.17 | 2503.75 ± 70.17 |
| | | | | 10000 | 90.02 ± 0.11 | 12543.61 ± 64.57 |
| Adult | 0.010 | 81.35 ± 1.22 | 12.51 ± 0.10 | 200 | 80.05 ± 1.36 | 10.50 ± 0.10 |
| | 0.025 | 83.64 ± 0.35 | 54.97 ± 0.25 | 500 | 82.41 ± 0.58 | 58.12 ± 1.46 |
| | 0.050 | 84.35 ± 0.28 | 199.76 ± 0.58 | 1000 | 83.62 ± 0.38 | 227.98 ± 8.40 |
| | 0.100 | 84.80 ± 0.27 | 774.11 ± 6.40 | 2000 | 84.08 ± 0.34 | 967.83 ± 34.18 |
| | 0.200 | 84.95 ± 0.26 | 3285.41 ± 36.97 | 3500 | 84.47 ± 0.16 | 3654.76 ± 137.48 |
| | 0.250 | 85.07 ± 0.29 | 5428.58 ± 45.47 | 5000 | 84.69 ± 0.15 | 9027.30 ± 833.47 |
| | | | | 10000 | – | – |
| Twonorm | 0.010 | 97.79 ± 0.08 | 5.69 ± 0.02 | 200 | 97.31 ± 0.43 | 3.71 ± 0.04 |
| | 0.025 | 97.79 ± 0.08 | 16.91 ± 0.07 | 500 | 97.52 ± 0.15 | 15.73 ± 0.08 |
| | 0.050 | 97.80 ± 0.08 | 52.51 ± 0.12 | 1000 | 97.53 ± 0.12 | 55.07 ± 0.82 |
| | 0.100 | 97.79 ± 0.07 | 185.27 ± 0.31 | 2000 | 97.60 ± 0.09 | 204.13 ± 1.66 |
| | 0.200 | 97.80 ± 0.10 | 667.53 ± 4.54 | 3500 | 97.62 ± 0.06 | 575.05 ± 10.08 |
| | 0.250 | 97.80 ± 0.08 | 1008.01 ± 7.60 | 5000 | 97.62 ± 0.05 | 1156.25 ± 10.82 |
| | | | | 10000 | 97.75 ± 0.11 | 4819.12 ± 37.73 |
| Threenorm | 0.010 | 86.87 ± 0.22 | 6.47 ± 0.04 | 200 | 85.10 ± 1.14 | 4.92 ± 0.06 |
| | 0.025 | 87.13 ± 0.14 | 22.15 ± 0.07 | 500 | 86.41 ± 0.66 | 22.90 ± 0.78 |
| | 0.050 | 87.59 ± 0.21 | 73.63 ± 0.97 | 1000 | 87.29 ± 0.44 | 107.42 ± 7.76 |
| | 0.100 | 88.14 ± 0.22 | 287.44 ± 3.79 | 2000 | 87.66 ± 0.43 | 403.86 ± 34.77 |
| | 0.200 | 88.57 ± 0.14 | 1142.24 ± 19.12 | 3500 | 88.32 ± 0.20 | 1159.19 ± 17.81 |
| | 0.250 | 88.58 ± 0.16 | 1806.76 ± 16.54 | 5000 | 88.46 ± 0.22 | 2456.30 ± 48.17 |
| | | | | 10000 | 88.78 ± 0.18 | 11923.65 ± 273.75 |
| Ringnorm | 0.010 | 98.47 ± 0.14 | 6.60 ± 0.03 | 200 | 98.24 ± 0.15 | 5.81 ± 0.07 |
| | 0.025 | 98.54 ± 0.12 | 20.44 ± 0.06 | 500 | 98.30 ± 0.25 | 21.06 ± 2.08 |
| | 0.050 | 98.53 ± 0.12 | 63.19 ± 0.27 | 1000 | 98.28 ± 0.30 | 69.25 ± 0.59 |
| | 0.100 | 98.52 ± 0.15 | 223.34 ± 2.53 | 2000 | 98.46 ± 0.15 | 251.93 ± 0.49 |
| | 0.200 | 98.51 ± 0.11 | 808.90 ± 3.21 | 3500 | 98.49 ± 0.12 | 733.09 ± 8.12 |
| | 0.250 | 98.51 ± 0.12 | 1238.11 ± 3.64 | 5000 | 98.49 ± 0.16 | 1459.79 ± 8.94 |
| | | | | 10000 | 98.51 ± 0.09 | 6163.33 ± 75.59 |

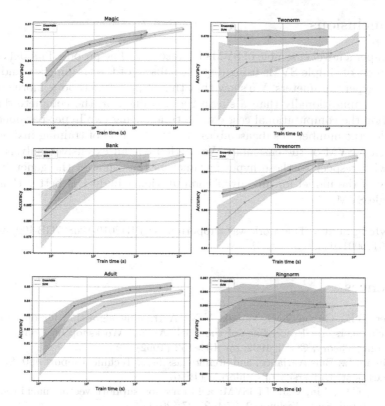

**Fig. 4.** Accuracy comparison between Structured Subbagging and single SVM. The vertical axis represents the score, the horizontal axis represents the training time in logarithmic scale. The shaded region represents the standard deviation of the scores.

time for the best accuracy of the ensemble for Magic04, Bank and Threenorm respectively (see Table 1). In any case, the difference between the best accuracies of each method in the different datasets are rather small (except maybe in Adult in which we could not run the $N_{train} = 10000$ for the single SVM) with a clear advantage of the proposed ensemble in terms of training speed.

Another interesting observation that can be made from Fig. 4 is that in four out of the six problems the accuracy of the ensemble improves when the value of $tp$ increases. In the other two datasets, Twonorm and Ringnorm, the ensemble achieves a similar accuracy for all values of $tp$. This tendency to achieve better accuracies for higher values of $tp$ indicates that the accuracy of the ensemble benefits from training the base models on larger training sets despite of the fact that less base models are combined. Note that, in this experiment, ensembles for all values of $tp$ have converged before reaching the given number for combined models. Hence, the differences in accuracy are not caused by lack of convergence of the models.

## 5  Conclusions

In this paper a novel ensemble of SVMs is presented. The proposed model creates a diverse set of simple SVMs using disjoint subsets of the training set and using different hyper-parameters. We show that the proposed method is more efficient to train computationally than a single SVM trained on the complete dataset. In addition the computational cost can be tuned using two hyper-parameters of the model: the number of subensembles and the fraction of training instances to use for each SVM of the ensemble. We carried out an extensive analysis of the model with respect to these hyper-parameters that showed the generalization accuracy of the model for any given computational budget is better than that of a single SVM.

**Acknowledgments.** This work was supported by PID2019-106827GB-I00/AEI/10. 13039/501100011033.

## References

1. Boser, B.E., Guyon, I.M., Vapnik, V.N.: A training algorithm for optimal margin classifiers. In: Proceedings of the Fifth Annual Workshop on Computational Learning Theory, COLT 1992, pp. 144–152 (1992)
2. Breiman, L.: Bias, variance, and arcing classifiers. Technical report 460, Statistics Department, University of California (1996)
3. Chang, C.C., Lin, C.J.: LIBSVM: a library for support vector machines. ACM Trans. Intell. Syst. Technol. **2**, 27:1–27:27 (2011)
4. Cherkassky, V., Ma, Y.: Practical selection of SVM parameters and noise estimation for SVM regression. Neural Netw. **17**(1), 113–126 (2004)
5. Cortes, C., Vapnik, V.: Support-vector networks. Mach. Learn. **20**(3), 273–297 (1995). https://doi.org/10.1007/BF00994018
6. Dua, D., Graff, C.: UCI machine learning repository (2017). http://archive.ics.uci.edu/ml
7. Kashef, R.: A boosted SVM classifier trained by incremental learning and decremental unlearning approach. Expert Syst. Appl. **167**, 114154 (2021)
8. Mayhua-López, E., Gómez-Verdejo, V., Figueiras-Vidal, A.R.: A new boosting design of Support Vector Machine classifiers. Inf. Fusion **25**, 63–71 (2015)
9. Moro, S., Cortez, P., Rita, P.: A data-driven approach to predict the success of bank telemarketing. Decis. Support Syst. **62**, 22–31 (2014)
10. Sabzevari, M., Martínez-Muñoz, G., Suárez, A.: Randomization vs optimization in SVM ensembles. In: Kůrková, V., Manolopoulos, Y., Hammer, B., Iliadis, L., Maglogiannis, I. (eds.) ICANN 2018. LNCS, vol. 11140, pp. 415–421. Springer, Cham (2018). https://doi.org/10.1007/978-3-030-01421-6_40
11. Snoek, J., Larochelle, H., Adams, R.P.: Practical Bayesian optimization of machine learning algorithms. In: Proceedings of the 25th NIPS, pp. 2951–2959 (2012)
12. Stork, J., Ramos, R., Koch, P., Konen, W.: SVM ensembles are better when different kernel types are combined. In: Lausen, B., Krolak-Schwerdt, S., Böhmer, M. (eds.) Data Science, Learning by Latent Structures, and Knowledge Discovery. SCDAKO, pp. 191–201. Springer, Heidelberg (2015). https://doi.org/10.1007/978-3-662-44983-7_17

# The Parallelization and Optimization of K-means Algorithm Based on MGPUSim

Zhangbin Mo, Yaobin Wang$^{(\boxtimes)}$, Qingming Zhang, Guangbing Zhang, Mingfeng Guo, Yaqing Zhang, and Chao Shen

School of Computer Science and Technology, Key Laboratory of Testing Technology for Manufacturing Process in Ministry of Education, Southwest University of Science and Technology, Mianyang 621010, China
wangyaobin@foxmail.com

**Abstract.** Although the k-means algorithm has been parallelized into different platforms, it has not yet been explored on multi-GPU architecture thoroughly. This paper presents a study of parallelizing k-means on a novel MGPUSim architecture, including its parallel execution mechanism, architecture design, etc. In addition, it proposes an optimization method "O-kmeans" to initialize the selection of clustering centers by first finding the centroids of the samples and then dividing the initialized clustering centers with centroids, thus solving the problem of poor clustering effect of the k-means algorithm when the data size is large. The performance of this algorithm is tested with both real and synthetic datasets. The experimental results show that:(1) The proposed O-kmeans algorithm performs well on the MGPUSim. It can achieve a $26.74\times$–$62.92\times$ speedup for real data sets, which is better than the CUDA implementation of kernel k-means. (2) In synthetic datasets, by conducting controlled variable experiments at varying data sizes and data dimensions, and different clustering centers. We find that the algorithm has higher stability and good processing speed on MGPUSim.

**Keywords:** K-means · GPU · MGPUSim · Data mining · Clustering

## 1 Introduction

Data mining is an emerging interdisciplinary field that incorporates concepts about machine learning, statistics, databases, and parallel computing which refers to all the integrated processes of discovering new patterns or building models from a given dataset [1]. Clustering is a process of classifying and organizing data members that are similar in some aspects of the dataset [2]. This algorithm has computational complexity and is suitable for small datasets, but there are still some disadvantages in clustering analysis, for example, the uncertainty of K values and the random selection of initial points make the results unstable leading to large errors in the final clustering results. The scalability of the algorithm becomes increasingly necessary with the rapid growth of dataset size, thus, parallel k-means is one of the solutions [3].

© The Author(s), under exclusive license to Springer Nature Switzerland AG 2022
E. Pimenidis et al. (Eds.): ICANN 2022, LNCS 13532, pp. 309–320, 2022.
https://doi.org/10.1007/978-3-031-15937-4_26

There are two main approaches to parallelization, one based on software platforms such as MPI (Message Passing Interface) and OpenMPI (open Message Passing Interface), and the other based on hardware accelerators, like FPGA (Field Programmable Gate Array) and GPU (Graphics Processing Unit) [4]. The algorithm is well suited to be accelerated with the massively parallel capabilities of the GPU since the k-means algorithm needs to perform many independent distance calculations [5, 6]. Generally speaking CUDA (Compute Unified Device Architecture) and OpenCL (Open Computing Language) are used to implement and optimize [7].

Parallelization of k-means has several research topics focusing on software implementation, but there is still a lot of work to be done to improve its hardware implementation. Parallel programs mainly take advantage of the parallelizability and independent parts of the target algorithm to increase the speed and we need to resort to a hardware simulator called MGPUSim while considering the limitations of the hardware used. MGPUSim [8] is a cycle-accurate, extensively validated GPU simulator tailored for multi-GPU platform simulation that simulates the AMD GCN3 ISA [9] with it has high flexibility, high scalability, and parallel simulation. Daisen [10] is a web-based visualization tool, the framework supports data collection from MGPUSim, and provides simulator-generated visualization of GPU execution traces, you can examine GPU execution traces, identify performance bottlenecks, and verify performance improvements.

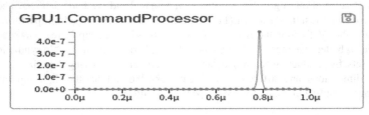

**Fig. 1.** On the x-axis, represents the execution time and on the y-axis, the Request Complete Rate, which represents the change in the number of requests as the execution time varies.

For the above problems, we propose a solution in this paper. We checked the CP (command processor) and improved the scheduling speed, and found out by Daisen that the CP was not running fast enough to schedule the working groups. In addition, the selection of the clustering center is one of the important factors affecting the algorithm to divide the clusters. The algorithm was improved by combining the characteristics of the algorithm to find out the central value of the samples first, and the method of dividing the initialized clustering center by the central point was optimized. Then complete the implementation of the k-means algorithm on MGPUSim, which uses the parallel GO language on the CPU side and OpenCL on the GPU side to implement the parallel part of its algorithm, configure the simulator, and perform data initialization. The GPU execution trace generated by the simulator is recorded using the visualization tool Daisen to identify the performance bottlenecks that exist, as shown in Fig. 1, where we selected the CP component and looked at the Request Complete Rates, which indicates the number of requests completed per second on a given component. Taking advantage of the fact that

MGPUSim has more computational resources and memory space than a single GPU, we have completed the design and optimization of the parallelization of the k-means algorithm in this system architecture.

We have made the following contributions:

(1) In MGPUSim, we parallelize the design and implementation of the k-means algorithm called "M-kmeans". Using the performance bottlenecks existing in Daisen analysis, we proposed a method for initial clustering center selection from the hardware level and combining algorithm characteristics. Compared with M-kmeans, the improved and optimized O-kmeans algorithm improves the speed by $1.4\times$–$13.7\times$ times.

(2) Under real data sets, we tested M-kmeans and O-kmeans to compare with CUDA implementation of kernel kmeans, and the results show that our parallelized implementation is effective in improving the efficiency and parallel computing capability of the algorithm. O-kmeans can achieve a $26.74\times$–$62.92\times$ speedup.

(3) Using synthetic datasets on MGPUSim, the operational efficiency of this algorithm is compared by control variables at different dataset sizes, several cluster centers, and sample point dimensions. It is also compared with the CPU execution results. The results show that our implementation method has better running efficiency.

## 2  Related Work

### 2.1  K-means Algorithm Implemented on GPU

In this research on parallel k-means, the aim is to improve the k-means algorithm or to provide enhanced parallel implementations on different platforms. Baydoun M et al. [11] provides the implementation of several enhanced multicore CPUs and it implements different accelerations based on the different sizes of the dataset used (data sample points, data dimensions, and the number of clustering centers). Meanwhile, GPU and the CUDA GPU speedup is over 20 times compared to a single-threaded CPU. Bhimani J et al. [12] considers the parallel implementation of K-means on MPI, OpenMP, and CUDA and concludes that for larger data, CUDA has the best speedup ratio. Nelson et al. [13] emphasize the importance of memory management and synchronization, and the lock-based GPU implementation of k-means algorithms on real and synthetic datasets can be faster than KMCUDA by a factor of 20 on average. Daoudi et al. [14] propose a parallel OpenCL-based k-means algorithm implementation for large datasets, with significant speedups compared to GPU-based implementations.

The literature on kernel K-means [15], starts with improving the accuracy of the K-means algorithm, and the GPU implementation developed by Baydoun et al. [16] CUDA on NVIDIA GPUs. uses multiple datasets with different numbers of features and patterns, and the CUDA implementation has a significant speedup [17].

### 2.2  MGPUSim System Architecture

The overall system architecture of MGPUSim [18], shown in Fig. 2 uses a discrete GPU framework consisting of four GPUs connected to a host CPU. The CPU side is responsible for data initialization and various preprocessing operations, while the GPU side mainly performs complex data computation. A GPU, for example, consists of a command processor (CP), an asynchronous computation engine (CU), a computation unit (CU), a cache, and a memory controller [19, 20].

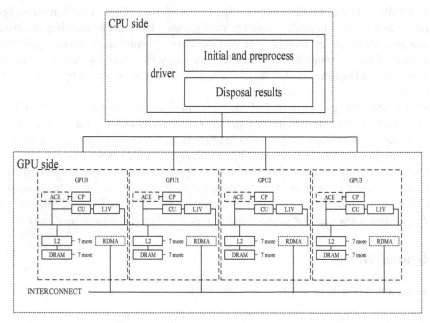

**Fig. 2.** MGPUSim system overall structure diagram

# 3   The Proposed Method

This subsection details the parallelization process of k-means algorithm implementation on MGPUSim based on the architectural advantages of the MGPUSim simulator, as well as the optimization of k-means implemented by parallelization design, performance analysis using Daisen, a GPU execution trajectory visualization tool, and an optimization method for initializing the clustering center by combining performance bottlenecks, which is implemented by parallelization scheme of MGPUSim platform.

## 3.1   Parallelized Design of the k-means Algorithm

As shown in Fig. 3, we first configure the environment of MGPUSim, then write the program start function main () and create a runner to initialize the multi-GPU platform, which code includes the simulation engine of the GPU driver and the benchmarks to be run, etc. [18]. Then initialize the workload and create the workload constructor and use "kernels.LoadProgramMemory" to extract the kernel binaries. Next, define the kernel parameters in kernels. cl and construct the kernel execution functions. The kernel is compiled using the clang-ocl, go-bindata, and esc tools. The "MemcopyH2D" function copies the data to the GPU, while cpukmeans, etc. is done on the CPU side. The "kernels. cl" file contains two kernels, one to calculate the distance from each input point to the cluster center of mass, and in the second kernel, each GPU processes its batch of data. Finally, the required memory data is allocated to the GPU and the program is run, completing the refactoring and parallelization of the application.

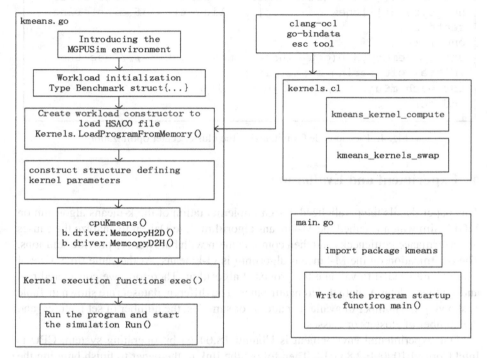

**Fig. 3.** Steps of k-means algorithm implementation on MGPUSim

## 3.2 Optimization of Initialized Clustering Centers

Since the method of randomly selecting the initial clustering, centers makes the results unstable, and to better adapt to the operation of MGPUSim, we'd better do as follows when we parallelize the implementation of the k-means algorithm: firstly, we need to find the centroids of the samples and then use the centroids to divide the k initial clustering centers to reduce the number of iterations of the algorithm and improve the clustering efficiency. The pseudo-code is shown in Fig. 4, which calculates the distance from each sample point to each cluster center and divides it into the corresponding cluster centers to be executed on the GPU side to update the clusters.

```
s=x1,x2,......,xm,  C=1,2,…,k
for each j∈µj, j=1,2, …,k
for each i∈xi, i=1,2,…,N //Calculate the distance of all
sample points
sum+=distance[xi];
end for
new_center[j]=sum/num_cluster*j //Find the sample center
new_cluster[i]=new_center[j]//Delineation of clustering
centers
end for
driver.MemCopyH2D(gpu_cluster, new_cluster);//Pass the
initial clustering center into the GPU
for each m∈µj, j=1,2, …,k parallel do
end for
```

**Fig. 4.** Pseudo-code for initializing the cluster center optimization

## 4 Experiment and Evaluation

This paper details the parallelized design implementation of the k-means algorithm on MGPUSim which is called the M-kmeans algorithm. Use Daisen to analyze the causes of performance bottlenecks and then combine them with hardware to provide solutions. The optimization on the M-kmeans algorithm is O-kmeans. At the same time, several datasets are needed to validate the proposed algorithm. Therefore, we considered real and synthetic datasets with different attributes. The different datasets are shown in Table 1, showing the number of available patterns or samples, the number of set features, and the number of clusters or classes.

Our experimental environment is Ubuntu 18.04 64-bit operating system, CPU is Intel Core i9-10900F 2.8 GHZ. Then follow the link to the paper to finish building the MGPUSim platform.

**Table 1.** Datasets used for clustering

| Dataset number | Dataset | Patterns | Features | Clusters |
|---|---|---|---|---|
| 1 | Bodyfat [21] | 252 | 13 | 2 |
| 2 | Blood transfusion [22] | 748 | 4 | 2 |
| 3 | Australian credit [21] | 690 | 14 | 2 |
| 4 | Haberman [21] | 306 | 3 | 2 |
| 5 | Breast cancer [21] | 683 | 10 | 2 |
| 6 | Flare [22] | 1389 | 13 | 2 |
| 7 | Iono [22] | 351 | 34 | 2 |
| 8 | Iris data | 150 | 4 | 2 |

### 4.1 Daisen Validation Performance Improvement Analysis

When we compare before and after the improvement, the improved CP starts to have requests earlier as shown in the figure, and the number of requests appears after 0.4 microseconds. By changing the scheduling speed from one workgroup per cycle to two workgroups per cycle, the scheduling speed is improved and the CP is more efficient. We at Daisen, a GPU visual execution trajectory tool, also analyzed other performance metrics, shown in the figure, denoting Number Concurrent Task and Average Request Latency, respectively. refers to the number of concurrent tasks and the duration of each requested task completed by a particular component. The number of concurrent tasks grows very fast as the execution time increases, and the combination of improvements to the algorithm helps to increase the number of concurrent tasks. As the execution time increases, the duration of each requested task decreases gradually, and the running speed increases. Overall, the Daisen findings and minor modifications to the GPU design have improved device utilization and reduced overall execution time. The modifications combined with the characteristics of the algorithm can further reduce the execution time (Figs. 5 and 6).

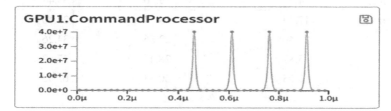

**Fig. 5.** The number of requests completed per second on the CP after the improvement. On the X-axis, it represents the execution time, and on the Y-axis, the request completion rate.

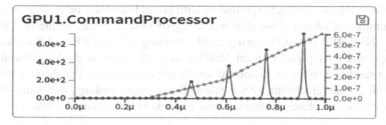

**Fig. 6.** As GPU execution time varies, the Number of Concurrent tasks (red) and Average Request Latency (blue) (Color figure online)

### 4.2 Experimental Analysis of the K-means Algorithm on the Real Data Set

The speedup of the serial CPU implementation and the parallelized design implementation and optimization on MGPUSim are done separately for different datasets. We also compared Baydoun et al. [17]. parallelized kernel k-means on GPU, a CUDA version implemented on NVIDIA GPUs, under the same experimental conditions of the dataset with clusters, sample points, and also data dimensions. Kernel kmeans is a kernelization method that uses specific functions to transform the data into a new feature vector representation. Through several experimental comparisons, M-kmeans have a maximum of 25 times improvement over CUDA implementation of kernel kmeans, but O-kmeans optimized by M-kmeans perform the best. It can achieve a 26.74×–62.92× speedup. Through the validation, we found that the parallelization on MGPUSim is better and the clustering results are stable (Table 2).

**Table 2.** Number of speedup in comparison with the serial implementation

| Dataset | #Speedups by CUDA | #Speedups by M-kmeans | #Speedups by O-kmeans |
|---|---|---|---|
| Bodyfat | 5.77 | 16.44 | 26.74 |
| Blood transfusion | 22.07 | 24.62 | 28.67 |
| Australian credit | 19.67 | 37.87 | 51.10 |
| Haberman | 4.3 | 49.70 | 58.44 |
| Breast cancer | 17.39 | 19.14 | 24.40 |
| Flare | 20.46 | 22.86 | 34.26 |
| Iono | 5.87 | 28.43 | 37.62 |
| Iris data | 2.25 | 50.53 | 62.92 |

### 4.3 Experimental Analysis of K-means Algorithm on Synthetic Data

In this subsection, we conduct experiments with control variables on the size of sample points, number of clusters, and dimensionality of sample points of the dataset, and calculate the RMSE of the clustering results running on the CPU and the clustering results optimized for parallelism on MGPUSim as the evaluation of the parallelized clustering results. And the experimental results are compared and analyzed with those of the serial-kmeans algorithm. we use a data set of random floating-point numbers up to 1 and with 8 decimal places as sample points to package the data and ensure consistency in data size.

#### 4.3.1 The k-means Algorithm is Implemented in Different Data Sizes.

According to Table 3, the performance of parallelization is significantly better than the performance of serial execution at different data sizes. Because of the obvious parallelism advantage of this system architecture, it can greatly improve operation efficiency. By the value of RMSE, we can conclude that as the number of samples increases the value of RMSE has a tendency to become smaller. Analysis of the reason for this reveals that as the number of cluster centers remains the same while the number of samples

**Table 3.** Runtime of serial k-means and M-kmeans and O-kmeans at varying data sizes

| d = 2,<br>k = 10\n | 100,000 | 200,000 | 400,000 | 800,000 | 1,600,000 | 3,200,000 |
|---|---|---|---|---|---|---|
| Serial_time | 0.05932 | 0.11267 | 0.22494 | 0.44092 | 0.87294 | 1.78684 |
| M-kmeans | 0.001454 | 0.004361 | 0.008554 | 0.016360 | 0.036400 | 0.058000 |
| O-kmeans | 0.00028741 | 0.00071311 | 0.00139468 | 0.00253138 | 0.00529005 | 0.00812950 |
| RMSE | 0.105236 | 0.053132 | 0.053124 | 0.053189 | 0.052988 | 0.053046 |

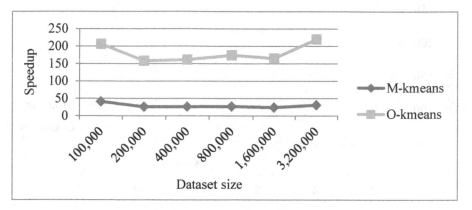

**Fig. 7.** Speedup of M-kmeans and O-kmeans at different data sizes

becomes denser in the clusters, the similarity of clusters increases, and the value of RMSE becomes smaller.

Figure 7 shows that the performance of O-kmeans consistently outperforms that of M-kmeans. When increasing the size of the data, the maximum speedups of M-kmeans can reach 40.8, and the optimized O-kmeans are 5–7 times higher than M-kmeans. By analyzing the acceleration ratio of the two, we can see that the optimized O-kmeans algorithm shows a trend to be more suitable for the MGPUSim platform, which also reflects the stable design of the MGPUSim architecture, the high accuracy of the test, and the stable results of the multiple tests.

### 4.3.2  The k-means Algorithm Implemented in Different Data Dimensions

Table 4 and Fig. 8 the running efficiency of O-kmeans is obviously due to M-kmeans. with the doubling of the data dimension, the running time of M-kmeans increases rapidly and the acceleration ratio becomes smaller and smaller, which indicates that the data dimension has more influence on M-kmeans. However, O-kmeans are not affected and the acceleration effect is obvious, which indicates that the stability of the clustering effect in O-kmenas is higher than that of M-kmeans.

**Table 4.** Runtime of serial k-means and M-kmeans and O-kmeans at Varying data dimension.

| n = 20000, k = 2\d | 2 | 4 | 8 | 16 | 32 |
|---|---|---|---|---|---|
| Serial_time | 0.01180 | 0.01811 | 0.03027 | 0.05515 | 0.11337 |
| M-kmeans | 0.000282 | 0.000399 | 0.000893 | 0.003654 | 0.007050 |
| O-kmeans | 0.000090703 | 0.000110975 | 0.000136781 | 0.000280991 | 0.000514937 |
| RMSE | 0.069629 | 0.081338 | 0.083303 | 0.083488 | 0.083407 |

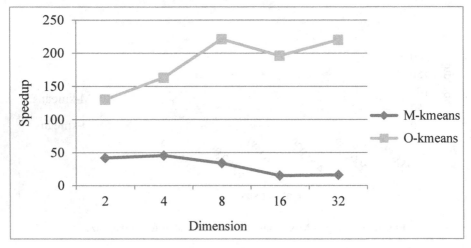

**Fig. 8.** Speedup of M-kmeans and O-kmeans at Varying the data dimension

### 4.3.3   The k-means Algorithm Implemented in Different Clustering Centers

**Table 5.** Runtime of serial k-means and M-kmeans and O-kmeans at Varying cluster size.

| n = 60000, d = 2\k | 10 | 20 | 40 | 80 | 160 | 320 |
|---|---|---|---|---|---|---|
| Serial_time | 0.03327 | 0.06430 | 0.12203 | 0.23826 | 0.45676 | 0.89639 |
| M-kmeans | 0.000741 | 0.000806 | 0.000894 | 0.001075 | 0.001432 | 0.002145 |
| O-kmeans | 0.00019193 | 0.00023641 | 0.00032388 | 0.00049699 | 0.00084416 | 0.00153575 |
| RMSE | 0.052706 | 0.052719 | 0.052719 | 0.052719 | 0.054226 | 0.054226 |

The number of clustering centers has a large impact on the algorithm running efficiency during serial execution, and in Table 5 the speedup of M-kmeans is increasing with the increase of the number of clustering centers. In Fig. 9, O-kmeans perform better than M-kmeans, and its clustering effect remains stable as the number of clustering centers increases. Because we use fine-grained parallelization and allocate the number of work items in this system architecture, the division of each clustering center to each work item is executed in parallel, which greatly improves the computational efficiency.

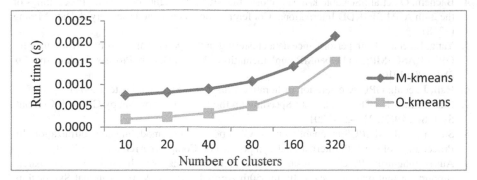

**Fig. 9.** The running time of M-kmeans and O-kmeans with Varying the cluster size k

## 5 Conclusion and Future Work

In this paper, by making improvements at the hardware level and combining the algorithm characteristics An optimization method for initializing clustering centers is proposed and implemented in parallel based on MGPUSim, a GPU simulator. The problem of too many aggregated or too scattered initialized clustering centers is solved, the efficiency of clustering is improved, and the operation suitable for the MGPUSim system architecture is completed. The algorithm is analyzed in a multi-dimensional comparison in terms of different data sets, running time, the accuracy of clustering results, acceleration ratio, etc. The experimental results show that the improved algorithm proposed in this paper can effectively improve the execution efficiency and reduce the running time under various types of data sets. Comparing the parallel computing performance with the CUDA implemented version demonstrates that the improved algorithm has better performance. In future work, we will continue to explore the performance impact of the multithreading mechanism on the classification algorithm.

**Acknowledgment.** This work has been supported by a grant from the National Natural Science Foundation of China General Program (61672438) and the Special Project of the China Association of Higher Education (21SZYB16).

## References

1. Zaki, M.J.: Parallel and distributed data mining: an introduction. In: Zaki, M.J., Ho, C.-T. (eds.) LSPDM 1999. LNCS (LNAI), vol. 1759, pp. 1–23. Springer, Heidelberg (2000). https://doi.org/10.1007/3-540-46502-2_1

2. Cuomo, S., et al.: A GPU-accelerated parallel K-means algorithm. Comput. Elect. Eng. **75**, 262–274 (2017)
3. Wang, Z., et al.: The parallelization and optimization of k-means algorithm based on spark. In: 2020 15th International Conference on Computer Science & Education (2020)
4. Bachem, O., et al.: Scalable k-means clustering via lightweight coresets. In: Proceedings of the 24th ACM SIGKDD International Conference on Knowledge Discovery & Data Mining (2018)
5. Yang, L., et al.: High performance data clustering: a comparison analysis of performance for GPU, RASC, MPI, and OpenMP implementation. Parallel Distrib. Process. Techn. App. **70**, 284–300 (2010)
6. Hall, J., et al.: GPU Acceleration of Iterative Clustering. Siggraph Poster (2004)
7. Li, Y., Zhao, K., Chu, X., Liu, J.: Speeding up the k-means algorithm by GPUs. J. Comput. Syst. Sci. **79**(2), 216–229 (2013)
8. Sun, Y., et al.: MGPUSim: enabling multi-GPU performance modeling and optimization. In: Proceedings of the 46th International Symposium on Computer Architecture (2019)
9. Ausavarungnirun, R., et al.: Mosaic: a GPU memory manager with application-transparent support for multiple page sizes. In: the 50th Annual IEEE/ACM International Symposium ACM (2017)
10. Sun, Y., et al.: Daisen: a framework for visualizing detailed GPU execution. Comput. Graph. Forum. **40**(3), 1–12 (2021)
11. Baydoun, M., Dawi, M., Ghaziri, H.: Enhanced parallel implementation of the K-means clustering algorithm. In: Advances in Computational Tools for Engineering Applications (ACTEA), 2016 3rd International Conference on IEEE, pp. 7–11 (2016)
12. Bhimani, J., Leeser, M., Mi, N.: Accelerating K-means clustering with parallel implementations and GPU computing. In: High Performance Extreme Computing Conference (HPEC), pp. 1–6 (2015)
13. Nelson, J., and Roberto, P.: Don't forget about synchronization! A case study of K-means on GPU. In: Proceedings of the 10th International Workshop on Programming Models and Applications for Multicores and Manycores- PMAM'192019, pp. 11–20 (2019)
14. Daoudi, S., et al.: A Comparative study of parallel CPU/GPU implementations of the K-means algorithm. In: 2019 International Conference on Advanced Electrical Engineering (ICAEE). IEEE (2019)
15. Salvatore, C., De Angelis, V., Gennaro, F., Livia, M., Gerardo, T.: A GPU-accelerated parallel K-means algorithm. Comput. Elect. Eng. **75**, 262–274 (2019)
16. Baydoun, M., Ghaziri, H., Al-Husseini, M.: CPU and GPU parallelized kernel K-means. J. Supercomput. **74**(8), 3975–3998 (2018). https://doi.org/10.1007/s11227-018-2405-7
17. Kruliš, M., Miroslav, K.: Detailed analysis and optimization of CUDA K-means algorithm. In: 49th International Conference on Parallel Processing-ICPP (2020)
18. Sun, Y., et al.: MGSim+MGMark: a framework for multi-GPU system research. arXiv preprint arXiv:1811.02884 (2018)
19. Young, V., et al.: Combining HW/SW mechanisms to improve NUMA performance of multi-GPU systems. In: 2018 51st Annual IEEE/ACM International Symposium on Microarchitecture (MICRO), IEEE (2018)
20. Lee, S., Won, W.R.: Parallel gpu architecture simulation framework exploiting architectural-level parallelism with timing error prediction. IEEE Trans. Comput. **65**(4), 1253–1265 (2015)
21. Michie, D., Spiegelhalter, D.J., Taylor, C.C.: Machine Learning, Neural and Statistical Classification. Ellis Horwood, Amsterdam (1994)
22. Blake, C., Merz, C.J.: UCI repository of machine learning databases. University of California, Irvine

# Two-Dimensional Encoding Method for Neural Synthesis of Tabular Transformation by Example

Yoshifumi Ujibashi[1,2](✉) [ID] and Atsuhiro Takasu[2,3] [ID]

[1] Fujitsu Limited, 4-1-1 Kamikodanaka, Nakahara-ku, Kawasaki, Kanagawa, Japan
ujibashi@fujitsu.com
[2] The Graduate University for Advanced Studies, SOKENDAI, Chiyoda-ku, Tokyo, Japan
[3] National Institute of Informatics, 2-1-2 Hitotsubashi, Chiyoda-ku, Tokyo, Japan
{ujibashi,takasu}@nii.ac.jp

**Abstract.** Programming by example (PBE) is a technology that makes data transformation tasks, especially tabular data transformation, easier for data analysts by automatically generating transformation programs from user-given input–output examples. In recent years, PBE research using machine learning (ML) has emerged because of the recent success of ML in various research fields. We developed an ML-based PBE system for tabular data transformation in previous work. The system is based on the Transformer model that fits sequential data and not two-dimensional structured data like tabular data. Inspired by recent work applying a Transformer model to tasks using two-dimensional data, such as the query answering task for tables or the image computer vision task, we propose a Transformer-based model with positional encoding for two-dimensional tabular data, called tabular positional encoding, to improve the Transformer-based model developed in our previous work. We implemented our proposed model and conducted various experiments. The experimental results show that the Transformer-based model with tabular positional encoding achieves much higher performance than our previous work.

**Keywords:** Programming by example · Transformer · Positional encoding

## 1 Introduction

The data transformation from raw data into well-formatted data is a time-consuming and labor-intensive task for data analysts, engineers, or domain specialists. Many data transformation tasks are composed of string transformations and table layout transformations, as described in [6]. Such a transformation is called *tabular transformation* in this paper.

E. Pimenidis et al. (Eds.): ICANN 2022, LNCS 13532, pp. 321–332, 2022.
https://doi.org/10.1007/978-3-031-15937-4_27

An example of tabular transformation is illustrated in Table 1 and 2[1]. Unstructured tabular data as shown in Table 1 is often seen in data analysis scenarios and cannot be used directly in downstream processing. To use this data, data analysts need to transform the data into a relational form, as seen in Table 2. Such a transformation task is difficult for data analysts who have limited coding skills.

A variety of approaches have been studied, aiming to make the data transformation task easier and to eventually remove the barrier that it constitutes.

**Table 1.** An unstructured spreadsheet

| Name | Numbers |
|------|---------|
| Alice | Tel: (03)7345-3850 |
| | Fax: (03)7001-1400 |
| Bob | Tel: (045)873-9639 |
| | Fax: (045)873-8762 |
| Carol | Tel: (06)2340-0987 |
| | Fax: (06)2340-6701 |

**Table 2.** A relational form of Table 1

| | Tel | Fax |
|------|-----|-----|
| Alice | (03)7345-3850 | (03)7001-1400 |
| Bob | (045)873-9639 | (045)873-8762 |
| Carol | (06)2340-0987 | (06)2340-6701 |

Programming by example (PBE) is one of these approaches. PBE accepts a pair of input–output examples given by users as the specification condition, generates a program consistent with the input–output examples, and results in removing the coding efforts of users.

In our previous work, we proposed a new machine learning (ML) approach to achieve PBE for tabular transformation [7]. This system is based on the Transformer model [8] and achieved better performance than the conventional PBE system using the search-based method [3].

Transformer is a state-of-the-art neural model for solving natural language processing (NLP) tasks and handles a sequence of words in documents or sentences. However, it is difficult for Transformer to handle two-dimensional structured data because of a lack of ability to embed two-dimensional positions.

In this paper, we propose a new technique to handle two-dimensional structured data using a Transformer-based model, and thereby improve accuracy compared with our previous work. The contributions are as follows.

- We designed tabular positional encoding to handle tabular data in the Transformer-based model, inspired by techniques used in a query answering model for tables and two-dimensional image computer vision models.
- We empirically show that the proposed tabular positional encoding effectively embeds two-dimensional positions and achieves better performance than the Transformer-based model without tabular positional encoding.

---

[1] This example is cited from our previous work [7].

## 2    Problem Formulation

We formally define the PBE problem discussed in this paper. This definition is cited from our previous work [7].

### 2.1    Problem

Given a pair of input–output tabular data $(T_i, T_o)$, the requirement is to synthesize a tabular transformation program $P$ that satisfies $T_o = P(T_i)$. The program $P$ is composed of a sequence of tabular transformation operations $(P_1, P_2, \ldots P_n)$. Each operation $P_i$ is a unit of tabular data transforms. The program $P$ is synthesized by chaining operations that satisfy the following expression.

$$T_1 = P_1(T_i), \quad T_2 = P_2(T_1), \quad \ldots \quad T_o = P_n(T_{n-1})$$

### 2.2    Program Components

Each operation is parameterized by arguments that specify, for example, column(s) to be manipulated or delimiters for dividing cells. We use the operators and their arguments listed in Table 3 similarly in our previous work [7].

## 3    Related Work

### 3.1    ML-Based PBE for Tabular Transformation

We propose a Transformer-based model that uses the ML-based PBE for tabular transformation developed in our previous work [7]. To handle two-dimensional tabular data in the Transformer-based model, we designed a tabular data linearization method that linearizes input–output tabular data into a sequence concatenated with each cell of tabular data Sect. 4.2.

Although the Transformer-based model achieved better performance than the conventional search-based method, its performance for large tabular data was poorer than that for smaller tabular data. Our main motivation to study this work was to improve the performance of the Transformer-based model for larger tabular data.

### 3.2    Two-Dimensional Positional Encoding

Transformer was originally designed for NLP tasks and for application to sequences of words. Some recent studies [1,2,9] leverage its high performance for tasks dealing with two-dimensional structured data like tabular data or two-dimensional images. We examined these studies to improve the Transformer-based model developed in our previous work.

Herzig et al. [2] developed TaPas, a system resembling bidirectional encoder representations from transformers (BERT), to answer natural language questions regarding tables. This system uses a Transformer-based architecture with additional positional embedding to encode tabular structures. Our proposed method in Sect. 5.1 was designed based on this work.

The work by Wnag et al. [9] and the work on Vision Transformer [1] examined Transformer models to encode two-dimensional images to translate math formula images to LaTeX codes [9] and to solve computer vision tasks [1]. Our proposed method in Sect. 5.1 was designed based on these works.

**Table 3.** Operators and their arguments used for tabular data transformation

| Operator | Description |
|---|---|
| MoveToEnd(*pos*) | Moves a column next to the last column |
| MoveFromEnd(*pos*) | Moves the last column |
| Drop(*pos*) | Drops a column |
| Copy(*pos*) | Duplicates a column |
| CopyToDest(*pos*, *pos*) | Duplicates a column |
| Fill(*pos*) | Fills empty cells |
| Split(*delim*\|*delimregex*, *pos*) | Splits a column at a delimiter or the match of a regex |
| MergeToOne(*delim*, *pos*) | Merges two or more columns after a position by a delimiter |
| Divide(*predicate*, *pos*) | Divides a column whereby one satisfies the predicate and the other does not |
| Extract(*regex*, *pos*) | Extracts the first match of a regex |
| Fold(*pos*) | Folds all the columns after a column |
| Unfold() | Expands folded columns of the table |
| FoldHeader(*pos*) | Folds the column names and the values after the specified position |
| UnFoldHeader(*pos*) | Expands the folded columns into a relational form |
| Delete(*pos*) | Deletes rows empty in a column |
| DeleteEmptyCols | Deletes empty columns |
| Transpose() | Transposes rows and columns |
| Wrap(*pos*) | Concatenates rows of same values in a column |
| WrapToOne() | Concatenates all rows of the table to one |
| WrapEveryKRows(*k*) | Concatenates every $k$ row into a row |
| **Numeric arguments** | **Description** |
| *pos* | Position of a column |
| *k* | Number of rows wrapped |
| **Non-numeric arguments** | **Description** |
| *delimregex* | `[-_!@#$%^&*\|  ,./:;<>\(\)\[\]]` |
| *delim* | One delimiter from: -, _, @, #, \$, &, *, \|, ' ', ',', '.', /, :, ;, <, >, [, ], (, ) |
| *regex*, *predicate* | One regular expression from: \w+, \d+, \W+, [^\d]+, \d+\.*\d+, [^\d\.]+, ^0+\$, \d{1,2}:\d{1,2}, (\d{1,4}/)?\d{1,2}/\d{1,2} |

# 4   Our Previous Work

In this paper, we propose tabular positional encoding, which improves the Transformer-based model proposed in our previous work. We provide an overview of the Transformer-based model in our previous work in this section.

## 4.1   The Transformer-Based Model

Transformer is a state-of-the-art ML model for NLP tasks [8]. The architecture is based on attention mechanisms and achieves high performance through high-level parallelization and short training times. This is realized by dispensing with recurrent and convolutional processing entirely.

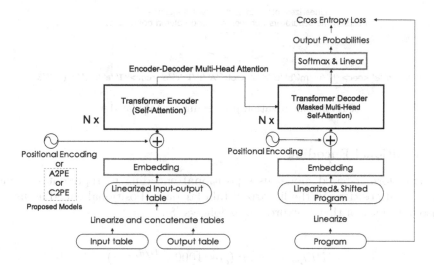

**Fig. 1.** The Transformer-based model

Figure 1 illustrates our Transformer-based model. A pair of input–output tables is linearized to token sequences in order to feed them into the Transformer model (linearization is described in detail in Sect. 4.2).

Once token sequences of the I/O tables are fed into the model, they are embedded in the embedding layer. After that, the positional encoding (see Sect. 4.3) is added to the embedded sequence in order to embed the position of each embedded token.

## 4.2   Tabular Data Linearization

We linearize tabular data into a serialized structure to feed the tabular data into the Transformer-based model. Figure 2 shows an example of this processing. First, each string in each cell of the input table is separated into character-level tokens with special characters <eoc> and <eol> that represent the boundaries of columns and rows, respectively, and then linearized to a sequence of tokens. In addition, we concatenate the input table and output table by introducing the special token <sep> to represent the separation point between the two tables.

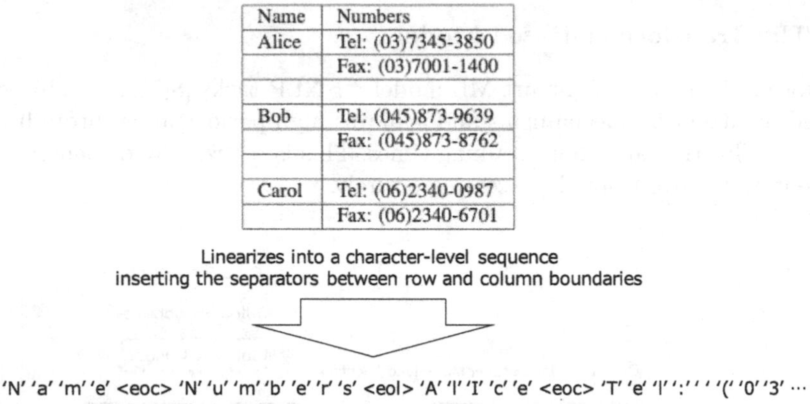

| Name | Numbers |
|---|---|
| Alice | Tel: (03)7345-3850 |
| | Fax: (03)7001-1400 |
| | |
| Bob | Tel: (045)873-9639 |
| | Fax: (045)873-8762 |
| | |
| Carol | Tel: (06)2340-0987 |
| | Fax: (06)2340-6701 |

Linearizes into a character-level sequence
inserting the separators between row and column boundaries

'N' 'a' 'm' 'e' <eoc> 'N' 'u' 'm' 'b' 'e' 'r' 's' <eol> 'A' 'l' 'I' 'c' 'e' <eoc> 'T' 'e' 'l' ':' ' ' '(' '0' '3' ⋯

**Fig. 2.** Linearization processing for tabular data

### 4.3  Positional Encoding

The Transformer-based model uses positional encoding to represent the one-dimensional positions in the linearized tabular data. Positional encoding uses a sinusoidal function that is expressed as follows [8].

$$PE_{(pos,2i)} = sin(pos/10000^{2iD/d_{model}})$$
$$PE_{(pos,2i+1)} = cos(pos/10000^{2iD/d_{model}}) \tag{1}$$

Here, $2i$, $2i - 1$ are the dimension indexes of the model, $pos$ is the position, $d_{model}$ is the dimension size of the model, and $D = 1$. Positions are embedded by adding the $PE$ into the linearized input–output table at each position $pos$.

## 5  Proposed Approach

In this paper, we propose to apply tabular positional encoding (see Sect. 5.1) into the Transformer-based model in our previous work. Replacing the positional encoding to proposed tabular positional encoding Fig. 1, we introduce the encoding method that embeds the positions of two-dimensional structured tabular data and thereby accommodates a pair of I/O tables well in the Transformer-based model.

## 5.1  Tabular Positional Encoding

We propose two types of tabular positional encoding that represent the positions in two-dimensional tabular data.

– Additive Tabular Positional Encoding (ATPE)
– Concatenative Tabular Positional Encoding (CTPE)

Positional encoding is replaced by either ATPE or CTPE. It is added to the embedded linearized input–output table at the former step of the Transformer encoder layers. Both types of tabular positional encoding are composed of four kinds of indexes in tabular data, as shown in Fig. 3.

– **Row** represents the indexes of rows in a table
– **Column** represents the indexes of columns in a table
– **Separator** denotes input table or output table
– **Local Position** represents the indexes of strings inside a table cell

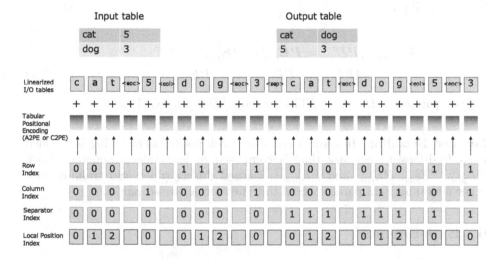

**Fig. 3.** Tabular positional encoding

**Additive Tabular Positional Encoding (ATPE).** Our ATPE design was inspired by the work on TaPas [2]. The vector of ATPE $PE_{pos}^{A}$ is computed by the addition of all positional encoding. Let the vector of the positional encoding of the row, column, separator, and local position be $PE_{pos}^{r}$, $PE_{pos}^{c}$, $PE_{pos}^{s}$, and $PE_{pos}^{l}$, respectively, then

$$PE_{pos}^{A} = PE_{row}^{r} + PE_{col}^{c} + PE_{sep}^{s} + PE_{local}^{l} \qquad (2)$$

Each *row*, *col*, *sep*, and *local* represent row index, column index, index denoting input or output table, and the local position of a table cell, respectively, at position *pos*.

**Concatenative Tabular Positional Encoding (CTPE).** We also designed CTPE, inspired by the work of Wang et al. [9]. The vector of CTPE $PE_{pos}^C$ is computed by concatenating all positional encoding, namely

$$PE_{pos}^C = [PE_{row}^r; PE_{col}^c; PE_{sep}^s; PE_{local}^l] \tag{3}$$

### 5.2 Positional Encoding Implementations

There are two types of implementation for positional encoding, namely fixed encoding and learned encoding. In our experiments, we evaluated each tabular positional encoding (ATPE, CTPE) with each encoding implementation (fixed, learned).

**Fixed Encoding.** In fixed encoding, each positional encoding, namely $PE_{pos}^r$, $PE_{pos}^c$, $PE_{pos}^s$, and $PE_{pos}^l$, is encoded into a fixed value as expressed by sinusoidal function in Eq. 1.

$$
\begin{aligned}
PE_{pos}^r = PE_{pos}^c &= PE_{pos}^s = PE_{pos}^l \\
&= (PE_{(pos,0)}, PE_{(pos,1)}, \ldots, PE_{(pos,d_{model}/D-1)})
\end{aligned} \tag{4}
$$

The parameter $D = 1$ for ATPE, whereas $D = 4$ for CTPE.

**Learned Encoding.** In learned encoding, each positional encoding is encoded by a feed-forward network that is composed of learnable parameters. Each $PE_{pos}^r$, $PE_{pos}^c$, $PE_{pos}^s$, and $PE_{pos}^l$ is learned during supervised training with other neural network parameters of the Transformer-based model.

## 6   Experiments

### 6.1   Experimental Settings

**Training Datasets.** Preparing a large-scale training dataset for the PBE ML model is rather difficult because such a dataset is composed of many input–output pairs of tabular data with corresponding transformation programs. We therefore synthesized the training datasets as in our previous work [7].

The maximum sizes for cell strings, rows, and columns of each input table are set as 10, 5, and 5, respectively. Each program is synthesized from operators and its arguments are randomly sampled from Table 3. The length of each program is up to the predefined maximum size parameterized to 6 in our experiments.

We prepared training datasets of size 10,240,000 (10M), where each item comprises an input–output table pair and the corresponding program. Each training dataset was partitioned, with 90% used for training and 10% for validation.

We selected the same sizes for the training datasets as those described in our previous work, because these achieved the best performance in experiments.

**Benchmark Datasets.** We evaluated our models using the evaluation benchmark used in our previous work [7] and on Foofah [3][2]. We divided the benchmark into two parts according to the size of the table. The "small" benchmark for each test involves tables with rows smaller than 5 and columns smaller than 5, whereas the remaining ones are referred to as "large".

The "small" benchmark was composed of 73 tests, as opposed to 177 for the "large" benchmark. The "all" benchmark includes both "small" and "large" benchmarks.

**Hardware and Software Settings.** We trained our model and evaluated it using one GPU slot of an NVIDIA Tesla P100-PCIE GPU with 16 GB memory. CPU jobs are run on an Intel(R) Xeon(R) CPU E5-2680 v4 @ 2.40 GHz with 132 GB memory. We developed our proposed models using the Pytorch library [5][3] and the fairseq toolkit [4][4].

## 6.2 Experimental Results

We empirically evaluated our proposed models and the baseline systems in terms of accuracy (see Table 4). We set a timeout to 30 s. Each experiment aborts when it exceeds the timeout. Because the performance for a beam size of 500 was better than other beam sizes, we evaluated the results with a beam size of 500. These are listed in Table 4.

We compared our proposed model with two types of baselines in our experiments. The first baseline was a search-based (non-neural) method that simulates that of Foofah [3]. It is referred to as "Search-based" in the experimental results. The second one was the Transformer-based model that was proposed in our previous work [7]. It is referred to as "Transformer" in the experimental results.

Our models proposed in Sect. 5.1 are referred as "ATPE" and "CTPE". Each model is implemented both by the fixed encoding with a sinusoidal function referred to as "(sinusoidal)" and by the learned encoding denoted as "(learned)."

First, the experimental results show the ML-based models, namely Transformer, ATPE, and CTPE, outperform the search-based method in both the large and the small datasets, and there is a large advantage in the small datasets. This shows that ML-based models can accommodate small-size tabular data well, resulting in better performance in the small datasets than the conventional search-based method.

---

[2] https://github.com/markjin1990/foofah_benchmarks.
[3] https://pytorch.org/.
[4] https://github.com/pytorch/fairseq.

**Table 4.** Accuracy performance (%). The bold number represents the best performance over a benchmark set.

| Model | Accuracy (small data) | Accuracy (large data) | Accuracy (all data) |
|---|---|---|---|
| Search-based [3] | 73.9 | 63.2 | 66.4 |
| Transformer [7] | **94.5** | 64.4 | 73.1 |
| ATPE (sinusoidal) | **94.5** | **72.3** | **78.8** |
| ATPE (learned) | 93.1 | 70.0 | 76.8 |
| CTPE (sinusoidal) | 91.7 | 69.4 | 76.0 |
| CTPE (learned) | 91.7 | **72.3** | 78.0 |

Second, our proposed models, ATPE and CTPE, are comparable to the Transformer in the small datasets, and significantly better than Transformer in the large datasets. This result shows that our proposed models represent the vertical and horizontal dependencies between tabular cells by directly embedding the positions of two-dimensional structures and are promising models for encoding two-dimensional tabular data.

We did not find remarkable differences in the accuracy between ATPE and CTPE and between sinusoidal and learned, and their performances are comparable. The model that achieved the best performance among all models was ATPE with a sinusoidal function.

Finally, we compared our proposed models and the baselines in terms of their response-time performance. We chose the ATPE with a sinusoidal function that achieved the best performance in Table 4 as our proposed model in this experiment. The bottom panel (c) of Fig. 4 compares the response performance of the search-based method and ML-based models with beam sizes of 100 and 500 with all datasets. Our proposed model, ATPE with a beam size of 100, achieved the best performance in the time range from start to about 15 s. ATPE with a beam size of 500 outperforms that with a beam size of 100 when the time lapse is longer than 15 s. This means that a larger beam size expands the solution space of beam search and takes a longer time to solve the problem.

Thus, we suggest that our proposed model with a beam size of 500 is better if the final accuracy is the preferred metric, whereas our proposed model with a beam size of 100 would be better if a rapid response is more desirable.

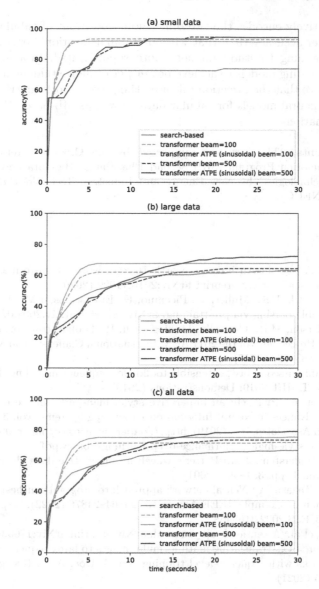

**Fig. 4.** Accuracy with respect to the elapsed time. The top panel (a) shows the performance in terms of the response with the small benchmark datasets, the center panel (b) shows the results with the large benchmark datasets, and the bottom panel (c) shows the results with all benchmark datasets.

## 7    Conclusion

We proposed tabular positional encoding for the Transformer-based model to accommodate tabular transformations in a sophisticated manner in the Transformer. We empirically showed that the Transformer with tabular positional encoding effectively encodes the two-dimensional positions of tabular data and results in better accuracy than that without tabular positional encoding.

We are planning to study further, more sophisticated, tabular positional encoding/embedding models to achieve better performance than achieved in this work. We believe that the direction taken by the present work contributes to the studies of the neural models for tabular data as well as ML-based PBE for tabular transformations.

**Acknowlegments.** This work was supported by the Cross-ministerial Strategic Innovation Promotion Program (SIP) Second Phase and "Big-data and AI-enabled Cyberspace Technologies" by New Energy and Industrial Technology Development Organization (NEDO).

# References

1. Dosovitskiy, A., et al.: An image is worth $16 \times 16$ words: transformers for image recognition at scale. arXiv preprint arXiv:2010.11929 (2020)
2. Herzig, J., Nowak, P.K., Müller, T., Piccinno, F., Eisenschlos, J.M.: TaPas: weakly supervised table parsing via pre-training. arXiv preprint arXiv:2004.02349 (2020)
3. Jin, Z., Anderson, M.R., Cafarella, M., Jagadish, H.: Foofah: transforming data by example. In: Proceedings of the 2017 ACM International Conference on Management of Data, pp. 683–698 (2017)
4. Ott, M., et al.: fairseq: a fast, extensible toolkit for sequence modeling. In: Proceedings of NAACL-HLT 2019: Demonstrations (2019)
5. Paszke, A., et al.: PyTorch: an imperative style, high-performance deep learning library. In: Advances in Neural Information Processing Systems, vol. 32, pp. 8024–8035. Curran Associates, Inc. (2019). http://papers.neurips.cc/paper/9015-pytorch-an-imperative-style-high-performance-deep-learning-library.pdf
6. Raman, V., Hellerstein, J.M.: Potter's wheel: an interactive data cleaning system. In: VLDB, vol. 1, pp. 381–390 (2001)
7. Ujibashi, Y., Takasu, A.: Neural network approach to program synthesis for tabular transformation by example. IEEE Access **10**, 24864–24876 (2022). https://doi.org/10.1109/ACCESS.2022.3155468
8. Vaswani, A., et al.: Attention is all you need. arXiv preprint arXiv:1706.03762 (2017)
9. Wang, Z., Liu, J.C.: Translating math formula images to latex sequences using deep neural networks with sequence-level training. Int. J. Doc. Anal. Recogn. (IJDAR) **24**(1), 63–75 (2021)

# Variational Autoencoders for Anomaly Detection in Respiratory Sounds

Michele Cozzatti, Federico Simonetta(iD), and Stavros Ntalampiras(✉)(iD)

LIM – Music Informatics Laboratory, Department of Computer Science,
University of Milano, Milan, Italy
michele.cozzatti@studenti.unimi.it, stavros.ntalampiras@unimi.it
https://www.lim.di.unimi.it/

**Abstract.** This paper proposes a weakly-supervised machine learning-based approach aiming at a tool to alert patients about possible respiratory diseases. Various types of pathologies may affect the respiratory system, potentially leading to severe diseases and, in certain cases, death. In general, effective prevention practices are considered as major actors towards the improvement of the patient's health condition. The proposed method strives to realize an easily accessible tool for the automatic diagnosis of respiratory diseases. Specifically, the method leverages Variational Autoencoder architectures permitting the usage of training pipelines of limited complexity and relatively small-sized datasets. Importantly, it offers an accuracy of 57%, which is in line with the existing strongly-supervised approaches.

## 1 Introduction

The human respiratory system may be affected by pathological conditions which typically alter the patterns of the emitted sound events [31]. Recently, due to the COVID-19 pandemic, such kind of diseases became of primary importance for the public health, being a novel cause of death for large part of the population [25]. Interestingly, medical acoustics, i.e. the scientific field using audio signal processing and pattern recognition methods for health diagnosis [1], can play a fundamental role in the development of user-friendly tools to prevent and limit the spread of respiratory diseases [18]. The ability to create automatic methods to detect anomalies is useful for both patients and physicians. If the first ones can take advantage from automatic diagnosis methods, physicians can save time and minimize potential errors in the performed diagnoses, improving the treatment path for the patients. Importantly, such solutions may also reduce the overall pressure on public health systems.

Respiratory/breathing cycle is the result of the combined operation of the diaphragm and rib muscles enabling inhalation and exhalation, i.e. breathing in and out. Breathing cycles are evaluated by physicians with the aid of a stethoscope to spot abnormalities that can represent the onset of a disease. Unfortunately, stethoscopes can suffer from external noises, sounds emitted by a variety of organs, etc.

© The Author(s), under exclusive license to Springer Nature Switzerland AG 2022
E. Pimenidis et al. (Eds.): ICANN 2022, LNCS 13532, pp. 333–345, 2022.
https://doi.org/10.1007/978-3-031-15937-4_28

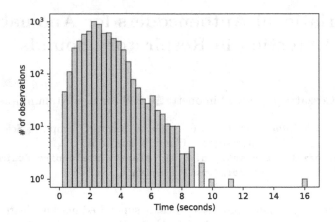

**Fig. 1.** Breathing cycle length versus number of observations. The lengths vary from a minimum of 0.2 s to a maximum of 16 s.

A respiratory cycle can be classified as normal or abnormal. Abnormal breathing cycles can mainly contain two types of abnormal sounds: *crackles* and *wheezes*. *Crackles* are mostly found in the inhalation phase, although in some cases, they appear in the exhalation phase [4]. They are characterized by a short duration and they are explosive. *Wheezes* are longer than crackles, around 80–100 ms, and the frequency can be 100 Hz. They are usually between 100 Hz and 1000 Hz and rarely exceed 1000 Hz [4].

The literature includes various works focusing on the creation of automatic systems that can detect abnormalities in respiratory cycles. Usually, feature extraction is performed to capture significant properties of the signals (audio features) in order to train machine learning models, such as Hidden Markov Model [12], Support Vector Machine [28] or boosted decision tree [6]. Recently, deep learning has been introduced in the audio signal processing community, bringing advances to medical acoustics as well. In this case, typical features are matrix-like representations of the signal in a frequency-time space. Usually, FFT-based representations are extracted and used as an input for training deep learning networks, such as MLP [9], CNN [8,9,21], RNN [22], and other neural architectures [23,24]. In some works, multiple type of features are used with exceptional results [9,29].

Most of the existing works dealing with the classification of respiratory cycles assume availability of data representing every potential class, thus modeling the specific task as a multi-class classification problem. In this paper, instead, we propose an anomaly detection approach. The underlying idea is that abnormalities in respiratory cycles are difficult to record and can vary between different patients, due to different ages and/or sexes. To account for such variability, a sophisticated modeling would be required, which is a hard requirement given the little amount of available data. Therefore, we decided to opt for an anomaly detection task that requires fewer data for training. Interestingly, Variational

Autoencoders have been successfully employed for anomaly/change/novelty detection tasks, such as bird species [19], ultrasounds [16], time series [14], computer networks [11], etc.

The main contribution of this article is to investigate how Variational Autoencoders (VAE) can be effectively employed for detecting anomalies existing in respiratory sounds. The proposed method achieves state-of-art results, while only requiring recordings of normal cycles for training, and as such improving considerably the model's generalization abilities. To distinguish the abnormalities, a threshold must be set, which can be optimally computed from a set of abnormalities. The following sections describe the a) employed dataset of respiratory sounds, b) audio signal preprocessing, c) VAE's architecture and training procedure, d) experimental set-up and results, as well as e) our conclusions.

## 2   The Dataset of Respiratory Sounds

We used the Respiratory Sound database provided by the 2017 International Conference on Biomedical and Health Informatics (ICBHI) [26]. The database consists of 5.5 h of audio: 6898 breathing cycles from 920 audio recordings of 126 patients. Audio recordings last from 10 to 90 s and the audios include different types of noises typical of real-world conditions. Moreover, the audio samples were acquired using various equipments, sampling rates and detection methods. Each respiratory cycle is categorized into four classes: *crackles, wheezes, crackles and wheezes*, and *normal*.

The creators of the challenge predefined train and test subsets of data which permits the reliable comparison between different approaches. Such division is performed at the level of recordings – i.e. the 920 records from which the respiratory cycles are extracted. In this way, a patient's observations can be either in the train set or in the test set, but not in both of them. As such, any patient-specific bias is eliminated. The direct consequence is that using the predefined division, the generalization abilities of the models are better assessed.

The predefined division is shown in the Table 1. Overall, the train set accounts for the 60% of the whole dataset, while the test part consists of the remaining 40%. In addition to the predefined division, several works in literature used random splits defined at the breathing cycle levels. To compare the proposed method to existing works, we tested our method in this setting as well. Namely, we used 80% of the cycles for training and the remaining 20% for testing – see Table 2.

**Table 1.** ICBHI Dataset 60%/40% splitting (statistics at the cycle level). Note that in the train set abnormal cycles are excluded.

|            | Crackles | Wheezes | Both | Normal | Total |
|------------|----------|---------|------|--------|-------|
| *Training*   | 962      | 401     | 281  | 1669   | **3313** |
| *Validation* | 253      | 100     | 89   | 394    | **829**  |
| *Testing*    | 649      | 385     | 143  | 1579   | **2756** |
| **Total**    | **1864** | **886** | **506** | **3642** | **6898** |

**Table 2.** ICBHI Dataset 80%/20% splitting. Note that in the train set, abnormal classes are excluded.

|            | Crackles | Wheezes | Both | Normal | Total |
|------------|----------|---------|------|--------|-------|
| *Training*   | 1192     | 572     | 325  | 2325   | **4414** |
| *Validation* | 290      | 144     | 93   | 577    | **1104** |
| *Testing*    | 382      | 170     | 88   | 740    | **1380** |
| **Total**    | **1864** | **886** | **506** | **3642** | **6898** |

Finally, since the proposed method performs anomaly detection, we grouped all the anomalies in one class ($anomalies = \{crackles, wheezes, both\}$) and the normal observations in another class ($normal = \{normal\}$). Moreover, for the sake of evaluating the generalization abilities of the proposed model, we used a validation set randomly drawn from the train set. Since the proposed method is weakly supervised, in the training set we disregarded the abnormal respiratory cycles and only employed the normal ones. We still used the abnormal cycles in the validation and test sets following both of the above-mentioned divisions.

## 3  Preprocessing of Respiratory Sounds

All recordings were resampled at 4 KHz since, according to the literature [12,28], most of the relevant information is below 2 KHz. As such, according to the Nyquist Theorem, 4 KHz is the minimum-sample rate that allows to reconstruct the important information content. Subsequently, we extracted each breathing cycle from each audio file using the annotations available in the dataset; in the example shown in Table 3, we extracted 9 audio excerpts, disregarding the remaining non-useful portions of audio. The available audio excerpts varied in duration, with the average being 2.7 s. Figure 1 shows the distribution of the obtained audio duration.

**Table 3.** Example of breathing cycles recorded in one audio file. 0 means "absence", 1 means "presence".

| ID | Start  | End    | Crackles | Wheezes |
|----|--------|--------|----------|---------|
| 1  | 2.3806 | 5.3323 | 1        | 0       |
| 2  | 5.3323 | 8.2548 | 0        | 0       |
| 3  | 8.2548 | 11.081 | 1        | 1       |
| 4  | 11.081 | 14.226 | 1        | 1       |
| 5  | 14.226 | 17.415 | 1        | 1       |
| 6  | 17.415 | 20.565 | 1        | 1       |
| 7  | 20.565 | 23.681 | 0        | 1       |
| 8  | 23.681 | 26.874 | 0        | 1       |
| 9  | 26.874 | 30     | 0        | 1       |

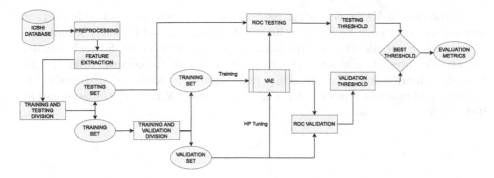

**Fig. 2.** Block diagram of the proposed anomaly detection approach. Starting from the database, a pre-processing phase is performed which is followed by a feature extraction step. The model is then trained with samples belonging to the normal class learning how to reconstruct the input, the optimal hyper-parameters are determined and tested. Finally, the optimal thresholds for the validation and test sets are determined.

To ease the processing of the audio excerpts, and similarly to previous works, we used a fixed-length for each excerpt [27]. Specifically, respiratory cycles lasting less than 3 s were wrap-padded while those that lasted more 3 s were truncated. To represent the audio characteristics of each excerpt and their evolution in time, we extracted Mel-Frequency Cepstral Coefficients (MFCCs) on moving windows. MFCCs are widely used in audio signal processing, including speech emotion recognition [13], acoustic scene analysis [20], music analysis [10], and medical acoustics [17]. First, the audio signal was converted in a log-amplitude spectrogram using windows lasting 40ms and overlapping by 50%; Hamming windowing function was applied before of computing the FFT-based log-amplitude spectrum. Then, the Mel filter banks are applied to each spectrogram column in order to extract perceptually relevant audio characteristics. Finally, the Discrete Cosine Transform (DCT) is used to compress the extracted information; the first component, which is proven to be highly correlated with the energy of the signal [32], was removed to prevent the model of learning information strongly correlated to the recording conditions. As such, 12 MFCCs were considered.

## 4   Anomaly Detection Model

Variational Autoencoders (VAE) are neural networks that unify variational inference approaches with autoencoders. Autoencoders are neural networks composed by two parts: the first part, named *encoder*, learns a mapping from the input sample $x$ to a latent representation $z$; the second part, instead, is named *decoder* and learns to map a point from $z$ to $x$.

In variational inference, instead, a distribution is inferred via point-estimation methods to approximate Bayesian inference when the number of parameters or the size of datasets makes the problem intractable with Monte Carlo methods [3].

In the case of VAEs, the latent representation $z$ must satisfy two important properties, i.e. it must be a) a continuous distribution, and b) easily samplable.

Usually, $z$ is modeled as a Gaussian distribution. In this case, for each sample, the encoder predicts a mean and a variance, defining the corresponding latent Gaussian distribution. Then, a single point from the predicted distribution is sampled and passed to the decoder. Figure 3 depicts a VAE with Gaussian latent distribution.

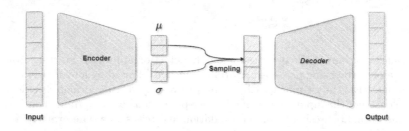

**Fig. 3.** Structure of the proposed VAE consisting of 4 convolutional layers.

Compared to basic autoencoders, VAEs allow to draw random samples at inference time, making them suitable for generation tasks, such as creativity in music applications [30]. Moreover, they allow to mimic Bayesian models, which by construction predict distributions. Indeed, when multiple samples are drawn from $z$, one can analyze a set of outputs that constitute a distribution by themselves, allowing to analyze the epistemic certainty measure of the model regarding its own prediction. In other words, VAEs can be used to help the final user with an estimation of the certainty of the prediction; for instance, a medical expert could decide if the probability score predicted by the model should be trusted or not.

As regards to the loss function, we used the sum of Mean Squared Error between the reconstructed matrix and the input, and the Kullback-Leibler Divergence between the unit Gaussian and the latent distribution. We defined each layer as the sequence of a convolutional layer, a batch-normalization layer, a ReLU function, and a dropout layer while training. The encoder is then built from a sequence of such layers, while the decoder is composed by the corresponding layers with transposed convolutions instead of simple convolutions. The latent means and standard deviations are computed with pure convolutional layers. Figure 2 illustrates the whole anomaly detection pipeline.

## 4.1   VAE Training

**Table 4.** Hyper-parameters and the optimal value found for each of them. BH indicates the best hyperparameters while HS indicates the hyperparameter space that has been considered.

|  | BH | HS |
|---|---|---|
| Loss function | MSE + $D_{KL}$ | {MAE,MAPE,MSE, MSLE} |
| Optimizer | Adam | {SGD, RMSprop, Adam, Adadelta} |
| Learning rate | $1 \times 10^{-4}$ | {$1 \times 10^{-5}$,$1 \times 10^{-4}$,$1 \times 10^{-3}$} |
| Epochs | 1000 | - |
| Patience | 10 epochs | {5,10,15} |
| Batch size | 32 | {32,64,128} |
| Activation functions hidden layer | ReLU | {LeakyReLU, ReLU, sigmoid, tanh} |
| Activation functions output layer | Linear | {linear, sigmoid} |
| Dropout rate | 0.3 | {0.1,0.2,0.3,0.4,0.5} |

**Table 5.** Results obtained on the testing set using two different thresholds, one computed on the validation and one computed on the testing set.

|  |  | Validation threshold | | |
|---|---|---|---|---|
|  |  | TPR | TNR | ACC |
| 60%/40% split | Validation threshold | 0.33 | 0.80 | 0.57 |
|  | Test threshold | 0.44 | 0.70 | 0.57 |
| 80%/20% split | Validation threshold | 0.48 | 0.71 | 0.60 |
|  | Test threshold | 0.58 | 0.61 | 0.60 |

During training, we first searched for the optimal hyper-parameters using Bayesian Optimization method [5] with a Gaussian Process as surrogate model, 2.6 as exploration-exploitation factor $k$, and Lower Confidence Bound (LCB) as acquisition function. The hyper-parameters and their optimal values are shown in Table 4. We then trained the model using the Adam optimization algorithm with a learning rate equal to $1 \times 10^{-4}$.

Training is performed in a weakly-supervised fashion by using the anomaly labels of the validation set only. Specifically, the model is trained to reconstruct samples from the normal class, thus when the input is an excerpt from the abnormal class, we expect that the model will not be able to efficiently reconstruct the input. Since the network is trained to minimize the Mean Squared Error (MSE) between the input and the output, we expect a small MSE for normal respiratory cycles and larger MSEs for abnormal ones. Consequently, the MSE computed on the training set observations can be used as a threshold to spot anomalies.

Since the dataset is not fully balanced, the threshold is chosen so that it maximizes the balanced accuracy on the validation set. Balanced accuracy, compared to Matthews Correlation Coefficient [15], allows for an easy interpretation, being the average between true-positive-rate (TPR) and true-negative-rate (TNR). In our case, TPR is the rate of correctly identified anomalies, while TNR is the rate of correctly identified normal observations [2,7].

## 5   Experimental Set-up and Results

In the context of the ICBHI challenge, the multi-class accuracy is computed as the average of TPR for each class. Having combined all the anomalous classes into one, we calculated TPR for two classes (*anomalies* and *normals*) and from there, the ICBHI score, which corresponds to the balanced accuracy. Moreover, we assessed the performance of the model using ROC curves and AUC values which are well-established figures of merit in the related literature.

We first observed the distribution of the MSE values in the validation set – see Fig. 4 – finding that MSE allowed to partially separate excerpts coming from the two classes. We also observed the ROC and AUC while training, discovering that an optimal threshold could successfully separate the two classes. Figure 5 shows the performance of the trained model on the validation set.

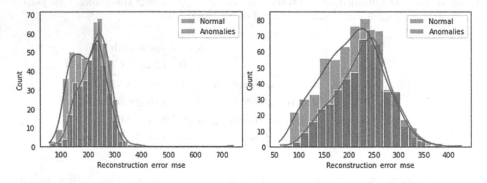

**Fig. 4.** Distributions of normal and anomalous samples existing in the validation set. The figure on the left is related to the division in 60%/40%, while the one on the right in 80%/20%.

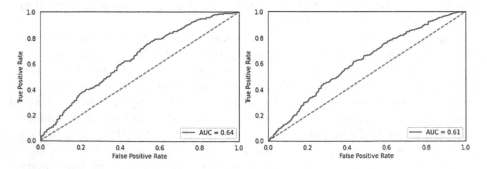

**Fig. 5.** ROC and AUC computed on the validation set. The left image is related to the 60%/40% division, while the one on the right to the 80%/20% one.

We performed the same evaluation on the testing set to assess the generalization abilities of the model – see Figs. 6 and 7. It is particularly interesting comparing the optimal threshold computed on the validation set and the corresponding one computed on the testing set. Using the 80%/20% division, the proposed method identified a slightly smaller threshold than using the 60%/40% division.

However, by comparing the results obtained using the two thresholds – see Table 5 – we observe that the validation threshold is an effective approximation of the testing one, proving the generalization abilities of the model.

A fundamental aspect that must be considered when comparing different works is the data division into training and testing sets. As explained in Sect. 2, the creators of the database offer a subdivision (60%/40%) at the level of audio recordings, so that observations associated with a given patient can be either in train or test set. The division into 80%/20% used by some authors is instead extracted randomly at the level of the excerpts in which each audio recording is segmented (respiratory cycles). Unfortunately, such a division may be biased due

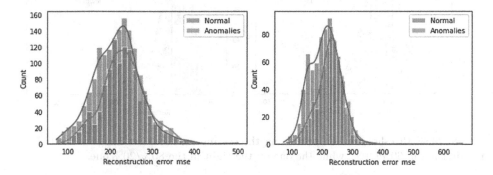

**Fig. 6.** Distributions of normal and anomalous respiratory sounds as regards to the testing set. The left image is related to the division in 60%/40%, while the one on the right to the 80%/20% one.

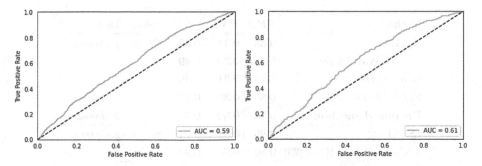

**Fig. 7.** ROC and AUC computed on the testing set. The left image is related to the division in 60%/40%, while the one on the right in the 80%/20% one.

to patient dependency. Using such a division, the performance measure increases essentially for two reasons:

– there is a greater amount of data in the training phase, and
– observations of the same patient can be both in training and in testing.

Moreover, the usage of random seeds can generate dataset division that are particularly successful, thus hiding a pre-bias – i.e. searching good random splits to boost the final scores.

Overall, the proposed approach offers performance which is in line with the state of the art even though it employs respiratory sounds representing only healthy conditions. Interestingly, such a line of thought addresses the problem in a more realistic way since it is unreasonable to assume availability of abnormal respiratory sounds representing the entire gamut of such diseases (Fig. 8).

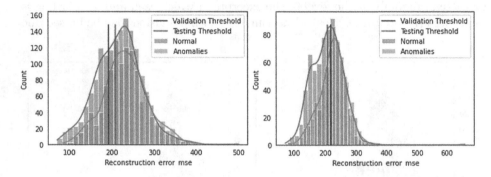

**Fig. 8.** MSE thresholds when processing the testing set. The left image is related to the division in 60%/40%, while the one on the right in the 80%/20% one.

**Table 6.** ICBHI challenge results on the detection of crackles and wheezes (four-class anomaly detection-driven prediction) with the proposed method. $TPR$ is the true-positive-rate, $TNR$ is the true-negative-rate and $ACC$ is the balanced accuracy (corresponding to the ICBHI score).

| Method | $TPR$ | $TNR$ | $ACC$ | Split | Task |
|---|---|---|---|---|---|
| HMM [12] | 0.38 | 0.41 | 0.39 | *60/40* | *4 classes* |
| STFT+Wavelet [28] | 0.78 | 0.20 | 0.49 | | |
| Boosted tree [6] | 0.78 | 0.21 | 0.49 | | |
| Ensemble DL [24] | 0.86 | 0.30 | 0.57 | | |
| **Proposed method** | 0.33 | 0.80 | 0.57* | | *2 classes* |
| LSTM [22] | 0.85 | 0.62 | 0.74 | *80/20* | *4 classes* |
| CNN-MoE & C-RNN [23] | 0.86 | 0.73 | 0.80 | | |
| LSTM [22] | - | - | 0.81 | | *2 classes* |
| CNN-MoE & C-RNN [23] | 0.86 | 0.85 | 0.86 | | |
| **Proposed method** | 0.58 | 0.61 | 0.60* | | |

# 6   Conclusions

In this work we presented a framework modeling the MFCCs extracted from healthy respiratory sounds using a fully convolutional Variational Autoencoder. To the best of our knowledge, this is the first time that the detection of respiratory diseases is faced from an anomaly detection perspective. Interestingly, the proposed model achieved state of the art results in a patient-independent experimental protocol even though it is only weakly-supervised (Table 6).

The small size of the available dataset poses the problem of overfitting and model generalization abilities. To this end, we employed Variational Inference, which allows the model to estimate its own epistemic confidence, in addition to the estimation of the anomaly probability.

In order to improve the performance of the presented anomaly detection system, data augmentation could be a fundamental addition, as it will provide additional training samples. Moreover, different architectures could be tested including networks able to take into account time dependencies, such as attention-based nets and Recurrent Neural Networks. Finally, multiple features could be used to improve the reconstruction abilities [9, 29].

# References

1. Beach, K.W., Dunmire, B.: Medical acoustics. In: Rossing, T.D. (ed.) Springer Handbook of Acoustics, pp. 877–937. Springer, New York (2014). https://doi.org/10.1007/978-1-4939-0755-7_21
2. Bekkar, M., Djemaa, D.H.K.: Evaluation measures for models assessment over imbalanced data sets. J. Inf. Eng. Appl. **3**(10), 13 (2013)
3. Blei, D.M., Kucukelbir, A., McAuliffe, J.D.: Variational inference: a review for statisticians. J. Am. Stat. Assoc. **112**(518), 859–877 (2017)
4. Bohadana, A., Izbicki, G., Kraman, S.S.: Fundamentals of lung auscultation. N. Engl. J. Med. **370**(8), 744–751 (2014)
5. Brochu, E., Cora, V.M., de Freitas, N.: A tutorial on Bayesian optimization of expensive cost functions, with application to active user modeling and hierarchical reinforcement learning. Technical report (2010)
6. Chambres, G., Hanna, P., Desainte-Catherine, M.: Automatic detection of patient with respiratory diseases using lung sound analysis. In: CBMI Conference, pp. 1–6, September 2018
7. Chicco, D., Tötsch, N., Jurman, G.: The Matthews correlation coefficient (MCC) is more reliable than balanced accuracy, bookmaker informedness, and markedness in two-class confusion matrix evaluation. BioData Mining **14**(1), 13 (2021)
8. Demir, F., Sengur, A., Bajaj, V.: Convolutional neural networks based efficient approach for classification of lung diseases. Health Inf. Sci. Syst. **8**(1), 1–8 (2019). https://doi.org/10.1007/s13755-019-0091-3
9. Do, Q.T., Lipatov, K., Wang, H.Y., Pickering, B.W., Herasevich, V.: Classification of respiratory conditions using auscultation sound. In: 2021 43rd Annual International Conference of the IEEE Engineering in Medicine Biology Society (EMBC), pp. 1942–1945 (Nov 2021)
10. Simonetta, F., Ntalampiras, S., Avanzini, F.: Context-aware automatic music transcription (2022)

11. Hannan, A., Gruhl, C., Sick, B.: Anomaly based resilient network intrusion detection using inferential autoencoders. In: 2021 IEEE International Conference on Cyber Security and Resilience (CSR), pp. 1–7 (2021)

12. Jakovljević, N., Lončar-Turukalo, T.: Hidden Markov model based respiratory sound classification. In: Maglaveras, N., Chouvarda, I., de Carvalho, P. (eds.) Precision Medicine Powered by pHealth and Connected Health. IP, vol. 66, pp. 39–43. Springer, Singapore (2018). https://doi.org/10.1007/978-981-10-7419-6_7

13. Li, C.: Robotic emotion recognition using two-level features fusion in audio signals of speech. IEEE Sens. J. 1 (2021)

14. Matias, P.A., Folgado, D., Gamboa, H., Carreiro, A.V.: Robust anomaly detection in time series through variational autoencoders and a local similarity score. In: BIOSIGNALS (2021)

15. Matthews, B.: Comparison of the predicted and observed secondary structure of t4 phage lysozyme. Biochimica et Biophysica Acta (BBA) - Protein Struct. **405**(2), 442–451 (1975)

16. Milković, F., Filipović, B., Subašić, M., Petković, T., Lončarić, S., Budimir, M.: Ultrasound anomaly detection based on variational autoencoders. In: 2021 12th International Symposium on Image and Signal Processing and Analysis (ISPA), pp. 225–229 (2021)

17. Ntalampiras, S.: Collaborative framework for automatic classification of respiratory sounds. IET Signal Process. **14**(4), 223–228 (2020)

18. Ntalampiras, S., Potamitis, I.: Classification of sounds indicative of respiratory diseases. In: Macintyre, J., Iliadis, L., Maglogiannis, I., Jayne, C. (eds.) EANN 2019. CCIS, vol. 1000, pp. 93–103. Springer, Cham (2019). https://doi.org/10.1007/978-3-030-20257-6_8

19. Ntalampiras, S., Potamitis, I.: Acoustic detection of unknown bird species and individuals. CAAI Trans. Intell. Technol. **6**(3), 291–300 (2021)

20. Paseddula, C., Gangashetty, S.V.: DNN based acoustic scene classification using score fusion of MFCC and inverse MFCC. In: 2018 IEEE 13th International Conference on Industrial and Information Systems (ICIIS), pp. 18–21 (2018)

21. Perna, D.: Convolutional neural networks learning from respiratory data. In: IEEE BIBM Conference, pp. 2109–2113, December 2018

22. Perna, D., Tagarelli, A.: Deep auscultation: Predicting respiratory anomalies and diseases via recurrent neural networks. In: IEEE CBMS Symposium, pp. 50–55, June 2019

23. Pham, L., McLoughlin, I., Phan, H., Tran, M., Nguyen, T., Palaniappan, R.: Robust deep learning framework for predicting respiratory anomalies and diseases. In: EMBC Conference, pp. 164–167, July 2020

24. Pham, L., Ngo, D., Hoang, T., Schindler, A., McLoughlin, I.: An ensemble of deep learning frameworks applied for predicting respiratory anomalies. arXiv:2201.03054 Cs Eess, January 2022

25. Rao, S., Narayanaswamy, V., Esposito, M., Thiagarajan, J., Spanias, A.: Deep learning with hyper-parameter tuning for COVID-19 cough detection. In: 2021 12th International Conference on Information, Intelligence, Systems Applications (IISA), pp. 1–5 (2021)

26. Rocha, B.M., et al.: An open access database for the evaluation of respiratory sound classification algorithms. Physiol. Meas. **40**(3), 035001 (2019)

27. Rocha, B.M., Pessoa, D., Marques, A., Carvalho, P., Paiva, R.P.: Influence of event duration on automatic wheeze classification. In: 2020 25th International Conference on Pattern Recognition (ICPR), pp. 7462–7469 (2021). https://doi.org/10.1109/ICPR48806.2021.9412226

28. Serbes, G., Ulukaya, S., Kahya, Y.P.: An automated lung sound preprocessing and classification system based onspectral analysis methods. In: Maglaveras, N., Chouvarda, I., de Carvalho, P. (eds.) Precision Medicine Powered by pHealth and Connected Health. IP, vol. 66, pp. 45–49. Springer, Singapore (2018). https://doi.org/10.1007/978-981-10-7419-6_8

29. Tariq, Z., Shah, S.K., Lee, Y.: Feature-based fusion using CNN for lung and heart sound classification. Sensors **22**(4), 1521 (2022)

30. Yamshchikov, I.P., Tikhonov, A.: Music generation with variational recurrent autoencoder supported by history. SN Appl. Sci. **2**(12), 1–7 (2020). https://doi.org/10.1007/s42452-020-03715-w

31. Zak, M., Krzyżak, A.: Classification of lung diseases using deep learning models. In: Krzhizhanovskaya, V.V., et al. (eds.) ICCS 2020. LNCS, vol. 12139, pp. 621–634. Springer, Cham (2020). https://doi.org/10.1007/978-3-030-50420-5_47

32. Zheng, F., Zhang, G., Song, Z.: Comparison of different implementations of MFCC. J. Comput. Sci. Technol. **16**(6), 582–589 (2001)

# An Innovate Hybrid Approach for Residence Price Using Fuzzy C-Means and Machine Learning Techniques

Antonios Papaleonidas[1]($\boxtimes$) (iD), Konstantinos Lykostratis[2],
Anastasios Panagiotis Psathas[1] (iD), Lazaros Iliadis[1] (iD), and Maria Giannopoulou[2]

[1] Department of Civil Engineering, Lab of Mathematics and Informatics (ISCE), Democritus University of Thrace, 67100 Xanthi, Greece
{papaleon,anpsatha,liliadis}@civil.duth.gr
[2] Department of Civil Engineering, Democritus University of Thrace, 67100 Xanthi, Greece
{klykostr,mgian}@civil.duth.gr

**Abstract.** House price forecasting is an important topic of real estate. The excessive increase of housing price will affect not merely the quality of life, but also the business cycle dynamics. However, the factors influencing residential real estate prices are complex and the selection of effective features is vague, which leads many of the traditional housing price prediction approaches to lower accuracy results. Housing price is strongly correlated to other factors such as location, area, population. In this research, the authors propose an innovate hybrid approach that consists of (i) Fuzzy C-Means (FCM) Algorithm and (ii) Coarse Tree, to predict the cluster that the residence price belongs. The innovation of this research stands to the use of FCM for data-handling and at the exhaustive search for the best Machine Learning (ML) Algorithm. The proposed approach achieves promising results achieving an overall accuracy of 78.8% for Train Data and 79.37% for Test Data. Furthermore, all indices range to relatively high levels and confusion matrix indicate a stability and consistency in the forecast. The algorithm can generalize and therefore, could be utilized as a benchmark for a variety of groups that could benefit from housing price prediction.

**Keywords:** Residence pricing · Fuzzy C-Means · Coarse tree · Clusters · Hybrid

## 1 Introduction

The decoding of the housing market price is one of the most important research subjects in urban economics, with the Hedonic Price Modeling [31] being the most frequently used method of analysis and interpretation of housing values and characteristics. Decoding housing value is significant for a variety of people involved: from land-lords, realtors and banks, to town planners and the state, in order to achieve sales, loans, financing and investment plans [5].

Although urban features seem to be important factors in shaping the value of a property and urban morphology has also a key role in real estate market structure [8], parameters such as building density and land uses or geometric accessibility which quantifies urban morphology, have gained little attention in land value literature [6, 7].

E. Pimenidis et al. (Eds.): ICANN 2022, LNCS 13532, pp. 346–357, 2022.
https://doi.org/10.1007/978-3-031-15937-4_29

According to the literature review, several attempts were performed for the prediction of residence price. In 2015, Park et Bae [11], use C4.5, RIPPER, Bayesian and AdaBoost Machine learning algorithms for the housing data of 5359 townhouses in Fairfax County, VA. Applying 10-fold cross-validation RIPPER outperformed these other housing price prediction models achieving average error of 0.2488 and Standard Deviation of 0.0254. In 2010, Kuşan et al. [12], propose fuzzy logic in predicting house selling price, located in different regions of Eskişehir city in Turkey. More specifically, they achieve RMSE, $R^2$ and MAPE accuracy at 0.0375, 0.9305 and 3.65%, respectively. In 2021, Imran et al. [13], perform eleven machine learning algorithms for regressions models for House price prediction of the capital of Islamabad achieving promising results. In 2019, Piao et al. [14], present a novel prediction model based on CNN for the estimation of housing price. Furthermore, they propose a feature selection process, claiming that their work can obtain a better performance using actual data of property transaction. In 2019, SungHo et al. [15], propose a machine-learning method to overcome the limitation of conventional linear regression model. The analysis targets of this study are apartments transacted in Busan region for three years from 2013 to 2015. The best results were achieved by using models of extreme gradient boost (XGboost), random forest, and support vector machine. Similar studies achieved suchlike results in [16–18].

Although there are several research attempts on the regression problem of residence price prediction, there is a lack of scientific attempts for the classification problem of the housing price prediction. The goal of this paper is to predict the price cluster that the residence belongs. More specifically, the authors propose a hybrid approach, which comprises of a combination of (1) Fuzzy C-Means (FCM) and (2) Coarse Tree. FCM was applied for both the creation of residence price clusters and independent variables, through the pre-processing of the dataset. The Machine Learning (ML) Algorithm was chosen through an exhaustive application of 29 ML algorithms on the processed dataset. To the best of our knowledge, this is the first time that such a combination for housing price prediction is exploited. The innovation also stands to the way the FCM used to generate the independent variables. The hybrid approach achieves promising results, paving the way for further research on this area.

The rest of the manuscript is organized as follows; Sect. 2, describes the variables achieved by the dataset. Section 3, present the data handling using the FCM algorithm and the final form of the dataset. Section 4 provides the classification methodoly, including the applying ML algorithms and the evaluation Indices. Section 5 analyze the experimental results of the research and Sect. 6 concludes the paper.

## 2 Dataset Description

The dataset considered in this research is not publicly available and was created by researchers of the Department of Civil Engineering, Democritus University of Thrace, Xanthi, Greece. The data set of this research effort consists of 313 residencies in the city of Xanthi, in the northeastern part of Greece. Xanthi is considered an ideal city for this study, as it has a great variety and diversity of buildings (modern, traditional and preserved construction). Figure 1 presents the 313 houses considered in this research, along with the boundaries of the building blocks and the traffic network as they were digitized on a GIS.

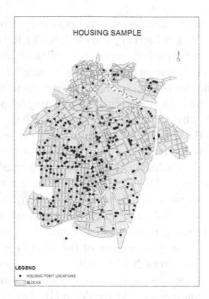

**Fig. 1.** The 313 sample residences in Xanthi, Greece

For each one of the 313 records, a total number of 12 variables were obtained. The name and description of each variable is being presented in Table 1.

**Table 1.** Name and description of 12 variables considered in this research

| Name | Description |
|------|-------------|
| Price | The price per m$^2$ of the house |
| Size | The size of the house in m$^2$ |
| Age | The age of the building in which the residence is located, in years |
| Floor | The floor where the housing is located |
| Material | 1 if the bearing body is made of reinforced concrete, metal or wood and 0 otherwise |
| View | 1 if the residence has a street view and 0 otherwise |
| Type | 1 if the residence is a detached house and 0 if it is an apartment |
| DistSchool | The minimum distance from primary school in m |
| DistTransport | The minimum distance from a public transportation stop in m |
| GreenSpace | The minimal distance from the entrance of a park or square in m |
| PopDensity | The building density of the block in which the residence is located |
| Criminality | The crime density per square kilometer in a radius of 400 m |

Additionally to the aforementioned variables, 4 calculated variables used for the exploitation of this task.

Using DepthMap Software to calculate the geometric accessibility variables, "Integration" and "Choice" were used. Those variables describe the relationship that develops between an axial line (road segment) and all the other axial lines of the system [1] in terms of topology and geometry [2], based on the concept of distance and direction [3]. Integration measures the distance of a line in relation to the others, with most "integrated" axes being those that can be reached more easily than the other lines of the system. Choice measures the degree to which a part of the network participates in all the shortest routes, with the highest values axes being those that will be selected most often for each possible movement / path (for the specific analysis radius). Geometric accessibility, as it is alternatively called, emerges as a statistically significant parameter of land and housing value [9, 10]. The calculation of integration is based on the following formula [2]:

$$Integration_i = \frac{1}{\sum_j d_{ij}}$$ (1)

where $d_{ij}$ is the shortest route between lines i and j. Choice is based on the following formula [4]:

$$Choice_i = \sum_m \sum_j n_{mj}$$ (2)

where $n_{mj}$ is the number of times line i was accessed in the set of shortest paths between lines m and j. Analysis results (global and local integration and choice values) are assigned for each observation to its nearest segment.

Lastly, the variables Point_X and Point_Y were used, due the fact that the location of the residence. These 2 variables were utilized from GIS to digitize Fig. 2. Although they do not represent the actual geographical coordinates, the mapping of the specific variables in the Cartesian coordinate system simulates the geographical distribution with great accuracy.

Finally our dataset comprises of 313 observation with 16 variables each. From these 16 variables, Price will be used to create the Dependent variable and the rest of them will be exploited for the creation of the Independent Variables.

## 3   Dataset Pre-processing

After a statistical analysis of the previously explained data, we notticed that some variables such as price, size and age of the house, as well as the distance of the residence from schools, means of transport and parks show large fluctuations. There are some extreme high or extreme low values that could affect the model. For this reason, the natural logarithm function $\ln(x)$ was applied to those variables in order to smooth out any spikes [19].

After applying the $\ln(x)$ function, data handling continued. The first step was the creation of clusters for the price per $m^2$. The second step was the generation of the independent variables from the variables described in Sect. 2 (except price per $m^2$). The rest of the data pre-processing was perform using the FCM algorithm as described below.

### 3.1 Fuzzy C-Means

**FCM Theoretical Foundation.** Fuzzy clustering (a well-known soft computing method) is an approach in which each data point can belong to more than one cluster. One of the most widely used fuzzy clustering algorithms is the Fuzzy C-means clustering (FCM) Algorithm. This method, developed by Dunn in 1973 [20] and improved by Bezdek [21], is frequently used in pattern recognition. It is based on minimization of the following objective function:

$$J_m = \sum_{i=1}^{N} \sum_{j=1}^{C} u_{ij}^m \|x_i - c_j\|^2, \ 1 \le m < \infty \tag{3}$$

where $m$ is the fuzzifier (the fuzzifier $m$ determines the level of cluster fuzziness), $u_{ij}$ is the degree of membership of $x_i$ in the cluster $j$, $x_i$ is the $i$th of d-dimensional measured data, $c_j$ is the d-dimension center of the cluster, and $\|*\|$ is any norm expressing the similarity between any measured data and the center. Fuzzy partitioning is carried out through an iterative optimization of the objective function shown above, with the update of membership $u_{ij}$ and the cluster centers $c_j$ by:

$$u_{ij} = \frac{1}{\sum_{k=1}^{C} \left( \frac{\|x_i - c_j\|}{\|x_i - c_k\|} \right)^{\frac{2}{m-1}}}, \quad c_j = \frac{\sum_{i=1}^{N} u_{ij}^m \cdot x_i}{\sum_{i=1}^{N} u_{ij}^m} \tag{4}$$

This iteration will stop when $\max_{ij} \left\{ \left| u_{ij}^{(k+1)} - u_{ij}^k \right| \right\} < \varepsilon$, where $\varepsilon$ is a termination criterion between 0 and 1, whereas $k$ are the iteration steps. This procedure converges to a local minimum or a saddle point of $J_m$.

Parameters used for the FCM algorithm are presented in Table 2 while columns Perimeter and Surface, from source data set, were chosen as input parameters. Exponent (*m fuzzier*) controls the degree of fuzzy overlap between clusters. A large $m$ results in smaller membership values, $u_{ij}$, and hence, fuzzier clusters. In the limit $m = 1$, the memberships, $u_{ij}$, converge to 0 or 1, which implies a crisp partitioning. Max_Iterations is the maximum number of optimization iterations and Min_Improvement is the minimum improvement in the objective function between successive iterations. When the objective function improves by a value below this threshold, the optimization stops. A smaller value produces more accurate clustering results, but the clustering can take longer to converge. For parameters' values, the ones most used in the relevant literature were selected [22].

**FCM on Housing Price Variables.** The first step was to create clusters for the variable Price. After a trial-and-error process, the authors ended up to 5 clusters as for the specific number of classes that could achieve the best results. FCM algorithm was applied using the variable Price for both axes. Name, label and instances of each cluster derived from FCM is presented in Table 3, while Fig. 2 sketches them.

Regarding the generation of the independent variables, the 15 variables (except Price) described in Sect. 2 were used. FCM was applied to all possible pairs of the 15 variables. To be more precise, FCM was utilized for all combination of each variable with

**Table 2.** FCM's Hyperparameters with their corresponding value

| Hyperparameter | Value |
|---|---|
| Exponent (*m fuzzier*) | 2 |
| Max_Iterations | 100 |
| Min_Improvement | 0.00001 |

**Table 3.** Name, label and instances of each cluster

| Clusters | Very low-priced | Low-priced | Normal | Expensive | Very expensive | Total |
|---|---|---|---|---|---|---|
| Label | 1 | 2 | 3 | 4 | 5 | |
| Instances | 35 | 77 | 93 | 74 | 34 | 313 |

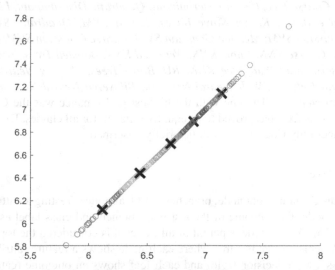

**Fig. 2.** The 5 clusters for price: (i) Blue/very low-priced, (ii) yellow/low-priced, (iii) normal, (iv) red/expensive, (v) orange/very expensive (Color figure online)

the rest 14 variables (e.g. Size-Age, Size-Floor, Size-Material, etc.). So far, there are 14 independent variables resulting from the 14 applications of the FCM algorithm. Thereinafter, FCM was employed for all combinations of the variable Age with the rest 13 variables (e.g. Age-Floor, Age-Material, Age-View, etc.). Someone may note that there is one less variable (and therefore one less combination), as the Size-Age pair has already been explored before. This results to 13 more independent variables resulting from the applications of FCM, thus, 27 independent variables in total. The above process continues until all possible combinations of pairs of all 15 variables are exhausted, resulting in a number of 105 independent variables. Thus, the number of independent variables considering in this research is 105.

In relation with the dependent variable (which was divided in 5 clusters), the FCM algorithm for the 105 combinations was also configured to classify the data set into 5 clusters. The exception is the combinations of the variables Material-View, Material-Type and View-Type, in which 4 clusters were used, as the variables take only values 0 and 1. Thus, it is impossible to create 5 clusters.

After applying all FCMs, the final dataset was derived. It consists of 313 records with 106 features, 105 of which are the independent variables and 1 is the cluster of *Price*. The dataset was split in **Train Data** (80% of the Final Data) and **Test Data** (20% of the Final Data). Both **Train** and **Test Data** contain records of every cluster. **Train Data** is a 250 × 106 table and **Test Data** is a 63 × 106 table.

# 4   Classification Methodology

A total of 29 classification algorithms were employed on the final dataset: *Fine Tree, Medium Tree, Coarse Tree, Linear Discriminant, Quadratic Discriminant, Linear SVM, Gaussian Naïve Bayes, Kernel Naïve Bayes, Linear SVM, Quadratic SVM, Cubic SVM, Fine Gaussian SVM, Medium Gaussian SVM, Coarse Gaussian SVM, Fine KNN, Medium KNN, Coarse KNN, Cubic KNN, Weighted KNN, Boosted Trees, Bagged Trees, Subspace Discriminant, Subspace KNN, RUSBoost Trees, Narrow Neural Network, Medium Neural Network, Wide Neural Network, Bilayered Neural Network and Trilayered Neural Network*. The one with the highest performance was the Coarse Tree Algorithm. Coarse Tree, has proved to be equally efficient for all classes. Due to limited area of the paper only Coarse Tree will be briefly described.

## 4.1   Coarse Tree

Tree algorithms contain a root node, branches, and leaf nodes. Testing an attribute is on every internal node, the outcome of the test is on branch and class label as a result is on leaf node [26]. A root node is parent of all nodes it is considered the topmost node of the Tree. A decision tree is a tree where each node shows a feature (attribute), each link (branch) shows a decision (rule) and each leaf shows an outcome (categorical or continues value) [27].

To predict a response of a tree, one should follow the tree from the root node down to a leaf node. The leaf node contains the value of the response. At each node, check the values of the predictors to decide which branch to follow. When the branches reach a leaf node, the response is set to the value corresponding to that node. A fine tree with many small leaves is usually highly accurate on the training data. However, the tree might not show comparable accuracy on an independent test set. A very leafy tree tends to overfit, and its validation accuracy is often far lower than its training (or resubstitution) accuracy. In contrast, a coarse tree with fewer large leaves does not attain high training accuracy. But a coarse tree can be more robust in that its training accuracy can be near that of a representative test set [28].

According to the values of the splitting attribute, the training data are partitioned into several subsets. Until all instances in a subset belong to the same class in any

Decision Tree the algorithm proceeds recursively [29]. The most used Splitting Criteria are Information Gain, Gain Ratio and Gini Index.

In the present research the Coarse Tree algorithm achieved the best values for all evaluation indices. The Optimizer used is Grid Search [30], the number of maximum splits was set at 4 and for split criterion, Gini's diversity index was set. All ML algorithms were trained using the *k-fold Cross Validation* [23] method on the **Train Data** for hyperparameter tuning for the optimal values of hyperparameters.

### 4.2 Evaluation of Model Classifier

Confusion Matrix will be used for visualization of the results. Furthermore, 5 classification indices were used for the evaluation of all Machine Learning Classifiers. The name, abbreviation and calculation type [24] of these 5 indexes are Presented in Table 4. TP, TN, FP and FN corresponds to True Positives, True Negatives, False Positives and False Negatives values of the Confusion Matrix. Due to the fact that the clusters of *Price* are 5, the authors deal with a Multi-Class Classification Problem. Thus, the "One Versus All" Strategy was followed [25].

**Table 4.** Name, abbreviation and Calculation Type for the 5 classification indices

| Name | Abbreviation | Calculation |
|------|-------------|-------------|
| Accuracy | ACC | $\frac{TP+TN}{TP+FP+FN+TN}$ |
| Sensitivity | SNS | $\frac{TP}{TP+FN}$ |
| Specificity | SPC | $\frac{TN}{TN+FP}$ |
| Precision | PREC | $\frac{TP}{TP+FP}$ |
| F1 Score | F1 | $2 \cdot \frac{PREC \cdot SNS}{PREC+SNS}$ |

## 5 Experimental Results

The training of the model was performed for 30 epochs using 5-fold Cross-Validation Method. The reason why 5-fold and not the common 10-fold was used, is due to the fact that in training model the total amount of records is just 250 observations. The model performs relatively well during the training process. 192 records were correctly classified and 58 were misclassified achieving an overall accuracy of 78.8% for **Train Data**. To be assured that the model can generalize, the authors examined whether the model is efficient in data that has not been trained (**Test Data**). The algorithm performs significantly well in **Test Data** too, achieving and overall accuracy of 79.37%. Surprisingly, the algorithm seems to generalize with high accuracy achieving greater results in **Test Data** than in **Train Data**. Confusion Matrixes for the **Train** and **Test Data** are presented in Tables 5 and the corresponding indices are displayed in Table 6.

**Table 5.** Confusion matrix for train and test data

| | | Predicted Class | | | | | | | | | | |
|---|---|---|---|---|---|---|---|---|---|---|---|---|
| | | Train Data | | | | | | Test Data | | | | |
| | Label | 1 | 2 | 3 | 4 | 5 | Label | 1 | 2 | 3 | 4 | 5 |
| True Class | 1 | *21* | 6 | 1 | 0 | 0 | 1 | *6* | 1 | 0 | 0 | 0 |
| | 2 | 6 | *48* | 6 | 2 | 0 | 2 | 1 | *12* | 2 | 0 | 0 |
| | 3 | 1 | 9 | *57* | 7 | 0 | 3 | 0 | 1 | *15* | 3 | 0 |
| | 4 | 0 | 0 | 8 | *46* | 5 | 4 | 1 | 0 | 0 | *11* | 3 |
| | 5 | 0 | 1 | 3 | 3 | *20* | 5 | 0 | 0 | 0 | 1 | *6* |

**Table 6.** Evaluation indices for the train and test data

| Index | Train Data | | | | | Test Data | | | | |
|---|---|---|---|---|---|---|---|---|---|---|
| | 1 | 2 | 3 | 4 | 5 | 1 | 2 | 3 | 4 | 5 |
| SNS | 0.75 | 0.774 | 0.77 | 0.78 | 0.74 | 0.857 | 0.8 | 0.79 | **0.733** | 0.857 |
| SPC | 0.966 | 0.915 | *0.898* | 0.937 | 0.978 | 0.964 | 0.958 | 0.954 | 0.917 | 0.946 |
| ACC | 0.944 | 0.88 | *0.86* | 0.9 | 0.952 | 0.952 | 0.921 | 0.905 | *0.873* | 0.937 |
| PREC | 0.75 | 0.75 | 0.76 | 0.793 | 0.8 | 0.75 | 0.857 | 0.882 | **0.733** | **0.667** |
| F1 | 0.75 | 0.761 | 0.765 | 0.786 | 0.769 | 0.8 | 0.828 | 0.833 | **0.733** | 0.75 |

Following the *"One Versus All"* Strategy the proposed approach shows promising results. If we attempt a more detailed insight to the results, one can note from the Confusion Matrix, that when the algorithm misclassifies records it assigns them to close clusters. For example, let an observation belongs to class 4. If the algorithm incorrectly classifies the observation, it is more likely to classify it into classes 3 and 5, which are closer to class 4 than to classes 1 and 2, which are farther away. This fact is perceived in both the Confusion Matrix of **Train Data** and the **Test Data**. A closer look to evaluation indices shows that the algorithm classifies the records more accurately, facing a negligible problem in class 3 of the **Train Data** table, and a more significant issue in cluster 5 of the **Test Data**. The misclassified instances of the 5th cluster occur due to the fact that cluster 5 is the minority class. However, in future research the authors will try to explore deeper the reasons why the algorithm does not correctly classify the observations of class 5. Regarding the Test Data, the algorithm seems to have some difficulty in correctly classifying observations in class 4. Furthermore, it seems that the algorithm classifies several records of class 2 and 4 in it. This may occur due to fact that the middle class has the most values. Although it seems that the overall Accuracy is not high enough, only 78%, all the indicators, but also the confusion matrix, show a stability and consistency in the forecast.

## 6    Conclusion

In this research, an innovate hybrid approach for prediction of the price cluster of residences in Xanthi has been presented. After applying the natural logarithm function to the data set variables, the authors exploit FCM algorithm for creating clusters for the *Price* variable and to generate the independent variables. The final dataset consists of 313 records with 106 features (105 independent variables and 1 dependent variable). Continuing, the dataset was split at **Train Data** (80% of records) and **Test Data** (20% of records). Using 5-fold Cross-Validation for validation method, a vast amount of 29 ML techniques was employed to achieve the best results. Coarse Tree is the algorithm with the highest performance of evaluation indices, achieving an overall accuracy of 78.8% for **Train Data** and of 79.37% for **Test Data.** The algorithm seems to be able to generalize with great accuracy, achieving promising results.

The results could be used as a benchmark by real-estaters, land-lords, realtors, banks, town planners and the state and could also be exploited as a benchmark study for further research in the field of housing price. The innovation of this research stands for the use of FCM for data-handling, the exhaustive search for the best ML algorithm and that there are not many studies that confront with the classification problem of residence price prediction.

Although the results look very promising, there is always room for further improvement. One of the future goals of the authors is to solve the regression problem of the dataset, i.e. to predict the exact value (or logarithmic value) of the price per $m^2$ for the residences. Further research will focus on deployment of deep learning algorithms for the confrontation of either classification or regression problem. Last but not least, the authors could explore a different combination of hyperparameters of ML and FCM algorithm in order to increase the accuracy of the proposed approach.

# References

1. Cutini, V.: Centrality and land use: three case studies on the configurational hypothesis. Cybergeo: Eur. J. Geogr. (2001)
2. Hillier, B., Iida, S.: Network effects and psychological effects: a theory of urban movement. In: Proceedings of the 5th International Symposium on Space Syntax, vol. 1, pp. 553–564. TU Delft, June 2005
3. Hillier, B., Vaughan, L.: The city as one thing. Prog. Plan. **67**(3), 205–230 (2007)
4. Shen, Y., Karimi, K.: Understanding the roles of urban configuration on spatial heterogeneity and submarket regionalisation of house price pattern in a mix-scale hedonic model: the case of Shanghai, China. In: SSS 2015-10th International Space Syntax Symposium, vol. 10. Space Syntax Laboratory, the Bartlett School of Architecture, UCL University College London, July 2015
5. Abidoye, R.B., Chan, A.P.: Critical review of hedonic pricing model application in property price appraisal: a case of Nigeria. Int. J. Sustain. Built Environ. **6**(1), 250–259 (2017)
6. Lykostratis, K., Giannopoulou, M.: Land value hot-spots defined by urban configuration. In: Calabrò, F., Della Spina, L., Bevilacqua, C. (eds.) New Metropolitan Perspectives. ISHT 2018. Smart Innovation, Systems and Technologies, vol. 100, pp. 590–-598. Springer, Cham (2018). https://doi.org/10.1007/978-3-319-92099-3_66
7. Lykostratis, K., Giannopoulou, M., Roukouni, A.: Measuring urban configuration: a GWR approach. In: Calabrò, F., Della Spina, L., Bevilacqua, C. (eds.) New metropolitan perspectives. ISHT 2018. Smart innovation, systems and technologies, vol. 100, pp. 479–488. Springer, Cham (2018). https://doi.org/10.1007/978-3-319-92099-3_54
8. Desyllas, J.: The Relationship Between Urban Street Configuration and Office Rent Patterns in Berlin. University of London, University College London (United Kingdom) (2000)

9. Hansen, W.G.: Accessibility and residential growth, Doctoral dissertation, Massachusetts Institute of Technology (1959)
10. Bertolini, L., Le Clercq, F., Kapoen, L.: Sustainable accessibility: a conceptual framework to integrate transport and land use plan-making. Two test-applications in the Netherlands and a reflection on the way forward. Transp. Policy 12(3), 207–220 (2005)
11. Park, B., Bae, J.K.: Using machine learning algorithms for housing price prediction: the case of Fairfax County, Virginia housing data. Expert Syst. Appl. 42(6), 2928–2934 (2015)
12. Kuşan, H., Aytekin, O., Özdemir, İ: The use of fuzzy logic in predicting house selling price. Expert Syst. Appl. 37(3), 1808–1813 (2010)
13. Imran, I., Zaman, U., Waqar, M., Zaman, A.: Using machine learning algorithms for housing price prediction: the case of Islamabad housing data. Soft Comput. Mach. Intell. 1(1), 11–23 (2021)
14. Piao, Y., Chen, A., Shang, Z.: Housing price prediction based on CNN. In: 2019 9th International Conference on Information Science and Technology (ICIST), pp. 491–495. IEEE, August 2019
15. SungHo, P., SangHa, S., Kangbae, L., ByungKwon, P., Doo-hwan, K., HyunSoo, K.: A Study on an apartment price prediction model using machine learning: an example from Busau Metropolitan area. In: Proceedings on the International Conference on Artificial Intelligence (ICAI), pp. 79–85. The Steering Committee of the World Congress in Computer Science, Computer Engineering and Applied Computing (WorldComp) (2019)
16. Kim, H., Kwon, Y., Choi, Y.: Assessing the impact of public rental housing on the housing prices in proximity: based on the regional and local level of price prediction models using long short-term memory (LSTM). Sustainability 12(18), 7520 (2020)
17. Gao, G., Bao, Z., Cao, J., Qin, A.K., Sellis, T.: Location-centered house price prediction: a multi-task learning approach. ACM Trans. Intell. Syst. Technol. 13(2), 1–25 (2022)
18. Henriksson, E., Werlinder, K.: Housing Price Prediction over Countrywide Data: A comparison of XGBoost and Random Forest Regressor models (2021)
19. Polyakova, A.G., Akhmetshin, E.M., Goloshchapova, L.V., Rakhmeeva, I.I., Noeva, E.E., Rakovskiy, V.I.: A model of regional economic space modernization. Eur. Res. Stud. 21, 624–634 (2018)
20. Dunn, J.C.: A fuzzy relative of the ISODATA process and its use in detecting compact well-separated clusters. J. Cybernet. 3, 32–57 (1973)
21. Bezdek, J.C.: Pattern Recognition with Fuzzy Objective Function Algorithms. Springer, New York (2013). https://doi.org/10.1007/978-1-4757-0450-1
22. Khalilia, M.A., Bezdek, J., Popescu, M., Keller, J.M.: Improvements to the relational fuzzy c-means clustering algorithm. Pattern Recogn. 47(12), 3920–3930 (2014)
23. Fushiki, T.: Estimation of prediction error by using K-fold cross-validation. Stat. Comput. 21(2), 137–146 (2011)
24. Psathas, A. P., Iliadis, L., Papaleonidas, A., Bountas, D.: COREM2 project: a beginning to end approach for cyber intrusion detection. Neural Comput. Appl. 1–20 (2022)
25. Milgram, J., Cheriet, M., Sabourin, R.: "One against one" or "one against all": Which one is better for handwriting recognition with SVMs?. In: Tenth International Workshop on Frontiers in Handwriting Recognition. Suvisoft, October 2006
26. Gershman, A., Meisels, A., Lüke, K.H., Rokach, L., Schclar, A., Sturm, A.: A decision tree based recommender system. In: 10th International Conference on Innovative Internet Community Systems (I2CS)–Jubilee Edition 2010 (2010)
27. Jadhav, S.D., Channe, H.P.: Efficient recommendation system using decision tree classifier and collaborative filtering. Int. Res. J. Eng. Technol 3(8), 2113–2118 (2016)
28. Patel, H.H., Prajapati, P.: Study and analysis of decision tree based classification algorithms. Int. J. Comput. Sci. Eng. 6(10), 74–78 (2018)

29. Zhang, X., Jiang, S.: A splitting criteria based on similarity in decision tree learning. J. Softw. 7(8), 1775–1782 (2012)
30. Liashchynskyi, P., Liashchynskyi, P.: Grid search, random search, genetic algorithm: A big comparison for NAS. arXiv preprint arXiv:1912.06059 (2019)
31. Brown, J.N., Rosen, H.S.: On the estimation of structural hedonic price models Econometrica 50, 765–68 (1982)

# Contrastive Learning for Session-Based Recommendation

Yan Chen[1,2], Wanhui Qian[1,2], Dongqin Liu[1,2], Yipeng Su[2], Yan Zhou[2(✉)], Jizhong Han[2], and Ruixuan Li[2]

[1] School of Cyber Security, University of Chinese Academy of Sciences, Beijing, China
[2] Institute of Information Engineering, Chinese Academy of Sciences, Beijing, China
{chenyan1,qianwanhui,liudongqin,suyipeng,zhouyan,hanjizhong, liruixuan}@iie.ac.cn

**Abstract.** Session-based recommendation predicts the next item to recommend by modeling session sequences. Existing methods usually treat this task as a sequential prediction task. Though these methods have achieved promising results, they still suffer from the data sparsity problem. Inspired by recent success of contrastive learning on natural language processing and recommendation, we propose a novel multi-task model called Contrastive Learning for Session-based Recommendation (CLSR). Based on the sequential prediction task, CLSR performs a contrastive learning task to get more accurate session representations. CLSR constructs augmented data from original data according to a global item transition graph to maintain users' intentions. Extensive experiments performed on three public datasets demonstrate the effectiveness of our proposed approach.

**Keywords:** Contrastive learning · Data augmentation · Session-based recommendation

## 1 Introduction

Recommendation systems are widely applied on various online shopping and service platforms, for the reason that they can help address information explosion problem by helping users find what they are interested in. Conventional recommendation methods are usually based on matrix factorization [8] or collaborative filtering [9] and do not take users' behavior sequences into consideration. However, users' interactions with items (items can be news, products, videos and so on) are behavior sequences in chronological order. At the same time, users' interests can change very fast, therefore mining this kind of behavior sequence pattern is valuable for recommendation.

To address the above issue, Session-based Recommendation (SR) is first introduced to capture users' behavior tendencies by modeling behavior sequence dependency in a session. A session is defined as a continuous interaction sequence

E. Pimenidis et al. (Eds.): ICANN 2022, LNCS 13532, pp. 358–369, 2022.
https://doi.org/10.1007/978-3-031-15937-4_30

of items in close proximity [12]. In this situation, users' preferences are usually captured by mining sequential transition patterns in a session [11]. Given a user's behavior sequence in the current session, session-based recommendation aims to predict the next item that she/he might be interested in [16].

Existing methods view session-based recommendation as a sequence predicting task. Specially, these methods recommend the next item to users according to users' session behavior sequences. Although recent methods for session-based recommendation have achieved encouraging results, they are easy to confront data sparsity problem. Most of methods approach this recommendation task under a supervised learning paradigm, where the supervision signal comes from the observed session sequences. However, users generally only interact with limited items compared with the item gallery which can easily reach 100 million [24]. As a result, these supervised methods are inclined to learn low quality representations due to data sparsity [18].

Recently, contrastive learning techniques have made a great breakthrough for representation learning in the fields of computer vision (CV) and natural language processing (NLP). They get better downstream task performances with more accurate representations. In detail, the idea is first to perform data augmentation from original input, then set an auxiliary contrastive loss to help optimize model parameters. Remind that the core of contrastive learning is designing a suitable data augmentation according to the task and data features. For example, SimCLR [2] gets augmented data from original input by doing image rotation and color distortion. CLEAR [20] augments data by word deletion, span deletion, reordering and synonym substitution. More accurate representations are finally learned with a common encoder.

Along this line, many works try to take advantage of contrastive learning to improve recommendation performance. SGL [18] executes data augmentation on user interaction graph structure by node dropout and edge dropout. SGL recommends to users without considering users' behavior sequences, thus fails to capture users' dynamic interests. CL4SRec [22] and CauseRec [24] attempt to make use of contrastive learning for sequential recommendation. Both of them gain performance promotion. CauseRec introduces a model to build positive and negative samples thus increases training costs and may cause error propagation. CL4SRec randomly deletes items in the sequence. Though it reduces computing costs, it may change users' intentions by randomly changing items in sequences. CL4SRec and CauseRec are typical methods for sequential recommendation. However, when it comes to session-based recommendation, few works have tried to use contrastive learning. In SR, users' session sequence lengths differ a lot [13]. We argue it is more suitable for short session sequences to insert items to get augmented data rather than deleting items. Moreover, the augmented data ought to maintain users' intentions in original session sequences.

In this paper, we propose a novel model called Contrastive Learning for Session-based Recommendation (CLSR). Specifically, it consists of two key components: (1) data augmentation, which generates augmented session sequences for each session, and (2) contrastive learning, which maximizes the agreement between original and augmented sessions. Our main innovation lies in the data augmentation: we construct augmented data in terms of session length and a global item transition graph, which can help keep users' intentions unchanged to the maximum extent. It is worthwhile mentioning that our CLSR is model-agnostic and can be applied to any session-based recommendation model.

Our contributions are summarized as follows:

1. We propose a novel model called Contrastive Learning for Session-based Recommendation (CLSR), which learns more accurate session representations by constructing augmented data and contrastive loss.
2. We come up with simple but effective data augmentation method to maintain users' intentions in order to get more accurate session representations.
3. Extensive experiments on three public datasets demonstrate the effectiveness of our CLSR model.

## 2    Related Works

**Session-Based Recommendation:** Existing methods take session-based recommendation as a sequence prediction task. Naturally, recurrent neural networks (RNNs) are preferred to model item transition patterns in sessions [4,6]. As the pioneering work, in [5], Hidasi et al. propose GRU4Rec with a multi-layered Gated Recurrent Unit (GRU) model, which is a variant of RNN to capture sequential dependencies in sessions. Following Hidasi's work, Neural Attentive Recommendation Machine (NARM) [10] extends GRU4Rec with an attention mechanism to reduce noise item impact and focus on users' main purposes. Since Convolutional Neural Networks (CNNs) have achieved excellent results in computer vision, some works try to take CNNs into consideration to model sequential dependencies [14,15]. NextItNet [23] attempts to use a dilated CNN with a stack of holed convolutional layers to learn high-level representation from both short- and long-range item dependencies. Graph Neural Networks (GNNs) recently have drawn increasing attention and have shown promising results in a large number of tasks besides session-based recommendation [7,25]. SR-GNN [19] exploits gated graph neural networks to analyze the complex item transitions within a session. These methods usually depend on the sequential prediction task to optimize model parameters. They usually suffer from the data sparsity problem, which makes models learn less accurate user representations.

**Contrastive Learning:** Contrastive learning can be regarded as a kind of self-supervised learning paradigm. Instead of building supervised signals, it first constructs augmented samples (positive samples) from original data, then adopts a contrastive learning framework to make a comparison between original and positive samples. Contrastive learning has shown superior ability on learning useful representations from unlabeled data. It has been widely applied in CV and NLP. SimCLR [2] proposes a simple framework for contrastive learning. It first performs image transformation to get augmented data by image rotation and color distortion. Then it optimizes models using a contrastive loss. CLEAR [20] utilizes a similar contrastive learning framework, while the data augmentation methods are different. Unlike image, data augmentation in NLP is usually based on sentences like word insertion and deletion. When it comes to contrastive learning for session-based recommendation, few works consider this method. However, there are still some attempts made for recommendation. CauseRec [24] proposes a contrastive learning model for sequential recommendation. CauseRec samples user sequences from the counterfactual data distributions by replacing dispensable and indispensable items within the original sequence. Since it requires extra computation before building positive and negative samples, it increases training costs and may cause error propagation for the following task. Inspired by data augmentation in NLP, CL4SRec [22] comes up with some simple but useful data augmentation methods, which randomly delete items in the sequence. CL4SRec does not increase computing costs, but it is likely to alter users' intentions in sequences.

## 3 Preliminaries

### 3.1 Problem Statement

Formally, let $V = \{v_1, v_2, ...v_N\}$ denote as the set of items, where $N$ is the number of items. $S = \{s^1, s^2, ...s^M\}$ is defined as the universal set of sessions. A session $s = \{v_1^i, v_2^i, ..., v_t^i, ...v_L^i\}$ is a sequence of items ordered by time, where $v_t^i \in V$ is the item at time step $t$ and $L$ is the length of session $s$. Given a new session, the goal of session-based recommendation aims to recommend the top-$K$ items ($1 \leq K \leq N$) from all items $V$ that are most likely to be clicked by the user in the current session.

### 3.2 Supervised Recommendation Model Optimization

In session-based recommendation, a model or encoder $f(x)$ is always designed to mine users' behavior patterns, where $f(x)$ may be RNN-based, CNN-based, GNN-based or other neural network-based models. Based on users' historical session sequences, the model is expected to learn dense vectors representing users' interests in sessions. Given a new session $s$, the trained encoder generates a vector $h$ to imply the user's intention in the session $s$. Then we compute scores $z$ for all the candidate items $i \in V$ by doing inner product between the item embedding $X$ and $h$:

$$z = h^T X. \tag{1}$$

Then, the probability of each item being the next one in the session is obtained by a softmax function:

$$y = softmax(z). \tag{2}$$

We apply a cross-entropy of the prediction and the ground truth as the loss function, which is defined as:

$$L_{main} = -\sum_{i=1}^{N} y_i log(\hat{y}_i) + (1 - y_i)log(1 - \hat{y}_i), \tag{3}$$

where $\hat{y}$ denotes the one-hot encoding vector of the ground truth item.

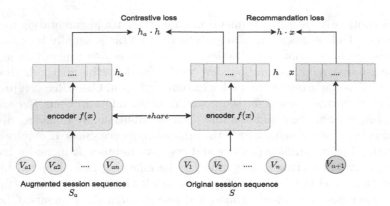

**Fig. 1.** An overview of CLSR architecture. For each session sequence $S$, augmented session sequence $S_a$ is constructed based on the original session sequence $S$. $S_a$ and $S$ are regarded as two views of each session sequence. Then the original and augmented session sequences are embedded to the latent space by a shared encoder $f(x)$. Contrastive loss and recommendation loss are joinly applied to train the encoder $f(x)$.

It can be observed that existing model optimization methods are typical supervised learning paradigm. Thus they may meet with performance degradation due to the data sparsity.

## 4   Methods

Inspired by the CLEAR framework [20] for learning sentence representation, we explore applying contrastive learning to session-based recommendation to obtain a powerful session representation. Figure 1 illustrates the working flow of CLSR, which is composed of three modules: a data augmentation module, a session encoder and a contrastive loss function. Since our CLSR is model-agnostic, any deep learning model can be applied as the session encoder. We introduce how to perform data augmentation in session-based recommendation, followed by the contrastive learning loss function.

### 4.1   Data Augmentation

Data Augmentation operators differ in terms of session lengths. Sessions are totally divided into three classes [17]: short sessions (length $< 4$), medium sessions and long sessions (length $> 9$). For short sessions, session sequences are augmented by item insertion. Items are deleted to make an augmented sequence for medium and long sessions. It is worthwhile mentioning that our CLSR constructs a global item transition graph on the whole user session sequences. We select items from the transition graph to insert or delete to generate augmented session sequences, which can protect users' intentions from being destroyed. We first introduce the construction of item transition graph, then present data augmentation operators in detail.

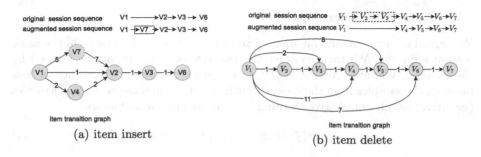

(a) item insert

(b) item delete

**Fig. 2.** A brief illustration of augmentation operations in CLSR.

The item transition graph is constructed as a directed graph $G = (U, E)$. In the graph, each node represents an item $v_i \in V$. Each edge $(v_i, v_j) \in E$ means that a user clicks item $v_j$ after $v_i$ in any session. In other words, there is an edge $(v_i, v_j)$ if item $v_i$ transmits directly to item $v_j$. And the weight of item-item $(v_i, v_j)$ is the times of item $v_i$ transmitted to $v_j$ in total session sequences.

After the item transition graph is built, we design an augmented session sequence for each original session sequence. To better understand our method, we introduce data augmentation operators by instances.

For a short session sequence, an item is inserted after the first item based on the original session sequence. As is shown on the left side of Fig. 2, the directed graph is the item transition graph. For the original short session sequence $s = (v_1, v_2, v_3)$, we first find out the entire paths for sequence $(v_1, I, v_2)$, that is to say, there are edges from node $v_1$ to $I$ and node $I$ to $v_2$. Then we choose the item $v_7$ from the largest weight edges $(v_1, I)$ as the final item to insert. For $s$, the augmented session sequence is $(v_1, v_7, v_2, v_3)$. We can see that such data augmentation can maintain user's intentions as the original sequence. We note that if there exists no such node $I$, a random item is selected from $V$.

For a long session sequence, items (except the first and the last in the session sequence) are chosen to be deleted to obtain an augmented session sequence based on the original session sequence. As is shown on the right side of Fig. 2, the directed graph is the item transition graph. For the original long session sequence $s = (v_1, v_2, v_3, v_4, v_5, v_6, v_7)$, we first find out if there is an edge between $v_1$ and $I$. $I$ can be any item in $s$ except the first and the last in the session sequence, namely $v_1$ and $v_7$. Then we seek out the item $v_4$ from the largest weight edges $(v_1, I)$. Finally, items between $v_1$ and $I$ are deleted. For $s$, the augmented session sequence is $(v_1, v_4, v_5, v_6, v_7)$. We can see that such data augmentation does not destroy user's intentions compared with the original sequence. We note that if there exists no such node $I$, a random item is selected to delete from $s$ except the first and the last in the session sequence $s$.

For a medium session sequence $s$, we randomly choose an item to delete except the first and the last in the session sequence $s$.

## 4.2  Contrastive Learning

We regard the original and augmented session sequence as two views of the same session sequence. We then contrast the two session representations learned by the encoder. We adopt infoNCE [21] with a standard binary cross-entropy loss between the samples from the ground-truth (positive) and the corrupted samples (negative) as our contrastive learning loss and defined it as follows:

$$L_{cl} = -log\sigma(f_D(h, h_a)) - log\sigma(1 - f_D(h, h_n)), \tag{4}$$

where $h$ and $h_a$ denote the session sequence representations learned by an encoder, and $h_n$ is the negative sample obtained by corrupting $h$ with row-wise and column-wise shuffling. $f_D$ is a function that takes two vectors as the input and then scores the agreement between them. specifically, the dot product between two vectors is implemented as the $f_D$ function.

## 4.3  Multi-task Training

To improve the performance of session-based recommendation, we leverage a multi-task training strategy where the main sequence prediction task and the additional contrastive learning task are jointly optimized. Formally, the joint learning objective is defined as:

$$L = L_{main} + \alpha L_{cl}, \tag{5}$$

where $\alpha$ controls the magnitude of the contrastive learning task.

# 5  Experiments

## 5.1  Experimental Setup

**Datasets.** We evaluate our proposed method on three public datasets:

(1) **Delicious**: Delicious[1] is an online bookmarking system. We consider a sequence of tags a user has marked to a book as a session (marking time is recorded).
(2) **Gowalla**: Gowalla[2] is a widely used check-in dataset from the Gowalla platform. Records are regarded as different sessions if interval is longer than a day.
(3) **Foursquare**: The Foursquare[3] dataset is a public available online dataset which consists of users' check-in records on different venues in a period of time. Sessions are extracted by the same way as Gowalla.

---

[1] https://grouplens.org/datasets/hetrec-2011/.
[2] https://snap.stanford.edu/data/loc-gowalla.html.
[3] https://sites.google.com/site/yangdingqi/home/foursquare-dataset.

For dataset preprocessing, following [19], sessions containing only one item and items appearing less than five times are filtered out in all datasets. We follow the same strategy described in [1] to split the sessions into training, validation and testing set with a ratio of 6:2:2. Then we apply a data augmentation technique which is often used in session-based recommendation [19], and generate multiple labeled sequences with the corresponding labels $([v_1], v_2), ([v_1, v_2], v_3), ..., ([v_1, v_2, ..., v_{n-1}], v_n)$, for each session sequence $S = (v_1, v_2, v_3, ..., v_n)$. And the last-clicked item in the session is treated as the label.

Note that our contrastive learning framework is conducted on the above-mentioned augmented data. The statistics of datasets after preprocessing are summarized in Table 1.

**Table 1.** Datasets statistics.

| Dataset | Delicious | Gowalla | Foursquare |
|---|---|---|---|
| #Users | 1313 | 33,661 | 39,302 |
| #Items | 5793 | 41,229 | 45,595 |
| #Interactions | 266,190 | 1,218,599 | 3,627,093 |
| #Sessions | 60,397 | 258,732 | 888,798 |
| Density | 0.03500 | 0.00088 | 0.00202 |

**Evaluation Metrics.** To evaluate the performance of the proposed CLSR, the same evaluation metrics used in previous work are adopted for fair comparisons:

(1) **Hit Ratio (HR)@K:** In session-based recommendation, HR focuses on whether the positive items are in the top-$K$ ranked items of the recommendation list over all the testing instances.
(2) **Mean Reciprocal Rank(MRR)@K:** MRR takes the rank position information into account, and the target item is expected to rank ahead. In this work, we report HR and MRR with $K = 10, 20$.

## 5.2 Baseline Methods

In order to verify the effectiveness and flexibility of our CLSR, we choose the following methods as baseline methods. They are representative and/or state-of-the-art methods based on a variety of models, such as RNN, CNN, attention and graph neural networks respectively.

(1) **NARM:** an RNN-based method for SR that integrates attention into Gated Recurrent Unit (GRU) to reduce noise item impact and focus on users' main purposes [10].
(2) **NextItNet:** a CNN-based method for SR that proposes a stack of holed convolutional layers to learn high-level representation from both short- and long-range item dependencies [23].

(3) **SSRM:** the state-of-the-art method for streaming SR. Its MF-based attentive session recommender can be used for SR [3].
(4) **SRGNN:** a GNN-based method for SR that employs a gated graph neural network to extract item transition patterns within sessions [19].

**Table 2.** Performance on three datasets.

| Model | Delicious | | | | Gowalla | | | | Foursquare | | | |
|---|---|---|---|---|---|---|---|---|---|---|---|---|
| | H@10 | M@10 | H@20 | M@20 | H@10 | M@10 | H@20 | M@20 | H@10 | M@10 | H@20 | M@20 |
| SRGNN | 37.01 | 19.57 | 45.74 | 20.20 | 41.31 | 22.39 | 49.31 | 22.94 | 53.12 | 28.55 | 61.90 | 29.17 |
| SRGNN+CLSR | 38.12 | 20.14 | 47.24 | 20.92 | 43.24 | 23.57 | 51.22 | 24.12 | 53.23 | 28.84 | 62.10 | 29.45 |
| Improv. (%) | 3.00 | 2.91 | 3.28 | 3.56 | 4.67 | 5.27 | 3.87 | 5.14 | 0.21 | 1.02 | 0.32 | 0.96 |
| NARM | 37.18 | 19.76 | 46.39 | 20.40 | 41.56 | 22.50 | 49.55 | 23.04 | 53.89 | 29.35 | 62.47 | 29.95 |
| NARM+CLSR | 37.82 | 20.14 | 47.15 | 20.78 | 42.39 | 22.94 | 50.42 | 23.48 | 53.91 | 29.40 | 62.43 | 30.00 |
| Improv. (%) | 1.72 | 1.92 | 1.64 | 1.86 | 2.00 | 1.96 | 1.76 | 1.91 | 0.04 | 0.17 | -0.06 | 0.17 |
| SSRM | 37.51 | 19.83 | 46.57 | 20.46 | 41.63 | 22.45 | 49.64 | 22.98 | 53.83 | 29.33 | 62.50 | 29.93 |
| SSRM+CLSR | 37.83 | 20.09 | 47.28 | 20.75 | 42.31 | 23.04 | 50.13 | 23.58 | 53.97 | 29.44 | 62.69 | 30.05 |
| Improv. (%) | 0.85 | 1.31 | 1.52 | 1.42 | 1.63 | 2.63 | 0.99 | 2.61 | 0.26 | 0.38 | 0.30 | 0.40 |
| NextItNet | 35.14 | 18.04 | 44.62 | 18.69 | 39.87 | 21.51 | 47.80 | 22.04 | 52.02 | 27.67 | 60.83 | 28.28 |
| NextItNet +CLSR | 35.91 | 18.86 | 44.98 | 19.50 | 40.60 | 21.93 | 48.60 | 22.47 | 52.70 | 28.47 | 61.34 | 29.08 |
| Improv. (%) | 2.19 | 4.55 | 0.81 | 4.33 | 1.83 | 1.95 | 1.67 | 1.95 | 1.31 | 2.89 | 0.84 | 2.83 |

**Implementation Details.** We utilize the public implementation and report performance of baseline methods provided by [1]. Our CLSR is implemented by PyTorch. Generally, items are made an embedding into low dimensional latent spaces with dimensionality 128. The models are optimized by the Adam optimizer with mini-batch size of 128. We test CLSR's performance under different values of learning rate and its performances are reported under its optimal hyper-parameter settings.

### 5.3   Experimental Results

**Overall Performance.** To prove the effectiveness of CLSR, we present the results of the original models and our framework. Table 2 shows the performance comparison results of baselines and models combined with the CLSR for session-based recommendation on three datasets. The models combined with the CLSR include NARM+CLSR, NextItNet+CLSR, SSRM+CLSR and SRGNN+CLSR. We can draw the following conclusions.

(1) In a nutshell, experimental results clearly show that the models combined with CLSR outperform the baselines by a margin, and the improvement is consistent on all the datasets and evaluation metrics. This verifies the effectiveness of incorporating the contrastive learning task.
(2) As a whole, the improvements on Gowalla are more significant than those on Delicious and Foursqure. This might be caused by the characteristics of

datasets. Specifically, in Gowalla, supervision signal from user-item interactions in sessions is too sparse to guide the representation learning in supervised models. Benefiting from the contrastive learning task, CLSR obtains auxiliary supervisions to assist the representation learning.

(3) We find the performance of GNN-based models is better than that of other models on Delicious and Gowalla. We attribute this observation to global item transition graph, from which models can learn more complex item transition patterns. And this observation also help demonstrate that augmenting data on the basis of item transition graph is feasible. For Foursquare, the advantage of GNN-based models is not very obvious due to the rich user-item interactions in the dataset.

**Impact of the Magnitude of Contrastive Learning.** We introduce a hyperparameter $\alpha$ to CLSR to control the magnitude of contrastive learning. To investigate the influence of contrastive learning, we report the performance of NextItNet+CLSR with a set of representative $\alpha$ values $(0.00005, 0.0001, 0.0005, 0.001, 0.005, 0.01)$. According to the results shown in Fig. 3, performance achieves decent gains when jointly optimized with the contrastive learning task. For both datasets, learning with smaller $\alpha$ values can promote both HR and MRR, but when $\alpha$ gets larger, the performance declines. We think it may result from the gradient conflicts between the two tasks. In a nutshell, we suggest to tune $\alpha$ in the range of $(0.00005, 0.01)$ carefully.

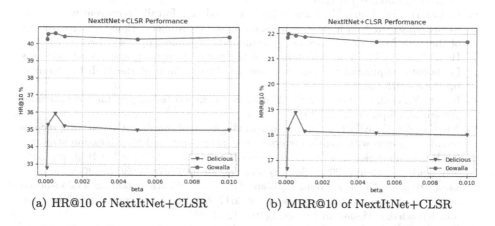

(a) HR@10 of NextItNet+CLSR     (b) MRR@10 of NextItNet+CLSR

**Fig. 3.** The impact of the magnitude of contrastive learning.

## 6   Conclusion

In this work, we recognize the limitations of existing session-based recommendation under general supervised learning paradigm and explore the potential of contrastive learning to solve the limitations. In particular, we propose a model-agnostic framework CLSR to supplement the supervised recommendation task with contrastive learning task. In addition, we construct augmented data from original session sequence in line with the global item transition graph and session length. And such a data augmentation method can help keep users' intentions unchanged. The proposed method is verified on three public datasets. Extensive experiment results show that our CLSR can obtain better performance compared with the existing representative SR methods.

# References

1. Chen, T., Wong, R.C.W.: An efficient and effective framework for session-based social recommendation. In: Proceedings of the 14th ACM International Conference on Web Search and Data Mining. pp. 400–408 (2021)
2. Chen, T., Kornblith, S., Norouzi, M., Hinton, G.: A simple framework for contrastive learning of visual representations. In: International conference on machine learning, pp. 1597–1607. PMLR (2020)
3. Guo, L., Yin, H., Wang, Q., Chen, T., Zhou, A., Quoc Viet Hung, N.: Streaming session-based recommendation. In: Proceedings of the 25th ACM SIGKDD International Conference on Knowledge Discovery & Data Mining, pp. 1569–1577 (2019)
4. Hidasi, B., Karatzoglou, A.: Recurrent neural networks with top-k gains for session-based recommendations. In: Proceedings of the 27th ACM international conference on information and knowledge management. pp. 843–852 (2018)
5. Hidasi, B., Karatzoglou, A., Baltrunas, L., Tikk, D.: Session-based recommendations with recurrent neural networks. In: 4th International Conference on Learning Representations, ICLR (2016)
6. Hidasi, B., Quadrana, M., Karatzoglou, A., Tikk, D.: Parallel recurrent neural network architectures for feature-rich session-based recommendations. In: Proceedings of the 10th ACM Conference on Recommender Systems, pp. 241–248 (2016)
7. Hsu, C., Li, C.T.: RetaGNN: relational temporal attentive graph neural networks for holistic sequential recommendation. In: Proceedings of the Web Conference, pp. 2968–2979 (2021)
8. Koren, Y., Bell, R., Volinsky, C.: Matrix factorization techniques for recommender systems. Computer **42**(8), 30–37 (2009)
9. Kużelewska, U.: Effect of dataset size on efficiency of collaborative filtering recommender systems with multi-clustering as a neighbourhood identification strategy. In: Krzhizhanovskaya, V.V., et al. (eds.) ICCS 2020. LNCS, vol. 12139, pp. 342–354. Springer, Cham (2020). https://doi.org/10.1007/978-3-030-50420-5_25
10. Li, J., Ren, P., Chen, Z., Ren, Z., Lian, T., Ma, J.: Neural attentive session-based recommendation. In: Proceedings of the 2017 ACM on Conference on Information and Knowledge Management, pp. 1419–1428 (2017)
11. Pan, Z., Cai, F., Ling, Y., de Rijke, M.: Rethinking item importance in session-based recommendation. In: Proceedings of the 43rd International ACM SIGIR Conference on Research and Development in Information Retrieval, pp. 1837–1840 (2020)
12. Ren, P., Chen, Z., Li, J., Ren, Z., Ma, J., De Rijke, M.: RepeatNet: a repeat aware neural recommendation machine for session-based recommendation. In: Proceedings of the AAAI Conference on Artificial Intelligence, pp. 4806–4813 (2019)
13. Song, W., Wang, S., Wang, Y., Wang, S.: Next-item recommendations in short sessions. In: Fifteenth ACM Conference on Recommender Systems, pp. 282–291 (2021)

14. Tuan, T.X., Phuong, T.M.: 3D convolutional networks for session-based recommendation with content features. In: Proceedings of the Eleventh ACM Conference on Recommender Systems, pp. 138–146 (2017)
15. Twardowski, B., Zawistowski, P., Zaborowski, S.: Metric learning for session-based recommendations. In: Advances in Information Retrieval - 43rd European Conference on IR Research, ECIR 2021, pp. 650–665 (2021)
16. Wang, M., Ren, P., Mei, L., Chen, Z., Ma, J., de Rijke, M.: A collaborative session-based recommendation approach with parallel memory modules. In: Proceedings of the 42nd International ACM SIGIR Conference on Research and Development in Information Retrieval, pp. 345–354 (2019)
17. Wang, S., Cao, L., Wang, Y., Sheng, Q.Z., Orgun, M.A., Lian, D.: A survey on session-based recommender systems. ACM Comput. Surv.) **54**(7), 1–38 (2021)
18. Wu, J., et al.: Self-supervised graph learning for recommendation. In: Proceedings of the 44th International ACM SIGIR Conference on Research and Development in Information Retrieval, pp. 726–735 (2021)
19. Wu, S., Tang, Y., Zhu, Y., Wang, L., Xie, X., Tan, T.: Session-based recommendation with graph neural networks. In: Proceedings of the AAAI Conference on Artificial Intelligence, pp. 346–353 (2019)
20. Wu, Z., Wang, S., Gu, J., Khabsa, M., Sun, F., Ma, H.: Clear: contrastive learning for sentence representation. arXiv preprint arXiv:2012.15466 (2020)
21. Xia, X., Yin, H., Yu, J., Wang, Q., Cui, L., Zhang, X.: Self-supervised hypergraph convolutional networks for session-based recommendation. In: Thirty-Fifth AAAI Conference on Artificial Intelligence, pp. 4503–4511. AAAI Press (2021)
22. Xie, X., et al.: Contrastive learning for sequential recommendation. arXiv preprint arXiv:2010.14395 (2020)
23. Yuan, F., Karatzoglou, A., Arapakis, I., Jose, J.M., He, X.: A simple convolutional generative network for next item recommendation. In: Proceedings of the Twelfth ACM International Conference on Web Search and Data Mining. pp. 582–590 (2019)
24. Zhang, S., Yao, D., Zhao, Z., Chua, T.S., Wu, F.: Causerec: Counterfactual user sequence synthesis for sequential recommendation. In: Proceedings of the 44th International ACM SIGIR Conference on Research and Development in Information Retrieval. pp. 367–377 (2021)
25. Zhou, H., Tan, Q., Huang, X., Zhou, K., Wang, X.: Temporal augmented graph neural networks for session-based recommendations. In: SIGIR '21: The 44th International ACM SIGIR Conference on Research and Development in Information Retrieval, pp. 1798–1802 (2021)

# Discriminative and Robust Analysis Dictionary Learning for Pattern Classification

Kun Jiang[✉], Lei Zhu, and Zheng Liu

School of Computer Science and Engineering,
Xi'an University of Technology, Xi'an, China
jk_365@126.com, {leizhu,zhengliu}@xaut.edu.cn

**Abstract.** Analysis dictionary learning (ADL) model has attracted much interest from researchers in representation-based classification due to its scalability and efficiency in out-of-sample classification. However, the discrimination of the analysis representation is not fully explored when roughly consider the supervised information with redundant and noisy samples. In this paper, we propose a discriminative and robust analysis dictionary learning model (DR-ADL), which explores the underlying structural information of data samples. Firstly, the supervised latent structural term is first implicitly considered to generate a roughly block-diagonal representation for intra-class samples. However, this discriminative structure is fragile and weak in the presence of noisy and redundant samples. Concentrating on both intra-class and inter-class information, we then explicitly incorporate an off-block suppressing term on the ADL model for discriminative structure representation. Moreover, non-negative constraint is incorporated on representations to ensure a reasoning explanation for the contributions of each atoms. Finally, the DR-ADL model is alternatively solved by the K-SVD method, iterative re-weighted method and gradient method efficiently. Experimental results on four benchmark face datasets classification validate the performance superiority of our DR-ADL model.

**Keywords:** Analysis dictionary learning · Off-block suppression · K-SVD method · Latent space classification

## 1 Introduction

Classification over large-amounts of data samples is a fundamental and indispensable problem in many real-world applications [7,18]. The extracted sample features and its label information are used to train a discriminative and robust classification model [6,16,22]. However, data samples collected from various modern sensing system maybe composed of high-dimensional, noisy/corrupted, redundant features. To obtain reliable classification models, sparse representation has attracted much attention, due to its discriminative and compact characteristics, with which an input sample can be coded as a linear combination of

E. Pimenidis et al. (Eds.): ICANN 2022, LNCS 13532, pp. 370–382, 2022.
https://doi.org/10.1007/978-3-031-15937-4_31

a few atoms in an over-complete dictionary [17]. The dictionary learning (DL) methods play a vital role in sparse representation, which can be classified into two categories by the way of encoding samples, i.e., synthesis dictionary learning (SDL) model and analysis dictionary learning (ADL) model [1,10]. A SDL model expects to learn an over-completed dictionary by minimizing the reconstruction errors such that it can exactly represent the samples. However, the basic SDL model focuses on the representation ability, but lacks of discrimination. Plenty of research on exploring the discrimination of SDL model have been proposed for pattern classification [6,7,19,22].

As a dual viewpoint of SDL model, the ADL model mainly focuses on learning a projection matrix, and constructing sparse analyzed vectors in transformation subspace [5]. The ADL model has aroused much attention as it has a more intuitive illustration for the role of analysis atoms and has a lower classification complexity. With ADL models, the coefficients of training samples are used as transformed space features for the jointly learned classifier. Then, the testing samples can also be efficiently projected into transformed feature space by analysis dictionary, leading to lower classification complexity. Shekhar et al. [12] performs a two-step ADL+SVM model which learns a transformed dictionary which is then used to obtain analysis coefficients for samples. The classification process acts as a post-step for the analysis representation. The basic ADL model mainly focuses on the representational ability of the dictionary without considering its discriminative capability for classification [9].

To achieve a global optimum solution for discriminative ADL model, Guo et al. incorporated the structural code consistent term and topology preserving term (DADL) into the conventional ADL model to yield a discriminative representation [4]. By introducing a synthesis-linear-classifier to map the label information into feature space, Wang et al. [14] presented a synthesis linear classifier-based ADL (SLC-ADL) algorithm. At the same period, Wang et al. [16] designed a synthesis K-SVD based ADL (SK-DADL) model by jointly learning ADL and a linear classifier through K-SVD method. After that, Tang et al. [13] incorporated a class characteristic structure of independent subspaces term and classification error term into the framework of ADL (SADL). However, the above research work are all performed in a ideal ambient space without noises or corruptions. Since data samples usually contain noisy or redundant features, the coding coefficients would be contaminated and the discrimination of the ADL model may be degraded [15].

To remedy these limitations, we joint incorporate the sparse representation error term, robust latent space structural term and off-block suppression term into one unified framework (DR-ADL) with non-negative representation constraint. The constraint terms can weaken the adverse effect of noisy and redundant features, and inter-class correlation of block-diagonal representation, which guarantee comprehensive interpretability and discrimination. The main contribution of this paper is as follows. Firstly, we integrate the latent space structural term and off-block suppression term into the ADL model with non-negative constraint for discriminative and robust sparse representation. Secondly, we exploit an alternating direction solution to optimize the proposed model, including K-SVD method, adaptive iterative re-weighted method and gradient method for each subproblem. Thirdly, we present an efficient and robust classification scheme in the latent label space. Empirical study on four benchmark databases show the efficacy and efficiency of our DR-ADL model.

The rest of this paper is organized as follows. The preliminary theory is presented in Sect. 2. The discriminative and robust ADL model and the solution are presented in Sect. 3. Section 4 presents a robust classification scheme. Experimental results on pattern classification are presented in Sect. 5. Relevant conclusions are finally given in Sect. 6.

## 2   Preliminary

**Notations.** Suppose $Y = [y_1, y_2, \cdots, y_n] \in R^{m \times n}$ is the sample set, let $D = [d_1, d_2, \cdots, d_k] \in R^{m \times k}$ and $\Omega = [w_1, w_2, \cdots, w_k]^T \in R^{k \times m}$ be a synthesis and analysis dictionary with a serials of atom $d_i$ and $w_i$ respectively, and $X = [x_1, x_2, \cdots, x_n] \in R^{k \times n}$ be the sparse representation, and $H = [h_1, h_2, \cdots, h_n] \in R^{c \times n}$ be the label matrix with each column $h_i = [0, \cdots, 0, 1, 0, \cdots, 0]^T$ describes the label vector of the $j$th sample; the non-zero value of $h_i$ occur at the index $j$ where training sample belong to class $j (1 \leq j \leq c)$.

### 2.1   Analysis Dictionary Learning

The ADL model aims to learn an analysis dictionary $\Omega \in R^{k \times m}$ with $k > m$ to implement the approximately sparse representation of the signal $y \in R^m$ in transformed domain [9,10]. Specifically, it assumes that the product of $\Omega$ and $y$ is sparse, i.e., $x = \Omega y$ with $\|x_i\|_0 = k - t$, where $0 \leq t \leq k$ is the number of zeros in $x \in R^k$. The sparse optimization problem can be formulated as follows.

$$\min_{\Omega, X} \|X - \Omega Y\|_F^2$$
$$s.t. \ \Omega \in \Gamma, \ \|x_i\|_0 \leq T_0, \ i = 1, 2, \ldots, \mathrm{n} \tag{1}$$

where the representation error term $\|X - \Omega Y\|_F^2$ shows the disparity between representations in transformed space and the coefficients with sparsity level $T_0$.

To enhance the discriminative power and efficiency of ADLs, there are various classification task-oriented improvements with well-conditioned regularizers, such as SK-DADL [16], DADL [4], CADL [15] and SADL [13]. For example, the recent proposed SK-DADL [16] and SADL [13] models combine the classification error term with the basic ADL framework, in which the supervised class label information is utilized to guide the generation of representation. However, the discrimination of these ADL models are not fully exploited due to the implicit transformation of label information under noisy and redundant ambient space.

### 2.2   Non-negative Representation

The negative coefficient in DL models lacks a reasonable interpretation as the substraction of sample contribution should be physically prohibited. The non-negative constraint is widely applied in non-negative matrix factorization [20], subspace clustering [2,23], representation-based classification [18] et al., for explanative part-based representation. Specifically, among representation based classification methods, there still exists controversy between sparsity and collaborative mechanism [17,21]. Nevertheless, Xu et al. further [18] found that without non-negative constraint, a sample will be represented by both heterogeneous and homogeneous samples, which brings about a difficult physical interpretation. By restricting the values of representation vector to be non-negative, the contributions of homogeneous samples can be enlarged, meanwhile, eliminating the adverse effects caused by heterogeneous samples. Motivated by the conjecture that the non-negativity constraint can boost the selection of representative atoms, we consider the non-negative representation to ADL model, so that the learned analysis dictionary atoms are more high-quality and discriminative.

## 3    Discriminative and Robust ADL Model

### 3.1    Model Formulation

As mentioned above, the discriminative ability of the analysis dictionary cannot be fully exploited only with the label matrix of training samples [4]. Recently, the labels of atoms also have been used to improve the discriminative ability of dictionary [6,8]. Inspired by [6,8], we explore the discriminative structural properties in the analysis representation model by leveraging the class-wise label information of analysis dictionary. However, as there is only one nonzero element $h_{ij}$ in each label vector $h_j$ of the label matrix $H$, the class of a sample is only determined by one element's location $i$ in a label vector $h_j$, which may easily drift a lot during the training procedure. Therefore, we extend the label matrix $H$ into a latent space $L$ by a Kronecker product to improve its robustness to some extent [14]. Specifically, given an all ones vector $1$ with length $l$, the extended class label matrix $L$ is defined as

$$L \equiv H \otimes 1 = \begin{bmatrix} h_{1,1}1 \cdots h_{1,n}1 \\ \vdots \quad \ddots \quad \vdots \\ h_{c,1}1 \cdots h_{c,n}1 \end{bmatrix} \in R^{lc \times n} \tag{2}$$

To this end, we further incorporate $\|L - WX\|_F^2$ as the latent space transformation term for implicit block-diagonal constraint on representation, where $W \in R^{lc \times k}$ is the transformation matrix. Note that the latent space transformation term can be viewed as a label-consistent term of the dictionary atoms if we set the number of dictionary atoms $k = lc$, which means that there are $l$ atoms chosen from each class and arranged sequentially. This indicates the latent space transform term roughly leads to a ideal structural representation.

When there are noisy and redundant samples, the fragile block-diagonal structure would be destroyed with the implicit ideal structural constraint. Thus the discrimination of representation and the performance of classification may be degraded. To this end, we further present a discriminative off-block diagonal suppression term $\|X \odot S\|_F^2$ to the coefficients $X$, where $\odot$ means the Hadamard product (element-wise multiplication) operator. The $S \in R^{k \times n}$ is defined as

$$S = \begin{cases} 0, & \text{if } \omega_i \text{ and } x_j \text{ belong to the same class} \\ 1, & \text{otherwise} \end{cases} \quad (3)$$

where $\omega_i$ is the $i$th row of the dictionary $\Omega$, and $x_j$ is the $j$th column of training samples matrix $X$. This off-block diagonal suppressing term can proved to be equal to the class-wise multiplication of $i$th sub-dictionary and the complementary matrix of $i$th class training samples [3].

Finally, the objective function of our proposed Discriminative and Robust ADL (DR-ADL) model is formulated as follows

$$\min_{\Omega, W, X} \|X - \Omega Y\|_F^2 + \alpha \|L - WX\|_F^2 + \beta \|X \odot S\|_F^2$$

$$s.t. \quad \Omega \in \Gamma, X \geq 0, \|x_i\|_0 \leq T_0, i = 1, 2, \ldots, \text{n} \quad (4)$$

where the first term is the representation error term of ADL model, the second term is the latent space structural term which combines the virtues of classification error term and ideal structural term, and the third term yields discriminative suppression on the off-block representation.

## 3.2  Solution to DR-ADL

The optimization problem (4) is a multiple variables optimization problem, and it is non-convex w.r.t. $\Omega$, $X$ and $W$ jointly. We first add one variable $Z = X$ to make the problem separable, and then problem (8) can be rewritten as

$$\min_{\Omega, W, X, Z} \|X - \Omega Y\|_F^2 + \alpha \|L - WX\|_F^2 + \beta \|Z \odot S\|_F^2$$

$$s.t. \ \Omega \in \Gamma, Z = X, Z \geq 0, \|x_i\|_0 \leq T_0, i = 1, 2, \ldots, \text{n} \quad (5)$$

Then, we can get the following objective function of the problem by the ALM method. Here, the augmented Lagrangian function of problem (9) is

$$\mathcal{L}(\Omega, W, X, Z, C_1) = \|X - \Omega Y\|_F^2 + \alpha \|L - WX\|_F^2 + \beta \|Z \odot S\|_F^2$$
$$+ <C_1, Z - X> + \frac{\mu}{2} \|Z - X\|_F^2 \quad (6)$$

where $<P, Q> = tr(P^T Q)$, $C_1$ is the Lagrangian multipliers, and $\mu > 0$ is a penalty parameter. The problem can be divided into three convex sub-problems.
(1) Fix $\{\Omega, Z\}$ and update $\{W, X\}$. The sub-problem for updating $\{W, X\}$ is

$$\min_{W, X} \|\Omega Y - X\|_F^2 + \alpha \|L - WX\|_F^2 + \frac{\mu}{2} \left\|Z - \frac{C_1}{\mu} - X\right\|_F^2 \quad (7)$$

which is equivalent to

$$\min_{W, X} \left\| \begin{pmatrix} \Omega Y \\ \sqrt{\alpha} L \\ \sqrt{\mu/2}(Z - C_1/\mu) \end{pmatrix} - \begin{pmatrix} R_1 \\ \sqrt{\alpha} W \\ \sqrt{\mu/2} R_2 \end{pmatrix} X \right\|_F^2 \quad (8)$$

$$s.t. \quad \|x_i\|_0 \leq T_0, \ i = 1, 2, \ldots, \text{n}$$

where $R_1$ and $R_2$ is initialized as an identity matrix $I$.

The above equation can be solved by K-SVD method. Specifically, Let $Y_{new} = \left(Y^T \Omega^T, \sqrt{\alpha} L^T, \sqrt{\mu/2}(Z^T - C_1^T/\mu)\right)^T$, $D_{new} = \left(R_1^T, \sqrt{\alpha} W^T, \sqrt{\mu/2} R_2^T\right)$, then Eq. (6) is equivalent to the following problem:

$$\min_{D_{new}, X} \|Y_{new} - D_{new}X\|_F^2$$

$$s.t. \|x_i\|_0 \le T_0, i = 1, 2, \ldots, n$$

(9)

The optimization problem in (9) can be solved by K-SVD method [1]. After convergence, we could take out $W$ from $D_{new}$ with a column-wise $l_2$ normalization respectively.

(2) Fix $\{\Omega, W, X\}$ and update $Z$. The sub-problem for updating $Z$ is

$$\mathcal{L} = \min_{Z} \beta\|Z \odot S\|_F^2 + <C_1, Z - X> + \frac{\mu}{2}\|Z - X\|_F^2 \quad s.t. \ Z \ge 0 \quad (10)$$

The above subproblem is difficult to be solved due to the Hadamard product. We propose an iterative re-weighted method to capture the block-diagonal elements of $Z$, thus the subproblem is equivalent to

$$\mathcal{L} = \min_{Z} \beta\|Z - Q_1\|_F^2 + \frac{\mu}{2}\|Z - X - \frac{C_1}{\mu}\|_F^2 \quad s.t. \ Z \ge 0 \quad (11)$$

where $Q_1 = Q \odot Z^{(t)}$ represents the block-diagonal elements of $Z$ in last iteration, and $Q = [q_1, q_2, \cdots, q_n] \in R^{k \times n}$ is a predefined ideal representation matrix and $q_i \in R^k$ has a form of $[0, \cdots, 0, 1, \cdots, 1, 0, \cdots, 0]^T$, which can be viewed as a coding vector for sample $y_i \in R^m$. If sample $y_i$ belongs to class $k$, the coefficients in $q_i$ associated with the row vectors in $\Omega_k$ are all 1s, whereas others are all 0s.

By setting the derivation $(\partial\mathcal{L}/\partial Z) = 0$, the closed-form solution of $Z$ is

$$Z = (2\beta Q_1 + \mu X + C_1)/(2\beta + \mu) \quad s.t. \ Z \ge 0 \quad (12)$$

In each iteration, all the negative elements and the lowest values in $Z$ are set to 0, thus generating non-negative representations.

(3) Fix $\{W, X, Z\}$ and update $\Omega$. For simplicity, we constrain the set $\Gamma$ to be matries with relatively small Frobenius norm and unity row-wise norm. Thus, we add a regularization term into the sub-problem for updating $\Omega$ as

$$\min_{\Omega} \|X - \Omega Y\|_F^2 + \gamma\|\Omega\|_F^2 \quad (13)$$

where $\gamma > 0$ is a parameter which weighs the penalty term to avoid singularity and over-fitting issues as well as ensuring a stable solution.

By setting the derivative of the objective function w.r.t. $\Omega$ be zero, we can finally obtain the analytical solution of $\Omega$ as follows.

$$\Omega = XY^T\left(YY^T + \gamma I\right)^{-1} \quad (14)$$

where $I$ is an identity matrix with appropriate size and $\gamma$ is a small positive scalar for regularizing the solution. Finally, each row of $\Omega$ is normalized to unit norm to avoid trivial solution.

## 3.3   Initialization

As latent space label matrix can be viewed as the ideal structural representations for all training samples, we adopt the initialization metric used in [14] to improve its robustness, in which the latent space label matrix is used as the initialization of sparse analysis representation $X_{ini}$ for training data, i.e., $X_{ini} = L$. The classifier $W$ is initialized to by solving a multivariant ridge regression model, and the solution can be referred to [4] as

$$W_{ini} = \alpha H X_{ini}{}^T \left( \alpha X_{ini} X_{ini}{}^T + \delta_0 I \right)^{-1} \tag{15}$$

Thus, the above training procedure is summarized in Algorithm 1.

---

**Algorithm 1.** Algorithm for solving our proposed model (4)

---

**Input:** Training data $Y$, label matrix $H$, latent space matrix $L$, model parameter $\alpha, \beta$,
    sparsity level $T_0$ and convergence tolerance $\varepsilon = 1e - 6$, maximum iteration $T_{max}$.
**Output:** The analysis dictionary $\Omega$ and classifier $W$.
1:  Initialize $\Omega$ by (14), $W$ by (15), $Z = X = L$, $C_1 = \mathbf{0}^{k \times n}$, $\rho = 1.01$, $\mu = 10^{-8}$,
    $\mu_{max} = 10^8$, $t = 1$.
2:  **while** not converge and $t < T_{max}$ **do**
3:      fixing $\Omega, Z$, update $W, X$ by solving model (9) using K-SVD method;
4:      fixing $\Omega, W, X$, update $Z$ by Eq. (12);
5:      fixing $W, X, Z$, update $\Omega$ by Eq. (14);
6:      update $C_1 = C_1 + \mu(Z - X)$, $\mu = min(\rho\mu, \mu_{max})$
7:      check the convergence condition: $\left\| Z^t - X^t \right\|_\infty < \varepsilon$, and $t = t + 1$
8:  **end while**

---

## 4   Robust Classification Scheme

For classification of test samples on DR-ADL model, preliminary representation coefficient $x_i$ is efficiently obtained via the operation of multiplying analysis $\Omega$ by the testing sample $y_i$. Keeping in view that the proposed method imposes sparsity and non-negativity on coefficients, we apply a hard thresholding operator $x_i = HT(\Omega y_i, T_0)$ to maintain the sparse and non-negative characteristic of $x_i$, where $T_0$ is an adjustable sparsity parameter for test samples in classification step. The operator reserves elements with $T_0$ biggest non-negative values and sets the others to be zero. We can easily obtain the latent space label vector for each testing sample by $\mathbf{lp}_i = W x_i$.

We predefine a desired latent space label matrix $L' \in R^{k \times k}$, in which the extended label vector for each class as $\mathbf{l}_j \in L'(1 \leq j \leq c)$. We utilize the $k$ Nearest Neighbor (kNN) for the latent space classification, as it does not require training effort and mainly depends on the distance metrics among samples. The classification of a test sample is determined by the category labels of its $k = 1$ nearest training samples. So we only need to solve each testing sample's representation in the classification stage, and the latent space label vector of test sample

$\mathbf{lp}_i$. Then, the final category of each testing sample is determined robustly by contrasting each obtained label vector $\mathbf{lp}_i$ with its nearest column vector $\mathbf{l}_j$ in the latent space label matrix $L'$.

## 5 Experiments

### 5.1 Experimental Settings

We extensively evaluate our DR-ADL model on four benchmark databases, including Extended Yale B (EYaleB), AR, LFW, Scene15 and UCF50. The above databases are widely used in evaluating the performance of sparse representation-based classification methods. The features we use are publicly provided by [6] and [11]. We randomly select the training and testing sets with fixed proportion that is consistent with previous paper [8]. On EYaleB and AR face databases, random face features are extracted by the projection with a randomly generated matrix. The LFW face image database contains more than 13,000 images of faces collected from the Web. We selected a subset of the LFW face database consisting of 1251 images of 86 persons. On Scene15 databases, features are achieved by extracting SIFT descriptors, max pooling in spatial pyramid and reducing dimensions via PCA for convenient processing. UCF50 is a large-scale and challenging action recognition database. It has 50 action categories and 6680 realistic human action videos collected from YouTube.

We compare our DR-ADL model with some state-of-the-art DL approaches: SRC [17], LC-KSVD [6], ADL+SVM [12], SK-DADL [16] and SLC-ADL [14]. To be fair, we use the released codes of all the compared models and finely tune the parameters, or directly adopt the results reported in the literatures with the same parameter setting. We repeat the experiments 5 times on randomly selected training and testing samples, and the mean accuracies are reported. There are four parameters in the proposed DR-ADL model, i.e., $\alpha$, $\beta$, $\gamma$ and $\delta$, where $\gamma$ and $\delta$ are set to $3e-3$ and $1e-6$ empirically to avoid over fitting and singular values, and the dominant parameters $\alpha$ and $\beta$, which weigh the two regularizers in objective function, are obtained by cross validation. The parameters we set in each database are listed in Table 1. For fair comparison, the sparsity is set as 45 in all the methods, and the dictionary atom is set around 600 which is the integral multiple of the number of classes in different databases. All experiments are run with MATLAB R2019a under Windows10 on a PC with Intel Core i5-8400 2.80 GHz 2.81 GHz CPU and 8 GB RAM.

**Table 1.** Best parameter settings for DR-ADL model by cross validation.

|          | EYaleB | AR | LFW | Scene15 | UCF50 |
|----------|--------|----|-----|---------|-------|
| $\alpha$ | 50     | 60 | 4   | 20      | 20    |
| $\beta$  | 12     | 20 | 1   | 14      | 11    |

## 5.2 Results and Analysis

Table 2 shows the mean classification accuracy results on different datasets. As can be seen, our method achieves notably higher accuracy than SRC and LC-KSVD on all four databases. This is mainly due to the structured non-negative representation ability and discrimination ability achieved in our method for ADL model, which is a further improvement on the LC-KSVD that only considers the label-consistent term and classification error term on SDL model. The SRC model that directly uses all training samples as the dictionary will introduce noisy and redundant features for sparse representation. The non-negative constraint on representation coefficients can boost the selection of representative analysis atoms, and this may help to overcome the above noise disadvantage. Our DR-ADL method also achieves favorable results compared with all three ADL-based methods. This proves the availability of adding robust structural constraints can further exploring the discriminative representation ability compared with conventional ADL models in complex noisy and redundant ambient space.

**Table 2.** Classification accuracy (%) comparison on different datasets. The best results are in bold.

|         | SRC  | LC-KSVD | ADL+SVM | SK-DADL | SLC-ADL | DR-ADL |
|---------|------|---------|---------|---------|---------|--------|
| EYaleB  | 96.5 | 96.7    | 95.4    | 96.7    | 97.0    | **97.3** |
| AR      | 97.5 | 97.8    | 96.1    | 97.7    | 97.2    | **98.1** |
| LFW     | 38.1 | 36.7    | 32.6    | 38.7    | 38.9    | **40.4** |
| Scene15 | 91.8 | 92.9    | 90.1    | 97.4    | 97.5    | **98.7** |
| UCF50   | 68.4 | 70.1    | 72.3    | 74.6    | 78.1    | **78.5** |

Table 3 shows the time for classifying one testing image on different datasets. As can be seen, our method is approximately one order of magnitude faster than LC-KSVD method. This mainly owns to the low classification complexity of ADL which uses efficient feature transformation and the robust structural constraints for compact representations. Also, our method performs slightly better than SK-DADL, due to the robust kNN classifier in Euclidean space and the non-negative constraint on sparse coding, which limits the number of dictionary atoms in projection of heterogeneous samples.

The dominant parameter $\alpha$ and $\beta$ in the objective function are tuned by 5-fold cross validation and optimized by using grid search. We firstly search in the larger range of $[10^{-3}, 10^{-2}, \cdots, 10^2, 10^3]$ for each parameter and then search a smaller grid with proper interval size determined by preliminary classification results. In Fig. 1, two 3D histograms show that the classification accuracy vary

**Table 3.** The time (ms) for classifying one testing image.

|         | EYaleB | AR    | LFW   | Scene15 | UCF50 |
|---------|--------|-------|-------|---------|-------|
| SRC     | 39.93  | 41.24 | 38.12 | 70.66   | 92.37 |
| LC-KSVD | 0.426  | 0.442 | 0.351 | 0.675   | 0.794 |
| SK-DADL | 0.029  | 0.078 | 0.052 | 0.113   | 0.169 |
| DR-ADL  | 0.024  | 0.063 | 0.050 | 0.105   | 0.157 |

as parameter $\alpha$ and $\beta$ change on AR and UCF50 databases respectively. We can observe that the best performance is achieved at $\alpha = 60$ and $\beta = 20$ on AR database and $\alpha = 20$ and $\beta = 14$ on UCF50 database. The results are consistent with the intuitive view that both regularization terms are crucial for a discriminative and robust ADL model.

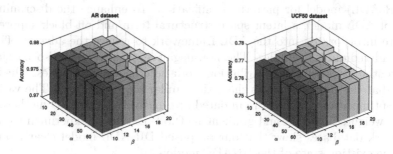

**Fig. 1.** Results of parameter selection of $\alpha$ and $\beta$ on AR and UCF50 databases.

Table 4 shows the average classification accuracy of different DL algorithms with different numbers of atoms on the LFW dataset. The other parameters remain the same as the best parameter settings in the above model comparison experiments. It can be seen that the average accuracy of the DR-ADL algorithm significantly outperformed other algorithms as the number of atoms increased. When the atom number becomes larger, its performance is roughly stable for ADL models. For SDL models as LC-KSVD model, the larger the number of dictionary atoms is, the more negative effect on discriminative dictionary learning it has. As dictionary atoms may be contaminated by more and more noisy or redundant samples. The analysis dictionary transforms the raw samples into representation space, and is somewhat more robust to noises or corruptions with the increase of atom num. The accuracies and time costs in tables demonstrate that our robust DR-ADL model has a huge potential in classification tasks.

**Table 4.** Classification accuracy (%) of different DL algorithms with different numbers of atoms on the LFW dataset.

| Atoms# | LC-KSVD | ADL+SVM | SK-DADL | SLC-ADL | DR-ADL |
|--------|---------|---------|---------|---------|--------|
| 86     | 29.3    | 27.9    | 29.6    | 31.4    | 32.3   |
| 172    | 34.1    | 29.7    | 34.3    | 34.6    | 35.7   |
| 258    | 34.8    | 30.3    | 36.1    | 36.8    | 37.5   |
| 344    | 35.4    | 31.1    | 37.0    | 37.9    | 38.9   |
| 430    | 36.9    | 31.7    | 38.2    | 38.6    | 39.9   |
| 516    | 36.7    | 32.6    | 38.7    | 38.9    | 40.4   |

# 6   Conclusion

In this paper, we propose a discriminative and robust analysis dictionary learning (DR-ADL) model for pattern classification. To enhance the discriminative ability of ADL model, a latent space structural term and off-block suppression term are incorporated into the ADL framework to relieve the adverse effect of noisy and redundant samples. The non-negative constraint is also considered to prevent substraction of contribution from heterogeneous samples, which can ensure that the similar samples share the similar representations. The variables in our optimization problem are updated alternatively by K-SVD method, iterative re-weighted method and gradient method. Extensive experiments on four benchmark databases show that our proposed DR-ADL model clearly outperforms the existing state-of-the-art ADL models.

**Acknowledgement.** This work is supported by the Natural Science Basic Research Program of Shaanxi, China (Program No. 2021JM-339).

# References

1. Aharon, M., Elad, M., Bruckstein, A.: K-SVD: an algorithm for designing overcomplete dictionaries for sparse representation. IEEE Trans. Signal Process. **54**(11), 4311–4322 (2006)
2. Chen, Z., Wu, X.J., Cai, Y.H., Kittler, J.: Sparse non-negative transition subspace learning for image classification. Signal Process. **183** (2021)
3. Chen, Z., Wu, X.J., Kittler, J.: Relaxed block-diagonal dictionary pair learning with locality constraint for image recognition. In: IEEE Transactions on Neural Networks and Learning Systems, pp. 1–15 (2021)
4. Guo, J., Guo, Y., Kong, X., Zhang, M., He, R.: Discriminative analysis dictionary learning. In: Schuurmans, D., Wellman, M.P. (eds.) Proceedings of the Thirtieth AAAI Conference on Artificial Intelligence, 12–17 February 2016, Phoenix, Arizona, USA, pp. 1617–1623. AAAI Press (2016)

5. Hawe, S., Kleinsteuber, M., Diepold, K.: Analysis operator learning and its application to image reconstruction. IEEE Trans. Image Process. **22**(6), 2138–2150 (2013)
6. Jiang, Z., Lin, Z., Davis, L.S.: Label consistent k-SVD: learning a discriminative dictionary for recognition. IEEE Trans. Pattern Anal. Mach. Intell. **35**(11), 2651–2664 (2013)
7. Kong, S., Wang, D.: dictionary learning approach for classification: separating the particularity and the commonality. In: Fitzgibbon, A., Lazebnik, S., Perona, P., Sato, Y., Schmid, C. (eds.) ECCV 2012. LNCS, vol. 7572, pp. 186–199. Springer, Heidelberg (2012). https://doi.org/10.1007/978-3-642-33718-5_14
8. Li, Z., Lai, Z., Xu, Y., Yang, J., Zhang, D.: A locality-constrained and label embedding dictionary learning algorithm for image classification. IEEE Trans. Neural Netw. Learn. Syst. **28**(2), 278–293 (2017)
9. Ravishankar, S., Bresler, Y.: Learning sparsifying transforms. IEEE Trans. Signal Process. **61**(5), 1072–1086 (2013)
10. Rubinstein, R., Peleg, T., Elad, M.: Analysis k-SVD: a dictionary-learning algorithm for the analysis sparse model. IEEE Trans. Signal Process. **61**(3), 661–677 (2013)
11. Sadanand, S., Corso, J.J.: Action bank: a high-level representation of activity in video. In: 2012 IEEE Conference on Computer Vision and Pattern Recognition, pp. 1234–1241 (2012)
12. Shekhar, S., Patel, V.M., Chellappa, R.: Analysis sparse coding models for image-based classification. In: 2014 IEEE International Conference on Image Processing (ICIP), pp. 5207–5211 (2014)
13. Tang, W., Panahi, A., Krim, H., Dai, L.: Analysis dictionary learning based classification: Structure for robustness. IEEE Trans. Image Process. **28**(12), 6035–6046 (2019)
14. Wang, J., Guo, Y., Guo, J., Li, M., Kong, X.: Synthesis linear classifier based analysis dictionary learning for pattern classification. Neurocomputing **238**, 103–113 (2017)
15. Wang, J., Guo, Y., Guo, J., Luo, X., Kong, X.: Class-aware analysis dictionary learning for pattern classification. IEEE Signal Process. Lett. **24**(12), 1822–1826 (2017)
16. Wang, Q., Guo, Y., Guo, J., Kong, X.: Synthesis k-SVD based analysis dictionary learning for pattern classification. Multim. Tools Appl. **77**(13), 17023C17041 (2018)
17. Wright, J., Yang, A.Y., Ganesh, A., Sastry, S.S., Ma, Y.: Robust face recognition via sparse representation. IEEE Trans. Patt. Anal. Mach. Intell. **31**(2), 210–227 (2009)
18. Xu, J., An, W., Zhang, L., Zhang, D.: Sparse, collaborative, or nonnegative representation: which helps pattern classification? Patt. Recogn. **88**, 679–688 (2019)
19. Yang, M., Zhang, L., Feng, X., Zhang, D.: Fisher discrimination dictionary learning for sparse representation. In: 2011 International Conference on Computer Vision, pp. 543–550 (2011)
20. Yi, Y., Wang, J., Zhou, W., Zheng, C., Kong, J., Qiao, S.: Non-negative matrix factorization with locality constrained adaptive graph. IEEE Trans. Circ. Syst. Video Technol. **30**(2), 427–441 (2020)
21. Zhang, L., Yang, M., Feng, X.: Sparse representation or collaborative representation: which helps face recognition? In: Proceedings of the 2011 International Conference on Computer Vision, ICCV 2011, pp. 471–478, IEEE Computer Society, USA (2011)

22. Zhang, Q., Li, B.: Discriminative k-svd for dictionary learning in face recognition. In: 2010 IEEE Computer Society Conference on Computer Vision and Pattern Recognition, pp. 2691–2698 (2010)
23. Zhuang, L., Gao, H., Lin, Z., Ma, Y., Zhang, X., Yu, N.: Non-negative low rank and sparse graph for semi-supervised learning. In: 2012 IEEE Conference on Computer Vision and Pattern Recognition, pp. 2328–2335 (2012)

# Domain Adaptative Semantic Segmentation by Fine-Grained Alignment

Zhixin Li[✉], Wei Li, and Jia Zhang

Guangxi Key Lab of Multi-source Information Mining and Security,
Guangxi Normal University, Guilin 541004, China
lizx@gxnu.edu.cn

**Abstract.** To alleviate the domain gap, we propose an improved domain adaptative network for semantic segmentation. Specifically, we use the method of distinguishing alignment between foreground and background classes for fine-grained adaptating diffrent type of categories. Furthermore, we use a channel and spatial paraller attention module to acquire the rich spatial and channel information from features. However, it will still causes a large inter-domain difference due to the different feature distributions between different domains. We use the self-supervised learning method to generate pseudo labels for better aligning target domain. Finally, we use focal loss in the target domain to alleviate the impact of categories imbalance on the adaptation process. Experiments show that our method achieves better segmentation performance in unsupervised domain adaptative semantic segmentation.

**Keywords:** Domain adaptative · Distinguish alignment · Self-supervised learning

## 1 Introduction

To effectively alleviate the domain gap is the key point to improve the performance of domain adaptative semantic segmentation tasks. At present, widely approaches [2, 4, 19, 23] are to use adversarial learning method to align the global semantic features between different domains, e.g., [17] construct a multi-level adversarial network to effectively perform output space domain adaptation at different feature levels. [12] proposes to apply different adversarial weights to different regions to solve the problem of class-level alignment. Different with them, we consider to align for the background and foreground classes.

Moreover, the unsupervised domain adaptative semantic segmentation method based on pseudo-labels uses high-confidence prediction as the pseudo ground truth of unlabeled data in the target domain, thus, does fine-tune the model trained on the source domain. In [8], a self-supervised learning method of combining different outputs of the model is proposed, and then pseudo-labels are generated for unlabeled data to train the model. CBST [25] achieves domain

© The Author(s), under exclusive license to Springer Nature Switzerland AG 2022
E. Pimenidis et al. (Eds.): ICANN 2022, LNCS 13532, pp. 383–394, 2022.
https://doi.org/10.1007/978-3-031-15937-4_32

adaptation by generating class-balanced pseudo-labels from images, and introduces a spatial prior to guide adaptation processing. After comprehensive analysis and consideration, we adopt the self-supervised learning (SSL) method proposed by bidirectional learning (BDL) [9]. The target domain with pseudo-labels is used to update the adaptative network, while excluding low-confidence prediction labels. This method combines the two domains better than existing methods to generate pseudo-labels through only one learning.

We notice that the spatial context is important to segmentation task, however, the balance of capturing rich context information and consuming complexity of computation needs our consideration. A lot of work has made great improvements on the joint encoding of spatial and channel information. The self-attention map in SAGAN [22] shows a good balance between the ability to simulate long-range dependencies and computational efficiency. Moreover, the self-attention module takes the weighted sum of the features at all positions on the feature map as the response of the position, and the calculation cost of the attention vector is small. The squeenze and excitation (SE) [5] module improves the expressive ability of the network by modeling the dependency between the channels of the convolutional features. The model selects and amplifies valuable channels from global information and suppresses useless feature channels. SAGAN focuses on obtaining the spatial position relationship between pixels, while the channel attention SE module discards spatial correlation through global average pooling. However, for semantic segmentation, which is a intensive prediction classification task, the dependence between the acquisition spatial and the channel is equally important. We introduce the spatial and channel parallel attention module (scSE) [15] to obtain the dependency relationship between the channels and the spatial position information. In order to reduce the impact of class imbalance on the domain adaptation process. We consider adding Focal Loss [10] to our overall loss.

Our main contributions are summaried as follow:

- We distinguish the foreground class from the background class and align them separately for finer-grained semantic alignment.
- We adapt the self-supervised learning (SSL) stategy for converting the unsuprvised learning to semi-suprvised learning which alignes different domains in global processing, thus, achieves a better performance.
- We propose an improved parallel attention module of spatial and channel to capture the spatial position information and the dependence between channels.

The proposed method is evaluated on two unsupervised domain adaptation tasks GTA5 [13] to Cityscapes [3] and SYNTHIA [14] to Cityscapes. And a high performance is achieved in these two domain adaptation tasks.

## 2   Methods

### 2.1   Overview

Our overall framework is shown in Fig. 1, which mainly includes segmentation network $G$ and discriminator network $D$. The same as AdaptSeg is that we adopt

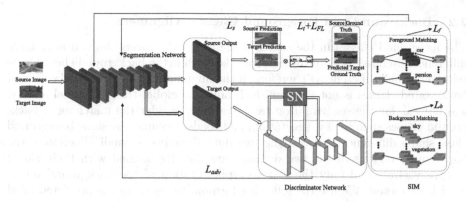

**Fig. 1.** Overview of our proposed framework.

a two-lever adversarial approach. Use the features of 4th convolution layer and 5th convolution layer to predict the segmentation results of the output space, and then input them into the discriminator for discrimination.

Feature-level adversarial training relies on the binary domain discriminator $D$ to align the features extracted by the segmentation network $G$ in two domains. In addition, in order to improve readability, $h$, $w$, $c$ denote the height, width and channel of the feature map respectively. While the discriminator tries to distinguish which domain the feature is from by optimizing the discriminator target function in Eq. (1):

$$\min_{D} L_D = -\sum_{h,w} \log\left(D\left(P_t\right)^{h,w}\right) + \log\left(1 - D\left(P_s\right)^{h,w}\right) \tag{1}$$

where $P_s$ and $P_t$ are respectively based on the predicted probability of the source domain and target domain output by the segmentation network.

For any image $x_s$ and given ground truth label $Y_s$ in the labeled source domain dataset, and the predicted probability $P_s$ output by the corresponding segmentation network, the cross entropy loss of the source domain can be obtained as follows:

$$L_s\left(x_s, y_s\right) = -\sum_{h,w,c} y_s^{h,w,c} \log\left(P_s^{h,w,c}\right) \tag{2}$$

In the training process, the adversarial loss obtained by the discriminator $D$ is used to optimize the segmentation network module to reduce the difference between the generated source domain probability and the target domain distribution. The adversarial loss is defined as follows:

$$L_{adv}\left(x_t\right) = -\sum_{h,w} \log\left(D\left(P_t\right)^{h,w}\right) \tag{3}$$

## 2.2   Background and Foreground Classes Alignment

The foreground classes in the source domain and the target domain have large differences even in the shape of the same class, while the background classes have relatively small differences. Therefore, if the alignment of foreground classes and background classes is not distinguished, only the global training signal against loss is weak for the segmentation task. We first consider the matching of background classes such as sky, vegetation, and roads. Because the same background class shape difference between the two data domains is small. Therefore, the background regions of the two domains are directly aligned with their global feature vectors, and only the feature representation of the background image level is extracted. We use the following formula to generate the predicted label map for each image in the source domain $X_s$ and its corresponding ground true label map to access the correctly classified label map:

$$T_{E_i}^s = T_{g_i}^s \bigcap T_{p_i}^s \qquad (4)$$

where $i \in \{1 \ldots |X_s|\}$, $T_{E_i}^s$ is the correctly classified label map, $T_{g_i}^s$ is the ground true label map, and $T_{p_i}^s = \mathrm{argmax}\left(E\left(f_s\right)^c\right)$ is the source domain image prediction label map. We assume that the background classes $b \in B$, then the features belonging to the same background class are averaged on the height and width of the image by the following formula, which is used as the instance feature representation of each background class:

$$H^b(T, f) = \frac{\sum_{h,w} \delta\left(T^{h,w} - b\right) f^{h,w}}{\max\left(\varepsilon, \sum_{h,w} \delta\left(T^{h,w} - b\right)\right)} \qquad (5)$$

$$S_j^b = H^b\left(T_{E_i}^s, f_i^s\right) \qquad (6)$$

where $\delta$ is the Dirac delta function, $\varepsilon$ is the regular term, and $S_j^b$ is the $j$'th source domain semantic feature sample of class $b$. In addition, $j = i\%w$, $w$ is the number of feature samples to be stored in each class. Because the initial target domain has no ground truth labels, the predicted label map is used to generate instance feature representations for each background class. Then we minimize the distance between the instance representation of each background class and the source instance feature representation of the class. Therefore, training on the target domain can adapt to the instance feature representation of the background classes through the following background classes loss function:

$$L_b = \sum_{i,b} \min_j \left\| H^b\left(T_{P_i}^t, f_i^t\right) - S_j^b \right\|_1^1 \qquad (7)$$

where $i \in \{1 \ldots |X_t|\}$, $T_{p_i}^t$ target domain image prediction label map, $b \in T_{P_i}^t \cap B$.

It is necessary to find disconnected regions for each foreground class in the label map $T$ to generate an instance mask of the foreground classes. Thus, the semantic regions within the class can be roughly divided into multiple foreground classes instances. Let $n \in N$ be the foreground class, and $o_{n_i}$ be the $i$'th ($i \in$

$\{1, \ldots, m\}$) binary mask of the connected area of the foreground class $n$. The instance-level feature representation of each foreground class is generated for each image by the following formula:

$$O_n = \{o_{n_1}, o_{n_2}, \ldots, o_{n_m}\} = I(T, n) \tag{8}$$

$$Q(o, f) = \frac{\sum_{h,w} o^{h,w} f^{h,w}}{\max\left(\varepsilon, \sum_{h,w} o^{h,w}\right)} \tag{9}$$

where $I$ is the operation of finding disconnected regions of foreground class $n$ in label map $T$, and $Q$ is used to generate the instance-level feature representation of foreground classes. Finally, by minimizing the following foreground classes loss functions, the instance-level features of the foreground classes of the target domain can be pulled to the vicinity of the instance-level feature samples in the classes closest to the source domain:

$$L_f = \sum_i \sum_{n \in N} \frac{1}{O_n^t} \sum_{o^t \in O_n^t} \min_j \left\| Q\left(o^t, f_i^t\right) - S_j^n \right\|_1^1 \tag{10}$$

where $S_j^n$ is the $j$'th semantic feature sample of foreground class $n$ in the source domain, $i \in \{1 \ldots |X_t|\}$, $O_n^t = I\left(T_{p_i}^t, n\right)$.

## 2.3  Self-supervised Learning

We use a self-supervised learning method to generate pseudo labels for the unlabeled target domain to improve the adaptation of the segmentation network to the source domain. As shown in Fig. 2, we first need to train a model based on the source image $x_s$ and its ground truth labels $y_s$ and the target image $x_t$ to generate pseudo labels for the target domain. Then, using the trained model, for the image $x_t$ in the target domain, the one-hot encoding pseudo labels $\hat{y}_t$ is generated by assigning the label of each pixel to the class with the largest prediction probability.

$$\hat{y}_t = \arg\max_{c \in C} \|_{[P_t^c > y_t^c]} \left(E\left(f_t\right)^c\right) \tag{11}$$

where $\|$ is a function, which means that when the condition is true, it returns the input; if the condition is false, it returns an irrelevant symbol. $y_t^c$ is the confidence threshold of class $c$. After we add pseudo labels to the target domain, we retrain our model. For the target domain, there is the following segmentation loss based on cross entropy:

$$L_t\left(x_t, \hat{y}_t\right) = -\sum_{h,w,c} \hat{y}_t^{h,w,c} \log\left(P_t^{h,w,c}\right) \tag{12}$$

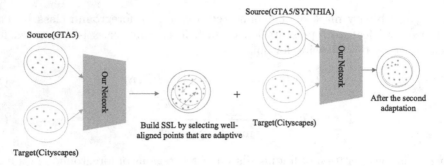

**Fig. 2.** Construction of SSL collection and training process.

## 2.4   Spatial and Channel Parallel Attention Module

At present, the convolutional neural network is used as the standard method of image classification. Its convolutional layer captures the local spatial features of all input channels through convolution kernels, and jointly encodes the feature maps of the channels and spatial information. Although there has been work to improve the joint encoding of channel and spatial information. However, little work has been done to explore the independent encoding of channels and spatial patterns. The SE [5] module eliminates spatial dependence through the operation of global average pooling, and excites and reweights along the channel. However, this attention method only explicitly models the dependency relationship between channel features. However, spatial location information is also important for dense prediction tasks such as semantic segmentation.

As shown in Fig. 3, we introduced the parallel spatial and channel attention module scSE, where cSE is adjusted on the basis of the SE module, and a spatial attention module sSE is added. In this way, the feature map is recalibrated along the channel and spatial direction respectively, which stimulates more information on the channel and spatial of the feature map. We assume that $X \in R^{H \times W \times C}$ is the feature map group obtained through a series of convolutional layers, and $H$, $W$ and $C$ correspond to its height, width and number of channels respectively. In addition, the visible feature map group $X = \{X_1, X_2, \ldots, X_c\}$ along the channel direction, where $x_i \in R^{H \times W}$ is represented as each single channel feature map.

To avoid the evaluation of the weight of the channel, due to the size of the convolution kernel, the extraction information range of the local receptive field is too small, and the amount of reference information is insufficient, which makes the evaluation inaccurate. Therefore, it is necessary to fuse the position information of the entire map of a single channel feature map. For the spatial squeeze and channel excitation module cSE in Fig. 3(a), the feature map group $X$ is first subjected to a spatial squeeze operation, which uses global average pooling to change the feature map spatial size to $1 \times 1$, and the channel is still $C$ Feature map. This global pooling produces channel statistics. The statistics

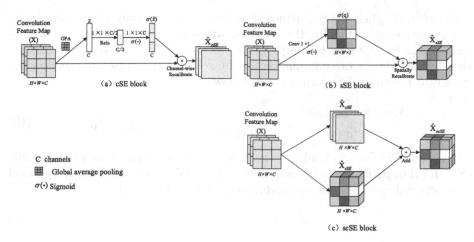

**Fig. 3.** Spatial and channel parallel attention module network structure. (a) is the spatial Squeeze and channel excitation module (cSE), (b) is the channel Squeeze and spatial excitation module (sSE), (c) scSE is the parallel structure of cSE and sSE.

$z \in R^{1 \times 1 \times C}$ is generated by scaling $X$ with $H \times W$ dimensions. Here, the calculation process of the $k$'th element of $z$ is as follows:

$$z_k = \frac{1}{H \times W} \sum_i^H \sum_j^W x_k(i, j) \tag{13}$$

In order to capture the dependencies between channels, prevent the model from becoming too complex and enhance its generalization ability. The vector $z$ obtained by global average pooling is passed through a fully connected layer $W_1 \in R^{1 \times 1 \times C/2}$ and a Relu activation layer $\delta(\cdot)$, and then through a fully connected layer $W_2 \in R^{1 \times 1 \times C}$. The channel dependency is encoded. Finally, the activation value is obtained by the sigmoid activation function $\sigma(\cdot)$, and the value in the channel is recalibrated using the activation value, thereby ignoring the unimportant channel. The formula is as follows:

$$\hat{X}_{cSE} = F_{cSE}(z, W) = \sigma\left(W_2 \delta\left(W_1 z\right)\right) \tag{14}$$

The structure of the channel squeeze and spatial excitation module scSE, which is important for fine-grained image semantic segmentation, is shown in Fig. 3(b). We consider an alternative slicing of the input tensor $X = \left(X^{1,1}, X^{1,2}, \ldots X^{i,j}, \ldots X^{H,W}\right)$, where $x$ is corresponding to the spatial location (i,j) with $i \in \{1, 2, \ldots, H\}$ and $j \in \{1, 2, \ldots, W\}$. The process first uses $1 \times 1$ convolution $q = W_{sq} * X$ to perform squeeze dimensionality reduction in the channel direction, so that its dimension changes from $H \times W \times C$ to $H \times W \times 1$ features, the weight $W_{sq} \in R^{1 \times 1 \times C}$, the generated projection tensor $q \in R^{H \times W}$ and each $q^{i,j}$ represents the linear combination of all channels $C$ at the spatial position $(i, j)$. Then use the sigmoid function $\sigma(\cdot)$ to activate the obtained spatial attention map. Finally, the obtained attention map is directly applied to the original feature map to complete the calibration of the spatial information, thereby providing more information for the relevant positions and ignoring the irrelevant positions. The formula is as follow:

$$
\begin{aligned}
\hat{X}_{sSE} &= F_{sSE}(q, x) \\
&= \left[ \sigma\left(q^{1,1}\right) x^{1,1}, \ldots, \sigma\left(q^{i,j}\right) x^{i,j}, \ldots, \sigma\left(q^{H,W}\right) x^{H,W} \right]
\end{aligned}
\tag{15}
$$

As shown in Fig. 3(c), adding the elements of the channel attention module cSE and the spatial attention module sSE obtained above, the following parallel channels and spatial attention module scSE can be obtained:

$$
\hat{X}_{scSE} = \hat{X}_{cSE} + \hat{X}_{sSE}
\tag{16}
$$

## 3   Experiments

### 3.1   Experimental Results

To reflect the superiority of the proposed method, we conducted the experiments on two domain adaptative segmentation benchmarks. The experimental results are compared with the existing advanced methods. All experiments are carried out under standard settings and mIoU metric is used.

Table 1 shows the comparison between our method and existing domain adaptative semantic segmentation methods in GTA5 to Cityscapes. After introducing the spatial and channel parallel attention module scSE and adding the pseudo labels SSL, compared with the baseline model AdaptSegNet, its segmentation performance is improved by 6.2%. After adding foreground and background loss SIM, its performance is improved by 6.7% compared with the baseline model. It is worth noting that although we have adopted the same method as BDL [9] to produce pseudo labels for the target domain. But in the BDL method, CycleGAN is used to translate source domain images into target domain images for training, thereby reducing the difference between the source domain and the target domain. But this conversion method is very cumbersome and adds a lot of training time. Therefore, we did not use this translated source image and achieved better segmentation results than the BDL method. Figure 4 shows the visualization results we got using each part separately. The red box marks the better part of our method segmentation. It can be seen from the figure that our method has greater advantages compared with the baseline model AdaptSeg.

Table 2 lists the comparison between our proposed method in SYNTHIA to Citycapes and some existing methods. We give the segmentation results of 16 classes $(mIoU_{16})$ and 13 classes $(mIoU_{13}^*)$ respectively. It can be seen that after introducing the scSE module and adding pseudo labels to the target domain, the performance of our segmentation results on 13 classes is improved by 10.4% compared with the baseline model AdaptSeg. After the introduction of foreground and background loss and Focal Loss, the segmentation performance on

**Table 1.** Semantic segmentation performance results (mIoU) for GTA5 to Cityscapes

| Models | Road | SW | Build | Wall | Fence | Pole | TL | TS | Veg. | Terrain | Sky | PR | Rider | Car | Truck | Bus | Train | Motor | Bike | mIoU |
|---|---|---|---|---|---|---|---|---|---|---|---|---|---|---|---|---|---|---|---|---|
| Luo et al. [11] | 88.5 | 35.4 | 79.5 | 26.3 | 24.3 | 28.5 | 32.5 | 18.3 | 81.2 | 40.0 | 76.5 | 58.1 | 25.8 | 82.6 | 30.3 | 34.4 | 3.4 | 21.6 | 21.5 | 42.6 |
| Luo et el. [12] | 87.0 | 27.1 | 79.6 | 27.3 | 23.3 | 28.3 | 35.5 | 24.2 | 83.6 | 27.4 | 74.2 | 58.6 | 28.0 | 76.2 | 33.1 | 36.7 | **6.7** | 31.9 | 31.4 | 43.2 |
| Chen et al. [1] | 89.4 | 43.0 | 82.1 | 30.5 | 21.3 | 30.3 | 34.7 | 24.0 | **85.3** | 39.4 | 78.2 | 63.0 | 22.9 | 84.6 | 36.4 | 43.0 | 5.5 | **34.7** | 33.5 | 46.4 |
| Tsai et al. [18] | 92.3 | **51.9** | 82.1 | 29.2 | 25.1 | 24.5 | 33.8 | 33.0 | 82.4 | 32.8 | 82.2 | 58.6 | 27.2 | 84.3 | 33.4 | 46.3 | 2.2 | 29.5 | 32.3 | 46.5 |
| Subhani et al. [16] | 90.2 | 40.0 | 83.5 | 31.9 | 26.4 | 32.6 | 38.7 | 37.5 | 81.0 | 34.2 | 84.6 | 61.6 | 33.4 | 82.5 | 32.8 | 45.9 | **6.7** | 29.1 | 30.6 | 47.5 |
| Li et al. [9] | 91.0 | 44.7 | 84.2 | **34.6** | 27.6 | 30.2 | 36.0 | 36.0 | 85.0 | **43.6** | 83.0 | 58.6 | 31.6 | 83.3 | 35.3 | 49.7 | 3.3 | 28.8 | 35.6 | 48.5 |
| Huang et al. [6] | **92.4** | 55.3 | 82.3 | 31.2 | 29.1 | 32.5 | 33.2 | 35.6 | 83.5 | 34.8 | 84.2 | 58.9 | 32.2 | 84.7 | 40.6 | 46.1 | 2.1 | 31.1 | 32.7 | 48.6 |
| Baseline [17] | 86.5 | 36.0 | 79.9 | 23.4 | 23.3 | 23.9 | 35.2 | 14.8 | 83.4 | 33.3 | 75.6 | 58.5 | 27.6 | 73.7 | 32.5 | 35.4 | 3.9 | 30.1 | 28.1 | 42.4 |
| Ours (scSE+SSL) | 89.4 | 42.6 | 84.4 | 26.8 | 31.6 | 32.2 | 40.7 | 33.3 | 85.0 | 39.2 | 84.7 | 60.9 | 33.3 | 80.6 | 36.8 | 49.0 | 0.7 | 32.9 | 39.2 | 48.6 |
| Ours (scSE+SSL+SIM) | 91.0 | 45.6 | 84.4 | 30.6 | **32.6** | 32.7 | 39.3 | 32.1 | 83.1 | 32.1 | **86.0** | 59.9 | **33.7** | 81.6 | **40.7** | **54.6** | 4.5 | 33.2 | 37.2 | **49.1** |

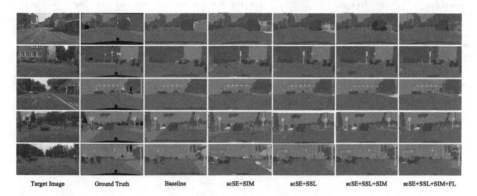

Target Image   Ground Truth   Baseline   scSE+SIM   scSE+SSL   scSE+SSL+SIM   scSE+SSL+SIM+FL

**Fig. 4.** Qualitative result

13 classes is improved by 11.1% compared with the baseline model. Judging from the segmentation results of 16 classes and 13 classes, our model has greater advantages than existing advanced methods. As shown in Fig. 2, the pseudo labels mainly added for the target domain are generated based on the model trained from GTA5 to Cityscapes, instead of directly using the model trained on SYNTHIA to Cityscapes to produce pseudo labels for the target domain. This has the advantage of using the migration method and making more use of the knowledge learned in GTA5 to Cityscapes training to generate pseudo labels for the target domain, so as to guide the training on SYNTHIA to Cityscapes.

### 3.2 Ablation Studies

We show in Table 3 the impact of each part on GTA5 (mIOU 19 classes) and SYNTHIA (mIOU* 13 classes) to Cityscapes tasks. On the two source domain datasets, the use of the spatial and channel attention module scSE and the pseudo labels SSL brings 6.2% and 10.4% improvement in segmentation accuracy compared with the baseline model AdaptSeg. When the SIM is used to distinguish the foreground classes and the background classes, the adaptation task of GTA5 to Cityscapes has increased by 0.3%, and the 13 classes on the task of SYNTHIA to Cityscapes have increased by 0.4%.

**Table 2.** Semantic segmentation performance results (mIoU) for SYNTHIA to Cityscapes

| Models | Road | SW | Build | Wall | Fence | Pole | TL | TS | Veg. | Sky | PR | Rider | Car | Bus | Motor | Bike | mIoU₁₆ | mIoU*₁₃ |
|---|---|---|---|---|---|---|---|---|---|---|---|---|---|---|---|---|---|---|
| SIBAN [11] | 82.5 | 24.0 | 79.4 | - | - | - | 16.5 | 12.7 | 79.2 | 82.8 | 58.3 | 18.0 | 79.3 | 25.3 | 17.6 | 25.9 | - | 46.3 |
| Tsai et al. [18] | 82.4 | 38.0 | 78.6 | 8.7 | 0.6 | 26.0 | 3.9 | 11.1 | 75.5 | 84.6 | 53.5 | 21.6 | 71.4 | 32.6 | 19.3 | 31.7 | 40.0 | 46.5 |
| CLAN [12] | 81.3 | 37.0 | 80.1 | - | - | - | 16.1 | 13.7 | 78.2 | 81.5 | 53.4 | 21.2 | 73.0 | 32.9 | 22.6 | 30.7 | - | 47.8 |
| Chen et al. [1] | 82.9 | 40.7 | 80.3 | 10.2 | 0.8 | 25.8 | 12.8 | 18.2 | 82.5 | 82.2 | 53.1 | 18.0 | 79.0 | 31.4 | 10.4 | 35.6 | 41.4 | 48.2 |
| LSE [16] | 82.9 | 43.1 | 78.1 | 9.3 | 0.6 | 28.2 | 9.1 | 14.4 | 77.0 | 83.5 | 58.1 | 25.9 | 71.9 | 38.0 | 29.4 | 31.2 | 42.6 | 49.4 |
| CrCDA [6] | 86.2 | 44.9 | 79.5 | 8.3 | 0.7 | 27.8 | 9.4 | 11.8 | 78.6 | 86.5 | 57.2 | 26.1 | 76.8 | 39.9 | 21.5 | 32.1 | 42.9 | 50.0 |
| Zou et al. [26] | 67.7 | 32.2 | 73.9 | 10.7 | 1.6 | **37.4** | 22.2 | 31.2 | 80.8 | 80.5 | 60.8 | 29.1 | 82.8 | 25.0 | 19.4 | 45.3 | 43.8 | 50.1 |
| BDL [9] | 86.0 | 46.7 | 80.3 | - | - | - | 14.1 | 11.6 | 79.2 | 81.3 | 54.1 | 27.9 | 73.7 | 42.2 | 25.7 | 45.3 | - | 51.4 |
| Wang et al. [20] | 84.5 | 40.1 | 83.1 | 4.8 | 0.0 | 34.3 | 20.1 | 27.2 | **84.8** | 84.0 | 53.5 | 22.6 | 85.4 | 43.7 | 26.8 | 27.8 | 45.2 | 52.5 |
| Yang et al. [21] | 86.4 | 41.3 | 79.3 | - | - | - | 22.6 | 17.3 | 80.3 | 81.6 | 56.9 | 21.0 | 84.1 | 49.1 | 24.6 | 45.7 | - | 53.1 |
| Zheng et al. [24] | 83.1 | 38.2 | 81.7 | 9.3 | 1.0 | 35.1 | **30.3** | 19.9 | 82.0 | 80.1 | **62.8** | 21.1 | 84.4 | 37.8 | 24.5 | **53.3** | 46.5 | 53.8 |
| Kang et al. [7] | 82.6 | 29.0 | 81.0 | 11.2 | 0.2 | 33.6 | 24.9 | 18.3 | 82.8 | 82.3 | 62.1 | 26.5 | **85.6** | 48.9 | 26.8 | 52.2 | 46.8 | 54.0 |
| Baseline [17] | 84.3 | 42.7 | 77.5 | - | - | - | 4.7 | 7.0 | 77.9 | 82.5 | 54.3 | 21.0 | 72.3 | 32.2 | 18.9 | 32.3 | - | 46.7 |
| Ours (SSL+scSE) | 89.0 | 43.6 | 83.6 | 31.2 | 25.7 | 30.4 | 28.3 | 26.5 | 82.9 | **87.0** | 60.8 | **33.4** | 81.9 | 52.2 | **34.0** | 38.6 | 51.8 | 57.1 |
| Ours (scSE+SSL+SIM+FL) | **90.4** | **47.7** | **84.0** | **33.3** | **26.4** | 31.0 | 29.2 | **32.2** | 83.3 | 84.3 | 61.0 | 32.8 | 82.2 | **56.1** | 31.2 | 36.0 | **52.6** | **57.8** |

**Table 3.** Ablation study on the adaptation from GTA5 and SYNTHIA dataset to Cityscapes dataset.

| GTA5 and SYNTHIA to Cityscapes | | | | |
|---|---|---|---|---|
| scSE | SSL | SIM | mIoU₍GTA5₎ | mIoU*₍SYN₎ |
| | | | 42.4 | 46.7 |
| ✓ | | ✓ | 44.5 | 48.0 |
| ✓ | ✓ | | 48.6 | 57.1 |
| ✓ | ✓ | ✓ | 49.1 | 57.8 |

### 3.3 Hyperparameters Analysis

We discuss the influence of the hyperparameter $\lambda_{FL}$ on the experiment when $\gamma = 3$ is set in Table 4. The value of $\gamma$ is obtained through experiments. From the experimental results, when the value of $\lambda_{FL}$ is 0.1, it has the best effect. A value that is too small will make the Focal Loss account for a relatively small portion of the overall loss, which will not contribute much to the difficult-to- segment samples. Furthermore, we discussed in Table 5 the attention degree of different values of $\gamma$ to the difficult-to-segment sample classes when $\lambda_{FL} = 0.1$. When $\gamma = 0$, Focal Loss is the cross entropy loss, so this value is useless to us. As $\gamma$ increases, the modulation factor also increases. The smooth adjust- ment of the parameter $\gamma$ reduces the weight ratio of the easy-to-segment sam- ple classes, so more attention is paid to the difficult-to-segment sample classes.But a too large $\gamma$value will excessively restrict easy-to-classify samples. It is found through experiments that a value of 3 for $\gamma$ is the best for our method.

**Table 4.** Ablation studies the influence of hyperparameter $\lambda_{FL}$.

| GTA5 to Cityscapes | | | | |
|---|---|---|---|---|
| $\lambda_{FL}$ | 1 | 0.5 | 0.1 | 0.05 | 0.01 |
| $mIoU$ | 47.8 | 48.5 | 49.1 | 48.7 | 48.9 |

**Table 5.** Influence of parameter $\gamma$.

| GTA5 to Cityscapes | | | | |
|---|---|---|---|---|
| $\gamma$ | 1 | 2 | 3 | 4 | 5 |
| $mIoU$ | 48.6 | 48.8 | 49.1 | 48.4 | 47.6 |

## 4  Conclusion

We present an adaptative semantic segmentation method based on fine-grained alignment is proposed, which is based on the original two-level adversarial network. First, we use a self-supervised learning method to generate pseudo labels for the target domain, and use the pseudo labels to better align the two domains. Then the foreground classes and the background classes are aligned separately, which takes a more detailed account of the inter-domain difference in the spatial distribution between the source domain and the target domain. Finally, the channel and spatial parallel attention module not only enables the feature extractor to capture the dependency between useful channels in the convolution process, but also pays more attention to the spatial position information, which is more important for fine-grained semantic segmentation, in the spatial direction. Experiments prove that our method has obvious advantages over the existing advanced methods.

**Acknowledgment.** This work is supported by the National Natural Science Foundation of China (Nos. 61966004,61866004), the Guangxi Natural Science Foundation (No. 2019GXNSFDA245018), the Guangxi "Bagui Scholar" Teams for Innovation and Research Project.

## References

1. Chen, M., Xue, H., Cai, D.: Domain adaptation for semantic segmentation with maximum squares loss. In: ICCV, pp. 2090–2099 (2019)
2. Chen, Y., Li, W., Van Gool, L.: Road: reality oriented adaptation for semantic segmentation of urban scenes. In: CVPR, pp. 7892–7901 (2018)
3. Cordts, M., et al.: The cityscapes dataset for semantic urban scene understanding. In: CVPR, pp. 3213–3223 (2016)
4. Hoffman, J., Wang, D., Yu, F., Darrell, T.: FCNs in the wild: pixel-level adversarial and constraint-based adaptation. arXiv preprint arXiv:1612.02649 (2016)
5. Hu, J., Shen, L., Sun, G.: Squeeze-and-excitation networks. In: CVPR, pp. 7132–7141 (2018)
6. Huang, J., Lu, S., Guan, D., Zhang, X.: Contextual-relation consistent domain adaptation for semantic segmentation. In: ECCV, pp. 705–722 (2020)
7. Kang, G., Wei, Y., Yang, Y., Zhuang, Y., Hauptmann, A.G.: Pixel-level cycle association: a new perspective for domain adaptive semantic segmentation. arXiv preprint arXiv:2011.00147 (2020)

8. Laine, S., Aila, T.: Temporal ensembling for semi-supervised learning. arXiv preprint arXiv:1610.02242 (2016)
9. Li, Y., Yuan, L., Vasconcelos, N.: Bidirectional learning for domain adaptation of semantic segmentation. In: CVPR, pp. 6936–6945 (2019)
10. Lin, T.Y., Goyal, P., Girshick, R., He, K., Dollár, P.: Focal loss for dense object detection. In: ICCV, pp. 2980–2988 (2017)
11. Luo, Y., Liu, P., Guan, T., Yu, J., Yang, Y.: Significance-aware information bottleneck for domain adaptive semantic segmentation. In: ICCV, pp. 6778–6787 (2019)
12. Luo, Y., Zheng, L., Guan, T., Yu, J., Yang, Y.: Taking a closer look at domain shift: category-level adversaries for semantics consistent domain adaptation. In: CVPR, pp. 2507–2516 (2019)
13. Richter, S.R., Vineet, V., Roth, S., Koltun, V.: Playing for data: ground truth from computer games. In: ECCV, pp. 102–118 (2016)
14. Ros, G., Sellart, L., Materzynska, J., Vazquez, D., Lopez, A.M.: The synthia dataset: a large collection of synthetic images for semantic segmentation of urban scenes. In: CVPR, pp. 3234–3243 (2016)
15. Roy, A.G., Navab, N., Wachinger, C.: Concurrent spatial and channel 'squeeze & excitation 'in fully convolutional networks. In: ICMICCAI, pp. 421–429 (2018)
16. Subhani, M.N., Ali, M.: Learning from scale-invariant examples for domain adaptation in semantic segmentation. arXiv preprint arXiv:2007.14449 (2020)
17. Tsai, Y.H., Hung, W.C., Schulter, S., Sohn, K., Yang, M.H., Chandraker, M.: Learning to adapt structured output space for semantic segmentation. In: CVPR, pp. 7472–7481 (2018)
18. Tsai, Y.H., Sohn, K., Schulter, S., Chandraker, M.: Domain adaptation for structured output via discriminative patch representations. In: ICCV, pp. 1456–1465 (2019)
19. Tzeng, E., Hoffman, J., Saenko, K., Darrell, T.: Adversarial discriminative domain adaptation. In: CVPR, pp. 7167–7176 (2017)
20. Wang, H., Shen, T., Zhang, W., Duan, L.Y., Mei, T.: Classes matter: a fine-grained adversarial approach to cross-domain semantic segmentation. In: ECCV, pp. 642–659 (2020)
21. Yang, J., Xu, R., Li, R., Qi, X., Shen, X., Li, G., Lin, L.: An adversarial perturbation oriented domain adaptation approach for semantic segmentation. In: Proceedings of the AAAI Conference on Artificial Intelligence, vol. 34, pp. 12613–12620 (2020)
22. Zhang, H., Goodfellow, I., Metaxas, D., Odena, A.: Self-attention generative adversarial networks. In: ICML, pp. 7354–7363 (2019)
23. Zhang, J., Li, Z., Zhang, C., Ma, H.: Stable self-attention adversarial learning for semi-supervised semantic image segmentation. J. Vis. Commun. Image Represent. **78**, 103170 (2021)
24. Zheng, Z., Yang, Y.: Rectifying pseudo label learning via uncertainty estimation for domain adaptive semantic segmentation. Int. J. Comput. Vis. **129**, 1106–1120 (2021)
25. Zou, Y., Yu, Z., Kumar, B., Wang, J.: Unsupervised domain adaptation for semantic segmentation via class-balanced self-training. In: ECCV, pp. 289–305 (2018)
26. Zou, Y., Yu, Z., Liu, X., Kumar, B., Wang, J.: Confidence regularized self-training. In: ICCV, pp. 5982–5991 (2019)

# Hypergraph Variational Autoencoder for Multimodal Semi-supervised Representation Learning

Jingquan Liu, Xiaoyong Du, Yuanzhe Li, and Weidong Hu[✉]

National Key Laboratory of Science and Technology on Automatic Target Recognition, National University of Defense Technology, Changsha, China
wdhu@nudt.edu.cn

**Abstract.** In many real-world settings, the external environment is perceived through multi-modal information, such as visual, radar, lidar, etc. Naturally, the fact motivates us to exploit interaction intra modals and integrate multiple source information using limited labels on the multimodal dataset as a semi-supervised task. A challenging issue in multimodal semi-supervised learning is the complicated correlations under pairwise modalities. In this paper, we propose a hypergraph variational autoencoder (HVAE) which can mine high-order interaction of multimodal data and introduce extra prior knowledge for inferring multimodal fusion representation. On one hand, the hypergraph structure can represent high-order data correlation in multimodal scenes. On the other hand, a prior distribution is introduced by mask-based variational inference to enhance multi-modal characterization. Moreover, the variational lower bound is leveraged to collaborate semi-supervised learning. We conduct experiments on semi-supervised visual object recognition task, and extensive experiments on two datasets demonstrate the superiority of our method against the existing baselines.

**Keywords:** Hypergraph · Multimodal · Semi-supervised

## 1 Introduction

Multimodal machine learning becomes increasing prevailing in community with the explosion of data, and multimodality comes in many different manifestations such as multi-source information, multi-sensor data, multi-view object, etc. For example, the visual question answering (VQA) [1] task attended to leverage two modalities, visual and textual, to jointly represent a complicated scene. Multimodal objection detection [2] enhanced the performance of model with fusing the information from different sensors, and multiview objection classification [3] observed the target by different views to model different modalities. However, the labeling of multimodal data is more time-consuming and more expansive than normal unimodal data. So it is necessary to study how to mine the interaction of multimodal data under missing labels as a semi-supervised task. The

E. Pimenidis et al. (Eds.): ICANN 2022, LNCS 13532, pp. 395–406, 2022.
https://doi.org/10.1007/978-3-031-15937-4_33

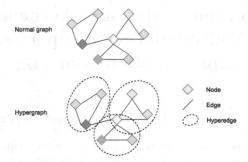

**Fig. 1.** High-order interactions between datapoints. Each node denotes a datapoint feature, and a hyperedge linking several nodes represent higher-order correlation than normal graph.

challenge of this work focus on two aspects: 1) how to effectively mine high-order correlation of multimodal samples in the absence of large supervision labels; 2) how to introduce the extra prior information for multimodal fusion to enhance representational capacity of data.

Multimodal semi-supervised learning has been researched widely in various application areas, e.g., an early work [4] combined Multiple Kernel Learning (MKL) and support vector machines (SVM) to train a classifier with tags for image classification task, where labeled and unlabeled images are associated with keywords to improve the performance of classifier. And a recent work [5] proposed a semi-supervised multi-modal emotion recognition model, which matched the cross-modality distribution. Moreover, an end-to-end semi-supervised multi-modal deep learning framework [6] was designed to recognize the RGB-D object by training on limited labeled data. All the above work belongs to inductive methods, but recently, a number of work emphasized on semi-supervised learning as a transductive method [7]. For example, in [8,9], a spectral convolution was integrated with neural network called graph convolution network (GCN) to predict attribute of node or linking relationship on graph-structures data. In [10], transductive zero-shot learning was introduced to reduce model-bias of unseen classes for object detection.

Multimodal fusion is the core question of multimodal learning, past works fuse features of different modalities by leveraging deep network to learn a latent representation [11–14]. Recently, hypergraph has been employed to model high-order correlation among data as show in Fig. 1. For example, in [15], a hypergraph neural network(HGNN) was presented which handles the data interaction by learning a hidden layer representation and conducting on visual object recognition task. In [16,17], the attention mechanism was introduced in hypergraph to resolve disparity between modalities. In [18], a multi-channel hypergraph convolutional network was proposed to enhance relationship in social recommendation. Moreover, in [19], Sun *et al.* proposed a representation learning framework for heterogeneous hypergraphs which can characterize high-order non-pairwise relationships. In [30], Chen *et al.* explored a multimodal fusion method to integrate multimodal data with incompleteness in heterogeneous graph structure. Nevertheless, most of them neglected the prior knowledge of correlation that can be introduced in the process to improve representational capacity on multimodal data.

A joint representation can be learned from latent space using multimodal generative models, such as variational autoencoder [20], deriving a meaningful latent representation from each modality. On one hand, generative models not only get a low dimensional representation from high dimensional modalities, but also can transfer into semi-supervised task as an unsupervised method [21]. On the other hand, it is important that an extra prior is introduced utilizing variational inference technology by fitting a distribution. But traditional variational autoencoder is hard to encode higher-order correlation of multi-modal data, and it also ignored this relationship between multimodal data.

Therefore, to cope with these challenging issues, we propose a novel hypergraph variational autoencoder (HVAE) for multimodal semi-supervised representation learning as shown in Fig. 2. Similar to a normal graph, a hypergraph is considered as a more superior method when learning from multi-modal data, which can integrate the high-order interaction in hypergraph structure and map the correlationship among different modalities to a latent correlation matrix. First, contrast to traditional generative models, HVAE encodes the latent fusion vector through multiple hypergraph convolution networks, the convolution operation is defined by the Laplacian matrix which map node feature to latent space. Then, a standard Gaussian distribution is introduced by mask-based inference model as the prior of latent joint representation of multi-modal fusion. Besides, we reconstruct hypergraph structure from latent fusion features in generative model, and the variational lower bound is verified to narrow the gap between training set and validation set.

To sum up, the main contribution of this paper are:

- A transductive model HVAE is proposed for multimodal representation learning on hypergraph, in which the high-order interaction among modalities is constructed.
- By leveraging a mask-based inference model, the prior distribution of latent variables is introduced to effectively infer the representation of multimodal fusion.
- The variational lower bound is collaborated to boost the performance of semi-supervised learning as an unsupervised loss function, and the experiments validate its effectiveness.

## 2    Preliminary

### 2.1    Introduction of Hypergraph

The hypergraph structure is a special form of topological graph in which a hyperedge has several vertexes, a hypergraph is defined as $\mathcal{G} = (\mathcal{V}, \mathcal{E}, \mathbf{W})$. Here, the

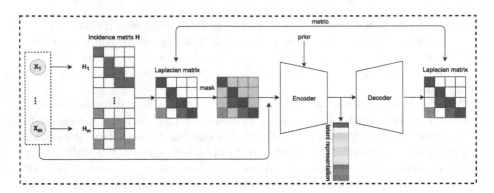

**Fig. 2.** Overall of the proposed Hypergraph Variational Autoencoder (HVAE), the bright color in matrix denote the linking relationship between nodes. The goal of HVAE is to infer an effective latent representation, so that the weak correlationship which the white color element denotes is masked when encoding latent variables, and reconstruct the original Laplacian matrix utilizing decoder.

$\mathcal{V}$ and $\mathcal{E}$ denote a set of vertexes and a set of hyperedges, and the hyperedge weight is represented by the diagonal matrix $\mathbf{W}$. Generally, the linking relationship on hypergraph $\mathcal{G}$ can be described by an incidence matrix, and the every entry defined as:

$$h(v,e) = \begin{cases} 1, & v \in e \\ 0, & otherwise \end{cases} \quad (1)$$

where the $h(v,e)$ is interpreted to the possibility of a vertex $v$ belongs to the hyperedge $e$. The degree of the hyperedge $e$ is defined as $\delta(e) = \sum_{v \in \mathcal{V}} h(v,e)$, similarity, the degree of the vertex is defined as $d(v) = \sum_{e \in \mathcal{E}} w(e)h(v,e)$. Respectively, let $\mathbf{D}_e$ and $\mathbf{D}_v$ denote diagonal matrices of the hyperedge's degrees and the vertex's degrees. Further, the hypergraph convolution(hgcn) can be formulated as a Laplacian mapping as introduced by [22]:

$$\mathbf{X}^{l+1} = \mathbf{D}_v^{-1/2}\mathbf{H}\mathbf{W}\mathbf{D}_e^{-1}\mathbf{H}^\mathsf{T}\mathbf{D}_v^{-1/2}\mathbf{X}^l\boldsymbol{\Theta} \quad (2)$$

Let $\mathbf{L} = \mathbf{D}_v^{-1/2}\mathbf{H}\mathbf{W}\mathbf{D}_e^{-1}\mathbf{H}^\mathsf{T}\mathbf{D}_v^{-1/2}$ is a Laplacian matrix representing a latent correlationship among nodes. Here, $\mathbf{X}$ is the input features with n vertexes, $\boldsymbol{\Theta}$ is the learned parameter for training, and the obtained result can be leveraged for predicting classification. For writing convenience, we denote hypergraph convolution operation using notation $hgcn(\cdot)$ in the following paragraphs.

## 2.2 Constructing Hypergraph with Multimodal Data

The high-order relationship of multimodal data can be denoted by constructing a hypergraph. Given M modalities $\mathbf{X} = (\mathbf{X}_1, ..., \mathbf{X}_m)$, each modality can construct an incidence matrix $\mathbf{H}_i \in (\mathbf{H}_1, ..., \mathbf{H}_m)$. The multimodal hypergraph structure is represented by combining the incidence matrices of M modalities. For very vertex $v \in \mathcal{V}$ and hyperedge $e \in \mathcal{E}$, its linking relationship can be inferred by the distance between two neighbor features. Assume we have one modal feature of N data points be represented as $\mathbf{X}_i = [x^1, ..., x^n]$, the euclidean distances of features $d(x^i, x^j)$ need be first calculated. For constructing hyperedge, the K nearest neighbors(Knn) algorithm is performed to select a certain number of vertexes linking to each hyperedge [15]. It means each hyperedge has K+1 vertexes and N hyperedges are constructed from unimodal data. And the final multimodal hypergraph representation $\mathbf{H}$ is implemented by concatenating all $\mathbf{H}_i$ matrix, which denotes an adjacency relationship on multimodal hypergraph.

## 3  Method

### 3.1  Problem Statement

Assume we have an object from two different modalities: $x_1$ and $x_2$, we now derive a probabilistic modeling where the purpose is learning a posterior distribution $p(y|x_1, x_2)$ of label y from bimodal data. The model is achieved with introduction of latent variables z such that $p(y|x_1, x_2) = \int p(z|x_1, x_2)p(y|z, x_1, x_2)dz$. Firstly, $p(z|x_1, x_2)$ is the distribution of fusing bimodal $x_1$ and $x_2$ by an encoder module, which can capture high-order interaction, and $p(y|z, x_1, x_2)$ is the posterior probability for predicting label. Then, the inference model aim to learn a latent representation from multimodal data points parameterized by $\theta$, we also can rewrite formulation as

$$p(z|x_1, x_2) = \int p(\theta|x_1, x_2)p(z|x_1, x_2, \theta)d\theta \tag{3}$$

where $p(z|x_1, x_2, \theta)$ is the distribution of latent variables z learned by parameter $\theta$. According to Bayes rule, we infer the learnable latent representation of multimodal fusion as:

$$p(z|x_1, x_2, \theta) = \frac{p(x_1, x_2, \theta|z)p(z)}{p(x_1, x_2)} \\ \propto p(x_1, x_2, \theta|z)p(z) \tag{4}$$

Here $p(z)$ is a prior about fusing representation z. Therefore, we wish to introduce the prior information of latent variables to improve fusing performance of multimodal data. So the variational inference as a based method is leveraged to design our inference model for introducing prior knowledge, which is also our motivation of why considering inference model.

### 3.2  Mask-Based Inference Model

Inspired by variational graph autoencoder (VGAE) [23], a generative model for graph representation learning as the base model to infer our HVAE model for multimodal learning. Hypergraph convolution can be viewed as the Laplacian mapping which can map high-dimensional feature to low-dimensional space.

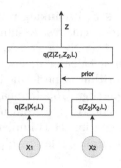

**Fig. 3.** Inference model for HVAE.eps

Actually, the sparse Laplacian matrix integrates a latent correlationship among indice matrices of hypergraph built by multimodal data, and the dense zeros value bring redundancy during training process. For better mining a latent correlation of multimodal data, we mask the weak link relationship in Laplacian matrix $\mathbf{L}$.

$$\overline{\mathbf{L}} = mask(l_{ij} < m), \ where \ l_{ij} \in (0,1) \tag{5}$$

Here $\overline{\mathbf{L}}$ denotes a masked Laplacian matrix which mask the tiny value and zeros value in matrix elements, and $mask(\cdot)$ represent a mask operation where $m$ is an upper bound of masking. As shown in Fig. 3, the proposed inference model generates latent representation by using two hgcn layers. We first extract multimodal initial representation as a hidden correlation, where $\mathbf{Z}_1$, $\mathbf{Z}_2$ is the hidden relevance representation, and $\mathbf{Z}_1 = hgcn_1(\mathbf{X}_1, \overline{\mathbf{L}})$, $\mathbf{Z}_2 = hgcn_2(\mathbf{X}_2, \overline{\mathbf{L}})$. Similar to VGAE, our inference model consider extra prior information of latent fusing representation by fitting a standard Gaussian distribution.

$$\begin{aligned} \mu &= hgcn_\mu(concat(\mathbf{Z}_1, \mathbf{Z}_2), \overline{\mathbf{L}}) \\ log\sigma &= hgcn_\sigma(concat(\mathbf{Z}_1, \mathbf{Z}_2), \overline{\mathbf{L}}) \end{aligned} \tag{6}$$

Here $\mu$ is the matrix of mean vector and $\sigma$ is the variance matrix, and the $concat(\cdot)$ denotes concatenation operation. For introducing prior of latent representation $\mathbf{Z}$, we also perform reparameterization trick [20] for training by sampling from $\epsilon \in \mathcal{N}(0,1)$.

### 3.3   Generative Model

Given an inferred latent variable Z, we reconstruct hyper-structure by inner product with itself:

$$p(\mathbf{L}|\mathbf{Z}) = \prod_{i=1}^{N} \prod_{j=1}^{N} p(l_{ij}|z_i, z_j) \tag{7}$$

Here $l_{ij} = \sigma(z_i^T z_j)$ and $\sigma(\cdot)$ is a sigmoid function. For achieving the hypergraph reconstructure, we leverage hypergraph Laplacian matrix which can denote the linking relationship on hypergraph and reconstruct Laplacian matrix by generative model. Similar to variational autoencoder(VAE) [20], the variational lower bound of hyper-structure generative model $\mathcal{L}_h$ is defined as

$$\mathcal{L}_h = \mathbb{E}_{q(\mathbf{Z}|\mathbf{X},\mathbf{L})}[\log p(\mathbf{L}|\mathbf{Z})] - \text{KL}[q(\mathbf{Z}|\mathbf{X},\mathbf{L})||p(\mathbf{Z})] \qquad (8)$$

where $\text{KL}(\cdot||\cdot)$ is the Kullback-Leibler divergence, which can reduce the gap between distribution $q(\cdot)$ and Gaussian prior $p(\cdot)$. And $\mathbb{E}_{q(\cdot)}[\log p(\cdot)]$ is the reconstructing error of hypergraph, the final loss function we optimized is:

$$\mathcal{L} = \lambda \mathcal{L}_s + (1 - \lambda)\mathcal{L}_h \qquad (9)$$

Here $\mathcal{L}_s$ is the cross-entropy loss of the semi-supervised label, and $\lambda$ is a hyperparameter for training.

## 4    Experiments

In this section, we evaluate our proposed HVAE on semi-supervised visual object classification task against other state-of-the-arts methods. Our experiments focus on two aspects: 1) The performance of HVAE for multimodal classification tasks with different percentages of labels. And, 2) The performance of HVAE compared with other baselines.

### 4.1    Dataset

In this experiments, our purpose is to verify the performance of fusion among multimodal features under few labels, so we use extracted features of data to deploy our experiments. We conduct our experiments on multi-view dataset ModelNet40 [24] and NTU datasets [25] to model multimodalities. ModelNet40 is a multi-view 3D dataset including 12311 CAD shapes across 40 different object categories. In ModelNet40 dataset, 80% objects are used for training and validation and 20% objects are used for testing. And NTU dataset is a multiple view description against 3D models containing 2012 objects from 67 categories where 603 datapoints are used for training and 373 datapoints are used for testing. Based on previous work [15], two different networks Multi-view Convolutional Neural Network (MVCNN) [28] and Group-View Convolutional Neural Network (GVCNN) [29] are used to extract different features of the same visual object, which can simulate two different modalities.

### 4.2    Experimental Settings

In the experiment, we deploy a transductive semi-supervised scenario on the hypergraph structure and compare our proposed HVAE against two categories of neural multimodal fusion method: inductive models including Tensor Fusion Network (TFN) [26], Low-rank Fusion Network (LFM) [27], and tranductive model including Graph Convolution Network (GCN) [8], Hypergraph Neural Network (HGNN) [15], Graph Auto-Encoder (GAE), Variational Graph Auto-Encoder (VGAE) [23]. We evaluate our method on different rates of labels compared to other model for future deploying on our application scene, and the test accuracy is calculated to show performance of model. We set ratio of labels in data sample as 30%, 20%, 15%, 10%, 2% for NTU dataset, and 0.2% to 1% with intermittent 0.2% for ModelNet40 dataset, which are implemented by randomly selecting the subset of labels from the training set. Since the dataset itself have no graph structure, so we manually construct multimodal hypergraph structure using extracted features and calculate linking relationship by Knn algorithm as described in Sect. 2.2, and K = 10 is set according our test. The dimension of hidden layer of HVAE is set as 128 and the dimension of latent representation is the number of category. And the drop rate p = 0.5 is employed to prevent overfitting, and the $\lambda$ is set as 0.4, we implement our model based on Pytorch1.7 and utilize Adam algorithm to optimize our loss function with the learning rate of 0.001.

**Table 1.** Experiments on NTU dataset with different ratio of labels

| Method | 30% | 20% | 15% | 10% | 2% |
|---|---|---|---|---|---|
| HGNN [15] | 83.1% | 80.6% | 78.5% | 75.8% | 46.9% |
| TFN [26] | 82.5% | 79.8% | 76.4% | 73.5% | 45.2% |
| LFM [27] | 82.8% | 79.3% | 77.4% | 72.9% | 44.7% |
| GCN [8] | 77.2% | 72.9% | 69.1% | 65.1% | 37.8% |
| GAE [23] | 73.5% | 70.5% | 67.8% | 64.1% | 42.4% |
| VGAE [23] | 77.7% | 74.3% | 69.2% | 66.2% | 39.4% |
| HVAE (ours) | **84.2%** | **81.2%** | **80.1%** | **76.9%** | **48.7%** |

**Table 2.** Experiments on Modelnet40 dataset with different ratio of labels

| Method | 1% | 0.8% | 0.6% | 0.4% | 0.2% |
|---|---|---|---|---|---|
| HGNN [15] | **95.1%** | 80.3% | 71.5% | 63.4% | 45.8% |
| TFN [26] | 92.1% | 76.5% | 67.7% | 62.4% | 43.5% |
| LFM [27] | 91.3% | 76.4% | 66.7% | 60.5% | 44.6% |
| GCN [8] | 67.3% | 56.5% | 51.3% | 47.6% | 34.1% |
| GAE [23] | 66.9% | 51.9% | 52.9% | 48.7% | 37.2% |
| VGAE [23] | 66.9% | 61.8% | 59.8% | 54.4% | 36.2% |
| HVAE (ours) | **95.1%** | **81.2%** | **72.4%** | **66.6%** | **48.5%** |

## 4.3    Result Analyses and Discussions

The experimental results show that the effectiveness of our proposed method on visual object semi-supervised classification task as shown in Table 1, Table 2 and Fig. 4. Compared to baselines, HVAE achieves best performance in different ratio of labels as shown in Fig. 4, for example, with 30% rates of labels, HVAE achieves gains of 1.1%, 1.8%, 7% compared with HGNN, LFM and GCN on NTU dataset. With 2% rates of labels, the HVAE achieves gains of 1.8% over the best baseline and 6.3% over the GAE on NTU dataset. For ModelNet40 dataset, the proposed HVAE method outperforms all presenting baselines methods. As shown in Table 2, when only 1% labels is used for training to fuse multimodal features, HVAE achieves 95.1% result nearing to completing labels. Compared to GCN, the HVAE achieves gains of 27.8% and 14.4% with 1% and 0.2% labels.

The hypergraph is constructed by employing Knn algorithm and can better represent complex correlations among data. Compared to traditional topological graph, a high-order relationship between different modalities can be captured. Besides, the mask-based inference model can infer effectively latent fusion representation of multimodal data. In our experiment, a standard Gaussian distribution is leveraged as prior knowledge, nevertheless, which may be unsuitable for other real scenes. So it is necessary to exploit how to introduce appropriate prior according to designed features and different settings for the future work.

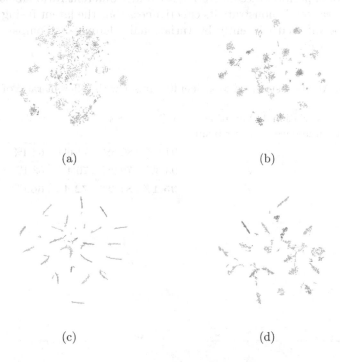

(a)                                          (b)

(c)                                          (d)

**Fig. 4.** 2D t-SNE visualization of data points choosing from testing set in ModelNet40 dataset, where contains forty classes in 2468 data points and the rates of labels is 1%. (a) Original features of mode one modeled by MVCNN. (b) Original features of mode two modeled by GVCNN. (c) Latent fusing representation obtained by HVAE. (d) Latent fusing representation without mask operation

## 4.4  Ablation

In this work, our contribution focuses on how to introduce prior information for fusing multimodel data and exploit high-order correlationship. Besides, the variational lower bound is collaborated to decrease the gap between training and testing. On one hand, mask-based variational inference can introduce a prior knowledge to improve fusing representation ability. On the other hand, hypergraph reconstructure can mine high-order interaction to exploit complicated relationship among data. So there are two questions: 1) Does introduced prior information for fusing representation and mask operation benefit to improve model's performance? 2) Is the variational inference beneficial for reduce the gap between training and testing? To investigate the effect of these parts, we evaluate our model on the condition without variational inference or variational lower bound under different ratio labels, and test the variational inference model with no mask. As shown in Table 3 and Fig. 5, the mask-based variational inference shows that the introduced prior information can improve the performance of model under semi-supervised situation. Further, the variational lower bound contribute to boost performance on testing set under different ratio labels. Besides, the mask operation demonstrate its effectiveness that the latent fusing representation can be inferred efficiently by variational inference as compared on Fig. 4(d) and Fig. 4(c).

**Table 3.** Ablation study on Modelnet40 dataset with different ratio of labels

| Mask operation | Variational inference | Variational lower bound | 1% | 0.8% | 0.6% | 0.4% | 0.2% |
|---|---|---|---|---|---|---|---|
| ✓ | | | 94.8% | 80.5% | 71.6% | 64.4% | 44.9% |
| | ✓ | ✓ | 93.3% | 79.2% | 70.4% | 63.1% | 45.9% |
| ✓ | ✓ | ✓ | **95.1%** | **81.2%** | **72.4%** | **66.6%** | **48.5%** |

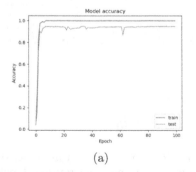

(a)

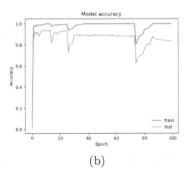

(b)

**Fig. 5.** Comparison on Moldelnet40 dataset. The left is the accuracy curve for training and testing with variational lower bound, and the right is accuracy curve without variational lower bound.

# 5    Conclusion

In this paper, we present a novel model named hypergraph variational autoencoder (HVAE) for multimodal semi-supervised representation learning, which is able to encode high-order correlations of modalities and fuse features of different modalities only using few labels. HVAE is a more general framework which can cope with the complex multimodal data and a latent correlation matrix is fully utilized to reconstruct representation of hypergraph through mask-based variational inference. We evaluate the proposed methods on 3D-visual dataset under semi-supervised condition, and the results perform better in terms of accuracy under different ratio labels than existing inductive and transductive methods.

# References

1. Antol, S., et al.: VQA: visual question answering. In: Proceedings of the IEEE International Conference on Computer Vision, pp. 2425–433 (2015)
2. Chen, Y.-T., Shi, J., Mertz, C., Kong, S., Ramanan, D.: Multimodal object detection via Bayesian fusion. arXiv preprint arXiv:2104.02904 (2021)
3. Qi, C.R., Su, H., Nießner, M., Dai, A., Yan, M., Guibas, L.J.: Volumetric and multi-view CNNs for object classification on 3D data. In: Proceedings of the IEEE Conference on Computer Vision and Pattern Recognition, pp. 5648–5656 (2015)
4. Guillaumin, J.V., Schmid, C.: Multimodal semi-supervised learning for image classification. In: IEEE Computer Society Conference on Computer Vision and Pattern Recognition, pp. 902–909. IEEE (2010)
5. Liang, J., Li, R., Jin, Q.: Semi-supervised multi-modal emotion recognition with cross-modal distribution matching. In: Proceedings of the 28th ACM International Conference on Multimedia, pp. 2852–2861 (2020)
6. Cheng, Y., Zhao, X., Cai, R., Li, Z., Huang, K., Rui, Z., et al.: Semi-supervised multimodal deep learning for RGB-D object recognition. In: IJCAI, pp. 3345–3351 (2016)
7. van Engelen, J.E., Hoos, H.H.: A survey on semi-supervised learning. Mach. Learn. **109**(2), 373–440 (2019). https://doi.org/10.1007/s10994-019-05855-6
8. Kipf, T.N., Welling, M.: Semi-supervised Classification with Graph Convolutional Networks. Toulon, France (2017)
9. Chiang, W.-L., Liu, X., Si, S., Li, Y., Bengio, S., Hsieh, C.-J. Cluster-GCN: an efficient algorithm for training deep and large graph convolutional networks. In: Proceedings of the 25th ACM SIGKDD International Conference on Knowledge Discovery & Data Mining, pp. 257–266 (2019)
10. Rahman, S., Khan, S., Barnes, N.: Transductive learning for zero-shot object detection. In: Proceedings of the IEEE/CVF International Conference on Computer Vision, pp. 6082–6091 (2019)
11. Gao, J., Li, P., Chen, Z., Zhang, J.: A survey on deep learning for multimodal data fusion. Neural Comput. **32**(5), 829–864 (2020)
12. Lee, M., Pavlovic, V.: Private-shared disentangled multimodal VAE for learning of latent representations. In: Proceedings of the IEEE/CVF Conference on Computer Vision and Pattern Recognition, pp. 1692–1700 (2021)
13. Xu, X., Lin, K., Gao, L., Lu, H., Shen, H.T., Li, H.T.: Learning cross-modal common representations by private-shared subspaces separation. In: IEEE Trans. Cybern. **52**, 3261–3275 (2020)

14. Prakash, A., Chitta, K., Geiger, A.: Multi-modal fusion transformer for end-to-end autonomous driving. In: Proceedings of the IEEE/CVF Conference on Computer Vision and Pattern Recognition, pp. 7077–7087 (2021)
15. Feng, Y., You, H., Zhang, Z., Ji, R., Gao, Y.: Hypergraph neural net-works. Proc. AAAI Conf. Artif. Intell. **33**(01), 3558–3565 (2019)
16. Kim, E.-S., Kang, W.Y., On, K.-W., Heo, Y.-J., Zhang, B.-T.: Hypergraph attention networks for multimodal learning. In: Proceedings of the IEEE/CVF Conference on Computer Vision and Pattern Recognition, pp. 14 581–14 590 (2020)
17. Bai, S., Zhang, F., Torr, P.H.: Hypergraph convolution and hyper-graph attention. Pattern Recogn. **110** (2021)
18. Yu, J., Yin, H., Li, J., Wang, Q., Hung, N.Q.V., Zhang, X.: Self-supervised multi-channel hypergraph convolutional network for social recommendation. In: Proceedings of the Web Conference 2021, pp. 413–424 (2021)
19. Sun, X., et al.: Heterogeneous hypergraph embedding for graph classification. In: Proceedings of the 14th ACM International Conference on Web Search and Data Mining, pp. 725–733 (2011)
20. Kingma, D.P., Welling, M.: Auto-encoding Variational Bayes. Banff, AB, Canada (2014)
21. Hui, B., Zhu, P., Hu, Q.: Collaborative graph convolutional networks: Unsupervised learning meets semi-supervised learning. In: Proceedings of the AAAI Conference on Artificial Intelligence, vol. 34, pp. 4215–4222 (2020)
22. Gao, Y., Zhang, Z., Lin, H., Zhao, X., Du, S., Zou, C.: Hypergraph learning: methods and practices. IEEE Trans. Pattern Anal. Mach. Intell. **44**, 2548–2566 (2020)
23. Kipf, T.N., Welling, M.: Variational graph auto-encoders. arXiv preprint arXiv:1611.07308 (2016)
24. Wu, Z., et al.: 3D SshapeNets: a deep representation for volumetric shapes. In: Proceedings of the IEEE Conference on Computer Vision and Pattern Recognition, pp. 1912–1920 (2015)
25. Chen, D.-Y., Tian, X.-P., Shen, Y.-T., Ouhyoung, M.: On visual similarity based 3D model retrieval. Comput. Graph. Forum **22**(3), 223–232 (2003)
26. Zadeh, A., Chen, M., Poria, S., Cambria, E., Morency, L.-P.: Tensor fusion network for multimodal sentiment analysis. In: Proceedings of the 2017 Conference on Empirical Methods in Natural Language Processing, pp. 1103–1114 (2017)
27. Liu, Z., Shen, Y., Lakshminarasimhan, V.B., Liang, P.P., Zadeh, A.B., Morency, L.-P.: Efficient low-rank multimodal fusion with modality-specific factors. In: Proceedings of the 56th Annual Meeting of the Association for Computational Linguistics (Volume 1: Long Papers), pp. 2247–2256 (2016)
28. Su, H., Maji, S., Kalogerakis, E., Learned-Miller, E.: Multi-view convolutional neural networks for 3D shape recognition. In: Proceedings of the IEEE International Conference on Computer Vision, pp. 945–953 (2015)
29. Feng, Y., Zhang, Z., Zhao, X., Ji, R., Gao, Y.: GVCNN: group-view convolutional neural networks for 3D shape recognition. In: Proceedings of the IEEE Conference on Computer Vision and Pattern Recognition, pp. 264–272 (2018)
30. Chen, J., Zhang, A.: HGMF: heterogeneous graph-based fusion for multimodal data with incompleteness. In: Proceedings of the 26th ACM SIGKDD International Conference on Knowledge Discovery & Data Mining, pp. 1295–1305 (2020)

# Intention-Aware Frequency Domain Transformer Networks for Video Prediction

Hafez Farazi[✉] and Sven Behnke

Computer Science Institute VI, Autonomous Intelligent Systems, University of Bonn,
Friedrich-Hirzebruch-Allee 5, 53115 Bonn, Germany
{farazi,behnke}@ais.uni-bonn.de

**Abstract.** The ultimate goal of video prediction is not to predict pixel-perfect future images. Instead, it is desired to extract a valuable internal representation to solve downstream tasks. One of the essential downstream tasks is to understand the semantic composition of the scene and later use it for decision making. For example, an observer robot can anticipate human activities and collaborate in a shared workspace. However, one of the biggest challenges in human-robot collaboration remains understanding human intentions and movements. This paper focuses on predicting future frame pose activities given a pre-trained off-the-shelf pose estimation model (i.e., shelf-supervised). We propose a lightweight and interpretable model based on the Frequency Domain Transformer Networks to solve semantic prediction, given that we have multiple plausible futures. We show that the proposed model outperforms other well-known video prediction models on the pose prediction task extracted from the Human3.6M dataset and a synthetically created dataset with multiple plausible futures.

## 1 Introduction

Video prediction is about predicting future unseen image sequences based on some initial observed image sequence. A video prediction model that is useful in real-world scenarios should not only take into account the dynamics and content of the observed scene but also have a notion of multiple plausible futures to account for the inherent uncertainty of the dynamics of the world. For example, in human-robot collaboration scenarios, given some observed frames of a human working in a shared human-robot workspace, the robot should not only have a notion of what the most likely next movement of the human is but also what the possible future movements and intentions are. Based on this notion of multiple plausible futures, the robot can plan its following actions. Given a real-world video sequence, a classical pixel-level prediction of the video leads to a blurry prediction that represents the average of all possible futures. We argue that such a representation is only valuable for deterministic or semi-deterministic situations where the past completely or mostly determines the future. For instance, several possible futures exist when a person performs a movement in front of the

© The Author(s), under exclusive license to Springer Nature Switzerland AG 2022
E. Pimenidis et al. (Eds.): ICANN 2022, LNCS 13532, pp. 407–419, 2022.
https://doi.org/10.1007/978-3-031-15937-4_34

camera. Suppose the person is walking in the initially observed frames. They may continue the walking sequence, decrease or increase walking speed, stop walking, start walking backward, and many other possibilities. It is not feasible to formulate all these possible futures in advance. Instead, they must be derived from the data, preferably in a self-supervised manner. It is also essential for the future latent space to be interpretable and easy to sample from because this directly impacts how well the robot can plan its future actions.

The task we are mainly concerned with in this paper is the prediction of future semantic frames, which is a variant of video prediction. Here we are not interested in predicting the signal level but in predicting future semantics based on some observed semantics. In general, semantic prediction refers to predicting the output of another network. Therefore, the prediction model must not only learn to make predictions but also cope with imperfect seed input frames. Semantic prediction is more valuable than video prediction at the signal level because we predict the scene's essence, not just some insignificant pixel-level details. For example, in one of our experimented datasets, we predict the motion of a human subject and discard irrelevant information such as the person's hairstyle and color.

In our particular use case, the ultimate goal is to predict the human pose in a shared human-robot workspace using multiple smart edge sensors with different viewing angles. Later, we collect and fuse these short-term predictions for further processing and decision making with a more computationally powerful centralized backend server. The backend will merge the short-term local predictions into an allocentric semantic map. To enable short-term predictions, we train our model with human poses from the Human3.6M dataset [1]. The human poses were extracted using a pre-trained off-the-shelf state-of-the-art model developed by Bultmann et al. [2]. Note that the short-term prediction has to be done in real-time on the edge sensor, so models with a massive number of parameters are not suitable for this task.

Most other human skeleton prediction works are unsuitable for the described use case. Human skeleton prediction models are typically formulated as time series of 3D points corresponding to human joint positions and developed with the intention of predicting long sequences into the future [3]. Much of the recent work on this topic uses a graph neural network approach [4,5]. These models usually cannot deal with occlusions, missing joints, and the ambiguity of human joint positions. Furthermore, they assume a perfect skeleton extractor, which is not realistic considering that the human joint extractor is also a deep learning model that looks at natural images and does not have access to the ground truth. Although such models can be used in our backend server, which has access to a fused and near-perfect 3D skeleton, they are not suitable for short-term local predictions in the sensor space, which is the purpose of this work.

Our work is an extension of our lightweight and fully interpretable FDTN-based models [6,7] and follows our recent findings [8], which suggest that when semantic prediction is the goal, first extracting semantics followed by video prediction yields a better result compared to first performing video prediction followed by semantic extraction. We address the multiple plausible futures problem by proposing a lightweight intention model to extract very low-dimensional stochastic latent variables, pass them to the FDTN-based prediction model, and train them jointly in an end-to-end fashion. Note that the intention model proposed in this paper is not limited to semantic predictions and can also be used for video predictions. The code and dataset of this paper will be publicly available on GitHub[1]. The main contributions of this paper are as follows:

- We extend the existing frequency-domain-based transformer models to account for multiple plausible future scenarios.
- We propose a lightweight model to extract different variants of the predictions in a very low-dimensional latent space.
- We show that the output space of our intention model is interpretable and meaningful while capturing a wide range of plausible predictions.

## 2 Related Work

While there are many different approaches to video prediction, the most effective ones use deep learning to create abstract representations of scene content and observed transformations. A successful example is Video Ladder Network (VLN) [9], an extension of Ladder Networks that uses a recurrent lateral link at each level and models transformations at that level of abstraction, with the lowest level representing video frames. Conversely, PredRNN++ [10] consists of a stack of LSTM modules, with the output of each module fed into the subsequent module, forming a frame prediction at the top. PredNet [11], which aims to improve neural plausibility, implements a hierarchical architecture that learns a generative model of the input per layer. Only deviations from the expected input are propagated upward, actualizing the concepts of predictive coding. In an extension of this idea, HPNet [12] also resorts to associative coding and adds a direct upstream of spatio-temporal feature encodings extracted by 3D convolution. Here, the feedback path is routed to an LSTM at each level. In addition to generating plausible future images, the above two ideas highlight the exciting potential of video prediction tasks in studying models of cortical processing. In contrast, other approaches mostly ignore image content and focus on the dynamics of the scene. For example, PGP [13,14] integrates a gated autoencoder and the transformation model of RAE [15] to learn encodings of global linear image transformations between successive frames.

Most of the existing video prediction models are suitable for deterministic datasets, do not fully capture the distribution of outcomes, and provide blurry predictions in stochastic datasets. The blurry prediction is the result of not explicitly modeling multiple plausible futures, so the model is forced to produce the aggregate of multiple predictions to reduce the loss. Recently, loss functions that specify a distribution of the outcome have been explored. One such approach is the adversarial loss [16]. Still, the difficulty of training, the overhead of using a discriminator, and the mode collapse make GAN-based approaches not ideal for

---

[1] https://github.com/AIS-Bonn/Intention-Aware-Video-Prediction.

real-time video prediction. Variational inference is another solution to the problem. While there are few previous works dealing with multiple plausible futures in the form of variational inference frameworks [17,18], they are often difficult to train and require a complex freezing and training scheme [18]. Moreover, these models typically require a high-dimensional stochastic latent space, complicating their interpretation because it is impossible to gain insight by exploring the fully formed latent space. Finally, these models often use hundreds of random samples in hopes of finding the best matching future prediction when reporting their test performance.

We argue that the desired model should use a very low-dimensional latent space with a known range while generating a diverse future outcome. Furthermore, if the latent variables have low dimensionality with a known range, we can iterate through the latent space and gain insight into the model's predictive ability. Finally, it is also desirable to group the latent variable across multiple frames to force it to form a concept of the variability of the possible motions, rather than encoding meaningless jitter-like variations on each prediction frame. In the following sections, we propose our model that meets these criteria.

## 3  Models

In this section, we introduce the components used in our experiments.

**Local Frequency Domain Transformer Networks (LFDTN):** The core functionality of Local Frequency Domain Transformer Networks is the ability to describe changes in an observed image like signal as a collection of local linear transformations, transport inferred shifts into the future, and consequently apply them to make a prediction for the content of the next frame. The first part of these three distinct tasks is performed by a process that can be described as *Local Fourier Transform* (LFT), a Fourier-based transform similar to STFT for a 2D signal. For a given image $x_t$, overlapping tiles are extracted and windowed with a function $w$ to produce $x_{t,u,v}$, a collection of tapering windows on $x_t$ around the image coordinates $\{u, v\}$. For each, the FFT $\mathcal{X}_{t,u,v}$ is computed. For $\mathcal{X}_{t-1,u,v}$ and $\mathcal{X}_{t,u,v}$ (the LFTs of two consecutive images $x_{t-1}$ and $x_t$), the *local phase difference* is then defined element-wise as:

$$\mathcal{PD}_{t-1,u,v} := \frac{\mathcal{X}_{t,u,v}\overline{\mathcal{X}_{t-1,u,v}}}{|\mathcal{X}_{t,u,v}\overline{\mathcal{X}_{t-1,u,v}}|}. \tag{1}$$

The local phase differences encode the image shift observed around $\{u, v\}$ and serve as a content-independent description of the local image transformation. Since local adversities sometimes perturb the phase differences, in addition to the fact that the shifts are generally not spatiotemporally constant, a lightweight learnable convolutional network $\mathcal{MM}$ filters and transports them one time-step ahead. We call this the "transform model" and apply it as:

$$\widehat{\mathcal{PD}}_{t,u,v} = \mathcal{MM}(\mathcal{PD}_{t-1,u,v}). \tag{2}$$

It should be noted that $\mathcal{MM}$ was designed with an intentional bottleneck that forces the representation of $\widehat{\mathcal{PD}}_{t,u,v}$ as a vector field in the output layer that can be easily accessed and that can well explain the final prediction results.

Next, a prediction of the local views on $x_{t+1}$ is formed via the *local phase addition* given by:

$$\hat{\mathcal{X}}_{t+1,u,v} = \mathcal{X}_{t,u,v} \cdot \widehat{\mathcal{PD}}_{t,u,v} \tag{3}$$

and subsequently to obtain their inverse Fourier transforms $\hat{x}_{t+1,u,v}$. In addition, the effects of local displacements on the tapering windows are considered by repeating this step for the Fourier transform of the window function $\mathcal{W}$:

$$\hat{w}_{t,u,v} := \mathrm{iFFT}(\mathrm{phase}_{\mathrm{add}}(\mathcal{W}, \widehat{\mathcal{PD}}_{t,u,v})). \tag{4}$$

Using both, the next video frame $x_{t+1}$ is reconstructed by inverse local Fourier Transform in the presence of shifted windows. The sequence of analysis, then transport and prediction, and finally synthesis described above can also be applied on a channel-by-channel basis. This means that any spatial signal, e.g., a segmented video or human keypoints activity maps, is also a valid input. For more details on LFDTN, we encourage the reader to read the original LFDTN paper [6].

**Global Frequency Domain Transformer Networks (GFDTN):** Here we present a special case of LFDTN, which for clarity, we call Global Frequency Domain Transformer Networks (GFDTN). This model is similar to LFDTN and analyzes the signal globally. We set the size of the analysis window to the full input resolution and replace the window function with the identity. Because the LFDTN uses positional encoding channels, it can infer the location of each local transform and use it for prediction. Since in GFDTN, we only have a global window, the location-dependent features are not needed. To compensate for this, we replace the positional encodings with each input channel's Center of Mass.

Evidently GFDTN is limited and can only model one global transformation per specified channel. Consequently, although using GFDTN cannot make predictions at the signal level in natural videos, it can predict simple signals, such as blob-like semantics separated in different channels, into the future. Furthermore, due to the rigid assumption of a single global motion, this model converges faster than LFDTN. When the difference between LFDTN and GFDTN is not the focus of discussion, we refer to both models as FDTN in this paper.

**Intention Aware Network:** The core idea behind this model is to encode different variations in the dataset and produce a latent variable, which we call the $z$ vector. During training, this model has access to the future frames to extract the essence of the future changes. We then feed the $z$ vector into the FDTN model by concatenating $z$ as an additional channel to the "transform model". The $z$ vector is a very low-dimensional representation of these future variations that helps the prediction model decouple stochasticity from prediction. Unlike the SVG-LP model [17], which computes the posterior distribution for each time step, the $z$ latent variable is time-invariant, i.e., it encodes the variations once for all future frames. Note that during testing, instead of computing the $z$ vector using the intention model, we can iterate through different possible $z$ values to generate diverse prediction frames. The experiments section shows that we can generate different plausible predictions by changing the $z$ variable. The $z$ latent space can be continuous or discrete. The discrete version is motivated by the recent success of discrete generative models like video VQ-VAE [19]. Note that one can utilize both discrete and continuous latent variables simultaneously.

The intention model is a copy of the "transform model" with some modifications. Some functions, such as the extraction of local phase differences, are computed once between each successive frame and then used in both the prediction and intention models to avoid redundant computations. The last layer is the difference between the "transform model" in FDTN and the intention model. The intention model's last layer is a fully-connected layer followed by non-linearity that outputs $z$. In the continuous space, the nonlinearity is a tanh activation, and in the discrete case, it is a softmax layer.

In contrast, in the FDTN, the last layer is a convolutional layer that generates two-dimensional vectors that are then used in the phase addition process. Due to the similarity between the "transform model" in FDTN and the intention model, and to save learnable parameters and speed up the training process, the FDTN model shares weights with the intention model in the human joint prediction experiments. We also experimented with replacing the affine layer in the intention model with a global average pooling layer, and the results were slightly worse, so we decided to use the affine layer.

As it can be seen in the Fig. 1, without this model, the FDTN model, when faced with a stochastic dataset, will produce a blurry outcome which is a superposition of all different variations. Finally, note that the idea of an intention-aware network is not limited to FDTN based models and can also be applied to other deterministic video prediction models to enable them to model multiple plausible futures.

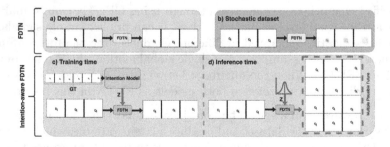

**Fig. 1.** An overview of the difference between the original FDTN model and the proposed intention-aware FDTN. a) The FDTN model is generating sharp future frames when trained on the deterministic "Moving MNIST" dataset. b) The FDTN model is producing a blurry result on the stochastic version of "Moving MNIST" dataset. c) The proposed intention-aware model during training. d) The proposed model while testing. Note that we can generate multiple plausible futures by sampling multiple times from the $z$ vector in test time.

# 4   Experimental Results

**Datasets and Training:** We use a variant of the synthetic Moving MNIST dataset to evaluate our proposed architecture and show the effect of stochasticity in video prediction. We call it "Stochastic Moving MNIST". It contains six frames with one MNIST image moving within a $64 \times 64$ frame. After three seed frames, the digit can maintain the initial velocity direction or reverse the velocity in $X$ and/or $Y$ directions. The choice between these four discrete random variants is made uniformly. This dataset is ideal for studying multiple plausible future scenarios with finite options.

We also created another dataset for the 2D human pose prediction task. We extracted this dataset from the Human3.6M dataset [1] using an off-the-shelf pre-trained model by Bultmann et al. [2]. The "Human3.6M Joints" dataset contains a sequence of ten frames with the shape $64 \times 64$. Each frame has 14 channels representing different human joints. The time difference between each frame is about $100ms$, and we predict the last five frames given the first five seed frames. This dataset has a very diverse range of actions captured from many different human subjects with multiple camera viewing angles.

Our models were trained end-to-end using backpropagation through time. In addition, we used AdamW optimizer and MSE prediction loss. For training the discrete intention model, we scheduled the softmax temperature by starting with a high temperature and gradually decreasing it to a very low temperature simulating one-hot-encoded argmax.

**Table 1.** Results for "Stochastic Moving MNIST" and "Human3.6M Joints" datasets.

| Model | "Stochastic Moving MNIST" | | | | "Human3.6M Joints" | | | |
|---|---|---|---|---|---|---|---|---|
| | L1 | MSE | DSSIM | Params | L1 | MSE | DSSIM | Params |
| Conv-PGP [14] | 0.01318 | 0.00507 | 0.06239 | 313K | 0.00074 | 0.00015 | 0.00380 | **640K** |
| HPNET [12] | 0.01330 | 0.00489 | 0.06140 | 1.5M | 0.00093 | 0.00020 | 0.00585 | 12.3M |
| SVG-LP-1D-$Best_{100s}$ [17] | 0.00390 | 0.00102 | 0.01016 | 12.6M | 0.00105 | 0.00023 | 0.00531 | 12.6M |
| SVG-LP-10D-$Best_{100s}$ [17] | 0.00451 | 0.00136 | 0.01233 | 12.6M | 0.00148 | 0.00037 | 0.00903 | 12.6M |
| SVG-LP-10D-$Best_{1000s}$ [17] | 0.00321 | 0.00062 | 0.00717 | 12.6M | 0.00144 | 0.00035 | 0.00881 | 12.6M |
| Our-GFDTN-Det | 0.01347 | 0.00503 | 0.06497 | **45K** | 0.00064 | 0.00012 | 0.00296 | **390K** |
| Our-LFDTN-Det | - | - | - | - | 0.00071 | 0.00015 | 0.00344 | **390K** |
| Our-GFDTN-C1D-$Best_{11s}$ | 0.00339 | 0.00133 | 0.00695 | 78K | **0.00057** | **0.00011** | 0.00249 | **390K** |
| Our-GFDTN-C1D-$Best_{21s}$ | 0.00175 | 0.00038 | 0.00239 | 78K | **0.00055** | **0.00010** | **0.00241** | **390K** |
| Our-LFDTN-C1D-$Best_{11s}$ | - | - | - | - | 0.00058 | 0.00012 | 0.00258 | **390K** |
| Our-LFDTN-C1D-$Best_{21s}$ | - | - | - | - | 0.00057 | 0.00011 | 0.00251 | **390K** |
| Our-GFDTN-D4 | **0.00067** | **0.00004** | **0.00033** | 82K | - | - | - | - |
| Our-GFDTN-D6 | **0.00059** | **0.00003** | **0.00025** | 85K | 0.00061 | 0.00012 | 0.00278 | **390K** |
| VLN-ResNet [20] | 0.01220 | 0.00467 | 0.05536 | 1.3M | 0.00078 | 0.00014 | 0.00368 | 1.3M |
| VLN-LDC [21] | 0.01241 | 0.00470 | 0.05565 | 1.3M | 0.00078 | 0.00014 | 0.00366 | 1.3M |
| PredRNN [22] | 0.01142 | 0.00434 | 0.05173 | 1.8M | 0.00070 | 0.00015 | 0.00345 | 3M |
| PredRNN++ [10] | 0.01167 | 0.00431 | 0.05222 | 2.8M | 0.00070 | 0.00014 | 0.00344 | 4M |
| Copy last frame | 0.01440 | 0.01000 | 0.04105 | - | 0.00085 | 0.00028 | 0.00441 | - |
| SVG-LP-1D-$Approx$ [17] | 0.00289 | 0.00043 | 0.00628 | 12.6M | 0.00099 | 0.00021 | 0.00464 | 12.6M |
| SVG-LP-10D-$Approx$ [17] | 0.00275 | 0.00038 | 0.00594 | 12.6M | 0.00080 | 0.00011 | 0.00303 | 12.6M |
| Our-GFDTN-C1D-$Approx$ | 0.00090 | 0.00008 | 0.00055 | 78K | 0.00055 | 0.00010 | 0.00238 | 390K |
| Our-LFDTN-C1D-$Approx$ | - | - | - | - | 0.00056 | 0.00011 | 0.00249 | 390K |

**Evaluation:** We compared our model against many well-known models, including Conv-PGP [14], VLN-ResNet [20] VLN-LDC [21], HPNet [12], PredRNN [22], PredRNN++ [10], and SVG-LP [17]. We also showed the result if we simply copy the last seed frame. Table 1 reports the outcomes on the "Stochastic Moving MNIST" and on the "Human3.6M Joints" datasets. Figures 2 and 4 depict two sample results on each dataset for each tested baseline.

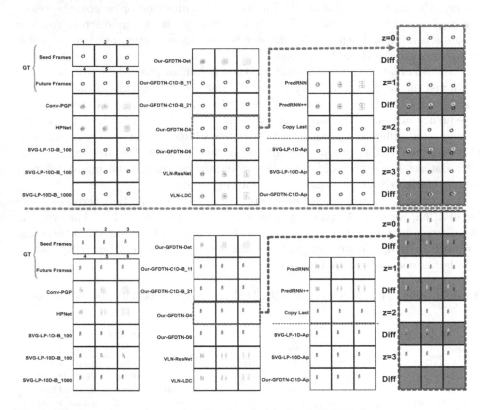

**Fig. 2.** Two sample results on the "Stochastic Moving MNIST" dataset were tested on different baselines. On the right, multiple plausible future predictions are generated by using different discrete choices of $z$ on the Our-GFDTN-D4 model. The variations are plausible and reflect the stochasticity of the dataset.

In these tables for SVG-LP [17] model, **1D** and **10D** indicate the dimensionality of the used latent space. At the same time, **Approx** means that the posterior is computed by accessing future frames, and $\mathbf{Best_{100s}}, \mathbf{Best_{1000s}}$ means that we draw random samples from the latent space 100 and 1000 times, respectively, and report the best loss. For our models, **C1D** means that the $z$ vector has dimensionality one and is continuous, while **D6** and **D4** means that the $z$ vector is discrete with 6 and 4 discrete choices, respectively. The word **Det** represents the deterministic version of the FDTN models without using the intention model. In our models, $\mathbf{Best_{11s}}$ and $\mathbf{Best_{21s}}$ mean that we can obtain these results by iterating through the $z$ vector with the range $[-1,1]$ with a fixed interval of 0.2 and 0.1 respectively and report the best test loss. Note that all results with the word **Approx** require access to the future test images and are therefore not realistic. We reported them here to compare the results among themselves but not with other baselines and also to show the best possible results when the sample size approaches infinity. Unlike the SVG-LP model, we can easily show the different choices for the $z$ vector by iterating through discrete choices or by choosing a fixed interval. Two example results for different $z$ choices are shown in Fig. 2 for the synthetic dataset, which indicates that the model successfully captures all four possible plausible futures. Furthermore, Fig. 4 depicts different $z$ values which exhibit that the model has arranged the latent variable $z$ in a highly interpretable and organized manner, which is a direct consequence of using a bounded low-dimensional latent variable.

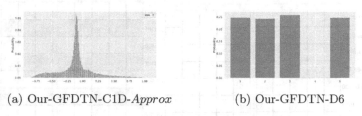

(a) Our-GFDTN-C1D-*Approx*          (b) Our-GFDTN-D6

**Fig. 3.** The histogram of the learned $z$ vector during training. a) Is the result of the continuous $z$ vector in the Our-GFDTN-C1D-*Approx* model, trained on "Human3.6M Joints". b) Is the result of discrete $z$ for the Our-GFDTN-D6 model trained on "Stochastic Moving MNIST". Note that the discrete index of zero and four is not utilized by the model.

We can constrain our choices during inference time by examining the gathered histogram of the $z$ vector during training. Two example histograms are shown in Fig. 3. It is to be observed that, in Fig. 3:b, the model with six discrete options only utilized four of the available options. This is due to a small L2 regularization used during training to encourage fewer choices. Since it is not always possible to determine the exact dimensions of the discrete variables in advance, we can choose a large enough dimension and force the model to select a minimal number of choices by increasing the regularization term.

We specified four metrics, including L1, MSE, and DSSIM, to compare our model against other baselines. Overall, experimental results indicate that our models perform well compared to other deterministic and stochastic models. We require much fewer sample iterations than SVG-LP while obtaining better results. Moreover, we need very few learnable parameters because we share the weights between the intention model and FDTN and also use lightweight FDTN models. Although we experimented with both the discrete and continuous versions of our intention model on both datasets, it is evident from the results that the discrete model works best in the synthetic dataset, which has clear and distinct plausible futures. On the other hand, the continuous model works best in the "Human3.6M Joints" dataset, where stochasticity is inherently continuous. Note that continuous variable models are easier to train compared to discrete latent variables, mainly because the gradient flows much better in the continuous version. Also, temperature scheduling is a critical part of training, and the range of the parameter and the decay rate is not a trivial hyper-parameter to tune.

SVG-LP is a model developed to address multiple plausible futures using a variational inference framework that requires a prior distribution. However, the Gaussian prior in SVG-LP, which is enforced by an additional KLD loss, is a strong assumption and leads to inferior results when the stochasticity in the dataset has a different distribution. For instance, the uniformly distributed

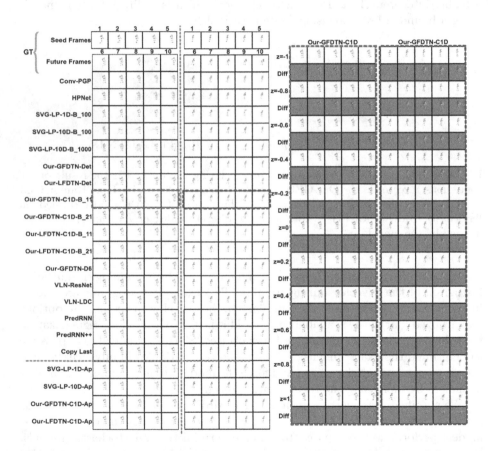

**Fig. 4.** Two sample results on the "Human3.6M Joints" dataset which were tested on different baselines. Right two columns show multiple plausible future predictions, given different values of *z* on the Our-GFDTN-C1D model. Note that all predictions are plausible, and the *z* dimension is organized in an interpretable manner. For example, changing the *z* vector can produce different walking directions in the left sample and change the amount of bending in the right.

stochasticity in our synthetic dataset makes Gaussian prior a problem for the SVG-LP model. To remedy this, we utilized a lower $\beta$ hyperparameter than the value originally proposed in the paper. In addition, time-variant stochasticity makes it unrealistic to iterate all possible plausible futures in SVG-LP. The required large dimensions of the latent variable combined with the time-variant stochasticity enable the SVG-LP model to essentially memorize the predictions and leak the future frames into the latent vector, leading to good training loss but inferior test performance. Although SVG-LP produces multiple plausible futures and generally outperforms most basic deterministic models after sampling multiple times and reporting the best result, the number of samples required is very high due to two main reasons. One reason is that the range of latent variables is not strictly bounded and is merely enforced with KLD loss. The second reason is that latent variables are generated per sample, which exponentially increases the number of samples required. Our proposed model does not have these problems. Therefore, we can achieve a diverse and plausible prediction with very few samples. Another problem with the SVG-LP model is that many aspects of the prediction, including the motion and content, are entangled in multiple LSTM layers. Hence the latent variable that is supposed to capture the stochasticity of the motions may also encode some variations of the content shapes (see Fig . 2 for an example of this problem). On the other hand, in our FDTN models, motion and content are clearly separated, so shape variations do not contaminate the motion stochasticity.

A fixed iteration interval works very well in our experimented datasets. Nevertheless, one can use k-means clustering in training time to find $K$ clusters and iterate over the midpoints of the clusters at inference time. Although more sophisticated sampling methods such as beam search or top-k sampling can be used depending on the computational budget, the maximum gain would not exceed **Approx** methods that have access to the approximated latent variables given the future frames. Note that if a bell curve-like shape is required in the $z$ variables, we can add an explicit regularization loss computed on the batch of $z$. On the other hand, if uniform distribution is desired, it can be enforced by a suitable additional loss term such as the label smoothing loss.

Our GFDTN model was successfully deployed to the Nvidia Jetson Xavier NX board, and we ran it in parallel with the human keypoint extraction model on the same board. We achieved about 8–10 Hz for single-person semantic prediction on this computationally limited GPU.

## 5 Conclusion and Future Work

We proposed Intention-aware Frequency Domain Transformer Networks (IFDTN), a fully interpretable and lightweight differentiable model for the video and semantic prediction tasks. The intention network encodes the stochasticity of the dataset in a vector with very low dimensionality. By multiple sampling of the latent space, we can generate a diverse set of plausible predictions. The latent representation formed is highly organized and interpretable. Furthermore, our models require very few learnable parameters, making them highly generalizable to unforeseen data. Experiments with synthetic data and human joints extracted from real data indicate that our models can outperform other baselines with far fewer parameters. In the future, we would like to fuse our short-term predictions with the semantic extraction model to improve the overall performance of semantic extraction.

**Acknowledgment.** This work was funded by grant BE 2556/16-2 (Unit FOR 2535 Anticipating Human Behavior) of the German Research Foundation (DFG). The authors would like to thank the open-source community and Mark Prediger for providing baseline methods and Simon Bultmann for providing the "Human3.6M Joints" dataset.

# References

1. Ionescu, C., Papava, D., Olaru, V., Sminchisescu, C.: Human3.6M: large scale datasets and predictive methods for 3D human sensing in natural environments. IEEE Trans. Pattern Anal. Mach. Intell. **36**, 1325–1339 (2014)
2. Bultmann, S., Behnke, S.: Real-time multi-view 3D human pose estimation using semantic feedback to smart edge sensors. In: RSS (2021)
3. Hernandez, A., Gall, J., Moreno-Noguer, F.: Human motion prediction via spatio-temporal inpainting. In: ICCV (2019)
4. Cui, Q., Sun, H., Yang, F.: Learning dynamic relationships for 3D human motion prediction. In: CVPR (2020)
5. Li, M., Chen, S., Zhao, Y., Wang, Y., Tian, Q.: Dynamic multiscale graph neural networks for 3D skeleton-based human motion prediction. In: CVPR (2020)
6. Farazi, H., Nogga, J., Behnke, S.: Local frequency domain transformer networks for video prediction. In: IJCNN (2021)
7. Farazi, H., Behnke, S.: Frequency domain transformer networks for video prediction. In: ESANN (2019)
8. Farazi, H., et al.: Semantic prediction: which one should come first, recognition or prediction? (2021)
9. Cricri, F., Ni, X., Honkala, M., Aksu, E., Gabbouj, M.: Video ladder networks. CoRR abs/1612.01756 (2016)
10. Wang, Y., Gao, Z., Long, M., Wang, J., Yu, P.S.: PredRNN++: towards a resolution of the deep-in-time dilemma in spatiotemporal predictive learning. In: ICML (2018)
11. Lotter, W., Kreiman, G., Cox, D.: Deep predictive coding networks for video prediction and unsupervised learning. arXiv preprint arXiv:1605.08104 (2016)
12. Qiu, J., Huang, G., Lee, T.: A neurally-inspired hierarchical prediction network for spatiotemporal sequence learning and prediction. arXiv preprint arXiv:1901.09002 (2019)
13. Michalski, V., Memisevic, R., Konda, K.: Modeling deep temporal dependencies with recurrent grammar cells. In: NeurIPS (2014)
14. Roos, F.D.: Modeling spatiotemporal information with convolutional gated networks. Master's thesis, Chalmers University of Technology (2016)
15. Memisevic, R.: Learning to relate images: mapping units, complex cells and simultaneous eigenspaces. arXiv:abs/1110.0107 (2011)

16. Kwon, Y.-H., Park, M.-G.: Predicting future frames using retrospective cycle GAN. In: CVPR (2019)
17. Denton, E., Fergus, R.: Stochastic video generation with a learned prior. In: ICML (2018)
18. Babaeizadeh, M., Finn, C., Erhan, D., Campbell, R.H., Levine, S.: Stochastic variational video prediction. arXiv preprint arXiv:1710.11252 (2017)
19. Yan, W., Zhang, Y., Abbeel, P., Srinivas, A.: VideoGPT: video generation using VQ-VAE and transformers. arXiv preprint arXiv:2104.10157 (2021)
20. Cricri, F., Ni, X., Honkala, M., Aksu, E., Gabbouj, M.: Video ladder networks. arXiv:1612.01756 (2016)
21. Azizi, N., Farazi, H., Behnke, S.: Location dependency in video prediction. In: ICANN (2018)
22. Wang, Y., Long, M., Wang, J., Gao, Z., Yu, P.S.: PredRNN: recurrent neural networks for predictive learning using spatiotemporal LSTMS. In: NPIS (2017)

# Knowledge-Aware Self-supervised Graph Representation Learning for Recommendation

Yeheng Sun, Jinghua Zhu[✉], and Heran Xi

School of Computer Science and Technology, Heilongjiang University,
Harbin 150080, China
{zhujinghua,xiheran}@hlju.edu.cn

**Abstract.** Representation learning improves the accuracy of recommendation through mining high-order neighbors information on the user-item graph, but still suffers the data sparsity and cold start problems. Although knowledge-aware representation learning can alleviate the above problems to some certain extent by using knowledge graphs to capture rich addition information of the items, this method relies heavily on a large amount of training data and annotations in a supervised learning manner. Self-supervised learning has been proved to be a good substitute because of its ability to avoid the cost of annotating large-scale datasets.

In this paper, we explore the self-supervised contrastive learning on the hybrid structure of the knowledge graph and user-item graph to solve above problems. We design a Knowledge-aware Self-supervised Graph Contrastive Learning model called KSGL. The core idea is to learn the representation of users and items effectively by pulling the augmented versions of the same users/items close to each other while pushing away different ones. Specifically, KSGL first performs data enhancement on the input hybrid graph, generates multiple views of the target node, and then refines the node embedding in each view through Graph Convolutional Networks (GCN), and finally updates the model by contrast loss. We conduct experiments on three benchmark datasets to demonstrate the effectiveness of KSGL and the results of the experiment show that our model can not only improve recommendation accuracy but also obtain robustness against interactive noise.

**Keywords:** Self-superviesd learning · Knowledge graph · Graph convolutional networks · Recommendation

## 1 Introduction

With the development of Internet technology, people can obtain a large amount of online content [4] on the Internet. A notorious problem with online platforms, however, is that the information overload. To alleviate the impact of information overload, recommender systems (RS) are proposed to search and recommend a

E. Pimenidis et al. (Eds.): ICANN 2022, LNCS 13532, pp. 420–432, 2022.
https://doi.org/10.1007/978-3-031-15937-4_35

small set of items to satisfy users' personalized interests. Collaborative filtering (CF) is widely used in RS which learns user(item) representations from interaction data and predicts user preferences. However, traditional CF-based methods usually suffer from the sparsity of user-item interactions and the cold-start problem. To address these limitations, researchers typically turn to feature-rich scenarios, where user and item attributes are used to compensate for sparsity and improve recommendation performance [13].

Some researchers [13] pointed out that the attributes are not isolated but interconnected, which forms the knowledge graph (KG). In general, a KG is a heterogeneous graph consisting of a large number of entity-relation-entity triples $(h, r, t)$, where $h \in \mathcal{E}$, $r \in \mathcal{R}$, $t \in \mathcal{E}$ denote head, relation, and tail of the triplet, $\mathcal{E}$ and $\mathcal{R}$ represent the entity set and relation set on the KG, respectively. The existing approaches that exploit KG information have achieved great success because KG can provide rich semantic information for RS, which enhances the representation learning ability. KGCN [14] is one typical information aggregation model on knowledge graph structure. KGCN effectively captures the correlation between items by mining the relevant attributes on the KG, and combines the neighbors' information with the biases when calculating the representation of an entity, so as to learn users and items representation.

But the supervised learning models [14,16], for knowledge-aware recommendation based on GCNs have the following limitations: **(1) Sparse supervision signal.** Most models complete the recommendation task in a supervised learning model, where the supervision signal comes from the observed interactions between users and items. However, the observed interactions are very sparse compared to the entire interaction space, making it insufficient to learn high-quality representations [1]. **(2) Skewed data distribution.** With the long tail consisting of unpopular items that lack supervisory signals. In contrast, popular items appear more frequently in neighborhood aggregation and supervised loss and thus have a greater impact on representation learning. Therefore, supervised graph recommendation can easily bias popular items [2], sacrificing the performance of unpopular items. **(3) Noise in the interaction.** Since most of the users' feedback is implicit (e.g. clicks, browses) rather than explicit (e.g. ratings, likes/dislikes), for example, a user is misled to click on an item and finds it uninteresting after consuming it [15]. Neighborhood aggregation schemes in GCNs amplify the impact of interactions on representation learning, making learning more susceptible to interaction noise.

To address the above issues, in this work we focus on exploring self-supervised learning (SSL) in RS. While self-supervised learning is popular in computer vision (CV) [5] and natural language processing (NLP) [3], there are relatively few implementations in RS. The idea is to set up an auxiliary task that distills additional signals from the input data itself, especially by exploiting the unlabeled data space. The auxiliary task consists of two key parts: (1) Data augmentation, we perform edge dropout and node dropout on the hybrid graph to generate multiple views for each node, which is constructed by changing the adjacency matrix of the graph to build "no label" data space. (2) Contrastive learning, we perform Graph Attention Network (GAT)-based contrastive learning on the changed structure. Maximize consistency between different views of the same node compared to views of other nodes.

We summarize the contributions of this work as follows:

- We design a model KSGL, which takes the self-identification of nodes as a self-supervised task, improves the influence of labeling bias, improves the robustness to interaction noise, and learns node representations better.
- We incorporate knowledge graphs into the paradigm of self-supervised graph learning, enlarging user and item attributes, mitigating data sparsity, and improving recommendation accuracy.
- We conduct extensive experiments on three benchmark datasets (Amazon-Book, Last-FM, Yelp2018) to demonstrate the superiority of KSGL.

## 2   Related Work

The recommendation methods based on graph can be divided into model-level and graph-level methods. Model-level approaches focus on model design for mining graphs. Research has evolved from random walks that encode graph structure as transition probabilities to GCNs that propagate node embeddings over graphs [14,16] now. Graph-level approaches enriche user-item graphs by considering additional information beyond user-item interactions, including user social relations [19], user and item attributes [10]. Recently, Knowledge Graph has also been unified with user-item graph, which can consider detailed connection types between items. Recommendation models combined with KG are mainly divided into two categories: (1) Path-based methods utilize different connection modes between entities on KG to manually set meta-paths or meta-graphs to provide additional guidance for RS. (2) Embedding-based methods [6] consider the combination of KG and RS in representation learning. In recent years, the use of information aggregation to process graph-structured data has attracted the attention of many researchers [20]. KGCN maps the user's interaction history to KG for information aggregation.

Research on self-supervised learning can be roughly divided into two branches: generative models [3] and contrastive models [7]. Contrastive models learn comparisons through a noise contrastive estimation objective, which can be a global-local contrast [8] or a global-global contrast [7] approach. Kaveh et al. [6] adopted a contrastive model to learn node and graph representations, comparing the node representation of one view with the graph representation of another view. Furthermore, GCC [11] utilizes instance recognition as a prerequisite task for pre-training with graph structure information. These studies focus on general graphs without taking into account the inherent properties of hybrid graphs. There has been very limited work on combining SSL with recommendations. A recent one is SGL [17], which explores self-supervised learning of user-item graphs. Although SGL applies contrastive learning to achieve good recommendation results in user-item graphs with sparse interaction data, the improvement of this method is still limited compared to the large amount of item-affiliated information in knowledge graphs.

# 3  KSGL Model

## 3.1  Framework

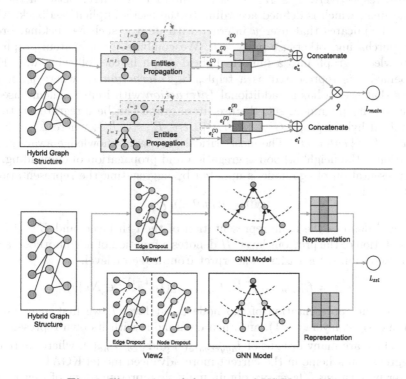

**Fig. 1.** Illustration of the proposed KSGL model.

We propose KSGL model for self-supervised knowledge-aware graph representation learning, which supercharges the knowledge-aware supervised task with
self-supervised learning. Figure 1 shows the framework of the model, the upper
figure shows a classical supervised knowledge-aware recommendation, the supervised signals come from observed interactions. The bottom figure shows the
self-supervised learning, the self-supervised task is to construct supervision signal from correlation within the input data. Specifically, we generate multiple
representational views through data augmentation, followed by the contrastive
learning based on the generated representations to build the self-supervised task.
Then, self-supervised learning is combined with classical supervised knowledge-
aware recommendation in a multi-task learning manner. Through joint training,
we optimize the model parameters to learn user and item representations better.
In the following sections, we will elaborate on this process.

## 3.2  Supervised Learning Model

In this section, we summarize the supervised knowledge-aware graph recommendation model. $\mathcal{U} = \{u_1, u_2, ..., u_M\}$ and $\mathcal{I} = \{i_1, i_2, ..., i_N\}$ denote $M$ users and $N$ items, respectively. $Y \in R^{M \times N}$ is the interaction matrix between the user and the item, which is defined according to the user's implicit feedback, where $y_{(u,i)} = 1$ indicates that user $u$ interact with item $i$, such as clicking, browsing or purchasing, otherwise $y_{(u,i)} = 0$. We combine the user-item graph and the knowledge graph into a uniform hybrid graph in the following way. First, user behavior is represented as a triple, $(u, Interaction, i)$, where $y_{(u,i)} = 1$ denotes that user $u$ has an additional $Interaction$ with item $i$. Then, based on the item-entity alignment set, the user-item graph can be integrated with KG as a unified hybrid graph $G = \{(h, r, t) | h, t \in E', r \in R'\}$, where $E' = E \cup U$ and $R' = R \cup \{Interact\}$. The most critical process in knowledge-aware recommendation is the neighborhood aggregation and propagation of embedding, and the representation of ego-node is updated by aggregating the representation of neighbor nodes:

$$E^{(l)} = H(E^{(l-1)}, G), \tag{1}$$

where $E^{(l)}$ denotes the node representation of the $l$-th layer, and $E^{(l-1)}$ is the representation of the previous layer. $H$ denotes a function of neighborhood aggregation. Equation (1) is easier to interpret from a vector level:

$$e_h^{(l)} = f_{combine}(e_h^{(l-1)}, f_{aggregate}(\{e_t^{(l-1)} | t \in N_h\})), \tag{2}$$

to update the representation of ego node $e_h$ at layer $l$, we first aggregate its neighbors $N_h$ at layer $(l-1)$, and then combine it with its own representation $e_h^{(l-1)}$. There are many designs of $f_{aggregate}(\cdot)$ and $f_{combine}(\cdot)$, where we refer to the aggregation scheme in the current more advanced model KGAT.

After performing $L$ layer, we obtain multiple representations of user node $u$, namely $\{e_u^{(1)}, \cdots, e_u^{(L)}\}$; item node $i$, $\{e_i^{(1)}, \cdots, e_i^{(L)}\}$ are obtained analogous to user. Since the output of the $l$-th layer is the node representation of the aggregation of messages at different levels with $u$ (or $i$) as the root shown in Fig. 1, the outputs of different layers emphasize the connectivity information of different orders. Therefore, we employ a layer aggregation mechanism to concatenate the representations at each step into a single vector as follows:

$$e_u^* = e_u^{(0)} || \cdots || e_u^{(L)}, \quad e_i^* = e_i^{(0)} || \cdots || e_i^{(L)}. \tag{3}$$

We conduct inner product the user and item representations, to predict their matching scores:

$$\hat{y}_{(u,i)} = e_u^{*\top} e_i^*. \tag{4}$$

To optimize model parameters, existing work usually sets the task as supervised learning and uses the pairwise Bayesian Personalization Ranking loss, which enforces the prediction of an observed interaction with a higher score than its unobserved interaction:

$$\mathcal{L}_{main} = \sum_{(u,i,j) \in O} -\ln \sigma(\hat{y}_{(u,i)} - \hat{y}_{(u,j)}), \tag{5}$$

where $O = \{(u,i,j)|(u,i) \in O^+, (u,j) \in O^-\}$ is the training data, and $O^- = \mathcal{U} \times \mathcal{I}\backslash O^+$ is the unobserved interaction. In this work, we choose it as the main supervision task.

### 3.3   Self-supervised Learning Model

**Data Augmentation on Hybrid Graph.** The data augmentation methods employed by self-supervised learning in CV and NLP tasks are not feasible for graph-based recommendations. CV and NLP task treat each data instance as an isolated, however, nodes in hybrid graphs are inherently interconnected and interdependent. Therefore, we need to design new data augmentation methods for graph-based recommendation.

The hybrid graph contains collaborative filtering signals. Specifically, the first-hop neighborhood directly describes ego user and item nodes—that is, historical items of a user (or interacted users of an item) can be viewed as pre-existing features of user (or item). The second-hop neighborhoods are entities on the knowledge graph associated with users (or items). Furthermore, the higher-order paths from a user to an item reflect the user's potential interest, so mining the inherent patterns in the hybrid graph is helpful for representation learning. We design two data augmentation, node dropout and edge dropout on the graph to create different node views. These operators can be expressed as:

$$E_1^{(l)} = H(E_1^{(l-1)}, s_1(G)), \quad E_2^{(l)} = H(E_2^{(l-1)}, s_2(G)),$$
$$E_3^{(l)} = H(E_3^{(l-1)}, s_3(G)), \quad E_4^{(l)} = H(E_4^{(l-1)}, s_4(G)), \quad s_1, s_2, s_3, s_4 \sim S, \tag{6}$$

where selected $s_1$, $s_2$, $s_3$ and $s_4$ are independently applied to the hybrid graph $G$ and establish correlated views of nodes $E_1^{(l)}$, $E_2^{(l)}$, $E_3^{(l)}$ and $E_4^{(l)}$. Our formulation of data augmentation is shown as follows:

- Node dropout (ND): With probability $\rho$, node is dropped from the graph along with its connected edges. In particular, $s_1$ and $s_2$ can be modeled as:

$$s_1(G) = (M' \odot \mathcal{V}, \mathcal{E}), \quad s_2(G) = (M'' \odot \mathcal{V}, \mathcal{E}), \tag{7}$$

where $M', M'' \in \{0,1\}^{|\mathcal{V}|}$ are two masking vectors that are applied to the node set $\mathcal{V}$ to generate two subgraphs. Therefore, this augmentation is expected to identify influential nodes from different augmented views.
- Edge dropout (ED): Drops edges in the graph with a dropout rate $\rho$. The two independent processes are expressed as:

$$s_3(G) = (\mathcal{V}, M_1 \odot \mathcal{E}), \quad s_4(G) = (\mathcal{V}, M_2 \odot \mathcal{E}), \tag{8}$$

where $M_1, M_2 \in \{0,1\}^{|\mathcal{E}|}$ are two masking vectors on the edge set $\mathcal{E}$, and only partial connections within the neighborhood contribute to the node representation. Thus, this data augmentation captures useful patterns of a node's local structure and further imparts more robustness to the representation against noisy interactions.

For simplicity, we make these augmentations to the graph in each epoch, that is, we produce different views for each node at the start of a new training epoch. Only dropout and masking operations are involved here, and no model parameters are added.

**Contrastive Learning.** Contrastive learning is an effective method for capturing similarities from data. In NLP, Word2vec models use co-occurring words and negative sampling to learn word embeddings. In CV, a large number of studies learn self-supervised image representations by minimizing the distance between two views of the same image. In this work, after building an augmented view of a node, we treat the view of the same node as a positive pair, (*i.e.* $\{(e'_u, e''_u)|u \in U\}$), while the view of any different node are all negative pairs (*i.e.* $\{(e'_u, e''_v)|u \in U, u \neq v\}$). Auxiliary supervision of positive pairs encourages consistency between different views of the same node, while supervision of negative pairs enforces divergence between different nodes. Formally we follow SimCLR and employ a contrastive loss, i.e. InfoNCE, to maximize the consistency of positive pairs and minimize the consistency of negative pairs:

$$\mathcal{L}_{ssl}^{user} = \sum_{u \in \mathcal{U}} - \log \frac{exp(s(e'_u, e''_u))}{\sum_{u \in \mathcal{U}} exp(s(e'_u, e''_v))}, \tag{9}$$

where $s(\cdot)$ measures the similarity between two vectors and is set as a cosine similarity function; $\tau$ is a hyperparameter, known as *temperature* in softmax. Similarly, we get the item-side contrast $\mathcal{L}_{ssl}^{item}$. Combining these two losses, we obtain the objective function for the self-supervised task as:

$$\mathcal{L}_{ssl} = \mathcal{L}_{ssl}^{user} + \mathcal{L}_{ssl}^{item}. \tag{10}$$

### 3.4 Multi-tasking Optimization

To improve the recommendation effect of self-supervised learning tasks, we utilize a multi-task training strategy to jointly optimize traditional knowledge-aware recommendation tasks and self-supervised learning tasks.

$$\mathcal{L} = \mathcal{L}_{main} + \lambda_1 \mathcal{L}_{ssl} + \lambda_2 \|\Theta\|_2^2, \tag{11}$$

where $\Theta$ is the set of model parameters in $\mathcal{L}_{main}$ ($\mathcal{L}_{ssl}$ introduces no extra parameters); $\lambda_1$ and $\lambda_2$ are hyperparameters that control the strength of the regularization of SSL and $L_2$, respectively.

## 4    Experiment

### 4.1    Experimental Setup

**Datasets.** To evaluate the effectiveness of KSGL, we use three benchmark datasets. Amazon-review is a widely used product recommendation dataset, and we choose Amazon-book from this collection. Last-FM is a music listening dataset collected from the Last.fm online music system, where music tracks are considered items. Yelp2018 is adopted from the 2018 edition of the Yelp Challenge. We consider local businesses such as restaurants and bars as items.

**Table 1.** Statistics of the datasetstables.

|               |              | Amazon-book | Last-FM   | Yelp2018  |
|---------------|--------------|-------------|-----------|-----------|
| User-item     | #Users       | 70,679      | 23,566    | 45,919    |
| interaction   | #Items       | 24,915      | 48,123    | 45,538    |
|               | #Interactions| 847,733     | 3,034,796 | 1,185,068 |
| Knowledge     | #Entities    | 88,527      | 58,266    | 90,961    |
| graph         | #Relations   | 39          | 9         | 42        |
|               | #Triplets    | 2,557,746   | 464,567   | 1,853,704 |

In addition to user-item interactions, we need to build item knowledge for each dataset. For Amazon-book and Last-FM, if a mapping is available, we map items to Freebase entities by title matching. In particular, we consider triples that are directly related to an item-aligned entity, whether it acts as a subject or an object. We consider triplets involving two-hop neighbor entities of an item. For Yelp2018, we extract item knowledge from local business information networks as KG data. We summarize the statistics of the three datasets in Table 1. For each dataset, we randomly select 80% of each user's interaction history to form the training set, the rest as the test set, and from the training set we randomly select 10% as a validation set.

**Baseline.** To demonstrate the effectiveness, we compare KSGL model with baseline methods, FM and SVD are KG-free and supervised methods, KGCN and KGAT are supervised methods about using knowledge graphs for recommendation, and SGL is a self-supervised method without KG, as follows:

- FM [12]: This is a model in which second-order feature interactions between inputs are considered. The IDs of users, items and their knowledge are input features in this work.
- SVD [9]: This is a classic CF-based model that uses inner products to simulate the interaction between users and items.
- KGCN [14]: KGCN is a representative of hybrid methods. It utilizes graph convolutional neural networks to aggregate information about items on KGs.
- KGAT [16]: An approach which explicitly models higher-order connections in KGs. To refine the node embedding, this methos employs an attention mechanism to distinguish the importance of neighbors.
- SGL [17]: A model-agnostic framework SGL that complements supervised recommendation tasks with self-supervised learning of user-item graphs.

**Parameter Settings.** We implement our model KSGL in Tensorflow. The embedding size is fixed to 64 for all models. We optimize all models with Adam optimizer, where the batch size is fixed at 1024. The default Xavier initializer with learning rate of 0.001 to initialize the model parameters. The proposed SGL methods inherit the optimal values of the shared hyper-parameters. For the unique ones of KSGL, we tune $\lambda_1$, $\tau$, and $\rho$ within the ranges of $\{0.005, 0.01, 0.05, 0.1, 0.5, 1.0\}$, $\{0.1, 0.2, 0.5, 1.0\}$, and $\{0, 0.1, 0.2, ..., 0.5\}$, respectively. We set $K = 50$ in top-$K$ recommendation.

### 4.2   Performance Comparison

We compare KSGL model with the aforementioned baseline methods, performance comparison results are shown in Table 2 and Fig. 2, we have the following observations:

Table 2. Overall performance comparison.

| Dataset | Amazon-book | | Last-FM | | Yelp2018 | |
|---|---|---|---|---|---|---|
| Method | Recall | NDCG | Recall | NDCG | Recall | NDCG |
| FM | 0.1345 | 0.0886 | 0.0778 | 0.1181 | 0.0627 | 0.0768 |
| SVD | 0.1366 | 0.0913 | 0.0829 | 0.1214 | 0.066 | 0.081 |
| KGCN | 0.1401 | 0.0998 | 0.0848 | 0.1276 | 0.0693 | 0.0834 |
| KGAT | 0.1489 | 0.1006 | 0.087 | 0.1325 | 0.0682 | 0.0867 |
| SGL | 0.1445 | 0.0963 | 0.0851 | 0.1279 | 0.0712 | 0.0855 |
| **KSGL** | **0.1501** | **0.1025** | **0.0896** | **0.1347** | **0.0769** | **0.0902** |
| *%Improv.* | 3.88% | 6.44% | 5.29% | 5.32% | 8.01% | 5.50% |

- Overall, we can see that KSGL consistently produces the best performance on all datasets. In particular, the recommendation accuracy on Amazon-Book and Yelp2018, two relatively sparse datasets, has been greatly improved. This shows that the introduction of knowledge graphs improves the effect of data sparsity, and the experimental results of knowledge graph-based recommendation methods (KGCN, KGAT) also show that they outperform the general supervised recommendation methods without knowledge graphs in most cases.
- Compared with traditional supervised learning, the introduction of knowledge graph increases many attributes of users and items, improving the data sparsity problem caused by only user interaction. Compared with knowledge-aware recommender systems, the setting of unsupervised auxiliary tasks learn user and item representations better, which solves the impact of inaccurate data labeling and improves recommendation performance.
- Compared with self-supervised graph learning, we combine the knowledge graph with the user-item graph, and perform data augmentation on the hybrid

graph structure, which not only increases the system robustness but also provides rich information for better representations of users and items.

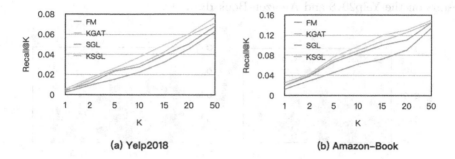

(a) Yelp2018                    (b) Amazon–Book

**Fig. 2.** The result of *Recall@K* Top-K recommendation.

### 4.3 Study of KSGL

**Effect of Aggregators.** In the process of graph representation learning, many researchers have proposed different graph convolutional neural networks, and most of the differences between them are in the aggregation scheme. In order to explore the influence of the aggregator, we consider the use of different aggregators. Specifically GCN, GraphSage, and GAT. Table 3 summarizes the experimental results. We have the following findings:

**Table 3.** Effect of aggregators.

| Dataset | Amazon-book | | Last-FM | | Yelp2018 | |
|---|---|---|---|---|---|---|
| Aggreator | Recall | NDCG | Recall | NDCG | Recall | NDCG |
| GCN | 0.1483 | 0.0971 | 0.0844 | 0.1318 | 0.0728 | 0.0878 |
| GraghSage | 0.1472 | 0.0959 | 0.0842 | 0.1308 | 0.0706 | 0.0861 |
| GAT | **0.1493** | **0.0988** | **0.0854** | **0.1326** | **0.0743** | **0.0892** |

- GCN is always better than GraphSage. One possible reason is that Graph-Sage abandons the interaction between entity representations and their ego-network representations. Thus, it illustrates the importance of feature interaction when performing information aggregation and propagation.
- Compared to GCN, the performance of GAT validates that incorporating additional feature interactions can improve representation learning. It illustrates the rationality and effectiveness of adding attention mechanism in neighborhood aggregation, while GCN treating neighborhoods equally may cause noise and mislead the propagation process.

**Robustness to Noise Interactions.** We conduct experiments to verify the robustness of KSGL to noise interactions. We pollute the training set by adding a certain percentage of adversarial examples (i.e., 5%, 10%, 15%, 20% of negative user-item interactions), while keeping the test set unchanged. Figure 3 shows the results on the Yelp2018 and Amazon-Book datasets:

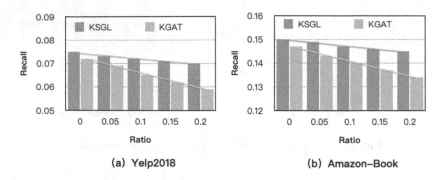

(a) Yelp2018          (b) Amazon–Book

**Fig. 3.** Model performance *w.r.t.* noise ratio.

- We found that adding noise data degrades the performance of KSGL and KGAT. However, the performance drop of KSGL is lower than that of KGAT; moreover, the gap between the two curves become more pronounced as the noise ratio increases. This shows that by comparing different node-enhanced views, KSGL can find useful patterns.
- Taking Amazon-Book as an example, KSGL with 20% more noise interaction still outperforms the noise-free dataset of KGAT. This demonstrates the superiority and robustness of KSGL over KGAT.
- We found that KSGL performed more robustly on Yelp2018. The possible reason is that Amazon-Book is much sparser than Yelp2018, and adding noise data has a greater impact on the graph structure of Amazon-Book than Yelp2018.

**Affection of Negative Sampling in Contrastive Learning.** In addition, we design two variants to explore the effect of selecting negative samples. (1) KSGL-only, only one data augmentation method is selected for the selection of negative samples, that is, only the data in one view is used as data augmentation; (2) KSGL-both, two data augmentation methods are used, both the edge dropout and node dropout views are taken as negative samples. The comparison results are shown in Table 4. KSGL-both performs better than KSGL-only, this indicates that combining different data augmentation methods can greatly improve the algorithm effect. The use of different data augmentation methods avoids the learned features from overfitting the low-level "shortcut" [18], making the features more generalizable.

**Table 4.** Effect of negatives.

| Dataset | Yelp2018 | | Amazon-Book | |
|---|---|---|---|---|
| Method | Recall | NDCG | Recall | NDCG |
| KSGL-only | 0.0728 | 0.0873 | 0.1489 | 0.1008 |
| KSGL-both | **0.0761** | **0.0901** | **0.1495** | **0.1015** |

## 5    Conclusion and Future Work

In this work, we explore self-supervised node representation learning on a hybrid structure of knowledge graphs and user-item graphs for knowledge-aware recommendations. We design a knowledge hybrid graph contrastive learning model KSGL, which is a self-supervised graph neural network model that generates multiple views of the target node by performing edge dropout and node dropout data augmentation on the hybrid graph, refines the node embeddings in each view by GAT, and finally updates the model by contrastive loss. Extensive experiments on three real datasets demonstrate the effectiveness and accuracy of KSGL in combating data sparsity and labeled data volume, as well as its advantages in improving long-tail recommendations and robustness against noisy interactions.

In the future, we will consider to incorporate dynamic knowledge graphs to assist recommendation since the knowledge graphs is usually evolving with time in real world. Another future work is to explore new perspectives on graphs, such as counter factual learning to identify influential data points to create more powerful data augmentation.

## References

1. Bayer, I., He, X., Kanagal, B., Rendle, S.: A generic coordinate descent framework for learning from implicit feedback. In: WWW, pp. 1341–1350 (2017)
2. Chen, J., Dong, H., Wang, X., Feng, F., Wang, M., He, X.: Bias and debias in recommender system: a survey and future directions. arXiv preprint arXiv:2010.03240 (2020)
3. Devlin, J., Chang, M.W., Lee, K., Toutanova, K.: Bert: pre-training of deep bidirectional transformers for language understanding. arXiv preprint arXiv:1810.04805 (2018)
4. Feng, Y., Hu, B., Lv, F., Liu, Q., Zhang, Z., Ou, W.: ATBRG: adaptive target-behavior relational graph network for effective recommendation. In: SIGIR, pp. 2231–2240 (2020)
5. Gidaris, S., Singh, P., Komodakis, N.: Unsupervised representation learning by predicting image rotations. arXiv preprint arXiv:1803.07728 (2018)
6. Hassani, K., Khasahmadi, A.H.: Contrastive multi-view representation learning on graphs. In: ICML, pp. 4116–4126. PMLR (2020)
7. He, K., Fan, H., Wu, Y., Xie, S., Girshick, R.: Momentum contrast for unsupervised visual representation learning. In: CVPR, pp. 9729–9738 (2020)
8. Hjelm, R.D., et al.: Learning deep representations by mutual information estimation and maximization. arXiv preprint arXiv:1808.06670 (2018)

9. Koren, Y.: Factorization meets the neighborhood: a multifaceted collaborative filtering model. In: SIGKDD, pp. 426–434 (2008)

10. Li, Z., Cui, Z., Wu, S., Zhang, X., Wang, L.: Fi-GNN: modeling feature interactions via graph neural networks for CTR prediction. In: CIKM, pp. 539–548 (2019)

11. Qiu, J., et al.: GCC: graph contrastive coding for graph neural network pre-training. In: SIGKDD, pp. 1150–1160 (2020)

12. Rendle, S., Gantner, Z., Freudenthaler, C., Schmidt-Thieme, L.: Fast context-aware recommendations with factorization machines. In: SIGIR, pp. 635–644 (2011)

13. Wang, H., Zhang, F., Xie, X., Guo, M.: DKN: deep knowledge-aware network for news recommendation. In: WWW, pp. 1835–1844 (2018)

14. Wang, H., Zhao, M., Xie, X., Li, W., Guo, M.: Knowledge graph convolutional networks for recommender systems. In: WWW, pp. 3307–3313 (2019)

15. Wang, W., Feng, F., He, X., Nie, L., Chua, T.S.: Denoising implicit feedback for recommendation. In: WSDM, pp. 373–381 (2021)

16. Wang, X., He, X., Cao, Y., Liu, M., Chua, T.S.: KGAT: knowledge graph attention network for recommendation. In: SIGKDD, pp. 950–958 (2019)

17. Wu, J., et al.: Self-supervised graph learning for recommendation. In: SIGIR, pp. 726–735 (2021)

18. You, Y., Chen, T., Sui, Y., Chen, T., Wang, Z., Shen, Y.: Graph contrastive learning with augmentations. Adv. Neural. Inf. Process. Syst. **33**, 5812–5823 (2020)

19. Yuan, F., He, X., Karatzoglou, A., Zhang, L.: Parameter-efficient transfer from sequential behaviors for user modeling and recommendation. In: SIGIR, pp. 1469–1478 (2020)

20. Zhu, J., Guo, X.: Deep neural model for point-of-interest recommendation fused with graph embedding representation. In: Biagioni, E.S., Zheng, Y., Cheng, S. (eds.) WASA 2019. LNCS, vol. 11604, pp. 495–506. Springer, Cham (2019). https://doi.org/10.1007/978-3-030-23597-0_40

# Meta-Style: Few-Shot Learning Dataset for Social Media Field

Yuncong Peng[1,2] , Boyi Fu[1,2] , and Xiaolin Qin[1,2](✉)

[1] Chengdu Institute of Computer Applications, Chinese Academy of Sciences,
Chengdu, China
qinxl2001@126.com

[2] University of Chinese Academy of Sciences, Beijing, China

**Abstract.** The research on few-shot learning has received extensive attention because there are few labeled samples in real application scenarios, which could promote the transformation of industrial intelligence. However, the existing datasets for few-shot learning mainly focus on common objects, which limits the application of few-shot learning to specific domains like the social media field. In this paper, we construct a few-shot learning dataset Meta-Style for the social media field, which is composed of the photos of different styles of online celebrities. Compared with the existing general few-shot datasets, it can better reflect the performance and application value of few-shot learning algorithm in the field of social media. In addition, to evaluate the performance of few-shot learning algorithms in this field, the performance of common few-shot learning algorithms on Meta-Style is reproduced and reported. More importantly, a baseline method is proposed, that is, latent prototype estimation based on global perception and neighborhood adaptation, which obtains the state-of-the-art result on Meta-Style. The algorithm was also awarded the fifth place in the few-shot learning track of the 2021 iFLY-TEK A.I. Developer Competition. Meta-Style and subsequent updates will be released at https://github.com/pcchvol/Meta-StyleV1.

**Keywords:** Few-shot learning · Meta-style · Global perception · Neighborhood adaptation · Latent prototype estimation

## 1 Introduction

Few-shot learning aims to learn with limited supervised information [3,8,14], which has played a key role in promoting the intelligent transformation of traditional industries. Existing few-shot datasets and benchmarks are mainly targeted

Supported by The National Natural Science Foundation of China (No. 61402537), Sichuan Science and Technology Program (Nos. 2019ZDZX0006, 2020YFQ0056), the West Light Foundation of Chinese Academy of Sciences (201899) and the Talents by Sichuan provincial Party Committee Organization Department, and Science and Technology Service Network Initiative (KFJ-STS-QYZD-2021-21-001).

E. Pimenidis et al. (Eds.): ICANN 2022, LNCS 13532, pp. 433–444, 2022.
https://doi.org/10.1007/978-3-031-15937-4_36

at general-purpose object classification, such as miniImageNet [15], which is a good choice as a way to evaluate the performance of general-purpose few-shot algorithms, but the performance on this kind of datasets is difficult to reflect the application value in specific fields.

In order to study the performance of few-shot learning in a specific domain, the few-shot dataset Meta-Style is constructed for the social media domain, which is composed of the photos of different styles of online celebrities in social media. Image classification in the social media domain has significant research value, such as accurate style recognition is important for users to get good recommendation results in social media software.

Algorithm researchers in related industries usually define various classification standards, such as dress classification, atmosphere classification and temperament classification, according to the actual business needs at different stages, and then train the corresponding classification models. This process involves large-scale data collection and data annotation that are labor-intensive and frequent, so the corresponding needs can be better solved by the few-shot learning.

More importantly, for the social media space, tracking and creating hot topics is a significant task. For example, during 2021, the "pure-and-sexy" bloggers in TikTok suddenly became popular. So relevant algorithm engineers need to push similar style bloggers and short videos on a large scale as soon as they discover the omen of the popularity of this style. It is noteworthy that only small samples of "pure-and-sexy" style may be labeled at this time, so a few-shot learning algorithm is a reasonable way to handle the situation.

In addition, we propose a baseline method that achieves state-of-the-art results on Meta-Style, which was also awarded the fifth place in the few-shot learning track of the 2021 iFLYTEK A.I. Developer Competition.

The main contributions in this paper are as follows:

(1) A challenging few-shot learning dataset Meta-Style is constructed, which better reflects the performance and application value of few-shot learning algorithms in the social media domain and is scalable compared to existing datasets.
(2) The latent prototype estimation based on global perception and neighborhood adaptation is proposed, which obtains the SOTA result on Meta-Style.
(3) The comparative results substantiate the superiority of the proposed method to existing approaches on Meta-Style, and the effectiveness of the proposed method is proved through ablation experiments.

## 2   Related Work

### 2.1   Prototype Estimation

Prototype estimation is very important for few-shot learning. Many algorithms usually obtain category prototypes based on metric learning, iterative updating [5] and so on. However, the existing algorithms do not pay attention to the huge deviation between the observed distribution of support samples and the original category distribution. Therefore, how to reasonably estimate the prototype rather than through simple mean aggregation is particularly significant.

## 2.2 Related Dataset

Common datasets for few-shot learning include miniImageNet [15], CUB [16], tieredImageNet [11] and Omniglot [7]. Among them, miniImageNet is the most commonly used to evaluate the performance of the few-shot learning algorithm, which has a total of 60000 color images with 100 classes, where each class has 600 images of size 84 × 84.

However, the performance on this kind of datasets is difficult to reflect the application value of specific fields in the actual scene, because these datasets are oriented to the universal object so that they are difficult to commercialize.

# 3  Meta-Style Dataset

## 3.1  Data Collection and Annotation

**Taxonomic System Establishment.** Style is not defined in a definitive way, which may be affected by many factors, such as dressing and makeup. Therefore, it is difficult to manually define the style classification standard of the dataset. In addition, if deterministic style criteria are used as categories, the dataset is less scalable.

A more fine-grained way to define the style is needed to construct the training dataset. And for the test dataset, there is an option to scale, i.e. to specific classification tasks as per actual needs.

The meta-style which is a more atomic style is used as a classification label. The relationship between meta-style and style is similar to the relationship between atoms and molecules. In other words, based on artificial definitions, some similar meta styles can be classified as a certain style. Meta-style is mainly proposed based on two assumptions:

(1) Every girl has her own unique atomic style, just as there are no two identical leaves in the world, even though they look similar in some way.
(2) During a period of time, online celebrities with numerous fans usually have a stable atomic style.

Specifically, in the latest period, the filtered photos of each online celebrity whose fans exceed a certain threshold are classified into one category, i.e. each category is exclusive to that celebrity's style (meta-style).

**Dataset Split.** The dataset is randomly divided into three parts, namely the training set, the validation set and the test set. The training set consists of 75 categories, the validation set consists of 23 categories, and the test set consists of 25 categories.

In order to be closer to the actual implementation, a scalable test set can be constructed, which evaluates the business achievement effect with small samples. For example, there is a business requirement for clothing classification, a scalable test set can be built that contains categories such as Chinese clothes, uniforms and sportswear, each using a few annotations for training, and then testing the algorithm's performance, so that the algorithm can be evaluated for practical business implementation under small sample conditions. The scalable test set will be demonstrated and tested in future work (Fig. 1).

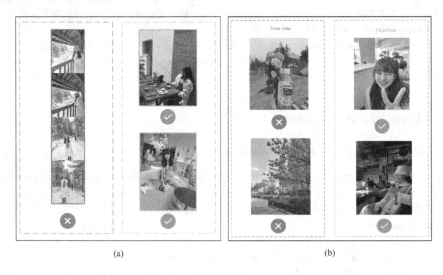

**Fig. 1.** Image filtering. (a) shows filtering based on image size ratio, and (b) shows that irrelevant images are filtered out.

**Image Collection.** Photo crawling on social media platforms for the filtered relevant users is performed. First, the crawling time interval is fixed to the last 6 months. Second, only a single image analysis is considered, so refer to the size ratio and filter out long images. Images with an aspect ratio of more than 3 times will be filtered out. Finally, considering that the size of individual images may have a large gap due to the source camera and image crop, we scale all images down so that the long side of the image is equal to 1024 pixels.

**Data Filtering Based on CLIP.** It is worth noting that there are usually many unrelated pictures of users in personal social media pictures to express their mood or share other interesting things. Therefore, it is necessary to filter out irrelevant images and only retain the user's personal style photos to avoid the impact of label noise.

Label noise can greatly affect model performance. Considering the cross-entropy loss function, for a noisy sample $(x, y')$ with a true label of $y^\star$, the loss for this single noisy sample is $-\log q_{y'}$, where $q_i = p(y = y_i \mid x, \theta)$, and assuming that the model was previously trained without label noise, $q_{y^*} > q_{y'}$ and $q_{y'}$ is close to 0. Since the loss function is a negative logarithmic function of $q_{y'}$, the loss will be very large at this point and will seriously affect the model training.

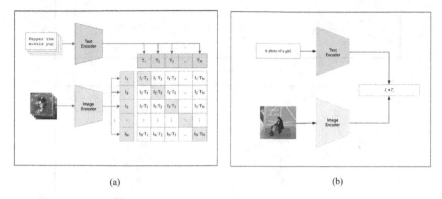

(a)                                                    (b)

**Fig. 2.** The framework of data filtering based on CLIP. (a) shows the pre-training task in CLIP [9], and (b) shows that the process of image filtering based on CLIP.

Therefore, CLIP-based [9] data filtering is used to reject irrelevant images. Specifically, based on the text description, the required samples can be selected from numerous potentially noisy data, as shown in Fig. 2. For example, given the text description $text$ = "a photo of girl", the image $img$ and the threshold $\delta$, the photo satisfies the text constraint when $f(img, text) > \delta$.

According to all filtering methods, the number of images was reduced from 88954 to 36567.

## 3.2 Dataset Analysis

**Sample-Level and Image-Level Analysis.** The Meta-Style dataset has a total of 36,567 color images, divided into 123 categories, of which each category has at least 100 images. The distribution of the number of images in each category is shown in Fig. 3, which shows a skewed distribution, i.e. most of the categories have less than 400 images. The kernel density estimate of the number of fans is close to the degree distribution of the actual social network nodes, showing a power-law distribution pattern, as shown in Fig. 3.

The resolution of the original image exceeds 1024 pixels on the long side, and the image of the dataset is scaled down so that the long side is 1024 pixels. The lowest width and lowest height of the image in the dataset are 426 pixels and 401 pixels.

Kmeans clustering is used to cluster all image size proportions similarly to YOLOV3 [10], using $1 - IOU$ as the distance. The three most typical image size proportions as shown in the Fig. 3.

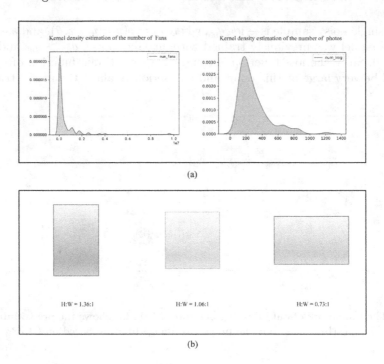

(a)

(b)

**Fig. 3.** Sample-Level and Image-Level Analysis. (a) shows the kernel density estimation of fans and images, and (b) shows the clustering results of image proportion.

**Comparison with Other Datasets.** Table 1 shows the basic information of common few-shot learning datasets and Meta-Style. It is obvious from the table that most of the existing datasets are either oriented to general object categories or more scientific categories of birds or fonts, which are difficult to apply to real tasks. The Meta-Style dataset is oriented to the style category, which has important application value for algorithm research in social platforms.

**Table 1.** Comparison of common few-shot datasets

| Dataset | Class | Sample | Size | Object |
|---|---|---|---|---|
| Meta-Style | 123 | 36567 | 224 × 224 | Style of online celebrities |
| miniImageNet [15] | 100 | 60000 | 84 × 84 | Common object |
| CUB-200 [16] | 200 | 11788 | 84 × 84 | Subcategories of birds |
| tieredImageNet [11] | 608 | 779165 | 84 × 84 | Common object |
| Omniglot [7] | 1623 | 32460 | 28 × 28 | Categories of handwritten characters |

# 4 Latent Prototype Estimation Based on Global Perception and Neighborhood Adaptation

## 4.1 Latent Prototype Estimation

The estimation of prototypes has been the top priority of few-shot learning. It is worth noting that the query set of samples provides rich information. LaplaceShot [18], GCN [12], EGNN [6] and other methods make use of samples that will be predicted to perform transductive learning. The proposed method also refers to this idea, assuming that the support set sample is the sample of category distribution, and then combines with the unlabeled data to be predicted to jointly infer the category prototype.

Specifically, it is assumed that the overall distribution of each category is a multivariate Gaussian distribution $N(\mu, \Sigma)$, where $\mu$ is the category prototype, the distribution of labeled samples in the support set is an observed distribution, and the samples in the query set may be picked from different category distributions.

For N-way K-shot task with Q query samples, note that the support set samples are $\{(x_i, y_i)\}_{i=1,...,NK}$, and the query set samples are $\{(x'_j)\}_{j=1,...,NQ}$, the attribution of the latent distribution of the query set samples is denoted as $z_j$, the parameters $\theta_n = \{\mu_n, \Sigma_n\}$, and $\theta = \{\theta_n\}_{n=1,...,N}$.

Thus, the log-likelihood function is given in the following equation.

$$
\begin{aligned}
L(\theta) &= \ln(\prod_{i=1}^{NK} p(x_i, y_i|\theta) \prod_{j=1}^{NQ} p\left(x'_j|\theta\right)) \\
&= \sum_{i=1}^{NK} \ln p\left(y_i \mid \theta\right) p\left(x_i \mid y_i, \theta\right) + \sum_{j=1}^{NQ} \ln \sum_{n=1}^{N} p\left(x'_j \mid z_j = n, \theta\right) p(z_j = n \mid \theta) \\
&= \sum_{i=1}^{NK} \ln \frac{1}{N} \frac{1}{(2\pi)^{d/2}|\Sigma_{y_i}|^{1/2}} e^{-\frac{1}{2}(x_i - \mu_{y_i})^T \Sigma_{y_i}^{-1}(x_i - u_{y_i})} + \sum_{j=1}^{NQ} \ln \sum_{n=1}^{N} p\left(x'_j \mid z_j = n, \theta\right) p(z_j = n \mid \theta)
\end{aligned}
\tag{1}
$$

It is worth noting that considering the inclusion of hidden variables, the $L(\theta)$ is usually approximated by an iterative method to gradually maximize $L(\theta)$. Suppose the estimate of $\theta$ after the $s$th iteration is $\theta^{(s)}$, we need to ensure that the new estimate $\theta$ satisfies $L(\theta) > L\left(\theta^{(s)}\right)$.

Considering that the antecedent term has no hidden variables, it should focus on the right term $L'(\theta)$ in the above equation.

$$
\begin{aligned}
L'(\theta) &= \sum_{j=1}^{NQ} \ln \sum_{n=1}^{N} p\left(x'_j \mid z_j = n, \theta\right) p(z_j = n \mid \theta) \\
&= \sum_{j=1}^{NQ} \ln \sum_{n=1}^{N} p\left(z_j = n \mid x'_j, \theta^{(s)}\right) \frac{p\left(x'_j \mid z_j = n, \theta\right) p(z_j = n \mid \theta)}{p\left(z_j = n \mid x'_j, \theta^{(s)}\right)}
\end{aligned}
\tag{2}
$$

Using Jensen's inequality, the following deflations can be performed:

$$
L'(\theta) \geqslant \sum_{j=1}^{NQ} \sum_{n=1}^{N} p\left(z_j = n \mid x'_j, \theta^{(s)}\right) \ln \frac{p\left(x'_j \mid z_j = n, \theta\right) p(z_j = n \mid \theta)}{p\left(z_j = n \mid x'_j, \theta^{(s)}\right)}
\tag{3}
$$

Let $B'\left(\theta, \theta^{(s)}\right)$ be the right term of the above inequality, it is obvious that the function $B'\left(\theta, \theta^{(s)}\right)$ is a lower bound of $L'(\theta)$. It further follows:

$$L(\theta) \geqslant \sum_{i=1}^{NK} \ln \frac{1}{N} \frac{1}{(2\pi)^{d/2}|\Sigma_{y_i}|^{1/2}} e^{-\frac{1}{2}(x_i - \mu_{y_i})^T \Sigma_{y_i}^{-1}(x_i - u_{y_i})} + B'\left(\theta, \theta^{(s)}\right) \quad (4)$$

Let the right term of the inequality be $B(\theta, \theta^{(s)})$, we can obtain $\theta^{(s+1)}$ by optimizing the lower bound of $L(\theta)$, which can be transformed into maximizing $B\left(\theta, \theta^{(s)}\right)$ to obtain $\theta^{(s+1)}$.

$$
\begin{aligned}
\theta^{(s+1)} &= \arg\max_{\theta} \left( \sum_{i=1}^{NK} \ln \frac{1}{N} \frac{1}{(2\pi)^{d/2}|\Sigma_{y_i}|^{1/2}} e^{-\frac{1}{2}(x_i - \mu_{y_i})^T \Sigma_{y_i}^{-1}(x_i - u_{y_i})} + B'\left(\theta, \theta^{(s)}\right) \right) \\
&= \arg\max_{\theta} \left( \sum_{i=1}^{NK} \ln \frac{1}{N} \frac{1}{(2\pi)^{d/2}|\Sigma_{y_i}|^{1/2}} e^{-\frac{1}{2}(x_i - \mu_{y_i})^T \Sigma_{y_i}^{-1}(x_i - u_{y_i})} + \right. \\
&\qquad \left. \sum_{j=1}^{NQ} \sum_{n=1}^{N} p\left(z_j = n \mid x'_j, \theta^{(s)}\right) \ln \frac{p\left(x'_j \mid z_j = n, \theta\right) p(z_j = n \mid \theta)}{p\left(z_j = n \mid x'_j, \theta^{(s)}\right)} \right) \\
&= \arg\max_{\theta} \left( \sum_{i=1}^{NK} \ln \frac{1}{N} \frac{1}{(2\pi)^{d/2}|\Sigma_{y_i}|^{1/2}} e^{-\frac{1}{2}(x_i - \mu_{y_i})^T \Sigma_{y_i}^{-1}(x_i - u_{y_i})} + \right. \\
&\qquad \left. \sum_{j=1}^{NQ} \sum_{n=1}^{N} p\left(z_j = n \mid x'_j, \theta^{(s)}\right) \ln p\left(x'_j \mid z_j = n, \theta\right) p(z_j = n \mid \theta) \right)
\end{aligned}
\quad (5)
$$

Denote $\hat{z}_{jn}^{(s)} = p\left(z_j = n \mid x'_j, \theta^{(s)}\right)$. For the above formula, It can find the partial derivative and make it equal to 0, so that $\theta^{(s+1)}$ can be obtained.

$$
\begin{aligned}
\mu_n^{(s+1)} &= \frac{1}{\sum_{j=1}^{NQ} \hat{z}_{jn}^{(s)} + K} \left( \sum_{j=1}^{NQ} \hat{z}_{jn}^{(s)} x'_j + \sum_{y_i = n} x_i \right) \\
\Sigma_n^{(s+1)} &= \frac{1}{\sum_{j=1}^{NQ} \hat{z}_{jn}^{(s)} + K} \left( \sum_{j=1}^{NQ} \hat{z}_{jn}^{(s)} \left(x'_j - \mu_n\right)\left(x'_j - \mu_n\right)^T + \sum_{y_i = n} (x_i - \mu_n)(x_i - \mu_n)^T \right)
\end{aligned}
\quad (6)
$$

It can iterate the category subordination probabilities $\hat{z}_{jn}^{(s)}$, and the latent distribution parameters $\theta^{(s)}$ to gradually update and finally obtain the latent prototype vector.

## 4.2   Global Perception and Neighborhood Adaptation

From the previous analysis, it is clear that $\hat{z}_{jn}^{(s)}$ is the key of the latent prototype estimation. In general, it can be measured by the distance between the sample $x'_j$ and the current prototype $\mu^{(s)}$. Thus, one of the simplest estimation methods is as follows.

$$\hat{z}_{jn}^{(s)} = \frac{||x'_j - \mu_n^{(s)}||_2^2}{\sum_{i=1}^{N} ||x'_j - \mu_i^{(s)}||_2^2} \quad (7)$$

It can be found that the above formula has some problems, namely, the probability of belonging to each category is close when the distance between the sample to be measured and each prototype is not very different. Therefore, we try to use the temperature control coefficient $T$ for the sharpening probability. Let $d_n(x', \mu) = \frac{||x'_j - \mu_n||_2^2}{\sum_{i=1}^{N} ||x'_j - \mu_i||_2^2}$, then

$$\hat{z}_{jn}^{(s)} = \frac{\exp(d_n/T)}{\sum_{i=1}^{N} \exp(d_i/T)} \tag{8}$$

Further analysis shows that the above estimation only considers the distance of the query samples from $N$ prototype vectors (centers of category distribution), which is only local information. Global perception should also be considered, that is, for all samples, if they are close in the feature space, their categories should also be similar.

Assuming that $y_q$ is the calculated per-class probability that $x'_q$ belongs to, and $w\left(x'_q, x'_p\right)$ refers to the similarity of $x'_q$ to $x'_p$. When $\mu^{(s)}$ is a deterministic value, then we need to optimize the following problem.

$$\min_{y_q} \overbrace{y_q^t \left(\log\left(y_q\right) + d\right)}^{L_1(y_q)} + \underbrace{\left(-\sum_{q,p} w\left(x'_q, x'_p\right) y_q^t y_p\right)}_{L_2(y_q)} \quad \forall q \tag{9}$$

where the former term $L_1(y_q)$ represents the local distance cost of adding the information entropy regularization and the latter term $L_2(y_q)$ represents the cost based on global perception. Thus solving the above problem is equivalent to solving $\hat{z}_{jn}^{(s)}$ based on global perception with neighborhood adaptation.

The above formula is a very complex optimization problem. We simplify it as follows:

(1) Firstly, calculate the initial probability $y_q = [y_{q1}, ..., y_{qN}]$ for the current round based on local information, where $y_{qn}$ satisfies the following definition:

$$y_{qn} = \frac{\exp(d_n/T)}{\sum_{i=1}^{N} \exp(d_i/T)} \tag{10}$$

(2) Secondly, do a one-step gradient descent to fine-tune the initial probability, which will guarantee a certain regularity.

$$y_q^* = y_q - \lambda \frac{\partial L_1(y_q)}{\partial y_q} \tag{11}$$

(3) Finally, approximate the global perception based on the label propagation algorithm to obtain the probability $y'_q$ that the query sample belongs to, and then derive the final estimate.

$$\hat{z}_q = \alpha y_q^* + (1 - \alpha) y'_q \tag{12}$$

### 4.3  Overview

The proposed method updates the latent prototype vector with reference to the momentum update method, which makes the algorithm more stable. The current process is as follows.

---

**Algorithm 1.** Latent Prototype Estimation Algorithm

---

**Input:** input parameters $\{(x_i, y_i)\}_{i=1,\dots,NK}$ $\{x'_j\}_{j=1,\dots,NQ}$ $f_{\hat{z}}$
**Output:** output result
1: $\mu^{(0)} = \frac{1}{K}\sum_{y_i=n} x_i$
2: **for** $s = 1$ to $S$ **do**
3:   $\hat{Z} = f_{\hat{z}}(X', \mu^{(s)})$
4:   $\hat{\mu}^{(s+1)} = \frac{1}{\sum_{j=1}^{NQ}\hat{z}_j+K}\left(\sum_{j=1}^{NQ}\hat{z}_j x'_j + \sum_{y_i=n} x_i\right)$
5:   $\mu^{(s+1)} = (1-\gamma)\mu^{(s)} + \gamma\hat{\mu}^{(s+1)}$
6: **end for**

---

where $f_{\hat{z}}(x'_q, \mu) = \hat{z}_q = \alpha y_q^\star + (1-\alpha)y'_q$, $X' = [x'_1, x'_2, \dots, x'_{NQ}]^T$, $\hat{Z} = [\hat{z}_1, \hat{z}_2, \dots, \hat{z}_{NQ}]^T$.

## 5  Experimental Evaluation

### 5.1  Implementation Details

The 2000 5-way 5-shot classification tasks on Meta-Style are evaluated by different algorithms, and the query set in the task contains 15 images per class. The average accuracy of these few shot tasks is reported along with the 95% confidence interval based on the Gaussian distribution hypothesis.

All methods utilize the ResNet12 as backbone. The proposed latent prototype estimation algorithm uses representation vectors provided by Baseline++ [1].

After fine-tuning on the validation set, the tuned hyperparameters of the latent prototype estimation algorithm are $\alpha = 0.8, T = 0.05, \gamma = 0.2, S = 20$.

### 5.2  Quantitative Comparison

The following Table 2 provides the comparative results of the various algorithms on the Meta-Style. It can be clearly observed that the proposed method outperforms the existing methods that also use ResNet12 as the backbone network in both 5-way 5-shot, 5-way 1-shot settings and obtains consistent improvements.

On the 5-way 1-shot task, the proposed method improves about 29%, 25% compared to the MAML [4] and Prototype Network [13], respectively. Notably, our latent prototype estimation algorithm uses the representation vector provided by Baseline++ [1], but outperforms Baseline++ by about 10%.

On the 5-way 5-shot task, the proposed method still performs the best, but it is worth noting that the latent prototype estimation algorithm has a diminishing gain and outperforms Baseline++ by only about 5% in accuracy.

## 5.3   Ablation Experiments

In this subsection, an ablation study to quantitatively investigate the effectiveness of latent prototype estimation was conducted. By comparing with the SimpleShot [17] which simply aggregates support set samples, it shows whether the latent prototype estimation is effective. Both algorithms use normalized and power-law transformed feature extracted from Baseline++.

**Table 2.** Few-shot classification accuracy on Meta-Style

| Method | Reference | backbone | 5-way 1-shot | 5-way 5-shot |
|---|---|---|---|---|
| MAML [4] | ICML-2017 | ResNet12 | $31.05 \pm 0.35\%$ | / |
| Prototypical Networks [13] | NIPS-2018 | ResNet12 | $35.33 \pm 0.37\%$ | $57.62 \pm 0.37\%$ |
| Baseline++ [1] | ICLR-2019 | ResNet12 | $50.26 \pm 0.43\%$ | $72.41 \pm 0.35\%$ |
| Meta-Baseline [2] | ICCV-2021 | ResNet12 | $30.53 \pm 0.80\%$ | $42.36 \pm 0.35\%$ |
| Our method | | ResNet12 | $\mathbf{60.66 \pm 0.59\%}$ | $\mathbf{77.00 \pm 0.37\%}$ |

The results of the ablation experiments are shown in the Table 3. It can be found that the latent prototype estimation is significantly better than Simpleshot that directly obtains the class prototypes through the mean, which proves the effectiveness of the latent prototype estimation.

It is clear from the analysis that it is not a good method to directly obtain the category prototype through mean aggregation, because the distribution of the observed samples is likely to have a huge deviation from the original category distribution. As a contrast, collaborative estimation based on query set samples can alleviate the distribution offset, so as to obtain a reasonable category prototype.

**Table 3.** Ablation study for our method

| Feature From | with LPE | 5-way 1-shot | 5-way 5-shot |
|---|---|---|---|
| Baseline++ | | 52.03 | 72.87 |
| | √ | **60.66** | **77.00** |

## 6   Conclusion

In this work, a few-shot learning dataset Meta-Style for the social field is constructed, which is more representative of the performance and application value of few-shot learning algorithms in the social media domain. In addition, a powerful baseline method is proposed, which obtains the state-of-the-art result on Meta-Style. This work has promoted the exploration of the application value of few-shot learning algorithm in specific business scenarios.

# References

1. Chen, W.Y., Liu, Y.C., Kira, Z., Wang, Y.C.F., Huang, J.B.: A closer look at few-shot classification. In: International Conference on Learning Representations (2019)
2. Chen, Y., Liu, Z., Xu, H., Darrell, T., Wang, X.: Meta-baseline: exploring simple meta-learning for few-shot learning. In: Proceedings of the IEEE/CVF International Conference on Computer Vision, pp. 9062–9071 (2021)
3. Fei-Fei, L., Fergus, R., Perona, P.: One-shot learning of object categories. IEEE Trans. Pattern Anal. Mach. Intell. **28**(4), 594–611 (2006)
4. Finn, C., Abbeel, P., Levine, S.: Model-agnostic meta-learning for fast adaptation of deep networks. In: International Conference on Machine Learning, pp. 1126–1135. PMLR (2017)
5. Hu, Y., Gripon, V., Pateux, S.: Leveraging the feature distribution in transfer-based few-shot learning. In: Farkaš, I., Masulli, P., Otte, S., Wermter, S. (eds.) ICANN 2021. LNCS, vol. 12892, pp. 487–499. Springer, Cham (2021). https://doi.org/10.1007/978-3-030-86340-1_39
6. Kim, J., Kim, T., Kim, S., Yoo, C.D.: Edge-labeling graph neural network for few-shot learning. In: Proceedings of the IEEE/CVF Conference on Computer Vision and Pattern Recognition, pp. 11–20 (2019)
7. Lake, B.M., Salakhutdinov, R., Tenenbaum, J.B.: Human-level concept learning through probabilistic program induction. Science **350**(6266), 1332–1338 (2015)
8. Munkhdalai, T., Yuan, X., Mehri, S., Trischler, A.: Rapid adaptation with conditionally shifted neurons. In: International Conference on Machine Learning, pp. 3664–3673. PMLR (2018)
9. Radford, A., et al.: Learning transferable visual models from natural language supervision. In: International Conference on Machine Learning, pp. 8748–8763. PMLR (2021)
10. Redmon, J., Farhadi, A.: Yolov3: an incremental improvement (2018). https://doi.org/10.48550/ARXIV.1804.02767
11. Ren, M., et al.: Meta-learning for semi-supervised few-shot classification. In: International Conference on Learning Representations (2018)
12. Satorras, V.G., Estrach, J.B.: Few-shot learning with graph neural networks. In: International Conference on Learning Representations (2018)
13. Snell, J., Swersky, K., Zemel, R.: Prototypical networks for few-shot learning. In: Proceedings of the International Conference on Neural Information Processing Systems, pp. 4080–4090 (2017)
14. Tang, K.D., Tappen, M.F., Sukthankar, R., Lampert, C.H.: Optimizing one-shot recognition with micro-set learning. In: Computer Society Conference on Computer Vision and Pattern Recognition, pp. 3027–3034. IEEE (2010)
15. Vinyals, O., Blundell, C., Lillicrap, T., Kavukcuoglu, K., Wierstra, D.: Matching networks for one shot learning. In: Proceedings of the International Conference on Neural Information Processing Systems, pp. 3637–3645 (2016)
16. Wah, C., Branson, S., Welinder, P., Perona, P., Belongie, S.: The Caltech-UCSD birds-200-2011 dataset. California Institute of Technology (2011)
17. Wang, Y., Chao, W.L., Weinberger, K.Q., van der Maaten, L.: Simpleshot: revisiting nearest-neighbor classification for few-shot learning. arXiv preprint arXiv:1911.04623 (2019)
18. Ziko, I., Dolz, J., Granger, E., Ayed, I.B.: Laplacian regularized few-shot learning. In: International Conference on Machine Learning, pp. 11660–11670. PMLR (2020)

# Problem Classification for Tailored Helpdesk Auto-replies

Reece Nicholls, Ryan Fellows, Steve Battle[(✉)], and Hisham Ihshaish

Computer Science Research Centre (CSRC),
University of the West of England (UWE), Bristol, UK
steve.battle@uwe.ac.uk

**Abstract.** IT helpdesks are charged with the task of responding quickly
to user queries. To give the user confidence that their query matters,
the helpdesk will auto-reply to the user with confirmation that their
query has been received and logged. This auto-reply may include generic
'boiler-plate' text that addresses common problems of the day, with relevant information and links. The approach explored here is to tailor the
content of the auto-reply to the user's problem, so as to increase the
relevance of the information included. Problem classification is achieved
by training a neural network on a suitable corpus of IT helpdesk email
data. While this is no substitute for follow-up by helpdesk agents, the
aim is that this system will provide a practical stop-gap.

**Keywords:** Helpdesk · Supervised learning · Data augmentation

## 1 Introduction

The university IT helpdesk system studied in this research uses a "call" ticket
system to manage requests and incidents from students and staff. These tickets
are usually generated by requests from self-service web services, email, phone,
web chats, and walk-in advice points. Currently, a generic acknowledgement
email is sent back with the most frequently asked issues (for example, guidance
on resetting passwords). Ultimately, these tickets are processed by human agents
who will assign the ticket to the relevant agent or team for resolution.

Many of these tickets are requests for information, which may already be
available on help pages or FAQ pages. An automated system that can process
these emails and automatically reply with the appropriate information may provide useful interim support, and in the best-case scenario may even resolve the
query raised by the user.

The dataset used in this paper is a real-world corpus of IT helpdesk interactions between University students & staff, and helpdesk assistants. This dataset
consists of 600 email threads and 5697 follow-up emails, including the direction
(incoming or outgoing), subject line, email body and time-stamp. A small selection of emails can be seen in Table 1. For this study we use only incoming emails,
and for simplicity the subject line and email body have been concatenated. All

© The Author(s), under exclusive license to Springer Nature Switzerland AG 2022
E. Pimenidis et al. (Eds.): ICANN 2022, LNCS 13532, pp. 445–454, 2022.
https://doi.org/10.1007/978-3-031-15937-4_37

punctuation has been removed and the time-stamp has been discarded. The interactions consist of a wide range of natural language queries that helpdesk staff must try to resolve. The dataset is fully anonymised at source, so that the identity of individuals is not revealed. In addition we attempt to remove any additional contextual information about the locale that could provide clues about their identity.

**Table 1.** Examples of uncategorised emails from the dataset. Each one is a concatentation of the subject line and email body, anonymised, and with punctuation removed.

---

"creative cloud Hi I can no longer load any of the adobe products on my PC as It says licence has expired Is this a known issue"

"Solidworks Good Morning I tried installing solidworks off the appsanywhere cloudpaging player but whenever i go to launch it gets removed straight away and i cant install it Please advise Cheers"

"Hi I tried to access my blackboard and it kept giving me an error message Hi I tried to access my blackboard and it kept giving me an error message"

"Forgotten password Hi Im having trouble logging in to my student account Ive forgotten my login and password Can you help please Kind regards"

"Temporary login ID for visitor needs wifi access would like to process a temporary ID for external visitor that needs to connect to wifi Event is tomorrow but shehe may come again after lockdown"

---

# 2   Natural Language Processing

Natural Language Processing (NLP) is a field of Computer Science where the goal is to make machines understand our spoken and written languages. NLP must cope with the complexity of grammar, syntax, and vocabulary of languages, as well as the semantics of words used in sentences [3, p.22]. Humans are able to read an email and determine which category the email falls into, such as problems with WiFi or passwords etc. Natural Language Processing is used to train a neural network on a corpus of email content, identified as *patterns*. Supervised learning is the task of learning a function that maps an input to an output based on a sample of input-output pairs [10]. Every email in the dataset is labelled with the category it belongs to. The training algorithm uses this to learn to classify new incoming queries.

However, the raw data comprises uncategorised emails, so establishing categories for supervised learning is problematic. It's possible to use clustering methods, but without access to a 'ground truth', the resulting categories must still be verified by helpdesk agents. Methods like Latent Dirichlet Allocation (LDA) [2] produce a statistical model that allows sets of observations to be explained by a number of *unobserved* categories, known as a *topic model*. LDA can be used to cluster data, using the presence of words as weighted signifiers of any given category. It enables the top-ranking words for any given category to be listed explicitly, providing the means for users to inspect, verify, and even revise the resulting clusters manually.

# 3   Methodology

This study side-steps the issues around the initial data categorisation, assuming instead that users are directly able to define categories using a set of keywords, such as may be produced by LDA. Emails in the raw data that match any of these keywords are assigned to that category to produce the training set. The categories and their associated keywords are ordered so that any given email is assigned only to the first matching category, though we strive (manually) to minimise the overlap. This provides a convenient method of categorisation, and because it is user-defined, establishes a ground-truth for supervised learning.

The five categories used in this study, and the keywords associated with them are listed in Table 2. Using these keywords to select data and assign a category produces a smaller subset of 265 emails used for training and testing as described in Sect. 3.1.

**Table 2.** Five user-defined categories and their associated keywords

| | |
|---|---|
| Adobe | { 'Adobe', 'Creative Cloud' } |
| AppsAnywhere | { 'AppsAnywhere', 'license', 'cloudpaging'} |
| Blackboard | { 'blackboard' } |
| Password | { 'password', 'mfa', 'multifactor', 'multi-factor', 'multi factor' } |
| WiFi | { 'wifi', 'wi-fi', 'network', 'eduroam', 'connection', 'internet', 'remote access' } |

This keyword based approach to defining categories begs the question, "why not use the keywords directly as a classifier, bypassing the neural network?" This is a valid approach, so in the evaluation section we compare the neural network solution with a simple classifier based on a *decision tree* – as a baseline estimator – trained on a binary vector indicating the presence or otherwise, of each keyword in any given email. This approach echoes the way we search for the samples in the first place, based on keyword matching.

## 3.1   Training/Test Data Split

The data is split into training data and testing data, and for these experiments an 80% training to 20% test ratio is used throughout. The available data is divided into a training set containing 212 emails, leaving 53 emails for testing. Because we have multi-category data, *stratified sampling* is used to split each category proportionally. This minimises sampling bias in the training set and helps to create a test set which best represents the entire population of data [7].

## 3.2   Data Augmentation

Following the training/test data split, the training data contains 212 different emails used for training the model. This is a relatively small dataset which is at risk of overfitting by the learning algorithm. To minimise overfitting and increase the accuracy of the model, we use a process called *data augmentation* which Shahul [11] describes as a way of generating brand new sentences to train the model. By preventing overfitting, the model is encouraged to generalise [12]. We use a technique known as *synonym replacement* [8] which generates new sentences from existing sentences, effectively re-expressing them.

Not only do we have limited data, but the data is imbalanced in terms of the number of samples in each category. This class imbalance [4] may create a learning bias towards the categories with more emails. We use a form of *Stratified* Data augmentation that allows us to re-balance the training data so that each category receives equal representation. The email data is augmented so as to present 200 emails per category, which involves augmenting some categories more than others. This produces a training set with 1000 samples, distributed equally over the five categories.

In the evaluation section, we compare classifiers with and without data-augmentation to see if the expected improvement is present.

### 3.3  Stemming and Stop-Word Removal

Before training the model, the data must first be prepared for processing. Word tokenisation chops up a sentence into individual tokens, stripping out punctuation leaving only the individual words or terms of a sentence [5]. After tokenisation, we take each word (or token) in the patterns and perform *lemmatisation*, converting it into its equivalent base word [5]. The process of lemmatisation allows for greater prediction accuracy as it removes all the various tenses and combinations of the same base word. For example, the words 'changed', 'changes' and 'changing' would all be lemmatised to their base word, 'change'. This enables the model to generalise, as a model trained on the word 'change' would correctly recognise the word 'changing' in an email, because they share a common base.

After lemmatisation, the final pre-processing step is to remove stop-words. Stop-words are common words which provide little value to a computer in representing a sentence [5]. Examples of English stop-words are 'and', 'are', 'from', 'he', 'is', 'the', 'it', 'the' and 'to'. The sentence, "the internet is not working" after stop-words are removed is reduced to "internet not working", and "internet not work" when combined with lemmatisation; both preserving the underlying semantics and both providing a simple sentence representation for supervised learning.

## 4  Problem Classification

Classification is the process of assigning items to a limited set of categories [1]. Given the text of a user query, we must classify it one of a predefined set of categories, each one of which is associated with a different response that to be included in the helpdesk auto-reply.

The bag-of-words model (BoW) is commonly used for text classification problems, and is the method selected for this research. The frequency of occurrence of each word is represented as a vector and used for training a classifier [6]. Each email is represented as a bag, or *multiset*, of its words, disregarding grammar and word order, but retaining the number of occurrences.

This bag of words representation is then used to train the neural network model. We build a sequential model, conventionally known as fully connected feed-forward neural net, comprising a stack of three main layers, where each layer has exactly one input tensor and one output tensor. The input layer is a tensor, a vector representing the bag of words. We allocate 40 units to a single intermediate (hidden) layer. The number of hidden units is determined by starting low, and then incrementing this by stages until no appreciable improvement in accuracy is seen during the learning phase. Finally we have an output layer with one unit for each output category. This *softmax* layer converts the output scores to a normalized probability distribution. Dropout layers, sandwiched between these principal layers, randomly clear their inputs to minimise over-fitting.

The number of epochs - the number of cycles through the training set - is set to 50 epochs, as the improvement in accuracy during the learning phase shows no appreciable improvement beyond this point.

## 5   Solution

Our solution uses the NLTK library (natural language toolkit), NumPy and TensorFlow to perform the machine learning and language processing required to train the model and classify emails. The NLPAug library is used to perform data augmentation on the training data. For the model evaluation, we use scikit-learn, Pandas and matplotlib libraries. Following data preparation, the neural network is built using TensorFlow. The result is a trained model used to classify emails into their respective categories.

The classifier is based on the trained model, and uses the NumPy and Tensor-Flow libraries to predict which category the email belongs to. During evaluation, the classifier tests the trained model against the test data. For the application of this model to incoming emails, currently in prototype, the classification model is applied to individual emails and the response associated with the predicted category is embedded within a generic auto-reply email template. If the prediction error is below a certain threshold (25%) the system reverts to a standard auto-reply, rather than risk sending out irrelevant information.

## 6   Evaluation

Data augmentation is applied not only to reduce over-fitting, but also to re-balance the training data. We would expect to see improved results. Figure 1 shows a *confusion matrix* for the neural network trained on the data without augmentation. A confusion matrix is a table showing the performance and quality of the model, with each row representing the true categories, and the columns

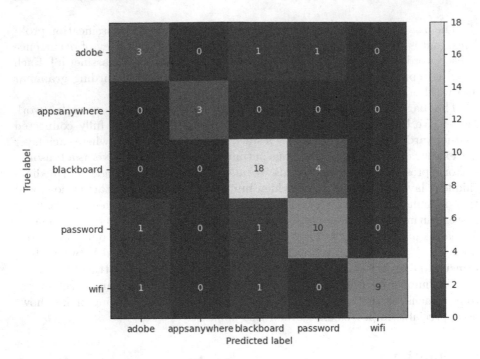

**Fig. 1.** Confusion matrix for neural network without data augmentation.

representing the predicted categories [9]. It literally allows you to see if the model is confusing one category with another. A similar confusion matrix for the neural net trained on the augmented data can be seen in Fig. 2. The results reported here reflect the median accuracy achieved over a small number of test runs.

It's possible to make out greater number of *true positives* in the leading diagonal of the confusion matrix for the model trained on the augmented data. The differences are clearer in the classification reports for each in Tables 3 and 4. For the model without data augmentation we see lower overall accuracy and lower average precision.

The accuracy is the number of correct predictions divided by the number of samples, expressed as a percentage. The neural net trained on the augmented data set has an overall accuracy of 85%, compared to 81% accuracy for the model trained on the unaugmented data. This percentage difference is borne out across a number of test runs. The average precision for the neural net trained on the augmented data set is 85%, versus 82% for the model trained on the unaugmented data. The model trained on the augmented data performs better in all respects.

**Table 3.** Classification report for neural network without data augmentation.

|             | Precision | Recall | f1-score | Support |
|-------------|-----------|--------|----------|---------|
| Adobe       | 0.60      | 0.60   | 0.60     | 5       |
| Appsanywhere| 1.00      | 1.00   | 1.00     | 3       |
| Blackboard  | 0.86      | 0.82   | 0.84     | 22      |
| Password    | 0.67      | 0.83   | 0.74     | 12      |
| WiFi        | 1.00      | 0.82   | 0.90     | 11      |
| Accuracy    |           |        | 0.81     | 53      |
| Macro avg   | 0.82      | 0.81   | 0.82     | 53      |

**Table 4.** Classification report for neural network with data augmentation.

|             | Precision | Recall | f1-score | Support |
|-------------|-----------|--------|----------|---------|
| Adobe       | 0.75      | 0.60   | 0.67     | 5       |
| Appsanywhere| 1.00      | 1.00   | 1.00     | 3       |
| Blackboard  | 0.91      | 0.91   | 0.91     | 22      |
| Password    | 0.79      | 0.92   | 0.85     | 12      |
| WiFi        | 0.80      | 0.73   | 0.76     | 11      |
| Accuracy    |           |        | 0.85     | 53      |
| Macro avg   | 0.85      | 0.83   | 0.84     | 53      |

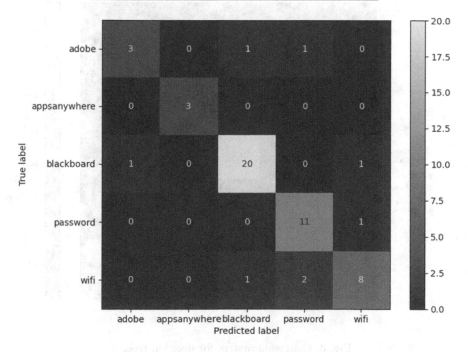

**Fig. 2.** Confusion matrix for neural network with data augmentation.

Now we turn our attention to comparing the neural network model with a simpler decision tree model. The confusion matrix for this is shown in Fig. 3. Looking at the classification report in Table 5, we see that the decision tree is outperforming the neural net in *accuracy*, 91% compared to 85%, respectively. However, as we have an imbalanced sample this is a biased metric in favour of the most frequent helpdesk queries about blackboard (a Virtual Learning Environment), as can be seen in the *support* column of the classification reports. We require our email auto-replies to be accurate across the whole range of possible queries so, for this application, a measure that treats each category with equal weight is favoured. We can see by inspection that the decision tree performs particularly badly on the small number of queries about AppsAnywhere (a higher-ed app-store). The precision (the ratio of true positives to the total number of positive predictions) is zero because there are no true positives at all. Similarly, the recall for this category is also zero, which indicates the complete inability of the classifier to identify the positive samples in this case. This in fact emphasises the well-known high variance (or overfitting) downside to decision tree induction, especially in learning problems with a limited sample size and explicit under-representation of some target categories.

The (macro) averages of these results are therefore a better indicator of performance in this application, and we can see that these are better for the neural network (with data augmentation) than for the decision tree (a weighted

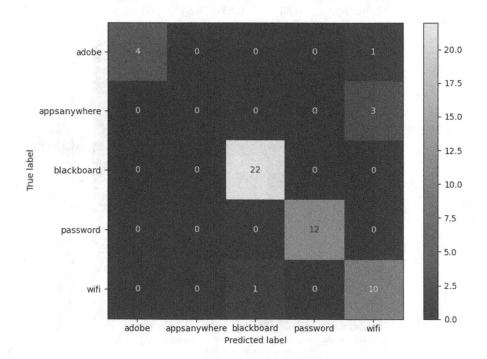

**Fig. 3.** Confusion matrix for decision tree.

average of scores would produces a similar imbalance as the accuracy, so is not considered here). The results for precision and recall are combined in a *harmonic mean* as the F-measure, or f1 score, which gives us the percentage of positive predictions that were correct. Comparing the (macro) average F-measure for the neural net and decision tree we see that it is greater for the neural net than for the decision tree, 84% compared to 73%, despite the fact that the decision tree achieves greater accuracy.

The methods and findings explored here are preliminary, and it is hard to draw general conclusions based on the limited data available. Nonetheless, we see the application of a 'light' neural net approach outperforming simpler learning methods on a small data set. Their ability to perform classification tasks in such conditions is further enhanced by data augmentation. In short, the neural net has learned better on all categories whereas the simpler model (the decision tree) focuses primarily on the majority cases.

**Table 5.** Classification report for decision tree

|              | Precision | Recall | f1-score | Support |
|--------------|-----------|--------|----------|---------|
| Adobe        | 1.00      | 0.80   | 0.89     | 5       |
| Appsanywhere | 0.00      | 0.00   | 0.00     | 3       |
| Blackboard   | 0.96      | 1.00   | 0.98     | 22      |
| Password     | 1.00      | 1.00   | 1.00     | 12      |
| WiFi         | 0.71      | 0.91   | 0.80     | 11      |
| Accuracy     |           |        | 0.91     | 53      |
| Macro avg    | 0.73      | 0.74   | 0.73     | 53      |

# 7   Conclusion

The helpdesk system described in this paper produces reliable responses based on classification of the user's initial query. These results provide positive evidence towards the use of data augmentation for small data sets, and demonstrate the improved precision of neural network models, over simpler models such as decision trees. However, they should be treated with caution as the size of dataset is currently too small to draw any strong conclusions, limiting our study in relation to generalisability as well as statistical significance. However, we continue to actively collect data, and are encouraged that tailored auto-replies can provide a useful stop-gap measure until helpdesk agents are able to step in and take over.

# References

1. Alpaydin, E.: Introduction to Machine Learning. The MIT Press, Cambridge (2014)

2. Blei, D.M., Ng, A.Y., Jordan, M.I.: Latent Dirichlet allocation. J. Mach. Learn. Res. **3**(4–5), 993–1022 (2003)
3. Ganegedara, T.: Natural Language Processing with TensorFlow: Teach Language to Machines Using Python's Deep Learning Library. Packt Publishing (2018)
4. López, F.: Class imbalance: random sampling and data augmentation with imbalanced-learn. https://towardsdatascience.com/class-imbalance-random-sampling-and-data-augmentation-with-imbalanced-learn-63f3a92ef04a, February 2021. Accessed 09 Apr 2022
5. Manning, C., Raghavan, P., Schütze, H.: Introduction to Information Retrieval. Cambridge University Press, Cambridge (2008). https://nlp.stanford.edu/IR-book/
6. McTear, M.: The Conversational Interface. Springer, Cham (2016). https://doi.org/10.1007/978-3-319-32967-3
7. Menon, S.: Stratified sampling in machine learning. https://medium.com/analytics-vidhya/stratified-sampling-in-machine-learning-f5112b5b9cfe, December 2020. Accessed 04 Apr 2022
8. Nayak, R.: Hands on data augmentation in NLP using NLPAUG python library. https://medium.com/codex/hands-on-data-augmentation-in-nlp-using-nlpaug-python-library-ad323c22908, April 2022. Accessed 09 Apr 2022
9. Powers, D.M.W.: Evaluation: from precision, recall and f-factor to ROC, informedness, markedness & correlation. Technical report SIE-07-001, Flinders University of South Australia, Adelaide, Australia (2007). https://www.researchgate.net/publication/228529307_Evaluation_From_Precision_Recall_and_F-Factor_to_ROC_Informedness_Markedness_Correlation
10. Russell, S.J., Norvig, P.: Artificial Intelligence: A Modern Approach, 3rd edn. Prentice Hall, Hoboken (2010)
11. Shahul, E.: Data augmentation in NLP: best practices from a Kaggle master. https://neptune.ai/blog/data-augmentation-nlp, November 2021. Accessed 03 Mar 2022
12. Wang, J., Luis, P.: The effectiveness of data augmentation in image classification using deep learning, report number: 300 (2017). http://cs231n.stanford.edu/reports/2017/pdfs/300.pdf. Accessed 04 Apr 2022

# Self-Enhancer: A Self-supervised Framework for Low-Supervision, Drifted Data with Significant Missing Values

Yu Chen[✉] and Peter Flach

University of Bristol, Bristol, UK
{yc14600,Peter.Flach}@bristol.ac.uk

**Abstract.** In this paper, we introduce a self-supervised framework for enhancing regular machine learning methods in scenarios that have: 1. very limited labeled data, 2. drifted data distributions, 3. significant missing values in both training and testing sets. These issues commonly exist in real world data and cause performance degradation to a large extent when directly applying supervised machine learning methods. We propose a multitask self-supervised framework to take care of all those issues by utilising a large amount of unlabeled data, which can bring promising improvements on downstream tasks.

**Keywords:** Self-supervised learning · Distribution drift · Missing values · Unlabeled data

## 1 Introduction

Modern machine learning methods, especially deep learning methods, have shown strong performance in applications that often have easy access to substantial amounts of data with full supervision as well as huge pre-trained models for better generalization. However, applications in many other fields (such as digital health care, medical diagnosis, fraud detection, etc.) often require expensive cost for data labeling and encounter difficulties in generalization between training and testing data sets. Moreover, large proportions of missing values may appear due to inevitable reasons in practice, for instance, hardware malfunctioning, drained batteries, privacy concerns, etc. These issues commonly exist in real world data and dampen the performance of many successful machine learning methods.

To deal with small training sets, few-shot learning focuses on transferring knowledge from a pre-trained model to new classes using a few instances of the new classes [4–6]. This would require that the pre-trained model has been trained on a similar classification task with a large related dataset that have general structures shared with the new classes. For data that are difficult to meet these

Supported by EPSRC-funded SPHERE IRC EP/K031910/1, EP/R005273/1.

requirements, few-shot learning is infeasible to solve the problem. Self-supervised learning makes efforts to learn better representations from unlabeled data for a downstream task with limited labeled data [1–3]. It fits situations that have easy access to large amounts of unlabeled data but expensive cost to labeled data. The key idea is producing supervision from the data itself. Prior work of self-supervised learning has shown promising results in improving the performance of downstream tasks.

In this paper, we propose a framework of self-supervised learning for solving the following problems in a downstream task: 1. very limited labeled data, 2. drifted data distributions, 3. significant missing values in both training and testing sets. We use data collected from real smart homes [7] in our experiments. The experimental results show that the proposed self-supervised methods can significantly improve the performance of the downstream task.

## 2 Problem Setting

In this section we clarify the problem setting of our work. Figure 1 demonstrates how to apply the self-supervised model for a downstream task. In our settings, the data has the following properties: 1). the training and testing sets for the downstream task model are both small due to very limited labeled data; 2). the training and testing sets are from different data distributions due to data distribution drift; 3). one or multiple features of the data (including the unlabelled data) may contain significant missing values.

In our experiments with data from smart homes, the downstream task is indoor localization, i.e. predicting the resident's location in the smart home. The labeled data were generated by a technician who had a few walk-around in the house on an installation day and a removal day. The labels were manually added by the technician whilst the walk-around. The training set is the labeled data from

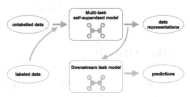

**Fig. 1.** Demonstration of applying self-supervised models for a downstream task.

the installation day and the testing set is from the removal day. The unlabeled data were collected from the period in between and generated by the resident of the smart home. A large proportion of missing values exist in both labeled and unlabeled data due to hardware malfunctioning.

## 3 The Self-supervised Framework: Self-Enhancer

In this section we briefly introduce Self-Enhancer: the self-supervised framework for jointly handling missing values and self-supervised tasks. Here we assume the self-supervised task is a classification task, however, it could be regression task as well. Figure 2 shows the architecture of Self-Enhancer, which enables jointly training on a chain of regressors and a classifier. The regressors aim to

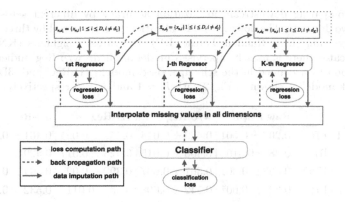

**Fig. 2.** The architecture of Self-Enhancer: a multitask self-supervised framework. It enables jointly training on a chain of regression tasks and a classification task. The classification loss will help with the regression tasks through gradient back propagation (green dot lines). $\tilde{x}_{n,d_j}$ denotes the $n$-th input data to the $j$-th regressor and $d_j$ is the index of the missing feature (i.e. the regression target) of the $j$-th regressor. $D$ is the number of total features. $K$ is the number of regressors. This multi-task model is trained by unlabelled data and the classification task is a self-supervised task that is different with the downstream task. (Color figure online)

interpolate missing values of multiple features in a chain, where the first regressor is applied to the feature with least missing values and the last regressor is for the feature with most missing values. The input data to later regressors will contain interpolated missing values from early regressors. During the training phase, the early regressors will receive gradients back propagated by the later regression losses; the classification task will affect the regression tasks through gradient back propagation too.

The final loss of this multitask model combines the losses of regression tasks and the classification task as given in Eq. (1). $\lambda_r$ is a hyperparameter for tuning the weights of both parts. When $\lambda_r = 0$, only the classification task is trained, the missing values are filled with zeros.

$$\mathcal{L}_{MT} = \lambda_r \sum_{k=1}^{K} L_{reg}^{(k)} + (1 - \lambda_r)\mathcal{L}_{clf}, \quad 1 > \lambda_r \geq 0. \tag{1}$$

The regression tasks and the classification task may not be consistent in updating the model parameters. When $\lambda_r$ is larger, the strength of regression tasks is larger and the classification task may get a worse performance. Similarly, the classification task may lead to a worse regression performance when $\lambda_r$ is smaller. In general, the performance of the downstream task would be better when the self-supervised model is less overfitted to its training data.

The self-supervised classification task in our experiments with data from smart homes[1] is using the real-numbered features to predict the binary features.

---

[1] https://www.bristol.ac.uk/engineering/research/digital-health/research/sphere/.

**Table 1.** Comparing downstream localization accuracy by different self-supervised models on two datasets. The downstream localization task is trained by three baselines: Logistic Regression (LR), Random Forest (RF), K-Nearest Neighbors (KNN). 'Raw feature' indicates there is no self-supervised model applied. 'w/o Reg' indicates there is no regression task trained in the self-supervised model. '1D-Reg' and '3D-Reg' use the multitask model as shown in Fig. 2 with $K = 1$ and $K = 3$ respectively.

|         |     | Raw feature | w/o Reg | 1D-Reg | 3D-Reg |
|---------|-----|-------------|---------|--------|--------|
| House 1 | LR  | $0.207 \pm 0.001$ | $0.429 \pm 0.014$ | $0.452 \pm 0.025$ | $0.461 \pm 0.015$ |
|         | RF  | $0.38 \pm 0.016$ | $0.403 \pm 0.015$ | $0.423 \pm 0.017$ | $0.429 \pm 0.022$ |
|         | KNN | $0.333 \pm 0.001$ | $0.367 \pm 0.007$ | $0.392 \pm 0.02$ | $0.394 \pm 0.015$ |
| House 2 | LR  | $0.328 \pm 0.001$ | $0.542 \pm 0.008$ | $0.55 \pm 0.011$ | $0.532 \pm 0.007$ |
|         | RF  | $0.474 \pm 0.017$ | $0.525 \pm 0.009$ | $0.51 \pm 0.01$ | $0.485 \pm 0.01$ |
|         | KNN | $0.476 \pm 0.001$ | $0.493 \pm 0.016$ | $0.504 \pm 0.016$ | $0.493 \pm 0.018$ |

More specifically, the real-numbered features include: the Received Signal Strength Indications (RSSI) of wearable sensors that were recorded by several Bluetooth access point installed in each smart home; the binary features include: binary readings of Passive Infra-Red (PIR) sensors that were installed in different locations of each smart home. We give experimental results of two smart homes in Table 1, which demonstrate the effectiveness of the proposed method.

# References

1. Chen, T., Kornblith, S., Swersky, K., Norouzi, M., Hinton, G.E.: Big self-supervised models are strong semi-supervised learners. Adv. Neural. Inf. Process. Syst. **33**, 22243–22255 (2020)
2. Jing, L., Tian, Y.: Self-supervised visual feature learning with deep neural networks: a survey. IEEE Trans. Pattern Anal. Mach. Intell. **43**(11), 4037–4058 (2020)
3. Misra, I., Maaten, L.V.D.: Self-supervised learning of pretext-invariant representations. In: Proceedings of the IEEE/CVF Conference on Computer Vision and Pattern Recognition, pp. 6707–6717 (2020)
4. Snell, J., Swersky, K., Zemel, R.: Prototypical networks for few-shot learning. In: Advances in Neural Information Processing Systems, vol. 30 (2017)
5. Sun, Q., Liu, Y., Chua, T.S., Schiele, B.: Meta-transfer learning for few-shot learning. In: Proceedings of the IEEE/CVF Conference on Computer Vision and Pattern Recognition, pp. 403–412 (2019)
6. Wang, Y., Yao, Q., Kwok, J.T., Ni, L.M.: Generalizing from a few examples: a survey on few-shot learning. ACM Comput. Surv. (CSUR) **53**(3), 1–34 (2020)
7. Zhu, N., et al.: Bridging e-health and the internet of things: the sphere project. IEEE Intell. Syst. **30**(4), 39–46 (2015)

# Self-supervised Anomaly Detection by Self-distillation and Negative Sampling

Nima Rafiee[1], Rahil Gholamipoor[1], Nikolas Adaloglou[1], Simon Jaxy[1],
Julius Ramakers[1], and Markus Kollmann[1,2]($\boxtimes$)

[1] Department of Computer Science, Heinrich Heine University, Düsseldorf, Germany
{rafiee,rahil.gholamipoorfard,nikolaos.adaloglou,simon.jaxy,
ramakers,kollmann}@hhu.de
[2] Department of Biology, Heinrich Heine University, Düsseldorf, Germany

**Abstract.** Detecting whether examples belong to a given in-distribution or are out-of-distribution (OOD) requires identifying features that are specific to the in-distribution. In the absence of labels, these features can be learned by self-supervised representation learning techniques under the generic assumption that the most abstract features are those which are statistically most over-represented in comparison to other distributions from the same domain. This work shows that self-distillation of the in-distribution training set together with contrasting against negative examples derived from shifting transformation of auxiliary data strongly improves OOD detection. We find that this improvement depends on how the negative samples are generated, with the general observation that negative samples that keep the statistics of lower level features but change the global semantics result in higher detection accuracy on average. For the first time, we introduce a sensitivity score using which we can optimise negative sampling in a systematic way in an unsupervised setting. We demonstrate the efficiency of our approach across a diverse range of OOD detection problems, setting new benchmarks for unsupervised OOD detection in the visual domain.

**Keywords:** Anomaly detection · Self-supervised learning · Self-distillation · Negative sampling

## 1 Introduction

OOD detection or anomaly detection is the problem of deciding whether a given test sample is drawn from the same in-distribution as a given training set or belongs to an alternative distribution. Many real-world applications require highly accurate OOD detection for secure deployment, such as in medical diagnosis. Despite the advances in deep learning, neural network estimators can generate systematic errors for test examples that are far from the training set [22]. For example, it has been shown that Deep Neural Networks (DNNs) with ReLU activation functions can make false predictions for OOD samples with arbitrarily high confidence [10].

© The Author(s), under exclusive license to Springer Nature Switzerland AG 2022
E. Pimenidis et al. (Eds.): ICANN 2022, LNCS 13532, pp. 459–470, 2022.
https://doi.org/10.1007/978-3-031-15937-4_39

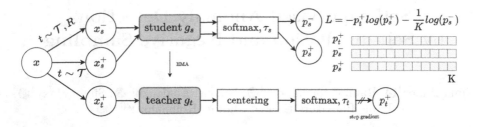

**Fig. 1.** An overview of the proposed contrastive self-distillation framework, consisting of student and teacher networks, $g_s$ and $g_t$, that map two random transformations of the same image, $x_s^+ \sim \mathcal{T}(x)$ and $x_t^+ \sim \mathcal{T}(x)$ to the same class. Negative views, $x^-$, arise from first applying a shifting transformation $R$, such as random rotation, followed by $\mathcal{T}$ to either an in-distribution image $x$ or an auxiliary image $x_{aux}$.

A major challenge in OOD detection is the case where the features of outlier examples are statistically close to the features of in-distribution examples, which is frequently the case for natural images. In particular, it has been shown that deep density estimators like Variational Autoencoders (VAEs) [14], PixelCNNs [28], and normalising flow models [24] can on average assign higher likelihood to OOD examples than to examples from the in-distribution [19]. This surprising finding can be partially attributed to an inductive bias from upweighting local pixel correlations as a consequence of using convolutional neural networks.

A challenging scenario of anomaly detection is near OOD detection [30], where the OOD distribution samples are similar to the in-distribution. A particular challenging OOD detection task is given by CIFAR10 and CIFAR100 [16] as in-distribution and OOD respectively, where the larger number of classes in CIFAR100 makes it harder to identify in-distribution specific features. For the cases where the in and out distributions are not closely related, we refer to as far OOD. State-Of-The-Art (SOTA) performance has been obtained for the CIFAR10/CIFAR100 near OOD detection task, using supervised pretrained models on ImageNet-21K [8]. However, CIFAR100 and CIFAR10 share many of their classes with ImageNet but the classes among themselves are mutually exclusive. The advantage of using supervised pretrained models as OOD detectors drops if there is no class overlap between pretrain dataset and the OOD test set, such as for SVHN [8]. To overcome these limitations, a plethora of self-supervised pretext tasks have been proposed that provide a richer learning signal that enables abstract feature learning [4]. These advancements in self-supervised learning have shown remarkable results on unsupervised anomaly detection [26,27,30] by solely relying on the in-distribution data. More recently, it has been suggested to include dataset-specific augmentations that shift the in-distribution – so-called negative samples. The core idea behind using shifting transformations is to concentrate the learned representation in feature space. This can result in a more conservative decision boundary for the in-distribution [12]. However, in-distribution shifting requires dataset-specific prior knowledge

[18]. Therefore, a bad choice of augmentations may result in rejecting the in-distribution test samples, which reduces the OOD detection performance. In this paper, we propose an improved version of the DINO [3] framework together with a sensitivity score for the problem of OOD detection. Figure 1 depicts an overall view of our framework. The main contributions of this work are summarized as follows:

- We propose a self-supervised self-distillation method that leverages unlabelled data for OOD detection which aims at drawing a tight, not necessary simply connected, decision boundary between the in-distribution data and an auxiliary negative distribution.
- We introduce an auxiliary loss that encourages unlabeled negative samples to be uniformly assigned to the existing in-distribution soft-classes.
- To the best of our knowledge, for the first time we introduce a sensitivity score defined by the AUROC value between the in-distribution training set and the in-distribution test set. Using sensitivity score, we can intuitively compare the effect of different negative auxiliary sets and to find optimal values by grid search for training hyperparameters without the access to OOD validation set.
- Finally, we show that the proposed framework does not only improve OOD detection performance but also improves representation learning for the in-distribution, as measured by the K-Nearest Neighbour (K-NN) accuracy.

## 2   Related Works

**Supervised OOD Detection Methods.** In-distribution classification accuracy is highly correlated with OOD performance [8]. This has motivated supervised OOD detection approaches to learn representations from classification networks [11]. This can be achieved by directly training a classifier on the in-distribution or by pre-training on a larger dataset. Fine-tuning pretrained transformers [29] has shown promising OOD scores. In computer vision, Koner et al. [15] leveraged the contextualization capabilities of pretrained Vision Transformer (ViT) [7] by exploiting the global image context. Such models heavily rely on the classes of the pretrained dataset, which often include classes from both the in and out distribution. Although, supervised pretraining can form a good boundary for OOD detection, it has two limitations, firstly the pretraining dataset should share labels with both in and out distributions, and secondly impeded OOD performance is observed when the distributions have overlapping classes. Mohseni et al. [18] recently presented a 2-step method that initially learns how to weight the in-distribution transformations based on a supervised objective. Then, the selected shifting transformations are applied in a self-supervised setup for OOD detection. Human-level supervision is still required to learn the best shifting transformations for each training dataset. In *Geometric* [13], Hendrycks et al. defined a self-supervised task to predict geometric transformations to improve the robustness and uncertainty of deep learning models. They further improve their self-supervised technique with supervision through outlier exposure.

**Unsupervised OOD Detection Methods.** Existing label-free OOD detection approaches can be separated in density-based [20], reconstruction-based [23], and self-supervised learning [13] methods. Density-based methods aim to fit a probability distribution (e.g. Gaussian) to the training data and then use it for OOD detection. Reconstruction-based methods assume the network would generalize less for unseen OOD samples. Meanwhile, recent studies [19] revealed that probabilistic generative models can fail to distinguish between training data and OOD inputs. Self-supervised methods have recently shown that adopting pretext tasks results in learning general data representations [1] for OOD detection. Choi et al. [5] used blurred data as adversarial examples to discriminate the training data from their blurred versions. In *CSI* [27], Tack et al. leverage shifting data transformations in contrastive learning for OOD detection, combined with an auxiliary task that predicts which shifting transformation was applied to a given input. In *SSD* [26], the authors further improved contrastive self-supervised training by developing a cluster-conditioned OOD detection method in the feature space.

**Outlier Exposure (OE).** OE leverages auxiliary data that are utterly disjoint from the ODD data [12]. Furthermore, OE assumes that the provided auxiliary samples are always OOD. To guarantee this, one needs human supervision to remove the overlap between auxiliary and in-distribution. OE has been successfully applied to training classifiers, by enforcing the auxiliary samples to be equally distributed among the in-distribution classes. In contrast to [12], we attempt to teach the network better representations for OOD detection by incorporating auxiliary data into a self-distillation soft-labeling framework. Finally, since the proposed method does not require labels, there is no information whether the in-distribution data are meaningfully similar to the auxiliary ones. In this aspect, this work is different from OE, as it only requires the in-distribution to be sufficiently statistically underrepresented. To ensure the latter an additional transformation is applied on the auxiliary data (e.g. rotation).

## 3    Proposed Method

### 3.1    The Vanilla DINO Framework

The DINO framework uses two identical networks $g_s$ and $g_t$ called student and teacher, with parameters $\theta_s$ and $\theta_t$, respectively. For each input image $x$, both networks produce $K$-dimensional output vectors, where $K$ is the number of soft-classes. Both outputs enter a temperature-scaled softmax functions defined by:

$$p^i(x) = \frac{\exp\left(g^i(x)/\tau\right)}{\sum_{k=1}^{K} \exp\left(g^k(x)/\tau\right)},\tag{1}$$

where $p^i(x)$ is the probability of $x$ falling in soft-class $i$ and $\tau_s, \tau_t$ are the student and teacher temperatures. For $\tau_t < \tau_s$, the training objective is given by the cross entropy loss for two non-identical transformations $x'', x'$ of an image $x$ drawn from the in-distribution training set $\mathcal{D}_{train}^{in}$

**Table 1.** The Area Under the Receiver Operating Characteristic Curve (AUROC) scores for OOD detection without label supervision

| $\mathcal{D}_{train}^{in}$ | $\mathcal{D}_{test}^{out}$ | Geometric* [13] | SSD [26] | CSI [27] | MTL† [18] | Ours Rot.ImgN | Combined |
|---|---|---|---|---|---|---|---|
| CIFAR10 | CIFAR100 | 91.91 | 90.63 | 89.20 | 93.24 | 92.51 | **94.20** |
| | SVHN | 97.96 | 99.62 | 99.80 | **99.92** | 99.69 | **99.92** |
| | ImageNet30 | – | 90.20 | 87.92 | – | **94.16** | 93.40 |
| | TinyImageNet | 92.06 | 92.25 | 92.44 | 92.99 | **96.28** | 95.02 |
| | LSUN | 93.57 | 96.51 | 91.60 | 95.03 | **98.08** | 97.52 |
| | STL10 | – | 70.28 | 64.25 | – | **77.29** | 74.34 |
| | Places365 | 92.57 | 95.21 | 90.18 | 93.72 | **97.14** | 96.01 |
| | Texture | 96.25 | 97.61 | 98.96 | – | **99.16** | 98.69 |
| CIFAR100 | CIFAR10 | 74.73 | 69.60 | 58.87 | **79.25** | 69.96 | 67.63 |
| | SVHN | 83.62 | 94.90 | 96.44 | 87.11 | 96.00 | **97.17** |
| | ImageNet30 | – | 75.53 | 71.82 | – | **84.82** | 75.36 |
| | TinyImagenet | 77.56 | 79.52 | 79.28 | 80.66 | **81.41** | 79.75 |
| | LSUN | 71.86 | 79.50 | 61.83 | 74.32 | **85.03** | 74.55 |
| | STL10 | – | 72.76 | 64.26 | – | **79.96** | 71.70 |
| | Places365 | 74.57 | 79.60 | 65.48 | 77.87 | **81.67** | 72.79 |
| | Texture | 82.39 | 82.90 | **87.47** | – | 80.65 | 77.33 |

* Requires labels for the supervised training loss. Results reported from [18].
† Requires labels to select the optimal transformations.

$$\mathcal{L}_{pos} = - \sum_{x'' \in G} \sum_{\substack{x' \in V \\ x' \neq x''}} p_t(x'') \log(p_s(x')). \qquad (2)$$

Additionally, DINO uses the multi-crop strategy [2], wherein $M$ global views $G = \{x_1^g, ..., x_M^g\}$ and $N$ local views, $L = \{x_1^l, \cdots, x_N^l\}$, are generated based on a set of transformations $\mathcal{T}$, e.g. crop and resize, horizontal flip, Gaussian blur, and color jitter. Global views are crops that occupy a larger region of the image (e.g. $\geq 40\%$) while local views cover small parts of the image (e.g. $\leq 40\%$). All $V = G \cup L$ views are passed through the student network, while the teacher has only access to the global views such that local-to-global correspondences are enforced. The trained teacher network is used for evaluation.

## 3.2 Negative Samples

The learning objective (Eq. 2) assigns two transformed views of an image to the same soft-class. The applied transformations $\mathcal{T}$ are chosen to be sufficiently strong and diverse, such that the generated images generalise well over the training set but keep the semantics of the image they were derived from. The transformations are designed to learn higher-level features such as labels that represent semantic information and avoid learning lower-level features, such as edges or the color statistics over pixels [4]. The quality of the learned representation can be quantified by evaluating the K-NN accuracy for an in-distribution test set $\mathcal{D}_{test}^{in}$, using as higher-level feature vector an activity map of the network near the last layer. For OOD detection, the feature vector representation should be enriched by in-distribution-specific features and depleted by features that frequently appear in other distributions from the same domain. This can be achieved by designing a negative distribution $D_{neg}$ that keeps most of the low-level features of the in-distribution but changes the high-level semantics. For example, a negative distribution for natural images can be realised by addition-ally rotating in-distribution images or images from a related auxiliary distri-bution by $r \sim R = \mathcal{U}(\{90°, 180°, 270°\})$, where $\mathcal{U}$ is the uniform distribution. It has been shown that using rotation as an additional positive transformation degrades the performance in the contrastive learning [4]. Motivated by this, authors in [27] report a performance gain for OOD detection by using rotation to generate negative examples.

### 3.3   Auxiliary Objective

In addition to the self-distillation objective Eq. 2 we define an auxiliary task to encourage the student to have a uniform softmax response for negative exam-ples. This task can be realised by a similar objective as Eq. 2 but with changed temperature $\tau_t \rightarrow \infty$ and transformations $\mathcal{T}$ applied to examples $x$ from the negative set $\mathcal{D}_{neg}$, defined as:

$$\mathcal{L}_{neg} = -\frac{1}{K} \sum_{x' \in V} \log p_s(x').$$  (3)

The total loss of our proposed method is defined by a linear combination of the two objectives

$$\mathcal{L}_{total} = \mathcal{L}_{pos} + \lambda \mathcal{L}_{neg},$$  (4)

where $\lambda > 0$ is a balancing hyperparameter.

### 3.4   Sensitivity Score

Intuitively the sensitivity score is the degree of rejection of in-distribution exam-ples which gives us a measure about the sensitivity of the OOD score to examples that have very similar feature statistics to $\mathcal{D}_{train}^{in}$. To calculate the sensitivity score we randomly extract $B$ samples from $\mathcal{D}_{train}^{in}$ without replacement as $\mathcal{D}_{train}^{sens}$ and denote the remaining train samples as $\mathcal{D}_{train}^{ref}$. We define the sensitivity score as the AUROC value between $\mathcal{D}_{train}^{sens}$ and $\mathcal{D}_{test}^{in}$, where $\mathcal{D}_{train}^{ref}$ is used as new train data during the evaluation.

## 4   Experiments

The proposed method is based on the vanilla DINO [3] implementation[1]. Unless otherwise specified, we use ViT-Small (ViT-S) with a patch size of 16. We use

---

[1] https://github.com/facebookresearch/dino.

$N = 8$ local views for both positives and negatives, but two global positive views and one global negative view. Global views are resized to $256 \times 256$ while local views to $128 \times 128$. The temperatures are set to $\tau_t = 0.01$ and $\tau_s = 0.1$. In each epoch, we linearly decrease $\tau_t$ starting from 0.055 for CIFAR10 and from 0.050 for CIFAR100 to 0.01 during training. Sensitivity score is used to find optimal $\lambda = 1$. We set $K = 4096$ for all experiments. We use the Adamw optimizer [17] with an effective batch size of 256. The learning rate $lr$ follows the linear scaling rule of $lr = lr_{base} \times$ batchsize $/256$, where $lr_{base} = 0.004$. All models are trained for 500 epochs. Experiments were conducted using 4 NVIDIA-A100 GPUs with 40 GB of memory. The image augmentation pipeline $\mathcal{T}$ is based on [3,9]. Finally, weight decay and learning rate are scaled with a cosine scheduler.

**Table 2.** AUROC scores for OOD Detection with CIFAR10 as $\mathcal{D}_{train}^{in}$ and different $\mathcal{D}_{neg}$. ImgN denotes ImageNet samples.

| Negative Sampling: | None | Auxiliary | | | | | | | | | In-Dist |
|---|---|---|---|---|---|---|---|---|---|---|---|
| $\mathcal{D}_{test}^{out}$ | DINO $\lambda = 0$ | ImgN | Rot. ImgN | Rot. 360 ImgN | DTI | Perm-16 ImgN | Perm-4 ImgN | Rot.DTI | Pix. Perm. | Rot. In-Dist. |
| CIFAR100 | 90.29 | 90.46 | 92.51 | 88.62 | 93.77 | 88.32 | 89.57 | 93.77 | 87.67 | **93.96** |
| SVHN | 99.38 | 99.50 | 99.69 | 99.42 | 99.86 | 99.59 | 99.13 | 99.86 | 99.62 | **99.92** |
| ImageNet30 | 88.81 | 89.96 | 94.16 | 88.95 | 93.39 | 89.17 | 84.71 | **96.04** | 87.46 | 91.69 |
| TinyImageNet | 91.07 | 94.14 | **96.28** | 91.60 | 94.53 | 89.72 | 91.27 | 95.64 | 89.39 | 94.27 |
| LSUN | 92.20 | 93.41 | 98.08 | 93.24 | 98.56 | 94.58 | 89.32 | **99.12** | 93.33 | 94.93 |
| STL10 | 66.50 | 77.65 | 77.29 | 72.41 | 72.01 | 69.22 | 68.81 | **81.49** | 68.55 | 69.11 |
| Places365 | 91.28 | 93.12 | 97.14 | 92.58 | 97.03 | 92.77 | 87.63 | **98.12** | 91.89 | 93.53 |
| Texture | 96.21 | 95.01 | **99.16** | 93.93 | 97.55 | 93.38 | 89.86 | 95.11 | 93.08 | 98.29 |
| Average | 89.47 | 91.66 | 94.29 | 90.09 | 93.34 | 89.59 | 87.54 | **94.89** | 88.87 | 91.96 |

## 4.1 Datasets and Negative Sample Variants

We evaluate our method on CIFAR10 and CIFAR100 as in-distribution data. For auxiliary datasets, we use ImageNet [25] and Debiased 300K Tiny Images (DTI) [12]. To avoid shortcut learning (due to different image resolutions), we resize the auxiliary data to the size of the in-distribution data before applying any augmentation. For OOD detection, we consider common benchmark datasets, such as SVHN [21], Places365, Texture [6] and STL10. To generate negative samples we consider cases where (1) no negatives are included ($\lambda = 0$) (2) samples from ImageNet (ImgN) (3) samples from Debiased Tiny Images (DTI) (4) samples randomly rotated by $r \sim R = \mathcal{U}(\{90°, 180°, 270°\})$ (Rot.) (5) samples rotated by an angle randomly sampled from range $(0°, 360°)$ (Rot.360) (6) randomly permuting each part of the evenly partitioned image in $N$ patches (Perm-$N$) (7) randomly shuffling all the pixels in the image (Pix. Perm.) (8) applying a random rotation $r \sim R$ to the in-distribution data (Rot. In-Dist.) and (9) samples from both Rot. In-Dist. and Rot. ImageNet (Combined).

## 4.2   Evaluation Protocol for OOD Detection

The DINO network structure $g(x)$ used in this work consists of a ViT-S as backbone, which maps the input $x$ to a $d$-dimensional feature vector $f \in \mathbb{R}^d$, and two fully connected layers as head, which converts the feature vector $f$ to a $K$-dimensional output vector that enters the softmax layer. We define an anomaly detection score, $\mathcal{S}$, for the OOD test data $\mathcal{D}_{test}^{out}$ by computing the cosine similarity between the feature vector for a test image $f_{test}$ and all feature vectors $f_m$ of the in-distribution training set. Instead of taking the maximum cosine similarity as a OOD score, we opt for a temperature weighted non-linear score,

$$\mathcal{S}(x) = -\frac{1}{M} \sum_{m=1}^{M} \exp \left( \frac{1}{\tau} \cdot \frac{f_{test}^T f_m}{\|f_{test}\| \|f_m\|} \right), \tag{5}$$

with $\tau = 0.04$ which is found by maximizing the sensitivity score. The value $\tau = 0.04$ is the average over optimal values for different datasets that typically lie in the range $[0.02, 0.08]$. The score is used to evaluate OOD performance by reporting AUROC between a given OOD test set and the in-distribution test set.

## 4.3   Experimental Results

In Table 1, quantitative results are reported for CIFAR10 and CIFAR100 as in-distribution. When using CIFAR10 as $\mathcal{D}_{train}^{in}$, the proposed method shows superior performance in 6 out of 8 (75%) OOD datasets compared to current SOTA self-supervised methods. Surprisingly, we surpass hybrid methods, where self-supervised training is combined with human-labelled images. By further leveraging in-distribution negatives, we are able to surpass all other self-supervised and supervised methods. Our results are roughly consistent for CIFAR100 as $\mathcal{D}_{train}^{in}$. We report superior performance in 6 out of 8 (75%) OOD datasets. Far OOD datasets have a substantial benefit, such as LSUN where we report a 5.53% gain against the best self-supervised method. Our results on near OOD, CIFAR10, are on par with self-supervised methods [27], while lacking behind supervised methods. In Table 2, we investigate several ways to generate negative samples, as detailed in Sect. 4.1. It can be observed that by rotating both ImageNet and DTI with $R$, both distributions demonstrate an average performance gain of 2.63% and 1.55% respectively compared to no additional transformation.

It is worth noting that we abstain from reporting the performance of DTI in Table 1, since labels were used to form this subset of 300K images. Finally, we report an inferior (or on par) average AUROC score when employing Pix. Perm, Perm-4, and Perm-16 against the vanilla DINO method using ImageNet as the auxiliary dataset.

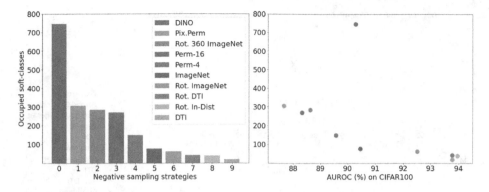

**Fig. 2.** We define a soft-class as "occupied" if the probability assigned to that soft-class is greater than the average probability of all $K$ soft-classes. Colors indicate multiple $\mathcal{D}_{neg}$ and are shared within the two plots. The teacher network $g_t$ is used to generate $p_t$ from $\mathcal{D}_{test}^{in}$. Training is performed on CIFAR10. **Left**: $\mathcal{D}_{test}^{in}$ occupy less soft-classes with negative sampling compared to the DINO baseline. **Right**: relationship of occupied soft-classes with respect to AUROC score on CIFAR100.

## 5   Discussion

**Do negative samples lead to more condensed in-distribution representations?** To understand the impact of the introduced negative sampling methods, we investigate how many of the $K = 4096$ soft-classes are "occupied" by the $\mathcal{D}_{test}^{in}$ after training on CIFAR10. A soft-class is considered occupied if the probability assigned to the intended soft-class computed from test data is greater than the average soft-class probability. As depicted in Fig. 2 (left), negative sampling reduces the occupied classes compared to the DINO baseline. This observation is independent of how $\mathcal{D}_{neg}$ is created. More specifically, Rot. ImageNet, Rot. DTI, and Rot. In-Dist use roughly the same number of soft-classes and achieve SOTA AUROC scores on CIFAR100. By combining the aforementioned qualitative evaluations with Table 2, we claim that by contrasting $\mathcal{D}_{train}^{in}$ against $\mathcal{D}_{neg}$ a more condensed representation can be learnt. **Is OOD detection related to in-distribution classification?** To answer this question, we investigate if there is a relationship between the OOD detection performance and the K-NN accuracy, determined from human-generated labels. To do so, we use CIFAR10 as $\mathcal{D}_{train}^{in}$ and CIFAR100 and Texture as $\mathcal{D}_{test}^{out}$, as representative cases of near OOD and far OOD, respectively. We find that the OOD AUROC score is positively correlated with K-NN accuracy for both near and far OOD detection (Fig. 3, top row). **Is the performance gain from use of transformers or auxiliary loss function?** The performance gain stems from a more compact representation of high-level features for the in-distribution. This can be seen from the high K-NN values, that can be partially attributed to the DINO self-distillation framework (CIFAR10 K-NN accuracy of 93.2% for vanilla DINO vs 87.1% for CSI) and in part due to the negative loss (4.82% AUROC improvement with Rot.ImgN compared to vanilla DINO on CIFAR10).

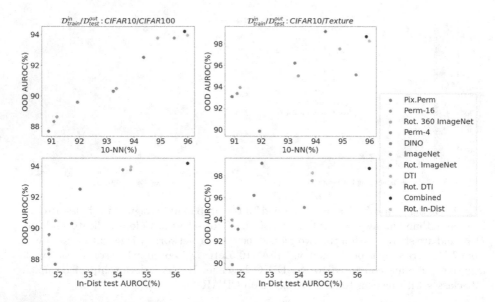

**Fig. 3.** We evaluate different models trained on CIFAR10 for two OOD datasets, CIFAR100 (left column) and Texture (right column). In each plot, points indicate different negative sampling strategies (colors are shared). **Top row**: correlation between OOD detection AUROC and K-NN accuracy on $\mathcal{D}_{test}^{in}$. **Bottom row**: correlation between OOD detection AUROC and AUROC score of $\mathcal{D}_{train}^{in}$ vs. $\mathcal{D}_{test}^{in}$. We observe models with higher sensitivity to detect $\mathcal{D}_{test}^{in}$ as outliers have higher OOD detection performance.

We highlight that K-NN correlates positively with OOD AUROC values (Fig. 3, top row). **Can an arbitrary auxiliary dataset be detrimental?** Auxiliary negative datasets can be detrimental if they are semantically too close to the in-distribution, which explains why non-rotated ImgN gives worse AUROC than Rot. ImgN for CIFAR10, despite the former being closer to the in-distribution. However, this effect can be detected by our sensitivity score, which is higher for Rot. ImgN (Fig. 3, bottom row). **How to choose good negative examples?** We use the sensitivity score to select $\mathcal{D}_{neg}$ (dataset + augmentation). Sensitivity values significantly higher than 0.5 indicate that negative examples are close enough to induce a difference between $\mathcal{D}_{train}^{in}$ and $\mathcal{D}_{test}^{in}$, but far enough to avoid a significant overlap of $\mathcal{D}_{train}^{in}$ with $\mathcal{D}_{neg}$ (see sensitivities of ImgN vs. Rot. ImgN, Fig. 3, bottom row).

## 6    Conclusion

In this work, we presented a new general method for self-supervised OOD detection. We demonstrated how self-distillation can be extended to account for positive and negative examples by introducing an auxiliary objective. The proposed objective introduces a form of contrastive learning, which pushes negative samples to be uniformly distributed among the existing in-distribution soft-classes. Additionally, we introduced a sensitivity analysis technique with which we can compare negative datasets and find the optimal values for the negative loss weight and the evaluation temperature without accessing the OOD validation set. The proposed method outperforms current SOTA for self-supervised OOD detection methods in the majority of OOD benchmark datasets for both CIFAR10 and CIFAR100 as $\mathcal{D}_{train}^{in}$. We hope that the provided insights of our analysis will shed light on how to choose negative samples in more challenging vision domains.

# References

1. Alexey, D., Fischer, P., Tobias, J., Springenberg, M.R., Brox, T.: Discriminative, unsupervised feature learning with exemplar convolutional, neural networks. IEEE TPAMI (2016)
2. Caron, M., Misra, I., Mairal, J., Goyal, P., Bojanowski, P., Joulin, A.: Unsupervised learning of visual features by contrasting cluster assignments (2020)
3. Caron, M., et al.: Emerging properties in self-supervised vision transformers. In: Proceedings of the International Conference on Computer Vision (ICCV) (2021)
4. Chen, T., Kornblith, S., Norouzi, M., Hinton, G.: A simple framework for contrastive learning of visual representations. In: International Conference on Machine Learning, pp. 1597–1607. PMLR (2020)
5. Choi, S., Chung, S.Y.: Novelty detection via blurring. In: International Conference on Learning Representations (2020)
6. Cimpoi, M., Maji, S., Kokkinos, I., Mohamed, S., Vedaldi, A.: Describing textures in the wild. In: Proceedings of the IEEE Conference on Computer Vision and Pattern Recognition, pp. 3606–3613 (2014)
7. Dosovitskiy, A., et al.: An image is worth 16x16 words: transformers for image recognition at scale. In: 9th International Conference on Learning Representations, ICLR 2021, Virtual Event, Austria, 3–7 May 2021 (2021)
8. Fort, S., Ren, J., Lakshminarayanan, B.: Exploring the limits of out-of-distribution detection. In: NeurIPS (2021)
9. Grill, J.B., et al.: Bootstrap your own latent-a new approach to self-supervised learning. Adv. Neural. Inf. Process. Syst. **33**, 21271–21284 (2020)
10. Hein, M., Andriushchenko, M., Bitterwolf, J.: Why relu networks yield high-confidence predictions far away from the training data and how to mitigate the problem. In: CVPR (2019)
11. Hendrycks, D., Gimpel, K.: A baseline for detecting misclassified and out-of-distribution examples in neural networks. In: Proceedings of International Conference on Learning Representations (2017)
12. Hendrycks, D., Mazeika, M., Dietterich, T.: Deep anomaly detection with outlier exposure. In: Proceedings of the International Conference on Learning Representations (2019)
13. Hendrycks, D., Mazeika, M., Kadavath, S., Song, D.: Using self-supervised learning can improve model robustness and uncertainty. In: Advances in Neural Information Processing Systems, vol. 32 (2019)
14. Kingma, D.P., Welling, M.: Auto-encoding variational bayes. arXiv preprint arXiv:1312.6114 (2013)

15. Koner, R., Sinhamahapatra, P., Roscher, K., Günnemann, S., Tresp, V.: Ood-former: out-of-distribution detection transformer. arXiv preprint arXiv:2107.08976 (2021)
16. Krizhevsky, A., Hinton, G.: Learning multiple layers of features from tiny images. Technical report, University of Toronto, Toronto, Ontario (2009)
17. Loshchilov, I., Hutter, F.: Fixing weight decay regularization in adam (2018)
18. Mohseni, S., Vahdat, A., Yadawa, J.: Shifting transformation learning for out-of-distribution detection (2021)
19. Nalisnick, E.T., Matsukawa, A., Teh, Y.W., Görür, D., Lakshminarayanan, B.: Do deep generative models know what they don't know? In: 7th International Conference on Learning Representations, ICLR (2019)
20. Nalisnick, E.T., Matsukawa, A., Teh, Y.W., Lakshminarayanan, B.: Detecting out-of-distribution inputs to deep generative models using a test for typicality (2019)
21. Netzer, Y., Wang, T., Coates, A., Bissacco, A., Wu, B., Ng, A.: Reading digits in natural images with unsupervised feature learning (2011)
22. Nguyen, A., Yosinski, J., Clune, J.: Deep neural networks are easily fooled: high confidence predictions for unrecognizable images. In: Proceedings of the IEEE Conference on Computer Vision and Pattern Recognition, pp. 427–436 (2015)
23. Pidhorskyi, S., Almohsen, R., Doretto, G.: Generative probabilistic novelty detection with adversarial autoencoders. In: Advances in Neural Information Processing Systems, vol. 31 (2018)
24. Rezende, D.J., Mohamed, S.: Variational inference with normalizing flows. In: Bach, F.R., Blei, D.M. (eds.) Proceedings of the 32nd International Conference on Machine Learning, ICML (2015)
25. Russakovsky, O., et al.: Imagenet large scale visual recognition challenge. Int. J. Comput. Vision **115**(3), 211–252 (2015)
26. Sehwag, V., Chiang, M., Mittal, P.: SSD: a unified framework for self-supervised outlier detection. In: International Conference on Learning Representations (2021)
27. Tack, J., Mo, S., Jeong, J., Shin, J.: CSI: novelty detection via contrastive learning on distributionally shifted instances. Adv. Neural. Inf. Process. Syst. **33**, 11839–11852 (2020)
28. Van Oord, A., Kalchbrenner, N., Kavukcuoglu, K.: Pixel recurrent neural networks. In: International Conference on Machine Learning, pp. 1747–1756. PMLR (2016)
29. Vaswani, A., et al.: Attention is all you need. In: Advances in Neural Information Processing Systems, pp. 5998–6008 (2017)
30. Winkens, J., et al.: Contrastive training for improved out-of-distribution detection. arXiv preprint arXiv:2007.05566 (2020)

# Self-supervised Detransformation Autoencoder for Representation Learning in Open Set Recognition

Jingyun Jia$^{(\boxtimes)}$ and Philip K. Chan

Florida Institute of Technology, Melbourne, FL 32901, USA
jiaj2018@my.fit.edu, pkc@fit.edu

**Abstract.** The objective of Open set recognition (OSR) is to learn a classifier that can reject the unknown samples while classifying the known classes accurately. In this paper, we propose a self-supervision method, Detransformation Autoencoder (DTAE), for the OSR problem. This proposed method engages in learning representations that are invariant to the transformations of the input data. Experiments on several standard image datasets indicate that the pre-training process significantly improves the model performance in the OSR tasks. Moreover, our analysis indicates that DTAE can yield representations that contain some class information even without class labels.

**Keywords:** Open set recognition · Self-supervised learning · Representation learning

## 1 Introduction

Deep learning has shown great success in recognition and classification tasks in recent years. However, there is still a wide range of challenges when applying deep learning to the real world. Most deep neural networks and other machine learning models are trained under a static close-set scenario. However, the real world is more of an open-set scenario, in which it is difficult to collect samples that exhaust all classes. The problem of rejecting the unknown samples meanwhile accurately classifying the known classes is referred as Open Set Recognition (OSR) [1] or Open Category Learning [3]. The OSR problem defines a more realistic scenario and has drawn significant attention in applications such as face recognition [10], malware classification [6] and medical diagnoses [14].

In this paper, we bring self-supervised pre-training to the OSR problem and fine-tune the pre-trained model with different types of loss functions: classification loss and representation loss. Particularly, we propose Detransformation Autoencoder (DTAE) for self-supervision. DTAE consists of three components: an encoder, a decoder, and an input transformation module. The encoder encodes all transformed images to representations, and the decoder reconstructs the representations back to the original images before transformations. Compared to

© The Author(s), under exclusive license to Springer Nature Switzerland AG 2022
E. Pimenidis et al. (Eds.): ICANN 2022, LNCS 13532, pp. 471–483, 2022.
https://doi.org/10.1007/978-3-031-15937-4_40

the traditional autoencoder, DTAE learns the representations that describe the pixels and are invariant to the transformations. Our contribution in this paper is threefold: First, we introduce DTAE as a self-supervised pre-training method for the OSR tasks. Second, our experiment results show that DTAE significantly improves the model performances for different down-streaming loss functions on several image datasets. Third, our analysis indicates that DTAE is able to capture some cluster information for both known and unknown samples even without class labels.

We organize the paper as follows. In Sect. 2, we give an overview of related work. Section 3 presents the self-supervision method, DTAE, in pre-training for the OSR tasks. Section 4 shows that the pre-training process can significantly improve the model performance in several standard image datasets. Meanwhile, the models pre-trained with DTAE achieve the best performance in detecting the unknown class and classifying the known classes.

## 2   Related Work

We can divide neural network based OSR techniques into three categories based on the training set compositions. The first category borrows additional data as the unknown samples in the training set. To better discriminate known class and unknown class, Shu et al. [16] and Saito et al. [12] introduce unlabeled data during the training phase as the unknown class. The second category generates additional data as the unknown class, Ge et al. [4] introduce a conditional GAN to generate unknown samples followed by an OpenMax classifier. The third category does not use additional data. Bendale and Boult [1] propose OpenMax for the OSR problems. OpenMax adapts Meta-Recognition concepts to the activation patterns in the representation layer of the network and then estimates the probability of an input being from an unknown class. Hassen and Chan [6] propose ii loss for the OSR problem. It first finds the representations for the known classes during training and then recognizes an instance as unknown if it does not belong to any known classes. Jia and Chan [7] propose MMF as a loss extension to further separate the known and unknown representations for the OSR problem. CROSR in [18] trains networks for joint classification and reconstruction of the known classes to combine the learned representation and decision in the OSR task. Perera et al. [11] adopt a self-supervision framework to force the network to learn more informative features when separating the unknown class. Specifically, they used the output of the autoencoder as auxiliary features for the OSR task.

Self-supervision in representation learning generally uses a pretext task that is different from the primary task. The pretext task includes reconstructing the input based on a smaller number of features (autoencoders), classifying transformations such as rotations [5], intra-sample vs inter-sample transformations in contrastive loss [2], redundancy reduction in learned features from transformations [19]. In an Autoencoder, the "labels" are the input samples themselves, and the network learns the representations of the inputs by minimizing the dissimilarity between the input and output. Denoising autoencoder (DAE) corrupts

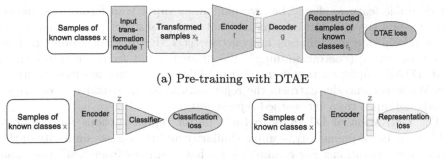

(a) Pre-training with DTAE

(b) Fine-tuning with classification loss    (c) Fine-tuning with representation loss

**Fig. 1.** The two stage training process of the OSR problem.

the input samples first, then the network is trained to denoise corrupted versions of their inputs to reconstruct back to the their original forms. RotNet in [5] uses image rotations as the pretext task, and the model is trained on the classification task of recognizing the rotation classes. SimCLR in [2] introduces contrastive loss to improve the quality of learned representations. Given transformed samples, the contrastive loss reduces the intra-sample distances meanwhile increase the inter-sample distances. Barlow twins in [19] feeds distorted versions of a sample to two identical networks, and proposes an objective function that makes the cross-correlation matrix between their outputs as close to the identity matrix to minimize the redundancy between components of the representations.

Our proposed method uses a self-supervision approach to learning the features of the known classes without using additional unknown samples. Unlike DAE, our proposed method includes the original input samples in the training process. Moreover, we augment the input samples with different rotation transformations. The network learns the representations that are invariant to the transformations of the input data by decoding all the transformed images back to the original ones before transformations.

## 3    Approach

We propose a two-step training process (pre-training step and fine-tuning step) for the OSR problems, thus better separating different classes in the feature space. As illustrated in Fig. 1, the training process includes two steps: 1) pre-training step uses detransformation autoencoder (DTAE) to learn features for all the input data; 2) fine-tuning step uses representation loss functions or classification loss functions to learn discriminative features for different classes.

### 3.1    Pre-training Step

The objective of the self-supervised pre-training process is to learn some meaningful representations via pretext tasks without semantic annotations.

The desirable features should be invariant under input transformations, meanwhile, contain the essential information that can reconstruct the original input. We propose a detransformation autoencoder (DTAE) to learn representations by reconstructing ("detransforming") the original input from the transformed input. DTAE employs a transformation module and an encoder-decoder structure. While the encoder extracts the representations, the decoder reconstructs the original input from the learned representations.

The motivation of DTAE is to learn better representations for the OSR problem via encouraging intra-sample similarity and intra-class similarity of the learned representations. For example, if we have samples from "cat" class and "dog" class, given sample "cat1" and its transformation "cat1a", we can learn their representations $z_{c1}$ and $z_{c1a}$. Similarly, we can learn the representations of "cat2" and "dog1" as $z_{c2}$ and $z_{d1}$. The intra-sample similarity describes the similarity between the representations of the original input and its transformations, as $z_{c1}$ and $z_{c1a}$ in our example, and we denote this similarity as $sim(z_{c1}, z_{c1a})$. As the decoder in DTAE reconstructs the *same* original samples from the learned representations of *both* original and transformed samples, the learned representations are of high intra-sample similarity. Thus the learned representations are invariant to the transformations and contain important features of the samples. The intra-class similarity describes the similarity among the learned representations of the same class, as $z_{c1}$ and $z_{c2}$ in our example, and we denote this similarity as $sim(z_{c1}, z_{c2})$. The encoder-decoder structure in DTAE is a generative model that embeds crucial features in lower dimensions. Compared to a discriminate model, the representations learned by a generative model contain more comprehensive information to reconstruct the inputs. Thus, for a generative model, the learned representations of samples from the same class should be more similar than those of different classes. Overall, the desired representation space should satisfy $sim(z_{c1}, z_{c1a}) > sim(z_{c1}, z_{c2}) > sim(z_{c1}, z_{d1})$.

As shown in Fig. 1a, in the pre-training stage with DTAE, the input transformation module $T$ transforms any given data example $x$ to several correlated views of the same example, denoted as $x_t = T(x)$. The network-based encoder $f(\cdot)$ extracts representation vectors from transformed data examples. Furthermore, decoder $g(\cdot)$ reconstructs the original data examples from the representation vectors. Let $r_t$ denotes the reconstructed data example from transformed input $x_t$, then the detransformation loss function becomes:

$$\mathcal{L}(x, r_t) = \mathcal{L}(x, g(f(x_t))) \tag{1}$$

where $r_t = g(f(x_t))$. Specifically, we use MSE (Mean Squared Error) loss and have a total of $M$ transformations, the loss function can be defined as:

$$\mathcal{L}_{\text{DTAE}} = \frac{1}{2} \sum_{t=0}^{M-1} \sum_{i=1}^{N} (x_i - r_{it})^2 \tag{2}$$

Each of the $N$ data points has $M$ transformations, and there are $M \times N$ data points after the input transformation module. In this work, we consider four transformations for each data example, i.e. $t \in \{0, 1, 2, 3\}$ for all $N$ input examples, resulting in $4N$ data points. For this paper, the four transformations in our experiments are rotations of an image: 0, 90, 180, and 270°.

## 3.2   Fine-Tuning Step

While the pre-trained network can be fine-tuned by different loss functions, we focus on two types of loss functions in this paper: the classification loss and the representation loss. The objective of classification loss is to lower the classification error of the training data explicitly in the decision layers. One of the widely used classification loss functions is cross-entropy loss. The objective of representation loss functions is to learn better representations of training data. The representation loss functions are normally applied to the representation layers, such as triplet loss [15] and ii loss [6].

The fine-tuning network shares the same encoder and representation layer with the pre-training network. However, compared with the pre-training process, the fine-tuning process does not contain the input transformation module, which means the training examples are sent directly into the encoder. Moreover, instead of connecting to a decoder, the representation layer connects to a classification loss function or a representation loss function as shown in Fig. 1b and Fig. 1c. In this work, we consider both classification loss (cross-entropy loss) and representation loss (triplet loss [15] and ii loss [6]) in the OSR task.

## 3.3   Open Set Recognition (OSR)

A typical OSR task solves two problems: classifying the known classes and identifying the unknown class. From the representation level, the instances from the same class are close to each other, while those from different classes are further apart. Under this property, we propose the outlier score:

$$outlier\_score(x) = \min_{1 \leq i \leq C} \|\mu_i - z\|_2^2, \tag{3}$$

where $z$ is the learned representation of test sample $x$, $\mu_i$ is the representation centroid of the known class $i$. There are multiple ways to set the outlier threshold. Here, we sort the outlier score of the training date in ascending order and pick the 99 percentile outlier score value as the outlier threshold. Then, for the $C$ known classes, we predict the class probability $P(y = i|x)$ for each class. When a network is trained on classification loss, the $P(y = i|x)$ is the output of the classification layer. Whereas in the case of a network without classification layer such as Fig. 1c, we calculate $P(y = i|x)$ as:

$$P(y = i|x) = \frac{e^{-\|\mu_i - z\|_2^2}}{\sum_{j=1}^{C} e^{-\|\mu_j - z\|_2^2}} \tag{4}$$

In summary, a test instance is recognized as "unknown" if its outlier score is greater than the threshold $t$, otherwise it is classified as the known class with the highest class probability:

$$y = \begin{cases} unknown, & \text{if } outlier\_score(x) > t \\ \underset{1 \leq i \leq C}{\arg\max} P(y = i|x), & \text{otherwise} \end{cases} \tag{5}$$

## 4    Experimental Evaluation

We evaluate the proposed pre-training method: Detransformation Autoencoder (DTAE) with simulated open-set datasets from the following datasets.

**MNIST** [9] contains 60,000 training and 10,000 testing handwritten digits from 0 to 9, which is 10 classes in total. Each example is a $28 \times 28$ grayscale image. To simulate an open-set dataset, we randomly pick six digits as the known classes participant in the training, while the rest are treated as the unknown class only existing in the test set.

**Fashion-MNIST** [17] is associated with 10 classes of clothing images. It contains 60,000 training and 10,000 testing examples. Same as the MNIST dataset, each example is a $28 \times 28$ grayscale image. To simulate an open-set dataset, we randomly pick six digits as the known classes participant in the training, while the rest are treated as the unknown class for testing.

**CIFAR-10** [8] contains 60,000 $32 \times 32$ color images in 10 classes, with 6,000 images per class. There are 50,000 training images and 10,000 test images. We first convert the color images to grayscale and randomly pick six classes out of the ten classes as the known classes, while the remaining classes are treated as the known class only existing in the test set.

### 4.1    Evaluation Network Architectures and Evaluation Criteria

In the proposed method, we use self-supervision in the pre-training stage, and then in the second stage, we fine-tune the pre-trained model with two types of loss functions: classification loss and representation loss. Specifically, we use the cross-entropy loss as the example of classification loss, and use ii loss [6] and triplet loss [15] as the examples of representation loss. We first trained the model from scratch as a baseline (no pre-training) for each loss function and compared it with the corresponding fine-tuned models after self-supervision. Second, to evaluate our proposed self-supervision technique DTAE, we compare the model performance using DTAE with traditional Autoencoder (AE) and RotNet [5] in the pre-training stage. We also compare the proposed method with OpenMax [1] to show that it is effective to OSR problems.

Figure 1a illustrates the network architecture of the DTAE. Moreover, the hyper-parameters are different based on datasets. For the encoder of the MNIST

**Table 1.** The average ROC AUC scores of 30 runs at 100% and 10% FPR of Open-Max and a group of 5 methods (without pre-training as baseline, pre-training with AE, RotNet, DTAE and TAE) for each of the 3 loss functions (ce, ii, triplet). The under-lined values are statistically significantly better than the baselines via t-test with 95% confidence. The values in bold and in brackets are the highest and the second-highest values in each group.

| FPR OpenMax | | MNIST | | Fashion-MNIST | | CIFAR-10 | |
|---|---|---|---|---|---|---|---|
| | | 100% | 10% | 100% | 10% | 100% | 10% |
| | | 0.9138 | 0.0590 | 0.7405 | 0.0160 | 0.6750 | 0.0060 |
| ce | No pre-training | 0.9255 | 0.0765 | 0.7175 | 0.0300 | 0.5803 | 0.0070 |
| | AE | 0.9410 | **0.0805** | 0.7346 | 0.0300 | 0.6114 | [0.0084] |
| | RotNet | 0.9367 | 0.0769 | 0.7364 | [0.0316] | [0.6124] | 0.0083 |
| | DTAE (ours) | **0.9523** | [0.0801] | **0.7490** | 0.0324 | **0.6183** | **0.0086** |
| | TAE | [0.9477] | 0.0799 | [0.7389] | 0.0298 | 0.6012 | 0.0075 |
| ii | No pre-training | **0.9578** | 0.0821 | 0.7684 | 0.0399 | 0.6392 | 0.0103 |
| | AE | 0.9560 | **0.0828** | 0.7636 | 0.0377 | 0.6320 | 0.0098 |
| | RotNet | 0.9530 | 0.0813 | [0.7703] | [0.0404] | [0.6478] | [0.0106] |
| | DTAE (ours) | [0.9566] | [0.0825] | **0.7802** | **0.0410** | **0.6520** | **0.0108** |
| | TAE | 0.9515 | 0.0815 | 0.7657 | 0.0387 | 0.6214 | 0.0091 |
| triplet | No pre-training | 0.9496 | 0.0750 | 0.7160 | 0.0211 | 0.6106 | 0.0089 |
| | AE | **0.9563** | **0.0772** | 0.7254 | 0.0220 | 0.6251 | 0.0090 |
| | RotNet | 0.9342 | 0.0702 | [0.7435] | **0.0252** | [0.6285] | [0.0095] |
| | DTAE (ours) | [0.9543] | [0.0758] | **0.7441** | [0.0234] | **0.6327** | 0.0096 |
| | TAE | 0.9531 | 0.0757 | 0.7271 | 0.0215 | 0.6114 | 0.0081 |

and the Fashion-MNIST datasets, the padded input layer is of size (32, 32), followed by two non-linear convolutional layers with 32 and 64 nodes. We also use the max-polling layers with kernel size (3, 3) and strides (2, 2) after each convolutional layer. We use two fully connected non-linear layers with 256 and 128 hidden units after the convolutional component. Furthermore, the representation layer is six dimensions in our experiments. The representation layer is followed by a decoder, which is the reverse of the encoder in our experiments. We use the Relu activation function and set the Dropout's keep probability as 0.2. We use Adam optimizer with a learning rate of 0.001. The encoder network architecture of the CIFAR-10 experiment is similar to the MNIST dataset, except the padded input layer is of size (36, 36). We use batch normalization in all the layers to prevent features from getting excessively large. And as mentioned in Sect. 3.3, we use contamination ratio of 0.01 for the threshold selection. The encoder and representation layer maintain the same architecture and hyper-parameters in the fine-tuning network. Meanwhile, the decoder is replaced with different fully connected layers associated with different loss functions.

We simulate three different groups of open sets for each dataset then repeat each group 10 runs, so each dataset has 30 runs in total. When measuring the model performance, we use the average AUC scores under 10% and 100% FPR (False Positive Rate) for recognizing the unknown class. We chose the 10% FPR limit as higher FPR is generally undesirable, particularly when negative instances are much more abundant than positive instances. We measure the F1 scores for known and unknown classes separately as one of the OSR tasks is to classify the known classes. Moreover, we perform t-tests with 95% confidence in the AUC scores and F1 scores to see if the proposed DTAE pre-training method can significantly improve different loss functions.

**Table 2.** The average F1 scores of 30 runs of OpenMax and a group of 5 methods (without pre-training as baseline, pre-training with AE, RotNet, DTAE and TAE) for each of the 3 loss functions (ce, ii, triplet). The underlined values show statistically significant improvements (t-test with 95% confidence) comparing to the baselines. The values in bold and in brackets are the highest and the second highest values in each group.

| | | MNIST | | | Fashion-MNIST | | | CIFAR-10 | | |
|---|---|---|---|---|---|---|---|---|---|---|
| | | Known | Unknown | Overall | Known | Unknown | Overall | Known | Unknown | Overall |
| OpenMax | | 0.8964 | 0.7910 | 0.8814 | 0.7473 | 0.5211 | 0.7150 | 0.6456 | 0.5407 | 0.6307 |
| ce | No pre-training | 0.7596 | 0.7561 | 0.7591 | 0.6858 | 0.5591 | 0.6677 | 0.5672 | 0.3697 | 0.5390 |
| | AE | 0.7735 | 0.7894 | 0.7757 | 0.7264 | 0.5481 | 0.7009 | 0.5729 | 0.4605 | [0.5569] |
| | RotNet | [0.8931] | [0.8447] | [0.8862] | 0.7117 | **0.5694** | 0.6914 | 0.5616 | **0.4729** | 0.5489 |
| | DTAE (ours) | **0.8967** | **0.8579** | **0.8912** | [0.7335] | [0.5692] | [0.7100] | **0.5911** | [0.4728] | **0.5742** |
| | TAE | 0.8804 | 0.8420 | 0.8749 | **0.7482** | 0.5364 | **0.7179** | [0.5815] | 0.3889 | 0.5540 |
| ii | No pre-training | 0.9320 | 0.8833 | 0.9250 | 0.7720 | 0.5870 | 0.7456 | 0.6206 | 0.3570 | 0.5829 |
| | AE | **0.9387** | **0.8950** | **0.9325** | 0.7669 | 0.5745 | 0.7394 | 0.6241 | 0.2527 | 0.5711 |
| | RotNet | 0.9300 | 0.8761 | 0.9223 | **0.7771** | 0.6108 | 0.7533 | 0.6442 | [0.3980] | [0.6090] |
| | DTAE (ours) | [0.9344] | [0.8885] | [0.9279] | [0.7768] | [0.6064] | [0.7524] | [0.6421] | **0.4252** | **0.6111** |
| | TAE | 0.9308 | 0.8830 | 0.9240 | 0.7625 | 0.5869 | 0.7374 | 0.6135 | 0.2103 | 0.5559 |
| triplet | No pre-training | 0.9103 | 0.8302 | 0.8989 | 0.7491 | 0.5055 | [0.7208] | 0.5798 | 0.4515 | 0.5614 |
| | AE | [0.9144] | 0.8356 | [0.9032] | 0.7505 | 0.5051 | 0.7154 | [0.6086] | [0.4800] | 0.5902 |
| | RotNet | 0.9012 | 0.8182 | 0.8893 | [0.7514] | [0.5376] | [0.7208] | 0.6037 | **0.4978** | [0.5886] |
| | DTAE (ours) | **0.9166** | **0.8513** | **0.9073** | 0.7558 | [0.5459] | **0.7259** | 0.6205 | 0.4724 | **0.5993** |
| | TAE | 0.9126 | [0.8387] | 0.9021 | 0.7472 | 0.5092 | 0.7132 | 0.5926 | 0.4220 | 0.5682 |

## 4.2 Experimental Results

**Model Performance.** We compare the model performances of cross-entropy loss, ii loss, and triplet loss with and without pre-training. Table 1 are the averaged ROC AUC scores of the model performances in three datasets under different FPR values. Comparing "RotNet", "DTAE" and "AE" rows with "No pre-training" rows, we observe that using self-supervision techniques for pre-training significantly improved the model performance. The results also show that our proposed self-supervision method DTAE achieves the top two ROC AUC scores for all the cases. Moreover, with our proposed pre-training method, all three loss functions perform better than OpenMax in 5 out of 6 cases (3 datasets × 2 FPR limits).

To evaluate the detransformation component of DTAE, we performed an ablation study on our method without detransformation, which is denoted as TAE. Although both DTAE and TAE use transformed instances as input, TAE reconstructs the transformed instances as output, while DTAE reconstructs the original instances as output. Comparing the "TAE" rows and "DTAE" rows, we observe that the detransformation component in DTAE plays a key role in improving the model performance. That is, our results indicate that learning features invariant to transformations, via detransformation, can yield more effective features than those learned from reconstructing the same samples.

Table 2 shows that the OSR performances of different methods are measured by F1 scores in known and unknown class domains. We first calculate the F1 scores for each known class and the unknown class, then average all the classes as the Overall F1 scores. The results show that models with pre-training achieve statistically significant improvements. Moreover, Our proposed method also achieves the top two F1 scores in 26 out of 27 cases (3 loss functions $\times$ 3 datasets $\times$ 3 domains).

**Table 3.** The training time (in seconds) for the self-supervision methods in different datasets.

|               | AE | RotNet | DTAE |
|---------------|----|--------|------|
| MNIST         | 75 | 132    | 137  |
| Fashion-MNIST | 70 | 118    | 145  |
| CIFAR-10      | 86 | 147    | 182  |

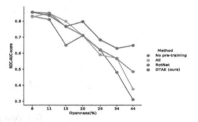

**Fig. 2.** AUC-ROC scores against varying Openness.

**Training Time.** While the pre-training step benefits the model performances and does not affect the final model complexity and inference time, it takes extra time during the training phase. Table 3 shows the comparison of the training time of the self-supervised networks in different datasets via NVIDIA RTX 2080. Because RotNet and DTAE both include transformed data as input, they took a longer training time than AE. We observe that DTAE takes a slightly longer training time than RotNet. The reason is that the network structure of DTAE is more complex than that of RotNet. While both RotNet and DTAE share the same encoder and representation layer structures, RotNet uses a softmax layer after the representation layer. Meanwhile, DTAE connects the representation layer with a decoder module. The decoder is the reverse of the encoder, which contains more layers than a softmax layer and needs a longer time in the forward and backward propagations.

**Openness Study.** We also study the model performances against vary Openness [13]. Let $n_{train}$ be the number of known classes participant in the training phase, with $n_{test}$ denotes the number of classes in the test set, and $n_{target}$ denotes the number of classes to be recognized in the testing phase. Openness can be defined as: $Openness = 1 - \sqrt{\frac{2 \times n_{train}}{n_{test} + n_{target}}}$.

In our experiments with the Fashion-MNIST dataset, we use all the ten classes in testing phase ($n_{test} = 10$) and varying the number of known classes from 2 to 9 ($n_{train} = 2, \ldots, 9$) in the training phase, and remaining classes together are treated as the unknown class to be recognized along with the known classes during inference ($n_{target} = n_{train} + 1$). That is, the openness is varied from 8% to 44%. We evaluate the AUC ROC scores of different models using cross-entropy loss: without pre-training (baseline), pre-training with AE, pre-training with RotNet, and pre-training with our proposed DTAE. The results are shown in Fig. 2. We observe that the three different models have similar performances when the openness is small. However, the AUC ROC scores of the baseline (No pre-training) degrade rapidly as the Openness increases. Moreover, the trend is alleviated by pre-training with self-supervision methods. Overall, the model pre-trained with DTAE is relatively more robust to openness and achieves the best performance.

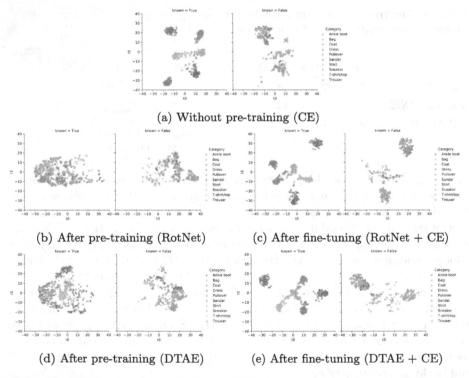

(a) Without pre-training (CE)

(b) After pre-training (RotNet)     (c) After fine-tuning (RotNet + CE)

(d) After pre-training (DTAE)     (e) After fine-tuning (DTAE + CE)

**Fig. 3.** The t-SNE plots of the Fashion-MNIST test set using cross-entropy loss. The left subplots are the representations of the known class, and the right plots are the representations of the unknown classes. (Color figure online)

## 4.3    Analysis

To analyze the differences in representations after pre-training and after fine-turning, we plot 1000 samples from the Fashion-MNIST test set in Fig. 3. In these experiments, classes "T-shirt/top", "Pullover", "Dress", "Coat", "Shirt" and "Ankle boot" are known classes while the remaining classes are unknown and absent from the training set. Figure 3a shows the t-SNE plot of the representations learned from cross-entropy loss without pre-training. Figures 3b and 3c are the learned representations of the model pre-trained by RotNet and fine-tuned by cross-entropy in different stages. Figures 3d and 3e are the learned representations of the model pre-trained by DTAE and again, fine-tuned by cross-entropy. From all the final representations of the three models in Figs. 3a, 3c and 3e, we observe overlaps between the known class "Ankle boot" (blue) and one component of the unknown class "Sneaker" (gray) as well as class "Dress" (red) and class "Trouser" (cyan). And the pre-training reduces the overlaps between "Shirt" (pink) and "Bag" (orange). Moreover, for the representations after pre-training, it shows that the representations learned by DTAE in Fig. 3b are more separable than those learned by RotNet in Fig. 3d for different classes. Note that DTAE, similar to RotNet, is not provided with class labels, but it can find representations that are more separable among the classes than RotNet. Moreover, we find that the representations learned by DTAE contain more fashion (target) information than those learned by RotNet (see supplementary material: https:// tinyurl.com/4amjev3m for more details).

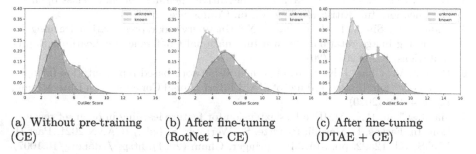

(a) Without pre-training    (b) After fine-tuning    (c) After fine-tuning
(CE)                        (RotNet + CE)            (DTAE + CE)

**Fig. 4.** The distributions of outlier scores for the known and unknown classes of the Fashion-MNIST dataset in different experiments using cross-entropy loss.

Figure 4 shows distributions of the outlier scores in experiments on the Fashion-MNIST test set. Compared with the model without pre-training in Fig. 4a, the pre-training steps in Figs. 4b and Fig. 4c increase the outlier scores in the unknown classes, which pushes their score distributions further away from the known classes. The fact that there are fewer overlaps between the known classes and the unknown class makes them more separable. The results indicate that the model pre-trained with DTAE has the fewest overlaps between the known and unknown classes.

# 5  Conclusion

In this work, we introduce the self-supervision technique to OSR problems. We provide experiments across different image datasets to measure the benefits of the pre-training step for OSR problems. Moreover, we have presented a novel method: Detransformation Autoencoder (DTAE) for self-supervision. The proposed method engages in learning the representations that are invariant to the transformations of the input data. We evaluate the pre-trained model with both classification and representation loss functions. The experiments on several standard image datasets show that the proposed method significantly outperforms the baseline methods and other self-supervision techniques. Our analysis indicates that DTAE can yield representations that contain some target class information even without class labels.

# References

1. Bendale, A., Boult, T.E.: Towards open set deep networks. In: Proceedings of the IEEE Conference on Computer Vision and Pattern Recognition, pp. 1563–1572 (2016)
2. Chen, T., Kornblith, S., Norouzi, M., Hinton, G.E.: A simple framework for contrastive learning of visual representations. In: Proceedings of the 37th International Conference on Machine Learning, ICML 2020, pp. 1597–1607 (2020)
3. Dietterich, T.G.: Steps toward robust artificial intelligence. AI Mag. **38**(3), 3–24 (2017)
4. Ge, Z., Demyanov, S., Garnavi, R.: Generative openmax for multi-class open set classification. In: British Machine Vision Conference (2017)
5. Gidaris, S., Singh, P., Komodakis, N.: Unsupervised representation learning by predicting image rotations. In: 6th International Conference on Learning Representations, ICLR 2018 (2018)
6. Hassen, M., Chan, P.K.: Learning a neural-network-based representation for open set recognition. In: Proceedings of SIAM International Conference on Data Mining, pp. 154–162 (2020)
7. Jia, J., Chan, P.K.: MMF: a loss extension for feature learning in open set recognition. In: Farkaš, I., Masulli, P., Otte, S., Wermter, S. (eds.) ICANN 2021, Part II. LNCS, vol. 12892, pp. 319–331. Springer, Cham (2021). https://doi.org/10.1007/978-3-030-86340-1_26
8. Krizhevsky, A., Hinton, G., et al.: Learning multiple layers of features from tiny images (2009)
9. LeCun, Y., Cortes, C., Burges, C.J.: The MNIST database (1999). http://yann.lecun.com/exdb/mnist/
10. Ortiz, E.G., Becker, B.C.: Face recognition for web-scale datasets. Comput. Vis. Image Underst. **118**, 153–170 (2014)
11. Perera, P., et al.: Generative-discriminative feature representations for open-set recognition. In: 2020 IEEE/CVF Conference on Computer Vision and Pattern Recognition, pp. 11811–11820 (2020)
12. Saito, K., Yamamoto, S., Ushiku, Y., Harada, T.: Open set domain adaptation by backpropagation. In: Proceedings of the European Conference on Computer Vision (ECCV), pp. 153–168 (2018)

13. Scheirer, W.J., de Rezende Rocha, A., Sapkota, A., Boult, T.E.: Toward open set recognition. IEEE Trans. Pattern Anal. Mach. Intell. **35**(7), 1757–1772 (2013)
14. Schlegl, T., Seeböck, P., Waldstein, S.M., Schmidt-Erfurth, U., Langs, G.: Unsupervised anomaly detection with generative adversarial networks to guide marker discovery. In: Information Processing in Medical Imaging - 25th International Conference, pp. 146–157 (2017)
15. Schroff, F., Kalenichenko, D., Philbin, J.: Facenet: a unified embedding for face recognition and clustering. In: Conference on Computer Vision and Pattern Recognition, pp. 815–823. IEEE (2015)
16. Shu, L., Xu, H., Liu, B.: Unseen class discovery in open-world classification. arXiv preprint arXiv:1801.05609 (2018)
17. Xiao, H., Rasul, K., Vollgraf, R.: Fashion-MNIST: a novel image dataset for benchmarking machine learning algorithms (2017)
18. Yoshihashi, R., Shao, W., Kawakami, R., You, S., Iida, M., Naemura, T.: Classification-reconstruction learning for open-set recognition. In: Conference on Computer Vision and Pattern Recognition, pp. 4016–4025 (2019)
19. Zbontar, J., Jing, L., Misra, I., LeCun, Y., Deny, S.: Barlow twins: self-supervised learning via redundancy reduction. In: Proceedings of the 38th International Conference on Machine Learning, ICML 2021, Virtual Event, vol. 139, pp. 12310–12320. PMLR (2021)

# Supervised Learning for Convolutional Neural Network with Barlow Twins

Ramyaa Murugan[1], Jonathan Mojoo[2], and Takio Kurita[3]([✉])

[1] Graduate School of Advanced Science and Engineering, Department of Informatics and Data Science Engineering, Hiroshima University, Higashi-Hiroshima, Japan
[2] Graduate School of Advanced Science and Engineering, Department of Information Engineering, Hiroshima University, Higashi-Hiroshima, Japan
[3] Graduate School of Advanced Science and Engineering, Hiroshima University, Higashi-Hiroshima, Japan
tkurita@hiroshima-u.ac.jp

**Abstract.** Supervised learning has found many applications as one of the fundamental techniques in machine learning. Recently, Barlow Twins loss has been used in self-supervised learning to train Convolutional Neural Networks to extract invariant features by introducing perturbations to the input data and encouraging the network to learn features that are invariant to these perturbations. It has been shown that the extracted features can achieve good performance for new tasks. However, this kind of 'perturbation-invariance' is also necessary for the models trained with supervised learning. The main contribution of this research is to explicitly introduce the perturbation-invariance in supervised learning. To do this, we propose to train a pair of identical networks using the standard classification loss and an additional Barlow Twins loss. The different sets of transformations are applied to the two network branches as the perturbations. We show empirically that the proposed method can learn invariant features and results in a higher classification accuracy than the baseline method.

## 1 Introduction

Supervised learning is a subcategory of machine learning algorithms that construct the model trained using labeled datasets. The trained model can accurately classify new samples or predict outcomes for the new samples. Usually, the accuracy of the model is measured through a loss function, and the best parameters are searched during the training until the loss has been sufficiently minimized.

Image classification is a computer vision task where the trained model must accurately assign test images into specific categories. Convolutional neural networks (CNNs) have proven to be an excellent performance for image classification. The cross-entropy loss is the most widely used loss function for supervised learning of deep classification models. A number of works have explored shortcomings of this loss, such as lack of robustness to noisy labels and the possibility of poor margins, leading to reduced generalization performance. However,

E. Pimenidis et al. (Eds.): ICANN 2022, LNCS 13532, pp. 484–495, 2022.
https://doi.org/10.1007/978-3-031-15937-4_41

in practice, most proposed alternatives have not worked better for large-scale datasets, such as ImageNet, as evidenced by the continued use of cross-entropy to achieve state of the art results.

In recent years, a resurgence of work in contrastive learning has led to major advances in self-supervised representation learning. The common idea in these works is the following: pull together an anchor and a "positive" sample in embedding space, and push apart the anchor from many "negative" samples. Since no labels are available, a positive pair often consists of data augmentations of the sample, and negative pairs are formed by the anchor and randomly chosen samples from the minibatch.

Recently research on self-supervised learning [1] becomes popular and have achieved almost similar accuracy to the supervised learning. In self-supervised learning, the samples without labels are used in the training and the perturbation-invariant features are extracted by contrastive mechanism [2] which reduce the distance between the representations of differently augmented views of the same image (positive pairs), and increase the distance between the representations of the augmented views from different images (negative pairs).

One of the self-supervised learning methods, named Barlow Twins [3] uses an objective function that computes the cross-correlation matrix between the outputs of two identical networks fed with distorted versions of the same sample, and makes it as close to the identity matrix as possible. This causes the embedding vectors of the distorted versions of the same sample to be similar, while minimizing the redundancy between the components of these vectors. Barlow Twins does not require large batches nor asymmetry between the network twins such as a predictor network, gradient stopping, or a moving average on the weight updates.

In this work, we propose a supervised learning method for image classification with CNN by combining the loss function of the supervised learning (cross-entropy loss) with the loss of the self-supervised learning (Barlow Twins loss). Perturbations (augmentations) are applied to the input data. The perturbed images are first fed into the two networks with the same parameters and then the Barlow Twins loss is measured at a small neural network projection heads that give the embedding features. The embedding features from the same class are pulled closer together than embedding features from different classes and are represented as 1's and 0's in cross correlation matrix. The main goal is to encourage the network to learn the perturbation invariant embeddings. We experimentally confirmed that the cross entropy (CE) loss with Barlow Twins loss can achieve the best classification accuracy in the Supervised classification problems. Our main contributions are summarized below:

1. We propose a perturbation-invariant feature extraction mechanism in the Supervised Learning for Classification with CNN using Barlow Twins loss function.

2. We show that the proposed approach provides consistent improvements in classification accuracy for different baseline CNNs, VGG-16 and ResNet-18, on different datasets, CIFAR-10 and STL-10.

## 2 Related Work

Self-supervised learning aims to learn useful representations of the input data without relying on human annotations. Recent advances in self-supervised learning for visual data show that it is possible to learn self-supervised representations that are competitive with supervised representations. A common underlying theme that unites these methods is that they all aim to learn representations that are invariant under different distortions (also referred to as 'data augmentations'). This is typically achieved by maximizing similarity of representations obtained from different distorted versions of a sample using a variant of Siamese networks.

Contrastive methods like SIMCLR [5] define 'positive' and 'negative' sample pairs which are treated differently in the loss function. Additionally, they can also use asymmetric learning updates wherein momentum encoders are updated separately from the main network.

In another recent line of works, BYOL [6] and SIMSIAM [7], both the network architecture and parameter updates are modified to introduce asymmetry. The network architecture is modified to be asymmetric using a special 'predictor' network and the parameter updates are asymmetric such that the model parameters are only updated using one distorted version of the input, while the representations from another distorted version are used as a fixed target. SIMSIAM conclude that the asymmetry of the learning update, 'stop-gradient', is critical to preventing trivial solutions.

Among discriminative methods, contrastive methods [11,12] currently achieve the state-of-the-art performance in self-supervised learning [13,14]. Contrastive approaches avoid a costly generation step in pixel space by bringing representation of different views of the same image closer ('positive pairs'), and spreading representations of views from different images ('negative pairs') apart [15]. Contrastive methods often require comparing each example with many other examples to work well [8,9] prompting the question of whether using negative pairs is necessary.

DeepCluster [10] partially answers this question. It uses bootstrapping on previous versions of its representation to produce targets for the next representation; it clusters data points using the prior representation, and uses the cluster index of each sample as a classification target for the new representation. While avoiding the use of negative pairs, this requires a costly clustering phase and specific precautions to avoid collapsing to trivial solutions.

In the new method, Barlow Twins [3], which applies redundancy reduction, a principle first proposed in neuroscience to self-supervised learning. This principle has been fruitful in explaining the organization of the visual system, from the retina to cortical areas and has led to a number of algorithms for supervised and unsupervised learning. Based on this principle, they propose the objective function which tries to make the cross-correlation matrix computed from twin embeddings as close to the identity matrix as possible. Barlow Twins is conceptually simple, easy to implement and learns useful representations as opposed to trivial solutions. Intriguingly, Barlow Twins strongly benefits from the use of very high-dimensional embeddings. The network architecture of Barlow Twins is shown in Fig. 1. Barlow Twins outperforms previous methods on ImageNet for semi-supervised classification in the low-data regime, and is on par with current state of the art for ImageNet classification with a linear classifier head, as well as for a number of transfer tasks of classification and object detection.

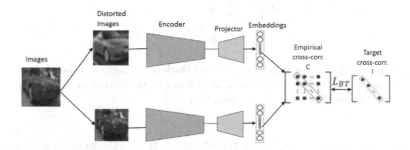

**Fig. 1.** Barlow Twins's objective function computes the cross-correlation matrix between the embeddings of two identical networks fed with distorted versions of a batch of samples, and tries to make this matrix close to the identity matrix. Barlow Twins is competitive with state-of-the-art methods for self-supervised learning while being conceptually simpler, naturally avoiding trivial constant (i.e. collapsed) embeddings, and being robust to the training batch size.

## 3   Proposed Method

### 3.1   Architecture for Supervised Learning with Barlow Twins

The architecture of the proposed supervised learning is shown in Fig. 2. There are two networks with the same parameters and two branches for classifiers and feature embedding for each network.

Let $\{(x_n, t_n)|n = 1, \ldots, N\}$ be the set of training samples, where $t_n = \left[t_{n1} \cdots t_{nK}\right]^T$ is the one-hot vector representation of the target class of the image $x_n$. The number of classes is assumed to be $K$. Then we apply two different perturbations to each of the training sample $x_n$. The perturbed images are denoted as $\tilde{x}_n^{(1)}$ and $\tilde{x}_n^{(2)}$ and they are fed into the upper and the lower networks in Fig. 2. The outputs for two classifiers are denoted as $y_n^{(1)}$ and $y_n^{(2)}$. Also, the embedding features for two networks are denoted as $z_n^{(1)}$ and $z_n^{(2)}$.

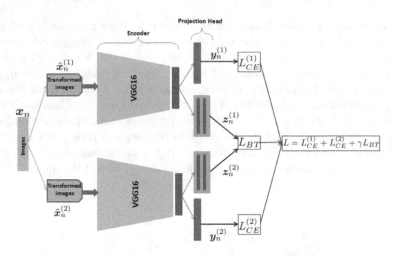

**Fig. 2.** Supervised CNN Architecture, where Barlow Twins loss function and Cross Entropy Loss are calculated from the embeddings of projection head layers and are combine together to form a single loss function

Each input image is randomly transformed during training to produce the two distorted views $\tilde{x}_n^{(1)}$ and $\tilde{x}_n^{(2)}$ as shown in Fig. 2. The image augmentation pipeline consists of the following transformations: random resize crop, random horizontal flip, random grayscale, and random solarize. We investigate the performance of our framework when applying augmentations individually or in pairs. Specifically, we always first randomly crop images and resize them to the same resolution, and then we apply the targeted transformations only to one branch of the framework, while randomly applying transformations to the other branch. The first two transformations (cropping and flipping) are always applied, while the random grayscale, and random solarize are applied randomly, with desired probability.

## 3.2    Cross Entropy Loss

Cross-entropy loss measures the similarity between the given one-hot vector and the estimated output vector (probabilities) and it is used to calculate how accurate the trained deep learning model is. Since we have two networks the cross entropy losses for each network can be defined as

$$L_{CE}^{(1)} = -\sum_{n=1}^{N} \sum_{k=1}^{K} t_{nk} \log y_{nk}^{(1)} \tag{1}$$

$$L_{CE}^{(2)} = -\sum_{n}^{N} \sum_{k=1}^{K} t_{nk} \log y_{nk}^{(2)} \tag{2}$$

### 3.3  Barlow Twins Loss

Like other recent methods for self-supervised learning, Barlow Twins operates on a joint embedding of distorted images. In the proposed method, the Barlow Twins loss is defined by using the embedding feature vectors in mini-batch. Let

$$\mathbb{Z}^{(1)} = \left\{ z_n^{(1)} = \left[ z_{n1}^{(1)} \cdots z_{nM}^{(1)} \right]^T \middle| n = 1, \ldots, B \right\}$$

$$\mathbb{Z}^{(2)} = \left\{ z_n^{(2)} = \left[ z_{n1}^{(2)} \cdots z_{nM}^{(2)} \right]^T \middle| n = 1, \ldots, B \right\}$$

be the sets of embedding feature vectors in a given mini-batch, where $M$ is the length of the feature vectors and $B$ is the number of samples in mini-batch. Then the Barlow Twins loss is defined as

$$L_{BT} = \sum_i \left( 1 - C_{ii} \right)^2 + \lambda \sum_i \sum_{j \neq i} \left( C_{ij} \right)^2 \tag{3}$$

where $\lambda$ is a positive constant trading off the importance of the first and second terms of the loss. The cross-correlation matrix $C = [C_{ij}]$ is computed between the sets of outputs of the two identical networks $\mathbb{Z}^{(1)}$ and $\mathbb{Z}^{(2)}$ along the batch dimension as

$$C_{ij} = \frac{\sum_{b=1}^{B} z_{bi}^{(1)} z_{bj}^{(2)}}{\sqrt{\sum_{b=1}^{B} \left( z_{bi}^{(1)} \right)^2} \sqrt{\sum_{b=1}^{B} \left( z_{bj}^{(2)} \right)^2}} \tag{4}$$

where $b$ indexes batch samples and $i, j$ index the vector dimension of the network's outputs. The cross-correlation matrix $C$ is a square matrix with size $M \times M$. Each of the elements of the matrix $C$ have the value between $-1$ (i.e. perfect anti-correlation) and 1 (i.e. perfect correlation).

Intuitively, the first term of Barlow Twins loss forces the diagonal elements of the cross-correlation matrix to be equal to 1. This makes the embedding features invariant to the perturbations applied to the input images. On the other hand, the second term forces the off-diagonal elements of the cross-correlation matrix to be equal to 0. This decorrelates the different elements of the embedding feature vectors. This decorrelation reduces the redundancy between the elements in the embedding feature vector, so that the output units contain non-redundant information.

### 3.4  Barlow Twins in Supervised Classification CNN

In the proposed methods, we combine the standard cross-entropy loss with the Barlow Twins loss. As shown in Fig. 2, we have two classifiers. Thus the total loss can be defined as

$$L = L_{CE}^{(1)} + L_{CE}^{(2)} + \gamma L_{BT}, \tag{5}$$

where $\gamma$ is a hyper-parameter to control the strength of the Barlow Twins loss. By introducing the Barlow Twins loss, it is expected that the each of the classifiers becomes robust to the perturbation and the generalization performance of the trained model is improved.

In test phase, we can use one of the backbone networks with classification head as one simple CNN.

## 4    Experiments

To confirm the effectiveness of the proposed approach, we have performed experiments using different data sets (CIFAR-10 and STL-10) and different baseline CNNs (VGG-16 and ResNet-18).

### 4.1    Datasets

We evaluated our method on two datasets, CIFAR-10 and STL-10 [4]. The CIFAR-10 dataset consists of 60000 $32 \times 32$ color images in 10 classes, with 6000 images per class. There are 50000 training images and 10000 test images. The dataset is divided into five training batches and one test batch, each with 10000 images. The test batch contains exactly 1000 randomly-selected images from each class. The training batches contain exactly 5000 images from each class. The STL-10 dataset is inspired by the CIFAR-10 dataset but with some modifications. In particular, each class has fewer labeled training examples than in CIFAR-10, but a very large set of unlabeled examples is provided to learn image models prior to supervised training. This dataset consist of 10 classes with $96 \times 96$ pixels colour images. There are 500 training images (10 pre-defined folds), 800 test images per class and 100000 unlabeled images for unsupervised learning.

### 4.2    Experimental Setup

**Network Architecture.** For the encoder, we use VGG-16 and ResNet-18 networks without pre-trained weights. We change the output size of the last layer to 2048 output units, following the original work on Barlow Twins. The encoder network is followed by two parallel projection head networks, where the first projection head has one linear layer with 10 output units for classification and the second projection head has two linear layers with 2048 hidden units and 128 output units for the transformation-invariant embedding. The first layer is followed by a ReLU activation.

**Optimization.** We use the SGD optimizer with a momentum of 0.9 and train the model for 1000 epochs at a learning rate of 0.01. We also add some weight decay with a rate of 0.0001. We run experiments with the values of $\gamma$ 0.0001, 0.001 and 0.01, and our results show that the optimal value for this parameter changes under different configurations. We use a batch size of 512 for VGG-16 and 128 for ResNet-18.

Training time taken for VGG-16 network in GPU is approximately 22 h for each experiment. For ResNet-18 network, the training time takes approximately 5 h for each experiments.

## 4.3  Evaluation on CIFAR-10 Dataset

We train VGG-16 network model without pretrained weights with our proposed method on CIFAR-10 dataset. The network is trained with different gamma parameters ranging from 0.0001 to 0.01. The gamma parameter value which results in the best accuracy is compared with the cross entropy loss (baseline model), where the baseline cross entropy loss accuracies are calculated from the transformed train and test data. Additionally, we show evaluations on augmented data to directy confirm our method's ability to learn transformation-invariant features. We perform the same process when training the ResNet-18 network model. The same experiments are conducted for multiple times and the performance variance is reported with the mean accuracy and standard deviation to all tables of ResNet-18 architecture. The classification accuracies obtained on the CIFAR-10 dataset with VGG-16 network for train data, test data and augmented test data are reported in Table 1. The gamma parameter of 0.001 consistently gives the best accuracy, outperforming the baseline (standard classification training with cross entropy loss). Figure 3 and Fig. 4 shows the 2-dimensional PCA and t-SNE visualizations of augmented train embeddings for baseline cross entropy loss and different gamma parameter values. The visualizations of embeddings from our proposed method show cleaner class separation than the baseline method. The classification accuracies obtained on the CIFAR-10 dataset with ResNet-18 network for train data, test data and augmented test data are reported in Table 2. The gamma parameter of 0.001 shows the best accuracy under all configurations. Figure 5 shows the 2-dimensional t-SNE visualizations of augmented train embeddings for baseline cross entropy loss and different gamma parameter values.

**Table 1.** Classification accuracy results on CIFAR-10 dataset with VGG-16 architecture

|  | Proposed method | | | Cross entropy loss (baseline) |
|---|---|---|---|---|
| Gamma parameter ($\gamma$) | 0.0001 | 0.001 | 0.01 | |
| Train Acc | 99.48 | **99.74** | 99.57 | 99.16 |
| Test Acc-test data | 88.78 | **89.52** | 89.34 | 88.67 |
| Test Acc-Aug test data | 88.36 | **88.71** | 88.08 | 87.19 |

## 4.4  Evaluation on STL-10 Dataset

For STL-10 dataset, we consider 5000 labelled train samples and 5000 unlabelled train samples to train VGG-16 network model without pretrained weights with

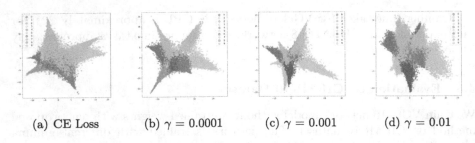

(a) CE Loss        (b) $\gamma = 0.0001$        (c) $\gamma = 0.001$        (d) $\gamma = 0.01$

**Fig. 3.** 2-dimensional PCA visualizations of augmented train embeddings from CIFAR-10 dataset with VGG-16 architecture

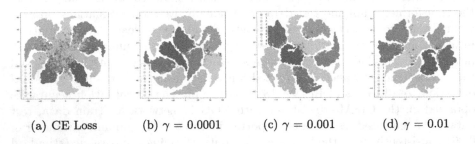

(a) CE Loss        (b) $\gamma = 0.0001$        (c) $\gamma = 0.001$        (d) $\gamma = 0.01$

**Fig. 4.** 2-dimensional t-SNE visualizations of augmented train embeddings from CIFAR-10 dataset with VGG-16 architecture

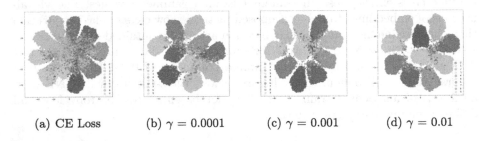

(a) CE Loss        (b) $\gamma = 0.0001$        (c) $\gamma = 0.001$        (d) $\gamma = 0.01$

**Fig. 5.** 2-dimensional t-SNE visualizations of augmented train embeddings from CIFAR-10 dataset with ResNet-18 architecture

our proposed method. We used only the 5000 labelled train samples to train the baseline cross entropy loss. The classification accuracies obtained on the STL-10 dataset with VGG-16 network for train data, test data and augmented test data are reported in Table 3. The gamma value of 0.01 shows the best accuracy under all configurations, outperforming the baseline by over 2% on the test data. Figure 6 and Fig. 7 shows the 2-dimensional PCA and t-SNE visualizations of augmented train embeddings for baseline cross entropy loss and different $\gamma$ parameter values. The visualizations of embeddings for $\gamma$ value 0.01 is more

**Table 2.** Classification accuracy results on CIFAR10 dataset with ResNet-18 architecture

| | Proposed method (mean acc ± std.deviation) | | | Cross entropy loss (baseline) |
|---|---|---|---|---|
| Gamma parameter ($\gamma$) | 0.0001 | 0.001 | 0.01 | |
| Train Acc | 98.29 ± 0.25 | **98.58 ± 0.19** | 98.53 ± 0.5 | 97.39 ± 0.25 |
| Test Acc-test data | 81.78 ± 1.51 | **83.63 ± 0.38** | 82.86 ± 0.33 | 82.78 ± 0.26 |
| Test Acc-Aug test data | 80.13 ± 2.61 | **81.3 ± 0.14** | 80.84 ± 0.92 | 80.85 ± 0.43 |

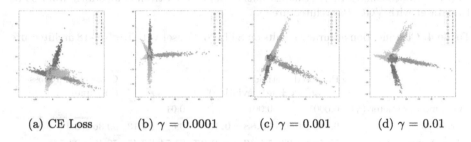

|     (a) CE Loss     |     (b) $\gamma = 0.0001$     |     (c) $\gamma = 0.001$     |     (d) $\gamma = 0.01$     |

**Fig. 6.** 2-dimensional PCA visualizations of augmented train embeddings from STL-10 dataset with VGG-16 architecture

**Table 3.** Classification accuracy results on STL-10 dataset with VGG-16 architecture

| | Proposed method | | | Cross entropy loss (baseline) |
|---|---|---|---|---|
| Gamma parameter ($\gamma$) | 0.0001 | 0.001 | 0.01 | |
| Train Acc | 99.44 | 99.88 | **99.92** | 99.9 |
| Test Acc-test data | 73 | 73.93 | **78.96** | 76.32 |
| Test Acc-Aug test data | 72.95 | 74.78 | **78.85** | 73.54 |

clearly clustered than the baseline cross entropy. The classification accuracies obtained on the STL-10 dataset with ResNet-18 network for train data, test data and augmented test data are reported in Table 4. The gamma parameter of 0.001 gives the best accuracy, again outperforming the standard classification baseline. Figure 8 shows the 2-dimensional t-SNE visualizations of augmented train embeddings for baseline cross entropy loss and different gamma parameter values.

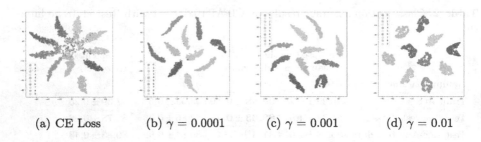

| (a) CE Loss | (b) $\gamma = 0.0001$ | (c) $\gamma = 0.001$ | (d) $\gamma = 0.01$ |

**Fig. 7.** 2-dimensional t-SNE visualizations of augmented train embeddings from STL-10 dataset with VGG-16 architecture

**Table 4.** Classification accuracy results on STL-10 dataset with ResNet-18 architecture

|  | Proposed method (mean acc ± std.deviation) | | | Cross entropy loss (baseline) |
|---|---|---|---|---|
| Gamma parameter ($\gamma$) | 0.0001 | 0.001 | 0.01 | |
| Train Acc | $99.86 \pm 0.02$ | $\mathbf{99.88 \pm 0.13}$ | $99.17 \pm 1.13$ | $99.36 \pm 0.33$ |
| Test Acc-test data | $72.78 \pm 1.06$ | $\mathbf{73.66 \pm \pm 0.37}$ | $71.74 \pm 3.45$ | $70.46 \pm 0.87$ |
| Test Acc-Aug test data | $72.34 \pm 0.33$ | $\mathbf{73.51 \pm 0.46}$ | $71.33 \pm 2.49$ | $71.28 \pm 0.27$ |

| (a) CE Loss | (b) $\gamma = 0.0001$ | (c) $\gamma = 0.001$ | (d) $\gamma = 0.01$ |

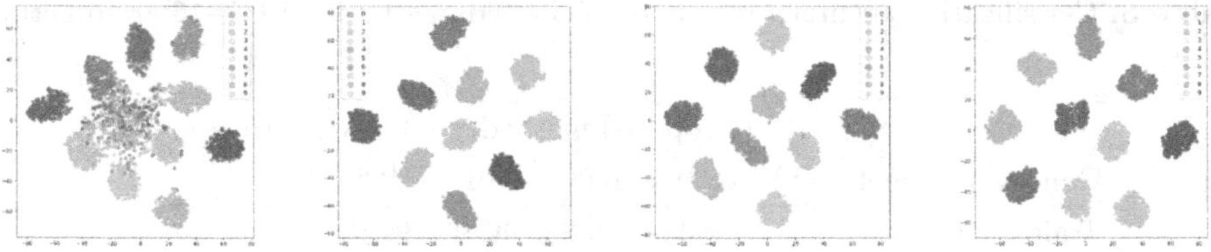

**Fig. 8.** 2-dimensional t-SNE visualizations of augmented train embeddings from STL-10 dataset with ResNet-18 architecture

## 5    Conclusion

In this paper, we propose a method of supervised learning for Convolutional Neural Network with Barlow Twins to learn useful features that are invariant to distortions applied to the input data. This method uses a cross entropy loss in a siamese setting, where the Barlow Twins function is used as an additional loss term with a weighting hyper-parameter $\gamma$, and can recover better learnable features from the transformed input image samples. Through our experiments, We show that the proposed method makes it possible to achieve higher classification accuracy and learns a better feature space (proven by visualization of the features) by tuning the weighting hyper-parameter. The proposed method achieves better results in classification accuracy than the baseline method, which uses a cross entropy loss with augmented input.

# References

1. Ohri, K., Kumar, M.: Review on self-supervised image recognition using deep neural networks. Knowl. Based Syst. **224**, 107090 (2021)
2. Zhang, T., Qiu, C., Ke, W., Süsstrunk, S., Salzmann, M.: Leverage Your Local and Global Representations: A New Self-Supervised Learning Strategy. Computer Vision and Pattern Recognition arXiv:2203.17205 (2022)
3. Zbontar, J., Jing, L., Misra, I., LeCun, Y., Deny, S.: Barlow Twins: Self-Supervised Learning via Redundancy Reduction. arXiv:2103.03230v3, 14 June 2021
4. Coates, A., Ng, A., Lee, H.: An analysis of single-layer networks in unsupervised feature learning. In: Proceedings of the Fourteenth International Conference on Artificial Intelligence and Statistics, pp. 215–223. JMLR Workshop and Conference Proceedings (2011)
5. Chen, T., Kornblith, S., Norouzi, M., Hinton, G.: A Simple Framework for Contrastive Learning of Visual Representations. arXiv:2002.05709v3, 1 July 2020
6. Grill, J.-B., et al.: Bootstrap your own latent: a new approach to self-supervised Learning. Machine Learning, Computer Vision and Pattern Recognition, Machine Learning, arXiv:2006.07733 (2020)
7. Zhang, C., Zhang, K., Zhang, C., Pham, T.X., Yoo, C.D., Kweon, I.S.: How Does SimSiam Avoid Collapse Without Negative Samples? A Unified Understanding with Self-supervised Contrastive Learning. Machine Learning, Artificial Intelligence, arXiv:2203.16262 (2022)
8. Chen, T., Kornblith, S., Norouzi, M., Hinton, G.E.: A simple framework for contrastive learning of visual representations. arXiv preprint arXiv:2002.05709 (2020)
9. He, K., Fan, H., Wu, Y., Xie, S., Girshick, R.B.: Momentum contrast for unsupervised visual representation learning. arXiv preprint arXiv:1911.05722 (2019)
10. Caron, M., Bojanowski, P., Joulin, A., Douze, M.: Deep clustering for unsupervised learning of visual features. In: European Conference on Computer Vision (2018)
11. Misra, I., van der Maaten, L.: Self-supervised learning of pretext-invariant representations. arXiv preprint arXiv:1912.01991 (2019)
12. Li, J., Zhou, P., Xiong, C., Hoi, S.C.H.: Prototypical contrastive learning of unsupervised representations. arXiv preprint arXiv:2005.04966 (2020)
13. Chen, X., Fan, H., Girshick, R., He, K.: Improved baselines with momentum contrastive learning. arXiv preprint arXiv:2003.04297 (2020)
14. Chen, T., Kornblith, S., Swersky, K., Norouzi, M., Hinton, G.E.: Big self-supervised models are strong semi-supervised learners. arXiv preprint arXiv:2006.10029 (2020)
15. Wu, Z., Xiong, Y., Yu, S.X., Lin, D.: Unsupervised feature learning via non-parametric instance discrimination. In: Computer Vision and Pattern Recognition (2018)

# Using Multiple Heads to Subsize Meta-memorization Problem

Lu Wang[✉] and K. L. Eddie Law

Faculty of Applied Sciences, Macao Polytechnic University, Macao, China
{lu.wang,eddielaw}@ipm.edu.mo

**Abstract.** The **memorization problem** is a meta-level overfitting phenomenon in meta-learning. The trained model prefers to remember learned tasks instead of adapting to new tasks. This issue limits many meta-learning approaches to generalize. In this paper, we mitigate this limitation issue by proposing multiple supervisions through a multi-objective optimization process. The design leads to a Multi-Input Multi-Output (MIMO) configuration for meta-learning. The model has multiple outputs through different heads. Each head is supervised by a different order of labels for the same task. This leads to different memories, resulting in meta-level conflicts as regularization to avoid meta-overfitting. The resulting MIMO configuration is applicable to all MAML-like algorithms with minor increments in training computation, the inference calculation can be reduced through early-exit policy or better performance can be achieved through low cost ensemble. In experiments, identical model and training settings are used in all test cases, our proposed design is able to suppress the meta-overfitting issue, achieve smoother loss landscapes, and improve generalisation.

**Keywords:** Meta-overfitting · Meta-learning · Multi-head

## 1  Introduction

Meta-learning aims to improve the ability on learning new tasks through experiencing a range of other tasks [1]. As research interest grows, many new approaches and insights in meta-learning are being developed among the machine learning community [2].

Today, there are some successful stories in artificial intelligence [3–5], but modern machine learning algorithmic designs still exhibit many constraints [6], and the meta-learning may possibly mitigate some of these limitations. However, there are also many problematic issues in meta-learning, such as the meta-overfitting, or the *memorization problem* [7]. The meta-trained model prefers to "remember" learned tasks instead of adapting to new tasks. It affects a model to generalize, and limits the depth of a model [8].

K. L. E. Law would appreciate the financial support provided by Macao Polytechnic University through the research funding programme (#RP/ESCA-09/2021).

Optimization-based meta-learning methods, such as those belong to the class of Model-Agnostic Meta-Learning (MAML) algorithms [1,9,10], are easy to use on new scenarios due to their effectiveness with fewer constraints. In fact, the MAML-like algorithm obtains initialization parameters through a bi-level gradient-based optimization method, as a pre-train model to fast adaptation to new tasks. During the training stage, the meta-learning algorithm learns on a series of tasks, and evaluates the learning ability on a new task. In contrast to conventional machine learning, meta-learning treats a task (dataset) as a single data point.

The overfitting issue in machine learning has been well studied, and some effective solutions are available [11,12]. However, apart from the overfitting problem of data points in meta-learning, there is an overfitting issue on a given set of training tasks. This implies that a model may adapt well to the tasks in training datasets, but severely suffer from overfitting tasks in the test datasets. This problem is called the memorization problem [7]. This indicates that during meta-overfitting, a model prefers to remember learned tasks rather than to adapt to new tasks.

Some solutions exist resolving the conventional overfitting problem, examples include meta-augmentation [13] and meta-regularization [14]. There are also approaches which may mitigate the meta-overfitting through reducing the model capacity [15,16]. In general, the perception is that a better performance can be effectively achieved by simply using a larger scaled model. It is thus desirable to develop methods that do not reduce the model capacity upon dealing with the meta-overfitting issue.

The core issue of the memorization problem is that a developed model is biased towards trained tasks. Hence, using conventional regularization methods that focus only on data points may not work well. Meta-level regularization can enhance the generalization capability, but we concern more that the model still tend to remembering a single supervision material. If the model can be motivated to form different or even conflicting memories using approximate meta-objectives, it should be better in avoiding the formation of *memories*.

The recent work on Multi-Input Multi-Output (MIMO) configuration [17] enables low-cost ensemble learning using a single model. In contrast to the use of one head in a conventional meta-learning configuration, multiple heads design can form different memories and then obtain regularization. In this paper, we propose and construct a MIMO configuration for MAML-like algorithms with a goal in reducing the meta-overfitting problem.

In this paper, our contributions are: (1) the MIMO is extended to meta-learning as a regularization method for improving the performance of the MAML-like algorithms; (2) the proposed approach effectively obtains better generalization with the loss landscape observation; (3) through testing with the CIFAR-FS dataset, our proposed approach can effectively mitigate the meta-overfitting problem.

## 2    Related Works

Typically, it is desirable that machine learning algorithms can use more input training data to create more knowledge [18,19]. Meta-learning is an important research area because its aim is to leverage more previous experiences to handle new tasks [1]. There are many latest results [2,20] reported in different fields, for example, the few-shot learning [21], the unsupervised learning [22], the reinforcement learning [23], the hyperparameter optimization [24], and the Neural Architecture Search (NAS) [25].

In [2], a novel taxonomy with three axes was developed to describe different meta-learning algorithms, and they were *meta-representation, meta-optimisation*, and *meta-objectives*. Among them, the MAML-like algorithms [26] used parametrization with initialization as the meta-representation, and used the gradient-based meta-optimizer. The resulting model was more effective with fewer constraints, and it could be used for a wide range of meta-objectives.

The memorization problem [7] is a common meta-overfitting phenomenon in the MAML-like algorithms that we focus in this paper. The overfitting problem of MAML was discovered in an earlier work [27], and was identified the limiting factor on the generalization capability of a meta-learning algorithm. Furthermore, it was not the conventional overfitting [28]. The meta-level overfitting got the MAML biased towards trained tasks instead of adapting to new tasks [29]. In dealing with this meta-level overfitting, some models based on entropy [29], Bayesian mechanisms [28], augmentation [30], meta-parameter decomposition [8,16] were proposed.

In [7], Yin *et al.* discussed the distinction between meta-overfitting and standard overfitting, as the memorization problem. Traditional overfitting solutions [11] at the data point level were ineffective at the task sets level. Some solutions to the memorization problem were proposed. In [13], meta-augmentation was suggested to add to meta-learning. Designs with meta-level dropouts [31,32], network pruning [15], task augmentation [33], and meta-regularization [14] approaches were proposed and discussed.

Dynamic neural networks [34] are our source of inspiration. Methods such as Early-Exiting [35] add supervision to the mid-layer of the model. This can also provide constraints on the meta-overfitting of the model.

## 3    MIMO-MAML

### 3.1    Meta Learning Problem

In a meta-learning algorithm, a gradient-based meta-optimizer is used for obtaining meta-trained initialization parameters. A model $f_\theta$ parametrized by $\theta$ is learned over a task distribution $p(\mathcal{T})$ by a meta-learning algorithm $\mathcal{A}$ to obtain an optimized model $f_\theta^*$. It has the ability to approximate a true mapping function $g(x)$ or a true conditional probability distribution $p(y|x)$ corresponding to any task $\mathcal{T}_i \sim p(\mathcal{T})$ on the distribution, as $|f_\theta^*(x) - g_\mathcal{T}(x)| < \varepsilon$ or $|f_\theta^*(x) - p(y|x)| < \varepsilon$.

Since the number of tasks and the amount of data are limited in real world, a feasible learning guideline is to use the Empirical Risk Minimization (EMP) described by loss function $\mathcal{L}$:

$$\mathcal{R}^{emp}_{p(\mathcal{T})}(f_\theta) = \sum_{\mathcal{T}_i \in \{\mathcal{T}\}} \mathcal{L}(f_\theta, \mathcal{T}_i) \tag{1}$$

We can split input datasets into $\mathcal{D}^{tr}_i$ and $\mathcal{D}^{test}_i$ for a task $\mathcal{T}_i$, the adaptation of MAML-like algorithm can be written as

$$arg\min_\theta \sum_{\mathcal{T}_i \in \{\mathcal{T}\}} \mathcal{L}(\theta - \alpha \nabla_\theta \mathcal{L}(\theta, \mathcal{D}^{tr}_{\mathcal{T}_i}), \mathcal{D}^{test}_{\mathcal{T}_i}) \tag{2}$$

For example, in the $N$-way $K$-shot learning problem, the $\mathcal{D}^{tr}_i$ is a dataset with $N$ categories and $K$ samples per category.

### 3.2 The Design

We extend the MIMO configuration to meta-learning and obtain regularization, as shown in Fig. 1. Since the output heads can be positioned in the middle layer, the over-thinking can be avoided. Upon combining the outputs from multiple heads, the low-cost ensemble can be obtained.

Using the classification problem as an example, when sampling a classification task from a task distribution, we usually label the different categories $[0, 1, \cdots, N]$ in the task. In order to construct more tasks, the sampling data of categories is usually repeated. If we keep the number of categories unchanged, the network model simply remembers the labels. Therefore, the sampled tasks are usually given new random labels, such as $[3, 1, 5, 2, 4]$.

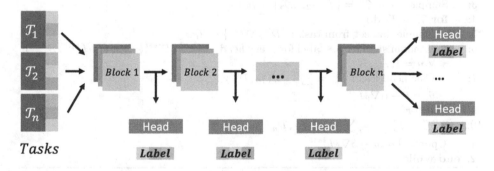

**Fig. 1.** Architecture overview

However, the classifier used by a learner is usually a linear or distance function layer, and the learner may update it several times during training on a task. This may still result in the model memorizing the category positions corresponding to the features. This memorization is likely created due to the label sequencing and the training method; therefore, the uses of common meta-regularization methods may only slow down but not prevent the memory generation. In this paper, we propose a MIMO configuration to avoid this memorization problem during the training phase. Firstly, given a set of assigned labels for the categories in the input data, we generate different randomly ordered labels for each task. This does not require any changes to the model input entries, but creating new multiple outputs in our model. For each output set, the output labels are randomly ordered. For example, a triple classification problem with three categories $\{A, B, C\}$ labeled with $\{0, 1, 2\}$ is denoted as $[0, 1, 2]$. For MIMO configuration, each output matches to a different label order, such as: $[2, 1, 0], [1, 0, 2], [0, 2, 1]$, etc.

There are multiple output heads in our proposed designs. The input dataset $\mathcal{D}$ has $N$ different labels. For each of these output heads, the output labels datasets $\{1, 2, \ldots, N\}$ are randomly shuffled on the labels. Hence, the same datasets $\{\mathcal{D}_1, \mathcal{D}_2, \ldots, \mathcal{D}_N\}$ are able to construct different label conflicted memories on different tasks. In the MAML-like algorithms, there are two-level optimizations: the inner and outer loop optimizations. The inner loop learns from the support sets $\{\mathcal{D}_i^{tr}\}_{i \in \{1, \ldots, N\}}$, in multiple tasks. The outer loop updates the model from the gradients using query sets $\{\mathcal{D}_i^{test}\}$ from these tasks. When meta-learning uses MIMO configuration, the details are outlined in Algorithm 1.

---

**Algorithm 1.** MIMO-MAML

---

**Require:** $p(\mathcal{T})$: task distribution
**Require:** $\alpha$, $\beta$: step size; $B$: batch size
**Require:** $N$: number of output heads
1: random initialization $\theta$
2: **while** not done **do**
3:     Sample tasks, $\mathcal{T}' = \{\mathcal{T}_1, \mathcal{T}_2, \ldots \mathcal{T}_j\} \sim p(\mathcal{T})$
4:     **for** $\mathcal{T}_i$ in $\mathcal{T}'$ **do**
5:         Sample dataset from task : $\{\mathcal{D}^{tr}, \mathcal{D}^{test}\} \sim \mathcal{T}_i$
6:         Random shuffle class label for every head $n$: $\{\mathcal{D}_n^{tr}, \mathcal{D}_n^{test}\} = shuffle(\mathcal{D}^{tr}, \mathcal{D}^{test})$,
            $\forall n = 1, \ldots, N$
7:         Calc head loss : $L_i^{tr} = \sum_{n=1}^N \mathcal{L}(f_\theta, \mathcal{D}_n^{tr})$
8:         $\theta_i' = \theta - \alpha \nabla_\theta L_i^{tr}$
9:     **end for**
10:    $L_i^{test} = \sum_{\mathcal{T}_i \in \{\mathcal{T}\}} \sum_{n=1}^N \mathcal{L}(f_{\theta_i'}, \mathcal{D}_n^{test})$
11:    Update $\theta \leftarrow \theta - \beta \nabla_\theta L_i^{test}$
12: **end while**

---

Generally, there are no needs to balance the losses carefully when the output heads are located at the same location [17]. However, when the output heads come out from the middle layers, i.e., in an early-exit configuration [35], then this requires loss balancing at different levels.

If the outer loop uses Eq. 3, it is the MIMO-Reptile [10]

$$\theta \leftarrow \beta \frac{1}{|\{\mathcal{T}_i\}|} \sum_{i=0}^{|\{\mathcal{T}_i\}|} (\theta_i' - \theta). \tag{3}$$

When the inner loop does not use any parameters, except the head parameter only, it is the Multi-Input Multi-Output Almost No Inner-Loop (MIMO-ANIL) algorithm [9].

$$\theta_{headi}' = \theta_{head} - \alpha \nabla_{\theta head} L_i^{tr}. \tag{4}$$

Considering that the computations of the second-order derivatives of multiple heads are complicated, the MIMO-ANIL is a compromise between balancing computational complexity and algorithmic performance.

## 3.3  Analysis

It is known that some architectures and training strategies may significantly affect the loss space, and a smooth loss space in general usually means easier optimization. Indeed, the flat minima [36,37] leads to better generalization performance.

To alleviate the memorization problem, our approach adds several supervisions to the training phase of the model. The design leads to a multi-headed model structure. A similar multiple output structure [17] makes the loss landscape smoother. Certainly, our proposed method uses different training methods and optimization objectives, this leads to different effects on the loss space. In the following, we shall examine the impact of our work on the loss space by comparing the loss spaces of different methods. By following the approach in [38], we can specifically visualize the loss landscape based on an open source implementation [39].

As shown in Fig. 2 and Fig. 3, we adopt the common baseline model ResNet12 [40] and train the model using the CIFAR-FS dataset [40] in our experiments. The model used in our approach is shown in Fig. 5.

In Fig. 2, a loss landscape is shwon for taking new tasks before carrying out any further adaptation to it. Since the skip connections in ResNet smooth out the loss space [38], there are no dramatic ups and downs in all the plots. The right-hand side is smoother than the subgraphs on the left, which implies that it is easier to optimize. The low loss region on the right is closer to the center. It means that the model is already close to the optimal parameters before taking on any new task, and can therefore be adapted to the new task with only a few parameter updates.

After adapting to the new task, the loss landscape is shown in Fig. 3. Similar interpretations to the previous ones can be observed. In addition to a smoother loss space, the current parameters are again closer to the centre of the lowest loss region. Although observing the loss space through random low latitude does not imply that it is accurate, it is a smooth visualization curve that can be used to observe and compare to the loss spaces of other designs.

## Loss Landspace 2D

**Fig. 2.** Loss landscape in new task before adaptation. Left: ANIL, Right: MIMO-ANIL

## Loss Landspace 2D

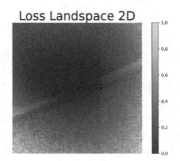

**Fig. 3.** Loss landscape in new task after adaptation. Left: ANIL, Right: MIMO-ANIL

### 3.4    Early-Exiting or Ensemble

Our proposed design does not restrict where in the model multiple supervision can be added. This leads to at least two possible approaches. One is to add supervision to the middle layer(s) in the model. The other option is to add multiple supervision(s) at the back end of the model.

**Early-Exiting.** Adding supervision to the side of the model results in adding multiple heads to the side of the network. This leads to our model being available with the early-exiting strategy [35].

The model $f$ can be thought of as consisting of several blocks or layers $\mathcal{F}_i$. The output layer, e.g., a classifier in a classification problem, can be expressed as $\mathcal{F}^{cls}$. For each exit $\mathcal{F}_i$, there is a dedicated classifier $\mathcal{F}_i^{cls}$. The model can be expressed as $f = \mathcal{F}_1 \circ \cdots \circ \mathcal{F}_i \circ \mathcal{F}_i^{cls}$.

The core idea of the early-exit strategy is to determine the inference path of the model. Because this design reduces the inference time of the model, when the prediction can be output earlier.

Furthermore, we use a confidence-based early-exit strategy [35]. The model infers through each head from shallow to deep layers. When the confidence level of the output of a header exceeds a preset threshold value $\gamma$, the model takes the result of this header as the final output and stops further inferences on subsequent layers. In the case of classification problems, for example, the confidence level of the model output is the output after the Softmax operations.

The model is ResNet12 with three output headers in the middle layer for evaluating the impact of the early-exit strategy. The structure of the model is shown in the Fig. 4. The model is trained using the CIFAR-FS dataset. The concerned threshold for the early-exit strategy is $\gamma = 0.85$. An output exits at a head when the corresponding confidence level reaches 0.85, and it is the final result.

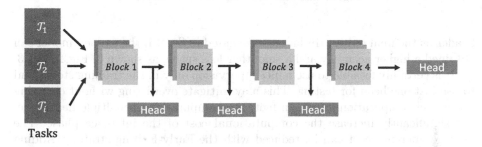

**Fig. 4.** Early-Exiting using ResNet12.

We use a "cost score" to estimate computational costs. The model inference per ResNet block takes 3 points. It is because each block contains three convolutional layers. Each header contains a fully connected layer, hence the cost of each output header is approximately 1 point. By counting the number of output samples from different heads on the test set, we can get the proportion of output from different heads and calculate the overall inference cost. In our early estimate, after several experiments, the early-exit strategy cost is about 807.33 while the conventional method cost reaches 1000 points. The early-exit strategy leads to a lower inference cost.

**Ensemble.** Upon adding multiple supervisions at the end of the model, the multiple heads of the model are located at the back end of the model. Different heads are trained using different labels, this is similar to having the model learning on multiple tasks. A similar structure is thought to enable low-cost ensemble learning, by prompting the model to form different sub-networks [17]. According to the Lottery Ticket Hypothesis [41], these sub-networks can achieve similar performance to the original network, which brings in multiple different learners, and higher performance can be achieved using an appropriate integration strategy.

A typical structure of the model is shown in Fig. 5. To evaluate the impact of our approach on the ensemble model setting, we shall use a ResNet12-based backbone network with multiple heads. The model is trained on the CIFAR-FS dataset. We propose a simple ensemble strategy with the highest confidence

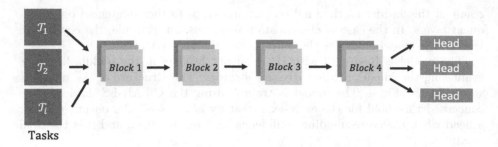

**Fig. 5.** Ensemble learning using ResNet12.

header as the final output. In fact, as discussed in Sect. 4, the trained model can obtained a higher accuracy and a smoother loss space, as shown in Fig. 2, Fig. 3.

It is certainly feasible to use multi-supervision only in the training stages and to use just one head for testing. This may mitigate overfitting without changing the model computation graph. In fact, the computation of multiple heads may not significantly increase the computational cost of the inference phase. The average inference cost can be reduced with the Early-Exiting strategy. Adding multiple headers to the backbone only increases the computational cost slightly, but also leads to higher performance through ensemble. In general, our approach gains advantages on several commonly used model structures.

## 4    Experiment

**Dataset.** CIFAR-FS (CIFAR100 few-shots) dataset [40] is used for few-shot image classification problem. It is sampled from the CIFAR100 dataset [42].

The models and datasets used are the usual baseline settings. The MAML-like algorithm is no longer used in recent State-of-the-Art methods due to the performance deficiencies of the meta-overfitting problem. However, since the MAML-like algorithm can be easily applied to other machine learning problems, we are interested in improving its overall performance.

**Table 1.** Experiment in CIFAR-FS 5-way 5-shot classification

| Method | Setting | Accuracy |
|---|---|---|
| MAML [1] | Original | 71.5% |
| ANIL | Our impl | 65.73% |
| MIMO-ANIL | One head | 70.26% |
| MIMO-ANIL | Early-exiting | 71.07% |
| MIMO-ANIL | Ensemble | 72.19% |

As shown as Table 1, we compared the performance of different settings. The proposed method achieved a higher test accuracy. The model fit the training data quickly, the improved test performance indicated that our proposed approach reduced the effects of meta-overfitting. Our proposed approach would have potential to achieve better performance if more strategies would be added.

Our implementation of ANIL was based on PyTorch [43] and followed the learn2learn [44] library. For a fair comparison, the algorithm implementation and hyperparametric search strategy were identical. Throughout the experiments, we did not use any data enhancement techniques or other training tricks. The hyperparameters were derived using a simple grid search strategy.

During the testing phase, our proposed method improved the accuracy when only one head was used. Our approach could be used without adding any restrictions to the model during the inference phase. Then upon using early-exit strategies (with a multi-headed structure), our approach could achieves faster overall inference with higher accuracy. When the ensemble learning strategy would be added, our model could even achieve higher accuracy.

## 5   Conclusion

The meta-overfitting problem in gradient-based meta-learning algorithms is well known. In general the memorization problem limits the generalisation capability of a model. In this paper, a Multi-Input Multi-Output Model-Agnostic Meta-Learning algorithm (MIMO-MAML) has been proposed by introducing multiple supervision operations at different layers in the network. Different supervisions of the same task may use different labels, which can construct different *memories* to obtain regularization in the system. In contrast to the meta-learning algorithms that place no restrictions on a model, we recommend the use of a multi-supervised structure, not necessary at the inference stage. Through experiments, advantages can be gained from the multi-supervised structure. Through comparisons and visualizations, our proposed design offers an improved effective meta-regularization.

## References

1. Finn, C., Abbeel, P., Levine, S.: Model-agnostic meta-learning for fast adaptation of deep networks. In: ICML, vol. 70, pp. 1126–1135 (2017). http://proceedings.mlr.press/v70/finn17a.html
2. Hospedales, T.M., Antoniou, A., Micaelli, P., Storkey, A.J.: Meta-learning in neural networks: a survey. IEEE Trans. Pattern Anal. Mach. Intell. (2021). https://ieeexplore.ieee.org/document/9428530
3. He, K., Zhang, X., Ren, S., Sun, J.: Deep residual learning for image recognition. In: CVPR (2016)
4. Silver, D., et al.: Mastering the game of go with deep neural networks and tree search. Nature **529**(7587), 484–489 (2016)
5. Devlin, J., Chang, M., Lee, K., Toutanova, K.: BERT: pre-training of deep bidirectional transformers for language understanding. In: NAACL-HLT (2019)

6. Marcus, G.: Deep learning: a critical appraisal. CoRR abs/1801.00631 (2018). https://arxiv.org/abs/1801.00631

7. Yin, M., Tucker, G., Zhou, M., Levine, S., Finn, C.: Meta-learning without memorization. In: ICLR (2020)

8. Doveh, S., et al.: MetAdapt: meta-learned task-adaptive architecture for few-shot classification. Pattern Recognit. Lett. **149**, 130–136 (2021)

9. Raghu, A., Raghu, M., Bengio, S., Vinyals, O.: Rapid learning or feature reuse? towards understanding the effectiveness of MAML. In: ICLR (2020)

10. Nichol, A., Achiam, J., Schulman, J.: On first-order meta-learning algorithms. CoRR abs/1803.02999 (2018). https://arxiv.org/abs/1803.02999

11. Srivastava, N., Hinton, G.E., Krizhevsky, A., Sutskever, I., Salakhutdinov, R.: Dropout: a simple way to prevent neural networks from overfitting. J. Mach. Learn. Res. **15**(1), 1929–1958 (2014)

12. Ioffe, S., Szegedy, C.: Batch normalization: accelerating deep network training by reducing internal covariate shift. In: ICML (2015)

13. Rajendran, J., Irpan, A., Jang, E.: Meta-learning requires meta-augmentation. In: NeurIPS (2020)

14. Pan, E., Rajak, P., Shrivastava, S.: Meta-regularization by enforcing mutual-exclusiveness. CoRR abs/2101.09819 (2021)

15. Tian, H., Liu, B., Yuan, X.-T., Liu, Q.: Meta-learning with network pruning. In: Vedaldi, A., Bischof, H., Brox, T., Frahm, J.-M. (eds.) ECCV 2020. LNCS, vol. 12364, pp. 675–700. Springer, Cham (2020). https://doi.org/10.1007/978-3-030-58529-7_40

16. Zintgraf, L.M., Shiarlis, K., Kurin, V., Hofmann, K., Whiteson, S.: Fast context adaptation via meta-learning. In: ICML (2019)

17. Havasi, M., et al.: Training independent subnetworks for robust prediction. In: ICLR (2021)

18. Pan, S.J., Yang, Q.: A survey on transfer learning. IEEE Trans. Knowl. Data Eng. **22**(10), 1345–1359 (2010)

19. Raffel, C., et al.: Exploring the limits of transfer learning with a unified text-to-text transformer. J. Mach. Learn. Res. **21**, 140:1–140:67 (2020). https://jmlr.org/papers/v21/20-074.html

20. Thrun, S., Pratt, L.Y.: Learning to learn: introduction and overview. In: Thrun, S., Pratt, L.Y. (eds.) Learning to Learn, pp. 3–17. Springer, Boston (1998). https://doi.org/10.1007/978-1-4615-5529-2_1

21. Snell, J., Swersky, K., Zemel, R.S.: Prototypical networks for few-shot learning. In: NeurIPS (2017)

22. Metz, L., Maheswaranathan, N., Cheung, B., Sohl-Dickstein, J.: Meta-learning update rules for unsupervised representation learning. In: ICLR (2019)

23. Alet, F., Schneider, M.F., Lozano-Pérez, T., Kaelbling, L.P.: Meta-learning curiosity algorithms. In: ICLR (2020)

24. Franceschi, L., Frasconi, P., Salzo, S., Grazzi, R., Pontil, M.: Bilevel programming for hyperparameter optimization and meta-learning. In: ICML (2018)

25. Elsken, T., Staffler, B., Metzen, J.H., Hutter, F.: Meta-learning of neural architectures for few-shot learning. In: CVPR (2020)

26. Finn, C.: Learning to Learn with Gradients. Ph.D. thesis, University of California, Berkeley, USA (2018). https://escholarship.org/uc/item/0987d4n3

27. Mishra, N., Rohaninejad, M., Chen, X., Abbeel, P.: A simple neural attentive meta-learner. In: ICLR (2018)

28. Yoon, J., Kim, T., Dia, O., Kim, S., Bengio, Y., Ahn, S.: Bayesian model-agnostic meta-learning. In: NeurIPS (2018)

29. Jamal, M.A., Qi, G.: Task agnostic meta-learning for few-shot learning. In: CVPR, pp. 11719–11727 (2019)
30. Lee, K., Maji, S., Ravichandran, A., Soatto, S.: Meta-learning with differentiable convex optimization. In: CVPR (2019)
31. Tseng, H., Chen, Y., Tsai, Y., Liu, S., Lin, Y., Yang, M.: Regularizing meta-learning via gradient dropout. In: ACCV (2020)
32. Lee, H., Nam, T., Yang, E., Hwang, S.J.: Meta dropout: learning to perturb latent features for generalization. In: ICLR (2020)
33. Yao, H., et al.: Improving generalization in meta-learning via task augmentation. In: ICML (2021)
34. Han, Y., Huang, G., Song, S., Yang, L., Wang, H., Wang, Y.: Dynamic neural networks: a survey. CoRR abs/2102.04906 (2021). https://arxiv.org/abs/2102.04906
35. Teerapittayanon, S., McDanel, B., Kung, H.T.: Branchynet: fast inference via early exiting from deep neural networks. In: ICPR (2016)
36. Keskar, N.S., Mudigere, D., Nocedal, J., Smelyanskiy, M., Tang, P.T.P.: On large-batch training for deep learning: generalization gap and sharp minima. In: ICLR (2017)
37. Xie, Z., Sato, I., Sugiyama, M.: A diffusion theory for deep learning dynamics: Stochastic gradient descent exponentially favors flat minima. In: Keskar (2021)
38. Li, H., Xu, Z., Taylor, G., Studer, C., Goldstein, T.: Visualizing the loss landscape of neural nets. In: Bengio, S., Wallach, H.M., Larochelle, H., Grauman, K., Cesa-Bianchi, N., Garnett, R. (eds.) NeurIPS (2018)
39. De Bernardi, M.: Loss-landscapes. https://pypi.org/project/loss-landscapes/3.0.6/
40. Bertinetto, L., Henriques, J.F., Torr, P.H.S., Vedaldi, A.: Meta-learning with differentiable closed-form solvers. In: ICLR (2019)
41. Frankle, J., Carbin, M.: The lottery ticket hypothesis: finding sparse, trainable neural networks. In: ICLR (2019)
42. Krizhevsky, A.: Learning multiple layers of features from tiny images. Technical report, University of Toronto (2009)
43. Paszke, A., et al.: Pytorch: an imperative style, high-performance deep learning library. In: Wallach, H., Larochelle, H., Beygelzimer, A., d' Alché-Buc, F., Fox, E., Garnett, R. (eds.) Advances in Neural Information Processing Systems 32, pp. 8024–8035. Curran Associates, Inc. (2019). https://proceedings.neurips.cc/paper/2019/file/bdbca288fee7f92f2bfa9f7012727740-Paper.pdf
44. Arnold, S.M.R., Mahajan, P., Datta, D., Bunner, I., Zarkias, K.S.: learn2learn: a library for meta-learning research. CoRR abs/2008.12284 (2020). https://arxiv.org/abs/2008.12284

# Video Motion Perception for Self-supervised Representation Learning

Wei Li[1,2], Dezhao Luo[1,2], Bo Fang[1,2], Xiaoni Li[1,2], Yu Zhou[1(✉)], and Weiping Wang[1]

[1] Institute of Information Engineering, Chinese Academy of Sciences, Beijing, China
zhouyu@iie.ac.cn
[2] School of Cyber Security, University of Chinese Academy of Sciences, Beijing, China

**Abstract.** The motion of a video contains two factors: magnitude and direction, but most of the existing video self-supervised methods ignored the motion direction information. In this paper, we propose a Video Motion Perception (**VMP**) self-supervised framework, simultaneously taking account of the above two key factors. Specifically, a Motion Direction Perception Module (MDPM) is applied to asking the network to predict the moving direction of the video objects by using two well-designed handcraft strategies. Additionally, we analyze the characteristic of video motion in natural scenes and propose the Motion Change Perception Module (MCPM) accordingly for motion magnitude learning. Experimental results show that VMP achieves competitive performance on different benchmarks, including action recognition, video retrieval, and action similarity labeling.

**Keywords:** Self-supervised learning · Action recognition · Video motion perception

## 1 Introduction

With the development of convolutional neural networks (CNNs), many computer vision tasks have achieved great progress in recent years. Even though supervised learning shows promising results, it suffers from demanding large labeled datasets like ImageNet [4] and Kinetics [9]. Furthermore, annotating large-scale datasets is expensive and time-consuming, especially for those dense prediction tasks, *e.g.*, semantic segmentation and action detection. Therefore, training CNNs in a self-supervised manner is of great significance.

Recently, self-supervised learning is proposed to utilize unlabeled data to learn representations. Typically, it automatically generates labels from the raw

Supported by the Beijing Municipal Science & Technology Commission (Z191100007119 002), the Key Research Program of Frontier Sciences, CAS, Grant NO ZDBS-LY-7024. W. Li and D. Luo—Equal contribution.

data itself and designs a proxy task to predict the corresponding labels. In this manner, CNNs are encouraged to learn representative features without manual annotations. The pre-trained models are then further used to finetune downstream tasks. For video self-supervised learning, many researchers focused on modeling the motion patterns of videos. SpeedNet [1], PRP [28] randomly speed up the video and ask the network to predict the speediness. [8] investigated 4 temporal transformations to extract spatio-temporal representations.

While promising results have been achieved, we believe that the above works have not sufficiently exploited the information provided by videos. We reduce the motion in videos to two key factors, i.e., magnitude (describing the intensity of the object's movement) and direction (depicting the direction in which the object moves). These works modify the magnitude of the motion as the learning target but ignore the motion direction, which contains discriminative semantics.

In this paper, we propose Video Motion Perception (**VMP**), a simple yet effective self-supervised method that can fully exploit the motion information in videos, which is important for video understanding. We discuss how VMP can capture meaningful motion information in videos from two perspectives: the direction and magnitude of the motion.

For motion direction learning, we propose the Motion Direction Perception Module (MDPM). We adopt two well-designed transforming strategies to change the video motion direction quantitatively, which are then taken as the learning target. In this way, information sensitive to the motion direction can be perceived by the model. For video motion magnitude learning, we analyze the characteristic of video motion in natural scenes and propose the Motion Change Perception Module (MCPM) to capture motion magnitude changes. We verify VMP's effectiveness on four backbones and three tasks, which demonstrate that VMP achieves competitive performance on different benchmarks.

## 2   Related Work

### 2.1   Self-supervised Representation Learning

By generating pseudo labels from the raw data, self-supervised learning methods can learn rich representations without leveraging expensive human-annotated labels. Self-supervised image representation learning has witnessed rapid progress. Various proxy tasks have been proposed such as jigsaw puzzle [15], inpainting [17], and context prediction [5], to name a few. Existing self-supervised learning methods in image classification can be directly applied to video representation learning due to the fact that video frames are images in essence.

Based on 2D-CNNs, [27] took temporally shuffled frames as inputs and trained a ConvNet to sort the shuffled sequences. [25] exploited the arrow of time as a supervisory signal. Recently, video self-supervised learning performance has been largely boosted due to 3D-CNNs (e.g. C3D [20]). [10] trained 3D-CNNs by completing space-time cubic puzzles. VCP [13] designed the video cloze procedure task to learn the spatio-temporal information from videos.

[14] solves action recognition towards untrimmed videos by exploring the relationship between video clips. These works have made great progress, but they lack the mining of motion information.

The critical difference between video and image is that video frames contain rich motion information. How to utilize the motion information by self-supervised learning has always attracted much attention. In SpeedNet [1] and PRP [28], the model was trained to predict the video playback rate, which was proved to be effective in learning the foreground moving objects. Similarly, [22] introduced a pace prediction task that fused the additional option of slow motion. [2] proposed the RSP task and exploited the relative playback speed between two video clips as the learning target. [8] investigated 4 temporal transformations and demonstrated their effectiveness to guide representation learning. [3] used variable playback speeds as the learning targets. These methods use the playback speed of the video to construct pseudo labels, thereby learning the motion intensity information in the video, but they ignore the motion direction information, which is also an important factor of video motion. Unlike the existing works, VMP makes use of the MDP module to explore the motion direction information, which can help the model discriminate between different actions.

## 2.2   Video Action Recognition

Action recognition is one of the most important tasks for video understanding. It takes a video clip as the input and outputs the specific action category of the video. Since the dynamic information is complex to understand, action recognition is challenging.

Based on the 2D CNNs feature extractor, [18] proposed two-stream convolutional networks where the results of RGB and optical flow were fused. TSN [24] extracted multiple clips for a video and utilized the whole video level supervision. [29] built temporal dependencies among video frames for action recognition.

Recently, 3D CNNs have attracted much attention due to their strong ability for temporal modeling. C3D [20] designed 3D convolutional kernels, which can model spatial and temporal features simultaneously. R3D [21] extended C3D with ResNet [7]. S3D-G [26] replaced 3D CNNs at the bottom of the network with low-cost 2D CNNs. In this paper, we verify the proposed VMP's effectiveness on four backbones: C3D [20], S3D-G [26], R3D [21] and R(2+1)D [21].

## 3   Methods

### 3.1   Motion Direction Perception Module

We propose the Motion Direction Perception Module (MDPM) to explore motion direction information in videos. Video motion direction is the direction in which the object in the video moves over a period of time, and the motion direction information can help the model discriminate different actions. For example, the human can easily discriminate between throwing the baseball and catching the baseball by perceiving the direction of the baseball's motion. In the action of catching the baseball, the baseball's motion direction is towards the person, while the latter is in the opposite direction. Similarly, shooting the basketball and passing the basketball also have different motion directions, although both are throwing. Consequently, we argue that if the model can perceive the motion direction, it can better discriminate different actions.

To explore motion direction information in videos, we propose two strategies: scale and projection, to change the motion direction of a video and use it as the learning target. Let $I(x, y)$ be the original frame, $I(u, v)$ be the transformed frame. There is a conversion formula which maps $(x, y)$ to $(u, v)$:

$$u = \frac{m_0 * x + m_1 * y + m_2}{m_6 * x + m_7 * y + 1}, v = \frac{m_3 * x + m_4 * y + m_5}{m_6 * x + m_7 * y + 1}. \tag{1}$$

$\begin{bmatrix} m_0 \ m_1 \ m_2 \\ m_3 \ m_4 \ m_5 \\ m_6 \ m_7 \ 1 \end{bmatrix}$ is calculated by solving linear system:

$$\begin{bmatrix} x_0 \ y_0 \ 1 \ 0 \ 0 \ 0 \ -x_0*u_0 \ -y_0*u_0 \\ x_1 \ y_1 \ 1 \ 0 \ 0 \ 0 \ -x_1*u_1 \ -y_1*u_1 \\ x_2 \ y_2 \ 1 \ 0 \ 0 \ 0 \ -x_2*u_2 \ -y_2*u_2 \\ x_3 \ y_3 \ 1 \ 0 \ 0 \ 0 \ -x_3*u_3 \ -y_3*u_3 \\ 0 \ 0 \ 0 \ x_0 \ y_0 \ 1 \ -x_0*v_0 \ -y_0*v_0 \\ 0 \ 0 \ 0 \ x_1 \ y_1 \ 1 \ -x_1*v_1 \ -y_1*v_1 \\ 0 \ 0 \ 0 \ x_2 \ y_2 \ 1 \ -x_2*v_2 \ -y_2*v_2 \\ 0 \ 0 \ 0 \ x_3 \ y_3 \ 1 \ -x_3*v_3 \ -y_3*v_3 \end{bmatrix} \cdot \begin{bmatrix} m_0 \\ m_1 \\ m_2 \\ m_3 \\ m_4 \\ m_5 \\ m_6 \\ m_7 \end{bmatrix} = \begin{bmatrix} u_0 \\ u_1 \\ u_2 \\ u_3 \\ v_0 \\ v_1 \\ v_2 \\ v_3 \end{bmatrix}, \tag{2}$$

where $(x_i, y_i), (u_j, v_j)(i, j = 1, 2, 3, 4)$ are the coordinates of the four vertices of the original and the transformed image. To explain it in detail, we first obtain the coordinates $(x, y)$ of four vertices in the original frame, and then calculate the coordinates $(u, v)$ of vertices after transformation. Then, $m_i(i = 0, ..., 7)$ is calculated by the above formula. Thus, every pixel in the original image can find the corresponding location in the transformed frame.

To make it simple, we set $(x_0, y_0) = (0, 0), (x_1, y_1) = (0, H), (x_2, y_2) = (W, H), (x_3, y_3) = (W, 0)$, where $W, H$ denotes the width and the height of the original image. We also set $(u_0, v_0) = (0, 0)$. In the following, we are going to describe the detail of the transformations.

**Scale:** In order to change the motion direction of the video, we modify the height or width of the video frame. It should be noted that we do not scale the height and width equally, because this only changes the resolution of the image, which is trivial to learn. In scale, we set $(u_1, v_1) = (0, b * H), (u_2, v_2) = (a * W, b * H), (u_3, v_3) = (a * W, 0)$. It denotes that the width and height of the transformed video frame are $a$ and $b$ times of that of the original video frame. In our implementation, $(a, b)$ is the hyperparameter and the learning target.

Figure 1 shows the example of a three-frame video. (a) shows a video of a star moving in a northeast direction, in (b) we change the speed of this video, and the motion magnitude changes accordingly. In (c), we stretch the video vertically through the scale transformation, which causes the motion direction of the star to be shifted to the north.

**Projection**: Projection transforms a cuboid into a trapezoid. We randomly choose one side as the head end and shorten the length. For example, we take the right side as the head end and set $(u_1, v_1) = (0, H)$, $(u_2, v_2) = (W, (H + c * H)/2)$, $(u_3, v_3) = (W, (H - c * H)/2)$. It denotes that the transformed frame is a trapezoid that takes the left side as the bottom end and the right as the head end. The length of the head end is $= c * H$. For projection transformation, $c$ and the head end side is the learning target.

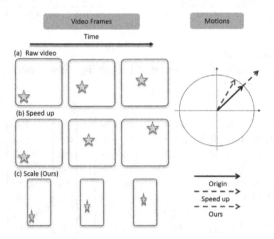

**Fig. 1.** The left (video frames) shows moving objects in videos. The right (motions) shows the magnitude and direction of the motions. VMP can leverage the direction of motions as the learning target.

Compared to scale transformation, projection transformation can distort the video in a non-uniform way. Some regions of the video are zoomed in and others are zoomed out, and the model needs to analyze the magnitude and position of the distortion to get the way of the projection transformation. Similarly, by analyzing the size and position of the object, we humans can assess the distance between the object and us, as close objects always appear larger than distant objects. We believe that through the projection transformation, the model can learn a better feature representation rich in spatial information.

### 3.2   Motion Change Perception Module

In Fig. 2, we show the speediness curve [1] of cliff diving action. This curve can reflect the change of the motion magnitude. As one can see, the motion magnitude of a video is not constant, but constantly changing, and the motion magnitude change contains semantic information that is helpful for action recognition.

Take the cliff diving action as an example, there is a rapid rise of the motion magnitude at stage 2, which corresponds to the moment of the jumping. The motion magnitude of videos of the same action tends to change similarly. For example, the motion magnitude of jumping jacks always fluctuates periodically, while the motion magnitude of cliff diving is often a process of gradual increase.

We argue that if the model can perceive the changes of motion magnitude, it can better recognize actions. To capture the changes of motion magnitude, we propose the Motion Change Perception Module (MCPM). MCPM uses two temporal transformations to change the video's playback speed, namely single-stage speed-up and multi-stage speed-up.

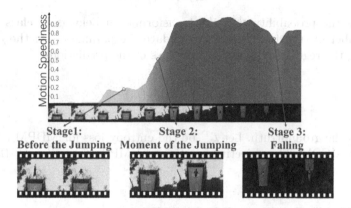

**Fig. 2.** Visualization of the speediness curve.

**Single-Stage Speed-Up.** For single-stage speed-up, we speed up a video by interval sampling, and the interval is saved as the learning target. Specifically, let $s$ be the speed, the interval is $s - 1$. Given a video $V = \{v_i\}$, where $v_i$ is the $i$-$th$ frame in $V$. We generated $V^s$, which is s times speed of $V$ as $V^s = [v_r, v_{r+s-1}, v_{r+2(s-1)}, ..., v_{r+l(s-1)}]$, where $r + l(s - 1) \leq$ the length of $V$, $r$ is a random start frame in $V$ and $l$ is the length of $V^s$. In our implementation, $l = 16$. For single-stage speed-up, the speed $s$ is the learning target.

**Multi-Stage Speed-Up.** The multi-stage speed-up progressively speed up a video so that it has different playback rates in different stages, which means the video has multiple speeds in the same video. To generate the training samples, when a video $V$ is given, we first sample $l_1$ frames at $s_1 - 1$ intervals, then $l_2$ frames at $s_2 - 1$ intervals. The total length of $V^p$ $l = l_1 + l_2$. In our implementation, $l_1 = l_2 = 8$. Given a specific speed pattern $p = (s_1, s_2)$ and $V$, we generate $V^p$ as $V^{s_1,s_2} = [V^{S_1}, V^{S_2}]$, and $p$ is the learning target.

### 3.3 Representation Learning

Given a video clip, we first change its motion direction and then change its motion magnitude. Then we feed it to a backbone to extract features and use a multi-task model to predict the learning target. To extract video representations, we choose C3D [20], R3D [21], R(2+1)D [21], and S3D-G [26] as backbones.We take VMP as a classification task. For each module, we fix its transformations' parameters and take them as a specific category for classification. Given the feature extracted by 3D CNNs, it is then fed to two fully connected (FC) layers, which completes the prediction. The output of each FC layer is a probability distribution over different categories. With $a_i$ is the $i$-th output of the fully connected layer for transformation, the probabilities are as follows:

$$p_i = \frac{\exp(a_i)}{\sum_{j=1}^{n} \exp(a_j)} \tag{3}$$

where $p_i$ is the probability that the transformation belongs to class $i$, and $n$ is the number of transformations. We update the parameters of the model by minimizing the regularized cross-entropy loss of the predictions:

$$\mathcal{L} = -\sum_{i=1}^{n} y_i \log(p_i) \tag{4}$$

where $y_i$ is the groundtruth. Let $\mathcal{L}^{\mathcal{D}}$ be the entropy loss for MDPM and $\mathcal{L}^{\mathcal{C}}$ be the loss for MCPM. The objective function of VMP is $\mathcal{L} = \mathcal{L}^{\mathcal{D}} + \mathcal{L}^{\mathcal{C}}$ (Fig. 3).

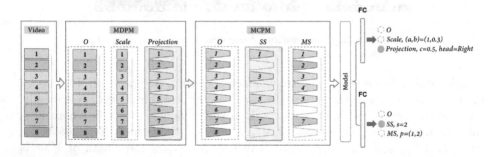

**Fig. 3.** Illustration of VMP framework. SS denotes single-stage speed-up, MS denotes multi-stage speed-up.

## 4    Experiment

**Implementation Details.** In our experiments, we use four datasets: the UCF101 [19], the HMDB51 [12], the Kinetics-400(K-400) [9] and the ASLAN [11] to evaluate the effectiveness of our method. To construct VMP's training, we firstly transform the raw video with proposed modules and then sample a 16-frame clip from it. Each frame is resized to 224 × 224 and randomly cropped to 112 × 112. Specially for projection transformation, if the head end is shorter than 224, we simply crop the frame by $l \times l$, where $l$ is the length of the head end, then it is resized to $112 \times 112$. We set the learning rate to be 0.01, momentum to be 0.9, and batch size to be 32. Our pre-training process stops after 300 epochs for UCF101 and 70 epochs for Kinetics-400 and the best validation accuracy model is used for downstream tasks. Specially, to match the requirement of S3D-G, the input size is set to $224 \times 224$.

## 4.1   Ablation Study

In this section, we evaluate the effectiveness and discuss the hyperparameters of the designed two modules on the first split of UCF101. For simplicity, we choose R(2+1)D as the backbone for our ablation studies.

As shown in Table 1, we conduct extensive experiments for the selection of each parameter. In Table 1 (top), we discuss the influence of *Scale* and *projection* for MDPM. For *Scale*, we select scale magnitude $(a, b) \in \{(1,1.15), (1,1.3), (1,1.45), (1.15,1), (1.3,1), (1.45,1)\}$, as it demonstrates the best performance among the settings (73.2% to 71.1%\72.8%). For *Projection*, we accordingly select projection magnitude $c \in \{0.8, 0.65, 0.5\}$ in the following experiments.

In Table 1 (bottom), we discuss the hyperparameters for MCPM, which are $s$ for single-stage speed-up($SS$) and $p$ for multi-stage speed-up($MS$). For $SS$, we randomly select $s$ from $\{1,2\}$, $\{1,2,3\}$ or $\{1,2,3,4\}$. When sampling $s \in \{1,2,3\}$, it demonstrates the best performance (76.4% to 71.0%\76.3%). We thus set a sampling speed $s \in \{1,2,3\}$ in the following experiments. For $MS$, we accordingly select the speed pattern $p \in \{(1,2), (2,3), (3,4), (4,5), (2,1), (3,2), (4,3), (5,4)\}$.

To combine the designed transformations, we integrate *Scale*, *Projection*, $SS$, $MS$ in Table 2. After combining *Scale* and *Projection*, VMP achieves 73.8%. VMP also shows better performance when combining $SS$ and $MS$. After

**Table 1.** Evaluation of VMP with R(2+1)D under different parameters. $SS$ denotes single-stage speed-up, $MS$ denotes multi-stage speed-up.

| Method | Value | Acc. |
|---|---|---|
| *Scale* | $\{(1,1.15), (1,1.3), (1,1.45), (1.15,1), (1.3,1), (1.45,1)\}$ | 73.2 |
| *Scale* | $\{(1,1.3), (1,1.6), (1,1.9), (1.3,1), (1.6,1), (1.9,1)\}$ | 71.1 |
| *Scale* | $\{(1,1.45), (1,1.9), (1,2.35), (1.45,1), (1.9,1), (2.35,1)\}$ | 72.8 |
| *Projection* | $\{0.8, 0.75, 0.7\}$ | 73.5 |
| *Projection* | $\{0.8, 0.7, 0.6\}$ | 73.6 |
| *Projection* | $\{0.8, 0.65, 0.5\}$ | 73.7 |
| $SS$ | $\{1, 2\}$ | 71.0 |
| $SS$ | $\{1, 2, 3\}$ | 76.4 |
| $SS$ | $\{1, 2, 3, 4\}$ | 76.3 |
| $MS$ | $\{(1,2) ,(2,3), (2,1), (3,2)\}$ | 75.0 |
| $MS$ | $\{(1,2), (2,3), (3,4), (2,1), (3,2), (4,3)\}$ | 76.8 |
| $MS$ | $\{(1,2), (2,3), (3,4), (4,5), (2,1), (3,2), (4,3), (5,4)\}$ | 77.0 |

**Table 2.** Combining MDPM and MCPM. VMP denotes $MDPM + MCPM$.

| Method | Scale | Projection | MDPM | SS | MS | MCPM | VMP |
|---|---|---|---|---|---|---|---|
| Acc. | 73.2 | 73.7 | 73.8 | 76.4 | 77.0 | 78.0 | 79.1 |

combining MDPM and MCPM, the accuracy of 79.1% is achieved, which surpasses the accuracy of the individual module. In summary, the MDPM and MCPM are complementary, thus with the combination as the final proxy task, more powerful representations can be learned.

### 4.2    Action Recognition

Utilizing self-supervised pre-training to initialize action recognition models is an established and effective way for evaluating the representation learned via self-supervised tasks. To verify the effectiveness of our method, we conduct experiments on the action recognition task. We initialize the backbone with VMP pre-trained model and initialize the fully connected layer randomly. Following [27], we train backbones for 300 epochs during training and make the fine-tuning

**Table 3.** Action recognition accuracy on UCF101 and HMDB51.

| Method | Backbone | Pre-train | UCF101 | HMDB51 |
|---|---|---|---|---|
| Random | C3D | UCF101 | 63.7 | 24.7 |
| VCP [13] | C3D | UCF101 | 68.5 | 32.5 |
| PRP [28] | C3D | UCF101 | 69.1 | 34.5 |
| VMP (Ours) | C3D | UCF101 | **74.8** | **34.9** |
| Random | R3D | UCF101 | 54.5 | 23.4 |
| ST-puzzle [10] | R3D | K400 | 65.8 | 33.7 |
| VCP [13] | R3D | UCF101 | 66.0 | 31.5 |
| PRP [28] | R3D | UCF101 | 66.5 | 29.7 |
| VideoMoCo [16] | R3D | K400 | 74.1 | **43.6** |
| VMP (Ours) | R3D | UCF101 | **76.3** | 38.0 |
| Random | R(2+1)D | UCF101 | 55.8 | 22.0 |
| VCP [13] | R(2+1)D | UCF101 | 66.3 | 32.2 |
| PRP [28] | R(2+1)D | UCF101 | 72.1 | 35.0 |
| PacePred [22] | R(2+1)D | UCF101 | 75.9 | 35.9 |
| PacePred [22] | R(2+1)D | K400 | 77.1 | 36.6 |
| VideoMoCo [16] | R(2+1)D | K400 | 78.7 | **49.2** |
| VMP (Ours) | R(2+1)D | UCF101 | **79.1** | 38.7 |
| VMP (Ours) | R(2+1)D | K400 | **81.0** | 41.4 |
| SpeedNet [1] | S3DG | K400 | 81.1 | 48.8 |
| CoCLR [6] | S3D | UCF101 | 81.4 | 52.1 |
| VMP (Ours) | S3DG | UCF101 | **85.4** | **53.2** |

procedure stop after 160 epochs. For testing, we sample 10 clips for each video and average the possibility of predictions to obtain the final action category.

Table 3 shows the split-1 accuracy on UCF101 and HMDB51 for action recognition task. With S3D-G pretrained on UCF101, VMP obtains 85.4% and 53.2% on UCF101 and HMDB51 respectively, outperforms CoCLR [6] by 4.0% and 1.1%. With R(2+1)D pretrained on kinetics-400, VMP achieves 81.0% on UCF101 which outperforms VideoMoCo [22] by 2.3%. With C3D, R3D, VMP obtains 74.8%\34.9% and 76.3%\38.0%.

### 4.3   Video Retrieval

To further validate the effectiveness of VMP, we adopt video retrieval as another downstream task. In the process of retrieval, we generate features at the last pooling layer of extractors. For each clip in the testing split, we query top-K nearest videos from the training set by computing the cosine similarity between two feature vectors. When the testing video and a retrieved video are from the same category, a correct retrieval is counted. Video retrieval results on UCF101 and HMDB51 are listed in Table 4. The experimental results demonstrate the competitive performance of our method with different backbones from Top1 to Top50. These results indicate that in addition to providing a good weight initialization for the downstream model, VMP can also extract high-quality and discriminative spatio-temporal features.

**Table 4.** Video retrieval performance on UCF101. Methods marked with * are pretrained with Kinetics-400.

| Method | Top1 | Top5 | Top10 | Top20 | Top50 |
|---|---|---|---|---|---|
| C3D(random) | 16.7 | 27.5 | 33.7 | 41.4 | 53.0 |
| C3D(VCP [13]) | 17.3 | 31.5 | 42.0 | 52.6 | 67.7 |
| C3D(PRP [28]) | **23.2** | 38.1 | 46.0 | 55.7 | 68.4 |
| C3D(PacePred [22]) | 20.0 | 37.4 | 46.9 | **58.5** | **73.1** |
| C3D(VMP) | 21.8 | **39.0** | **47.7** | 57.0 | 69.2 |
| R3D(random) | 9.9 | 18.9 | 26.0 | 35.5 | 51.9 |
| R3D(VCP [13]) | 18.6 | 33.6 | 42.5 | 53.5 | 68.1 |
| R3D(PRP [28]) | 22.8 | 38.5 | 46.7 | 55.2 | 69.1 |
| R3D(PacePred [22]) | 19.9 | 36.2 | 46.1 | 55.6 | 69.2 |
| R3D(VMP) | **28.3** | **43.7** | **51.3** | **60.1** | **71.9** |
| R(2+1)D(random) | 10.6 | 20.7 | 27.4 | 37.4 | 53.1 |
| R(2+1)D(VCP [13]) | 19.9 | 33.7 | 42.0 | 50.5 | 64.4 |
| R(2+1)D(PRP [28]) | 20.3 | 34.0 | 41.9 | 51.7 | 64.2 |
| R(2+1)D(PacePred [22]) | 17.9 | 34.3 | 44.6 | 55.5 | 72.9 |
| R(2+1)D(VMP) | 23.1 | **40.5** | 48.7 | 58.5 | 72.4 |
| R(2+1)D(VMP*) | **23.5** | 40.0 | **49.4** | **59.7** | **73.9** |
| S3DG(SpeedNet* [1]) | 13.0 | 28.1 | 37.5 | 49.5 | 65.0 |
| S3DG(VMP) | **16.6** | **32.2** | **41.8** | **52.3** | **68.0** |

### 4.4  Action Similarity Labeling

In this section, we exploit the action similarity labeling task [11] to verify the quality of the learned spatio-temporal representations from another perspective on the ASLAN dataset [11]. Unlike the action recognition task, the action similarity labeling task focuses on action similarity (same/not-same). The model needs to determine whether the action categories of the two videos are the same. This task is quite challenging as the test set contains never-before-seen actions.

Action similarity results on ASLAN are listed in Table 5. The results show that the accuracy of VMP on R3D outperforms that of the previous methods, and it further shortens the gap between supervised and unsupervised methods. It demonstrates that the features extracted by the VMP have excellent intra-class similarity and inter-class dissimilarity.

**Table 5.** Action similarity accuracy on ASLAN.

| Features | Hand-crafted | Supervised | Self-supervised | Acc. |
|---|---|---|---|---|
| C3D | | ✓ | | 78.3 |
| HOF | ✓ | | | 56.7 |
| HNF | ✓ | | | 59.5 |
| HOG | ✓ | | | 59.8 |
| STS [23], R3D | | | ✓ | 60.9 |
| VMP, R3D | | | ✓ | **65.4** |

## 5  Conclusion

In this paper, we have proposed a self-supervised method referred to as VMP to exploit rich spatio-temporal features from videos. In VMP, to fully utilize the motion information in videos, the MDPM has been utilized to change the motion direction of the video and as the learning target. In addition, we have designed MCPM to progressively speed up a video and took the motion magnitude changes as the learning target. Experimental results have shown the effectiveness of our VMP when transferred to downstream tasks such as action recognition, video retrieval, and action similarity labeling, which demonstrates that our method captures the motion direction information containing discriminative semantics. Recently, self-supervised learning contrastive learning [2,16,22] has demonstrated promising results. In future work, we plan to explore the combination of proxy task methods and contrastive learning methods.

## References

1. Benaim, S., et al.: SpeedNet: learning the speediness in videos. In: Proceedings of the IEEE Conference on Computer Vision and Pattern Recognition, pp. 9922–9931 (2020)

2. Chen, P., et al.: RSPNet: relative speed perception for unsupervised video representation learning. In: AAAI. vol. 1, p. 5 (2021)
3. Cho, H., Kim, T., Chang, H.J., Hwang, W.: Self-supervised spatio-temporal representation learning using variable playback speed prediction, vol. 2, pp. 13–14. arXiv preprint arXiv:2003.02692 (2020)
4. Deng, J., et al.: ImageNet: a large-scale hierarchical image database. In: Proceedings of the IEEE Conference on Computer Vision and Pattern Recognition, pp. 248–255 (2009)
5. Doersch, C., Gupta, A., Efros, A.A.: Unsupervised visual representation learning by context prediction. In: Proceedings of the IEEE International Conference on Computer Vision, pp. 1422–1430 (2015)
6. Han, T., Xie, W., Zisserman, A.: Self-supervised co-training for video representation learning. NeurIPS **33**, 5679–5690 (2020)
7. He, K., Zhang, X., Ren, S., Sun, J.: Deep residual learning for image recognition. In: Proceedings of the IEEE Conference on Computer Vision and Pattern Recognition, pp. 770–778 (2016)
8. Jenni, S., Meishvili, G., Favaro, P.: Video representation learning by recognizing temporal transformations. In: Proceedings of the European Conference on Computer Vision, pp. 425–442 (2020)
9. Kay, W., et al.: The kinetics human action video dataset. arXiv preprint arXiv:1705.06950 (2017)
10. Kim, D., Cho, D., Kweon, I.S.: Self-supervised video representation learning with space-time cubic puzzles. In: AAAI, vol. 33, pp. 8545–8552 (2019)
11. Kliper-Gross, O., Hassner, T., et al.: The action similarity labeling challenge. IEEE Trans. Pattern Anal. Mach. Intell. **34**(3), 615–621 (2011)
12. Kuehne, H., Jhuang, H., Garrote, E., Poggio, T., Serre, T.: HMDB: a large video database for human motion recognition. In: Proceedings of the IEEE International Conference on Computer Vision, pp. 2556–2563. IEEE (2011)
13. Luo, D., et al.: Video cloze procedure for self-supervised spatio-temporal learning. In: AAAI, pp. 11701–11708 (2020)
14. Luo, D., Zhou, Y., Fang, B., Zhou, Y., Wu, D., Wang, W.: Exploring relations in untrimmed videos for self-supervised learning. ACM Trans. Multimed. Comput. Commun. App. (TOMM) **18**(1s), 1–21 (2022)
15. Noroozi, M., Favaro, P.: Unsupervised learning of visual representations by solving jigsaw puzzles. In: Leibe, B., Matas, J., Sebe, N., Welling, M. (eds.) ECCV 2016. LNCS, vol. 9910, pp. 69–84. Springer, Cham (2016). https://doi.org/10.1007/978-3-319-46466-4_5
16. Pan, T., et al.: VideoMoCo: contrastive video representation learning with temporally adversarial examples. In: Proceedings of the IEEE Conference on Computer Vision and Pattern Recognition, pp. 11205–11214 (2021)
17. Pathak, D., Krahenbuhl, P., Donahue, J., Darrell, T., Efros, A.A.: Context encoders: feature learning by inpainting. In: Proceedings of the IEEE Conference on Computer Vision and Pattern Recognition, pp. 2536–2544 (2016)
18. Simonyan, K., Zisserman, A.: Two-stream convolutional networks for action recognition in videos. In: NeurIPS, pp. 568–576 (2014)
19. Soomro, K., Zamir, A.R., Shah, M.: UCF101: a dataset of 101 human actions classes from videos in the wild. arXiv preprint arXiv:1212.0402 (2012)
20. Tran, D., Bourdev, L., Fergus, R., Torresani, L., Paluri, M.: Learning spatiotemporal features with 3D convolutional networks. In: Proceedings of the IEEE International Conference on Computer Vision, pp. 4489–4497 (2015)

21. Tran, D., Wang, H., Torresani, L., Ray, J., LeCun, Y., Paluri, M.: A closer look at spatiotemporal convolutions for action recognition. In: Proceedings of the IEEE Conference on Computer Vision and Pattern Recognition, pp. 6450–6459 (2018)

22. Wang, J., Jiao, J., Liu, Y.-H.: Self-supervised video representation learning by pace prediction. In: Vedaldi, A., Bischof, H., Brox, T., Frahm, J.-M. (eds.) ECCV 2020. LNCS, vol. 12362, pp. 504–521. Springer, Cham (2020). https://doi.org/10.1007/978-3-030-58520-4_30

23. Wang, J., et al.: Self-supervised spatio-temporal representation learning for videos by predicting motion and appearance statistics. In: Proceedings of the IEEE Conference on Computer Vision and Pattern Recognition, pp. 4006–4015 (2019)

24. Wang, L., et al.: Temporal segment networks: towards good practices for deep action recognition. In: Leibe, B., Matas, J., Sebe, N., Welling, M. (eds.) ECCV 2016. LNCS, vol. 9912, pp. 20–36. Springer, Cham (2016). https://doi.org/10.1007/978-3-319-46484-8_2

25. Wei, D., Lim, J.J., Zisserman, A., Freeman, W.T.: Learning and using the arrow of time. In: Proceedings of the IEEE Conference on Computer Vision and Pattern Recognition, pp. 8052–8060 (2018)

26. Xie, S., Sun, C., Huang, J., Tu, Z., Murphy, K.: Rethinking spatiotemporal feature learning: speed-accuracy trade-offs in video classification. In: Ferrari, V., Hebert, M., Sminchisescu, C., Weiss, Y. (eds.) ECCV 2018. LNCS, vol. 11219, pp. 318–335. Springer, Cham (2018). https://doi.org/10.1007/978-3-030-01267-0_19

27. Xu, D., Xiao, J., Zhao, Z., Shao, J., Xie, D., Zhuang, Y.: Self-supervised spatiotemporal learning via video clip order prediction. In: Proceedings of the IEEE Conference on Computer Vision and Pattern Recognition, pp. 10334–10343 (2019)

28. Yao, Y., Liu, C., Luo, D., Zhou, Y., Ye, Q.: Video playback rate perception for self-supervised spatio-temporal representation learning. In: Proceedings of the IEEE Conference on Computer Vision and Pattern Recognition, pp. 6548–6557 (2020)

29. Zhou, B., Andonian, A., Oliva, A., Torralba, A.: Temporal relational reasoning in videos. In: Ferrari, V., Hebert, M., Sminchisescu, C., Weiss, Y. (eds.) ECCV 2018. LNCS, vol. 11205, pp. 831–846. Springer, Cham (2018). https://doi.org/10.1007/978-3-030-01246-5_49

# A Differentiable Architecture Search Approach for Few-Shot Image Classification

Chunmao He[1,2], Lingyun Zhang[3], Songqing Huang[2],
and Pingjian Zhang[3(✉)]

[1] Guangdong Provincial Key Laboratory of High Performance Servo System,
Zhuhai, China
[2] GREE Electric Appliances Inc. of Zhuhai, Zhuhai, China
[3] South China University of Technology, Guangzhou, China
pjzhang@scut.edu.cn

**Abstract.** Few-shot image classification is to learn models to distinguish between unseen categories, even though only a few labeled samples are involved in the training process. To alleviate the over-fitting problem caused by insufficient samples, researchers typically utilize artificially designed simple convolutional neural networks to extract features. However, the feature extraction capability of these networks is not strong enough to extract abstract semantic features, which will affect subsequent feature processing and significantly degrade performance when transferred to other datasets. This paper aims to design a general feature extraction network for few-shot image classification by improving the differentiable architecture search process. We propose a search space regularization method based on DropBlock and an early-stopping strategy based on pooling operation. Through the end-to-end search on the few-shot image dataset CUB, we obtain a light-weighted model FSLNet with excellent generalization ability. In addition, we propose a spatial pyramid self-attention mechanism to optimize the feature expression capability of FSLNet. Experiments show that the FSLNet searched in this paper achieves significant performance. The optimized FSLNet reaches state-of-the-art accuracy on the standard few-shot image classification datasets and in a cross-domain setting.

**Keywords:** Few-shot image classification · Differentiable architecture search · Spatial pyramid self-attention mechanism · Convolutional neural networks

## 1 Introduction

The powerful performance of deep learning relies heavily on training the models with a wealth of labeled samples. However, the human annotation cost and data scarcity greatly limit the generalization ability of existing models to effectively

E. Pimenidis et al. (Eds.): ICANN 2022, LNCS 13532, pp. 521–532, 2022.
https://doi.org/10.1007/978-3-031-15937-4_44

learn from sample diversity. Recently, few-shot learning has evolved to figure out this issue.

The general methods for few-shot image classification can be divided into three categories: meta-learning, metric learning, and transfer learning. Meta-learning methods [7–9,19,23] aim to utilize the meta-learning framework to optimize the initialization of model parameters to adapt the optimal classifier weights of the novel classes with few gradient updates. Metric learning methods [14,24,26,27] typically employ cosine similarity, Euclidean distance, or distance based on graph neural networks to compare the similarity between two images to classify unseen categories. The main idea of the transfer learning methods [4,12,18] is training a model that can effectively segregate novel classes that are never seen before after a few fine-tuning epochs. However, these few-shot image classification methods usually utilize artificially designed convolutional neural networks containing only ordinary $3 \times 3$ convolution and $5 \times 5$ convolution to extract image features. The feature extraction capability of these networks is not strong enough to extract abstract semantic features, which will affect subsequent feature processing and significantly degrade performance when transferred to other datasets.

Network architecture search [32] is based on the search strategy, combining with constraints (such as accuracy and latency), to explore the optimal network structure within the search space (set of candidate operations or blocks). The search process typically searches for architectures on a proxy dataset and then transfers the searched architecture to the target dataset for retraining, which can also achieve significant performance. The appearance of differentiable architecture search (DARTS) [17] reduces the overhead of architecture search and improves the practical application value of architecture search. In this paper, we investigate the combination of differentiable architecture search with few-shot image classification and realize the rapid search of a few-shot image classification baseline model by improving the architecture search process. We propose a search space regularization method based on DropBlock [10] and an early-stopping strategy based on pooling operation. Through an end-to-end search on the CUB [28] dataset, we obtain a baseline model FSLNet with fewer parameters and strong generalization ability. Furthermore, we propose a spatial pyramid self-attention mechanism (SP-SAM) to improve the feature expression capability of FSLNet. Our main contributions include three aspects:

- We investigate the combination of differentiable architecture search with few-shot image classification. We propose a search space regularization method based on DropBlock and an early-stopping strategy based on pooling operation. A baseline model FSLNet with excellent generalization performance is obtained by searching.
- We propose a spatial pyramid self-attention mechanism to improve the generalization ability of the FSLNet model.
- Experimental results demonstrate that our proposed method outperforms previous methods on multiple publicly available few-shot image datasets and under cross-domain configuration.

# 2  Related Work

## 2.1  Few-Shot Learning

**Meta-learning Methods.** MAML [9] algorithm aims to find more easily transferable representations with sensitive parameters. A first-order optimization-based approach named Reptile [19] is proposed by Nichol et al., which is more convenient to implement than first-order MAML. MetaNAS [8] combines DARTS and Reptile to train and optimize model parameters and network architecture parameters simultaneously. MetAdapt [7] combines DARTS with meta-learning and introduces a weight correction structure that achieves certain performance improvements. However, MetaNAS searches in the way of task training, and the long search time is not conducive to algorithm optimization. MetAdapt searches based on the artificial neural network ResNet-12, which limits the freedom of search.

**Metric Learning Methods.** Vinyals et al. [27] propose a Matching Network that utilizes a differentiable nearest neighbor classifier to perform label matching on samples of unseen classes. The Prototype Networks [26] first calculates the prototype feature vectors of the novel categories and then implements the label assignment of test samples based on distance comparison. Garcia and Bruna [24] implement a graph neural network to transfer the label information of the label-supported samples to the unlabeled query samples. Kim et al. [14] propose a novel edge-labeling graph neural network that learns edge labels instead of node labels on prediction graphs.

**Transfer Learning Methods.** Chen et al. [4] present a baseline approach that trains backbones using distance-based classifiers and achieves competitive performance. S2M2_R [18] jointly trains an additional rotating classifier to output distinguishing features through self-supervised learning, which enhances the feature extraction capabilities of the model. Hu et al. propose the PT+MAP [12] method, which first preprocesses the original feature vector to make it more consistent with Gaussian distribution, and then designs an iterative algorithm inspired by the optimal transmission to estimate the class center.

## 2.2  Differentiable Architecture Search

The mainstream neural architecture search methods mainly include reinforcement learning, evolutionary learning, etc. Liu et al. [17] propose DARTS, which relaxes the discrete search space so that the entire search can be optimized by gradient descent. The search efficiency is dozens of times faster than previous non-differentiable methods. Although DARTS is effective, the researchers found some shortcomings, and its performance crashes are always documented in the literature. Specifically, after a period of searching, the number of skip-connect operations increases dramatically, resulting in performance degradation. To solve this problem, Chen et al. [5] propose P-DARTS applying Dropout to alleviate the advantage of skip-connect. Fair-DARTS [6] believes that this collapse is caused by an unfair advantage in a competitive environment so they turn competition into cooperation and each operation is independent of other operations.

## 3    Methodology

### 3.1    Preliminary

The few-shot image classification method is evaluated applying the $N$-way $K$-shot classification framework, selecting $N$ classes from classes that have never been seen, with $K$ samples for each category. The transfer-based approach has two stages: training and fine-tuning. Specifically, train the classification network of the base classes first, and then freeze the feature extraction layer, and fine-tune with a linear classification head to quickly generalize to complete the classification of the novel classes. The whole flowchart is shown in Fig. 1.

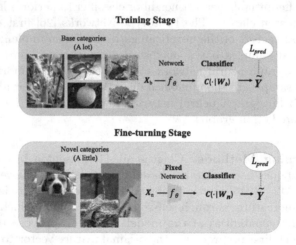

**Fig. 1.** The transfer learning methods first apply the data of base classes training $f_\theta$ and classifier $C(\cdot \mid W_b)$ and then fix the parameters $\theta$ in $f_\theta$ and utilize the data of novel classes to train a new classifier $C(\cdot \mid W_n)$.

Previously non-differentiable neural architecture search methods will predefine a search space (such as $3 \times 3$ and $5 \times 5$ convolution operations). Each layer of the neural network selects an operation from the search space to form a model, verify the performance of the model, and then constantly verify the combination of other neural networks, which requires a lot of repeated work. DARTS integrates the search strategy into the model training, which greatly reduces the search time. Specifically, a super network stacked by two kinds of cell structures (normal cell and reduction cell) is constructed. Each cell structure is composed of seven nodes. The edge connecting nodes will compute all the candidate operations in search space. The final output is calculated by multiplying the softmax result of structural parameter matrix $\alpha$ and output of candidate operation, as shown in Eq. 1, where $x$ means the input feature map, $\mathcal{O}$ means the operation set. Both architecture parameter $\alpha$ and operation weights $\omega$ can be optimized simultaneously through gradient descent back-propagation. Finally, these two types of cell structures are obtained through the architecture parameter matrix $\alpha$, thereby obtaining the final model.

$$\bar{o}_{i,j}(x) = \sum_{o \in \mathcal{O}} \frac{exp(a_{o_{i,j}})}{\sum_{o' \in \mathcal{O}} exp(a_{o'_{i,j}})} o(x) \tag{1}$$

## 3.2   Improved Search Strategy

In this section, we implement an improved search process suitable for few-shot image classification. Through the end-to-end search on the CUB [28] dataset, we obtain a light-weighted baseline model with strong transfer learning ability, which we name it FSLNet. In addition, we propose a spatial pyramid self-attention mechanism to optimize the accuracy of the FSLNet model.

**Eliminate the Depth Gap Issue.** Due to resource constraints, DARTS can only search for architectures in shallow networks and evaluate architectures in deep networks, which leads to a problem called the *depth gap*. Specifically, the architecture search is performed on a network with eight cells, and the discovered cell structure is evaluated on a network with twenty cells. However, the feature extraction capabilities of shallow networks and deep networks are significantly different, so the cell structure searched in shallow networks may not be optimal when applied to deep networks. To avoid this issue, considering that the overfitting phenomenon is prone to occur when the network complex is too high in the few-shot scenario, we set the search and evaluation to a network with six cells to make the feature extraction capabilities of the search and evaluation network similar, ensure that the architecture we searched for is optimal.

**Search Space Regularization Based on DropBlock.** DARTS [17] tends to reserve skip-connect operations during architecture search to speed forward/backward propagation. However, since the skip-connect has no parameters, it is difficult for our model to extract abstract visual feature representation. PDARTS adds a Dropout operation to each skip-connect to alleviate the enrichment of skip-connect, but the number of skip-connect still needs to be manually controlled after the search is complete. We believe that Dropout is effective at the fully connected layer, but features in the convolutional layer are strongly correlated, semantic information can still be transmitted to the next layer even if Dropout operation is employed, resulting in insufficient punishment for skip-connect. Therefore, we propose to add DropBlock operation to each skip-connect to better mitigate the advantages of skip-connect.

**Early-Stopping Strategy Based on Pooling Operation.** After adding the search space regularization method based on DropBlock proposed above, the number of skip-connect operations is controlled, but we find that the pooling operation will gradually increase in the later stage of the search. Like skip-connect, these pooling operations are parameter-free and will also lead to significant performance degradation. We believe that skip-connect operation enrichment in DARTS is a problem of parameter-free operation enrichment, but the advantage of skip-connect operation covers the number of pooling operations. To verify our idea, we remove skip-connect from the search space and construct a search experiment. The experimental results are shown in Table 1. It can be seen that, as we thought, a lot of pooling does occur in the later stages of the search, and the accuracy of the validation set gradually decreases. To control the number of parameter-free operations, we propose an early-stopping strategy based on pooling operations considering the gradual convergence of parameter operations in the later training period. Specifically, when the total number of pooling operations in the normal cell and reduction cell exceeds one, the search is terminated.

**Table 1.** Enrichment experiment of pooling operation.

|  | Epoch 26 | Epoch 27 | Epoch 28 | Epoch 30 |
|---|---|---|---|---|
| Number of pooling operations | 3 | 4 | 5 | 6 |
| Accuracy of validation set | 85.97 | 84.63 | 81.61 | 80.67 |

The improved search algorithm in this paper is shown in Algorithm 1. In the algorithm, $\omega$ represents the model weight, $\alpha$ represents the architecture parameters, $E$ represents the number of early-stopping, $p$ represents the probability of DropBlock, $k$ represents the size of DropBlock, and $S$ represents the current number of pooling.

### 3.3    Spatial Pyramid Self-attention Mechanism

Attention plays a vital role in the human visual system. Humans do not try to process all the scenes at once, but take full advantage of local information, selectively focusing on prominent features to grasp better visual concepts. The visual attention mechanism is a module designed to simulate the human visual system to extract more representative features. To enhance the ability of the model to express the effective information of the image, we propose a spatial pyramid self-attention mechanism (SP-SAM) based on the fusion of local and global features, as shown in Fig. 2. SP-SAM consists of a channel attention module and spatial attention module. In the channel attention module, the feature map with an input resolution of 21 will first go through the spatial pyramid pooling with the pooling kernel size of 7, 13, and 21, and then use $1 \times 1$ convolution for feature aggregation. Finally, the obtained feature map will be sent to an SE module [11]

**Algorithm 1.** Proposed algorithm

---

**Parameter:**
$\omega, \alpha, n_{steps}, s, p, k$
**Initialization:**
$E \Leftarrow 1, n_{steps} \Leftarrow 50, p \Leftarrow 1.0, k \Leftarrow 5, s \Leftarrow 0$
1: **for** $i = 1; i \leq n_{steps}; i = i + 1$ **do**
2:    $p \Leftarrow p \times (n_{steps} - i)/n_{steps}$
3:    adding DropBlock in the skip-connect operation.
4:    $\omega \Leftarrow \omega - \nabla_\omega \mathcal{L}_{train}(\omega, \alpha)$
5:    $\alpha \Leftarrow \alpha - \nabla_\alpha \mathcal{L}_{val}(\omega - \nabla_\omega \mathcal{L}_{train}(\omega, \alpha), \alpha)$
6:    $s \Leftarrow$ count the pooling operations.
7:    **if** $s \geq E$ **then**
8:        break
9:    **end if**
10: **end for**
11: Derive the final architecture based on the learned $\alpha$.

---

to obtain the feature map weighted by channel attention score. In the spatial attention module, we will utilize a non-local module [29] to extract global spatial information to establish long-distance inter-pixel dependencies.

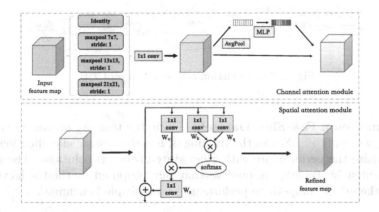

**Fig. 2.** Spatial pyramid self-attention mechanism. The upper part is the channel attention module, and the lower part is the spatial attention module.

## 4    Experiments

### 4.1    Datasets

We conduct experiments on four publicly available few-shot image classification datasets: miniImageNet [27], tieredImageNet [21], CUB [28], and CIFAR-FS [1]. The baseline model is searched on the CUB training set and validated on these four datasets.

## 4.2    Results

**Effectiveness of Our Search Strategy.** We split the CUB into 1:1 for training and validation. The total number of epochs in the search process is 50, and the batch size is 64. Candidate operations in the search space include: *DilatedConv*3 × 3, *DilatedConv*5 × 5, *SepConv*3 × 3, *SepConv*5 × 5, *Skip-Connect, MaxPool*3 × 3, *AvgPool*3 × 3 and *Conv*1 × 3–3 × 1. The whole search process can be completed in about an hour on one 3080 with 10G memory. Figures 3 and 4 show the normal cell and the reduction cell searched by the improved search strategy. It can be seen that there is no enrichment problem of parameter-free operation in the cell structure obtained by search. We stack six cells to get the final architecture FSLNet, with only 1.1 million parameters.

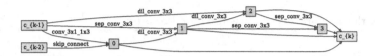

**Fig. 3.** The normal cell searched on CUB.

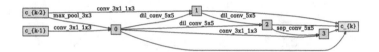

**Fig. 4.** The reduction cell searched on CUB.

**Performance on Few-Shot Datasets.** Using the training process of transfer learning, we apply FSLNet to the training of few-shot image classification tasks and compare the performance with other state-of-the-art solutions. The results are presented in Table 2, we observe that our proposed method achieves the state-of-the-art or competitive performance on multiple benchmarks.

**Ablation Experiments with SP-SAM.** To verify the effectiveness of the SP-SAM proposed in this paper, we add SP-SAM and CBAM [30] after the last cell structure of FSLNet for retraining and compare the results, as shown in Table 3. The first line is the result of the original FSLNet, the second line is the result after adding CBAM, and the third line is the result of adding the SP-SAM proposed in this paper. It can be seen that after adding spatial pyramid pooling for local and global feature fusion and using the self-attention mechanism to extract global spatial information, the SP-SAM attention mechanism proposed in this paper achieves better results than CBAM, and the optimized model achieves state-of-the-art results on all three datasets.

**Table 2.** Comparison of 1-shot and 5-shot accuracy (%) on four few-shot image datasets.

| Method | Backbone | miniImageNet | |
|---|---|---|---|
| | | 1-shot | 5-shot |
| DSN [25] | ResNet12 | 62.64 ± 0.66 | 78.83 ± 0.45 |
| MetaNAS [8] | DAG | 63.10 ± 0.30 | 79.50 ± 0.20 |
| MetAdapt [7] | Block | 64.05 | 79.97 |
| S2M2_R [18] | WRN | 64.93 ± 0.18 | 83.18 ± 0.11 |
| DeepEMD [31] | ResNet12 | 65.91 ± 0.82 | 82.41 ± 0.56 |
| SSFormers [3] | ResNet12 | 67.25 ± 0.24 | 82.75 ± 0.20 |
| Invariance [22] | ResNet12 | 67.28 ± 0.80 | **84.78 ± 0.52** |
| RENet [13] | ResNet12 | 67.60 ± 0.44 | 82.58 ± 0.30 |
| iLPC [15] | WRN | **68.17 ± 0.60** | 84.33 ± 0.43 |
| Ours | FSLNet | 67.77 ± 0.94 | 84.51 ± 0.72 |
| Method | Backbone | CUB | |
| | | 1-shot | 5-shot |
| Baseline++ [4] | ResNet18 | 67.02 ± 0.90 | 83.58 ± 0.54 |
| Neg-Margin [16] | ResNet18 | 72.66 ± 0.85 | 89.40 ± 0.43 |
| DeepEMD [31] | ResNet12 | 75.65 ± 0.83 | 88.69 ± 0.50 |
| RENet [13] | ResNet12 | 79.49 ± 0.44 | 91.11 ± 0.24 |
| S2M2_R [18] | WRN | 80.68 ± 0.81 | 90.85 ± 0.44 |
| Ours | FSLNet | **84.85 ± 0.81** | **94.77 ± 0.41** |
| Method | Backbone | CIFAR-FS | |
| | | 1-shot | 5-shot |
| RENet [13] | ResNet12 | 74.51 ± 0.46 | 86.60 ± 0.32 |
| S2M2_R [18] | WRN | 74.81 ± 0.19 | 87.47 ± 0.13 |
| Invariance [22] | ResNet12 | 76.83 ± 0.82 | **89.26 ± 0.58** |
| DSN [25] | ResNet12 | 75.60 ± 0.90 | 86.20 ± 0.60 |
| iLPC [15] | ResNet12 | 77.14 ± 0.95 | 85.23 ± 0.55 |
| Ours | FSLNet | **77.23 ± 0.94** | 88.74 ± 0.66 |
| Method | Backbone | tieredImageNet | |
| | | 1-shot | 5-shot |
| DSN [25] | ResNet12 | 67.39 ± 0.82 | 82.85 ± 0.56 |
| DeepEMD [31] | ResNet12 | 71.16 ± 0.87 | 83.95 ± 0.58 |
| RENet [13] | ResNet12 | 71.61 ± 0.51 | 85.28 ± 0.35 |
| Invariance [22] | ResNet12 | 72.21 ± 0.90 | 87.08 ± 0.58 |
| SSFormers [3] | ResNet12 | 72.52 ± 0.25 | 86.61 ± 0.18 |
| S2M2_R [18] | WRN | 73.71 ± 0.22 | 88.59 ± 0.14 |
| Ours | FSLNet | **75.80 ± 0.99** | **89.51 ± 0.94** |

**Table 3.** 1-shot and 5-shot accuracy (%) of ablation experiments with SP-SAM.

| miniImageNet | | CUB | | CIFAR-FS | |
|---|---|---|---|---|---|
| 1-shot | 5-shot | 1-shot | 5-shot | 1-shot | 5-shot |
| 67.77 ± 0.94 | 84.51 ± 0.72 | 84.85 ± 0.81 | 94.77 ± 0.41 | 77.23 ± 0.94 | 88.74 ± 0.66 |
| 68.07 ± 0.93 | 84.73 ± 0.67 | 85.28 ± 0.79 | 95.01 ± 0.39 | 77.59 ± 0.94 | 88.91 ± 0.68 |
| 68.79 ± 0.95 | 85.35 ± 0.68 | 85.94 ± 0.77 | 95.43 ± 0.37 | 78.15 ± 0.99 | 89.36 ± 0.66 |

**Table 4.** Comparison of 5-way 1-shot and 5-way 5-shot accuracy (%) in cross-domain scenarios.

| Method | Backbone | 1-shot | 5-shot |
|---|---|---|---|
| Baseline++ [4] | ResNet18 | - | 56.64 ± 0.72 |
| Neg-Margin [16] | ResNet18 | - | 66.03 ± 0.71 |
| TIM [2] | ResNet18 | - | 66.03 ± 0.71 |
| OCD [20] | ResNet18 | - | 66.03 ± 0.71 |
| S2M2_R [18] | WRN | 48.24 ± 0.84 | 70.44 ± 0.75 |
| Ours | FSLNet | 50.61 ± 1.01 | 71.93 ± 0.89 |
| Ours | FSLNet* | **55.65 ± 1.01** | **75.43 ± 0.85** |

**Performance on Cross-Domain Settings.** In the practical application of few-shot image classification, base classes and novel classes are likely to come from different domains and have certain domain offsets. Therefore, we conduct experiments to validate the performance of FSLNet and FSLNet* optimized with SP-SAM under cross domain setting. We train our FSLNet and FSLNet* on miniImageNet and validate them on CUB. Results are presented in Table 4. It can be seen that the architecture searched using our improved search strategy shows excellent transfer learning ability. The optimized FSLNet* model achieves the state-of-the-art performance under cross-domain scenarios, and also validate the effectiveness of the SP-SAM attention mechanism proposed in this paper in the cross-domain configuration.

## 5    Conclusions

In this paper, we investigate the integration of differentiable architecture search and few-shot image classification. As for the search strategy, we propose a search space regularization method based on DropBlock and an early-stopping strategy based on pooling operation. Through searching, FSLNet, a light-weighted model is obtained, which is suitable for few-shot scenarios with superior performance. In addition, we propose a spatial pyramid self-attention mechanism to enhance the ability of the model to express local discriminant information and global effective information of pictures. Experimental results show that the model obtained by our improved search strategy achieves remarkable performance on the standard few-shot image classification datasets, and achieves state-of-the-art results in 5way-1shot, 5way-5shot, and cross-domain scenarios after the attention mechanism optimization. We believe that other few-shot learning methods can achieve further performance improvements using our FSLNet. Later we shall concentrate on enriching the design of the search space and further improving the capabilities of the obtained architecture.

# References

1. Bertinetto, L., Henriques, J.F., Torr, P.H.S., Vedaldi, A.: Meta-learning with differentiable closed-form solvers. In: International Conference on Learning Representations (2019)
2. Boudiaf, M., Ziko, I.M., Rony, J., Dolz, J., Piantanida, P., Ayed, I.B.: Transductive information maximization for few-shot learning. arXiv:abs/2008.11297 (2020)
3. Chen, H., Li, H., Li, Y., Chen, C.: Sparse spatial transformers for few-shot learning. arXiv:abs/2109.12932 (2021)
4. Chen, W., Liu, Y., Kira, Z., Wang, Y.F., Huang, J.: A closer look at few-shot classification. In: International Conference on Learning Representations (2019)
5. Chen, X., Xie, L., Wu, J., Tian, Q.: Progressive differentiable architecture search: bridging the depth gap between search and evaluation. In: IEEE/CVF International Conference on Computer Vision, pp. 1294–1303 (2019)
6. Chu, X., Zhou, T., Zhang, B., Li, J.: Fair DARTS: eliminating unfair advantages in differentiable architecture search. In: Vedaldi, A., Bischof, H., Brox, T., Frahm, J.-M. (eds.) ECCV 2020. LNCS, vol. 12360, pp. 465–480. Springer, Cham (2020). https://doi.org/10.1007/978-3-030-58555-6_28
7. Doveh, S., et al.: MetAdapt: meta-learned task-adaptive architecture for few-shot classification. Pattern Recogn. Lett. **149**, 130–136 (2021)
8. Elsken, T., Staffler, B.S., Metzen, J.H., Hutter, F.: Meta-learning of neural architectures for few-shot learning. In: 2020 IEEE/CVF Conference on Computer Vision and Pattern Recognition (CVPR), pp. 12362–12372 (2020)
9. Finn, C., Abbeel, P., Levine, S.: Model-agnostic meta-learning for fast adaptation of deep networks. In: International Conference on Machine Learning, vol. 70, pp. 1126–1135 (2017)
10. Ghiasi, G., Lin, T.Y., Le, Q.V.: DropBlock: a regularization method for convolutional networks. In: NeurIPS (2018)
11. Hu, J., Shen, L., Sun, G.: Squeeze-and-excitation networks. In: 2018 IEEE/CVF Conference on Computer Vision and Pattern Recognition, pp. 7132–7141 (2018)
12. Hu, Y., Gripon, V., Pateux, S.: Leveraging the feature distribution in transfer-based few-shot learning. In: International Conference on Artificial Neural Networks, vol. 12892, pp. 487–499 (2021)
13. Kang, D., Kwon, H., Min, J., Cho, M.: Relational embedding for few-shot classification. In: 2021 IEEE/CVF International Conference on Computer Vision (ICCV), pp. 8802–8813 (2021)
14. Kim, J., Kim, T., Kim, S., Yoo, C.D.: Edge-labeling graph neural network for few-shot learning. In: IEEE Conference on Computer Vision and Pattern Recognition, pp. 11–20 (2019)
15. Lazarou, M., Avrithis, Y., Stathaki, T.: Iterative label cleaning for transductive and semi-supervised few-shot learning. In: 2021 IEEE/CVF International Conference on Computer Vision (ICCV), pp. 8731–8740 (2021)

16. Liu, B., et al.: Negative margin matters: understanding margin in few-shot classification. In: Vedaldi, A., Bischof, H., Brox, T., Frahm, J.-M. (eds.) ECCV 2020. LNCS, vol. 12349, pp. 438–455. Springer, Cham (2020). https://doi.org/10.1007/978-3-030-58548-8_26

17. Liu, H., Simonyan, K., Yang, Y.: DARTS: differentiable architecture search. In: International Conference on Learning Representations (2019)

18. Mangla, P., Singh, M., Sinha, A., Kumari, N., Balasubramanian, V.N., Krishnamurthy, B.: Charting the right manifold: manifold mixup for few-shot learning. In: IEEE Winter Conference on Applications of Computer Vision, pp. 2207–2216 (2020)

19. Nichol, A., Achiam, J., Schulman, J.: On first-order meta-learning algorithms. arXiv preprint arXiv:1803.02999 (2018)

20. Qi, G., Yu, H., Lu, Z., Li, S.: Transductive few-shot classification on the oblique manifold. In: 2021 IEEE/CVF International Conference on Computer Vision (ICCV), pp. 8392–8402 (2021)

21. Ren, M., et al.: Meta-learning for semi-supervised few-shot classification. arXiv:abs/1803.00676 (2018)

22. Rizve, M.N., Khan, S.H., Khan, F.S., Shah, M.: Exploring complementary strengths of invariant and equivariant representations for few-shot learning. In: 2021 IEEE/CVF Conference on Computer Vision and Pattern Recognition (CVPR), pp. 10831–10841 (2021)

23. Rusu, A.A., et al.: Meta-learning with latent embedding optimization. In: International Conference on Learning Representations (2019)

24. Satorras, V.G., Estrach, J.B.: Few-shot learning with graph neural networks. In: International Conference on Learning Representations (2018)

25. Simon, C., Koniusz, P., Nock, R., Harandi, M.T.: Adaptive subspaces for few-shot learning. In: 2020 IEEE/CVF Conference on Computer Vision and Pattern Recognition (CVPR), pp. 4135–4144 (2020)

26. Snell, J., Swersky, K., Zemel, R.S.: Prototypical networks for few-shot learning. In: Advances in Neural Information Processing Systems, pp. 4077–4087 (2017)

27. Vinyals, O., Blundell, C., Lillicrap, T., Kavukcuoglu, K., Wierstra, D.: Matching networks for one shot learning. In: Advances in Neural Information Processing Systems, pp. 3630–3638 (2016)

28. Wah, C., Branson, S., Perona, P., Belongie, S.J.: Multiclass recognition and part localization with humans in the loop. In: IEEE International Conference on Computer Vision, pp. 2524–2531 (2011)

29. Wang, X., Girshick, R.B., Gupta, A.K., He, K.: Non-local neural networks. In: 2018 IEEE/CVF Conference on Computer Vision and Pattern Recognition, pp. 7794–7803 (2018)

30. Woo, S., Park, J., Lee, J.-Y., Kweon, I.S.: CBAM: convolutional block attention module. In: Ferrari, V., Hebert, M., Sminchisescu, C., Weiss, Y. (eds.) ECCV 2018. LNCS, vol. 11211, pp. 3–19. Springer, Cham (2018). https://doi.org/10.1007/978-3-030-01234-2_1

31. Zhang, C., Cai, Y., Lin, G., Shen, C.: Deepemd: few-shot image classification with differentiable earth mover's distance and structured classifiers. In: IEEE/CVF Conference on Computer Vision and Pattern Recognition (CVPR), pp. 12200–12210 (2020)

32. Zoph, B., Le, Q.V.: Neural architecture search with reinforcement learning. In: International Conference on Learning Representations (2017)

# AFS: Attention Using First and Second Order Information to Enrich Features

Yan Zuo, Junjie Lv, and Huiwei Wang[⊠] [iD]

College of Electronic and Information Engineering, Southwest University,
Chongqing 400715, China
hwwang@swu.edu.cn

**Abstract.** Convolutional Neural Network (CNN) is the basis of many computer vision tasks. In order to depict complex boundaries in visual tasks, it is essential to fully explore the feature distribution to realize the potential of CNN. However, most of the current research focuses on the design of deeper architectures, and rarely explores high-level feature statistics. To solve this problem, we propose a simple and effective neural network attention insertion module, named Attention Module using First and Second order information fusion (AFS). Our method combines the first-order pooling and the second-order pooling, corresponding to the two independent dimensions of space and channel respectively, and verifies the effectiveness of our AFS through the two connection ways. The feature map outputed by the middle convolutional layer infers the attention map in turn along the channel and space, and then multiplies the attention map with the input feature map for adaptive feature refinement. Our AFS can be integrated with any feedforward CNNs and can be trained end-to-end with negligible overhead. We have conducted a large number of experiments on CIFAR-10 and CIFAR-100, and the experimental results show that our AFS module significantly improves the classification and detection performance on different models.

**Keywords:** Convolutional neural network · First-order spatial attention · Second-order channel attention · Feature map end-to-end

## 1 Introduction

CNN is a type of feedforward neural network that includes convolutional calculations and has a deep structure. Based on its rich representation capabilities, it significantly improves the performance of visual tasks, for example, object detection [1], semantic segmentation [2] and video classification [3], etc. To improve network performance, various models have been proposed such as Le-Net [4], VGG-Net [5], GoogLe-Net [6], Res-Net [7]. The development from Le-Net to Res-Net

Supported in part by the Natural Science Foundation of Chongqing under Grant cstc2020jcyj-msxmX0057.

E. Pimenidis et al. (Eds.): ICANN 2022, LNCS 13532, pp. 533–545, 2022.
https://doi.org/10.1007/978-3-031-15937-4_45

shows that stacking more layers to make the network deeper can improve the performance of the network. VGG-Net shows that stacking layers of the same shape can perform better. Res-Net has 22 times more layers than VGG-Net, it builds an extremely deep architecture by stacking the same residual blocks and skipping connections, and obtains excellent characterization. However, most of these models focus on the design of deeper architectures, and rarely explore high-level feature statistics. Learning high-level representation is a feasible solution. In recent years, the image recognition architecture using the second-order statistics of deep CNNs has attracted widespread attention, and has achieved advanced results in a variety of visual tasks [8–10], significantly superior in average pooling.

To obtain a deeper network, we have also focused on another aspect of architecture design, attention. Our goal is to add attention to the network, which can help to improve the representational ability of the network, that is, emphasizing important information while suppressing unimportant information. The attention mechanism has been extensively studied in past years [4,11–13]. SE-Net [14] employed the relationship between channels and proposed a channel attention module, which brought significant performance improvements to the existing deep architecture.

Since the convolution operation extracts features by mixing cross-channel and spatial information, in this article, we propose a novel attention module, named AFS. AFS is designed to plug in the existing CNN architecture, including the channel attention sub-module using the second-order pooling and the spatial attention sub-module using the first-order pooling, which can emphasize the along-channel and significant characteristics of the 2D space. In addition, we also propose two connection ways of channel and space to infer the 3D feature map, namely Serial-AFS (S-AFS) and Parallel-AFS (P-AFS). Finally, we conducted a large number of comparative experiments using various baseline architectures on CIFAR-10 and CIFAR-100 to verify the effectiveness of S-AFS and P-AFS and verified them through extensive ablation studies. As a summary, the main contributions of this article are two points:

1. This article proposes a plug-and-play attention module - AFS that combines first-order and second-order statistics to improve the characterization ability of CNN, which can be easily inserted into any position of the existing network architecture with low computational complexity, and further improve its performance with less overhead.
2. This article provides two connection ways of channel and space to emphasize important information, that is, S-AFS and P-AFS, which have achieved performance improvements relative to the baseline network by inserting S-AFS and P-AFS modules in the classification tasks.

## 2    Related Work

**Attention Mechanisms.** Many studies [15–17] have shown that attention plays an important role in human perception. In the human visual system, in order to process visual information efficiently and adaptively, it will not get the global information at one time, but will selectively focus on the salient area

[18]. The attention mechanism in the network is to score the information flowing through the network and assign higher scores to the most relevant parts [19–21]. At present, there are several ways to integrate attention into CNN, and training to generate attention in an end-to-end manner to extract and optimize better features is an effective solution for general classification tasks, such as Squeeze-and-Excitation in SE-Net proposed by Hu et al. [14]. This is an attention mechanism using first-order feature statistics (global average pooling) provides recalibration weights for the channel feature maps generated by the convolution kernel. However, they only introduced the first-order pooling on the spatial axis, which has certain limitations and cannot obtain the second-order feature statistics of the feature map. At the same time, it is worth noting that spatial attention is also an important factor in inferring the feature map. Compared with SE-Net, our AFS uses additionally second-order feature statistics (correlation between channels) and spatial attention modules, combined with first-order pooling and second-order pooling, and has stronger modeling capabilities.

**Second-Order Feature Statistics.** The first-order statistics have been successfully applied to classic and deep learning-based classification scenarios. In the field of low-level patch descriptors, local Gaussian descriptors have shown better performance than descriptors using first-order statistics [22]. Wang et al. used the global Gaussian distribution [23] as an image representation, and used the convolutional features of a pre-trained convolutional network for material recognition. In recent years, the global second-order pooling has received great attention and has achieved significant performance improvements [15,24,25], which is inserted on the network and is end-to-end trainable. In [14], a high-order kernel (HoK) descriptor is proposed for video recognition. Mo-Nets [26] presented a sub-matrix square root layer, making G2De-Net a compact representation. Traditional networks rely heavily on linear convolution operations. In order to improve the nonlinear modeling capabilities of deep networks, some researchers have further explored higher-order transformations. The second-order response transform (SORT) developed a two-branch network module that combines the response of two convolutional blocks and the multiplication of the response. They elementize the square root of the second-order term. In contrast, our AFS is aimed at collecting second-order statistics of the overall image on the channel axis to enhance the nonlinearity of the deep network.

## 3 Methods

### 3.1 AFS

The AFS described in Fig. 1 can be easily inserted after any convolutional layer. By introducing this module in the middle layer, the overall image can be extracted and combined with first-order and second-order features at early stage, which enhances the nonlinear modeling capabilities of deep neural networks. In the AFS module, it is divided into two sub-modules, the first-order space module (FS) and the second-order channel module (SC).

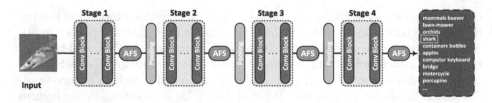

**Fig. 1.** Integrating AFS into a general CNN architecture.

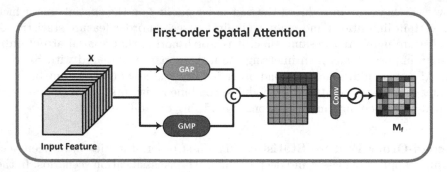

**Fig. 2.** First-order spatial attention module (FS).

**First-Order Spatial Attention (FS).** FS aims to take advantage of the first-order spatial dependence of convolutional features, whose detailed structure is shown in Fig. 2. We use the spatial relationship of features to generate a first-order spatial attention map to recalibrate the incoming feature map feature map $\mathbf{X} \in \mathbb{R}^{H \times W \times C}$, where $H$ and $W$ are the height and width of the space, and $C$ is the number of channels. In order to calculate the first-order spatial attention, we first perform global average pooling and maximum pooling operations on $\mathbf{X}$ along the channel dimension, representing the average pooling characteristics and maximum pooling characteristics of each pixel on all channels. And output a feature descriptor with a size of $H \times W \times 2$, which is used to emphasize or suppress the features at different positions in space. Finally, after $3 \times 3$ convolution, our first-order spatial attention map $\mathbf{M}_f \in \mathbb{R}^{H \times W \times 1}$ is generated. In short, the attention weight of the first-order spatial attention module is:

$$\mathbf{M}_f = f_{3 \times 3}(\mathbf{Avg}(\mathbf{X}) \copyright \mathbf{Max}(\mathbf{X})) \tag{1}$$

where $\copyright$ represents a convolution operation with the filter size of $3 \times 3$ and denotes a stack of feature map dimensions.

**Second-Order Channel Attention (SC).** SC aims to collect second-order statistics of the overall image on the channel axis to enhance the nonlinearity of the deep network, whose detailed structure is shown in Fig. 3. Firstly, for given a feature map $\mathbf{X} \in \mathbb{R}^{H \times W \times C}$ as input, the correlation between channels is calculated through the second-order pooling operation. Suppose $\mathbf{X}$ is a 3D matrix.

The covariance matrix represents the correlation statistics between channels, which is generated after the second-order pooling operation $\mathbf{P}(\mathbf{X})$ and can be viewed as a feature map whose length and height are both $C$. The method of calculating the covariance matrix $\mathbf{P}(\mathbf{X})$ is:

$$\mathbf{P}(\mathbf{X}) = \mathbf{X}\hat{\mathbf{I}}\mathbf{X}^\top \tag{2}$$

$$\hat{\mathbf{I}} = \frac{1}{C}\left(\mathbf{I} - \frac{1}{C}\mathbf{1}\mathbf{1}^\top\right) \tag{3}$$

where $\mathbf{I}$ is the $C \times C$ identity matrix, $\mathbf{1} = [1, \cdots, 1]^\top$ is a $C$-dimensional vector, and 'T' represents the transpose of the matrix. The $i^{th}$ row of the covariance matrix represents the statistical correlation between channel $i$ and all channels. Since the secondary operations involved in calculating the covariance matrix change the order of the data, we normalized the covariance matrix row-by-row to maintain the original structure information. Finally, linear convolution and nonlinear activation are performed on the covariance matrix. In order to maintain the structure of the information, we treat each row as a group in the grouped convolution, and convolve the covariance matrix row-by-row. Finally, we use the sigmoid function as a nonlinear activation, and output a first-order channel weight vector of size $\mathbf{M}_s \in \mathbb{R}^{1 \times 1 \times C}$.

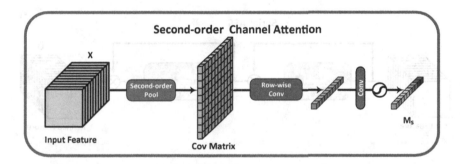

**Fig. 3.** Second-order channel attention module (SC).

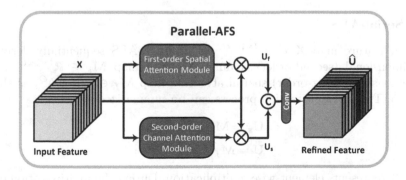

**Fig. 4.** The overview of Parallel-AFS.

## 3.2 Parallel-AFS

For any given feature map $\mathbf{X} \in \mathbb{R}^{H \times W \times C}$ as input, P-AFS connects the first-order spatial attention module (FS) and the second-order channel attention module (SC) in parallel, whose detailed structure is shown in Fig. 4. P-AFS is to obtain two-dimensional (first-order) spatial feature weights and one-dimensional (second-order) channel feature weights that are given to $\mathbf{X}$ to enhance the expression. Subsequently, a standard convolutional layer is used to stack them to generate our feature map with a channel number of $2C$. Finally, the dimension is reduced to $C$ to obtain the attention graph of P-AFS. In short, the calculation process of P-AFS are:

$$\mathbf{U}_f = \mathbf{M}_f(\mathbf{X}) \otimes \mathbf{X} \tag{4}$$

$$\mathbf{U}_s = \mathbf{M}_s(\mathbf{X}) \otimes \mathbf{X} \tag{5}$$

$$\widehat{\mathbf{U}} = f_{1 \times 1}(\mathbf{U}_f \copyright \mathbf{U}_s) \tag{6}$$

where $\otimes$ represents element-wise multiplication, $\copyright$ represents the dimensional stacking of the corrected first-order space attention map $\mathbf{U}_f$ and the second-order channel attention map $\mathbf{U}_s$, $f_{1 \times 1}$ represents a convolution operation with the filter size of $1 \times 1$, and $\widehat{\mathbf{U}}$ is the final refined output.

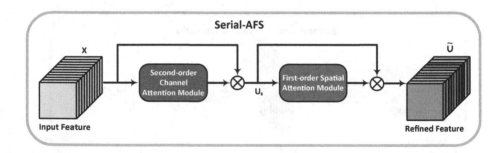

**Fig. 5.** The overview of Serial-AFS.

## 3.3 Serial-AFS

Given a feature map $\mathbf{X} \in \mathbb{R}^{H \times W \times C}$ as input, S-AFS sequentially derives a one-dimensional (second-order) channel attention map $\mathbf{M}_s \in \mathbb{R}^{1 \times 1 \times C}$ and a two-dimensional (first-order) spatial attention map $\mathbf{M}_f \in \mathbb{R}^{H \times W \times Q}$, as shown in Fig. 5. The overall attention process can be summarized as:

$$\mathbf{U}_s = \mathbf{M}_s(\mathbf{X}) \otimes \mathbf{X} \tag{7}$$

$$\widetilde{\mathbf{U}} = \mathbf{M}_f(\mathbf{U}_s) \otimes \mathbf{X}_s \tag{8}$$

where $\otimes$ represents element-wise multiplication. During the multiplication operation, the attention value is copied and propagated accordingly, and vice versa.

$\tilde{\mathbf{U}}$ is the final refined output. For the arrangement of the sub-module $\mathbf{M}_f$ and sequential $\mathbf{M}_s$ process, our experimental results show that the priority order of the second-order channel attention module is slightly better than that of the first-order spatial attention module. We will discuss the experimental results of network engineering in Sect. 4.

# 4 Experiments

In this section, we will explore the experimental results of integrating AFS into various CNN architectures for various tasks and data sets. We evaluate AFS on standard benchmarks: CIFAR-10, CIFAR-100 [27] are used for image classification, and MS COCO [28] is used for target detection. All our programs are implemented under the PyTorch framework [29].

## 4.1 Ablation Studies on CIFAR-100

In this section, we conduct ablation experiments on the AFS block structure to explore the meaning of the design choices we made. In this ablation study, we used the CIFAR-100 dataset and adopted ResNet-50 [30] as the infrastructure. We adopt a standard data augmentation method of random cropping with 4-pixel padding and horizontal flipping for this dataset. The learning rate starts at 0.1 and decreases every 60 epochs. We train the network for 200 epochs. After that, we report the classification error rate on the validation set. Our module design process is divided into three parts. We first look for effective ways to calculate channel attention, and then spatial attention. Finally, we consider how to combine channel and spatial attention modules. Below we will explain each experiment in detail.

**Channel Attention.** We conduct the experiments that using first-order pooling via average pooling and maximum pooling, and second-order pooling via covariance matrix, can achieve the effect of strengthening important features. We compare the following: average pooling, maximum pooling, average pooling & maximum pooling, and second-order pooling. Please note that the channel attention module with average pooling is the same as the SE-Net [14] module.

The experimental results of various pooling methods are shown in Table 1. Comparing the accuracy improved from the baseline, we observe that each pooling method brings different degrees of improvement. However, in [14], authors only used the characteristics of first-order pooling to strengthen the weights of different channels, unable to obtain the second-order feature statistics of feature mapping, and ignored the correlation between each channel. These comparisons between our network and SE-Net as well as its variants show that the use of second-order pooling modeling can capture richer statistical data than first-order modeling, resulting in more significant features.

**Table 1.** Comparison of different channels of attention. Our second-order pooling characteristics are better than the recently proposed Squeeze-and-Excitation method [14] and other first-order pooling characteristics.

| Description | Top-1 err (%) |
|---|---|
| ResNet-50 (baseline) | 22.34 |
| ResNet-50 + AvgPool (SE-Net [14]) | 21.42 |
| ResNet-50 + MaxPool | 21.53 |
| ResNet-50 + AvgPool & MaxPool | 21.39 |
| ResNet-50 + 2nd - Pool (SC) | **21.23** |

**Spatial Attention.** We further explored an effective method of calculating spatial attention. The design concept is similar to the first-order channel attention. In order to generate a two-dimensional spatial attention map, we first calculate a two-dimensional descriptor that encodes channel information on each pixel of all spatial positions. Then we apply a convolutional layer to the two-dimensional descriptor to obtain the original attention map. The final attention map is normalized by the sigmoid activation function. We studied the effect of kernel size in the following convolutional layers: convolution kernel sizes are 3, 5, and 7. In the experiment, we placed the first-order spatial attention module after the previously designed second-order channel attention module, and the final goal is to use the two modules together.

**Table 2.** Comparison of spatial attention with different convolution kernel sizes.

| Description | Top-1 err (%) |
|---|---|
| ResNet-50 + SE | 21.42 |
| ResNet-50 + SC | 21.23 |
| ResNet-50 + SC + FS (k = 7 × 7) | 20.89 |
| ResNet-50 + SC + FS (k = 5 × 5) | 20.25 |
| ResNet-50 + SC + FS (k = 3 × 3) | **19.73** |

The experimental results are shown in Table 2. We can observe that pooling between channels produces better accuracy. By comparing convolution kernels of different sizes, we find that using a $3 \times 3$ convolution kernel can produce better accuracy. This means that when deciding an important area in space, a smaller receptive field is needed to filter the weights on the feature map more finely.

**Arrangement of the Channel and Spatial Attention.** In this part, we compared three different ways for connecting attention modules: serial connection of second-order channels and first-order space, and crossing connection of first-order space and second-order channel as well as two attention sub-modules are connected in parallel. Due to the different functions of each module, different arrangements may affect the overall performance. Note that the outputs of the two attention modules are added and normalized by the sigmoid function.

**Table 3.** Methods of combining second-order channel and first-order spatial attention.

| Description | Top-1 err (%) | Params |
|---|---|---|
| ResNet-50 (baseline) | 22.34 | 25.56M |
| ResNet-50 + SE | 21.42 | 28.79M |
| ResNet-50 + FS + SC | 20.47 | – |
| ResNet-50 + SC & FS in parallel (P-AFS) | **19.86** | 30.15M |
| ResNet-50 + SC + FS (S-AFS) | **19.73** | 29.34M |

Table 3 summarizes the experimental results of different attention arrangements, we found that the attention map generated by the sequential connection and the parallel connection are more refined. It should be noted that all permutation methods perform better than using second-order channels or first-order spatial attention alone, which shows that the use of two attentions is crucial, and the best permutation strategy can further promote performance. From the experimental results, we can see that the image will generate more parameters in the process of second-order feature extraction, which makes the model more complex to a certain extent. We can observe that using the second-order pooling method can obtain better classification accuracy at a very small cost.

## 4.2 CIFAR Classification

In this subsection, we rigorously evaluate our module through CIFAR-10 and CIFAR-100 classification tasks. We use the same settings mentioned in [14] and evaluate our modules in ResNet [7,30], VGG network [5] and GoogLeNet [6] of different depths. In addition to the above work, this paper also compares the results of P-AFS and S-AFS with SE module. In the experiments, in order to maintain standard conditions, additional tricks used by SE blocks, such as repeated training at a lower learning rate when loss platforms and additional augmentation techniques (such as pixel dithering, image rotation) are not used. Various experimental results are shown in Table 4.

As shown in Table 4, on the CIFAR-100 dataset, integrating AFS module into different networks significantly improves the performance compared to the baseline and the network that integrates the SE module [14]. A more significant effect, i.e., lower error, can be obtained by serially connecting the two submodules proposed in this paper. The identical conclusion is drawn on the CIFAR-10 dataset through experimental results. It is worth noting that the performance of

ResNet-56 after integrating AFS module is even better than the deeper ResNet-164 base model. In addition, it is also found that the effect of serial is better than that of parallel.

Figure 6 shows the error curves of integrating the AFS module into different networks, which are trained and tested on the CIFAR-100 dataset. It can be clearly seen that the AFS module shows the lowest training and testing errors during training. The results show that AFS has a stronger ability to improve the generalization of the baseline model compared to SE module [14].

**Table 4.** Classification errors of different networks on the CIFAR dataset (%)

| Architecture | Original | SE [14] | **P-AFS** | **S-AFS** |
|---|---|---|---|---|
| CIFAR-100 | | | | |
| ResNet-34 [30] | 23.24 | 22.07 | **21.69** | **21.17** |
| ResNet-101 [30] | 22.22 | 20.98 | **19.63** | **19.25** |
| ResNet-152 [30] | 22.31 | 20.66 | **18.9** | **18.73** |
| VGG11 [5] | 31.36 | 29.12 | **27.83** | **27.37** |
| VGG16 [5] | 27.12 | 25.83 | **24.76** | **24.23** |
| VGG19 [5] | 27.77 | 26.27 | **25.35** | **24.98** |
| GoogLeNet [6] | 21.97 | 20.89 | **19.77** | **19.34** |
| CIFAR-10 | | | | |
| ResNet-56 [30] | 6.54 | 5.67 | **5.35** | **5.27** |
| ResNet-164 [7] | 5.56 | 4.65 | **4.44** | **4.36** |

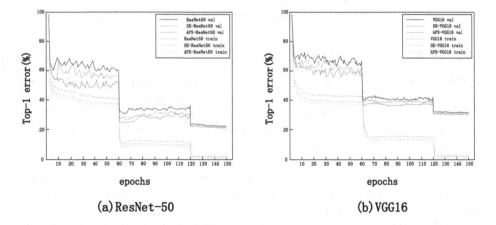

(a) ResNet-50                    (b) VGG16

**Fig. 6.** Error curves during CIFAR-100 training.

### 4.3  Object Detection

In this part, we will further evaluate the generalization performance of AFS module on the MS-COCO dataset. Table 5 shows the performance of the validation set of the object detector using the ResNet-50 base model and the ResNet-50 integrating AFS and SE module. Under COCO's standard measurement AP and AP@IoU = 0.5, AFS ResNet-50 is better than ResNet-50 by 1.9% and SE ResNet-50 by 0.6%. After integrating AFS, ResNet-50 is better than the baseline and SE models.

From these experiments, we can conclude that AFS module brings better network performance improvements than other existing methods in many architectures, data sets, and tasks.

**Table 5.** MS-COCO detection tasks.

| Base model | AP@IoU = 0.5 | AP |
|---|---|---|
| ResNet-50 | 45.2 | 25.1 |
| SE ResNet-50 | 46.8 | 26.4 |
| **AFS ResNet-50** | **47.3** | **27.0** |

## 5  Conclusion

We propose a simple and effective method that combines first-order pooling and second-order pooling to capture the overall statistical correlation of the image through a deep CNN. Using the global second-order pooling statistics to obtain more relevant channel features, and combining the first-order spatial attention mechanism to further strengthen the feature representation, this method can learn more feature representations. The performance of our proposed AFS network is better than SE-Net [14] (i.e. first-order correspondence). The proposed AFS module can be easily inserted into residual network architectures of different depths. Of course, our module is also applicable to other neural networks, such as WideResNet [31] and MobileNet [32], which will be our future work.

## References

1. Redmon, J., Farhadi, A.: YOLO9000: better, faster, stronger. In: CVPR, pp. 7263–7271 (2017)
2. Long, J., Shelhamer, E., Darrell, T.: Fully convolutional networks for semantic segmentation. In: CVPR, pp. 3431–3440 (2015)
3. Wang, X., Girshick, R., Gupta, A., et al.: Non-local neural networks. In: CVPR, pp. 7794–7803 (2018)
4. LeCun, Y., Bottou, L., Bengio, Y., et al.: Gradient-based learning applied to document recognition. Proc. IEEE **86**(11), 2278–2324 (1998)

5. Simonyan, K., Zisserman, A.: Very deep convolutional networks for large-scale image recognition. arXiv preprint arXiv:1409.1556 (2014)
6. Szegedy, C., Liu, W., Jia, Y., et al.: Going deeper with convolutions. In: CVPR, pp. 1–9 (2015)
7. He, K., Zhang, X., Ren, S., Sun, J.: Identity mappings in deep residual networks. In: Leibe, B., Matas, J., Sebe, N., Welling, M. (eds.) ECCV 2016. LNCS, vol. 9908, pp. 630–645. Springer, Cham (2016). https://doi.org/10.1007/978-3-319-46493-0_38
8. Ionescu, C., Vantzos, O., Sminchisescu, C.: Matrix backpropagation for deep networks with structured layers. In: ICCV, pp. 2965–2973 (2015)
9. Wang, Y., Xie, L., Liu, C., et al.: SORT: second-order response transform for visual recognition. In: ICCV, pp. 1359–1368 (2017)
10. Li, P., Xie, J., Wang, Q., Zuo, W.: Is second-order information helpful for large-scale visual recognition? In: ICCV, pp. 2070–2078 (2017)
11. Gregor, K., Danihelka, I., Graves, A., et al.: DRAW: a recurrent neural network for image generation. In: ICML, pp. 1462–1471. PMLR (2015)
12. Jaderberg, M., Simonyan, K., Zisserman, A.: Spatial transformer networks. In: NIPS 28 (2015)
13. Xu, K., Ba, J., Kiros, R., et al.: Show, attend and tell: neural image caption generation with visual attention. In: ICML, pp. 2048–2057. PMLR (2015)
14. Hu, J., Shen, L., Sun, G.: Squeeze-and-excitation networks. In: CVPR, pp. 7132–7141 (2018)
15. Itti, L., Koch, C., Niebur, E.: A model of saliency-based visual attention for rapid scene analysis. IEEE TPAMI **20**(11), 1254–1259 (1998)
16. Rensink, R.A.: The dynamic representation of scenes. Vis. Cogn. **7**(1–3), 17–42 (2000)
17. Corbetta, M., Shulman, G.L.: Control of goal-directed and stimulus-driven attention in the brain. Nat. Rev. Neurosci. **3**(3), 201–215 (2002)
18. Larochelle, H., Hinton, G.E.: Learning to combine foveal glimpses with a third-order Boltzmann machine. In: NIPS (2010)
19. Mnih, V., Heess, N., Graves, A., et al.: Recurrent models of visual attention. In: NIPS 27 (2014)
20. Chen, L., Zhang, H., Xiao, J., et al. : SCA-CNN: spatial and channel-wise attention in convolutional networks for image captioning. In: CVPR, pp. 5659–5667 (2017)
21. Vaswani, A., Shazeer, N., Parmar, N., et al.: Attention is all you need. In: NIPS 30 (2017)
22. Li, P., Wang, Q., Zeng, H., et al.: Local log-Euclidean multivariate Gaussian descriptor and its application to image classification. IEEE TAPMI **39**(4), 803–817 (2016)
23. Wang, Q., Li, P., Zuo, W., et al.: RAID-G: robust estimation of approximate infinite dimensional Gaussian with application to material recognition. In: CVPR, pp. 4433–4441 (2016)
24. Cui, Y., Zhou, F., Wang, J., et al.: Kernel pooling for convolutional neural networks. In: CVPR (2017)
25. Li, P., Xie, J., Wang, Q., et al.: Towards faster training of global covariance pooling networks by iterative matrix square root normalization. In: CVPR, pp. 947–955 (2018)
26. Xiao, H., Feng, J., Lin, G., et al.: MoNet: deep motion exploitation for video object segmentation. In: CVPR, pp. 1140–1148 (2018)
27. Krizhevsky, A., Hinton, G.: Learning multiple layers of features from tiny images. Technical report, Citeseer (2009)

28. Lin, T.-Y., et al.: Microsoft COCO: common objects in context. In: Fleet, D., Pajdla, T., Schiele, B., Tuytelaars, T. (eds.) ECCV 2014. LNCS, vol. 8693, pp. 740–755. Springer, Cham (2014). https://doi.org/10.1007/978-3-319-10602-1_48
29. Pytorch. http://pytorch.org/
30. Cui, Y., Zhou, F., Wang, J., et al.: Kernel pooling for convolutional neural networks. In: CVPR, pp. 2921–2930 (2017)
31. Zagoruyko, S., Komodakis, N.: Wide residual networks. arXiv preprint arXiv:1605.07146 (2016)
32. Howard, A.G., Zhu, M., Chen, B., et al.: MobileNets: efficient convolutional neural networks for mobile vision applications. arXiv preprint arXiv:1704.04861 (2017)

# Autonomous Driving Model Defense Study on Hijacking Adversarial Attack

Kabid Hassan Shibly[1]([✉]), Md. Delwar Hossain[1], Hiroyuki Inoue[2],
Yuzo Taenaka[1], and Youki Kadobayashi[1]

[1] Division of Information Science, Nara Institute of Science and Technology,
Ikoma, Nara, Japan
{shibly.kabid_hassan.sl1,delwar.hossain,yuzo,youki-k}@is.naist.jp
[2] Faculty of Information Science and Engineering,
Kyoto Sangyo University, Kyoto, Japan
hinoue@cc.kyoto-su.ac.jp

**Abstract.** Modern Connected and Autonomous Vehicle (CAV) has several innovative embedded devices aimed at enhancing driving comfort. However, the most advanced embedded equipment did not address security features at the time of development; as a result, it enlarged the attack surfaces of CAVs. Consequently, an attacker can easily compromise the CAV system even with limited hacking capabilities. In case the CAV system is compromised, that can raise significant concerns about safe driving and human safety. We know that the CAV driving model is mainly based on artificial intelligence and deep learning algorithms. Despite deep learning methods being successfully used in Connected and Autonomous Vehicles, slight perturbations of the driving model can be crucial and mislead the driving system. Henceforth, a robust defense mechanism is imperative for safe driving as a countermeasure. This research proposed an effective defense mechanism based on an autoencoder. We study FGSM and AdvGAN for hijacking adversarial attack injection, and simultaneously we use the Nvidia Dave-2 Driving model for our experimentation. Our experiment results demonstrate that the proposed solution outperformed compared with the recent and most typically used defensive strategies; it achieves 93.8% and 91.2% defense success rate in the Whitebox setup and 71.3% and 63.1% defense success rate in the Blackbox setup by FGSM and AdvGAN, respectively.

**Keywords:** Connected and Autonomous Vehicle · Hijacking Adversarial Attack · Defense study · Automotive security

## 1 Introduction

Connected and Autonomous Vehicles (CAVs) combine connection, and automated technology supports or substitutes people in the driving activity. As per the online survey report, during 2021–2027, the Autonomous (Driverless) Car Market is estimated to grow at a CAGR (Compound Annual Growth Rate)

E. Pimenidis et al. (Eds.): ICANN 2022, LNCS 13532, pp. 546–557, 2022.
https://doi.org/10.1007/978-3-031-15937-4_46

of 22.75%; from USD 22.22 billion in 2021 to USD 75.95 billion in 2027. As a result, the rise of these level 2 and level 3 automobiles will boost the market by 2030. Since autonomous vehicles do not require human involvement for driving, many advanced sensor technologies, machine learning, on-board, remote processing capabilities, GPS, telecommunications networks, etc., are used to function in autonomous driving. However, safety has become a significant concern for the autonomous driving system. Recently, the remarkable advancement in deep learning has proposed ways that are a natural fit for incorporating into autonomous control. Whereas the deep learning model immediately transforms perceptual inputs into control decisions such as vehicle steering angles [1], which is one of the approaches to employ end-to-end learning for autonomous driving control (e2e). A recent study has demonstrated that this strategy is incredibly effective, particularly when we learn to emulate human drivers. Although deep learning systems have enabled greater autonomy, they are vulnerable to minor antagonistic interference in inputs - such as images in parallel research.

Several approaches have been offered to defending against adversarial examples. In general, there are two types of defense tactics for countermeasures for adversarial instances, where the first type is used to improve the network model or training set [2,3]. The fundamental objective of this technique is to train more resilient deep learning models by altering the network topology, the model's loss function, increasing the dataset, and so on, in order to increase defense against adversarial attacks. However, the key disadvantage of this technique is that the network must be retrained and cannot defend against unknown threats. Another defensive approach is to adjust adversarial inputs to make them comparable to clean inputs, rather than the network and training process; subsequently, the model does not need to be retrained [4]. Wherein the most adversarial cases are found in low probability zones [5,6]. Henceforth, an effective defense mechanism is imperative to mitigate the limitations of the existing defense approaches.

In this research, we intend to demonstrate the performance of the most prevalent defense approaches, such as auto-encoder [7], block switching, adversarial training, defensive distillation, feature squeezing, etc. However, the diversity of generative models can lead reconstructed pictures to diverge from the originals, and CNNs' high representation capacity allows for the reconstruction of adversarial perturbations. The aforementioned defense mechanism is intricate and certainly results in the defense failing. Hence, we do not train the model with adversarial examples to overcome the limitation of the defense ability against unknown threats. Rather, we attempt to make a system that cleans the adversarial inputs and makes them similar to the original inputs captured with CAV's camera. Additionally, we propose a memory module to store the original data features. We intend to develop an Auto-Encoder-based model by merging Auto-Encoder with GAN through a memory module with the items recorded in the memory, which will contain the features of clean samples. Our major objective is to merge an Auto Encoder's decoder with a GAN generator by combining parameters and training them together to reduce the loss during the process of cleaning and reconstructing adversarial images. We contend to study the Hijacking Adversarial Attack from several adversarial attacks for further experimentation.

The major contribution of this paper is addressed as follows:

– We proposed a defense mechanism to the adversarial attack in an autonomous driving model, which purifies the adversarial samples into clean samples.
– In this study we use a memory module to improve the model's ability to capture and maintain the features of the input examples.
– Our proposed method achieves a reasonable performance compared to the most common defense approaches.

## 2   Background and Related Work

Pomerleau's groundbreaking work in 1989 on the Autonomous Land Vehicle in a Neural Network (ALVINN) [8] technology inspired DAVE-2 [1]. It reveals that a fully trained neural network can successfully guide a car on public highways. DAVE-2 is distinguished by the fact that the progress of 25 years has significantly enabled us to apply more data and compute the capacity of the task.

Adversarial attacks can fool a target model into making wholly incorrect predictions by introducing slight disturbances to the source pictures. An adversarial attack generates an undetectable adversarial perturbation to form an adversarial example and causes the target model to categorize the original class as a different class, which is different from its class, given a target model and an original picture with its actual class [15]. Existing adversarial attacks can be classified as Whitebox [9] or Blackbox [10] attacks based on the knowledge necessary to carry out the attack. In order to perform a Whitebox attack, all features of the target model must be known, including training data, neural network architecture, parameters, hyperparameters, and the ability to gather the model's gradients and prediction outcomes. On the other hand, Blackbox attacks on a query merely involve querying the model with arbitrary input data and a predicted result. Attackers can develop a replacement model based on the target model's inputs and outputs and execute Whitebox attacks on their model to perform a Blackbox attack. The transferability of adversarial examples refers to the ability to employ adversarial examples on the replacement model to attack the target Blackbox model. In this study, we are experimenting with Hijacking Adversarial Attack where the attacker changes the actual trajectory of the model differently, as we can see in Fig. 1.

Adversarial training has shown to be the most successful method for increasing robustness so far. However, it often requires the generation of a large number of adversarial examples, along with huge computation costs; additionally, it's also difficult to ensure if the effects of unknown adversarial threats are avoided. Researchers have discovered that any degree of picture manipulation, adding noise to the image [11], scaling the image [4], JPEG compression [12], and so on, can break the structure of the adversarial attack. One more extensively used technique is image denoising. To eliminate the adversarial perturbation, the easiest way is to train an Auto-Encoder and then feed it into the target model [13]. Using generative networks, Defense-GAN [14] and PixelDefend [5] adversarial samples can be converted into clean ones. The issue of this strategy is that it requires solving an optimization problem in order to discover a clean example, which is computationally hard and vulnerable to increasingly powerful attack methods. Using latent encoding, Defense-GAN generates pictures directly and gives clean samples that are beyond the decision boundary of the classifier. Despite the purification of the source pictures, the classifier is unable to identify the purified samples effectively which results in a loss in model accuracy. Our solution depends on the clean features stored in the memory module to assist the model to reconstruct clean pictures by using the input image as a prior. We use the discriminator in the generative network to assist the model in the process of reconstruction and adjust the weight of reconstruction loss based on the dataset, after ensuring clean input images and matched output images.

# 3 Methodology

## 3.1 Dataset

For this experiment, we trained Nvidia DAVE-2 autonomous driving model and created adversarial instances using the Udacity dataset [16]. This dataset comprises real-world road photos captured by a vehicle's front camera, which Udacity has divided into two sets: training and testing. There are 33805 frames in the training set and 5614 frames in the test set. Each frame's steering angle is normalized from a degree to a value between $-1$ and $1$.

## 3.2 Attack Scenarios - Hijacking Adversarial Attacks

An adversarial attack on an image classification model is counted successful if the adversarial images can be classified as a different class than the original image. Autonomous driving models, on the other hand, are regression models that forecast continuous values. Therefore, adversarial attacks on driving models are described in terms of a tolerable error range, which is referred to as the adversarial threshold. As a result, if the difference between the original forecast and the prediction of an adversarial example is larger than the adversarial threshold, an adversarial attack on a driving model is considered successful.

Based on the perturbation generation mechanism, current adversarial attacks on the automotive driving model can be divided into two categories. By adding the sign of the loss gradient concerning each pixel on original pictures, the Fast Gradient Sign-based technique immediately produces adversarial instances. The generative model-based technique suggests using generative models such as the *Generative Adversarial Network (GAN)* to produce adversarial instances.

In this paper, we implemented two adversarial attacks on regression models to create a full collection of adversarial attacks. We used *Fast Gradient Sign Method* (FGSM) and AdvGAN [15], a state-of-the-art generative model-based attack. Below, we go through each of the attack methods in more detail.

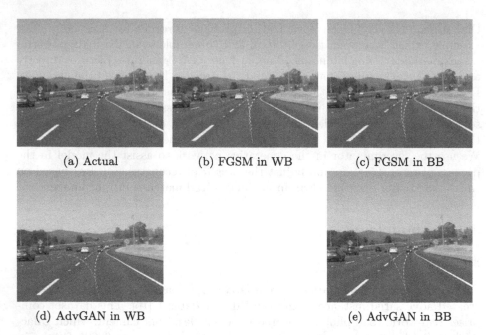

(a) Actual            (b) FGSM in WB            (c) FGSM in BB

(d) AdvGAN in WB                          (e) AdvGAN in BB

**Fig. 1.** Hijacking Adversarial Attack in Nvidia DAVE-2 autonomous driving model using FGSM and AdvGAN in both Whitebox and Blackbox setup.

**Fast Gradient Sign Method.** On original frames, this approach simply adds the sign of the loss gradient to each pixel. To provide a more potent adversarial scenario, we applied the targeted FGSM numerous times.

**Adversarial GAN.** By incorporating another goal ($L_y = J_\theta(G(x); f(x) + \alpha)$ into the objective function ($LAdvGAN = L_y + \alpha LGAN$), AdvGAN constructs an adversarial example $G(x)$ from an original picture. Following training, the generator $G$ might produce an adversarial example $x'$ that is identical to the original picture but makes a prediction $f(x')$ that differs $\Delta$ from $f(x)$.

### 3.3   Defense Mechanism Against Adversarial Attack

From the Fig. 2 we observe the defense model consists of a generator, a discriminator, and a memory module, with the generator being a hybrid of the original Auto-Encoder's encoder and decoder.

Three convolutional layers compensate for the encoder and decoder. The encoder gathers higher-level characteristics from the input picture over time via convolutional techniques and finally encodes it into a high-level latent encoding. A deconvolution process is used by the decoder to restore the latent encoding to the original picture. Through the memory module, the first and second layers of the encoder are linked to the second and third layers of the decoder, respectively.

In the Fig. 2 the downsampling is performed first, and then the pixels are masked, and finally sent to the input layer. A traditional decoder merely

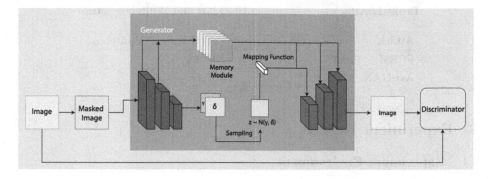

**Fig. 2.** The structure of the defense model.

gets the encoder's latent code z to create images. However, when the decoder depth increases, the influence of the latent code z decreases as it is transferred upstream, which causes the feature information supplied via the skip link to become dominant and lowers the quality of the output images. Inspired by the layered structure, we have included the latent coding z in each layer of the decoder. The newly created potential encoding is divided into three parts: the first is fed directly into the first layer of the decoder, and the second and third portions are fed into the second and third levels of the decoder after connecting the memory module features.

Several components in the memory module are utilized to store the regular characteristics in clean pictures. We use a softmax technique to determine the similarity score ($s = Softmax(c(i, a))$ between each query and all items before reading them. Where $s$ is similarity score, $c$ represents cosine similarity, $i$ denotes items in memory and a is query in memory. Each item has a one-to-many connection with the query vector, which means that each item might have several query vectors which are similar to it mostly. As a result, while updating items, we use all of the query vectors that are closest to the item. We employ two operations, forget and update, to update the memory. The forget action, in particular, defines which feature information in the memory is wiped, and the updated operation ($i \leftarrow w; i + u$) specifies which feature information is put into the memory. Where $w$ and $u$ represent wipe and update in the memory respectively. The contribution of each query vector is calculated using the softmax function.

We integrate the GAN and Autoencoder loss functions to reduce the impact of reconstruction loss while increasing the model's generated image quality. The mechanism of reading memory resembles that of grouping. Each memory item may be thought of as a cluster center, and the query vector as the clustering sample. As a result, we hope that a cluster center can accurately represent the query vector. We need to increase inter-class dispersion and intra-class compactness to limit the influence of other memories.

**Table 1.** Attack success rate in Blackbox and Whitebox setup

| Attack | Success rate (Blackbox) | Success rate (Whitebox) |
|--------|--------------------------|--------------------------|
| FGSM   | 26.4%                    | 33.2%                    |
| AvdGAN | 87.7%                    | 97.2%                    |

## 4    Experiment Results

### 4.1    Experiment Environment

For our proposed experiment, we used python Jupyter Notebook 4.8 and Keras with TensorFlow as the backend. We did our experiment on an AMD Ryzen 5 5600H CPU 3.30 GHz, 16 GB RAM, Windows 11 (64-bit), and NVIDIA GeForce RTX 3050.

### 4.2    Attack Injection and Success Against Autonomous Driving

The Nvidia DAVE-2 autonomous driving model is well-known and widely used. This model is implemented and trained using PyTorch. The input picture size for the driving model is consistently set to $128 \times 128$. Table 1 illustrates the specifics of such models.

Root Mean Square Error, as given in column RMSE, is used to calculate the model's error rate. If an autonomous driving model predicts 0 for all frames by default on the test dataset, the RMSE between the predictions and the ground truth is 0.20678. Our customized model Nvidia DAVE-2 has an RMSE of 0.1055.

Experiments are performed in both Whitebox and Blackbox environments. The approaches have full knowledge of a driving model in a Whitebox context, allowing them to produce adversarial cases directly. Attackers have commonly tried to train a proxy driving model offline in a Blackbox situation. The AdvGAN model might potentially be trained on the proxy model for AdvGAN attacks. Then, AdvGAN might be embedded into malicious activity to perform Blackbox attacks. The performance of adversarial attacks and countermeasures is measured using the attack success rate. The attack is declared successful if the steer angle deviation is larger than the adversarial threshold delta $= 0.3$. The attack's success rate is calculated from the number of attacks generated from all adversarial examples to be the percentage of success.

The AvdGAN has achieved a higher success rate compared with FGSM. The FGSM achieved the success rate of 33.2%, wherein AvdGAN's success rate is 97.2%. AvdGAN learns the internal features of colored road lines, that have an effect on steer angle predictions, causing adversarial disturbances.

As we can see in the Fig. 3(a), in the Whitebox setup, the AdvGAN performs very well. The AvdGAN achieved a higher success rate compared with the FGSM, the same as Whitebox settings. FGSM achieved 26.4% where AvdGAN is 87.7%. The techniques create adversarial perturbations that are customized for specific models and hence lose their advantages when utilized across models.

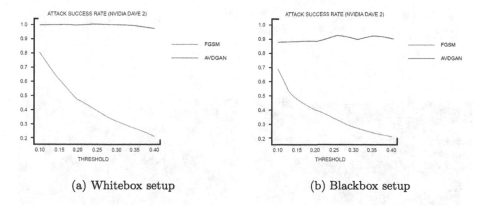

(a) Whitebox setup                    (b) Blackbox setup

**Fig. 3.** Attack success rate of FGSM and AdvGAN in both Whitebox and Blackbox setup with different threshold.

As we can see in the Fig. 3(b), in the Blackbox setup, the AdvGAN performs better than FGSM; however, in this setup, the performance drops to the Whitebox setup. In summary, adversarial attacks on autonomous vehicles are possible, making apprehension about safe driving and may render the driving system. AdvGAN might produce adversarial instances to obtain a high attack success rate in a Whitebox situation. AdvGAN appears to be the most hazardous of the attacks since it uses inherent properties gained by driving models. The Blackbox settings results indicate that the transferability of adversarial cases is linked to fundamental aspects of driving models, such as network architectural complexity. Attacks in a Blackbox situation do not perform well on autonomous driving models. The outcome shows that adversarial examples' transferability to driving models isn't as excellent as in Whitebox situations.

### 4.3   Defense Performance Result - Proposed

Regarding the FGSM and AdvGAN attacks, we applied some common defensive methods, Autoencoder, Block Switching, Adversarial Training, Defense Distillation, and Feature Squeezing respectively; and compared them with our proposed study.

Table 2 displays the results of defense success rate in Whitebox and Blackbox settings on the Udacity dataset.

The adversarial training's generalization ability is poor, and it cannot withstand many attacks; Defense Distillation, Feature Squeezing, and Autoencoder cannot effectively fight AdvGAN attacks. Blockswitching works well, although it affects the original image's categorization accuracy.

Though our technique isn't tailored to certain attacks, it can withstand a variety of them. Our technology is employed for good reconstruction capabilities and eliminates the impact of malicious disruption on image generation during the reconstruction phase. As a result, the model's robustness is enhanced by keeping highly accurate on the original images. The results show that the proposing

(a) Prediction on cleaned image in White-  (b) Prediction on cleaned image in Blackbox setup                                 box setup

**Fig. 4.** Prediction of cleaned image in both Whitebox and Blackbox setup.

**Table 2.** Defense success rate in Whitebox and Blackbox setup.

| Mechanisms | Whitebox | | Blackbox | |
|---|---|---|---|---|
| Defensive | FGSM | AdvGAN | FGSM | AdvGAN |
| Autoencoder | 78.4% | 45.2% | 45.4% | 23.5% |
| Block switching | 31.8% | 17.3% | 49.2% | 37.3% |
| Adversarial training | 89.7% | 66.5% | 50.1% | 40.4% |
| Defense distillation | 76.5% | 45.3% | 40.6% | 25.7% |
| Feature squeezing | 67.1% | 54.2% | 35.7% | 31.6% |
| Proposed | 93.8% | 91.2% | 71.3% | 63.1% |

method improves the model's robustness while having little effect on the accuracy of clean images. From Fig. 4 we can observe the predicted trajectory of our model in cleaned images.

### 4.4 Performance of Autoencoder - Whitebox Setup

Table 2 displays the defense success rate of Blackbox and Whitebox setup on the Udacity dataset. The attacker knows not just the specifics of the classifier, but also the details of the defensive mechanism in a Whitebox attack. In Whitebox setup, Autoencoder, Adversarial training, and Defense Distillation perform better in defending FGSM attacks. Similarly, in the AdvGAN attack, Adversarial Training performs better. Our proposed study performs best among our experimented defense mechanisms, 93.8% against FGSM and 91.2% against AdvGAN.

## 4.5    Performance of Proposed Method - Blackbox Setup

In the Blackbox setup, the utmost probable thing the attacker may know is about the classifier. Subsequently, the defense success rate is lower compared with the Whitebox setup. The Feature Squeezing method performance is inadequate, wherein it achieved the defense success rate of 35.7% against FGSM and 31.6% in AdvGAN. The rest of the defense methods, Block switching, Adversarial Training, Defense Distillation, etc. have a defense success rate of 40–50%, which is also not reasonable compared with the proposed method. The proposed methods outperformed compared with the above-mentioned methodologies wherein the proposed method achieved a defense success rate of 71.3% against FGSM and 63.1% against AdvGAN.

Since our technique is non-differentiable, we employ Adversarial training to estimate the classifier's gradient. We utilized similar attack parameters and datasets throughout the experiments. The experimental findings demonstrate that when the purification model and the classifier are trained simultaneously using adversarial training, the proposed strategy is reasonably successful in resisting the attacks of adversarial examples. As a result, the samples cleaned by our model are highly similar to the original clean samples, which increases the model's robustness without compromising its accuracy.

## 4.6    Time and Computation Overhead on Defense Mechanism

Table 3 demonstrates the overhead incurred by various defense approaches in terms of Time (delay), GPU usage, and GPU memory cost.

**Table 3.** Time and computation overhead on defense mechanism

| Defensive | Time overhead (s) | GPU overhead (utilization %) | GPU overhead (memory %) |
|---|---|---|---|
| Autoencoder | 0.0039 | 4 | 0.73 |
| Block switching | 0.0037 | 4 | 1.75 |
| Adversarial training | 1.124 | 7 | 40.1 |
| Defense distillation | 0.74 | 3 | 20.4 |
| Feature squeezing | 0.0102 | 4 | 3.75 |
| Proposed | 0.0056 | 4 | 1.21 |

Adversarial Training and defense distillation has the highest time overhead or delay which is 1.124 s and 0.74 s respectively. The GPU memory overhead is also too high. The Adversarial training used more than 50% of GPU memory when predicting an attack. While the other defenses performed well keeping the time overhead under 1 s, GPU utilization and memory usage are also better than Adversarial training. However, our proposed method has 0.0056 s time overhead, 4% GPU overhead on utilization, and 1.21% GPU Memory overhead.

## 5    Discussion

With recent breakthroughs in the AI, IoT, and data analytics domains, digital transformation has gained traction in the automobile sector during the previous 20 years. Automotive businesses are being pushed to adapt their product design processes and start designing cars with new features and services as a result of digital revolutions in consumers' lives. Self-driving technology, for example, will be practical and commonplace in the near future. Advanced algorithms evaluate data from cameras and sensors, which allows individuals to drive safely. On the other hand, data privacy and cyber security might be difficult in this domain. The safety of autonomous cars can be easily compromised in various instances. As a result, protecting against an attack is critical for human life protection. In this research, our primary intent is to analyze adversarial hijacking attacks and defense mechanisms against the autonomous driving system. Wherein we use FGSM and AdvGAN model regarding attack injection and we employ a memory module with autoencoder which will contain the features of the input image and clean the adversarial examples. The major limitation of this study is, that we experiment with one common autonomous driving model, two most common adversarial approaches, and a few defense mechanisms. In the future, we want to enhance the quality of image reconstruction and improve the memory module while also experimenting with the most advanced autonomous driving models and state-of-the-art attack-defense mechanisms.

## 6    Conclusion

In this paper, we proposed a defense method against Hijacking adversarial attacks on the autonomous driving model and compared it with some other commonly used defense systems. We used FGSM and AdvGAN to perform a Hijacking Adversarial Attack in the Whitebox and the Blackbox setup. Our proposed defense method uses a memory module to store the input image features of the Autonomous Driving model. It converts the input pictures to a high-probability image manifold in latent space and reconstructs it using the memory module's normal features. The proposed model achieved 93.8% and 91.2% defense success rates in the Whitebox setup and 63.1% and 71.3% is the defense success rates in the Blackbox setup. According to our findings, this strategy considerably improves the classification performance of adversarial cases.

**Acknowledgement.** Part of this study was funded by the ICSCoE Core Human Resources Development Program and MEXT Scholarship, Japan.

## References

1. Bojarski, M., et al.: End to end learning for self-driving cars, **140**. arXiv preprint arXiv:1604.07316 (2016)

2. Papernot, N., McDaniel, P., Wu, X., Jha, S., Swami, A.: Distillation as a defense to adversarial perturbations against deep neural networks. In: 2016 IEEE Symposium on Security and Privacy (SP), pp. 582–597 (2016)
3. Tramèr, F., Kurakin, A., Papernot, N., Goodfellow, I., Boneh, D., McDaniel, P.: Ensemble adversarial training: attacks and defenses. arXiv preprint arXiv:1705.07204 (2017)
4. Guo, C., Rana, M., Cisse, M., Van Der Maaten, L.: Countering adversarial images using input transformations. arXiv preprint arXiv:1711.00117 (2017)
5. Song, Y., Kim, T., Nowozin, S., Ermon, S., Kushman, N.: PixelDefend: leveraging generative models to understand and defend against adversarial examples. arXiv preprint arXiv:1710.10766 (2017)
6. Zhou, J., Liang, C., Chen, J.: Manifold projection for adversarial defense on face recognition. In: Vedaldi, A., Bischof, H., Brox, T., Frahm, J.-M. (eds.) ECCV 2020. LNCS, vol. 12375, pp. 288–305. Springer, Cham (2020). https://doi.org/10.1007/978-3-030-58577-8_18
7. Wang, W., Huang, Y., Wang, Y., Wang, L.: Generalized autoencoder: a neural network framework for dimensionality reduction. In: Proceedings of the IEEE Conference on Computer Vision and Pattern Recognition Workshops, pp. 490–497 (2014)
8. Pomerleau, D.: ALVINN: an autonomous land vehicle in a neural network. In: Advances in Neural Information Processing Systems, vol. 1 (1988)
9. Huang, S., Papernot, N., Goodfellow, I., Duan, Y., Abbeel, P.: Adversarial attacks on neural network policies. arXiv preprint arXiv:1702.02284 (2017)
10. Papernot, N., McDaniel, P., Goodfellow, I., Jha, S., Celik, Z., Swami, A.: Practical black-box attacks against machine learning. In: Proceedings of the 2017 ACM on Asia Conference on Computer and Communications Security, pp. 506–519 (2017)
11. Gu, S., Rigazio, L.: Towards deep neural network architectures robust to adversarial examples. arXiv preprint arXiv:1412.5068 (2014)
12. Buckman, J., Roy, A., Raffel, C., Goodfellow, I.: Thermometer encoding: one hot way to resist adversarial examples. In: International Conference on Learning Representations (2018)
13. Jalal, A., Ilyas, A., Daskalakis, C., Dimakis, A.: The robust manifold defense: adversarial training using generative models. arXiv preprint arXiv:1712.09196 (2017)
14. Samangouei, P., Kabkab, M., Chellappa, R.: Defense-GAN: protecting classifiers against adversarial attacks using generative models. arXiv preprint arXiv:1805.06605 (2018)
15. Goodfellow, I., Shlens, J., Szegedy, C.: Explaining and harnessing adversarial examples. arXiv preprint arXiv:1412.6572 (2014)
16. Udacity: An open source self-driving car dataset (2017). https://github.com/udacity/self-driving-car/tree/master/datasets. Accessed 11 Mar 2022

# Chinese Character Style Transfer Model Based on Convolutional Neural Network

Weiran Chen, Chunping Liu, and Yi Ji[✉]

School of Computer Science and Technology, Soochow University, Suzhou, China
{cpliu,jiyi}@suda.edu.cn

**Abstract.** With various styles, Chinese characters are one of the most important cultural symbols in China. Designing a set of new fonts with a specific style is a very tedious and massive task. It usually relies on traditional manual methods or computer-aided design for each Chinese character, which is time-consuming and labor-intensive. And the products are often not ideal. Therefore, it is necessary to design a model that can automatically generate new Chinese characters in a specified style. In this paper, a convolutional neural network model is proposed to be applied into the Chinese character style migration. To train the network, we exploit the root mean square optimizer to automatically adjust the deep learning rate and gradually reduce the difference values. Experiments are conducted based on the Chinese character datasets. Ultimately the resulting character style is basically close to the manually designed one, which reaches the target of the font style transfer.

**Keywords:** Chinese characters font · Style transfer · Convolutional neural network · Automatic generation

## 1 Introduction

In computer vision, style transfer refers to the combination of the content of one image with the style of another image. It aims to generate an image with a specific style [1]. At present, the transfer of color style has achieved good results through continuous development, but there is still almost no satisfactory scheme for the transfer of line, contour and edge style, because the style transfer based on line level is very different from that based on color level. The key factors of line style are the edge of the pixel position, length, and the specific shape contour. Therefore, most solutions of color style transfer cannot be applied in the line style transfer.

The research topic of this paper is the transfer of Chinese font style. Chinese character represents an important form of Chinese culture. Compared with the English alphabet, the extensive and profound Chinese characters are ideographic with a large number of characters, complex structures, many similar graphemes and diversified writing styles. Different characters in one font style should have the same style. Therefore, related experts need to spend a lot of time and energy

E. Pimenidis et al. (Eds.): ICANN 2022, LNCS 13532, pp. 558–569, 2022.
https://doi.org/10.1007/978-3-031-15937-4_47

designing different Chinese character fonts. And the result is sometimes not satisfactory. Therefore, in this paper we put forward a novel approach of Chinese character style transfer, and realize the migration of style through convolutional neural network. Its main purpose is to generate a whole set of Chinese characters with the same style based on a small number of Chinese characters samples, as is shown in Fig. 1.

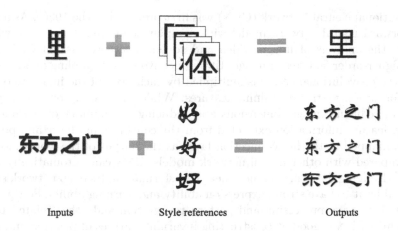

Fig. 1. The main purposes are twofold. 1) It can realize one-to-one style transfer. 2) It can realize many-to-many style transfer.

## 2    Related Work

At present, the research on style transfer mainly focuses on images [2]. Gatys et al. [2] first proposed the use of convolutional neural network to achieve the integration of picture content and style. Although the methods of image style conversion have been studied extensively for many years [2–6], font and text style transfer has only been studied in recent years. As a sub-topic of image style transformation, font style transformation aims to generate new font and text effects using the idea of neural network migration. Nowadays, the research on font style transfer mainly focuses on Chinese characters and English fonts. For the study of Chinese characters, Yang et al. [7,8] first studied this task and designed a patch-based text style transfer model. It suggested that style elements should be represented first and then extracted features should be used to guide the generation of text effects. Zhang et al. [9] proposed a recursive neural network model that could realize the basic read and write operations of Chinese characters. Lyu et al. [10] proposed a deep neural network model that can directly generate calligraphy images from standard font images. Lu et al. [11] proposed a neural network architecture for Chinese font transfer, which can directly use Chinese character images as input.

In terms of English alphabet, Baluja [12] used deep learning models to successfully differentiate fonts and generate the same style of fonts by analyzing only a small number of English letters. Azadi et al. [13] proposed a model of English style transfer based on deep generative adversarial network.

# 3   Algorithm Design

## 3.1   Concept and Principle of Convolutional Neural Network

Convolutional Neural Network (CNN) was first proposed in the 1990s. As a deep feed forward neural network model with complex structure, it has been widely used in the analysis of image, video and so on. The core task of CNN is to learn higher-order features in images through convolutional pooling operation, in which the convolutional kernel is multiplied by each pixel of the image to obtain the information matrix containing features. While the pooling operation plays a role in reducing image dimensions and reducing the number of parameters. Finally, feature information extracted from the convolutional layer and pooling layer is mapped to the full connection layer as the output of the whole model.

Compared with other neural network models, CNN can automatically learn features from big data through nonlinear transformation. Its deep network structure enables it to have strong expression ability and learning ability. So it is very suitable for image processing and pattern recognition and other related tasks. Meanwhile, CNN is good at constructing invariant features of position and rotation from original image data [14], which provides a strong driving force for the development of Chinese character style transfer.

## 3.2   Overview of Transfer Model

Figure 2 shows the basic idea of the whole architecture. First, we preprocess the images of the two input Chinese fonts samples (content font and style font), then extract the corresponding features of the preprocessed Chinese font samples. Next we analyze and process them using the CNN model. Finally, the model outputs the generated target fonts.

Specifically, the whole font design process is a matter of style transformation from standard appearance fonts to stylized target fonts. The main network is trained by pairs to convert between two fonts. The average absolute error method is used to measure the performance. So the style difference between the generated font and the ground-truth font can be obtained. The root mean square optimizer is used to automatically adjust the learning rate and gradually reduce the difference value. Once the training process is complete, our model can be used to infer the shapes of the rest of the characters.

## 3.3   Image Preprocessing

In the task of Chinese character style transfer, the image quality of the input font will directly affect the design of the whole model and the effect of the output font. Therefore, the preprocessing is a crucial step, whose main purpose is

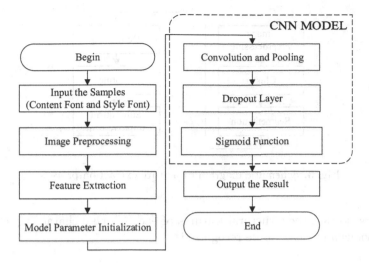

**Fig. 2.** Specific flow of whole architecture

to eliminate irrelevant information in the image and enhance the detect-ability of important information. This will improve the reliability of feature extraction, image segmentation, matching and recognition [15]. In our model, the preprocessing mainly includes the following four aspects: geometric transformation, image enhancement, image filtering and histogram equalization. Meanwhile, the size and gray values of all images are normalized, so as to enhance the generalization ability of the model.

### 3.4    Feature Extraction of Chinese Character Samples

During the whole process of Chinese font style transfer, accurate feature extraction of images is the most core and key link, which aims to extract its unique internal features from the original Chinese character samples. For Chinese characters, according to different methods of feature extraction, the features are generally divided into two categories: structural features and statistical features (global features and local features) [16]. Among them, structural features are mainly analyzed and extracted from the overall character and stroke, while statistical features are mainly calculated by some statistical methods, such as direction features [17–19]. Most traditional feature extraction methods, such as the Hough transform, Canny edge detection and unicom area detection [19], have a series of problems, like sensitivity to noise, small sample problem, extraction of image features exist in the redundancy and so on [19]. Therefore, we use a new feature extraction method, through a series of steps such as clustering, segmentation, and so on, to get a better feature set as in Fig. 3.

Among them, clustering and segmentation are mainly to extract the statistical features of Chinese characters. The process of de-noising, pooling and subsequent improvement is mainly to extract the structural features of Chinese

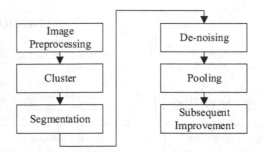

**Fig. 3.** Schematic diagram of feature extraction process

characters, so that the structural features of each Chinese character picture are more obvious and easier to be recognized.

### 3.5   Main Architecture

Figure 4 shows the main architecture of Chinese character style transfer. The main part adopts a top-down deep convolutional neural network structure to transfer and transform Chinese font styles. It consists of 1 input layer, 14 convolution layers, 1 maximum pooling layer, 1 random discarding layer, 1 activation layer and 1 output layer. The specific model structure and parameter configuration are shown in Table 1.

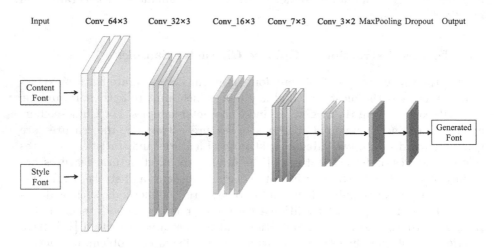

**Fig. 4.** Schematic diagram of main model

Table 1. Detailed parameters of CNN network model

| The Network Layer | Parameters |
|---|---|
| Input | $160 \times 160 \times 1$ |
| Conv_64 × 3 | The Number of Kernel: 16 ; Kernel Size: $64 \times 64$ |
| Conv_32 × 3 | The Number of Kernel: 32 ; Kernel Size: $32 \times 32$ |
| Conv_16 × 3 | The Number of Kernel: 64 ; Kernel Size: $16 \times 16$ |
| Conv_7 × 3 | The Number of Kernel: 128 ; Kernel Size: $7 \times 7$ |
| Conv_3 × 2 | The Number of Kernel: 128 ; Kernel Size: $3 \times 3$ |
| Max_pooling | The Number of Kernel: 1 ; Kernel Size: $2 \times 2$ |
| Output | $80 \times 80 \times 1$ |

In the main architecture, there is a Batch Normalization layer (BN) followed by each of the convolutional layers. The BN layer aims to normalize the input of each layer to effectively make the data obey a certain distribution. At the same time, BN layer also increases the overall convergence speed of the neural network model [20], and the network model can maintain a high initial learning rate in the training process without manual intervention and adjustment.

In our method, the addition of BN layer allows each time using the formula 1 and formula 2 for the mean and variance of bulk data normalization of more accord with normal distribution, which $m$ represents the number of $x$, $\mu_\beta$ is the mean of each feature in the calculated small batch sample, $\sigma_\beta$ stands for the characteristic variance of each sample in the calculated small batch total, and then by scaling and translating variables $\gamma$ and $\beta$, the normalized value $y^i$ is calculated by using formula 3, where $x^{ii}$ represents the normalized value.

$$\mu_\beta \leftarrow \frac{1}{m} \sum_{i=1}^{m} x^{(i)} \tag{1}$$

$$\sigma_\beta^2 \leftarrow \frac{1}{m} \sum_{i=1}^{m} (x^{(i)} - \mu_\beta)^2 \tag{2}$$

$$y^i \leftarrow \gamma \bigotimes x^{ii} + \beta \tag{3}$$

After the convolution layer, the pooling layer can be used to extract the feature with a wider range. The maximum pooling algorithm is adopted in the experiments, and the filter is set to $2 \times 2$ and the step value is 2. In the experiments, a random discarding layer was set, and some neural units were discarded randomly during model training to prevent the occurrence of over-fitting.

In terms of the activation function at the network layer, ReLU (Rectified Linear Unit) is adopted as the activation function. Compared with other activation functions, ReLU has no saturation zone and no complex exponential, logarithm and other mathematical operations, making calculation simple and efficient. Meanwhile, ReLU function converges much faster than tanh and other functions. It can also effectively alleviate the problem of gradient disappearance, and trains the deep neural network in a supervised way without relying on unsupervised layer-by-layer pre-training, which significantly improves the performance of the deep neural network [21].

For our system, the output layer creates the forecast output with dimension $80 \times 80$ and compared with the real image, calculate the loss value between each other.

In the aspect of loss function and model optimization, our approach adopts MAE as the loss function to realize the real-time evaluation of the model. At the same time of model training, Adam Optimizer is used as the Optimizer to optimize and improve the model, with the main purpose of improving the robustness and accuracy of the whole model framework.

### 3.6    Model Algorithm Description

The algorithm description of this model is shown below.

---

**Algorithm 1.** Chinese character style transfer algorithm

---

**Input:**
Dataset: content font $I_n$ and style font $I_t$;
Number of training iterations: $iter$;
Network layer weight value: $w_i$;
Loss ratio weight: $A,B$;
Number of convolutional network layers: $L$;
**Output:**
Chinese font after style transfer: $I_o$;
1: Input the content font $I_n$ and style font $I_t$
2: $N_j$ is the content feature map of random white noise images at each layer of the network. $T_j$ is the style feature map of random white noise images at each layer of the network.
3: **for** $i = 1, 2, 3, ..., iter$ **do**
4:     **for** $j = 1, 2, 3, ..., L$ **do**
5:         Calculate the content loss $L_n$
6:         $L_n = \frac{1}{i} \sum_{i=1}^{iter} w_i \sum_{j=1}^{iter} |N_j - I_n|$
7:         Calculate the style loss $L_t$
8:         $L_t = \frac{1}{i} \sum_{i=1}^{iter} w_i \sum_{j=1}^{iter} |T_j - I_t|$
9:         Calculate the whole loss $L$
10:        $L = AL_n + BL_t$
11:        Optimize the model parameters
12:        $w_i = w_i - \lambda \frac{\delta L}{\delta w_i}$
13:     End for
14: End for
15: **return** result

---

# 4    Experimental Analysis

## 4.1    Dataset

Samples used in this model are all bitmap images of $160 \times 160 \times 1$ formed by OTF and TTF files after image preprocessing, which represent 2D images composed of multiple pixels. Simkai font and huangkaiti font are selected for training, in which the first one is used as content font and the second one is used as style font. 6500 pieces from two characters fonts were selected as datasets. Among them 6000 pieces were used as training sets and the remaining 500 pieces were used as validation set.

## 4.2    Experimental Analysis

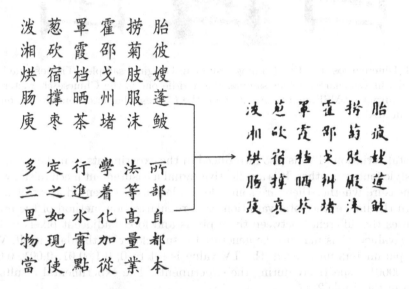

**Fig. 5.** Experimental results, in which the left figure is the input image (one is the content font, the other is the style font), the right figure is the output image.

In this setting, simkai font is used as the content font and huangkaiti font is used as the style font. During the experiments, the two fonts are simultaneously input into the CNN network structure, analyzed and processed. It can be seen from Fig. 5 that the convolutional neural network built in this paper finally achieves a good effect of Chinese style transfer.

**Loss Function Analysis.** The mean absolute error loss function (MAE) and mean square error loss function (MSE) were used in the experiments. Figure 6 includes the results of the training of the mean absolute error loss function and mean square error loss function models respectively. It can be seen from the figure that after MAE training, both the font style and content are clear, and the generated effect is basically close to the original picture. However, after MSE training, the font display is incomplete, the handwriting is blurred, and the background noise is large. From what has been discussed above, the average absolute error loss function is used in the experiments to reduce the pixel error value between the predicted image and the real image, so that the effect of font style after migration is more neat and beautiful.

**Fig. 6.** Different loss function training results and original samples. The left one is the original Chinese character font sample, the middle one is the Chinese character font sample output by MSE, and the right one is the Chinese character font sample output by mean MAE.

Total variation (TV) is also introduced in the experiments to make the generated style fonts smoother. It is an effective signal measurement mechanism, which can measure whether there are some close relations between adjacent elements [22]. In the image, the total variation, as a regularization method of the image, measures the difference between these pixels and forces adjacent pixels to have similar values, thus making the generated result closer to the data itself. With other parameters unchanged, the TV value is set to 0, 0.1, 0.01, 0.001, 0.0001 and 0.00001 respectively during the experiments. The experimental results are shown in the Table 2.

As can be seen from the table, when the TV value is 0, the training time is the longest and the convergence effect is very poor. When the TV value is 0.01 and 0.001, although the training time is similar, the latter model has better convergence effect. When its value is 0.0001 or 0.00001, the training time is longer, and the convergence speed is slow. After comprehensive analysis, we can come to the conclusion that if the TV value is too high or too low, the experimental effect is not ideal. Therefore, 0.001 is selected as the TV value in our final model.

**Error Curve Analysis.** In the training process of the deep learning model, the change of the error curve represents the convergence state of the whole network model. In the convolutional neural network model of Chinese character font style

**Table 2.** Comparison between different values of total variation

| Parameter setting | Total variation | Training time | Convergence effect |
|---|---|---|---|
| Iters: 5000 | 0 | 5 | Worse |
| Alpha: 1.0 | 0.1 | 3 | Worse |
| keep_prob: 0.9 | 0.01 | 3 | Better |
| Training set: 6000 | 0.001 | 3 | Best |
| Test set: 500 | 0.0001 | 3.5 | Worse |
| Batch_size: 64 | 0.00001 | 4 | Worse |

transfer, the experiments recorded the change curve of the error on the training set and the error on the verification set respectively, and the results are shown in Fig. 7.

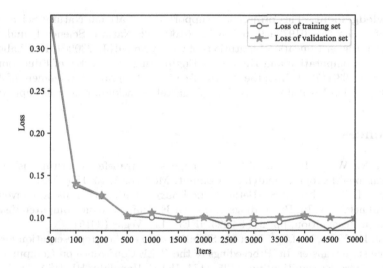

**Fig. 7.** Error variation curve during model training

As can be seen from the experimental results, in the first 500 iterations of training, both on the training set and on the validation set, the loss rate decreased significantly. However, with the increasing number of iterations, the error value tended to be near 0.1, without too much fluctuation, and closed to a stable value. At this point, the model converges.

**Generalization Ability Analysis.** In the field of machine learning, generalization ability is one of the key indicators to evaluate a model. Generalization Ability refers to the adaptability of the model algorithm to fresh samples [23].

From the experimental results, it can be seen that the font generated by our proposed approach has a good effect, which is very clear and beautiful both in terms of font structure and font outline. Therefore, our model has good generalization ability.

## 5   Conclusion

This paper proposes a Chinese character style transfer model based on convolutional neural network. During the whole process, the model was trained and improved by a series of technical means and mechanisms, such as image preprocessing, image feature extraction and CNN. At the same time, we carried out exhaustive experiments with different loss functions and total variation values. Finally, the transfer task of Chinese character style from simkai font to huangkaiti font was successfully completed. The experimental results on the dataset also proved the validity and reliability of our model.

**Acknowledgement.** This project was supported by National Natural Science Foundation of China Nos 61972059, 61773272, 61602332; Natural Science Foundation of the Jiangsu Higher Education Institutions of China No 19KJA230001, Key Laboratory of Symbolic Computation and Knowledge Engineering of Ministry of Education, Jilin University No 93K172016K08; the Priority Academic Program Development of Jiangsu Higher Education Institutions (PAPD). We gratefully acknowledge this support.

## References

1. Li, Y.N., Wang, P., Xiao, J.L.: An image style transfer algorithm using multi-dimensional histogram matching. Comput. Modern. **2**, 15–18 (2019)
2. Gatys, L.A., Ecker, A.S., Bethge, M.: Image style transfer using convolutional neural networks. In: Proceedings of the IEEE Conference on Computer Vision and Pattern Recognition, pp. 2414–2423. IEEE, Las Vegas (2016)
3. Chen, D., Yuan, L., Liao, J., et al.: StyleBank: an explicit representation for neural image style transfer. In: Proceedings of the IEEE Conference on Computer Vision and Pattern Recognition, pp. 1125–1134. IEEE, Honolulu, HI, USA (2017)
4. Isola, P., Zhu, J.Y., Zhou, T., et al.: Image-to-image translation with conditional adversarial networks. In: Proceedings of the IEEE Conference on Computer Vision and Pattern Recognition, pp. 5967–5976. IEEE, Honolulu, HI, USA (2017)
5. Zhu, J.Y., Park, T., Isola, P., et al.: Unpaired image-to-image translation using cycle-consistent adversarial networks. Proceedings of the IEEE international conference on computer vision, pp. 2223–2232. IEEE, Venice, Italy (2017)
6. Choi, Y., Choi, M., Kim, M., et al.: StarGAN: unified generative adversarial networks for multi-domain image-to-image translation. In: Proceedings of the IEEE Conference on Computer Vision and Pattern Recognition, pp. 8789–8797. IEEE, Salt Lake City (2018)
7. Yang, S., Liu, J., Lian, Z., et al.: Awesome typography: statistics-based text effects transfer. In: Proceedings of the IEEE Conference on Computer Vision and Pattern Recognition, pp. 7464–7473. IEEE, Honolulu, HI, USA (2017)

8. Yang, S., Liu, J., Yang, W., et al.: Context-aware unsupervised text stylization. In: Proceedings of the 26th ACM international conference on Multimedia, pp. 1688–1696. ACM, Seoul in Korea (2018)

9. Zhang, X.Y., Yin, F., Zhang, Y.M., et al.: Drawing and recognizing Chinese characters with recurrent neural network. IEEE Trans. Patt. Anal. Mach. Intell. **99**, 849–862 (2018)

10. Lyu, P., Bai, X., Yao, C., et al.: Auto-encoder guided GAN for Chinese calligraphy synthesis. In: The 14th IAPR International Conference on Document Analysis and Recognition, pp. 1095–1100. IEEE, Kyoto, Japan (2017)

11. Lu, S.Y., Hsiang, T.R.: Generating Chinese typographic and handwriting fonts from a small font sample set. In: 2018 International Joint Conference on Neural Networks, pp. 1–8. IEEE, Rio de Janeiro, Brazil (2018)

12. Baluja, S.: Learning typographic style: from discrimination to synthesis. Mach. Vis. Appl. 551–568 (2017). https://doi.org/10.1007/s00138-017-0842-6

13. Azadi, S., Fisher, M., et al.: Multi-content GAN for few-shot font style transfer. In: Proceedings of the IEEE Conference on Computer Vision and Pattern Recognition, pp. 7564–7573. IEEE, Salt Lake City, UT, USA (2018)

14. Krizhevsky, A., Sutskever, I., Hinton, G.: ImageNet classification with deep convolutional neural networks. Adv. Neural Inf. Proces. Syst. **25**(2), 1–9 (2012)

15. Jiang, R.L., Liu, Y., et al.: Image based detection method of vibrating screen materials existence. J. Image Signal Process. **9**(1), 57–64 (2020)

16. Jing, Y.L., Jiang, X., Ming, G.H.: Comparative study on several feature extraction methods of handwritten Chinese characters. Acad. Res. **30**(10), 12–13 (2009)

17. Zhang, H.G., Guo, J., et al.: HCL2000: a large scale handwritten Chinese character database for handwritten character recognition. In: Proceedings of the 10th International Conference on Document Analysis and Recognition, pp. 286–290. IEEE, Barcelona, Spain (2009)

18. Yang, Y.L., Lin, X.S., et al.: Design and implementation of basic database for Chinese information processing and intelligent man-machine Interface in 863 Program. High-tech. Commun. **15**(1), 107–110 (2005)

19. Jin, L.W., Gao, Y., et al.: CUT-COUCH2009: a comprehensive online unconstrained Chinese handwritten database and benchmark evaluation. Int. J. Doc. Anal. Recogn. **14**, 53–54 (2011)

20. Li, J., Gao, J., et al.: Mongolian style transfer model based on convolutional Neural network. J. Inner Mongolia Agric. Univ. **42**(5), 94–99 (2021)

21. Jiang, A.B., Wang, W.W.: Optimization of activation function ReLU. Sens. Microsyst. **37**(2), 50–52 (2018)

22. Rudin, L.I., Osher, S., Fatemi, E.: Nonlinear total variation based noise removal algorithms. Phy. D Nonlinear Phenom. **60**(1–4), 259–268 (1992)

23. Huang, L., Li, W.B.: Generalization ability improvement method and application of BP network. J. Shijiazhuang Railway Inst. **18**(3), 94–97 (2005)

# CNN-Transformer Hybrid Architecture for Early Fire Detection

Chenyue Yang[1,2], Yixuan Pan[1,2], Yichao Cao[1,2], and Xiaobo Lu[1,2](✉)

[1] School of Automation, Southeast University, Nanjing 210096, China
[2] Key Laboratory of Measurement and Control of Complex Systems of Engineering, Ministry of Education, Nanjing 210096, China
xblu2013@126.com

**Abstract.** Fire hazards bring great harm to human beings and nature. Advances in computer vision technology have made it possible to detect fire early through surveillance videos. In recent works, CNN is widely used in fire detection but it cannot model long-range dependencies and its capability of global feature processing is poor. When dealing with the problem of early fire detection, the flame target is small and the color characteristics are not obvious, so the effect of the previous fire detection methods is poor. Transformer's strong capacity of feature processing and growing success in visual field highlight its potential and provide us with new ideas, but its large calculation has a certain impact on the detection speed. Therefore, in this paper, we design a network combining CNN and Transformer, (GLCT), which can model global and local information and achieve a balance between accuracy and speed. In the backbone MobileLP, linear highlighted attention mechanism is used to reduce the amount of computation, and locality is introduced in the feed forward network. Feature fusion is carried out by combining the designed backbone with BiFPN. Equipped with YOLO Head, the whole fire detection model is constructed. By detecting the surveillance video images of early fire, our network outperforms some representative and excellent object detection works, including YOLOv4, MobileViT, PVTv2 and its variants, showing its reliability in early fire detection.

**Keywords:** Fire detection · MobileLP · CNN · Vision transformer

## 1  Introduction

Fire hazards are burning out of control, causing great harm to public safety, social development and natural ecology, so setting up monitoring equipment in all kinds of places, timely noticing, and fighting the fire in the early stage are the most effective ways to deal with the fire. Traditional fire monitoring equipment is mostly based on temperature or smoke particle sensor, which is susceptible to height, dust, air velocity and other factors. At the same time, when the monitoring scene is large, such sensors cannot provide detailed information such as the burning degree of the fire and the specific location of the flame. In recent years, with the development of computer vision, fire detection technology can overcome the limitations of traditional methods. As long as the flame appears in the monitoring range, it can immediately identify the flame information, and alarm. The advantages of this type of computer vision based fire detection technology are as follows: (1) It is less affected by the surrounding environment and can detect fire in the early stage. (2) HD video surveillance covers a large area and the detection system outputs detailed information about the location and size of the flame. (3) With the gradual improvement of computer performance and the further improvement of the object detection algorithms, we can achieve more accurate and fast identification. Therefore, more accurate and faster fire detection algorithms have also received the attention of many researchers. At present, most fire detection methods adopt dividing image into blocks first and then classifying them. In some direct detection methods, the flame target in the data set is large and the color is obvious, so when the model is used to detect initial flame, considering the domain of it is different, the accuracy is low.

The research content of this paper is mainly the early fire detection algorithm in the fire monitoring system, and the monitoring scene covers a variety of indoor and outdoor environments. The contributions of our work are as follows:

1. We propose a new network combining CNN and Transformer to achieve the balance between high accuracy and speed. This model overcomes the problems of CNN model's limited ability to capture long-range dependencies and Transformer model's large amount of computation and limited detection speed.
2. A backbone with linear highlighted attention mechanism and local feed forward network, -MobileLP is designed. MobileLP block is used to process global features, and the inverted residual block is used for downsampling. In Transformer architecture, adaptive max pooling is used to reduce the size of the input space and highlight the main features. Locality is added to the feed forward network by introducing depth-wise convolution, and we add activation function to improve the performance. These operations make the model learn the global and local features of the image better while reducing the computational load.
3. SPP and BiFPN are combined to enhance feature fusion, and YOLO Head is introduced to build the whole fire detection model GLCT. By comparing on early fire surveillance video image dataset, the proposed network can be applied to early fire detection and achieve better detection results in speed and accuracy.

The structure of the whole paper is as follows. Section 2 discusses the current application of computer vision in fire detection. Section 3 describes the structure and principle of the entire network. The experimental results and comparative analysis are presented in Sect. 4. Finally, the conclusion is presented in Sect. 5.

## 2 Related Works

### 2.1 Feature Analysis Based Fire Detection Methods

Feature analysis based methods mainly obtain the flame region first, calculate several flame features from it, and then use the rules designed to judge and classify. Qureshi et al. [1] detected the flame by performing growth rate analysis and Luca-Kanade pyramid optical flow analysis on candidate regions. Celik et al. [2] obtained statistical color information by manually marking flame pixels to help judge whether the foreground target is flame. The universality of these methods is poor, and detection accuracy is low. Later, a learning method based on extracted flame features emerged. Multiple flame features are calculated to form a feature vector, and then classified by learning methods. Dimitropoulos et al. [3] used background subtraction and color analysis to define candidate flame regions. For each candidate fire block, six features such as flame color probability, spatial wavelet energy etc. are calculated. Finally, SVM is used for classification. In this kind of methods, the effect of feature extraction and the rules have great influence on the detection results, and these methods have poor universality and low detection accuracy.

### 2.2 CNN Based Fire Detection Methods

In recent years, feature extraction methods based on deep learning have been rapidly applied to various fields due to their powerful expression ability. Huang et al. [4] proposed a color-guided fire detection method based on Faster R-CNN, which reduced the number of anchors by using flame color zone constraints when generating initial anchors. Zhao et al. [5] adopted K-means++ clustering algorithm to initialize the candidate box, improved the multi-scale feature fusion structure based on YOLOv3 algorithm, and proposed the densely connected structure of the same scale features and the spatial pyramid convolution operation. Muhammad et al. [6] fine-tuned GoogleNet to adapt to fire detection through transfer learning. Zhang et al. [7] proposed multi-linear principal component analysis (MPCA) deep learning algorithm for feature extraction of tensor objects, and used MPCANet to establish fire image recognition model. Although CNN has been applied in the field of fire detection to a certain extent, it has poor ability to capture long-range dependencies [8], and the accuracy of detecting initial flames in images with high resolution is limited.

### 2.3 Transformer Based Fire Detection Methods

Although CNN can realize fire detection, it still has some limitations in modeling global context information. With the introduction of ViT [9], a great deal of researches on Transformer's application in the field of vision have flourished, including all kinds of Transformer based backbone, such as LocalViT [10]. At the same time, a series of pyramid structure networks such as PVT [11] and Swin Transformer [12] emerged, and Transformer neck was proposed, such as

DETR [13] and Deformable DETR [14]. Shahid et al. [15] used ViT for detection on open flame datasets, but the model required lightweight improvement. Ghali et al. [16] used two visual based Transformer networks, TransUNet and MedT, to segment forest flames on visible spectral images. However, Transformer used in object detection has the problem of large computation and slow detection speed. Therefore, some studies focus on the combination of Transformer and CNN, such as MobileViT [17], to achieve a balance between accuracy and speed in visual tasks. At present, there are relatively few studies on fire detection using Transformer, and there is still a lot of room for improvement in the research on early fire detection based on Transformer and its hybrid.

## 3    Methods

### 3.1    Locality Feed Forward Network

Transformer consists of self-attention mechanism and feed forward network. In our network, the design of feed forward network is mainly based on LocalViT [10], and the locality mechanism is introduced into Transformer by adding depth-wise convolution to FFN.

The input image is $X \in R^{C \times H \times W}$, where C and H × W represent the number of channels and the spatial dimension of the input image. The input image is first transformed into a sequence of tokens, and tokens can be aggregated into a matrix $X \in R^{N \times d}$, where $d = C \times p^2$ and $N = HW/p^2$. FFN is applied to it by position and can rearrange the token sequence into a 2D lattice first. The process can be expressed as:

$$X^r = Seqto\mathrm{Img}(X), \tag{1}$$

where $X^r \in R^{h \times w \times d}$, $h = H/p$, $w = W/p$. This step converts the token sequence into a 2D feature representation, restoring the proximity between tokens. Therefore, the full connection layer in the previous FFN can be replaced with $1 \times 1$ convolution layer, and we add activation function after it.

In order to make the Transformer model local and global dependencies, referring to the idea of inverted residual block in MobileNets [18], depth-wise convolution is introduced into the network. That is, applying K × K (K >1) convolution kernel to each channel, the features are aggregated and computed to generate new features. Locality can be introduced into the network in an efficient manner, i.e.

$$Y^r = f(f(f(X^r * W_1) * W_d) * W_2), \tag{2}$$

where $W_1 \in R^{d \times \varepsilon d \times 1 \times 1}$, $W_2 \in R^{d \times \varepsilon d \times 1 \times 1}$ represents $1 \times 1$ convolution kernel, $W_d \in R^{\varepsilon d \times 1 \times k \times k}$ is depth-wise convolution kernel, $\varepsilon$ is dimensional expansion rate, usually set to 4, $f(\cdot)$ is nonlinear activation function, and $Y^r \in R^{h \times w \times d}$ is the output feature representation. Then, the output feature representation is converted into token sequence for the next self-attention layer, i.e.

$$Y = \mathrm{Img}toSeq(Y^r). \tag{3}$$

The network structure is shown in the Fig. 1(c). Because the nonlinear activation function is very important for improving the network capacity, the h-swish [19] activation function is selected after the $1 \times 1$ convolution. The h-swish activation function and the Squeeze-and-Excitation (SE) module [20] are combined for the $3 \times 3$ depth-wise convolution.

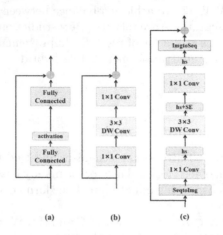

**Fig. 1.** (a) Fully connected layers of the feed forward network in Vision Transformers, (b) inverted residual blocks, (c) the final feed forward networks that brings locality.

### 3.2  Linear Highlighted Attention

For the self-attention mechanism of Transformer block, referring to PVTv2 [21], linear highlighted attention (LHA) layer is designed to replace the traditional multi-head attention (MHA) layer. Similar to MHA, LHA receives a Query Q, a key K, and a value V as input, but reduces the spatial scale of K and V before attention operation, greatly reducing the memory overhead, and outputs improved features. LHA can be expressed as:

$$LHA(Q,K,V){=}Concat(h_1,h_2,\ldots h_N)W^O,$$
$$h_i = Attention(QW_i^Q, SR(K)W_i^K, SR(V)W_i^V), \tag{4}$$

where $Concat(\cdot)$ is the concatenation operation as in [22]. $W_i^Q \in \mathbb{R}^{C \times d_h}$, $W_i^K \in \mathbb{R}^{C \times d_h}$, $W_i^V \in \mathbb{R}^{C \times d_h}$, $W^O \in \mathbb{R}^{C \times C}$ are linear projection parameters. N is the head number of the attention layer. The dimension of each head $d_h$ is equal to $C/N$. $SR(\cdot)$ is the operation that reduces the spatial dimension of the input sequence K and V, and can be written as

$$SR(x) = Act(Norm(Conv(MaxPool(x)))), \tag{5}$$

where $x \in \mathbb{R}^{(HW) \times C}$ represents an input sequence. By using adaptive max pooling, the input sequence is reshaped to the sequence of $p^2 \times C$. $p$ is the pooling size, and its default is 7. This process retains the main features and highlights the foreground, improving the detection accuracy of the network. The $1 \times 1$ convolution is applied next. $Norm(\cdot)$ refers to layer normalization [23], and $Act(\cdot)$ refers to GELU activation function [24]. The specific structure is shown in Fig. 2(b). The operation of attention calculation $Attention(\cdot)$ is same as multi-head attention.

LHA has linear computation cost, which is lower than MHA, and it can process larger input feature map or longer sequence with limited resources.

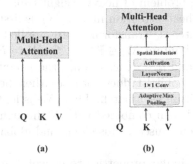

(a)                           (b)

**Fig. 2.** Comparison of (a) Multi-head attention (MHA) and (b) Linear highlighted attention (LHA).

### 3.3 GLCT

This part introduces the overall structure of the network. The core idea of the network is to learn global and local feature representation and build a lightweight and efficient fire detection network combining CNN and Transformer.

**MobileLP Block.** Considering the idea of MobileViT block [17], the structure of MobileLP block is shown in Fig. 3. Its core idea is to model global and

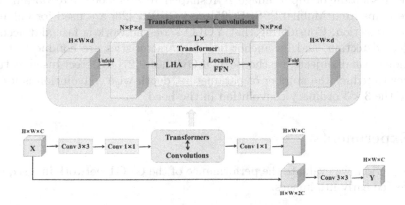

**Fig. 3.** Architecture of MobileLP block. Here, conv $3 \times 3$ and conv $1 \times 1$ represent standard convolution, kernel size is 3 or 1. The size of each tensor is labeled in the figure.

local information in an input tensor with fewer parameters. In the Transformer structure of MobileLP block, we replace multi-head attention with LHA, and locality is introduced into the feed forward network to build a new lightweight Transformer structure.

Theoretically, for a given input tensor $X \in \mathbb{R}^{H \times W \times C}$, MobileLP blocks use an n × n convolution layer to encode local spatial information, and then use a point-wise convolution layer to map the tensor to a higher-dimensional space, generating $X_L \in \mathbb{R}^{H \times W \times d}$, where $d > C$.

In order to solve the problem of heavy weight caused by the lack of spatial inductive bias for multi-head attention in ViT, $X_L$ is first expanded into N non-overlapping flattened patches, Transformers are applied to encode the relation between the patches, and obtain $X_G \in \mathbb{R}^{P \times N \times d}$, where $P = wh$, $N = HW/P$ is the number of patches, and $h \leq n$, $w \leq n$ are the height and width of a patch respectively. In this way, MobileLP does not lose either the order of patches or the spatial order of pixels within each patch. Then $X_G$ is folded and mapped to low C-dimensional space and then combined with X through connection operation. Another n × n convolution is used to fuse local and global features in connected tensors.

MobileLP block has similar properties to convolution because its operation is similar to convolution, requiring unfolding and folding, except that it uses Transformer to replace local feature processing with global feature processing. The module can also be used in other deep networks.

**Overall Architecture.** The network structure is shown in Fig. 4. The backbone is MobileLP, and the first layer of the network is the 3 × 3 standard convolution with stride of 2, followed by inverted residual blocks [18]. The main role of these blocks in MobileLP is to downsample, and their parameter contribution is relatively small compared to the overall backbone network. After the CNN section, we use MobileLP blocks for a better representation of learning features. We set h = w = 2 and L of the two blocks to 2 and 4, respectively.

The resolution of input image is reshaped to 608 × 608. We obtain three feature maps from MobileLP. SPP [25] and BiFPN [26] are used for enhanced feature extraction. Considering that YOLO series network is fast and accurate in object detection, and its anchor-based characteristics are conducive to the detection of small objects, we choose YOLOv3 head [27] to detect fused features. In order to reduce the number of parameters, depth-wise convolution is used to replace the 3 × 3 ordinary convolution in the head.

## 4    Experiments

In this section, we evaluate the performance of the GLCT network in a sequence of collected early fire images.

## 4.1   Implementation Details

We collected a total of 3717 early fire video images in different scenarios, with a size of $1920 \times 1080$. The images contain various indoor and outdoor environments, with objects of similar color, moving people, cars, floating leaves, shielding and other disturbances. They are all images in the early stage of the fire. Part of the images are interfered by light, and contains reflection, etc., which can basically cover all kinds of complex scenes. The images were randomly divided into 3345 images in the training set and 372 images in the test dataset.

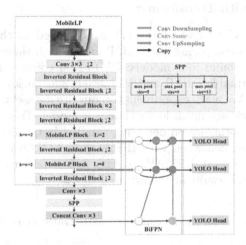

**Fig. 4.** GLCT. Here, blocks for downsampling are marked with $\downarrow 2$, $\times 2$ refers that the block is repeated twice, Conv$\times 3$ refers to a cubic convolution block, which firstly uses $1 \times 1$ convolution to raise dimension, then uses $3 \times 3$ depth-wise convolution to extract feature, and then uses $1 \times 1$ convolution to reduce dimension.

The GPU used is a GeForce GTX 1080. We use the annotated data set to train the network, including 100 epochs. The initial learning rate is set to $7 \times 10^{-4}$ following a StepLR learning rate scheduler. The resolution of input image is reshaped to 608×608, Adam optimization algorithm is used, and loss function is the same as YOLOv4 algorithm [28]. The model's performance will be evaluated by AP and FPS, and compared to popular CNN and Transformer networks.

## 4.2   Compared with CNN

We choose the CNN object detection algorithm commonly used at present with different backbone to conduct experiments on our early fire data set. All the experimental results are shown in Table 1. GLCT achieves 80.71 AP and 26.27 FPS, and our network is more accurate and faster than YOLOv4, which is the most accurate CNN network in our experiments.

**Table 1.** Fire detection results compared with CNN.

| Networks | Backbone | AP | FPS |
|---|---|---|---|
| YOLOv4 | CSPDarknet53 | 79.89 | 20.8 |
| CenterNet | ResNet50 | 46.41 | 60.06 |
| MobileNetv3-YOLOv4 | MobileNetv3 | 72.60 | 51.60 |
| **GLCT** | **MobileLP** | **80.71** | **26.27** |

### 4.3   Compared with Transformer

Since the idea of PVTv2 and MobileViT are referred in the network, so we conduct experiments comparing our GLCT model with these Transformer network structures. We build four models: PVTv2-b0 combined with RetinaNet, YOLOv4, and Deformable DETR and MobieNetv2 as backbone combined with Deformable DETR. We make experiments on our fire datasets. The accuracy and speed of these models are much lower than our model. Transformer based networks have poor performance on detecting small objects. Also, we take Mobile-ViT as the backbone, combined with BiFPN and YOLOv4, experiments show that our model exceeds it 1.95 AP, proving the superiority of our network. Detailed experimental results are shown in Table 2.

**Table 2.** Fire detection results compared with Transformer based networks

| Networks | Backbone | AP | FPS |
|---|---|---|---|
| PVTv2-b0-RetinaNet | PVTv2-b0 | 56.80 | 6.2 |
| PVTv2-b0-YOLOv4 | PVTv2-b0 | 72.50 | 7.3 |
| PVTv2-b0-Deformable DETR | PVTv2-b0 | 56.00 | 7.4 |
| MobileNetv2-Deformable DETR | MobileNetv2 | 55.30 | 9.5 |
| MobileViT-YOLOv4 | MobileViT | 78.76 | 30.27 |
| **GLCT** | **MobileLP** | **80.71** | **26.27** |

Table 3 compares the number of parameters and GFLOPs of all the reference models, which is sorted by the number of model parameters from the lowest to the highest. It can be seen that our model achieves the best performance while the number of parameters is small.

The visualization results are shown in Fig. 5. Our model can detect the early fire object in multiple indoor and outdoor scenarios, overcome the interference of lighting and reflection, and achieve a more accurate and faster detection.

**Table 3.** Parameters and flops of reference models

| Networks | Input size | #Param (M) | GFLOPs | AP |
|---|---|---|---|---|
| MobileNetv3-YOLOv4 | (608, 608) | 8.96 | 4.84 | 72.60 |
| PVTv2-b0-YOLOv4 | (1280, 800) | 9.47 | 40.43 | 72.50 |
| PVTv2-b0-RetinaNet | (1280, 800) | 11.31 | 126.91 | 56.80 |
| MobileNetv2-Deformable DETR | (1280, 800) | 13.31 | 57.56 | 55.30 |
| **GLCT** | **(608, 608)** | **15.63** | **16.69** | **80.71** |
| MobileViT-YOLOv4 | (608, 608) | 15.98 | 11.3 | 78.76 |
| PVTv2-b0-Deformable DETR | (1280, 800) | 16.85 | 130.16 | 56.00 |
| CenterNet | (512, 512) | 32.66 | 35.02 | 46.41 |
| YOLOv4 | (608, 608) | 63.94 | 63.83 | 79.89 |

**Fig. 5.** Visualization of fire detection results.

## 5   Conclusion

In this paper, we propose a new fire detection network combining CNN and Transformer–GLCT. The backbone of the network is mainly composed of inverted residual blocks responsible for sampling and MobileLP blocks responsible for feature processing. MobileLP blocks unfold tensors, encode the relationships between blocks using Transformer structures, and fold them to perform operations. In Transformer structure, LHA is used and locality is introduced in feed forward network, which enables the network to process both global and local features and reduces the amount of computation. Combining MobileLP with BiFPN, and using YOLO Head as the detection head, we built the whole model of early fire detection. Experiments on multi-scenarios early fire images show that our network achieves good results in both accuracy and speed. Compared with other CNN and Transformer networks, it is found that the constructed model is superior to other reference networks. Future research will focus on improving the model speed, as well as the model's generalization performance to achieve fire detection in more complex and interference conditions.

**Acknowledgement.** This work was supported by the National Natural Science Foundation of China (No. 61871123), Key Research and Development Program in Jiangsu Province (No. BE2016739) and was funded by the Priority Academic Program Development of Jiangsu Higher Education Institutions. We thank the Big Data Center of Southeast University for providing facility support for the numerical calculations in this paper.

# References

1. Qureshi, W.S., Ekpanyapong, M., Dailey, M.N., et al.: QuickBlaze: early fire detection using a combined video processing approach. Fire Technol. **52**(5), 1293–1317 (2016)
2. Celik, T., Demirel, H., Ozkaramanli, H.: Automatic fire detection in video sequences. Fire Saf. J. Nurnal **6**(3), 233–240 (2006)
3. Dimitropoulos, K., Barmpoutis, P., Grammalidis, N.: Spatio-temporal flame modeling and dynamic texture analysis for automatic video-based fire detection. IEEE Trans. Circ. Syst. Video Technol. **25**(2), 339–351 (2015)
4. Huang, J., Chaoxia, C.Y., Dong, X.Y., et al.: Faster R-CNN based color-guided flame detection. J. Comput. Appl. **40**(05), 1470–1475 (2020)
5. Zhao, F.Y., Luo, B., Lin, G.J., et al.: Flame detection based on improved YOLOv3. China Sciencepaper **15**(07), 820–826 (2020)
6. Muhammad, K., Ahmad, J., Mehmood, I., et al.: Convolutional neural networks based fire detection in surveillance videos. IEEE Access **2018**, 18174–8183 (2018)
7. Zhang, X.L., Hou, D.B., Zhang, C.C., et al.: Design of MPCANet fire image recognition model for deep learning. Infrared Laser Eng. **47**(02), 49–54 (2018)
8. Wang, X., Girshick, R., Gupta, A., He, K.: Non-local neural networks. In: Proceedings of the CVPR, pp. 7794–7803 (2018)
9. Dosovitskiy, A., et al.: An image is worth 16x16 words: transformers for image recognition at scale. arXiv preprint arXiv:2010.11929 (2020)
10. Li, Y, Zhang, K., Cao, J., et al.: LocalViT: bringing locality to vision transformers. arXiv:2104.05707
11. Wang, W., et al.: Pyramid vision transformer: a versatile backbone for dense prediction without convolutions. In: Proceedings of the ICCV, pp. 568–578 (2021)
12. Liu, Z., et al.: Swin transformer: hierarchical vision transformer using shifted windows. In: Proceedings of ICCV, pp. 10012–10022 (2021)
13. Carion, Nicolas, Massa, Francisco, Synnaeve, Gabriel, Usunier, Nicolas, Kirillov, Alexander, Zagoruyko, Sergey: End-to-end object detection with transformers. In: Vedaldi, Andrea, Bischof, Horst, Brox, Thomas, Frahm, Jan-Michael. (eds.) ECCV 2020. LNCS, vol. 12346, pp. 213–229. Springer, Cham (2020). https://doi.org/10.1007/978-3-030-58452-8_13
14. Zhu, X., Su, W., Lu, L., Li, B., Wang, D., Dai, J.: Deformable DETR: deformable transformers for end-to-end object detection. In: Proceeding of ICLR (2021)
15. Shahid, M., Hua, K.-L.: Fire detection using transformer network. In: Proceeding of ICMR, pp. 627–630 (2021)

16. Ghali, R., Akhloufi, M.A., Jmal, M., Souidene Mseddi, W., Attia, R.: Wildfire segmentation using deep vision transformers. Remote Sens. **13**, 3527 (2021). https:// doi.org/10.3390/rs13173527'

17. Mehta, S., Rastegari, M.: MobileViT: light-weight, general-purpose, and mobile-friendly vision transformer. arXiv:2110.02178

18. Sandler, M., Howard, A., Zhu, M., Zhmoginov, A., Chen, L.-C.: Mobilenetv 2: inverted residuals and linear bottlenecks. In: Proceedings of the IEEE Conference on Computer Vision and Pattern Recognition, pp. 4510–4520 (2018)

19. Howard, A., et al.: Searching for mobilenetv3. In: Proceedings of the ICCV, pp. 1314–324 (2019)

20. Hu, J., Shen, L., Sun, G.: Squeeze-and-excitation networks. In: Proceedings of the IEEE Conference on Computer Vision and Pattern Recognition, pp. 7132–7141 (2018)

21. Wang, W., et al.: PVT v2: improved baselines with pyramid vision transformer. arXiv:2106.13797 (2021)

22. Vaswani, A., et al.: Attention is all you need. In: Proceedings of the Advances in Neural Information Processing System (2017)

23. Ba, J.L., Kiros, J.R., Hinton, G.E.: Layer normalization. arXiv preprint arXiv:1607.06450 (2016)

24. Hendrycks, D., Gimpel, K.: Gaussian Error Linear Units (GELUs). arXiv:1606.08415

25. He, K., Zhang, X., Ren, S., Sun, J.: Spatial pyramid pooling in deep convolutional networks for visual recognition. IEEE Trans. Patt. Analy. Mach. Intell. **37**(9), 1904–1916 (2015)

26. Tan, M., Pang, R., Le, Q.V.: EfficientDet: scalable and efficient object detection. In: Proceedings of the IEEE Conference on Computer Vision and Pattern Recognition (CVPR) (2020)

27. Redmon, J., Farhadi, A.: YOLOv3: an incremental improvement. arXiv preprint arXiv:1804.02767 (2018)

28. Alexey, B., Wang, C.Y., Liao, H.Y.: YOLOv4: optimal speed and accuracy of object detection. arXiv:2004.10934v1 (2004)

# DeepArtist: A Dual-Stream Network for Painter Classification of Highly-Varying Image Resolutions

Doron Nevo[✉], Eli O. David, and Nathan S. Netanyahu

Department of Computer Science, Bar-Ilan University, 5290002 Ramat-Gan, Israel
doron_nevo@hotmail.com, mail@elidavid.com, nathan@cs.biu.ac.il

**Abstract.** Painter classification is a well-researched problem, which has been pursued mainly during the past two decades via traditional approaches of image processing and machine learning. In this paper, we propose a novel *dual-stream architecture* designed for capturing in parallel both global elements (*e.g.*, scenery) and local structures (*e.g.*, brushstrokes) in images of highly-varying resolutions and aspect ratios. Our proposed method yields 93.39% accuracy, which comprises an improvement of 1.66% (and an error rate reduction of 20%), compared to the previous state-of-the-art (SOTA) method on the same extensive dataset.

**Keywords:** Image classification · Convolutional neural networks · Digital humanities

## 1 Introduction

Over the past two decades, the transfer of art work to a digital environment has increased significantly, and digital collections have been made available across the Internet. With such massive collections of digital artworks, automated painting analysis has become essential in assisting curators in their daily work routine.

Painter classification is especially challenging due to rather small amounts of training data; furthermore, classification of a multi-style artist is harder than that of a single-style artist. In the last two centuries, many painters experimented with several styles (*e.g.*, Picasso painted over 760 paintings in more than 10 different styles). As a result, the number of an artist's paintings per style can be rather small (*e.g.*, Picasso produced just 21 Impressionist paintings and 15 paintings in Art Nouveau). Painter classification is all the more challenging, as the number of paintings of most artists from earlier periods is even smaller.

Nathan Netanyahu is also affiliated with the Department of Computer Science at the College of Law and Business, Ramat-Gan 5257346, Israel.

D. Nevo—The support of the Israeli Innovation Authority and Defender Cyber Technologies LTD under File No. 69098 of the NOFAR *Academic Knowledge Guidance Program* is gratefully acknowledged.

E. Pimenidis et al. (Eds.): ICANN 2022, LNCS 13532, pp. 582–593, 2022.
https://doi.org/10.1007/978-3-031-15937-4_49

While many works use *transfer learning* and *data augmentation* to overcome the issue of small datasets, one needs to consider also the highly-varying resolutions and aspect ratios of the image dataset. Resizing merely all images to the same dimensions results in severe degradation of image proportionality and texture, which could have a negative impact on the classification accuracy.

To overcome (both issues of small datasets and) highly-variable image resolutions and aspect ratios, we pursue in this work a novel *dual-stream architecture* designed for a set of digital artworks, which achieves 93.39% accuracy, *i.e.*, a 1.66% improvement (or a 20% error reduction), compared to the previous state-of-the-art (SOTA) method, trained and tested on the same extended dataset (to be described).

## 2    Background

Painter classification is the task of determining the artist of a given painting (from a certain group of artists). The input consists of several painting images of each artist, and the objective is to automatically classify a given painting to the artist. One of the challenges in solving this problem is to define a specialized set of rules that the painting has to conform to, in order to classify it to the subgroup of the correct artist. Thus, basic computer vision (CV) techniques, capable of identifying shapes and objects in an image, may not be sufficiently effective for solving the problem.

### 2.1    Early Painting Classification

Formerly there have been attempts to harness the strength of image analysis tools to classify historical art paintings into categories of artists or genres.

Kroner and Lattner [11] classified drawings by using image histograms and pattern recognition methods. Herik and Postma [6] surveyed image features relevant to the historic art domain, and concluded that neural network (NN) techniques combined with domain knowledge were most suitable for the task of automatic painter classification. Natural language processing (NLP) techniques, using a naive-Bayes classifier and the coefficients of a discrete cosine transform (DCT), were used by Keren [9] to classify local features in an image. Under-drawing strokes in infrared reflectograms were analyzed by Kammerer *et al.* [7] in order to classify how and by what tools paintings are painted. Shamir *et al.* [18] used various types of image descriptors to identify useful visual features for artist recognition, given paintings of three different styles.

Levy *et al.* [13,14] applied feature extraction to paintings using generic image processing (IP) operators (e.g., fractal dimension, Fourier spectra coefficients, texture coefficients, etc.). They also employed a restricted Boltzmann machine (RBM), followed by a genetic algorithm (GA)-based learning of the weights of a weighted nearest neighbor classifier. Their approach achieved 90.44% classification accuracy on a self-generated digital collection of Rembrandt, Renoir, and van Gogh paintings.

## 2.2    CNN-Based Extraction of Painting Features

*Convolutional neural networks* (CNNs) have been frequently employed as typical features extractors. For example, Bar *et al.* [1] utilized a pre-trained CNN model on ImageNet [16] to extract specialized features and fuse them with additional low-level descriptors, such as PiCoDes [2].

Karayev *et al.* [8] extended the "target domain" from merely fine-art paintings to images, in general, including but not limited to, landscape and portrait photography, in order to recognize image style in a more generic sense. Target labels encompass atmospheric terms to describe images (*e.g.,* sunny), color (*e.g.,* pastel), intensity (*e.g.,* bright), cinematic terms (*e.g.,* noir, vintage, romantic), etc. Their research is motivated by the potential practicality in visual tools (*e.g.,* style), by capturing similarities of various visual elements (*e.g.,* intensity, color, pattern, etc.).

Saleh and Elgammal [17] introduced a shallow CNN as a feature extractor coupled with one-versus-all support vector machine (SVM) artist and style classifiers. They trained their model on the WikiArt dataset [15] extract, consisting of 19,050 images from 23 artists, and achieved 63.06% accuracy on the designated test set.

Note that in the above studies CNN models were used for feature extraction only, since their use as classifiers was not common practice at that time.

**Table 1.** Comparative classification rates due to different methods

| Reference | Method | # of Paintings | Acc. [%] |
|---|---|---|---|
| Saleh et al. '15 [17] | Feature fusion & SVM | 19,050 | 68.25 |
| Tan et al. '16 [20] | CNN fine-tuning (AlexNet) | 19,050 | 76.11 |
| Cetinic et al. '18 [3] | CNN fine-tuning (CaffeNet) | 19,050 | 81.94 |
| Zhong et al. '20 [23] | 2-Channel dual path (ResNet131) | 9,766 | 88.38 |
| Zhao et al. '21 [22] | EfficientNet | 19,050 | 91.73 |

## 2.3    CNN-Based Painter Classification

Transfer learning has become a key element in deep learning (DL)-based CV. Its objective is to transfer knowledge acquired by a model that has been trained on some large dataset to a smaller dataset of a target problem. The technique is especially useful where there is a lack of training data. The smaller the distance between the source and target domains, the better performance on the new task (see, *e.g.* Yosinski *et al.* [21]).

Tan *et al.* [20] used AlexNet [10] as a pre-trained CNN on ImageNet for style, genre, and artist classification. Their study compared the effect of transfer learning with fine-tuning. Specifically, they showed that transfer learning leads to better generalization when working with datasets of limited size, and that its combination with fine-tuned parameters results in further improvement. They

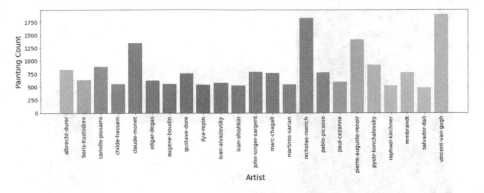

**Fig. 1.** Number of paintings per artist in WikiArt subset, which consists of 19,050 paintings from 23 artists; artist classes are highly unbalanced.

trained on the WikiArt extract, consisting of 19,050 images from 23 artists, and achieved 76.11% accuracy on the designated test set.

David and Netanyahu [4] pursued a different approach to address the issue of small training data. Instead of using ImageNet as in above study, they introduced a novel unsupervised training using a deep convolutional auto-encoder (CAE) network and trained it on a small dataset of 5000 paintings images (retrieved from the WebMuseum collection). The learned parameters (weights) of the CAE were used to initiate a CNN classifier. They achieved 96.52% accuracy on the 3-painter classification problem involving 3×40 paintings downloaded from the WebMuseum. Their approach underscored the importance of the data domain used for pre-training, $i.e.$, using "artistic" data, in this case, enabled effective pre-training on relatively small datasets.

Lecoutre $et\ al.$ [12] extended the work of Tan $et\ al.$ [20], using a residual neural network (ResNet) architecture. They investigated the optimal number of layers required for style classification. Also, they demonstrated the effectiveness of transfer learning by comparing models retrained from a pre-trained network and models trained from scratch on painting data. Specifically, a model optimized for object classification (on ImageNet) produced superior results to a model whose weights were initialized at random, regardless of the layers the weights were copied from. Likewise, their study supported the argument that the two learning tasks were related, since the features of the former contributed to the target task.

Cetnik $et\ al.$ [3] used CafeNet (a variant of AlexNet), and tuned the training by using, for example, a non-constant learning rate and by skipping the first convolutional layer, to improve previous SOTA results. Training was performed on the WikiArt extract experimented previously by Tan $et\ al.$ [20], and their model achieved 81.94% accuracy on the designated test set.

Elgammal $et\ al.$ [5] studied the similarities between art style classification and object recognition. They employed a similar transfer learning technique to that of Lecoutre $et\ al.$ [12], combining the top dense layers of a baseline model

**Fig. 2.** Four paintings by Picasso, in super resolution (5472 × 3648), low resolution (380 × 307), landscape orientation (443 × 1113) and portrait orientation (1088 × 427). All paintings are in the public domain (courtesy wikiart.org); images are shown in different scale.

with various additional high-level image object features. Their improved results suggested that transferability was also applicable to the high-level features used. In addition, they observed that deeper models provided only marginal precision gain against shallower ones, at the sacrifice of additional computational time resources, due to the use of additional high-level object features.

Zhong *et al.* [23] pointed out that similarly to handwriting, an artist can be identified by their unique brush stroke technique. Therefore, they proposed a dual path classification scheme of 131-layer networks; one for color (RGB) information (as with a conventional CNN), and the other for brush strokes information, captured initially by the four-directional gray-level co-occurrence matrix (GLCM). Training was done on the WikiArt extract containing 9,766 images from 19 artists, and testing resulted in 88.38% accuracy on the test set. (This benchmark was thus non-applicable, as all other works compared against used 19,050 images from 23 artists.) A drawback of their dual path architecture is that it is based on the same resized input image, which implies loss of original information required for accurate local structure representation.

Recently, Zhao *et al.* [22] used the EfficientNet architecture [19], which provided top results on standard image classification benchmarks. Training was performed on the same WikiArt extract of 19,050 images from 23 artists, and their model achieved 91.73% accuracy on the designated test set.

Table 1 summarizes the comparative performance of the above key models with state-of-the-art results. Four of the models used the same WikiArt dataset as we do.

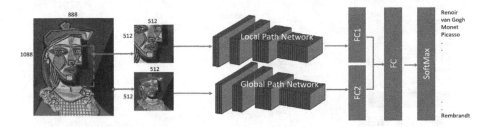

**Fig. 3.** Dual input stream architecture; all paintings are in the public domain (courtesy wikiart.org).

# 3    Proposed Method

## 3.1    The WikiArt Dataset

We adopted the WikiArt dataset by wikiart.org, the largest online fine-art painting collection available in the public domain for educational use. The dataset consists of more than 250,000 artworks by 3,000 artists. To ensure a fair comparison with other models, we adopted the very same wikiart subset used in [3,17,20,22] for our study. The subset consists of 19,050 paintings from 23 artists, and can be found on github.com/cs-chan/ArtGAN. Figure 1 depicts the number of paintings per artist in the subset. Note that the classes are highly unbalanced (*e.g.*, there are 1,888 paintings by van Gogh, compared to only 585 paintings by Cezanne). A 70-30 split between training and testing was applied.

## 3.2    Local Structures and Global Elements of a Painting

An artist can be recognized by a combination of local structures (*e.g.*, brushstrokes, texture, blurriness, etc.) and global elements, such as scenery (*e.g.*, cityscape, landscape, abstract, etc.). To exploit these elements effectively, we need to consider that digital representations of paintings often result in highly-varying resolutions and aspect ratios. For example, Fig. 2 shows four paintings of Picasso in super resolution ($5472 \times 3648$) low resolution ($380 \times 307$), landscape orientation ($443 \times 1113$), and portrait orientation ($1088 \times 427$).

## 3.3    Network Architecture

There are two main approaches for handling image datasets of highly-varying resolutions:

1. Resize the images to some fixed size (*e.g.*, $512 \times 512$ pixels). This has two drawbacks; first, the original aspect ratio of the image is lost, causing a distortion. Secondly, fine details such as texture may be degraded, especially in high-resolution images.

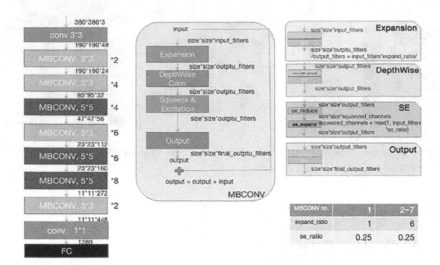

**Fig. 4.** EfficientNet-B4 architecture, based on inverted bottleneck residual blocks (MBConvs), for image models with inverted structure for efficiency. Source: [24].

2. Use, alternatively, a *fully convolutional network* (FCN), which preserves the image dimensions. A serious drawback is that training would require, in this case, a very large amount of resources, which would make it impractical. For example, the super-resolution $5472 \times 3648$ image (in Fig. 2) would require a very large amount of GPU memory allocated to parameter storage utilized along the forward and backward paths of the automatic differentiation engine during network training. (Note that our actual model, which handles only input images of $512 \times 512$ pixels, already utilizes 15 GB GPU memory.) Batch training is not feasible either, in this case, as it would require input images of the same size, or training with a trivial batch size of 1, which would result in a highly-computational GPU load.

To alleviate the above difficulties, we propose a new architecture composed of two (identical) convolutional networks, each having its own weights (see Fig. 3). The two networks, based on Google's EfficientNet model [19] pre-trained on ImageNet, realize the following input streams (Fig. 4):

1. **Local Path Network:** This network inputs a $512 \times 512$ center cropped patch (from the original image without any resizing), and learns the local structures contained in the subimage. It outputs a feature vector representing these local structures. (We picked the above dimensions as a tradeoff between subimage size and memory constraints.)

2. **Global Path Network:** Similarly to Zhao *et al.*, this network inputs the entire image resized to $512 \times 512$ pixels, and learns the global elements

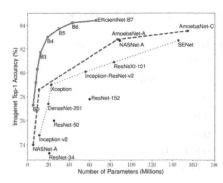

| | Top1 Acc. | #Params |
|---|---|---|
| ResNet-152 (He et al., 2016) | 77.8% | 60M |
| **EfficientNet-B1** | **79.1%** | **7.8M** |
| ResNeXt-101 (Xie et al., 2017) | 80.9% | 84M |
| **EfficientNet-B3** | **81.6%** | **12M** |
| SENet (Hu et al., 2018) | 82.7% | 146M |
| NASNet-A (Zoph et al., 2018) | 82.7% | 89M |
| **EfficientNet-B4** | **82.9%** | **19M** |
| GPipe (Huang et al., 2018) [†] | 84.3% | 556M |
| **EfficientNet-B7** | **84.3%** | **66M** |

[†]Not plotted

**Fig. 5.** ImageNet accuracy vs. model size for different networks. Source: [19].

contained in the image. It outputs a feature vector representing these global elements.

Our approach is advantageous over that of Zhong *et al.* [23], as it is based on two input streams originated from two sources (Fig. 3), each with a different resolution, while their dual-path architecture is based on the same resized source image. This difference helps to reduce information loss, thereby obtaining a higher classification accuracy. In addition, our architecture backbone is based on a modern EfficientNet variant, which provides better general classification, compared to that obtained with a ResNet131-based backbone.

Similarly, the added value of our approach with respect to that of Zhao *et al.* [22], is the capability of learning *in parallel* local structures directly from the original, unresized image, as well as global features from the resized image.

**EfficientNet Architecture.** The EfficientNet model [19] shown in Fig. 4 is based on a CNN architecture and a uniform scaling method. Unlike conventional practice, where network parameters, such as depth, width, and resolution, are scaled arbitrarily, the EfficientNet scaling method uniformly scales such network parameters with a set of fixed scaling coefficients. The compound scaling method is justified by the intuition that for a larger input image the network requires additional layers to increase the receptive field and additional channels to capture more fine-grained patterns in the larger image.

The EfficientNet network is based on the notion of *inverted bottleneck residual block* (known as an MBConv block), which is a type of residual block used for image models that uses an inverted structure for efficiency purposes. See https://paperswithcode.com/method/efficientnet, for a more detailed description of EfficientNet's architecture. The added value of EfficientNet-B4, as illustrated in Fig. 5 [19], is that it provides the best tradeoff between performance and required resources (*i.e.,* the number of model parameters).

**Table 2.** Classification summary for test set of WikiArt extract

| Painter | Precision | Recall | $F_1$-score | Support |
|---|---|---|---|---|
| Albrecht Durer | 0.967 | 0.952 | 0.959 | 248 |
| Boris Kustodiev | 0.892 | 0.921 | 0.906 | 189 |
| Camille Pissarro | 0.913 | 0.902 | 0.907 | 266 |
| Childe Hassam | 0.945 | 0.939 | 0.942 | 165 |
| Claude Monet | 0.968 | 0.910 | 0.938 | 402 |
| Edgar Degas | 0.964 | 0.870 | 0.914 | 184 |
| Eugene Boudin | 0.859 | 0.994 | 0.922 | 166 |
| Gustave Dore | 0.978 | 0.982 | 0.980 | 225 |
| Ilya Repin | 0.812 | 0.832 | 0.822 | 161 |
| Ivan Aivazovsky | 0.971 | 0.971 | 0.971 | 173 |
| Ivan Shishkin | 0.937 | 0.955 | 0.946 | 155 |
| John Singer Sargent | 0.852 | 0.936 | 0.892 | 234 |
| Marc Chagall | 0.973 | 0.947 | 0.960 | 228 |
| Martiros Saryan | 0.876 | 0.928 | 0.901 | 167 |
| Nicholas Roerich | 0.969 | 0.923 | 0.945 | 545 |
| Pablo Picasso | 0.938 | 0.864 | 0.900 | 228 |
| Paul Cezanne | 0.914 | 0.909 | 0.912 | 176 |
| Pierre Auguste Renoir | 0.959 | 0.948 | 0.953 | 420 |
| Pyotr Konchalovsky | 0.953 | 0.953 | 0.953 | 275 |
| Raphael Kirchner | 0.956 | 0.987 | 0.971 | 154 |
| Rembrandt | 0.921 | 0.961 | 0.941 | 231 |
| Salvador Dali | 0.878 | 0.853 | 0.865 | 143 |
| Vincent van Gogh | 0.937 | 0.973 | 0.955 | 566 |
| Accuracy | | | **0.934** | 5701 |
| Macro Avg. | 0.928 | 0.931 | 0.929 | 5701 |
| Weighted Avg. | 0.935 | 0.934 | 0.934 | 5701 |

## 4  Experimental Results

We have conducted various empirical studies to learn simultaneously both local structures and global elements of labeled artworks, separately.

To enlarge the dataset, each of the two networks was first pre-trained on ImageNet. After cropping for the local structures path and resizing for the global elements path, we then applied the following augmentations, yielding eight times as many training samples. (The augmentation results in a relative gain of 1% accuracy.)

**Table 3.** 5-fold cross-validation evaluation

| Painter | Support | Run 1 | Run 2 | Run 3 | Run 4 | Run 5 | Avg. | StD |
|---|---|---|---|---|---|---|---|---|
| Albrecht Durer | 110 | 0.930 | 0.950 | 0.943 | 0.943 | 0.949 | 0.943 | 0.007 |
| Boris Kustodiev | 152 | 0.957 | 0.964 | 0.955 | 0.951 | 0.944 | 0.954 | 0.006 |
| Camille Pissarro | 96 | 0.867 | 0.890 | 0.806 | 0.840 | 0.880 | 0.857 | 0.028 |
| Childe Hassam | 104 | 0.977 | 0.958 | 0.961 | 0.951 | 0.962 | 0.962 | 0.008 |
| Claude Monet | 118 | 0.915 | 0.936 | 0.929 | 0.936 | 0.942 | 0.932 | 0.008 |
| Edgar Degas | 154 | 0.890 | 0.882 | 0.852 | 0.891 | 0.893 | 0.882 | 0.014 |
| Eugene Boudin | 376 | 0.953 | 0.957 | 0.943 | 0.962 | 0.954 | 0.954 | 0.006 |
| Gustave Dore | 110 | 0.922 | 0.943 | 0.932 | 0.957 | 0.969 | 0.945 | 0.015 |
| Ilya Repin | 107 | 0.840 | 0.910 | 0.830 | 0.824 | 0.910 | 0.863 | 0.035 |
| Ivan Aivazovsky | 184 | 0.967 | 0.936 | 0.972 | 0.957 | 0.967 | 0.960 | 0.012 |
| Ivan Shishkin | 268 | 0.944 | 0.947 | 0.940 | 0.946 | 0.954 | 0.946 | 0.004 |
| John Singer Sargent | 104 | 0.943 | 0.931 | 0.922 | 0.946 | 0.971 | 0.943 | 0.015 |
| Marc Chagall | 124 | 0.885 | 0.922 | 0.897 | 0.945 | 0.915 | 0.913 | 0.019 |
| Martiros Sarian | 280 | 0.957 | 0.954 | 0.964 | 0.946 | 0.961 | 0.956 | 0.006 |
| Nicholas Roerich | 158 | 0.940 | 0.909 | 0.930 | 0.936 | 0.913 | 0.926 | 0.011 |
| Pablo Picasso | 364 | 0.955 | 0.956 | 0.954 | 0.965 | 0.975 | 0.961 | 0.007 |
| Paul Cezanne | 166 | 0.956 | 0.933 | 0.961 | 0.953 | 0.970 | 0.955 | 0.011 |
| Pierre Auguste Renoir | 115 | 0.964 | 0.996 | 0.974 | 0.969 | 0.974 | 0.975 | 0.010 |
| Pyotr Konchalovsky | 126 | 0.878 | 0.881 | 0.864 | 0.875 | 0.933 | 0.886 | 0.022 |
| Raphael Kirchner | 154 | 0.962 | 0.944 | 0.952 | 0.946 | 0.955 | 0.952 | 0.006 |
| Rembrandt | 110 | 0.932 | 0.921 | 0.920 | 0.905 | 0.917 | 0.919 | 0.008 |
| Salvador Dali | 152 | 0.974 | 0.960 | 0.977 | 0.987 | 0.980 | 0.976 | 0.008 |
| Vincent van Gogh | 178 | 0.907 | 0.911 | 0.893 | 0.915 | 0.910 | 0.907 | 0.007 |
| Accuracy | | 0.937 | 0.938 | 0.932 | 0.939 | 0.947 | **0.939** | |
| StD | | 0.036 | 0.028 | 0.046 | 0.040 | 0.028 | | |

1. Apply an affine transformation with a randomly selected rotation in the range [−45, +45] degrees and random horizontal and vertical shifts (of up to 0.2 of the image dimensions), with respect to the image center;
2. Apply at random a horizontal flip with 50% probability;
3. Similarly, apply at random a vertical flip with 50% probability.

We used the Adam optimizer with an initial rate of 1E–4 and a ReduceLROnPlateau learning rate scheduling with a reduction factor of 0.5, up to a minimal learning rate of 1E–6. An early stopping criterion of five epochs without improvement was applied.

We ran the model over 25 epochs with early stopping in epoch 21, and obtained 93.39% accuracy on the designated test set. This comprises a 1.66% precision improvement compared to the previous SOTA (by Zhao *et al.* [22]), *i.e.*, a 20% decrease in error rate (from 8.73% to 6.61%). Table 2 below summarizes the precision, recall, and $F_1$-score values for the designated test set. (The support column consists of 5,701 images, which comprise 30% of the dataset.) The scores (for each artist) are based on the number of correctly classified images (of the painter) versus ground truth over all of the painter's images. Note that for some individual artists (*e.g.*, Ilya Repin and Salvador Dali), the scores obtained are significantly smaller than those for most of the other painters. This deviation will be investigated as part of future research.

To further establish our model's validity, we applied a 5-fold cross-validation (CV) on the 19,050-image dataset. Specifically, the dataset was split randomly into five equal folds, four of which were used for training and the fifth for testing, for each run. Using the same set of hyperparameters as before, we obtained the following average precision values (and standard deviations). See Table 3.

## 5   Conclusions

In this paper, we presented a novel approach for painter classification. Specifically, we presented a dual-input stream architecture designed for a set of images, such as digital artworks, of highly-varying resolutions and aspect ratios, that achieves state-of-the-art results, compared to previous studies.

Our future work will focus on establishing further the enhanced performance of our proposed model by introducing *e.g.,* new augmentation techniques and new architectures. Moreover, we intend to explore additional domains, which are also characterized by datasets of multiple image resolutions and where the classification also depends on both global elements and local structures. An example for such a domain could be tree classification, where global elements correspond to the shape of the tree, and local structures correspond to leaf structures and trunk texture.

## References

1. Bar, Y., Levy, N., Wolf, L.: Classification of artistic styles using Binarized features derived from a deep neural network. In: Agapito, L., Bronstein, M.M., Rother, C. (eds.) ECCV 2014. LNCS, vol. 8925, pp. 71–84. Springer, Cham (2015). https://doi.org/10.1007/978-3-319-16178-5_5
2. Bergamo, A., Torresani, L., Fitzgibbon, A.: PiCoDes: learning a compact code for novel-category recognition. In: Proceedings of the Annual Conference on Advances in Neural Information Processing Systems, vol. 24, pp. 2088–2096 (2011)
3. Cetinic, E., Lipic, T., Grgic, S.: Fine-tuning convolutional neural networks for fine art classification. Exp. Syst. Appl. **114**, 107–118 (2018)
4. David, E., Netanyahu, N.: DeepPainter: Painter classification using deep convolutional autoencoders. In: Proceedings of the ENNS International Conference on Artificial Neural Networks. pp. 20–28 (2016)
5. Elgammal, A., Mazzone, M., Liu, B., Kim, D., Elhoseiny, M.: The shape of art history in the eyes of the machine. arXiv: 1801.07729 (2018)
6. van den Herik, H., Postma, E.: Discovering the visual signature of painters. In: Kasabov, N. (ed.) Future Directions for Intelligent Systems and Information Sciences, pp. 129–147. Springer-Verlag, Heidelberg (2000). https://doi.org/10.1007/978-3-7908-1856-7_7

7. Kammerer, P., Lettner, M., Zolda, E., Sablatnig, R.: Identification of drawing tools by classification of textural and boundary features of strokes. Pattern Recogn. Lett. **28**(6), 710–718 (2007)
8. Karayev, S., Hertzmann, A., Winnemoeller, H., Agarwala, A., Darrell, T.: Recognizing image style. arXiv:1311.3715 (2013)
9. Keren, D.: Painter identification using local features and naive bayes. In: Proceedings of the IEEE International Conference on Pattern Recognition, vol. 2, pp. 474–477 (2002)
10. Krizhevsky, A., Sutskever, I., Hinton, G.: ImageNet classification with deep convolutional neural networks. Commun. ACM **60**(6), 84–90 (2017)
11. Kroner, S., Lattner, A.: Authentication of free hand drawings by pattern recognition methods. In: Proceedings of the Fourteenth International Conference on Pattern Recognition. vol. 1, pp. 462–464 (1998)
12. Lecoutre, A., Negrevergne, B., Yger, F.: Recognizing art style automatically in painting with deep learning. In: Proceedings of the Ninth Asian Conference on Machine Learning. vol. 77, pp. 327–342 (2017)
13. Levy, E., David, E., Netanyahu, N.: Painter classification using genetic algorithms. In: Proceedings of the IEEE Congress on Evolutionary Computation, pp. 3027–3034 (2013)
14. Levy, E., David, E., Netanyahu, N.: Genetic algorithms and deep learning for automatic painter classification. In: Proceedings of the ACM Annual Conference on Genetic and Evolutionary Computation, pp. 1143–1150 (2014)
15. Pirrone, R., Cannella, V., Gambino, O., Pipitone, A., Russo, G.: WikiArt: an ontology-based information retrieval system for arts. In: Proceedings of the 2009 Ninth International Conference on Intelligent Systems Design and Applications, pp. 913–918 (2009)
16. Russakovsky, O., et al.: ImageNet large scale visual recognition challenge. Int. J. Comput. Vis. **115**(3), 211–252 (2015)
17. Saleh, B., Elgammal, A.: Large-scale classification of fine-art paintings: learning the right metric on the right feature. arXiv: 1505.00855 (2015)
18. Shamir, L., Macura, T., Orlov, N., Eckley, D., Goldberg, I.: Impressionism, expressionism, surrealism: automated recognition of painters and schools of art. ACM Trans. Appl. Percept. **7**(2), 1–17 (2010)
19. Tan, M., Le, Q.: EfficientNet: rethinking model scaling for convolutional neural networks. arXiv: 1905.11946 (2019)
20. Tan, W., Chan, C., Aguirre, H., Tanaka, K.: Ceci n'est pas une pipe: a deep convolutional network for fine-art paintings classification. In: Proceedings of the IEEE International Conference on Image Processing, pp. 3703–3707 (2016)
21. Yosinski, J., Clune, J., Bengio, Y., Lipson, H.: How transferable are features in deep neural networks? arXiv: 1411.1792 (2014)
22. Zhao, W., Zhou, D., Qiu, X., Jiang, W.: Compare the performance of the models in art classification. PLoS ONE **16**(3) (2021). https://doi.org/10.1371/journal.pone.0248414
23. Zhong, S., Huang, X., Xiao, Z.: Fine-art painting classification via two-channel dual path networks. Int. J. Mach. Learn. Cybern. **11**(1), 137–152 (2019). https://doi.org/10.1007/s13042-019-00963-0
24. Zhu, C., et al.: A deep learning based framework for diagnosing multiple skin diseases in a clinical environment. Front. Med. **8** (2021). https://doi.org/10.3389/fmed.2021.626369

# Dual Branch Network Towards Accurate Printed Mathematical Expression Recognition

Yuqing Wang(ID), Zhenyu Weng(ID), Zhaokun Zhou, Shuaijian Ji, Zhongjie Ye,
and Yuesheng Zhu(✉)(ID)

Communication and Information Security Lab, Shenzhen Graduate School,
Peking University, Shenzhen, China
{wyq,zhouzhaokun,2101212809,zhongjieye}@stu.pku.edu.cn,
{wzytumbler,zhuys}@pku.edu.cn

**Abstract.** Over the past years, Printed Mathematical Expression Recognition (PMER) has progressed rapidly. However, due to the insufficient context information captured by Convolutional Neural Networks, some mathematical symbols might be incorrectly recognized or missed. To tackle this problem, in this paper, a Dual Branch transformer-based Network (DBN) is proposed to learn both local and global context information for accurate PMER. In our DBN, local and global features are extracted simultaneously, and a Context Coupling Module (CCM) is developed to complement the features between the global and local contexts. CCM adopts an interactive manner so that the coupled context clues are highly correlated to each expression symbol. Additionally, we design a Dynamic Soft Target (DST) strategy to utilize the similarities among symbol categories for reasonable label generation. Our experimental results have demonstrated that DBN can accurately recognize mathematical expressions and has achieved state-of-the-art performance.

**Keywords:** Context jointly modeling · Dynamic soft label · Mathematical expression recognition

## 1 Introduction

Mathematics expression understanding has received much attention from both academia and industry due to its numerous applications such as arithmetical exercise correction [7], student performance prediction [14], and automatic marking [16]. Deep neural networks have made dramatic advances over the past few years, resulting in many inspiring ideas [5,19,22]. However, there is still large room for improvement when facing expressions containing semantically-correlated symbols.

Mathematics expression recognition takes a mathematical expression image as input and transforms the image into the format of MathML or LaTeX

E. Pimenidis et al. (Eds.): ICANN 2022, LNCS 13532, pp. 594–606, 2022.
https://doi.org/10.1007/978-3-031-15937-4_50

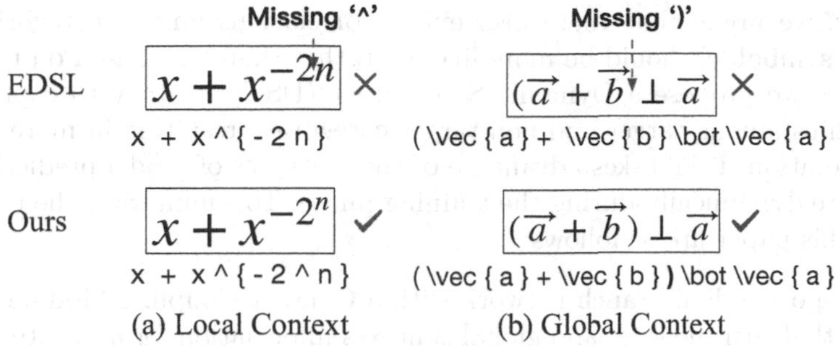

|  | Missing '^' | Missing ')' |
|---|---|---|
| EDSL | $x + x^{-2n}$ ✗ | $(\vec{a} + \vec{b} \perp \vec{a}$ ✗ |
|  | x + x ^ { - 2 n } | ( \vec { a } + \vec { b } \bot \vec { a } |
| Ours | $x + x^{-2^n}$ ✓ | $(\vec{a} + \vec{b}) \perp \vec{a}$ ✓ |
|  | x + x ^ { - 2 ^ n } | ( \vec { a } + \vec { b } ) \bot \vec { a } |
|  | (a) Local Context | (b) Global Context |

**Fig. 1.** The predicted LaTeX sequence from EDSL and our methods. We also rendered the predicted LaTeX sequence into images for better visualization. EDSL made some missing predictions while ours predictions are the correct results.

sequence. Due to the inherent complicated semantic correlation of the mathematical expression, learning the context information between symbols plays a crucial role in PMER. However, the context information captured by existing methods is still insufficient, which may result in suboptimal predictions. For example, EDSL [5], a representative transformer-based method which treats segmented symbols as image patches, will degrade when recognizing expressions containing semantically correlated symbols and result in incorrect results as depicted in Fig. 1. We argue that the reason is the insufficient context information which comes from two aspects: **1). Insufficient local context clues.** The symbol that determines the local spatial structure is highly related to its neighboring symbols, for instance, the exponent symbol '^' between the base number '2' and the exponent 'n', as depicted in Fig. 1(a). However, EDSL directly treats separated symbols as input, which destroys the local continuity between adjacent symbols and causes errors, as the missing exponent symbol depicted in Fig. 1(a). **2). Lack of global context information.** Symbols in expressions are also correlated to the global layout. For instance, the close parenthesis ')' usually appears with the open parenthesis '(', as shown in Fig. 1(b). However, EDSL neglects the context clues of the whole image, which only performs convolution on each local symbol. Even if the multi-head self-attention mechanism between local symbols can capture long-distance relationships, it fails to capture the context cross symbol boundary [20].

In this paper, we propose a novel Dual Branch Network, named DBN, to fully exploit the context information for accurate mathematical expression recognition. Specifically, DBN adopts a dual branch to simultaneously extract the local context of the symbol and the global context of the whole image. Moreover, we design a Context Coupling Module (CCM) to leverage the complementary advantages between the global and local contexts. CCM adopts an interactive manner so that the coupled context clues are highly correlated to each mathematical expression symbol. With CCM, our network is able to jointly reinforce local and global perception abilities, which is beneficial for recognizing mathematical expressions containing semantically-correlated symbols (e.g., paired braces).

Moreover, we argue that there also exists correlations among categories. For example, symbol 'c' should be more like 'C' rather than 'A'. Based on the analysis above, we propose a Dynamic Soft Target (DST) strategy to capture the relationships among target and non-target categories, resulting in more reliable label generation. DST takes advantage of the statistics of model prediction and can update dynamically during the training phase. To summarize, the contributions of this paper are as follows:

- We propose a dual branch network with a Context Coupling Module (CCM) to jointly learn the local and global contexts information for accurate PMER.
- We design a Dynamic Soft Target (DST) strategy to generate reliable target probability distribution by capturing the similarity among symbol categories.
- Extensive experiments prove that our proposed DBN has achieved state-of-the-art performance.

## 2    Related Work

The existing PMER methods can be classified into two categories: multi-stage methods and end-to-end methods.

The Multi-stage methods typically include two major steps: symbol recognition phase [10] and structural analysis phase [2]. The symbol recognition phase aims to determine the categories of symbols. The structural analysis is used to parse the symbols into a complete mathematical expression. Okamoto et al. [2] analyzed the expression by scanning each component and their relative positions. Moreover, [24] introduced a structure tree to describe the symbol and recognize expressions using tree transformation. However, multi-stage methods often require predefined expression grammar and suffer from symbol segmentation.

The end-to-end methods [5,19,22,27] often share an encoder-decoder architecture to recognize the expression. For example, WAP [27] proposed to use RNN equipped with an attention mechanism to generate LaTeX sequences. [4] introduced a coarse-to-fine attention layer to reduce the inference complexity. [23] adopted a GRU network to capture long-distance relationships. [26] proposed a multi-scale attention mechanism to recognize symbols in different scales. Despite the end-to-end design, the approach will still fall short when facing the mathematical expression containing semantically-correlated symbols.

## 3    Method

The pipeline of our proposed DBN is illustrated in Fig. 2, which follows an encoder-decoder architecture. The encoder includes two different branches: a local context branch extracts feature from local symbols, which are segmented from the given image by Connected-component labeling [12], and a global context branch extracts feature from the whole image. Then, a Context Coupling Module (CCM) is designed to couple the local and global contexts, as well as

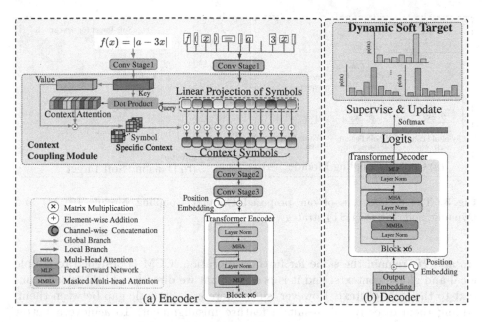

**Fig. 2.** The pipeline of our DBN. The inputs are the whole image and the symbol images segmented from the whole image by the Connected Component Labelling algorithm. Our DBN consists of an (a) encoder to extract image embeddings and a (b) decoder to parse the embeddings into LaTeX sequences. The encoder consists of a dual branch network to jointly learn the global and local context information, a Context Coupling Module (CCM) to couple the context clues for enriching context symbols, then a transformer-based encoder to extract symbol embeddings. The decoder transcribes the embeddings into a LaTeX sequence. Finally, the designed Dynamic Soft Target (DST) strategy updates label distribution for better supervision.

produce the enhanced context symbols. After that, the context symbols are sent to a transformer-based encoder to encode symbol tokens. Then, a decoder structure is used to decode the token features into a LaTeX sequence. Finally, the designed DST strategy uses model predictions as input and outputs more reliable label distributions at each training epoch to better supervise the model.

### 3.1 Context Coupling Module

In order to exploit both global image context and local symbol context, we propose a novel Context Coupling Module (CCM) to establish the correlative relationship between local and global contexts.

As illustrated in Fig. 3(a). The input of CCM is the global context extracted by the global branch, which is of shape $[C, H_0, W_0]$, and the local context extracted by the local branch, which is of shape $[C, H_1, W_1]$, where the $H_0, W_0$ and $H_1, W_1$ are the height and width of the global feature and local feature map, respectively. $C$ indicates the number of channels, set to 8, and the value of

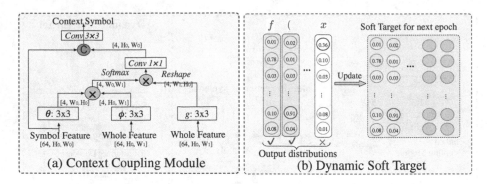

**Fig. 3.** The architecture of our proposed Context Coupling Module (CCM) and Dynamic Soft Target (DST) strategy.

$H_0$ and $H_1$ remain the same for further operation. CCM is designed to couple local and global contexts, and it is possible that we directly add the global context to the local context. However, since there is a semantic gap between them, adding them directly will result in feature misalignment. To achieve a better combination, we first align the global features with local features, given by:

$$\mathbf{y}_i = \frac{1}{\mathcal{C}(\mathbf{L})} \sum_{\forall j} f\left(\mathbf{L}_i, \mathbf{G}_j\right) g\left(\mathbf{G}_j\right)^T \qquad (1)$$

Here $\mathbf{L}$ is the local context of the symbol, and $\mathbf{G}$ is the global context of the whole image. $g$ computes a representation of the global context. $f$ is a pairwise function that interactively computes the relationship weight between $i$ and $j$. The relationship is used to reweight the global context information for feature alignment. The output feature $y$ is of the same size as $\mathbf{L}$. Finally, $y$ is normalized by a factor $\mathcal{C}(\mathbf{L})$, which is the feature dimension of local context $\mathbf{L}$. In this paper, function $f$ is formulated as:

$$f\left(\mathbf{L}_i, \mathbf{G}_j\right) = Softmax(\theta\left(\mathbf{L}_i\right)^T \phi\left(\mathbf{G}_j\right)) \qquad (2)$$

Here, we firstly learn a function $\theta$ that maps $\mathbf{L}$ into new representation, and $\Phi$ maps $\mathbf{G}$ into new representation. Then, we serve local context information as the query, and global information as key, to compute the relationship between local and global representation by matrix multiplication, followed by a Softmax function to normalize them into range $[0, 1]$. The relationship can reflect the correlation between the local symbol context and the global image context, ensuring that the aligned global context $y$ is highly correlated to each symbol.

Finally, we concatenate the aligned global context $y$ with the local context $\mathbf{L}$, and warp CCM into a block operation that can be incorporated into many existing architectures, given by:

$$\mathbf{z}_i = Conv_{1\times1}[\mathbf{L}_i, \mathbf{y}_i] \qquad (3)$$

where $z_i$ represents the output enhanced context symbols. $[\cdot, \cdot]$ denotes channel-wise concatenation, followed by a $1 \times 1$ convolution layer to improve representation.

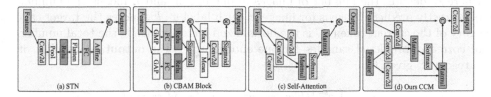

**Fig. 4.** Previous solutions for feature enhancement. (a) STN [8] explicitly predicted important regions. (b) CBAM [18] implicitly calculates the focus region for feature enhancement. (c) Self-attention mechanism [17]. (d) The proposed CCM builds a bridge between local features and global features for more information propagation. Notes: GAP (global average pooling), GMP (global max pooling), Mean (channel-wise mean operation), Max (channel-wise max operation).

Through CCM, we can better align and couple the global image context with the local symbol context, ensuring that more context information gets passed into the model. Moreover, compared with previous solutions in Fig. 4(a–c), which only utilize one branch feature for feature enhancement, our CCM can utilize two branches feature to perceive context information. We also conduct ablation studies to compare our CCM with previous solutions and discuss which convolution stage to add CCM operation in Sect. 4.2.

### 3.2 DST Strategy

Label Smoothing [15] is commonly used in PMER, which can generate soft labels by averaging over hard labels and uniform label distributions. Although such soft labels can provide regularization to prevent network over-fitting, it treats the non-target categories equally by assigning them with fixed probability. However, the non-target categories may convey useful information. For example, symbol 'c' should be more like 'C' rather than 'A'. According to knowledge distillation [6], the model predictions can reflect the similarities between categories. Inspired by [25], we use model predictions to capture the relationship among categories and update the soft labels during the training phase, as shown in Fig. 3(b).

Specifically, let $S = \{S^0, S^1, \ldots, S^{T-1}\}$ denote the collection of the class-level soft labels, and $T$ represents the number of training epochs. $S^t$ has $K$ rows and $K$ columns, where $K$ is the total number of categories, and each column in $S^t$ corresponds to the soft label for one category. In the $t$ th training epoch, given an input image $x_i$, and its ground truth $y_i = < y_i^1, y_i^2, \ldots, y_i^l >$, where $l$ means $l$-th target token in LaTeX sequence. We sum up all the distributions of correctly predicted samples to generate the soft target $S_k^{t-1}$ from $t-1$ epoch:

$$S_k^{t-1} = \frac{1}{C} \sum_{i=1}^{N} \sum_{j=1}^{L} p_{i,k}^j \tag{4}$$

where $N$ denotes the number of images in one epoch, and $L$ means the number of correctly predicted tokens for image $\boldsymbol{x}_i$ with label $y_i^l$. $k$ denotes the target category of the current token. $C$ is the normalized factor, which is the total number of correctly predicted samples for one epoch. $p_{i,k}^j$ is the output probability of category $k$, given by:

$$p_{i,k}^j = \begin{cases} p^{t-1}(k|\boldsymbol{x}_i, y_i^1, y_i^2, ..., y_i^{l-1}), & if \ \hat{y}_i^l = y_i^l \\ 0, & else \end{cases} \tag{5}$$

here, $\hat{y}_i^l$ and $y_i^l$ is the predicted and ground truth of token $y$ from image $\boldsymbol{x}_i$. $p^{t-1}$ is the output probability from the model prediction, given by:

$$p = \frac{\exp(z_i/\boldsymbol{T})}{\sum_j \exp(z_j/\boldsymbol{T})} \tag{6}$$

where $z_i$ represents the output logit from the model prediction, followed by a Softmax function to convert the logit into probabilities. Here, we add a temperature $\boldsymbol{T}$ to smooth the logits. Using a higher value for $\boldsymbol{T}$ produces a softer probability distribution over classes, which contains more knowledge to learn as proved in [6].

Moreover, in order to fully utilize the soft target generated at each epoch to achieve stable training, we propose to add a factor to adjust the weight between the soft target $S^{t-1}$ from historical epochs and the soft target $S^t$ from the current epoch, which is formulated as:

$$S^t = \beta * S^{t-1} + (1 - \beta) * S^t \tag{7}$$

where $\beta$ means the reweighting factor, and the larger $\beta$, the more important the distribution in history epochs.

Finally, the training loss of the model can be calculated by:

$$L_{soft} = - \sum_{k=1}^{K} S_k^{t-1} \cdot \log p^{t-1} \left( k \mid y_i^1, y_i^2, \ldots, y_i^{l-1} \right) \tag{8}$$

The proposed DST indicates that all historically correctly classified samples $x_n$ will constrain the current sample $x_i$, encouraging samples belonging to the same category to be much closer.

## 4    Experiment

Following EDSL, the performance of DBN is evaluated on two benchmark datasets: **ME-20K** dataset and **ME-98K** dataset. The **ME-20K** contains

20,834 expressions from high school math exercises, with a total categories number of 191. The **ME-98K** provides a challenging dataset with 98,676 images, which consists of real-world long mathematical expressions collected from published articles [4]. The "baseline" mentioned in our experiment refers to the model adapted from EDSL [5]. All ablation studies are conducted on the ME-20K dataset. We use BLEU-4, ROUGE-4, Match, and Match-ws as evaluation metrics in our experiments. Match and Match-ws [4] are the exact match accuracy and the exact match accuracy after deleting whitespace columns between the rendered image of ground truth LaTex and predicted LaTex, respectively.

**Table 1.** Ablation study of the proposed architecture on ME-20K. CCM and DST indicate Context Coupling Module and Dynamic Soft Target strategy, respectively.

| CCM | DST | BLEU-4 | ROUGE-4 | Match | Match-ws |
|-----|-----|--------|---------|-------|----------|
| ✗ | ✗ | 94.23 | 95.10 | 92.70 | 93.45 |
| ✓ | ✗ | 94.72 | 95.60 | 92.85 | 93.60 |
| ✗ | ✓ | 94.58 | 95.41 | **92.89** | 93.61 |
| ✓ | ✓ | **94.73** | **95.60** | 92.85 | **93.61** |

## 4.1 Implementation Details

During training, we resize the symbols into size $30 \times 30$, the same as EDSL [5] for a fair comparison. The embedding size of the transformer is 256. For the proposed CCM, the height of the input image is scaled to 30 while keeping the image aspect ratio. Each convolutional stage in CCM consists of two $3 \times 3$ convolution layers, followed by a $2 \times 2$ max-pooling layer to reduce the resolution. We use Adam optimizer with an initial learning rate of 3e–4. For all datasets, the training batch size is 16. The model is trained with 1 Tesla V100 GPU.

## 4.2 Abations Study

As shown in Table 1, we conduct some ablation experiments to illustrate the effectiveness of proposed modules, including the Context Coupling Module (CCM) and the Dynamic Soft Target (DST) Strategy.

**Table 2.** Ablation study of one CCM added to different convolutional stages.

| Stage | BLEU-4 | ROUGE-4 | Match | Match-ws |
|-------|--------|---------|-------|----------|
| 1 | **94.72** | **95.60** | **92.85** | 93.60 |
| 2 | 94.64 | 95.50 | 92.70 | 93.33 |
| 3 | 94.34 | 95.14 | 92.84 | **93.81** |

**Impact of CCM** is shown in Table 1. We can find that it is crucial to couple global and local contexts information. Moreover, we conducted an ablation study to compare our CCM with other feature enhancement modules which only utilize one branch information, and the result is shown in Table 3. CCM not only boosts the accuracy of baselines significantly but also achieves better performance compared with other methods, that is because the powerful feature representation comes from both local and global signals.

Moreover, Table 2 compares a single CCM module added to different convolution stages in Fig. 2(a). The block is added right after the last layer of a stage. We can find that CCM is more useful when added to the first convolutional stage since it enriches the features. When it is applied to deeper stages, the performance decreases slightly. One possible explanation is that features in deeper stages have a small spatial size due to the pooling layer, and it is insufficient to provide precise spatial information.

**Table 3.** Ablation study of different attention modules.

| Method | BLEU-4 | ROUGE-4 | Match | Match-ws |
|---|---|---|---|---|
| Baseline | 94.23 | 95.10 | 92.70 | 93.45 |
| w/STN | 94.28 | 95.27 | 91.93 | 92.85 |
| w/CBAM | 94.41 | 95.27 | 92.85 | 93.57 |
| w/Self-attn | 94.38 | 95.22 | 92.17 | 92.85 |
| w/CCM | **94.72** | **95.60** | **92.85** | **93.60** |

**Impact of DST** is shown in Table 1. We can find that DST stably boosts the performance of PMER, demonstrating that PMER models can benefit from the soft labels, which brings more knowledge to learn. Using DST to train the model encourages the samples belonging to the same category to be much closer.

### 4.3    Impact of Hyper-parameters

We enumerate possible values with $\beta \in \{0.1, 0.2, \ldots, 1.0\}$ for hyperparameter $\beta$ in Eq. 7. The experiment results are shown in Fig. 5(a). It can be seen that the model achieves the highest BLEU-4 score when $\beta$ is set to 0.5. It will decrease the performance when $\beta$ changes from 0.5 to 0. We argue that is caused by the insufficient use of historical labels. When $\beta$ changes from 0.5 to 1.0, the performance decreases sharply. We analyze that the predictions become better and better with the network's training. The accumulated historical labels will be outdated for the model in the current epoch.

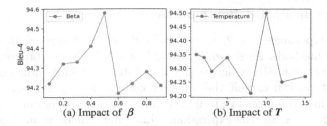

**Fig. 5.** Impact of hyper-parameters. The BLEU-4 of different $\beta$ and temperature $T$.

Then we analyze the hyperparameter $T$ in Eq. 6. A high value of $T$ softens the probability distribution. It can be seen that the model achieves the highest BLEU-4 score when $T$ is set to 10, as shown in Fig. 5(b). We also observe that the performance is very close when $T$ is less than 10. However, when the $T$ is higher than 10, the performance decreases sharply. We argue that this is because that too high $T$ will make the knowledge disappear, as proved in [13].

**Table 4.** Quantitative results on ME-20K.

| Method | BLEU-4 | ROUGE-4 | Match | Match-ws |
|---|---|---|---|---|
| DA [9] | 87.27 | 89.08 | 76.92 | 77.31 |
| LBPF [11] | 88.82 | 90.57 | 80.46 | 80.88 |
| SAT [21] | 89.77 | 91.15 | 82.09 | 82.65 |
| TopDown [1] | 90.55 | 91.94 | 83.85 | 84.22 |
| ARNet [3] | 91.18 | 92.50 | 85.40 | 85.84 |
| IM2Markup [4] | 92.83 | 93.74 | 89.23 | 89.63 |
| EDSL [5] | 94.23 | 95.10 | 92.70 | 93.45 |
| Ours | **94.73** | **95.60** | **92.85** | **93.61** |

$$\frac{a_1 + a_2 + a_3 + \ldots + a_n}{\boxed{nn}} \quad \times \qquad \frac{a_1 + a_2 + a_3 + \ldots + a_n}{\boxed{n}} \quad \checkmark$$

$$h(x) = \boxed{m}\{f(x), g(x)\} \quad \times \qquad h(x) = \boxed{min}\{f(x), g(x)\} \quad \checkmark$$

$$a_1 = -3.\boxed{1}a_5 = 5a_8 \quad \times \qquad a_1 = -3,\boxed{11}a_5 = 5a_8 \quad \checkmark$$

$$[x - (e + \frac{1}{e})\boxed{]}^2 + y^2 = 1 \quad \times \qquad [x - (e + \frac{1}{e})\boxed{]}^2 + y^2 = 1 \quad \checkmark$$

EDSL                                    Ours

**Fig. 6.** Comparisons of our method with EDSL. The red box illustrates the incorrectly predicted symbols from EDSL. The green box illustrates the correct symbols from ours. (Color figure online)

## 4.4    Results on PMER Benchmarks

We conduct experiments on 20K and 98K datasets to compare our DBN with other related methods. As shown in Table 4 and Table 5, our proposed method outperforms other methods across the two datasets, which indicates that the proposed method can exploit the inherent context among symbols. The comparison of rendered images in Fig. 6 also shows the priority of our model, which can accurately recognize the expression, while EDSL made some incorrect predictions. Overall, we can prove that jointly coupling global and local contexts is crucial for PMER, and the DST allows samples belonging to the same category to be much closer.

**Table 5.** Quantitative results on ME-98K.

| Method | BLEU-4 | ROUGE-4 | Match | Match-ws |
|---|---|---|---|---|
| DA [9] | 79.71 | 82.40 | 55.15 | 55.15 |
| LBPF [11] | 84.64 | 86.57 | 66.83 | 66.87 |
| SAT [21] | 86.56 | 87.86 | 70.85 | 71.04 |
| TopDown [1] | 87.56 | 89.32 | 72.65 | 72.85 |
| ARNet [3] | 86.04 | 88.27 | 68.55 | 68.98 |
| IM2Markup [4] | 91.47 | 92.45 | 84.96 | 85.16 |
| EDSL [5] | **92.93** | 93.30 | 89.00 | 89.34 |
| Ours | 92.90 | **93.34** | **89.71** | **90.01** |

## 5    Conclusion

This paper proposes a novel dual branch framework to jointly learn the local symbol-level and global image-level context for accurate PMER. Moreover, we propose a Context Coupling Module to interactively couple global context with local context so that the obtained context clues are highly correlated to each symbol. Additionally, we propose the DST strategy to capture the similarities among categories by the statistics during the training phase. The quantitative and qualitative experiments have demonstrated that the proposed approach can tackle mathematical expressions with semantically-correlated symbols and has achieved state-of-the-art results.

**Acknowledgement.** This work was supported in part by the National Innovation 2030 Major S&T Project of China under Grant 2020AAA0104203, and in part by the Nature Science Foundation of China under Grant 62006007.

## References

1. Anderson, P., He, X., Buehler, C., et al.: Bottom-up and top-down attention for image captioning and visual question answering. In: CVPR, pp. 6077–6086 (2018)

2. Blostein, D., Grbavec, A.: Recognition of mathematical notation. In: Handbook of Character Recognition and Document Image Analysis, pp. 557–582. World Scientific (1997)
3. Chen, X., Ma, L., Jiang, W., Yao, J., Liu, W.: Regularizing RNNs for caption generation by reconstructing the past with the present. In: CVPR, pp. 7995–8003 (2018)
4. Deng, Y., Kanervisto, A., Ling, J., Rush, A.M.: Image-to-markup generation with coarse-to-fine attention. In: ICML, pp. 980–989. PMLR (2017)
5. Fu, Y., Liu, T., Gao, M., Zhou, A.: EDSL: an encoder-decoder architecture with symbol-level features for printed mathematical expression recognition. arXiv preprint arXiv:2007.02517 (2020)
6. Hinton, G., Vinyals, O., Dean, J.: Distilling the knowledge in a neural network. Comput. Sci. 14(7), 38–39 (2015)
7. Hu, Y., Zheng, Y., Liu, H., et al.: Accurate structured-text spotting for arithmetical exercise correction. In: AAAI, vol. 34, pp. 686–693 (2020)
8. Jaderberg, M., Simonyan, K., Zisserman, A., et al.: Spatial transformer networks, vol. 28, pp. 2017–2025 (2015)
9. Luong, T., Pham, H., Manning, C.D.: Effective approaches to attention-based neural machine translation. In: EMNLP (2015)
10. Okamoto, M., Imai, H., Takagi, K.: Performance evaluation of a robust method for mathematical expression recognition. In: ICDAR. pp. 121–128. IEEE (2001)
11. Qin, Y., Du, J., Zhang, Y., Lu, H.: Look back and predict forward in image captioning. In: CVPR, pp. 8367–8375 (2019)
12. Samet, H., Tamminen, M.: Efficient component labeling of images of arbitrary dimension represented by linear bintrees. IEEE Trans. Pattern Anal. Mach. Intell. 10(4), 579–586 (1988). https://doi.org/10.1109/34.3918
13. Shin, S., Boo, Y., Sung, W.: Knowledge distillation for optimization of quantized deep neural networks. In: SiPS, pp. 1–6. IEEE (2020)
14. Su, Y., et al.: Exercise-enhanced sequential modeling for student performance prediction. In: AAAI, vol. 32 (2018)
15. Szegedy, C., Vanhoucke, V., Ioffe, S., Shlens, J., Wojna, Z.: Rethinking the inception architecture for computer vision. In: CVPR, pp. 2818–2826 (2016)
16. Ung, H.Q., Phan, M.K., Nguyen, H.T., et al.: Strategy and tools for collecting and annotating handwritten descriptive answers for developing automatic and semi-automatic marking-an initial effort to math. In: ICDARW, vol. 2, pp. 13–18. IEEE (2019)
17. Wang, X., Girshick, R., Gupta, A., He, K.: Non-local neural networks. In: CVPR, pp. 7794–7803 (2018)
18. Woo, S., Park, J., Lee, J.Y., Kweon, I.S.: CBAM: convolutional block attention module. In: ECCV, pp. 3–19 (2018)
19. Wu, C., Wang, Q., Zhang, J., et al.: Stroke based posterior attention for online handwritten mathematical expression recognition. In: ICPR, pp. 2943–2949. IEEE (2021)
20. Xie, E., Wang, W., Yu, Z., Anandkumar, A., Alvarez, J.M., Luo, P.: Segformer: simple and efficient design for semantic segmentation with transformers (2021)
21. Xu, K., Ba, J., Kiros, R., et al.: Show, attend and tell: Neural image caption generation with visual attention. In: ICML, pp. 2048–2057. PMLR (2015)
22. Yan, Z., Zhang, X., Gao, L., Yuan, K., Tang, Z.: ConvMath: a convolutional sequence network for mathematical expression recognition. In: ICPR, pp. 4566–4572. IEEE (2021)

23. Yin, Y., et al.: Transcribing content from structural images with spotlight mechanism. In: ACM SIGKDD, pp. 2643–2652 (2018)
24. Zanibbi, R., Blostein, D., Cordy, J.R.: Recognizing mathematical expressions using tree transformation. IEEE Trans. Pattern Anal. Mach. Intell. **24**(11), 1455–1467 (2002)
25. Zhang, C.B., Jiang, P.T., Hou, Q., et al.: Delving deep into label smoothing. IEEE Trans. Image Process. **30**, 5984–5996 (2021)
26. Zhang, J., Du, J., Dai, L.: Multi-scale attention with dense encoder for handwritten mathematical expression recognition. In: ICPR, pp. 2245–2250. IEEE (2018)
27. Zhang, J., Du, J., Zhang, S., et al.: Watch, attend and parse: an end-to-end neural network based approach to handwritten mathematical expression recognition. Pattern Recogn. **71**, 196–206 (2017)

# Efficient Search of Multiple Neural Architectures with Different Complexities via Importance Sampling

Yuhei Noda[1] , Shota Saito[1,2] , and Shinichi Shirakawa[1]( )

[1] Yokohama National University, Kanagawa, Japan
`saito-shota-bt@ynu.jp`, `shirakawa-shinichi-bg@ynu.ac.jp`,
`nodayuhei@gmail.com`
[2] SkillUp AI Co., Ltd., Tokyo, Japan
`s_saito@skillupai.com`

**Abstract.** Neural architecture search (NAS) aims to automate architecture design processes and improve the performance of deep neural networks. Platform-aware NAS methods consider both performance and complexity and can find well-performing architectures with low computational resources. Although ordinary NAS methods result in tremendous computational costs owing to the repetition of model training, one-shot NAS, which trains the weights of a supernetwork containing all candidate architectures only once during the search process, has been reported to result in a lower search cost. This study focuses on the architecture complexity-aware one-shot NAS that optimizes the objective function composed of the weighted sum of two metrics, such as the predictive performance and number of parameters. In existing methods, the architecture search process must be run multiple times with different coefficients of the weighted sum to obtain multiple architectures with different complexities. This study aims at reducing the search cost associated with finding multiple architectures. The proposed method uses multiple distributions to generate architectures with different complexities and updates each distribution using the samples obtained from multiple distributions based on importance sampling. The proposed method allows us to obtain multiple architectures with different complexities in a single architecture search, resulting in reducing the search cost. The proposed method is applied to the architecture search of convolutional neural networks on the CIAFR-10 and ImageNet datasets. Consequently, compared with baseline methods, the proposed method finds multiple architectures with varying complexities while requiring less computational effort.

**Keywords:** Neural architecture search · Convolutional neural network · Importance sampling · Natural gradient

## 1 Introduction

Architecture design is a key factor in accelerating the performance of deep neural networks (DNNs); however, the associated process is arduous for practitioners.

E. Pimenidis et al. (Eds.): ICANN 2022, LNCS 13532, pp. 607–619, 2022.
https://doi.org/10.1007/978-3-031-15937-4_51

Neural architecture search (NAS), aimed at automating the design of DNN architectures, has been actively studied in recent years [7]. Popular methods often optimize architectures using evolutionary algorithms [16, 21] or reinforcement learning [27]. These early NAS methods optimize the architecture in hyperparameter optimization frameworks, which requires a significant amount of time for architecture search due to the repetition of model training. *One-shot NAS*, e.g., [12, 15, 20], is a promising approach for reducing the computational cost of NAS. One-Shot NAS simultaneously optimizes the weight and architecture parameters considering an extensive network (supernetwork) that includes many candidate architectures as its subnetworks. Because the weight parameters are shared between subnetworks, one-shot NAS optimizes the weights in the supernetwork only once during the search process, thus significantly reducing the search cost.

DNNs are often implemented in devices with limited computational resources, such as embedded and mobile devices. In such cases, NAS methods are required to find an architecture with good prediction performance and low computation and memory usage. Therefore, NAS methods have been developed for optimizing the prediction performance and architecture complexity, such as FLOPs, latency, and the number of weight parameters. The method proposed in [24] includes a term related to the latency in the objective function and successfully finds a highly accurate architecture while suppressing latency. This study focuses on the one-shot NAS method proposed in [17], which introduces a regularization of the architecture complexity. This method uses binary variables to represent the architecture and a multivariate Bernoulli distribution as the law of binary variables. The architecture search is performed by updating the parameters of the Bernoulli distribution to minimize the weighted sum of the predictive loss and the regularization term related to the complexity of the architecture. Although this approach reduces the number of connections in a densely connected convolutional neural network (CNN), the architecture search space is limited because it must represent the architecture using binary variables. This implies that directly employing the state-of-the-art architecture search space represented by categorical variables [15, 28] is not straightforward. Additionally, obtaining multiple architectures with different complexities requires repeated architecture searches with different regularization coefficients in the objective function, which, in turn, increases computational cost.

This study extends the method proposed in [17] to overcome the limitation described above. We adopt categorical distributions as the architecture distribution and propose a regularization term for the architecture complexity. We also derive the analytical natural gradient of the proposed regularization term. Thereafter, we propose an efficient search method to simultaneously obtain multiple architectures with different complexities in a single architecture search using importance sampling. The proposed method is then evaluated by applying it to the architecture search of CNNs on the CIFAR-10 [11] and ImageNet [6] datasets. The experimental results indicate that the proposed method can obtain multiple architectures with different complexities in a single search, and its prediction performance is comparable with that demonstrated by baseline methods.

# 2  Probabilistic Model-Based One-Shot NAS with Complexity Regularization

This section details the one-shot NAS framework using the architecture complexity regularization proposed in [17]. We denote the DNN parameterized by architecture parameters $M$ and weights $W$ as $\phi(M, W)$ and assume that $\phi$ is differentiable with respect to (w.r.t.) $W$ but non-differentiable w.r.t. $M$. The architecture parameters $M$ determine the types of connections and operations in DNN. The architecture defined by $M$ corresponds to a subnetwork in the supernetwork and shares weights in the operations between different architectures.

Let us consider the optimization of $W$ and $M$ to minimize both the loss, for instance, the cross-entropy loss, and the regularization metric w.r.t. the complexity of the architecture. We denote the loss for the dataset $\mathcal{D}$ and the regularization term as $\mathcal{L}(M, W, \mathcal{D})$ and $\mathcal{R}(M)$, respectively. In [17], the weighted sum of the two terms, $\mathcal{F}(M, W) = \mathcal{L}(M, W, \mathcal{D}) + \epsilon \mathcal{R}(M)$, has been adopted as the objective function, where $\epsilon$ represents the regularization coefficient that balances the two terms. However, because the architecture parameters $M$ are non-differentiable and often discrete, we cannot optimize $M$ by a gradient method. To relax the problem, we introduce the parametric probability distribution of $M$ and denote it as $P_\theta(M)$, where $\theta$ denotes the distribution parameters. Instead of directly optimizing $\mathcal{F}(M, W)$, we optimize $\theta$ by minimizing the expected loss of $\mathcal{F}(M, W)$ under $P_\theta(M)$ as $\mathcal{G}(\theta, W) = \mathbb{E}_{P_\theta}[\mathcal{L}(M, W, \mathcal{D})] + \epsilon \mathbb{E}_{P_\theta}[\mathcal{R}(M)]$.

As the objective function $\mathcal{G}(\theta, W)$ is differentiable w.r.t. both $W$ and $\theta$, we can optimize it by a gradient method. We update the distribution parameters $\theta$ to the natural gradient direction [2], which is the steepest direction when considering the Kullback-Leibler divergence as the pseudo-distance in the distribution parameter space, and it is given by the product of the inverse of the Fisher information matrix (FIM) and Euclidean gradient. We use the vanilla gradient to optimize $W$ as usual DNN training. The gradients w.r.t. $W$ and $\theta$ are given by

$$\nabla_W \mathcal{G}(\theta, W) = \mathbb{E}_{P_\theta}[\nabla_W \mathcal{L}(M, W, \mathcal{D})] \tag{1}$$

$$\tilde{\nabla}_\theta \mathcal{G}(\theta, W) = \mathbb{E}_{P_\theta}\left[\mathcal{L}(M, W, \mathcal{D})\tilde{\nabla}_\theta \ln P_\theta(M)\right] + \epsilon \tilde{\nabla}_\theta \mathbb{E}_{P_\theta}[\mathcal{R}(M)] , \tag{2}$$

where $\tilde{\nabla}_\theta = F(\theta)^{-1}\nabla_\theta$ represents the natural gradient operator. Here, $F(\theta)$ indicates the FIM of $P_\theta(M)$. Optimizing $\theta$ using (2) with $\epsilon = 0$ operates in a manner similar to information geometric optimization [14], which is a unified framework for probabilistic model-based evolutionary algorithms. In most cases, it is difficult to compute the gradients (1) and (2). Therefore, the gradients (1) and (2) are approximated using Monte Carlo methods with $\lambda$ architecture parameters $M_1, M_2, \ldots, M_\lambda$ sampled from $P_\theta(M)$ as follows:

$$\nabla_W \mathcal{G}(\theta, W) \approx \frac{1}{\lambda}\sum_{i=1}^{\lambda} \nabla_W \mathcal{L}(M_i, W, \mathcal{D}) \tag{3}$$

$$\tilde{\nabla}_\theta \mathcal{G}(\theta, W) \approx \frac{1}{\lambda}\sum_{i=1}^{\lambda} \mathcal{L}(M_i, W, \mathcal{D})\tilde{\nabla}_\theta \ln p_\theta(M_i) + \epsilon \tilde{\nabla}_\theta \mathbb{E}_{P_\theta}[\mathcal{R}(M)] . \tag{4}$$

Because the scale of the loss affects the magnitude of the natural gradient, we transform $\mathcal{L}(M_i, W, \mathcal{D})$ into the quantile-based utility value under $P_\theta(M)$, as done in [14]. The probability of sampling a solution with a loss value less than or equal to $\mathcal{L}(M_i, W, \mathcal{D})$ is estimated as $\bar{q}_\theta^\leqslant(M_i) = \lambda^{-1} \sum_{k=1}^\lambda \mathbb{I}\{\mathcal{L}(M_k, W, \mathcal{D}) \leqslant \mathcal{L}(M_i, W, \mathcal{D})\}$, where $\mathbb{I}\{\cdot\}$ denotes the indicator function. We use the utility function of $\hat{s}_i = w(\bar{q}_\theta^\leqslant(M_i))$, instead of $\mathcal{L}(M_i, W, \mathcal{D})$, to update the distribution parameters $\theta$.[1] Specifically, we use the following function for $w$.

$$w(x) = \begin{cases} -2 & (x \leqslant 0.25) \\ 0 & (0.25 < x \leqslant 0.75) \\ 2 & (0.75 < x) \end{cases}$$

Consequently, the update rule for $\theta$ at the $t$-th iteration is given by

$$\theta^{(t+1)} = \theta^{(t)} - \eta \left( \frac{1}{\lambda} \sum_{i=1}^\lambda \hat{s}_i \tilde{\nabla}_\theta \ln p_\theta(M_i) + \epsilon \tilde{\nabla}_\theta \mathbb{E}_{P_\theta} \left[ \mathcal{R}(M) \right] \right), \tag{5}$$

where $\eta$ represents the learning rate for $\theta$. We note that the weights $W$ can be updated using any stochastic gradient descent (SGD) method with (3).

## 3    Proposed Method

In [17], the binary vector has been adopted as the architecture parameter. However, state-of-the-art architecture search spaces, such as [12,15], are defined using categorical variables. In addition, repeating the architecture search is required to obtain multiple architectures with different complexities. We first introduce the categorical distribution as $P_\theta(M)$ in the framework considered in [17]. Subsequently, we propose simultaneously optimizing multiple categorical distributions, each corresponding to a different regularization coefficient, to obtain multiple architectures with varying complexities in a single search. Each categorical distribution is updated by exploiting samples from other distributions to realize an efficient search process.

### 3.1    Introducing Categorical Distributions

The DNN architecture is represented by the following $D$ dimensional categorical variables: $h = (h_1, \ldots, h_D)$. The $d$-th categorical variable $h_d$ possesses $K_d$ candidate categories and determines operations or connections in the DNN. For instance, one can determine the kernel size of a convolution layer. We denote categorical variables by one-hot vectors as $M = (m_1, \ldots, m_D)$, where $m_d = (m_{d,1}, \ldots, m_{d,K_d})^\mathrm{T} \in \{0, 1\}^{K_d}$. When $h_d$ is the $k$-th category,

---

[1] This utility definition does not assume the possibility of sampling architectures with the same loss value. Although it could happen in our case, we use this utility definition for simplicity. A rigorous definition can be found in [14,19].

$m_{d,k} = 1$, and other elements of $m_d$ are zero. We consider the categorical distribution as the distribution of the architecture parameters, which is described as $P_\theta(M) = \prod_{d=1}^{D} \prod_{k=1}^{K_d} (\theta_{d,k})^{m_{d,k}}$, where $\theta_{d,k} \in [0,1]$ is the probability of being $m_{d,k} = 1$.

We choose the number of weight parameters as the complexity metric for the regularization term $\mathcal{R}(M)$ to penalize the complicated architecture. Let us denote the number of weight parameters in the operation corresponding to $m_{d,k}$ as $c_{d,k}$; then, we define the regularization term as $\mathcal{R}(M) = \sum_{d=1}^{D} \sum_{k=1}^{K_d} c_{d,k} m_{d,k}$. The expected value of $\mathcal{R}(M)$ under $P_\theta(M)$ is described as

$$\mathbb{E}_{P_\theta}[\mathcal{R}(M)] = \sum_{d=1}^{D} \sum_{k=1}^{K_d} c_{d,k} \theta_{d,k} \ . \tag{6}$$

It should be noted that the distribution parameter of the last category can be given by $\theta_{d,K_d} = 1 - \sum_{k=1}^{K_d-1} \theta_{d,k}$ owing to $\sum_{k=1}^{K_d} \theta_{d,k} = 1$; consequently, we can introduce the notation of the distribution parameter vector without the last category's parameter as $\bar{\theta}_d = (\theta_{d,1}, \theta_{d,2}, \ldots, \theta_{d,K_d-1})^{\mathrm{T}}$.

Next, we derive the natural gradient of $\mathbb{E}_{P_\theta}[\mathcal{R}(M)]$. The vanilla gradient of $\mathbb{E}_{P_\theta}[\mathcal{R}(M)]$ w.r.t the $d$-th distribution parameters $\bar{\theta}_d$ is given by $\nabla_{\bar{\theta}_d} \mathbb{E}_{P_\theta}[\mathcal{R}(M)] = \bar{c}_d - c_{d,K_d}\mathbf{1}$, where $\bar{c}_d = (c_{d,1}, c_{d,2}, \ldots, c_{d,K_d-1})^{\mathrm{T}}$, and $\mathbf{1}$ represents the all-ones vector. The FIM is a block diagonal matrix because our categorical variables are independent. The inverse of the $d$-th block in the FIM is given by $F(\bar{\theta}_d)^{-1} = \mathrm{diag}(\bar{\theta}_d) - \bar{\theta}_d\bar{\theta}_d^{\mathrm{T}}$. Then, we can obtain the natural gradient of (6) as $\tilde{\nabla}_{\bar{\theta}_d} \mathbb{E}_{P_\theta}[\mathcal{R}(M)] = \bar{c}_d \odot \bar{\theta}_d - (\bar{c}_d^{\mathrm{T}}\bar{\theta}_d + c_{d,K_d}(1 - \bar{\theta}_d^{\mathrm{T}}\mathbf{1})) \bar{\theta}_d = (\bar{c}_d - \mathcal{Q}_d\mathbf{1}) \odot \bar{\theta}_d$, where $\odot$ indicates the element-wise product and $\mathcal{Q}_d = \sum_{k=1}^{K_d} c_{d,k}\theta_{d,k}$. According to [1], the natural gradient of the log-likelihood is given by $\tilde{\nabla}_{\bar{\theta}_d} \ln P_\theta(M) = \bar{m}_d - \bar{\theta}_d$, where $\bar{m}_d = (m_{d,1}, \ldots, m_{d,K_d-1})^{\mathrm{T}}$. We then obtain the update rule of $\bar{\theta}_d$ as

$$\bar{\theta}_d^{(t+1)} = \bar{\theta}_d^{(t)} - \eta \left( \frac{1}{\lambda} \sum_{i=1}^{\lambda} \hat{s}_i (\bar{m}_d^{(i)} - \bar{\theta}_d^{(t)}) + \epsilon (\bar{c}_d - \mathcal{Q}_d\mathbf{1}) \odot \bar{\theta}_d^{(t)} \right) \ , \tag{7}$$

where $\bar{m}_d^{(i)}$ indicates the $d$-th one-hot vector without the last element of the $i$-th sample. Additionally, $\theta_{d,K_d}^{(t+1)} = 1 - \sum_{k=1}^{K_d-1} \theta_{d,k}^{(t+1)}$ is given by

$$\theta_{d,K_d}^{(t+1)} = \theta_{d,K_d}^{(t)} - \eta \left( \frac{1}{\lambda} \sum_{i=1}^{\lambda} \hat{s}_i \left( m_{d,K_d}^{(i)} - \theta_{d,K_d}^{(t)} \right) + \epsilon (c_{d,K_d} - \mathcal{Q}_d) \theta_{d,K_d}^{(t)} \right) \ . \tag{8}$$

According to (7) and (8), we can replace $\bar{\theta}_d$ in (7) with $\theta_d = (\theta_{d,1}, \theta_{d,2}, \ldots, \theta_{d,K_d})^{\mathrm{T}}$ and update the distribution parameter $\theta_d$ using the replaced update rule.

## 3.2  Searching Multiple Architectures via Importance Sampling

In existing methods [3,17], a search for the architecture must be performed multiple times by altering the regularization coefficient to obtain multiple architectures with different complexities. Herein, we propose a method for finding

---

**Algorithm 1.** Architecture Search Procedure of the Proposed Method

---
**Require:** Dataset $\mathcal{D} = \{\mathcal{D}_W, \mathcal{D}_\theta\}$
1: Initialize $W$ and $\theta^{(1)}, \theta^{(2)}, \ldots, \theta^{(N)}$
2: **for** $t = 1, \ldots, T_W$ **do**
3:     Sample mini-batch $\tilde{\mathcal{D}}_W$ from $\mathcal{D}_W$
4:     Sample $\lambda$ architectures from uniform distribution and update $W$ using (3)
5: **end for**
6: **for** $t = 1, \ldots, T_\theta$ **do**
7:     Sample mini-batch $\tilde{\mathcal{D}}_\theta$ from $\mathcal{D}_\theta$
8:     Sample $\lambda$ architectures from $P_\theta(M)$ and update $\theta^{(n)}$ for $n = 1, \ldots, N$ by (10)
9: **end for**

---

multiple architectures within a single search, thereby reducing the search cost. The idea is to jointly update the multiple distributions corresponding to different complexities by exploiting the samples drawn from other distributions via importance sampling. Let us consider $N$ distribution parameters, $\boldsymbol{\theta} = (\theta^{(1)}, \ldots, \theta^{(N)})$, corresponding to different regularization coefficients $\epsilon_1, \ldots, \epsilon_N$. The objective function of each distribution is defined by $\mathcal{G}(\theta^{(n)}, W) = \mathbb{E}_{P_{\theta^{(n)}}}[\mathcal{L}(M, W, \mathcal{D})] + \epsilon_n \mathbb{E}_{P_{\theta^{(n)}}}[\mathcal{R}(M)]$. We sample $\lambda$ architecture parameters from the mixture distribution $P_\theta(M) = N^{-1} \sum_{n=1}^{N} P_{\theta^{(n)}}(M)$ at each iteration and update each distribution using the samples obtained from the mixture. Based on the importance sampling technique used in [18,19], the probability $\bar{q}_{\theta^{(n)}}^{\leqslant}(M_i)$ is estimated by

$$\bar{q}_{\theta^{(n)}}^{\leqslant}(M_i) = \frac{1}{\lambda} \sum_{k=1}^{\lambda} r_k^{(n)} \mathbb{I}\{\mathcal{L}(M_k, W, \mathcal{D}) \leqslant \mathcal{L}(M_i, W, \mathcal{D})\} \ , \tag{9}$$

where $r_k^{(n)} = \frac{P_{\theta^{(n)}}(M_k)}{P_\theta(M_k)}$ indicates the likelihood ratio. Then, the utility of $\hat{s}_i^{(n)} = w(\bar{q}_{\theta^{(n)}}^{\leqslant}(M_i))$ is used to update $\theta^{(n)}$. Similarly, the natural gradient can be approximated via importance sampling, and we obtain the update rule of $\theta_d^{(n)}$ as

$$\theta_d^{(n)} \leftarrow \theta_d^{(n)} - \eta \left( \frac{1}{\lambda} \sum_{i=1}^{\lambda} \hat{s}_i^{(n)} r_i^{(n)} \left( m_d^{(i)} - \theta_d^{(n)} \right) + \epsilon_n \left( c_d - \mathcal{Q}_d \mathbf{1} \right) \odot \theta_d^{(n)} \right) \ . \tag{10}$$

Here, we ignore the notation of the time step $t$ for simplicity.

### 3.3   Overall Algorithm

The architecture search procedure followed by the proposed method is presented in Algorithm 1. The dataset $\mathcal{D}$ is divided into $\mathcal{D}_W$ and $\mathcal{D}_\theta$, and the resulting datasets are used to update the weights and distribution parameters, respectively. Although the method in [17] jointly optimizes the weights $W$ and distribution parameters $\theta$, the proposed method separates the optimization of $W$

and $\theta$. That is, we first optimize $W$ under a uniform distribution and then optimize $\theta$ using the trained weights $W$. A separate (two-stage) optimization of the weight and architecture parameters has been conducted in recent NAS-related studies [4,8,10], and the approach has demonstrated promising performance.

In the optimization phase of $W$, $\lambda$ architecture parameters $M_1, \ldots, M_\lambda$ are sampled from a discrete uniform distribution, and the weight parameters of $W$ are updated using (3). This update of $W$ is repeated $T_W$ times. Then, in the optimization phase of $\theta$, $\lambda$ architecture parameters $M_1, \ldots, M_\lambda$ are sampled from the mixture distribution $P_\theta(M)$, and the distribution parameters $\theta = (\theta^{(1)}, \ldots, \theta^{(N)})$ for different regularization coefficients $\epsilon_1, \ldots, \epsilon_N$ are updated using (10). Following the architecture search, we determine the final architectures by $M_{(n)}^* = \mathrm{argmax}_M P_{\theta^{(n)}}(M)$ for $n = 1, \ldots, N$ and obtain multiple architectures with different complexities. Then, we retrain the weights of the final architecture $M_{(n)}^*$ from scratch using the dataset $\mathcal{D}$.

# 4  Experiment and Results

This section evaluates the proposed method on image classification tasks. Our algorithms were run using NVIDIA Tesla V100 GPUs (32 GB memory).

## 4.1  CIFAR-10

**Experimental Settings.** The CIFAR-10 [11] dataset contains 50,000 training and 10,000 test images, and each image is labeled using one class out of 10. We adopt the cell-based CNN architecture search space used in [1,15] and follow the experimental setting in [1]. In the architecture search phase, we stack six normal and two reduction cells and set the number of channels in the first cell to 16. The architectures of the normal and reduction cells are searched by NAS algorithms. The training data $\mathcal{D}$ are divided into $\mathcal{D}_W$ and $\mathcal{D}_\theta$, which are then used to update the weights and distribution parameters, respectively. Both mini-batch sizes $|\tilde{\mathcal{D}}_W|$ and $|\tilde{\mathcal{D}}_\theta|$ are set to 64. We set the sample size of the architecture $\lambda$ to 2. The weights and distribution parameters are both updated for 200 epochs, respectively, i.e., $T_W = T_\theta = 200$. For updating the weights $W$, we use SGD with a momentum of 0.9 and set the weight decay to $3 \times 10^{-4}$. According to the cosine schedule [13], the learning rate gradually decreases from 0.025 to 0. For updating the distribution parameters $\theta$, we set the learning rate to $\eta_\theta = (\sum_{d=1}^{D} K_d)^{-1} = 1/180$ and the regularization coefficient $\epsilon_n$ to $\{0.0, 0.1, 0.3, 0.5\}$. In the retraining phase, we set the number of normal cells to 10 and the number of channels in the first cell to 50. The other retraining settings are the same as [1].

We compare the proposed method with two baseline one-shot NAS methods. The first method, presented in Algorithm 2 and termed Method 1 (Simultaneous), is a straightforward extension of the method considered in [17]. This algorithm simultaneously updates the weights and distribution parameters and performs the architecture search several times with different regularization coefficients $\epsilon$ to obtain multiple architectures. The second method, presented in

| **Algorithm 2.** Method 1 (Simultaneous) | **Algorithm 3.** Method 2 (Separate) |
|---|---|
| **Require:** Dataset $\mathcal{D} = \{\mathcal{D}_W, \mathcal{D}_\theta\}$ | **Require:** Dataset $\mathcal{D} = \{\mathcal{D}_W, \mathcal{D}_\theta\}$ |
| 1: Initialize $\theta^{(1)}, \theta^{(2)}, \ldots, \theta^{(N)}$ | 1: Initialize $W$ and $\theta^{(1)}, \theta^{(2)}, \ldots, \theta^{(N)}$ |
| 2: **for** $n = 1, \ldots, N$ **do** | 2: **for** $t = 1, \ldots, T_W$ **do** |
| 3:    Initialize $W$ | 3:    Sample mini-batch $\tilde{\mathcal{D}}_W$ from $\mathcal{D}_W$ |
| 4:    **for** $t = 1, \ldots, T$ **do** | 4:    Sample $\lambda$ architectures from uniform distribution and update $W$ using (3) |
| 5:       Sample mini-batch $\tilde{\mathcal{D}}_W$ from $\mathcal{D}_W$ | 5: **end for** |
| 6:       Sample $\lambda$ architectures from $P_{\theta^{(n)}}(M)$ and update $W$ using (3) | 6: **for** $n = 1, \ldots, N$ **do** |
| 7:       Sample mini-batch $\tilde{\mathcal{D}}_\theta$ from $\mathcal{D}_\theta$ | 7:    **for** $t = 1, \ldots, T_\theta$ **do** |
| 8:       Sample $\lambda$ architectures from $P_{\theta^{(n)}}(M)$ and update $\theta^{(n)}$ by (7) | 8:       Sample mini-batch $\tilde{\mathcal{D}}_\theta$ from $\mathcal{D}_\theta$ |
| 9:    **end for** | 9:       Sample $\lambda$ architectures from $P_{\theta^{(n)}}(M)$ and update $\theta^{(n)}$ by (7) |
| 10: **end for** | 10:    **end for** |
|  | 11: **end for** |

Algorithm 3 and termed Method 2 (Separate), separates the weight optimization and architecture search, similar to the proposed method, but performs the architecture search several times with different $\epsilon$. The second method is advantageous compared to Method 1 (Simultaneous) because it performs the weight optimization only once; however, it is still inefficient compared to the proposed method because it requires multiple runs during the architecture search phase. The experiment uses the same number of epochs to optimize the weights and distribution parameters in a single search as in the proposed method, i.e., $T = T_W = T_\theta = 200$ in Algorithms 2 and 3. Moreover, we perform the random search as the simplest baseline, which randomly samples architectures from the search space and retrains them. We sample architectures with weight parameters of 2.5M (million), 3.0M, 4.0M, and 5.0M. We reported the median values among three independent trials for all algorithms.

**Results and Discussions.** Figure 1 and Table 1 show the test error of the obtained architectures and search cost, respectively. The proposed method achieves better accuracies than those obtained by Method 1 (Simultaneous). In Method 1, the weight and distribution parameters are updated simultaneously. As the convergence speed of the operations in the cells differs, the distribution parameters converge to select the architecture that minimizes the loss early, resulting in a search failure. This difficulty associated with one-shot NAS during simultaneous optimization of weights and architectures has been pointed out in [5, 26]. In comparison with Method 1, the proposed method selects well-performed architectures because all operations are equally selected and trained during the weight training stage. Table 1 shows that the proposed method obtains

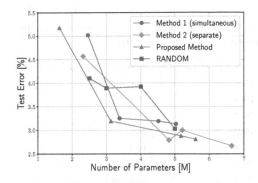

**Fig. 1.** Relationship between the number of parameters and test error in CIFAR-10.

**Table 1.** Search cost to obtain 4 architectures in CIFAR-10. The search cost excludes the architecture retraining cost.

| Method | Search cost [GPU hours] |
|---|---|
| Method 1 (simultaneous) | 16.4 |
| Method 2 (separate) | 5.2 |
| Proposed method | **3.4** |

four architectures in approximately one-fifth of the search time required by Method 1. While Method 1 requires as many searches as the number of architectures to be obtained, the proposed method obtains multiple architectures in a single search.

Comparing the proposed method with Method 2 (Separate), the proposed method obtains multiple architectures with different parameters without causing a degradation of the prediction accuracy. Both methods require a single optimization of the weights, but the proposed method updates multiple distribution parameters using the architecture samples from the mixture distribution. Therefore, the proposed method does not need to repeat the architecture search. Consequently, the proposed method reduces the search cost compared to Method 2. Finally, the architectures obtained by the proposed method exhibit better prediction accuracies than those obtained via a random search, suggesting that the architecture search is effective.

### 4.2 ImageNet

**Experimental Settings.** ImageNet [6] is a large-scale image classification dataset consisting of 1,000 classes containing approximately 1.28 million training images and 50,000 validation images. We use the CNN architecture search space proposed in ProxylessNAS [3] and evaluate the performance of the obtained architectures using the validation data. For the training data, we follow the pre-processing and data augmentation methods in [10].

During the search phase, we update the distribution parameters $\theta$ with 50,000 randomly selected images from the training data $\mathcal{D}$ and update the weights $W$ with the remaining training data. We update the weights and distribution parameters for 60 epochs. We set the mini-batch sizes $|\tilde{\mathcal{D}}_W|$ and $|\tilde{\mathcal{D}}_\theta|$ to 350 and the number of samples $\lambda$ to 8. For updating the weights $W$, we use SGD with a momentum of 0.9 and set the weight decay to $5 \times 10^{-5}$. According to the cosine schedule [13], the initial learning rate decreases from 0.068 to 0. For updating the

**Table 2.** Result of ImageNet. $N$ represents the number of architectures to be searched. The values of the existing methods are referred from the literature.

| Method | Params [M] | Top-1 Accuracy [%] | Search Cost [GPU hours] |
|---|---|---|---|
| MnasNet-A2 [23] | 4.8 | 75.6 | 40,000$N$ |
| ProxylessNAS [3] | 4.4 | 75.3 | 200$N$ |
| GreedyNAS-C [25] | 4.7 | 76.2 | 168+24$N$ |
| SGNAS-C [10] | 4.7 | 76.2 | 285 |
| Proposed method ($\epsilon = 1.0$) | 4.3 | 75.8 | **164** |
| MnasNet-A3 [23] | 5.2 | 76.7 | 40,000$N$ |
| GreedyNAS-B [25] | 5.2 | 76.8 | 168+24$N$ |
| SGNAS-B [10] | 5.5 | 76.8 | 285 |
| Proposed method ($\epsilon = 0.5$) | 5.4 | 76.8 | **164** |
| SCARLET-A [4] | 6.7 | 76.9 | 240+48$N$ |
| GreedyNAS-A [25] | 6.5 | 77.1 | 168+24$N$ |
| SGNAS-A [10] | 6.0 | 77.1 | 285 |
| Proposed method ($\epsilon = 0.0$) | 6.5 | 77.2 | **164** |

distribution parameters, we set the learning rate and regularization coefficient to $\eta_\theta = (\sum_d^D K_d)^{-1} = 1/141$ and $\epsilon_n \in \{0.0, 0.5, 1.0\}$, respectively.

In the retraining phase, we update the weights for 350 epochs with a mini-batch size of 768. We use RMSProp and set the weight decay to $1 \times 10^{-5}$. In the first five epochs, the learning rate increases linearly from 0 to 0.192. Thereafter, the learning rate gradually decreases by multiplying 0.963 every three epochs. We use the label smoothing technique [22] and introduce the squeeze and excitation module [9] into the MBConv operations. During inference, the model exponential moving average (EMA) is applied to calculate the prediction accuracy of the test data. These retraining settings are based on [10].

**Results and Discussions.** Table 2 shows the results of the proposed method and the existing NAS methods. The search cost indicates the cost to obtain $N$ optimized architectures. The proposed method ($\epsilon = 1.0$) demonstrates a prediction accuracy of 75.8% with 4.4M parameters. This accuracy is worse than that of the existing methods; however, the number of parameters is lower than that in the existing methods. The prediction accuracies of the proposed method ($\epsilon = 0.5$ and $0.0$) are 76.8% and 77.2%, respectively, indicating that these prediction accuracies are equal to or superior to those of existing methods. The search cost of the proposed method is lower than that of existing NAS methods. MnasNet and ProxylessNAS require $N$ architecture searches to obtain $N$ architectures with varying complexities, similar to Method 1 described in Sect. 4.1. Greedy-NAS and SCARLET-NAS perform the architecture search multiple times after optimizing the supernet weights, similar to Method 2 described in Sect. 4.1. Similar to the proposed method, SGNAS can obtain multiple structures in a single architecture search. However, SGNAS needs to train a DNN as the structure generator, which is more expensive than the proposed method. Our method results in a lower search cost compared with that in existing methods because it simultaneously updates multiple distributions by sharing the samples via importance sampling and realizes an efficient architecture search.

## 5   Conclusion

This paper has proposed a method for one-shot NAS that can efficiently find multiple architectures with different architecture complexities. We extended the method proposed in [17] to be able to use categorical variables and have derived the natural gradient of the regularization term. Subsequently, we have proposed an efficient method to search multiple architectures via importance sampling. The experimental results produced using CIFAR-10 and ImageNet show that the proposed method obtains multiple well-performed architectures with different complexities by incurring less computational cost than the baseline methods. Most NAS methods use fixed training hyperparameters, despite their impact on the performance. A possible future work could be developing a method for the joint optimization of both the architecture and training parameters, further improving the NAS performance.

**Acknowledgments.** This work was partially supported by NEDO (JPNP18002), JSPS KAKENHI Grant Number JP20H04240, and JST PRESTO Grant Number JPMJPR2133.

## References

1. Akimoto, Y., Shirakawa, S., Yoshinari, N., Uchida, K., Saito, S., Nishida, K.: Adaptive stochastic natural gradient method for one-shot neural architecture search. In: International Conference on Machine Learning (ICML) (2019)
2. Amari, S.: Natural gradient works efficiently in learning. Neural Comput. **10**(2), 251–276 (1998)
3. Cai, H., Zhu, L., Han, S.: ProxylessNAS: direct neural architecture search on target task and hardware. In: International Conference on Learning Representations (ICLR) (2019)
4. Chu, X., Zhang, B., Li, Q., Xu, R., Li, X.: SCARLET-NAS: bridging the gap between scalability and fairness in neural architecture search. In: ICCV Workshops (2021). https://arxiv.org/abs/1908.06022
5. Chu, X., Zhou, T., Zhang, B., Li, J.: Fair DARTS: eliminating unfair advantages in differentiable architecture search. In: Vedaldi, A., Bischof, H., Brox, T., Frahm, J.-M. (eds.) ECCV 2020. LNCS, vol. 12360, pp. 465–480. Springer, Cham (2020). https://doi.org/10.1007/978-3-030-58555-6_28
6. Deng, J., Dong, W., Socher, R., Li, L.J., Li, K., Fei-Fei, L.: ImageNet: a large-scale hierarchical image database. In: IEEE Conference on Computer Vision and Pattern Recognition (CVPR) (2009)
7. Elsken, T., Metzen, J.H., Hutter, F.: Neural architecture search: a survey. J. Mach. Learn. Res. **20**(55), 1–21 (2019)

8. Guo, Z., et al.: Single path one-shot neural architecture search with uniform sampling. In: Vedaldi, A., Bischof, H., Brox, T., Frahm, J.-M. (eds.) ECCV 2020. LNCS, vol. 12361, pp. 544–560. Springer, Cham (2020). https://doi.org/10.1007/978-3-030-58517-4_32

9. Hu, J., Shen, L., Sun, G.: Squeeze-and-excitation networks. In: IEEE/CVF Conference on Computer Vision and Pattern Recognition (CVPR) (2018)

10. Huang, S., Chu, W.: Searching by generating: flexible and efficient one-shot NAS with architecture generator. In: IEEE/CVF Conference on Computer Vision and Pattern Recognition (CVPR) (2021)

11. Krizhevsky, A.: Learning multiple layers of features from tiny images. Technical report, Department of Computer Science, University of Toronto (2009)

12. Liu, H., Simonyan, K., Yang, Y.: DARTS: differentiable architecture search. In: International Conference on Learning Representations (ICLR) (2019)

13. Loshchilov, I., Hutter, F.: SGDR: stochastic gradient descent with warm restarts. In: International Conference on Learning Representations (ICLR) (2017)

14. Ollivier, Y., Arnold, L., Auger, A., Hansen, N.: Information-geometric optimization algorithms: a unifying picture via invariance principles. J. Mach. Learn. Res. 18(18), 1–65 (2017)

15. Pham, H., Guan, M.Y., Zoph, B., Le, Q.V., Dean, J.: Efficient neural architecture search via parameter sharing. In: International Conference on Machine Learning (ICML) (2018)

16. Real, E., et al.: Large-scale evolution of image classifiers. In: International Conference on Machine Learning (ICML) (2017)

17. Saito, S., Shirakawa, S.: Controlling model complexity in probabilistic model-based dynamic optimization of neural network structures. In: Tetko, I.V., Kůrková, V., Karpov, P., Theis, F. (eds.) ICANN 2019. LNCS, vol. 11728, pp. 393–405. Springer, Cham (2019). https://doi.org/10.1007/978-3-030-30484-3_33

18. Shirakawa, S., Akimoto, Y., Ouchi, K., Ohara, K.: Sample reuse in the covariance matrix adaptation evolution strategy based on importance sampling. In: Genetic and Evolutionary Computation Conference (GECCO) (2015)

19. Shirakawa, S., Akimoto, Y., Ouchi, K., Ohara, K.: Sample Reuse via Importance Sampling in Information Geometric Optimization. arXiv:1805.12388 (2018). https://arxiv.org/abs/1805.12388

20. Shirakawa, S., Iwata, Y., Akimoto, Y.: Dynamic optimization of neural network structures using probabilistic modeling. In: 32nd AAAI Conference on Artificial Intelligence (AAAI) (2018)

21. Suganuma, M., Shirakawa, S., Nagao, T.: A genetic programming approach to designing convolutional neural network architectures. In: Genetic and Evolutionary Computation Conference (GECCO) (2017)

22. Szegedy, C., Vanhoucke, V., Ioffe, S., Shlens, J., Wojna, Z.: Rethinking the inception architecture for computer vision. In: IEEE/CVF Conference on Computer Vision and Pattern Recognition (CVPR) (2016)

23. Tan, M., et al.: MnasNet: platform-aware neural architecture search for mobile. In: IEEE/CVF Conference on Computer Vision and Pattern Recognition (CVPR) (2019)

24. Wu, B., et al.: FBNet: hardware-aware efficient ConvNet design via differentiable neural architecture search. In: IEEE/CVF Conference on Computer Vision and Pattern Recognition (CVPR) (2019)

25. You, S., Huang, T., Yang, M., Wang, F., Qian, C., Zhang, C.: GreedyNAS: towards fast one-shot NAS with greedy supernet. In: IEEE/CVF Conference on Computer Vision and Pattern Recognition (CVPR) (2020)

26. Zhou, P., Xiong, C., Socher, R., Hoi, S.C.H.: Theory-inspired path-regularized differential network architecture search. In: Advances in Neural Information Processing Systems (NeurIPS), vol. 33, pp. 8296–8307 (2020)
27. Zoph, B., Le, Q.V.: Neural architecture search with reinforcement learning. In: International Conference on Learning Representations (ICLR) (2017)
28. Zoph, B., Vasudevan, V., Shlens, J., Le, Q.V.: Learning transferable architectures for scalable image recognition. In: IEEE/CVF Conference on Computer Vision and Pattern Recognition (CVPR) (2018)

# End-to-End Large-Scale Image Retrieval Network with Convolution and Vision Transformers

Qing Zhang[1,2,3], Feilong Bao[1,2,3]([✉]), Xiangdong Su[1,2,3], Weihua Wang[1,2,3], and Guanglai Gao[1,2,3]

[1] College of Computer Science, Inner Mongolia University, Hohhot, China
{csfeilong,cssxd,wangwh,csggl}@imu.edu.cn
[2] Inner Mongolia Key Laboratory of Mongolian Information Processing Technology, Hohhot, China
[3] National & Local Joint Engineering Research Center of Intelligent Information Processing Technology for Mongolian, Hohhot, China

**Abstract.** There has been significant progress in content-based image retrieval with the development of convolutional neural networks and visual transformers. However, there are semantic gaps between high-level semantic information and low-level visual features. To solve this problem, we propose a high-performance image retrieval method based on the convolutional neural network (CNN) and vision transformers, which takes advantage of the local characteristics of the CNN and the long-range dependence characteristics of vision transformers. The proposed convolution and vision transformers network (CVTNet) firstly uses the CNN backbone network to extract the feature representation of the image. Secondly, it uses the vision transformers to enhance the semantic relationship among the feature layer to reduce the semantic gap. Finally, we propose an adaptive weight loss function that fuses triplet loss and second-order similarity loss to capture more image structure information. Extensive experimental results demonstrated that CVTNet achieves significant performance improvement on Revisited Oxford and Paris datasets compared with the baselines.

**Keywords:** Image retrieval · Vision transformer · Content based image retrieval · CNN

Supported by the National Key Research and Development Program (2018YFE0122 900), the National Natural Science Foundation of China (61773224, 62066033), the Applied Technology Research and Development Foundation of Inner Mongolia Autonomous Region (2019GG372, 2020GG0046, 2021GG0158, 2020PT0002), the Achievements Transformation Project of Inner Mongolia Autonomous Region (2019CG028), the Natural Science Foundation of Inner Mongolia Autonomous Region (2020BS06001), the Science Foundation of Inner Mongolia College and University (NJZY20008).

E. Pimenidis et al. (Eds.): ICANN 2022, LNCS 13532, pp. 620–632, 2022.
https://doi.org/10.1007/978-3-031-15937-4_52

# 1    Introduction

Content-based image retrieval (CBIR) plays a fundamental role in computer vision and multimedia and has substantial potential application in a variety of fields. The CNN has become a standard technique in image retrieval because of its ability to robust feature representation. At the same time, inspired by the successful use of the transformer [1] self-attention mechanism model in natural language processing, many recent works have attempted to use the transformer in computer vision, such as image classification [2], and image retrieval [3].

However, the ViT model proposed by Dosovitskiy et al. [4] shows that the generalization performance of the transformer is low when the training data is insufficient. Subsequently, a lot of work was carried out to improve the performance of the ViT model, such as the DeiT [5] model that introduced the distillation training strategy, and the VTs [6] model that combined CNN and transformer. The above models are all focused on the image classification task, and how to effectively combine CNN and transformer in the image retrieval is still under researched.

In the train time, the image retrieval network can obtain each image's feature descriptor [7]. In the test time, we use the feature descriptors of the query image and the feature descriptors of each image in the dataset to calculate the similarity, and the retrieval results are output in the order of similarity from high to low. Therefore, feature descriptors are significant for image retrieval. The off-the-shelf end-to-end image retrieval network includes single-pass schemes [7] and multiple-pass schemes [8]. Despite single-pass or multiple-pass schemes, there exists a semantic gap when obtaining an image descriptor.

The CNN has translation invariance and local characteristics [9]. The transformer can establish long-distance dependencies, but it is difficult to effectively extract low-level features [10]. At present, CNN is used as the image descriptor extracted by the backbone in image retrieval. The descriptor is obtained by extracting the low-level visual features of the image, and its discriminability needs to be improved. Therefore, we focus on how to use transformer characteristics of capturing long-range dependence to explore the relationship among the different spatial frequency feature maps in convolutional neural networks (CNNs). So that the descriptor can represent the target building, improve the distinguishing ability of the descriptor, and reduce the semantic gap. The main contributions are summarized as follows:

1. We propose a novel end-to-end triplet image retrieval network CVTNet, which uses the transformer to capture the semantic correlation among the feature images.
2. We propose an effective adaptive weighting loss, which automatically updates the weights of the triplet loss and second-order similarity loss.
3. Extensive experiments are conducted on two public image retrieval datasets to verify the effectiveness of our method, and the performance is significantly improved compared with the baseline model.

## 2   Related Work

In the early CBIR system, local features and global features often used brightness, shape, texture, and other information to describe the image as a representation. Sivic et al. [11] proposed a Bag-of-Words model based on quantification of local features to compact representation for image retrieval. In particular, scale-invariant feature transform [12] is highly descriptive and discriminative to capture visual content in various scenes, so it is used for image representation.

In the early CNN-based image retrieval, researchers used the activated fully connected layer (FC) as the global image description [13]. The FC lacks geometric invariance and spatial information, so the subsequent work uses the convolutional layer as the global description. When clustering convolution layers into a global image description, a global pooling operation is needed. Researchers have proposed a variety of pooling methods, such as MAC [14], SPoC [15], Crow [16], R-MAC [17], DAME [18]. In particular, the Generalized-Mean (GeM) pooling proposed by Radenovic et al. [19] effectively combines global maximum pooling (MAC [14]) and average pooling (SPoC [15]) into a paradigm. It is widely used in image retrieval.

In order to further improve the performance of image retrieval, many researchers have focused on the selection of the loss function, design of the network structure, and feature representation, respectively. At present, image retrieval mainly uses contrast loss [19] and triplet loss [17] for network training. For the design of the network structure, Radenovic et al. [19] used VGG [9] and ResNet [20] as the backbone for image retrieval, respectively. The experiment showed that the ResNet network achieved the best results. In order to obtain a significant feature representation, Cao et al. [21] proposed a unified model for jointly extracting global and local features. In addition, some researchers improved the accuracy of image retrieval by introducing more visual mechanisms and regularization. Nie et al. [22] used the self-attention mechanism to fuse the information between different layers, effectively extracting more relevant features. Ng et al. [7] used second-order spatial attention and combined second-order similarity loss (SOLAR) to learn global image representation for image retrieval.

The transformer has demonstrated excellent capabilities and have made significant progress on vision tasks [2,3]. El-nouby et al. [8] proposed an image retrieval model based on the visual transformer, which used the visual transformer to generate image descriptors. In addition, Messina et al. [23] proposed an image-text retrieval model based on the transformer, which mapped the image and text modal information into the common space to preserve the relationship between the two modalities. Miech et al. [3] used ResNet to extract image features and transformer decoder to calculate the similarity between image features and text features. Therefore, the transformer has made significant progress in both single-modal and multi-modal computer vision tasks.

Our method is motivated by the work of Ng et al. [7] and El-Nouby et al. [8]. Both of them proposed an end-to-end architecture for image retrieval tasks, while their networks only use CNN or transformer. This paper proposes an end-to-end image retrieval model based on CNN and vision transformers, and our method further improves the performance of image retrieval. At the same time, our method is motivated by Kendall et al. [24], who propose weighing multiple loss functions by considering the homoscedastic uncertainty of each task.

## 3 Proposed Method

### 3.1 Network Architecture

We propose an end-to-end large-scale image retrieval network combining CNN and vision transformer (CVTNet), which pipeline is shown in Fig. 1. The CVT-Net uses the CNN removed the fully connected layer as the backbone to extract the image representation, and the CNN backbone uses the ResNet. Meanwhile, transformer encoder blocks can be inserted into any stage of the CNN to obtain the semantic correlation among the feature maps and enhance the feature semantic representation. Each transformer encoder blocks consists of positional encoding, multi-head self-attention, add & norm, and feed-forward networks (FFN). The global single-pass image retrieval tasks need to capture high-level semantic information. In addition, the complexity of the transformer is $O(n^2)$. Therefore, this paper inserts the transformer block after the fifth stage of the CNN, and the transformer block is only used once. Next, we process the feature map from transformer with GeM pooling, whitening, and $\ell_2$ normalization to obtain the 1024 dimension image descriptor. In each mini-batch, an image of the one class as the anchor is selected as a positive example. Some images of different classes from the anchor are selected as negative examples. Given a set of triplets formed by anchor, positive and negative images, their corresponding global descriptors

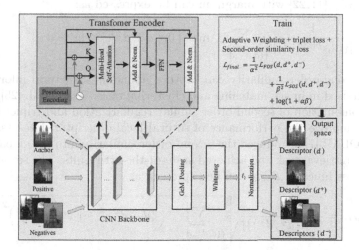

**Fig. 1.** The pipeline of proposed end-to-end global single-pass image retrieval network CVTNet. The blue box represents the transformer encoder module. The CNN and transformer map the input images into an output space. At training time, the triplet loss and second-order similarity loss are constrained network. (Color figure online)

are denoted as $\{(d, d^+, d^-)\}$. In the training process, all triplets share the network weights. In particular, as shown in the upper right corner of Fig. 1, we use adaptive weight combined with triplet loss and second-order similarity (SOS) loss to enhance the representation of feature descriptors.

## 3.2 Improved Triplet Loss and SOS Loss

Current image retrieval models usually combine multiple loss functions to constrain the network training. However, manually tuning the weights of these loss functions is a time-consuming and challenging process, and the weights cannot be optimized with the training of the network simultaneously. Inspired by the work [24], we propose an adaptive weight loss based on maximising the Gaussian likelihood with homoscedastic uncertainty. In practice, we set the auxiliary term as $log(1 + \alpha\beta)$ rather than $log(\alpha\beta)$ due to its numerical stability. The adaptive weight loss (Awloss) is as follows:

$$\mathcal{L}_{\text{final}} = \frac{1}{\alpha^2}\mathcal{L}_{\text{FOS}} + \frac{1}{\beta^2}\mathcal{L}_{SOS} + log(1 + \alpha\beta) \tag{1}$$

where, $\mathcal{L}_{FOS}$ and $\mathcal{L}_{SOS}$ denote the triplet loss and the second-order similarity loss, respectively. $\alpha$ and $\beta$ are the adaptive weight parameters, which are initialized and optimized by the training of the network simultaneously.

Given an anchor, we select an image related to the anchor as a positive sample and five images unrelated to the anchor as a negative sample pair. In the training stage, we make the distance between anchor (d) and the positive example $(d^+)$ closer, and widen the distance between the anchor (d) and the negative example $(d^-)$. At the same time, the whole network shares weight, and the triplet loss function $\mathcal{L}_{FOS}$ [11,22] with margin m can be expressed as:

$$\mathcal{L}_{FOS} = \frac{1}{|\{(d, d^+, d^-)\}|} \sum_{\{(d,d^+,d^-)\}} \max\left(0, \|d - d^+\|^2 - \|d - d^-\|^2 + m\right). \tag{2}$$

Since second-order similarity can capture abundant structural information, it has been used in image matching and clustering tasks. Tian et al. [25] showed that the combination of second-order similar regularization and triplet loss can effectively improve the performance of several local descriptor datasets. Subsequently, SOLAR [7] introduced the second-order similarity into the global single-pass image retrieval task and achieved state-of-the-art results. The second-order similarity loss function $\mathcal{L}_{SOS}$ can be expressed as:

$$\mathcal{L}_{SOS} = \frac{1}{|\{(d, d^+, d^-)\}|} \sqrt{\sum_{\{(d,d^+,d^-)\}} \left(\|d - d^-\|^2 - \|d^+ - d^-\|^2\right)^2}. \tag{3}$$

The SLOAR [7] balances the triplet loss and second-order similarity loss functions with the parameter $\lambda$, and its expression is:

$$\mathcal{L} = \mathcal{L}_{FOS} + \lambda\mathcal{L}_{SOS} \tag{4}$$

The Eq. (4) adopts the method of manually selected loss weights. However, we adopts the adaptive weight loss (Awloss) as shown in Eq. (1) ($\mathcal{L}_{final}$) in this paper, and verify the effectiveness of the Awloss in the experiment.

# 4    Experiment and Discussion

This section describes the details of the experimental. Section 4.1 describes the datasets and evaluation metrics. Section 4.2 describes the implementation details. Section 4.3 describes experiments on two public large-scale image retrieval datasets, including Revisited Oxford (ROxf) and Revisited Paris (RPar) [11], and compares CVTNet with peer methods. Section 4.4 describes ablation experiments on the ROxf and RPar to verify the effectiveness of each component.

## 4.1    Datasets and Evaluation Metrics

The Google Landmarks 18 (GL18) [7] dataset is the largest dataset of instance image retrieval, which contains over 1.2 million photos from 15k landmarks around the world. As reference [7], it serves as a semi-automatically labeled training dataset. The ROxf and RPar dataset is commonly used for evaluating the performance of global single-pass descriptors on large-scale CBIR systems. The ROxf and RPar datasets are composed of 4993 and 6322 images, respectively, and each with 70 query images. About the evaluation criteria [7,19], we use standard evaluation metrics, namely mean average precision (mAP) and mean precision at rank 10 (mP@10), and report performance on the Medium and Hard levels. We also conduct experiments on the 1M-distractors (R1M) datasets to test the robustness of descriptors. This dataset contains 1-million extra images.

## 4.2    Implementation Details

At the train time, following [7], we start with ResNet101-GeM [19] pre-trained on GL18. We train for a maximum of 100 epochs to fine-tune the transformers block and whitening layer on the same GL18 dataset using Adam. For each epoch, 2,000 anchors and 20,000 negative samples are randomly selected. For every anchor, the triplet loss contains 1 positive and 5 negatives. In Eq. (2), the margin m is 1.25 for triplet loss. For train, the hyperparameters of CVTNet included: batch-size (4), initial learning rate (1e−6), learning rate exponential decay (0.01). The whole training procedure takes about 42 h using 4×P100 GPUs. Since the number of images included in the revisitop1m.txt file does not match the number of images in the R1M dataset, we removed the extra images in the revisitop1m.txt file. We construct an image pyramid to achieve multi-scale retrieval results in the test time, as used in previous works [7,19]. First, we use to 1, 2, $1/\sqrt{2}$ resize the image to build an image pyramid, and each of these images are separately inputted into the CVTNet. Then, we averaged these descriptors to obtain the final retrieval descriptor. The FLOPS (G) is 126.15 and computed for input images of size 1024 × 768.

## 4.3  Comparison with Baseline and State-of-the-Art Methods

We choose to use the triplet loss and GeM [19] method in the GL18 dataset as the baseline. We define it as GeM [SOTA] in Table 1. To evaluate the performance of the CVTNet, we have compared the performance of CVTNet with the state-of-the-art image retrieval methods on ROxf, RPar, and ROxf+R1M (O+R1M), RPar+R1M (P+R1M) dataset in Table 1. We show the Medium and Hard protocols performance of the state-of-the-art global single-pass methods using mAP and mP@10 evaluation criteria in Table 1.

It can be seen from Table 1, compared with GeM [SOTA] [19], the CVTNet of mAP performance with a boost of up to 2.2% on ROxf-Medium, 3.6% on ROxf-Hard, 0.3% on RPar-Medium, and 1.5% on RPar-Hard. It is worth noting that compared with the state-of-the-art ResNet+SOLAR [11] (SOLAR), CVTNet improves mP@10 performance by 1.7% on ROxf-Medium, 1.3% on ROxf-Hard, and 0.2% on RPar-Medium. Therefore, the proposed method can effectively improve the performance of global single-pass image retrieval. In the R1M dataset, compared with the baseline method, the mAP performance of CVTNet in O+R1M-Medium, P+R1M-Medium, O+R1M-Hard, and P+R1M-Hard increases to 8.2% and 2.8%, 11.9%, 5.8%, respectively. Compared with SOLAR [7], mAP performance improves by 4.2%, 0.9%, 7.7% and 2.2%, respectively. Therefore, CVTNet obtains significant results on multiple retrieval datasets.

In Fig. 2, given a query image, we show the top-10 retrieval results of baseline [19], SOLAR [7], and CVTNet. The yellow box represents the query area, the green box represents the positive retrieval results, and the red box represents the negative retrieval results. The retrieval result suggests that CVTNet can return more positive retrieval samples than baseline [19] method and the state-of-the-art SOLAR [7] method. This is because that the transformer can capture semantic information between feature layers and improve the feature representation.

**Table 1.** Performance (mAP and mP@10) compared the proposed method with state-of-the-art methods on ROxf-Rpar and their respective R1M-distractors datasets. [O] denotes results from off-the-shelf networks pre-trained on ImageNet.

| Method | Medium | | | | | | Hard | | | | | |
|---|---|---|---|---|---|---|---|---|---|---|---|---|
| | ROxf | | O+R1M | RPar | | P+R1M | ROxf | | O+R1M | RPar | | P+R1M |
| | mAP | mP@10 | mAP | mAP | mP@10 | mAP | mAP | mP@10 | mAp | mAP | mP@10 | mAP |
| AlexNet-GeM [19] | 43.3 | 62.1 | 24.2 | 58.0 | 91.6 | 29.9 | 17.1 | 26.2 | 9.4 | 29.7 | 67.6 | 8.4 |
| VGG16-GeM [19] | 61.9 | 82.7 | 42.6 | 69.3 | 97.9 | 45.4 | 33.7 | 51.0 | 19 | 44.3 | 83.7 | 19.1 |
| ResNet-R-MAC [17] | 60.9 | 78.1 | 39.3 | 78.9 | 96.9 | 54.8 | 32.4 | 50.0 | 12.5 | 59.4 | 86.1 | 28 |
| ResNet-SPoC [13] [O] | 39.8 | 61.0 | 21.5 | 69.2 | 96.7 | 41.6 | 12.4 | 23.8 | 2.8 | 44.7 | 78.0 | 15.3 |
| ResNet-CroW [16] | 41.4 | 58.8 | 22.5 | 62.9 | 94.4 | 34.1 | 13.9 | 25.7 | 3 | 36.9 | 77.9 | 10.3 |
| ResNet-GeM [19] [O] | 45.8 | 66.2 | 25.6 | 69.7 | 97.6 | 46.2 | 18.1 | 31.3 | 4.7 | 47.0 | 84.9 | 20.3 |
| ResNet-GeM [19] | 64.7 | 84.7 | 45.2 | 77.2 | 98.1 | 52.3 | 38.5 | 53.0 | 19.9 | 56.3 | 89.1 | 24.7 |
| GeM+DAME [18] | 65.3 | 85.0 | 44.7 | 77.1 | 98.4 | 50.3 | 40.4 | 56.3 | 22.8 | 56.0 | 88.0 | 22 |
| GeM [SOTA] [19] | 67.3 | 84.7 | 49.5 | 80.6 | 96.7 | 57.3 | 44.3 | 53.0 | 25.7 | 61.5 | 90.7 | 29.8 |
| GeM+SOS [7] | 67.6 | 84.7 | 50 | 80.9 | 96.6 | 57.6 | 44.9 | 60.1 | 26.2 | 61.9 | 91.0 | 30.3 |
| ResNet+SOA [7] | 68.6 | 85.7 | 51.3 | 81.4 | 96.6 | 58.8 | 46.9 | 62.7 | 28.3 | 63.7 | 91.9 | 32.4 |
| ResNet+SOLAR [7] | **69.9** | 86.7 | 53.5 | **81.6** | 97.1 | 59.2 | **47.9** | 63.0 | 29.9 | **64.5** | **93.0** | 33.4 |
| CVTNet | 69.5 | **88.4** | **57.7** | 80.9 | **97.3** | **60.1** | 47.9 | **64.3** | **37.6** | 63 | 91.7 | **35.6** |

## 4.4    Ablation Studies

To verify our design choices, Sect. 4.4.1 describes the impact of transformers block and adaptive weighting loss (Awloss) performance, respectively. Section 4.4.2 describes the impact of the different number of encoder layers and multi-head self-attention performance. Section 4.4.3 describes the manually selected loss weights and Awloss methods.

**Fig. 2.** Demonstration of top-10 retrieval results. Results of Baseline [19], SOLAR [7], and CVTNet are shown from top to bottom. The green and red boxes represent positive and negative retrieval images, respectively.

**Impact of Transformers and Adaptive Weighting Loss (Awloss).** In Table 2, following [7], SOS means second-order similarity loss, SOA means second-order attention. We select GeM [19] trained on GL18 dataset with the triplet loss as our baseline. When introducing the transformer block to baseline [19], we observe that the mAP of ROxf-Medium and ROxf-Hard is improved from 67.3% to 68.2% and 44.3% to 44.7%, respectively. Meanwhile, mP@10 of ROxf-Medium and ROxf-Hard is improved from 84.7% to 85.6% and 59.7% to 61.6%, respectively. Therefore, the transformer block can improve the retrieval performance of the ROxf dataset.

When using Awloss, we observe that the mAP of ROxf-Medium and ROxf-Hard is improved from 67.3% to 68.1% and 44.3% to 46.5%, respectively. When we use transformers and Awloss simultaneously, the performance of CVTNet in ROxf and RPar datasets are better than the baseline. At the same time, we also compared with the SOLAR [7] method because the Awloss function is improved based on SOS [7]. As shown in Table 2, compared it with SOLAR method using SOS and SOA, mP@10 of ROxf-Medium and ROxf-Hard increased by 1.7% and 1.3%, respectively. As a result, CVTNet obtains significant performance improvement on both ROxf and RPar datasets.

To demonstrate the performance of Awloss and transformer, we selected an image from the ROxf dataset shown in Fig. 3. The first column of Fig. 3 show the query image. The second and eleventh columns show the top10 retrieval results. The second row show the CVTNet with Awloss without transformer

(CVTNet W/o transformers) retrieval results. The third row show the CVTNet with transformer without Awloss (CVTNet W/o Awloss) retrieval results. The last row show the CVTNet with Awloss and transformer retrieval results.

**Table 2.** Ablation studies of each method and component.

| Method | Transformers block | Awloss | SOS | SOA | Medium | | | | Hard | | | |
|---|---|---|---|---|---|---|---|---|---|---|---|---|
| | | | | | ROxf | | RPar | | ROxf | | RPar | |
| | | | | | mAP | mP@10 | mAP | mP@10 | mAP | mP@10 | mAP | mP@10 |
| baseline [19] | × | × | × | × | 67.3 | 84.7 | 80.6 | 96.7 | 44.3 | 59.7 | 61.5 | 90.7 |
| SOLAR [7] | × | × | √ | × | 67.6 | 84.7 | 80.9 | 96.6 | 44.9 | 60.1 | 61.9 | 91.0 |
| | × | × | × | √ | 68.6 | 85.7 | 81.4 | 96.6 | 46.9 | 62.7 | 63.7 | 91.9 |
| | × | × | √ | √ | **69.9** | 86.7 | **81.6** | 97.1 | 47.9 | 63.0 | **64.5** | **93.0** |
| CVTNet | √ | × | × | × | 68.2 | 85.6 | 80.0 | 97 | 44.7 | 61.6 | 60.6 | 90.4 |
| | × | √ | × | × | 68.1 | 85.4 | 80.2 | 97.3 | 46.5 | 63.4 | 61.4 | 91.7 |
| | √ | √ | × | × | 69.5 | **88.4** | 80.9 | **97.3** | **47.9** | **64.3** | 63.0 | 91.7 |

It can be seen from the second row of Fig. 3, compared with baseline [19], the Awloss (CVTNet W/o transformers) can return more positive retrieval results. The experiments demonstrated that the proposed Awloss is robust. It can be seen from the third row of Fig. 3, the transformer (CVTNet W/o Awloss) also returns more positive retrieval results than baseline [19]. This is attributed to the advantage of the transformer based on the self-attention. It make the image descriptor pay attention to the target object, thus reducing the semantic gap.

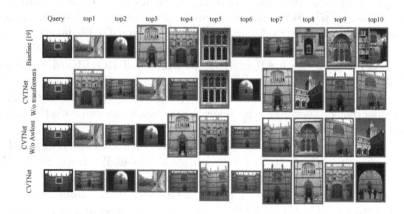

**Fig. 3.** Effect of the qualitative results of the adaptive weight Loss and transformer on the example image from the ROxf dataset. The rows from up to down represent the baseline [19], corresponding CVTNet W/o transformers, CVTNet W/o Awloss and CVTNet, respectively.

**Comparison with Different Number of Encoder Layers and Multihead Self-attention.** In Table 3, 2L-8N represents the number of encoder layers is 2, and the number of multi-head self-attention in each encoder layer is 8. When we fixed encoder layers and increased the number of multi-head self-attention, such as 4L-8N to 4L-16N, the performance of CVTNet in ROxf and RPar datasets decreased. When we fixed encoder layers and reduced the number of multi-head self-attention, such as 4L-8N to 4L-2N, the performance of CVTNet also reduced. Furthermore, in the case of fixing the number of multi-head self-attention, and increased or decreased the number of encoder layers respectively, such as 4L-8N to 8L-8N, 4L-8N to 2L-8N, the performance of CVTNet in ROxf-Hard and RPar-Hard is reduced. Therefore, the selection number of encoder layers and multi-head self-attention in the transformers has a significant influence on the performance. As can be seen from Table 3, when select the 4L-8N in the transformers, the proposed method achieve a significant retrieval performance. Therefore the combined parameter 4L-8N is finally selected.

**Table 3.** Comparison with different number of encoder layers and multi-head self-attention.

| Setting | Medium | | | | Hard | | | |
|---------|--------|--------|--------|--------|--------|--------|--------|--------|
| | ROxf | | RPar | | ROxf | | RPar | |
| | mAP | mP@10 | mAP | mP@10 | mAP | mP@10 | mAP | mP@10 |
| 2L-8N | 68.1 | 85.4 | 80.2 | 97.3 | 44.5 | 62.1 | 61.4 | 91.3 |
| 4L-2N | 68.4 | 87.4 | 78.9 | 97.3 | 45.7 | 63.9 | 59.5 | 90.1 |
| **4L-8N** | **69.5** | **88.4** | **80.9** | 97.3 | **47.9** | 64.3 | **63.0** | 91.7 |
| 8L-8N | 65.3 | 85.1 | 76.5 | 97.3 | 42.0 | 57.3 | 56.6 | 91.6 |
| 4L-16N | 69.4 | 87.9 | 80.8 | **97.4** | 47.8 | **64.4** | 62.9 | **91.9** |

**Comparison of Manually Selected Loss Weights and Awloss Methods.** We compare the performance of manually selected weight of the loss function and Awloss method. The experimental results are shown in Table 4. We set three manually selected loss function weight. It can be seen from Table 4 that in Eq. (4), when $\lambda = 5$ achieves better retrieval performance. When using the Awloss method, we can further improve the mP@10 performance of ROxf-RPar. For example, the mP@10 performance of Awloss compared with $\lambda = 5$ is increased by 1% and 0.2% in ROxf-Hard and RPar-Medium respectively, which verifies the effectiveness of Awloss. For the setting of the initial value in Awloss, we take $\alpha = 1$, $\beta = 0.45$, where $\alpha$ and $\beta$ are trainable parameters. Specifically, these two parameters are updated with the training and regulated by the last term in Eq. (1). Therefore both terms mutually interact and restrict each other.

**Table 4.** Comparison of loss weights that were selected manually or using the proposed Awloss method.

| Setting | Medium | | | | Hard | | | |
|---------|--------|--------|--------|--------|--------|--------|--------|--------|
| | ROxf | | RPar | | ROxf | | RPar | |
| | mAP | mP@10 | mAP | mP@10 | mAP | mP@10 | mAP | mP@10 |
| $\lambda = 1$ | 69.1 | 86.4 | 80.1 | 97 | 44.9 | 61.3 | 61.1 | 90.9 |
| $\lambda = 5$ | **70.0** | 87.9 | **81.0** | 97.1 | 47.7 | 63.3 | **63.1** | 91.7 |
| $\lambda = 10$ | 67.6 | 85.7 | 77.9 | 97.1 | 44.0 | 59.6 | 58.8 | 90.6 |
| **Awloss** | 69.5 | **88.4** | 80.9 | **97.3** | **47.9** | **64.3** | 63 | **91.7** |

## 5   Conclusion

In this paper, we propose a novel network which CNN and vision transformers combined network, called CVTNet. The network uses CNN to extract feature layers of images, and adopts transformer to obtain the semantic relationship among the features layer to enhance the feature representation. In particular, we further use adaptive weighting methods combined with multiple loss functions to effectively improve the retrieval results. The proposed CVTNet combing the advantages of CNN and transformer, can capture local and global information and enhance the representation ability of the network. The adaptive weight method can update the weight parameters with the training, so that multiple loss functions can be jointly optimized. Compared with the baseline [19] method, the CVTNet improves the mAP performance by 3.6% and 1.5% in ROxf-Hard and RPar-Hard, respectively. Compared with the state-of-the-art SOLAR [7], the CVTNet improves the mP@10 performance by 1.7% and 1.3% in ROxf-Medium and ROxf-Hard, respectively. Therefore, combination of CNN and vision transformers can obtain significant improvement of the image retrieval performance.

## References

1. Vaswani, A., et al.: Attention is all you need. In: Advances in Neural Information Processing Systems, vol. 30 (2017)
2. Lanchantin, J., Wang, T., Ordonez, V., Qi, Y.: General multi-label image classification with transformers. In: Proceedings of the IEEE/CVF Conference on Computer Vision and Pattern Recognition, pp. 16478–16488 (2021)
3. Miech, A., Alayrac, J.B., Laptev, I., Sivic, J., Zisserman, A.: Thinking fast and slow: efficient text-to-visual retrieval with transformers. In: Proceedings of the IEEE/CVF Conference on Computer Vision and Pattern Recognition, pp. 9826–9836 (2021)
4. Dosovitskiy, A., et al.: An image is worth 16x16 words: transformers for image recognition at scale. arXiv preprint arXiv:2010.11929 (2020)
5. Touvron, H., Cord, M., Douze, M., Massa, F., Sablayrolles, A., Jégou, H.: Training data-efficient image transformers & distillation through attention. In: International Conference on Machine Learning, pp. 10347–10357. PMLR (2021)

6. Wu, B., et al.: Visual transformers: token-based image representation and processing for computer vision. arXiv preprint arXiv:2006.03677 (2020)

7. Ng, T., Balntas, V., Tian, Y., Mikolajczyk, K.: SOLAR: second-order loss and attention for image retrieval. In: Vedaldi, A., Bischof, H., Brox, T., Frahm, J.-M. (eds.) ECCV 2020. LNCS, vol. 12370, pp. 253–270. Springer, Cham (2020). https://doi.org/10.1007/978-3-030-58595-2_16

8. El-Nouby, A., Neverova, N., Laptev, I., Jégou, H.: Training vision transformers for image retrieval. arXiv preprint arXiv:2102.05644 (2021)

9. Simonyan, K., Zisserman, A.: Very deep convolutional networks for large-scale image recognition. arXiv preprint arXiv:1409.1556 (2014)

10. Yuan, K., Guo, S., Liu, Z., Zhou, A., Yu, F., Wu, W.: Incorporating convolution designs into visual transformers. In: Proceedings of the IEEE/CVF International Conference on Computer Vision, pp. 579–588 (2021)

11. Sivic, J., Zisserman, A.: Video google: a text retrieval approach to object matching in videos. In: IEEE International Conference on Computer Vision, vol. 3, pp. 1470–1470. IEEE Computer Society (2003)

12. Lowe, D.G.: Distinctive image features from scale-invariant keypoints. Int. J. Comput. Vision **60**(2), 91–110 (2004)

13. Babenko, A., Slesarev, A., Chigorin, A., Lempitsky, V.: Neural codes for image retrieval. In: Fleet, D., Pajdla, T., Schiele, B., Tuytelaars, T. (eds.) ECCV 2014. LNCS, vol. 8689, pp. 584–599. Springer, Cham (2014). https://doi.org/10.1007/978-3-319-10590-1_38

14. Tolias, G., Sicre, R., Jégou, H.: Particular object retrieval with integral max-pooling of CNN activations. arXiv preprint arXiv:1511.05879 (2015)

15. Babenko, A., Lempitsky, V.: Aggregating local deep features for image retrieval. In: Proceedings of the IEEE International Conference on Computer Vision, pp. 1269–1277 (2015)

16. Kalantidis, Y., Mellina, C., Osindero, S.: Cross-dimensional weighting for aggregated deep convolutional features. In: Hua, G., Jégou, H. (eds.) ECCV 2016. LNCS, vol. 9913, pp. 685–701. Springer, Cham (2016). https://doi.org/10.1007/978-3-319-46604-0_48

17. Gordo, A., Almazán, J., Revaud, J., Larlus, D.: Deep image retrieval: learning global representations for image search. In: Leibe, B., Matas, J., Sebe, N., Welling, M. (eds.) ECCV 2016. LNCS, vol. 9910, pp. 241–257. Springer, Cham (2016). https://doi.org/10.1007/978-3-319-46466-4_15

18. Yang, T.Y., Kien Nguyen, D., Heijnen, H., Balntas, V.: Dame web: dynamic mean with whitening ensemble binarization for landmark retrieval without human annotation. In: Proceedings of the IEEE/CVF International Conference on Computer Vision Workshops (2019)

19. Radenović, F., Tolias, G., Chum, O.: Fine-tuning CNN image retrieval with no human annotation. IEEE Trans. Pattern Anal. Mach. Intell. **41**(7), 1655–1668 (2018)

20. He, K., Zhang, X., Ren, S., Sun, J.: Deep residual learning for image recognition. In: Proceedings of the IEEE Conference on Computer Vision and Pattern Recognition, pp. 770–778 (2016)

21. Cao, B., Araujo, A., Sim, J.: Unifying deep local and global features for image search. In: Vedaldi, A., Bischof, H., Brox, T., Frahm, J.-M. (eds.) ECCV 2020. LNCS, vol. 12365, pp. 726–743. Springer, Cham (2020). https://doi.org/10.1007/978-3-030-58565-5_43

22. Nie, X., Lu, H., Wang, Z., Liu, J., Guo, Z.: Weakly supervised image retrieval via coarse-scale feature fusion and multi-level attention blocks. In: Proceedings of the 2019 on International Conference on Multimedia Retrieval, pp. 48–52 (2019)
23. Messina, N., Falchi, F., Esuli, A., Amato, G.: Transformer reasoning network for image-text matching and retrieval. In: 2020 25th International Conference on Pattern Recognition (ICPR), pp. 5222–5229. IEEE (2021)
24. Kendall, A., Gal, Y., Cipolla, R.: Multi-task learning using uncertainty to weigh losses for scene geometry and semantics. In: Proceedings of the IEEE Conference on Computer Vision and Pattern Recognition, pp. 7482–7491 (2018)
25. Tian, Y., Yu, X., Fan, B., Wu, F., Heijnen, H., Balntas, V.: Sosnet: second order similarity regularization for local descriptor learning. In: Proceedings of the IEEE/CVF Conference on Computer Vision and Pattern Recognition, pp. 11016–11025 (2019)

# Ensemble Ranking for Image Retrieval via Deep Hash

Donggen Li, Dawei Dai, Hongyuan Shan, Shunyin Xia[✉], and Yulong Xia

Key Laboratory of Computational Intelligence,
Chongqing University of Posts and Telecommunications, Chongqing, China
xiasy@cqupt.edu.cn

**Abstract.** In recent years, convolutional neural networks (CNNs) have achieved remarkable success in computer vision applications. Deep hashing combines feature extraction or representation with hash coding jointly; it can extract high-quality image features and generate approximate hash codes containing rich semantic information. Because an image is represented by binary codes instead of a high-dimensional floating-point-number feature matrix, the hashing method can significantly improve the speed of large-scale image retrieval. However, we notice that compared with traditional retrieval methods, image retrieval through binary hash encoding induces performance degradation to a certain extent, and most existing hash retrieval algorithms focus only on the semantic similarity between image pairs, the returned image samples should not only match the ground truth, but also the correct image should be in the front of the result list, they ignore the ranking information of the returned samples, limiting their performance. For this issue, this paper proposes a multimodel ensemble image retrieval framework which can learn compact hash codes containing rich semantic information through hash constraints. The ensemble strategy is introduced, and the weighted voting is applied to integrate the ranking list. Comprehensive experiments on three benchmark datasets show that the proposed method achieves very competitive results.

**Keywords:** Convolutional neural networks · Image retrieval · Hash coding · Ensemble learning

## 1 Introduction

Images convey a massive amount of information in a concise and intuitive way, and it is an important source for human to obtain information about the objective world. Large-scale image retrieval is an important and fundamental task in computer vision. In the field of image retrieval, the critical steps are image feature extraction and hash coding. In the feature extraction step, compared

---

Supported by Key Laboratory of Computational Intelligence, Chongqing University of Posts and Telecommunications.

with manual feature extraction, the method based on a deep convolutional neural network (CNN) can extract high-level features with better expressive ability. The hash-based image retrieval method approach maps the high-dimensional feature vector space of the input image to the Hamming space with values of 0 and 1, achieving data dimensionality reduction and greatly reducing the time complexity and spatial complexity of the retrieval process.

One of the main challenges encountered when utilizing hash methods for large-scale image retrieval is mapping from the original feature space to the binary codes in the hash code space while preserving semantic similarity. Many deep hashing methods have demonstrated impressive performance. However, most existing hash retrieval algorithms pay attention only to the semantic similarity between the query image and the database image and ignore the ranking information of the retrieval result, that is, the position of the correct image in the result list, which limits their performance.

This paper proposes a hash-based image retrieval framework based on ensemble learning, which combines the advantages of deep CNNs and hashing algorithms. First, a hidden hash layer is added to the end of the deep CNN. This hash layer not only extract high-level semantic features, but also obtains approximate hash codes, which are quantized to obtain strict binary hash codes. Second, we apply a weighted voting strategy to image retrieval by integrating the location information of the returned image to ensure the similarity between the top image in the query result ranking list and the query image. Experimental results on three widely used benchmark datasets: CIFAR-10, SUN397 and ILSVRC2012 show that our method is superior to the state-of-the-art methods and has excellent performance. The main contributions of this paper are summarized as follows:

1) This paper provides a novel framework based on ensemble learning for hash retrieval. The feature expression ability of a single model is insufficient, and the advantages of ensemble learning are considered to compensate for the deficiency of a single model.
2) The position information of the returned sample list is integrated to preserve the semantic similarity between the top images in the ranking list and query images.
3) This paper fill the gap in image hash retrieval field by proposing a general ensemble retrieval method for the first time to solve the problem that existing hash image retrieval can only adopt a single network model.

## 2    Related Work

### 2.1    Unsupervised Hashing Methods

The unsupervised hashing method is independent of the input data during the process of designing feature data mapping schemes. The main research directions regarding traditional unsupervised hashing methods are hash function learning and hash quantization coding. The most classic hashing method is locality-sensitive hashing (LSH [1]), which is considered the baseline algorithm for binary coding methods; it maps the data points in the feature space into a hyperplane to generate binary hash codes.

## 2.2 Semi-supervised Hashing Methods

A semi-supervised hashing method uses a small number of dataset labels and unlabeled image data to learn a hash function. The most representative semi-supervised hashing method is semi-supervised hashing (SH [2]), which uses labeled data to learn hash functions to preserve semantic similarity and improve the quality of the resulting hash codes. By optimizing the errors between the labeled data point pairs, the generated hash codes are as small as possible while balanced and independent, and only a portion of the data contains supervision information. The algorithm has strong robustness and can prevent the occurrence of overfitting to a certain extent.

## 2.3 Supervised Hashing Methods

A supervised hashing method aims to use supervision information (labeled data) for hash function training. Minimal loss hashing (MLH [3]) evaluates the similarities between data based on label information and obtains effective hash codes. The typical method is CCA-ITQ, an extension of ITQ, which uses the canonical correlation analysis method [4] to analyze data correlations and then minimizes the quantization error. Supervised hashing with kernels (KSH [5]), based on the kernel function, uses a nonlinear kernel function as the hash function and uses the characteristics of the Hamming distance and the inner product of the code to train the hash function to generate compact hash codes. Supervised discrete hashing (SDH [6]) uses a bit-by-bit optimization method to obtain efficient hash codes.

## 2.4 Deep Hash-Based Retrieval Method

With the breakthrough of deep learning theory, the ability of deep learning models to express high-level semantic information contained in images has become increasingly prominent. Therefore, methods based on deep learning, especially CNNs, have achieved impressive results. During 2010 and 2017, some classic CNN models emerged, such as VGG [7], ResNet [8], and DenseNet [9]. Semantic hashing (SH [10]) was the first approach to link deep neural networks with hashing methods. Based on this new methodology, academia began to pay attention to the combination of deep learning and hashing algorithms. With hashing (CNNH) and CNNH+ [11], which are two of the early fusions of deep neural networks with hash coding. These networks can perform image feature extraction and hash code generation simultaneously. Semisupervised deep hashing (SSDH) [12] assumes that the label of an image can be represented by a set of potential attributes, and the classification results depend on these attributes, limiting the output of a particular layer to close to 0 or 1, making the generated hash codes more discriminative.

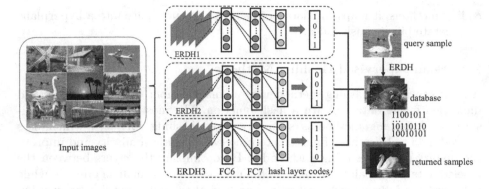

**Fig. 1.** In the proposed ERDH method for hashing-based learning, each of the three individual learners adds a hidden layer that is used to generate approximate binary code, and they are all obtained by fine-tuning the classic network.

## 3    Ensemble Learning and Deep Hashing CNNs

### 3.1    Motivation

The existing hashing methods pay attention only to the semantic similarities between image pairs and ignore the position information of the result list. Furthermore, the feature extraction capabilities of each network are different. The direct voting method cannot reflect the influence of the network weight, and cannot fully adjust the location information of the returned image.

Therefore, this paper proposes an ensemble weighting method based on a deep CNN named ERDH to generate compact hash codes and use the accuracy of the network and the Hanming distance to calculate the score of the returned image. The ERDH network is based on three backbone networks: VGG, ResNet and DenseNet, each individual learner adds a hidden layer that is used to generate approximate binary code, and the overall structure is shown in Fig. 1.

### 3.2    Ensemble Learning

Ensemble learning [13] completes the learning task by constructing and combining multiple individual learners; this method involves using a certain strategy to integrate the results of each individual learner to obtain a better learning effect than that of the individual learner. Ensemble strategies mainly include the averaging method, weighted voting method and learning method. The underlying idea of ensemble learning is that even if a certain weak classifier (referring to a classifier with low accuracy) obtains an incorrect prediction, other strong classifiers can correct the error. Our goal is to train a model that is stable and performs well in all aspects, but the actual situation is often not ideal, and sometimes we can only obtain a few models with given preferences. To obtain a good ensemble, individual learners should be "good but different"; that is, individual learners must have a certain degree of "accuracy", and there must be diversity (there must be differences between individual learners).

In this paper, three individual learners are used, which are models based on the classic VGG, Resnet, and DenseNet backbone networks. In different tasks, they can be regarded as feature extractors guided by an objective function designed specifically for a single task. The successful application of CNNs in various tasks shows that although the appearance of an image changes greatly, the features learned by a CNN can effectively capture the underlying semantic structure of the image. At the same time, when the learners perform feature extraction on the same image, their focuses are different, so they are very suitable as individual learners. CNNs have strong autonomous learning capabilities and feature expression capabilities. Therefore, using the image features extracted by a CNN as image descriptors can describe image content accurately. Reference [14] showed that the features output by the second fully connected layer $fc_7$ of a neural network can be regarded as image features and used for subsequent image classification tasks. However, these features are high-dimensional vectors. For image retrieval with large-scale databases, the high computational cost of this approach leads to low retrieval efficiency; a suitable method to avoid massive calculations is to convert high-dimensional vectors into binary hash codes. Therefore, we introduce a hash layer between the last two fully connected layers, which can reduce the loss of image feature information and generate hash codes with rich semantic information; thus, the input of the hash layer is divided into two parts: one part comes from $fc_7$, and the other part comes from $fc_6$.

### 3.3   Hidden Hash Layer

The hidden hash layer maps the high-dimensional feature space of the image output by the deep CNN to the Hamming space and can be used for efficient retrieval. The hash layer is added after the fully connected layer $fc_7$. The classification layer $fc_8$ in the model express the high-level semantic information of the input image and complete the classification task. The hash layer is not only a generalization of the features of the fully connected layers $fc_6$ and $fc_7$; the neurons of the hash layer also receive feedback from the classification layer $fc_8$ during backpropagation. Therefore, the hash layer can be regarded as a bridge between $fc_7$ and $fc_8$ to a certain extent. It connects the middle-level features of the deep convolutional network with the high-level semantic features, so the generated hash codes have rich semantic information. The hash function can be formulated as:

$$h(x : w) = \delta \left( w^T \left[ fc_6(x); fc_7(x) \right] \right) \tag{1}$$

where $\delta(t)$ is logistic function, $w$ represents the weight of the hash layer, $fc_6(x)$ and $fc_7(x)$ represent the feature vectors output by fully connected layers $fc_6$ and $fc_7$, respectively. To obtain k-bit binary codes, the hash layer is set as a k-dimensional fully connected layer. The output range of the sigmoid function is a continuous value between 0 and 1, which is naturally close to 0 or 1; and the function is symmetric at approximately 0.5, which is convenient for the subsequent quantization of the hash codes.

Hash codes with rich semantic information require that after the image is encoded, the hash codes with similar Hamming distances should be semantically similar, and vice versa. Suppose that there are N images $[X_1 \dots X_N]$, the corresponding labels are $[Y_1 \ldots Y_N]$, and the labels predicted by the model are $[\hat{Y}_1 \ldots \hat{Y}_N]$. After the sigmoid activation function of the hash layer is executed, for each image, the approximate hash codes $[B_1 \ldots B_N]$ can be obtained. For each bit of the hash codes, to generate compact hash codes, a loss function should be added to the classification layer. Furthermore, in the hash layer, a loss function is needed to guide the learning of the target task. Two hash functions are used to constrain the hash layer. One is the binary hash loss function because the output value of the hash layer obtained through the sigmoid activation function is continuously distributed between 0 and 1. To obtain binary hash codes that can be used for efficient image retrieval, the loss function must constrain the output value as close to 0 or 1 as possible so that the hash codes lose a minimal amount of semantic information during the quantization process. The binary hash loss function is expressed as:

$$L_1 = \theta - \frac{1}{2N} \sum_{i=1}^{N} (B_i - \varsigma)^2 \tag{2}$$

where $\theta$ is 0.25, $B_i$ is the output of the hash layer and $\varsigma$ is 0.5. The second hash loss function makes 0 and 1 each compose half of the generated hash codes; this is expressed as:

$$L_2 = \frac{1}{2N} \sum_{i=1}^{N} \left( \left[ \frac{\sum_{j=1}^{K} b_j}{K} \right]_i - \xi \right)^2 \tag{3}$$

where $\left[ \frac{\sum_{j=1}^{K} b_j}{K} \right]_i$ denotes the $B_i$ mentioned above and $\xi$ is 0.5. During the model training process, to maintain semantic information, we also use a classification loss function. In the last layer of the model, the cross-entropy loss function is used; it is defined as follows:

$$L_c = -\frac{1}{N} \sum_{i} \sum_{c=1}^{M} y_{ic} \log p_{ic} \tag{4}$$

where $i$ represents the $i$th sample, $N$ represents the number of images, $M$ represents the number of label categories, and $y_{ic}$ is an indicator function. To ensure that the hash codes of images contain rich semantic information while ensuring the classification accuracy, the overall optimization goal must include both of these aspects, and the overall loss function is defined as:

$$L_{all} = \alpha L_c + \beta L_1 + \gamma L_2 \tag{5}$$

where $\alpha$, $\beta$ and $\gamma$ are hyperparameters.

### 3.4   Ensemble Learning Methods

In this part, for each image, the weighted voting method is used to determine the result for the image predicted returned by each of the three individual learners. Assuming that we have $N$ query images, for each query image, the quantized binary hash codes are compared with the image in the database, which not only

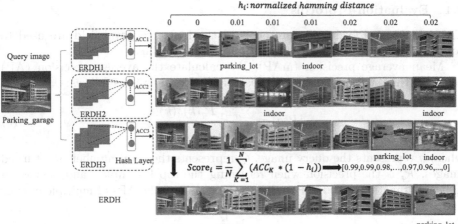

**Fig. 2.** Examples of the top eight retrieved images for a given query image from the SUN397 dataset. We calculate the score for each image and then adjust its position. The images with green borders are the matched images, while those with red borders are incorrect matches. (Color figure online)

contains the hash code but also records the name of the image corresponding to the hash code and the true label of the image. Generally, after sorting the Hamming matrix in ascending order, the top-k query results can be obtained, but in this paper, the accuracy of each individual learner and the top-k Hamming distances returned to participate in the score calculation process for each image. The score of each returned image can be formulated as follows:

$$Score_i = \left( \frac{1}{N} \sum_{k=1}^{N} ACC_k * \left( 1 - \frac{h_i}{\max(H)} \right) \right) \tag{6}$$

$$S_i = descort(Score_i) \tag{7}$$

where $ACC_k$ represents the classification accuracy of each individual learner, $h_i$ represents the normalized Hamming distance between the $i$-th returned image and the query image, $H$ represents the Hamming distance matrix and $N$ represents the number of individual learners. We sort these scores in descending order and obtain the final score ranking; that is, the k query results returned at the end are ranked. The overall idea of the reordering method is shown in Fig. 2.

## 4   Experiments

We compared ERDH with the existing methods on several benchmark datasets, including CIFAR-10 [15] and SUN397 [16]. We also verified the stability of our method on a large-scale dataset containing about 1.2M images, such as ILSVRC2012 [17]. The evaluation indicators and datasets are summarized as follows.

## 4.1  Evaluation Protocols

Two widely used evaluation protocols in the image retrieval field are used to compare the performance of different hashing algorithms.

Mean average precision (mAP): We calculate the average precision (AP) values of the retrieved images. The calculation formula is as follows:

$$AP(q) = \frac{\sum_{r=1}^{Q} P_q(k)\delta(k)}{\sum_{r'=1}^{Q} \delta(k')} \tag{8}$$

where $q$ represents the query image, $Q$ represents the total number of returned images, $P_q$ is the precision when returning the top k samples, and $\delta(*)$ is an indicator function. The mAP is the average value of the APs of multiple queries and is formulated as:

$$mAP = \frac{1}{Q} \sum_{i=1}^{Q} AP(q_i) \tag{9}$$

Precision at $k$ samples: This is the percentage of true image labels among the top k retrieved images, it reflects the proportion of the correct image returned.

## 4.2  Retrieval Results on CIFAR-10

In the experiment, following the previous method, our binary hash code lengths are 12 bits, 32 bits and 48 bits, and the results are shown in Table 1. It can be observed that, in general, supervised hashing methods have better performance than unsupervised hashing methods. In addition, the hashing method based on deep learning can provide better performance, which shows that deep learning methods have strong feature extraction capabilities and are more suitable as image feature descriptors.

**Table 1.** The mAP values of different methods with 12 bits, 32 bits and 48 bits on CIFAR-10.

| Bits | 12 bits | 32 bits | 48 bits |
|---|---|---|---|
| ERDH | **0.9623** | **0.9627** | **0.9643** |
| DTH | 0.9214 | 0.9372 | 0.9488 |
| DIHN | 0.8916 | 0.9330 | 0.9456 |
| SSDH | 0.9072 | 0.9128 | 0.9145 |
| CNNH+ | 0.9193 | 0.9210 | 0.9578 |
| CNNH | 0.8901 | 0.9204 | 0.9430 |
| CCA-ITQ | 0.7972 | 0.7972 | 0.7970 |
| MLH | 0.8675 | 0.8591 | 0.8255 |
| BRE | 0.8597 | 0.8348 | 0.8161 |
| ITQ | 0.8260 | 0.7904 | 0.7499 |
| SH | 0.7794 | 0.7130 | 0.5497 |
| DPSH | 0.7130 | 0.7440 | 0.7570 |
| LSH | 0.5497 | 0.5124 | 0.4201 |

**Table 2.** The precision rates obtained with different numbers of retrieved samples on the CIFAR-10 dataset at 48 bits

| Top-k | Top100 | Top200 | Top400 | Top600 | Top800 | Top1000 |
|---|---|---|---|---|---|---|
| ERDH | **0.9520** | **0.9521** | **0.9522** | **0.9522** | **0.9522** | **0.9522** |
| SSDH | 0.9123 | 0.9119 | 0.9117 | 0.912 | 0.9121 | 0.9122 |
| CNNH+ | 0.6010 | 0.6178 | 0.6198 | 0.6201 | 0.6219 | 0.6286 |
| CNNH | 0.6043 | 0.6145 | 0.6186 | 0.6200 | 0.6200 | 0.6251 |
| CCA-ITQ | 0.4076 | 0.4065 | 0.3987 | 0.3906 | 0.3896 | 0.3868 |
| MLH | 0.3842 | 0.3794 | 0.3705 | 0.3716 | 0.3684 | 0.3634 |
| BRE | 0.3245 | 0.3213 | 0.3201 | 0.3198 | 0.3176 | 0.3146 |
| ITQ | 0.3203 | 0.3213 | 0.3201 | 0.3198 | 0.3176 | 0.3149 |
| SH | 0.2475 | 0.2214 | 0.2108 | 0.2089 | 0.1986 | 0.1895 |
| LSH | 0.1974 | 0.1905 | 0.1912 | 0.1931 | 0.1932 | 0.1957 |

Compared to the unsupervised hashing methods such as LSH and ITQ, when the hash code length is 12 bits, ERDH outperforms LSH and ITQ by substantial margins of 75.06% and 16.50%, respectively. Compared to some supervised methods such as DTH [18], DIHN [19] and SSDH, ERDH achieves absolute boosts of 4.44%, 7.93% and 6.07% in terms of the mAP, respectively. Even if the hash code length is different, ERDH can provide more stable performance than other approaches.

Table 2 shows the precision achieved with different numbers of retrieved samples on CIFAR-10 at 48 bits, where the number of returned images, which represents the proportion of returned samples to correct samples, ranges from 100 to 1,000. In the evaluation, the length of each hash code is 48 bits. It can be seen from the table that ERDH has more stable performance than other hashing methods, and the label information used in the hash function can help generate more compact hash codes.

### 4.3 Retrieval Results on SUN397

SUN397 is a dataset containing 397 scene categories with a total of 108754 images. Compared with CIFAR-10, it is a more difficult dataset. We use 48-bit, 128-bit, and 1024-bit encoding lengths for comparison with existing hash methods such as SSDH, FastHash [20], CCA-ITQ, ITQ, and LSH. The results are shown in Table 3. Even if the dataset contains numerous complicated scenarios, ERDH can still provide stable performance, and the mAP values of ERDH are significantly better than those of SSDH under different hash code lengths, with ERDH achieving performance boosts of 52.93%, 38.59%, and 29.74%. Table 4 shows the performance with different numbers of returned samples (from 100 to 1,000) for various hash methods on SUN397. As shown in the table, under the condition that the length of hash code is 1024 bits, when the number of returned samples is less than 200, the precision of ERDH is better than that of the other hashing methods, the performance of ERDH is better than the

**Table 3.** The mAP values of various hashing methods under different code lengths on SUN397

| Bits | ERDH | SSDH | FastHash | CCA-ITQ | ITQ | LSH |
|---|---|---|---|---|---|---|
| 48 bits | **0.7570** | 0.4950 | 0.2010 | 0.1460 | 0.0800 | 0.0700 |
| 128 bits | **0.7373** | 0.5320 | 0.2120 | 0.1500 | 0.0700 | 0.0690 |
| 1024 bits | **0.6993** | 0.5390 | 0.2200 | 0.1550 | 0.1100 | 0.1010 |

**Table 4.** The precision rates obtained by various hashing methods with different numbers of returned samples on SUN397 at 1024 bits.

| Top-k | Top100 | Top200 | Top400 | Top600 | Top800 | Top1000 |
|---|---|---|---|---|---|---|
| ERDH | **0.6450** | **0.5850** | **0.4854** | **0.4104** | **0.3542** | **0.3104** |
| SSDH | 0.4950 | 0.4430 | 0.3370 | 0.2850 | 0.2380 | 0.1940 |
| FastHash | 0.1870 | 0.1480 | 0.1240 | 0.1150 | 0.0960 | 0.0870 |
| CCA-ITQ | 0.1280 | 0.0980 | 0.0860 | 0.0740 | 0.0650 | 0.0570 |
| ITQ | 0.0420 | 0.0390 | 0.0330 | 0.0300 | 0.0260 | 0.0200 |
| LSH | 0.0400 | 0.0360 | 0.0310 | 0.0320 | 0.0210 | 0.0220 |

precision of SSDH by 30.30%, and ERDH performs better than the other hash methods regardless of the number of returned images, which indicates the success of ERDH in learning the hash loss function.

## 4.4   Retrieval Results on ILSVRC2012

To further prove effectiveness and stability of ERDH, we apply ERDH to ILSVRC2012, which has 1,000 categories and a total of approximately 1.2M images. Table 5 shows the mAP values of ERDH on ILSVRC2012 when the lengths of the hash codes are 512 bits and 1024 bits. It can be seen from the table that ERDH has a stable effect; compared with those of SSDH, the mAP values of ERDH increase by 18.53% and 12.13%. It appears that ERDH is applicable not only to large-scale datasets but also to datasets with massive numbers of labels. Table 6 shows the precision obtained under numbers of returned samples ranging from 100 to 1,000 on ILSVRC2012 at 512 bits. When only the top 400 returned images are considered, compared to SSDH, ERDH performs better than the other hashing methods. When the top 1000 returned samples are considered, ERDH still has comparable performance.

**Table 5.** The mAP values of various hashing methods under different code lengths on ILSVRC2012

| Bits | ERDH | SSDH | ITQ | CCA-ITQ |
|---|---|---|---|---|
| 512 bits | **0.7278** | 0.6140 | 0.4710 | 0.1280 |
| 1024 bits | **0.6795** | 0.6060 | 0.4680 | 0.0570 |

**Table 6.** The precision rates obtained by various hash methods under different numbers of returned samples on ILSVRC2012 at 512 bits.

| Top-k | Top100 | Top200 | Top400 | Top600 | Top800 | Top1000 |
|---|---|---|---|---|---|---|
| ERDH | **0.7223** | **0.7173** | **0.7129** | **0.7085** | **0.7038** | **0.6986** |
| SSDH | 0.6370 | 0.6290 | 0.6120 | 0.5940 | 0.5720 | 0.5440 |
| ITQ | 0.5160 | 0.4900 | 0.4530 | 0.4210 | 0.3910 | 0.3620 |
| CCA-ITQ | 0.5480 | 0.5390 | 0.5170 | 0.4960 | 0.4730 | 0.4470 |

## 5  Conclusion

This paper proposes a supervised hashing network named ERDH, which retains the semantic information of the labels between images and learns binary hash codes with rich semantic information by jointly optimizing a classification loss function and a hash loss function. ERDH has the following advantages: (1) ERDH is simple to implement, and it can be achieved only by fine-tuning the existing deep networks. (2) The ensemble learning method enables other individual learners to compensate for the shortcomings encountered when the performance of an individual learner of ERDH is slightly poor. (3) ERDH not only pays attention to the semantic similarity between the returned image and the query image but also integrates the ranking information to ensure the similarity between the top image and the query image. (4) ERDH provides an image retrieval framework based on deep hashing, which is versatile and can be combined with efficient hashing methods to achieve better performance.

**Acknowledgements.** This work was supported in part by the National Natural Science Foundation of China under Grant Nos. 62176033 and 61936001, the Natural Science Foundation of Chongqing under Grant No. cstc2019jcyj-msxmX0380.

## References

1. Datar, M., Immorlica, N., Indyk, P., Mirrokni, V.S.: Locality-sensitive hashing scheme based on p-stable distributions. In: Proceedings of the Twentieth Annual Symposium on Computational Geometry, pp. 253–262 (2004)
2. Wang, J., Kumar, S., Chang, S.-F.: Semi-supervised hashing for large-scale search. IEEE Trans. Pattern Anal. Mach. Intell. **34**(12), 2393–2406 (2012)
3. Norouzi, M., Fleet, D.J.: Minimal loss hashing for compact binary codes. In: ICML (2011)

4. Thompson, B.: Canonical correlation analysis. In: Encyclopedia of Statistics in Behavioral Science (2005)
5. Liu, W., Wang, J., Ji, R., Jiang, Y.-G., Chang, S.-F.: Supervised hashing with kernels. In: 2012 IEEE Conference on Computer Vision and Pattern Recognition, pp. 2074–2081. IEEE (2012)
6. Shen, F., Shen, C., Liu, W., Shen, H.T.: Supervised discrete hashing. In: Proceedings of the IEEE Conference on Computer Vision and Pattern Recognition, pp. 37–45 (2015)
7. Simonyan, K., Zisserman, A.: Very deep convolutional networks for large-scale image recognition. arXiv preprint arXiv:1409.1556 (2014)
8. He, K., Zhang, X., Ren, S., Sun, J.: Deep residual learning for image recognition. In: Proceedings of the IEEE Conference on Computer Vision and Pattern Recognition, pp. 770–778 (2016)
9. Huang, G., Liu, Z., Van Der Maaten, L., Weinberger, K.Q.: Densely connected convolutional networks. In: Proceedings of the IEEE Conference on Computer Vision and Pattern Recognition, pp. 4700–4708 (2017)
10. Salakhutdinov, R., Hinton, G.: Semantic hashing. Int. J. Approx. Reason. **50**(7), 969–978 (2009)
11. Xia, R., Pan, Y., Lai, H., Liu, C., Yan, S.: Supervised hashing for image retrieval via image representation learning. In: Proceedings of the AAAI Conference on Artificial Intelligence, vol. 28 (2014)
12. Yang, H.-F., Lin, K., Chen, C.-S.: Supervised learning of semantics-preserving hash via deep convolutional neural networks. IEEE Trans. Pattern Anal. Mach. Intell. **40**(2), 437–451 (2017)
13. Dietterich, T.G., et al.: Ensemble learning. In: The Handbook of Brain Theory and Neural Networks, vol. 2, pp. 110–125 (2002)
14. Girshick, R., Donahue, J., Darrell, T., Malik, J.: Rich feature hierarchies for accurate object detection and semantic segmentation. In: Proceedings of the IEEE Conference on Computer Vision and Pattern Recognition, pp. 580–587 (2014)
15. Krizhevsky, A., Hinton, G., et al.: Learning multiple layers of features from tiny images (2009)
16. Xiao, J., Hays, J., Ehinger, K.A., Oliva, A., Torralba, A.: Sun database: large-scale scene recognition from abbey to zoo. In: 2010 IEEE Computer Society Conference on Computer Vision and Pattern Recognition, pp. 3485–3492. IEEE (2010)
17. Russakovsky, O., et al.: ImageNet large scale visual recognition challenge. Int. J. Comput. Vision **115**(3), 211–252 (2015)
18. Zhai, H., Lai, S., Jin, H., Qian, X., Mei, T.: Deep transfer hashing for image retrieval. IEEE Trans. Circuits Syst. Video Technol. (2020)
19. Wu, D., Dai, Q., Liu, J., Li, B., Wang, W.: Deep incremental hashing network for efficient image retrieval. In: Proceedings of the IEEE/CVF Conference on Computer Vision and Pattern Recognition, pp. 9069–9077 (2019)
20. Lin, G., Shen, C., Shi, Q., Van den Hengel, A., Suter, D.: Fast supervised hashing with decision trees for high-dimensional data. In: Proceedings of the IEEE Conference on Computer Vision and Pattern Recognition, pp. 1963–1970 (2014)

# Examining the Proximity of Adversarial Examples to Class Manifolds in Deep Networks

Štefan Pócoš[✉], Iveta Bečková, and Igor Farkaš

Faculty of Mathematics, Physics and Informatics, Comenius University in Bratislava, Bratislava, Slovak Republic
stefan.pocos@fmph.uniba.sk

**Abstract.** Deep neural networks achieve remarkable performance in multiple fields. However, after proper training they suffer from an inherent vulnerability against adversarial examples (AEs). In this work we shed light on inner representations of the AEs by analysing their activations on the hidden layers. We test various types of AEs, each crafted using a specific norm constraint, which affects their visual appearance and eventually their behavior in the trained networks. Our results in image classification tasks (MNIST and CIFAR-10) reveal qualitative differences between the individual types of AEs, when comparing their proximity to the class-specific manifolds on the inner representations. We propose two methods that can be used to compare the distances to class-specific manifolds, regardless the changing dimensions throughout the network. Using these methods, we consistently confirmed that some of the adversarials do not necessarily leave the proximity of the manifold of the correct class, not even in the last hidden layer of the neural network. Next, using UMAP visualisation technique, we projected the class activations to 2D space. The results indicate that the activations of the individual AEs are entangled with the activations of the test set. This, however, does not hold for a group of crafted inputs called the rubbish class. We confirm the entanglement of adversarials with the test set numerically using the soft nearest neighbour loss.

**Keywords:** Adversarial examples · Manifold · $L_p$ norm · Entanglement

## 1 Introduction

Studies of the past years have shown that a carefully crafted minor perturbation can be added to an input to alter the prediction. Such modified inputs are called adversarial examples (AEs) [16]. Their existence poses a serious security risk not only in the domain of image classification, but also for malware detection [9], automatic speech recognition [4] and many more applications. For that reason, the study of robustness became a hot topic. Earlier experiments

[17] suggested that obtaining networks, which are both accurate and robust is not possible. However, some studies argue that robust and accurate networks are indeed achievable [7,15]. They claim that defence against AEs is basically a good generalisation, so robustness and accuracy may not necessarily be contradicting goals. Numerous defence mechanisms have been proposed, but most of them yield only seemingly better results, due to the gradient obfuscation [1]. So far, the most promising one is adversarial training [11] (based on enhancing the training set with adversarial inputs), but it is computationally demanding, cannot guarantee absolute robustness and the defender is bounded to a specific attack type.

In our work we focus on adversarial examples from the perspective of data manifolds, formed by the hidden-layer activations of the training set, test set, the set of generated AEs and the rubbish class examples (Sect. 2). We conduct a computational analysis, where we compare the average distances of AEs vs original images to different classes (Sect. 3). To eliminate the issues when comparing distances in spaces with different dimensions, we propose two methods of assessing and comparing the class correspondences of AEs in hidden-layer representations and show consistent distinctions between inner representations of different types of AEs and rubbish class examples (Sect. 4). Next, we show that AEs are entangled with the test set and their entanglement gradually decreases progressing through the network (Sect. 5). We conclude that these results provide novel qualitative insights into the geometry of AEs (Sect. 6).

## 2    Experimental Setup

### 2.1    Models

For evaluations of adversarial examples and their behaviour during the classification we use MNIST and CIFAR-10 datasets. We train two different types of networks on MNIST: a fully connected feed-forward with two hidden layers, each containing 128 neurons followed by ReLU, and a convolutional network with two convolutional layers, each containing 16 filters followed by max-pooling and ReLU activation function.

In order to classify CIFAR-10, we use a deep convolutional network, consisting of three VGG-type blocks, after which an additional fully connected layer of 256 neurons is applied (before the output layer). In the case of CIFAR-10, we also use dropout and batch normalisation.

To eliminate the effects of additional factors on internal representations and behaviours of the networks, we deliberately do not work with the state-of-the-art networks for classifying the datasets. Although, we achieve satisfying average accuracies for our purposes, i.e. 98.0% using a fully connected network, 98.9% for the convolutional network, both trained on MNIST using SGD, and 87.2% for the network trained on CIFAR-10 using Adam optimizer.

## 2.2  Attack Methods

Usually, a method for generating AEs is dependent on a set of hyperparameters, such as $L_p$ norm used to measure the perturbation, the number of iterations, confidence of resulting adversarial examples, and the perturbation magnitude.

When considering the perturbation magnitude, the selection of a distance metric is crucial. A common choice is $L_p$ metric. Surprisingly, the resulting AEs for different $p$ are not universal and generating the examples using different $L_p$ norm usually yields a completely different kind of AEs. To ensure the diversity of studied AEs, we use the following four types of attacks, optimized for a specific norm constraint:[1]

- **$L_\infty$ constraint:** In this case, we utilise projected gradient descent (PGD) introduced in [11]. Given a perturbation magnitude $\epsilon$, PGD finds the most fooling image, with perturbation no greater than $\epsilon$. The attack usually finds a perturbation of magnitude close to $\epsilon$, so in order to have various perturbations, we generate AEs for MNIST $\epsilon \in \{0.01, 0.02, ..., 0.15\}$ and for CIFAR-10 $\epsilon \in \{0.01, 0.02, ..., 0.05\}$.
- **$L_2$ constraint:** To generate AEs with a low $L_2$ perturbation, we use the Carlini & Wagner (CW) attack [3] which belongs to the state-of-the-art methods for generating AEs with minimal perturbation. The optimization procedure is aimed at creating an AE from input $x$, with the smallest possible perturbation $\delta$ while finding the value of scaling parameter $c$, according to:

$$\begin{aligned} \text{minimize} \quad & c \cdot f(\mathbf{x} + \boldsymbol{\delta}) + \|\boldsymbol{\delta}\|_2, \\ \text{subject to} \quad & \mathbf{x} + \boldsymbol{\delta} \in [0, 1]^n. \end{aligned} \tag{1}$$

- **$L_1$ constraint:** In [5] it was argued that $L_1$ norm accounts for the total variation of perturbation, thus by replacing the $L_2$ term in CW attack with $L_1$ constraint, we can create qualitatively different set of AEs.
- **$L_0$ constraint:** In this attack the goal is to change the smallest number of pixels, in order to achieve misclassification. For that reason, we construct $L_0$ AEs as follows. First, we calculate the gradient of loss w.r.t. the input image and choose a pixel with the greatest absolute gradient. Second, we perform a grid search for pixel values and choose the one, which yields the maximal decrease of the output probability for the correct class. This procedure is then repeated (perturbing one pixel at a time), until misclassification occurs, or the stopping criterion is met (perturbation of 50 pixels).

In our studies we also include **rubbish class** (RC) examples [8] e.g. seemingly random noise patterns which are classified by the network as one of the target classes with high confidence, in our case at least 95%. We generate rubbish class examples in two distinct ways. The first is based on sampling from a uniform distribution for each pixel value and using PGD to find an AE with a small perturbation, so the noise pattern does not change a lot. The second method

---

[1] Rubbish class examples (also called fooling examples or false positives) do not meet the definition of AEs, however they also provide useful insights into robustness.

only differs in the initialisation, where the color value of each pixel is sampled from the probability distribution function of the pixels in the same position – we use a random selection of a pixel from the training data. In the following text, we denote these groups as $RC_{rnd}$ and $RC_{distrib}$, respectively.

We generate a body of AEs for each attack type, $\approx$12,000 AEs for each of the three used networks.[2] In most of the cases $(L_0, L_1, L_2, L_\infty)$ we use a non-targeted attack, i.e., it does not matter what kind of misclassification occurs as long as the adversarial image is not classified correctly. However, to support the diversity of the generated inputs, for the rubbish class we use a targeted attack, where we set the target step by step to all classes. Using a targeted attack for the analysis of rubbish class examples is favourable, because without that the networks tend to classify a big margin of rubbish class inputs as belonging to the same class (for MNIST as '8' and for CIFAR-10 as 'frog').

A random sample of the generated AEs for the two used datasets is shown in Fig. 1. The differences between AEs generated by the mentioned methods are easy to see by a naked eye, and they can also be demonstrated using distances of AEs to their original images in individual norms (shown in Table 1).

**Table 1.** Average distances of the AEs crafted using different attacks. We can see that the individual attacks indeed minimize the distance of an AE to the original input in the norm, which was chosen as a constraint for them.

| | MNIST FC | | | | MNIST Conv. | | | | CIFAR-10 | | | |
|---|---|---|---|---|---|---|---|---|---|---|---|---|
| | $L_0$ | $L_1$ | $L_2$ | $L_\infty$ | $L_0$ | $L_1$ | $L_2$ | $L_\infty$ | $L_0$ | $L_1$ | $L_2$ | $L_\infty$ |
| Our $(L_0)$ | **10.42** | 8.50 | 2.69 | 1.00 | **13.14** | 9.91 | 2.86 | 1.00 | **9.78** | 10.01 | 2.19 | 0.81 |
| EAD $(L_1)$ | 51.88 | **8.28** | 1.68 | 0.73 | 42.14 | **7.82** | 1.83 | 0.84 | 66.34 | **1.97** | 0.29 | 0.11 |
| CW $(L_2)$ | 286.52 | 13.21 | **1.13** | 0.26 | 180.21 | 11.83 | **1.38** | 0.43 | 428.98 | 3.85 | **0.21** | 0.04 |
| PGD $(L_\infty)$ | 493.27 | 47.06 | 2.21 | **0.11** | 516.68 | 49.28 | 2.35 | **0.12** | 1022.81 | 76.83 | 1.46 | **0.03** |

## 3 Distances to Classes

A typical neural network classifier takes an input (an image in our case) and returns the predicted class label. However, the process of how the input image gets transformed into a certain output class is highly non-linear and more importantly, non-transparent. This is one of the drawbacks of modern machine learning. Not only are the representations hard to interpret, but in addition, the inherent dimensionalities of the spaces (i.e. hidden layers) are usually too high, preventing the use of multiple methods for their analysis.

In this section we focus on the question why AEs end up yielding wrong output. Is it a continuous process of a slow divergence from the correct class manifold, a sudden leap to the wrong class in the activation space (at hidden layers), or only wrong generalization caused at the last layer in the network?

We inspect this phenomenon by comparing the distances in the activation spaces. To be more general, we create triples $O_i, A_i, R_i$, where $O_i$ denotes the

---

[2] We use ART (Adversarial Robustness Toolbox) [13] for all attacks except $L_0$.

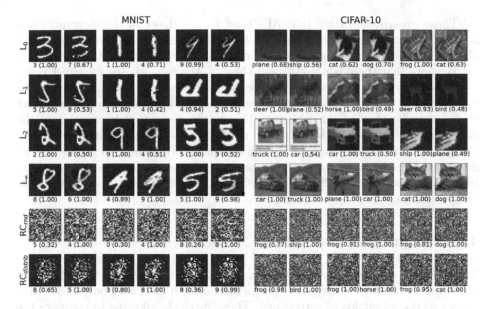

**Fig. 1.** An illustration of all 6 types of attacks crafted for convolutional networks on MNIST and CIFAR-10. For each attack, three pairs of original (left) vs. adversarial (right) images are shown with their corresponding predicted classes and confidence.

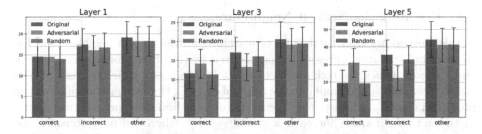

**Fig. 2.** The y-axis shows the average distance of specific input activation (original image, AE or original modified by random noise) to three categories of data – the correct class, the class found by the attack (incorrect) and the other classes. The data were generated by modifying the MNIST dataset and for AEs we used the PGD attack. Due to varying number of neurons used in hidden layers, we cannot compare the scale of the y-axis across layers.

original image, $A_i$ the adversarial image and $R_i$ represents original image modified by random noise, where the perturbation magnitude is the same as the one used for creating $A_i$. Having these triples, we systematically calculated the average distances to three different groups of data in the activation space. The first is the distance to the correct class, second is the distance to the incorrect (incorrectly predicted) class, which was found by adversarial attack and the third is the average distance to the activations of the rest of the examples in the training set. An exemplar visualisation is depicted in Fig. 2.

These experiments show that AEs tend to get closer to the incorrect class later in the network and their distance to the original class is slowly rising. We also see that on average, the "incorrect" class is closer than the rest of the classes.

We note that there is a non-trivial shift of AEs towards the incorrect class, which is not visible when analyzing the original examples. Another interesting observation is that on average, the distance of original examples to the incorrect class is smaller than to other classes. This might mean that in most cases the adversarial attack causes the output to shift towards the closest incorrect class.

Unfortunately, using statistical comparison experiments such as the one we described above cannot capture this process of movement from one manifold towards another, due to different dimensionalities of the activation spaces. These comparisons would be inconsistent.

## 4    Proximity to Manifolds

To illuminate the process of how an adversarial image is gradually mapped onto an incorrect output, we propose two methods. Each of them analyses the distances to the manifolds of activations. These methods allow us to compare the distances throughout the network, even though the dimensionalities of the layers (activation spaces) differ significantly.

### 4.1    Counting the Nearest Neighbours

In this method, we leverage the idea of searching for the nearest neighbours in the space of hidden-layer representations, inspired by [14]. First, for a given network and a chosen attack, we pick a subset of AEs ($Adv_{C_o \to C_p}$), which consists of AEs crafted from images belonging to the original class $C_o$ that are misclassified as the predicted class $C_p$, where $p \neq o$. The next step is to find the $k$ nearest neighbours in the activation space for each $\mathbf{x} \in Adv_{C_o \to C_p}$, where we only consider the activations of those data from the training set, which belong to $C_o$ or $C_p$. Then we calculate the $k_o/k$ ratio, where $k_o$ refers to the number of points from the manifold of the original, correct class. This way, we can visualise the average ratio (considering $\forall \mathbf{x} \in Adv_{C_o \to C_p}$) and see how this value develops throughout the network.

To provide statistically sound results, we choose initial and target class (i.e. $o, p$) according to the confusion matrix of the generated AEs. We pick such combinations $(o, p)$, which have a lot of occurrences ($\approx 100$) in the table. To compare different attack methods we can fix the pair $(o, p)$ thanks to the fact that distinct attacks tend to have similar success rate for all possible pairs.

Results in Fig. 3 illustrate that in the first layers the AEs usually have a lot of neighbours belonging to the correct class. Surprisingly, this often holds for the successive layers as well. Individual attacks have their own behaviour, regarding the distance to the manifolds. AEs crafted using $L_0$ tend to eventually have more neighbours from the incorrect class, however only by a small margin. $L_1$ and $L_2$ attacks show very similar behaviours, since these AEs often have more

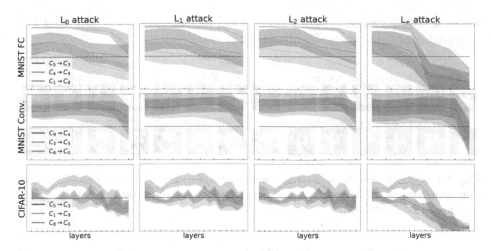

**Fig. 3.** Development of the $k_o/k$ ratio ($y$-axis) across the networks ($x$-axis) for three chosen pairs of $(o, k)$ for each network, using different attacks. The dashed horizontal line in the middle of the plot helps to visualise, where the number of neighbours to the correct class is lower than those to the predicted class.

neighbours from the correct class, even near the last hidden layer. $L_\infty$ attack invokes the strongest reaction, since the AEs have the tendency to completely flip the number of neighbours, in case of the fully connected network and the network trained on CIFAR-10, after several layers almost all neighbours are from the incorrect class. For the convolutional network trained on MNIST this flip is only visible at the end. We also observe that each of the explored pairs $(o, p)$ has its unique behaviour, but follow a certain trend.

### 4.2 Computing Distances to Class-Specific Manifolds

This method is based on the idea of measuring the distances between AE activations and class-specific manifolds (of the classes $C_o$ and $C_p$) of the train-set activations, so we apply it to a fixed attack and a subset of AEs ($Adv_{C_o \to C_p}$). A class-specific manifold is approximated as the convex hull of $k$ nearest neighbours (of a given AE activation) belonging to the given class. The distance to this manifold is the Euclidean distance to the (orthogonal) projection onto the convex hull. The projection is easily expressed as a constrained convex minimisation problem

$$\text{minimize}_{\alpha_1, \alpha_2, \ldots, \alpha_k} \left\| \left( \sum_{i=1}^{k} \alpha_i \mathbf{x}_i \right) - \mathbf{x} \right\|_2,$$

$$\text{subject to} \quad \sum_{i=1}^{k} \alpha_i = 1, \quad \alpha_i \geq 0, \ i \in \{1, 2, \ldots, k\}, \tag{2}$$

where $\mathbf{x}_i$ are the nearest neighbours of $\mathbf{x}$ approximating the manifold and $k$ is the number of data points considered in the manifold.

**Fig. 4.** Convex combinations of inputs computed using the coefficients from the projections of activations of AEs from $Adv_{C_4 \to C_9}$ (a fully-connected network) and $Adv_{C_3 \to C_5}$ (a convolutional network).

However, the dimensionality of hidden layers varies, so the comparison of distances between different layers would be inconsistent. In order to avoid this problem, we proceed as follows: for each layer and each AE activation, we first compute the projection onto the manifold of the entire train-set activations (i.e., we do not require them to belong to a specific class) but instead of computing the distance to this projection, we only remember the indices of the $k$-NN and their respective coefficients $\alpha_i$ (Eq. 2). These are used to compute the corresponding convex combination of images in the input space (a few examples of such projections across network layers are shown in Fig. 4), which is then projected onto the class-specific manifolds of inputs belonging to classes $C_o$ and $C_p$. Then we can reliably monitor the development of these distances across the network. Results are shown in Fig. 5. Both chosen pairs $(o, p)$ were also used in the first method, allowing a better comparison. The results are quite consistent, the PGD attack has the greatest influence on the distances to the class manifolds. In almost all cases, the distance to the predicted class decreases through the network layers. In the fully-connected MNIST network, the change is gradual, in the other two networks, it happens mostly on the last few hidden layers.

## 5    Assessment of Entanglement

The manifold disentanglement theory states that the manifolds of individual classes tend to separate (disentangle) during the classification, although they are entangled in the earlier layers [2]. In this section we shed light on what happens during the manifold disentanglement with adversarial examples, applying two methods: First, we visualise the projections of manifolds using the state-of-the-art nonlinear dimensionality reduction method UMAP [12] and second, we numerically determine the exact "rates" of AEs disentanglement. We focus on the differences between the representations of the AEs and ordinary test set examples.

Our experiment proceeds in the following manner: we start with the whole set of AEs together with the test set, and feed them into the trained network.

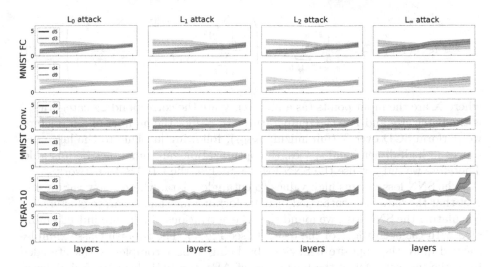

**Fig. 5.** Development of the distances ($y$-axis) of convex combinations of input images, corresponding to AEs activation projections, to the class-specific manifolds of $C_o$ (dark) and $C_p$ (light). The $x$-axis denotes individual layers. In general, we observe a trend of AEs activations moving away from the original class manifold towards the predicted class manifold.

Usually, to classify an image, one only needs to care about the last layer, but here we are interested in activations on each hidden layer. Next, a dimensionality of representations on each hidden layer is reduced into two dimensions using UMAP. For the final step, the resulting points are depicted in 2D space, where each type of adversarial has its unique color, in order to highlight their distributions. The output of the mentioned method can be seen in Fig. 6. We observe the following phenomena:

1. On most of the layers, all 4 types of AEs are close to the activations of the test set, one could say they are entangled. This observation is valid for all three networks.
2. The only visual distinction between the clusters of AEs and the test set can be seen towards the last layers. The attack with $L_\infty$ constraint shows the biggest deviation.
3. Rubbish class examples are well separated on all layers, where usually $RC_{rnd}$ is a bit further from the rest of the data than $RC_{distrib}$. Towards the end layers, both rubbish class sets are progressively split into ten clusters, corresponding to classes. This indicates a certain specificity for each class even in the seemingly random patterns.

To verify whether the statements 1 and 2 also hold for high-dimensional representations on the hidden layers, we measure the entanglement of adversarial vs. non-adversarial inputs. The standard methods to do so are the triplet loss [10], the soft nearest neighbour (SNN) loss [6] or the comparison of interclass/intraclass distances. For our analysis, we employ the SNN loss defined as

$$l_{\text{SNN}}(\mathbf{X}, \mathbf{y}, T) = -\frac{1}{b} \sum_{i \in \{1..b\}} \log \left( \frac{\sum_{\substack{j \in \{1..b\} \setminus i \\ y_i = y_j}} \exp(-\|\mathbf{x}_i - \mathbf{x}_j\|^2 / T)}{\sum_{k \in \{1..b\} \setminus i} \exp(-\|\mathbf{x}_i - \mathbf{x}_k\|^2 / T)} \right) \quad (3)$$

where $\mathbf{X}$ are the input points (as a matrix), $\mathbf{y}$ are the corresponding categories, $b$ is the batch size and $T$ is the temperature. To reduce the number of parameters, we perform SGD over $T$ (minimizing $l_{\text{SNN}}$), following [6]. Due to the large distances in high-dimensional spaces, the optimization can sometimes be unstable. Therefore we did not use the SNN loss to analyse the CIFAR-10 network.

The SNN loss assigns high values to entangled data, whereas low values suggest that the data is disentangled, usually forming nice and separate clusters. By calculating the SNN loss, we found that the activations of AEs are indeed entangled with the activations of the test set (see Fig. 7). The rubbish class examples showed quite the opposite behaviour by being almost completely disentangled from the test set. Out of the four types of AEs, the PGD leads to faster disentanglement in the network, the others start to disentangle only towards the final layer. We also see big differences between the individual types of networks. In the fully-connected network the process of disentangling is gradual, whereas in the convolutional one the disentangling is only visible on the last few layers.

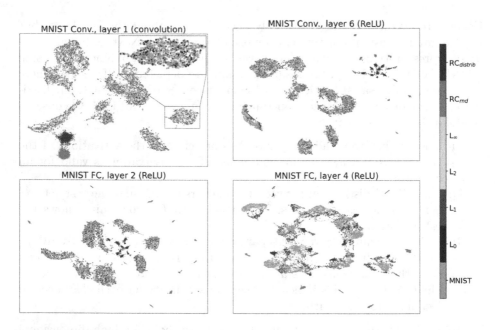

**Fig. 6.** Visualisation of activations of four types of adversarial examples, two types of rubbish class examples and the test set, using UMAP. Distinctive behaviours depend on the network and the layer: very high entanglement of AEs with the test set (top left) is contrasted with a minimum entanglement (bottom right).

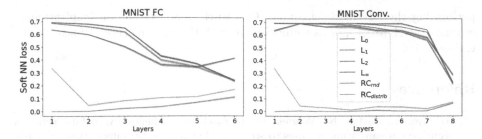

**Fig. 7.** Visualisation of the soft nearest neighbour loss scores between malicious inputs (AEs and the rubbish class) and the test set (averaged across 4 runs) throughout the networks trained on MNIST.

## 6   Conclusion

We studied the behaviour of adversarial examples in the hidden layers of neural networks trained on MNIST and CIFAR-10 datasets. We confirmed that AEs generated using different $L_p$ norm constraints invoke various effects in the neural network, thus the cause of the misclassification can also differ.

Following a simple statistical analysis of distances of AEs to different classes, we proposed two novel methods of analysing these distances on hidden layers, allowing for a more consistent comparison throughout the studied networks. The first method is based on the deep $k$-NN, where we count the number of nearest neighbours only from specific classes and monitor their ratio. The second method also utilizes the nearest neighbours, but they are used to approximate the manifold, onto which the AEs are projected. After the projection is calculated, we perform the distance measurement in the input space, thus alleviating the problem of comparison of distances with spaces of different dimensions. Both methods showed consistent results that some of the AEs (mainly those generated using PGD) tend to approach the manifold of the predicted (incorrect) class faster in the network. In the other cases, the misclassification often occurs even though the activations of AEs are closer to the manifold of the correct class even in the last layers.

Our analysis using the SNN loss reveals that AEs are entangled with the test set. This is the case of hidden-layer representations as well, where AEs showed a high level of entanglement which slightly decreased towards the last layers of the studied networks. This does not hold for the rubbish class examples, where the opposite is true. They begin disentangled in the input space, and gradually get a little entangled with the test set. However they do not get entangled too much before they reach the last layer. We also confirmed the entanglement visually, using UMAP, where after the transformation of the activation space into 2D we see that AEs co-occupy the areas with the test set examples.

To extend our work, it would be interesting to see, how the measured behaviour changes using adversarially trained networks and whether it is possible for AEs to have similar behaviour as in adversarially trained ones, without performing the adversarial training. Our work may serve as an inspiration to evaluate novel attacks, or as a guideline to pick the right methods of adversarial training.

# References

1. Athalye, A., Carlini, N., Wagner, D.: Obfuscated gradients give a false sense of security: circumventing defenses to adversarial examples. In: International Conference on Machine LearningProceedings of Machine Learning Research, vol. 80, pp. 274–283 (2018)
2. Brahma, P.P., Wu, D., She, Y.: Why deep learning works: a manifold disentanglement perspective. IEEE Trans. Neural Netw. Learn. Syst. 27(10), 1997–2008 (2016). https://doi.org/10.1109/TNNLS.2015.2496947
3. Carlini, N., Wagner, D.: Towards evaluating the robustness of neural networks. In: 2017 IEEE Symposium on Security and Privacy, pp. 39–57 (2017)
4. Carlini, N., Wagner, D.: Audio adversarial examples: targeted attacks on speech-to-text. In: 2018 IEEE Security and Privacy Workshops, pp. 1–7 (2018)
5. Chen, P.Y., Zhang, H., Yi, J., Hsieh, C.J.: EAD: elastic-net attacks to deep neural networks via adversarial examples (2017). arXiv:1709.04114
6. Frosst, N., Papernot, N., Hinton, G.: Analyzing and improving representations with the soft nearest neighbor loss. In: Proceedings of the 36th International Conference on Machine Learning, vol. 97, pp. 2012–2020 (2019)
7. Gilmer, J., et al.: Adversarial spheres (2018). arXiv:1801.02774
8. Goodfellow, I., Shlens, J., Szegedy, C.: Explaining and harnessing adversarial examples. In: International Conference on Learning Representations (2015)
9. Grosse, K., Papernot, N., Manoharan, P., Backes, M., McDaniel, P.: Adversarial examples for malware detection. In: Foley, S.N., Gollmann, D., Snekkenes, E. (eds.) ESORICS 2017. LNCS, vol. 10493, pp. 62–79. Springer, Cham (2017). https://doi.org/10.1007/978-3-319-66399-9_4
10. Hoffer, E., Ailon, N.: Deep metric learning using triplet network. In: Feragen, A., Pelillo, M., Loog, M. (eds.) SIMBAD 2015. LNCS, vol. 9370, pp. 84–92. Springer, Cham (2015). https://doi.org/10.1007/978-3-319-24261-3_7
11. Madry, A., Makelov, A., Schmidt, L., Tsipras, D., Vladu, A.: Towards deep learning models resistant to adversarial attacks. In: International Conference on Learning Representations (2018)
12. McInnes, L., Healy, J., Saul, N., Großberger, L.: UMAP: Uniform manifold approximation and projection. J. Open Source Softw. 3(29), 861 (2018)
13. Nicolae, M.I., et al.: Adversarial robustness toolbox v1.2.0 (2018). https://arxiv.org/pdf/1807.01069
14. Papernot, N., McDaniel, P.: Deep k-nearest neighbors: towards confident, interpretable and robust deep learning (2018). arXiv:1803.04765
15. Stutz, D., Hein, M., Schiele, B.: Disentangling adversarial robustness and generalization. In: IEEE Conference on Computer Vision and Pattern Recognition (2019)
16. Szegedy, C., et al.: Intriguing properties of neural networks. In: International Conference on Learning Representations (2014)
17. Tsipras, D., Santurkar, S., Engstrom, L., Turner, A., Madry, A.: Robustness may be at odds with accuracy (2019). arXiv:1805.12152

# Gesture MNIST: A New Free-Hand Gesture Dataset

Monika Schak[(✉)] and Alexander Gepperth

Fulda University of Applied Sciences, Leizpiger Str. 123, 36037 Fulda, Germany
{monika.schak,alexander.gepperth}@cs.hs-fulda.de

**Abstract.** We present a unimodal, comprehensive, and easy-to-use dataset for visual free-hand gesture recognition. We call it GestureM-NIST because of the 28 × 28 grayscale format of its images, and because the number of samples is approximately 80,000, similar to MNIST. Each of the six gesture classes is composed of a sequence of 12 images taken by a 3D camera. As a peculiarity w.r.t. other datasets, all sequences are recorded by a single person, ensuring high sample uniformity and quality. A particular focus is to provide a vision-based dataset that can be used "out of the box" for sequence classification without any preprocessing, segmentation, and feature extraction steps. We present classification experiments on GestureMNIST with different types of DNNs, establishing a performance baseline for sequence classification algorithms. We place particular emphasis on ahead-of-time classification, i.e., the correct identification of a gestures class *before* the gesture is completed. It is shown that CNN and LSTM-based deep learning achieves near-perfect performance, whereas ahead-of-time classification performance offers ample scope for future research with GestureMNIST. GestureM-NIST contains visual samples only, but other modalities, namely acceleration and sound data, are available upon request.

**Keywords:** Hand gesture · Dataset · Sequence classification · LSTM · CNN · Outlier detection

## 1 Introduction

This work is in the context of free-hand gesture recognition, a field of machine learning that has profound application relevance in, e.g., human-machine-interaction (HMI). More generally, we target the wider field of *sequence classification*, where data samples consist of several elements that are presented one after the other. Typical sequence classifiers are given by Hidden Markov models (HMM) often used in speech classification. Recurrent neural networks (RNNs) have a long tradition in this domain as well. With the advances in Deep Learning, deep recurrent neural networks have been proposed, perhaps most prominently represented by bi-directional LSTM networks [3] which reach state-of-the-art performance in several application domains.

E. Pimenidis et al. (Eds.): ICANN 2022, LNCS 13532, pp. 657–668, 2022.
https://doi.org/10.1007/978-3-031-15937-4_55

RNNs offer the intriguing possibility to obtain a decision before a sequence has been completely presented, which we denote as **ahead-of-time** classification. Especially in free-hand gesture recognition, this ability seems crucial for seamless and intuitive interaction with humans.

Successful hand gesture recognition requires datasets that are large, diverse, and reliable. These requirements are partially conflicting since large and diverse datasets are usually ensured by involving many different persons. Although this promotes sample diversity, this diversity is, partially at least, an undesirable one, since each person performing the gestures needs to learn how to perform them correctly. As a consequence, the recorded data will contain many gestures that are inconsistent with others or even plain inappropriate. Thus, the **sample quality and quantity** of a dataset plays an important role in successfully training gesture classifiers.

Free-hand gesture recognition is often performed on RGB images, which requires extensive **image pre-processing** and **feature extraction** techniques to be applied. In particular, these steps are necessary if robustness to illumination and background is a goal.

Lastly, the acquisition of a **sufficiently large number** of gesture samples is a tedious and expensive process, which maybe explains why most public gesture recognition datasets are rather small as compared to image classification benchmarks.

### 1.1   Related Work

Hand gesture recognition is a long-standing subject of academic and industrial interest and thus has a long history in machine learning, please see [5,10,14] for surveys. Surprisingly, the number of large-scale public datasets is rather low. Concretely, the nvGesture dataset [8] contains 1,532 samples grouped in 25 categories (~60 samples per category). The EgoGesture dataset [14] contains ~24,000 samples in 83 classes (~300 samples/class). Lastly, the ChaLearn ISO/ConGD 2016 datasets [13] contains ~47,000 gesture samples grouped into 249 classes, or ~200 samples per class. In most of these datasets, the emphasis is on realistic settings, so background, clutter, and subject diversity form an integral part of the problems addressed in these work, namely robustness and subject invariance. On the other hand, given the low number of gesture samples per class, it may be asked whether this is actually sufficient for training DNNs, which require a large number of data samples for training. All of these datasets (except [14]) require significant pre-processing of images since the full background is included and no foreground/background segmentation is provided.

### 1.2   Contribution

We present GestureMNIST, a large, publicly available dataset of high-quality visual hand gesture samples (see Fig. 1 for a visualization of typical samples). All gestures are recorded from a single person to ensure uniformity and sample quality. Two of the gesture classes are very similar visually ("one snap"

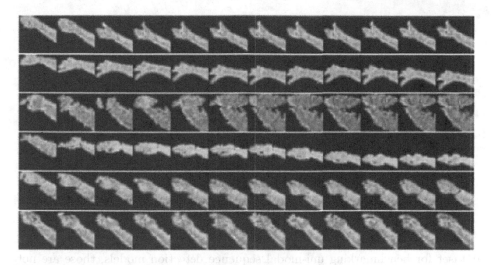

**Fig. 1.** Samples taken from each GestureMNIST class. From top to bottom: thumbs up, thumbs down, swipe left, swipe right, one snap, two snaps.

and "two snaps"), which poses strong challenges on ahead-of-time classification. We place great emphasis on providing a sufficient amount of gesture samples per class (~13,000) to enable efficient training of DNN models. The hand has already been segmented and the background has been removed, so the dataset can be directly used for machine learning, without having to resort to complex image processing pipelines. We describe experiments with deep CNN and LSTM sequence classifiers that establish a performance baseline for this new dataset. As a particular focus of the examination of LSTM classifiers, we investigate ahead-of-time classification for different time points in the sequence.

## 2  Dataset

Gesture MNIST is an MNIST-like [7] dataset of six free-hand gestures, consisting of 79,881 samples. Each sample is a sequence of twelve $28 \times 28$ grayscale images. All gestures are performed by a single person to ensure carefully curated data with little to no errors in how the correct gesture for each class is performed.

The samples for this dataset are recorded in a fixed setting to ensure that the hand gesture is always performed in a predefined volume of interest. For this reason, we built a setup: We bolted the camera to a board and marked the area in which to conduct the gesture. This setup can be seen in Fig. 2.

Every recording consists of ten repetitions $r$ of one gesture before continuing to the next gesture class $c$. Therefore, each recording produces $r \cdot c = 10 \cdot 6 = 60$ samples. The samples are simultaneously assigned class labels while saving them to the disk. For this dataset, we only used the 3D point clouds obtained by an Orbbec Astra 3D sensor. In fact, we also record three other modalities – RGB images, audio, and acceleration data. Since this is supposed to be an MNIST-like

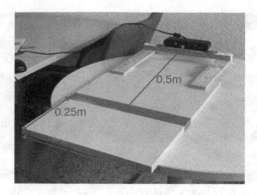

**Fig. 2.** The fixed setup to record hand gestures for our gesture dataset.

dataset for benchmarking uni-modal sequence detection models, those are not used here but are available upon request for further research on multi-modal models.

The Gesture MNIST dataset consists of six classes $C_i$ with $i = [1, 6]$ as follows: Thumbs Up, Thumbs Down, Swipe Left, Swipe Right, One Snap, Two Snaps. Both swiping gestures are performed with the whole hand instead of one or multiple fingers. The snapping gestures focus on the thumb and middle finger to make one or two snapping sounds, respectively.

To record our data, we use the stream of depth images provided by an Orbbec Astra 3D sensor. The depth images have a size of $640 \times 480$ pixels and are converted to point clouds, then stored. Each gesture lasts for two seconds. During this time frame, we receive a total of twelve depth images. Therefore, the length of each sample is twelve frames.

After recording the gestures, we conducted an automated preprocessing step. At first, we downsample the point cloud. We create a 3D-voxel grid over the input data. Then, we compute the centroid of all the points in that voxel and use this to represent the voxel. Thus, we reduce the size to lower computational costs. In the next step, we crop the point cloud to a predefined volume of interest to remove unnecessary data. That is the reason why performing the gesture in a predefined area during recording is so important. By performing a Principal Component Analysis [12], we determine which points belong to the hand and remove all others. After these steps, we only keep the downsampled points that describe the hand performing the gesture.

Afterward, we project these points onto a 2D plane and remove all color information. Thus, we receive a grayscale image of just the hand. This image is further processed: We resize the image to $28 \times 28$ pixels and invert the colors to correspond to the MNIST data format and style. A randomly picked sequence for each gesture class is shown in Fig. 1.

In total, the Gesture MNIST dataset contains approximately 13,300 recordings of each gesture class, totaling almost 80,000 samples. Table 1 shows the exact distribution of each class. All gestures are performed by a single person to ensure a consistently high quality of the data. Since this person is well-instructed and experienced, mistakes or incorrect gestures are very unlikely to happen. That is not necessarily a sign of invariability since all background and size data are removed during preprocessing and there are strict guidelines on how to perform a gesture to ensure consistency. Experiments with a live demonstrator [11] show that an LSTM model trained on our dataset is able to correctly classify most gestures performed by users that are not the one who recorded the dataset.

**Table 1.** Distribution of the six gesture classes in the Gesture MNIST dataset.

| Class | $C_1$ | $C_2$ | $C_3$ | $C_4$ | $C_5$ | $C_6$ | **Total** |
|---|---|---|---|---|---|---|---|
| Samples | 13,440 | 13,410 | 13,228 | 13,233 | 13,308 | 13,262 | **79,881** |

The dataset will be publicly available to be used for research at the following website: http://data.informatik.hs-fulda.de/. We provide the data in dependence on the format given by the well-known MNIST dataset. The data are available in a Numpy-Array of shape $(N, 12, 28, 28)$, where $N = 79,881$ is the total number of samples, 12 is the number of frames per sequence, and $28 \times 28$ is the size of each frame. The labels are also available in a Numpy-Array of shape $(N, 6)$ in one-hot-encoded format.

## 3 Experiments

We conduct benchmark experiments with state-of-the art classification networks for sequence detection: a deep Long Short-Term Memory (LSTM) network [4] and a deep Convolutional Neural Network (CNN) [6].

### 3.1 LSTM Network

By using preliminary experiments to establish network parameters that lead to the highest classification accuracy, we choose a deep LSTM network with 5 hidden layers, 800 cells per layer, a learning rate of 0.001, a batch size of 1,000, and we run 1,000 iterations. We train the network on 80% randomly picked samples and test the performance on the remaining 20%.

After training the network, we get the predictions on the test data for each frame of the sequence to receive the gesture classification accuracy for the whole gesture along with the gesture classification accuracy for ahead-of-time classification.

Figure 3 shows the gesture classification accuracy at each frame in a graph. It can be seen that after five frames the accuracy is already over 50%. After two-thirds of the gesture has been processed, the correct class can be predicted with an accuracy of over 80%. And, after nine of twelve frames, we achieve a classification accuracy of almost 90%. After processing the whole gesture, we can predict the correct gesture class with an accuracy of 99,04%.

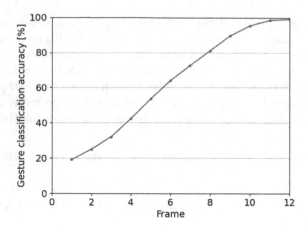

**Fig. 3.** Gesture classification accuracies on our test data [in %] for the ahead-of-time classification at each of the twelve frames.

Table 2 shows the confusion matrix after half the gesture has been processed (frame 6 of 12). Here, we achieve classification accuracies of 84%, 86%, 79%, 66%, 10% and 63% for the six classes. Therefore, it is visible that the classification of class 5 (Snap Once) seems to be most difficult and requires more frames for reliable classification.

**Table 2.** Confusion matrix for the ahead-of-time classification at frame 6 of 12.

| | Predicted class [1–6] | | | | | |
|---|---|---|---|---|---|---|
| Target [1–6] | 1,987 | 0 | 0 | 27 | 726 | 0 |
| | 4 | 2,032 | 0 | 618 | 18 | 5 |
| | 7 | 0 | 1,796 | 370 | 356 | 91 |
| | 4 | 0 | 103 | 1,805 | 738 | 38 |
| | 0 | 1 | 1 | 0 | 259 | 2,325 |
| | 0 | 0 | 1 | 1 | 330 | 2,333 |

Table 3 shows the confusion matrix after eight of twelve frames have been processed. Now, the first four classes achieve classification accuracies of over 90%, while classes five and six only achieve accuracies of 34% and 65% respectively. This is not surprising, since those two classes are specifically designed to be very difficult to distinguish. Adding additional modalities like acceleration data or sound can help improve the classification.

Finally, Table 4 shows the confusion matrix after all twelve frames have been processed. After being able to see the whole gesture, the LSTM model achieves an average classification accuracy over all gesture classes of 99.04%. Still, the accuracy for the first four classes is marginally higher than the gesture classification

**Table 3.** Confusion matrix for the ahead-of-time classification at frame 8 of 12.

| | Predicted class [1–6] | | | | | |
|---|---|---|---|---|---|---|
| Target [1–6] | 2,586 | 0 | 0 | 8 | 146 | 0 |
| | 1 | 2,579 | 0 | 96 | 0 | 1 |
| | 4 | 0 | 2,478 | 82 | 52 | 4 |
| | 0 | 0 | 79 | 2,365 | 213 | 31 |
| | 0 | 1 | 0 | 0 | 716 | 1,869 |
| | 0 | 0 | 0 | 1 | 468 | 2,196 |

accuracy achieved on the two snapping gestures. Overall, it can be said that an LSTM model can achieve near-perfect results on the Gesture MNIST dataset when classifying the whole gesture. Ahead-of-time classification still requires further research to improve results.

**Table 4.** Confusion matrix for the gesture classification after all twelve frames of the gesture have been processed.

| | Predicted class [1–6] | | | | | |
|---|---|---|---|---|---|---|
| Target [1–6] | 2,739 | 0 | 0 | 1 | 0 | 0 |
| | 0 | 2,673 | 0 | 4 | 0 | 0 |
| | 0 | 0 | 2,603 | 16 | 0 | 1 |
| | 0 | 0 | 6 | 2,682 | 0 | 0 |
| | 0 | 1 | 0 | 0 | 2,538 | 47 |
| | 0 | 1 | 0 | 1 | 75 | 2,589 |

## 3.2  CNN

Since a Convolutional Neural Network is not specifically designed to classify sequential data we concatenate the twelve frames of each Gesture MNIST sample to create one big image of size $28 \times 28 \cdot 12 = 28 \times 336$ pixels comparable to the ones shown in Fig. 1. We choose a standard Deep CNN architecture consisting of the following 17 layers: 3 Conv2D layers, 4 ReLU layers, 3 Max Pooling layers, 4 Dropout layers, 1 Flatten layer, and 2 Dense layers. Further information about each layer and how the model is designed is shown in Fig. 4.

We train the model with a batch size of 64 for a total of 10 epochs. 80% randomly picked samples from the Gesture MNIST dataset are used for training while the remaining 20% are used to validate the model and evaluate the performance. Since all frames are fed into the network as one big image, ahead-of-time classification is not possible in this case.

```
Layer (type)                    Output Shape           Param #
=================================================================
conv2d_1 (Conv2D)               (None, 28, 336, 32)    320
_____
leaky_re_lu_1 (LeakyReLU)       (None, 28, 336, 32)    0
_____
max_pooling2d_1 (MaxPooling2    (None, 14, 168, 32)    0
_____
dropout_1 (Dropout)             (None, 14, 168, 32)    0
_____
conv2d_2 (Conv2D)               (None, 14, 168, 64)    18496
_____
leaky_re_lu_2 (LeakyReLU)       (None, 14, 168, 64)    0
_____
max_pooling2d_2 (MaxPooling2    (None, 7, 84, 64)      0
_____
dropout_2 (Dropout)             (None, 7, 84, 64)      0
_____
conv2d_3 (Conv2D)               (None, 7, 84, 128)     73856
_____
leaky_re_lu_3 (LeakyReLU)       (None, 7, 84, 128)     0
_____
max_pooling2d_3 (MaxPooling2    (None, 4, 42, 128)     0
_____
dropout_3 (Dropout)             (None, 4, 42, 128)     0
_____
flatten_1 (Flatten)             (None, 21504)          0
_____
dense_1 (Dense)                 (None, 128)            2752640
_____
leaky_re_lu_4 (LeakyReLU)       (None, 128)            0
_____
dropout_4 (Dropout)             (None, 128)            0
_____
dense_2 (Dense)                 (None, 6)              774
=================================================================
Total params: 2,846,086
Trainable params: 2,846,086
Non-trainable params: 0
```

**Fig. 4.** Description of the 17 layers of the CNN model used for our experiments including layer type, output shape and number of parameters.

After training the deep Convolutional Neural Network model, we achieve a gesture classification accuracy of 99.61% on the test set. The training and test accuracies during the ten epochs are shown in Fig. 5. It can be seen that the test accuracy is already very high after just one epoch of training and then hardly improves. Therefore, it can be said that a CNN model adapts to the GestureMNIST dataset really fast which can reduce computational costs for training the network.

Tables 5 and 6 show the confusion matrix, and the classification report for the test data after the training process is finished. A nearly perfect gesture classification accuracy can be achieved which is not surprising since deep convolutional neural networks are specifically designed to classify images. It can also be seen that the most difficulties – albeit they are not really significant either – happen with gestures from the last two gesture classes: Snapping once or twice. This, as explained above already, is due to the fact of their nature to be designed to add some challenge when only classifying visual modalities.

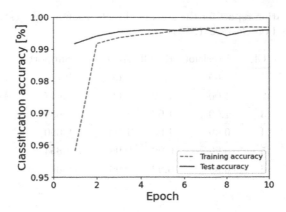

**Fig. 5.** Gesture classification accuracy for each of the ten epochs during training, comparing the accuracy on the training data and the testing data.

**Table 5.** Confusion matrix for the gesture classification on our test set using a deep CNN model trained on GestureMNIST.

| | Predicted class [1–6] | | | | | |
|---|---|---|---|---|---|---|
| Target [1–6] | 2,710 | 0 | 0 | 0 | 0 | 1 |
| | 0 | 2,617 | 0 | 0 | 0 | 0 |
| | 0 | 0 | 2,627 | 12 | 0 | 0 |
| | 0 | 0 | 3 | 2,687 | 0 | 0 |
| | 0 | 0 | 0 | 4 | 2,636 | 14 |
| | 0 | 0 | 0 | 0 | 30 | 2,635 |

# 4  Outlier Detection

Outlier detection arguably constitutes another important functionality in the context of gesture recognition, since relevant gestures are often embedded into a continuous stream of non-gestures, or else there may be irrelevant frames before and after a meaningful gesture that need to be ignored. In addition, there should be an additional safeguard against spurious gestures or adversarial attacks, where unknown or absurd gestures may be used to confident classification results. Outlier detection usually relies on unsupervised methods such as Gaussian Mixture Models (GMMs) or k-means (which is really an approximation to GMMs). Here, we report results for GMMs that are fed entire sequences in concatenated form. Based on a thresholding operation performed on the returned score, a gesture is classified as an inlier or an outlier. Notably, GMM training is performed on inliers only.

**Table 6.** Classification report for the gesture classification on our test set using a deep CNN model trained on GestureMNIST.

| Class | Precision | Recall | Accuracy | Support |
|-------|-----------|--------|----------|---------|
| 1 | 1.00 | 1.00 | 1.00 | 2,711 |
| 2 | 1.00 | 1.00 | 1.00 | 2,617 |
| 3 | 1.00 | 1.00 | 1.00 | 2,639 |
| 4 | 0.99 | 1.00 | 1.00 | 2,690 |
| 5 | 0.99 | 0.99 | 0.99 | 2,654 |
| 6 | 0.99 | 0.99 | 0.99 | 2,665 |

### 4.1 Gaussian Mixture Models (GMMs)

GMMs [1] are unsupervised generative models that directly model the data distribution, which is represented as a weighted mixture of $K$ multi-variate Gaussian densities $\mathcal{N}(\vec{x}; \Sigma_k, \vec{\mu}_k) \equiv \mathcal{N}_k(\vec{x})$, each of which is parameterized by a centroid $\vec{\mu}_k$ and a covariance matrix $\Sigma_k$. GMM training aims at maximizing the *log-likelihood* $\mathcal{L}$ of the data under the model, with:

$$\mathcal{L} = \sum_n \log \sum_k \pi_k \mathcal{N}_k(\vec{x}_n). \tag{1}$$

The vector $\vec{\pi}$ represents the mixture weights, which are adapted together with the set of all centroids $\{\vec{\mu}_k\}$ and covariance matrices $\{\Sigma_k\}$.

Once a GMM has been trained on data, the log-likelihood computed from a single inlier or outlier sample is taken to be a measure of the GMMs familiarity with that sample. Consequently, the sample is classified as an inlier if $\mathcal{L}(\vec{x}) \geq \theta_{\text{GMM}}$. For each value of this threshold, we can now compute the percentage $p_I$ of inliers (in a test set) that would be accepted as inliers, and a corresponding percentage $p_O$ of outliers that are rejected. By plotting pairs of $p_I(\theta_{\text{GMM}}), p_O(\theta_{\text{GMM}})$ into a 2D plot while varying the threshold $\theta_{\text{GMM}}$, we obtain receiver-operator-characteristics (ROCs) as shown in Fig. 6a and Fig. 6b.

### 4.2 Results

We train a GMM with $K = 100$ mixture components on all classes but one and then perform outlier detection using the remaining class, which, by definition, contains outliers only. The GMM is trained for 10 epochs by SGD using the procedure and the default parameters given in [2]. Table 7 shows the results for these experiments. As can be seen, the best results were achieved performing outlier detection on class 4 (Swipe Right) with an AUC of 0.802. The corresponding ROC can be seen in Fig. 6a. The lowest results were achieved performing outlier detection on class 5 (One Snap) with an AUC of 0.480. The corresponding ROC curve can be viewed in Fig. 6b.

**Table 7.** Outlier detection results for each class on a GMM trained on the other five classes.

| T1 | T2 | AUC |
|---|---|---|
| $\{2,3,4,5,6\}$ | 1 | 0.613 |
| $\{1,3,4,5,6\}$ | 2 | 0.758 |
| $\{1,2,4,5,6\}$ | 3 | 0.772 |
| $\{1,2,3,5,6\}$ | 4 | 0.802 |
| $\{1,2,3,4,6\}$ | 5 | 0.480 |
| $\{1,2,3,4,5\}$ | 6 | 0.592 |

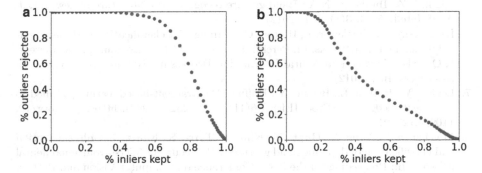

**Fig. 6.** (a) ROC curve for outlier detection with $T1 = \{1,2,3,5,6\}$ and $T2 = 4$. The AUC is 0.802. (b) ROC curve for outlier detection with $T1 = \{1,2,3,4,6\}$ and $T2 = 5$. The AUC is 0.480.

## 5    Discussion and Conclusion

Summarizing the presented experiments, we observe that Gesture MNIST can be used "out of the box" for machine learning, without requiring any pre-processing or feature extraction steps. Sequence classification performance of LSTM and CNN-based sequence classifiers is high, indicating that Gesture MNIST is a rather easy classification problem. This does not impair its value as a benchmark, since ahead-of-time classification remains unsatisfactory, and other applications such as outlier detection, video modeling, or continual learning (see, e.g., [9]) can be performed relying on Gesture MNIST. We emphasize again the value of a visual sequence classification dataset that contains a large number of high-quality samples per class, and in which variability is mainly contributed by the intrinsic differences between the classes, in contrast to background variability, inconsistently performed gestures, and differences in gesture onset.

# References

1. Dempster, A.P., Laird, N.M., Rubin, D.B.: Maximum likelihood from incomplete data via the EM algorithm. J. Roy. Statis. Soc. Ser. B **39**, 1–38 (1977). http://web.mit.edu/6.435/www/Dempster77.pdf
2. Gepperth, A., Pfülb, B.: Image modeling with deep convolutional gaussian mixture models. In: International Joint Conference on Neural Networks (IJCNN) (2021)
3. Graves, A., Jaitly, N., Mohamed, A.R.: Hybrid speech recognition with deep bidirectional LSTM. In: 2013 IEEE Workshop on Automatic Speech Recognition and Understanding, pp. 273–278. IEEE (2013)
4. Hochreiter, S., Schmidhuber, J.: Long short-term memory. Neural Comput. **9**, 1735–80 (1997). https://doi.org/10.1162/neco.1997.9.8.1735
5. Khan, R.Z., Ibraheem, N.A.: Hand gesture recognition: a literature review. Int. J. Artif. Intell. Appl. **3**(4), 161 (2012)
6. Krizhevsky, A., Sutskever, I., Hinton, G.E.: ImageNet classification with deep convolutional neural networks. In: Pereira, F., Burges, C.J.C., Bottou, L., Weinberger, K.Q. (eds.) Advances in Neural Information Processing Systems, vol. 25. Curran Associates, Inc. (2012)
7. LeCun, Y., Bottou, L., Bengio, Y., Haffner, P.: Gradient-based learning applied to document recognition. Proc. IEEE **86**(11), 2278–2324 (1998). https://doi.org/10.1109/5.726791
8. Molchanov, P., Yang, X., Gupta, S., Kim, K., Tyree, S., Kautz, J.: Online detection and classification of dynamic hand gestures with recurrent 3D convolutional neural network. In: Proceedings of the IEEE Conference on Computer Vision and Pattern Recognition, pp. 4207–4215 (2016)
9. Pfülb, B., Gepperth, A.: A comprehensive, application-oriented study of catastrophic forgetting in DNNs. In: International Conference on Learning Representations (2019). http://openreview.net/forum?id=BkloRs0qK7
10. Rautaray, S.S., Agrawal, A.: Vision based hand gesture recognition for human computer interaction: a survey. Artif. Intell. Rev. **43**(1), 1–54 (2015). https://doi.org/10.1007/s10462-012-9356-9
11. Schak, M., Gepperth, A.: Gesture recognition on a new multi-modal hand gesture dataset. In: ICPRAM (2022)
12. Tharwat, A.: Principal component analysis - a tutorial. Int. J. Appl. Pattern Recogn. **3**(3), 197–240 (2016). https://doi.org/10.1504/IJAPR.2016.079733, www.inderscienceonline.com/doi/abs/10.1504/IJAPR.2016.079733, pMID: 79733
13. Wan, J., Zhao, Y., Zhou, S., Guyon, I., Escalera, S., Li, S.Z.: Chalearn looking at people RGB-D isolated and continuous datasets for gesture recognition. In: Proceedings of the IEEE Conference on Computer Vision and Pattern Recognition Workshops, pp. 56–64 (2016)
14. Zhang, Y., Cao, C., Cheng, J., Lu, H.: EgoGesture: a new dataset and benchmark for egocentric hand gesture recognition. IEEE Trans. Multimedia **20**(5), 1038–1050 (2018). https://doi.org/10.1109/TMM.2018.2808769

# GH-CNN: A New CNN for Coherent Hierarchical Classification

Mona-Sabrine Mayouf[✉][iD] and Florence Dupin de Saint-Cyr[iD]

IRIT, Université Paul Sabatier, Toulouse, France
{mouna-sabrine.mayouf, florence.bannay}@irit.fr
http://www.irit.fr

**Abstract.** Hierarchical multi-label classification is a challenging task implying the encoding of a high level constraint in the neural network model. Before the rise of this field, the classification was done without paying attention to the hierarchical links existing between data. Nevertheless, information relating the classes and subclasses may be very useful for improving the network performances. Recently, some works have integrated the hierarchy information by proposing new neural network architectures (called B-CNN or H-CNN), achieving promising results. However with these architectures, the network is separated into blocks where each block is responsible for predicting only the classes of a given level in the hierarchy. In this paper, we propose a novel architecture such that the whole network layers are involved in the prediction of the entire labels of a sample, i.e., from its class in the top level of the hierarchy to its class in the bottom level. The proposed solution is based on a Bayesian adjustment encoding the hierarchy in terms of conditional probabilities, together with a customized semantic loss function that penalizes drastically the hierarchy violation. A teacher forcing strategy learning is used to enhance the learning quality. Thanks to this approach, we could outperform the state of the art results in terms of accuracy (improved for all levels) and also in terms of hierarchy coherence.

**Keywords:** Multi-label classification · Artificial neural networks · Hierarchical classification · Semantic loss function

## 1 Introduction

Classification is a crucial task in everyday life, it is the first thing that is learned by any living being in order to survive. A smarter task is hierarchical classification since it involves high-level structural knowledge. As recalled in the survey [10], hierarchical classification is used in many applications such as text categorization (where knowing the hierarchy associated to a word may help a user to disambiguate polysemous terms), protein function prediction (where the functions are naturally organized into hierarchies like the Enzyme Commission class hierarchy and the Gene ontology), music genre classification, phoneme classification, 3D shape classification (where some semantic meaning can be assigned to geometry by using an existing class hierarchy like e.g. Princeton Shape Benchmark), classification of emotional speech (Berlin emotional speech database).

© The Author(s), under exclusive license to Springer Nature Switzerland AG 2022
E. Pimenidis et al. (Eds.): ICANN 2022, LNCS 13532, pp. 669–681, 2022.
https://doi.org/10.1007/978-3-031-15937-4_56

In this study we adopt the point of view defended by Silla and Freitas in their survey [10] which defines hierarchical classification as the process of doing classification under the guidance of a pre-established taxonomy, in the context of supervised learning. For instance hierarchical classification is a particular case of structured classification where meta-data is available about the classes organization. The approaches of hierarchical classification can be distinguished according to the depth where it is performed. For instance some works always classify at the level of leaves nodes, these approaches are called *mandatory leaf-node prediction* (MLNP) and others classify at any level of the hierarchy (non mandatory leaf-node prediction). In non-MLNP approaches, a sample can be assigned a label of any level in the hierarchy, it is often done by using a confidence threshold under which no further digging inside the sub-levels of the classification is done.

Another distinction is done about the way the classifier uses the hierarchy:

- *flat classifiers* only aim to give the leaf class, then the hierarchy maybe used a posteriori to deduce all the implicitly assigned ancestor. The drawback of this kind of approaches is that it requires to discriminate among a large number of classes (the leaves of the taxonomy), moreover, the hierarchy is not used to guide the learning.
- *local classifiers* are using the predicted upper-class to narrow the choices of the current class. A disadvantage of these approaches is that an error at a given level will propagate to the sub-levels.
- *global classifiers* are trained on the entire class hierarchy at once and do not perform local training.

In this paper, in order to overcome some limitations of local classifiers and based on the idea that conditional probabilities should play a role to constrain the links between a class and its subclasses, we propose a new architecture called "Globally Hierarchically Coherent"-CNN (GH-CNN) which exploits Bayes' rule and branching CNN yielding a powerful architecture with a well-designed semantic loss function that penalizes the hierarchy violation. The classifier can be considered as global since in the architecture that we propose the whole network is involved in the prediction of the entire label of a sample, i.e., from its class in the top level of the hierarchy to its class in the bottom level. A teacher forcing strategy learning (which uses the ground truth class in order to predict one of its subclass) is used to enhance the learning quality. Thanks to this approach, we could outperform the state of the art results in terms of accuracy and hierarchy coherence for both BreakHis and Fashion MNIST datasets.

## 2   State of the Art About Hierarchical Classification

Hierarchical multi-label classification (HMC) aims at classifying objects with a set of labels that respects a given hierarchy constraint. In HMC, the classes of objects are organized as a tree where the edges correspond to superclass-subclass links. The goal of HMC is to assign to each object a set of labels corresponding to a path in this hierarchy. We expose in this state of the art some works dealing with the hierarchical classification. These approaches can be categorized into three sets: the branch based CNN approaches, the local approaches, the approaches that translate the hierarchical constraint inside the loss function.

In the field of branch based CNN approaches, Zhu and Bain [15] introduce the Branch Convolutional Neural Network (B-CNN) which is a CNN with a particular architecture where the first layers are dedicated to coarse class predictions and the last layers to fine class prediction according to a given hierarchical structure of the target classes. The predictions of the different hierarchical levels are then aggregated with a weighted sum of the loss functions associated to each of them. Moreover the learning phase is done by following a curriculum incremental strategy (as in [4]) consisting in successively learning coarse to fine concepts. The authors experiments show that B-CNN improves over the corresponding baseline CNN on the benchmark datasets MNIST, CIFAR-10 and CIFAR-100. This approach is related to the one developed in this article because the structure of the network is a little bit similar, however the loss function used by Zhu and Bain is not used to adjust the output as we do. Similarly, Seo and Shin [9] are using hierarchical classification for recognizing and classifying people's clothing in apparel images. Their proposal is a VGG19 architecture with additional intermediary outputs: the network is able to give three predicted values for a given sample: one at the top level of the hierarchy ("coarse 1 level", "coarse 2 level" and "fine level"). In the approach of Kolisnik et al. [2]: a new architecture, called H-CNN, is introduced based on B-CNN and designed on VGG16 model to classify with hierarchy constraint the images of FashionImage dataset. The model is an extension of the solution proposed in Seo and Shin [9] which separates the neural network into connected blocks where each block is responsible for predicting a class at a given level. The novelty of this article is the conditional probability update where the probabilities of the super-classes are multiplied by a Conditional Probability Weight Matrix (CPWM) in order to guide the classification of the subclasses. The conditional probability update was previously used by Phan et al. [7] to highlight the relationships among diseases in classification of chest X-rays, and also by Taoufiq et al. [13] for urban structure classification. Most of these works exploit the hierarchy structure. The experiments done on Kaggle Fashion Product Images dataset have promising results and enhance the accuracy of fine-classes prediction compared to a simple model and to a B-CNN model without conditional probability adjustment. Note that the primary goal of these approaches is to fine-tune the prediction of the fine-granular classes, it contrasts with our own goal which is to guarantee a respect of the hierarchy and to obtain accuracy both on superclasses and subclasses; moreover our method is different since we are not partitioning the network in blocks dedicated to some precise level of the hierarchy.

Concerning the local approaches, in [5], Murtaza et al. propose to use hierarchical classification on the BreakHis dataset (described in Example 1), for this aim, they build three classifiers: a binary classifier for predicting if the tissue is benign or malignant, a multi-class classifier for the benign subclasses (A, F, TA, PT) and a second multi-class classifier for the malignant ones (DL, LC, MC, PC). The architecture is a cascade network where the output of the binary classifier guides the choice of the second classifier to use. The approach is a local approach in the taxonomy of Silla and Freitas [10], it separates the network in three parts, our approach takes a different point of view since it uses a single global architecture for all levels which provides more accurate results.

Nevertheless, even if [5] makes mistake on some predictions, its results are completely coherent with the hierarchy (by construction).

Lots of articles deal with using semantic loss function for translating high level knowledge. Among them we can mention the work of Xu et al. [14] which proposes to integrate a Boolean logical constraint into a loss function, called semantic loss function. The article focuses on constraints expressing the exclusive membership to a unique class when using a layer of sigmoid activation functions. In this article, for each sample $s$, the network provides a vector of $n$ probabilities $x = (\hat{y}_1, \ldots, \hat{y}_n)$ where $\hat{y}_k$ represents the predicted probability that the variables $X_k$ is true for the input $s$. The semantic loss function $Loss^s$ associated to the constraint (called $\alpha$) that only one variable $X_k$ should be true (denoted $x \models \alpha$) is defined by $Loss^s = -\log \sum_{x \models \alpha} \prod_{k:x \models X_k} \hat{y}_k \prod_{k:x \models \neg X_k} (1 - \hat{y}_k)$. In the same vein, Giunchiglia and Lukasiewicz propose to impose a hierarchical constraint by designing an appropriate loss function in [1]. Their solution is based on enforcing inclusion between the objects of a class to its superclass: if an object is assigned to a category $A$, it should also be assigned to its supercategory $B$ ($A \subseteq B$). For that, they adjust the output $z_B$ of the superclass $B$ wrt the output $\hat{y}_A$ of $A$, by defining $\hat{y}_B = \max(z_B, \hat{y}_A)$. The final loss function is a sum of the loss function concerning the output $\hat{y}_A$ and the loss function concerning the adjusted output $\hat{y}_B$. Even if [1] imposes the respect of the hierarchy, this approach is using a sigmoïd function which is incompatible with the intra-category exclusivity constraint (ICE) presented below.

## 3   Notations

We consider a dataset $D = \{s_1, s_2, \ldots, s_n\}$ of $n$ samples, with a hierarchy of labels $\mathscr{C} = \mathscr{C}^1 \cup \mathscr{C}^2 \cup \ldots \cup \mathscr{C}^C$, the labels are organized in a tree of depth $C$, where the more general labels are in the first stratum (or level) $\mathscr{C}^1$ and the most specific ones are in the stratum $\mathscr{C}^C$. Strata are called categories (or levels in the hierarchy). Each stratum $\mathscr{C}^i$ is composed of a number $\mathscr{N}_i$ of classes: $|\mathscr{C}^i| = \mathscr{N}_i$. The classes are uniquely identified by two numbers: the number $i$ of the level and the absolute number of the class in this level (in $[1, \mathscr{N}_i]$): $c_j^i$ denotes the $j$th class of the hierarchy level $i$. The hierarchical relations between classes are described by two functions $ch$ (for children) and $pa$ (for parent) where $ch(c_j^i)$ gives the list of the numbers of the classes of level $i + 1$ that are subclasses of the class $c_j^i$, and $pa(c_j^i)$ is the number associated to the superclass of $c_j^i$ in level $i - 1$.

The aim of the classification task is to assign to each sample $s$ a multi-label with $C$ labels: $s.label = (c^1, \ldots, c^C)$ where for all level $i$, $c^i \in \mathscr{C}^i$. It means that the sample $s$ is assigned to the class $c^C$ which is a subtype of the class $c^{C-1}$ which itself is a subtype of $c^{C-2}$ and so on until $c^2$ is a subtype of $c^1$.

**Example 1.** *BreakHis [12] stands for "Breast Cancer Histopathological Images". It is a public dataset of histopathological biopsy images of breath observed by different microscopic magnifications. In BreakHis dataset, $D$ is the set of histopathological images with $|D| = n = 7909$. Each sample $s$ of this dataset is double-labeled. Benign subtypes are Adenosis (A), Fibro Adenoma (F), Tubular Adenoma (TA) and Phyllodes*

*Tumor (PT). Malignant sub-types are Ductal Carcinoma (DC), Lobular Carcinoma (LC), Mucinous Carcinoma (MC) and Papillary Carcinoma (PC). The hierarchy has two levels: the category $\mathscr{C}^1$ which represents the tumor type, and the category $\mathscr{C}^2$ which is the category of the tumor subtype. More precisely, $\mathscr{C}^1 = \{B, M\}$ with $\mathcal{N}_1 = 2$ and $\mathscr{C}^2 = \{A, F, TA, PT, DC, LC, MC, PC\}$ with $\mathcal{N}_2 = 8$.*

*Here, $c_1^1 = B$ and $ch(c_1^1) = \{1, 2, 3, 4\}$, i.e., the subtypes of the benign class are the four first classes of category $\mathscr{C}^2$ namely: A, F, TA and PT respectively corresponding to $c_1^2$, $c_2^2$, $c_3^2$ and $c_4^2$. Similarly $ch(c_2^2) = \{5, 6, 7, 8\}$ contains the number of the classes of the malign subtypes. Moreover Fibroadenoma is a benign tumor, is translated into $pa(c_2^2) = 1$, while Lobular Carcinoma is malign is translated into $pa(LC) = pa(c_5^2) = 2$.*

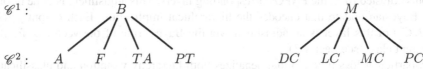

$\mathscr{C}^1 :$         B                     M

$\mathscr{C}^2 :$    A    F    TA    PT          DC    LC    MC    PC

The following definition expresses two constraints that a hierarchical classifier should respect:

**Definition 1 (ICE and ICH constraints).** *A classifier is a function that maps a sample s to a vector of **sets** of classes $s.label = (sc^1, sc^2, \ldots, sc^C)$ where for all $i \in [1, C]$ the set $s.label(i) = sc^i$ is the set of classes of the category $\mathscr{C}^i$ that are assigned to s ($sc^i \subseteq \mathscr{C}^i$). A classifier complies with* the intra-category exclusivity constraint *(ICE) if each sample s of the dataset D has a unique label per category:*

$$\forall s \in D, \forall i \in [1, C], \quad |s.label(i)| = 1, \tag{ICE}$$

*An ICH classifier[1] complies with the* inter-categories hierarchical constraint *(ICH) if for any sample s, $s.label = (c_{j_1}^1, c_{j_2}^2, \ldots, c_{j_C}^C)$ with $j_i \in [1..\mathcal{N}_i]$ is s.t.:*

$$\forall i \in [2, C], j_i \in ch(c_{j_{i-1}}^{i-1}) \tag{ICH}$$

In other words, ICH imposes that at each level $i$ the label of the sample is a number which correspond to a subtype of the label of the sample at level $i - 1$, this means that for each sample, its label represents a path from the root to a leaf in the hierarchy.

**Example 2.** *If the classifier assigns the sample s the vector $s.label = (\{c_1^1\}, \{c_5^2, c_7^2\})$ (i.e., assigns both DC and MC to s), ICE is violated. Moreover if $s.label = (\{c_1^1\}, \{c_8^2\})$ then ICH is violated but ICE is respected.*

---

[1] In the following, we consider ICE classifiers, hence labels are vectors of singleton sets of classes, thus they are abbreviated into C-uplets of classes (with no curly brackets) instead of C-uplets of singletons of classes.

## 4   An Architecture Compliant with ICE and ICH

The GH-CNN architecture (see Fig. 1) is designed in order to ensure that the hierarchical constraint existing between classes and subclasses (ICH) and the exclusivity in the same category constraint (ICE) hold. The network is composed as follows:

- A set of hidden layers described in Sect. 4.1.
- A penultimate primary output layer (PNPO) with $C$ outputs: $z^1, z^2, \ldots, z^C$, each output $z^i$ is a vector of length $\mathcal{N}_i$ (containing the $\mathcal{N}_i$ membership probabilities for the sample to belong to each class of $\mathscr{C}^i$), See Sect. 4.2.
- The final adjusted finer output layer (FAFO) is a layer composed of $C - 1$ outputs adjusted from the PNPO corresponding layers. This adjustment is done through a Bayesian update that encodes the hierarchical implication. Each output $\hat{y}^i$ ($i \in [2, C]$) of this layer is an adjustment via the Bayes' rule of the vector $z^i$ from its parent class (see Sect. 4.3).
- A particular loss function that penalizes both hierarchy violation and classification errors (weighted wrt the depth in the hierarchy), see Sect. 4.4.

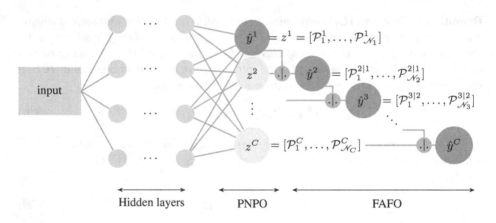

**Fig. 1.** The GH-CNN architecture. The nodes ⊕ represent the Bayesian adjustement (see (3)).

### 4.1   The Hidden Layers

Any neural network backbone can be used for the first layers, the particularity of GH-CNN architecture only appears at the penultimate and last layers of the network. In practice, we opted for the VGG19 model as a skeleton for the hidden layers. Our choice is justified by the great performances of this network in several classification tasks [11] (cited more than 70 000 times). This model is a pre-trained CNN, with 19 learnable layers: 16 convolutional layers followed by 3 fully connected layers, with a total of 144M parameters. It was primary used to classify images during the ImageNet competition (http://www.image-net.org). The competition's aim is to truly classify an image among 1000 daily-object classes. The huge training set containing millions of images trained for a long training time, gave to VGG19 the powerful ability to recognize daily-objects achieving landmark results [8]. As recalled in Sect. 2, VGG was also used for fashion images hierarchical classification by Kolisnik et al. [2] and by Seo and Shin [9] with a promising learning behavior.

## 4.2    The Penultimate Layer of Primary Outputs (PNPO)

In the GH-CNN architecture, the PNPO layer produces $C$ penultimate outputs called $(y^i)$ with $i \in [1, C]$, one for each category $\mathscr{C}^i$ present in the dataset. The inputs of PNPO are activated with a softmax function[2]. Each obtained output $z^i$ is a vector of probabilities of $\mathscr{N}_i$ values: $z^i = (\mathcal{P}_1^i, \mathcal{P}_2^i, \dots \mathcal{P}_{\mathscr{N}_i}^i)$ where $\mathcal{P}_j^i$ corresponds to the probability $\mathcal{P}(s \in c_j^i)$ for a sample $s$ to be classified into the $j^{th}$ class of the level $\mathscr{C}^i$ (this class being called $c_j^i$).

## 4.3    Updating the Probability of a Subclass in the Layer FAFO

The aim of the FAFO layer is to adjust the vector $z^i$ such that it corresponds to the probability of assigning classes at level $i$ under the ICH constraint, the new output vector is denoted $\hat{y}^i$. This is done iteratively on the levels by stating that $z^1$ is already adjusted i.e., $\hat{y}^1 = z^1$ then the adjusted probabilities of level $i + 1$: $\hat{y}^{i+1}$ are computed from $z^{i+1}$ accordingly to the adjusted probabilities of the super classes (at level $i$) $\hat{y}^i$. Indeed, it is clear that the probability vectors $z^i$ and $z^{i+1}$ obtained in the penultimate layer which represent the probability for the sample to be classified by the network into the two consecutive levels $i$ and $i + 1$ in the hierarchy, do not take into account the fact that a class $c_j^i$ of the level $i$ is the parent of a set of classes at level $i + 1$.

Let us denote by $\boxed{s_j^i}$ the event that the sample $s$ is associated (by the network) to the $j$th class of the level $i$ in the hierarchy, i.e., $s.label(i) = c_j^i$. Due to the partition of the class into its subclasses, the events of associating a sample $s$ to one **subclass of** the class $c_j^i$ is an EME[3]. Hence, for coherence purpose, the layer FAFO is designed to adjust each probability vectors $z^i$ in order to enforce that each adjusted probability vector $\hat{y}^i$ should verify the EME law. Intuitively, the knowledge of the superclass must condition the knowledge of its subclasses. In terms of probabilities, it translates into:

$$\begin{aligned} \mathcal{P}(s_j^i) &= \sum_{k \in ch(c_j^i)} \mathcal{P}(s_j^i | s_k^{i+1}) \times \mathcal{P}(s_k^{i+1}) \\ &= \sum_{k \in ch(c_j^i)} \mathcal{P}(s_k^{i+1}) \end{aligned} \tag{1}$$

Note that the second equality is due to $\mathcal{P}(s_j^i | s_k^{i+1}) = 1$ when $k \in ch(c_j^i)$, since when a sample belongs to a **subclass of** $c_j^i$, then this sample should belong to $c_j^i$ itself, which is denoted $s_j^i$. Now, given a level of the hierarchy $i \in [2, C]$, let us consider the conditional probability, abbreviated $\mathcal{P}_j^{i|i-1}$, for a sample $s$ to belong to a class $c_j^i$ (for

---

[2] Softmax is an activation function that takes $\mathscr{N}$ inputs $(x_k)_{k=1\dots\mathscr{N}}$ and gives a probability vector $z$ of dimension $\mathscr{N}$ s.t. its $k$th component is $z(k) = \frac{\exp^{x_k}}{\sum_{j=1}^{\mathscr{N}} \exp^{x_j}}$.

[3] EME = exhaustive mutually exclusive set of events.

any $j \in [1, \mathcal{N}_i]$) knowing that this sample belongs to the parent class of $c_j^i$ (indexed by the number $pa(c_j^i)$ in the level $i - 1$). The knowledge about the fact that the sample belongs to the parent class $c_{pa(c_j^i)}^{i-1}$ is assumed to incompass the fact that the sample belongs also to the grand-parent class and to the great-grand-parent class and so on until the root of the hierarchy. Hence, this conditional probability can be expressed:

$$\mathcal{P}_j^{i|i-1} = \mathcal{P}(s_j^i|s_{pa(c_j^i)}^{i-1}, s_{pa(pa(c_j^i))}^{i-2}, \dots, s_{pa(pa(..(c_j^i))..))}^{1}) \tag{2}$$

According to the softmax function done in layer PNPO, $\forall j \in [1, \mathcal{N}_i]$, $z_j^i$ can be viewed as the probability of $s$ to be attributed a label for the level $i$ equal to $c_j^i$, in short $z_j^i = \mathcal{P}(s_j^i)$, then due to Bayes theorem, we get the equation of the FAFO layer:

$$\hat{y}_j^i = P_j^{i|i-1} = \frac{\hat{y}_{pa(c_j^i)}^{i-1} \times z_j^i}{\sum_{t \in ch(pa(c_j^i))} z_t^i} \tag{3}$$

Finally, the output of FAFO is a vector $(\hat{y}^i)_{i \in [1..C]}$ of vectors such that for any $i$ in $[2, C]$, $\hat{y}^i = [\mathcal{P}_1^{i|i-1}, \dots, \mathcal{P}_{\mathcal{N}_i}^{i|i-1}]$ and $\hat{y}^1 = z^1 = [\mathcal{P}_1^1, \dots \mathcal{P}_{\mathcal{N}_1}^1]$ (see Fig. 1).

**Example 3.** *Suppose that, forwarding a sample through a network associated with the hierarchy of Example 1 yields to a probability distribution $\mathcal{P}^1$ of the tumor type equal to 0.6 for the Benign class and 0.4 for the malignant one: $\mathcal{P}^1 = (0.6, 0.4)$ and $\mathcal{P}^2 = (0.3, 0.025, 0.025, 0.05, 0.2, 0.2, 0.1, 0.1)$.*

*After the Bayesian update of $\mathcal{P}^2$, we obtain $\mathcal{P}^{2|1} = (0.45^4, 0.0375, 0.0375, 0.075, 0.13, 0.14, 0.066, 0.068)$ and $\mathcal{P}^{2|1}(1) + \mathcal{P}^{2|1}(2) + \mathcal{P}^{2|1}(3) + \mathcal{P}^{2|1}(4) = \mathcal{P}^1(1)$.*

At the end of the forward pass through the network, the sample $s$ is assigned to the predicted classes of each category having the maximal probability. The final predicted class inside category $\mathscr{C}^i$ is thus $\hat{c}^i = \mathrm{argmax}(\hat{y}^i)$ where $\mathrm{argmax}(v)$ selects the index $i$ in the vector $v$ such that $v(i)$ is the maximum value in $v$, and in case of equal maximal values in $v$, one index is chosen randomly among the maxima. Hence, the definition of $\hat{c}^i$ guarantees ICE.

## 4.4 Hierarchical Loss Function

In order to support the ICH constraints and to take into account the different levels of robustness required at different levels of the hierarchy, the loss hierarchical loss function $Loss^{h.v}$ is composed of two parts $Loss^h$ that penalizes the errors with respect to the ground truth, this penalty is weighted according to the hierarchy level, and $Loss^v$ that translates the semantic constraint ICH.

$$Loss^{hv} = Loss^h + Loss^v \tag{4}$$

---

[4] $0.45 = 0.3 \times 0.6/(0.3 + 0.025 + 0.025 + 0.05)$.

**Hierarchically Weighted Loss Function:** $Loss^h$ is the part that guarantees the learning of the classification at each level of the hierarchy. It is a linear combination of the cross-entropy distance between the prediction and the ground truth at each level:

$$Loss^h = \sum_{i=1}^{C} \alpha_i \times d(y^i, \hat{y}^i), \text{ with } \alpha_i \in \mathbb{N} \tag{5}$$

where $d(v, \hat{v})$ is the cross-entropy between the two vectors $v$ and $\hat{v}$ defined by $d(v, \hat{v}) = \sum_k v(k) \log(\hat{v}(k)) + (1 - v(k)) \log(1 - \hat{v}(k))$. According to the nature of the hierarchy, several configurations of the weights $\alpha_i$ are worth noticing:

- **Egalitarian penalty**: all $\alpha_i$ are equal. The loss function considers equally important the errors done on superclasses or on subclasses (in Sect. 5, it is implemented with $\alpha_i = 1$ for all $i$).
- **Superclass/subclass enhanced penalty** These variants are proposed when superclasses (respectively subclasses) are considered as more important than the subclasses (respectively superclasses) for guiding the learning, the weights should be decreasing (respectively increasing) along the hierarchy. In Sect. 5, it is implemented with $\alpha_i = C - i + 1$ (or $\alpha_i = i$ respectively) for all $i$.
- **Finest/Coarsest basic model**: We remark that (without the Bayesian update) by setting $(\alpha_1, \ldots, \alpha_{C-1}, \alpha_C) = (0, \ldots, 0, 1)$ (or respectively by setting $(\alpha_1, \alpha_2, \ldots, \alpha_C) = (1, 0, \ldots, 0)$), we obtain the basic neural network that classifies the finest class (respectively the coarsest class) without taking into account its superclasses (respectively its subclasses)

**Hierarchy Violation Loss Function.** We introduce a loss term that penalizes the hierarchy violation: it is the greatest error done on a prediction at a level where the predicted class and subclass are not coherent, (the subclass is not a child of the class).

$$Loss^v = \max_{i \in [1,C] \text{ s.t. } \hat{c}^{i+1} \text{ not child of } \hat{c}^i} \max(d(y^i, \hat{y}^i), d(y^{i+1}, \hat{y}^{i+1})) \tag{6}$$

where $d(v, \hat{v})$ is the cross-entropy distance.

## 5 Experiments and Results

In this section we expose the experiments done on the BreakHis dataset and on Fashion MNIST. The BreakHis dataset is described in Example 1. The Kaggle Fashion MNIST, is one of the largest hierarchical dataset, with more than 40k images and 3 hierarchy levels. The coarsest category contains 4 classes, its subcategory contains 21 classes, and the finest category contains 45 classes. The algorithms were implemented using the Keras library with Python 3 on Osirim platform [6]. The training period of each experiment contains 1000 epochs, with Adam optimizer, and a train batch size of 128. For both datasets, the images were resized to $250 \times 250$, the chosen operators were label conservative (Horizontal and vertical flip, HSV coloration and color inversion). The datasets were split into 70% for training, 10% for validation and 20% for test.

The training phase is divided into three parts: 1) a preliminary warm-up (during 15% of the training phase) where the model is only trained on the coarsest category to ensure a more accurate classification at this level (which will guide the next levels). 2) a teacher forcing strategy[5] (during 25% of the training phase), to adapt the $Loss^{hv}$. 3) a training with one variant of $Loss^{hv}$ (during the remaining time).

We define **the hierarchy violation rate metric (HV)** in order to evaluate the variants of GH-CNN: HV is the number of predicted samples disrespecting the hierarchy divided by the total number of samples in the test set.

Table 1 represents the results obtained using GH-CNN with the different loss functions, with teacher forcing strategy and Bayesian adjustment. The parameters of the Loss functions are inside parenthesis, ($\alpha_1$, $\alpha_2$[, $\alpha_3$]). **Acc**$^i$ and **F1S**$^i$ are the accuracy

**Table 1.** Performances of GH-CNN

| Dataset | Loss variant | Acc$^1$ | Acc$^2$ | Acc$^3$ | F1S$^1$ | F1S$^2$ | F1S$^3$ | HV | ($L_{\min}$, $L_{\max}$)% |
|---|---|---|---|---|---|---|---|---|---|
| BreakHis | CNN [5] | **95.48** | – | – | – | **94.62** | – | – | – |
| | Loss$^h$ (1, 0) | 97.03 | 76.45* | – | 98.69 | 70.64* | – | 58.13 | **(0.0035**, 1.8744) |
| | Loss$^h$ (0, 1) | 85.83* | 95.49 | – | 83.54* | 94.26 | – | 65.14 | (0.0058, 1.9201) |
| | Loss$^h$ (1, 1) | 97.65 | 94.91 | – | 98.45 | 91.67 | – | 11.06 | (0.0120, 2.1352) |
| | Loss$^h$ (2, 1) | 98.43 | 96.78 | – | 99.01 | **95.57** | – | 9.15 | (0.0177, 3.5138) |
| | Loss$^v$ | 67.03 | 58.91 | – | 64.30 | 52.13 | – | 66.25 | (0.2344, **7.3807**) |
| | Loss$^{hv}$ (2, 1) | **98.46** | **96.81** | – | **99.11** | 95.45 | – | **4.39** | (0.0037, 6.7671) |
| Fashion MNIST | B-CNN [9] | – | – | **93.33** | – | – | – | – | – |
| | B-CNN [2] | **99.75** | 98.06 | 91.04 | – | – | – | – | – |
| | Loss$^h$ (1, 0, 0) | **99.98** | 85.14* | 69.03* | 99.12 | 80.62* | 65.64* | 69.45 | (0.0002, 1.0322) |
| | Loss$^h$ (0, 0, 1) | 80.13* | 78.02* | 93.12 | 83.62* | 75.64* | 93.12 | 71.43 | (0.0091, 1.7610) |
| | Loss$^h$ (1, 1, 1) | 99.47 | 86.63 | 91.79 | 93.12 | 99.53 | 84.35 | 18.67 | (0.3546, 6.2380) |
| | Loss$^h$ (3, 2, 1) | 99.81 | 88.95 | 94.61 | 99.81 | 86.11 | 95.41 | 10.19 | (0.0031, 7.1092) |
| | Loss$^v$ | 71.15 | 58.21 | 69.43 | 69.61 | 60.03 | 68.53 | 78.84 | (2.0451, 8.2751) |
| | Loss$^{hv}$ (3, 2, 1) | 99.31 | **98.74** | **95.06** | **99.62** | **99.01** | **94.64** | **3.45** | (0.01984, 7.8924) |

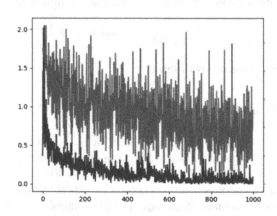

**Fig. 2.** Training loss curves (HG-CNN with/without Bayesain update in blue/green) (Color figure online)

---

[5] The teacher forcing strategy uses the ground truth of the superclass (and not its prediction) to guide the learning of a subclass. It is commonly used with RNNs [3].

and F1S percentages for classes of level $i$. ($L_{min}$, $L_{max}$) are the minimal and maximal training loss values. The * means that the model was only tested (but not trained) for this level. The lines CNN and B-CNN indicate some state of the art results.

For both datasets, the *coarsest basic model* approach (with $Loss^h$ (1, 0) or (1, 0, 0)) is less accurate for classifying in the finest class than the *finest basic model* approach (trained only on the finest class i.e., with $Loss^h$ (0, 1) or (0, 0, 1)), even if the first approach has a greater performance on the coarsest level. It seems that the approach needs to be fine-tuned on finer classes in order to be more efficient. Besides, for both *basic model* approaches, the hierarchy violation rate HV is the highest compared to other loss function variants since there is no information learned about the hierarchical links between classes during the training.

The *egalitarian* loss function increases the accuracy on both datasets. However, in the first half of the training period the loss values are higher than for the basic models. It can be interpreted by saying that the model is learning a more difficult combined task. Note that the HV rate drastically decreases compared with the basic models, since the network is learning simultaneously superclasses and classes, an implicit link has to be discovered. The *superclass enhanced penalty* loss function improves the performances on the superclasses, then improves the performances on subclasses due to the Bayesian adjustment. The *hierarchy violation* loss function can only be used as a complement it is not useful per se in terms of classification because the model does not have any feedback about the accuracy of the class predictions. However, the model GH-CNN trained with $Loss^{hv}$ has the greatest performances in term of accuracy and F1-score for all the levels because the hierarchy violation loss forces the CNN to discover and respect the hierarchical link between labels (the hierarchy violation rate is the lowest reaching 4.39% ($< \alpha_{risk} = 5\%$). Hence $Loss^{hv}$ is achieving an accurate and confident classification with coherent hierarchical links.

Experiments done *without the warm-up phase* showed unstable Loss values which leads us to believe that warm-up helps the network to find the right starting weights for classifying the coarsest classes, then the teacher forcing strategy improves the learning of the subclasses. We observe that the highest loss is reached with the $Loss^{hv}$ for both datasets, but this high error deceases during the last 25% training time attesting that the network manages the classification of each category separately and integrates the hierarchy between the levels. Experiments done *without the Bayesian update* using the $Loss^{hv}$ showed a very disturbed training loss curve (the green curve in Fig. 2[6]) compared to training with the Bayesian update (the blue one in Fig. 2) attesting the crucial role of the Bayesian update.

Comparing with state of the art works, we can remark that, for BreakHis dataset, almost all of the approaches did not pay attention to the hierarchical link between classes, except for [5] where the hierarchy question was addressed (achieving an accuracy of 95.48% of the tumors type detection and 94.62% for the subtypes), while we obtained with $Loss^{hv}$ 98.46% and 96.81% accuracy rates respectively. Concerning the Fashion MNIST dataset, in [9] a B-CNN model was used (giving an accuracy of 93.33% for the finest level). In [2], a conditional probability update was used also with a B-CNN (achieving an accuracy of 99.75%, 98.06% and 91.04%) for the three levels

---

[6] The vertical axis of Fig. 2 is scaled by 3 (e.g. at the first epoch the loss value is 6.76).

respectively. While we achieved, thanks to the global architecture of HG-CNN, to the Bayesian update and to the well designed loss function, a greater accuracy of 99.71%, 98.94% and 95.06% respectively.

## 6    Conclusion and Perspectives

This paper presents the GH-CNN, a novel architecture, that encodes the labels hierarchy inside the network using both a Bayesian adjustment and a particular loss function penalizing hierarchy violations. GH-CNN outperforms the state of the art results for both BreakHis and Fashion MNIST datasets. As a conclusion, GH-CNN is well designed such that all the layers of the network are involved in the determination of the classes at all the levels. Also, the hierarchical coherence is imposed by the Bayesian adjustment before the back-propagation and guarantied thanks to the well-designed loss function. An additional novelty of this paper is the flexibility of $Loss^{hv}$ which can be customized accordingly to the nature of the task. A first perspective of this work is to compare GH-CNN to a CNN where the loss function contains an encoding of the hierarchical constraint as proposed in [14] and a second perspective is about exploring the different combinations of $Loss^h$.

## References

1. Giunchiglia, E., Lukasiewicz, T.: Coherent hierarchical multi-label classification networks. Adv. Neural. Inf. Process. Syst. **33**, 9662–9673 (2020)
2. Kolisnik, B., Hogan, I., Zulkernine, F.: Condition-CNN: a hierarchical multi-label fashion image classification model. Expert Syst. Appl. **182**, 115195 (2021)
3. Lyu, H., Sha, N., Qin, S., Yan, M., Xie, Y., Wang, R.: Advances in neural information processing systems. In: Advances in Neural Information Processing Systems 32 (2019)
4. Mayouf, M.S., Dupin de Saint-Cyr, F.: Formalizing data preparation in curriculum incremental deep learning on breakhis dataset. Technical report, IRIT (2022)
5. Murtaza, G., Shuib, L., Mujtaba, G., Raza, G.: Breast cancer multi-classification through deep neural network and hierarchical classification approach. Multimedia Tools Appl. **79**(21), 15481–15511 (2020)
6. Osirim (observatory of systems information retrieval and indexing of multimedia contents) platform description. https://osirim.irit.fr/site/. Accessed 18 Jun 2020
7. Pham, H.H., Le, T.T., Tran, D.Q., Ngo, D.T., Nguyen, H.Q.: Interpreting chest x-rays via CNNs that exploit hierarchical disease dependencies and uncertainty labels. Neurocomputing **437**, 186–194 (2021)
8. Russakovsky, O., et al.: Imagenet large scale visual recognition challenge. Int. J. Comput. Vision **115**(3), 211–252 (2015)
9. Seo, Y., Shin, K.S.: Hierarchical convolutional neural networks for fashion image classification. Expert Syst. Appl. **116**, 328–339 (2019)
10. Silla, C.N., Freitas, A.A.: A survey of hierarchical classification across different application domains. Data Min. Knowl. Disc. **22**(1), 31–72 (2011)
11. Simonyan, K., Zisserman, A.: Very deep convolutional networks for large-scale image recognition. In: International Conference on Learning Representations (2015)
12. Spanhol, F.A., Oliveira, L.S., Petitjean, C., Heutte, L.: A dataset for breast cancer histopathological image classification. IEEE Trans. Biomed. Eng. **63**(7), 1455–1462 (2016)

13. Taoufiq, S., Nagy, B., Benedek, C.: Hierarchynet: hierarchical CNN-based urban building classification. Remote Sens. **12**(22), 3794 (2020)
14. Xu, J., Zhang, Z., Friedman, T., Liang, Y., Broeck, G.: A semantic loss function for deep learning with symbolic knowledge. In: International Conference on Machine Learning, pp. 5502–5511 (2018)
15. Zhu, X., Bain, M.: B-CNN: branch convolutional neural network for hierarchical classification. arXiv preprint arXiv:1709.09890 (2017)

# Hyperspectral Endoscopy Using Deep Learning for Laryngeal Cancer Segmentation

Felix Meyer-Veit[1(✉)], Rania Rayyes[1], Andreas O. H. Gerstner[2], and Jochen Steil[1]

[1] Technische Universität Braunschweig, Institut für Robotik und Prozessinformatik, Braunschweig, Germany
{f.meyer-veit,r.rayyes,j.steil}@tu-bs.de
[2] Klinikum Braunschweig, ENT-Clinic, Braunschweig, Germany
gerstaoh@web.de

**Abstract.** We propose an efficient hyperspectral imaging (HSI) Deep Learning system for laryngeal cancer prediction. An in-vivo data set with 13 hyperspectral (HS) cubes of malignant laryngeal tumors has been collected directly from 13 different patients at Klinikum Braunschweig using a HS camera. In such medical applications, the data set is usually very sparse, limited, complex and noisy. Therefore, an efficient HSI Deep Learning system is highly needed. First, a relevant wavelength analysis has been done in order to detect the most informative channels in the HS cubes to speed up the prediction and reduce the noise. Based on the results, a new UNet, called Efficient Exception UNet (EFX-UNet), is devised and the two channels No. 13 and No. 14 from each cube are used for training and prediction. The EFX-UNet predicts the probability of the patient having a malignant tumor and yields an initial segmentation. After that a deeper analysis is carried on for the detected patients using the 8 channels No. 9 to No. 16 with our modified Deep UNet to precisely segment the tumor. The system is tested on real patient data. With EFX-UNet we could reduce the prediction time from 60 s with Deep UNet to only 5 s. Although the data set is very limited and very complex, we could achieve a dice score test of 68.6% with EFX-UNet for initial segmentation and 88% with the Deep UNet in our system.

**Keywords:** Deep Learning · Hyperspectral imaging · Cancer detection

## 1 Introduction

Most forms of head and neck cancers occur in the larynx [2], whereas early detection of larynx tumors is crucial for treatment, for instance according to the National Cancer Plan in Germany [7]. Yet, early detection of larynx tumors is challenging. The current standard diagnostic procedure uses white light laryngoscopy in combination with a biopsy for the evaluation of laryngeal tumors and

E. Pimenidis et al. (Eds.): ICANN 2022, LNCS 13532, pp. 682–694, 2022.
https://doi.org/10.1007/978-3-031-15937-4_57

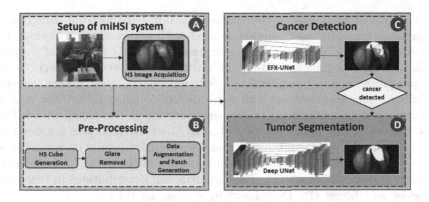

**Fig. 1.** Efficient HSI Deep Learning system.

precancerous lesions, which often leads to false detection of malignant lesions at an early stage. Tissues have to be carefully analyzed by human doctors, which is time-consuming and prone to errors, while it typically takes years to train a physician for this task to gain enough experience. Furthermore, modern diagnostic imaging often leads to an underestimation of the tumor stage and the treatment of tumors during surgery can also lead to a spread of cancer cells [6,24]. Hence, it is important to accurately determine the position of a malignant tumor, which needs to be removed as early as possible, and assistance through technical means is highly desired and well motivated. The recent progress of Deep Learning offers such means and Convolutional Neural Networks (CNN) have demonstrated good results for cancer detection [15]. One of the most promising CNN architectures for efficient and fast tumor detection from small data sets is the well-known U-Net architecture [17], which we also used. Beyond, hyperspectral imaging (HSI) can provide spectral information over multiple wavelength channels that is relevant to diagnoses.

In this paper, we focus on designing an efficient HSI Deep Learning system for fast tumor segmentation that can support the doctors during the endoscopic procedure and help to avoid overlooking critical information. Therefore, a 100% perfect segmentation is not necessary, but a high confidence of detection is needed. For this purpose, we investigate how to minimize the prediction time while maintaining a good prediction accuracy. The preprocessing and training for HSI are very time-consuming. Hence, a wavelength analysis is carried out in order to detect the most informative channels in the hyperspectral (HS) cubes to reduce the prediction time, improve the segmentation performance, and efficiently train and test the networks. Accordingly, the best 2 and 8 channels are determined from 24 available. The results support the medically motivated expectation that the longer wavelengths are more relevant and accordingly HSI is highly recommended for that.

To the best of our knowledge, we present the first work on segmenting efficiently in-vivo larynx tumor from diverse, clinical images in form of HS cubes at a low spatial resolution in the visible-near infrared spectrum using the U-Net architecture. The most relevant related work is presented in Sect. 2. Our proposed efficient HSI Deep Learning system (cf. Fig. 1) consists of 4 stages: (A) in-vivo data acquisition within the miHSI system setup (cf. Sect. 3), (B) data pre-processing and augmentation (cf. Sect. 4), (C) fast cancer detection and initial tumor segmentation with a specifically designed EFX-UNet, and (D) if a tumor is detected, a more precise segmentation is performed with a Deep UNet tailored to the processing of HSI. The UNet architectures are described in Sect. 5, and the wavelength analysis and preliminary results on segmentation accuracy are evaluated and discussed in Sect. 6. Finally, Sect. 7 concludes and gives an outlook on future work. To summarize our contributions in this paper: We devise an efficient HSI Deep Learning system, for this:

- The first time to use HSI for laryngeal cancer with diverse, clinical images.
- Wavelength analysis to detect the most informative channels for fast and efficient prediction.
- Metathesizing with results the medical hypothesis that HSI and long wavelength yield better results.
- EFX-UNet and modified Deep UNet for tumor segmentation are devised.

## 2    Related Work

Although HSI is promising, there are relatively few works in HSI Deep Learning for larynx cancer detection. Bengs et al. [4] present multiple CNNs for in-vivo laryngeal cancer detection based on HSI. They achieved an average accuracy of 81% for predicting cancer and a normal tissue within a spectral range of 380 nm to 680 nm in the visible spectrum with a 3D densenet. However, specifically, the longer wavelength range is auspicious because the penetration depth into the tissue is higher and the relevant interaction between a malignant tumor and a healthy environment does not take place at the tumor surface, but at the tumor invasion front in the depth of the tissue [1, 23]. In another study, a CNN classifier was developed by Halicek et al. [8] to classify head and neck cancer using HSI with 80% accuracy within a spectral range of 450 nm to 900 nm. However, the conducted tumor classification is ex-vivo in contrast to [4] and to our study. Note that none of these previous studies consider the prediction time, nor a real-time segmentation. Furthermore, none of these works which use HSI considered the U-Net, although it is the most promising architecture to deal with sparse data. The benefits of using U-Net on a small data set with consideration of only the relevant channels of the HS cube to speed up inference and improve performance has been demonstrated by the study of Trajanovski et al. [21]. They achieved 96% accuracy using the 128 most relevant channels in the wavelength range 400 to 1700 nm. However, the study is demonstrated on ex-vivo tongue tumors and conducted with an HS camera, which does not enable real-time cancer detection. Lastly, Azam et al. [3] conducted a study on the detection of laryngeal cancer in real-time for white light and narrow band imaging video laryngoscopy. They achieved a precision of 66% based on the YOLO deep learning CNN, which needs only 26 ms to analyze a video frame. Nevertheless, it does not take into account HSI and the NIR wavelength range for improved detection.

## 3   Mobile Intraoperative HSI (miHSI) Acquisition

### 3.1   Clinical Hardware Setup

Figure 2 shows the clinical setup of the data acquisition at Klinikum Braunschweig and Fig. 3 illustrates the mobile intraoperative hyperspectral imaging (miHSI) system. The hyperspectral snapshot camera[1] is utilized for real-time image acquisition and accordingly offers the opportunity for real-time prediction. Most of the time, a halogen 150 Twin cold light source (Karl Storz, Germany) is utilized for lighting, which is attached to a rigid optic through a fiber optic light cable. In some images for clinical reasons a further light source is used, which also contains halogen but only has a power of 80 W. Halogen has a bell-shaped spectrum that reaches far into the infrared range. Hence, this light

source used is ideal for the camera, as it captures the environment in the visible and near-infrared range. To simplify the focus adjustment and to reduce motion artifacts, an endoscope is fixed in an endoscopic holding system consisting of a pipe and a support. If available, a rigid endoscope with 0° optics and a large diameter is used. However, due to operational constraints some HSIs are recorded with a smaller diameter (all endoscopy devices: Karl Storz GmbH & CoKG, Tuttlingen, Germany). The endoscope is connected to the camera via a dedicated C-mount adapter. It is noteworthy that heat sinks are attached to the camera to ensure longevity and high-precision operation, as recommended by the manufacturer [22].

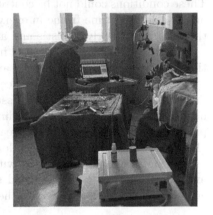

**Fig. 2.** Live setup of miHSI system.

### 3.2   Image Acquisition and Data Set

The camera is connected to a Laptop via a GigE Cable *X-Coded M12* and a *DPE-101GI* Gigabit PoE Injector. The laptop runs the software *PFviewer* provided by Photonfocus AG for image acquisition. The camera deploys the *IMEC snapshot mosaic CMV2K-SM5x5-NIR* sensor which is based on the *CMOSIS CMV2000 V3 CMOS* image sensor. The 25 pass bands of the snapshot sensor are within the visible and near-infrared spectral region, ranging from 665 nm to 975 nm in a $5 \times 5$ mosaic, such that HS data is recorded in a single shot. The total spatial resolution of the sensor is $2048 \times 1088$ pixels, which corresponds to $409 \times 217$

---

[1] *MV0-D2048x1088-C01-HS02-160-G2* (Photonfocus AG, Switzerland).

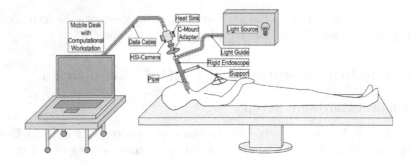

**Fig. 3.** Schematic illustration of miHSI system.

pixels per spectral band due to mosaicing. Additional care is taken to ensure that the setup is sterile. Note that the differing conditions and hardware equipment and the different involved physicians result in a varying and complex data set. These conditions could not be controlled for, as the image acquisition was carried out in a limited time frame in everyday clinical practice. However, this renders the data particularly realistic and application-oriented.

The HSI data set was collected from 13 different patients. The image acquisition was performed under general anesthesia and consequently on the operating table. This minimized the influence of possible confounding variables. Furthermore, it was performed before tissue samples were collected for further diagnostic examination. Image recording took place within the framework of the project "Early detection of laryngeal cancer by means of Hyperspectral Imaging (109825110275)" funded by the German Cancer Aid. Since the conditions varied during the image acquisition with regard to light source and endoscope, the exposure time had to be adjusted so that the bands are illuminated similarly across different HSIs. Therefore, the respective HSIs are all comparably bright.

## 4   Pre-processing

After an image has been captured, pre-processing is necessary before it can be considered for training and validation. First, the spectral corrected HS cube is generated from the captured raw image. Second, glare points are removed to reduce noise. Lastly, patch generation and data augmentation are performed to artificially increase the size of the data set.

**Hyperspectral Cube Generation.** The acquired image is a raw sensor image with a resolution of 2048 × 1088 pixels. The mosaic structure of the sensor is visible in this image because of capturing all bands in one shot. In order to generate the spectral corrected reflectance HS cube from the raw sensor image, three processing steps have to be carried out. First, demosaicing is used to remove the effects of the mosaic pattern from the data by resampling the data of each band in the same regular grid. The demosaicing algorithm translates each band of the spectral image so that all bands of the spectral image are aligned using bilinear interpolation of each band [10]. Second, a reflectance calculation is applied to compute the reflectance signal from the captured radiance of an object. In this way, the saturation at any spectral band is avoided and the maximum dynamic range of the sensor is ensured. Lastly, a spectral correction is conducted which removes higher-order and cross-talk spectral information from the spectrum. Consequently, instead of 25 bands that are within the wavelength range 665 nm to 975 nm, the created HS cube has now 24 bands within the wavelength range 668.86 nm to 948.54 nm.

**Glare Removal.** Glare points cannot provide accurate information about the human tissue and appear to the learning algorithm as outliers. To eliminate glare spots, the inpainting algorithm [20] has been used. For detection of glaring spots, bi-dimensional histograms are applied because they do not require denoising and post-processing and are very reliable [16,19].

**Data Augmentation and Patch Generation.** Attaining acceptable performance with a very small data set is challenging. Therefore, patch generation and data augmentation are very important to increase the data set size and avoid overfitting. First, patch generation can be used to duplicate the given dataset. In this work, half of all patches are cut out of the data cube with an overlap of 50%. Using the overlap, the data is even further augmented. The other half is taken randomly around the perimeter of the lesion. This oversampling counteracts the imbalance between pixels of a lesion and background pixels. The generated patches are then randomly flipped, mirrored, and rotated. This results in a data set of 1100 patches for training and 100 patches for validation with a patch size of $128 \times 128$. The patches are generated from 11 different HS cubes for training and 1 cube for validation, leaving one cube for final testing.

**Data Labeling.** A binary mask was created from the images labeled by the lead physician based on the pathologist's findings and then augmented in the same way as the HS images. This mask is used to train and validate the model and is sufficient as gold standard in the sense that a malignant property of the tumor has been verified in advance by the pathologist. Note that there is no pixel-wise ground truth in the image because it is hand-labeled by the expert.

# 5  Efficient HSI Deep Learning System

We employ the U-Net architecture [17] which recently has been very successful in medical image segmentation [18]. This section describes the U-Net, it's modification to obtain the EFX-UNet and the Deep UNet architectures for our efficient HSI Deep Learning system (cf. Fig. 1) and finally their loss function.

## 5.1  U-Net

The U-Net architecture comprises an encoder and decoder, which are also known as the contracting and expanding paths. To capture the context in the image, the encoder is used. Two convolutional layers with a $3 \times 3$ kernel are followed by one max-pooling layer with a $2 \times 2$ kernel in each convolutional block. Additionally, a Rectified Linear Unit acts as a non-linear activation function after each convolutional layer. This method is also known as downsampling. The decoder, is used to enable precise localization. There are two convolutional layers with a $3 \times 3$ kernel in each deconvolutional block, followed by one up convolutional layer with a $2 \times 2$ kernel. Similar to the encoder, one Rectified Linear Unit is added after each convolutional layer. In a nutshell, this process is known as upsampling. In addition, the UNet combines the low and higher resolution features from different layers numerous times with skip connections to obtain a more exact pixel-wise segmentation [17].

## 5.2   The EFX-UNet and the Deep UNet Architectures

Since HS images introduce multiple channels, a deeper network is needed to reveal the characteristics of the channels through an increased number of convolutional blocks in the contracting path and corresponding deconvolutional blocks in the expanding path (cf. Fig. 4a). Our modified convolutional block consists of two convolutional layers, two batch normalization layers, and a dropout layer, which enhances the generalization of the model and reduces overfitting. To avoid artifacts, we implement reflective padding and insert a cropping layer at the end of the UNet (cf. Fig. 4a) in order to ensure the correct adjustment of the weights during the backpropagation process and smoothing during inference to enhance the final heat map result. These operations were inspired by the work of B. Huang et al. [9]. The size of the network increases with the number of channels which in turn increases the training costs and execution time. Therefore, we first investigated which wavelength channels are the most informative without jeopardizing the accuracy of detection and segmentation (details see cf. Sect. 6). It preliminary turned out that No. 9 to No. 16 yielded the best results and using more channels did not enhance the results. Among these 8 channels, the channels No. 13 to No. 14 turned out to provide enough information to make an initial tumor prediction.

This motivated the final two-stage approach with two nets tailored to use two channels for detection and eight for semantic segmentation. To process full 8 channels for the pixel-wise semantic segmentation, 6 (de-) convolutional blocks are used (cf. Fig. 4a). It starts with 32 feature maps in the first convolutional block and it doubles the number after each block. This leads to 2048 feature maps at the bottleneck of the proposed Deep UNet in Fig. 4a.

For faster detection, a flatter network EFX-UNet with 3 (de-) convolutional blocks for only 2 channels is designed (cf. Fig. 4b). One advantage of this simpler UNet is that the padding can be neglected, thus simplifying processing. Furthermore, training and prediction of this network are accelerated by using depthwise separable convolutional layers [5] instead of convolutional layers. The EFX-UNet is used for a fast cancer examination in the real-time deep learning system (cf. Fig. 1) to detect the malign lesion and to assist the decision if a deeper analysis is needed.

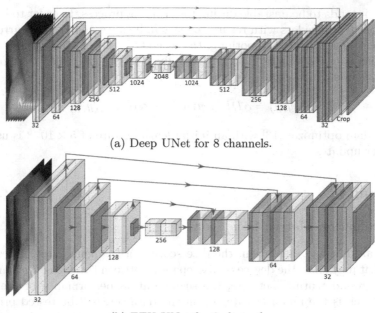

(a) Deep UNet for 8 channels.

(b) EFX-UNet for 2 channels.

**Fig. 4.** EFX-UNet and Deep UNet architectures, visualized using [11].

## 5.3   Loss Function and Optimizer

In the data set, the distribution between the background and lesion pixels is rather unbalanced. Therefore, a weighted sum of binary cross-entropy and dice loss function was used to deal with this issue.

The binary cross-entropy is given in Eq. (1).

$$L_{BCE}(\hat{y}, y) = -(y \log(\hat{y}) + (1 - y) \log(1 - \hat{y})) \tag{1}$$

Each category contributes equally to the loss function in Eq. (1), which is suitable for a balanced data set but not for the given skewed data set. If simply binary cross-entropy is used as the loss function, the neural network may be prone to classifying the majority of pixels as background pixels and fail to categorize the lesion pixels correctly.

In order to handle the skewed class data set correctly, a dice loss (cf. Eq. (2)) can be implemented. It derives from the dice score, which is a metric for comparing the similarity of two images.

$$DL(\hat{y}, y) = 1 - \frac{2y\hat{y} + 1}{y + \hat{y} + 1} \tag{2}$$

However, it tends to be unstable during the training process. In order to leverage the flexibility of dice loss with regard to class imbalance and the concurrent use of cross-entropy for curve smoothing, the weighted sum of both is used in this work which is called Combo Loss [12] and given in Eq. (3). The factor $\alpha = 0.7$ is chosen heuristically.

$$CL(\hat{y}, y) = \alpha DL(\hat{y}, y) + (1 - \alpha)L_{BCE}(\hat{y}, y) \tag{3}$$

The adam optimizer [13] with an initial learning rate of $5 \times 10^{-5}$ is used for parameter updates.

## 6    Results

### 6.1    Evaluation Metric: Dice Score

In medical image segmentation, the dice score is a frequently used assessment metric that may show the degree of discrepancy between the segmentation result and the ground truth. Therefore, the segmentation performance of the lesion region, which is the minority category in the data set, will be tested primarily on the dice score (cf. Eq. (4)). The results are shown in Table 1 and Fig. 6.

$$DSC = \frac{2|Y \cap \hat{Y}|}{|Y| + |\hat{Y}|} = \frac{2TP}{2TP + FP + FN} \tag{4}$$

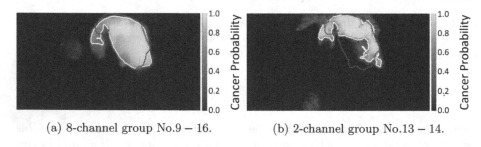

(a) 8-channel group No.9 − 16.          (b) 2-channel group No.13 − 14.

**Fig. 5.** Heat map with ground truth contour of the malignant lesion determined with the red line marked by the expert. (Color figure online)

## 6.2    Wavelength Analysis

The channel group analysis of the HS dataset is performed using a test set derived from one HSI showing a malignant lesion. The lesion is a moderately differentiated, keratinized Squamous Cell Carcinoma. This type of malignant lesion is one of the most common in the larynx, which is why it is a suitable test case for the following analysis. The segmentation performance is analyzed by evaluating heat maps. They show the probability of cancer ranging from 0.0 (blue) to 1.0 (yellow) for each pixel (cf. Fig. 5). The

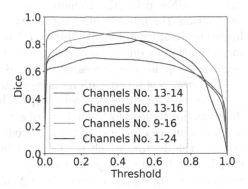

**Fig. 6.** Dice-Threshold curves for the best 2-, 4-, 8-, and 24-channel group.

label of the doctor is marked as a red line and the predicted lesion contour with a probability of at least 50% is marked as a white line.

One HS cube has 24 bands after it has been created. Subsequently, the 24 bands are divided into three equally sized 8-channel groups. The 8-channel group No. 9–16 (780–862 nm) performs best as the entire lesion is predicted with a high probability with only a few false positives using the proposed Deep UNet.

In a further step, the respective 8-channel groups are split into 4-channel groups. When observing all 4-channel groups, it can be seen that channel group No. 13–16 (826–862 nm) performs best regarding the dice score values in Table 1. Since the 4-channel group No. 13–16 performs best, the 2-channel group No. 13–14 (826–840 nm) is selected as a sufficient subgroup. The EFX-UNet is applied to this 2-channel group for fast prediction and the initial segmentation result is

**Table 1.** Dice score of different channel groups for the test malignant lesion.

| Channel groups | | Dice score at threshold >0.5 |
|---|---|---|
| 2-channel group | No. 13–14 | 0.686 |
| 4-channel group | No. 1–4 | 0.496 |
| | No. 5–8 | 0.815 |
| | No. 9–12 | 0.775 |
| | No. 13–16 | 0.818 |
| | No. 17–20 | 0.729 |
| | No. 21–24 | 0.108 |
| 8-channel group | No. 1–8 | 0.49 |
| | No. 9–16 | **0.88** |
| | No. 17–24 | 0.738 |
| 24-channel group | No. 1–24 | 0.815 |

shown in Fig. 5b. Compared to the heat map result of the Deep UNet (cf. Fig. 5a), the EFX-UNet using the 2-channel group has more false positives (cf. Fig. 5b). In addition, the number of true positives is lower, but they are endowed with a higher probability in Fig. 5b. However, the EFX-UNet reduces computation time for evaluation by one order of magnitude from 60 s to only 5 s. This was achieved using an i5 quad-core processor, 16 GB RAM and a GPU with 850–1100 MHz.

The previous investigations have shown that the 8-channel group No. 9–16 performs best among 8-channel groups. This can also be seen in the dice score at different thresholds plotted in form of a curve diagram (cf. Fig. 6). The threshold has an influence on the shape of the predicted lesion and how similar it is to the label of the doctor, which is measured by the dice score. The dice score from threshold 0.2 to 0.8 always remains above 80% for the 8-channel group No. 9–16 when observing its green curve. The 2-channel group performs also well and is stable at all thresholds. What was described as true positives, which are endowed with a high probability on the heat map before, is noticeable in Fig. 6 by the blue curve that does not flatten out early.

### 6.3   Preliminary Evaluation of Accuracy and Discussion

In the previous, only one HS image stack was used for testing and the evaluation of generalization, which consequently allows only for intermediate results on the segmentation accuracy. Table 1 shows a summary of the dice score of all the channel groups at a threshold of 0.5. Consequently, it can also be concluded from this that channel group No. 9–16 performs best with a dice score of 0.88. Looking at the dice score of all the 4-channel groups, the poor results of the first and last 4-channel groups are particularly striking. These are due to the overexposed channels. Their result also has an effect on the first and last 8-channel group, as well as the 24-channel group, since they are included. This supports the intention to focus on the most informative channels, which was also concluded in the work of Trajanovski et al. [21]. This is realized in our system (cf. Fig. 1) by means of channels 13 and 14 with the EFX-UNet and channels 9 to 16 with the Deep UNet.

While the presented results are very encouraging and confirm that hyperspectral imaging is beneficial for larynx tumors, the presented study focuses on establishing the technological basis and investigating which range of wavelengths is most promising. However, there are clear limitations, that must be addressed in further work. First, data labeling was performed by one doctor, second, the data set is still relatively small, and therefore only one test image was used for generalization, and third, the effect of different exposure times is not further analyzed. The effect of the exposure times, as well as the complexity of the limited data set, are analyzed and evaluated in our continuing work [14]. Nevertheless, the overall approach shows great potential to be implemented as a clinical application to enhance the standard procedure.

# 7  Conclusion and Outlook

In this paper, a new HSI Deep Learning system for efficient and fast laryngeal tumor segmentation and detection was designed. The results of our wavelength analysis emphasize clearly the medical assumption that the longer wavelength range is more relevant for tumor detection and hence HSI are the most relevant images to be used. Based on this result, we were able to reduce the number of HSI channels from 24 to 8 without reducing the accuracy. Additionally, the best 2 channels were identified for faster prediction and efficiently providing an initial tumor segmentation. With our EFX-UNet, we were able to reduce the prediction time from 60 s to only 5 s.

With these very encouraging results, we are already in the range where it can be applied practically in clinical treatment. In order to further reduce the prediction time, it is worthwhile to quantize the trained model for real-time applications and more investigation is currently carried out. Note that these results provide only primarily results on the achieved accuracy since the focus was more on the efficiency since the data set is very limited (only 13 images) and very complex as well as the changing conditions of the data acquisition. Still, the preliminary results of the accuracy are very promising. In our continuing work [14] extended testing procedures with cross-validation considering the exposure time are addressed. In future work, we would like to put more emphasis on the accuracy of segmentation, which requires establishing a gold standard through multiple labeling. Additionally, we are investigating how to enhance the performance of EFX-UNet by adding residual connections [5] which can significantly improve the performance of its model.

# References

1. Arens, C., et al.: Fortschritte der endoskopischen diagnostik von dysplasien und karzinomen des larynx. HNO **60**(1), 44–52 (2012)
2. Aupérin, A.: Epidemiology of head and neck cancers: an update. Curr. Opin. Oncol. **32**(3), 178–186 (2020)
3. Azam, M., et al.: Deep learning applied to white light and narrow band imaging videolaryngoscopy: toward real-time laryngeal cancer detection. Laryngoscope (2021). https://doi.org/10.1002/lary.29960
4. Bengs, M., et al.: Spatio-spectral deep learning methods for in-vivo hyperspectral laryngeal cancer detection. In: Medical Imaging 2020: Computer-Aided Diagnosis (2020). https://doi.org/10.1117/12.2549251
5. Chollet, F.: Xception: Deep learning with depthwise separable convolutions (2016). https://doi.org/10.48550/ARXIV.1610.02357
6. Date, K., et al.: Inhibition of tumor growth and invasion by a four-kringle antagonist (hgf/nk4) for hepatocyte growth factor. Oncogene **17**(23), 3045–3054 (1998)
7. Gerstner, A.O.H.: Früherkennung von kopf-hals-tumoren. entwicklung, aktueller stand und perspektiven. Laryngo-Rhino-Otologie **87 Suppl 1**(S 1), S1–S20 (2008)
8. Halicek, M., et al.: Deep convolutional neural networks for classifying head and neck cancer using hyperspectral imaging. Biomed. Opt. **22**(6), 1–4 (2017)

9. Huang, B., et al.: Tiling and stitching segmentation output for remote sensing: basic challenges and recommendations (2018). https://doi.org/10.48550/ARXIV.1805.12219

10. HyperSpectral Imaging: Photonfocus (2021)

11. Iqbal, H.: Harisiqbal88/plotneuralnet (2018). https://doi.org/10.5281/zenodo.2526396

12. Jadon, S.: A survey of loss functions for semantic segmentation. In: CIBCB, pp. 1–7. IEEE (2020)

13. Kingma, D.P., Ba, J.: Adam: A method for stochastic optimization. CoRR (2015)

14. Meyer-Veit, F., et al.: Hyperspectral Wavelength Analysis with U-Net for Larynx Cancer Detection. In: ESANN (2022)

15. Munir, K., et al.: Cancer diagnosis using deep learning: a bibliographic review. Cancers 11(9), 1235 (2019)

16. Ortiz, F., et al.: Automatic detection and elimination of specular reflectance in color images by means of ms diagram and vector connected filters. IEEE Trans. Syst. Man Cybern. Part C (Applications and Reviews) 36(5), 681–687 (2006)

17. Ronneberger, O., Fischer, P., Brox, T.: U-Net: convolutional networks for biomedical image segmentation. In: Navab, N., Hornegger, J., Wells, W.M., Frangi, A.F. (eds.) MICCAI 2015. LNCS, vol. 9351, pp. 234–241. Springer, Cham (2015). https://doi.org/10.1007/978-3-319-24574-4_28

18. Siddique, N., et al.: U-net and its variants for medical image segmentation: a review of theory and applications. IEEE Access 9, 82031–82057 (2021)

19. Tchoulack, S., et al.: A video stream processor for real-time detection and correction of specular reflections in endoscopic images. In: IEEE NEWCAS-TAISA, pp. 49–52 (2008)

20. Telea, A.: An image inpainting technique based on the fast marching method. J. Graphics Tools 9(1), 23–34 (2004)

21. Trajanovski, S., et al.: Tongue Tumor Detection in Hyperspectral Images Using Deep Learning Semantic Segmentation. IEEE Trans. Biomed. Eng. 68(4), 1330–1340 (2021). https://doi.org/10.1109/TBME.2020.3026683

22. User Manual MV0/OEM0 CMOSIS Camera Series: Photonfocus (2020)

23. Wang, T.D., et al.: Optical biopsy: a new frontier in endoscopic detection and diagnosis. Clin. Gastroenterol. Hepatol. Official Clin. Ppract. J. Am. Gastroenterol. Assoc. 2(9), 744–753 (2004)

24. Yamada, T., et al.: Hepatocyte growth factor reduces susceptibility to an irreversible epidermal growth factor receptor inhibitor in egfr-t790m mutant lung cancer. Clin. Cancer Res. 16(1), 174–183 (2010)

# Image Super-Resolution Using Deep RCSA Network

Yuheng Cao[1] and Mengjie Zhou[2(✉)]

[1] School of Electronic Science and Engineering, Southeast University, Nanjing, China
220171326@seu.edu.cn
[2] Department of Computer Science, University of Bristol, Bristol, UK
mengjie.zhou@bristol.ac.uk

**Abstract.** The aim of image super-resolution (SR) is to reconstruct high-resolution images from low-resolution images. As a basic image-processing procedure, SR facilitates subsequent tasks. With the boom in deep learning (DL), DL-based image SR approaches have also attracted considerable interest. The main challenge for DL-based image SR is constructing a deep trainable network with powerful representation capability. To meet this challenge, we propose a residual channel-spatial attention (RCSA) network combining the dense module and attention module in the trunk component of the network. For the dense module, we use the sparse residual-dense connection to tackle the gradient-vanishing problem and, thereby, increase the depth of the network. For the attention module, we use the channel-spatial attention mechanism to rescale the importance across the channels and spaces in the feature maps. Both strategies can improve the learning and representational capability of the network. We conducted extensive comparisons with 9 other state-of-the-art methods on 5 standard benchmark datasets. The quantitative and qualitative results show the superior performance of our RCSA method.

**Keywords:** Image super-resolution · Deep convolutional neural network · Attention mechanism

## 1 Introduction

Image super-resolution (SR) refers to the task of reconstructing high-resolution (HR) images from one or more low-resolution (LR) observations of the same scene. To ensure the overall structure of the original LR image and enrich the details of the texture, SR generates the appropriate number of target pixels around each pixel to maintain the gray value jump in the high-frequency region and ensure the gray value gradient in the low-frequency region. The result is a reconstructed image that is clear, natural, and noise-free. As a means of image preprocessing, SR technology improves the performance of many advanced visual tasks such as small target detection [2], facial keypoint detection [10] and text recognition [20].

© The Author(s), under exclusive license to Springer Nature Switzerland AG 2022
E. Pimenidis et al. (Eds.): ICANN 2022, LNCS 13532, pp. 695–706, 2022.
https://doi.org/10.1007/978-3-031-15937-4_58

The first SR algorithm was proposed by Harris and Goodman in the 1960s [7, 9]. Currently, most mainstream algorithms fall into one of three categories, being either interpolation-based, reconstruction-based, or learning-based methods. In the push to achieve acceptable levels of both performance and efficiency, deep learning (DL) based methods have been attracting interest. These DL-based methods have yielded better results than reconstruction-based and conventional ML-based methods [4, 11, 12, 24, 25].

For image DL-based SR tasks, constructing very deep trainable network with powerful representation ability remains a challenge and a focus of research. Inspired by the development of network structure and attention mechanism, we have proposed a residual channel-spatial attention network (RCSA) to effectively resolve key problems. The two main components of our network are the dense module and the attention module. Similar to the residual dense block in RDN [25], our dense module also utilizes dense connections and residual learning, as shown in Fig. 2(a). The bypass enhances the reuse of features connections and residual learning, as shown in Fig. 2(a), and alleviates the problems of gradient vanishing and model degradation. The dense connected layers increase the depth of the network and facilitate the training. Unlike RDN, we discard some of the skip connections so as to reduce the number of feature channels and improve the computational efficiency. In the attention module, we use the channel-spatial attention mechanism to re-scale channel and spatial features adaptively and, thereby, increase the learning capability and representational power of the network further.

Unlike the original channel-spatial attention module, we replace the fully connected layers with $1 \times 1$ convolutional layers. This operation alleviates the limitation on the input size as well as the structural damage caused by the fully connected layer and improves computational efficiency. Attentive to the information loss, we discard the global pooling in the spatial attention mechanism block. Overall, our contributions are three-fold, including proposals for (1) the very deep residual channel-spatial attention network (RCSA) to reconstruct highly accurate SR images, (2) the sparse residual dense module to construct the very deep trainable network, and (3) use of the channel-spatial attention (CSA) mechanism to rescale features adaptively through consideration of inter-dependencies among feature channels and spaces.

## 2   Related Works

Most of the existing research on reconstructing high-resolution images has involved learning-based methods that continue to evolve in step with DL techniques. Because of the representative and learning ability, deep CNN has been widely used for image SR tasks. In the pioneering work on SRCNN [4], the mapping relationship between the LR and HR images was learned directly in an end-to-end manner within the CNN architecture. To fulfill the real-time demand, FSRCNN [5] was proposed in the form of a compact, hourglass-shaped CNN structure. With the introduction of a deconvolution layer, a downsampling-upsampling strategy, and a smaller filter size with more mapping layers, this method realized acceleration of more than 40-fold while maintaining good restoration quality. Using a very deep convolutional network, VDSR [11] achieved further improvements in accuracy and visual quality. The introduction of a residual learning strategy with adjustable gradient clipping served to increase the convergence speed and solve the gradient-disappearing problem. The LapSRN [14] proposed by the Laplacian Pyramid Super-Resolution Network to reconstruct the sub-band residuals of high-resolution images progressively further improved speed and accuracy. MemNet [19] introduced the memory block, which consists of a recursive unit and a gate unit. This kind of structure tackled the long-term dependency problem caused by very deep models. EDSR [15] also utilized residual learning to form an enhanced deep SR network with the elimination of some unnecessary modules. Expanding the model size improved performance and stabilized the training procedure.

For the purpose of extending the practicability to real-world tasks, SRMD proposed a general framework with a dimensionality stretching strategy to handle various types of degradation [23]. Similarly, to represent multiple types of image degradation, DBPN [6] exploited the mutual dependencies of low- and high-resolution images and constructed iterative upsampling and downsampling layers with an error feedback mechanism for projection errors. More recently, to make full use of the hierarchical features, RDN [25] proposed a dense feature fusion (DFF) model in which these features are extracted both locally and globally. Specifically, the abundant local features are extracted with dense, connected convolutional layers, after which local feature fusion serves to learn more efficient features from preceding and current local features and, lastly, to obtain the global hierarchical features. With the development of the attention mechanism, this efficient structure has also been used for image SR tasks.

Moreover, to improve the representational ability of CNNs, RCAN [24] proposed a very deep residual channel attention network. In this case, the residual in residual (RIR) structure serves to learn high-frequency information. Meanwhile, the channel attention mechanism is used to re-scale channel-wise features adaptively by considering the interdependencies among channels. Here, we propose a residual channel-spatial attention network (RCSA) that combines the advantages of residual learning, the dense connection, and the attention mechanism. Extensive experiments comparing the proposed methods just discussed with this network showed that it delivers superior performance.

## 3  Our Approach

In the existing work on DL-based image SR methods, the basic network structure is normally divided into head, trunk, and reconstruction components. As Fig. 1 shows, the head component performs the convolution operation to extract the shallow features of input images. The trunk component consists of some basic modules (BMs) to extract the deep features. Through the last component, reconstruction, the upscaling operation serves to acquire SR images with the same size of input HR images.

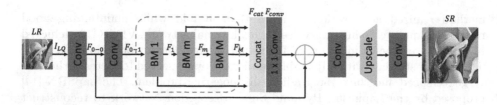

**Fig. 1.** The residual channel-spatial attention (RCSA) network.

## 3.1 Network Structure

As shown in Fig. 1, the head component of the proposed RCSA network uses two $3 \times 3$ convolution layers to extract the shallow features of the input LR image. Specially, given LR image $\mathbf{X}$, the shallow features $\mathbf{F}_{0-0}$ and $\mathbf{F}_{0-1}$ are obtained as follows:

$$\mathbf{F}_{0-0} = H_0(\mathbf{X}) \tag{1}$$

$$\mathbf{F}_{0-1} = H_1(H_0(\mathbf{X})) \tag{2}$$

where $H_0$ and $H_1$ donate the first and the second convolution operations, respectively. Then, the extracted feature $\mathbf{F}_{0-1}$ is fed into the trunk component with $M$ basic modules, each consisting of a dense block and $N$ attention blocks. The output feature $\mathbf{F}_m$ of each basic module can be calculated as:

$$\mathbf{F}_m = B_{cpa}(B_{des}(\mathbf{F}_{m-1})) \tag{3}$$

where $B_{des}$ and $B_{cpa}$ indicate the calculation procedures of dense block and attention block, respectively (further details in Sects. 3.2 and 3.3). Therefore, the final output feature $\mathbf{F}_M$, after the whole trunk component can be formulated as:

$$\mathbf{F}_\mathbf{M} = B_M(\mathbf{F}_{M-1}) = B_M(...(B_1(\mathbf{F}_{0-1}))...) \tag{4}$$

where $B_M$ is the function and $\mathbf{F}_{M-1}$ the input of the last basic module. Subsequently, the outputs of each basic module are jointly concatenated after the last basic module, followed by a $1 \times 1$ convolution operation to reduce the number of channels as follows:

$$\mathbf{F}_{cat} = [\mathbf{F}_1, \mathbf{F}_2, ..., \mathbf{F}_M] \tag{5}$$

$$\mathbf{F}_{conv} = H_{1 \times 1}(\mathbf{F}_{cat}) \tag{6}$$

Given that the number of features extracted by each basic module is $C$, $\mathbf{F}_{cat}$ represents the concatenated feature with $C \times M$ channels. $H_{1 \times 1}$ represents the $1 \times 1$ convolution operation, which reduces the number of channels from $C \times M$ to $C$. After the final reconstruction component $R$, the output of the entire module $\mathbf{Y}$ can be defined as:

$$\mathbf{Y} = R(\mathbf{F}_{conv} + \mathbf{F}_{0-0}) = g(\mathbf{X}) \tag{7}$$

where $g(\mathbf{X})$ represents the function of the SR network. To optimize the SR network, we use the $L1$ loss function to minimize the sum of the absolute differences between the HR image $\mathbf{I}_{HR}$ and the SR image $\mathbf{Y}$. The loss function is defined as:

$$loss = avg(\sum_i \|\mathbf{Y}^i - \mathbf{I}^i_{HR}\|_1) = avg(\sum_i \|g(\mathbf{X}^i) - \mathbf{I}^i_{HR}\|_1) \tag{8}$$

## 3.2   Dense Module

Figure 2(a) presents details of the dense module. As can be seen, each dense module consists of three convolution-ReLU units and a channel fusion module. In each unit, the $3 \times 3$ convolution operation serves to extract the local deep features. We chose the ReLU function for the benefits that it confers in terms of relatively few parameters, high training speed, and more spare models.

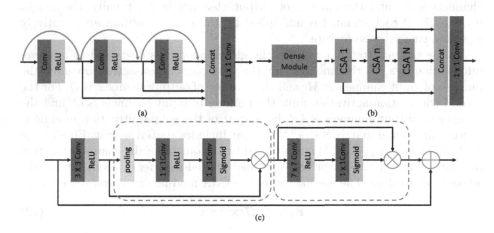

**Fig. 2.** The structure of the dense module (a) and the channel-spatial attention module (c) in the basic module (b) of the RCSA network.

Except for the first unit, the input and output from the previous unit are concatenated and then fed to the next unit. The output of each unit keeps the number of channels and their fusion after concatenation consistent. The fused module uses the $1 \times 1$ convolution kernel to make the input and output dimensions of the dense module the same. We define $U_i$ as the function of the $i$-th convolution-activation unit, $\mathbf{x}$ as the input of the dense module, and $\mathbf{D}$ as the output of the dense module. The function of the dense module can be calculated as

$$U_2(\mathbf{x}) = U_2[\mathbf{x}, U_1(\mathbf{x})] \tag{9}$$

$$U_3(\mathbf{x}) = U_3[U_1(\mathbf{x}), U_2(\mathbf{x})] \tag{10}$$

$$\mathbf{D} = H_{1\times1}[U_1(\mathbf{x}), U_2(\mathbf{x}), U_3(\mathbf{x})] \tag{11}$$

### 3.3   Channel Spatial Attention Module

Figure 2(c) presents the details of the channel-spatial attention (CSA) module. As can be seen, the CSA module consists of a channel attention unit and a spatial attention unit. The combination of the channel and spatial attention mechanisms maximizes the effectiveness of the CSA module and focuses the network on important channels and regions of interest.

The procedure consists of three steps. First, a convolution-ReLU unit is used to adjust the number of channels. Next, the output is fed into a channel attention module. In this module, an average global pooling is used to enlarge the receptive field and produce the pooled feature $\mathbf{F}_{pool} \in \mathbb{R}^{1 \times 1 \times c}$. For the first convolution-activation unit, the number of input channels is $M$, and the number of output channels is $N$. For the second convolution-activation unit, the number of input channels is $N$, and the number of output channels is $M$. Finally, the weight $w_c \in (0, 1)$ of each channel is multiplied by the $\mathbf{F}_{pool}$ to obtain an adaptively re-scaled channel-wise feature.

In the spatial attention module, the global pooling is discarded to mitigate information loss. In this module, for the first convolution-activation unit, the number of input channels is $M$, and the number of output channels is $Q$. For the second convolution-activation unit, the number of input channels is $Q$, and the number of output channels is 1. The output of the spatial attention module is a two-dimensional matrix $\mathbf{S} \in \mathbb{R}^{h \times w \times 1}$ that includes spatial weight. Finally, the spatial weight $w_{(h,w)} \in (0, 1)$ is multiplied by the output of the channel attention module to obtain the adaptively re-scaled spatial-wise feature output for the whole CSA module. The mechanism of the CSA module can be represented as

$$\mathbf{F}_1 = C(H(\mathbf{x})) * \mathbf{x} \tag{12}$$

$$\mathbf{F}_2 = P(\mathbf{F}_1) * \mathbf{F}_1 \tag{13}$$

$$\mathbf{F} = \mathbf{F}_2 + \mathbf{x} \tag{14}$$

where $\mathbf{x}$ is the input of the CSA module, $C$ and $P$ are the functions of the channel attention mechanism and spatial attention mechanism, respectively, and $H$ is the convolution-ReLU operation before the channel attention mechanism. $\mathbf{F}_1$ and $\mathbf{F}_2$ are the outputs of the channel attention and spatial attention mechanisms, respectively, and $\mathbf{F}$ is the output of the whole CSA module. As Fig. 2(b) shows, in the basic module of RCSA, multiple CSA modules are connected in series after the dense module. Eventually, a channel fusion module is used to concatenate the output channels of each CSA module.

## 4   Experiments and Results

### 4.1   Settings

For the training, we used 800 training images from DIV2K dataset [1]. For testing, we used five standard benchmark datasets, specifically, Set5 [3], Set14 [22],

BSD100 [16], URBAN100 [8], and MANGA109 [17]. We conducted the experiments with Bicubic (BI) degradation through bicubic downsampling of the original images with factors ×2, ×3 and ×4 to synthesize the LR input images. We evaluated the SR results by the Peak Signal to Noise Ratio (PSNR) and the Structural Similarity Index Measure (SSIM) [21] metrics on the Y channel of the transformed YCbCr space. Each training mini-batch generated 16 LR color patches measuring $32 \times 32$ inputs. We trained the model with the ADAM optimizer [13] with $\beta_1 = 0.5$, $\beta_2 = 0.99$, $\epsilon = 10^{-8}$. The learning rate was initialized as $10^{-4}$ and decreased by half every $2 \times 10^5$ iterations. We implemented our model on a Geforce 2080Ti GPU using the Pytorch framework.

As Fig. 1 shows, the RCSA model consisted of $M$ basic modules in the trunk component, which we set at 15 in our work. In each basic module, there were three CSA blocks. The filter size of all of the convolutional layers was clarified in Sect. 3 with stride = 1 and the number of filters = 64. For the upscaling module, we used the pixel shuffle operation proposed in [18].

**Table 1.** Ablation results of various CSA modules combined with the RCSA network.

| Number of modules | 1 | 2 | 3 |
|---|---|---|---|
| PSNR | 32.54 | 32.61 | 32.66 |
| Parameter [M] | 13.4 | 14.4 | 15.4 |

## 4.2 Study of the Basic Module

In our work, each basic module consisted of one dense module and several CSA modules. First, we studied the effect induced by varying the number of CSA modules on the Set5 dataset. As can be seen in Table 1, as the number of CSA modules increased, the SR performance of the image improved. When there was only one CSA module, the PSNR on the Set5 test set was 32.54 dB. With two or three CSA modules, the PSNR on Set5 reached 32.61 dB and 32.66 dB, respectively. However, an excess of modules increased the capacity and parameters of the model from one with 13.4 million parameters to three with 15.3 million parameters.

Furthermore, to show the kinds of features that our network was learning and focusing on, Fig. 3(c) presents the output of the feature maps with various layers. In this figure, each row displays 10 feature maps from the first convolutional layer, the second convolutional layer, the first basic module, the eighth basic module, and the final basic module. In the "Jet" colormap, the red regions indicate greater weight and attention, while the blue region indicates less weight and attention. As can be seen, the shallow layers focused more on low-level features, such as edges and areas. As the network depth increased, more texture details of

**Fig. 3.** Illustrations of (a) High-resolution image, (b) Super-resolution image and (c) feature maps. (Color figure online)

the input image were learned. As is widely recognized, the reconstruction of the details is critical for the image SR task. However, as the fourth row indicates, these details have comparatively equal weights. With the attention mechanism, the network focused on the detailed information but having different importance, as shown in the fifth row.

**Table 2.** Quantitative results with the BI degradation model (×2) (the best and second-best results being **highlighted** and <u>underlined</u>, respectively)

| Method | Scale | Set5 | | Set14 | | BSD100 | | URBAN100 | | MANGA109 | |
|--------|-------|-----------|--------|-----------|--------|-----------|--------|-----------|--------|-----------|--------|
| | | PSNR/SSIM | | PSNR/SSIM | | PSNR/SSIM | | PSNR/SSIM | | PSNR/SSIM | |
| Bicubic | x2 | 32.66 | 0.9299 | 30.24 | 0.8688 | 29.56 | 0.8431 | 26.88 | 0.8403 | 30.80 | 0.9399 |
| SRCNN | x2 | 36.66 | 0.9542 | 32.45 | 0.9067 | 31.36 | 0.8879 | 29.50 | 0.8946 | 35.60 | 0.9663 |
| FSRCNN | x2 | 37.05 | 0.9560 | 32.66 | 0.9090 | 31.53 | 0.8920 | 29.88 | 0.9020 | 36.67 | 0.9710 |
| VDSR | x2 | 37.53 | 0.9590 | 33.05 | 0.9130 | 31.90 | 0.8960 | 30.77 | 0.9140 | 37.22 | 0.9750 |
| LapSRN | x2 | 37.52 | 0.9591 | 33.08 | 0.9130 | 31.08 | 0.8950 | 30.41 | 0.9101 | 37.27 | 0.9750 |
| MemNet | x2 | 37.78 | 0.9597 | 33.28 | 0.9142 | 32.08 | 0.8978 | 31.31 | 0.9195 | 37.72 | 0.9740 |
| EDSR | x2 | 38.11 | 0.9602 | 33.92 | 0.9145 | 32.32 | 0.9013 | 32.93 | 0.9351 | 39.10 | 0.9773 |
| SRMD | x2 | 37.79 | 0.9601 | 33.32 | 0.9159 | 32.05 | 0.8985 | 31.33 | 0.9204 | 38.07 | 0.9761 |
| DBPN | x2 | 38.09 | 0.9600 | 33.85 | 0.9190 | 32.27 | 0.9000 | 32.89 | 0.9324 | 38.89 | 0.9775 |
| RDN | x2 | 38.24 | <u>0.9614</u> | 34.01 | 0.9212 | 32.34 | 0.9017 | 32.55 | 0.9353 | 39.18 | 0.9780 |
| RCAN | x2 | <u>38.27</u> | <u>0.9614</u> | <u>34.12</u> | <u>0.9216</u> | <u>32.41</u> | <u>0.9027</u> | <u>33.34</u> | <u>0.9384</u> | <u>39.44</u> | <u>0.9786</u> |
| OURS | x2 | **38.34** | **0.9622** | **34.27** | **0.9219** | **34.44** | **0.9031** | **33.42** | **0.9389** | **39.57** | **0.9798** |

**Table 3.** Quantitative results with the BI degradation model (×4) (the best and second-best results being **highlighted** and <u>underlined</u>, respectively)

| Method | Scale | Set5 | | Set14 | | BSD100 | | URBAN100 | | MANGA109 | |
|--------|-------|------|------|-------|------|--------|------|----------|------|----------|------|
| | | PSNR/SSIM | | PSNR/SSIM | | PSNR/SSIM | | PSNR/SSIM | | PSNR/SSIM | |
| Bicubic | x4 | 28.43 | 0.8104 | 26.00 | 0.7027 | 25.96 | 0.6675 | 23.14 | 0.6577 | 24.89 | 0.7866 |
| SRCNN | x4 | 30.48 | 0.8128 | 27.50 | 0.7513 | 26.90 | 0.7101 | 24.52 | 0.7221 | 27.58 | 0.8555 |
| FSRCNN | x4 | 30.72 | 0.8660 | 27.61 | 0.7550 | 26.98 | 0.7150 | 24.62 | 0.7280 | 27.90 | 0.8610 |
| VDSR | x4 | 31.35 | 0.8830 | 28.02 | 0.7680 | 27.29 | 0.7260 | 25.18 | 0.7540 | 28.83 | 0.8870 |
| LapSRN | x4 | 31.54 | 0.8850 | 28.19 | 0.7720 | 27.32 | 0.7270 | 25.21 | 0.7560 | 29.09 | 0.8900 |
| MemNet | x4 | 31.74 | 0.8893 | 28.26 | 0.7723 | 27.40 | 0.7281 | 25.50 | 0.7630 | 29.42 | 0.8942 |
| EDSR | x4 | 32.46 | 0.8968 | 28.80 | 0.7876 | 27.71 | 0.7420 | 26.64 | 0.8033 | 31.02 | 0.9148 |
| SRMD | x4 | 31.96 | 0.8925 | 28.35 | 0.7787 | 27.49 | 0.7337 | 25.68 | 0.7731 | 30.09 | 0.9024 |
| DBPN | x4 | 32.47 | 0.8980 | 28.82 | 0.7860 | 27.72 | 0.7400 | 26.38 | 0.7946 | 30.91 | 0.9137 |
| RDN | x4 | 32.47 | 0.8990 | 28.81 | 0.7871 | 27.72 | 0.7419 | 26.61 | 0.8028 | 31.00 | 0.9151 |
| RCAN | x4 | <u>32.63</u> | <u>0.9002</u> | <u>28.87</u> | <u>0.7889</u> | <u>27.77</u> | <u>0.7436</u> | <u>26.82</u> | <u>0.8087</u> | <u>31.22</u> | <u>0.9173</u> |
| OURS | x4 | **32.66** | **0.9004** | **28.91** | **0.7892** | **27.80** | **0.7437** | **26.93** | **0.8114** | **31.41** | **0.9237** |

## 4.3 Quantitative Analysis

To evaluate the performance of our RCSA network, we conducted comparative experiments with bicubic method and the other 9 state-of-the-art methods, namely, SRCNN [4], FSRCNN [5], VDSR [11], LapSRN [14], MemNet [19], EDSR [15], SRMD [23], DBPN [6], RDN [25] and RCAN [24]. Tables 2 and Table 3 present the quantitative results for ×2 and ×4 SR, respectively. As can be seen, when the scaling factor increased, the performance of all of the methods diminished. An explanation for this result is that the recovery of SR images from smaller LR images is especially challenging. However, our proposed RCSA still showed better performance than the other methods on all of the datasets with all of the scaling factors. This observation demonstrates that a dense connected deep network with CSA can definitely improve SR performance.

## 4.4 Visual Analysis

Figure 4 presents the visual comparisons of ×4 SR on various types of images. As can be seen, most methods encountered challenges with lattice recovery and the blurring of artifacts. Our proposed RCSA performed better in terms of restoring details. The visual analysis indicated that our network demonstrated great learning ability regarding the extraction of representational features from low-resolution images.

## 4.5 Model Complexity Analysis

Figure 5 presents the model complexity with the various SR methods. As can be seen, our proposed RCSA has fewer parameters but achieved better performance

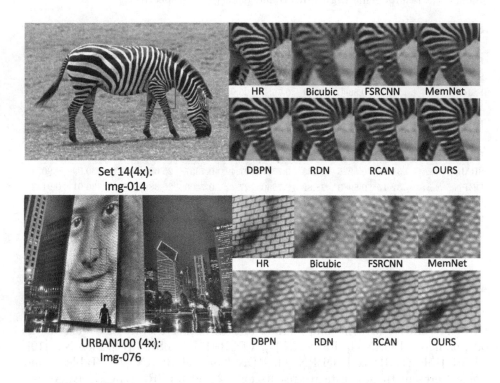

Set 14(4x):
Img-014

URBAN100 (4x):
Img-076

**Fig. 4.** Visual comparisons for ×4 SR with bicubic degradation model.

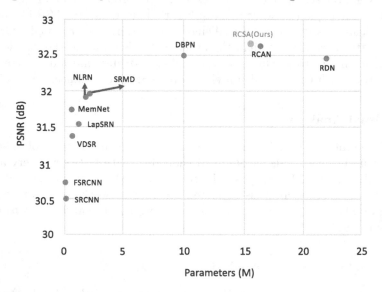

**Fig. 5.** Model complexity analysis on Set5 (×4).

than RDN [25] or RCAN [24]. Though the number of parameters in RCSA exceeded those of DBPN [6], the SR effect was better to some extent. The model complexity analysis indicated that our model maintained the desired balance between memory consumption and task performance.

## 5   Discussion

We have proposed a residual channel-spatial attention network (RCSA) for performing SR tasks with a high degree of accuracy. This method integrates a dense block and multiple attention blocks into the basic module of the trunk component. In the dense block, a residual sparse dense structure serves to extract the deep features. This kind of structure effectively mitigates the gradient-vanishing problem. In the attention block, a channel-spatial attention mechanism facilitates the focusing of the network on important information across the channels and spaces. Such mechanisms can significantly improve the learning ability of the network. To demonstrate the superior performance of our proposed method, we carried out extensive comparisons of SR tasks using the bicubic degradation model on various datasets. The quantitative and qualitative results proved that our method is effective.

## References

1. Agustsson, E., Timofte, R.: Ntire 2017 challenge on single image super-resolution: dataset and study. In: Proceedings of the IEEE Conference on Computer Vision and Pattern Recognition Workshops, pp. 126–135 (2017)
2. Bai, Y., Zhang, Y., Ding, M., Ghanem, B.: Sod-mtgan: small object detection via multi-task generative adversarial network. In: Proceedings of the European Conference on Computer Vision (ECCV), pp. 206–221 (2018)
3. Bevilacqua, M., Roumy, A., Guillemot, C., Alberi-Morel, M.L.: Low-complexity single-image super-resolution based on nonnegative neighbor embedding (2012)
4. Dong, C., Loy, C.C., He, K., Tang, X.: Learning a deep convolutional network for image super-resolution. In: Fleet, D., Pajdla, T., Schiele, B., Tuytelaars, T. (eds.) ECCV 2014. LNCS, vol. 8692, pp. 184–199. Springer, Cham (2014). https://doi.org/10.1007/978-3-319-10593-2_13
5. Dong, C., Loy, C.C., Tang, X.: Accelerating the super-resolution convolutional neural network. In: Leibe, B., Matas, J., Sebe, N., Welling, M. (eds.) ECCV 2016. LNCS, vol. 9906, pp. 391–407. Springer, Cham (2016). https://doi.org/10.1007/978-3-319-46475-6_25
6. Haris, M., Shakhnarovich, G., Ukita, N.: Deep back-projection networks for super-resolution. In: Proceedings of the IEEE Conference on Computer Vision and Pattern Recognition, pp. 1664–1673 (2018)
7. Harris, J.L.: Diffraction and resolving power. JOSA 54(7), 931–936 (1964)
8. Huang, J.B., Singh, A., Ahuja, N.: Single image super-resolution from transformed self-exemplars. In: Proceedings of the IEEE Conference on Computer Vision and Pattern Recognition, pp. 5197–5206 (2015)
9. Huggins, E.: Introduction to fourier optics. Phys. Teacher 45(6), 364–368 (2007)

10. Kim, D., Kim, M., Kwon, G., Kim, D.S.: Progressive face super-resolution via attention to facial landmark. arXiv preprint arXiv:1908.08239 (2019)

11. Kim, J., Lee, J.K., Lee, K.M.: Accurate image super-resolution using very deep convolutional networks. In: Proceedings of the IEEE Conference on Computer Vision and Pattern Recognition, pp. 1646–1654 (2016)

12. Kim, J., Lee, J.K., Lee, K.M.: Deeply-recursive convolutional network for image super-resolution. In: Proceedings of the IEEE Conference on Computer Vision and Pattern Recognition, pp. 1637–1645 (2016)

13. Kingma, D.P., Ba, J.: Adam: A method for stochastic optimization. arXiv preprint arXiv:1412.6980 (2014)

14. Lai, W.S., Huang, J.B., Ahuja, N., Yang, M.H.: Deep laplacian pyramid networks for fast and accurate super-resolution. In: Proceedings of the IEEE Conference on Computer Vision and Pattern Recognition, pp. 624–632 (2017)

15. Lim, B., Son, S., Kim, H., Nah, S., Mu Lee, K.: Enhanced deep residual networks for single image super-resolution. In: Proceedings of the IEEE Conference on Computer Vision and Pattern Recognition Workshops, pp. 136–144 (2017)

16. Martin, D., Fowlkes, C., Tal, D., Malik, J.: A database of human segmented natural images and its application to evaluating segmentation algorithms and measuring ecological statistics. In: Proceedings Eighth IEEE International Conference on Computer Vision, ICCV 2001, vol. 2, pp. 416–423. IEEE (2001)

17. Matsui, Y., Ito, K., Aramaki, Y., Fujimoto, A., Ogawa, T., Yamasaki, T., Aizawa, K.: Sketch-based manga retrieval using manga109 dataset. Multimed. Tools Appl. **76**(20), 21811–21838 (2017). https://doi.org/10.1007/s11042-016-4020-z

18. Shi, W., et al.: Real-time single image and video super-resolution using an efficient sub-pixel convolutional neural network. In: Proceedings of the IEEE Conference on Computer Vision and Pattern Recognition, pp. 1874–1883 (2016)

19. Tai, Y., Yang, J., Liu, X., Xu, C.: Memnet: a persistent memory network for image restoration. In: Proceedings of the IEEE International Conference on Computer Vision, pp. 4539–4547 (2017)

20. Wang, W., Xie, E., Sun, P., Wang, W., Tian, L., Shen, C., Luo, P.: Textsr: content-aware text super-resolution guided by recognition. arXiv preprint arXiv:1909.07113 (2019)

21. Wang, Z., Bovik, A.C., Sheikh, H.R., Simoncelli, E.P.: Image quality assessment: from error visibility to structural similarity. IEEE Trans. Image Process. **13**(4), 600–612 (2004)

22. Zeyde, R., Elad, M., Protter, M.: On single image scale-up using sparse-representations. In: Boissonnat, J.-D., et al. (eds.) Curves and Surfaces 2010. LNCS, vol. 6920, pp. 711–730. Springer, Heidelberg (2010). https://doi.org/10.1007/978-3-642-27413-8_47

23. Zhang, K., Zuo, W., Chen, Y., Meng, D., Zhang, L.: Beyond a gaussian denoiser: residual learning of deep CNN for image denoising. IEEE Trans. Image Process. **26**(7), 3142–3155 (2017)

24. Zhang, Y., Li, K., Li, K., Wang, L., Zhong, B., Fu, Y.: Image super-resolution using very deep residual channel attention networks. In: Ferrari, V., Hebert, M., Sminchisescu, C., Weiss, Y. (eds.) ECCV 2018. LNCS, vol. 11211, pp. 294–310. Springer, Cham (2018). https://doi.org/10.1007/978-3-030-01234-2_18

25. Zhang, Y., Tian, Y., Kong, Y., Zhong, B., Fu, Y.: Residual dense network for image super-resolution. In: Proceedings of the IEEE Conference on Computer Vision and Pattern Recognition, pp. 2472–2481 (2018)

# Lip Reading Using Deformable 3D Convolution and Channel-Temporal Attention

Chen Peng[1,2,3,4], Jun Li[2], Jie Chai[2], Zhongqiu Zhao[1,2,3,4(✉)],
Housen Zhang[1,2,3,4], and Weidong Tian[1,2,3,4]

[1] School of Computer Science and Information Engineering,
Hefei University of Technology, Hefei 230009, China
z.zhao@hfut.edu.cn
[2] Fiber Inspection Bureau of Anhui Province, Chunjiang, China
[3] Intelligent Manufacturing Institute of HFUT, Hefei, China
[4] Guangxi Academy of Sciences, Guangxi, China

**Abstract.** At present, for lip-reading with isolated words, the front-end networks mostly use a combination of 3D convolutional layer and 2D convolutional network to extract features, and the back-end networks mostly use a temporal processing network for classification. However, the convolution of the front-end does not comply with the lip structures to extract spatial information, and the back-end cannot exploit all correlations of global spatio-temporal features. Therefore, in this paper, we propose a network with deformable 3D convolution (D3D) and channel-temporal attention (CT), where D3D adjusts the sampling position adaptively according to the lip structures, thus making more efficient utilization of spatial information, and CT exploits the intrinsic correlation of features to make the network concentrate on valuable key frames. Experiments prove the effectiveness of the proposed method in information extraction and show that our network achieves state-of-the-art performance for lip reading.

**Keywords:** Lip-reading · Deformable convolution · Attention mechanism

## 1 Introduction

Lip reading, as the name implies, is to 'read' or 'partially read' what is said through the lips of the speaker. With the development of machine vision, lip reading has received more and more attention in recent years. Nowadays, machine lip reading is much more accurate than humans and is widely used in many fields such as assisting speech and sign language recognition [20], biometric recognition [14], and so on.

Since lip reading analyzes the speaker's lip movements to infer what he or she is saying, it's needed to extract more fine-grained information than other visual recognition tasks. In real life, the shape of lips is very irregular and diverse.

© The Author(s), under exclusive license to Springer Nature Switzerland AG 2022
E. Pimenidis et al. (Eds.): ICANN 2022, LNCS 13532, pp. 707–718, 2022.
https://doi.org/10.1007/978-3-031-15937-4_59

When a person speaks, the spatial structure of his lip is abundant and variable, which means that the network needs to fit the structure of lip movement and to extract more recognizable spatial information. At the same time, the network not only requires the capability of sequence processing and analysis but also needs to weigh the importance of different frames for recognition, since not all video frames correspond to the target word and some frames correspond to its context.

More recently, existing lip-reading methods based on deep learning have improved in different aspects and obtained good results. Martinez *et al.* [9] replaced the back-end network with a Multi-scale Temporal Convolution Network (MS-TCN), improving the sequence processing capability of the lip-reading network. Hao *et al.* [5] applied Temporal Shift Module (TSM) [7] to ResNet18 at the front-end of lip reading to improve the time processing capability of 2D convolution. Although these methods have greatly improved lip-reading performance, there are still some issues that deserve more consideration. Firstly, how to better fit the lip motion information in the front-end network to extract more identifiable spatial information. Secondly, how to recalibrate the importance of various frames to enable the network to concentrate on the target word.

In this paper, we propose a deformable 3D convolution block, which combines with 2D-ResNet18 from the front-end feature extractor. The proposed method is based on the fact that lips have abundant spatial structure changes during motion. The traditional convolution kernels cannot deal with this complex deformation well due to its own regularity and invariance. In our method, D3D block is used to fit the spatial structure of lips as much as possible without reducing the temporal information extraction capability. Considering key frames associated with words, we also use channel-temporal attention in the back-end to understand global information and to focus on critical information.

In summary, our contributions are as follows: (a) we propose a deformable 3D convolutional block at the front-end, which can extract more generalized and robust features and better represent spatial information; (b) we propose a channel-temporal attention block, which enables the network to focus on valuable key frames based on the inherent correlation of features.

## 2    Related Works

### 2.1    Lip Reading

With the rapid development of deep learning, more and more deep learning methods have been applied to lip reading. For example, convolutional neural networks (CNNs) have replaced most traditional methods for feature extraction, and Long-Short Term Memory (LSTM) [13] or Gate Recurrent Unit (GRU) [12] have replaced Support Vector Machines [15] and Hidden Markov Models [11] for classification. LipNet [1] is the first method that combines 3D CNN and BiGRU for statement-level lip reading. Stafylakis *et al.* [16] used a front-end of 3D convolution combined with 2D-ResNet and a back-end of LSTM to form a spatio-temporal deep learning network for word-level visual speech recognition

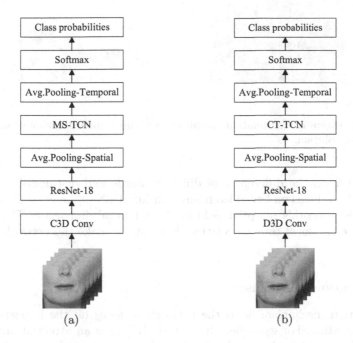

**Fig. 1.** (a) The overall structure of the baseline model; (b) The overall framework of our method. Both models use processed video frames as the network input.

and achieved good results. Martinez *et al.* [9] applied TCN to the lip-reading network and used MS-TCN instead of BiGRU, and achieved higher performance than before on two large lip reading datasets. Tian *et al.* [17] used the Whole-Part Collaborative Learning to help lipreading model make full use of both global and fine-grained spatial information of lip. Then Hao *et al.* [5] applied Temporal Shift Module [7] to lip reading and added it to 2D-ResNet18 to improve the temporal information processing capability of the front-end network. All these models achieve good results, but they ignore the influence of the complex and changeable lip structure on extracting spatial information.

## 2.2   Focus on Target Word

One video may contain multiple words. Therefore, how to effectively use global time information to make the network focus on key frames is a problem to be solved. The existing solutions can be divided into two categories. One is to input the boundary information of label words into the network during the data processing stage, which directly tells the network where the key frames are. The other is to make the network pay attention to the key frames automatically using some methods. Inputting the word boundary as additional information into the network can effectively improve the prediction accuracy, but the boundary information only exists in artificial datasets and does not exist in natural situations. Zhao *et al.* [22] used mutual information maximization to enable the

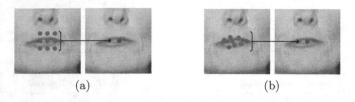

(a)                                      (b)

**Fig. 2.** Illustration of deformation sampling. (a) The standard convolution; (b) The deformed convolution.

network to learn the differences of different words and distinguish the target word, and then focus on key video frames. In MS-TCN [9], multi-scale is used to increase the network's receptive field in the temporal dimension. This method can enhance the local time correlation, but cannot make the network focus on keyframes.

### 2.3  Attention Mechanism

The attention mechanism helps the network to focus on the important parts of all information. For example, Mnih *et al.* [10] used an attention mechanism on the RNN model for image classification. In isolated words lip-reading tasks, considering that the spatial information of each frame is compressed on the channel, we propose a channel-temporal attention block, which captures the global spatio-temporal structure from the two dimensions of channel and temporal, and achieves the ability to pay attention to key channels and frames.

## 3  The Proposed Work

### 3.1  Overview

Figure 1(a) illustrates the architecture of the baseline model, which is improved from two aspects: feature extraction and temporal modeling. The overall framework of our method is shown in Fig. 1(b). The input of the network is the cropped gray mouth ROI with a size of $T \times 1 \times 88 \times 88$, where $T$ is the temporal dimension. We use the D3D block to extract the spatio-temporal feature of video frames, and get the output feature of $T \times C_1 \times H_1 \times W_1$, where $C_1$ refers to the number of feature channels and $H_1$, $W_1$ represent the height and width of the feature. Then we use the 2D-ResNet18 network to get the feature of size $T \times C_2 \times H_2 \times W_2$. After the front-end feature extraction, the spatio-temporal features are inputted to the average pooling layer to summarize the spatial information and reduce the dimensionality to $T \times C_2$. The obtained features are inputted into the CT-TCN network for modeling in the temporal dimension. Then, the output tensor ($T \times C_3$) is reduced to $1 \times C_4$ by the temporal average pooling layer. Finally, we use the SoftMax layer for probability prediction.

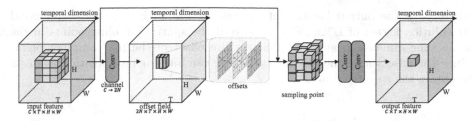

**Fig. 3.** A specific illustration of the D3D network with a $3 \times 3 \times 3$ deformed convolution. The tricolor cube in the input feature denoted the sampled grid of the original convolution. Sampling point indicates the sampled grid of the deformable convolution. Offset field is obtained by the convolution of $3 \times 3 \times 1$. The size of offset field is $2N \times T \times H \times W$. Offsets represent the deformation values of the sampled grid in space. Sampling point is passed through two convolutional layers to form the output feature.

### 3.2  Deformable 3D Convolution

The traditional convolution kernel is usually fixed in size, which makes the convolution kernel with poor adaptability to the change of lip-reading input information and with insufficient generalization ability. DConv [4] adds an offset variable to the location of each sampling point in the convolution kernel, allowing a larger and more appropriate range for the convolution kernel to be trained and improving the ability to model appearance deformation. Figure 2 shows an example of sampled points with deformable convolution. This dynamically variable sampling is more conducive to understanding the lip spatial structure than traditional conventional sampling and enables the network to extract spatial representation that is more suitable for lip structures. We replace the 3D convolution layer with the deformable 3D convolution block to obtain the flexibility of lip structure modeling.

The implementation of D3D is divided into two steps: the first step is to use the traditional convolution network to learn offsets; the second step is to use the learned offsets to guide the original sampling grid to generate a new sampling grid, and then to obtain the output feature based on the new sampling grid. Specifically, as shown in Fig. 3, taking a tensor of size $C \times T \times H \times W$ as an input feature, an offset feature of size $2N \times T \times H \times W$ is generated by 3D convolution. $N$ with a value of 9 denotes the size of the sampling grid in each time dimension. The number "2" represents the offsets in both the height and width directions. Then, the offset feature is used to update the original sampling grid, and the new sampling grid is convolved to obtain the output feature. Thus, the above processes can be formulated as:

$$x(p_m) = \sum_{n=0}^{N} w(p_n)x(p_m + p_n + \Delta p_n), \tag{1}$$

$$y(p_0) = \sum_{m=0}^{M} w(p_m)x(p_0 + p_m), \tag{2}$$

where $p_0$ is the output location of the feature, $M$ is the size of the temporal convolution kernel of D3D, $N$ is the size of the spatial sampling points in the same time dimension, and $\Delta p_n$ denotes the offset of the $n_{th}$ sampling point. Since the offsets are generally fractional, we use bilinear interpolation as in [4] to obtain the specific values.

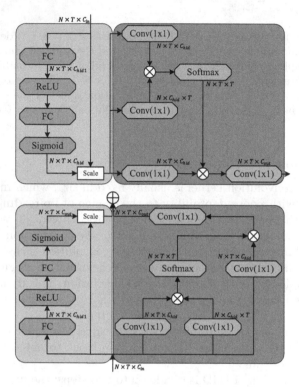

**Fig. 4.** Two structures of channel-temporal attention block. The top one is the sequential layout, and the bottom one is the parallel layout. The yellow part is the channel attention block and the blue part is the temporal attention block. (Color figure online)

### 3.3    Channel-Temporal Attention

In order to effectively use global information to make the network concentrated on key frames, we propose a channel-temporal attention block. This block pays attention to key information based on the intrinsic correlation of global spatio-temporal features. Since the spatial information of each frame is compressed on the channel, we focus on spatial information from the perspective of the channel. Specifically, we use channel attention block and temporal attention block to process global spatial and temporal information respectively. According to different layouts, we design two channel-temporal attention blocks shown in Fig. 4.

In the sequential layout, the input feature go through a fully connected layer for dimensionality reduction, then through a ReLu activation, then through a fully connected layer for dimensionality increment, and finally through Sigmoid activation to obtain the weight matrix. Here our treatment is consistent with the Excitation processing in [6]. The weight is assigned to the input feature to obtain the output $x_c$ of the channel attention block.

$$x_c = Sigmoid(W_2 \times ReLU(W_1x)) \times x, \tag{3}$$

where $x \in \mathbb{R}^{N \times T \times C_{in} \times 1 \times 1}$ refers to the input of the channel time attention block. $W_1$ and $W_2$ are the parameters of the linear layer to reduce and restore the channel dimension of the feature respectively.

In the temporal attention block, the channel attention feature is used as queries, keys, and values, The weight matrix is obtained by using the intrinsic correlation of the feature in temporal dimension. Then the weight is assigned to the channel attention feature to obtain output feature $x_{ct}$ as:

$$x_{ct} = \sigma(((W_q x_c) \times (W_k x_c)^T)/\sqrt{C}) \times W_v x_c, \tag{4}$$

where $x_c \in \mathbb{R}^{N \times T \times C_{hid} \times 1 \times 1}$ and $x_{ct} \in \mathbb{R}^{N \times T \times C_{out} \times 1 \times 1}$ denote the output feature of the channel attention block and the channel-temporal attention block respectively. $\sigma$ is SoftMax operator. $W_q$, $W_k$ and $W_v$ are the parameters of the linear layer.

In the parallel layout, both attention blocks can be applied in parallel, then the output features of the two blocks are added together. The expressions are as follows.

$$x_c = Sigmoid(W_2 \times ReLU(W_1x)) \times x, \tag{5}$$
$$x_t = \sigma(((W_q x) \times (W_k x)^T)/\sqrt{C}) \times W_v x. \tag{6}$$
$$x_{ct} = x_c + x_t, \tag{7}$$

where $x_c \in \mathbb{R}^{N \times T \times C_{out} \times 1 \times 1}$ and $x_t \in \mathbb{R}^{N \times T \times C_{out} \times 1 \times 1}$ denote the output features of the channel attention block and the temporal attention block respectively. $x_{ct} \in \mathbb{R}^{N \times T \times C_{out} \times 1 \times 1}$ is the output feature after addition.

# 4   Experiments

## 4.1   Datasets

We experimentally analyzed the proposed method on the LRW and LRW-1000 datasets. LRW [3] and LRW-1000 [21] are the largest publicly available English and Chinese lip reading datasets.

LRW dataset is a large lip-reading dataset in the wild. Each sequence of LRW is approximately 1.16 s of video footage (29 video frames) captured from BBC programs. LRW dataset has 500 word classes, each with approximately 1000 training samples, 50 validation samples, and 50 test samples. The main challenge of LRW is that the dataset contains up to 1000 speakers with diverse postures and appearances, and the speaker's realistic backgrounds and lighting conditions are different. Moreover, there is not only the target word but also the context of the target word in the video clip, which further increases the difficulty of recognition.

LRW-1000 is the first publicly available large Mandarin lip reading dataset. It contains approximately 600,000 training samples, 60,000 validation samples, and 50,000 test samples, covering 1000 Mandarin words and recording more than 2000 topics. The average duration of each sequence is 0.3 s, and the total length of all sequences is about 57 h. In contrast to LRW, each class corresponds to a Mandarin word consisting of one or several Chinese characters. This means that the duration of the sample is not constant. In terms of sample content, speaker attributes, lighting conditions and proportions are closer to natural conditions. Considering these factors, this dataset is even more challenging than LRW.

## 4.2   Implementation Details

In LRW we use face detection in [9] to locate 68 facial landmarks to adjust the image to the average face shape in each frame. Then cut out a $96 \times 96$ pixel fixed-size mouth ROI and convert it to grayscale. During the training process, the input images are subjected to random cropping, horizontal flipping with 50% probability, and data enhancement with a mixup of weight 0.4. Since LRW-1000 has cropped out the lip region, no cropping for facial landmark detection was performed.

**Table 1.** Comparison with other related work on LRW.

| Methods | Front-end | Back-end | Acc. (%) |
|---|---|---|---|
| Seq-to-Seq Wild [2] | VGGM | LSTM | 76.2 |
| ResNet+BiLSTM [16] | 3D Conv + ResNet34 | BiLSTM | 83.0 |
| End-to-End [13] | 3D Conv + ResNet34 | BiLSTM | 83.4 |
| Mutual Information GLMIM [22] | 3D Conv + ResNet18 | BiGRU | 84.4 |
| TSM+BiGRU [5] | 3D Conv + TSM_ResNet18 | BiGRU | 86.2 |
| Multi-Stage Distillation [8] | 3D Conv + ResNet18 | MS-TCN | 87.7 |
| MS-TCN [9] (Baseline) | 3D Conv + ResNet18 | MS-TCN | 85.3 |
| Ours | D3D Conv + ResNet18 | CT-TCN | **87.70** |

Our model is trained in an end-to-end manner, using Adam as the optimizer with an initial learning rate of $3e-4$ and a cosine scheduler with a weight decay of $1e-4$. We train 80 epochs on LRW and LRW-1000, and add variable-length broadening from [9] to enhance the robustness of the model in time. Finally using the standard Cross-Entropy loss for the model gradient descent is performed.

## 4.3 Experimental Results

In order to evaluate the effectiveness of our method, we compare the experimental effects of our model with some existing mainstream lip-reading models and the baseline model on two large lip reading datasets.

**Table 2.** Comparison with other related work on LRW-1000.

| Methods | Front-end | Back-end | Acc. (%) |
|---|---|---|---|
| Multi-Grained [18] | Multi-Grained + ResNet34 | Conv-BiLSTM | 36.9 |
| 3D + 2D [21] | 3D Conv + ResNet34 | LSTM | 38.2 |
| Deformation Flow DFTN [19] | Two-Stream + ResNet34 | BiGRU | 41.9 |
| TSM+BiGRU [5] | 3D Conv + TSM_ResNet18 | BiGRU | 44.6 |
| Multi-Stage Distillation [8] | 3D Conv + ResNet18 | MS-TCN | 46.6 |
| MS-TCN [9] (baseline) | 3D Conv + ResNet18 | MS-TCN | 41.4 |
| Ours | D3D Conv + ResNet18 | CT-TCN | **47.11** |

The results on the LRW dataset are shown in Table 1. Our method improves 2.4% on the baseline model and achieves comparable results to the best model. Since the best model needs to be trained four times by knowledge distillation, while our method is trained end-to-end and needs to be trained only once. Therefore, our model is more advantageous in terms of training strategy and time.

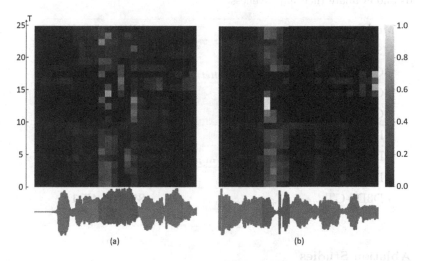

**Fig. 5.** The visualization of attention weight. The horizontal axis represents the temporal dimension of the audio, the green part of the audio denotes the word boundary of the target word. The vertical axis corresponds to the 25 frames, and the brightness of color represents the attention weight of the frame to frame. The pinyin of (a) label is *"er shi san"* and the pinyin of (b) label is *"gong min"*.

The experimental results on LRW-1000 dataset are shown in Table 2, Our method outperforms the baseline model and achieves an accuracy rate of 47.11%. It is obvious that our method has a much more significant improvement on LRW-1000 than on LRW. This is because the speaker is more unrestricted in LRW-1000 dataset and there is no face correction cropping step in the data processing. This requires the network to better fit the lips for modeling, which D3D can achieve. Moreover, the target word length is not fixed on the LRW-1000 dataset, which also places a higher demand on the network's capability to recognize key frames.

The visualization of the $N \times T \times T$ attention weight after SoftMax in CT block on the LRW-1000 dataset, is shown in Fig. 5. We randomly sample the videos from two labels(its corresponding pinyin are "er shi san", "gong min"). The key frames of Fig. 5(a) are 11–16, and the key frames of Fig. 5(b) are 8–11. Intuitively, the CT block adaptively performs keyframes recognition for different labeled videos. Each frame in the figure has a higher attention weight between the key time (the frames within the word boundary), indicating that CT block not only successfully learns the key frames, but also strengthens the association between each frame and the key frames.

It is a challenge to get better performance on LRW-1000 dataset, and our method obtains state-of-the-art results on LRW-1000 dataset. The more significant improvement over LRW reflects that our method is more advantageous and robust to lip reading in natural cases, which proves the effectiveness of our method.

**Table 3.** The ablation results on LRW and LRW-1000 dataset. We add the proposed methods and evaluate their effectiveness.

| Models | LRW | LRW-1000 |
|---|---|---|
| MS-TCN | 85.3 | 41.4 |
| +CT$_{(channel\ \&\ temporal\ in\ parallel)}$ | 86.48 | 45.47 |
| +CT$_{(temporal\ +\ channel)}$ | 86.64 | 45.74 |
| +CT$_{(channel\ +\ temporal)}$ | 86.78 | 45.89 |
| +D3D | 86.88 | 45.84 |
| +D3D+CT$_{(channel\ \&\ temporal\ in\ parallel)}$ | 87.26 | 46.67 |
| +D3D+CT$_{(temporal\ +\ channel)}$ | 87.54 | 46.83 |
| +D3D+CT$_{(channel\ +\ temporal)}$ | **87.70** | **47.11** |

## 4.4   Ablation Studies

To evaluate the effectiveness of different parts of our method, we conducted some evaluation experiments on LRW and LRW-1000. The influence of different attention layouts and different module matching strategies on the network model is shown in Table 3. From the experimental data, we can find that D3D block and different CT blocks all have better improvements to the baseline model. For different CT blocks, the sequential layout of the channel module in front is better than other layouts. This is due to the fact that the lip reading task is ultimately predicted by temporal relationships, and the enhancement of spatial information is beneficial to the identification of subsequent key frames, so the channel module is more appropriate in the front. The effect is better when D3D block is combined with the CT block. The experimental results show that our D3D block and CT block both perform their due role, which is consistent with our motivation and confirms the effectiveness of our method.

## 5  Conclusion

In this paper, we propose a lip reading network that utilizes deformable 3D convolutional and channel-temporal attention. We replace the original 3D convolutional layer with the deformable 3D convolutional block to enhance the lip motion modeling capability of the network. We also use channel-temporal attention block to enable the network to focus on effective spatio-temporal regions. Extensive experiments are conducted on two large lip reading datasets to validate the effectiveness of our method and achieve state-of-the-art performance for lip reading.

**Acknowledgements.** This work was supported in part by the National Natural Science Foundation of China under Grants 61976079, in part by Guangxi Key Research and Development Program under Grant 2021AB20147, and in part by Anhui Key Research and Development Program under Grant 202004a05020039.

## References

1. Assael, Y.M., Shillingford, B., Whiteson, S., Freitas, N.D.: Lipnet: end-to-end sentence-level lipreading. arXiv preprint arXiv:1611.01599 (2016)
2. Chung, J.S., Senior, A., Vinyals, O., Zisserman, A.: Lip reading sentences in the wild. In: The IEEE Conference on Computer Vision and Pattern Recognition (CVPR), pp. 3444–3453 (2017)
3. Chung, J.S., Zisserman, A.: Lip reading in the wild. In: Asian Conference on Computer Vision, pp. 87–103 (2016)
4. Dai, J., Qi, H., Xiong, Y., Li, Y., Zhang, G., Hu, H., Wei, Y.: Deformable convolutional networks. In: The IEEE International Conference on Computer Vision (ICCV), pp. 764–773 (2017)
5. Hao, M., Mamut, M., Yadikar, N., Aysa, A., Ubul, K.: How to use time information effectively? combining with time shift module for lipreading. In: The IEEE International Conference on Acoustics, Speech and Signal Processing (ICASSP), pp. 7988–7992 (2021)
6. Hu, J., Shen, L., Sun, G.: Squeeze-and-excitation networks. In: The IEEE Conference on Computer Vision and Pattern Recognition (CVPR), pp. 7132–7141 (2018)
7. Lin, J., Gan, C., Han, S.: Tsm: Temporal shift module for efficient video understanding. In: The IEEE International Conference on Computer Vision (ICCV), pp. 7083–7093 (2019)

8. Ma, P., Martinez, B., Petridis, S., Pantic, M.: Towards practical lipreading with distilled and efficient models. In: The IEEE International Conference on Acoustics, Speech and Signal Processing (ICASSP), pp. 7608–7612 (2021)

9. Martinez, B., Ma, P., Petridis, S., Pantic, M.: Lipreading using temporal convolutional networks. In: The IEEE International Conference on Acoustics, Speech and Signal Processing (ICASSP), pp. 6319–6323 (2020)

10. Mnih, V., Heess, N.M.O., Graves, A., Kavukcuoglu, K.: Recurrent models of visual attention. In: Advances in Neural Information Processing Systems (NIPS), pp. 2204–2212 (2014)

11. Papandreou, G., Katsamanis, A., Pitsikalis, V., Maragos, P.: Adaptive multimodal fusion by uncertainty compensation with application to audio-visual speech recognition. IEEE Trans. Audio Speech Lang. Process., 423–435 (2008)

12. Petridis, S., Stafylakis, T., Ma, P., Cai, F., Tzimiropoulos, G., Pantic, M.: End-to-end audiovisual speech recognition. In: The IEEE International Conference on Acoustics, Speech and Signal Processing (ICASSP), pp. 6548–6552 (2018)

13. Petridis, S., Wang, Y., Li, Z., Pantic, M.: End-to-end audiovisual fusion with lstms. In: International Conference on Auditory-visual Speech Processing (2017)

14. Rekik, A., Ben-Hamadou, A., Mahdi, W.: Human machine interaction via visual speech spotting. In: International Conference on Advanced Concepts for Intelligent Vision Systems, pp. 566–574 (2015)

15. Shaikh, A.A., Kumar, D.K., Yau, W.C., Azemin, M.C., Gubbi, J.: Lip reading using optical flow and support vector machines. In: 2010 3Rd International Congress on Image and Signal Processing, pp. 327–330 (2010)

16. Stafylakis, T., Tzimiropoulos, G.: Combining residual networks with lstms for lipreading. In: arXiv preprint arXiv:1703.04105 (2017)

17. Tian, W.D., Zhang, H.S., Peng, C., Zhao, Z.Q.: Lipreading model based on whole-parl collaborative learning. In: The IEEE International Conference on Acoustics, Speech and Signal Processing (ICASSP), pp. 2425–2429 (2022)

18. Wand, M., Koutník, J., Schmidhuber, J.: Lipreading with long short-term memory. In: The IEEE International Conference on Acoustics, Speech and Signal Processing (ICASSP), pp. 6115–6119 (2016)

19. Xiao, J., Yang, S., Zhang, Y., Shan, S., Chen, X.: Deformation flow based two-stream network for lip reading. In: IEEE International Conference on Automatic Face and Gesture Recognition (FG 2020), pp. 364–370 (2020)

20. Xu, K., Li, D., Cassimatis, N., Wang, X.: Lcanet: End-to-end lipreading with cascaded attention-ctc. In: IEEE International Conference on Automatic Face & Gesture Recognition (FG 2018), pp. 548–555 (2018)

21. Yang, S., Zhang, Y., Feng, D., Yang, M., Wang, C., Xiao, J., Long, K., Shan, S., Chen, X.: Lrw-1000: A naturally-distributed large-scale benchmark for lip reading in the wild. In: IEEE International Conference on Automatic Face & Gesture Recognition (FG 2019), pp. 1–8 (2019)

22. Zhao, X., Yang, S., Shan, S., Chen, X.: Mutual information maximization for effective lip reading. In: IEEE International Conference on Automatic Face and Gesture Recognition (FG 2020), pp. 420–427 (2020)

# Loop Closure Detection Based on Siamese ConvNet Features and Geometrical Verification for Visual SLAM

Zhe Chen, Xiaofeng Zhang$^{(\boxtimes)}$, Yaojun Ou, and Mei Wang

School of Information Science and Technology, Nantong University,
Nantong 226019, China
zxf@ntu.edu.cn

**Abstract.** Loop closure detection (LCD) is an important module in visual simultaneous location and mapping (VSLAM) because it can correctly recognize the previously visited places and reduce the accumulated localization errors. In this paper, a novel LCD method is proposed. First obtain the image intensity, depth and edge features of the RGB-D image. Then, the above image features are fused to generate a three-channel input and fed to the Siamese network to generate global features. Finally, the similarity between the images is quantified by calculating the Euclidean distance between the features, and the images with similarity scores greater than a specific threshold are selected as loop closure candidates. In addition, a real-time geometrical verification method is incorporated to eliminate mismatches. Experiments on several publicly datasets show that our method can achieve higher recall at 100% precision compared to other LCD methods.

**Keywords:** Siamese network · Global features · Geometrical verification · Loop closure detection

## 1 Introduction

Today, Visual Simultaneous Localization and Mapping (VSLAM) has become the most active research problem in the field of robotics. It means that a robot equipped with sensors moves in an unknown environment, and can perform attitude estimation and positioning through the observed environmental features, and realize map building [1]. Loop closure detection(LCD) is an important component in SLAM systems, aiming to correctly identify places the robot has visited before, reducing cumulative trajectory drift [2].

At present, the traditional LCD method adopts Bag-of-Words (BoW) structure [3]. The BoW framework quantifies the local feature descriptors extracted from the image into visual words. Common descriptors of local features include SURF [4], SIFT [5], ORB [6] and local difference binary (LDB) [7]. By using the technique of tf-idf (term frequency-inverse document frequency), the BoW model can use vectors that describe the word histogram to represent the image.

© The Author(s), under exclusive license to Springer Nature Switzerland AG 2022
E. Pimenidis et al. (Eds.): ICANN 2022, LNCS 13532, pp. 719–730, 2022.
https://doi.org/10.1007/978-3-031-15937-4_60

Then, through the combination of inverted index method to quickly calculate the similarity between the two vectors to find the loop closure image. Although the BoW method performs well, the local features it extracts are not robust to changes in illumination and weather, and there may be mismatches.

In recent years, a large number of researchers have used convolutional neural networks(CNNs) for image feature extraction and demonstrated that the features extracted by CNNs are superior to hand-crafted image descriptors [8,9]. However, they only use the original RGB image from the sensor, and the RGB information may be affected due to changes in illumination and viewpoint. Therefore, the performance of LCD systems implemented using the above methods may be limited. In fact, additional feature information, especially depth and edge, is robust and invariant to illumination changes and is clearly a good choice for improving performance.

Based on the above analysis, this paper proposes a novel and efficient LCD method based on Siamese ConvNet features. First, robust global features of the images are extracted using Siamese network with AlexNet [10] as a two branch. Then, the Euclidean distance is used to quantify the similarity between images, and the loop closure candidate frames are selected based on the similarity. After the above first stage, images with similar appearance to the query image may be added to the loop closure candidate frames because the spatial geometrical relationship between the global features is ignored. For this reason, in the second stage, we employ LDB descriptor matching and RANSAC for geometric verification. The proposed method is evaluated on several public datasets and compared with several typical methods. The contributions of this paper mainly include:

(1) The intensity, depth and edge features of the image are fused and used as the input of the Siamese network, aiming to better utilize the information from the environment to construct a more comprehensive image feature.
(2) An efficient geometrical verification method is proposed for verifying the loop closure candidates obtained from Siamese network.
(3) Experiments conducted on several publicly available datasets show that the method improves the performance of the LCD system under different illumination conditions.

## 2    Related Work

### 2.1    Hand-Crafted Features

At present, the LCD methods based on hand-crafted features all use the BoW model, which creates a visual dictionary by clustering the visual features extracted from the image [11]. However, most BoW methods generate fixed visual dictionaries offline before the loop is closed, so performance is affected by datasets that generate pre-trained visual dictionaries [12]. Therefore, many researchers use incremental methods to generate online visual dictionaries. Tsintotas et al. [13] used an online clustering algorithm to construct visual words. Local feature descriptors are first extracted from image sequences that are close in time and content, and then Growing Neural Gas clustering is performed on them to generate corresponding visual words. Sheraz Khan et al. [14] proposed to incrementally generate a vocabulary consisting of binary words online by tracking features between consecutive images without prior vocabulary learning.

## 2.2 CNN-Based Features

Nowadays, CNN-based features have been widely used in LCD. Gao et al. [15] proposed to use stacked denoising auto-encoder (SDA) to learn image feature representations, which showed better results than the FAB-MAP method. Yong Chen et al. [16] the effects of several popular pre-trained CNN models in LCD are analyzed, and it is proved that it is feasible to use deep neural network in LCD. However, none of the above methods make use of the depth information in the image and are sensitive to the change of illumination. Method [17] obtains depth information by adding an input channel, which provides information about scene structure and is independent of lighting. Method [18] proposes to separately train depth and RGB images on a CNN model, and then fuse them to obtain joint descriptors of the images to enhance place recognition.

However, the above methods only use the original RGB and depth image of the sensor. Due to the variation of illumination and viewpoint, the RGB and depth information may be ambiguous, so the image features cannot be described comprehensively and reliably.

## 3 Method

In this section, the proposed flow of LCD will be described in detail. The process of the proposed method is shown in Fig. 1.

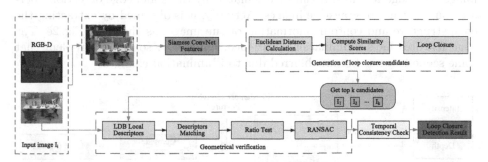

**Fig. 1.** An overview of the proposed LCD framework based on Siamese ConvNet Features and geometrical verification. When an input image enters the pipeline, its global feature is extracted by the Siamese network. Then the similarity between global feature is calculated by Euclidean distance, and the images with similarity greater than a threshold are used as loop closure candidates. The candidate pair is verified based on ratio test and RANSAC. Finally, a temporal consistency check further verifies the final loop closure pair.

### 3.1   Generation of Loop Closure Candidate Frames

**(1) Feature Information Fusion.** In the field of image processing, color, intensity, depth and edge features (see Fig. 2) are widely used [19]. Among them, color features describe the scene appearance and are robust to changes in size and viewpoint, but are susceptible to illumination changes. However, intensity, depth and edge features are insensitive to illumination changes and have great advantages in feature matching. Therefore, the above three low-level invariant feature cues are used to learn global features of images.

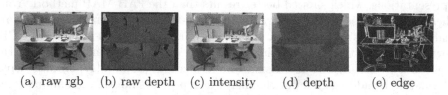

(a) raw rgb     (b) raw depth     (c) intensity     (d) depth     (e) edge

**Fig. 2.** (a) and (b) are raw RGB and depth images from the TUM dataset. (c), (d) and (e) denote the intensity, depth and edge features that represent the image, respectively, and the above three features are used to learn the global features of the image.

For intensity features, it can be obtained by converting the RGB image to grayscale image, as shown in Fig. 2a and 2c. For depth features, as shown in Fig. 2b, the original depth images in the TUM [24] dataset have noise and many holes and only provide depth information for some points, resulting in inaccurate center depths of objects. To alleviate this issue, we use the cross-bilateral filter method provided by [20] to fill depth information to obtain a completed and usable depth image. Figure 2d is the filled depth image of the original depth image. For edge features, it can be calculated by the Sobel edge detection operator on the basis of grayscale images. Actually, it is obtained by extracting the edge structure and contour information of the image, as shown in Fig. 2e. The edge features have illumination invariance, which can solve the problem that some scene features become blurred due to illumination changes.

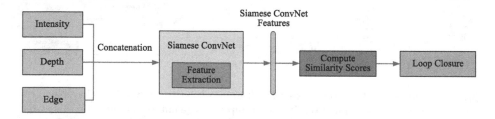

**Fig. 3.** Image feature information fusion pipeline.

To take full advantage of feature invariance and enable early interaction of feature information, we combine intensity, depth, and edge features at the beginning of the network, resulting in a three-channel input. Next, the combination of these features is fed to the Siamese network to generate the final global features. Figure 3 shows the flowchart of the feature information fusion pipeline.

**(2) Training Method.** We propose a new Siamese network for training, each branch structure is designed based on AlexNet [10], with an eight-layer network architecture including five convolutional layers and three fully connected layers. As shown in Fig. 4, it takes two images as input and feeds forward through two branched convolutional structures that share the same parameters. Since fully-connected layers do not perform as well as convolutional layers in tasks such as place recognition [21], we extract only the first fully-connected layer output as image features. This extracts and represents semantic information, enhancing the robustness of the features to viewpoint changes. Finally, we input a pair of images into the Siamese network for feature learning to obtain a 1024-dimensional feature vector, which is the global feature of the image.

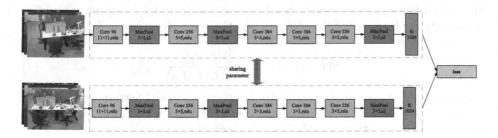

**Fig. 4.** The architecture of the Siamese convolutional neural network for training.

In the training we use the contrastive loss function and use the Euclidean distance as a similarity measure between the feature vectors. For the $k$-th input sample pair, assume that the feature vector output by the fully connected layer is $f_k = \{f_{k1}, f_{k2}\}$, and that the contrast loss function is:

$$L = \frac{1}{2N} \sum_{n=1}^{N} [y_k d_k^2 + (1 - y_k) max(0, m - d_k)^2] \tag{1}$$

where $N$ is the number of sample pairs, $y_k$ is the label of the $k$-th pair of samples, and $d_k = \|f_{k1} - f_{k2}\|_2$ represents the Euclidean distance between feature vectors. $y_k = 1$ represents a positive sample, indicating that $f_{k1}$ and $f_{k2}$ are from the same class, that is, the two pictures are similar. $y_k = 0$ is a negative sample, indicating that $f_{k1}$ and $f_{k2}$ are from different classes, that is, the two images are less similar. Because the contrastive loss function can represent the degree of match between two images, we use it for model training.

**(3) Similarity Calculation.** When the robot performs LCD task, because the images captured by the robot are continuous images, there is a high similarity between adjacent images, which may lead to LCD errors. Therefore, we introduce a constraint to limit the matching range of the query image. The matching range of the query image is as follows:

$$U = N - f \cdot T \tag{2}$$

where $U$ represents the matching range of the query image; $N$ represents the set of all images before the query image; $f$ is the frame rate of the camera; $T$ is the time constant; $f \cdot T$ is the set of $f \cdot T$ images before the query image. By adding this constraint, the problem of incorrect LCD can be avoided.

In addition, the feature vectors extracted by the Siamese network are normalized and the Euclidean distance between vectors is calculated as follows:

$$D(I_i, I_j) = \left\| \frac{f_i}{\|f_i\|_2} - \frac{f_j}{\|f_j\|_2} \right\|_2 \tag{3}$$

where $D(I_i, I_j)$ is the distance between images $I_i$ and $I_j$, $f_i$ and $f_j$ represent the global feature vectors extracted from images $I_i$ and $I_j$, respectively; $\|f_i\|_2$ represents the L2 norm of the vector. Then the similarity between images $I_i$ and $I_j$ is defined as:

$$S(I_i, I_j) = 1 - \frac{D(I_i, I_j)}{max(D(I_i, I_j))} \tag{4}$$

where $S(I_i, I_j)$ represents the similarity between two global feature vector, which lies between 0 and 1. If the similarity between images equals or exceeds the specified threshold, then we take it as the loop closure candidate frame.

## 3.2   Geometrical Verification

We adopt geometrical verification method to judge whether the query image $I_i$ and its corresponding loop closure candidate image $I_k$ constitute a real positive loop closure. Specifically, we extract ORB feature points and corresponding LDB descriptors from the query image and $k$ loop closure candidate images respectively, and then match the descriptors of the two images.

For the extraction of LDB descriptors, first, extract the ORB feature points of the query image $I_i$ and the loop closure candidate image $I_k$, and crop out an image patch of size $s \times s$ with each feature point as the center. Then, the image patch is divided into $c \times c$ grid cells of equal size, and the average intensity $I_{avg}$ and gradient $d_x$, $d_y$ of each grid cell are calculated respectively. A binary test is performed on any two grid cells $c_{ij}^m$ and $c_{ij}^n$ in each image patch, as defined in the following Eq. 5, and the resulting binary code is the LDB descriptor of the feature point $k_{ij}$.

$$\tau(func(m), func(n)) = \begin{cases} 1, & func(m) > func(n) \\ 0, & func(m) \le func(n) \end{cases} \tag{5}$$

where $func(m)$ and $func(n)$ represent the values of the average intensity $I_{avg}$ and the regional gradient $d_x$ and $d_y$ in grid cells $c_{ij}^m$ and $c_{ij}^n$, respectively. We set multiple $c$ values for image patch division, and concatenate the binary strings generated by all the divisions to form the final 256-bit LDB descriptor.

We adopt the binary ratio test [5] to match the LDB local descriptors $I_i$ and $I_k$, and the binary ratio test threshold $\varepsilon$ is defined as follows:

$$\frac{H(d_i^a, d_k^1)}{H(d_i^a, d_k^2)} < \varepsilon \tag{6}$$

where $d_i^a$ is the LDB descriptor of the query image $I_i$, and $d_k^1$ and $d_k^2$ are the two descriptors with the closest distance to $d_i^a$ found in the candidate image $I_k$ based on the Fast Approximate Nearest Neighbor (FLANN) algorithm. $H(\cdot)$ represents the Hamming distance, and $\varepsilon$ is the ratio of distance. Descriptor matches lower than $\varepsilon$ will be considered as good feature matches and feed into RANSAC to eliminate mismatches and compute the fundamental matrix $T$. If the fundamental matrix $T$ is successfully calculated, the one with the highest number of inliers is selected as the candidate for loop closure.

### 3.3 Temporal Consistency Check

As with the method used in [13], the image pair $I_i$ and $I_k$ will be recognized as a loop closure event if two consecutive camera measurements satisfy the above conditions.

## 4 Experiments

### 4.1 Experimental Settings

1) Datasets: To evaluate the effectiveness of the method, we test the method on three publicly available datasets. The KITTI [22] public dataset is collected by cameras mounted on a moving car in different challenging environments, such as different lighting conditions, viewpoint changes, and dynamic occlusions. KITTI 00, 05 are used as outdoor datasets in this experiment because these two datasets provide many examples of loop closures as well as real trajectories of sensors. The ground truths of KITTI were provided by authors in [13]. The dataset of New College [23] was recorded by the vision system installed on the wheeled robot platform. In the experiment, we use the left images of New College for evaluation, and use the ground truths provided in [23].

2) Parameters Setting: For the global feature extraction network, we train it using the dataset of TUM [24]. The training of the CNN adopts the Adam optimizer with a learning rate of 1e−4. The batch size is set to 16 and the maximum number of training is 40 epochs.

3) Evaluation Metrics: Precision and recall are important performance metrics for evaluating LCD tasks. Precision refers to the probability that the closed loops detected by the algorithm are true, while recall refers to the probability that all true closed loops are correctly detected. For SLAM systems, more

correct loop closure examples are better at eliminating accumulated errors and helping to modify the final robot pose, therefore, we choose to perform maximum recall evaluation at 100% precision.

### 4.2   Experiment Results

**(1) Evaluation on Siamese ConvNet Features.** To verify the effectiveness of our feature information fusion strategy and global feature extraction network, we compare the proposed method with a global feature extraction method (RGB method) that only uses RGB images. Table 1 shows the precision and recall results for the global feature descriptors extracted by different methods in the KITTI dataset with the specified threshold range. From the experimental results, it can be seen that our method has better recall than the methods that only use RGB images. This is because we not only use raw intensity and depth features, but also add edge features when training the network. They can be combined in advance to generate a three-channel input, which is then fed into the network to learn to describe the scene. The learned features inherit the global context of the scene and are insensitive to illumination and viewpoint changes.

**Table 1.** Comparison of proposed method with RGB method on KITTI dataset.

| Datasets | Methods | Precision (%) | Recall (%) |
|----------|---------|---------------|------------|
| KITTI00 | RGB method | 100 | 34.2 |
| KITTI00 | Proposed method | 100 | 38.9 |
| KITTI05 | RGB method | 100 | 37.4 |
| KITTI05 | Proposed method | 100 | 42.1 |

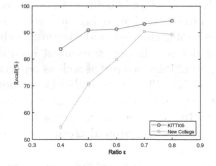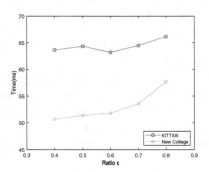

**Fig. 5.** The max recall rate at 100% precision(left) and average processing time(right) on KITTI05 and New College datasets using a different ratio $\varepsilon$.

**(2) Evaluation on Geometrical Verification.** The ratio $\varepsilon$ of the binary ratio test affects the precision and recall of LCD. For the ratio $\varepsilon$ of the binary ratio test, we increase it from 0.4 to 0.8 in steps of 0.1. The recall rate of the

KITTI05 and New College datasets increase with the ratio, and tend to be stable when $\varepsilon$ reaches 0.7, as shown in Fig. 5a. The average processing time increases as the ratio increases, as shown Fig. 5b. Therefore, we set the ratio to 0.7, which guarantees a higher recall at 100% precision.

Finally, we evaluate the recall and average processing time of the ORB and LDB descriptor at 100% precision, as shown in Table 2. We can see that the method using the LDB descriptor has a higher recall, but it has a longer average processing time. This is because the LDB descriptor computes image gradients and intensities, slightly increasing the processing time, but it enhances the stability and descriptive power of the LDB descriptor.

**Table 2.** Comparison of ORB descriptors and LDB descriptors.

| Datasets | Descriptor | Time (ms) | Recall (%) |
|---|---|---|---|
| KITTI00 | ORB | 55.46 | 95.31 |
| KITTI00 | LDB | 60.91 | 97.18 |
| KITTI05 | ORB | 52.25 | 90.58 |
| KITTI05 | LDB | 58.64 | 94.32 |
| New College | ORB | 47.34 | 84.25 |
| New College | LDB | 52.98 | 91.53 |

## 4.3   Comparative Result

We also compare our method with FabMap [23], FPSN [17] and RGB method that is using only RGB images. The precision and recall curves of these methods on the KITTI dataset were plotted by adjusting the threshold values of the similarity scores. As shown in Fig. 6, we can find that since we combine Siamese ConvNet Features with geometrical verification, our method performs better than other methods, and the recall rate is also improved to a certain extent while improving the precision rate.

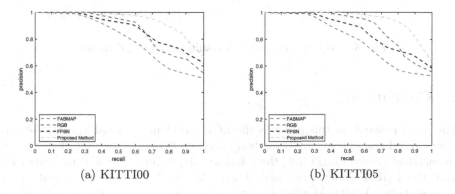

(a) KITTI00                    (b) KITTI05

**Fig. 6.** P-R curves of KITTI dataset under different methods.

## 4.4   Visualization of the Loop Detection Results

To further evaluate the effectiveness of our method, as shown in Fig. 7 and Fig. 8, in the first figure we plot moving trajectory of the camera corresponding to each keyframe of the image. At the same time, the keyframe points where the loop closure occurs are marked with red circles on the figure, and each circle refers to a loop closure pair. The second figure shows the loop closure pairs obtained by our method.

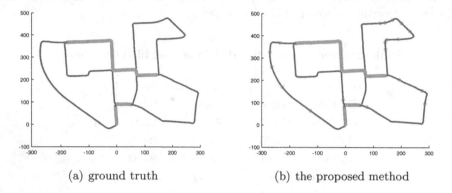

(a) ground truth                              (b) the proposed method

**Fig. 7.** Loop closure detection results on KITTI00 dataset.

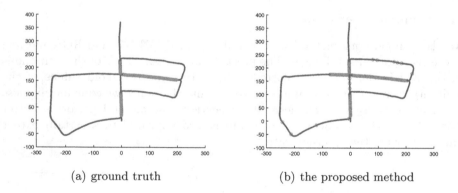

(a) ground truth                              (b) the proposed method

**Fig. 8.** Loop closure detection results on KITTI05 dataset.

## 5   Conclusion

The main research in this paper is the LCD problem in visual SLAM. We propose a novel and efficient LCD method based on Siamese ConvNet Features and geometrical verification. First, the intensity, depth and edge features extracted from the RGB-D image are fused. Then, the fused features are passed to the Siamese network with AlexNet as the two branch to extract the global features of the image. For global features, Euclidean distance is used to calculate the similarity, and loop closure candidate frames are selected according to the similarity. Finally, LDB descriptor matching and RANSAC are applied to examine the loop closure candidate pairs. The proposed method is evaluated on several public datasets, and the experimental results show that our method can significantly improve the performance of LCD and outperforms other LCD methods, especially in challenging scenarios with illumination and viewpoint variations.

**Acknowledgement.** This work is supported by the grant of National Natural Science Foundation of China (No. 62002179), Natural Science Foundation of Jiangsu Province (BK20191445), Natural Science Key Foundation of Jiangsu Education Department (21KJA510004) and Nantong Social Livelihood Science and Technology Project (MS12020078).

# References

1. Dong, Y., et al.: A novel texture-less object oriented visual SLAM system. IEEE Trans. Intell. Transp. Syst. **22**(1), 36–49 (2019). https://doi.org/10.1109/TITS.2019.2952159
2. Han, J., Kim, J., Shim, D.H.: Precise localization and mapping in indoor parking structures via parameterized SLAM. IEEE Trans. Intell. Transp. Syst. **20**(12), 4415–4426 (2018). https://doi.org/10.1109/TITS.2018.2885341
3. Garcia-Fidalgo, E., Ortiz, A.: IBOW-LCD: an appearance-based loop-closure detection approach using incremental bags of binary words. IEEE Robot. Autom. Lett. **3**(4), 3051–3057 (2018). https://doi.org/10.1109/LRA.2018.2849609
4. Bay, H., Tuytelaars, T., Van Gool, L.: SURF: speeded up robust features. In: Leonardis, A., Bischof, H., Pinz, A. (eds.) ECCV 2006. LNCS, vol. 3951, pp. 404–417. Springer, Heidelberg (2006). https://doi.org/10.1007/11744023_32
5. Lowe, D.G.: Distinctive image features from scale-invariant keypoints. Int. J. Comput. Vision **60**(2), 91–110 (2004). https://doi.org/10.1023/B:VISI.0000029664.99615.94
6. Rublee, E., Rabaud, V., Konolige, K., Bradski, G.: ORB: an efficient alternative to SIFT or SURF. In: 2011 International Conference on Computer Vision, pp. 2564–2571. IEEE (2011). https://doi.org/10.1109/ICCV.2011.6126544
7. Yang, X., Cheng, K.T.T.: Local difference binary for ultrafast and distinctive feature description. IEEE Trans. Pattern Anal. Mach. Intell. **36**(1), 188–194 (2013). https://doi.org/10.1109/TPAMI.2013.150
8. Hou, Y., Zhang, H., Zhou, S.: BoCNF: efficient image matching with Bag of ConvNet features for scalable and robust visual place recognition. Auton. Robot. **42**(6), 1169–1185 (2017). https://doi.org/10.1007/s10514-017-9684-3
9. Dai, K., Cheng, L., Yang, R., Yan, G.: Loop closure detection using KPCA and CNN for visual SLAM. In: 2021 40th Chinese Control Conference (CCC), pp. 8088–8093. IEEE (2021). https://doi.org/10.23919/CCC52363.2021.9550432
10. Krizhevsky, A., Sutskever, I., Hinton, G. E.: Imagenet classification with deep convolutional neural networks. In: Advances in Neural Information Processing Systems, vol. 25 (2012). https://doi.org/10.1145/3065386
11. Shin, D.W., Ho, Y.S.: Loop closure detection in simultaneous localization and mapping using learning based local patch descriptor. Electron. Imaging **2018**(17), 284-1 (2018). https://doi.org/10.2352/ISSN.2470-1173.2018.17.AVM-284

12. Mur-Artal, R., Tardós, J.D.: Orb-slam2: an open-source slam system for monocular, stereo, and RGB-D cameras. IEEE Trans. Rob. **33**(5), 1255–1262 (2017). https://doi.org/10.1109/TRO.2017.2705103

13. Tsintotas, K. A., Bampis, L., Gasteratos, A.: Assigning visual words to places for loop closure detection. In: 2018 IEEE International Conference on Robotics and Automation (ICRA), pp. 5979–5985. IEEE (2018). https://doi.org/10.1109/ICRA.2018.8461146

14. Khan, S., Wollherr, D.: IBuILD: incremental bag of binary words for appearance based loop closure detection. In: 2015 IEEE International Conference on Robotics and Automation (ICRA), pp. 5441–5447. IEEE (2015). https://doi.org/10.1109/ICRA.2015.7139959

15. Gao, X., Zhang, T.: Unsupervised learning to detect loops using deep neural networks for visual SLAM system. Auton. Robot. **41**(1), 1–18 (2015). https://doi.org/10.1007/s10514-015-9516-2

16. Zuo, L., Zhang, C. H., Liu, F.L., Wu, Y.F.: Performance evaluation of deep neural networks in detecting loop closure of visual SLAM. In: 2019 11th International Conference on Intelligent Human-Machine Systems and Cybernetics (IHMSC), vol. 2, pp. 171–175. IEEE (2019). https://doi.org/10.1109/IHMSC.2019.10136

17. Qianhao, Z., Mai, A., Menke, J., Yang, A.: Loop closure detection with RGB-D feature pyramid siamese networks. arXiv preprint arXiv:1811.09938 (2018)

18. Sizikova, E., Singh, V.K., Georgescu, B., Halber, M., Ma, K., Chen, T.: Enhancing place recognition using joint intensity - depth analysis and synthetic data. In: Hua, G., Jégou, H. (eds.) ECCV 2016. LNCS, vol. 9915, pp. 901–908. Springer, Cham (2016). https://doi.org/10.1007/978-3-319-49409-8_74

19. Pratondo, A., Chui, C.K., Ong, S.H.: Robust edge-stop functions for edge-based active contour models in medical image segmentation. IEEE Signal Process. Lett. **23**(2), 222–226 (2015). https://doi.org/10.1109/LSP.2015.2508039

20. Silberman, N., Hoiem, D., Kohli, P., Fergus, R.: Indoor segmentation and support inference from RGBD images. In: Fitzgibbon, A., Lazebnik, S., Perona, P., Sato, Y., Schmid, C. (eds.) ECCV 2012. LNCS, vol. 7576, pp. 746–760. Springer, Heidelberg (2012). https://doi.org/10.1007/978-3-642-33715-4_54

21. Sünderhauf, N., Shirazi, S., Dayoub, F., Upcroft, B., Milford, M.: On the performance of convnet features for place recognition. In: 2015 IEEE/RSJ International Conference on Intelligent Robots and Systems (IROS) pp. 4297–4304. IEEE (2015). https://doi.org/10.1109/IROS.2015.7353986

22. Geiger, A., Lenz, P., Stiller, C., Urtasun, R.: Vision meets robotics: the kitti dataset. Int. J. Robot. Res. **32**(11), 1231–1237 (2013). https://doi.org/10.1177/0278364913491297

23. Cummins, M., Newman, P.: FAB-MAP: probabilistic localization and mapping in the space of appearance. Int. J. Robot. Res. **27**(6), 647–665 (2008). https://doi.org/10.1177/0278364908090961

24. Sturm, J., Engelhard, N., Endres, F., Burgard, W., Cremers, D.: A benchmark for the evaluation of RGB-D SLAM systems. In: 2012 IEEE/RSJ international Conference on Intelligent Robots and Systems, pp. 573–580. IEEE (2012). https://doi.org/10.1109/IROS.2012.6385773

# Multi-Sensor Data Fusion for Short-Term Traffic Flow Prediction: A Novel Multi-Channel Data Structure Integrated with Mixed-Pointwise Convolution and Channel Attention Mechanism

Ruijun Feng[1]($\boxtimes$) (iD) and Mingzhou Chen[2]

[1] Zhejiang University of Finance and Economics, Hangzhou, China
fengruijun@zufe.edu.cn
[2] Tongji University, Shanghai, China
2010361@tongji.edu.cn

**Abstract.** Accurate short-term traffic flow prediction is critical to improving the reliability and efficiency of intelligent transportation systems. However, the complex spatio-temporal characteristics of traffic flow pose a great challenge. The latest methods usually use a multi-sensor data fusion approach to learn the spatio-temporal information. First, it represents the traffic flow data collected from different sensors as a single-channel data structure. Then, the single-channel data structure combined with the multi-branch feature fusion strategy is used to learn the periodic dependencies (recent, daily, and weekly). However, these branches add a massive usage of parameters, which tends to overparameterize the prediction model, resulting in model overfitting and performance degeneration. To address these issues, a novel deep learning-based prediction model is proposed, which consists of three components. First, a new multi-channel data structure is proposed to efficiently reconstruct periodic dependencies of traffic data. Then, a new mixed-pointwise convolution method is proposed to extract spatio-temporal correlations and periodic dependencies of traffic data without over-parameterization and information loss. Last, an improved channel attention mechanism is employed to quantify the contributions of different channels. Extensive experiments are conducted on two real-world traffic datasets. The results demonstrate the proposed method consistently outperforms other baseline methods and has strong robustness in different settings.

**Keywords:** Traffic flow prediction · Multi-channel data structure · 3D convolution · Pointwise convolution · Channel attention

## 1 Introduction

Short-term traffic flow prediction aims to predict the traffic flow for the next five to 30 min based on the historical traffic data. And it's of great significance to build the Intelligent Transportation Systems (ITS). Traditional prediction methods such as Historical Average (HA) [17], Auto-Regressive Integrated Moving Average (ARIMA) [17],

© The Author(s), under exclusive license to Springer Nature Switzerland AG 2022
E. Pimenidis et al. (Eds.): ICANN 2022, LNCS 13532, pp. 731–742, 2022.
https://doi.org/10.1007/978-3-031-15937-4_61

and Support Vector Regression (SVR) [18], only consider the intra-dependencies (i.e., temporal correlation across a single sequence), but ignoring the inter-information (i.e., spatio-temporal correlations across multiple sequences).

Recently, a modern solution that adopts the multi-sensor data fusion method has arisen. First, it converts traffic data collected from multiple sensors into different data formats that can represent spatial dependency. Then, deep learning-based methods are used to capture the spatio-temporal correlations, which include two types of methods: Convolutional Neural Network (CNN)-based methods and Recurrent Neural Network (RNN)-based methods. RNN-based methods [6] are good at capturing temporal dependencies but fail to consider spatial dependency without additional help, and usually suffered from low parallel efficiency and vanishing gradient due to recursive design. CNN-based methods, on the other hand, can capture the spatio-temporal correlations [2, 4, 15, 19] with high parallel efficiency and no vanishing gradient. In our previous work, CNN is used for its superior ability in capturing spatio-temporal correlations [20].

Traditional CNN-based methods reconstruct the traffic data into a two-dimensional matrix and apply a 2D-CNN for feature extraction [15]. This matrix stacks multiple one-dimensional sequences vertically, making spatial information very ambiguous because it can't represent the real geographic distribution of different sections. Further researches improve it by using a three-dimensional tensor, each two-dimensional matrix is a snapshot of the transportation network. And they further enhance temporal correlation by using three parallel tensors with three parallel branches, corresponding with three types of periodic dependency: recent, daily, and weekly (hereinafter referred it as multi-branch feature fusion strategy). In the beginning, a Spatio-Temporal Residual Network (ST-ResNet) [19] based on 2D convolution is proposed. But due to the limitations of 2D convolution, the temporal information will lose after the first layer. To improve that, a multiple local 3D CNN Spatio-Temporal Residual Network (LMST3D-ResNet) [4] is proposed by replacing the 2D convolution with 3D convolution. Compared with 2D convolution, 3D convolution can preserve more temporal information.

However, the aforementioned methods still have a huge research gap. First of all, the multi-branch feature fusion strategy is highly inefficient. It's not worth tripling the parameters or even more just to account for periodic dependencies, which is likely to cause over-parameterization. Second, they all suffered from information loss to some extent, due to the usage of max pooling layers or 2D convolution. Third, they all ignored the channel inter-dependencies, which are useful in terms of CNN-based methods.

To tackle these challenges, a novel multi-channel data structure integrated with mixed-pointwise convolution and channel attention mechanism (CAMPConv-MC) is proposed. The main contributions of this article are summarized as follows:

1. A new multi-channel data structure is proposed by reconstructing traffic data into a four-dimensional tensor. This data structure can make full use of the channel parallelism in CNN while representing the periodic dependencies of traffic data.
2. A new mixed-pointwise convolution method is proposed that integrates 3D convolution, 2D convolution, and their variants pointwise convolution to extract spatio-temporal correlations. No max pooling layer or 2D convolution is used in the middle, thus alleviating the information loss. And it removes the multi-branch feature fusion

strategy and fully connected (FC) layers, hence over-parameterization is avoided as well.

3. A channel attention mechanism is adapted from the squeeze and excitation (SE) unit [8] and employed to learn the channel inter-dependencies of 3D convolution with a mild parameter usage.

## 2  Related Work

### 2.1  Traditional Traffic Prediction Methods

Traditional traffic prediction methods include parametric methods and non-parametric methods. Some typical examples of parametric methods are HA and ARIMA [17]. These methods achieve satisfactory performance on short series that are stational and univariate. But the strong assumptions about data are not suitable for non-linear traffic data. These limitations have been improved by non-parametric methods. A typical example is SVR [18]. SVR uses a kernel function to project the traffic data to high dimensional space. This reconstruction makes non-linear traffic data linearly separable with hyperplanes. Other methods such as Bayesian Network [12] and K-Nearest Neighbor [12] all achieved a better forecast error by considering spatial dependency. However, these non-parametric methods still require some human intervention like feature engineering. In comparison with them, deep learning-based methods learn the features on their own with no human help required.

### 2.2  Deep Learning-Based Traffic Prediction Methods

In the age of big data, deep learning-based methods like Deep Belief Networks (DBF) [9], Stacked Auto Encoder (SAE) [14], Gated Recurrent Unit (GRU) [6], and Long Short-Term Memory (LSTM) [6] have been proposed for traffic data prediction. DBF and SAE focus on spatial dependency but ignore the long-term patterns while GRU and LSTM are the opposite. In addition, RNN-based methods (i.e., LSTM and GRU) have poor parallel efficiency and vanishing gradient problems as they are trained [2]. Subsequent methods have overcome these shortcomings with CNN-based models and multi-sensor data fusion to reconstruct and capture the spatio-temporal correlations. At an early stage, Ma et al. [15] proposed a traditional 2D-CNN with two-dimensional matrix. Later, Zhang et al. [19] extended it into three-dimensional tensor and proposed the ST-ResNet. However, 2D convolution used in ST-ResNet can't preserve temporal information after the first layer. To improve it, Chen et al. [4] proposed an LMST3D-ResNet by replacing the 2D convolution with 3D convolution and introducing the 3D max pooling layers and FC layers. In addition, ST-ResNet and LMST3D-ResNet adopt a multi-branch feature fusion strategy to enhance the modeling of temporal correlation. But this strategy and FC layers use a huge number of parameters, which is likely to cause over-parameterization that triggers overfitting and performance degeneration. What's more, these CNN-based methods with max pooling layers condense too much information when extracting features, resulting in information loss. Moreover, they all neglect the importance of channel inter-dependencies, which is crucial in CNN-based methods.

## 2.3  Pointwise Convolution and Channel Attention Mechanism

Pointwise convolution was proposed in fully convolutional methods like the Xception network [5]. Pointwise convolution refers to convolution with a kernel size of one. It's used to reduce channels before expensive filters while learning the channel inter-dependencies. Meanwhile, a channel attention mechanism was proposed to refine informative filter output. Chen et al. [3] used global mean pooling with softmax function and FC layers to find the informative channels. Liu et al. [13] applied it in traffic data prediction using multiple two-dimensional matrixes. However, apart from the drawbacks of the two-dimensional matrix, the FC layers are very computational expensive as the channels increase. SE unit [8] improved it with more flexible squeeze and excitation operations. Inspired by them, a mixed-pointwise convolution integrated with a channel attention mechanism is proposed to reduce computations and boost performance.

# 3  Methodology

## 3.1  Multi-channel Data Structure

In this article, a transportation network is defined as regular raster data [1] to fuse the spatio-temporal information collected from multiple traffic sensors. Apart from spatio-temporal correlations, the proposed method adds periodic dependencies into account.

**Definition 1: Rasterization.** The transportation network is partitioned into $I \times J$ grids based on latitude and longitude. Each sensor records at time point $t$ are assigned to the closest grid $(i, j)$ and averaged into a scalar denoted as $x_t^{i,j}$.

**Definition 2: Spatio-Temporal Raster Data.** First, a two-dimensional matrix denoted as $S_t \in \mathbb{R}^{I \times J}$ is used to represent the spatial information at time point $t$, as defined in Eq. (1):

$$S_t = \{x_t^{i,j} | i \in I, j \in J\} \tag{1}$$

Then, the temporal information is represented by $T_p \in \mathbb{R}^{d \times I \times J}$ as defined in Eq. (2) where $d$ refers to subsequence length and $p$ is sampling period.

$$T_p = \{S_{t-d \times p}, S_{t-(d-1) \times p}, ..., S_t\} \tag{2}$$

**Definition 3: Multi-Channel Data Structure.** The multi-channel data structure is denoted as $X_C \in \mathbb{R}^{C \times d \times I \times J}$, composed of $C$ types of periodic dependency: recent, daily, and weekly. $X_C$ can be rewritten as $X_C = \{T_r, T_d, T_w\}$. For each tensor $T$, $d$ is set to the same, and $p$ is set to five minutes, 24 h, and one week respectively.

**Definition 4: Traffic Flow Prediction.** As defined in Eq. (3). Given $X_C$, the goal is to predict the value at the time point $t + \Delta t$ denoted as $\widehat{X}_{t+\Delta t}$, where $\Delta t$ is the forecast time interval, and $\theta$ is the trainable parameters of the proposed CAMPConv.

$$\widehat{X}_{t+\Delta t} = f_\theta(X_C) \tag{3}$$

## 3.2   Mixed-Pointwise Convolution Integrated with Channel Attention Mechanism

In this section, a novel CAMPConv is proposed which contains two components: convolutional unit, and SE unit as shown in Fig. 1(b) and Fig. 1(c). Figure 1(a) is the overall structure of the proposed CAMPConv-MC. First, the input unit uses a 3D pointwise convolutional unit with 64 filters is used to project the proposed multi-channel data structure $X_C$ to a high-dimensional channel space. Then, the backbone uses multiple 3D convolutional units (same padding) with 64 filters and SE units are employed to extract the spatio-temporal correlations. After this, the output unit uses a 3D pointwise convolutional unit with one filter implemented to compress the channel space into one. At last, the 3D channel axis is removed so that a 2D pointwise convolutional unit can be employed to extract temporal information of the same region and make predictions.

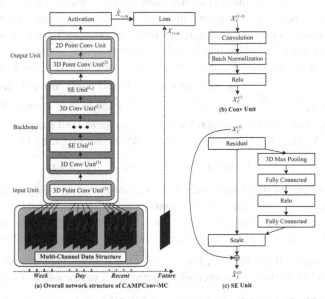

**Fig. 1.** Network structure and the details of the proposed CAMPConv-MC. (3D Conv Unit: 3D Convolutional Unit; 3D Point Conv Unit: 3D Pointwise Convolutional Unit; 2D Point Conv Unit: 2D Pointwise Convolutional Unit; SE Unit: Squeeze and Excitation Unit)

**Mixed-Pointwise Convolution.** Mixed-pointwise convolution is a hybrid method that adopts 3D convolution, 2D convolution, and their variants pointwise convolution. They are denoted as convolutional units as demonstrated in Fig. 1(b). First, a convolutional layer is used to extract spatio-temporal correlations. Then, a batch normalization [10] layer is implemented to avoid internal covariate shift. Finally, a relu function is used to add nonlinearity. As defined in Eq. (4), $X_C^{(l-1)} \in \mathbb{R}^{C_{l-1} \times d \times I \times J}$ denotes the input of the $l^{th}$ 3D convolutional layer, which is the output of the upper layer with $C_{l-1}$ channels. $W^{(l)}$ and $b^{(l)}$ are the weights and bias of the $l^{th}$ 3D convolutional layer, and $*$ denotes the operation of 3D convolution. $BN$ denotes the batch normalization operation and $\delta$

denotes the relu function. This design preserves the temporal information by keeping the sequence length $d$ unchanged during 3D convolution.

$$X_C^{(l)} = \delta(BN(W^{(l)} * X_C^{(l-1)} + b^{(l)})) \tag{4}$$

After 3D convolution, 2D pointwise convolution is used to extract temporal information for prediction. As defined in Eq. (5), $L$ refers to the last 3D pointwise convolutional units as shown in Fig. 1(a). $W$ and $b$ refer to the weights and bias of the 2D convolutional layer, $\circledast$ denotes the 2D convolutional operation.

$$\hat{X}_{t+\Delta t} = \delta(BN(W \circledast X_C^{(L)} + b)) \tag{5}$$

**Squeeze and Excitation Unit.** This article extends the traditional SE unit to meet the requirements of traffic prediction, as shown in Fig. 1(c). Unlike image data, spatio-temporal traffic raster data often contains many empty regions due to the sparsity of the transportation network. The global mean pooling used in traditional SE units will introduce too much noise. In this article, a simple adaption to 3D max pooling is used to pick out the most informative region in the spatio-temporal domain.

In the notion that follows, $F_{sq}$ denotes squeeze operation and $F_{ex}$ denotes excitation operation. $X_C^{(l)} \in \mathbb{R}^{C_l \times d \times I \times J}$ is the output of the $l^{th}$ 3D convolutional unit, which can be rewritten as $X_C^{(l)} = \{x_1^{(l)}, x_2^{(l)}, ..., x_{C_l}^{(l)}\}$ where $x_c^{(l)}$ refers to the output of the $c^{th}$ filter in $l^{th}$ layer. The global spatio-temporal information is squeezed out using 3D max pooling, denotes as *MAX*. The element $z_c$ of statistic $z \in \mathbb{R}^{C_l}$ is calculated by Eq. (6):

$$z_c = F_{sq}(x_c^{(l)}) = MAX(x_c^{(l)}) \quad c = 1, 2, ...C_l \tag{6}$$

After squeezing out the global spatio-temporal information, the excitation operation uses two FC layers to learn the non-linear interaction. To control network complexity, the first FC layer encodes $z$ into a smaller space and the next FC layer decodes it back to the original space. The reduction ratio is denoted as $r$, and the weights of these FC layers are denoted as $W_1 \in \mathbb{R}^{\frac{C_l}{r} \times C_l}$, $W_2 \in \mathbb{R}^{C_l \times \frac{C_l}{r}}$. $\sigma$ denotes the sigmoid function and $\delta$ denotes the relu function. After excitation operation, a vector $s \in \mathbb{R}^{C_l}$ is calculated as:

$$s = F_{ex}(z, W) = \sigma(W_2 \delta(W_1 z)) \tag{7}$$

In the end, as defined in Eq. (8), channel-wise multiplication and residual link [7] are conducted between $s$ and $X_C^{(l)}$ to get the refined feature maps denoted as $\tilde{X}_C^{(l)} \in \mathbb{R}^{C_l \times d \times I \times J}$. It can be rewritten as $\tilde{X}_C^{(l)} = \{\tilde{x}_1^{(l)}, \tilde{x}_2^{(l)}, ..., \tilde{x}_{C_l}^{(l)}\}$, where $\circ$ is the element-wise multiplication and $\tilde{x}_c^{(l)}$ refers to the refined output of the $c^{th}$ filter in the $l^{th}$ layer.

$$\tilde{x}_c^{(l)} = s_c \circ x_c^{(l)} + x_c^{(l)} \quad c = 1, 2, ...C_l \tag{8}$$

## 4 Experiments

### 4.1 Computing Environment and Datasets

In terms of the computing environment, the following experiments were conducted on a server with 16 physical cores (Intel Xeon Silver 4110 @ 2.10 GHz) and two

GPUs (RTX 2080Ti). The software environment uses python 3.8.5 with pytorch 1.7.1, pytorch-lightning 1.1.8, and statsmodels 0.12.2 with Windows10 20H1 to build models.

This article uses two high way traffic datasets collected by the Caltrans Performance Measurement System (PeMS). PeMS collects real-time data samples every 30-s and aggregated them into 5-min time interval. Table 1 shows the details of these datasets. The raster sizes are set to (42, 34) and (20, 36) so that each grid is 5 km × 5 km. At first, detectors with any empty records are eliminated from the dataset. After converting the traffic data into spatio-temporal traffic raster data, min-max normalization is adopted to scale the value between zero to one. Then, the raster data is converted to the multi-channel data structure. Finally, the dataset is divided into training data and testing data under the ratio of 8:2, then 20% of the training data is cut out as validation data.

**Table 1.** Descriptions of the two high way traffic datasets

| Dataset | PeMSD4 | PeMSD7 |
| --- | --- | --- |
| Location | San Francisco Bay Area | District 7 of California |
| Number of detectors | 3796 | 4817 |
| Time span | 1st Jun 2017–30th Jun 2017 | 1st Jun 2017–30th Jun 2017 |
| Time interval | 5-min | 5-min |
| Raster size | (42, 34) | (20, 36) |
| Available time points | 8640 | 8640 |

### 4.2 Baselines and Benchmarks

The proposed method is compared with the following six baseline methods:

- HA: The predicted values are estimated with four historical time points.
- ARIMA: A classic statical model for time series prediction. It uses the order of (0, 1, 1) according to the previous study [17].
- CNN: CNN uses two 2D convolutional layers (valid padding) with a kernel size of three, a filer num of 128 and 64, and a stride of one; two max pooling layers are used with a kernel size of two and a stride of two; and one FC layer with serval neurons.
- ConvLSTM: Convolutional LSTM is a variation of LSTM which is good at capturing spatio-temporal correlations [16]. It uses three layers (same padding) with a filter num of six, a kernel size of three, and a stride of two.
- ST-Resnet: A fully convolutional method uses 12 residual units; each contains a 2D convolutional layer (same padding) with a filter num of 64, a kernel size of three, and a stride of one. And a multi-branch feature fusion strategy is also used.
- LMST3D-ResNet: An improved version of ST-Resnet. It uses three residual units, each contains a 3D convolutional layer (same padding) with a filter num of 64, a kernel size of three, and a stride of one; and a 3D max pooling layer uses a kernel size of (2, 3, 3), the stride of one, and a padding size of (0, 1, 1). Two FC layers are used in the last. A dropout rate of 20% is used to avoid overfitting.

For fairness, all methods use the same computing environment with four historical time points to make future predictions. All deep learning-based methods share the same hyperparameter setting with a learning rate of 1e-4 and a batch size of 64. They are trained for 200 epochs by Adam optimizer [11] with $l1$ loss as defined in Eq. (9), where $I$ and $J$ are the width and height of the grid map, $\hat{x}^{i,j}_{t+\Delta t}$ refers to predicted value and $x^{i,j}_{t+\Delta t}$ is ground truth. The model with a minimal loss value is kept as final model.

$$Loss = \frac{1}{I \times J} \sum_{j=1}^{J} \sum_{i=1}^{I} \left| x^{i,j}_{t+\Delta t} - \hat{x}^{i,j}_{t+\Delta t} \right| \tag{9}$$

Root Mean Squared Error (RMSE) and Mean Absolute Error (MAE) are used to measure the forecast performance. As defined in Eq. (10) and Eq. (11), $n$ is the number of ground truths at time point $t + \Delta t$, $\hat{x}^i_{t+\Delta t}$ and $x^i_{t+\Delta t}$ are the rescaled predicted value and the corresponding ground truth.

$$RMSE = \sqrt{\frac{1}{n} \sum_{i=1}^{n} (x^i_{t+\Delta t} - \hat{x}^i_{t+\Delta t})^2} \tag{10}$$

$$MAE = \frac{1}{n} \sum_{i=1}^{n} \left| x^i_{t+\Delta t} - \hat{x}^i_{t+\Delta t} \right| \tag{11}$$

## 5   Results and Analysis

This section shows the results in predicting the traffic flow in the next 15-min with the grid size of 5 km × 5 km. The proposed CAMPConv-MC uses three 3D convolutional units and three SE units. All convolutional layers (same padding) use 64 filters, a kernel size of three, and a stride of one. The reduction ratio $r$ for SE units is four.

### 5.1   Experimental Results on PeMSD4

**Comparison with Baseline Methods.** The results on the PeMSD4 dataset are listed in Table 2, where the proposed CAMPConv-MC beats all other methods. The worst are HA and ARIMA due to the neglect of spatial dependencies. Despite CNN and ConvL-STM considering spatial dependencies, they have a significant drawback as they only consider spatial dependencies of nearby regions. On the contrary, ST-Resnet considers the long-distance spatial dependency using residual units. But 2D convolution fails to preserve temporal information for it treats the temporal axis as multiple channels. LMST3D-ResNet replaces 2D convolution with 3D convolution to preserve more temporal information. However, LMST3D-ResNet suffered from over-parameterization and information loss due to the multi-branch feature fusion strategy and massive usage of max pooling layers, even regularization techniques like dropout can't fundamentally

**Table 2.** Performance comparison on PeMSD4 (The best values are marked in bold)

| Methods | MAE | RMSE |
|---|---|---|
| HA | 21.425 | 28.406 |
| ARIMA | 20.221 | 27.410 |
| CNN | 15.540 | 21.027 |
| ConvLSTM | 18.689 | 25.047 |
| ST-Resnet | 14.822 | 20.399 |
| LMST3D-Resnet | 13.948 | 19.798 |
| **CAMPConv-MC** | **13.464** | **18.832** |

solve it. The proposed CAMPConv-MC capture the correlations between different periodic dependencies and the channel inter-dependencies. It achieves the best performance without any max pooling layers or a massive usage of parameters. To investigate the effectiveness of each part, an ablation study is conducted in next section.

**Ablation Study of CAMPConv-MC.** This section tests a few variants of the CAMPConv-MC with a new metric called Time, which refers to the training time. A fully convolutional network made up of multiple 3D convolutional units (M3D) trained on a single-channel data structure is used as a baseline. M3D-CA denotes baseline plus SE unit, M3D-MP denotes baseline plus mixed-pointwise convolution, and M3D-MC denotes baseline plus multi-channel data structure. Expect for M3D-MP, all models use the kernel of size $(2, 3, 3)$ and the padding of size $(0, 1, 1)$ to compress temporal channels into one. Table 3 proves that every part of the proposed model is effective compared with M3D. When compared to M3D, M3D-MC has superior MAE and RMSE with nearly equal training times while not using any branch, demonstrating the high efficiency of the proposed data structure. M3D-MC has a larger RMSE but a substantially lower MAE when compared to M3D-MP. This showed that the spatio-temporal correlations can improve forecast performance in extreme conditions thus increasing the robustness. Additionally, M3D-CA outperforms M3D proves the necessity of considering the channel inter-dependencies and the validity of the improved SE units.

**Table 3.** Effects of different components of the proposed method

| Methods | Time (Minutes) | MAE | RMSE |
|---|---|---|---|
| M3D | **9.666** | 16.926 | 26.174 |
| M3D-MC | 9.672 | 14.789 | 24.034 |
| M3D-CA | 12.219 | 15.801 | 24.987 |
| M3D-MP | 22.858 | 15.173 | 20.876 |
| CAMPConv-MC | 27.146 | **13.464** | **18.832** |

## 5.2   Experimental Results on PeMSD7

**Comparison with Baseline Methods.** The results of PeMSD7 are similar to PeMSD4. As shown in Table 4, CAMPConv-MC consistently outperforms other baseline methods. Because the raster size of PeMSD7 is smaller than PeMSD4, the forecast errors on PeMSD7 are smaller than PeMSD4. The proposed CAMPConv-MC performs well on both datasets, yielding strong robustness under different raster sizes. To further prove the advantages of CAMPConv-MC, a scalability analysis is conducted in the next section.

**Table 4.**  Performance comparison on PeMSD7

| Methods | MAE | RMSE |
|---|---|---|
| HA | 20.883 | 25.325 |
| ARIMA | 18.518 | 23.084 |
| CNN | 14.591 | 18.745 |
| ConvLSTM | 16.701 | 21.320 |
| ST-Resnet | 13.576 | 18.041 |
| LMST3D-Resnet | 13.497 | 17.752 |
| **CAMPConv-MC** | **12.408** | **16.126** |

**Scalability Analysis.** Table 5 and Table 6 show the results of RMSE under different grid sizes and time intervals. For fairness, one setting is changed while the other is kept unchanged. As shown in Table 5, forecast errors decrease as the grid size enlarges. This is because, given a fixed transportation network, a smaller grid size can generate more grids to be predicted. At the scale of 10 km × 10 km, ST-Resnet and LMST3D-Resnet don't vary a lot compared with CNN. This is due to the grid map becoming too small. At this scale, even CNN can discern the long-distance spatial dependencies. As shown in Table 6, forecast errors increase as time intervals enlarge. This is due to the fact that a larger time interval will result in more temporal uncertainty. For instance, when the time interval is 30-min, the increased temporal uncertainty narrowed the performance gap between LMST3D-Resnet and ST-Resnet. However, the proposed methods consistently outperform all other deep learning-based methods, displaying the highest robustness regardless of grid size and time interval.

**Table 5.** RMSE under different grid sizes (time interval of 15-min)

| Methods | 2.5 km × 2.5 km | 5 km × 5 km | 10 km × 10 km |
|---|---|---|---|
| CNN | 22.266 | 18.745 | 15.810 |
| ConvLSTM | 25.330 | 21.320 | 19.065 |
| ST-Resnet | 25.332 | 18.041 | 15.384 |
| LMST3D-Resnet | 19.931 | 17.752 | 15.556 |
| **CAMPConv-MC** | **18.524** | **16.126** | **15.242** |

**Table 6.** RMSE under different time intervals (grid size of 5 km × 5 km)

| Methods | 5-min | 15-min | 30-min |
|---|---|---|---|
| CNN | 18.244 | 18.745 | 19.981 |
| ConvLSTM | 19.822 | 21.320 | 23.840 |
| ST-Resnet | 18.093 | 18.041 | 18.645 |
| LMST3D-Resnet | 17.818 | 17.752 | 18.440 |
| **CAMPConv-MC** | **17.030** | **16.126** | **17.069** |

# 6 Conclusions and Future Work

In this article, a novel CAMPConv-MC is proposed for short-term traffic flow prediction. A novel multi-channel data structure is proposed to efficiently build periodic dependencies of traffic data. Then, a new mixed-pointwise convolution is proposed to capture the spatio-temporal correlations and periodic dependencies, and an improved channel attention mechanism adapted from traditional SE unit is used to learn the channel interdependencies. Extensive experiments on two real-world datasets show that the proposed method exceeds the state-of-the-art methods in robustness and performance.

However, there are some limitations to this article. As grid size goes up, the sparsification of grid maps is a problem. Moreover, the effects of external features and results on datasets from different countries are remains to be discussed in future work.

# References

1. Atluri, G., Karpatne, A., Kumar, V.: Spatio-temporal data mining: a survey of problems and methods. ACM Comput. Surv. **51**(4), Article. No. 83, 1–41 (2018)
2. Bai, S.J., Kolter, J.Z., Koltun, V.: An empirical evaluation of generic Convolutional and recurrent networks for sequence modeling. arXiv:1803.01271v2, https://arxiv.org/abs/1803.01271 (2018)
3. Chen, L., Zhang, H.W., Xiao, J., Nie, L.Q., Shao, J., Liu, W. et al.: SCA-CNN: spatial and channel-wise attention in convolutional networks for image captioning. In: Proceedings of the

2017 IEEE Conference on Computer Vision and Pattern Recognition (CVPR), 21–26 July, pp. 6298–6306. Honolulu, USA (2017)

4. Chen, Y.B., Zou, X.F., Li, K.L., Li, K.Q., Yang, X.L., Chen, C.: Multiple local 3D CNNs for region-based prediction in smart cities. Inf. Sci. **542**, 476–491 (2021)

5. Chollet, F.: Xception: deep learning with depthwise separable convolutions. In: Proceedings of the 2017 IEEE Conference on Computer Vision and Pattern Recognition (CVPR), 21–26 July, pp. 1800–1807. Honolulu, USA (2017)

6. Fu, R., Zhang, Z., Li, L.: Using LSTM and GRU neural network methods for traffic flow prediction. In: Proceedings of the 31st Youth Academic Annual Conference of Chinese Association of Automation (YAC), 11–13 November, pp. 324–328. Wuhan, China (2016)

7. He, K.M., Zhang, X.Y., Ren, S.Q., Sun, J.: Deep residual learning for image recognition. In: Proceedings of the 2016 IEEE Conference on Computer Vision and Pattern Recognition (CVPR), 27–30 June. pp. 770–778. Las Vegas, USA (2016)

8. Hu, J., Shen, L., Albanie, S., Sun, G., Wu, E.H.: Squeeze-and-excitation networks. IEEE Trans. Pattern Anal. Mach. Intell. **42**(8), 2011–2023 (2020)

9. Huang, W.H., Song, G.J., Hong, H.K., Xie, K.Q.: Deep architecture for traffic flow prediction: deep belief networks with multitask learning. IEEE Trans. Intell. Transp. Syst. **15**(5), 2191–2201 (2014)

10. Ioffe, S., Szegedy, C.: Batch normalization: accelerating deep network training by reducing internal covariate shift. In: Proceedings of the 32nd International Conference on Machine Learning (ICML), 6–11 July, pp. 448–456. Lille, France (2015)

11. Kingma, D.P., Ba, J.: Adam: a method for stochastic optimization. In: Proceedings of the 3rd International Conference on Learning Representations (ICLR), 7–9 May, pp. 1–15. San Diego, USA (2014)

12. Kuang, L., Yan, H., Zhu, Y.J., Tu, S.M., Fan, X.L.: Predicting duration of traffic accidents based on cost-sensitive Bayesian network and weighted K-nearest neighbor. J. Intell. Transp. Syst. **23**(2), 161–174 (2019)

13. Liu, Q.C., Wang, B.C., Zhu, Y.Q.: Short-term traffic speed forecasting based on attention convolutional neural network for arterials. Comput.-Aided Civil Infrast. Eng. **33**(11), 996–1016 (2018)

14. Lv, Y.S., Duan, Y.J., Kang, W.W., Li, Z.X., Wang, F.Y.: Traffic flow prediction with big data: a deep learning approach. IEEE Trans. Intell. Transp. Syst. **16**(2), 865–873 (2015)

15. Ma, X.L., Dai, Z., He, Z.B., Ma, J.H., Wang, Y., Wang, Y.P.: Learning traffic as images: a deep convolutional neural network for large-scale transportation network speed prediction. Sensors **17**(4), 818 (2017)

16. Shi, X.J., Chen, Z.R., Wang, H., Yeung, D.Y., Wong, W.K., Woo, W.C.: Convolutional LSTM network: A machine learning approach for precipitation nowcasting. In: Proceedings of the 28th International Conference on Neural Information Processing Systems (NIPS), 7–12 December, pp. 802–810, Montreal, Canada (2015)

17. Smith, B.L., Demetsky, M.J.: Traffic flow forecasting: comparison of modeling approaches. J. Transp. Eng. **123**(4), 261–266 (1997)

18. Wu, C.H., Ho, J.M., Lee, D.T.: Travel-time prediction with support vector regression. IEEE Trans. Intell. Transp. Syst. **5**(4), 276–281 (2004)

19. Zhang, J.B., Zheng, Y., Qi, D.K., Li, R.Y., Yi, X.W., Li, T.R.: Predicting citywide crowd flows using deep spatio-temporal residual networks. Artif. Intell. **259**, 147–166 (2018)

20. Zhang, S., Chen, Y., Zhang, W.Y., Feng, R.J.: A novel ensemble deep learning model with dynamic error correction and multi-objective ensemble pruning for time series forecasting. Inf. Sci. **544**, 427–445 (2021)

# Neural Architecture Search for Low-Precision Neural Networks

Binyi Wu[1,2]([✉])([iD]), Bernd Waschneck[2], and Christian Mayr[1]

[1] Dresden University of Technology, 01069 Dresden, Germany
{Binyi.Wu,Christian.Mayr}@tu-dresden.de
[2] Infineon Technologies AG, 01099 Dresden, Germany
{Binyi.Wu,Bernd.Waschneck}@infineon.com

**Abstract.** In our work, we extend the search space of the differentiable Neural Architecture Search (NAS) by adding bitwidth. The extended NAS algorithm is performed directly with low-precision from scratch without the proxy of full-precision. With our low-precision NAS, we can search for low- and mixed-precision network architectures of Convolutional Neural Networks (CNNs) under specific constraints, such as power consumption. Experiments on the ImageNet dataset demonstrate the effectiveness of our method, where the searched models achieve better accuracy (up to 1.2 percentage point) with smaller model sizes (up to 27% smaller) and lower power consumption (up to 27% lower) compared to the state-of-art methods. In our low-precision NAS, sharing of convolution is developed to speed up training and decrease memory consumption. Compared to the FBNet-V2 implementation, our solution reduces training time and memory cost by nearly 3× and 2×, respectively. Furthermore, we adapt the NAS to train the entire supernet instead of a subnet in each iteration to address the insufficient training issue. Besides, we also propose the forward-and-backward scaling method, which addresses the issue by eliminating the vanishing of the forward activations and backward gradients.

**Keywords:** Neural Architecture Search · Low- and mixed-precision · Convolutional Neural Network

## 1 Introduction

In edge AI applications, deploying Convolution Neural Networks (CNNs) is strictly constrained by latency, energy, and model size. To improve the efficiency of CNNs, different optimization methods have been proposed, for example quantization [7,22] and neural architecture search (NAS) [3,13,19]. The former optimizes the neural networks at the arithmetic level while the latter performs optimization on the architectural. Recent research [18,20,21,23] has started exploiting the power of NAS to search for hybrid precision network models. However, most have no or only a weak ability to search the network architecture, as shown in Table 1. Therefore, in this work, we introduce the bitwidth search space into

© The Author(s), under exclusive license to Springer Nature Switzerland AG 2022
E. Pimenidis et al. (Eds.): ICANN 2022, LNCS 13532, pp. 743–755, 2022.
https://doi.org/10.1007/978-3-031-15937-4_62

NAS while keeping the other search spaces, enabling network architecture search for low- and mixed-precision networks. With the introduction of the bitwidth space, the number of candidate networks grows exponentially. It increases the NAS cost dramatically and thus makes the training more difficult. The increased NAS cost is due to the convolutions of mixed-precision activations and weights. To reduce it, we propose the method of sharing convolutions, which executes only one convolution on different precision activations and weights.

Most previous works [18,20,21,23] require pre-trained full-precision models as a proxy. However, we hypothesize that low-precision networks prefer different network architectures than full-precision networks. Therefore, our proposed NAS is directly trained with low-precision, avoiding the proxy of full-precision NAS.

One of the difficulties of differentiable architecture search (DARTS) training arises from the dominance issue of simpler operations, which prevents NAS from choosing complex ones [26]. To tackle this issue, we train the entire supernet instead of subnets at each iteration, increasing the number of traversals of each operation. The therefore increased computation overhead can be addressed by the sharing of convolution. Besides, we propose the forward-and-backward scaling method to address the insufficient training through maintaining forward activations and backward gradients. The main contributions of our work are:

- We introduce the bitwidth search space into the current NAS algorithm without sacrificing other NAS search spaces, which enables NAS to explore mixed-precision networks. With sharing of convolutions, the formed supernet is more memory- and computation-efficient, compared to FBNet-V2 [19].
- We address the well-known issue of DARTS-based NAS converging to simpler operations by training the entire supernet in each iteration and proposing the forward-and-backward scaling method.

The rest of the paper is organized as follows: Sect. 2 introduces the background and related work. The sharing of convolution, insight into the dominance issue, and solutions will be in Sect. 3. Section 4 demonstrates the experimental results. The conclusion section completes the paper.

**Table 1.** Search space comparison: layers ($l$), channels ($c$), expansion rate ($e$), kernel size ($k$), nonlinearity ($f_a$), binarization (*binary*) and multi-bit quantization (*bultibit*).

| Method | $l$ | $c$ | $e$ | $k$ | $f_a$ | binary | multibit |
|---|---|---|---|---|---|---|---|
| ProxylessNAS (2018) [3] | | x | x | x | x | | |
| FBNetV2 (2020) [19] | x | x | x | x | x | | |
| BATS (2020) [2] | x | x | | x | x | x | |
| SPNAS (2020) [9] | | x | x | | | x | x |
| MixedDNNs (2020) [18] | | | | | | x | x |
| HAWQ-V3 (2021) [23] | | | | | | x | x |
| **Ours** | **x** | **x** | **x** | **x** | **x** | **x** | **x** |

## 2    Background and Related Work

Network quantization optimizes basic operation and compresses the model by reducing the computational complexity to integers. For 1-bit quantization, BNN [5] binarized the models but sacrificed accuracy. In Bi-Real-Net and its variants [1,14], the accuracy gap with the full-precision was closed by introducing shortcut connections for every convolution. ReActiNet [15] further improved the performance of binary networks with the help of dedicated networks and learned activation distribution changes. Multi-bit quantization from Esser et al. [7] utilized the power of gradients to quantize both activations and weights. It narrows the accuracy drop of 3-bit-quantization to be less than 1%. Wu et al. [22] presented the first work to apply the attention mechanism for activation quantization.

Neural Architecture Search (NAS) optimizes the network at the architecture level based on specific metrics, such as accuracy, latency, power consumption, etc. Early NAS approach [27] used reinforcement learning (RL) or evolutionary algorithms (EA). However, they consume thousands of GPU hours. Later, Liu et al. [13] proposed a differentiable architecture search (DARTS), which is gradient-based, to lower the computation cost. Gradient-based NAS requires instantiating all candidates in memory, increasing memory usage and limiting the search space. In FBNet-V2, Wan et al. [19] proposed channel and feature reuse to reduce memory consumption and thus increase the search space. Besides, DARTS-based NAS often prefers simpler operations over other candidates. Zhou et al. [26] proved this is because the supernet is undertrained. Thus the subnet with simpler operations converges faster to win the competition. They proposed a path-regularized DARTS to address this issue.

Mixed-precision quantization is a more popular method for quantizing networks recently. Wang et al. [20] proposed a framework that utilized reinforcement learning to automatically search for the best mixed-precision policy on MobileNet-V2 [17] while taking the latency into account. Furthermore, Wang et al. [21] proposed APQ that jointly searches the neural Architecture, Pruning policy, and Quantization policy through sampling from a pretrained network. In HAWQ-V3, Yao et al. [23] proposed a novel integer-only quantization framework for mixed-precision neural networks. While Uhlich et al. [18] parameterize the quantizer with step size and dynamic range for mixed-precision networks.

## 3    Method

In this section, we first explain how to share a convolution and the benefits it brings. Then we discuss why the simple candidate operations dominate in the competition and how to resolve it. Low-precision networks are mainly for edge applications, so in the final subsection, we introduce how to incorporate power consumption into NAS.

## 3.1   Shared Mixed-Precision Convolution Block

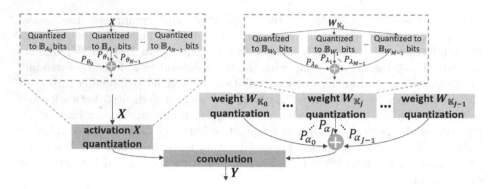

**Fig. 1.** The sharing of convolution on different precision activations and different precision weights with different kernel size

Figure 1 demonstrates the sharing of convolution on different precision activations and different precision weights with different kernel sizes. $\mathbf{X}$ and $\mathbf{Y}$ are the input and output activations, respectively. $\mathbb{B}_A$ is the activation bitwidth search space with $N$ options. $\mathbb{B}_W$ is the weight bitwidth search space with $M$ options. $\mathbb{K}$ is the kernel size search space with $J$ options. $\mathbf{W}_{\mathbb{K}_j}$ is the weight with kernel size $\mathbb{K}_j$. $\mathbf{P}_\theta = \{\mathbf{P}_{\theta_0}, \mathbf{P}_{\theta_1}...\mathbf{P}_{\theta_{N-1}}\}$, $\mathbf{P}_\lambda = \{\mathbf{P}_{\lambda_0}...\mathbf{P}_{\lambda_i}...\mathbf{P}_{\lambda_{M-1}}\}$, and $\mathbf{P}_\alpha = \{\mathbf{P}_{\alpha_0}, \mathbf{P}_{\alpha_1}...\mathbf{P}_{\alpha_{J-1}}\}$ are the sampling probabilities of activation bitwidth, weight kernel size and weight bitwidth, respectively.

$$\mathbf{Y} = \left(\sum_{n=0}^{N-1} P_{\theta_n} \mathcal{Q}\left(\mathbf{X}, \mathbb{B}_{A_n}\right)\right) \otimes \left(\sum_{j=0}^{J-1} P_{\alpha_j} \mathcal{E}\left(\sum_{m=0}^{M-1} P_{\lambda_m} \mathcal{Q}\left(\mathbf{W}_{\mathbb{K}_j}, \mathbb{B}_{W_m}\right)\right)\right), \quad (1)$$

where $\otimes$ is convolution, $\mathcal{Q}(\mathbf{T}, b)$ is the method that quantizes input $\mathbf{T}$ to $b$-bit integers while $\mathcal{E}(*)$ is the method that expands the quantized weights to the maximum kernel size by padding zero around the border. The corresponding activation and weight quantization methods are from STQ [22]. With sharing of convolution, we reduce the required convolutions from $N \times J \times M$ to only one. The corresponding output size is also reduced by a factor of $N \times J \times M$. The cost of the weight expansion operation $\mathcal{E}(*)$ only introduces marginal overhead, compared to the savings.

## 3.2   Forward-and-Backward Scaling

We observe that skip connections and small kernel convolutions account for a large proportion of the selected operations in the final model, whose achievable accuracy is far from the baseline models. It suggests that the dominance problem of DARTS-based NAS significantly limits the searched models. Due to insufficient training, simple operations show an advantage over other candidates in the competition [26]. To solve this problem, we propose another two methods.

**Firstly**, we train the entire supernet instead of a subnet in each iteration. One drawback of DARTS-based NAS is that it consumes massive memory since candidates must be explicitly instantiated. ProxylessNAS [3] first proposed to train only one subnet in each iteration, reducing the instantiated candidates. After that, training subnets became popular. However, our supernet contains much more candidate subnets and requires more iterations to converge, leading to a much longer training time. Therefore, we instead train the entire supernet. The resulting massive memory requirement is mitigated by the convolution sharing in Subsect. 3.1 and the activation-and-channel reuse proposed in FBNet-V2 [19].

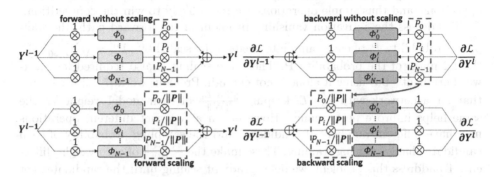

**Fig. 2.** Forward-and-backward scaling. $\mathbf{\Phi} = \{\Phi_0, ..., \Phi_i, ...\Phi_{N-1}\}$ is the candidate operation, whereas $\mathbf{\Phi}' = \{\Phi_0', ..., \Phi_i', ...\Phi_{N-1}'\}$ is the corresponding derivative. $\mathbf{P} = \{P_0, ..., P_i, ..., P_{N-1}\}$ is the sampling probability of candidate operations. $P_i = g_{w_i} = \frac{\exp[(w_i+n_i)/\tau]}{\sum_{j=1}^{N-1} \exp[(w_j+n_j)/\tau]}$, with architecture parameter $\mathbf{W_A} = \{w_0..w_{N-1}\}$, Gumbel noise $n_0..n_{N-1}$ (i.i.d samples drawn from Gumbel$(0,1)$) and temperature $\tau$.

**Secondly**, we propose forward-and-backward scaling shown in Fig. 2 to maintain the variance of forwarding activations and backward gradients across the entire supernet. Without scaling, the variance of the activations becomes smaller with forward propagation, while the gradient vanishes with backward propagation. We explain how they decay below. The widely used He initialization [10] ensures that a candidate in a searchable operation has

$$\text{Var}\left(\mathbf{Y}_i^l\right) = \text{Var}\left(\mathbf{Y}^{l-1}\right), \tag{2}$$

where $\mathbf{Y}^{l-1}$ is the output of the previous layer and $\mathbf{Y}_i^l$ is the output of the $i_{th}$ candidate. If $N$ candidate outputs of a searchable operation are independent, according to the rules of the sum of independent random variables, we have

$$\text{Var}\left(\mathbf{Y}^l\right) = \sum_{i=0}^{N-1} P_i^2 \text{Var}\left(\mathbf{Y}_i^{l-1}\right) = \text{Var}\left(\mathbf{Y}^{l-1}\right) \sum_{i=0}^{N-1} P_i^2. \tag{3}$$

Due to $\sum_{i=0}^{N-1} P_i^2 \leq \sum_{i=0}^{N-1} P_i = 1$, therefore

$$\text{Var}\left(\mathbf{Y}^l\right) \leq \text{Var}\left(\mathbf{Y}^{l-1}\right). \tag{4}$$

As the network deepens, the output variance gradually decreases. The lower magnitude of activations make the training harder.

Using the chain rule of backpropagation, the vanishing gradient can be concluded as follows

$$\text{Var}\left(\frac{\partial \mathcal{L}}{\partial \mathbf{Y}^{l-1}}\right) = \text{Var}\left(\frac{\partial \mathcal{L}}{\partial \mathbf{Y}^{l}}\right) \sum_{i=0}^{N-1} P_i^2 \le \text{Var}\left(\frac{\partial \mathcal{L}}{\partial \mathbf{Y}^{l}}\right). \tag{5}$$

Layers close to the final output are less affected, but layers close to the input will be severely affected. Vanishing gradient is not sufficient to optimize complex operations, and thus simple operations are more likely to win the competition.

To address the activation vanishing problem in the forward path, the sampling probability $P_i$ of each candidate needs to be scaled by $\|\mathbf{P}\| = \sqrt{\sum_{i=0}^{N-1} P_i^2}$, the L2 norm of the probability $\mathbf{P}$. The same scaling is also required for backward gradients, but using it alone is not enough. Previous work [7,24] has shown that for a network with loss $\mathcal{L}$, keeping $\frac{\|\nabla_{\mathbf{W}}\mathcal{L}\|}{\|\mathbf{W}\|}$ of each model weight $\mathbf{W}$ the same helps improve performance. However, in a supernet different operations may have different numbers of candidates and the sampling probability of each candidate changes during training. These make the $\frac{\|\nabla_{\mathbf{W}}\mathcal{L}\|}{\|\mathbf{W}\|}$ of each weight different. To address this problem, we defer gradient scaling until the candidates get gradients. The final proposed forward-and-backward scaling method is shown in Fig. 2.

### 3.3 Power Estimation

Power consumption is essential in edge applications. To estimate power consumption, we define a general machine learning accelerator similar to most current machine accelerators [25]. By estimating the number of MAC and memory operations required by the accelerator, then multiplying with the power consumption of each MAC and memory operation [16], respectively, the total power consumption can be roughly estimated. To let the search algorithm take this into account, we define the loss function used in the architecture training as

$$\mathcal{L} = CE\left(\mathbf{W}_M, \mathbf{W}_A\right) + \alpha \left(\frac{\mathcal{J}_{Exp}\left(\mathbf{W}_A\right) - \mathcal{J}_{ref}}{\mathcal{J}_{ref}}\right)^{\beta} \text{sigmoid}\left(\mathcal{J}_{Exp}\left(\mathbf{W}_A\right) - \mathcal{J}_{ref}\right).$$

The first term $CE(\mathbf{W}_M, \mathbf{W}_A)$ is the cross-entropy loss of the model parameters $\mathbf{W}_M$ and the architecture parameters $\mathbf{W}_A$. The second term is the loss caused by the power consumption. It is close to zero (no punishment) when the expected power of supernet $\mathcal{J}_{Exp}(\mathbf{W}_A)$ does not exceed the reference power $\mathcal{J}_{ref}$ defined by users. Hyperparameters $\alpha$ and $\beta$ control the contribution of the power loss to the total loss $\mathcal{L}$. The expected power of the supernet $\mathcal{J}_{Exp}(\mathbf{W}_A)$ is the weighted sum of the power of all operations. The corresponding weight is the sampling probability derived from $\mathbf{W}_A$.

# 4    Experiments

In this section, we provide experimental results to prove the feasibility of our method. To speed up the development, we first study the low-precision NAS on the small dataset CIFAR-10 [12]. When it performs well enough, we move on to the medium-sized Tiny ImageNet dataset. Finally, we move on to ImageNet [6]. Like previous work [3,19], the training data is randomly split into two parts, 80% of which is allocated for model training and the rest is for architecture training.

## 4.1    Effectiveness of Dominance Problem Solutions

Table 2 shows the effectiveness of the two solutions proposed in Subsect. 3.2. The searched result is indicated with "$(K_0, K_1, K_2), C_e, C_o$". $K_0$, $K_1$, $K_2$ are the kernel size of the three convolutions in the residual branch. $K = 0$ means skip connection. $C_e$ and $C_o$ are the expansion and output channels, respectively. Column $MAX$ shows the largest setting. Row "Accuracy" shows the top-1 accuracy in percentage of the full-precision and 1-bit models as "full/1-bit".

**Table 2.** Effectiveness of the methods (searching for 1-bit model on Tiny-ImageNet)

| Method | V1 | V2 | V3 | MAX |
|---|---|---|---|---|
| InputBlock | K=1, $C_o = 32$ | K=1, $C_o = 32$ | K=3, $C_o = 32$ | K=5, $C_o = 32$ |
| ResBlock | (1, 0, 1), 32, 32 | (3, 0, 1), 16, 16 | (5, 0, 5), 48, 64 | (5, 5, 5), 64, 64 |
| ResBlock | (1, 0, 1), 32, 32 | (3, 0, 3), 16, 16 | (5, 5, 5), 96, 128 | (5, 5, 5), 128, 128 |
| ResBlock | (1, 0, 1), 64, 64 | (3, 3, 5), 32, 224 | (5, 5, 5), 192, 256 | (5, 5, 5), 256, 256 |
| ResBlock | (1, 5, 5), 128, 256 | (5, 5, 5), 64, 512 | (5, 5, 5), 384, 448 | (5, 5, 5), 512, 512 |
| Accuracy | 21.53/21.65 | 56.07/39.15 | 60.45/55.84 | 60.7/56.45 |

Previous work has shown that larger models have stronger abstractions and therefore achieve higher accuracy [11,17]. In this experiment, no constraints on power consumption or model size are set. Therefore, the expected searched model should be close to the largest model. $V1$ uses the training method from ProxylessNAS [3], sampling one subnet in each iteration, whereas $V2$ trains the supernet instead. $V3$ adds the forward-and-backward scaling in addition to $V2$. As can be seen from the comparison of $V1$ and $V2$ training the entire supernet helps overcome the insufficient training problem (most kernel grows up to three), but there is still much room for improvement. With the forward-and-backward scaling in $V3$, most kernel sizes and output channels choose the largest configuration. The corresponding top-1 accuracy also corroborates the effectiveness of our methods in solving the dominance problem.

## 4.2    Search for Models

We apply our low-precision NAS to different datasets. After NAS, we first train the searched model with full precision and then quantize it. The quantization hyperparameter settings are the same as STQ [22].

The results on CIFAR-10 are shown in Table 3. Compared to the 1- and 2-bit baseline models, our searched 1- and 2-bit models (CI_B and CI_T) improve accuracy by 1.6 and 0.8 percentage points, respectively, while consuming less energy and taking up less storage. The mixed-precision model CI_M exhibits the highest efficiency, consuming less energy (42.6% reduction) than the 1-bit baseline model, and achieving similar accuracy to the full-precision baseline model (only 0.1 percentage point degradation).

**Table 3.** Models on CIFAR-10. Model CI_B, CI_T, and CI_M are 1-bit, 2-bit, and mixed-precision models, respectively. We abbreviate Top-1 accuracy as "Top-1", power consumption per inference as "Energy" (in µJ), and model size as "Size" (in MB). Column "Bitwidth" shows the activation and weight quantization bitwidth. "mixed" indicates the model is mixed precision. The full-precision ResNet-10 has a top-1 accuracy of **90.3%**. Its low-precision models are quantized with STQ [22].

| Model | 1-bit or equivalent | | | | 2-bit or equivalent | | | |
|---|---|---|---|---|---|---|---|---|
| | Bitwidth | Top-1 | Energy | Size | Bitwidth | Top-1 | Energy | Size |
| ResNet-10 | 1 | 87.6 | 85.6 | 0.66 | 2 | 89.6 | 281.8 | 1.25 |
| **CI_B (ours)** | **1** | **89.2** | **61.7** | **0.63** | - | - | - | - |
| **CI_T (ours)** | - | - | - | - | **2** | **90.4** | **216.6** | **1.10** |
| **CI_M (ours)** | - | - | - | - | **Mixed** | **90.2** | **49.1** | **0.60** |

Table 4 shows the comparison with the state-of-art methods on the ImageNet dataset. Compared to other methods, our 2- and 3-bit equivalent models (IM_M_1 and IM_M_2) exhibit the best classification accuracy while consuming the least amount of energy and occupying the least storage space. Specifically, the model IM_M_1 improves the accuracy by 1.2 percentage points while consuming 13.9% less energy and 26.9% less storage space. Model IM_M_2, on the other hand, improves accuracy by 0.4 percentage points, reduces power consumption by 26.8%, and reduces memory footprint by up to 24.0%.

**Table 4.** Comparison on ImageNet. "Energy" (in mJ) and "Size" (in MB) include the input and output layer. However, "Bitwidth" does not include them. All the comparison models are based ResNet-18, whose full-precision model has a top-1 accuracy of **69.7%**.

| Method | 2-bit or equivalent | | | | 3-bit or equivalent | | | |
|---|---|---|---|---|---|---|---|---|
| | Bitwidth | Top-1 | Energy | Size | Bitwidth | Top-1 | Energy | Size |
| PACT (2018) [4] | 2 | 64.4 | 2.37 | 4.69 | 3 | 68.1 | 4.37 | 6.02 |
| DSQ (2019) [8] | 2 | 65.2 | 2.37 | 4.69 | 3 | 68.7 | 4.37 | 6.02 |
| STQ (2021) [22] | 2 | 66.7 | 2.37 | 4.69 | 3 | 68.8 | 4.37 | 6.02 |
| LSQ (2020) [7] | 2 | 67.6 | 2.37 | 4.69 | 3 | 70.2 | 4.37 | 6.02 |
| Mixed (2020) [18] | - | - | - | - | Mixed | 70.0 | - | 5.40 |
| HAWQ-V3 (2021) [23] | - | - | - | - | Mixed | 70.4 | - | 6.70 |
| **IM_M_1 (ours)** | **Mixed** | **68.8** | **2.04** | **3.43** | - | - | - | - |
| **IM_M_2 (ours)** | - | - | - | - | **Mixed** | **70.8** | **3.20** | **5.09** |

A memory operation consumes much more energy than a MAC operation (10–100 times) [16]. Therefore, to search for an efficient model, reducing memory operations is more effective than reducing MAC operations. Convolution (the main operation of CNNs) reuses weights on activations, which requires multiple transfers of weights from memory. Therefore, a compact model with fewer parameters will be more energy efficient. As we can see, our models on CIFAR-10 and ImageNet are consistent with the rule: smaller models consume less power. The specific search space of the models in ImageNet is in Table 5. The supernet starts with InputBlock, then a $3 \times 3$ pooling with a stride of 2 for down sampling. The residual branch in a residual block (ResBlock) contains three convolutions, the middle one is skippable. The transition convolution in the residual connection is searchable. The network ends with a non-searchable block, which consists of an average pooling and a fully connected layer in full-precision.

**Table 5.** Search space of IM_M_1 and IM_M_2 with activation bitwidth space $\mathbb{B}_A$, weight bitwidth space $\mathbb{B}_W$, kernel size space $\mathbb{K}$, expansion space $\mathbb{E}$, channel space $\mathbb{C}$ and activation space $\mathbb{F}$, number of blocks n and stride s. A tuple of three values (min, max, step) represents minimum, maximum, and step of the option. The expansion channel space is $(\mathbb{E}_{min} * \mathbb{C}_{min}, \mathbb{E}_{max} * \mathbb{C}_{max}, \mathbb{E}_{step} * \mathbb{C}_{min})$. N.A. stands for not available. N, R and S in activation space $\mathbb{F}$ are none, ReLU and Swish, respectively.

| Block | $\mathbb{B}_A/\mathbb{B}_W$ | $\mathbb{K}$ | $\mathbb{E}$ | $\mathbb{C}$ | $\mathbb{F}$ | n | s |
|---|---|---|---|---|---|---|---|
| InputBlock | 32 | 3, 5, 7 | N.A. | (32, 64, 8) | N, R, S | 1 | 2 |
| ResBlock | 1, 2, 4, 8 | 1, 3 | (0.5, 2.0, 0.5) | (32, 64, 8) | N, R, S | 2 | 1 |
| ResBlock | 1, 2, 4, 8 | 1, 3 | (0.5, 2.0, 0.5) | (64, 128, 16) | N, R, S | 2 | 2 |
| ResBlock | 1, 2, 4, 8 | 1, 3 | (0.5, 2.0, 0.5) | (128, 256, 32) | N, R, S | 2 | 2 |
| ResBlock | 1, 2, 4, 8 | 1, 3 | (0.5, 2.0, 0.5) | (256, 512, 64) | N, R, S | 2 | 2 |

From the architecture of model IM_M_2 in Table 6, we observe that the low-precision NAS with an energy constraint prefers a network with narrower weight bitwidth and narrower layers compared to ResNet. In particular, some kernels in the last two residual blocks are reduced to one to lower the number of parameters. Due to fewer parameters, the activation bit width becomes wider to maintain the accuracy. However, the overall activation size does not grow significantly since the channels are reduced. The result also reveals wider activation bitwidths are more relevant to accuracy than wider weight bitwidths or wider layers, which is consistent with previous work [18,23]. The mixed-precision models CI_M, IM_M_1, and IM_M_2 demonstrate that mixed-low-precision have better performance compared to single-low-precision, which also aligns with the finding in previous work [18,23]. Below, we list the difference between IM_M_2 and ResNet to better understand the preferences of low-precision networks:

1. Model IM_M_2 reduces the computation in the residual branch and transfers them to the residual connection: The kernel size of convolution in the residual

connection grows up to three. This shows that the convolution in the residual connection is important for low-precision networks.

2. The number of expansion channels of the first four residual blocks in IM_M_2 is larger than the number of output channels, and vice versa, which reveals that the extracted features at the beginning are more important for improving performance, and compressing them will affect the classification accuracy.

3. In the residual block of ResNet, there is no activation function at the end of the two branches, only a ReLU after they merge. Whereas IM_M_2 is different. We manually remove the activation functions at the end of the two branches in each block of IM_M_2 to have the same settings as ResNet, which results in an accuracy drop of about 0.4%. We believe low-precision networks rely more on nonlinear functions to extract abstract features.

**Table 6.** Architecture of IM_M_2. $(B_A, B_W, K, F)$ with activation bitwidth $B_A$, weight bitwidth $B_W$, kernel size $K$ and activation function $F$ is for describing a not-skipped convolution. A skipped convolution is noted as "None". $\text{CONV}_{\text{tran}}$ is the convolution in residual connection. $E$ is the expansion channel. $C$ is the output channel. $F_b$ is the activation at the end of the block. $I$ is the input feature size.

| Block | Residual Branch | $\text{CONV}_{\text{tran}}$ | $E$ | $C$ | $F_b$ | $I$ |
|---|---|---|---|---|---|---|
| InputBlock | (32, 32, 5, R) | N.A. | N.A. | 56 | N.A. | 224 |
| ResBlock | (8, 4, 1, S),    None    (8, 4, 3, S) | None | 96 | 56 | S | 56 |
| ResBlock | (4, 4, 3, R), (2, 2, 3, R), (4, 4, 3, S) | None | 112 | 56 | S | 56 |
| ResBlock | (4, 4, 3, R),    None    (8, 4, 3, R) | (8, 4, 3, N) | 112 | 80 | R | 28 |
| ResBlock | (4, 4, 3, R), (4, 4, 3, R), (4, 4, 3, S) | None | 96 | 80 | R | 28 |
| ResBlock | (4, 4, 3, S),    None    (8, 4, 3, R) | (8, 4, 3, N) | 192 | 224 | R | 14 |
| ResBlock | (4, 4, 3, R),    None    (8, 4, 3, R) | None | 224 | 224 | R | 14 |
| ResBlock | (8, 4, 3, S),    None    (8, 4, 1, N) | (8, 4, 3, N) | 384 | 448 | R | 7 |
| ResBlock | (8, 4, 1, S), (8, 4, 3, S), (8, 2, 3, N) | None | 448 | 448 | S | 7 |

By sharing the convolution, the cost of our low-precision NAS is not increased but reduced even with the introduction of the bitwidth search space. We implement the FBNet-V2 [19] and execute the cost comparison with our NAS as shown in Table 7. The used supernet has four residual blocks and the same search space as Table 5 except for the bitwidth space $\{1, 2, 4\}$. The experiments are done on CIFAR-10 and Tesla P40. As we can see, the proposed convolution sharing helps reduce the time cost and memory cost by nearly $3\times$ and $2\times$, respectively.

**Table 7.** NAS cost comparison between FBNet-V2 and our method. "time" is the average time required by single epoch training. "memory" indicates the maximum GPU memory usage.

| Method | FBNet-V2 [19] | Ours |
|--------|---------------|------|
| Time   | 35.5 min      | 8.5 min |
| Memory | 9.0 GB        | 3.2 GB |

# 5  Conclusion

In this paper, we introduce bitwidth space into NAS for searching efficient low-precision neural networks and develop shared convolution lowering the computation and memory cost. To address the dominance issue of simple operation, we train the entire supernet instead of subnets and propose the forward-and-backward scaling method. The experiments demonstrate that our proposed NAS can search for high-quality low-precision models and achieves state-of-art results.

**Acknowledgment.** We are grateful to the Centre for Information Services and High Performance Computing [Zentrum für Informationsdienste und Hochleistungsrechnen (ZIH)] TU Dresden for providing its facilities for high throughput calculations.

# References

1. Bethge, J., Bartz, C., Yang, H., Chen, Y., Meinel, C.: MeliusNet: Can binary neural networks achieve mobileNet-level accuracy? arXiv (2020)
2. Bulat, A., Martinez, B., Tzimiropoulos, G.: BATS: binary ArchitecTure search. In: Vedaldi, A., Bischof, H., Brox, T., Frahm, J.-M. (eds.) ECCV 2020. LNCS, vol. 12368, pp. 309–325. Springer, Cham (2020). https://doi.org/10.1007/978-3-030-58592-1_19
3. Cai, H., Zhu, L., Han, S.: ProxylessNAS: direct neural architecture search on target task and hardware. arXiv pp. 1–13 (2018)
4. Choi, J., Wang, Z., Venkataramani, S., Chuang, P.I., Srinivasan, V., Gopalakrishnan, K.: PACT: parameterized clipping activation for quantized neural networks. CoRR (2018)
5. Courbariaux, M., Hubara, I., Soudry, D., El-Yaniv, R., Bengio, Y.: Binarized neural networks: training deep neural networks with weights and activations constrained to +1 or −1 (2016)
6. Deng, J., Dong, W., Socher, R., Li, L.J., Li, K., Fei-Fei, L.: ImageNet: a large-scale Hierarchical image database. In: CVPR09 (2009)
7. Esser, S.K., McKinstry, J.L., Bablani, D., Appuswamy, R., Modha, D.S.: Learned step size quantization. In: 8th International Conference on Learning Representations, ICLR. OpenReview.net (2020)
8. Gong, R., et al.: Differentiable soft quantization: Bridging full-precision and low-bit neural networks. In: 2019 IEEE/CVF International Conference on Computer Vision, ICCV 2019, Seoul, Korea (South), October 27 - November 2, 2019, pp. 4851–4860. IEEE (2019)

9. Guo, Z., et al.: Single path one-shot neural architecture search with uniform sampling. In: Vedaldi, A., Bischof, H., Brox, T., Frahm, J.-M. (eds.) ECCV 2020. LNCS, vol. 12361, pp. 544–560. Springer, Cham (2020). https://doi.org/10.1007/978-3-030-58517-4_32

10. He, K., Zhang, X., Ren, S., Sun, J.: Delving deep into rectifiers: surpassing human-level performance on ImageNet classification. In: Proceedings of the IEEE International Conference on Computer Vision, pp. 1026–1034 (2015)

11. He, K., Zhang, X., Ren, S., Sun, J.: Deep residual learning for image recognition. In: Proceedings of the IEEE Computer Society Conference on Computer Vision and Pattern Recognition, pp. 770–778 (2016)

12. Krizhevsky, A.: Learning multiple layers of features from tiny images, Technical Report (2009)

13. Liu, H., Simonyan, K., Yang, Y.: DARTS: differentiable architecture search. arXiv pp. 1–13 (2018)

14. Liu, Z., Luo, W., Wu, B., Yang, X., Liu, W., Cheng, K.-T.: Bi-Real Net: binarizing deep network towards real-network performance. Int. J. Comput. Vis. **128**(1), 202–219 (2020). https://doi.org/10.1007/s11263-019-01227-8

15. Liu, Z., Shen, Z., Savvides, M., Cheng, K.-T.: ReActNet: towards precise binary neural network with generalized activation functions. In: Vedaldi, A., Bischof, H., Brox, T., Frahm, J.-M. (eds.) ECCV 2020. LNCS, vol. 12359, pp. 143–159. Springer, Cham (2020). https://doi.org/10.1007/978-3-030-58568-6_9

16. Horowitz, M.: Computing's energy problem (and what we can do about it). In: Digest of technical Papers - IEEE International Solid-State Circuits Conference, pp. 10–14 (2014)

17. Sandler, M., Howard, A., Zhu, M., Zhmoginov, A., Chen, L.C.: MobileNetV2: inverted residuals and linear bottlenecks. In: Proceedings of the IEEE Computer Society Conference on Computer Vision and Pattern Recognition, pp. 4510–4520 (2018)

18. Uhlich, S., et al.: Mixed precision DNNs: all you need is a good parametrization. In: 8th International Conference on Learning Representations, ICLR 2020, Addis Ababa, Ethiopia, 26–30 April 2020. OpenReview.net (2020)

19. Wan, A., et al.: FBNetV2: differentiable neural architecture search for spatial and channel dimensions. In: Proceedings of the IEEE Computer Society Conference on Computer Vision and Pattern Recognition (2020)

20. Wang, K., Liu, Z., Lin, Y., Lin, J., Han, S.: HAQ: hardware-aware automated quantization with mixed precision. Proceedings of the IEEE Computer Society Conference on Computer Vision and Pattern Recognition, pp. 8604–8612 (2019)

21. Wang, T., et al.: APQ: joint search for network architecture, pruning and quantization policy. In: Proceedings of the IEEE Computer Society Conference on Computer Vision and Pattern Recognition, pp. 2075–2084 (2020)

22. Wu, B., Waschneck, B., Mayr, C.: Squeeze-and-threshold based quantization for low-precision neural networks. In: Iliadis, L., Macintyre, J., Jayne, C., Pimenidis, E. (eds.) EANN 2021. PINNS, vol. 3, pp. 232–243. Springer, Cham (2021). https://doi.org/10.1007/978-3-030-80568-5_20

23. Yao, Z., et al.: Hawq-v3: dyadic neural network quantization. In: Proceedings of the 38th International Conference on Machine Learning, pp. 11875–11886. PMLR (2021)

24. You, Y., Gitman, I., Ginsburg, B.: Large batch training of convolutional networks. arXiv pp. 1–8 (2017)

25. Zhou, G., Zhou, J., Lin, H.: Research on NVIDIA deep learning accelerator. In: Proceedings of the International Conference on Anti-Counterfeiting, Security and Identification, ASID (2018)

26. Zhou, P., Xiong, C., Socher, R., Hoi, S.C.: Theory-inspired path-regularized differential network architecture search. arXiv (2020)

27. Zoph, B., Le, Q.V.: Neural architecture search with reinforcement learning. In: 5th International Conference on Learning Representations, ICLR 2017, pp. 1–16 (2017)

# RegionDrop: Fast Human Pose Estimation Using Annotation-Aware Spatial Sparsity

Youki Sada[✉], Seiya Shibata, Yuki Kobayashi, and Takashi Takenaka

Digital Technology Development Laboratories, NEC Corporation, Kanagawa, Japan
{youkis,s-shibata,y-kobayashi.hq,takashi.t}@nec.com

**Abstract.** Convolutional neural networks (CNN) have been attracting attention for accurate scene parsing including a human pose estimation. However, CNN requires a massive amount of floating-point operations, so it is difficult to realize CNN on low-cost devices. Thus, we propose RegionDrop, an annotation-aware spatially sparse network, which skips computations of unnecessary spatial regions in activations. We present a novel loss that directly uses annotations so that important activation regions are retained. We also developed an efficient sparse GPU kernel to accelerate processing speed of both depthwise and general $K \times K$ convolutional layers. Our RegionDrop is evaluated by using two pose estimation networks, a modified stacked hourglass network, and an HRNet. RegionDrop using an hourglass network archived 3.2 times faster processing speed compared with a non-sparse network, and 1.8 times faster processing speed than a prior spatially sparse network, with no accuracy degradation. Moreover, the processing speed of RegionDrop using HRNet is increased by a factor of 2.0 with negligible accuracy loss.

**Keywords:** Convolutional neural networks · Pose estimation · Spatially sparse network · GPU

## 1 Introduction

Human pose estimation is the image processing task that predicts keypoint positions and classes of each person. The implementation of human pose estimation in edge/mobile environments is crucial in surveillance, human-computer interaction, medical industries, gaming ones, etc. Recently, by the rapid evolution of CNN [14]-based scheme, human pose estimation is getting more accurate, especially with a deeper network structure and higher resolution features [4,6,17,19]. However, under these trends, the computational complexity increases, and powerful machines and costly environments are required to execute those models in practical speed.

The most common approach to address this problem is to use lightweight convolutional networks. Most prior works rely on replacing a conventional convolutional building block [7] with the convolutions or the building block that has

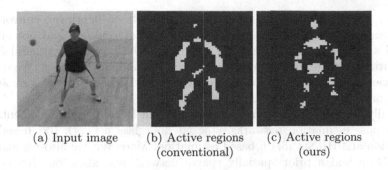

(a) Input image    (b) Active regions    (c) Active regions
                       (conventional)         (ours)

**Fig. 1.** Active regions. Yellow-colored regions represent active regions that are convolved, and purple ones denote inactive regions which are ignored on spatially sparse networks. **(a)** Input image. **(b)** The active regions in the conventional scheme. **(c)** The annotation-aware active regions by our scheme, yielding higher accuracy and faster overall processing speed than (b). (Color figure online)

a fewer amount of FLOPs (FLoating-point OPerations), such as depthwise convolutions [8], ShuffleNet [24], and dense modules [10]. However, non-negligible accuracy loss occurs, and the amount of FLOPs does not precisely affect the actual processing speed. Those networks require complex memory access or too low computational intensity, and they cannot be efficiently executed on generic GPUs.

The other approach eliminates the computation of unnecessary activations depending on the input. The technique focuses on the nature of the CNN-based image processing that there exist many spatially inactive regions in CNN feature maps. Since inactive regions correspond to the image background or unrelated objects, the calculations of those regions are unnecessary and do not affect prediction results. This technique modifies a base neural network by attaching additional tiny networks which predict active regions (i.e. image foregrounds), and then the base neural network calculates the only activations corresponding to active regions. However, most prior works [5,20,21] train the tiny networks by a loss criterion calculated from the area ratio of active regions, and prior networks don't refer to an annotation in a training phase. As shown in Fig. 1, in prior works, important spatial regions defect or unimportant regions remain, so accuracy loss and speed degradation occur.

Thus, we propose an annotation-aware spatially sparse network (RegionDrop), and a novel sparse loss to train RegionDrop. The sparse loss is calculated from ground-truth keypoints in an annotation, and RegionDrop generates more comprehensive active regions which are gathered around ground-truth keypoints or person pixels.

Furthermore, most prior works [5,20] reported only the reduction rate in FLOPs but did not provide actual speedup, or they require dedicated hardware such as ASIC to enable speedup. Therefore, they are not available on general GPUs or CPUs. A few works [18,21] proposed GPU implementations to take advantage of spatial redundancy and reported execution speedup.

However, those implementations are evaluated only on depthwise convolutions or 3D convolutions, and those convolutions are not common and not efficient on GPUs. Therefore, the difficulty of how to effectively compute general $K \times K$ convolutions with taking advantage of spatial redundancy remains. We develop the efficient implementation for both depthwise and general $K \times K$ convolutions and report actual speedup over generic GPUs.

Finally, we provide experimental results of our RegionDrop implementations on two pose estimation networks, stacked hourglass network [17] based pose estimation and HRNet [6,19] based estimation. Moreover, we also compare our RegionDrop and a prior spatially sparse network and show our RegionDrop achieves significant speedup without accuracy loss.

Our contributions are summarized as follows.

- We propose an annotation-aware spatially sparse network (RegionDrop). It archives better speed-accuracy trade-off compared with the state-of-the-art spatially sparse networks.
- We propose an efficient implementation of a spatially sparse network on low-cost GPUs. To the best of our knowledge, this is the first implementation of general CNN utilizing spatial sparsity on GPUs. We provide a speed comparison between our GPU implementation with the sparse approach and a cuDNN based implementation, which is one of the fastest implementations for dense (i.e. non-sparse) convolutions.

## 2    Related Work

### 2.1    Pose Estimation

There are two main schemes in human pose estimation, top-down [17,19] and bottom-up [4,6,16]. The top-down scheme first predicts the bounding boxes of each person and then performs single-person pose estimation for each image cropped by the box. The bottom-up scheme generally predicts all keypoint positions and then performs group assignment of the keypoints to each person. Recent grouping methods rely on affinity linking [2,13], associative embedding [16], or HigherHRNet [4]. In general, a top-down scheme is more accurate but more costly especially in crowded situation.

### 2.2    Spatial Sparsity

In [5], an adaptive number of ResNet layers are skipped within a residual block for unimportant regions in object classification. The skipping mechanism is controlled by halting scores predicted at branches to the output of each residual unit. However, most prior works [5,9] did not provide the evaluation of execution speed, or they require dedicated hardware such as ASIC to obtain execution speedup. Thus, they are not available on general GPUs or CPUs.

The closest work to our RegionDrop training scheme is [18]. They proposed the 3D object detector with two neural networks. The first small semantic segmentation network predicts the foreground pixels of a spatial space, and then the second object detection network processes only the foreground pixels. However, designing completely different neural networks to generate foreground masks is required and their two steps training scheme is costly. Additionally, they only evaluated it with 3D object detection with high-resolution LiDAR images.

[21] uses gumbel-softmax [12] to train the small gating unit to generate a binary mask. They provide the efficient implementation for depthwise convolution based networks with spatial sparsity. They modified the hourglass network with depthwise convolution for the evaluation of pose estimation, and it achieved 1.6 times faster throughput with no accuracy degradation. [23] proposed an interpolation scheme for inactive regions. They use gumbel-softmax while both training and inference. Their object detection models and semantic segmentation models achieved favorable FLOPs-accuracy trade-off, and the improvement of wall-clock time is evaluated on CPUs. However, the interpolation requires many depthwise operations and gumbel-softmax requires a random number generator, so it is not a suitable solution for general GPUs.

## 3    Annotation-Aware Spatial Sparsity

In this section, we introduce a spatially sparse network (SSN). Moreover, we describe the basics of our RegionDrop using annotation-aware spatial sparsity including its structure and training scheme.

### 3.1    Spatially Sparse Network

A convolutional layer calculates an output feature map $Z \in \mathbb{R}^{H \times W \times C_{out}}$ by performing MAC (Multiply ACcumulate operation):

$$Z(x, y, z) = f_{act}( \sum_{c=0}^{C_{in}-1} \sum_{k_h=-K'_h}^{K'_h} \sum_{k_w=-K'_w}^{K'_w}$$

$$X(x + k_w, y + k_h, c) \times F(k_w + K'_h, k_h + K'_h, c, z)), \tag{1}$$

where $X \in \mathbb{R}^{H \times W \times C_{in}}$ and $F \in \mathbb{R}^{K_h \times K_w \times C_{in} \times C_{out}}$ denote an input feature map and convolution weights, $K_h, K_w$ are kernel size and $K'_h, K'_W$ satisfy $K'_h = \lfloor K_h/2 \rfloor, K'_w = \lfloor K_w/2 \rfloor$. $H, W, C_{in}$, and $C_{out}$ represent height, width, the number of input channels, and output channels of a feature map, respectively. In general, ReLU (Rectified Linear Unit) is used as an activation function $f_{act}$.

A convolutional layer requires $K_h K_w C_{in} HW C_{out}$ MACs in total. However, spatially redundant computations exist on a convolutional layer when real-world images are used. Our approach is to first predict the inactive $(x, y)$ coordinates in an output feature map, where the corresponding activations will become zero or nearly zero, and then skip MACs of the coordinates.

Figure 2 represents the illustration of SSN. It is composed of SSConv (Spatially Sparse Convolutional layer) and a tiny prediction network called a mask unit. The mask unit firstly generates a binary mask $M \in \{0, 1\}^{H \times W}$ from

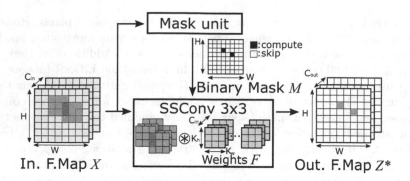

**Fig. 2.** Spatially sparse network by a single convolutional layer with kernel size 3 × 3. Black pixels on the binary mask are predicted as spatially important coordinates by a mask unit, and then SSConv computes only activations that correspond to the pixels. The other activations correspond to white pixels are filled as zero.

the input feature map. Then, SSConv calculates the output feature map $Z^* \in \mathbb{R}^{H \times W \times C_{out}}$ by:

$$Z^*(x, y, z) = \begin{cases} Z(x, y, z) & \text{if } M(x, y) = 1 \\ 0 & \text{if } M(x, y) = 0. \end{cases} \tag{2}$$

The height and width of the mask are the same as that of the output feature map. SSConv calculates only active regions where the corresponding mask value $M(x, y)$ is non-zero. In Fig. 2, the SSConv performs MACs using its weights and $16C_{in}$ input activations, and then generates $2C_{out}$ output activations. Therefore, only $2K_h K_w C_{in} C_{out}$ operations are required to obtain the output feature map out of $K_h K_w C_{in} H W C_{out}$ operations. The reduction rate of computation by SSN is calculated as:

$$1 - \frac{1}{H \cdot W} \sum_{y=0}^{H-1} \sum_{x=0}^{W-1} M(x, y). \tag{3}$$

Then the reduction rate in the example of Fig. 2 is equal to $1 - \frac{2}{8 \cdot 8} = 96.9$ [%].

## 3.2   Non-blind Mask Unit for Annotation-Aware Spatial Sparsity

We propose a non-blind mask unit to learn annotation-aware masks for higher accuracy. The difference between a conventional mask unit (blind mask unit) and our non-blind mask unit is illustrated in Fig. 3.

As shown in Fig. 3, a conventional blind mask unit is composed of typically a single convolutional layer and binarization by either or both of a thresholding function and a gumbel-softmax [12,23]. The prior sparse loss is computed from a 2D binary mask and desirable reduction rate [21], or from the L1 regularization of the convolutional layer output feature map [23]. However, the use of those

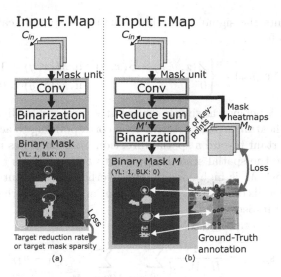

**Fig. 3.** (a) Conventional blind mask unit. (b) Our non-blind mask unit composed of a single convolutional layer (Conv), a reduce-sum, and a binarization.

losses makes binary masks difficult to retain important pixels, and sometimes difficult to eliminate unimportant background pixels.

Thus, we propose a non-blind mask unit to handle this problem. Firstly, in the non-blind mask unit, a convolutional layer generates mask heatmaps whose channel size is equal to the number of keypoints in the ground-truth annotation. And then, a "reduce sum" function shrinks the channel dimension of mask heatmaps $M_h \in \mathbb{R}^{J \times H \times W}$ into a 2D heatmap $M'$ by:

$$M'(x, y) = \sum_{z=0}^{J-1} M_h(x, y, z), \tag{4}$$

where $M' \in \mathbb{R}^{H \times W}$ denotes an intermediate 2D heatmap, and $J$ represents the number of joints (classes). Finally, a binarization calculates a binary mask $M$ from the 2D heatmap $M'$ as:

$$M(x, y) = \begin{cases} 1 & \text{if } M'(x, y) >= \rho \\ 0 & \text{if } M'(x, y) < \rho, \end{cases} \tag{5}$$

where $\rho$ represents a certain threshold. We increase $\rho$ stepwisely from 0.1 to 0.7 to maintain the accuracy, and adopt bypassing the gradient of binary mask to the upstream for a backpropagation by following the Binary Neural Networks [11] and prior work [21].

Moreover, we propose another non-blind mask unit which generates not only the binary mask but also a spatial scale $S \in \mathbb{R}^{H \times W}$ calculated by:

$$S(x, y) = \sigma(M'(x, y)), \tag{6}$$

where $\sigma$ represents the sigmoid function. Then, the spatial scale is applied to active regions as follows:

$$Z^*(x, y, z) = \begin{cases} Z(x, y, z) \times S(x, y) & \text{if } M(x, y) = 1 \\ 0 & \text{if } M(x, y) = 0. \end{cases} \tag{7}$$

The spatial scale $S$ behaves as simple spatial attention and facilitates predictions of accurate pose heatmaps [3,22]. Activations corresponding to active regions are not equally important toward a spatial direction, so $S$ amplifies more important activations. Since the spatial scale is applied to active regions and the sparsity of the binary mask $M$ is high enough, the overhead in computation is usually negligible. The details of accuracy improvement and speed overhead by the scale use are described in Sect. 4.

Our sparse loss is calculated by:

$$\text{Loss}_{\text{sparse}} = \frac{1}{H \cdot W \cdot J} \sum_{m} \sum_{v_1 \in M_h^m, v_2 \in \widehat{M_h}} (v_1 - v_2)^2, \tag{8}$$

where $M_h^m \in \mathbb{R}^{J \times H \times W}$ and $\widehat{M_h} \in \mathbb{R}^{J \times H \times W}$ denote mask heatmaps of $m$-th mask unit and ground-truth heatmaps. The ground-truth heatmaps are generated by applying 2D Gaussian with a standard deviation of 1 pixel centered on the ground-truth location of each keypoint. Finally, the sparse loss is added to the main task loss $\text{Loss}_{\text{main}}$ with a balancing parameter $\alpha$. The final loss $\text{Loss}_{\text{total}}$ is defined by:

$$\text{Loss}_{\text{total}} = \text{Loss}_{\text{main}} + \alpha \cdot \text{Loss}_{\text{sparse}}. \tag{9}$$

## 4    Experimental Results

In this section, we present experimental results on stacked hourglass network and HRNet, and we show RegionDrop achieves significant speedup on both a top-down pose estimation and a bottom-up one.

### 4.1    Experimental Setting for Hourglass Networks

**Dataset.** We use the MPII dataset [1] with standard test/validation split (22K/3K images). Images are resized to $256 \times 256$ and augmented with $\pm$ 30° rotation, $\pm$ 25% scaling and random horizontal flip during training. No flip augmentation is used during evaluation.

**Evaluation Metric.** The evaluation metric of an accuracy is the mean PCKh (Percentage of Correct Keypoints), normalized by a fraction of the head size (PCKh@0.5) [17].

**Models.** An inverted residual block based hourglass network [21] is used. We compared our RegionDrop with baseline non-sparse hourglass network and DynConv [21] as the prior spatially sparse scheme. We set the parameter $\alpha = 1.0$ for

**Table 1.** Comparison between our RegionDrop and the prior work on MPII dataset. $\rho_{1st}$ indicates the threshold parameter for the first hourglass network.

|  | #MACs | Throughput [persons/sec] | | PCKh [%] | |
|---|---|---|---|---|---|
|  |  | FP32 | FP16 | FP32 | FP16 |
| Baseline | 6.90 G | 31.1 | 37.5 | 88.1 | 88.1 |
| Baseline $\frac{C_{in}}{2}$, $\frac{C_{out}}{2}$ | 1.83 G | 69.5 | 86.0 | 85.2 | 85.2 |
| DynConv $\theta = 0.5$ | 3.78 G | 45.1 | 67.2 | 88.2 | 88.2 |
| DynConv $\theta = 0.25$ | 2.30 G | 67.2 | 96.9 | 87.4 | 87.4 |
| DynConv $\theta = 0.125$ | 1.71 G | 77.8 | 115.9 | 86.7 | 86.7 |
| Ours $\rho_{1st} = 0.1$ | 2.04 G | 80.1 | 114.1 | 88.3 | 88.3 |
| Ours $\rho_{1st} = 0.3$ | 1.95 G | 83.3 | 119.5 | 88.2 | 88.2 |
| Ours $\rho_{1st} = 0.5$ | 1.81 G | 89.7 | 124.3 | 87.7 | 87.6 |

hourglass based RegionDrop, which is the weight parameter for our sparse loss $Loss_{sparse}$, and train three RegionDrop models with different threshold settings for the first mask unit $\rho_{1st} = 0.1, 0.3, 0.5$ while $\rho = 0.7$ for the other mask units.

## 4.2    Experimental Setting for HRNet

**Dataset.** We evaluate the performance on the COCO keypoint detection task [15]. The train2017 set includes 57 K images and 150 K person instances annotated with 17 keypoints, and the val2017 set contains 5 K images. We train the models on the train2017 set and report the results on the val2017 sets.

**Evaluation Metric.** We follow the standard evaluation metric[1] and use OKS (Object Keypoint Similarity) [4] based metris for COCO pose estimation. We report mAP (mean Average Precision at OKS $= 0.50, 0.55, \dots, 0.90, 0.95$).

**Models.** A HRNet-w32 based DEKR [6] is used. A RegionDrop model for the HRNet DEKR has two mask units, and they make binary masks for latter 96 basic blocks out of 104 basic blocks. We use the parameters $\alpha = 0.8$ and $\rho = 0.7$, and then compare our RegionDrop and non-sparse model.

## 4.3    Accuracy and Execution Time Comparison for RegionDrop Using Hourglass Networks

Table 1 shows the comparison among our RegionDrop models, Baseline non-sparse models, and DynConv models[2] on a Jetson AGX Xavier embedded GPU

---

[1] http://cocodataset.org/#keypoints-eval.

[2] https://github.com/thomasverelst/dynconv is used to measure throughput of FP32 DynConv models and our implementation is used for FP16 DynConv models.

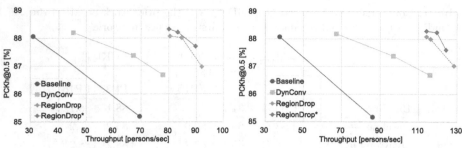

(a) Trade-off curves using FP32 models    (b) Trade-off curves using FP16 models

**Fig. 4.** Throughput–accuracy (PCKh@0.5) trade-off on Jetson AGX Xavier and MPII dataset. A curve of "Baseline" is drawn by two different models, one is a full-channel model and the other is half-channel model. The other curves are drawn by various parameters $\theta, \rho$ in sparse loss with the full-channel model.

**Table 2.** Comparison between our RegionDrop and a non-sparse model on a RTX 2080Ti GPU and COCO dataset.

|  | #MACs | #Params | mAP | Processing speed [ms] |
|---|---|---|---|---|
| Baseline | 51 G | 29.6 M | 62.7% | 42.9 |
| RegionDrop | 19 G | 29.6 M | 61.6% | 21.5 |

device with batch size $N_b = 128$. We used a power mode of MAXN, that enables all CPU and GPU cores, and the maximum frequencies for the CPU and the GPU. Moreover, we evaluated models in both FP32 (32-bit single precision floating-point) and FP16 (16-bit half precision floating-point) for convolutional operations. As shown in Table 1, in a FP32 evaluation, our RegionDrop $\rho_{1st} = 0.3$ achieved 2.7 times higher throughput than a baseline model and 1.8 times higher throughput than a prior DynConv $\theta = 0.5$ model without accuracy loss. In a FP16 evaluation, our RegionDrop achieved 3.2 times higher throughput than a baseline and 1.8 times higher throughput than DynConv. In other words, RegionDrop can process three and two persons per frame using FP16 and FP32 respectively with real-time speed ($\geq 30.0$ [FPS]), while the non-sparse model can infer only a single person per frame and DynConv $\theta = 0.5$ can infer only a 1–2 persons per frame.

Figure 4 shows the trade-off curves of accuracy and execution speed. "Region-Drop*" in Fig. 4 indicates a network that uses spatial scale $S$ multiplications explained at Sect. 3.2. The proposed RegionDrop achieved better throughput-accuracy trade-off compared to the conventional spatially sparse models. Table 1 also shows that RegionDrop models achieved higher throughput even if the number of MACs is more than DynConv models. It is because our non-blind mask units generates binary masks whose active regions are congregated to important keypoints in most of the layers. Figure 5 shows ponder costs which are layer-wise averaged heatmaps of the binary masks. As shown in Fig. 5, our ponder costs are

**Fig. 5.** Ponder cost on top-down pose estimation using MPII dataset. From top to bottom row, the images and heatmaps represent predicted skeletons and ponder costs of our RegionDrop $\rho = 0.5$ (87.7% mAP, 1.71G MACs), and the bottom two row denotes of DynConv $\theta = 0.125$ (86.7% mAP, 1.81G MACs) from [21].

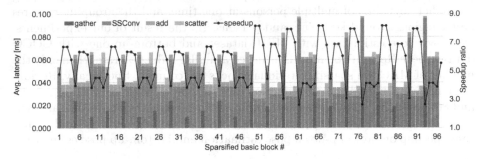

**Fig. 6.** Layer-wise execution time on the HRNet sparsified layers using COCO validation dataset. Black line indicates relative speed over non-sparse layers

significantly compact, while the clutter in ponder costs of conventional scheme causes layer-wise imbalance and low GPU utilization.

## 4.4 Accuracy and Execution Time Comparison for RegionDrop Using HRNet

Table 2 shows the comparison between our RegionDrop models and a non-sparse model evaluated on the RTX 2080Ti GPU with Core i7-8700 as the host CPU. We resized short side of the input image to 512 while keeping its aspect ratio, and we measured the execution speed with batch size $N_b = 1$. The latter part of a HRNet-w32 backbone are sparsified, since the #MACs in the backbone occupies 88% computation and the backbone is the dominant part in processing speed. Our RegionDrop reduced 63% of MACs and achieved 2.0 times faster processing speed with 1.1 point mAP degradation compared with cuDNN implementation of non-sparse models.

Figure 6 shows the layer-wise execution time of sparsified basic blocks. Gather denotes an operation which gathers active pixels and construct a 2D matrix. SSConv is matrix multiplication between the matrix and weights. Add indicates the add operation of a skip connection and scatter denotes the conversion operation from the 2D matrix to a tensor. Gather/scatter operation occupies 15% and SSConv/add occupies 85% execution time in average, so conversion overhead by gather/scatter is small. Moreover, the layer-wise speedup ratio resulted in × 5.5 on average over sparsified basic blocks.

### 4.5   Comparison Between Top-Down and Bottom-Up Pose Estimation

In top-down pose estimation by hourglass networks, spatially sparse pose estimators need to calculate small regions around keypoints, though the former object detector already eliminates most of the background regions. In contrast, spatially sparse bottom-up pose estimators by HRNet has potentially larger background regions. However, the bottom-up scheme needs to perform the grouping to predict keypoints of multiple persons at one time, and the grouping requires larger regions around keypoints and persons. As the result of our experiments, top-down pose estimation with MPII dataset and bottom-up one with COCO dataset, both RegionDrop models achieved a similar reduction rate when only the number of MACs on sparsified residual blocks are counted. Specifically, Region-Drop models achieved an 83% reduction rate on top-down scheme with $\rho_{1st} = 0.5$ and 86% reduction rate on the bottom-up scheme, while they have similar accuracy degradation. RegionDrop realized high spatially sparse networks and significant speedup on both top-down pose estimation and bottom-up pose estimation.

## 5   Conclusions

We introduced the reduction technique of CNN computations by exploiting the spatial redundancy on activations. We proposed RegionDrop trained directly by annotations to retain important active regions and developed an efficient GPU implementation of spatially sparse convolutions. Finally, we evaluated our RegionDrop models with both top-down and bottom-up schemes. In the top-down pose estimation, RegionDrop using an hourglass network achieved 3.2 times faster processing speed than the non-sparse hourglass network and achieved 1.8 times faster processing speed than the prior work without accuracy loss. In the bottom-up pose estimation, RegionDrop using HRNet achieved 2.0 times faster speed and 5.5 times faster layer-wise speed than the non-sparse HRNet with negligible accuracy loss. RegionDrop realized high spatially sparse networks and significant speedup on both top-down pose estimation and bottom-up pose estimation.

# References

1. Andriluka, M., Pishchulin, L., Gehler, P., Schiele, B.: 2D human pose estimation: new benchmark and state of the art analysis. In: IEEE Conference on Computer Vision and Pattern Recognition (CVPR) (2014)
2. Cao, Z., Simon, T., Wei, S.E., Sheikh, Y.: Realtime multi-person 2D pose estimation using part affinity fields. In: CVPR, pp. 7291–7299 (2017)
3. Chen, L., et al.: SCA-CNN: spatial and channel-wise attention in convolutional networks for image captioning. In: CVPR, pp. 5659–5667 (2017)
4. Cheng, B., Xiao, B., Wang, J., Shi, H., Huang, T.S., Zhang, L.: HigherHRNet: scale-aware representation learning for bottom-up human pose estimation. In: CVPR, pp. 5386–5395 (2020)
5. Figurnov, M., et al.: Spatially adaptive computation time for residual networks. In: CVPR, pp. 1039–1048 (2017)
6. Geng, Z., Sun, K., Xiao, B., Zhang, Z., Wang, J.: Bottom-up human pose estimation via disentangled keypoint regression. In: CVPR, pp. 14676–14686 (2021)
7. He, K., Zhang, X., Ren, S., Sun, J.: Deep residual learning for image recognition. In: CVPR, pp. 770–778 (2016)
8. Howard, A.G., et al.: MobileNets: efficient convolutional neural networks for mobile vision applications. arXiv preprint arXiv:1704.04861 (2017)
9. Hua, W., Zhou, Y., De Sa, C.M., Zhang, Z., Suh, G.E.: Channel gating neural networks. In: Advances in Neural Information Processing Systems, vol. 32 (2019)
10. Huang, G., Liu, Z., Van Der Maaten, L., Weinberger, K.Q.: Densely connected convolutional networks. In: CVPR, pp. 4700–4708 (2017)
11. Hubara, I., Courbariaux, M., Soudry, D., El-Yaniv, R., Bengio, Y.: Binarized neural networks. In: Advances in Neural Information Processing Systems, vol. 29 (2016)
12. Jang, E., Gu, S., Poole, B.: Categorical reparameterization with gumbel-softmax. arXiv preprint arXiv:1611.01144 (2016)
13. Kreiss, S., Bertoni, L., Alahi, A.: PifPaf: composite fields for human pose estimation. In: CVPR, pp. 11977–11986 (2019)
14. LeCun, Y., Bengio, Y., Hinton, G.: Deep learning. Nature $521$(7553), 436–444 (2015)
15. Lin, T.-Y., et al.: Microsoft COCO: common objects in context. In: Fleet, D., Pajdla, T., Schiele, B., Tuytelaars, T. (eds.) ECCV 2014. LNCS, vol. 8693, pp. 740–755. Springer, Cham (2014). https://doi.org/10.1007/978-3-319-10602-1_48
16. Newell, A., Huang, Z., Deng, J.: Associative embedding: end-to-end learning for joint detection and grouping. arXiv preprint arXiv:1611.05424 (2016)
17. Newell, A., Yang, K., Deng, J.: Stacked hourglass networks for human pose estimation. In: Leibe, B., Matas, J., Sebe, N., Welling, M. (eds.) ECCV 2016. LNCS, vol. 9912, pp. 483–499. Springer, Cham (2016). https://doi.org/10.1007/978-3-319-46484-8_29
18. Ren, M., Pokrovsky, A., Yang, B., Urtasun, R.: SBNet: sparse blocks network for fast inference. In: CVPR, pp. 8711–8720 (2018)
19. Sun, K., Xiao, B., Liu, D., Wang, J.: Deep high-resolution representation learning for human pose estimation. In: CVPR, pp. 5693–5703 (2019)
20. Veit, A., Belongie, S.: Convolutional networks with adaptive inference graphs. In: Ferrari, V., Hebert, M., Sminchisescu, C., Weiss, Y. (eds.) ECCV 2018. LNCS, vol. 11205, pp. 3–18. Springer, Cham (2018). https://doi.org/10.1007/978-3-030-01246-5_1

21. Verelst, T., Tuytelaars, T.: Dynamic convolutions: exploiting spatial sparsity for faster inference. In: CVPR, pp. 2320–2329 (2020)
22. Woo, S., Park, J., Lee, J.-Y., Kweon, I.S.: CBAM: convolutional block attention module. In: Ferrari, V., Hebert, M., Sminchisescu, C., Weiss, Y. (eds.) ECCV 2018. LNCS, vol. 11211, pp. 3–19. Springer, Cham (2018). https://doi.org/10.1007/978-3-030-01234-2_1
23. Xie, Z., Zhang, Z., Zhu, X., Huang, G., Lin, S.: Spatially adaptive inference with stochastic feature sampling and interpolation. In: Vedaldi, A., Bischof, H., Brox, T., Frahm, J.-M. (eds.) ECCV 2020. LNCS, vol. 12346, pp. 531–548. Springer, Cham (2020). https://doi.org/10.1007/978-3-030-58452-8_31
24. Zhang, X., Zhou, X., Lin, M., Sun, J.: ShuffleNet: an extremely efficient convolutional neural network for mobile devices. In: CVPR, pp. 6848–6856 (2018)

# SDCN: A Species-Disease Hybrid Convolutional Neural Network for Plant Disease Recognition

Yiqi Yang(✉)

School of Computer Science and Artificial Intelligence,
Wuhan University of Technology, Wuhan, China
yiqi_yang_21@163.com

**Abstract.** Crop diseases will cause serious yield reduction. Leaf disease identification methods based on Convolutional Neural Network (CNN) have achieved good results, but the cost of labeling disease images is very high. Image augment and Few-Shot Learning (FSL) reduced the demand for labeled data. Other than these methods, this paper designs a novel CNN performed very well, which can greatly reduce the demand for training images. Firstly, the idea of decreasing CNN is proposed to learn much more visual features of plant leaves with fewer parameters. According to it, a kind of lightly decreasing CNN (D-CNN) is proposed in this paper, while the traditional mainstream CNNs are no decreasing. Further, for learning more lesion features, a two branch Species-Disease hybrid Convolution neural Network (SDCN) is designed to learn plant species and lesions features respectively, each branch of which is decreasing CNN. Experiments on the popular dataset PlantVillage show that the classification accuracy of SDCN achieves 99.81% trained from scratch, while its parameters are only 13% of VGG11. And SDCN achieves 98.26% classification accuracy trained on 25% of the training data, which is equivalent to the performance of mainstream CNNs trained on 100% of the training data. Even when trained on 6.25% of training data (50 images/class), its classification accuracy still reaches 92.58%, while others do not exceed 80%. It shows that SDCN has much stronger feature learning ability, which can greatly reduce the demand for training data.

**Keywords:** Plant leaf disease recognition · Decreasing CNN · Convolution Neural Network (CNN) · Deep learning

## 1 Introduction

Leaf diseases will cause serious crop yield reduction, the automatic identification of leaf diseases can effectively reduce the risk of crop yield reduction [1]. Because plant diseases images with complicated noise and background, the traditional machine vision technology relying on manual design features is difficult to precisely identify diseases. Fortunately, Convolution Neural Network(CNN)

E. Pimenidis et al. (Eds.): ICANN 2022, LNCS 13532, pp. 769–780, 2022.
https://doi.org/10.1007/978-3-031-15937-4_64

be good at to identify crop leaf disease. With the deepening of convolution layers, the network can abstract richer visual features, and effectively overcome the difficulties [2,3]. Plant leaf disease recognition models based on deep learning have achieved good results, but they often need a large number of labeled data [4]. The labeling of crop disease images is highly cost and difficult owe to it is inseparable from the participation of agricultural experts [3]. Therefore, a novel lightly convolutional neural network model is proposed in this paper, which can greatly reduce the demand for training data. The main contributions of this paper are as follows:

1) The decreasing CNN is proposed in this paper, and it has significantly better disease classification ability than mainstream CNNs on the largest public dataset PlantVillage [5];
2) Using decreasing CNN (D-CNN), A two branch Species-Disease hybrid Convolution neural Network (SDCN) is proposed to learn the plant species and disease spot features in the image respectively, and then synthesize these features to classify plant diseases. Experiments indicate that SDCN can greatly reduce the demand for training data while keeping reasonable performance;
3) Trained on few images, the performance differences between SDCN and mainstream CNNs such as VGG, ResNet and MobileNet, are compared. It is found that the performance of these mainstream models on the plant disease images mainly benefits from the learning of plant species features rather than of disease features. SDCN has a significantly stronger ability to extract the visual features of plant diseases.

## 2   Related Works

CNN can learn the visual features including blade shape and lesion distribution, so as to achieve good performance [6–8]. For working on mobile devices, CNNs for identification plant disease tend to be lightweight [9], which are mainly divided into two categories. One is to identify or detect crop diseases with some popular CNNs, such as AlexNet [10], GooGleNet [11], VGG [12], ResNet [13], DenseNet [14] or MobileNet [15], and their variants [16]. The other is to introduce some novel structures into CNN to perfect from the specific characteristics of plant disease images [17]. For example, the attention mechanism is introduced into the convolution layer. Literature [18] is similar to ViT [19], which divides the input image into small patches, obtains the attention weight by clustering the feature vectors of global data, and improves the classification performance.

The labeling cost of crop disease image is very high, and some disease images are hard to collect. There are two main methods to reduce the demand for training data. One is to apply the few-shot learning (FSL) technology. With a general image feature extractor obtained through transfer learning or comparative learning, it can be carried out rapid training on the support set of a small number of samples [20,21]. The other is to preprocess or deform the labeled images to obtain new training samples through various image augment such as scaling, rotation, random clipping, changing brightness, sharply contrast, gamma trans-formation, translation, adding noise, geometric transformation and so on [22–24]. In addition, like literature [25], generative adversarial network (GAN) is used to generate new virtual samples, so as to reduce the demand for labeled data [26–28]. In fact, the training of the general feature extractor of FSL still needs a lot of labeled data, and the CNN models with image augment still need a lot of training data.

Different from the above methods, this paper proposes a Species-Disease hybrid CNN (SDCN) with stronger visual feature extraction ability, which reduces the demand of training samples by extracting more abundant and diverse visual features with fewer parameters. SDCN uses the species and diseases branches to extract the category features and disease spot features of plant leaves respectively, so that SDCN can get more and richer visual features; Fur-ther, each branch of SDCN uses a design idea called decreasing CNN proposed in this paper. By stacking more low-level convolution layers to expand the receptive field, it can extract more abundant texture features contained in plant leaves. At the same time, in order to reduce the amount of parameters, it uses as few high-level convolution layers as possible.

## 3    SDCN: Species-Disease Hybrid CNN

By enhancing the disease feature learning ability and reducing the amount of trainable parameters of the model, a new idea is proposed in this paper to reduce the demand for training data. First of all, the Species-Disease Hybrid CNN (SDCN) is proposed, which uses two branches to extract the species features and disease spot features of plant leaf images respectively. Species features or Disease features are learned separately, so each branch can learn more abundant visual features. From the model visualization, it can be found that the classic mainstream CNNs learned the shape characteristics reflecting plant species while learning the characteristics of disease spots during training. Experiments show that this method of learning these two decoupled features at the same time can not extract enough visual features. With two branches, SDCN can not only learn more abundant species and lesion features, but also further enhance the total features it can learn. Secondly, each branch of SDCN is designed as a model called Decreasing Convolution Neural Network (D-CNN), which not only enhances the ability of learning visual features, but also reduces the number of model parameters.

### 3.1    Decreasing CNN

**Definition 1.** *A convolutional neural network CNN denotes by*

$$CNN = \{CB_1, CB_2, \ldots, CB_k, \ldots, CB_n\},$$

*where $CB_k$ means the $k^{th}$ convolutional block, which composed of m neural network layers, it be denoted as follows:*

$$CB_k = \{X_k, L_k^1, L_k^2, \ldots, L_k^m, Y_k\}, and L_k^i = \{X_k^i, C_k^i, \delta_k^i, P_k^i, N_k^i, Y_k^i\}$$

*where $X_k$ and $Y_k$ denotes the input and output of $CB_k$ respectively, and $L_k^i$ means the $i^{th}$ neural network layer of $CB_k$, whose input is $X_k^i$, and the output of $L_k^i$ is $Y_k^i$, $C_k^i$ is its convolutional operation, $\delta_k^i$ is the activation function, $P_k^i$ is the pooling operation, and $N_k^i$ is normalization operation. set $U_k^i = N_k^i(X_k^i)$, $Z_k^i = C_k^i(U_k^i) = \sum_{j=1}^{s_i} U_k^i \odot F_k^{(i,j)}$, where $\odot$ denotes convolution, $F_k^{(i,j)}$ denotes the $j^{th}$ convolution kernel of $L_k^i$, and set $Y_k^i = P_k^i(\delta_k^i(Z_k^i))$. The convolution layer $L_k^i$ maintains the following properties:*
*1) $C_k^i$, $\delta_k^i$, $P_k^i$ and $N_k^i$ can't be null at the same time;*
*2) $X_k = X_k^1$; $Y_k = Y_k^m$; $Y_k^{i-1} = X_k^i (i = 2, \ldots, m)$.*
*At last, Let $|CB_k| = m$ be the length of convolutional block $CB_k$.*

**Definition 2.** *A convolution neural network $CNN = \{CB_1, \ldots, CB_k, \ldots, CB_n\}$ is decreasing CNN, If $i < j$, then $|CB_i| \geqslant |CB_j|$, otherwise is increasing CNN.*

### 3.2    A Lightly Decresing CNN for Plant Disease Recognition (D-CNN)

In fact, the mainstream CNNs such as AlexNet, GooLeNet, VGG, ResNet and DenseNet are increasing CNNs. According to the characteristics of plant disease image, a decreasing CNN is proposed in this paper, which contains 4 convolution blocks, D-CNN = $\{CB_1, CB_2, CB_3, CB_4\}$, and $| CB_4 | = 1$. $CB_k$ of D-CNN is composed of one or more convolution layers and end with a pool layer. $X_1$ and $Y_4$ is the input and output of D-CNN respectively. D-CNN stacks much more convolution layers in bottom $CB_k(1 \leqslant k \leqslant 2)$ to extract much more low-level texture and other visual features, at the same time it can expand the perceptive field. The following experiments show that this structure can effectively learn the shape and random distribution characteristics of plant disease spots, so that the classification network D-CNN has more powerful feature extraction ability. The main function of the bottom convolution layers is to learn the texture of the plant image, and the followed convolution layers continue to abstract the random distribution characteristics of the lesion or the shape of the plant leaves. So D-CNN needs no much more high-level convolution layers to learn the shape and lesions feature, so the top $CB_k(3 \leqslant k \leqslant 4)$ contains much less convolution layers. Therefore D-CNN can learn much more visual features for plant lesions with fewer trainable parameters.

Each convolution layer $L_k^i$ of D-CNN includes a convolution operation and nonlinear transform (realized by the activation function) and a normalization operation. Among them, normalization operation is not necessary, but batch normalization can significantly accelerate the convergence of the network and greatly reduce the training time of the model [29], and can also effectively improve the generalization ability of the model. Therefore, this paper suggests that each convolution layer contains a normalization operation. In this paper, the normalization operation of D-CNN convolution layer is Batch Normalization (BN), and the activation function is relu:

$$relu(x) = \begin{cases} 0, & x < 0 \\ x, & x \geqslant 0 \end{cases} \tag{1}$$

## 3.3  SDCN: Species-Disease Hybrid Convolutional Neural Network

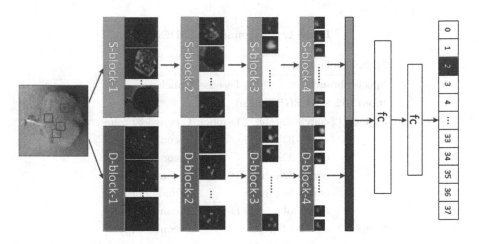

**Fig. 1.** The architecture of SDCN with two branches and a classifier (white). The species branch contains four CBDL blocks (green), such as the disease branch (blue). (Color figure online)

The disease image includes the species characteristic of plants, and the disease spot characteristics related to the disease class. Therefore, this paper proposes a new plant disease recognition model, which includes two branches, as Fig. 1. The species branch extracts the plant species features of the input image, and the disease branch extracts the disease features. Then, through a classifier composed of three full connection layers, the species and disease features are synthesized, and the final classification results are output. This recognition process is similar to human beings. When a picture $X_i$ is fed into SDCN and the species feature vector $\mathbf{c}_i = (c_i^1 \ldots, c_i^k)$ be extracted by species branch SDCN-c, at the same time the disease feature vector $\mathbf{d}_i = (d_i^1, \ldots, d_i^s)$ be extracted by disease branch SDCN-d, and then them be merged into $\mathbf{x}_i^t = (c_i^1, \ldots, c_i^k, d_i^1, \ldots, d_i^s)$, finally a 38 dimensional vector $\mathbf{y}_i^o = (y_{i,1}^o \ldots, y_{i,38}^o)$ is output by the classifier, the last prediction label $y_i = argmax_{j=1}^{38} \{y_{i,j}^o\}$.

SDCN-c is an D-CNN, whose $CB_1$ contains five convolution layers, and the length of $CB_k (2 \leqslant k \leqslant 4)$ is one. The main task of species branch is to extract more low level visual features of plant species, such as shape. Through more stacking convolution layers, it can not only expand the receptive field of the model, but also help it learn the shape features in the image data. The specific configuration is shown in Table 1, in which "conv3-$y$[relu]" means the convolution layer with $y$ $3 \times 3$ filters and *relu* activation.

SDCN-d is another D-CNN. The first to fourth convolutional block is composed of 4, 3, 2 and 1 convolution layers respectively. The visual characteristics of disease are mainly composed of disease spot texture and its distribution. Compared with the size of leaf, the size of the lesion is generally smaller than it. Therefore, the first convolutional block contains fewer convolution layers. The specific configuration is shown in Table 1.

**Table 1.** Configuration of SDCN

| SDCN configuration | | | |
|---|---|---|---|
| Species branch | | Disease branch | |
| Input ($62 \times 62$ RGB image) | | | |
| S-block 1 | conv3-32[relu] | D-block 1 | conv3-32[relu] |
| | conv3-32[relu] | | conv3-32[relu] |
| | conv3-32[relu] | | conv3-32[relu] |
| | conv3-32[relu] | | conv3-32[relu] |
| | conv3-64[relu] | | maxpool |
| | maxpool | D-block 2 | conv3-64[relu] |
| S-block 2 | conv3-128[relu] | | conv3-64[relu] |
| | maxpool | | conv3-128[relu] |
| S-block 3 | conv3-256[relu] | | maxpool |
| | maxpool | D-block 3 | conv3-128[relu] |
| S-block 4 | conv3-512[relu] | | conv3-256[relu] |
| | globalavgpool | | maxpool |
| | | D-block 4 | conv3-512[relu] |
| | | | globalavgpool |
| fc-1024[relu] | | | |
| fc-256[relu] | | | |
| fc-38[softmax] | | | |
| softmax | | | |

## 3.4   Training of SDCN

Firstly, the species branch SDCN-c is added with two full connection layers (100 [relu] - 38 [softmax]) to form a species classification network SDCN-cn, which is trained on the species dataset Species-PLD and save the model with the highest validation accuracy; Secondly, the disease branch SDCN-d is added with two full connection layers (100 [relu] - 38 [softmax]) to form the disease classification network SDCN-dn, which is trained on the disease dataset Disease-PLD and save the model with the highest validation accuracy; Finally, the species branch and disease branch are combined, followed by three full connection layers to form SDCN, which is divided into two stages for training. In the first stage, the parameters of the two branches are fixed, and only the parameters of the full connection layer are trained. In the second stage, all the parameters of the network are fine tuned (Table 2).

## 4    Experiment

### 4.1    Experimental Setting

**Table 2.** Detail of PLD

| Common name | # | Label | Common name | # | Label |
|---|---|---|---|---|---|
| Apple scab | 1000 | 0 | Pepper bell healthy | 1478 | 19 |
| Apple black rot | 1000 | 1 | Potato early blight | 1000 | 20 |
| Apple cedar rust | 1000 | 2 | Potato healthy | 1000 | 21 |
| Apple healthy | 1645 | 3 | Potato late blight | 1000 | 22 |
| Blueberry healthy | 1502 | 4 | Raspberry healthy | 1000 | 23 |
| Cherry healthy | 1000 | 5 | Soybean healthy | 5090 | 24 |
| Cherry powdery mildew | 1052 | 6 | Squash powdery mildew | 1835 | 25 |
| Corn gray leaf spot | 1000 | 7 | Strawberry healthy | 1000 | 26 |
| Corn common rust | 1192 | 8 | Strawberry leaf scorch | 1109 | 27 |
| Corn healthy | 1162 | 9 | Tomato bacterial spot | 2127 | 28 |
| Corn northern leaf blight | 1000 | 10 | Tomato early blight | 1000 | 29 |
| Grape black rot | 1180 | 11 | Tomato healthy | 1591 | 30 |
| Grape black measles | 1383 | 12 | Tomato late blight | 1909 | 31 |
| Grape healthy | 1000 | 13 | Tomato leaf mold | 1000 | 32 |
| Grape leaf spot | 1076 | 14 | Tomato leaf spot | 1771 | 33 |
| Orange citrus greening | 5507 | 15 | Tomato spider mites | 1676 | 34 |
| Peach bacterial spot | 2297 | 16 | Tomato target spot | 1404 | 35 |
| Peach healthy | 1000 | 17 | Tomato mosaic virus | 1000 | 36 |
| Pepper bell bacterial spot | 1000 | 18 | Tomato yellow leaf curl virus | 5357 | 37 |

PlantVillage is the largest open plant disease dataset, which contains 14 species and 26 kinds of diseases. Firstly, a dataset called PLD is setup. The background class is removed from original data, leaving 38 classes, a total of 60341 images. However, the number of images in each class in PlantVillage varies greatly. In order to ensure fairness, we randomly takes 1000 images from each class in PLD to form a new dataset PLD-base, a total of 38000. Further, for comparing the recognition performance of different models trained on different amount of train data, this paper makes five settings for the amount of training data. Test set test200 is obtained by randomly selecting 200 images from each class of PLD-base, and the remaining images are as the training set train800. Then, 800, 600, 400, 200 and 50 images are randomly selected from each class of train800 as training sets, named tr80, tr60, tr40, tr20 and tr05 respectively.

Just for comparing the feature extraction ability of these models, this paper only use three common image augments: (1) resize the original RGB image to $62 \times 62$; (2) flip left and right; (3) Rotate $90°$ counterclockwise. For fairness all models are trained from scratch without fine tune. In experiments, epoch is 150, learning rate is 1e−4, optimizer is Adam, and the loss function is the cross entropy. The recognition accuracy is calculated as follows:

$$accuracy = \frac{c}{n} \times 100\% \tag{2}$$

where $c$ represents the total number of correctly predicted samples and $n$ represents the total number of test samples.

Table 3. Configuration of Species-PLD and Disease-PLD

| PLD label | 0 | 1 | 2 | 3 | 4 | 5 | 6 | 7 | 8 | 9 | 10 | 11 | 12 | 13 | 14 | 15 | 16 | 17 | 18 |
|---|---|---|---|---|---|---|---|---|---|---|---|---|---|---|---|---|---|---|---|
| Species label | 0 | 0 | 0 | 0 | 1 | 2 | 2 | 3 | 3 | 3 | 3 | 4 | 4 | 4 | 4 | 5 | 6 | 6 | 7 |
| Disease label | 16 | 2 | 15 | 7 | 7 | 7 | 14 | 6 | 15 | 7 | 9 | 2 | 1 | 7 | 12 | 3 | 0 | 7 | 0 |
| PLD label | 19 | 20 | 21 | 22 | 23 | 24 | 25 | 26 | 27 | 28 | 29 | 30 | 31 | 32 | 33 | 34 | 35 | 36 | 37 |
| Species label | 7 | 8 | 8 | 8 | 9 | 10 | 11 | 12 | 12 | 13 | 13 | 13 | 13 | 13 | 13 | 13 | 13 | 13 | 13 |
| Disease label | 7 | 5 | 7 | 8 | 7 | 7 | 14 | 7 | 11 | 0 | 5 | 7 | 8 | 10 | 12 | 17 | 18 | 13 | 4 |

## 4.2 Experiments

**Performance Comparison Experiments on PLD.** As in Table 4, the accuracy of all convolution networks trained on PLD is more than or close to 99%, which may be due to image augment and the learning rate is very small, which makes it difficult to miss some better minimum points of loss. SDCN contains two branches, whose each branch is lightly decreasing CNN. The parameters of SDCN is only 13% of VGG11, and its performance achieves 99.81% on PLD. The parameters of SDCN-cn is only 4.78% of VGG11, 27.3% less than the typical lightweight network MobilNet, but the accuracy reaches 99.73%, 1.1% points higher than MobileNet.

From the experimental results in Table 4, it can be seen that with the reduction of training data, the accuracy of the mainstream CNNs decreased rapidly, while the performance of SDCN decreased slowly. When the training data is reduced to 20% of PLD-base, the recognition accuracy of each mainstream CNN is less than 95%. On the contrary, the accuracy of SDCN is still 98.26%, which is achieved by other CNNs trained on tr80. Even when trained on tr05 (50 images/class), the classification accuracy of SDCN still reaches 92.58%, while others do not exceed 80%. SDCN uses the species and diseases branches to extract the category features and disease spot features of plant leaves respectively, so that SDCN can get more and richer visual features; Further, each branch of SDCN uses a design idea called decreasing CNN proposed in this paper. By stacking more low-level convolution layers to expand the receptive field, it can extract more abundant texture features contained in plant leaves. At the same time, in order to reduce the amount of parameters, it uses as few high-level convolution layers as possible. These two branches not only prominently learned the species features, but also has a stronger ability to learn the disease spot features. We believe that this mostly maybe the main reason why SDCN can still achieve high plant disease recognition accuracy trained on few training data. It shows that SDCN has the stronger ability of feature extraction, and the amount of training data required by SDCN is greatly reduced.

**Table 4.** Performance of main stream CNNs on PLD

| Model | # Parameters (M) | Accuracy of test (%) | | | | | |
|---|---|---|---|---|---|---|---|
| | | PLD | tr80 | tr60 | tr40 | tr20 | tr05 |
| MobileNetv2 | 2.30 | 98.65 | 97.28 | 96.3 | 93.75 | 83.95 | 51.8 |
| ResNet18 | 11.33 | 99.20 | 98.14 | 97.45 | 96.46 | 92.30 | 74.57 |
| ResNet34 | 21.30 | 99.17 | 98.21 | 97.66 | 95.88 | 92.22 | 75.64 |
| VGG11 | 34.55 | 99.01 | 98.35 | 97.28 | 96.54 | 94.98 | 78.59 |
| CBDL-cn (ours) | **1.65** | 99.73 | 99.35 | 99.1 | 98.97 | 97.87 | 91.28 |
| CBDL-dn (ours) | 1.84 | 99.75 | 99.41 | 99.07 | 98.83 | 97.37 | 90.59 |
| SDCN (ours) | 4.70 | **99.81** | **99.46** | **99.29** | **98.93** | **98.26** | **92.58** |

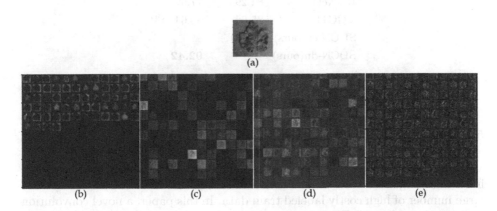

**Fig. 2.** The feature maps extracted from original image (a), by ResNet (b), VGG (c), SDCN-cn (d), and SDCN-dn (e).

**Comparative Experiment of Lesion Learning Ability.** SDCN is formed by SDCN-c and SDCN-d, and it needs few training data to achieve height accuracy, which is high probably due to its stronger learning ability of lesion features. In order to compare the lesion learning ability, the dataset Species05 and Disease05 are obtained from tr05 according to the configuration in Table 3 respectively. In this paper, SDCN-cn, SDCN-dn and mainstream CNNs are carried out comparative experiments on Disease05 and Species05.

According to the qualitative comparative experiment results shown in Fig. 2, these mainstream CNNs could extract few lesion features while much more species features such as the shape of plant leaves. On the contrary, SDCN-dn can learn more diverse and rich visual features of lesions, such as more and longer texture curves, more texture combinations, and so on. SDCN-cn and SDCN-dn in Table 5 represent the species and disease branch in SDCN respectively. From the quantitative comparative results in Table 5, it can be seen that in the case of few training data, the disease identification accuracy of SDCN-dn still maintains a high level, while the disease classification performance of other models is seriously reduced, but the classification accuracy of plant species is relatively high. It shows that other models do not better learn the disease spot features in the image, but mainly learn the species characteristics of plant leaves.

**Table 5.** Accuracy of main CNNs trained on little dataset

| Network | Accuracy of test (%) | |
|---------|----------|----------|
|  | Species05 | Disease05 |
| MobileNetv2 | 60.50 | 59.49 |
| ResNet34 | 83.46 | 75.62 |
| ResNet18 | 84.29 | 77.57 |
| VGG11 | 85.68 | 80.64 |
| SDCN-cn(ours) | **95.89** | – |
| SDCN-dn(ours) | – | **92.42** |

## 5   Conclusion and Future Work

Various diseases will seriously cause yield reduction. Deep learning based on CNN has achieved good results on plant disease recognition. However, CNN needs a large number of high costly labeled train data. In this paper, a novel convolution neural network model SDCN is proposed, not only achieves high recognition accuracy, but also greatly reduces the demand for the amount of train data. In the case of few training data, it can also achieve the recognition performance of the mainstream CNN trained on full train data. The experiment shows that it more effectively learned visual features of disease spots, while mainstream CNNs have weak ability to learn disease features. Therefore, the SDCN model proposed in this paper is more suitable for plant disease identification.

The future research work in this field can more deeply and systematically study the learning methods of disease spot features independent of plant species. And it is also of great significance to build a larger, more diverse and challenging public data set, as well as the model evaluation and comparative analysis.

# References

1. Li, Zheng et al.: Non-invasive plant disease diagnostics enabled by smartphone-based fingerprinting of leaf volatiles. Nature Plants **5**(8), 856–866 (2019). https://doi.org/10.1038/s41477-019-0476-y
2. Kamilaris, A., Prenafeta-Boldú, F.: A review of the use of convolutional neural networks in agriculture. J. Agric. Sci. **156**(3), 312–322 (2018). https://doi.org/10.1017/S0021859618000436
3. Li, L., Zhang, S., Wang, B.: Plant disease detection and classification by deep learning - a review. IEEE Access **9**, 56683–56698 (2021). https://doi.org/10.1109/ACCESS.2021.3069646
4. LeCun, Y., Bengio, Y., Hinton, G.: Deep learning, Nature **521**, 436–444 (2015). https://doi.org/10.1038/nature14539
5. Hughes, D., Salathé, M.: An open access repository of images on plant health to enable the development of mobile disease diagnostics. arXiv preprint arXiv:1511.08060 (2015)
6. Barbedo, J., Arnal, G.: A review on the main challenges in automatic plant disease identification based on visible range images. Biosyst. Eng. **144**, 52–60 (2016)
7. Duarte-Carvajalino, J.M., Alzate, D.F., Ramirez, A.A., Santa-Sepulveda, J.D., Fajardo-Rojas, A.E., Soto-Suárez, M.: Evaluating late blight severity in potato crops using unmanned aerial vehicles and machine learning algorithms. Remote Sens. **10**(10), 1513 (2018)
8. Kaur, S., Pandey, S., Goel, S.: Semi-automatic leaf disease detection and classification system for soybean culture. IET Image Proc. **12**(6), 1038–1048 (2018)
9. Ahmed, S., Hasan, M., Ahmed, T., Sony, R. K., and Kabir, M.: Less is more: lighter and faster deep neural architecture for tomato leaf disease classification. arXiv preprint arXiv:2109.02394. (2021)
10. Lu, Y., Yi, S., Zeng, N., Liu, Y., Zhang, Y.: Identification of rice diseases using deep convolutional neural networks. Neurocomputing **267**, 378–384 (2017)
11. Mohanty, S.P., Hughes, D.P., Salathé, M.: Using deep learning for image-based plant disease detection. Front. Plant Sci. **7**, 1419 (2016)
12. Lee, S.H., Go?au, H., Bonnet, P., Joly, A.: New perspectives on plant disease characterization based on deep learning. Comput. Electron. Agriculture **170**, 105220 (2020)
13. Zhang, Y., Song, C., Zhang, D.: Deep learning-based object detection improvement for tomato disease. IEEE Access **8**, 56607–56614 (2020)
14. Brahimi, M., Arsenovic, M., Laraba, S., Sladojevic, S., Boukhalfa, K., Moussaoui, A.: Deep learning for plant diseases: detection and saliency map visualisation. In: Zhou, J., Chen, F. (eds.) Human and Machine Learning. HIS, pp. 93–117. Springer, Cham (2018). https://doi.org/10.1007/978-3-319-90403-0_6
15. Bi, C., Wang, J., Duan, Y., Fu, B., Kang, J.R., Shi, Y.: MobileNet based apple leaf diseases identification. Mobile Networks and Applications, 1–9 (2020)

16. Geetharamani, G., Pandian, A.: Identification of plant leaf diseases using a nine-layer deep convolutional neural network. Comput. Electr. Eng. **76**, 323–338 (2019)

17. Yang, G., He, Y., Yang, Y., Xu, B.: Fine-grained image classification for crop disease based on attention mechanism. Front. Plant Sci. **2077** (2020)

18. Liu, X., Min, W., Mei, S., Wang, L., Jiang, S.: Plant disease recognition: a large-scale benchmark dataset and a visual region and loss reweighting approach. IEEE Trans. Image Process. **30**, 2003–2015 (2021)

19. Dosovitskiy, A., Beyer, L., Kolesnikov, A., et al.: An image is worth 16x16 words: Transformers for image recognition at scale. arXiv preprint arXiv:2010.11929 (2020)

20. Argüeso, D., et al.: Few-Shot Learning approach for plant disease classification using images taken in the field. Comput. Electron. Agric. **175**, 105542 (2020)

21. Li, Y., Chao, X.: Semi-supervised few-shot learning approach for plant diseases recognition. Plant Methods **17**(1), 1–10 (2021)

22. Chen, J., Chen, J., Zhang, D., Sun, Y., Nanehkaran, Y.A.: Using deep transfer learning for image-based plant disease identification. Comput. Electron. Agric. **173**, 105393 (2020)

23. Zhang, S., Zhang, S., Zhang, C., Wang, X., Shi, Y.: Cucumber leaf disease identification with global pooling dilated convolutional neural network. Comput. Electron. Agric. **162**, 422–430 (2019)

24. He, X., Li, S.-Q., Liu, B.: Grape leaf disease identification based on multi-scale residual network. Comput. Eng. **6**(4), 1–8 (2020)

25. Nazki, H., Yoon, S., Fuentes, A., Park, D.S.: Unsupervised image translation using adversarial networks for improved plant disease recognition. Comput. Electron. Agric. **168**, 105117 (2020)

26. Tian, Y., Yang, G., Wang, Z., Li, E., Liang, Z.: Detection of apple lesions in orchards based on deep learning methods of cyclegan and yolov3-dense. J. Sensors (2019)

27. Wu, Q., Chen, Y., Meng, J.: DCGAN-based data augmentation for tomato leaf disease identification. IEEE Access **8**, 98716–98728 (2020)

28. Liu, B., Tan, C., Li, S., He, J., Wang, H.: A data augmentation method based on generative adversarial networks for grape leaf disease identification. IEEE Access **8**, 102188–102198 (2020)

29. Ioffe, S., Szegedy, C.: Batch normalization: accelerating deep network training by reducing internal covariate shift. In: International Conference on Machine Learning, pp. 448–456. PMLR (2015)

# TFCNs: A CNN-Transformer Hybrid Network for Medical Image Segmentation

Zihan Li[1], Dihan Li[1], Cangbai Xu[1], Weice Wang[1], Qingqi Hong[1,4(✉)] ⓘ, Qingde Li[2]ⓘ, and Jie Tian[3]ⓘ

[1] Xiamen University, Xiamen 361005, China
{zihanli,dihanli,cangbaixu,wangweice}@stu.xmu.edu.cn, hongqq@xmu.edu.cn
[2] University of Hull, Hull HU6 7RX, UK
Q.li@hull.ac.uk
[3] Chinese Academy of Sciences, Beijing 100190, China
tian@ieee.org
[4] State Key Laboratory of Virtual Reality Technology and Systems, Beihang University, Beijing, China

**Abstract.** Medical image segmentation is one of the most fundamental tasks concerning medical information analysis. Various solutions have been proposed so far, including many deep learning-based techniques, such as U-Net, FC-DenseNet, etc. However, high-precision medical image segmentation remains a highly challenging task due to the existence of inherent magnification and distortion in medical images as well as the presence of lesions with similar density to normal tissues. In this paper, we propose TFCNs (Transformers for Fully Convolutional denseNets) to tackle the problem by introducing ResLinear-Transformer (RL-Transformer) and Convolutional Linear Attention Block (CLAB) to FC-DenseNet. TFCNs is not only able to utilize more latent information from the CT images for feature extraction, but also can capture and disseminate semantic features and filter non-semantic features more effectively through the CLAB module. Our experimental results show that TFCNs can achieve state-of-the-art performance with dice scores of 83.72% on the Synapse dataset. In addition, we evaluate the robustness of TFCNs for lesion area effects on the COVID-19 public datasets. The Python code will be made publicly available on https://github.com/HUANGLIZI/TFCNs.

**Keywords:** Medical image segmentation · CNN-Transformers · Attention mechanism

## 1 Introduction

Medical image segmentation plays a critical role in clinical diagnosis and assisting doctors to evaluate patient's reactions to treatment. Various algorithms based on convolutional neural networks (CNNs) [9] have been applied to image segmentation. And with a U-shaped network design, U-Net [15] has achieved great

---

Z. Li and D. Li—Means equal contribution.

© The Author(s), under exclusive license to Springer Nature Switzerland AG 2022
E. Pimenidis et al. (Eds.): ICANN 2022, LNCS 13532, pp. 781–792, 2022.
https://doi.org/10.1007/978-3-031-15937-4_65

success in various medical imaging applications. Following this technical route, many algorithms have been developed for medical image and volume segmentation, such as U-Net++ [27]. In order to solve the degradation problem, He et al. proposed ResNets [5], which aims to simplify very deep networks by introducing a residual block that sums two input signals. Then a new CNN architecture called DenseNets [7] has been developed by the composition of dense blocks and pooling operations. In FC-DenseNet [23], the up-sampling path was introduced to restore the input resolution. Recently, inspired by the great success of Transformers in the field of natural language processing (NLP) [3], researchers have tried to introduce Transformers into the field of computer vision [10,26]. Vision transformer (ViT) [4] has been proposed to achieve object detection tasks.

Currently, there are two problems: 1). As shown in Fig. 1, since the convolution operation collects information by layer, which leads to too much focus on local feature information. In the field of medical image segmentation, the lack of global information often leads to false category of segmentation. Therefore, a visual transformer was introduced, which can reflect complex spatial transformations and long-distance feature dependencies, which are regarded as global representations. Currently, although Chen et al. proposed Transunet [2] to solve problems such as lack of high-level details. However, we found that the direct feeding of CNN-style features into the transformer for recoding tends to bring limited improvement. 2). In U-shape networks, the skip connection between encoder and decoder is crucial. However, semantic-independent features tend to be fed to the decoder with direct transmission, which will interfere with image segmentation. Our main motivation is how to preserve image features more completely.

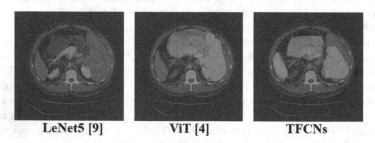

**LeNet5 [9]**          **ViT [4]**          **TFCNs**

**Fig. 1.** Class activation maps in LeNet5 [9], ViT [4] and TFCNs by using the CAM method [25]. In which we set a fixed value as the activation intensity threshold.

To tackle the problem 1), we utilize DenseBlocks to facilitate the propagation of feature information to the transformer part while adding a residual structure to the MLP to further effectively preserve the global representation information. To tackle the problem 2), we decide to fuse spatial and channel attention on the original skip connection to transmit information more efficiently. Our main contributions are as follows:

1. A new deep neural network framework (TFCNs) is proposed, to the best of our knowledge, which is the first network to introduce Transformers into FC-DenseNet and improve the internal structure of Transformers.

2. A general attention module CLAB (Convolutional Linear Attention Block) is proposed to improve segmentation performance, which includes two types of attentions: (a) attention over the spatial extent of image and (b) attention over the CNN-style feature channels.

## 2    Related Work

In the field of semantic segmentation, FCNs [13] innovatively proposed a model structure in the form of encoder-decoder. And to solve the problem of information loss in the encoding process, it utilized the form of residual connection to combine the encoding process. In addition to the semantic segmentation of real objects, more and more attention has also been paid to medical image segmentation. Based on FCNs, U-Net [15] was proposed and applied to medical image segmentation. This model makes use of a mutually symmetrical encoding-decoding design. Another example was FC-DenseNet [8], where they extended the work in DenseNets [7] by introducing the DenseBlock in the process of upsampling, which not only alleviated the problem of dimensional explosion in the deep encoder but also retained contextual information better. Some Transformer-based methods have also been proposed for semantic segmentation, object detection, and instance segmentation, such as SETR, DETR [1,24]. Inspired by the previous breakthroughs, TransUNet [2] embedded the Transformers in the down-sampling process to extract the information in the original image. More recently, a Gated Axial-Attention model was proposed in MedT [17] to extend some existing attention-based schemes. There are also other variants to the Transformers such as the Swin Transformer [12], which utilize a sliding window to limit self-attention calculations to non-overlapping partial windows.

## 3    Method

### 3.1    Overall Structure of TFCNs

As described in the first section, the conventional U-shaped structured network lacks global contextual information to perform high-precision medical image segmentation. Given this, we propose TFCNs (Fig. 2), which takes FC-DenseNet [23] as the backbone network, with an RL-Transformer Layer being added to the encoder to enhance the segmentation capability of the network. In addition, CLAB (Convolutional Linear Attention Block) in the skip connection part is introduced to enhance the spatial recovery of the focused segmentation region. The CNN-Transformer hybrid model acts as an encoder and CLAB as the upper and lower connecting part between DenseBlock and Transition-Down, which helps to filter non-semantic features. Compared with TransUNet [2], TFCNs not only replaces the traditional convolutional layers with Dense Blocks, but also changes the feature encoding method. The details of each part of the structure will be described in the next two subsections. More specifically, the RL-Transformer (ResLinear-Transformer) is described in Sect. 3.2, the CLAB (Convolutional Linear Attention Block) is described in Sect. 3.3.

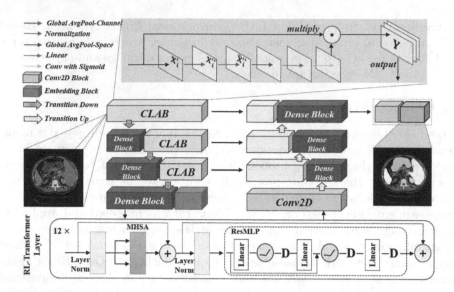

**Fig. 2.** Overview of the proposed TFCNs. RL-Transformer module at the end of encoder gives access to a receptive field containing images and CLAB modules are dedicated to filtering non-semantic features by including spatial and channel attention.

### 3.2   RL-Transformer

Referring to the ViT [4] implementation, we propose the ResLinear-Transformer (RL-Transformer) and apply it to the encoder of TFCNs. Of particular note is that the 2D patch $x_P^i$ is expanded linearly and its projection is mapped to the $D$ dimension using a trainable linear layer, as shown in Eq. 1. The output of this projection is called Patch Embedding.

$$z_0 = [x_{class}; x_P^1 E; x_P^2 E; \cdots ; x_P^N E] + E_{pos} \tag{1}$$

where $E$ is the patch embedding projection which is located before entering the RL-transform layer and $E_{pos}$ is the position embedding. RL-Transformer Layer consists of alternating ResMLP blocks and $L$ layers of Multi-Head Self-Attention (MHSA). The expressions are shown in Eq. 2 and Eq. 3, where LN denotes Layer Norm.

$$z_\ell' = MHSA(LN(z_{\ell-1})) + z_{\ell-1} \tag{2}$$

$$z_\ell = ResMLP(LN(z_\ell')) + z_\ell' \tag{3}$$

The RL-Transformer encoder consists of alternating multi-headed self-attentive layers and ResMLP blocks. As shown in Fig. 2, our proposed ResMLP consists of two GELU [6] nonlinear layers, three Linear layers, and three dropout layers alternating with a residual connection to the source input before the second GELU [6] layer. ResMLP can be expressed in Eq. 4 and Eq. 5 shown below:

$$z_\ell'' = LN(z_\ell') \tag{4}$$

$$y = z''_\ell + L(\alpha GELU(L(z''_\ell))) \tag{5}$$

where GELU represents the GELU [6] nonlinear layer, $L$ represents the Linear layer, and $\alpha$ represents the associated weight parameters which is a learned parameter. Finally, the state of the sequence at the output of the RL-Transformer encoder is utilized as the image features.

### 3.3 CLAB (Convolutional Linear Attention Block)

Inspired by TTD (Test-Time Dropout) [20] and TTA (Test-Time Augmentation) [11], we propose **Convolutional Linear Attention Block** (CLAB). Nowadays TTD [20] can utilize dropout layers in the reasoning process and generate multiple predictions for each data instance. Compared with CUAB [19], we change the order of extracting channel and spatial attention, as indicated by the experimental results of CBAM [21]. In addition, the normalization operation is utilized between the two attention operations to accelerate the training convergence process. Finally, inspired by the local field of view, the weak influence outside the local area is directly reduced to zero influence by using the linear layer.

As shown in Fig. 2, the global average pooling layer with the linear layer is added between the two convolutional layers. In CLAB, we first use $1 \times 1$ convolutional layers, where each convolutional layer has $K$ kernels to generate the sequence $X'_i = \mathbb{R}^{H \times W \times K}, i \in \{1, \ldots, N\}$. Then a global average pooling operation is performed on $X'_i$ in channel dimensions to obtain $X''_i$, and a normalization operation is performed on $X''_i$ to homogenize the data to obtain $\hat{X}''_i = \frac{X'_i - \mu_B}{\sqrt{\sigma_B^2 + \varepsilon}}$ to accelerate the convergence and accuracy improvement of the training process, where $\mu_B$ denotes the mean of a batch, $\sigma_B$ denotes the standard deviation of the batch, and $\varepsilon$ is a minimal positive value to ensure that the denominator is not zero. All $\hat{X}''_i = \mathbb{R}^{H \times W}, i \in \{1, \ldots, N\}$, are concatenated to form $X_m = \mathbb{R}^{H \times W \times N}$, which is then input sequentially into a submodule consisting of a global average pooling layer (with respect to dimensionality), a linear layer and a convolutional layer with sigmoid. The result is then multiplied with the source input to obtain the final output feature $Y$. We later perform ablation analysis for CLAB as well, and the experimental results show that CLAB has a significant effect on the model segmentation performance improvement.

## 4 Experimental Results and Discussion

### 4.1 Implementation Details

For all experiments, we perform a simple data augmentation, i.e., by performing random rotation or flipping operations. The optimizer chosen is the SGD optimizer, with a momentum of 0.9 and a weight decay of 1e-4. The learning rate selected for the experiment for our method is 0.005 and is set to 0.001 for other models. The learning rate is made to decay after 30,000 iterations. The batch size is set to 3 for Segtran [24], and 12 for all other models. The epoch is set to 150 on all datasets.

For Patch Size, it is worth noticing from Table 1 that the performance of the model is optimal when the patch size is set to 16. When the patch size is set to 8, the included area is too small, so some relatively large organs such as liver or kidney will be divided into many different patches for encoding, which splits some important information. This makes it difficult for the decoder to perform well, thereby reducing the performance of the model. When the patch size is set to 32, because the coding area is relatively large, it contains many interfering information that makes the model to misjudge. Although the CLAB module functions as a filter, the remaining redundant information is still greater than when the patch size is 16, so it also affects the judgments of the model.

**Table 1.** Ablation study on different patch sizes in transformer (Dice score% and Hausdorff distance in mm and Jaccard score%).

| Patch_Size | Dice↑ | Hd95↓ | Jaccard↑ |
|---|---|---|---|
| 8 | 78.79 | 38.11 | 65.95 |
| 16 | **83.72** | **17.26** | **72.78** |
| 32 | 80.00 | 24.41 | 67.84 |

Moreover, in our experiment, the combination of the Dice coefficient and cross-entropy is taken as the loss function for all methods. And the weight of these two components is 0.5.

## 4.2 Comparison with Other SOTA Methods

We conduct our experiments on Synapse[1] dataset and COVID-19[2] dataset. The experimental results are analyzed by taking the Dice coefficient, Hausdorff distance, and Jaccard coefficient as evaluation factors. All the State-of-the-art methods are implemented using original paper without any deviations.

**Synapse Dataset**
As shown in Table 2, these methods including Transformers, i.e. TransUNet [2], Segtran [24], and our TFCNs achieves better performance when compare with other methods. Especially, our method has a slight lead in terms of Dice coefficient and Jaccard coefficient when compared to TransUNet [2] and Segtran [24]. We believe this improvement is brought by the Dense Block we add, which is able to enhance the transmission of semantic information in the main pipeline.

From Table 2, it can be observed that our method achieves more accurate results than other approaches on some organs that are difficult to be segment, such as the Gallbladder and Pancreas. Since these tiny organs occupy a relatively small proportion in the original image, other approaches are easy to wrap other

---

[1] https://www.synapse.org/#!Synapse:syn3193805/wiki/217789.
[2] https://aistudio.baidu.com/aistudio/datasetdetail/34221.

**Table 2.** Performance comparison between our method and other state-of-the-art methods on Synapse dataset (Dice score% and Hausdorff distance in mm and Jaccard score%, and Dice score % for each organ). Avg means average result of all testing cases and the Dice coefficient% on each organ.

| Method | Dice (avg)↑ | Hd95 (avg)↓ | Jaccard (avg)↑ | Aorta↑ | Gallbladder↑ | Kidney (L)↑ | Kidney (R)↑ | Liver↑ | Pancreas↑ | Spleen↑ | Stomach↑ |
|---|---|---|---|---|---|---|---|---|---|---|---|
| U-Net [15] | 81.81 | 26.81 | 71.21 | 86.99 | 67.31 | 88.64 | 82.81 | 94.15 | 60.99 | 90.50 | 83.10 |
| Fc-DenseNet [23] | 81.62 | 21.83 | 70.62 | 86.68 | 66.31 | 88.14 | 82.07 | 95.26 | 61.73 | 92.11 | 80.68 |
| AttU-Net [14] | 81.05 | 29.09 | 70.71 | 89.63 | 67.05 | 88.46 | 77.08 | 94.52 | 56.89 | 92.13 | 82.69 |
| Res-UNet [22] | 78.33 | 58.66 | 66.61 | 86.16 | 59.63 | 86.55 | 83.93 | 94.49 | 48.94 | 86.96 | 79.96 |
| U-Net++ [27] | 81.60 | 28.31 | 70.48 | 88.15 | 67.29 | 86.31 | 83.62 | 94.00 | 61.71 | 89.51 | 82.18 |
| DDANet [16] | 79.60 | 21.29 | 67.87 | 83.74 | 64.93 | 88.93 | 83.83 | 94.99 | 51.99 | 90.68 | 77.69 |
| TransUNet [2] | 82.33 | 19.88 | 71.18 | 88.50 | 62.96 | 91.23 | 90.03 | 94.90 | 59.90 | 90.53 | 80.59 |
| Segtran [24] | 83.02 | 14.73 | 72.68 | 87.10 | 62.88 | 92.66 | 89.94 | 95.47 | 61.76 | 91.47 | 83.40 |
| TFCNs | **83.72** | 17.26 | **72.78** | **89.69** | **67.75** | 90.11 | 88.30 | 94.74 | **64.08** | **92.22** | 82.84 |

interfering information when extracting features from the areas containing these tiny organs. Conversely, through the utilization of the designed CLAB module, our model is able to pay more attention to these tiny organs themselves instead of those irrelevant areas. Meanwhile, for other organs, the results achieved by our method are also in the top 5 (Fig. 3).

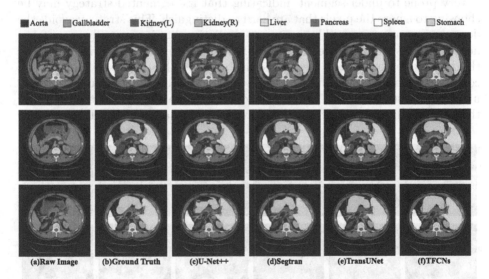

**Fig. 3.** Qualitative results on Synapse Dataset. All columns respectively represent: (a) Raw Image; (b) Ground Truth; (c) U-Net++ [27]; (d) Segtran [24]; (e) TransUNet [2]; (f) TFCNs. Top row describes corresponding color of each organ in raw image.

## Analysis of Segmentation for COVID-19 Infected Areas

The performance of our model at the fine-grained feature is explored using the second dataset, i.e. the COVID-19 dataset. Since lesion features normally are more refined and scattered than organs which cover a large proportion of the image. Table 3 indicates that the capability of our method on the fine-grained target also reaches the SOTA level.

**Table 3.** Performance comparison between our method and other state-of-the-art methods on Covid-19 dataset (Dice score% and Hausdorff distance in mm and Jaccard score%). Avg means result average of all testing cases.

| Method | Dice (Avg)↑ | Hd95 (Avg)↓ | Jaccard (Avg)↑ |
|---|---|---|---|
| Segtran [24] | 75.35 | 41.18 | 60.35 |
| Res-UNet [22] | 73.53 | 47.54 | 59.86 |
| DDANet [16] | 75.52 | 39.36 | 60.52 |
| U-Net [15] | 73.96 | 45.19 | 59.99 |
| FC-DenseNet [23] | 71.13 | 54.72 | 55.52 |
| AttU-net [14] | 74.70 | 48.36 | 60.26 |
| TransUNet [2] | 72.19 | 52.51 | 57.22 |
| TFCNs | **75.55** | **37.32** | **60.74** |

Combining with the results visualized in Fig. 4, it can be seen that DDANet [16], which is very close to our method in Dice coefficient and Jaccard coefficient, is very prone to under-segment, indicating that its segmented strategy may be choosing to ignore the pixels that are hard to distinguish. This strategy avoids the decrease inaccuracy caused by erroneous prediction, but it can easily cause false-negative that should be as least as possible in the diagnosis. TransUNet [2] shows the over-segmentation in all rows. This may be the result of excessive utilization of contextual information in the local area which is suitable for continuous and regular objects such as organs, but these pieces of information are still too coarse for the lesion features. However, we solve this problem by adding the CLAB module.

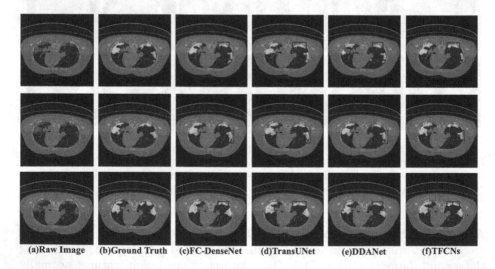

**Fig. 4.** Qualitative results on COVID-19 dataset. All columns respectively represent: (a) Raw Image; (b) Ground Truth; (c) FC-DenseNet [23]; (d) TransUNet [2]; (e) DDANet [16]; (f) TFCNs. Infected area in lung are labeled in yellow. (Color figure online)

### 4.3    Interpretability Analysis

Interpretability analysis is conducted on the COVID-19 dataset using Class Activation Mapping (CAM) [25] to explore what causes the model to make the decision on every pixel and which area of feature map the model pays the most attention to when it segments the infected area. As shown in Fig. 5, TFCNs focuses its attention on the lung area and pay least attention in the area surrounding the lung which means our model can act as an expert that focuses on the lung area at the beginning, and then pays more and more attention to the infected area gradually (in Fig. 5, the lung area is light red, and the infected area is dark red) when it predicts.

As for TransUNet [2], although it can also focus its attention on the infected area when predicting, it disperses other attention to the entire image instead of gathering it to the lungs. This reflects the importance of our CLAB module because it relocates the attention of the model to the key area.

Moreover, even though DDANet [16] achieves good results, it ignores most areas in the image except the infected area, indicating that it does not have the concept of lungs and only makes some mechanical predictions based on ground truth which will make it very difficult to predict at the edge of the infected area, resulting in a large number of false-negatives.

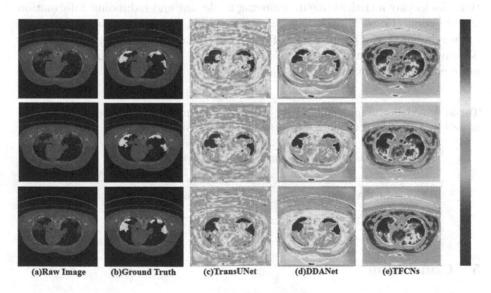

(a)Raw Image        (b)Ground Truth        (c)TransUNet        (d)DDANet        (e)TFCNs

**Fig. 5.** Heat map for interpretability analysis of different approaches on COVID-19 dataset. All columns respectively represents: (a) Raw Image; (b) Ground Truth; (c) TransUNet [2]; (d) DDANet [16]; (e) TFCNs. The colormap in right presents the degree of attention which increases from bottom to top. Infected area in lung are labeled using yellow in ground truth. (Color figure online)

### 4.4   Ablation Studies

**Effectiveness of ResMLP**

It can be seen from Table 4 that the Dice coefficient increases by 1.87% after using ResMLP. In addition, the Hausdorff distance drops by 8.38 mm, indicating that ResMLP makes the semantic features in the Transformers propagate more complete, thereby increasing the contextual information extracted by the encoder, which promotes the performance of the overall structure.

**Table 4.** Ablation study on verifying the effectiveness of ResMLP (Dice score% and Hausdorff distance in mm and Jaccard score%).

|        | Dice↑ | Hd95↓ | Jaccard↑ |
|--------|-------|-------|----------|
| ResMLP | **83.72** | **17.26** | **72.78** |
| MLP    | 81.85 | 25.64 | 70.57    |

**Type of Attention Block**

As shown in Table 5, the performance of the model is greatly improved after using the attention blocks (no matter what type it is), which means these attention blocks play a critical role in removing irrelevant and redundant information at skip connections. Moreover, it can be seen that after using the CLAB module we designed, the performance of the model is continuously improved, which demonstrates that our CLAB module can accurately locate the area containing more effective information in the feature map.

**Table 5.** Ablation study on different types of attention block in skip connection (Dice score% and Hausdorff distance in mm and Jaccard score%).

| Type of attention block | Dice↑ | Hd95↓ | Jaccard↑ |
|-------------------------|-------|-------|----------|
| None                    | 80.16 | 28.40 | 68.53    |
| CUAB [19]               | 81.83 | 25.68 | 70.72    |
| CLAB                    | **83.72** | **17.26** | **72.78** |

## 5   Conclusion

To improve the performance of medical image segmentation, in this paper, we propose TFCNs based on Transformer [18] and FC-DenseNet [23]. And the internal structure of Transformers is modified by introducing residual connections to form RL-Transformer. This change can help enhance the receptive field and improve the coding ability of the model. In addition, a common module-CLAB, which is mainly composed of global average pooling and linear mapping, is designed in the network to filter out non-semantic features. Experimental results show that TFCNs which is the best among the baselines achieves a score of 83.72% on the Dice coefficient and a score of 72.78% on the Jaccard coefficient in terms of the Synapse dataset. The experiments are also conducted on the COVID-19 public dataset, and results show that TFCNs also has the state-of-the-art performance.

**Acknowledgement.** This work was supported in part by the Natural Science Foundation of Fujian Province of China (No. 2020J01006), the National Natural Science Foundation of China (No. 61502402), and the Open Project Program of State Key Laboratory of Virtual Reality Technology and Systems, Beihang University (No. VRLAB2022AC04).

# References

1. Carion, N., Massa, F., Synnaeve, G., Usunier, N., Kirillov, A., Zagoruyko, S.: End-to-end object detection with transformers. In: Vedaldi, A., Bischof, H., Brox, T., Frahm, J.-M. (eds.) ECCV 2020. LNCS, vol. 12346, pp. 213–229. Springer, Cham (2020). https://doi.org/10.1007/978-3-030-58452-8_13
2. Chen, J., et al.: Transunet: transformers make strong encoders for medical image segmentation. arXiv preprint arXiv:2102.04306 (2021)
3. Chowdhury, G.G.: Natural language processing. Ann. Rev. Inf. Sci. Technol. **37**(1), 51–89 (2003)
4. Dosovitskiy, A., et al.: An image is worth 16x16 words: transformers for image recognition at scale. arXiv preprint arXiv:2010.11929 (2020)
5. He, K., Zhang, X., Ren, S., Sun, J.: Identity mappings in deep residual networks. In: Leibe, B., Matas, J., Sebe, N., Welling, M. (eds.) ECCV 2016. LNCS, vol. 9908, pp. 630–645. Springer, Cham (2016). https://doi.org/10.1007/978-3-319-46493-0_38
6. Hendrycks, D., Gimpel, K.: Gaussian error linear units (GELUs). arXiv preprint arXiv:1606.08415 (2016)
7. Iandola, F., Moskewicz, M., Karayev, S., Girshick, R., Darrell, T., Keutzer, K.: Densenet: implementing efficient convnet descriptor pyramids. arXiv preprint arXiv:1404.1869 (2014)
8. Jégou, S., Drozdzal, M., Vazquez, D., Romero, A., Bengio, Y.: The one hundred layers tiramisu: fully convolutional densenets for semantic segmentation. In: Proceedings of the IEEE Conference on Computer Vision and Pattern Recognition Workshops, pp. 11–19 (2017)
9. LeCun, Y., Bottou, L., Bengio, Y., Haffner, P.: Gradient-based learning applied to document recognition. Proc. IEEE **86**(11), 2278–2324 (1998)
10. Li, Z., et al.: LViT: language meets vision transformer in medical image segmentation. arXiv preprint arXiv:2206.14718 (2022)
11. Litjens, G., et al.: Evaluation of prostate segmentation algorithms for MRI: the promise12 challenge. Med. Image Anal. **18**(2), 359–373 (2014)
12. Liu, Z., et al.: Swin transformer: hierarchical vision transformer using shifted windows. In: Proceedings of the IEEE/CVF International Conference on Computer Vision, pp. 10012–10022 (2021)
13. Long, J., Shelhamer, E., Darrell, T.: Fully convolutional networks for semantic segmentation. In: Proceedings of the IEEE Conference on Computer Vision and Pattern Recognition, pp. 3431–3440 (2015)

14. Oktay, O., et al.: Attention u-net: learning where to look for the pancreas. arXiv preprint arXiv:1804.03999 (2018)
15. Ronneberger, O., Fischer, P., Brox, T.: U-Net: convolutional networks for biomedical image segmentation. In: Navab, N., Hornegger, J., Wells, W.M., Frangi, A.F. (eds.) MICCAI 2015. LNCS, vol. 9351, pp. 234–241. Springer, Cham (2015). https://doi.org/10.1007/978-3-319-24574-4_28
16. Tomar, N.K., et al.: DDANet: dual decoder attention network for automatic polyp segmentation. In: Del Bimbo, A., et al. (eds.) ICPR 2021. LNCS, vol. 12668, pp. 307–314. Springer, Cham (2021). https://doi.org/10.1007/978-3-030-68793-9_23
17. Valanarasu, J.M.J., et al.: Medical transformer: gated axial-attention for medical image segmentation. arXiv preprint arXiv:2102.10662 (2021)
18. Vaswani, A., et al.: Attention is all you need. In: Advances in Neural Information Processing Systems, vol. 30 (2017)
19. Wang, C.S., Su, F.Y., Lee, T.L.M., Tsai, Y.S., Chiang, J.H.: CUAB: convolutional uncertainty attention block enhanced the chest x-ray image analysis. arXiv preprint arXiv:2105.01840 (2021)
20. Wang, G., Li, W., Aertsen, M., Deprest, J., Ourselin, S., Vercauteren, T.: Aleatoric uncertainty estimation with test-time augmentation for medical image segmentation with convolutional neural networks. Neurocomputing **338**, 34–45 (2019)
21. Woo, S., Park, J., Lee, J.Y., Kweon, I.S.: CBAM: convolutional block attention module. In: Proceedings of the European Conference on Computer Vision (ECCV), pp. 3–19 (2018)
22. Xiao, X., Lian, S., Luo, Z., Li, S.: Weighted res-unet for high-quality retina vessel segmentation. In: 2018 9th International Conference on Information Technology in Medicine and Education (ITME), pp. 327–331. IEEE (2018)
23. Zhang, R., et al.: Automatic segmentation of acute ischemic stroke from DWI using 3-D fully convolutional densenets. IEEE Trans. Med. Imaging **37**(9), 2149–2160 (2018)
24. Zheng, S., et al.: Rethinking semantic segmentation from a sequence-to-sequence perspective with transformers. In: Proceedings of the IEEE/CVF Conference on Computer Vision and Pattern Recognition, pp. 6881–6890 (2021)
25. Zhou, B., Khosla, A., Lapedriza, A., Oliva, A., Torralba, A.: Learning deep features for discriminative localization. In: Proceedings of the IEEE Conference on Computer Vision and Pattern Recognition, pp. 2921–2929 (2016)
26. Zhou, D., et al.: Deepvit: towards deeper vision transformer. arXiv preprint arXiv:2103.11886 (2021)
27. Zhou, Z., Rahman Siddiquee, M.M., Tajbakhsh, N., Liang, J.: UNet++: a nested U-Net architecture for medical image segmentation. In: Stoyanov, D., et al. (eds.) DLMIA/ML-CDS -2018. LNCS, vol. 11045, pp. 3–11. Springer, Cham (2018). https://doi.org/10.1007/978-3-030-00889-5_1

# Author Index

Adaloglou, Nikolas 459
Araújo, Aluizio F. R. 285
Aydin, Mehmet Emin 1

Bao, Feilong 620
Battle, Steve 445
Bečková, Iveta 645
Behnke, Sven 407
Brinkrolf, Johannes 76

Cao, Yichao 570
Cao, Yuheng 695
Castellani, Andrea 260
Chai, Jie 707
Chan, Philip K. 471
Chen, Mingzhou 731
Chen, Weiran 558
Chen, Xiu-yan 27
Chen, Yan 358
Chen, Yu 455
Chen, Zhe 719
Chen, Zheng 101
Cheng, Xi 151
Cozzatti, Michele 333

da Silva Júnior, Marcondes R. 285
Dai, Dawei 633
Dai, Qiang 151
Dang, Hy 273
David, Eli O. 582
Du, Songlin 113
Du, Xiaoyong 395
Dupin de Saint-Cyr, Florence 669
Durgut, Rafet 1

Eddie Law, K. L. 496

Fang, Bo 508
Farazi, Hafez 407
Farkaš, Igor 645
Fellows, Ryan 445
Feng, Ruijun 731
Feng, Yuchao 14
Flach, Peter 455

Fu, Boyi 433
Fu, Yingxun 101
Futsæther, Cecilia Marie 163

Gao, Guanglai 620
Gao, Wenting 139
Gepperth, Alexander 657
Gerstner, Andreas O. H. 682
Gholamipoor, Rahil 459
Giannopoulou, Maria 346
Gu, Xiaodong 64
Gu, Yubin 14
Guo, Mingfeng 309

Hammer, Barbara 76, 248, 260
Han, Jizhong 358
Han, Yu 139
Hasenjäger, Martina 248
He, Chunmao 521
Helin, Runar 163
Hinder, Fabian 76
Hong, Qingqi 781
Hossain, Md. Delwar 546
Hu, Weidong 395
Huang, Songqing 521
Huang, Xinlei 187
Huynh, Bao Ngoc 163

Ihshaish, Hisham 1, 445
Ikenaga, Takeshi 113
Iliadis, Lazaros 346
Inoue, Hiroyuki 546
Ito, Yasuaki 212

Jaja, Joseph 236
Jakob, Jonathan 248
Jaxy, Simon 459
Jenul, Anna 163
Ji, Shuaijian 594
Ji, Yi 558
Jia, Jingyun 471
Jiang, Anyan 176
Jiang, Kun 370

Jiang, Linlin   224
Jiang, Ning   187

Kadobayashi, Youki   546
Kasagi, Akihiko   212
Kobayashi, Yuki   756
Kollmann, Markus   459
Kundu, Amit Kumar   236
Kurita, Takio   484

Li, Chunpeng   199
Li, Dihan   781
Li, Donggen   633
Li, Jianjun   88
Li, Jun   707
Li, Qingde   781
Li, Ruixuan   358
Li, Wei   383, 508
Li, Wen-tao   27
Li, Xiaojuan   139
Li, Xiaoni   508
Li, Yang   101
Li, Yuanzhe   395
Li, Zhixin   383
Li, Zhongtao   224
Li, Zihan   781
Liland, Kristian Hovde   163
Liu, Chunping   558
Liu, Dongqin   358
Liu, Jian-wei   27
Liu, Jie   51
Liu, Jingquan   395
Liu, Ran   176
Liu, Shuai   88
Liu, Yue   139
Liu, Zheng   370
Lu, Xiaobo   570
Luo, Dezhao   508
Lv, Junjie   533
Lykostratis, Konstantinos   346

Ma, Li   101
Martínez-Muñoz, Gonzalo   297
Mayouf, Mona-Sabrine   669
Mayr, Christian   743
Mei, Bo   273
Meyer-Veit, Felix   682
Mo, Zhangbin   309
Mojoo, Jonathan   484
Murugan, Ramyaa   484

Nakano, Koji   212
Netanyahu, Nathan S.   582
Nevado, David   297
Nevo, Doron   582
Nguyen, Minh   273
Nicholls, Reece   445
Niu, Tao   126
Noda, Yuhei   607
Ntalampiras, Stavros   39, 333

Ou, Yaojun   719

Pan, Yixuan   570
Papaleonidas, Antonios   346
Peng, Chen   707
Peng, Yuncong   433
Pócoš, Štefan   645
Poirè, Alessandro Maria   39
Psathas, Anastasios Panagiotis   346

Qian, Junhui   176
Qian, Wanhui   358
Qin, Xiaolin   433
Qing, Haifeng   187

Rafiee, Nima   459
Rakib, Abdur   1
Ramakers, Julius   459
Rayyes, Rania   682

Sada, Youki   756
Saito, Shota   607
Sasaki, Taiki   212
Schak, Monika   657
Schmitt, Sebastian   260
Schrunner, Stefan   163
Shan, Hongyuan   633
Shen, Chao   309
Shibata, Seiya   756
Shibly, Kabid Hassan   546
Shirakawa, Shinichi   607
Simonetta, Federico   39, 333
Steil, Jochen   682
Su, Xiangdong   620
Su, Yipeng   358
Suárez, Alberto   297
Sun, Yeheng   420

Taenaka, Yuzo   546
Takasu, Atsuhiro   321
Takenaka, Takashi   756
Tan, Chao   51

Tan, Zhenshan   64
Tang, Jialiang   187
Teng, Yinglei   126
Tian, Fengchun   176
Tian, Jie   781
Tian, Weidong   707
Tomic, Oliver   163

Ujibashi, Yoshifumi   321

Wang, Huiwei   533
Wang, Lu   496
Wang, Mei   719
Wang, Weice   781
Wang, Weihua   620
Wang, Weiping   508
Wang, Yaobin   309
Wang, Yuqing   594
Waschneck, Bernd   743
Weng, Zhenyu   594
Wu, Binyi   743

Xi, Heran   420
Xia, Shunyin   633
Xia, Yulong   633
Xiao, Xin   224
Xu, Cangbai   781
Xu, Jinshan   14

Yan, Yaping   113
Yang, Chenyue   570
Yang, Xiaoyan   187

Yang, Yiqi   769
Ye, Zhongjie   594
Yuan, Zhenxin   224
Yuan, Zhiwei   113

Zhang, Guangbing   309
Zhang, Housen   707
Zhang, Jia   383
Zhang, Li   151
Zhang, Lingyun   521
Zhang, Meiyu   14
Zhang, Pingjian   521
Zhang, Qing   620
Zhang, Qingming   309
Zhang, Xiaofeng   719
Zhang, Yaqing   309
Zhao, Leilei   176
Zhao, Shuai   224
Zhao, Zhongqiu   707
Zheng, Jianwei   14
Zhou, Boquan   199
Zhou, Mengdong   88
Zhou, Mengjie   695
Zhou, Yan   358
Zhou, Yu   508
Zhou, Zhaokun   594
Zhu, Honglin   187
Zhu, Jinghua   420
Zhu, Lei   370
Zhu, Yuesheng   594
Zou, Panpan   126
Zuo, Yan   533

Printed in the United States
by Baker & Taylor Publisher Services